The Stand
of the U.S. Army
at Gettysburg

The Stand of the U.S. Army at Gettysburg

Jeffrey C. Hall

INDIANA University Press

Bloomington & Indianapolis

Lyrics from Bob Dylan's "Paths of Victory" copyright © 1964 by Warner Bros., Inc. Copyright renewed 1992 by Special Rider Music. All rights reserved. International copyright secured. Reprinted by permission.

Lyrics from "(What a) Wonderful World" by Sam Cooke, Herb Alpert, and Lou Adler are reprinted by permission of ABKCO Music, Inc.

Lyrics from "Brothers in Arms" by Mark Knopfler copyright © 1985 by Chariscourt Limited and Rondor Music (London) Ltd. administered by Almo Music Corp. (PRS/ASCAP). International copyright secured. All rights reserved. Reprinted by permission.

Lyrics from "One Bullet" by Garnet Rogers are reprinted by permission of Snow Goose Songs.

This book is a publication of

Indiana University Press
601 North Morton Street
Bloomington, IN 47404-3797 USA

http://iupress.indiana.edu

Telephone orders   800-842-6796
Fax orders   812-855-7931
Orders by e-mail   iuporder@indiana.edu

Design by Emmy Ezzell, cartography by Bill Nelson, charts by Emmy Ezzell. Printed and bound by Thomson-Shore, Inc.

© 2003 by Jeffrey C. Hall

All rights reserved

No part of this book may be reproduced or utilized in any form or by any means, electronic or mechanical, including photocopying and recording, or by any information storage and retrieval system, without permission in writing from the publisher. The Association of American University Presses' Resolution on Permissions constitutes the only exception to this prohibition.

The paper used in this publication meets the minimum requirements of American National Standard for Information Sciences—Permanence of Paper for Printed Library Materials, ANSI Z39.48-1984.

Manufactured in the United States of America

Library of Congress Cataloging-in-Publication Data

Hall, Jeffrey C.
The stand of the U.S. Army at Gettysburg / Jeffrey C. Hall
   p.   cm.
Includes bibliographical references and index.
ISBN 0-253-34258-9 (alk. paper)
1. Gettysburg, Battle of, Gettysburg, Pa., 1863. 2. United States. Army of the Potomac. I. Title: Stand of the United States Army at Gettysburg. II. Title: Stand of the US Army at Gettysburg. III. Title.
E475.53.H215 2003
973.7'349—dc21   2003004407

1 2 3 4 5 08 07 06 05 04 03

Indiana University Press gratefully acknowledges
the generous support of the following sponsors:

Donald F. Carmony
Standiford H. Cox
Dr. and Mrs. George F. Rapp
Eli Lilly and Company
Martin Foundation
Alan T. and Jane Nolan
Margaret Cole Richards in memory of Ralph D. Richards
Frank E. and Nancy M. Russell
Martin D. Schwartz
Gordon L. and Beatrice St. Angelo
William A. Welsheimer, Sr.
Thomas W. and Bernadette Zoss

and

Friends of Indiana University Press

Publication of this book is also made possible in part
with the assistance of a Challenge Grant from
the National Endowment for the Humanities,
a federal agency that supports research, education,
and public programming
in the humanities.

For my father, Joseph W. Hall,
who taught me much about American history
when he was a newspaper reporter covering the U.S. Senate.
Born less than 50 years after the battle of Gettysburg,
he provided a link of sorts to that time;
120 years later, he took me there
and changed everything.

Contents

Preface xi

Acknowledgments xv

Introduction xix

Cast of Characters xxv

Key to Maps xxx

1. The Roads to Gettysburg: Virginia, Maryland, and Pennsylvania in June 1863 1
2. July 1: The Union Suffers a Setback but Gains a Great Position 35
3. July 2: The Climax of the Battle 79
4. July 3: The Great Gamble Lee Could Have Won and the Federals' Finest Hour 169
5. Aftermath: The Pursuit and Escape of the Army of Northern Virginia 245

Appendixes

A. The Cavalry Battle at Brandy Station (June 9) 267
B. The Loudoun Valley Cavalry Battles (June 17–21) 277
C. The Fighting Near Brinkerhoff's Ridge (July 2) 285
D. The Cavalry Battle East of Gettysburg (July 3) 289
E. The Fatal Cavalry Charge of Elon Farnsworth (July 3) 299
F. Organization of the Union and Confederate Armies at Gettysburg 309
G. The Potential and Problems of Small-Arms Fire at Gettysburg 325

Notes 333

Bibliographic Essay 371

Index of Military Units 395

Subject Index 401

Preface

Trails of troubles,
Roads of battles,
Paths of victory,
We shall walk

—Bob Dylan

Don't know much about history
Don't know much biology

—Sam Cooke

I am a biologist, but I claim to know as much history as biology on one subject: The Battle of Gettysburg. However, this may not be much, to paraphrase the late, great Sam Cooke.

What most fascinates me about this battle is that the Northern army had been traveling incredibly troubled trails before the cataclysm at Gettysburg in the summer of 1863. Yet the Army of the Potomac rose up and stood its ground, fighting "as they had never fought before," in the words of historian Bruce Catton.[1] One of his many books on the American Civil War is *Glory Road,* the second volume in Catton's trilogy on the Army of the Potomac. The title of this volume points to its final section, four glorious chapters about Gettysburg. Why am I writing about the roads of battle that led there—and to victory for the U.S. army? I do so for three reasons.

First, I wish to make the battle completely comprehensible for readers and battlefield visitors. The former may have found the large number of recent Civil War battle books tough pills to swallow. The writers delve deeply into the minutiae of these campaigns. It is altogether fitting and proper that they do so. However, I sense that readers often have no idea what piece of geography is involved and sometimes do not even know whether it is the Union or the Confederate army whose units are being described in terms of their location and actions. In contrast to the form of these increasingly standardized battle books, this work is intended for the basic student of the battle. Such a person is likely to know something about Gettysburg but realizes the desirability of understanding its details—if not all of them, then at least in terms of maximal clarity. Thus, this work is salted throughout with visual and charted aids. Each part of the battlefield is displayed in the context of the overall geography, and graphic depictions of the involved in a given action make it clear where they fit in the larger scheme of things.

Another feature of this book is the clarifying treatment of the three days at Gettysburg: I focus on a key element of each of them. These salient events are discussed briefly in the Introduction and are offered as mnemonic devices that may cut through some of the battle's complexities, even though some of these interpretations might be regarded as iconoclastic reaching.

My second aim is to reinterpret certain elements of the events and their meaning. A number of historians today debunk the idea that Gettysburg was *the* (or even *a*) turning point of the Civil War. They might be wrong. Some of my interpretive remarks address this issue. In any case, it is correct to say that the Union victory at Gettysburg did not make it inevitable that the Confederate rebellion would fail. Yet had the Federals—against expectations—not stood their ground with such courage and élan during those three days in July, the American Civil War might have turned out differently. This study of the Gettysburg campaign thus focuses renewed attention on whether it was one of the pivotal armed conflicts in human history. Was it "the battle that constituted America's hinge of fate"?[2]

The third impulse that prompted this book is connected with how easy it is to become obsessed with the Battle of Gettysburg. I probably have fallen prey to this. However, many participants in the campaign also exhibited a preoccupation with it starting not long after the war. Moreover, many historians subsequently implied a certain degree of obsession by their relentless studies of the campaign. My first communication about the battle with a professional historian—James M. McPherson, author of *Battle Cry of Freedom*—exemplifies how Gettysburg can dominate one's thoughts and feelings about the American Civil War.

McPherson's work, a superb narrative about this era of American history, seems to have started the "Civil War Boomlet," as some would have it.[3] This culminated in the early 1990s with the airing of Ken Burns's Public Broadcasting System series on the Civil War in the fall of 1990 and the release of the movie *Gettysburg* in the fall of 1993, five years after *Battle Cry of Freedom* appeared. Soon after reading that book, I wrote to its author:

> A few months ago, I read *Battle Cry of Freedom*. On the back cover was printed that it "is in every respect a deeply satisfying book." I, too, found this to be so. I am most grateful to you for having written it. I even thank your wife, as you did, for suggesting the title; this, as well, was perfect.... I did not become aware of *Battle Cry of Freedom* "at random." Instead, I was primed to notice a review of it, because of a weekend trip I took a few years ago. Thus, I learned some of the details of the battle [of Gettysburg]. Not long afterward, I began to read a bit and became dimly aware of the context of these three days in 1863. One result was that—to this day—I am completely fascinated by the bravery displayed by the Union troops and by the startling performance of the Union officers during that battle. As you wrote, the Union solders had previously performed with great valor, often to be undermined fatally by their officers (at least their Generals). Gettysburg was different.... Superficially ... this may account for the results of the 2nd and 3rd of July.... I also remember being struck ... by a sense of fright as to what could have happened on those days, and thus to the nation, had it not been for the 20th Maine, the 1st Minnesota, and for the fact that—at the top of that "gentle slope"—one regiment ran and *26 stood their ground*.[4]

Professor McPherson responded:

> Thank you for your letter of December 3 with its warm words of praise.... You were a discerning reader who, like me, apprehends viscerally as well as intellectually the meaning of the Civil War. And nowhere can this meaning be grasped more meaning-

fully than at Gettysburg. I take students there nearly every spring, and it is always a powerful experience for me as well as for them.[5]

These excerpts provide a caveat about this book: It may be an overly personal account of a historical event to which I have indeed reacted viscerally, but it is not a truly original one. It is largely a synthesis of what others have written about the campaign. What I hope is useful about this treatment is that many of the accounts and analyses I draw upon are recent ones that have uncovered much new information and present fresh insights.[6] I also found myself digging into primary sources to which I was guided by secondary works and interactions with valued colleagues whose contributions are described in the Acknowledgments. Following their lead, I include some of my own interpretations resulting from my modest forays into accounts written by participants in the campaign and my discussions with several Civil War historians.

An analogy to coming to grips with primary documents about Gettysburg was my seminal exposure to a firsthand source of sorts. This occurred in the summer of 1983, when I traveled from Boston to the Maryland suburbs of Washington because my sister and her then husband were coming in from the West Coast to visit my parents, my brother, and his family. The day we arrived, father announced: "Well, we will all go to Gettysburg tomorrow" (a Saturday in July almost exactly 120 years after the battle). We started our tour by seeing the "Electric Map" in the Visitors Center located on Cemetery Hill.[7]

For those of you who visit Gettysburg, whether or not you wade through the crowded Visitors Center: Bravo. Anyone interested in one of the reasons why this nation has *not yet* perished from the earth should go there. You will perceive in microcosm how ordinary Americans helped preserve that society (and what it may still stand for) for at least an additional 140 years. Perhaps you will find this volume to be a useful guidebook; one that has been produced by someone who not only is fascinated by the overall sweep of the battle, but who also claims to know the details of its venues and events like the back of his hand—which is shaking as he, a biologist, plunges into the writing of military history.

If you do visit Gettysburg and tour the battlefield, you may find it a fascinating, possibly moving, experience. You should cover the ground involving all three days of the battle. I learned as much in the late 1980s. When my family and I visited Gettysburg in July of 1983, however, we walked only parts of the field in a nonsystematic manner, confining our movements to the well-known venues on and just south of Cemetery Hill. Nevertheless, enough of the impact of the battle's events sank in for something to dawn on me late that Saturday afternoon. I thus cried out (although I think this was merely to myself): "My God, the Union could have lost this battle!"—and with it, possibly the war. But it did not. The goal of this book is to explain how and why.

Acknowledgments

James M. McPherson formally introduced me to the Gettysburg battlefield, permitting me to accompany his tour groups three times in 1989 and 1990. A few years later, Professor McPherson recommended me as a tour guide to a group of biologists who were going to Gettysburg for their yearly retreat. This forced me to dig deeper into the subject on my own in preparation for a lecture prior to my leading that regiment-sized organization over the battlefield.[1] Still later, McPherson read a draft of this book and provided suggestions for beefing up Chapter 4. He subsequently provided a useful document about the immediate aftermath of the Gettysburg battle.

David H. Fischer, who teaches a course at Brandeis University on the Civil War era, permitted me to audit it in the late 1980s and early 1990s and gave me the opportunity to lecture to one of his classes about Gettysburg. A few years later, Professor Fischer, on behalf of the Brandeis History Department, asked me to develop a course on the Gettysburg campaign. Trite as it may sound, nothing focuses the mind like having to hold forth semipublicly on a subject. This instructional pressure also made me think that I should write a book about the subject, at least to help students find their way through its complexities.

I met Dr. Thomas A. Desjardin in 1992 when he was a graduate student at the University of Maine. It took me ten seconds to realize that Tom is a gifted, knowledgeable, yet skeptical student of the Gettysburg campaign. Over the ensuing years, Dr. Desjardin has taken me over several sectors of the battlefield at the place he calls "Mecca."[2] Tom has also presented lectures to my Brandeis students (lending his wisdom as much to me as to them); discussed with me countless Gettysburg events and issues; and shared what seems kilograms' worth of research materials and information about the campaign. If all this were not enough, Dr. Desjardin performed a critical reading of the manuscript.

Alan T. Nolan read drafts of this book as well. I cannot thank him enough for the many comments and corrections he provided, along with several insightful questions. Mr. Nolan kindly recommended it to the publisher and supplied further comments on the manuscript as part of that process.

Major Dale E. Wilson, Ph.D. (U.S. Army, Ret.), edited this work extremely carefully and supplied a host of substantive corrections, augmentations, and insights. He not only knows what he is talking about in general, but also has studied Gettysburg and traversed the battlefield on numerous occasions while teaching military history at the United States Military Academy. I am most grateful for Major Wilson's remarkable thoroughness and how he improved the prose. Emmy Ezzell, Marvin Keenan, Jane Lyle, and Robert Sloan at Indiana University Press labored long, hard, and most effectively on behalf of the book's preparation and production.

Charles C. Fennel, James Clouse, and Wayne E. Motts taught me much about various components of the battle by leading me on densely verbal tours of portions of the battlefield. During several oral and electronic conversations, Mr. Motts also instructed me in exquisite, insightful detail about the actions of July 3.

Another consummate Gettysburg professional, D. Scott Hartwig, patiently absorbed my many e-mail requests for information and opinions. He came through with several facts and numerous insights from among the vast number he has accumulated over the years as a historian at the Gettysburg National Military Park. In 1999, he kindly sent me an excellent manuscript about the third day of the battle (two years before I became aware of the obscure group of published articles that included Hartwig's). I engaged in similar e-mail exchanges with Wayne Motts, Glenn LaFantasie, Eric Wittenberg, David Shultz, Carol Reardon, Paul Shevchuk, David Palmer, and Kent Gramm. These historians, all of whom have published on various aspects of the Gettysburg campaign, shared their knowledge and transmitted stimulating arguments related to their areas of expertise.

After I met him in Washington, D.C., Mr. LaFantasie set up a further meeting at Gettysburg. The insights he put forth there—near Little Round Top—were not only appreciated in particular, but drove home the point that there is nothing like studying the battle on the field.

General H. Norman Schwarzkopf (U.S. Army, Ret.), Dr. Jay Luvaas, Maj. Mark Stricker, Bevin Alexander, and Thomas K. Tate furnished me with letters and documents that helped me better understand given features of the campaign or its historiography.

The Brandeisians who opted to take History 150B, "Gettysburg: Its Context in the American Civil War," shared with me the results of their research because I required it of them. Several of their term papers told me more than I knew before about some aspects of the campaign. I single out the following students (in chronological order) whose papers were especially valuable: Rachel Klein, Jeremy Markowitz, Andrea Samber, William Shapiro, Brad Silverman, Cian Dane, Boris Klimovitsky, Lloyd Patashnick, Jake Steinmann, Seth Baylies, Josh Green, Mark Kestnbaum, Adam Weinstein, Seth Coffey, and Jeffrey Li.

There are many students of the battle who have neither taken a course on the subject nor written about it. I wanted the opinions of such persons as much as I wanted those of professionals. The latter may take me to task for failing to mention something they consider important or criticize my interpretations, but this work is not really aimed at them. Thus, my question for the "ordinary" but potentially avid pupil was: "Is it comprehensible and interesting, whether or not you can also fact-check a given page?" I appreciate the efforts of the following Gettysburg aficionados, all of whom know the story from their readings and from walking the battlefield, for taking the time to read the manuscript and respond: William F. Ingraham, Prof. Bambos Kyriacou, Burton R. Hall, and Comdr. Adele Langevin (U.S. Naval Reserve).

Mr. Ingraham also instructed me about Civil War weapons, teaching me how to shoot them so that I might gain a small appreciation of what the soldiers at Gettysburg were coping with when they used their rifled muskets. Bill also introduced me to Andrew H. Addoms III, a Civil War arms expert who has been a researcher and craftsman for forty years; he taught me about nineteenth-century small arms in general and about their usage at Gettysburg in particular. I have grown to appreciate not only the potential but also the problems associated with these weapons, leading me to the conclusion that Civil War shoulder arms were not the wonder weapons some historians have made them out to be. Scott Hartwig is one who does not quite claim that rifled muskets were wondrous. But he and I engaged in valuable e-mail exchanges in which he refuted the thesis developed by Mr. Addoms. Although Scott's knowledge cannot be denigrated in the least, I still wonder whether the firepower and accuracy of these famed weapons are not oft overstated. Such skepticism results in my claim that the "suicidal frontal assault" of Lee's army on July 3 *might* have succeeded. I thank the researchers just named for helping me to think about the issues that underlie this hypothesis.

Andy Addoms also introduced me to two of his colleagues, William O. Adams and Jack Richardson. They are Civil War arms experts in their own right.[3] This trio has been engaged in a ten-year study of the cavalry fighting east of Gettysburg on July 3. I have benefited from hearing their iconoclastic views about this action in both informal conversations and lectures. Mr. Addoms twice lectured to my Gettysburg course, deepening my appreciation of this battle within the battle.

I am grateful to Prof. Michael Ashburner for encouraging me to go to Hill 107 on the island of Crete. He subsequently helped me root around the lower reaches of a library at Cambridge University, where I found archival information on the military action that occurred there, and which led to an essay within Chapter 3. For an anecdote that comes into play within that chapter, I thank Dr. Joseph E. O'Tousa, who provided information about Notre Dame University, where he works. In Chapter 3 especially, the actions of Southern regiments from Alabama are notable. I always thought that those men should be called "Alabamans," but Dr. Michael K. Cooper, a native of that state, made it clear they are "Alabamians."

Finally, I wish to thank those who helped make the visual aids that take up almost as many pages as the text. Tom Desjardin, Bill Ingraham, and Wayne Motts provided starting materials for the maps; then Joshua Robbins and Bill Nelson digitized my drawings and scrawls and made numerous presentational improvements within the maps and charts. The aforementioned Maj. Dale Wilson, in conjunction with his extremely attentive editing efforts, pointed out many places where both the maps and charts needed substantive corrections and enhancements.

Introduction

The narrative that follows is meant to be a straightforward account of the Gettysburg campaign. My aim is to describe and explain the major events of the campaign and the battle that took place at Gettysburg in early July 1863. Although it is the centerpiece of the narrative, the story begins three weeks before the battle, when Gen. Robert E. Lee's Army of Northern Virginia began its second invasion of the North, and ends with its return to Virginia in mid-July.[1]

I provide little about the broad context of the campaign—which would require discussing several aspects of the Civil War up to that time (roughly its midpoint), including the reasons Lee may have invoked for invading the North after his victory at the Battle of Chancellorsville in early May 1863. Also, I do not pause to provide mini-biographies of participants in the campaign. My intent was to avoid going into excruciating detail about Gettysburg by writing "more and more about less and less."[2]

Even though this work is relatively limited in scope and depth, perhaps it is not thoroughly straightforward. The underlying theme is that Gettysburg was a battle that was *not* sitting there for the Confederates to win or lose. Many interpretive accounts of the Gettysburg campaign—starting soon after the Civil War and continuing into the 1990s—were, in effect, written from a Southern perspective: Why did the rebels "*lose* the battle of Gettysburg?" What were the critical "Confederate *mistakes*?" That is a reasonable way to view Gettysburg, but it should be equally appropriate to approach this subject from the Union standpoint. The Northern army in the East won the battle, thus the title of this book. Perhaps this work belongs under the heading "the victors write the history." That remark has been uttered many times, disparagingly so. However, it is arguably inapplicable to the history of the American Civil War in general and to the Battle of Gettysburg in particular.[3]

In an attempt to balance the scales, I suggest that the Army of the Potomac was much more than a passive participant that benefited solely from Confederate errors of strategy and tactics. Instead, the *actions* of the Northern officers and men made an enormous difference. For the rebels' part, the ordinary soldiers at Gettysburg fought with great skill and courage, and I believe their commanders planned and performed better than the conventional wisdom would have it. The Southerners did not flounder at Gettysburg; they were outfought. I am glad they were. This is not meant to be a smug snarl. I echo remarks made in 1880 by Woodrow Wilson about the Civil War as a whole. Wilson was born in the South fifty-seven years before he became president, and had previously expressed great admiration for the fighting spirit and achievements of the Confederate armies. Nevertheless he was relieved that their cause did not succeed.[4]

Some passages in this book are more overtly discursive than are others, whether or not they connect with the theme described above. The interpretive passages offer my opinions about what an event from the campaign or the battle might mean: why it happened, what supposedly would have happened had it *not* occurred, and what might have been in the mind of a key participant at a particular place and time. Some of these interpretations may be based on thin evidence, but they will frequently connect with some of the new scholarship about Gettysburg. Elements of that writing have reopened some old issues and controversies or attempted to modify our understanding of classic accounts. Some of those old stories within the story did not ring true anyway.

Certain remarks interspersed within the narrative offer analogies comparing aspects of the Gettysburg campaign to other events in military history. Such connections to battles in other wars could introduce unwanted distractions into the account, but maybe not. The historical interludes, involving military episodes ranging from 216 B.C. to 1991, have two potentially useful purposes. On one hand, they are object lessons that may make us dig deeper into the Gettysburg issue to which the analogy connects. On the other, they create rhetorical pauses—refreshing ones I hope, because the narrative can be pretty heavy going at times in terms of the Gettysburg details, explicated as they must be (I believe) by all the pictorial and diagrammatic aids that are previewed later in this Introduction. To lighten further the reader's burden, many details about some event or participant's actions in the campaign or the battle are relegated to the endnotes.

Since the appearance of Edwin B. Coddington's *The Gettysburg Campaign: A Study in Command* in 1968, few comprehensive works on the subject have been produced. His book was the Gettysburg bible for thirty-five years and may remain so (but see note 6 of the Preface). In addition to describing the entire campaign on a moment-to-moment basis, Coddington provides much wisdom about why it all came out the way it did. In fact, his account is the most salient exception to the notion that the South lost at Gettysburg. I follow Coddington's lead without coming anywhere near his level of detail. Whatever fresh insights I may have added are the result of researching material over the past fifteen years that was obviously unavailable to this author.

Contemporary Gettysburg scholarship involves three categories of works. First are the macro accounts, including Harry W. Pfanz's narratives about the fighting in the southern sector of the battlefield on July 2 and what happened in the northern reaches of the field; Dr. Pfanz's and David G. Martin's accounts of events on July 1; John Michael Priest's revisionist account of the events on July 3, buttressed significantly by the more orthodox but equally detailed works written by Jeffry D. Wert and Earl J. Hess (these are the first book-length treatments since the 1950s that cover the third day of the battle). Next come the micro accounts based on the authors' studies of particular events within the campaign. Third are a number of descriptive and interpretive essays collected within four books and twenty-eight issues (so far) of a periodical devoted entirely to the Gettysburg campaign.[5]

The three core chapters herein, covering the events of July 1–3, each commence with my analysis of the "phases of battle." It may be useful to return to these lists in order to keep things straight—which is especially difficult to do for July 2 (Chapter 3). Each of these chapters (2–4) contain explications of certain mnemonic devices, which purport to boil down the significance of each day's fighting to one simple point:

1. July 1 was a crucial prelude to what most people believe are the main components of the battle as they occurred on the next two days. The Confederates prevailed on the first day—but not really. The Union soldiers (comprising about 20 percent of the army) eventually gave way, but they had "fought like furies" for several hours and eventually rallied at a superb location elsewhere on the battlefield.[6] The occupation of this position by the Army of the Potomac was *not an accident*.

2. On July 2, the *blunder* of Maj. Gen. Daniel E. Sickles—a Union large-unit commander who dangerously redeployed his entire force—redounded to the Army of the Potomac's benefit. Sickles set in motion a series of *crises,* ultimately, *manageable* ones, which crucially accentuated the confidence of the Union commanders; this held them in such good stead during:

3. The destruction—*not the failure*—of Pickett's Charge on July 3. This was triggered by the results of a little-known component of the Federal artillery defense, and by the stand of Lt. Col. Franklin Sawyer's 8th Ohio Regiment. These events, which took place on one wing of the Union line, occurred well before the climax of the charge.

Several of the opinion-laden passages will perilously attempt to address the meaning of a particular micro event (such as that involving the Ohioans just mentioned). The purpose of most of these observations is to lay out the issues revolving around the various *what ifs* of the campaign. What if such-and-such an attack had been made? What if one defensive move or another had failed? Anguished interpretations revolving around these moments within the battle were first put forth shortly after the campaign ended. I have heard several contemporary students of the battle say, accompanied by figurative rending of their garments, "If only! . . . then it would have all come out differently." Yet certain less passionate interpreters say things like: "It really would not have mattered anywhere near as much you think." I will try to deal with what such old and newly unearthed bones of contention mean in the particular, as well as discuss why certain of these attempts at predicting the past are wrongheaded on general principles. Some of the aforementioned analogies to what *did* happen on pertinent occasions elsewhere in military history will be gingerly offered as object lessons, aimed at trying to get us unstuck from preoccupations with the *what ifs* of Gettysburg.

The maps that depict troop positions and movements are designed to take the reader from a given low-resolution diagram of a major portion of the field down to a subsequent series of high-magnification images. Within each such map, the main diagram is accompanied by a you-are-here image, permitting readers to orient themselves with regard to the battlefield as a whole.

Many explanatory charts identifying the units involved accompany the maps. Thus, the organizational location of a given small unit, whose actions are being described at the moment, will be referred to in the text. The ninety-four-thousand-man Union army at Gettysburg was divided into seven infantry corps, the Artillery Reserve, and a cavalry corps. The seventy-two-thousand-man Confederate army consisted of three infantry corps and a cavalry division.[7] To discern just where a regiment, say, comes from within its army, a series of vertical or horizontal arrows will so indicate. For example:

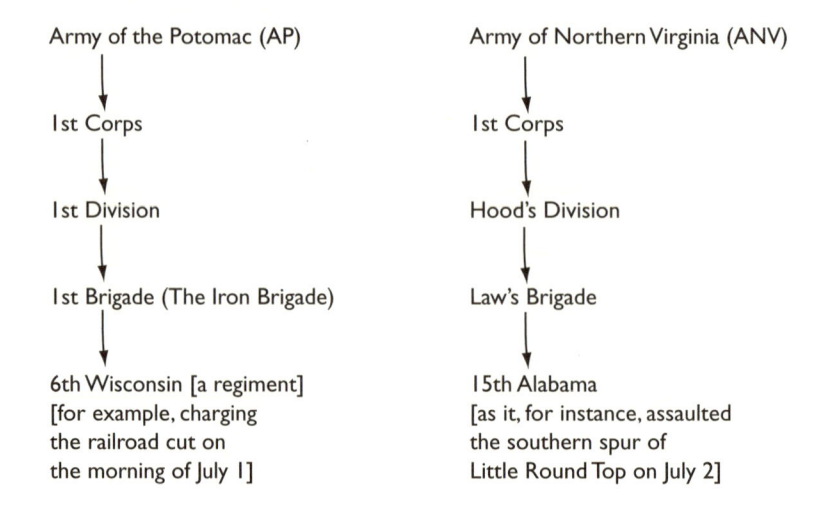

Army of the Potomac (AP)	Army of Northern Virginia (ANV)
↓	↓
1st Corps	1st Corps
↓	↓
1st Division	Hood's Division
↓	↓
1st Brigade (The Iron Brigade)	Law's Brigade
↓	↓
6th Wisconsin [a regiment] [for example, charging the railroad cut on the morning of July 1]	15th Alabama [as it, for instance, assaulted the southern spur of Little Round Top on July 2]

Some of these hierarchical diagrams will include branching arrays if the accompanying text describes the actions of several regiments together. Rarely is it necessary to describe the actions of units smaller than a regiment. However, occasionally, the activities of an intra-regimental company come into play.

The remainder of this introduction is devoted to a description of the organization of Civil War armies. This is designed to familiarize the reader with organizational rules for the two armies that fought at Gettysburg. Thus, for example, mention of a "division" of troops will trigger a quick appreciation of its numerical strength. What follows is rather dry, so the reader may wish to skip to the beginning of Chapter 1.

- The smallest of the armies' subunits were companies, which were supposed to be composed of a hundred men commanded by a captain. A ten-company regiment was led by a colonel. Brigades, generally commanded by a brigadier general (by definition), consisted of from three to five regiments. Some three to five brigades made up a division, which usually was commanded by a major general. Finally, there were two to three divisions per corps. Corps were led by major generals in the Union army and lieutenant generals in the Confederate army. The rationale for this is explained below.

- Many of these rules were honored only in the breach, especially in terms of the numbers of men per unit and the rank of the officer who commanded it. By 1863, virtually all regiments had been whittled down to far fewer than 1,000 men. Colonels routinely commanded 1,000–2,000-man brigades, and brigadier generals led some of the 3,000–7,000-man divisions. A quick scan of Appendix F will highlight these facts.

- Notwithstanding the violation of so many organizational rules during the Civil War, certain regularities are worth noting because they highlight differences between the Army of the Potomac and the Army of Northern Virginia. The Union infantry corps at Gettysburg were smaller than those in the Confederate army. The relevant importance of rebel corps is correlated with the command of these 20,000-man units by lieutenant generals in the Army of Northern Virginia (whereas this exalted rank was reserved for the commander of all the Union armies, Ulysses S. Grant, and was not conferred upon him until 1864). Robert E. Lee was the only full general in the Army of Northern Virginia (the rank did not exist in the Union army).

- Corps in both armies were numbered; divisions and brigades in the Union army likewise. Confederate divisions and brigades were named after their commanders. An idiosyncratic exception was that four Confederate brigades in each of two 3rd Corps divisions—those commanded by Maj. Gens. Henry Heth and W. Dorsey Pender—were numbered. However, this work will refer to those brigades by the names of the officers who led them. Volunteer regiments in both armies were given an ordinal number based on the chronological order in which they were formed, followed by the name of the state in which they were raised. It is not unusual to encounter regiments from large Northern states (such as New York and Pennsylvania) with numbers ranging above one hundred, a phenomenon not seen in Southern regiments or Northern ones from small to midsize states. Confederate and Union regiments were not dissimilar in size, but the range of the strengths of these units varied widely in both cases. Union Regular Army regiments were given an ordinal number followed by the designation "United States."

- In Confederate brigades, homogeneity with regard to state of origin was the rule (with some exceptions) due to the reorganization of the Army of Northern Virginia that occurred several months before Gettysburg. This was relatively rare in the Army of the Potomac. Indeed, many of its brigades contained a mixture of regiments from the West (any state off the eastern seaboard) and from the East. In this regard, regiments in the Army of the Potomac were drawn from all of the eastern states and half of the western ones.[8]

- Certain Union brigades were distinct in character, and took on what became almost formal names, as alluded to above. Examples include the Irish Brigade in the 1st Division of the Federal 2nd Corps (which was made up of regiments from three states) and the Philadelphia Brigade in the 2nd Division of the same corps.[9] Nicknamed Confederate brigades existed as well. The Texas Brigade (not all of which was from Texas) in Maj. Gen. John Bell Hood's Division of the 1st Corps took pride in its origin, whereas the Stonewall Brigade in Maj. Gen. Edward Johnson's Division of the 2nd Corps was named in honor of its former commander, Lt. Gen. Thomas J. "Stonewall" Jackson, who died after the Battle of Chancellorsville on May 10, 1863. Some regiments also were given nicknames (see Appendix F).

- Infantry divisions and brigades tended to be larger in the Army of Northern Virginia—including five regiments in most brigades; this was relatively rare in the Army of the Potomac. Such numerical differences contributed to each of the Confederate corps being much larger than those in the Army of the Potomac—although the overall Union forces outnumbered the Confederates at Gettysburg by approximately ninety thousand to seventy thousand.

- "Overall" takes into account artillerymen and cavalry troopers, as well as ordinary foot soldiers. The artillery units were attached to the infantry components of both armies in complex ways.[10] Each corps in the Army of the Potomac contained an artillery brigade; there was also a large, separate Artillery Reserve. Confederate divisions each had their own artillery units. Despite this widespread deployment of artillery units both armies had artillery chiefs. Colonel E. Porter Alexander, who performed essentially in that role on an ad hoc basis on July 3, is a prominent figure in both Gettysburg and Civil War history. The smallest artillery units in both armies, equivalent to infantry companies, are called batteries.

- Major General Alfred Pleasonton commanded the Army of the Potomac's Cavalry Corps, the creation of which was one of Maj. Gen. Joseph Hooker's innovations earlier that year (prior to Chancellorsville, during which campaign Hooker commanded the Army of the Potomac). The exploits of the semi-independent Confederate cavalry command, led by Maj. Gen. J. E. B. Stuart throughout much of the war in the East, are well known. The nature of that independence in the late spring and early summer of 1863 is a matter for renewed controversy with regard to the June phase of the Gettysburg campaign. The cavalry in the Union army was further subdivided into divisions, and in both armies into brigades and regiments in a manner similar to the infantry.[11] The free-ranging Union cavalry units, newly unleashed from attachment to the infantry corps, are most relevant to both the start of the campaign in early June 1863, and to the opening of the battle on July 1.

Cast of Characters

Officers who played a prominent or important role—at least at a certain moment during the battle, another stage of the campaign, or both—are listed alphabetically. In parentheses after the unit to which the officer belonged appears the date or dates during which that character's principal actions occurred.

The Army of the Potomac

Ames, Brig. Gen. Adelbert, brigade then division commander, 11th Corps (July 1, 2)

Barlow, Brig. Gen. Francis, division commander, 11th Corps (July 9)

Baxter, Brig. Gen. Henry, brigade commander, 1st Corps (July 1)

Bigelow, Capt. John, battery commander, Artillery Reserve (July 2)

Birney, Maj. Gen. David B., division commander, 3rd Corps (July 2)

Buford, Brig. Gen. John, division commander, Cavalry Corps (June 9, 30, July 1, 6–12)

Caldwell, Brig. Gen. John C., division commander, 2nd Corps (July 2)

Carroll, Col. Samuel S., brigade commander, 2nd Corps (July 2)

Chamberlain, Col. Joshua L., regimental commander, 5th Corps (July 2)

Colvill, Col. William, Jr., regimental commander, 2nd Corps (July 2)

Coster, Col. Charles R., brigade commander, 11th Corps (July 1)

Cowan, Capt. Andrew, battery commander, 6th Corps (July 3)

Crawford, Brig. Gen. Samuel W., division commander, 5th Corps (July 2)

Cushing, Lt. Alonzo H., battery commander, 2nd Corps (July 3)

Custer, Brig. Gen. George A., brigade commander, Cavalry Corps (June 30, July 3)

Cutler, Brig. Gen. Lysander, brigade commander, 1st Corps (July 1)

Devereux, Col. Arthur F., regimental commander, 2nd Corps (July 3)

Devin, Col. Thomas C., brigade commander, Cavalry Corps (July 1)

Doubleday, Maj. Gen. Abner, division, then corps, then division commander, 1st Corps (July 1)

Farnsworth, Brig. Gen. Elon, brigade commander, Cavalry Corps (June 30, July 3)

Gamble, Col. William, brigade commander, Cavalry Corps (July 1)

Gates, Col. Theodore B., regimental commander, 1st Corps, and led a "demi-brigade" on Cemetery Ridge (July 3)

Geary, Brig. Gen. John W., division commander, 12th Corps (July 2)

Gibbon, Brig. Gen. John, division commander, 2nd Corps (July 2, 3)

Gilsa, Col. Leopold von, brigade commander, 11th Corps (July 1, 2)

Graham, Brig. Gen. Charles K., brigade commander, 3rd Corps (July 2)

Greene, Brig. Gen. George S., brigade commander, 12th Corps (July 2)

Gregg, Brig. Gen. David McM., division commander, Cavalry Corps (June 9, July 2, 3)

Gregg, Col. J. Irwin, brigade commander, Cavalry Corps (June 9, July 3)

Hancock, Maj. Gen. Winfield S., 2nd Corps commander (July 1–3)

Hays, Brig. Gen. Alexander, division commander, 2nd Corps (July 2, 3)

Hazlett, Lt. Charles E., battery commander, 5th Corps (July 2)

Hooker, Maj. Gen. Joseph S. "Fighting Joe," army commander (June 9–28)

Howard, Maj. Gen. Oliver O., 11th Corps commander (July 1)

Humphreys, Brig. Gen. Andrew A., division commander, 3rd Corps (July 2)

Hunt, Brig. Gen. Henry J., chief of artillery (July 3)

Ireland, Col. David, regimental commander, 12th Corps (July 2)

Jones, Lt. Marcellus E., company commander, Cavalry Corps (July 1)

Kilpatrick, Brig. Gen. Judson, brigade then division commander, Cavalry Corps (June 9, 30, July 3)

McGilvery, Lt. Col. Freeman, brigade commander, Artillery Reserve (July 2, 3)

Meade, Maj. Gen. George G., 5th Corps, then army commander (June 11, June 28–July 14)

Merritt, Brig. Gen. Wesley, brigade commander, Cavalry Corps (July 3)

Morrill, Capt. Walter G., company commander, 5th Corps (June 21, July 2)

Newton, Maj. Gen. John, division commander, 6th Corps; then 1st Corps commander (July 1, 2)

O'Kane, Col. Dennis, regimental commander, 2nd Corps (July 3)

O'Rorke, Col. Patrick H., regimental commander, 5th Corps (July 2)

Osborn, Maj. Thomas W., artillery brigade commander, 11th Corps (July 3)

Paul, Brig. Gen. Gabriel R., brigade commander, 1st Corps (July 1)

Reynolds, Maj. Gen. John F., 1st Corps commander (July 1)

Rittenhouse, Lt. Benjamin F., battery commander, 5th Corps (July 3)

Robinson, Brig. Gen. John C., division commander, 1st Corps (July 1)

Ruger, Brig. Gen. Thomas H., brigade then division commander, 12th Corps (July 2)

Sawyer, Lt. Col. Franklin, regimental commander, 2nd Corps (July 3)

Schurz, Maj. Gen. Carl, division commander, 11th Corps (July 2, 3)

Sickles, Maj. Gen. Daniel E., 3rd Corps commander (July 2)

Smith, Capt. James E., battery commander, 3rd Corps (July 2)

Stannard, Brig. Gen. George J., brigade commander, 1st Corps (July 3)

Steinwehr, Brig. Gen. Adolph von, division commander, 11th Corps (July 1)

Stone, Col. Roy, brigade commander, 1st Corps (July 1)

Sykes, Maj. Gen. George, 5th Corps commander (July 2)

Trobriand, Col. P. Regis de, brigade commander, 3rd Corps (July 2)

Vincent, Col. Strong, brigade commander, 5th Corps (July 2)

Wadsworth, Brig. Gen. James S., division commander, 1st Corps (July 1)

Ward, Brig. Gen. J. H. Hobart, brigade commander, 3rd Corps (July 2)

Warren, Brig. Gen. Gouverneur K., Chief of Engineers (July 2)

Webb, Brig. Gen. Alexander, brigade commander, 2nd Corps (July 2, 3)

Weed, Brig. Gen Stephen H., brigade commander, 5th Corps (July 2)

Willard, Col. George L., brigade commander, 2nd Corps (July 2)

Williams, Brig. Gen. Alpheus S., division commander and temporary corps commander, 12th Corps (July 2)

The Army of Northern Virginia

Alexander, Col. E. Porter, artillery battalion commander, 1st Corps (July 2, 3)

Anderson, Brig. Gen. George T., brigade commander, 1st Corps (July 2)

Archer, Brig. Gen. James J., brigade commander, 3rd Corps (July 1)

Armistead, Brig. Gen. Lewis A., brigade commander, 1st Corps (July 3)

Avery, Col. Isaac E., brigade commander, 2nd Corps (July 2)

Barksdale, Brig. Gen. William, brigade commander, 1st Corps (July 2)

Benning, Brig. Gen. Henry L., brigade commander, 1st Corps (July 2)

Brockenbrough, Col. J. M., brigade commander, 3rd Corps (July 1, 3)

Chambliss, Col. John R., Jr., brigade commander, Cavalry Division (June 9, July 3)

Daniel, Brig. Gen. Junius, brigade commander, 3rd Corps (July 1)

Davis, Brig. Gen. Joseph R., brigade commander, 3rd Corps (July 1, 3)

Doles, Brig. Gen. George, brigade commander, 3rd Corps (July 1)

Early, Maj. Gen. Jubal A., division commander, 2nd Corps (June 26, July 1, 2)

Ewell, Lt. Gen. Richard S., 2nd Corps commander (June 10, 14–15, July 1–3)

Fry, Col. Birkett D., regimental then brigade commander, 3rd Corps (July 3)

Garnett, Brig. Gen. Richard B., brigade commander, 1st Corps (July 3)

Gordon, Brig. Gen. John B., brigade commander, 2nd Corps (July 1)

Hampton, Brig. Gen. Wade, brigade commander, Cavalry Division (June 9, July 3)

Harrison, James, civilian scout, 1st Corps (June 28)

Hays, Brig. Gen. Harry T., brigade commander, 2nd Corps (July 2)

Heth, Maj. Gen. Henry "Harry," division commander, 3rd Corps (July 1)

Hood, Major Gen. John B., division commander, 1st Corps (July 2)

Imboden, Brig. Gen. John D., commander of detached cavalry brigade (July 4–6)

Iverson, Brig. Gen. Alfred, brigade commander, 2nd Corps (July 1)

Jenkins, Brig. Gen. Albert G., brigade commander, Cavalry Division (June 15, July 2)

Johnson, Maj. Gen. Edward, division commander, 2nd Corps (July 2, 3)

Johnston, Capt. Samuel R., staff engineer (July 2)

Jones, Brig. Gen. William E. "Grumble," brigade commander, Cavalry Division (June 9)

Kemper, Brig. Gen. James L., brigade commander, 1st Corps (July 3)

Kershaw, Brig. Gen. Joseph B., brigade commander, 1st Corps (July 2)

Lane, Brig. Gen. James H., brigade commander, then temporarily a division commander, 3rd Corps (July 3)

Lang, Col. David, brigade commander, 3rd Corps (July 2, 3)

Latimer, Maj. J. W., artillery battalion commander, 2nd Corps (July 2)

Law, Brig. Gen. Evander McI., brigade then division commander, 1st Corps (July 2, 3)

Lee, Brig. Gen. Fitzhugh, brigade commander, Cavalry Division (July 3)

Lee, Brig. Gen. W. H. F. "Rooney," brigade commander, Cavalry Division (June 9)

Lee, Gen. Robert E., army commander (June 8–July 14)

Longstreet, Lt. Gen. James, 1st Corps commander (July 2, 3)

Mahone, Brig. Gen. William, brigade commander, 3rd Corps (July 2)

Marshall, Col. James K., regimental then brigade commander, 3rd Corps (July 3)

McClellan, Maj. Henry, staff officer, Cavalry Division (June 9)

McLaws, Maj. Gen. Lafayette, division commander, 1st Corps (July 2)

Oates, Col. William C., regimental commander, 1st Corps (July 2)

O'Neal, Col. Edward A., brigade commander, 2nd Corps (July 1)

Pender, Maj. Gen. William Dorsey, division commander, 3rd Corps (July 1, 2)

Perrin, Col. Abner M., brigade commander, 3rd Corps (July 1)

Pettigrew, Brig. Gen. James J., brigade then division commander, 3rd Corps (June 30, July 1, 3, 14)

Pickett, Maj. Gen. George E., division commander, 1st Corps (July 3)

Posey, Brig. Gen. Carnot, brigade commander, 3rd Corps (July 2)

Ramseur, Brig. Gen. Stephen Dodson, brigade commander, 2nd Corps (July 1)

Robertson, Brig. Gen. Beverly H., brigade commander, Cavalry Division (June 9)

Robertson, Brig. Gen. Jerome B., brigade commander, 1st Corps (July 2)

Rodes, Maj. Gen. Robert E., division commander, 2nd Corps (July 1, 2)

Scales, Brig. Gen. Alfred M., brigade commander, 3rd Corps (July 1, 3)

Semmes, Brig. Gen. Paul Jones, brigade commander, 1st Corps (July 2)

Steuart, Brig. Gen. George H. "Maryland," brigade commander, 2nd Corps (July 2)

Stuart, Maj. Gen. J. E. B. "Jeb," Cavalry Division commander (June 8, 9, 16–23, 28, 30, July 1–9)

Trimble, Maj. Gen. Isaac R., without field command (attached to Ewell's 2nd Corps), then "demi-division" commander (July 1, 3)

Wilcox, Brig. Gen. Cadmus M., brigade commander, 3rd Corps (July 2, 3)

Witcher, Lt. Col. Vincent A., battalion commander, Cavalry Division (July 3)

Wofford, Brig. Gen. William T., brigade commander, 1st Corps (July 2)

Wright, Brig. Gen. Ambrose R., brigade commander, 3rd Corps (July 2)

The Stand
of the U.S. Army
at Gettysburg

Map Key

- ▬ Confederate troops
- ▬ Union troops
- ▨ Confederate cavalry
- ▨ Union cavalry
- ⁞⁞⁞⁞ Initial troop positions
- ---→ Troop movements
- ⊔ or ⚶ Artillery
- ▦ Wooded area
- ▦ Orchard
- ═ Road
- ┝┿┥ Railroad
- ······ Fence
- ♦ Houses or buildings
- ⌒ Elevation contours
- ∼ Creeks or streams
- 🪨 Rocks

CHAPTER ONE

The Roads to Gettysburg

Virginia, Maryland, and Pennsylvania in June 1863

On June 15, the first troops of the Army of Northern Virginia ... slip across the Potomac ... and begin the invasion of the North. It is an army of seventy thousand men ... of remarkable unity, fighting for disunion.... Their main objective is to draw the Union army out into the open where it can be destroyed.... Late in June the Army of the Potomac, ever slow to move, turns north at last to begin the great pursuit which will end at Gettysburg. It is a strange new kind of army, a polyglot of vastly dissimilar men, fighting for union. There are strange accents and strange religions and many who do not speak English at all. Nothing like this army has been seen upon the planet. It is a collection of men from many different places who have seen much defeat and many commanders. They are volunteers: last of the great volunteer armies.... They have lost faith in their leaders but not in themselves. They think this will be the last battle, and they are glad that it is to be fought on their own home ground.

—Michael Shaara, *The Killer Angels*

Alpheus S. Williams rode his horse along a ridge south of the town of Gettysburg, Pennsylvania. The ridgeline ran in a north-south direction. He was exhausted, frazzled. It was early in the evening of July 2, 1863.

Willliams was a brigadier general in the Army of the Potomac. At the age of almost fifty-three, he was among the oldest officers in the army. He had received a generalship because of his military experience, having commanded a Michigan regiment in the Mexican War in the 1840s (Connecticut-born, Yale-educated, he wound up in Detroit where he had been a lawyer, judge, and newspaper owner). But Williams had no formal military training; he was a citizen soldier—one of a vast number of such men who fought in the American Civil War.

At Gettysburg, General Williams commanded a large unit of infantrymen, a five-thousand-man force known as a division. Part of his unit had been called from a northern sector of the battlefield to make an emergency reinforcement of the left of his army's line. The Union left had been embattled since the late afternoon by a ferocious attack made by a large force from the Army of Northern Virginia, the principal Southern army in the East during the Civil War.

Williams had led the reinforcements himself, deploying from a place known as Culp's Hill, down to a southern section of the low rise of ground that stretched below the town. That place would come to be called Cemetery Ridge, but it was nameless on this Thursday in July. The troops led by General Williams had helped to repel the Confederate attack as advanced elements of the rebels approached the ridge.

The defense of the Northern army's left wing had been a close-run thing, but Williams sensed that the Southerners' assault had at last lost its steam, narrowly failing to take its objective; the fighting seemed to be winding down on this part of the field.

The men of Williams's division were positioned near a house owned by a Pennsylvania farmer, George Weikert, north of a patch of woods located down the western slope of the ridge. As these Union soldiers had been posted at the Weikert farm after their counterattack in this vicinity, Williams searched for someone who could tell him of the situation. Was the army still in peril? Should he receive further orders?

Finally, General Williams came upon a large group of officers. They surrounded the commander of the Army of the Potomac, Maj. Gen. George Gordon Meade. Panting from physical exhaustion and apprehension, Williams learned that the Union army had repelled the enemy attacks all along the line. Relief flowed over him, mirroring the feelings expressed by his fellow officers. When someone remarked to General Meade how desperate the fight had been, the commander replied, "but it is all right now, it is all right now."[1]

Neither Williams, Meade, nor the others knew it as nightfall approached on the first Thursday in July, but the crisis of the Battle of Gettysburg had just passed. The Army of Northern Virginia's chance for victory in the campaign was gone.

The story of how the armies in the East got to this point—traveling the roads to Gettysburg and arriving at this crucial moment of the battle that happened there halfway through the war—will now be told. In this narrative we will see that the more famous fighting at Gettysburg was yet to come—during the afternoon of July 3. How the climax of the battle occurred on the previous day will be revealed as we contemplate the meaning of the vast number of events that took place in Virginia, Maryland, and Pennsylvania during the early summer in the third year of the Civil War.

As novelist Michael Shaara suggested in the passage quoted at the beginning of this chapter, Gettysburg *was* in some ways the last battle in the eastern theater of the American Civil War. North of the Mason-Dixon line in the summer of 1863, the final in a series of discrete clashes occurred between the Army of the Potomac and the Army of Northern Virginia. In the ensuing years of the Civil War the conflict in the East became one long, grinding horror. However, before and through the time of Gettysburg, seven distinct large battles were fought in Maryland, Pennsylvania, and Virginia.[2]

Winston Churchill once said, "In a war, the English army always manages to win one battle, and that is the last one."[3] This statesman also referred, however unwittingly, to a largely English-speaking army in the New World in the 1860s: the Army of the Potomac. In the foreword to *The Killer Angels*, Michael Shaara speaks intriguingly about that army's "last battle" in the summer of 1863. If this is meaningful, it is because it connects with a view of the Civil War in the East in 1864 and early 1865 as one relentless campaign: a given engagement proceeded directly into the next, as the Northern army drove the Southern one southward then finally west to Appomattox, Virginia. However, Shaara overstated the extent to which the emerging pluralism of the northern United States was represented within the Army of the Potomac.[4] Yet the novelist usefully alluded to the nature

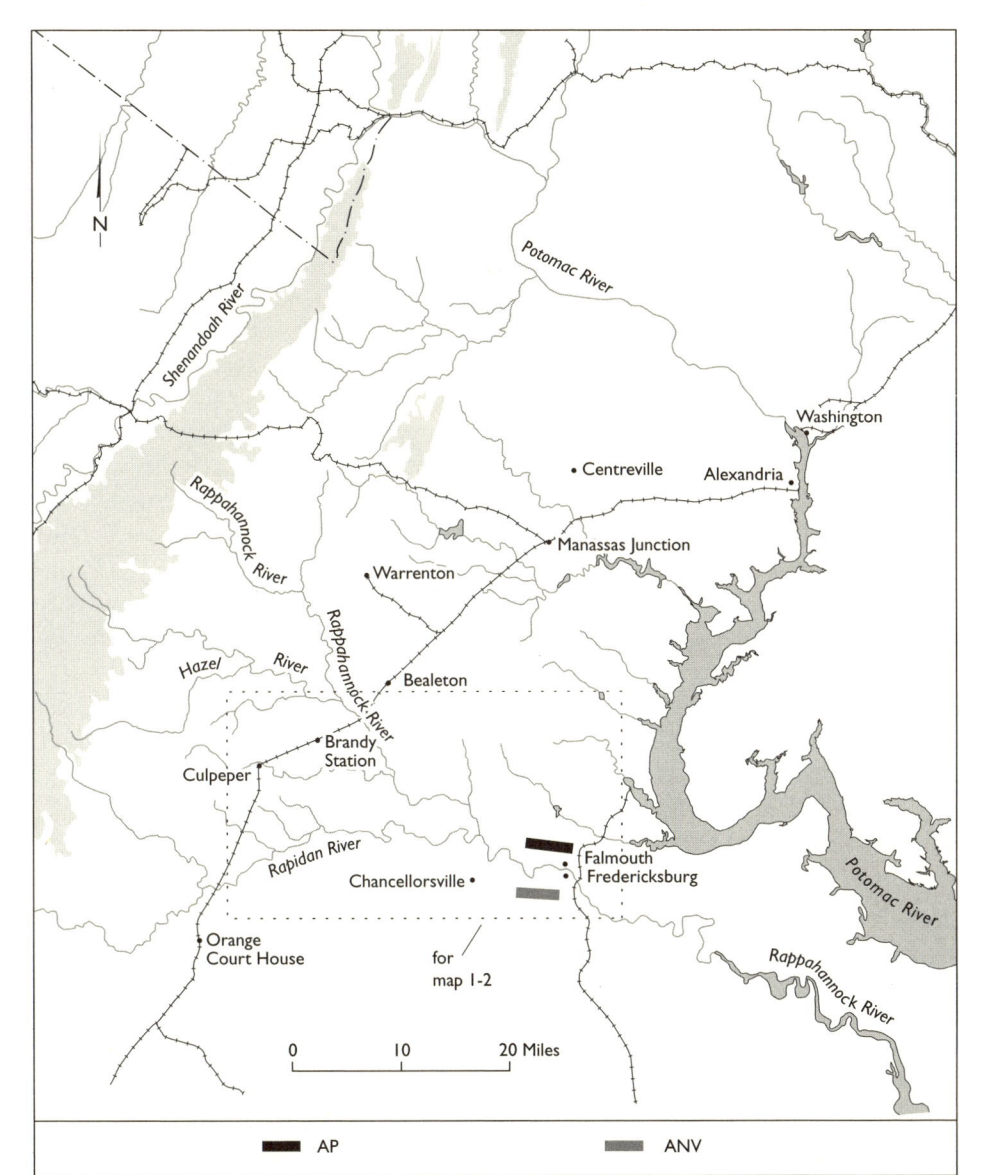

**Map 1-1
Fredericksburg and vicinity,
early June 1863**

of the Civil War in the East, before and up to the time of the Gettysburg campaign. The Union and Confederate armies would collide. One side would be defeated, or it would realize it had failed to win in the strategic sense. Then it would retreat across the nearest river.

In early June 1863, these two great armies faced each other across the Rappahannock River, which flows past the town of Fredericksburg, north of the York River, then into the sea at Virginia's eastern seaboard.[5]

The positions of the Federal and Confederate armies in the late spring of 1863 are diagrammed in map 1-1. The Army of Northern Virginia, commanded by Gen. Robert E. Lee, faced northward, and the Army of the Potomac, led by Maj. Gen. Joseph S. "Fighting Joe" Hooker, was oriented to the south. Additional details of the opposing forces are depicted in map 1-2.[6]

THE ROADS TO GETTYSBURG   3

The First Battle of Brandy Station

Phases of Campaign:

a. The First Battle of Brandy Station (described in detail in Appendix A)

b. Ewell moves north, taking the lead of the other corps and taking the town of Winchester

c. Fighting Joe Hooker fights—seemingly against moving north

d. Cavalry forces clash in Loudoun Valley (described in detail in Appendix B)

e. Stuart leaves Loudoun, moving counterclockwise then north—out of sight, out of mind?

f. Fighting Joe Hooker continues to fight—now, with his bosses—as the rebels range to the north and the east

g. Meade takes over: his cavalry finds Lee north of the Mason-Dixon line, where Stuart has strayed off to the east

In early June 1863 General Hooker ordered the army's cavalry to initiate a raid south of the nearby river. This meant fording the Rappahannock in a region northwest of Fredericksburg and Chancellorsville in the vicinity of Culpeper, Virginia, a town located between the Rappahannock and Rapidan Rivers (the latter flows into the former between Culpeper and Fredericksburg [map 1-1]). The result of this probe in force was the Battle of Brandy Station, which achieved fame as supposedly the largest cavalry battle ever fought in the New World.[7]

The details of this engagement—the first clash of arms in the Gettysburg campaign—are in Appendix A. In brief, the Federal cavalry was divided into two wings to make an aggressive reconnaissance against the Confederate cavalry. The latter was posted near Culpeper (map 1-1) in early June. The first move against General Stuart's troopers by the northern component of the mounted Union force surprised the Southerners early in the morning on June 9. However, the rebels mobilized a series of emergency defensive moves and stalled the Federal attacks in this sector. Then the southern wing of Northern cavalrymen came onto the field, but they too were blocked by further deployments of Confederate cavalry units. After vigorous mounted fighting took place in the southern sector of the field, the long day of battle ended when the Union force broke off the engagement. It retired "in good order" to the north bank of the Rappahannock River.

What are we to make of this cavalry battle? Although it involved the largest number of cavalrymen to fight in a distinct battle in the Civil War, 3,000 of the approximately 11,000-man Federal force at Brandy Station were infantrymen. One feature of the outcome of this June 9 battle was that it was not an utter bloodbath.[8] The Federals suffered 866 casualties: 81 dead, 403 wounded, 382 missing—not a huge proportion, and several of the "missing" were truly that, because they eventually staggered back into Union camps. The Federal losses were a higher number and percentage than the 433 inflicted on the approximately 9,000 Confederate cavalrymen who fought at Brandy Station. Although the Union troopers had withdrawn in good order, they left the field to the rebel defenders. Nevertheless, the conventional wisdom is that Brandy Station was a draw. In this sense, the Federals had taken the initiative as cavalrymen—for the first time in the East—and in so doing startled Stuart's elite troopers. They did so squarely in the context of behaving as an independent force—not rampaging completely on their own, but operating as a separate large unit of attacking horsemen. Major Henry B. McClellan, an officer on General Stuart's staff, wrote later: Brandy Station "*made* the Federal cavalry."[9] This remark, written by a Confederate participant in retrospect (1885), has been echoed many times. On the flip side of the coin—minted on one side with the confidence gained by these Union cavalrymen—was stamped Stuart's supposed anxiety about being "surprised" on the morning of June 9. Thus, he may have overreached in order to put the shine back on his tarnished legend, the positive features of which happened in his own time. Perhaps his subsequent performances in the campaign and the battle at Gettysburg suffered as a consequence. As we shall see, this component of Brandy Station's meaning is debatable.[10]

Just a few weeks later, Brig. Gen. John Buford's 1st Cavalry Division, which initiated the Union attack at Brandy Station, played an important role in the actions that led to Gettysburg and in the fighting that opened that momentous battle.

The Army of the Potomac further reorganized the Cavalry Corps after Brandy Station,[11] and Jeb Stuart was loudly rebuked in the Southern press in mid-June for being startled into defensive action on the morning of June 9.[12]

June 3

Map 1-2
Positions of the armies near Fredericksburg

FEDERAL
INFANTRY
CORPS:

1st REYNOLDS
2nd HANCOCK
3rd SICKLES
5th MEADE
6th SEDGWICK
11th HOWARD
12TH SLOCUM

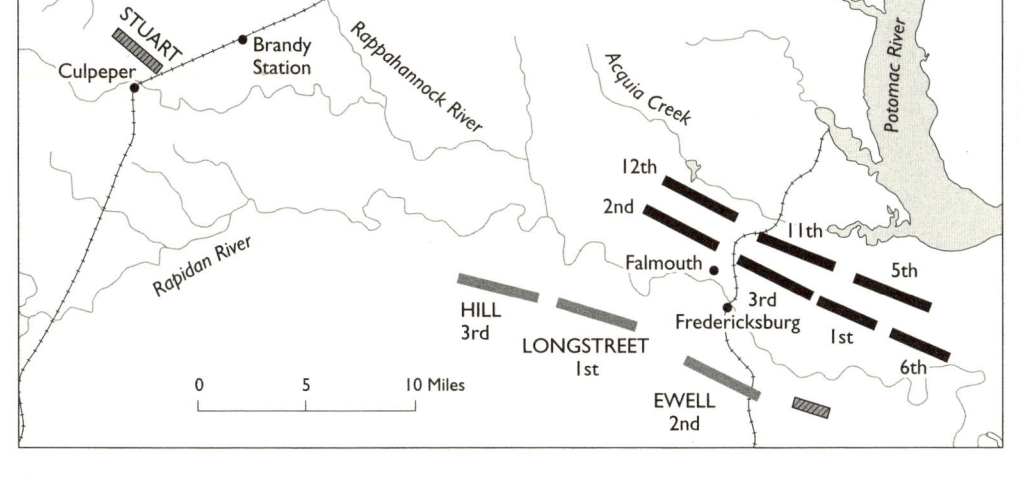

June 6–9

▨ Confederate Cavalry
▧ Union Cavalry

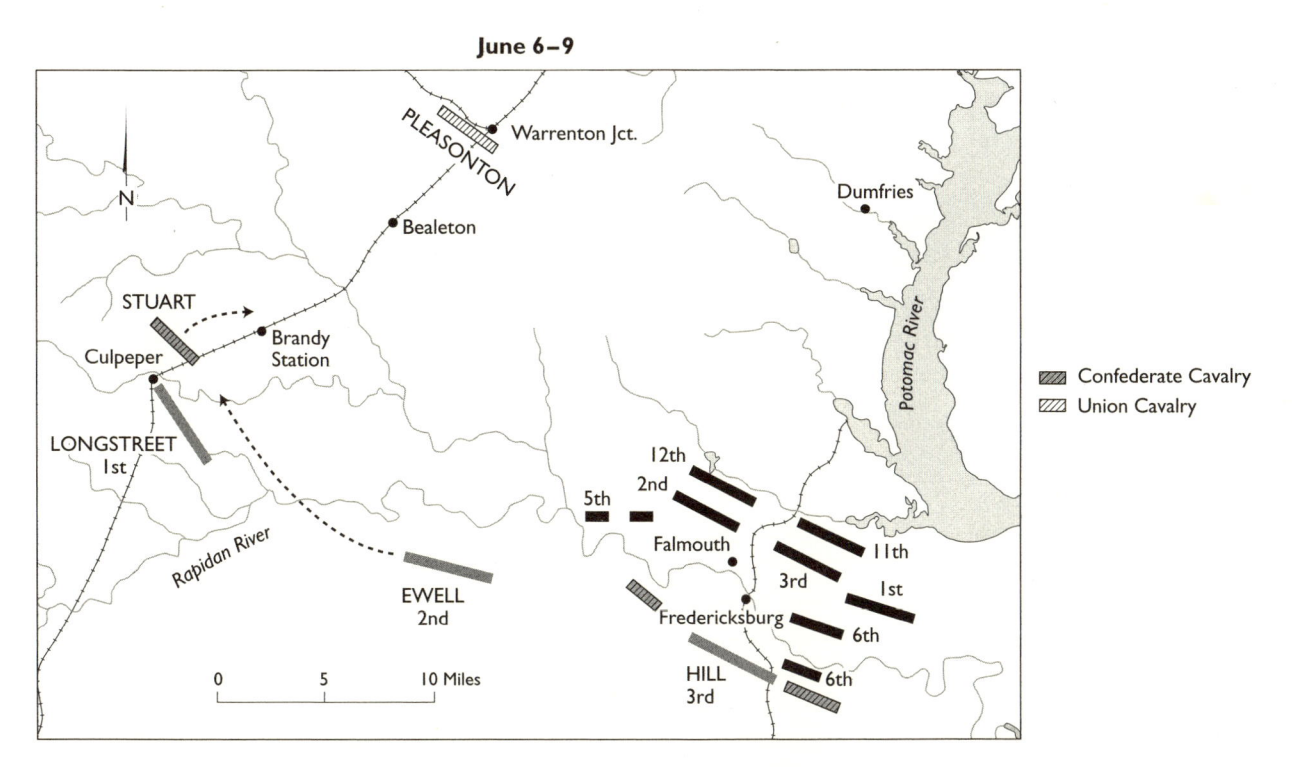

THE ROADS TO GETTYSBURG 5

Ewell Moves North, Taking the Lead of the Other Corps and Taking the Town of Winchester

We now shift our attention to infantry motions and actions. The northward advance of the Army of Northern Virginia was not to be delayed, the cavalry's surprise at Brandy Station notwithstanding. As planned, Lt. Gen. Richard S. Ewell's 2nd Corps, which had already swung round in a clockwise direction from Fredericksburg toward Culpeper, continued moving in this manner across the Rappahannock in the direction of the Shenandoah Valley (map 1-3). This crossing occurred on June 10. However, the *screening* movements that Stuart had originally been ordered to effect were delayed while his cavalry division recovered. Yet, Ewell *was* accompanied at the outset by one small cavalry unit, the 35th Virginia Battalion from Brig. Gen. William E. "Grumble" Jones's brigade (chart 1-1; see also chart A-3 in Appendix A).

One important feature of Ewell's assignment as the van of the three Confederate corps was that he was also ordered to take the town of Winchester, Virginia (maps 1-3 and 1-4), which was garrisoned by a force of some ten thousand Union soldiers who were not part of the Army of the Potomac (map 1-4). In addition to being a thorn in the side of the Confederacy in Virginia, the garrison force also posed a threat to the Army of Northern Virginia as it began to approach river crossing points into Maryland (maps 1-3 and 1-5).

Ewell attacked the Federals in and around Winchester, ultimately getting into their rear west and north of the town. He gobbled up much of the Union force, especially during its attempt to withdraw to Harper's Ferry, on June 14 and overnight into June 15. The actions included attacks on Union positions at Berryville and Martinsburg (map 1-4). Union casualties were 95 killed, 348 wounded, and 3,358 captured or missing (the remainder escaping northward to Harper's Ferry). In contrast, the rebels lost 47 killed, 219 wounded, and 3 captured in the Second Battle of Winchester. This Confederate success in the Shenandoah Valley was an auspicious beginning for the incipient invasion in general, and in terms of this newly minted corps commander's performance in particular.[13]

Another consequence of the movement toward Winchester was that General Ewell picked up Brig. Gen. Albert G. Jenkins's cavalry brigade (chart 1-1; map 1-4). This planned rendezvous occurred on approximately June 12–13 at Cedarville, a small town just north of Front Royal (map 1-3), shortly after Ewell passed westward through the Blue Ridge Mountains at Chester Gap on June 12 (maps 1-3 and 1-4). Jenkins's troopers had been on patrol in the Winchester area, keeping tabs on the Union garrison troops. Jenkins would accompany Ewell all the way into Pennsylvania (ultimately, well to the north and east of Gettysburg). This exemplifies an important fact: the invading Confederate infantrymen were not totally unscreened as they proceeded northward.

Ewell's corps crossed the Potomac at Shepherdstown, West Virginia, over the

Chart 1-1
Marches and positions of Confederate units, large and small, mid-June

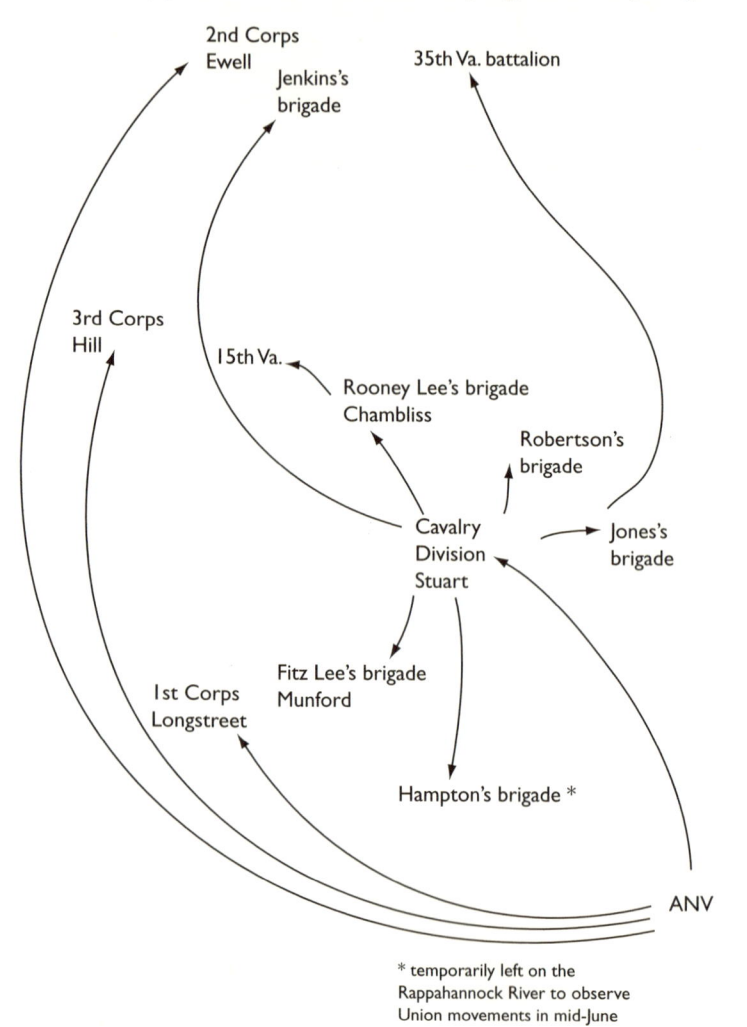

* temporarily left on the Rappahannock River to observe Union movements in mid-June

6   THE STAND OF THE U.S. ARMY AT GETTYSBURG

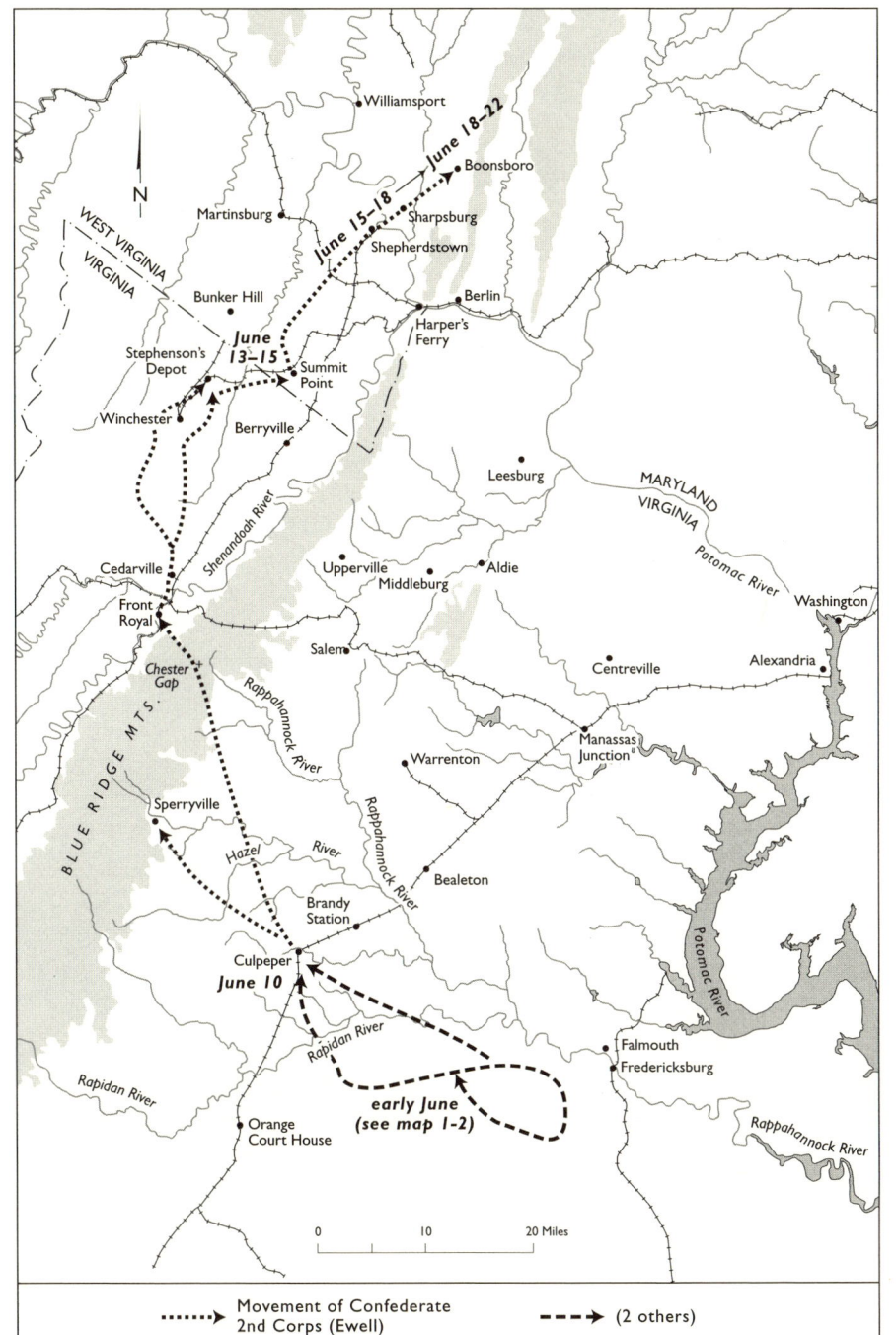

Map 1-3
Ewell's Confederate corps moves north

course of June 15–22 (map 1-3).[14] On June 22, under orders from Lee to range rather far to the north and the east, he began moving into Pennsylvania (maps 1-6 and 1-8).

The next large Confederate unit to escape from the Federal force facing it and join the Army of Northern Virginia's march north was Lt. Gen. Ambrose P. Hill's new 3rd Corps (chart 1-1). They were the last to leave Fredericksburg (maps 1-2 and 1-4), marching away from that town on June 15 along a route similar to the one taken by Ewell (map 1-5). Therefore, the Army of Northern Virginia was becoming quite strung out (Ewell was already crossing into Maryland on this date).

Finally, Lt. Gen. James Longstreet's 1st Corps (chart 1-1) took off from the vi-

THE ROADS TO GETTYSBURG   7

Map 1-4 Movements of various large units, June 12–13

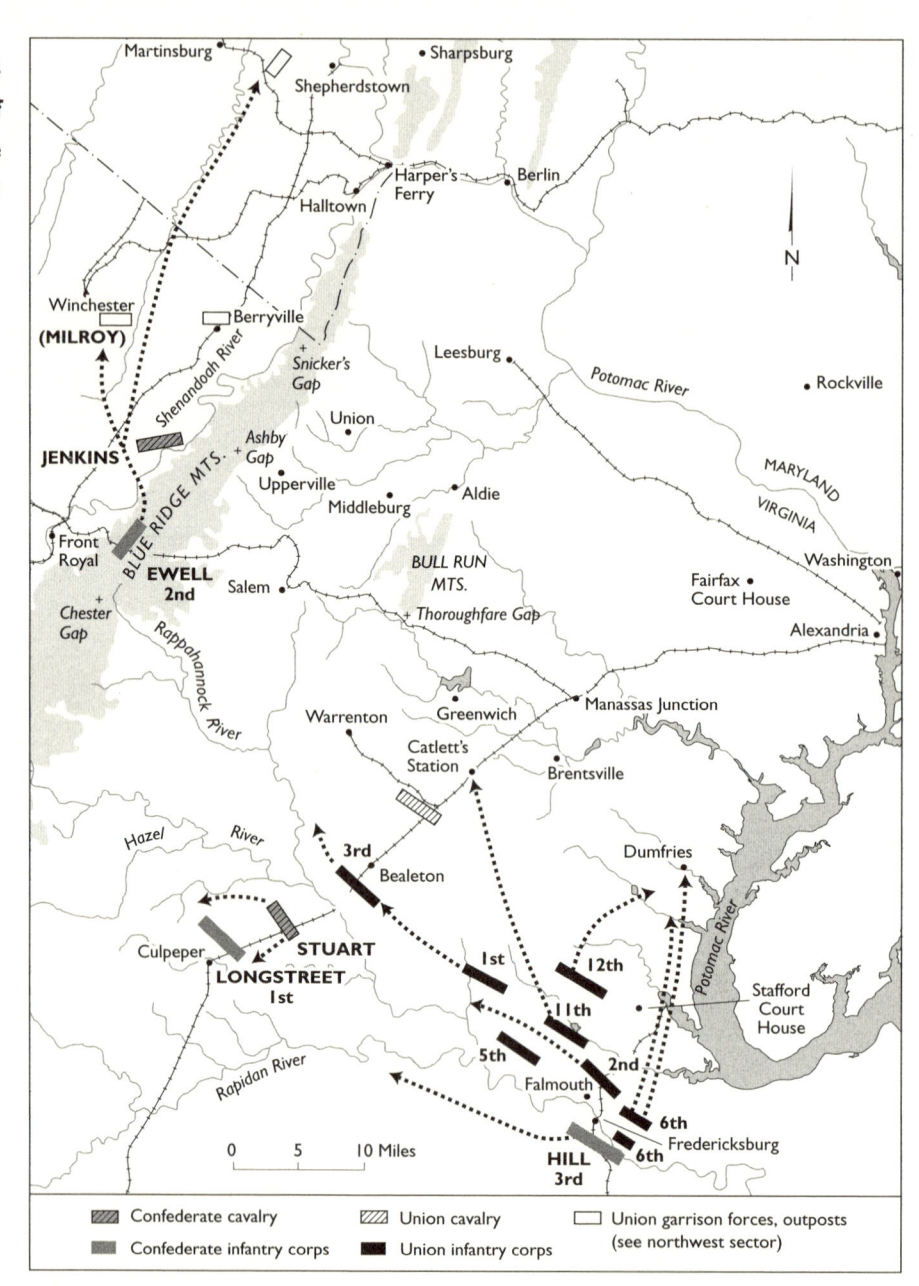

cinity of Culpeper (maps 1-4 and 1-5). He was ordered more directly northward from there, toward the eastern slopes of the Blue Ridge Mountains. Elements of Longstreet's corps then turned westward (map 1-5) and moved to occupy the mountain passes at Ashby's and Snicker's Gaps in the Blue Ridge (these rebels were at Ashby's by June 17–18). Stuart, whose troopers had by then rested and refitted after Brandy Station, covered this movement with several of his brigades (chart 1-1).[15] The passes just indicated were a short distance west of the Loudoun Valley, which is bordered on its east by the Bull Run Mountains (maps 1-4 and 1-5). With the Federal infantry beginning to move north and to the east of those mountains, Loudoun Valley was temporarily a no-man's-land—into which large numbers of opposing cavalry units were soon to move.

Longstreet was directed to march from Ashby's and Snicker's Gaps (map 1-5) into the Shenandoah Valley on June 19—but then moved quickly back into those passes to help Stuart defend them when the rebel cavalry came under pressure from Federal troopers trying to break westward through Stuart's screen west of

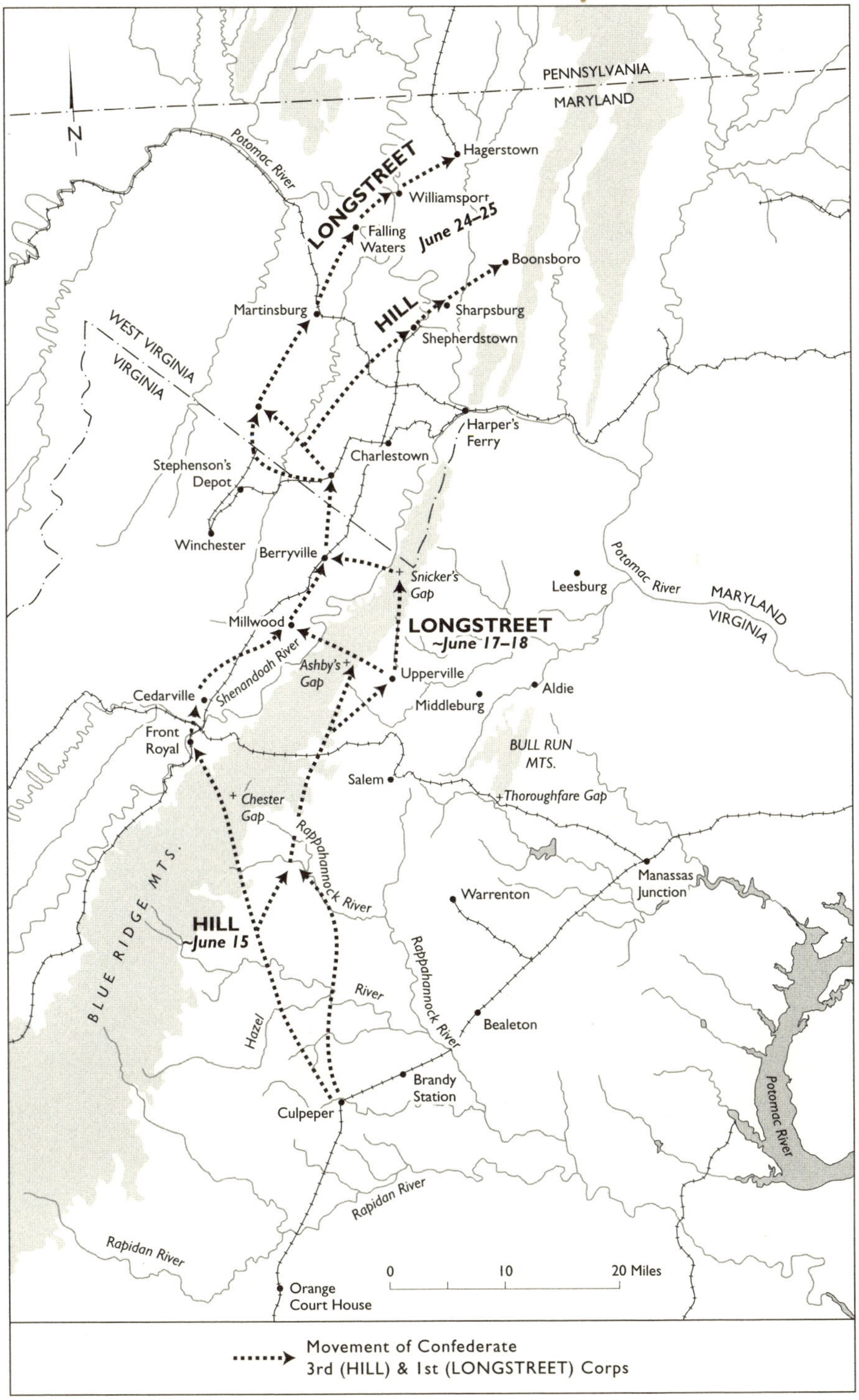

**Map 1-5
Confederate corps marching north**

Upperville, Virginia (Appendix B). While Longstreet guarded the mountain gaps, Hill was protected as he moved north through the Shenandoah Valley following the route taken by Ewell (maps 1-3 and 1-5).

Once the fighting in the Loudoun Valley subsided on June 21 (Appendix B), Generals Hill and Longstreet then were able to proceed with their northward marches in a fairly unimpeded manner. These two Confederate infantry corps began to cross the Potomac at Shepherdstown and Williamsport, with Hill fording the river near Shepherdstown on June 24 and Longstreet traversing it at Williamsport June 24–25 (maps 1-5 and 1-8).

THE ROADS TO GETTYSBURG   9

**Map 1-6
Positions of the armies, June 17**

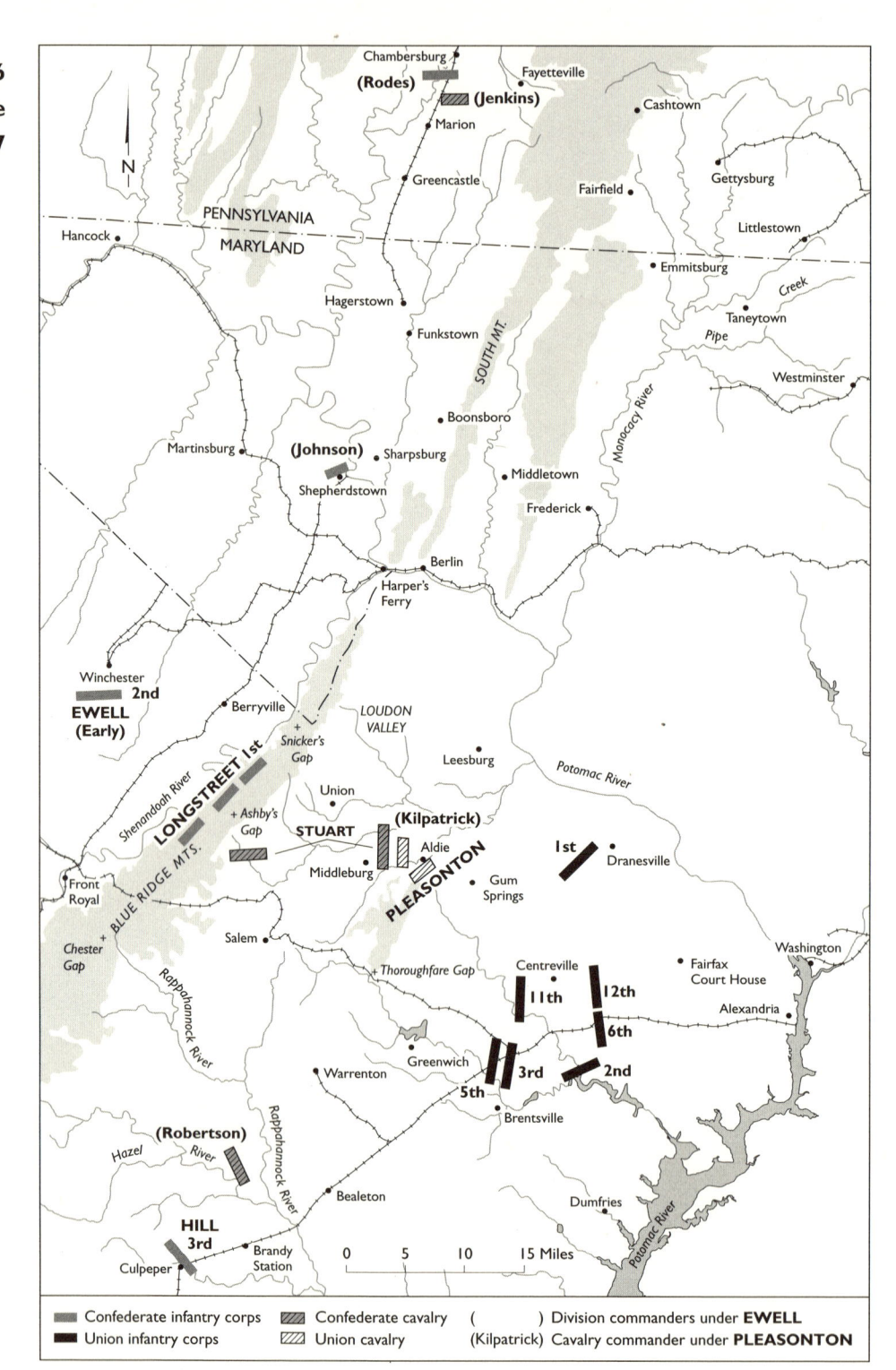

10 THE STAND OF THE U.S. ARMY AT GETTYSBURG

Fighting Joe Hooker Fights—Seemingly against Moving North

What was General Hooker and the Army of the Potomac up to as all this significant Confederate activity was occurring? Hooker sensed, in part as a result of Brandy Station, that the Army of Northern Virginia was on the move—and that it was proceeding northward. He also knew that his superiors would soon be yelling at him to both find Lee and protect Washington by keeping the Union army between the Confederate forces and the Federal capital. At this time (around mid-June), Hooker nevertheless wondered aloud whether he should move on Richmond since it was unprotected by Lee's army, which was headed in the opposite direction. However, by then President Lincoln was thoroughly aware of the importance of destroying that army and had lost interest in taking the Confederate capital.[16] The extent to which this is true ironically sidesteps the Federals' preoccupation with protecting *their* capital city, which thus more or less became the order of the day as it came down on Hooker's head from Lincoln's military high command.

This dithering on Hooker's part—the "on to Richmond" component of it being perhaps a way to *avoid* following Lee—contributed to his relatively late start northward. Yet, some of his units had left the banks of the Rappahannock by the night of June 13 (a Saturday).[17] By June 17, all of Hooker's corps had concentrated north of Fredericksburg in the vicinity of Centreville (maps 1-6 and 1-7). They languished there between Manassas and Leesburg for several days—not bestirring themselves to move farther northward until June 25 (map 1-8). On that day, the Army of the Potomac's vanguard—the 11th, 1st, and 3rd Corps—crossed the river (map 1-7). The remaining large Federal infantry units passed across the Potomac on the Twenty-sixth (2nd, 5th, and 12th Corps) and Twenty-seventh (6th Corps). Thus, the Army of the Potomac did not move into Maryland *that* much later than when the trailing Confederate corps did (map 1-5). However, the river crossing point used by the Union infantry was farther downstream (a pontoon bridge thrown across the Potomac at the location shown on map 1-7), so they were lagging in space if not in time. A loose corollary was that Hooker seemed during the first half of June to be in a Chancellorsville-like fog with regard to the positions and movements of the Confederate corps—although information on both of those matters was filtering into his headquarters.[18] Appreciating that at least some of those large rebel units were well out of Virginia as of the last week in June, Hooker's army finally left that state as well, but did not complete its crossing of the Potomac River until June 27 (map 1-7). By then the Union army commander was near the end of the line.

The slow progress and relative inactivity of Hooker's main body during the last two-thirds of June did not mean that all forces under his command were in that posture: the Union cavalry was on the move. As was previewed above, these activities involved elements of Brig. Gen. Alfred Pleasonton's command, pitted against elements of Stuart's cavalry division.

Cavalry Forces Clash in Loudoun Valley

The infantry was already on the move when the opposing cavalry forces shook themselves loose from the vicinity of the Rappahannock River. Map 1-9 diagrams the initial movements of these large units of horse soldiers—north from the Brandy Station on the part of the Confederates, and Warrenton plus Catlett

**Map 1-7
The Army of the Potomac's marches from the Rappahannock to the Potomac River**

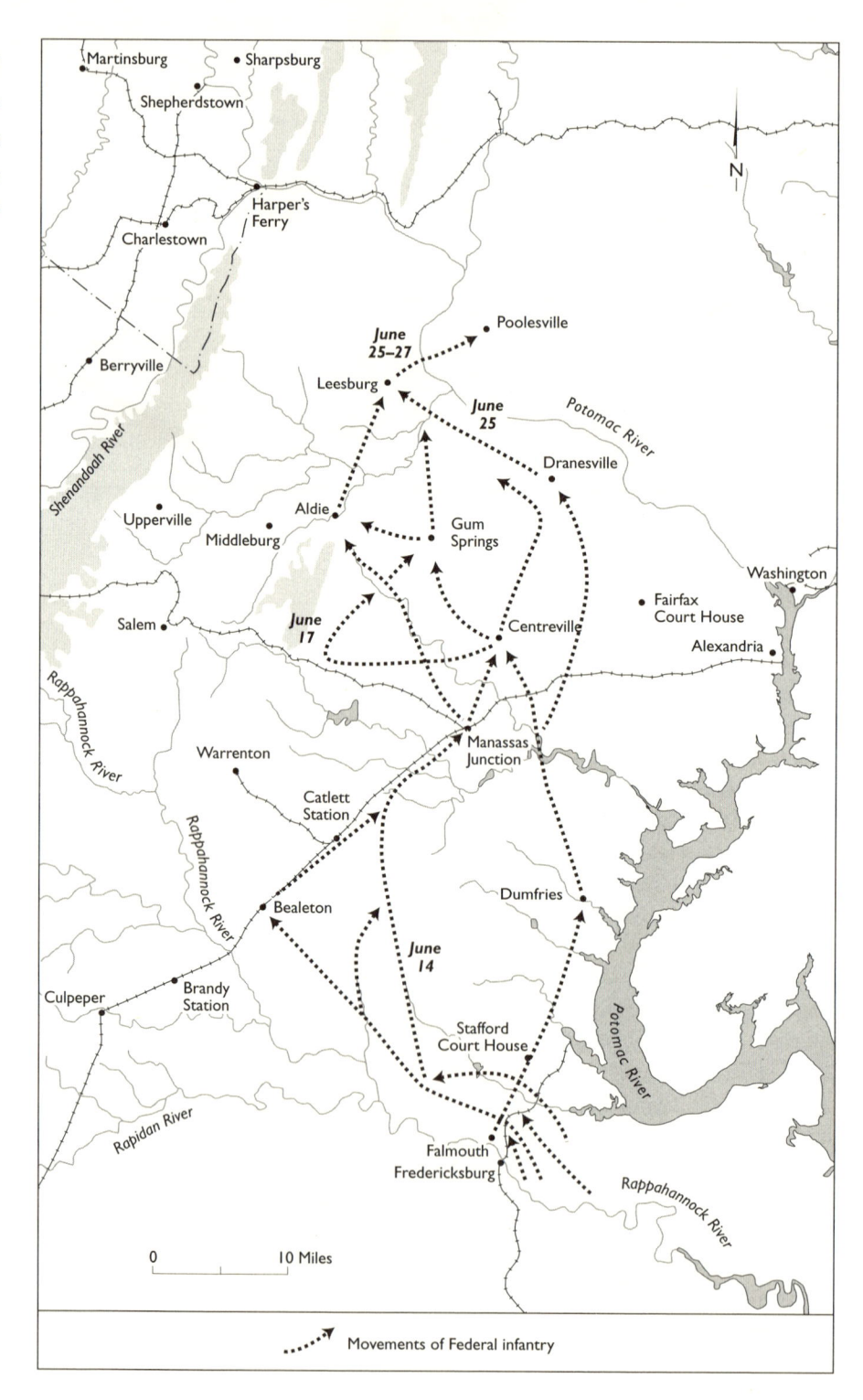

······▶ Movements of Federal infantry

Station on the part of the Federals (the latter location is just southeast of Warrenton and Warrenton Junction [maps 1-4 and 1-7]).[19]

General Stuart began his major northward rides an entire week after the Battle of Brandy Station, in conjunction with carrying out his formal duties: screening the rebel infantry's right flank as they moved across the Blue Ridge Mountains or toward the passes therein. The Union troopers, sensing that enemy foot soldiers were marching north, headed off after them. Their intent was not to stop the

Confederate infantrymen (assuming that was possible). Instead, General Pleasonton's aimed to poke their noses westward through certain of the Blue Ridge mountain passes in an effort to learn the Confederates' whereabouts and movements.

That both Confederate and Union cavalry were able to proceed with relative rapidity was unlikely to precipitate clashes between these mounted forces. What happened accordingly—in Loudoun Valley, between the two mountain ranges (maps 1-6 and 1-9)—is described in detail in appendix B.[20] It is enough to say here that the Federal troopers once again fought the Confederate horsemen to a series of drawn battles between June 17 and 21. However, Stuart's force did succeed, for the most part, in blocking the Union cavalrymen's attempts to reconnoiter west of the Blue Ridge. The opposing cavalry forces then recoiled from each other (in effect): The Federals rode east and then north, while Stuart moved south initially. Then the majority of his brigades swung round to the east before proceeding northward—into controversy.

Stuart Leaves Loudoun, Moving Counterclockwise Then North—Out of Sight, Out of Mind?

Jeb Stuart may have been frustrated, owing to the Battle of Brandy Station and those that occurred in the Loudoun Valley. These engagements cannot be designated "defeats" inflicted upon the rebel cavalry—and Stuart said as much, including what he proclaimed to his troopers.[21] Yet, the Federal cavalry had given Stuart a run for his money on June 9 and again from June 17 to 21. Following Brandy Station, he had been subjected to widespread criticism in the South, particularly in the newspapers. He was aware of these verbal attacks and the implication that the Union cavalry was coming into its own—although the public criticism mainly talked about Stuart having been surprised by the Federals' initiative. (Unanticipated attacks in the Civil War seemed constantly to invoke public outcries against commanders who were caught unaware.)

Some have argued that Stuart's actions after the Loudoun Valley battles were not influenced by the public outcry.[22] However, it seems possible that he was impatient to get north. The refitting necessitated by Brandy Station appears to have led to frustration on his part: on the one hand because elements of the infantry had taken off without his main body, and on the other because of the delay between the Brandy Station clash and the next opportunity to engage the Union Cavalry Corps. He finally got that opportunity on June 17, but the outcome of that day's fighting, and of the other Loudoun Valley battles occurring over the next four days, did not result in any kind of crushing blow being delivered to the mounted components of his foe. In fact, Civil War students who are not necessarily enamored of Jeb Stuart have wondered aloud as to whether that commander ever inflicted such a blow on any element of the Union forces.[23] In any case, the opportunity grasped by General Stuart as of June 24 was arguably influenced by at least subconscious frustration—absent any conscious admission on his part that he was being pushed around by the Federal cavalry.

In any event, General Stuart might well have stayed with and caught up with the northward marching Confederate infantry. He could have hugged their right in the Shenandoah Valley, or effected a looser screening operation by riding in a northeasterly direction to the east of the mountains. That he did not created a controversy that continues into the twenty-first century.

After the Battle of Upperville (June 21, Appendix B), Stuart's force rode a short distance south to Salem, Virginia (still within Loudoun Valley). After spending a couple days of battle recovery there, the bulk of Stuart's force then set out on a long, counterclockwise ride that would ultimately take him to Gettysburg on July 2 (map 1-10). This was too late to do any good—and not just because the battle in Pennsylvania started the day before. More important, as is argued throughout a cogent analysis of General Stuart's activities during late June, the Confederate cavalry commander should have had his force *in southern Pennsylvania* at least a day or two before the end of the month.[24] Whatever route Stuart chose—and whether or not there were certain psychological components to his choice—he needed to be in a position to "feel the right of Ewell's troops." These words formed part of an order sent to Stuart by General Lee himself on June 23.[25] We will see that Stuart was never to find General Ewell and his 2nd Corps as it marched eastward toward the Susquehanna River (map 1-11). The rebel cavalry would not approach this region of Pennsylvania until the waning hours of June, thus missing a meeting with *any* elements of Lee's main body.

What General Stuart did between the waning hours of June 24 and the early ones of the Twenty-fifth was to swing east and slightly south of Salem with the majority of his cavalry division, thus disengaging from the rebel infantry. He and three brigades of his troopers then turned northward to the east of Centreville and crossed the Potomac River between Leesburg and Washington (map 1-10). This maneuver placed him to the right of the Federal army—and he was not making good time. He was still in Virginia on June 27 and would spend all of that day getting to and crossing the Potomac River.[26] By this time, Hooker's infantry had bestirred itself and was marching toward and in a northerly direction to the east of Frederick, Maryland (map 1-12). The Union army was, in effect, interposing itself between Stuart's force and much of Lee's infantry (map 1-5).

On the next day, Stuart was riding into Maryland, taking an *eastward* tack, away from "everything" (map 1-10). While in Rockville on the Twenty-eighth, the Confederate troopers received a warm reception from the Marylanders in that town and captured a large train of Federal supply wagons, which tried to escape down the Rockville Pike toward Washington. Incidentally, Hooker's relatively northerly position left the Federal capital protected from Stuart only by a garrison force permanently assigned that duty. In principle, General Stuart could have sent his entire force down the pike from Rockville on a raid against Washington itself. However, this almost certainly did not enter his mind, because he would have been really flouting his orders to get north and rendezvous with Ewell.

Stuart's cavalrymen were nowhere in the vicinity of the rebel foot soldiers as the former rode north. But Stuart planned eventually to *rejoin* the Confederate infantry—in the sense that he had been very near it momentarily when Longstreet's 1st Corps encamped just to Stuart's west in the Loudoun Valley on June 17, right before Longstreet moved through the mountain passes into the Shenandoah Valley (see Appendix B). To fulfill his aim of finding elements of General Ewell's 2nd Corps of infantrymen, Stuart would have to range north of the Mason-Dixon line. Ewell's forces were by then marching above that line (the border between Maryland and Pennsylvania) in an arc that took them eastward toward York and the Pennsylvania capital at Harrisburg (map 1-14). The orders that told Stuart to meet up with Ewell contained additional instructions. These, as transmitted to him by Robert E. Lee, are one element of the controversy surrounding the cavalry general's ride.

Some believe that Stuart just took off on his own, aiming to ride around the Union army, as he had done before, once to great fanfare.[27] He certainly *did* so

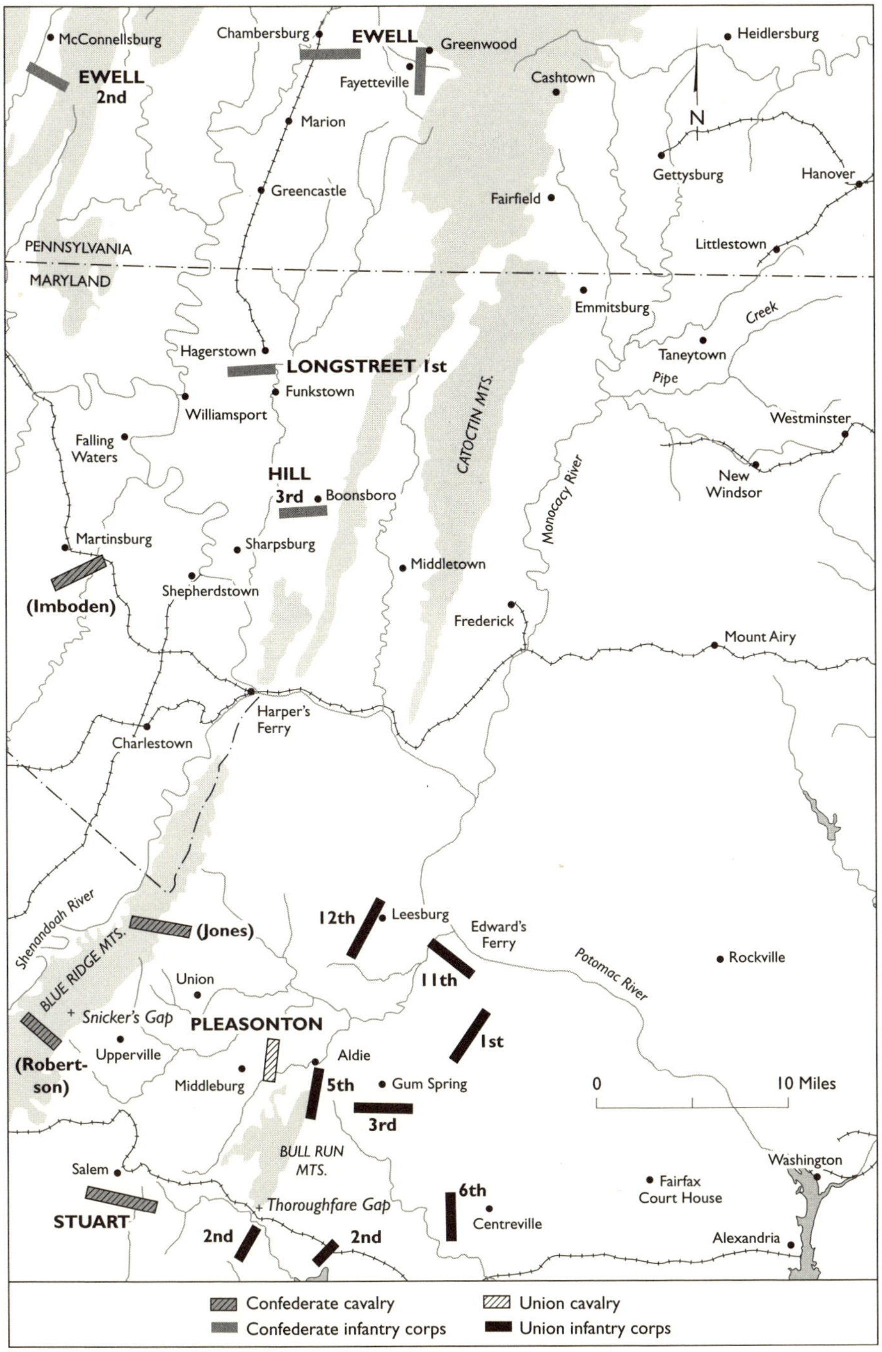

Map 1-8
Positions of the armies, June 24

ride in late June 1863, and the wisdom of that action as such will be discussed at the end of this section. However, he was not moving away from the two armies without authority. The order transmitted from Lee to Stuart on June 23 was poorly written and left ample room for the actions *and* the route taken by Stuart's troopers (as diagrammed in map 1-10).[28] As for the end product of whatever discretionary action Stuart might take—ultimately to join up with Ewell in Pennsylvania—he did try to do this and just missed, in a region northeast of Gettysburg. Along the way Stuart was told to raid and gather supplies, which he accomplished.

Returning to his movements through Maryland, two days after Stuart was in Rockville, he collided with a division of Federal cavalry. This led to a firefight at

THE ROADS TO GETTYSBURG 15

Map 1-9
Cavalry rides toward the Loudon Valley

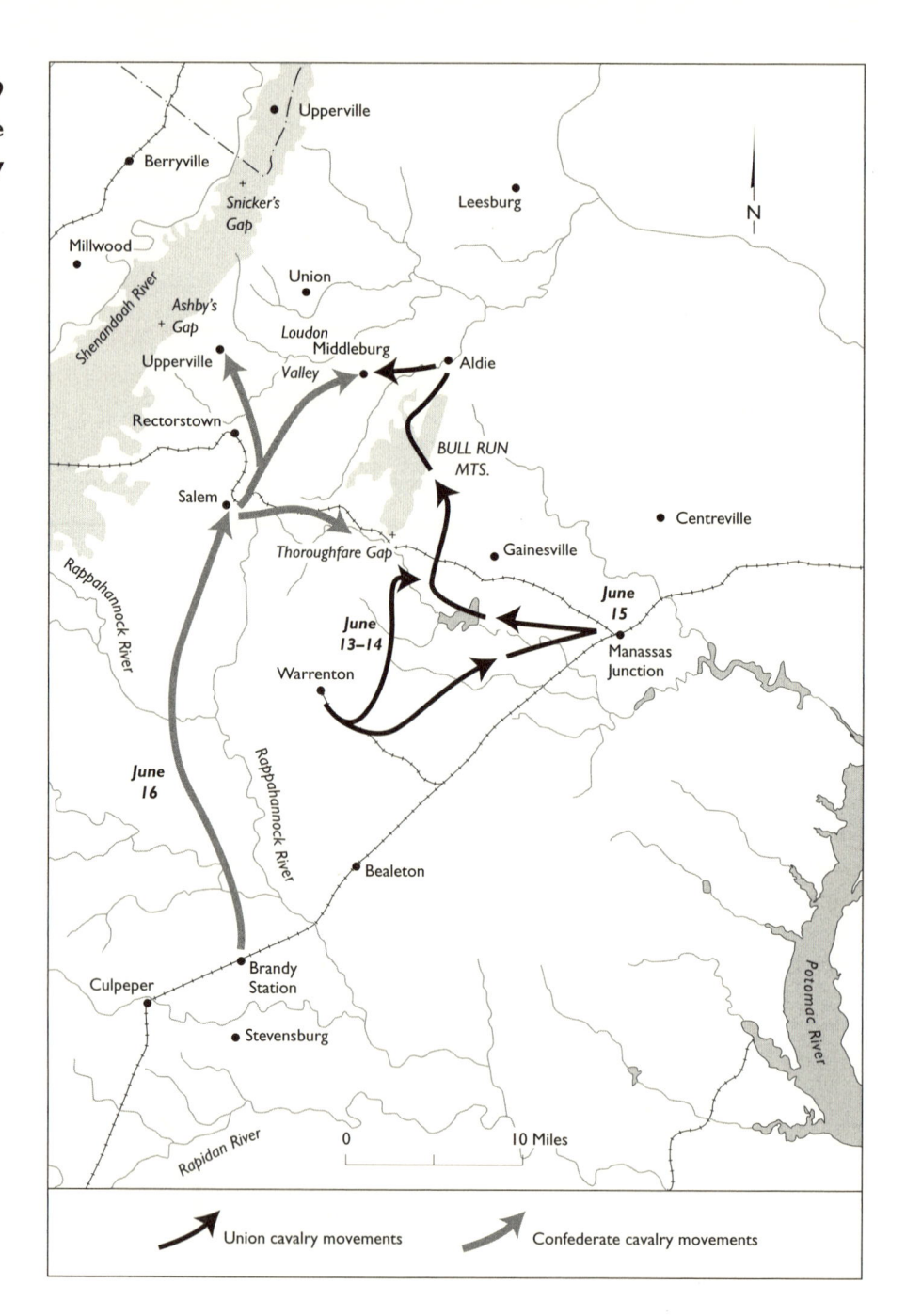

Hanover, Pennsylvania, which will be described in the next section. There, we will also pick up the threads of the various forces (infantry and cavalry on both sides) and their movements during late June and early July.[29]

Was Stuart's sweeping counterclockwise ride a piece of *negligence*, whereby he had left his army's infantry naked of cavalrymen? No. Recall that General Ewell had been given a cavalry battalion to cover his move when he left Culpeper on June 10.[30] Also, Jenkins's brigade joined Ewell's foot soldiers as they took the van northward through the Shenandoah and continued to provide cover as Ewell progressed through the two Northern states. Moreover, Brig. Gen. John D. Imboden was loosely guarding Lee's left or western flank (maps 1-10 and 1-15) as the other two Confederate infantry corps followed in Ewell's footsteps.[31]

Before Stuart did anything with his core brigades he *ordered* Brig. Gen. Beverly

16   THE STAND OF THE U.S. ARMY AT GETTYSBURG

H. Robertson to take a force of almost three thousand troopers and "inform Lee" of what was transpiring as the Army of Northern Virginia moved north.[32] In other words, Robertson's command, which included his regiments *and* those of General Jones, was to stay in reasonably close contact with Lee while Stuart went eastward and then northward with three brigades commanded by Brig. Gens. Wade Hampton, Fitzhugh Lee, and W. H. F. "Rooney" Lee (the latter two still under the temporary command of Cols. Thomas T. Munford and John R. Chambliss Jr., respectively).

Generals Robertson and Jones did not accomplish much by screening the approximate tail of the rebel infantry, doing so only as it moved northward within Virginia. However, it is arguable that the mission of these two brigades was mainly to stay near Lee's rear. By so doing, Robertson kept half of the six regiments in his command down in the southwest corner of the campaign theater (lower left portions of maps 1-6, 1-8, and 1-10), mostly removing his cavalrymen from any of the action. David Powell's analysis, on one hand, suggests that Robertson's actions (or lack thereof) were as directed, even necessary. Mark Nesbitt, on the other hand, is convinced that Robertson was essentially derelict in his duty—which would fit with his performance at Brandy Station.[33] During that battle, Robertson seemed to be in a stupor (Appendix A). In any case, General Lee could really have used Robertson's twenty-seven hundred troopers later in June, had they ridden north with the army and replaced the vanished Stuart.

However, the actions of that Confederate cavalry commander in late June did not approach dereliction of duty. Stuart's "Third Ride" (see note 27) was legitimate in the strictest sense: His orders gave him the leeway he exercised—to go *where* he wanted on his way north, if not *when*. That he arrived late in Pennsylvania was far less than a court-martialable offense.[34] Nevertheless, the far-ranging ride of the rebel horsemen was at best unwise, and it might have been worthless. Stuart's progression into Northern territory effected nothing *useful* in the Gettysburg campaign, whether or not it helped ruin that campaign insofar as the overall Confederate fortunes were concerned. It was not just that Stuart and his three best brigades (some forty-five hundred troopers) were out of touch with Lee and his infantry, but also that Stuart was out of touch with anything of real military consequence. Yes, he captured some supply wagons and cut some communication and transportation lines, but this did not help the rebel cause significantly in the summer of 1863. He did finally reengage with Federal forces at Hanover in late June, but that cavalry battle was of minimal consequence. Moreover, it helped further to delay and exhaust Stuart and his main force, to the point that they were unable to participate at all in the big battle on July 2. Their performance on July 3 was an ambiguous tactical outcome at best.[35]

What should Stuart have done during the week before the Battle of Gettysburg? Granting him the discretion to initiate his movements out of northern Virginia by a wide counterclockwise wheel, from then on he might have considered acting differently from his classically portrayed performances. These were to dart toward the Union forces and harass, fluster, and embarrass them; gather some on-the-run intelligence in conjunction with these thrusts and parries; and serve as the "eyes of his army."[36]

Instead of the activities just listed, Stuart could better have contributed by finding the Federal infantry units, ridden ahead of as many of them as his mounted force would allow, and then *really* harassed them by stopping to fight dismounted. He did not have enough weight to make all-out defensive stands, but he could have effected a series of fighting withdrawals and by so doing stalled the

Union advance into Pennsylvania. This could have given Lee a material advantage. Moreover, these sorts of deliberately sought-out contacts with the Army of the Potomac could have generated much useful intelligence. Thus, in conjunction with each dragoon-like defensive action (as is suggested here), he could have sent couriers off to the west to let Lee know where the Union infantry was located and what they were up to. The key word just stated—*dragoon,* the military term for a mounted infantryman—is something Jeb Stuart was not. He was a dashing "light saber" of a military figure and seemed constitutionally unable to use all those horses merely as a method to get mounted infantry from one defensive position to another. Fair enough.[37] But is this defense of Stuart thoroughly persuasive? Stuart expressed on enough occasions that he aimed to *hurt the enemy,* and he claimed afterward that he had done so—following Brandy Station and after some of the Loudoun Valley engagements. Thus, he did not seem to display the attitude that he was merely a will-o'-the-wisp gatherer of intelligence or a terrier-like hunter nipping at the enemy's heels. So, if he truly felt that he *could* hurt the Federal forces, he might have considered a plan to go right after them during the June phase of the Gettysburg campaign.

David Powell, who discusses analogous scenarios about the ride of Stuart's cavalry, provides a final fillip to this argument.[38] Had Stuart taken a more direct route northward—from Loudoun Valley through Sharpsburg, Maryland, let's say (map 1-10)—his troopers might have gotten into Pennsylvania within four days of his departure from Salem, Virginia, and established a screen on an east-west line ranging from the Gettysburg vicinity toward Hanover (map 1-13). Alternatively, a more efficient ride along the route Stuart *did* take could have achieved the same positioning of his force, had he *not* been delayed and *had* he been more concerned with fulfilling his mission—to "*feel the right of Ewell's troops*"—than with riding round the Union army again. In any case, the Gettysburg–Hanover line proposed would have achieved Stuart's appointed task by placing his troopers near the southern flank of Ewell's marching columns. Moreover, according to the proposal for more militarily aggressive action on Stuart's part, the "intended position" along this line *would have facilitated harassment of the Federal advance* and even temporary blockage of the Union columns, some of them anyway (compare map 1-12 to the bottom of map 1-13). Where Stuart intended to be by June 28—according to Powell—would also have permitted him to convey *information* he would naturally have absorbed about the Federal advance from the south. Such intelligence could have been readily sent to the Confederate infantry commanders, located a short distance to the north (map 1-13).

General Stuart's lack of accomplishments in June 1863 was exacerbated by the fact that he himself was exhausted to the point of "stress fatigue." Brandy Station, the Loudoun Valley engagements, and the wide-swinging, ever-delayed ride from that valley into Northern territory all resulted in more than elementary weariness. The mental exhaustion that accompanied Stuart's physically debilitated state militated against the Confederate cavalry commander's ability to fulfill his reconnaissance mission, let alone to mobilize anything in the way of significant military action. One wonders if Stuart's seemingly stressed-out state was influenced by mental pressure—a sense that his mission in *this* campaign was most important, in comparison to some of the riding around he had done earlier in the war. In any event, the seriously fatigued condition in which Jeb Stuart arguably found himself throughout most of June would undermine his capacity to accomplish much of anything during the Battle of Gettysburg itself, although he rallied afterward (Chapter 5).[39]

Map 1-10

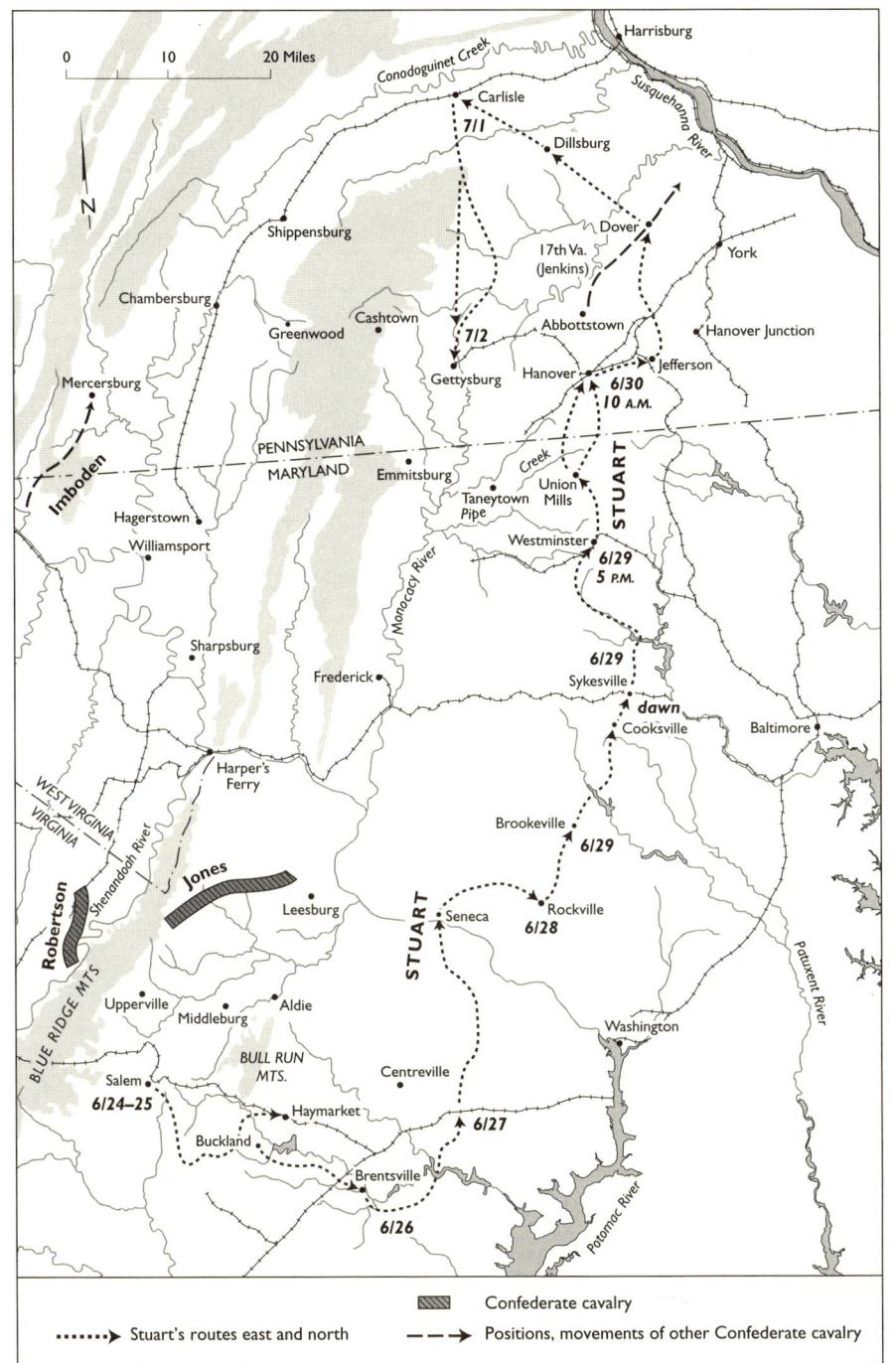

Stuart's rides from the Loudon Valley to Pennsylvania

FIGHTING JOE HOOKER CONTINUES TO FIGHT—NOW, WITH HIS BOSSES—AS THE REBELS RANGE TO THE NORTH AND THE EAST

What follows is a brief summary of where we are in the last days of June (in addition to the quick recapitulation of the rebel cavalry's activities just given). Both armies have moved across the Potomac River, the Confederates crossing sooner and upstream of the Yankees (maps 1-3–1-7). Ewell's 2nd Corps is north of the Maryland-Pennsylvania border and has begun swinging to the east as it proceeds northward. The Union cavalry is only as far north as Loudoun Valley (map 1-8).

THE ROADS TO GETTYSBURG   19

Map 1-11

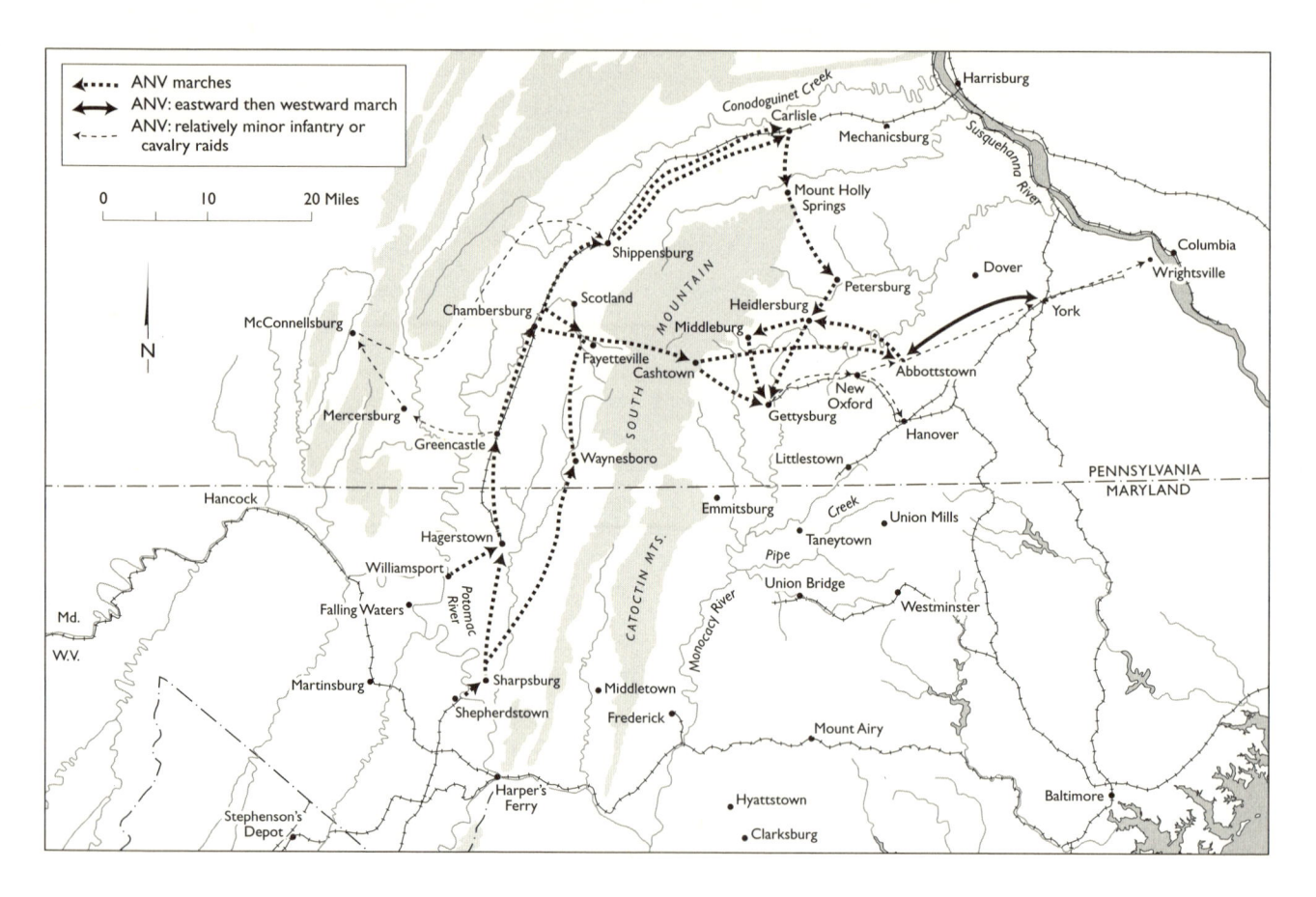

The Army of Northern Virginia's movements into and throughout southern Pennsylvania

The last of these movements, under Federal Cavalry Corps commander Alfred Pleasonton, was the slowest. Indeed, the Federal troopers languished at Aldie, Virginia (Appendix B), for no good reason for some four days after the battles between the mountains. It must be mentioned in this respect that Pleasonton's performance in the Gettysburg campaign was lackluster at best and probably worse than that of his counterpart, Jeb Stuart. Pleasonton was, at various key moments, slow, unimaginative, blustery, dishonest, and mean-spirited (as exemplified by elements of the Brandy Station story in Appendix A). Finally, Pleasonton moved northeastward into Maryland, met up with Hooker's infantry, and by June 27 these two components of the Army of the Potomac were converging on Frederick.

Map 1-12 diagrams the Federal infantry movements subsequent to their Potomac River crossing and proceeding into the waning hours of June. Map 1-11 summarizes the Confederate infantry marches over a similar time frame—although also projecting back to mid-June to give an overview of Ewell's 2nd Corps movements into Maryland and Pennsylvania. Recall the mention of Lee's orders to Ewell, transmitted on June 22. They included the suggestion that if the Pennsylvania capital of Harrisburg "comes within your means, capture it."[40] This quaint notion reflected nineteenth-century conventional military wisdom, which held that seizing an opponent's capital city would incapacitate his government, destroy enemy morale, and thus force his surrender.[41] While possession of this piece of Pennsylvania real estate might have caused further gnashing of Northern teeth, potentially more significant was that taking Harrisburg would have permitted the rebels to destroy the railroad bridge that crossed the Susquehanna there (maps 1-10 and 1-12).[42]

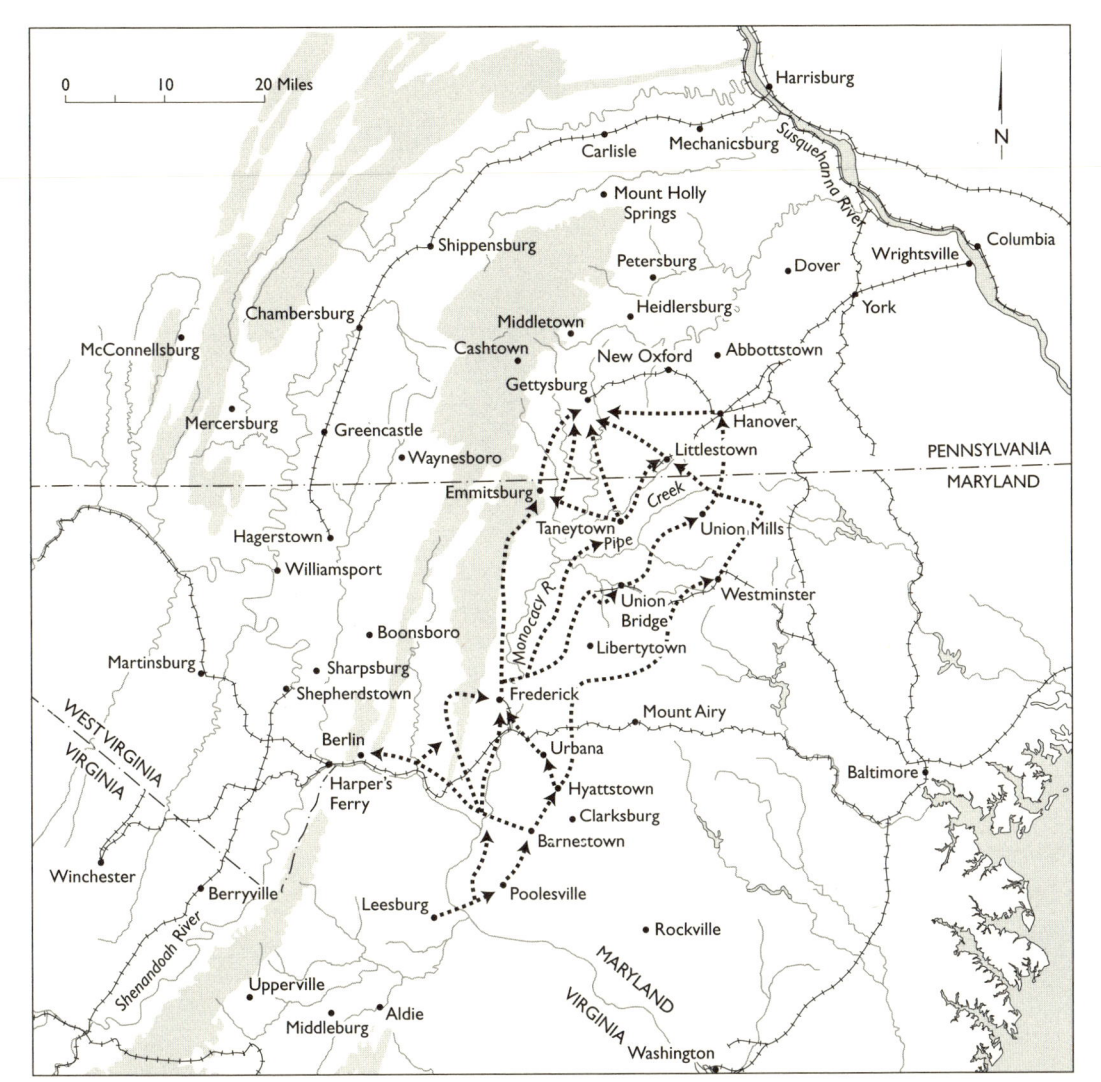

Map 1-12 The Army of the Potomac's marches through Maryland into southern Pennsylvania

In any case, General Ewell moved with good speed and on a broad front. He took some of his units in a clockwise arc toward Carlisle, in the direction of Harrisburg, while sending others in a more easterly direction not long after they crossed the Mason-Dixon line (map 1-11). An interesting feature of the latter marches was that Maj. Gen. Jubal A. Early's division passed through the town of Gettysburg while moving toward York. This occurred late in the afternoon on June 26, after Confederate cavalry and Pennsylvania militiamen clashed briefly on the road that goes northwest from the town.

Owing to the fact that Early moved through Gettysburg from west to east, *it is doubtful he learned about certain ridges and hills arrayed to the south of that town* (these later became known as Cemetery Ridge, Cemetery Hill, and the Round Tops). However, one of Early's brigade commanders, Brig. Gen. John B. Gordon, asserted in his postwar writings that he and his 2nd Corps comrades *had* been aware (five days before the battle) of the crucial strategic significance of the high ground below Gettysburg.[43] Such a retrospective claim should be viewed with suspicion.

Map 1-14 displays further details of the positions of Ewell's infantry units—and that of all the other major elements of the infantry on both sides, as of June

**Map 1-13
Stuart's ride into
Pennsylvania**

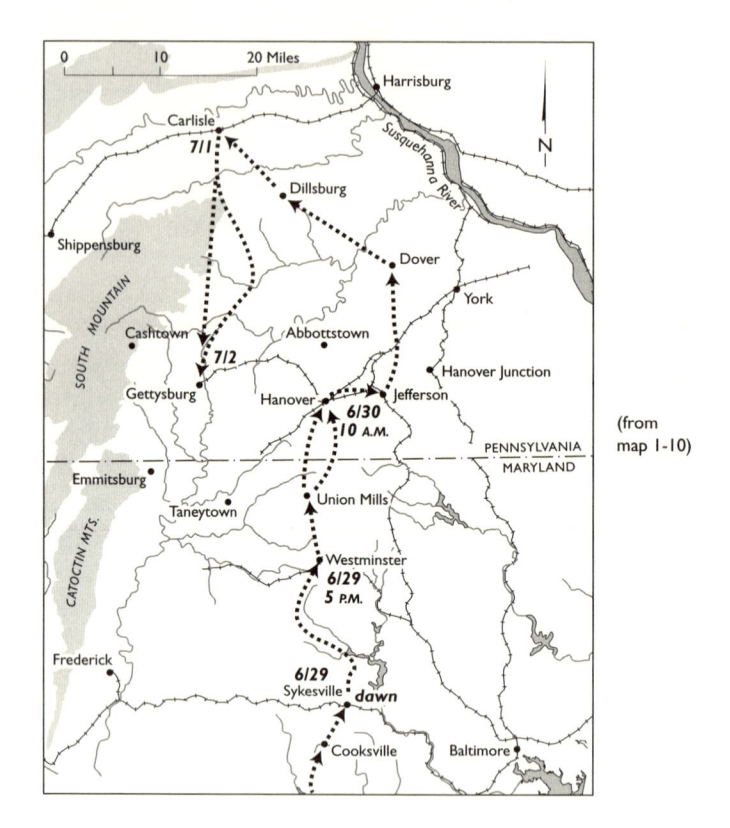

**Where Stuart might
have been in
Pennsylvania, well in
advance of the battle**

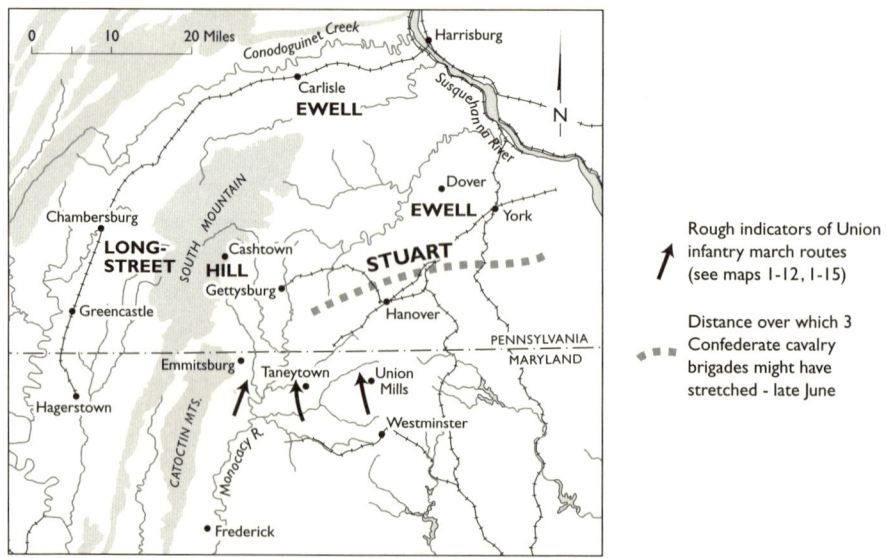

28. This is an important day in the Gettysburg campaign. One reason is that it signaled the end of General Hooker. President Lincoln and the Union general in chief, Henry W. Halleck, were already displeased with his slowness and hoped for an opportunity to remove the Army of the Potomac's commander. He gave it to them when he began asking for reinforcements. In particular, Hooker hoped to bolster his forces by gaining control of the ten-thousand-man garrison at Harper's Ferry. This was a demand similar to those repeatedly made by a previous army commander, Maj. Gen. George B. McClellan, the general Lincoln accused of always having a case of "the slows." In fact, Hooker's June request echoed McClellan's in September 1862, when the latter asked that his Army of the Potomac—which in McClellan's mind was outnumbered by the Confederates—

22 THE STAND OF THE U.S. ARMY AT GETTYSBURG

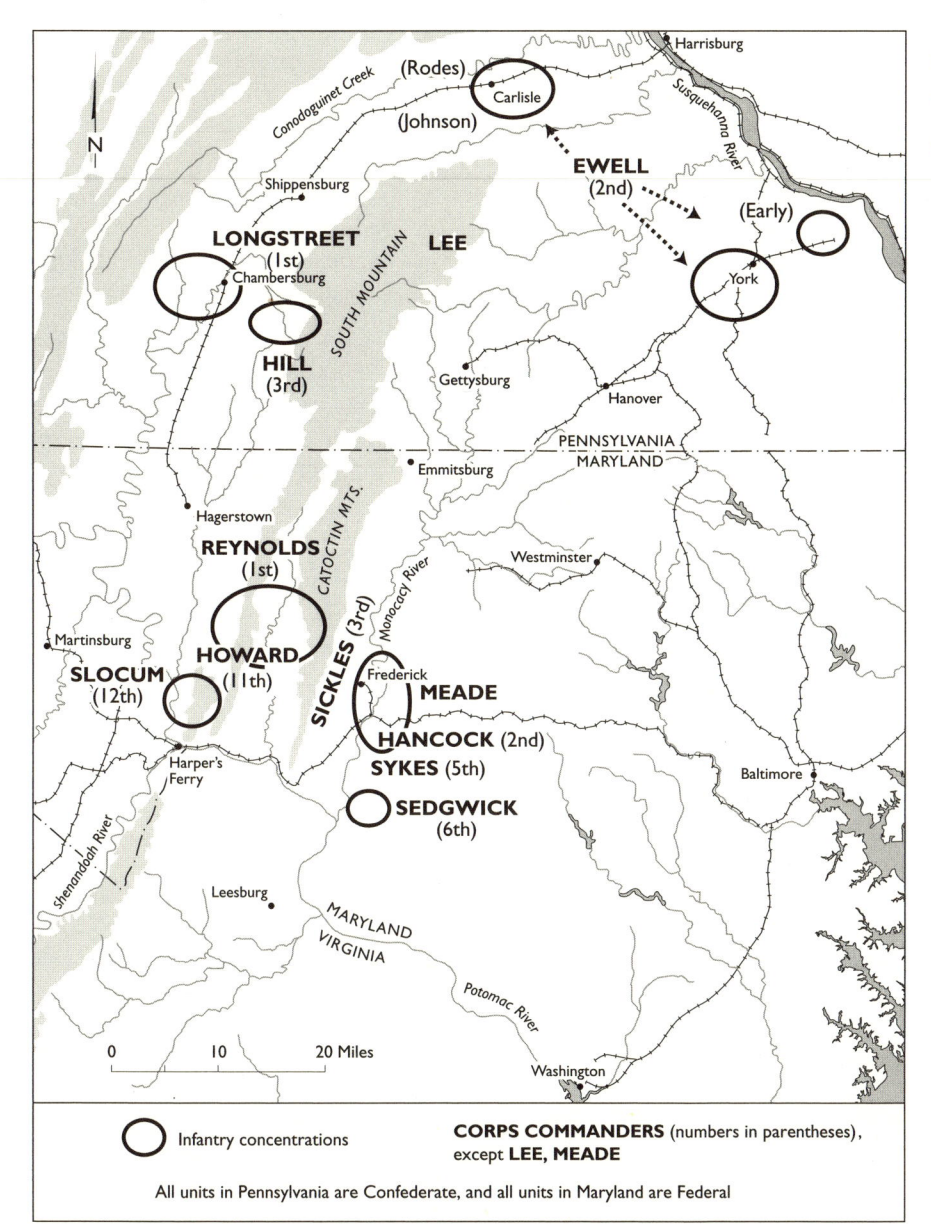

Map 1-14
Confederate and Union infantry positions, June 28

be bolstered by the Harper's Ferry garrison during the Antietam campaign. However, Hooker's request for more men during Lee's second invasion of the North was neither cantankerous nor based on self-hypnotism about being outnumbered by Lee's army. Instead, the Army of the Potomac's commander was formulating a plan that would involve Maj. Gen. William H. French's Harper's Ferry garrison joining Hooker's 12th Corps. General Hooker envisioned this combined force getting in Lee's rear and cutting his lines of communication to the south—possibly forcing the Confederate army to withdraw from Pennsylvania.[44] During that complicated redeployment, Hooker hoped to bring the rebels to battle on ground of his own choosing.

General Hooker's request was denied. He responded on June 27 by sending a telegram from his headquarters at Frederick asking that he be relieved of command. The result was that a colonel from the War Department took a train from Washington to Frederick. The orders he carried indeed called for the army commander's relief—probably not to his amazement. In fact, it is likely that this turn of events gave Hooker relief of the other kind. The orders also promoted Maj. Gen. George Gordon Meade from leadership of the 5th Corps to command of the entire army. This occurred when the colonel found General Meade's camp south of Frederick (map 1-14) at 3 A.M. on June 28. Meade—surprised, and not pleasantly so—accepted the new assignment, despite the foreboding it carried.[45] When he arrived at Hooker's headquarters (still in the early morning hours of that Sunday) to formalize the change in command, Fighting Joe accepted his firing with a fair degree of graciousness.

One can go overboard in ridiculing General Hooker's performance during the June portion of the Gettysburg campaign. The extent to which he was in a stupor has been overstated. By pulling together some supporting threads for this from some of the passages presented above, recall that he had given solid orders on occasion, or behaved on certain days with more irascibility than immobility. It *was* Hooker who got the Army of the Potomac well into northern Maryland, not far from the positions of Lee's army—in fact so close that the Union army's location seemed a distressing surprise to the Confederate high command on June 28. In all events, Hooker was out of the war for a while. He returned, however, within four months' time—when, as commander of a three-division force, he performed rather well in the Chattanooga campaign—as he had previously done as a corps commander in 1862.[46]

Meade Takes Over: His Cavalry Finds Lee North of the Mason-Dixon Line, Where Stuart Has Strayed Off to the East

When he took over the Army of the Potomac, Meade was already a seasoned commander. Elements of his 5th Corps had already participated in the Loudoun Valley actions (chart B-4 in Appendix B). Moreover, Meade had commanded this corps at Fredericksburg and Chancellorsville, where his actions and attitudes indicated competence and toughness. During the early days of the Gettysburg campaign, General Meade also offered an intriguing piece of judgment and foresight:

> The army is weakened, and its morale is not so good as at the last battle [Chancellorsville], and the enemy are undoubtedly stronger and in better morale. Still, I do not despair, but that *if they assume the offensive and force us into a defensive attitude,* that our own morale will be raised, and with a moderate degree of good luck and good management, we will give them better than they can send. War is very uncertain in its results, and often when affairs look the most desperate they suddenly assume a more hopeful state.

General Meade wrote these words to his wife Margaret; the letter was dated June 11, 1863.[47]

Seventeen days later, Meade needed a good measure of whatever ability and confidence he possessed, because he was about to command an entire army in a momentous battle. He must have guessed as much on the morning he took over, but he could not know that it would happen just three days later. Not surprisingly, he would behave somewhat like the corps commander he had just recently been. Some aspects of that behavior can be a good thing, as we shall see in Chapter 3. This is one feature of the idea that it may have been useful for General Meade not to be given the false luxury of thinking about it for weeks on end. Granted lots of time over the winter and spring of 1863, had Hooker subconsciously thought himself out of the willingness and ability to command an army, such that he collapsed at Chancellorsville in May and, as some would have it, swooned in June?

June 28 also marked the day that Lt. Gen. James Longstreet learned of the Federal infantry movements from a scout he had hired. Elements of this story have drifted into legend, but the balance of evidence indicates that "The Spy, Harrison" was a real person and his report of the Union army's imminent approach to southern Pennsylvania may have come as *somewhat* of a surprise to the rebel high command.[48] If Harrison's intelligence did cause Confederate consternation, Hooker deserves some credit, for he had gotten the Army of the Potomac in a position to threaten the rebels before Meade took over.

When the intelligence from Harrison reached Lee, we first reflect on the supposed absence of cavalry-generated information. Some have interpreted the strategic situation at the end of June to include the idea that Lee needed large numbers of horsemen closely associated with his infantry so that these thousands of troopers could truly scour the theater of war and have quick access to the army commander.[49] Others note that Lee did have *some* cavalry with him and thus, according to certain students of the battle, had to have been aware of the Army of the Potomac's proximity irrespective of Harrison. Do keep in mind, however, that most of the "non-Stuart" Confederate cavalry units were off to the southwest of the rebel infantry (Imboden's brigade) or had swung way around to the northeast (Jenkins's brigade). Maps 1-8, 1-10, and 1-15 exemplify these movements and positions. Perhaps Lee could have possessed a higher grade of intelligence had Stuart not been off to the east and north of the Federal forces—out of any significant contact with them, except for the Union cavalry division Stuart encountered on the last day in June at Hanover, Pennsylvania.

However Lee learned of the Union presence, the Confederate army commander ordered a rapid concentration of his forces, mainly in a westerly direction. Ewell was recalled from York and his approach to Harrisburg, and Hill was ordered to move southeast down the Chambersburg Pike, with Longstreet—arrayed behind Hill, in the vicinity of Chambersburg, Pennsylvania—to follow (map 1-14). These two wings of the Army of Northern Virginia were thus told to move toward the vicinity of Gettysburg, the place where all the roads converge (maps 1-15 and 1-19).[50]

For his part, General Meade had taken the reins of command firmly in hand, and he got his somewhat scattered corps moving with dispatch from the vicinity of Frederick. These movements are depicted in the top portion of map 1-12, with further details indicated on map 1-14. By the late stages of Monday, June 29, Meade had maneuvered his large units some twenty-five miles farther north (map 1-15). As of June 29–30, the Federal infantry was distributed along an approximately twenty-mile east-west front, between the Maryland towns of Emmitsburg and Westminster (map 1-15). They were poised to enter Pennsylvania, which they did not do, however, until July 1.

After the campaign, several of these Union soldiers wrote that their spirits lifted when they crossed the Mason-Dixon line. The citizens of Pennsylvania showed enthusiastic support as the Federals passed through towns in the southern sector of that state—the only free-soil one in which a major battle occurred in the Civil War. The Union solders were in a special situation, and they said so: They were on a mission to defend their "own home ground."[51]

In contrast, some have argued that the rebels' activities during this stage of the Gettysburg campaign were subtly sapping their morale. This contention is presented against a background of what seems to have been the usual mind-set of the Southern fighting man, placed in a situation where he felt obliged to throw back one Union encroachment into Southern territory after another. Thus, for most of

**Map 1-15
Positions of all forces, June 29**

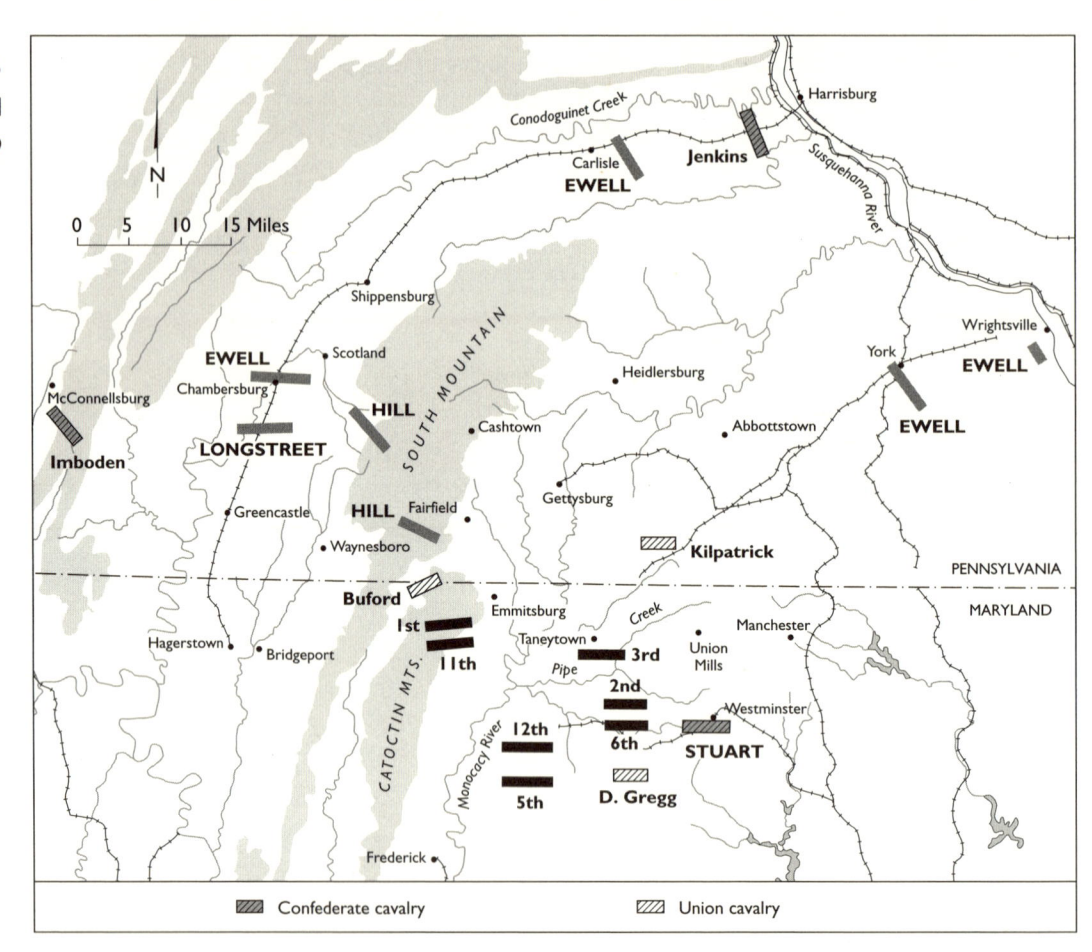

the Civil War, if any Southern soldier had been asked "Why are you fighting?" he might simply but insightfully have answered: "I'm fightin' because you're down here."[52] However, because of the nature of this campaign, many of the individual rebels may have instead felt themselves on a lark—at least on certain days during their march north in June 1863. Most of these Confederate infantrymen were unengaged with the enemy (except for Ewell's corps at Winchester). Yet however "pleased [they were] that their march to this point had been uncontested," some of these men expressed a nagging concern. "We have heard nothing of the Yankee army, which puzzles the boys very much"; and "The men are . . . rather anxious to meet the enemy, but I am afraid they are overconfident, and expect to accomplish too much in this rash movement into Pennsylvania" are two common themes. Perhaps they sensed that a determined foe (for once) was coming their way. In particular, certain rebels articulated worries about fighting outside of Virginia: "The thought of being wounded and falling into enemy hands filled us with sorrow of fighting so far from home and the vicinity of so many victories over our foes."

Now, back to the armies' northward movements. However, before dealing with the Union infantry marches and actions in southern Pennsylvania, we need to back up a couple of days and again grab the cavalrymen's reins. What these Federal horsemen did—including clashing with rebel cavalry at the end of June and *precipitating the Battle of Gettysburg* on the first day of July—was important. On June 28, the principal units of Federal cavalry (map 1-16) were moving away from the Frederick vicinity (these rides began the day before). On the Twenty-

26   THE STAND OF THE U.S. ARMY AT GETTYSBURG

Map 1-16

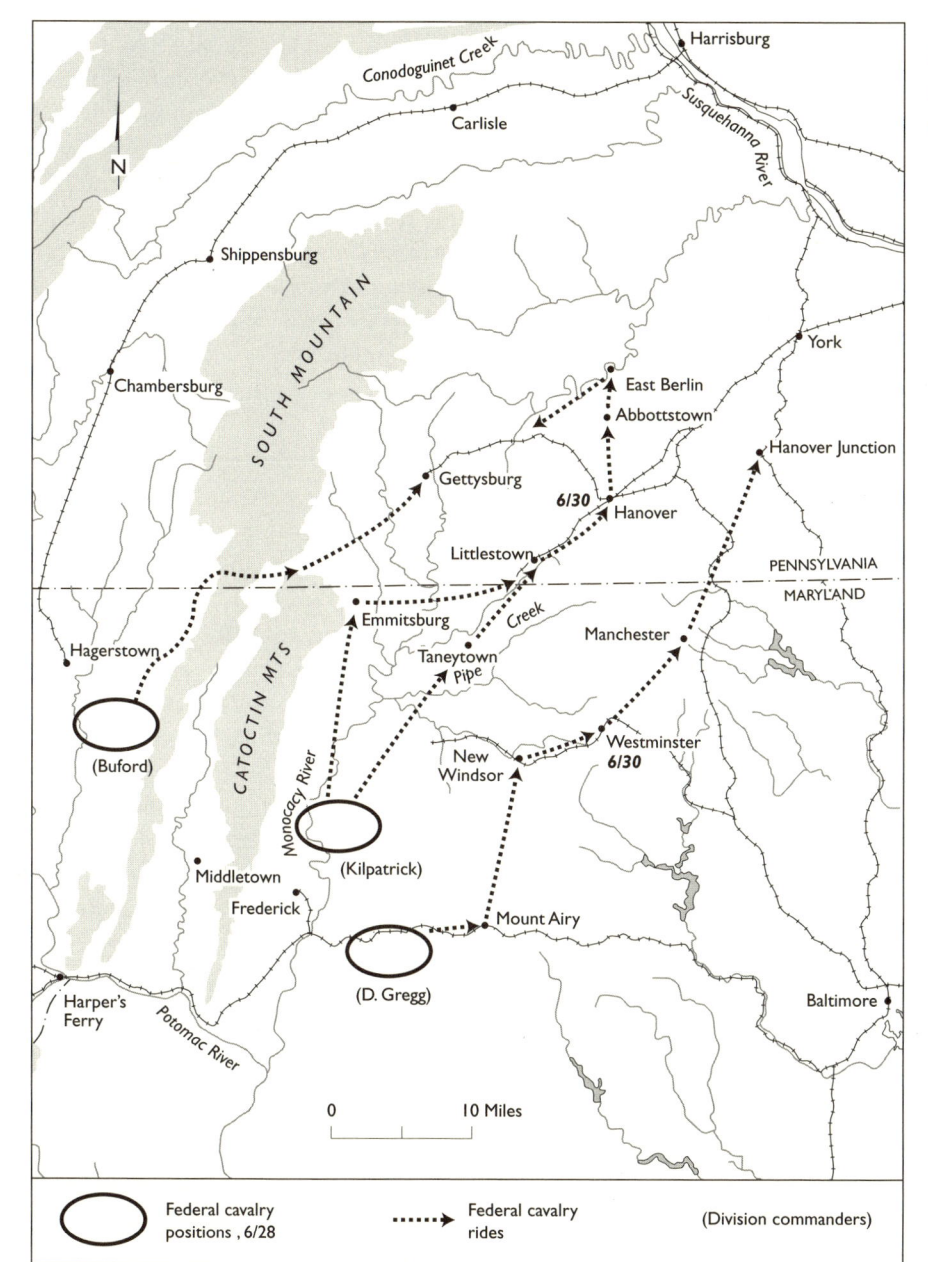

Union cavalry rides from Maryland to Pennsylvania

eighth, General Pleasonton was promoted to major general and he effected a *further* reorganization of his force. Regiments were reshuffled and a reconstituted 3rd Division, commanded by Brig. Gen. Judson Kilpatrick, was formed.[53]

Brigadier General John Buford's 1st Division formed the left wing of this next advance of the Federal cavalry, Kilpatrick the center, and David McM. Gregg the right rear (map 1-16; chart 1-2). On June 26, the three brigades of General Buford's Division rode from northern Virginia (vicinity Leesburg), moved across the Potomac at Edward's Ferry (map 1-17) to Jefferson, Maryland, and then went along the east edge of South Mountain (the northern extension of the Blue Ridge range), reaching Middletown by June 27. These Union troopers shoed horses and refit at that Maryland town through the Twenty-eighth.[54] The next day, Buford crossed South Mountain through Turner's Gap, headed westward toward Boonsboro, Maryland. He divided his force, sending the brigades commanded by

THE ROADS TO GETTYSBURG

**Chart 1-2
Cavalry in late June**

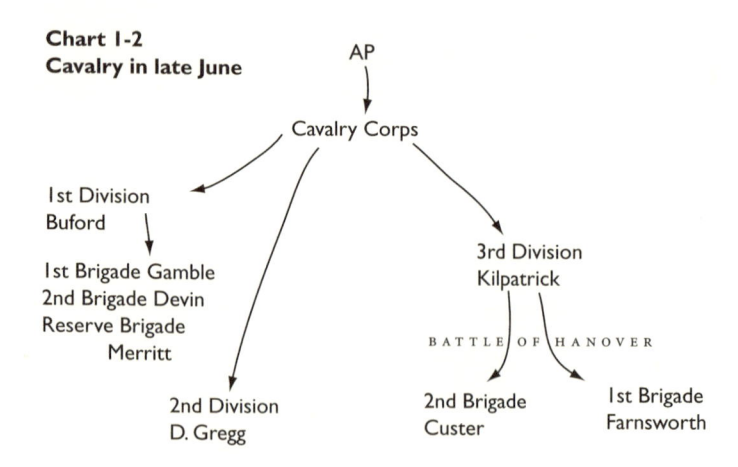

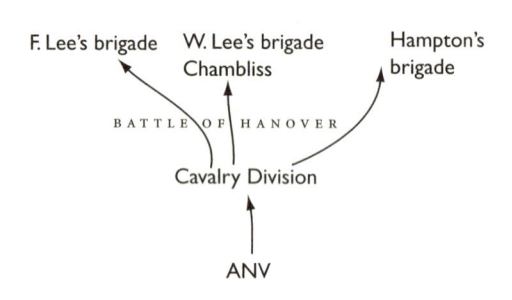

```
                    AP
                    ↓
              Cavalry Corps
              ↙     ↓     ↘
1st Division    3rd Division
Buford          Kilpatrick
  ↓                  
1st Brigade Gamble       BATTLE OF HANOVER
2nd Brigade Devin       ↙            ↘
Reserve Brigade     2nd Brigade    1st Brigade
Merritt             Custer         Farnsworth
       ↓
  2nd Division
  D. Gregg
```

```
F. Lee's brigade   W. Lee's brigade    Hampton's
                   Chambliss           brigade
       ↖              ↑              ↗
          BATTLE OF HANOVER
              Cavalry Division
                    ↑
                   ANV
```

Cols. William Gamble and Thomas C. Devin (chart 1-2) toward Fairfield, Pennsylvania, and his remaining brigade, led by Brig. Gen. Wesley Merritt, toward Mechanicsville, Virginia. The van of Buford's units reached a point ten miles south of Gettysburg on June 29 (map 1-17).[55] He would receive important orders on this day from the Army of the Potomac's new high command.

Moving over to the right wing of the Union cavalry rides, we find General Gregg near Frederick on June 28, his force riding roughly eastward (map 1-16). Gregg's 2nd Division was also divided, but the brigades reunited as they rode northeast toward New Windsor on June 29, continuing in this direction to Westminster, which they reached early the next day. Gregg may not have known it, but he was following General Stuart's three brigades at this time (map 1-13). General Gregg continued angling to the northeast through Manchester, Maryland, and was on the road to Hanover Junction, Pennsylvania, early on July 1 (map 1-16). The direction of his movements and his trailing position left him out of any fighting until the Battle of Gettysburg unfolded.

Stuart, meanwhile, was engaged by the Union cavalry situated in the center of this theater of the campaign. This was the force under General Kilpatrick, who had been ordered to locate the Confederate infantry under Ewell (given the Union high command's belief that elements of Ewell's 2nd Corps, accompanied by Confederate cavalry, were near York in late June). Kilpatrick, proceeding from Frederick early on June 29, advanced toward Littlestown, Pennsylvania (in a more direct northeasterly direction than that taken by Gregg). Littlestown is just across the state border and twenty-five miles southwest of York (map 1-16).

On the morning of June 30, Kilpatrick's division rode toward Hanover and then to Abbotstown, Pennsylvania. However, the van of Kilpatrick's advance had to be ordered back to Hanover when Stuart's cavalry collided with his rear just below that town. The Battle of Hanover ensued, with Kilpatrick's newly promoted brigadiers, George Armstrong Custer and Elon Farnsworth, facing southward. Custer was on the Federal right or west, and Farnsworth was arrayed from positions in the town eastward (chart 1-2). They were confronted by Stuart's brigades under Brig. Gens. Fitzhugh Lee, John R. Chambliss (commanding Rooney Lee's brigade), and Wade Hampton from left to right (chart 1-2). The indecisive battle swayed back and forth. At one point, Kilpatrick mounted a counterattack against Stuart's northward-facing forces. This resulted in the near capture of General Stuart, who escaped by urging his horse to jump over a ravine. Casualties for the Federal cavalry were 19 killed, 73 wounded, and 123 missing; the Confederates lost 9 dead, 50 wounded, and 58 missing.

The result of the action at Hanover was mainly to delay Stuart even further. Moreover, he swung out to the *east* after Hanover, moving toward Jefferson, in the direction of York (map 1-13) on the evening of June 30. Recall that Stuart's mis-

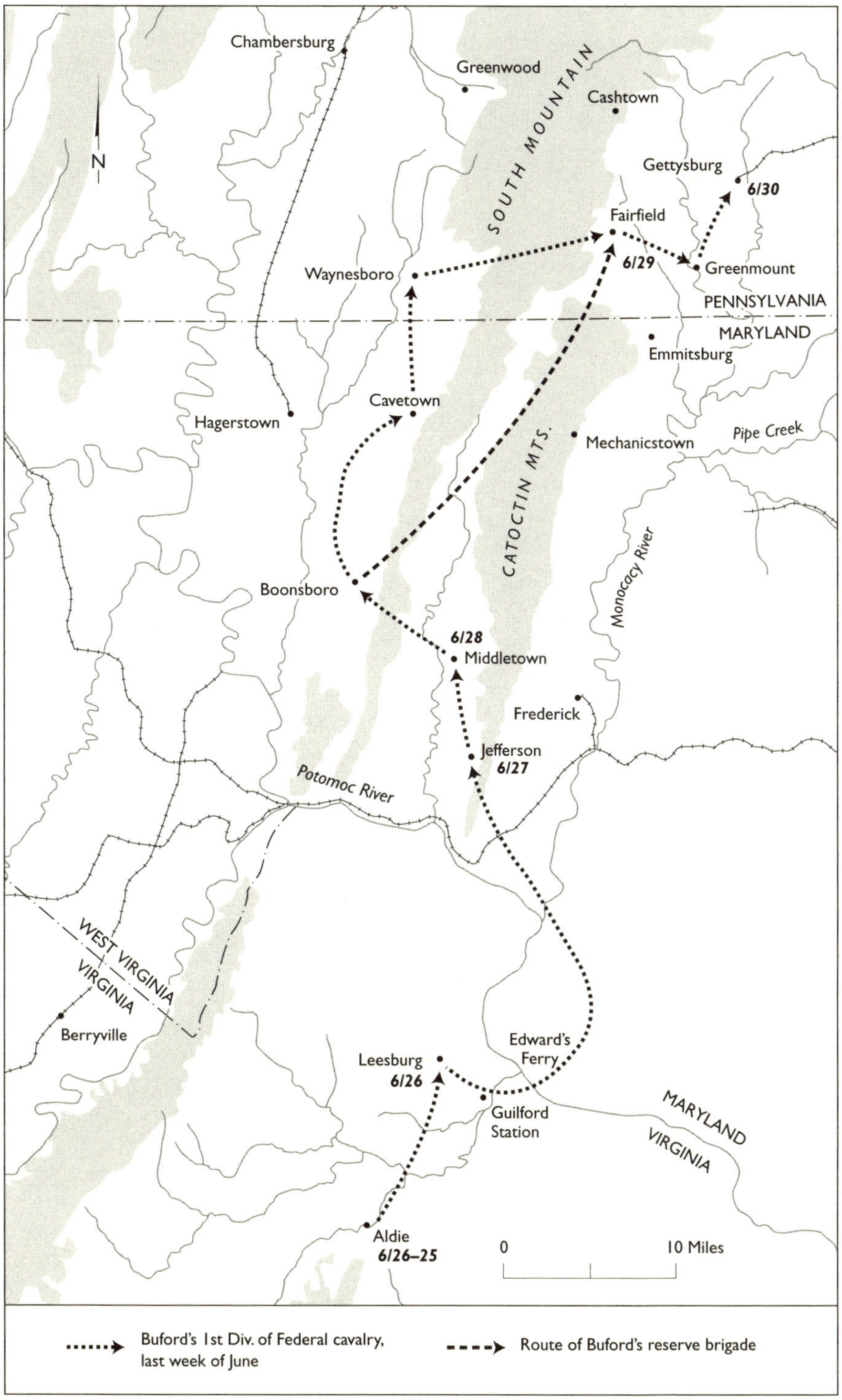

Map 1-17
Buford's rides

Legend: ......> Buford's 1st Div. of Federal cavalry, last week of June   ---> Route of Buford's reserve brigade

sion was to rendezvous with elements of Ewell's corps near that Pennsylvania town. However, as he skirted York to its west on July 1 (map 1-13), he learned that Early's division of 2nd Corps infantry had just left this area. Those infantrymen were on their way to a crucial rendezvous with the rest of the Confederate army, which occurred on the afternoon of July 1.

Stuart proceeded farther to the north—and at last somewhat in the direction of the Army of Northern Virginia—because his next destination was Carlisle (map 1-13). The Confederate cavalry encountered no forces there except some Union militiamen. Late on the night of July 1 a staff officer whom Stuart had sent to find

THE ROADS TO GETTYSBURG 29

Map 1-18 Buford's cavalry patrols, evening of June 30

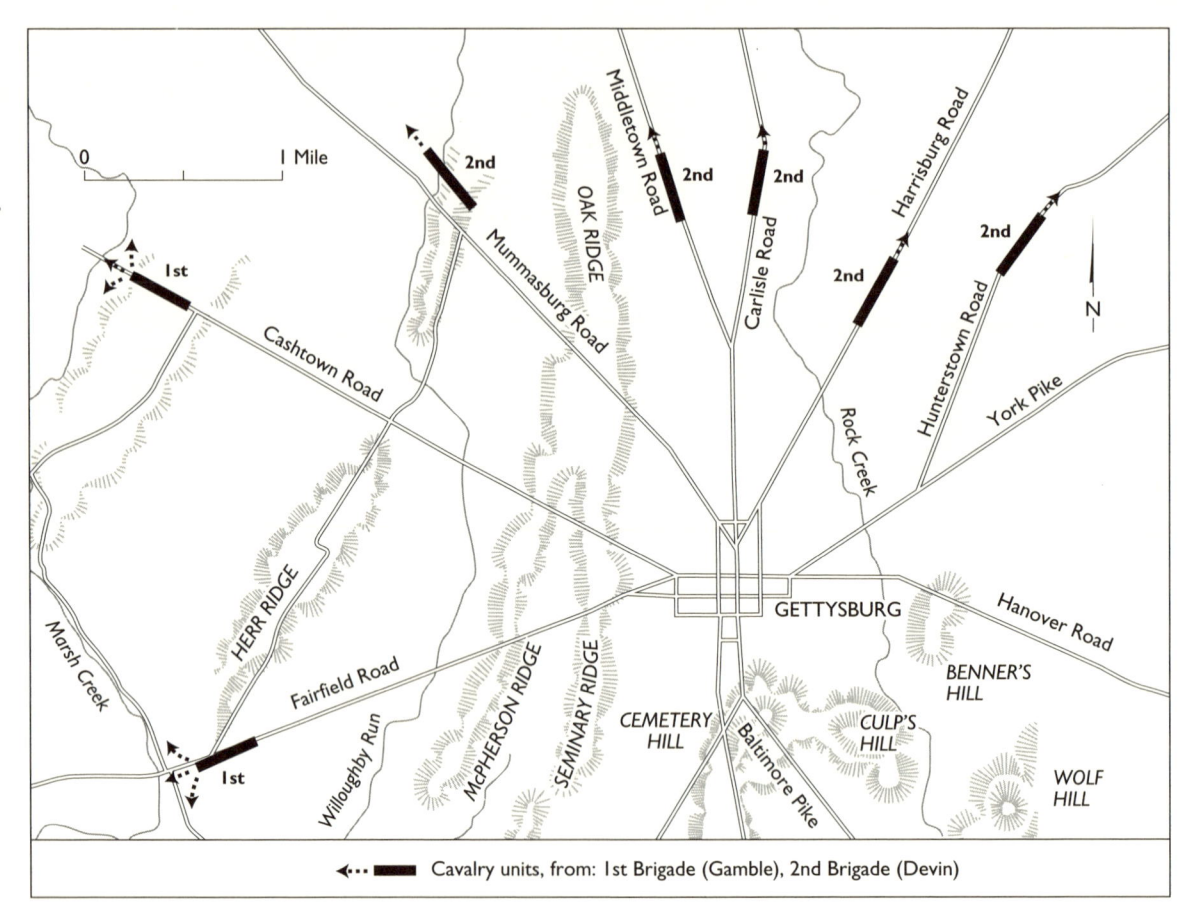

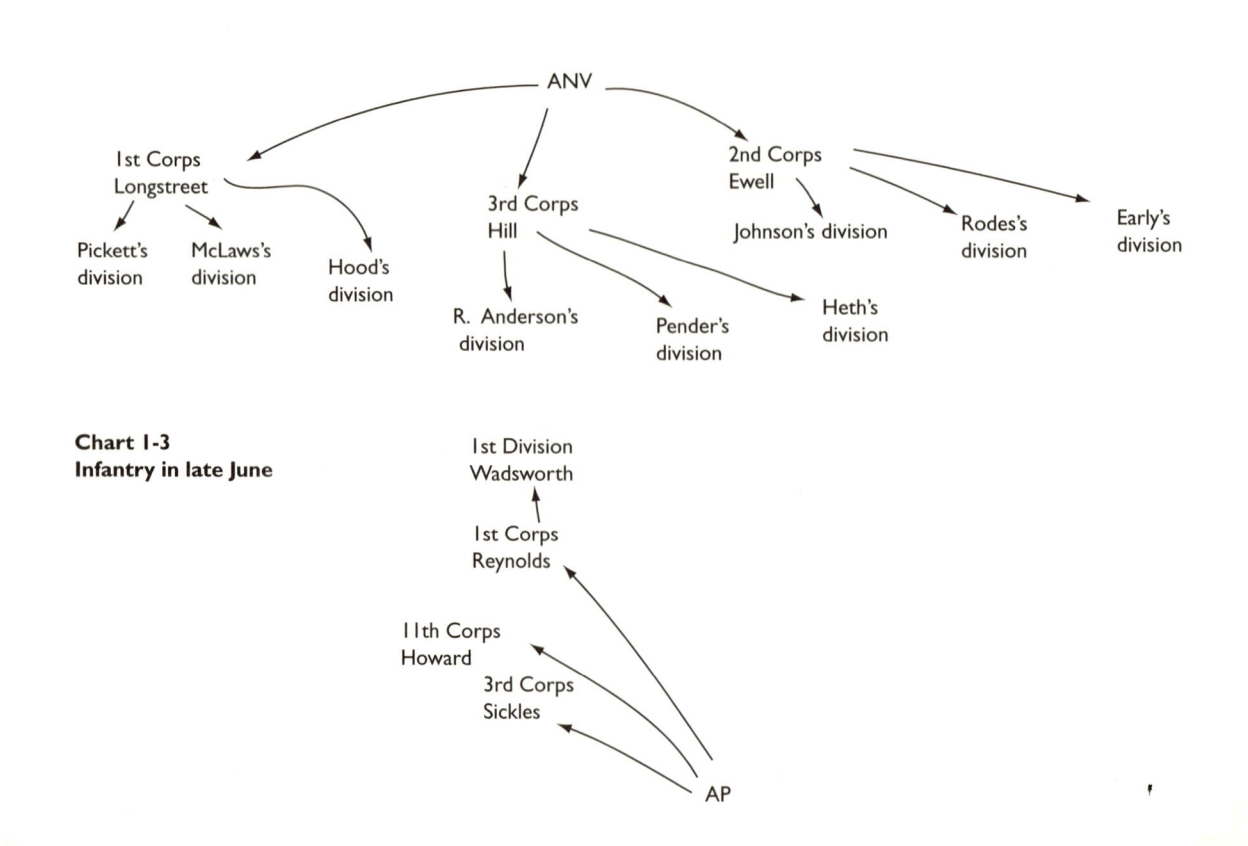

Cavalry units, from: 1st Brigade (Gamble), 2nd Brigade (Devin)

Chart 1-3 Infantry in late June

ANV
- 1st Corps Longstreet
  - Pickett's division
  - McLaws's division
  - Hood's division
- 3rd Corps Hill
  - R. Anderson's division
  - Pender's division
  - Heth's division
- 2nd Corps Ewell
  - Johnson's division
  - Rodes's division
  - Early's division

AP
- 1st Corps Reynolds
  - 1st Division Wadsworth
- 11th Corps Howard
- 3rd Corps Sickles

30 THE STAND OF THE U.S. ARMY AT GETTYSBURG

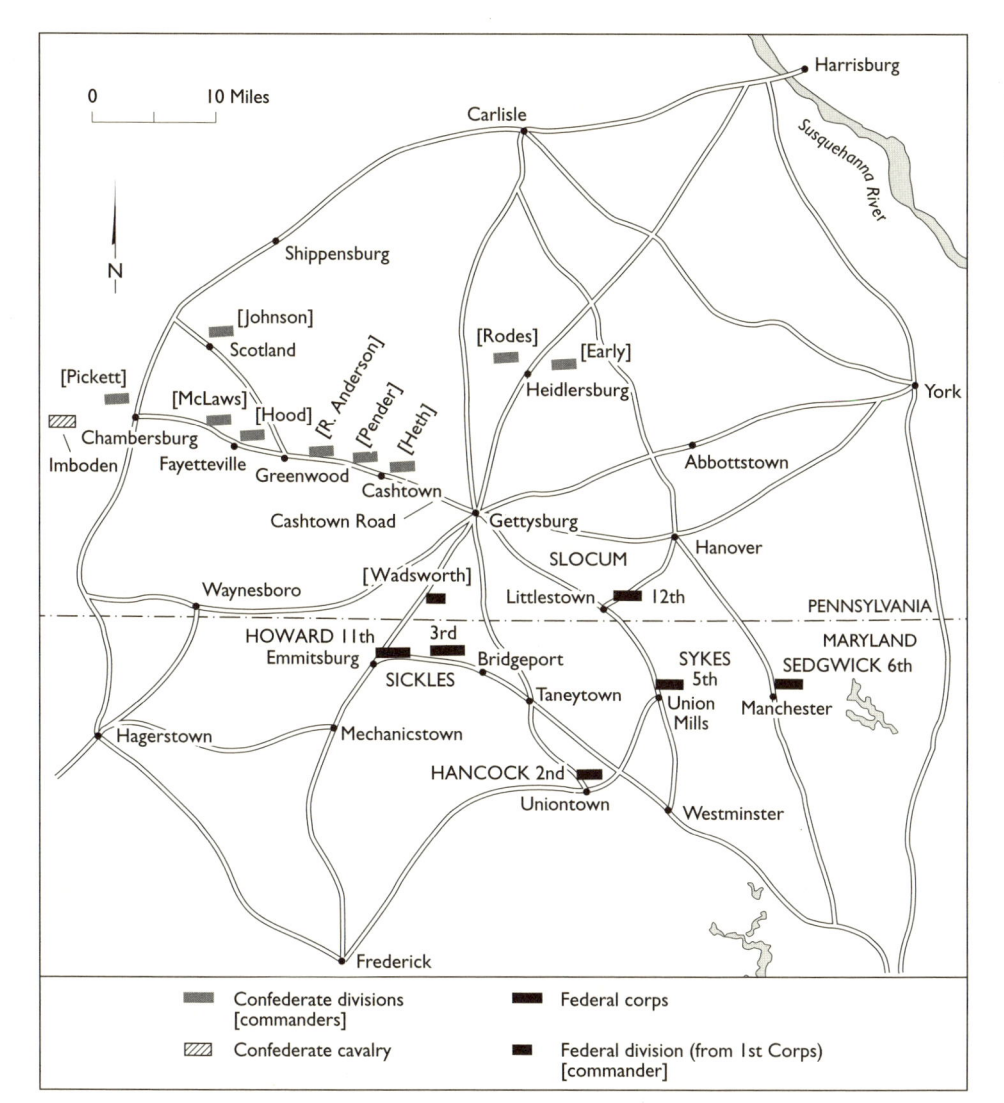

**Map 1-19
Infantry positions,
June 30, P.M.**

Lee—dispatching that man from Dover on June 30 (map 1-10)—returned carrying orders from the army commander. They described the action at Gettysburg on that day and directed General Stuart to join the Confederate concentration there (map 1-10). Exhausted and sleep deprived, Stuart's three brigades of troopers took off toward Gettysburg at 1 A.M. on July 2.

For his part, General Kilpatrick did not pursue Stuart after the Battle of Hanover. Because his Union troopers were outnumbered—so he can perhaps be excused for not nipping at the rebels' heels—Kilpatrick failed to do anything useful. By riding slowly away from Hanover on July 1 due northward toward East Berlin (map 1-16), he failed to keep tabs on Stuart's movements. Nor did he seek details of the Confederate infantry positions in this part of the campaign theater (in particular, the rebel infantry movements westward). Finally, on the morning of July 2, Kilpatrick's division was ordered to Gettysburg—where, unbeknownst to him, a great battle was under way. Kilpatrick progressed southwest from East Berlin, with Generals Custer and Farnsworth converging on Hunterstown, five miles northeast of Gettysburg (map 1-16). The brigades commanded by both of these "boy generals" would see heavy action the next day, but by then another element of the Union cavalry had long since initiated an engagement with the Army of Northern Virginia.

THE ROADS TO GETTYSBURG

Map 1-20
Buford's positions, and an outlying Confederate one, night of June 30

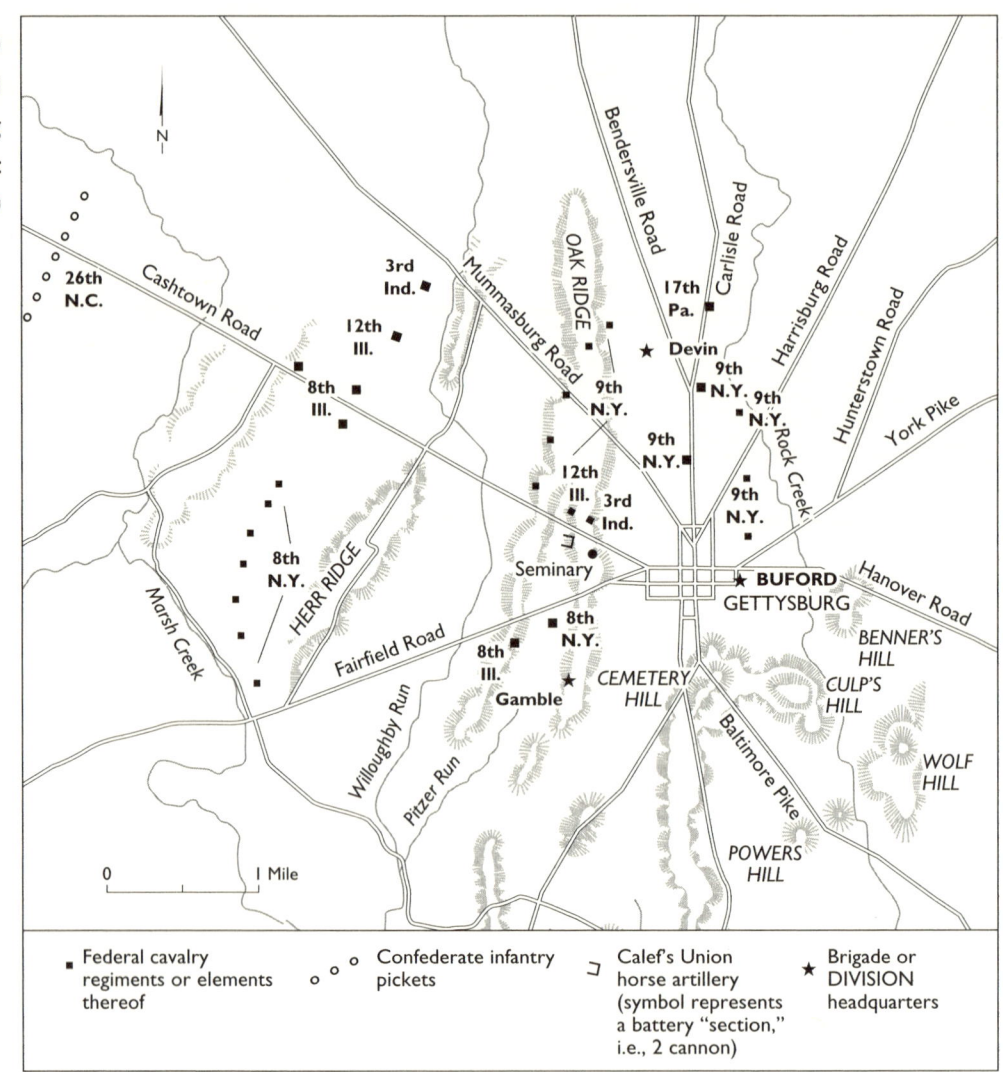

That unit, Buford's division, was ordered by General Meade to proceed to Gettysburg from its position west and just south of it (map 1-17).[56] Buford entered the town just before noon on Tuesday, June 30. Gettysburg was then a place of no consequence, at least in terms of what the Union high command knew about the Confederate positions and concentrations—next to nothing. Meade nevertheless ordered his infantry units to march in the direction of Gettysburg (where "all the roads converge"), and General Buford sought intelligence about the rebel army. He sent scouting parties north and west of town throughout the second half of June 30 (map 1-18). By that night, Buford knew that Confederate forces were all over the place and were coming (maps 1-15 and 1-19, chart 1-3). Moreover, the Gettysburg townspeople had informed Buford's men of a column of Confederate *infantry*, coming down Cashtown Road (maps 1-19 and 1-20) in the late morning. However, those soldiers had quietly retraced their footsteps back to the northwest.

Between 10 and 11 P.M. on June 30, General Buford sent couriers southward to the commander of the Federal 1st Corps, Maj. Gen. John F. Reynolds, and to his own cavalry commander, General Pleasonton.[57] Buford described explicitly that elements of Hill's Confederate corps were northwest of and close to Gettysburg,

32   THE STAND OF THE U.S. ARMY AT GETTYSBURG

and that Ewell's corps was marching toward that town from the north. Pleasonton in turn informed General Meade. Thus, the Union high command knew that its army might have to prepare for a fight.

General Reynolds commanded the lead element of Union infantry as it proceeded north from Frederick. Meade ordered Reynolds to move toward Gettysburg early on July 1, with the Federal 11th and 3rd Corps to follow (maps 1-14 and 1-19; chart 1-3). He ordered two of the other corps to advance toward Gettysburg as well, but no explicit orders were given to engage the enemy in the vicinity of that town. This was signified by General Meade leaving his headquarters in northern Maryland and holding two of his corps south of the Pennsylvania border.

That night, John Buford sent pickets out from Gettyburg. Advance Confederate infantry elements were surprisingly nearby (map 1-20; chart 1-4), although General Buford was not about to be surprised. As the situation unfolded, the two great armies moved toward a cataclysmic collision that "would become etched in the national memory."[58]

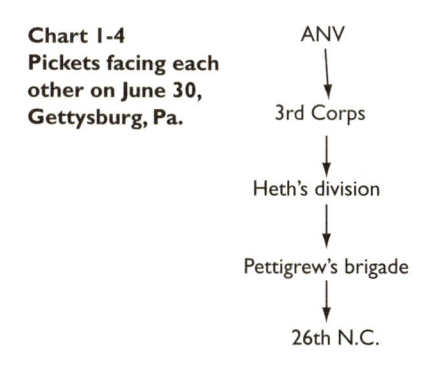

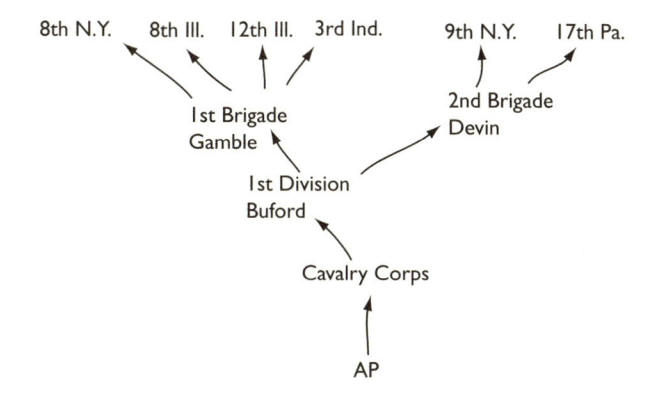

**Chart 1-4
Pickets facing each other on June 30, Gettysburg, Pa.**

ANV
↓
3rd Corps
↓
Heth's division
↓
Pettigrew's brigade
↓
26th N.C.

8th N.Y.　8th Ill.　12th Ill.　3rd Ind.　　　9th N.Y.　17th Pa.
　　　↖　↖　↑　↗　　　　　　↑　↗
　　　　1st Brigade　　　　2nd Brigade
　　　　Gamble　↖　　↗　Devin
　　　　　　　1st Division
　　　　　　　Buford
　　　　　　　↑
　　　　　　Cavalry Corps
　　　　　　　↑
　　　　　　　AP

THE ROADS TO GETTYSBURG   33

**Map 2-1
Model for Gettysburg
and vicinity**

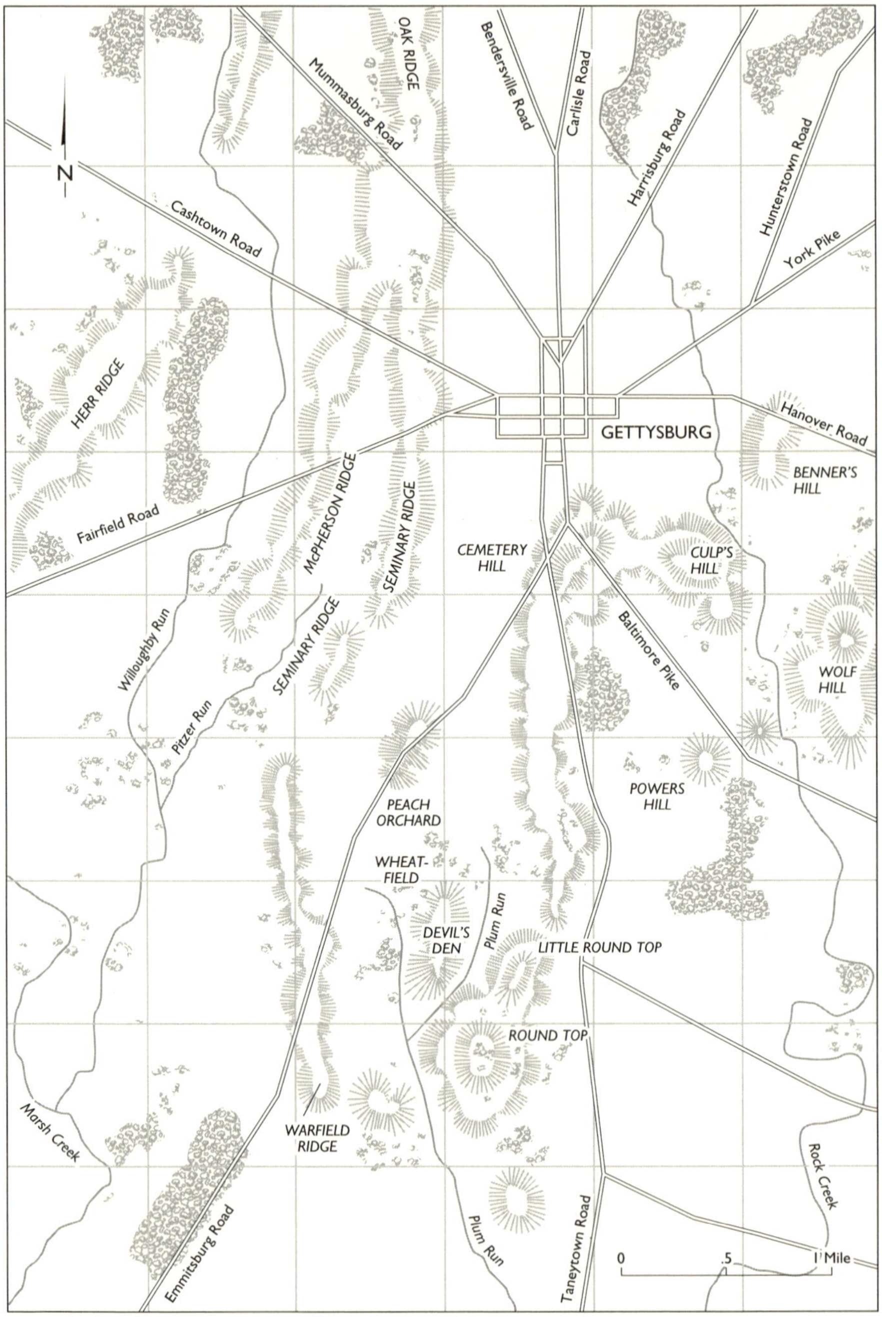

CHAPTER TWO

July 1: The Union Suffers a Setback but Gains a Great Position

Give me a firm place on which to stand.

—Archimedes

Stand on the right spot . . . be surely founded.

—Goethe

The Battle of Gettysburg commenced on July 1. However, before we begin the account of events on that Wednesday in the early summer of 1863, we need to become acquainted with the basic nature of the Gettysburg battlefield (map 2-1). This image will reappear repeatedly, as we will use it to orient ourselves with regard to many subsequent maps, which will show a portion of the field at higher magnification and higher resolution. Meanwhile, map 2-2 provides the first such orientation: Here, we see the theater of battle as it occurred on July 1—when essentially all of the fighting took place northwest and to the north of town. However, note that relevant portions of the field south of Gettysburg are also circumscribed on this map (2-2).

To help set the stage let us first consider what the weather, of all things, was like. July 1 began as a cloudy, relatively cool day. The early morning temperature was seventy-two degrees and would rise to seventy-six by 2 P.M., and there was a gentle southerly breeze.[1] This *is* worth mentioning, because some of the accounts seem to imply it was a hot and humid hell-on-earth during most of the Gettysburg campaign. In reality, it was generally cloudy, rainy, and on the cool side through most of the second half of June. Things did not really heat up in this mundane sense until July 3.

Cavalry Delaying Tactics and Accomplishments, Early Morning

The Battle of Gettysburg was triggered by what amounted to minor firefights that occurred early that Wednesday morning on the Cashtown and Carlisle Roads. How the fighting initially broke out was hinted at by specifying the positions of Union cavalry pickets, which had been ordered out from the town on the previous night. This was depicted at the end of the previous chapter in map 1-20. That diagram also coyly shows the portion of a Confederate infantry unit that was closest to the Federal defenders.

Phases of Battle:

a. Cavalry delaying tactics and accomplishments, early morning

b. Infantry clashes on the Union left and Confederate right: attack and counterattack

c. A late morning lull

d. The fighting resumes in the center of the field

e. Infantry action all along the lines: the rebel left enters the fray and the right resumes the attack

f. The Union lines give way from right to left and are pushed back below the town

g. The Federal defense coalesces on a hill south of Gettysburg, where the Confederate attacks could not have readily resumed

Map 2-2
Theater of battle, July 1

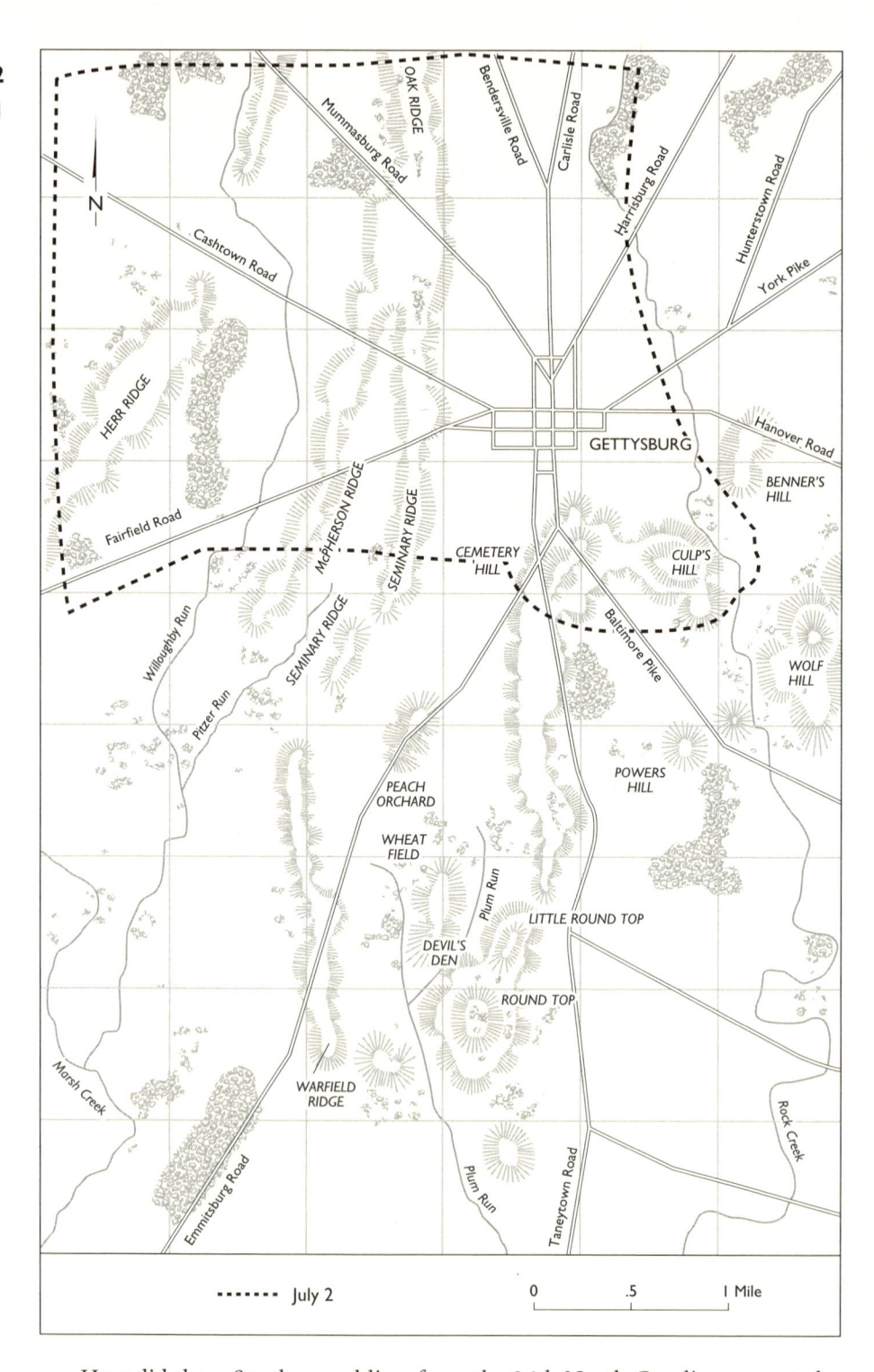

------- July 2   0   .5   1 Mile

How did these Southern soldiers from the 26th North Carolina come to be poised—along with larger elements of their brigade and division (chart 1-3)—to participate in the opening stages of an engagement that would eventually draw in significant portions of both armies that day?

The North Carolinians, and Pettigrew's brigade, were a part of Maj. Gen. Henry Heth's infantry division in the newly formed Confederate 3rd Corps commanded by Lt. Gen. Ambrose P. Hill (*barely* so commanded, it seemed, as the battle unfolded). Because Heth's division was the first large rebel infantry unit on the field, its path from northern Virginia to southern Pennsylvania is diagrammed in map 2-3.

Map 2-3

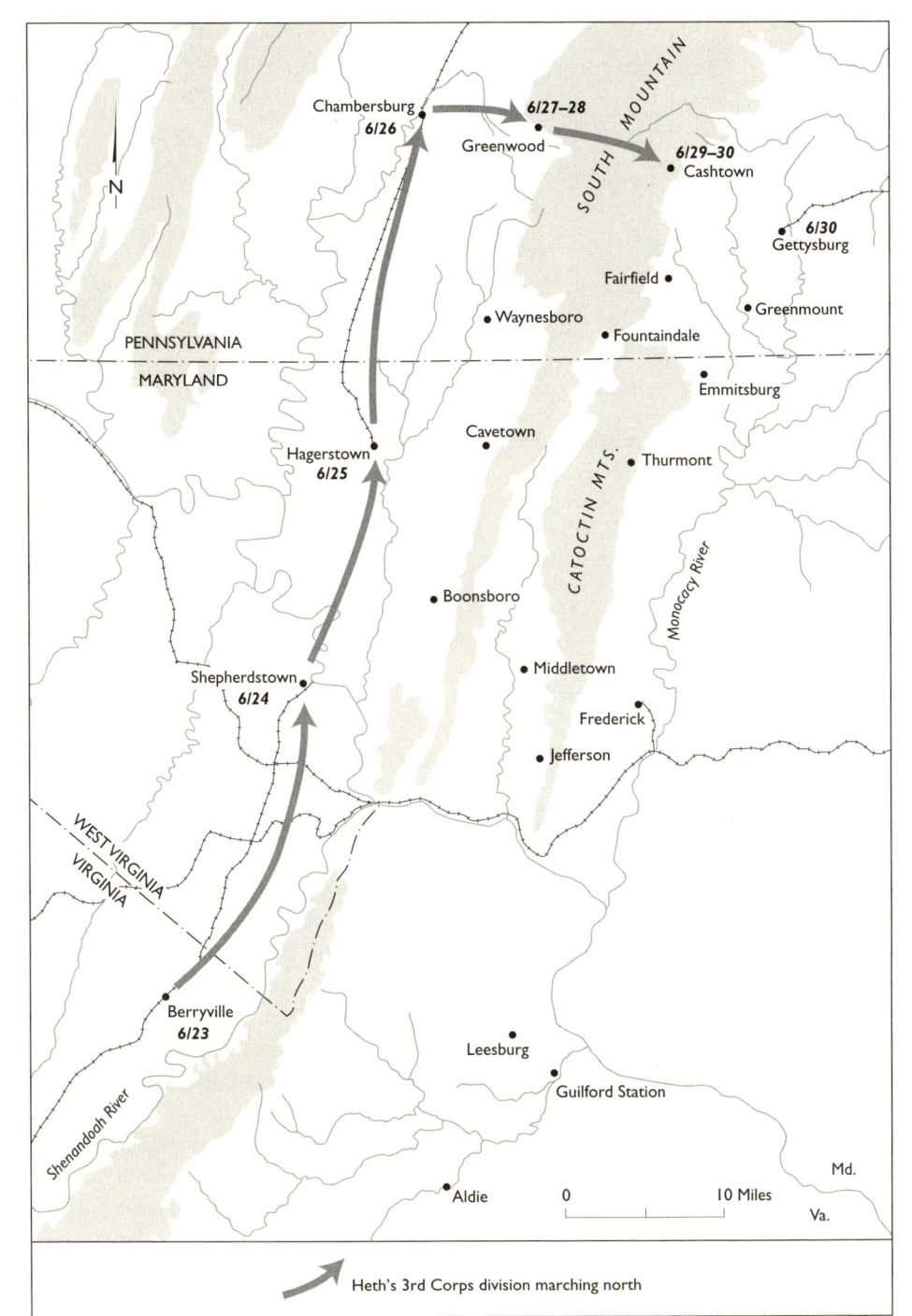

Northward marches of Heth's Confederate Division

→ Heth's 3rd Corps division marching north

Hill's corps formed the van of the Confederate forces arrayed northwest of Gettysburg in late June. Thus, Brig. Gen. J. Johnston Pettigrew's brigade found itself in a position to reconnoiter the immediate vicinity of that town. This it did, marching down the Cashtown Road on June 30. General Pettigrew sensed that the Army of Northern Virginia should not engage the enemy because the army as a whole was "not up."[2]

Legend has it that Pettigrew and his brigade marched to Gettysburg for the purpose of commandeering a supply of shoes. These were supposedly inventoried at some factory or another in Gettysburg. Some historians today view this part of the July 1 story as false. Gettysburg had no shoe factory in the 1860s and only a

THE UNION SUFFERS A SETBACK 37

Map 2-4
Heth's advance toward Gettysburg, July 1, early A.M.

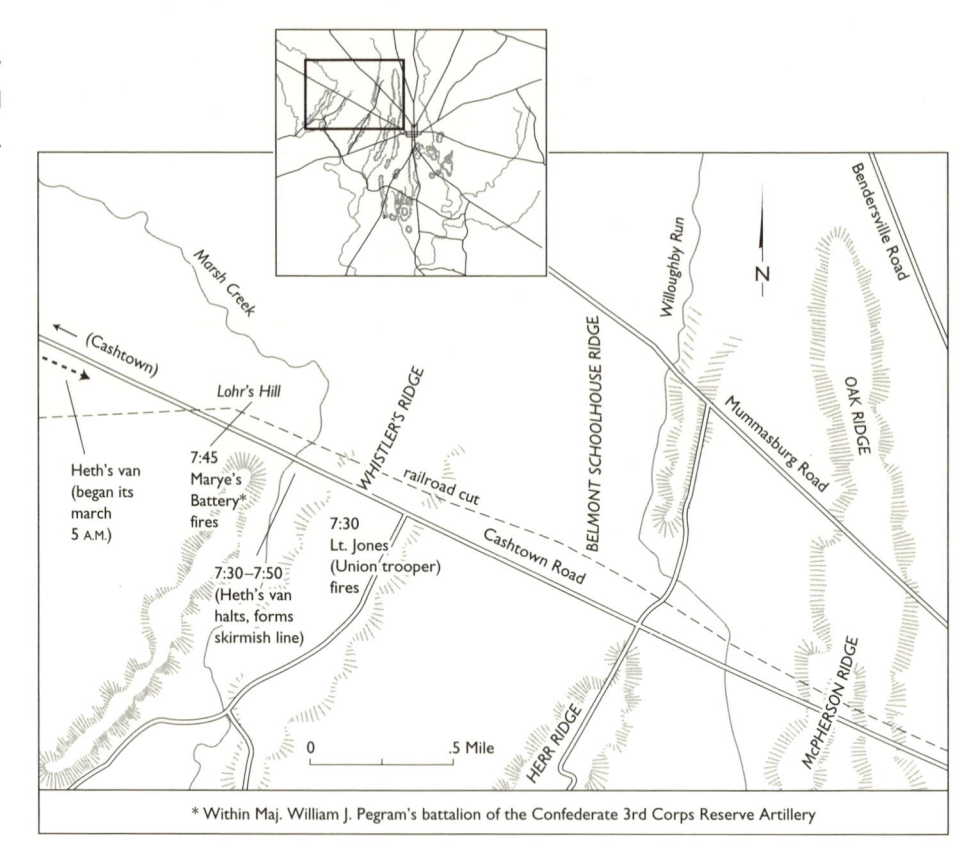

*Within Maj. William J. Pegram's battalion of the Confederate 3rd Corps Reserve Artillery

few citizens there listed their occupation as shoemaker. Recall that General Early's 2nd Corps division passed through Gettysburg on June 26. One of the "forage demands" Early had made upon the townspeople was for fifteen hundred pairs of shoes, but none were found. Even though there is no evidence that the Army of Northern Virginia was severely short of footwear during the campaign, it is conceivable that Pettigrew's soldiers thought they were on an important mission to commandeer shoes four days later. However, in his after-action report written in September 1863, Pettigrew's commander, General Heth, made only the barest mention of shoes. It was not until 1878, in a suspiciously excuse-ridden article he wrote for a Northern newspaper, that Heth invoked a more bloated claim about his footwear-finding mission at Gettysburg.[3]

On June 30, General Pettigrew had been simply reconnoitering—in force, mind you. The army was concentrating in the Gettysburg vicinity, and the question that needed to be answered was: What was there, in the town's *immediate* vicinity? General Lee almost certainly had received no information on the relevant details from cavalry reconnaissance.

As Pettigrew's infantrymen marched southeastward, he received word from an informant that "Buford's cavalry division, 3000 strong" occupied Gettysburg.[4] Some of Pettigrew's men, ranging east of Herr Ridge toward Willoughby Run (map 2-4), saw mounted Northern troopers on the crest of McPherson Ridge four hundred yards east of them. General Pettigrew, exercising good judgment, ordered a 180-degree turn and marched back toward Cashtown.

That night, Pettigrew's division and corps commanders, Heth and Hill, rather casually decided to send Pettigrew back to Gettysburg in the morning to complete his reconnaissance (chart 2-1).[5] General Pettigrew protested that he had observed Union cavalry near Gettysburg, but his superiors downplayed that report. They

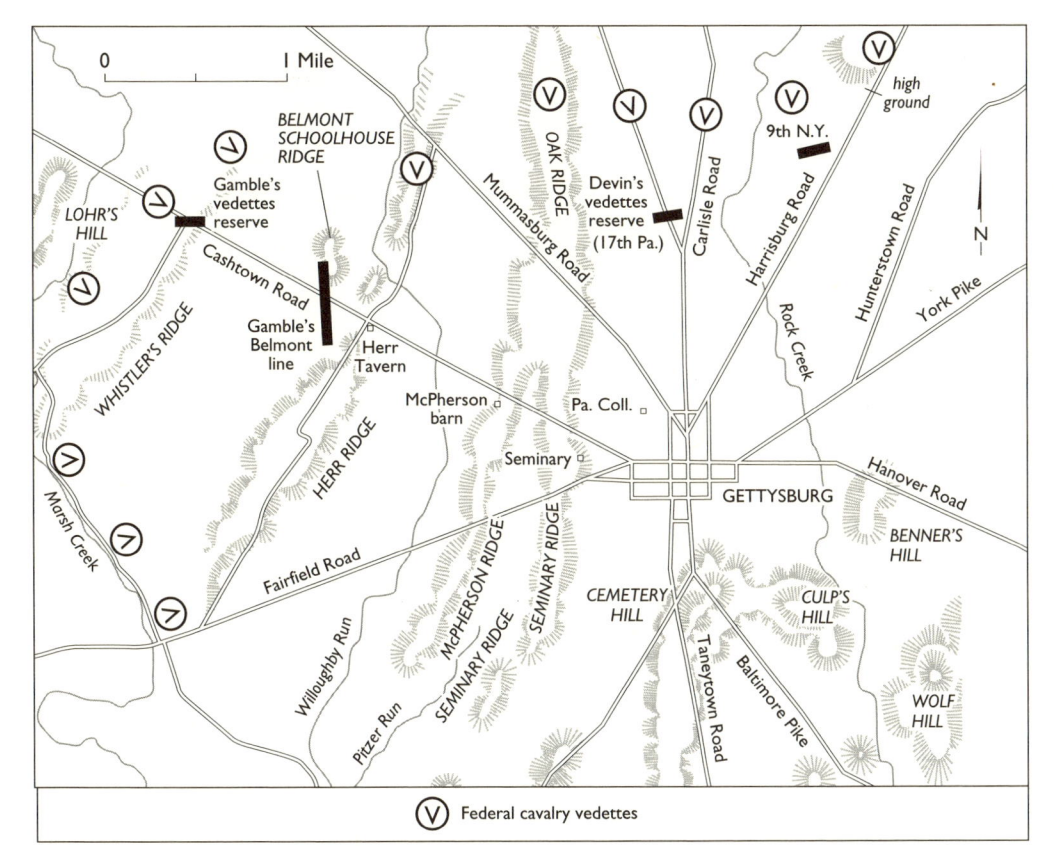

**Map 2-5
Buford's positions and actions, early July 1**

did not believe elements of the Army of the Potomac could be so near, so Pettigrew must have seen mere militia. (There *were* other Northern cavalry units roaming this part of Pennsylvania, but they were not attached to the Army of the Potomac.) Militiamen could, of course, be brushed aside with no problem. This was revealed by how readily such Union men were scattered when Early's troops passed through Gettysburg on June 26.

In any case, General Heth ordered his brigades, including Pettigrew's, back down that road. These 3rd Corps soldiers started off in column formation at 5 A.M. on July 1 (map 2-4). They were led by the five batteries of Maj. William J. Pegram's artillery battalion from the 3rd Corps Reserve, followed by infantry brigades commanded by Archer, Davis, Pettigrew, and Brockenbrough (chart 2-1). Buford's outlying pickets were not very far away. In particular, those cavalrymen were scattered about in an anticipatory defensive posture as vedettes, four- or five-man patrols (map 2-5). Most such cavalrymen would have dismounted, with one member holding the others' horses nearby, so that they could fall back quickly if they were engaged. However, other subunits in Buford's brigades and regiments were operating thoroughly dismounted, with their horses taken to the rear.

This signifies a problem with dismounted cavalry. As implied above, up to a quarter of the troopers are effectively removed from action, owing to the necessity of tending to the horses. These details lead to the mention of a larger matter: The *dismounted* fighting involving Buford's cavalry arrayed above and beyond Gettysburg in *small groups of mobile men*, describes most of what happened in the early morning hours on the first day of the battle.[6] Buford's troopers did not make an hours-long last-ditch stand in a defensive line of battle on that Wednes-

THE UNION SUFFERS A SETBACK   39

day morning. Buford's stand was brief, occurring at the very end of his division's contribution to the fighting.

Chart 2-1 lists the units that essentially opened the battle. Indeed, a scrape seemed inevitable during the early morning hours, given that Heth's infantrymen were heading straight for Buford's vedettes. The officer in charge of the farthest outlying pickets was Lt. Marcellus E. Jones of Company E, 8th Illinois Cavalry (chart 2-1). The men under him were on and just beyond Whistler's Ridge (map 2-5), which overlooked Marsh Creek. This is the fourth ridge out from Gettysburg in a westerly direction, including the famous ones: Seminary Ridge (closest to the town) and McPherson (the next one out). Lieutenant Jones was some three hundred yards in the rear, but was excitedly called to a vedette post. There, on Whistler's Ridge, Jones saw what his outposted men had already glimpsed: Confederate infantry marching down the road. He immediately notified his regimental commander and borrowed a Sharp's carbine from Sgt. Levi Shaffer. Thus, at 7:30 A.M. on July 1, 1863, Lieutenant Jones fired a shot up the road, at "an officer on a white or light gray horse" (map 2-4).[7]

As was often the case with such a short-barreled shoulder arm, this firing was to no effect (moreover, the distance from Whistler's Ridge to the position of the mounted rebel officer near the bridge at Marsh Creek was eight hundred yards). However, with that shot, the Battle of Gettysburg had begun.[8]

The lone shot from Sergeant Shaffer's carbine startled the advancing rebels. They paused while an artillery unit accompanying Heth's infantrymen unlimbered on Lohr's Hill and fired off in the direction of Whistler's Ridge (map 2-4). The Federal plan was beginning to work, in that all General Buford could really do was stall the Confederate's trek down the Cashtown Road. Heth outnumbered Buford by more than two-to-one even though one of Heth's four brigades, Col. John M. Brockenbrough's (chart 2-1), was well back at this time. Also, Heth had more firepower on a unit-by-unit basis (muskets outgun carbines, and Buford had minimal artillery support).

Referral to John Buford's plan speaks to his goals for July 1. "In memory, [has] Buford's day one fighting . . . been blown out of all proportion?"[9] Was Buford protecting the "good ground" south of the town of Gettysburg? One feature of it does come into play toward the end of July 1: Cemetery Hill (as circumscribed on map 2-2). However, it is *not* clear that this cavalry commander was explicitly aware of that hill or any other nearby prominent elevations. Some students of the battle have given General Buford credit for *specifically* protecting potential high-

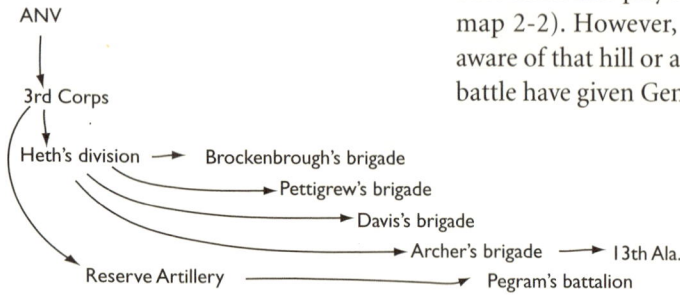

Chart 2-1
The opening of (what would become) the major engagements of July 1

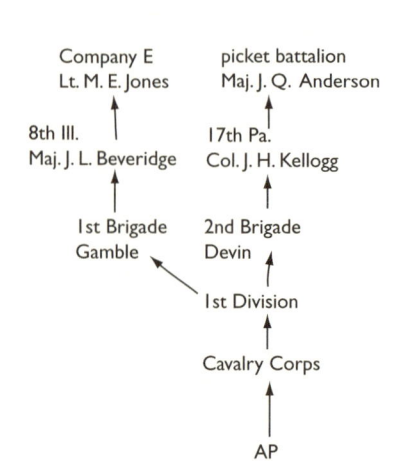

quality positions for the main body of the Army of the Potomac. They contend he knew that if he could stall the Confederate infantry moving toward him from two directions, the Union infantry corps might have time to come up and occupy all those areas of good ground south of the town. However, I can find no mention by Buford himself of any hill, ridge, or other such piece of high ground collectively (not that he could have referred to them by name).[10] Thus, I sense that Buford was not "protecting" anything in particular. Instead, he was defending *out front*, solely in the general sense of what that means. If he had set up defenses *south* of Gettysburg, it would not have given the Federal infantry much in the way of options when they arrived on the field, because Buford knew his cavalrymen could be forced to retreat from a given defensive position southward, thus minimizing the geographical options available to the Union infantry units arriving from that direction. Should the Union cavalry be compelled to retreat on the morning of July 1, Buford wanted his troopers to get pushed back from *outlying* locations north and west of town.

John Buford's decision to conduct a highly mobile fighting withdrawal—rather than simply form one defensive line that would have cracked soon after the initial assault upon it—maximized the amount of *time* that he could hold the enemy off north and northwest of Gettysburg, and maximized the amount of *space* that would be available to the main body when it arrived. Therefore, Buford's forward defense acted out a sound, generic military strategy: *do not* choose *at first* the *last* possible defensive position. Based on the evidence, this makes more sense than the arguments of those who credit Buford with prescient brilliance in which he envisioned his comrades in arms on Culp's Hill, Cemetery Hill, the ridge below, and a high place farther to the south called Little Round Top. The potential value of an out-front defense, followed by a fallback if necessary, will be reprised on July 2.

Returning now to July 1, Brig. Gen. James J. Archer, commander of Heth's lead brigade (chart 2-1), sent skirmishers out to flank the road to the north and south of it. But Heth's division was basically still strung out in a long column: Archer in the lead (the 13th Alabama on point), followed not far behind by Brig. Gen. Joseph R. Davis's and Pettigrew's brigades along with that of Col. Brockenbrough. Pettigrew's unit had been closest to the Federals overnight and at dawn, but had fallen into line behind Davis as the latter's regiments of Mississippians and North Carolinians passed.

Generals Heth, Davis, and Pettigrew were all new to the levels of command they held in the Gettysburg campaign. One wonders if this is why Heth did not move with much celerity on this Wednesday morning. He started out only five miles from the outlying Union cavalry vedettes. Heth's nominal start time was 5 A.M., but several of his units may have actually set out later, or they dawdled on the march to the extent that it took them two and a half hours to reach their foe. Time was of the essence, as it turned out in terms of the Federal infantry arrival. However, General Heth may have felt in no hurry to collide with any kind of Federal force, making him gingerly march toward Gettysburg. According to the postwar writings of former Confederates, he was *not* to engage the enemy. His corps commander, A. P. Hill, supposedly knew this and told Heth to exercise caution as he again advanced on that Pennsylvania town.[11]

Heth's leading units continued to advance from the area of Marsh Creek and Whistler's Ridge (map 2-6) as Col. William Gamble's cavalry vedettes maintained rapid harassing fire on the infantry moving toward them. They were deliberately falling back toward McPherson Ridge, the one closest to Gettysburg (about two miles from the original outposted positions of Buford's troopers). These cavalry-

Map 2-6

Heth's advance toward the town—later in the morning

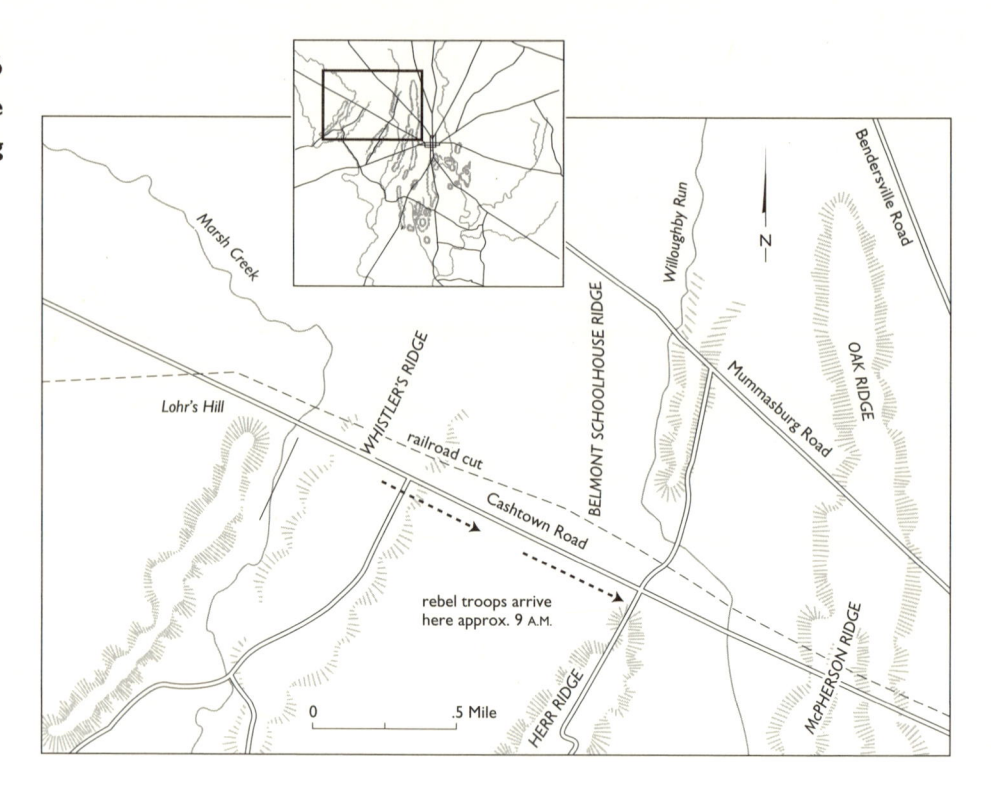

men were executing a fighting withdrawal in good order. It was a game of hide-and-seek involving small clusters of troopers firing their carbines up the Cashtown Road (and to either side of it) at Heth's lead brigades. An example is provided by the account of a cavalryman in the 8th Illinois who recalled being slowly driven from three successive positions between Belmont Schoolhouse Ridge and Herr Ridge, as he took cover, fired, and then was forced to keep withdrawing in the direction of the town.[12]

Thus, the Confederates were not making rapid headway. They were further slowed down when, as Heth's infantrymen approached Belmont Schoolhouse Ridge, Buford ordered Colonel Gamble to advance with a relatively large mass of troopers (map 2-5)—three hundred to four hundred of whom went to what was now the outer rim of the morning's defense (map 2-7).[13] With this, General Heth had enough of trying to advance toward Gettysburg largely in column. Instead of increasing his skirmishing pressure on Gamble's defenders, Heth had his lead brigades deploy from column formation into full lines of battle perpendicular to the Cashtown Road. This began about 9:30 A.M. and required about half an hour as Archer's brigade moved into battle line south of the road and Davis's brigade did the same on the north side. Buford was by now pulling back and concentrating most of the cavalrymen in his two brigades. The Confederates bombarded the line of defense Buford was forming with artillery fire from Pegram's batteries (chart 2-1), which had dropped trail on Herr Ridge.

The Confederates, attacking along a three-thousand-man front, finally reached Herr Ridge at about 10 A.M. General Buford knew that the game of hide-and-seek was over. By the time Archer and Davis passed Herr Ridge, Buford had established his last line along McPherson Ridge, where he arrayed approximately two thousand troopers between the Fairfield Road on his left and Oak Hill on his right (map 2-7). This was a long, thin defensive line (made thinner by the fact that more than five hundred of these cavalrymen had to tend to the horses).

Buford also knew that Federal infantry was near. The commander of the 1st

42   THE STAND OF THE U.S. ARMY AT GETTYSBURG

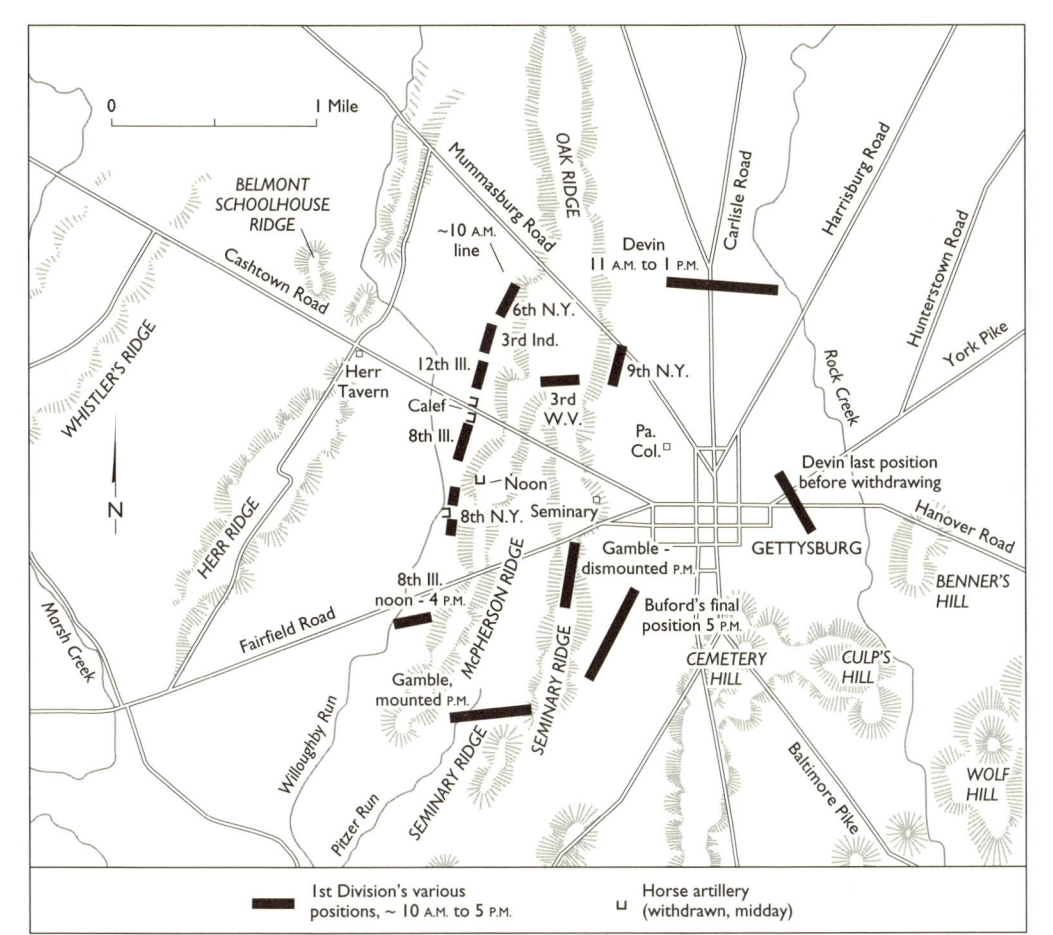

Map 2-7
Buford's actions and positions, late morning and afternoon of July 1

Corps, and in fact of the Army of the Potomac's entire left wing (forming the units closest to Gettysburg that morning), had ridden ahead of his foot soldiers to find the cavalry commander. Thus, Maj. Gen. John F. Reynolds conferred with Buford behind the latter's lines just before the Confederate artillery fire ceased and their infantry battle line rolled down Herr Ridge. After their brief conference, Reynolds rejoined his advancing infantrymen. Before they could get to the battlefield, however, the rebel attack commenced at a few minutes after ten. By 10:30, Heth's soldiers were almost on top of Buford's troopers and his one battery of horse artillery (map 2-7). The pressure was severe, and it was only a matter a time until the defending cavalrymen would be gobbled up or pushed off the ridge.

It was just about this time that General Reynolds reappeared on the field at the head of a column of Federal infantrymen moving across a meadow straight for McPherson Ridge. The 1st Corps had come at last.

The Infantry Clashes on the Union Left and Confederate Right: Attack and Counterattack

Among the Union soldiers arriving literally in the nick of time were the 1st Brigade of the 1st Division of the 1st Corps (chart 2-2). These were the hard fighters of the Iron Brigade, commanded by Brig. Gen. Solomon Meredith.[14] Since the 1st Division of the 1st Corps was the first Federal infantry force on the field, its paths to Gettysburg are shown in map 2-8. As it approached the town itself, the division's two brigades cut to the left across open fields to minimize the distance between the road on which they had been marching and the scene of the

THE UNION SUFFERS A SETBACK

**Map 2-8
Wadsworth's Federal
Division marches north**

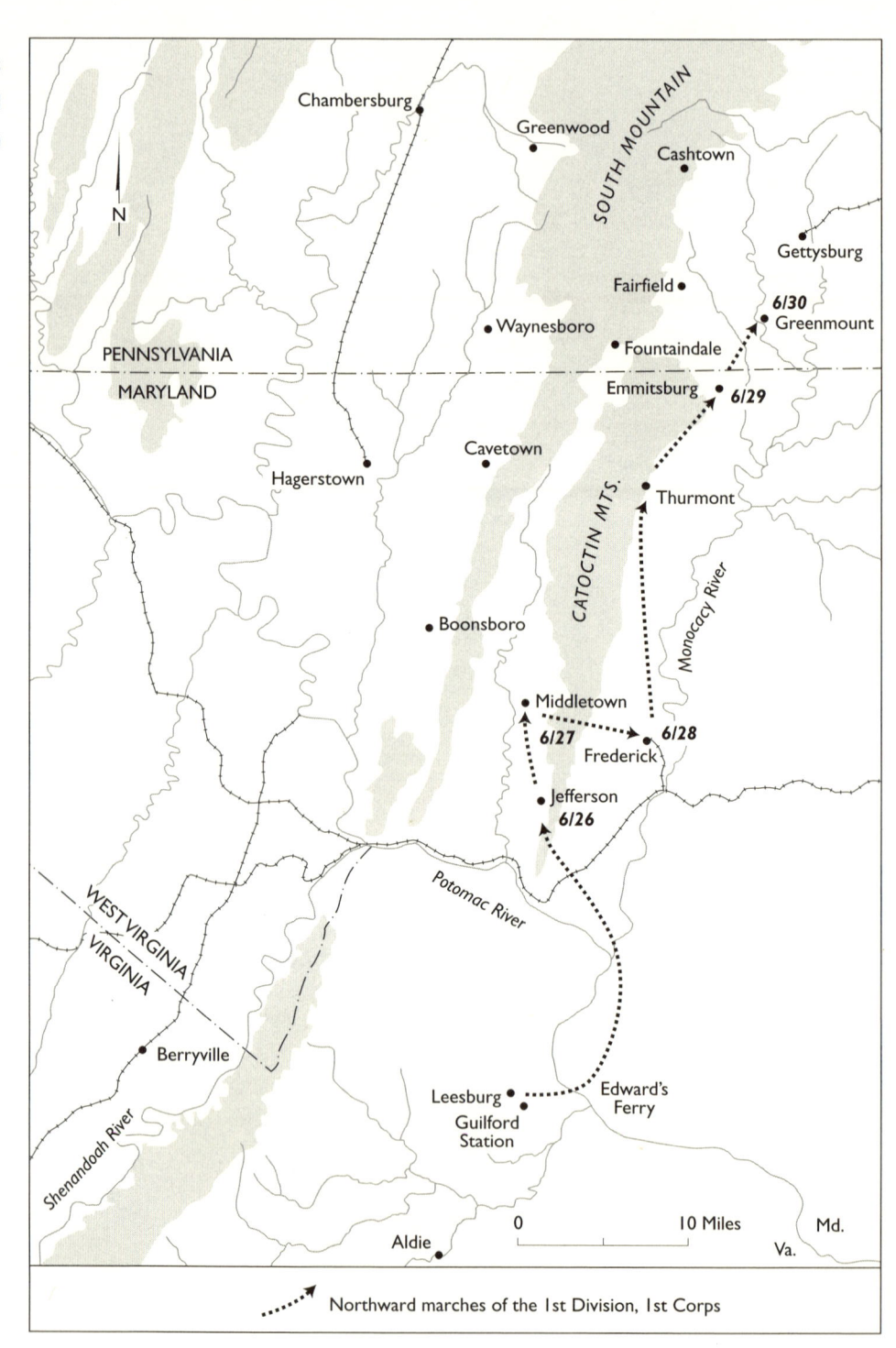

morning's battle. The Federal infantrymen took over the positions momentarily occupied by their cavalry mates, leading to the first major clash of foot soldiers. The units so poised are indicated on map 2-9.

The Iron Brigade did not just relieve the dismounted cavalry defenders on McPherson Ridge; it attacked. This action began slightly *later* than the fight that broke out just *north* of the Cashtown Road, but the action south of it is described first for the sake of a certain piece of continuity: Davis's attack against Cutler north of the road will be described shortly, followed immediately by an account of the battle for the railroad cut (maps 2-11 and 2-12).[15]

44   THE STAND OF THE U.S. ARMY AT GETTYSBURG

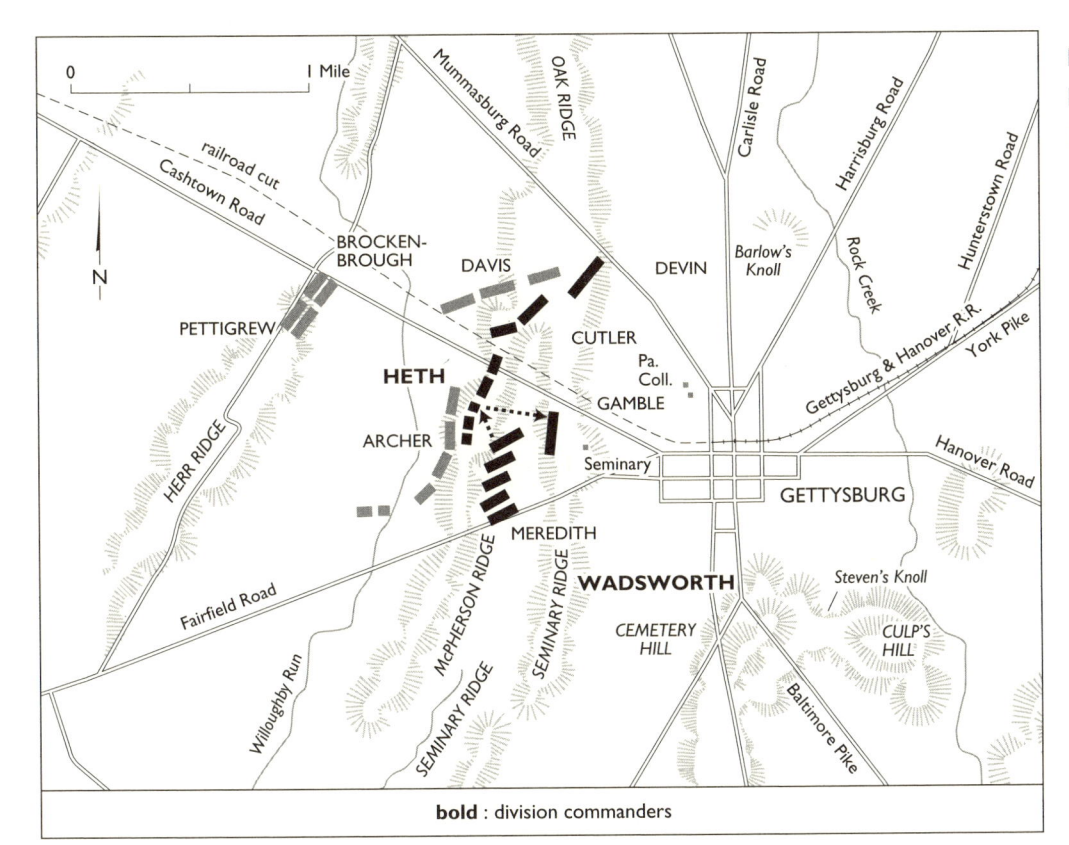

**Map 2-9
Infantry in position,
10–10:30 A.M.**

bold: division commanders

The Iron Brigade soldiers (chart 2-2) swept down from McPherson Ridge toward Willoughby Run (map 2-10) and went in against Archer's brigade *en echelon* (we will see this maneuver again on a larger scale in Chapter 3). The right-hand regiment (2nd Wisconsin) was engaged first, firing toward Archer's men near the Cashtown Road. Then the next Iron Brigade regiment (7th Wisconsin) went into position to the 2nd Wisconsin's left, followed by the 19th Indiana and the 24th Michigan on its left. When the turn of this fourth regiment came, the Michigan men advanced with their left wing extending almost to Fairfield Road (map 2-10). As elements of Archer's brigade became preoccupied with the 2nd Wisconsin in their front,[16] on the Iron Brigade's right, the left wing of this Union force found itself with the opportunity to *flank* Archer's men by overlapping the right side of the rebel advance into McPherson Woods. The Westerners achieved this (map 2-10), and in so doing sent the Alabama regiments tumbling back across the stream, with many of the Confederates being captured, including General Archer himself.[17]

This finished the Confederate advance south of the Cashtown Road on the morning of July 1. By now, the Union cavalry was well relieved. To oversimplify somewhat—Buford's brigades withdrew from harm's way and went to guard the infantry's flanks (maps 2-7 and 2-9). Not long afterward, this division of troopers was ordered to ride to Winchester, Maryland. Buford's command sustained 4 percent casualties on July 1 (110 of 2,780 men engaged).[18] This small figure reflects the way that General Buford had arranged and executed his defense that morning. By the end of the day, the losses suffered by several defending Federal infantry units would rise to horrifying proportions. One of the most significant losses occurred when General Reynolds was fatally shot in the head while on the back side of McPherson Ridge between 10:30 and 11 A.M. (map 2-10).[19] Command of Reynold's 1st Corps devolved to Maj. Gen. Abner Doubleday; he headed the 1st Corps's 3rd Division, which was still marching toward the sound of the guns.

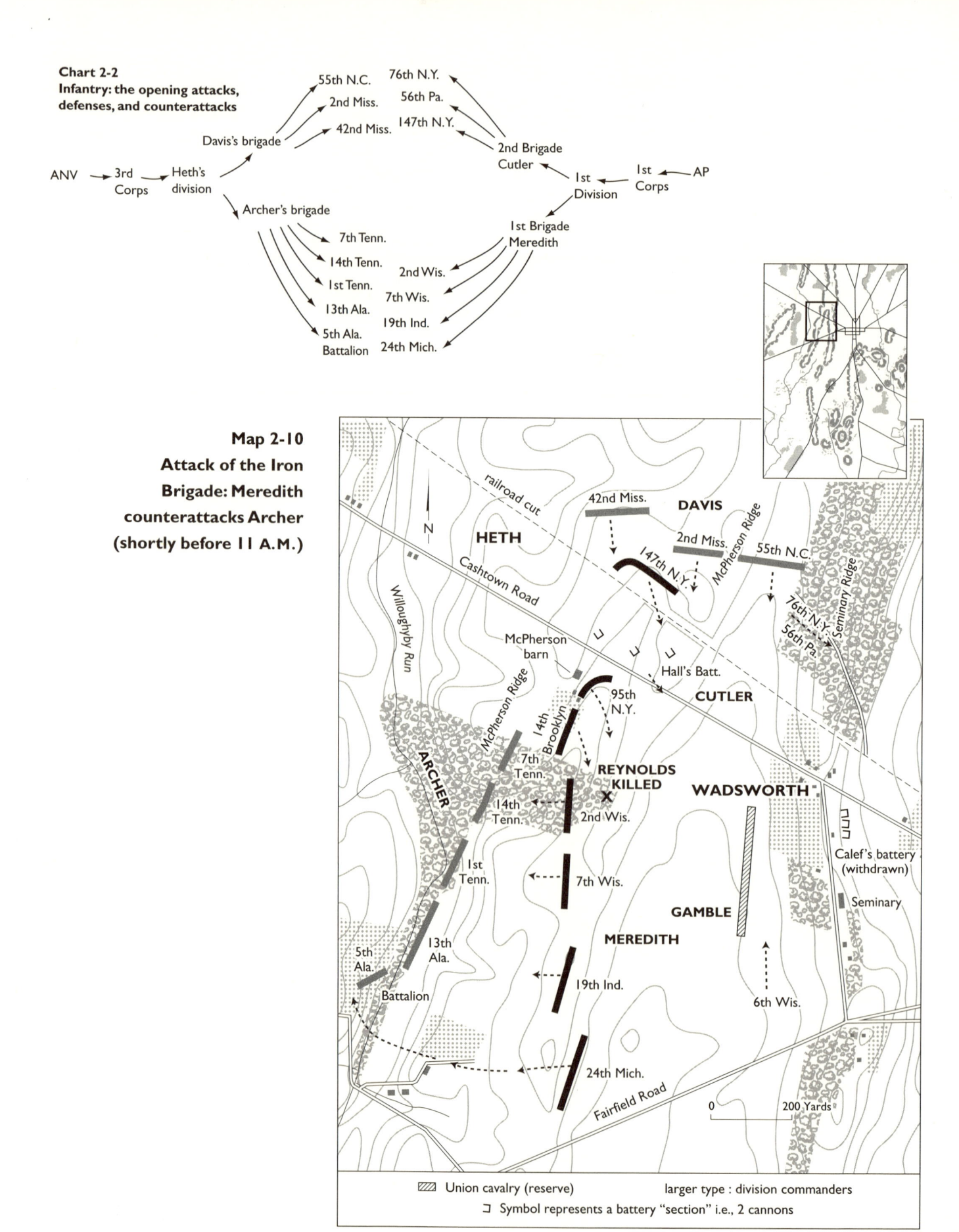

Chart 2-2
Infantry: the opening attacks, defenses, and counterattacks

ANV → 3rd Corps → Heth's division → Davis's brigade
- 55th N.C.
- 2nd Miss.
- 42nd Miss.

Heth's division → Archer's brigade
- 7th Tenn.
- 14th Tenn.
- 1st Tenn.
- 13th Ala.
- 5th Ala. Battalion

AP → 1st Corps → 1st Division → 2nd Brigade Cutler
- 76th N.Y.
- 56th Pa.
- 147th N.Y.

1st Division → 1st Brigade Meredith
- 2nd Wis.
- 7th Wis.
- 19th Ind.
- 24th Mich.

Map 2-10
Attack of the Iron Brigade: Meredith counterattacks Archer (shortly before 11 A.M.)

Union cavalry (reserve)
larger type: division commanders
⌐ Symbol represents a battery "section" i.e., 2 cannons

46 THE STAND OF THE U.S. ARMY AT GETTYSBURG

As the morning progressed, the seesaw battle between Heth's Confederates and the Union defenders in the 1st Division (1st Corps) continued north of the Cashtown Road. Recall that Davis's brigade was in the rebel van on that part of the field, its main body advancing behind its skirmishers abreast of Archer's line (map 2-9). Brigadier General Lysander Cutler's 2nd Brigade with three fresh regiments was moving in to meet Davis (chart 2-2). Cutler's unit had been marching in the lead as Reynolds's corps hurried toward Gettysburg. It arrived at McPherson Ridge shortly before the Iron Brigade did, and deployed north of the Cashtown Road (map 2-9).

In mirror-image symmetry to what had just happened below the road, General Davis got his left around Cutler's right. This is shown grossly in map 2-10 and at higher magnification in map 2-11. The left-most rebel regiment swung farther left as it advanced, moving past the Bender farm located well north of the Cashtown Road (map 2-11). The Confederate flanking attack caused Cutler's three regiments to give way and retreat in some disorder toward Seminary Ridge. The 147th New York was especially in peril in that they were unaware of the order to fall back and fought on, isolated near the north edge of the railroad cut (map 2-11, middle). Cutler's casualties were severe: 454 of 1,007 men lost; the highest percentage—56—was suffered by the 147th New York.

But a subset of the Federal force in this vicinity came to the rescue. The 6th Wisconsin was in a reserve position south of the Cashtown Road, roughly between the rest of the Iron Brigade (on its left) and the bulk of Cutler's brigade (to the north) (map 2-10).[20] Nearby were two additional regiments, the 95th and the 84th New York, which filled out Cutler's brigade. The latter was nicknamed the "14th Brooklyn" (chart 2-3). These three regiments could readily come to the fore from their reserve posture (map 2-9) because of a crucial rebel mistake on the morning of Gettysburg's first day: Heth had been feeding his units into the fight *piecemeal.* Thus, Archer alone had moved in first, threatening only the Union left and allowing the three regiments just mentioned to hold back. This permitted these bluecoats to go in *later,* when and where they might be needed elsewhere. Moreover, Archer advanced toward McPherson Ridge in a manner that was not very careful (was it arrogant?). Perhaps there were insufficient skirmishers sent out in advance of, for example, Archer's attack;[21] such a probe might have usefully informed the rest of that rebel brigade what the skirmishers would have found in the woods surrounding Willoughby Run: the black-hatted soldiers of the Iron Brigade (a Federal unit whose reputation preceded it).

So, the 6th Wisconsin was under no particular pressure during the early stages of the infantry clash, and it was readily able to generate flanking fire on Davis's right.[22] This slowed the rebel onslaught against Cutler. In fact, many of Davis's Mississippians and North Carolinians looked for cover as a result of this Federal fire. They found it in a—soon to be known as *the*—railroad cut. This feature of the terrain, running parallel to the Cashtown Road, has been shown in most of the maps with which we have been dealing (for now, see map 2-12).

After the 6th Wisconsin first fired on Davis's right, those rebels fairly disappeared into the unfinished cut, which was trackless in 1863. This trench became a *rifle pit* for a large fraction of Davis's brigade. With those rebels' attention being directed toward the road, the pressure on Cutler was relieved (in fact, though pushed off the field early on, his 1st Corps brigade would return to the vicinity of McPherson Ridge by early afternoon). But the pressure on Davis was to escalate sharply: The 6th Wisconsin, supported on its left by the aforementioned New York regiments, *attacked* from the Cashtown Road, storming over fences and

Map 2-11
Davis's brigade attacks
Cutler's (10:30–11 A.M.)

Chart 2-3
The first battle for the railroad cut

ANV
↓
3rd Corps
↓
Heth's division
↓
Davis's brigade
↙   ↓   ↘
42nd Miss. 2nd Miss. 55th N.C.

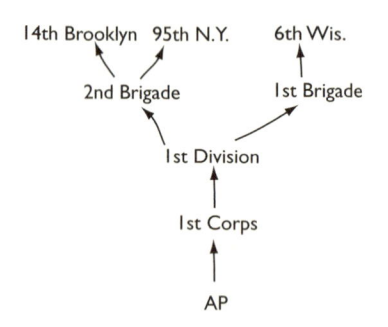

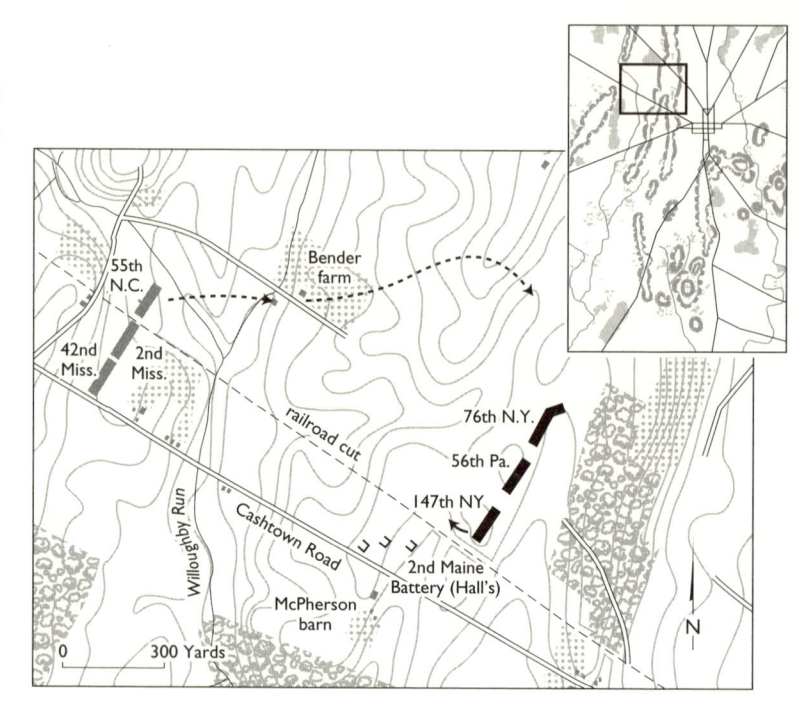

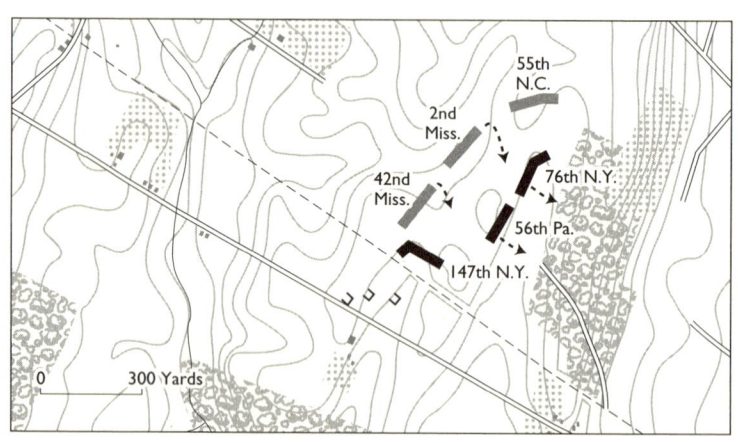

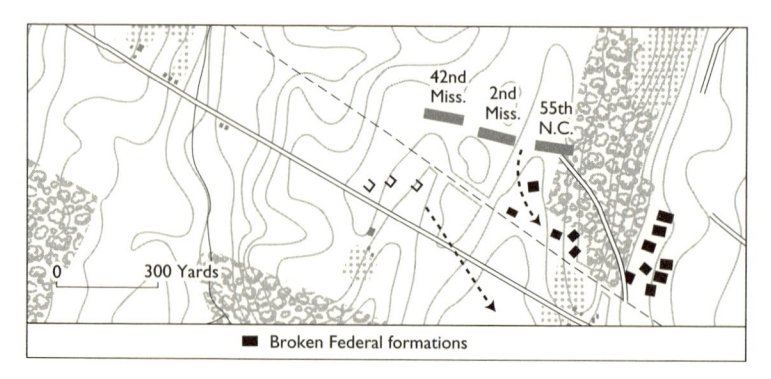

14th Brooklyn 95th N.Y.   6th Wis.
        ↖ ↑ ↗   ↑
        2nd Brigade   1st Brigade
              ↖   ↗
               1st Division
                   ↑
               1st Corps
                   ↑
                  AP

Broken Federal formations

48   THE STAND OF THE U.S. ARMY AT GETTYSBURG

**Map 2-12
The first battle for the railroad cut, late morning**

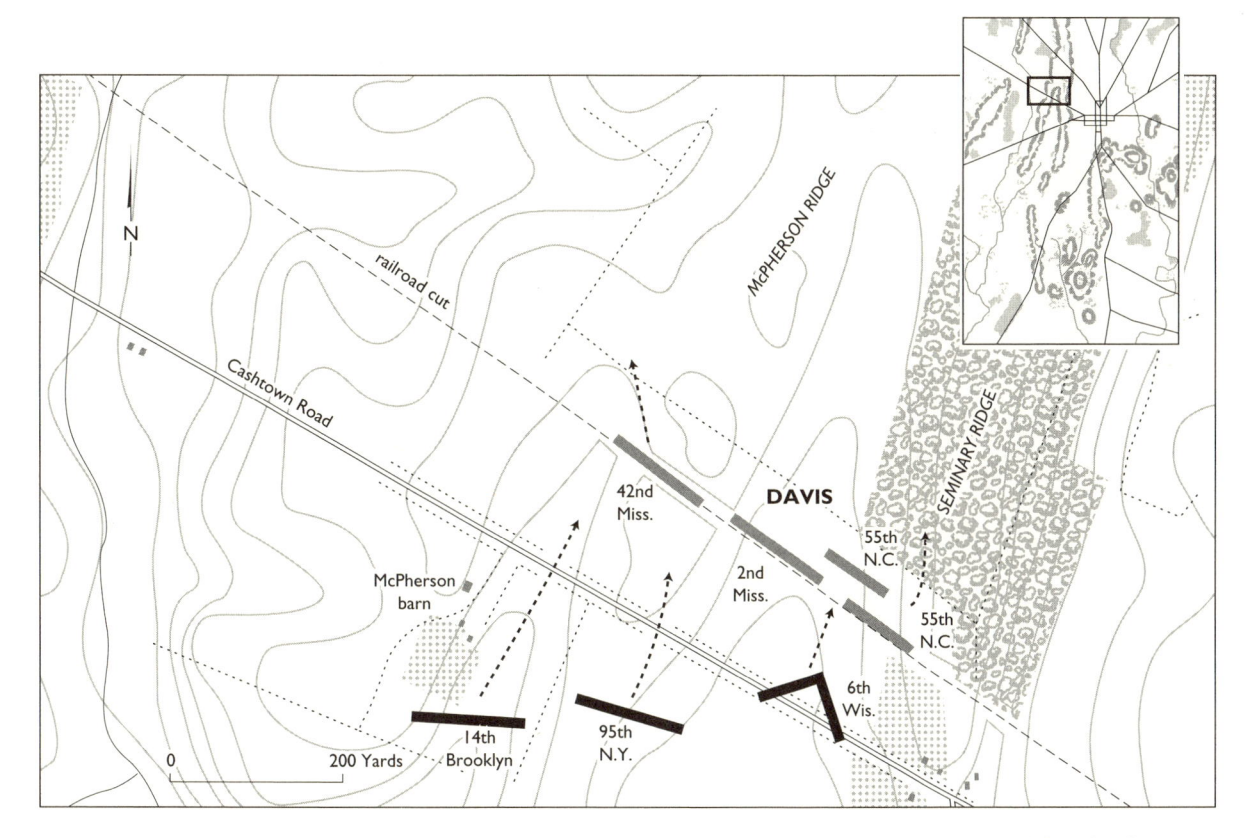

across an open field, toward the railroad cut (map 2-12).[23] The Federals, under great duress, made it to the edge of the cut.[24] The rifle pit had become a *trap*. Davis's brigade was thus defeated. Approximately 230 of his soldiers were captured—not as many as some have implied. Moreover, very few of Davis's soldiers were cruelly gunned down within the trap formed by the Federals who had charged the Southerners' position; many of these rebels escaped out the back (northwest) end of the railroad cut.

A Late Morning Lull

A cessation of hostilities settled over the field. It began before noon and would last—on the rebel right and Union left—until the afternoon was well under way.

The Confederate attack on July 1 had started tentatively in the early morning hours, escalated in intensity, and finally failed. General Heth had performed poorly in the narrow sense by committing his brigades in piecemeal attacks. He also had precipitated a battle in a situation that was not necessarily favorable in the broader sense: The Confederates did not choose the field; they plunged into a quasi-collision with cavalry, then a real one against the advance elements of Federal infantry.

This was a classic meeting engagement, an action in which the lead elements of opposing forces that are near to one another as they approach become embroiled in battle without having planned to do so. It follows that most of the remainder of the two armies are not on or even near the field during the battle's opening stages, and the high commanders are not necessarily nearby. All of this describes Gettysburg on the morning of July 1. The battle continued to develop as a meeting engagement after this lull ended—as more and more opposing units were drawn to the sounds of the guns—and the result was to the Confederates' short-

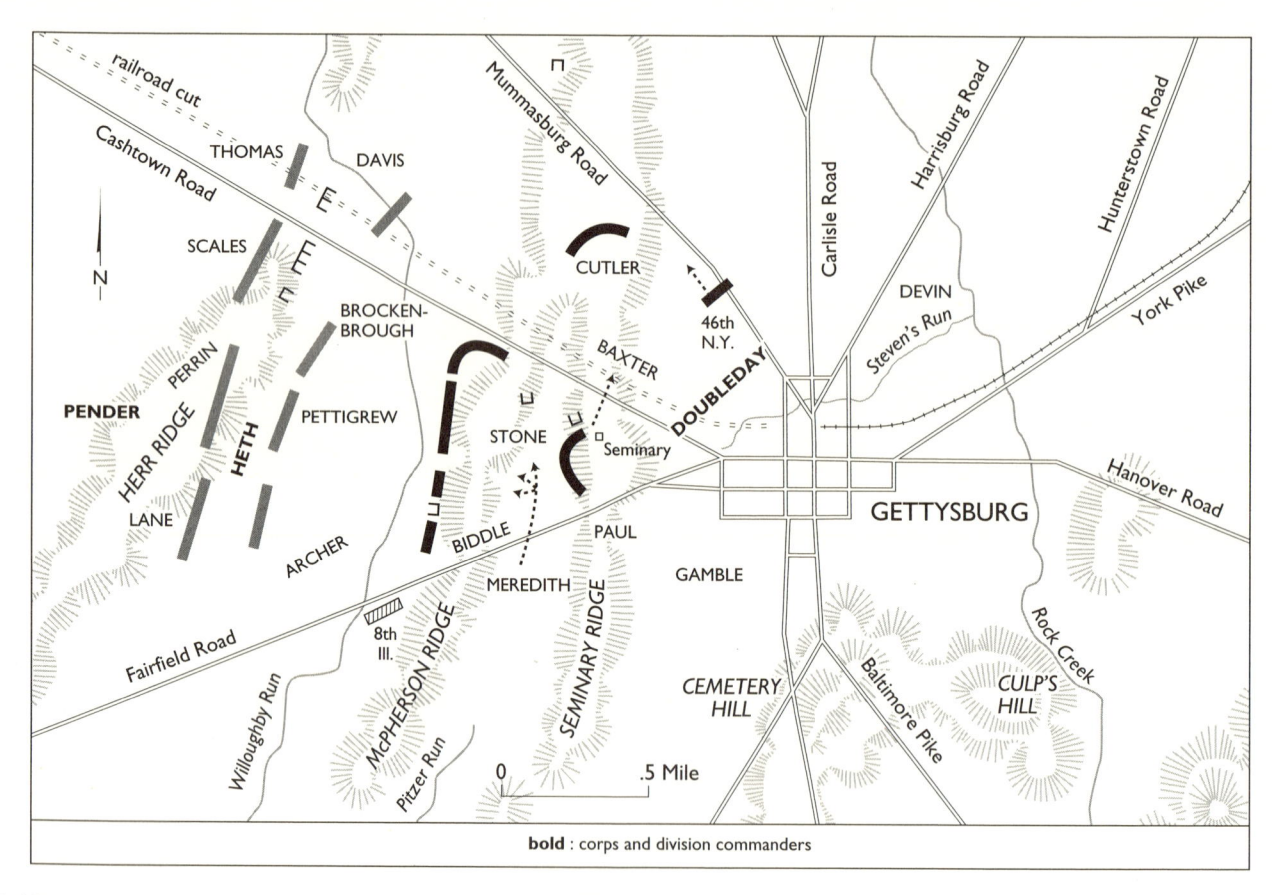

Map 2-13
Rebel 3rd Corps, Federal 1st Corps positions, early afternoon

Chart 2-4
Reinforcements for the Federal 1st Division, 1st Corps

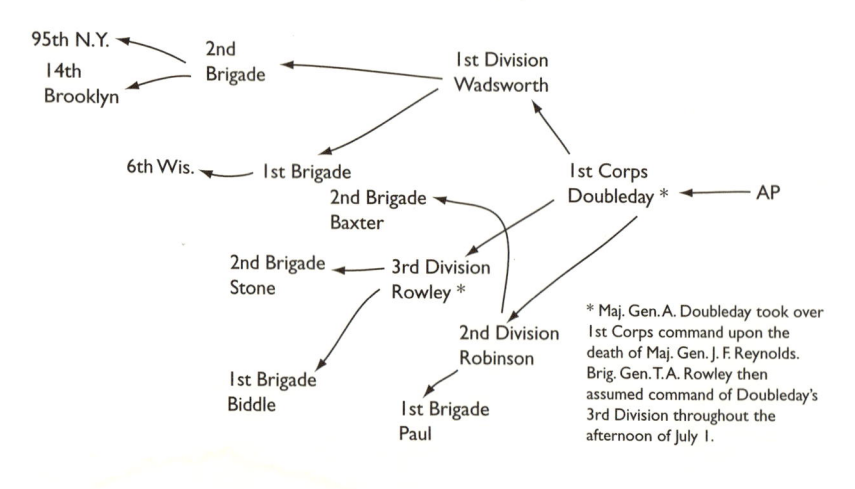

* Maj. Gen. A. Doubleday took over 1st Corps command upon the death of Maj. Gen. J. F. Reynolds. Brig. Gen. T. A. Rowley then assumed command of Doubleday's 3rd Division throughout the afternoon of July 1.

term advantage. However, the overall outcome of July 1's events was not favorable for them. If one wants to assign blame for this, perhaps General Heth deserves some for his precipitously thoughtless attitude. His commander, General Hill, had unwisely endorsed Heth's blind morning march. But Heth had also managed a mediocre tactical performance. Was it the cavalryman, General Stuart, who really put his army at a disadvantage in terms of how the next two days of the battle unfolded? Or was it instead Heth and Hill?

The lull in the fighting continued, but there was activity on and in the vicinity of the field. Major General W. Dorsey Pender's Confederate 3rd Corps division marched toward Gettysburg to support Heth as the Iron Brigade and General Cutler's brigade solidified their positions on either side of the Cashtown Road. Additional 1st Corps units moved into the vicinity of McPherson Ridge, with some 1st Division regiments filling in the areas between Meredith and Cutler (map 2-13, chart 2-4). Elements of the 1st Corps's 2nd Division eventually deployed to Cutler's right, extending well to the right of the Cashtown Road and the railroad cut, toward the Mummasburg Road and Oak Hill just beyond it (map 2-16).

Meanwhile, another Federal corps commander was approaching the battlefield. This was Maj. Gen. Oliver O. Howard of the 11th Corps. Upon arrival in the town, he took over the Union left wing, command of which had temporarily passed to General Doubleday

50 THE STAND OF THE U.S. ARMY AT GETTYSBURG

Map 2-14
The Federal 11th Corps and its foe

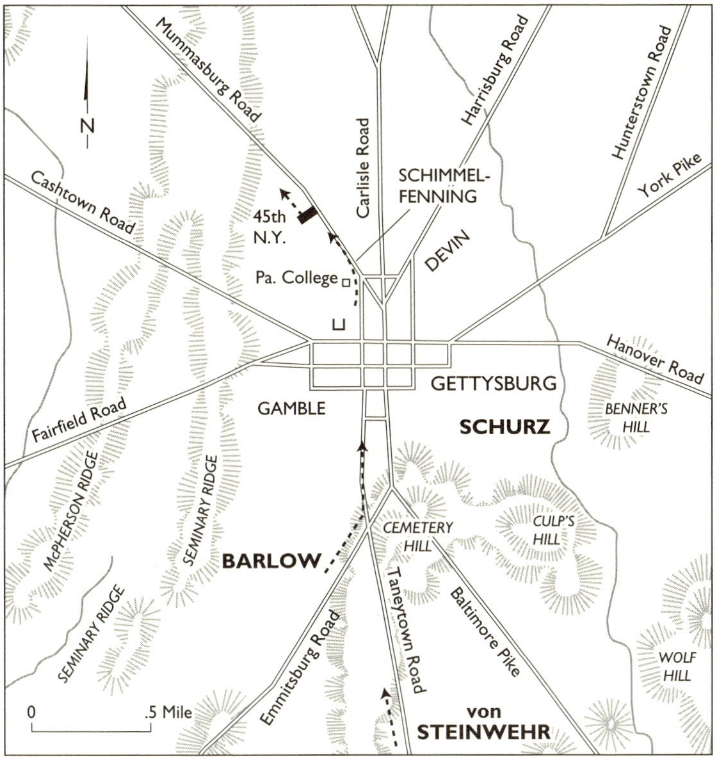

11th Corps movements early afternoon

(Federal 1st, rebel 3rd Corps positions not shown: see map 2-13)

↑ Movements of large 11th Corps Federal units

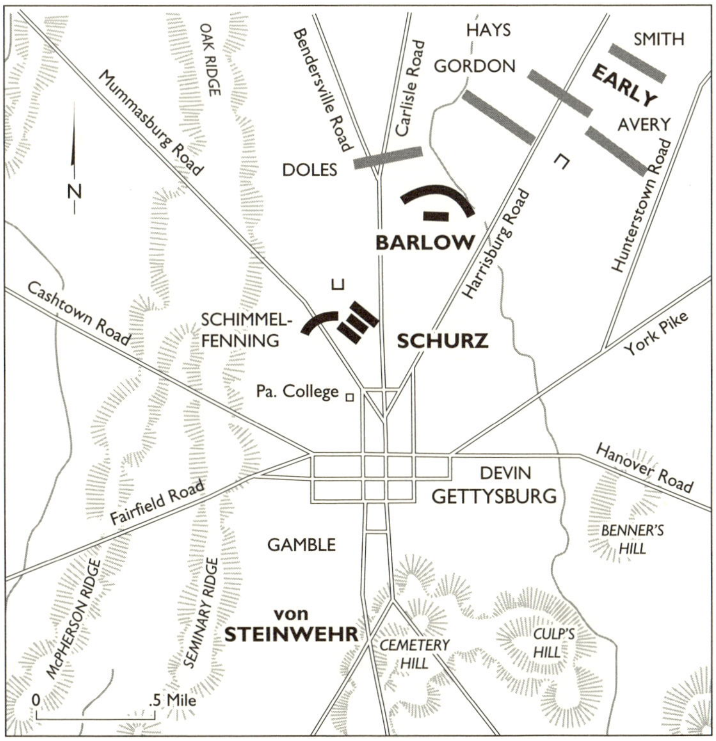

Union 11th Corps, and rebel 2nd Corps*, positions mid-afternoon

* Early's div. (Rodes div., except Doles's brig., not shown: see maps 2-18 to 2-20)

⊔ artillery

bold : division commanders

THE UNION SUFFERS A SETBACK   51

**Map 2-15
The Federal defense on Cemetery Hill, afternoon of July 1**

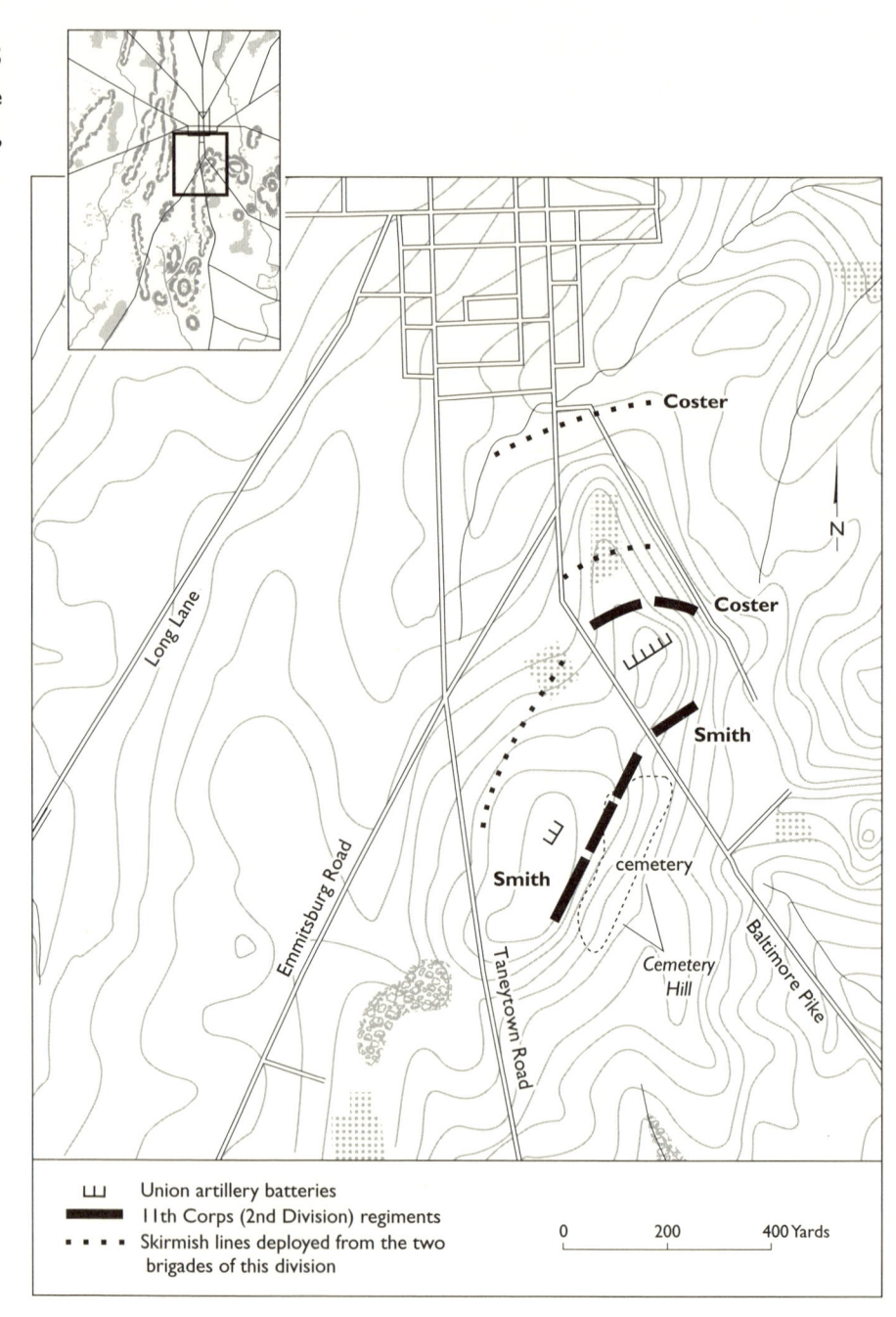

- ⊔⊓ Union artillery batteries
- ▬ 11th Corps (2nd Division) regiments
- ▪ ▪ ▪ Skirmish lines deployed from the two brigades of this division

(chart 2-4). Howard made his arrival an eventful one by making a certain pronouncement about what had transpired in the morning and by making a decision. Although the conclusion to which he leaped was wrong, the action he decided upon was fatefully positive.

From high up in a town building, Howard had observed Cutler apparently being swept from the field. Learning later that Doubleday had assumed command of the left wing, Howard blamed him for the ostensibly poor defensive performance he had observed from a distance.[25]

52   THE STAND OF THE U.S. ARMY AT GETTYSBURG

The most important job for Howard was to get the 11th Corps into position. He began to move his men northward (map 2-14) through the town and thus out onto the field, to form up on the right of the 1st Corps. This deployment of the 11th Corps units began in the early part of the afternoon. As these marching orders were being issued, Oliver Howard had his golden moment at Gettysburg. He ordered the twenty-eight hundred troops in the two brigades of Brig. Gen. Adolph von Steinwehr's 2nd Division (chart 2-5) to form hard defensive positions, skirmishers forward, on a broad rise of ground called Cemetery Hill, about a half-mile south of town (map 2-15).[26] Colonel Charles L. Coster's 1st Brigade faced north, and Col. Orland Smith's 2nd Brigade was placed on ground now occupied by the National Cemetery, facing northwest (map 2-15). Howard also supervised the placement of cannon on this hill, understanding "its strategic and tactical importance as an artillery platform. It commanded not only the town and surrounding fields but, perhaps more important, the converging roads."[27] Having said this, Howard's men were able to place only a small number of guns in firing positions on Cemetery Hill during the afternoon of July 1 (map 2-15).[28]

As General Howard sent the rest of his corps north to the battlefield under the command of Maj. Gen. Carl Schurz (map 2-14), Schurz's 3rd Division, temporarily commanded by Brig. Gen. Alexander Schimmelfennig, moved up on the 1st Corps's right—not really abutting it, but with a gap between the relevant units (chart 2-5) that gave a hinge configuration to the positions in the Union center (map 2-21).[29]

Howard's 1st Division was on the 3rd Division's right, hence forming the extreme right of the Union defense (map 2-14). Its commander, Brig. Gen. Francis Barlow, was another "boy general" (chart 2-5). Did his relative youth (twenty-nine years) contribute to the bad decision he was to make—involving a certain piece of tactical geometry—as the afternoon played out?

First we need to consider the ground that Barlow and his 11th Corps comrades had to occupy. Out on the right flank itself—near the intersection of the Harrisburg Road and Rock Creek, ranging most of the way to the right of the 1st Corps positions—is some of the worst defensive terrain imaginable. It is not possible to appreciate this by looking at a diagram (map 2-14), but this expanse (about six-tenths of a mile wide) is low *and* open. Yet, if the 11th Corps was to bolster the Federal defense north of the town, it had no choice but to occupy this lousy stretch of terrain.

As the 11th Corps troops deployed northward to assume their putative defensive positions, they were not engaged immediately. Thus, we are still within the lull in the battle, but it did not last long. General Howard felt that he had to rush two divisions forward to join the 1st Corps defenders in an emergency manner, taking positions to that unit's right, no matter what the ground was like. Perhaps Howard should have deployed his entire force closer to Cemetery Hill, rather than in such outward, exposed, and vulnerable locations. This could have avoided the near-rout of the 11th Corps that occurred during the afternoon. Yet had he not done so, there would have been no protection for the 1st Corp's right wing, which would have been left dangerously isolated. In any event, Howard made what he thought was the best decision under the circumstances. This is another difficult consequence of a meeting engagement.

Chart 2-5
11th Corps advances and positions

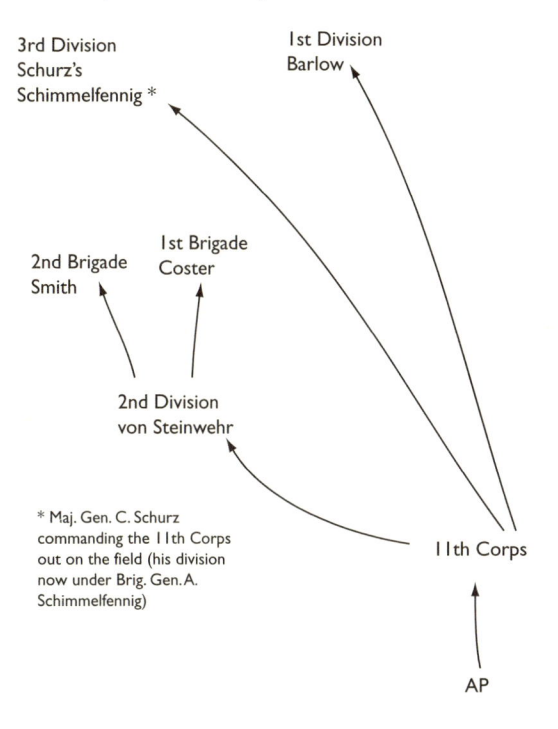

* Maj. Gen. C. Schurz commanding the 11th Corps out on the field (his division now under Brig. Gen. A. Schimmelfennig)

THE UNION SUFFERS A SETBACK   53

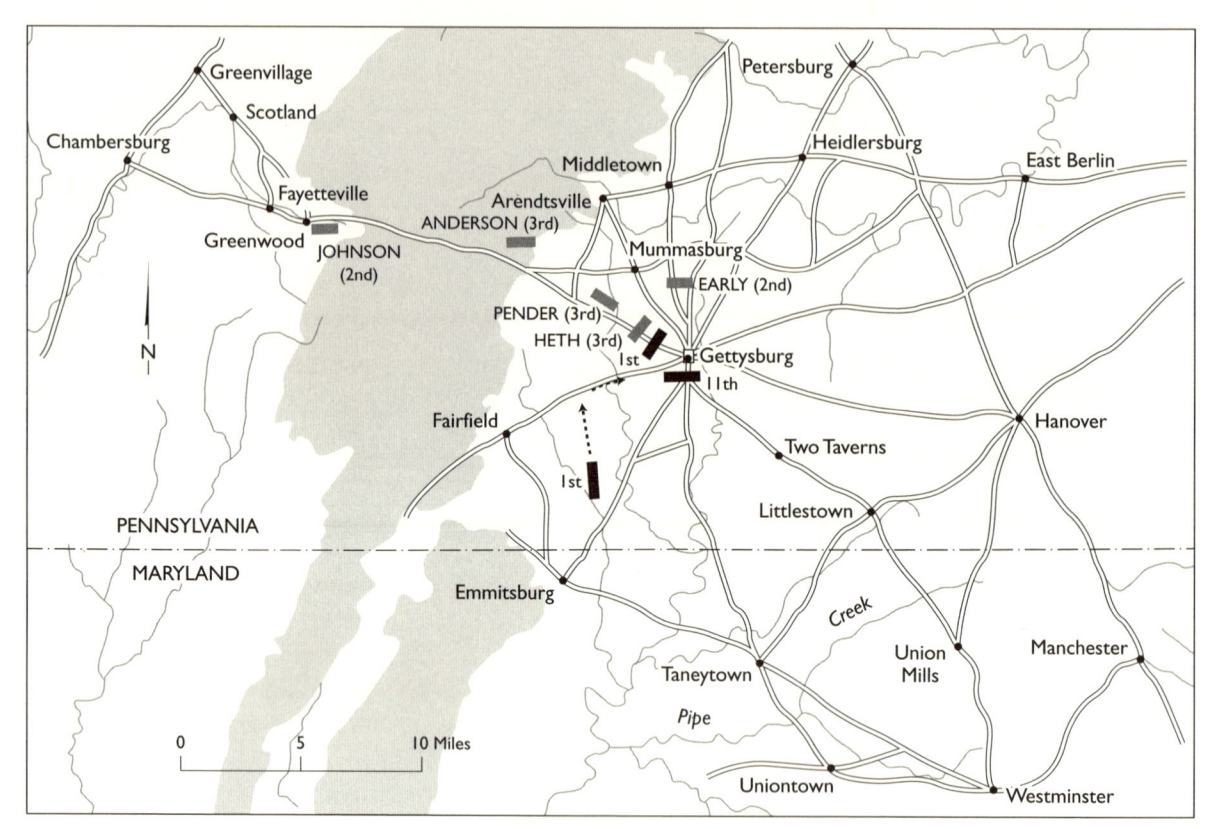

**Map 2-16
Infantry movements toward Gettysburg**

Infantry movements toward Gettysburg, relatively early July 1

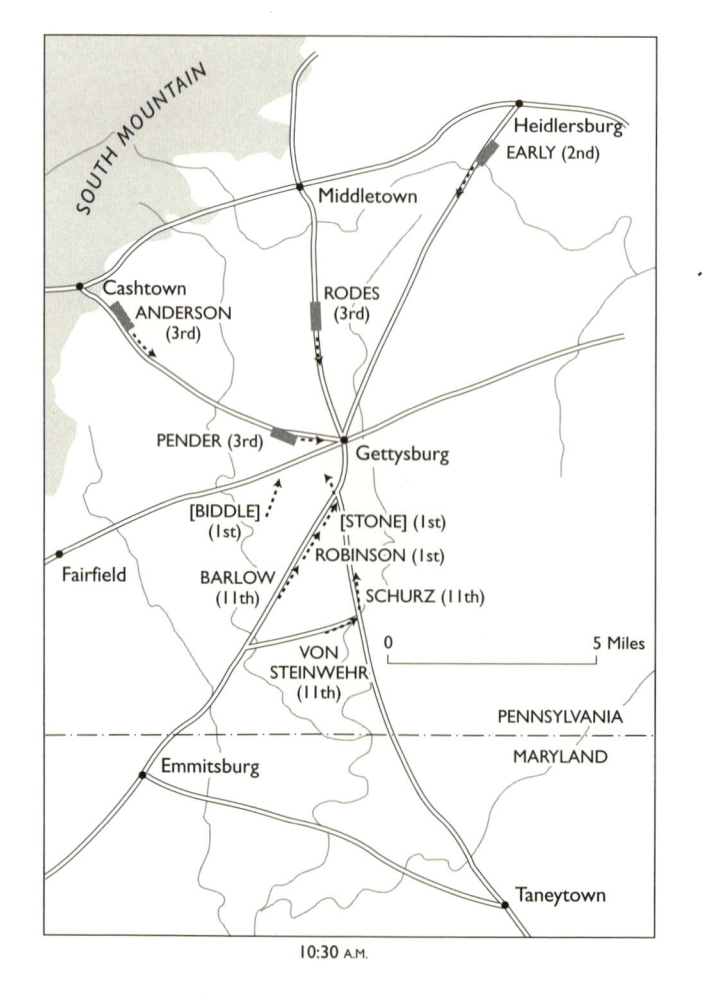

54 THE STAND OF THE U.S. ARMY AT GETTYSBURG

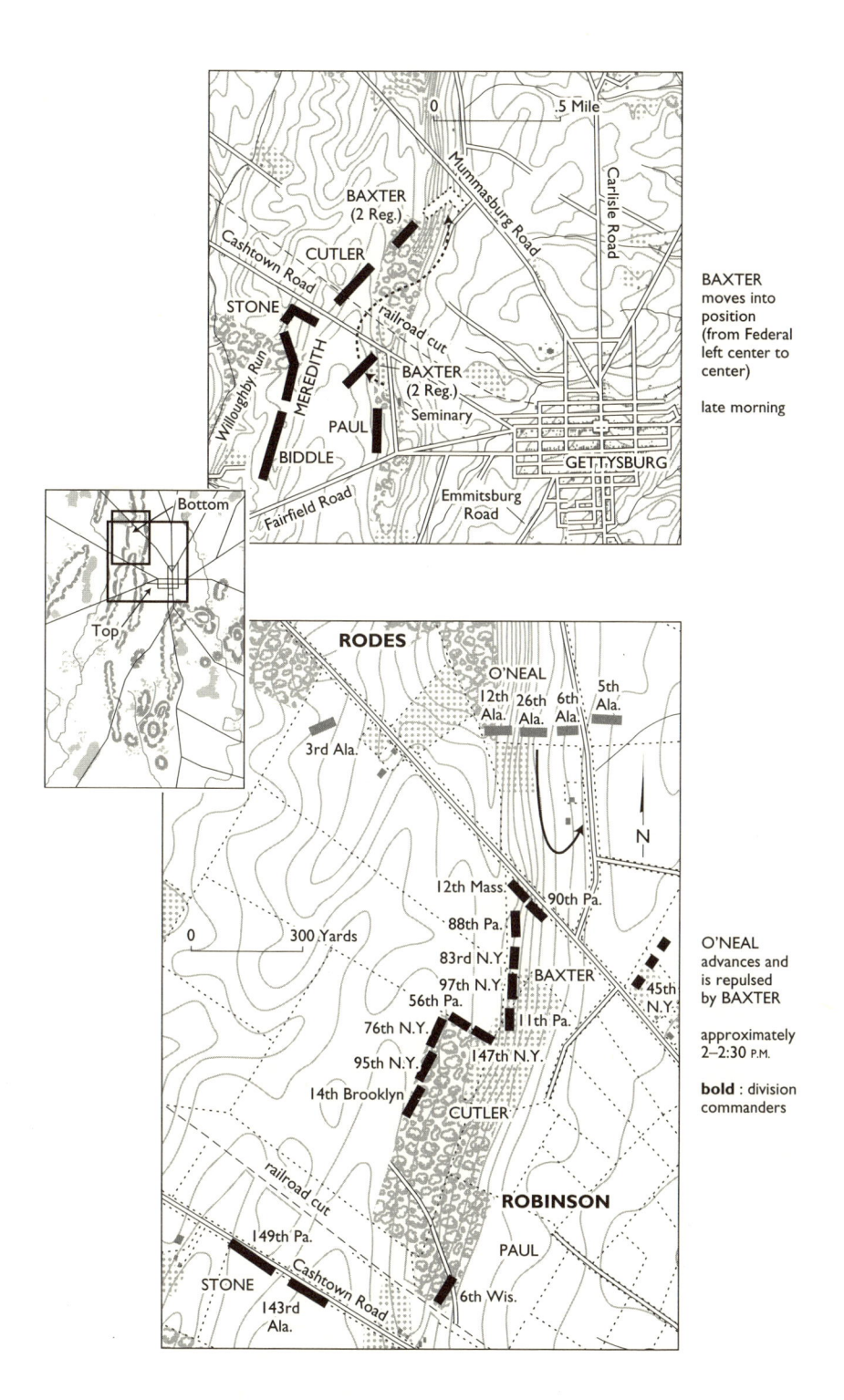

**Map 2-17
Opening of Rodes's attacks on the Union center**

BAXTER moves into position (from Federal left center to center)

late morning

O'NEAL advances and is repulsed by BAXTER

approximately 2–2:30 P.M.

bold: division commanders

THE FIGHTING RESUMES IN THE CENTER OF THE FIELD

The battle started again in the early afternoon with *further* collisions of infantry that were not very well planned.[30] The vanguard units of the Confederate 2nd Corps were now approaching the field, coming into the center of it from Middletown, Pennsylvania. This is shown on map 2-16. That diagram also shows how the initial two pairs of Union infantry corps (two Union, two Confederate) approached Gettysburg and the battlefields near it.

THE UNION SUFFERS A SETBACK   55

**Chart 2-6
Initial assaults of Rodes's division, Baxter's brigade defending**

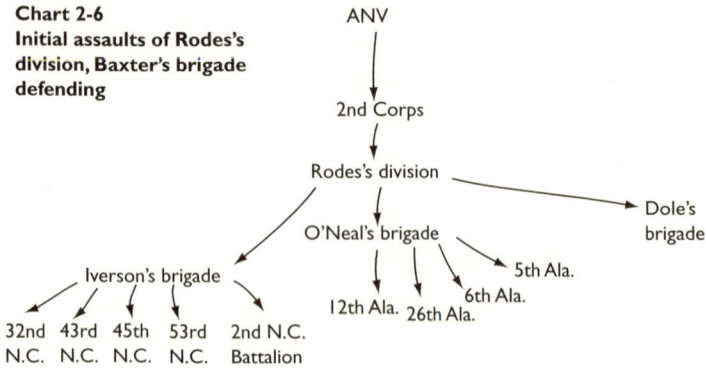

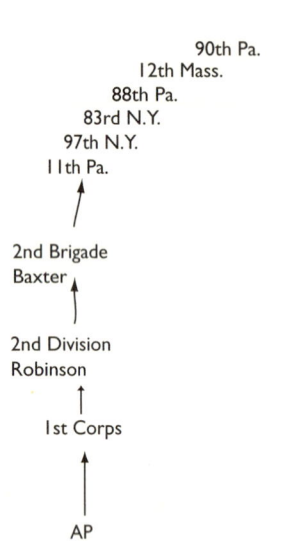

```
ANV
 ↓
2nd Corps
 ↓
Rodes's division ────────→ Dole's brigade
 ↓
O'Neal's brigade
 ↙    ↓  ↓  ↘
Iverson's  12th  6th  5th Ala.
brigade    Ala. 26th Ala.
                Ala.
 ↙  ↓  ↓  ↓  ↘
32nd 43rd 45th 53rd 2nd N.C.
N.C. N.C. N.C. N.C. Battalion
```

```
90th Pa.
12th Mass.
88th Pa.
83rd N.Y.
97th N.Y.
11th Pa.
  ↑
2nd Brigade
Baxter
  ↑
2nd Division
Robinson
  ↑
1st Corps
  ↑
AP
```

The 2nd Corps's van was Maj. Gen. Robert E. Rodes's division (chart 2-6), which came out of the woods north of Oak Hill (maps 2-17 and 2-18).[31] Rodes initiated his assault with artillery fire from this vicinity (at about 1 p.m.), training the guns on Cutler's right flank some eight hundred yards away. However, when Rodes's infantrymen went into action (shortly after he gave that order about 2:15 p.m.), they attacked the Federal center with no apparent regard to their companion corps and divisions. No effort was made to coordinate with the resting 3rd Corps units to Rodes's right; and, to his left, additional elements of the 2nd Corps were not yet up (maps 2-16 and 2-21). Rodes attacked nonetheless. In so doing, he conformed to the Confederate theme thus far: piecemeal assaults. Rodes's brigades went in one after the other, minimizing their effectiveness in principle and leading to disasters in particular.

Thus, the brigade of a ne'er-do-well officer, Col. Edward A. O'Neal (chart 2-6), came down off Oak Hill toward the Mummasburg Road (map 2-17). This was at about 2 p.m. Rodes had thought that these Alabamians would be hitting the 1st Corps's exposed right flank, some distance off to O'Neal's right as he began his brigade's advance with three of his five regiments. Waiting for O'Neal, however, were elements of Brig. Gen. Henry Baxter's 2nd Brigade from Brig. Gen. John C. Robinson's 2nd Division, 1st Corps (chart 2-6). Deploying from a reserve position near the Lutheran seminary, Baxter had recently arrived in the area just below the Mummasburg Road (map 2-17). Thus, the Federal 1st Corps's right extended that far by that time—significantly more north and east than would have been gleaned by Confederate skirmishers in this area in the morning.[32] Moreover, Baxter's force was bolstered on its right by a regiment of New Yorkers from the 11th Corps (bottom of map 2-17), which was moving into positions north of town as Rodes began to organize his attacks.[33]

Unknown to him, O'Neal's attack mirrored the manner in which General Archer had advanced toward McPherson Ridge in the morning—and into a trap. O'Neal's units went in possibly without exercising sufficient caution,[34] and without their commander, who stayed in the rear with a reserve regiment. Baxter's soldiers then rose up from behind a stone fence, behind which they were lurking just below and parallel to the Mummasburg Road (map 2-16). They inflicted severe casualties with surprise volley fire: O'Neal lost 696 of 1,688 men in the attacking regiments. This ruined the first Confederate attack in this area before it had put the Union center in any peril.

To O'Neal's right, the unit of another low-quality commander, Brig. Gen. Alfred Iverson (chart 2-6), went in as the next element in these piecemeal attacks. Iverson's regiments skirted the west slope of Oak Hill, proceeding southward at about 2:30 p.m. (map 2-18). This separate advance permitted elements of Baxter's force to shift position, and they reformed behind another nearby stone fence running perpendicular to the road, such that the barrels of these Union men's

56   THE STAND OF THE U.S. ARMY AT GETTYSBURG

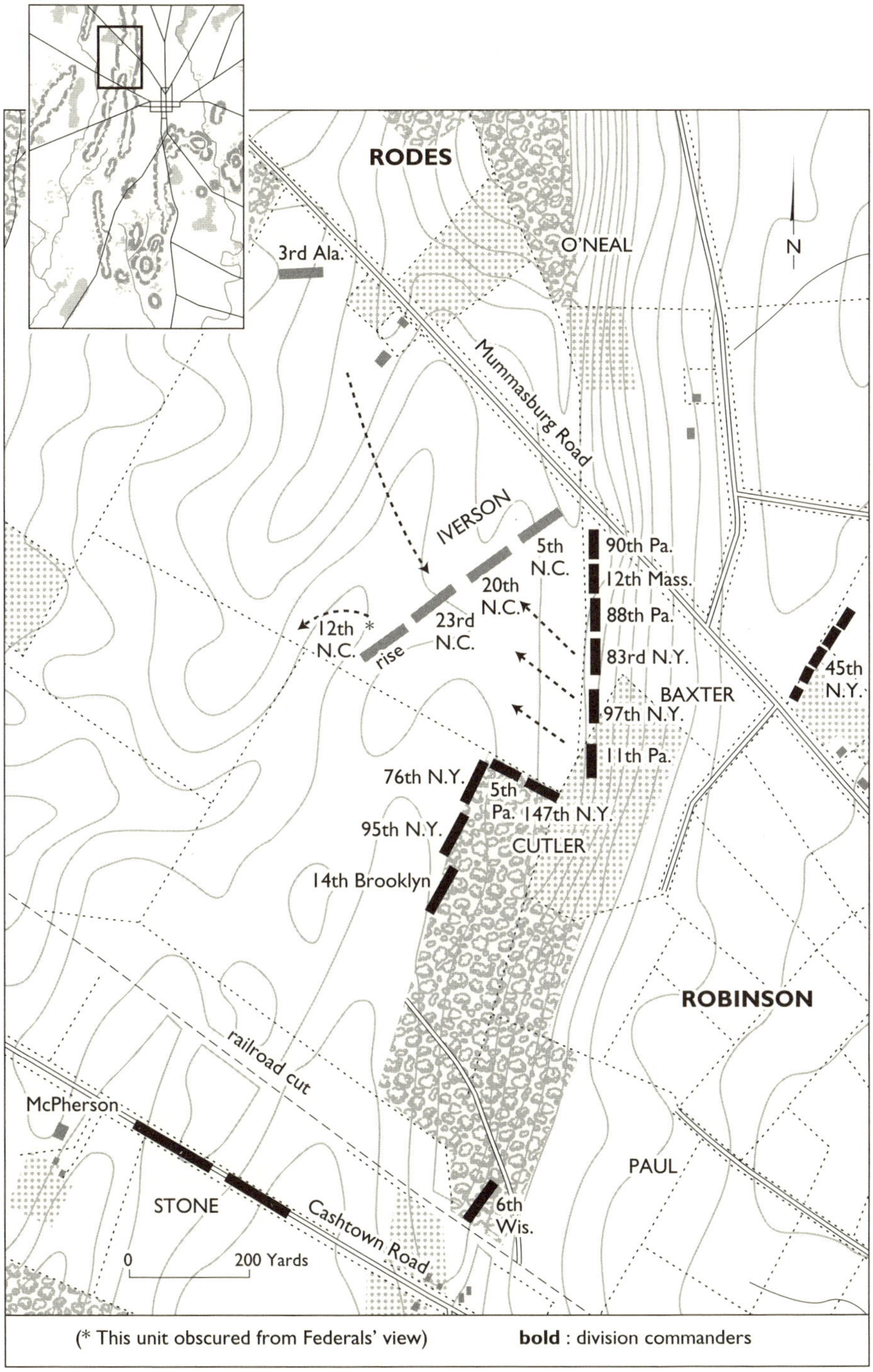

Map 2-18
Iverson advances and is repulsed by Baxter, mid-afternoon

(* This unit obscured from Federals' view)   **bold**: division commanders

muskets were pointing westward.[35] As Iverson's rebels advanced—once again, largely without an outlying advance probe[36]—the defenders hit them with devastating flanking fire. Approximately five hundred of Iverson's soldiers were mowed down—killed or wounded in only fifteen minutes of what can barely be called fighting. Actually, Baxter counterattacked as well, taking four hundred prisoners and leaving Iverson with losses amounting to more than 70 percent of the approximately fourteen hundred men who began the advance.

From the Confederates' perspective, this was *not* working. However, with the near destruction of Iverson's brigade, *the successes of the Federal defense on July 1 crested.* The beginning of the end transpired when Rodes continued his attack, and two higher-quality brigade commanders came to the fore (chart 2-7). Brig.

THE UNION SUFFERS A SETBACK   57

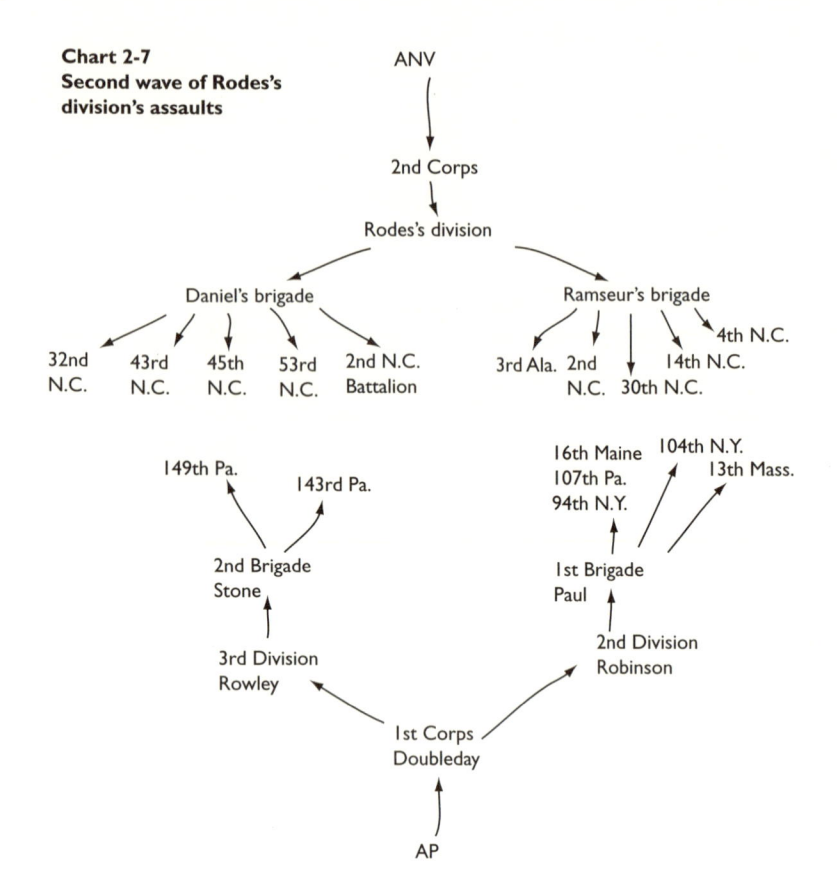

**Chart 2-7
Second wave of Rodes's division's assaults**

```
                                    ANV
                                     ↓
                                  2nd Corps
                                     ↓
                                Rodes's division
                              ↙               ↘
                    Daniel's brigade        Ramseur's brigade
                  ↙  ↓  ↓  ↓  ↘            ↙  ↓   ↓   ↘
              32nd 43rd 45th 53rd 2nd N.C.  3rd Ala. 2nd  14th N.C. 4th N.C.
              N.C. N.C. N.C. N.C. Battalion          N.C. 30th N.C.

                                              16th Maine   104th N.Y.
                                              107th Pa.    13th Mass.
              149th Pa.    143rd Pa.           94th N.Y.     ↗
                 ↖          ↗                      ↑
                  2nd Brigade                  1st Brigade
                    Stone                         Paul
                     ↑                             ↑
                 3rd Division                  2nd Division
                    Rowley                      Robinson
                       ↖                     ↗
                           1st Corps
                           Doubleday
                               ↑
                              AP
```

Gen. Junius Daniel aimed his five regiments toward a gap located between Cutler's left and the Cashtown Road (map 2-19). The plan was to curl around counterclockwise and hit Cutler's left flank. The railroad cut was in the way, however. As Daniel approached it (map 2-19), he took heavy fire from the other side of this trench—that is, from the aforementioned 1st Corps units positioned near the road. In this instance it was from Col. Roy Stone's 2nd Brigade, 2nd Division (chart 2-7), which had filled in a gap on the Iron Brigade's right during the late morning (maps 2-13 and 2-19).

Thus began the second battle for the railroad cut (map 2-19). The Federals under Stone attempted to counterattack Daniel, moving from the vicinity of the Cashtown Road then through the cut. Stone's troops were forced back *into* it by flanking fire on their left from elements of the Confederate 3rd Corps—which had been facing the Federal left for some time now and were finally getting back into action. Daniel's regiments (chart 2-7) attacked the railroad cut twice. Large numbers of casualties were inflicted on both sides in this area, with this second battle within the battle devolving to a deadly stalemate. However, the second of Daniel's attacks drove Stone from the railroad cut itself, leaving the Union brigade in a threatened position. After this attack, Daniel moved one of his regiments south of the cut between it and the Cashtown Road (map 2-20) so that this group of North Carolinians was on Stone's left flank.

Now the fourth of General Rodes's brigades entered the fray. This unit, commanded by Brig. Gen. S. Dodson Ramseur (chart 2-7), advanced along a path similar to the one taken by Iverson not long before (map 2-20). By this time, an additional 1st Corps unit, Brig. Gen. Gabriel R. Paul's 1st Brigade, 2nd Division (chart 2-7) had been sent to bolster Baxter's defenders in this area (below the Mummasburg Road on map 2-20). Ramseur, avoiding the fate that befell Iverson, was able to slide a bit to the east and hit Paul's brigade on its right flank. Ultimately, Paul was pushed back toward the Cashtown Road in the vicinity of the Lutheran Seminary (map 2-20). As Baxter's brigade withdrew (chart 2-7), his men paused and fired on Daniel's North Carolinians (who had been attacking Stone at the railroad cut). However, Baxter did not provide significant defensive help as he retreated. His soldiers were fought out, in part because they supposedly were low on ammunition.[37]

The Confederate pressure on the Union center north of Gettysburg was finally working.[38] As the defense steadily receded in this part of the field, General Robinson, the 2nd Division commander in the 1st Corps, ordered the 16th Maine in Paul's brigade (chart 2-7) to make a suicidal counterattack to protect the withdrawal of its companion regiments. The 16th Maine thus *advanced* toward the Mummasburg Road, into the face of Ramseur's assaulting rebels (map 2-20). They were hit hard, took casualties, and were pushed back along the ridge south

58   THE STAND OF THE U.S. ARMY AT GETTYSBURG

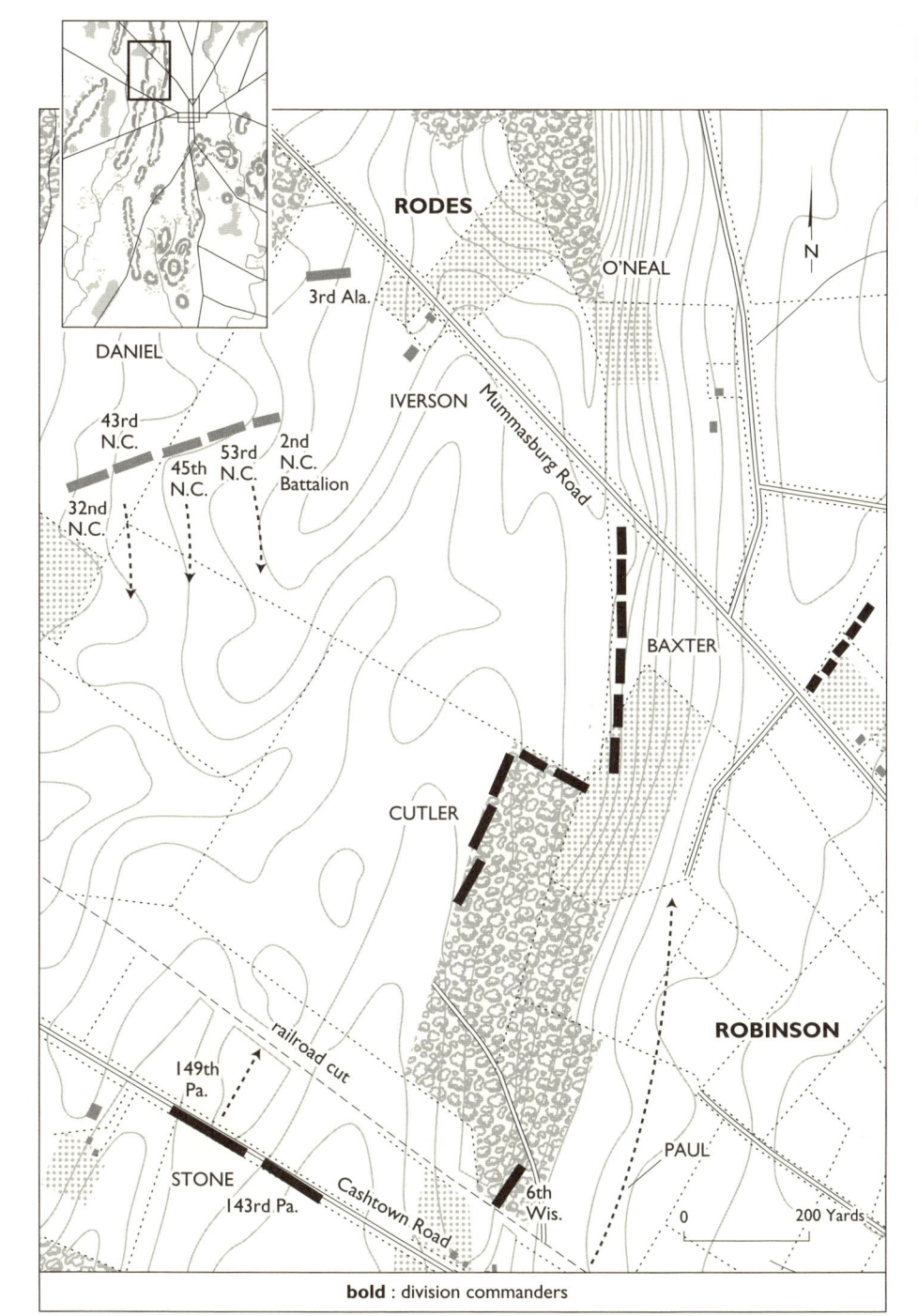

**Map 2-19
Daniel moves in, Stone advances toward him, and Paul reinforces the center**

of Oak Hill to the north edge of the railroad cut (map 2-20). There they were attacked on their front and left and ultimately overrun.[39] More than three-quarters of the 298 men in the 16th Maine who went into action became casualties (including 164 captured, almost two-thirds of these at the railroad cut). The Mainers paid a brutal price for slowing Ramseur's advance: sixty-one were killed or wounded. However, they had done the dirty work assigned to them in the midafternoon on July 1.[40] Late in the afternoon the *next* day, another group of Maine men would act in an analogous manner. This would lead to their lasting fame, though no more deserved than that which is due the 16th Infantry Regiment of Maine Volunteers.

THE UNION SUFFERS A SETBACK   59

**Map 2-20
Ramseur attacks Paul, supported by O'Neal and Daniel, mid-to-late-afternoon**

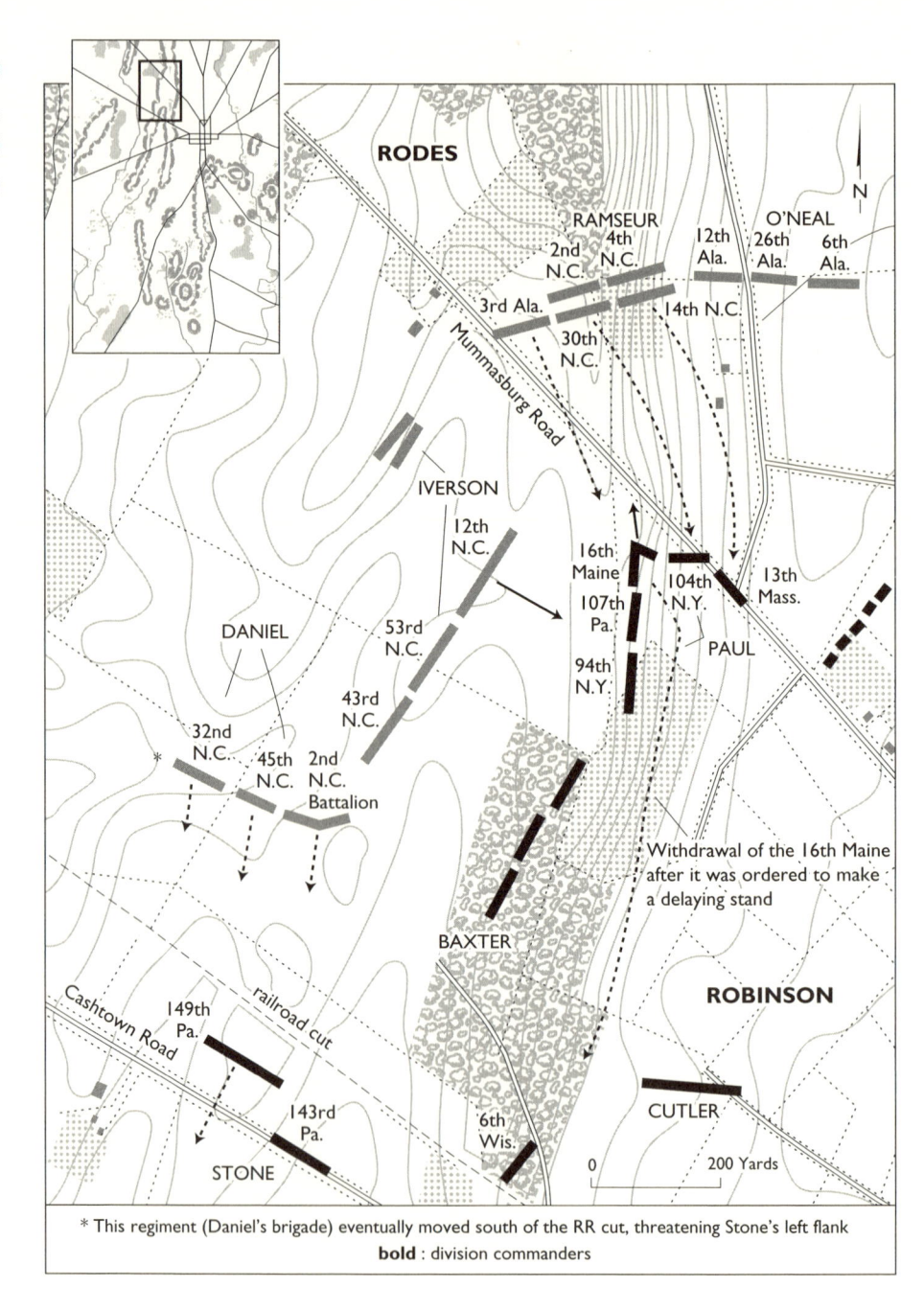

*This regiment (Daniel's brigade) eventually moved south of the RR cut, threatening Stone's left flank
bold: division commanders

INFANTRY ACTION ALL ALONG THE LINES: THE REBEL LEFT ENTERS THE FRAY AND THE RIGHT RESUMES THE ATTACK

Between 2 and 2:30 P.M. (before the action in the center culminated), Gen. Robert E. Lee arrived on the Gettysburg battlefield, riding to the crest of Herr Ridge northwest of town. He was by then aware that a major engagement, stemming from the clashes General Heth had initiated in the morning, was fast unfolding. However, the 3rd Corps in Lee's vicinity was largely inactive now, arrayed mostly south of the Cashtown Road (map 2-21). One suspects that General Lee and his staff officers saw many of Heth's men gathered around the campfires burning in the fields flanking the roadway.[41]

60   THE STAND OF THE U.S. ARMY AT GETTYSBURG

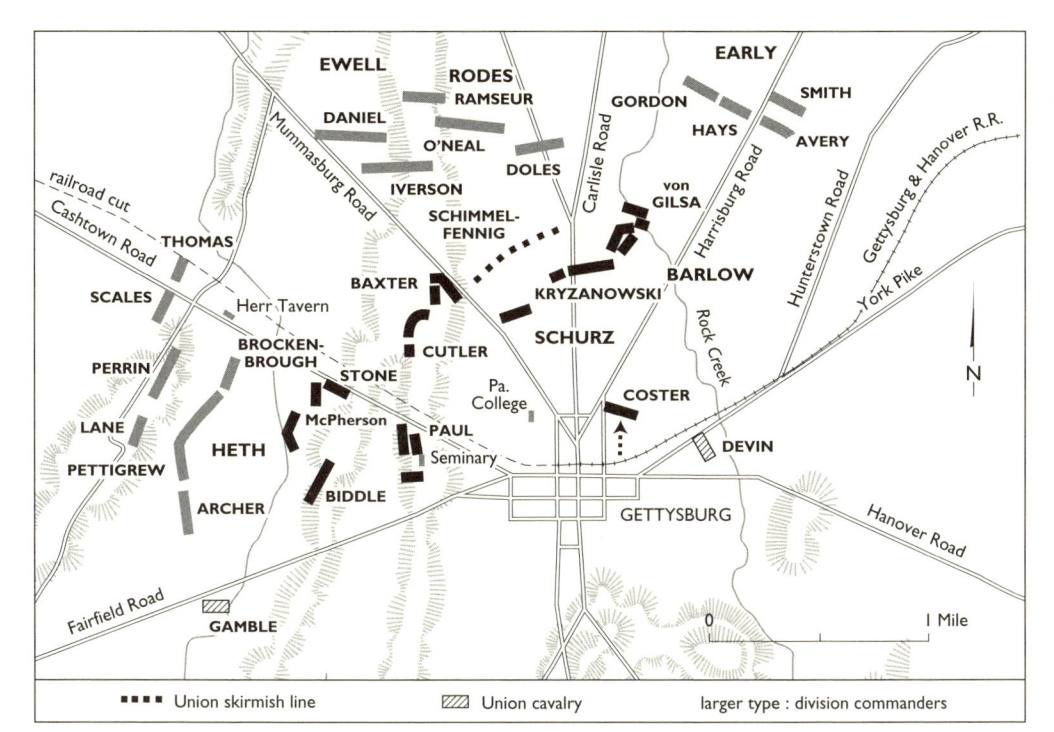

**Map 2-21
Confederate ring of impending attack, July 1, P.M.**

**Chart 2-8
Early's attacks on the 11th Corps**

General Lee was in the vicinity of General Hill, whose generally ill state during the first days of July left him pretty much on the sidelines.[42] Nevertheless, Hill had sent a courier to General Ewell with word that his units were moving toward Gettysburg. Ewell therefore sent the two divisions nearest him in a more southerly than westerly direction, toward Gettysburg.[43]

Lee was cognizant of the overall sweep of what had been developing—although he probably did not know that Rodes, too, had begun attacking piecemeal, as had Heth. In fact, as Lee approached the field, he became aware of the more successful attacks of Rodes's later advances to his left. Thus, Lee's late arrival at this meeting engagement left him with little appreciation of the quality of the Federal defense on this day—which included the timely arrival and aggressive defense by General Baxter against Rodes's two hapless brigade commanders, Iverson and O'Neal.

Lee thus acted on what he *did* know—spurred on by what he was probably *thinking*, thanks to Chancellorsville and other poor performances by his foe. In Lee's mind, the Army of the Potomac was just not a good enough force to withstand an attack from the Army of Northern Virginia, unplanned though it may have been on that day. And even though he had not expected Federal infantry to be nearby, Lee almost certainly realized that only a part of the Northern army was on the field. Thus, his force now outnumbered the Federals in front of him, because the van of Ewell's advancing corps was approaching from the northeast (to Lee's left as he looked toward the Union left wing down the Cashtown Road). The afternoon's attacks were already under way in the center, and soon Ewell's tough division commander, Maj. Gen. Jubal A. Early, would join in, attacking from an area of the field to the left of Rodes, who occupied the center of the sector. The superior force of the Army of Northern Virginia would overlap the Union defenders on both their flanks and could crush them.

The assault therefore would occur *all along the line* (map 2-21). General Lee unleashed his 3rd Corps, which soon resumed its attacks toward the defensive positions on the Union left (some of General Hill's units already had been fight-

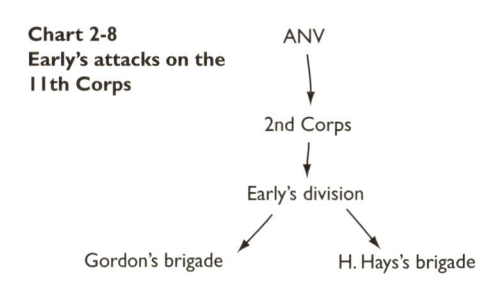

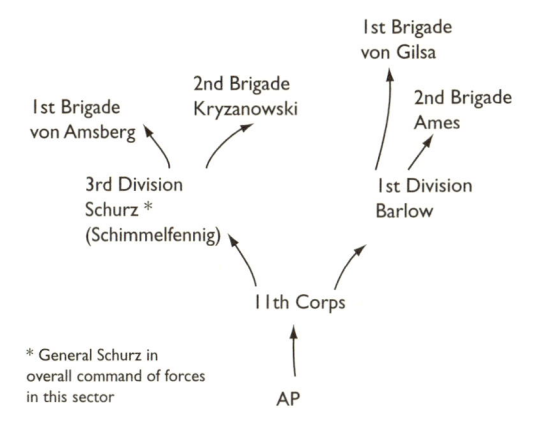

THE UNION SUFFERS A SETBACK   61

ing in the afternoon, but by long-range fire from stationary positions). General Pender's unbloodied division, now up and poised to attack, was to follow Heth. They were ordered to attack the Federal 1st Corps on McPherson Ridge.

The Union Lines Give Way from Right to Left and Are Pushed Back below the Town

The Confederate units that attacked next (Heth's brigades) were close to General Lee's position on the field, but this action will be described in the next section as part of a description of the overall assault by the Confederate right wing. Now we deal with what became the most severe blow that fell on the Federal defenders, inflicted by General Early's 2nd Corps division (chart 2-8). Early's division was on the rebel army's left flank at the end of a wide arc running from the Harrisburg Road in the east to below the Cashtown Road in the western sector of the field. The arc indeed overlapped the Federal defensive positions on both of its flanks (map 2-21).

General Early had advanced to Gettysburg (map 2-16) in almost perfect position to hit the Union right.[44] By overlapping it, he would be advancing not on a line of defenders, but on its exposed end (maps 2-21 and 2-22). Moreover, this part of the Federal defense turned out to be worse off than is implied by its position at one end of the line.

As previewed above, the right half of the Union defense was manned by the 11th Corps (charts 2-5 and 2-8). Those soldiers may have been jittery, given what had happened to them at Chancellorsville on May 2, where they had also been on the army's vulnerable right flank. At Gettysburg on July 1, the position on the extreme right—occupied by General Barlow's 1st Division, 11th Corps (chart 2-8)—was deliberately placed in an extremely vulnerable location by its commander. Recall that the ground arrayed between the Mummasburg and Harrisburg Roads was a terrible defensive position. However, there was a small piece of high ground in the right-hand sector of this portion of the field. This *knoll,* to which Barlow sent a fair fraction of his force, became the flank of the Federal defense in this area (maps 2-14 and 2-22). Reaching to take advantage of this high ground, Barlow extended his division too far north and to the right, such that he was not well connected with 3rd Division units to his left. Moreover, Barlow ruined the tentative plan that was then being improvised by General Schurz for the flank defense—which was to "refuse" the line, bending the extreme right-hand part of it clockwise, perhaps as far back as the vicinity of the county almshouse (map 2-22).[45] This could afford a measure of protection for a flank position that had no natural cover in the vicinity—that is, a flank that was "in the air," as the 11th Corps's right had been on that fateful evening in early May at Chancellorsville.[46] In a microcosm of sorts, we will learn on July 2 about the defensive power that can be provided by a refused line on an extreme flank (see map 3-20 in Chapter 3).

For now, the putative 11th Corps defenders were not in a good geometric position (map 2-21).[47] Although the Union right did have a momentary advantage—it outnumbered the rebel unit to its front, a brigade from Rodes's division led by Brig. Gen. George Doles (in position to the left of where O'Neal had advanced [maps 2-14 and 2-22])—General Early was on the verge of moving in, advancing to Doles's left (map 2-22, top). In this specific sector, Brig. Gen. John B. Gordon's men outnumbered the defenders to their front two to one. Early's soldiers launched their attack at about 3:30 P.M. When those rebels hit the Union

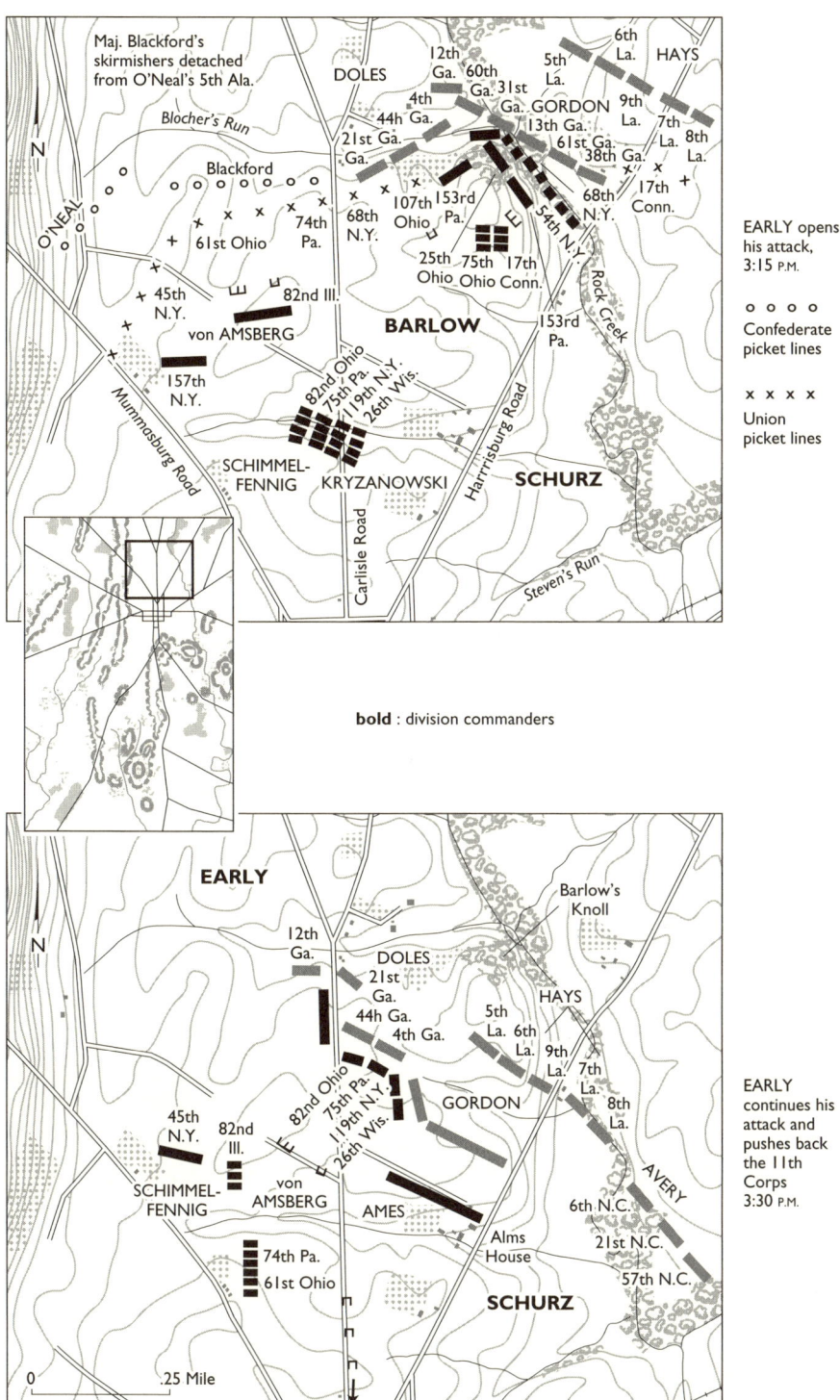

Map 2-22
Early's attack on the Federal right

defense on what became known as Barlow's Knoll, the Federal right flank caved in (map 2-22, bottom). This was in part because of the poor decision that had just been made by the 1st Division's youthful commander. Also, according to Barlow, some of the 11th Corps units in this area simply ran, retreating in disorder (maps 2-22 and 2-23). Others have disputed this, saying that elements of Barlow's force fought as they withdrew.[48]

THE UNION SUFFERS A SETBACK 63

**Map 2-23
Culmination of Early's attack**

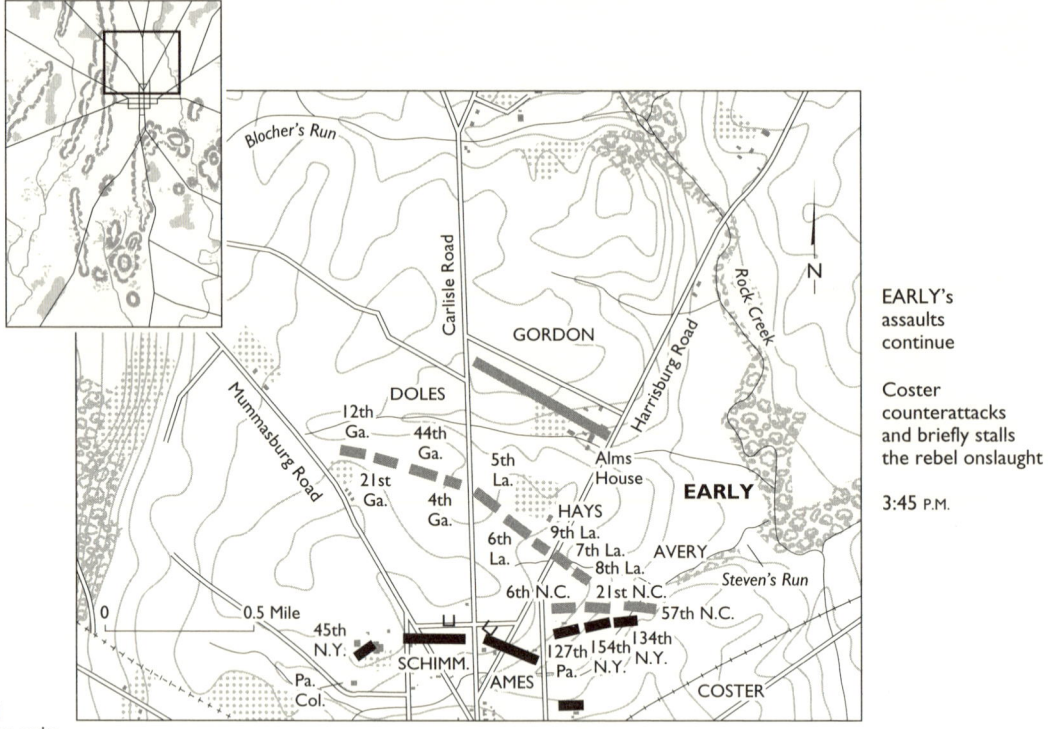

EARLY's assaults continue

Coster counterattacks and briefly stalls the rebel onslaught

3:45 P.M.

Confederate 3rd Corps and most 2nd Corps units not shown; nor are Federal 1st Corps ones (see maps 2-24, 2-25)

bold: division commanders

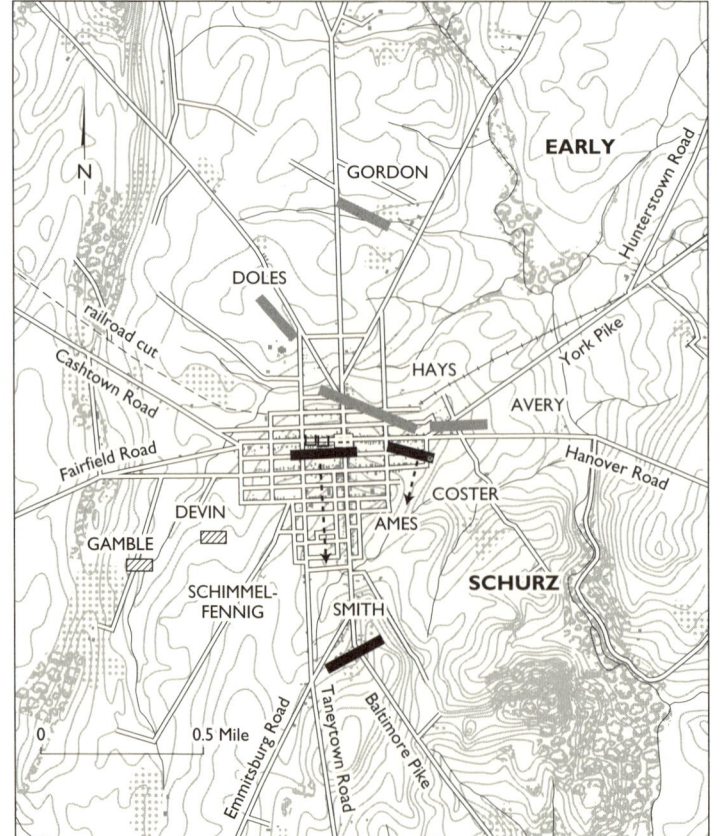

11th Corps retreats through and below the town

4 P.M.

▨ Union cavalry

64 THE STAND OF THE U.S. ARMY AT GETTYSBURG

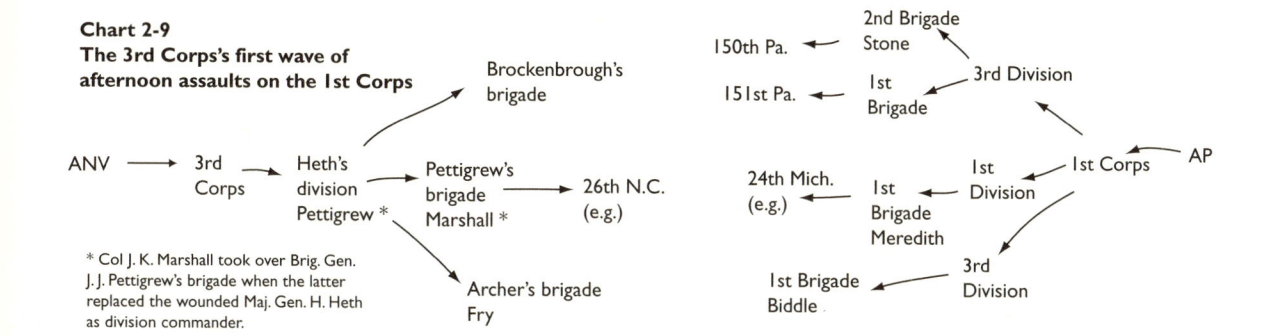

Chart 2-9
The 3rd Corps's first wave of afternoon assaults on the 1st Corps

ANV → 3rd Corps → Heth's division Pettigrew * → Brockenbrough's brigade

Heth's division Pettigrew * → Pettigrew's brigade Marshall * → 26th N.C. (e.g.)

Heth's division Pettigrew * → Archer's brigade Fry

150th Pa. ← 2nd Brigade Stone
151st Pa. ← 1st Brigade
2nd Brigade Stone → 3rd Division
1st Brigade → 3rd Division
3rd Division → 1st Corps
1st Corps → AP

24th Mich. (e.g.) ← 1st Brigade Meredith ← 1st Division ← 1st Corps
1st Brigade Biddle ← 3rd Division ← 1st Division

* Col J. K. Marshall took over Brig. Gen. J. J. Pettigrew's brigade when the latter replaced the wounded Maj. Gen. H. Heth as division commander.

In any case, the Union line began to buckle under escalating pressure as two additional brigades in Early's division (those of Hays and Avery) were ordered to attack soon after Gordon went in (map 2-22). The overall Union defense beyond the town gave way from its right wing, collapsing all the way to its left on McPherson Ridge. This does not mean that the line crumbled as dominoes, in an east-west direction. Instead, the 11th Corps units on the extreme right were pushed back southward toward Gettysburg (map 2-23).[49] This exposed the 3rd Division (11th Corps) brigades on the left, which likewise retreated back in the direction from which they had initially approached the field.[50] Recall that, by now, Ramseur had pushed the Federal center back from the approximate hinge position it had held near the Mummasburg Road. Thus, the one significant group of defenders left on the field was the 1st Federal Corps (map 2-21).

Heth's bloodied soldiers were the first to attack General Doubleday's men in the vicinity of McPherson Ridge (map 2-24). Thankfully, for Confederate fortunes, Heth was himself bloodied during this action (almost).[51] General Johnston Pettigrew assumed command of the division, with Colonel John M. Brockenbrough's brigade on the left, Pettigrew's own in the center, and what used to be Archer's on the right (map 2-24). Pettigrew turned his brigade over to Col. James K. Marshall; Col. Birkett D. Fry commanded the brigade formerly led by the captured Archer (chart 2-9). According to Heth's post-battle report, Fry's soldiers—as they moved in from the west on the right—veered farther in that direction, principally to tie up a group of Federal cavalrymen posted on the extreme left of this ephemeral defensive position (map 2-24).[52] However, the Confederate right wing was ultimately to attack the left flank of the Federal 1st Corps's infantry line (map 2-25).

Even though the units within that Union corps, including the Iron Brigade, gave ground grudgingly, they were forced to fall back to Seminary Ridge (map 2-24). This was a fighting withdrawal of another kind, not the hide-and-seek game that General Buford had played in the morning. By making the best stand they could before retiring in reasonably good order from McPherson Ridge to Seminary Ridge, these 1st Corps defenders continued to absorb casualties as several of these Union units had begun to do in the morning. This resulted, for example, in the loss of almost two-thirds of the Iron Brigade on July 1.

The faltering 1st Corps had little respite on Seminary Ridge. General Pender's fresh Confederate 3rd Corps division (chart 2-10) soon hit it there (map 2-25). More than three thousand rebels attacked, advancing against the backed-up Union defense deployed to both sides of the Cashtown Road. Below it, General Doubleday had anticipated that the ridge might have to be a final defensive position.[53] Hours earlier, breastworks of sorts had been thrown up in front of the

Map 2-24
First wave of Confederate 3rd Corps attacks, mid-afternoon

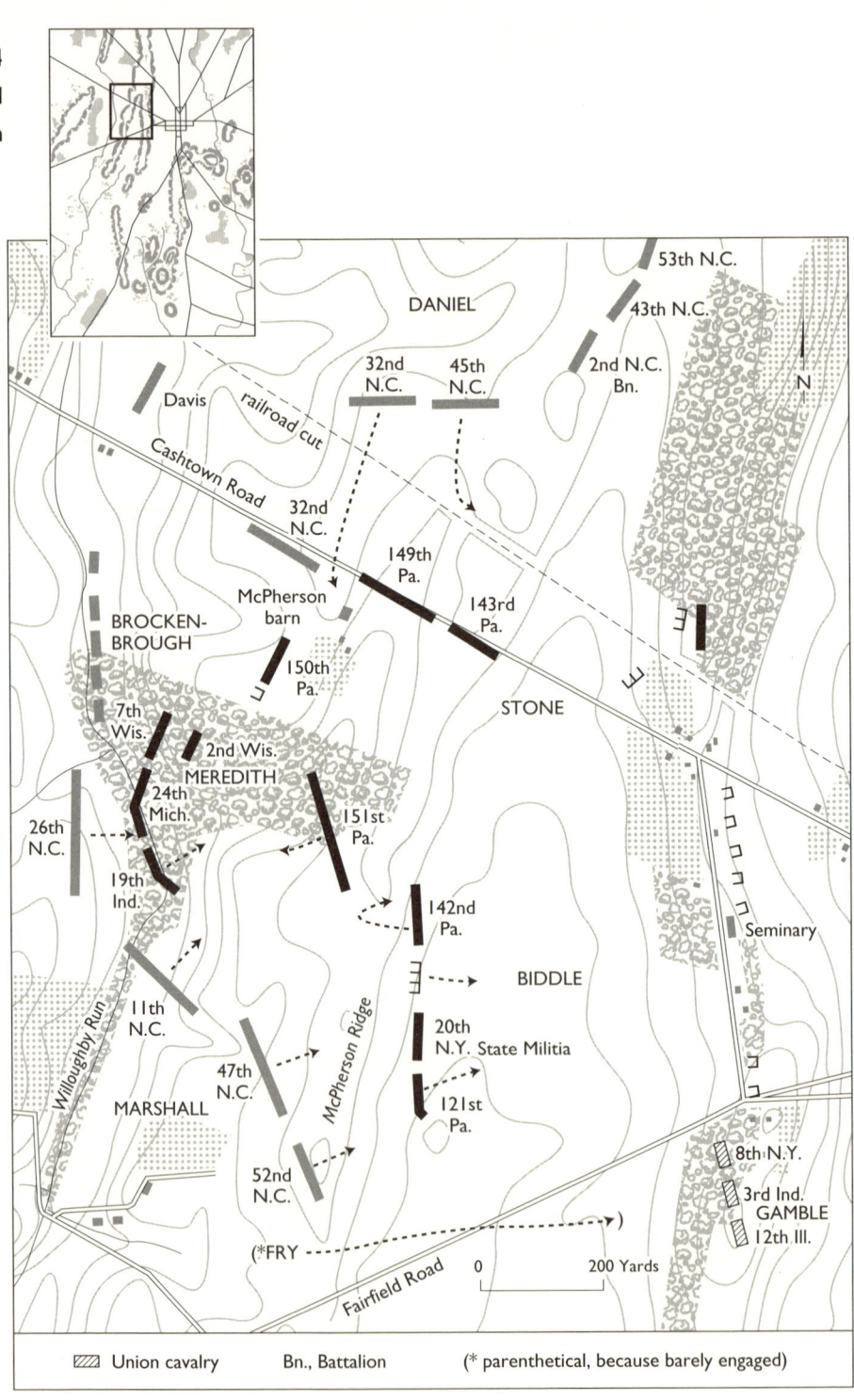

Lutheran seminary. Paul's brigade put these works together before it left this reserve position to reinforce Baxter on the Mummasburg Road (map 2-20). The semicircle of modest fortifications near the seminary was a rallying point for the 1st Corps units withdrawing from McPherson Ridge.

It was about 4 P.M., and both Federal flanks were about to be hit near the seminary. The Union right flank was across the road to the north. Bolstering this line

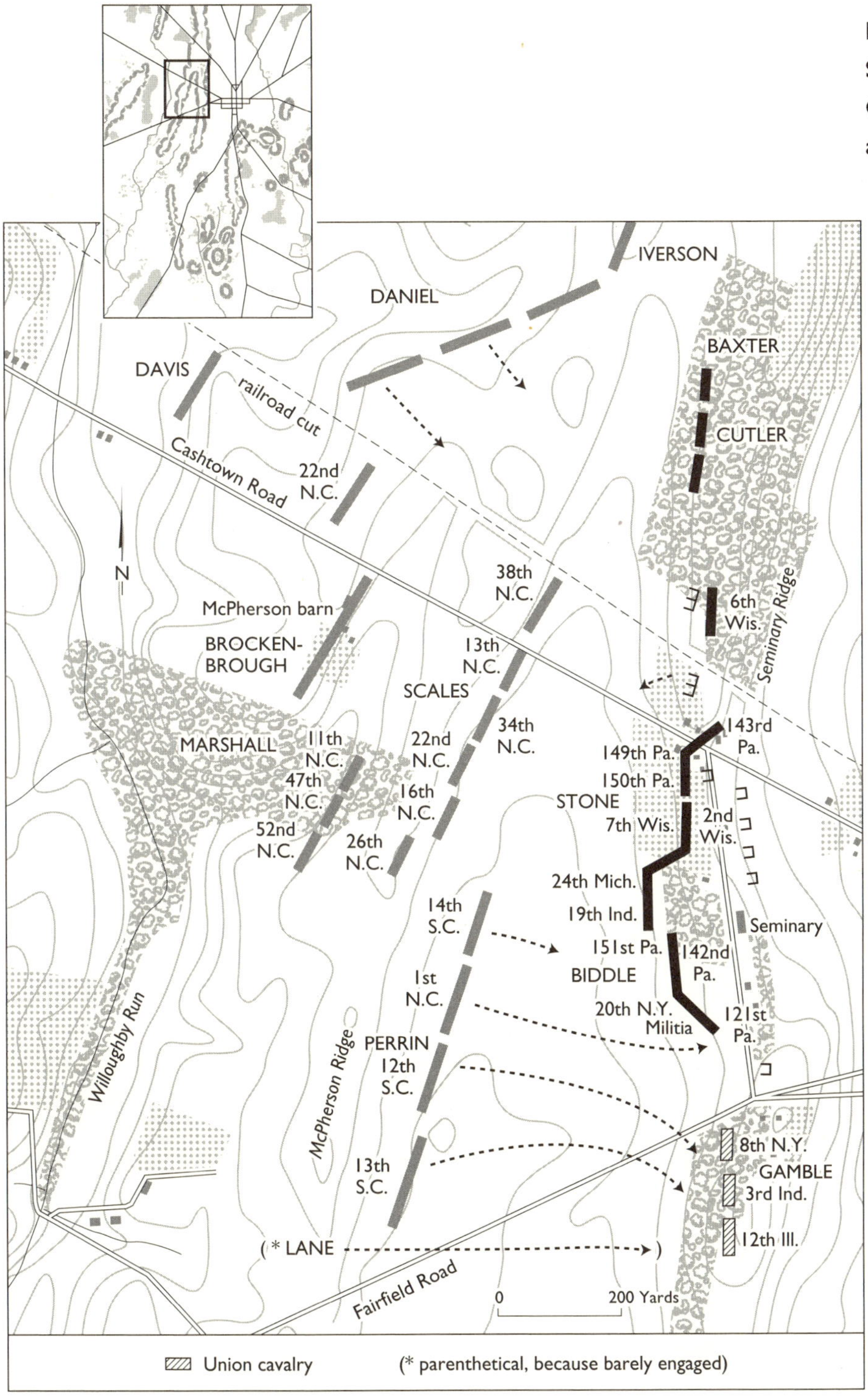

Map 2-25
Second wave of Confederate 3rd Corps attacks, mid-to-late-afternoon

were twenty-one artillery pieces, ranging from just north of the railroad cut to south of the seminary buildings (maps 2-24 and 2-25). As the rebels advanced toward Seminary Ridge, a battery north of the road ripped at the left flank of Scales's brigade, which formed the left wing of Pender's assault, straddling the Cashtown Road (map 2-25). Cannon fire also poured in from the center of the defensive line.

THE UNION SUFFERS A SETBACK

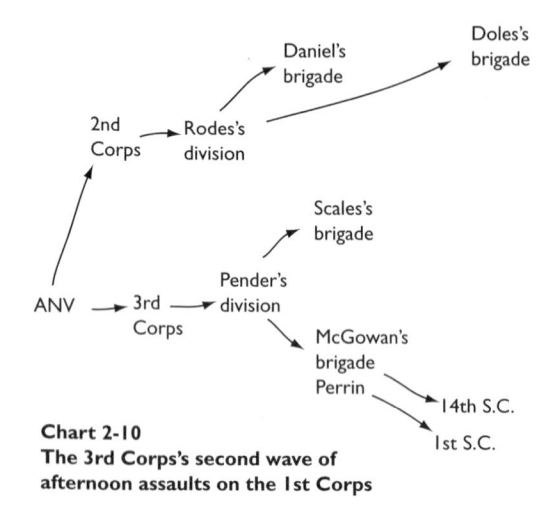

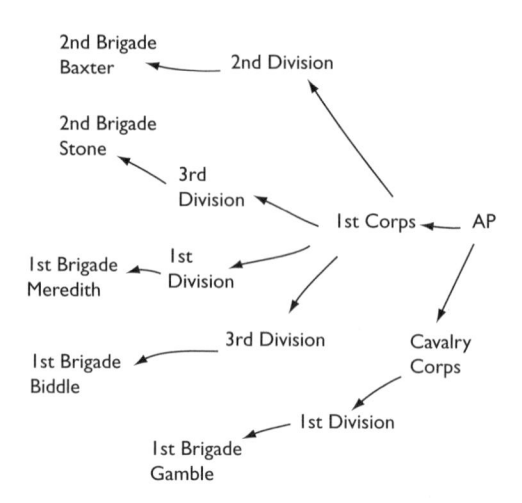

Chart 2-10
The 3rd Corps's second wave of afternoon assaults on the 1st Corps

The Union center was holding for the time being, but the flanks were under severe pressure. In this regard, Pender's attack was supported north of the road (map 2-25) by Daniel's brigade from Rodes's 2nd Corps division (chart 2-10), which had been fighting earlier in the second battle for the railroad cut (map 2-20).[54] On the other wing of the late afternoon attack, Col. Abner M. Perrin's brigade from Pender's division was slowed down by the defenders' artillery fire, and his advance was staggered by Federal musketry—in part because he was unsupported on his right flank.[55] However, Perrin's 1st South Carolina ultimately got around the Union left and enfiladed it. Simultaneously, the 14th South Carolina hit the left-center of the Union line from the front (map 2-25; chart 2-10).

The attack of the two South Carolina regiments on the left of Perrin's battle line broke through the defense near the seminary. The entire Union line along Seminary Ridge was beginning to crumble. Over on the Union right in this sector, General Daniel's troops were tearing into that flank (maps 2-25 and 2-26), while farther to the north the Federal 1st Corps's right wing—with Paul's brigade in the most advanced, northernmost position—was still under attack by Ramseur's brigade. Paul was giving way below Oak Hill (map 2-20). Ramseur had already pushed back Baxter's Federal brigade (map 2-20), now formed on Seminary Ridge to the north of the railroad cut (map 2-25). Also by this time, the 11th Corps's outer defense farther to the east had been wrecked by Early (maps 2-22 and 2-23).[56]

Finally, the Federal 1st Corps withdrew. General Doubleday, with no reserves left west of Gettysburg, ordered his troops to retreat. They streamed back toward town, many using the Cashtown Road. Heavy fire from Perrin's still-advancing regiments swept the road, forcing many of the retreating Federals over to their left, past the railroad cut, where it might be safer. It was not, and the withdrawing troops soon found themselves being hit by Confederates pushing south from north of the cut (maps 2-26 and 2-27). This included rebel artillery fire from pieces rolled up to assail the retreating masses of men. Doles's brigade, which had been positioned farther to the north (maps 2-22 and 2-23), entered the fray (map 2-26) and began moving toward the seminary, trying to cut off the withdrawing bluecoats. Doles's attack, in conjunction with the continuing advance of Perrin's brigade from the south, threatened to demolish the entire Federal 1st Corps.

This did not happen, but the converging Confederate troops created a horren-

Map 2-26

The Federal 1st Corps gives way on Seminary Ridge

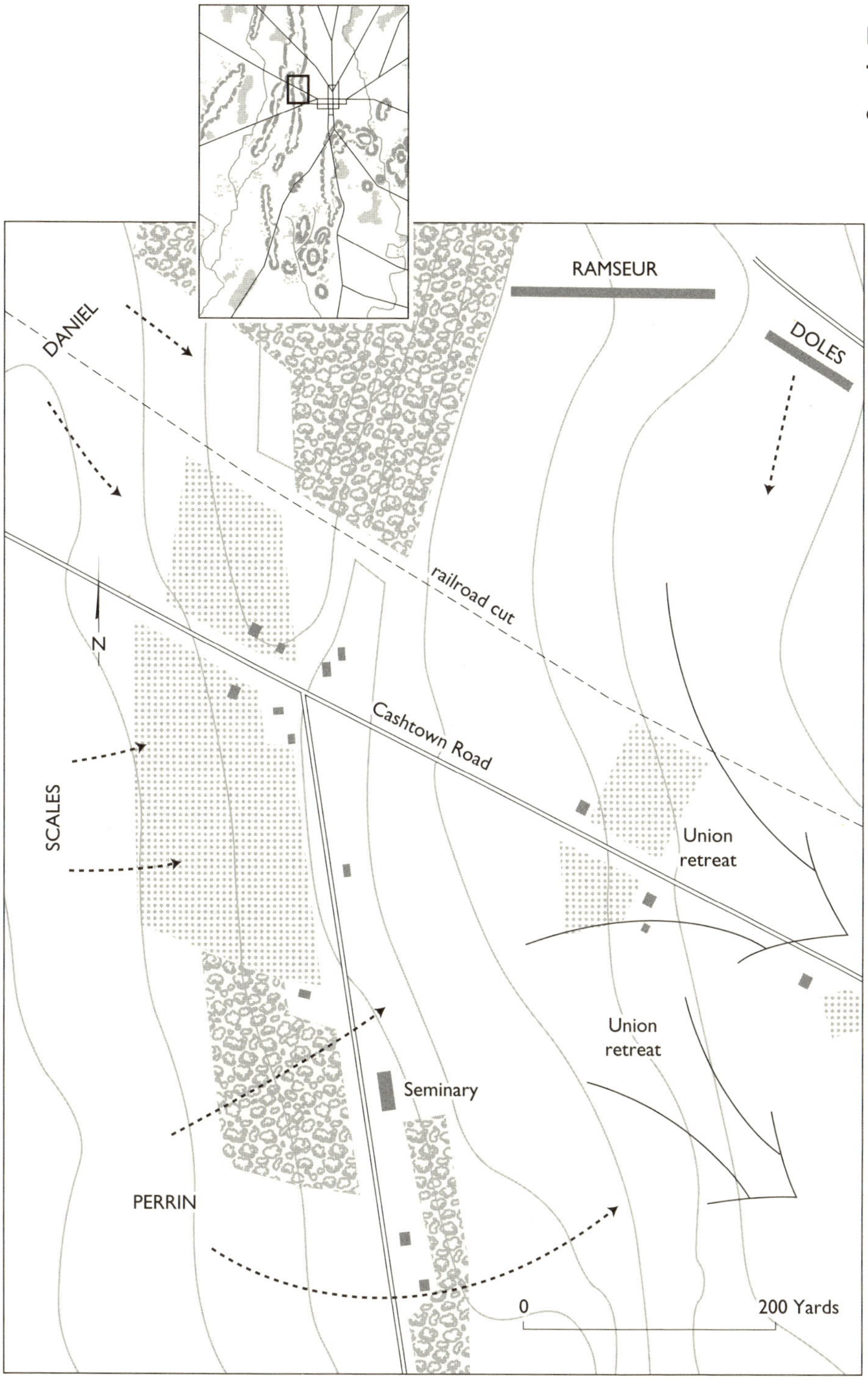

dous *gauntlet* through which the Union troops had to retreat (map 2-26). Their losses continued to mount. As they withdrew across Seminary Ridge and moved into the town, General Paul's brigade (chart 2-7), which had replaced Baxter's out near the Mummasburg Road, suffered the highest casualty rate of any 1st Corps brigade. Forty percent of Paul's troops were captured, the tip of the iceberg in terms of 1st Corps casualties in this category. Yet some of these men, and many of the other retreating Union units, made it through the gauntlet and into Gettys-

THE UNION SUFFERS A SETBACK

burg by the skin of their teeth. Some were able to bypass Gettysburg and cut across open fields between the Fairfield and Emmitsburg Roads in the direction of Cemetery Hill (maps 2-26 and 2-29). However, large numbers of 1st Corps infantrymen became intermingled inside the town limits with 11th Corps soldiers, who were retreating from the north.

Lest we get carried away by too much contrasting of the 1st Corps's fighting withdrawal and the 11th's disorderly retreat, it must be mentioned that an element of Howard's command was deployed from the vicinity of Cemetery Hill and did put up a last-ditch defense north of town.[57] Moreover, 2,200 1st Corps soldiers were captured, compared with 1,500 from the 11th Corps. Out of twenty-eight 1st Corps infantry regiments engaged on July 1, twenty-four had 50 or more men captured (see chart 2-13 for a list of all casualties for July 1). Many of the troops in these two Union corps became prisoners as they mixed together trying to retreat through town. However, about half of the 11th Corps casualties were killed and wounded, which implies that they put up a good fight. The 1st Corps's overall casualties (6,100 of 12,200 men engaged) were so horrendous that it ceased to exist. The same was so for the vaunted Iron Brigade, which lost 1,153 out of 1,829, and continued for the remainder of the war in name only.[58]

Confederate casualties were also heavy on July 1, such that the attacking rebel forces lost more men killed and wounded than did the Federals (although the number of the latter captured was far greater). For example, on the Confederate side, General Heth's division suffered more than 1,500 casualties out of 7,500 infantrymen. One regiment, the 26th North Carolina (map 2-24, chart 2-9), was left with only 25 percent of the approximately eight hundred men who had begun the day's actions.

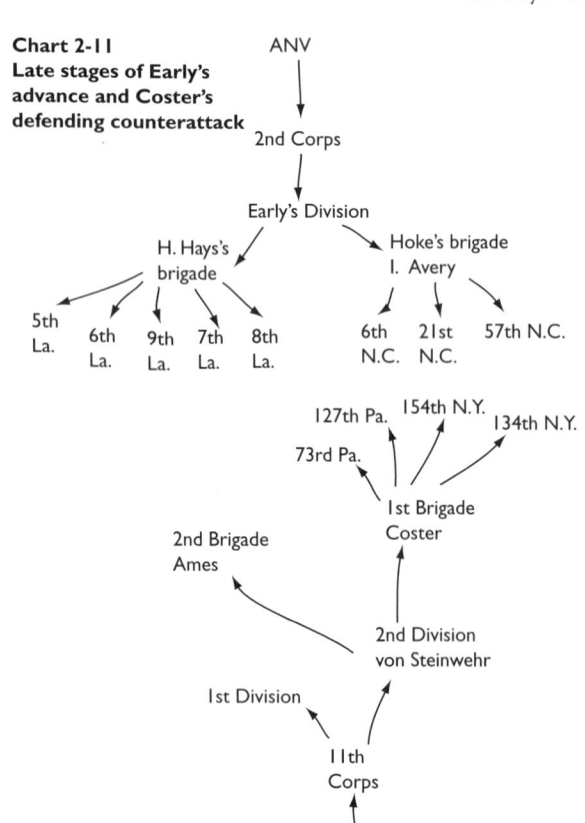

Chart 2-11
Late stages of Early's advance and Coster's defending counterattack

THE FEDERAL DEFENSE COALESCES ON A HILL SOUTH OF GETTYSBURG, WHERE THE CONFEDERATE ATTACKS COULD NOT HAVE READILY RESUMED

It was now between 4 and 5 P.M. It appeared that the Army of the Potomac had again been defeated—but how badly? In addition to holding out for most of the day, that the relevant *fraction* of the Federal force (less than two of its seven corps' worth of infantrymen) got pushed off the field to the north and northwest of Gettysburg was ultimately to their *advantage*. As they fell back to more defensible ground south of town (map 2-23) General Howard's prescience was borne out. The retreating 1st and 11th Corps infantry units were able to *rally round a defensive force* that was firmly in place and holding good ground on Cemetery Hill (map 2-27). The nominally defeated Federal forces thus did not have to locate this hill, a place they had never heard of and probably never seen, as a mere geographical rallying point. Instead, the retreating Union men were able to focus their withdrawal toward a large group of their mates who were holding a conspicuous, organized defensive position.[59]

General von Steinwehr's well-placed defenders on Cemetery Hill (chart 2-12) were joined by their fellow corps members and by what was left of the Federal 1st Corps (map 2-27). There had to be a fair amount of confusion in this area, notwithstanding the strong, artillery-augmented positions.

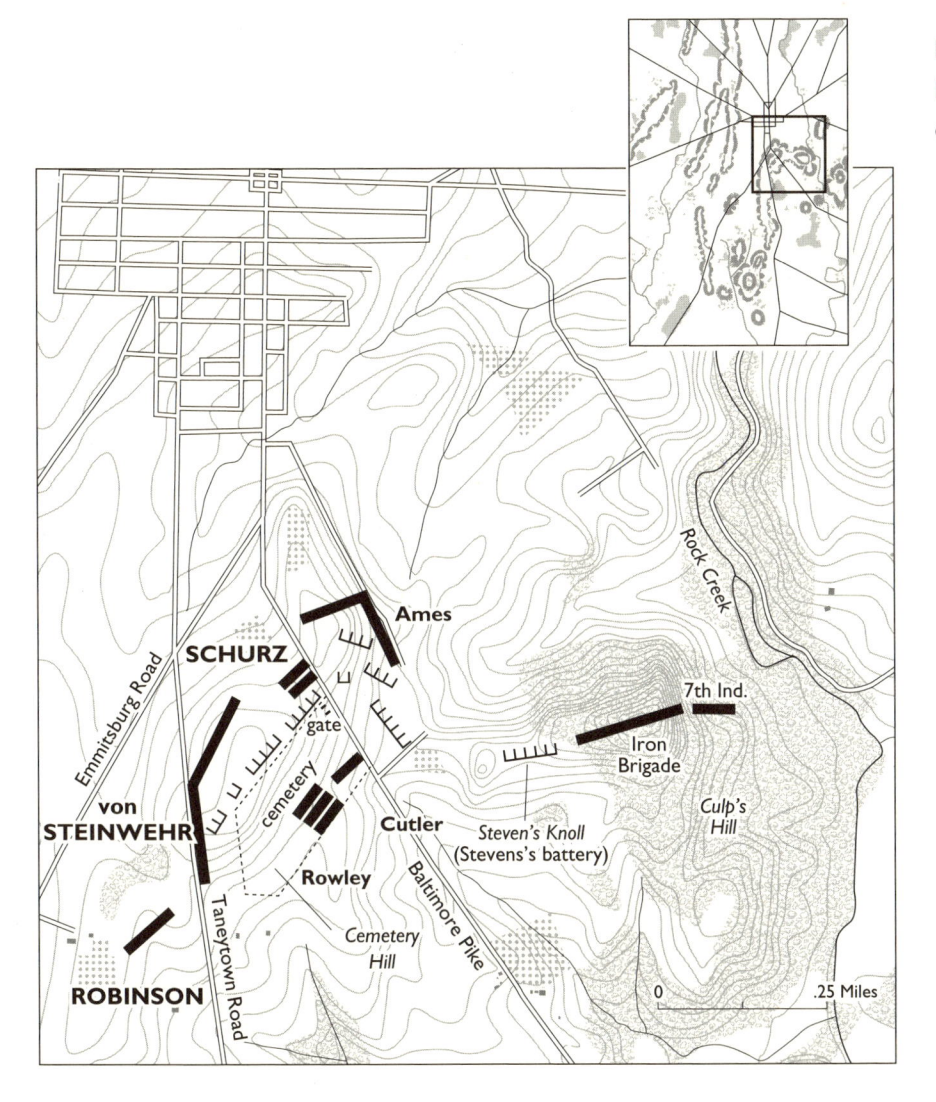

**Map 2-27
Final Federal defense forming, early evening**

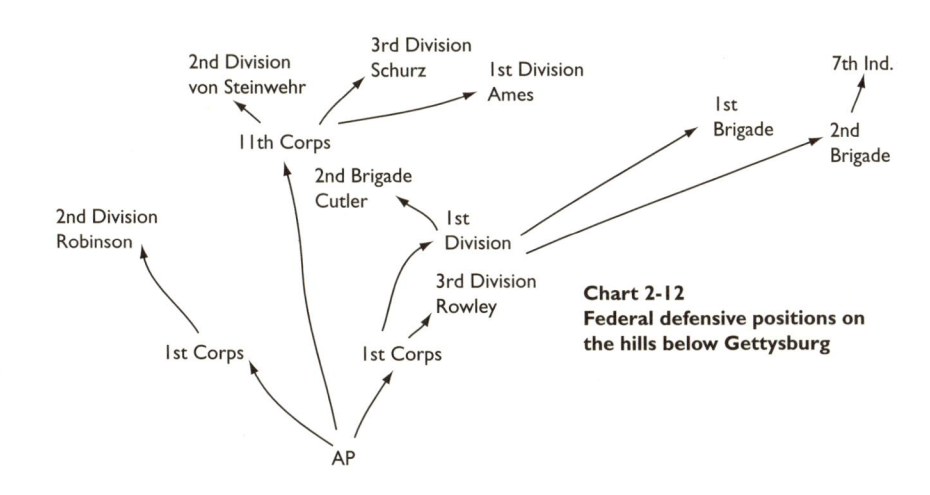

**Chart 2-12
Federal defensive positions on the hills below Gettysburg**

THE UNION SUFFERS A SETBACK

The disorder was ameliorated by the presence of a new general officer on the field, Maj. Gen. Winfield Scott Hancock, commander of the Union 2nd Corps. Hancock, who led the 2nd Corps's 1st Division before assuming command of the corps after the Battle of Chancellorsville, was well regarded by both his peers and by the common soldiers.[60] General Meade had sent Hancock from northern Maryland, ahead of his corps (map 2-28), to take overall command on the emerging battlefield at Gettysburg. One of Hancock's first actions was to send a report to Meade outlining what had happened there earlier in the day, what was going on in the late afternoon, and the prospects for fighting the battle near that Pennsylvania town and not, for example, at the "Pipe Creek line" in northern Maryland.[61]

In the midst of this activity, General Hancock got into a dispute with General Howard, who believed that he should be in charge of the Federal defense that was then forming on the battlefield, south of Gettysburg.[62] However, Hancock and Howard worked out an arrangement whereby they tacitly cooperated in placing the Union units arriving on Cemetery Hill (chart 2-12) to bolster von Steinwehr's positions (map 2-27).[63] Part of the 1st Corps (chart 2-12) was sent to man Culp's Hill—a higher, much more heavily wooded prominence to the east (map 2-27).[64] General Hancock "made his greatest contribution to the Federal rally . . . [when] he asked Doubleday to send Wadsworth [commander of the 1st Division, 1st Corps] and the Iron Brigade to the west slope of Culp's Hill beyond Stevens's battery" [map 2-27].[65]

Culp's Hill, with all its natural cover, could perhaps be more readily defended; but it was undermanned and vulnerable, despite Hancock's prescience. Only about a thousand Union defenders were there in the late afternoon of July 1: what was left of the Iron Brigade, along with the 7th Indiana, a large 1st Corps regiment that had been posted on Culp's Hill in reserve (map 2-27). This situation was exacerbated by the fought-out nature of most of the 1st Corps forces on the hill.

The Culp's Hill defenders, or the relative lack thereof, is one of several factors that brings us to one of the great controversies of Gettysburg, if not of the entire Civil War: Should the Confederates have *followed up the success they achieved in the fields above the town and taken the hills just south of it*?

Lieutenant General Richard S. Ewell has been relentlessly criticized for *not* pushing on against Cemetery and Culp's Hill. However, General Lee first asked Lt. Gen. A. P. Hill to continue attacking. Hill demurred, saying that he and his men were fought out by that time.[66] Perhaps this was so; or it could have been a symptom of A. P. Hill being *the* phantom large-unit commander during the Battle of Gettysburg. But if the majority of his 3rd Corps men were spent as of this Wednesday evening, why had Hill not brought up his fresh division, under Maj. Gen. Richard H. Anderson, and the thus far unengaged brigade of Brig. Gen. Edward Thomas from Pender's division?[67] If the bloodied units in Heth's and Pender's divisions were too exhausted to continue, Anderson could have been sent in to pursue the Federal 1st Corps from northwest of Gettysburg without getting tangled up in town as his division advanced toward Cemetery Hill.[68] Given Hill's performance later in the battle, it was, in retrospect, not surprising that he failed to mobilize Anderson and Thomas.

Thus, Lee sent one of his staff officers to the 2nd Corps headquarters to *ask* Ewell to "carry the hill occupied by the enemy, *if he found it practicable.*"[69] Like Hill, Ewell, too, demurred—and has been excoriated by Southerners ever since. In fact, Maj. Gen. Isaac R. Trimble, attached to the Army of Northern Virginia but without a command, claims to have protested to Ewell later that day about not

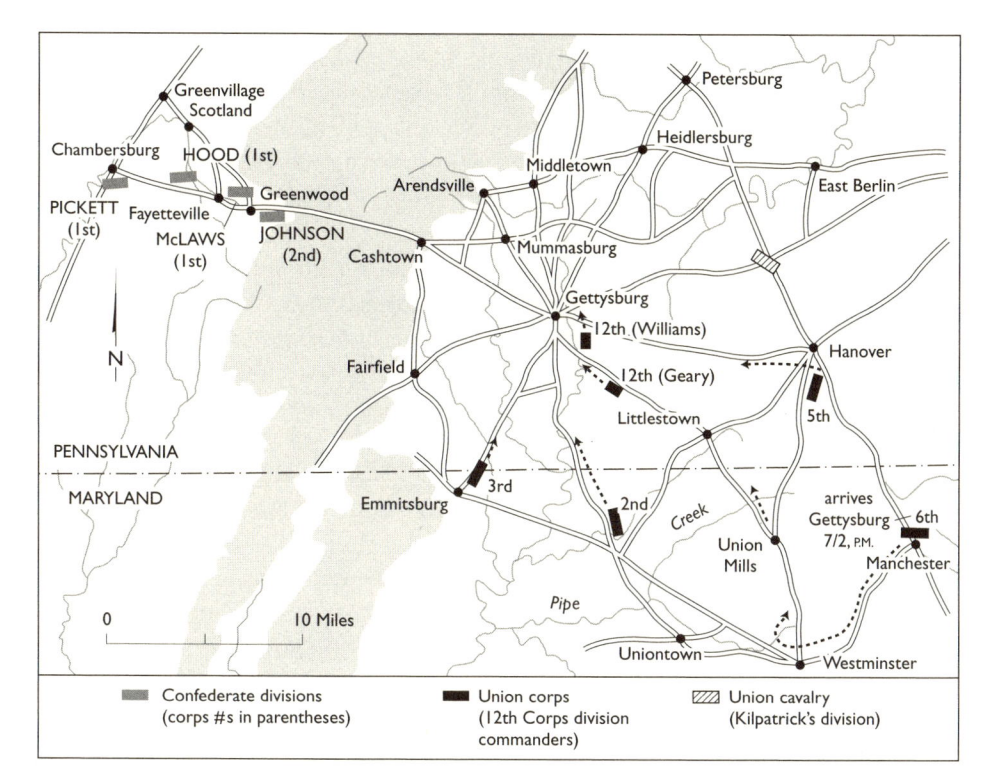

Map 2-28
Positions, movements of the opposing large units, arriving relatively late on July 1

being given units with which he could assail *Culp's* Hill, which at the time was only lightly defended (map 2-27).[70] Perhaps a 2nd Corps rebel force could have taken it. With difficulty, they could then have gotten artillery pieces up on the high ground there—cut down trees if necessary, to create fields of fire—and eventually blasted the Union positions off of Cemetery Hill just to the south and west (map 2-27).[71]

But most of the controversy about the events on July 1 centers on Cemetery Hill, which was supposedly there for the Confederates' taking. This is arguably false, but one must cut through the cacophony of criticism that came down on General Ewell's head and has continued to this day.

In brief, Ewell's units were not in terrific shape as evening approached on that Wednesday afternoon: They had had to march to the battle, and then struggle to some extent to push back the Federal right.[72] In so doing, many of the 2nd Corps's units became disorganized as they chased the retreating 11th Corps into Gettysburg. Could these Confederate soldiers have readily reformed their units in time to sweep southward then up the formidable slopes of Cemetery Hill before the Federal defense there had solidified? Gettysburg itself was a further impediment to this possibility. In addition to the fact that moving through its streets and among its houses broke up unit cohesion, it is not easy to bolt into an unfamiliar town and pop out on the other side, still fully organized. Even if the 2nd Corps units in this vicinity had accomplished this difficult task, they were not at full strength as Maj. Gen. Edward Johnson's division was still in the process of extricating itself from a traffic jam on the rebel's right wing (map 2-28), having become detached from the 2nd Corps's main body during the marches required to concentrate in the Gettysburg area (map 2-16).[73]

Thus, if General Ewell had assaulted the hills south of town, he would have been doing so in a far less than advantageous situation from the perspective of his own units. In addition, he would have been moving up the north and perhaps western slopes of Cemetery Hill over relatively open ground against defenders, many of whom had been there for hours—time enough to form fine defensive positions. Moreover, General von Steinwehr's Union soldiers were in the process of welcoming the aforementioned reinforcements (chart 2-12)—retreating though they were, but given some breathing space because of the difficulty the attackers had maintaining their momentum. Ewell also may have factored in the lack of offensive support in his vicinity, in case the hill's defenders had some fight left in them and an initial assault on it met with disaster. (Indeed, the 11th Corps defenders on Cemetery Hill did pretty well later in the battle.)

Here's another little-known concern that Ewell had to deal with as the evening of July 1 approached: About the time the Union 11th and 1st Corps were being driven through the town, a 12th Corps division was moving east toward Gettysburg on the Hanover Road (map 2-28).[74] General Ewell had to know he was embroiled in a meeting engagement, meaning that major components of the opposing army were not present but were coming. To where? Even if Ewell had no idea whether a Federal force, or what size of one, was arriving in his vicinity, the circumstances of July 1 would naturally create anxiety in a commander's mind: Might enemy elements arrive more or less out of nowhere *on his flank,* just as his own left wing hit the Union right shortly before?[75] Given all of these factors, Richard Ewell's decision not to attack was eminently reasonable.

However, let us imagine what might have happened had General Ewell cobbled together his 2nd Corps troops and attacked the hill.[76] Conceivably, the assault would have succeeded, a point that can be bolstered by the following.[77] Why not *try* to attack Cemetery Hill on July 1, when the Federals right there were in a *relatively* poor posture and significant components of the Army of the Potomac had not even reached the battlefield? Even if such a Confederate attack failed, would that have ruined rebel fortunes in the battle as a whole? The *eventual* assault on Cemetery Hill by elements of Ewell's corps failed the next day anyway (see Chapter 3), arguably because the Union defense was in better shape on July 2 compared with its quasi-confusion the previous evening.

Another corps commander made an important decision of his own as darkness descended on the battlefield. General Hancock had helped anticipate the emerging Federal defense, which was beginning to harden as additional Union units—the 3rd and 12th Corps (maps 2-27 and 2-28)—approached the field from the south to bolster the 11th and 1st Corps positions. After the Federal defense had solidified, thanks in part to Hancock's efforts, he rode to General Meade's headquarters in Taneytown, Maryland. They conferred at 9 P.M. and Hancock urged Meade to make a stand at Gettysburg. General Meade had already decided to do so, owing to the information carried by the courier sent to him by Hancock earlier that afternoon. Meade's and Hancock's nighttime discussion clinched the decision. The commander of the Army of the Potomac thus rode north to the battlefield, departing about ten P.M.

General George Meade had accomplished a lot on this day, even though he had done so in a partly passive or indirect manner. After he got the Army of the Potomac out of its Maryland doldrums in late June, he delegated key decisions to his northernmost large-unit commanders on July 1. Just recently a corps commander himself, Meade unleashed the general officers now holding that position under him while he properly hung back in case he decided to recall the advance units to the aforementioned defensive line along Pipe Creek in northern Maryland (see note 61). However, before any such decision was seriously considered, he had sent General Reynolds northward with the authority to run whatever operation was necessary with the van of the Union infantry. Reynolds got his corps to Gettysburg with but a few minutes to spare, and had he not acted with celerity the North surely would have suffered a disastrous defeat. Thus, Reynolds had his "golden hours" on the morning of July 1, just as Howard had his golden moment on Cemetery Hill a little later in the day. Then General Hancock was unleashed to supervise the late stages of the July 1 operations. He performed well, contributing superbly by steadying the shaky (albeit numerically significant) defense south of town. Then he exercised good judgment, both on the hills and in terms of the advice about the emerging power of the troop positions there. Finally, Hancock carried this assessment to his commander in a timely manner.

Was the Army of the Potomac at last *free* of a high command that would not act on its own or permit its potentially solid large-unit commanders to act? Meade, in his fourth day of running the army, implied that he was going to do the opposite: give quick, judicious orders and then trust that the corps commanders would perform well on their own, exploiting the autonomy granted them. General Meade therefore seemed more than *willing* to give them this authority, but he also implied that he was a novice who was *counting* on them. Would that General Hooker had so done at Chancellorsville, when the majority of his corps commanders urged him to unleash his entire force—much of which was never sent into that battle, while the rest of it was compelled to absorb the Confederate assaults and then retreat.[78]

Meade, of course, was not on the Gettysburg battlefield on July 1, and he has been criticized for holding back.[79] Yet neither he nor any of his principal subordinates could have known about the whereabouts of the rebel army as a whole, or about Lee's intentions, that day. Knowing the Pipe Creek line might become the place where the Union army would make its stand, Meade judiciously kept his headquarters at nearby Taneytown, Maryland, until it became clear that the battle would be fought in southern Pennsylvania.

In any event, Maj. Gen. George Gordon Meade had got most of this "last army of the Republic" into positions where its soldiers could make a stand.[80] Would they be doing so on the impending Thursday? Would the Confederates attempt to renew the momentum that had allowed them to prevail on Wednesday afternoon?

It seemed likely that Gen. Robert E. Lee would so order. He probably felt that he came within an ace of routing the Army of the Potomac, perhaps on a scale that would have superseded the Federal disasters on the first and second days at Chancellorsville two months earlier. This near miss at Gettysburg on July 1 may have caused Lee to downplay the increasingly strong Federal position on Cemetery and Culp's Hills, and on a low ridge running southward from Cemetery Hill (map 2-29). Troops of the 12th Corps were forming up on the part of the Union line just described, bolstering the northerly positions held by their 1st and 11th Corps mates, and the 3rd Corps was not far behind (map 2-28).[81]

General Lee was either *unaware* of or *discounted* the strong defensive stand made by the Federals during the early hours of July 1—a defense that did not crack until late in the afternoon. This was followed by the irony of the Union retreat putting Lee's opponents in a better position than that which they had defended for most of the day.

The two words emphasized in the previous paragraph may characterize the twin factors running together in Lee's mind, doing so because he had (by definition) arrived at this meeting engagement after more than half of the day's actions had taken place. He threw into the mix, at least subconsciously, his feelings about

**Map 2-29
General troop positions, end of July 1**

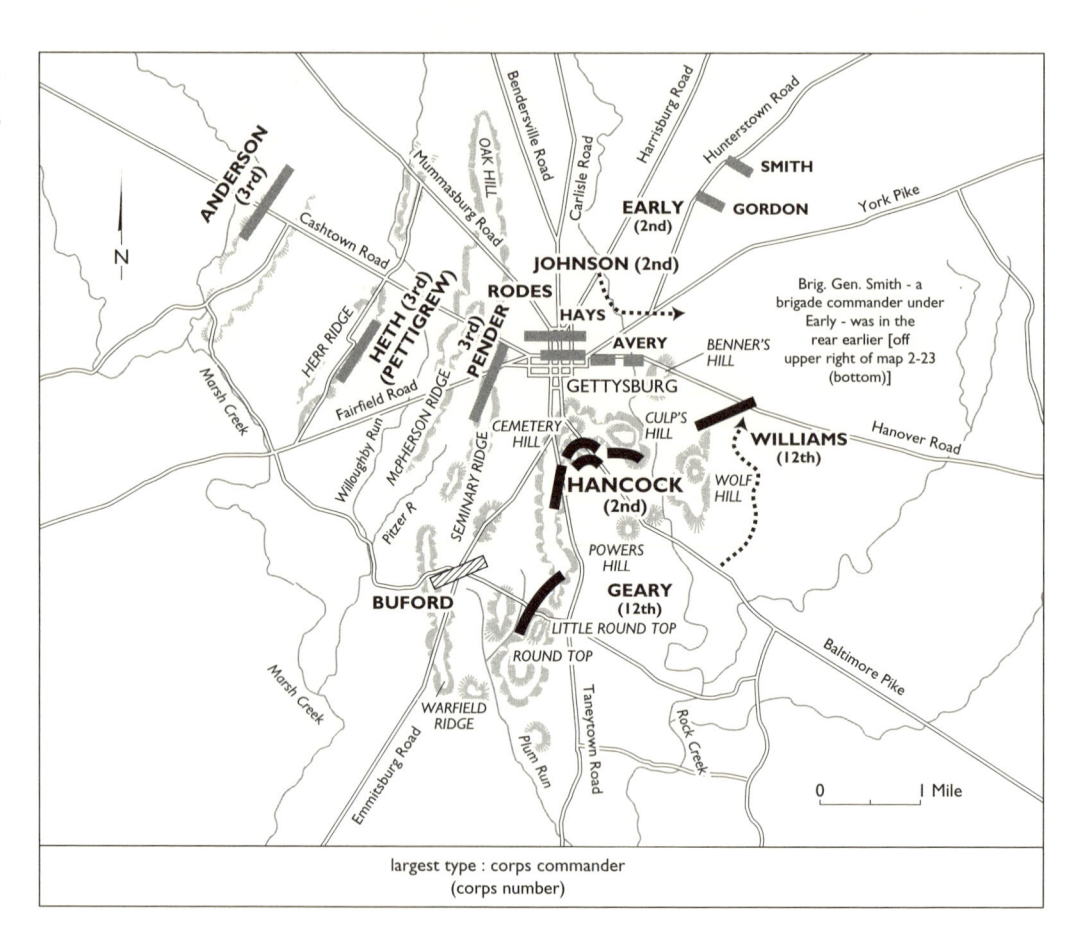

Chart 2-13
Estimates of casualties for July 1 *

	killed and wounded	missing / captured	total
Confederate	5,880	1,840	7,720
Union	5,360	3,600	8,960

*These estimates, and those given at the end of the next two chapters, are rather wild (even if educated) guesses made by J. M. Vanderslice in his book *Gettysburg, Then and Now* (1899, Dillingham Co., New York). Other estimates of Union losses on July 1 came from Generals Doubleday and Howard themselves: approximately 5,700 - 5,800 (1st Corps) and 3,200 (11th Corps), respectively, totaling more than 9,900 (Pfanz, *First Day*, p. 333). A separate estimate for Confederate casualties on this day of the battle is that the divisions of Heth, Pender, and a portion of Rodes's division lost 5,900 men during their assaults from the west and north; and that Early's division lost only 400 as they attacked from the northeast, supported by Doles who, along with O'Neal (two of Rodes's brigades), probably sustained 200 casualties (Pfanz, *First Day*, p. 351). In truth, it is difficult to imagine anyone (during that century or subsequent ones) accurately breaking down the losses day by day. There are surviving "morning reports" (made by certain unit commanders, who specified their losses from the previous day's fighting as best they could); but even these spotty records are not very reliable. The officers were too busy to record carefully their killed, wounded, and captured for a given day; and they could not do so with great accuracy after the battle ended. Nevertheless, other sources can be used to try to generate figures like those listed above: private letters and diaries, to augment what might be available for a given unit in the official reports. In them, per-day losses at Gettysburg are indicated for some of the units engaged. Others did nearly all their fighting during only one day of the battle, so the overall losses for such a unit permit a reasonable use of those numbers in a chart like this one (also see charts 3-37 and 4-32).

76   THE STAND OF THE U.S. ARMY AT GETTYSBURG

the temper of his soldiers *and his own*—looking back to the culmination of the previous battle in the eastern theater, which had occurred in the clearing near the Chancellorsville mansion on May 3, 1963.[82] Thus, barely two months later, he could well have jumped to a conclusion about the irresistible superiority of his force—and did so for reasons that went deeper than the mere events of the first day in July. Lee was predisposed to conclude that he should take an aggressive course of action whenever the facts as he knew them warranted it. These analytical and emotional forces joined in his mind, such that Lee itched to continue his attacks on July 2. If the Federals were *on the run today,* perhaps they could be *destroyed tomorrow.* In particular, the chance of achieving a truly annihilative tactical victory seems in general to be much higher for an *attacking* rather than a defending force. Yet in formulating this offensive plan General Lee was overconfident. He was in that state not only inherently, but also in the context of the rapidly improving quality of the Army of the Potomac, and especially the commanders within it.

Map 3-1
Theater of battle, July 2

Phases of Battle:

a. The armies move into position: the Confederates deploy southward with some difficulty, and the Federals solidify their fishhook line with a reserve force placed behind it

b. A Union corps moves out from its line, breaking the lower shank of the fishhook

c. The Confederates open the attack with two long right hooks moving eastward against one Federal corps, which is reinforced by elements of another

d. The battle for Little Round Top and the Charge of the 20th Maine

e. The south-to-north Confederate attack continues with a short right hook, and the Federals counterattack from Cemetery Ridge into the Wheatfield

f. The south-to-north attack continues as a Federal salient in the Peach Orchard is broken, leading to fighting withdrawals large and small

g. The south-to-north attack reaches the Union center, is stalled by a desperate counterattack, but achieves a mini-high-water mark just to the north

h. The Confederate left finally attacks Culp's and Cemetery Hills

i. Stands and repulses all along the lines

j. The climax

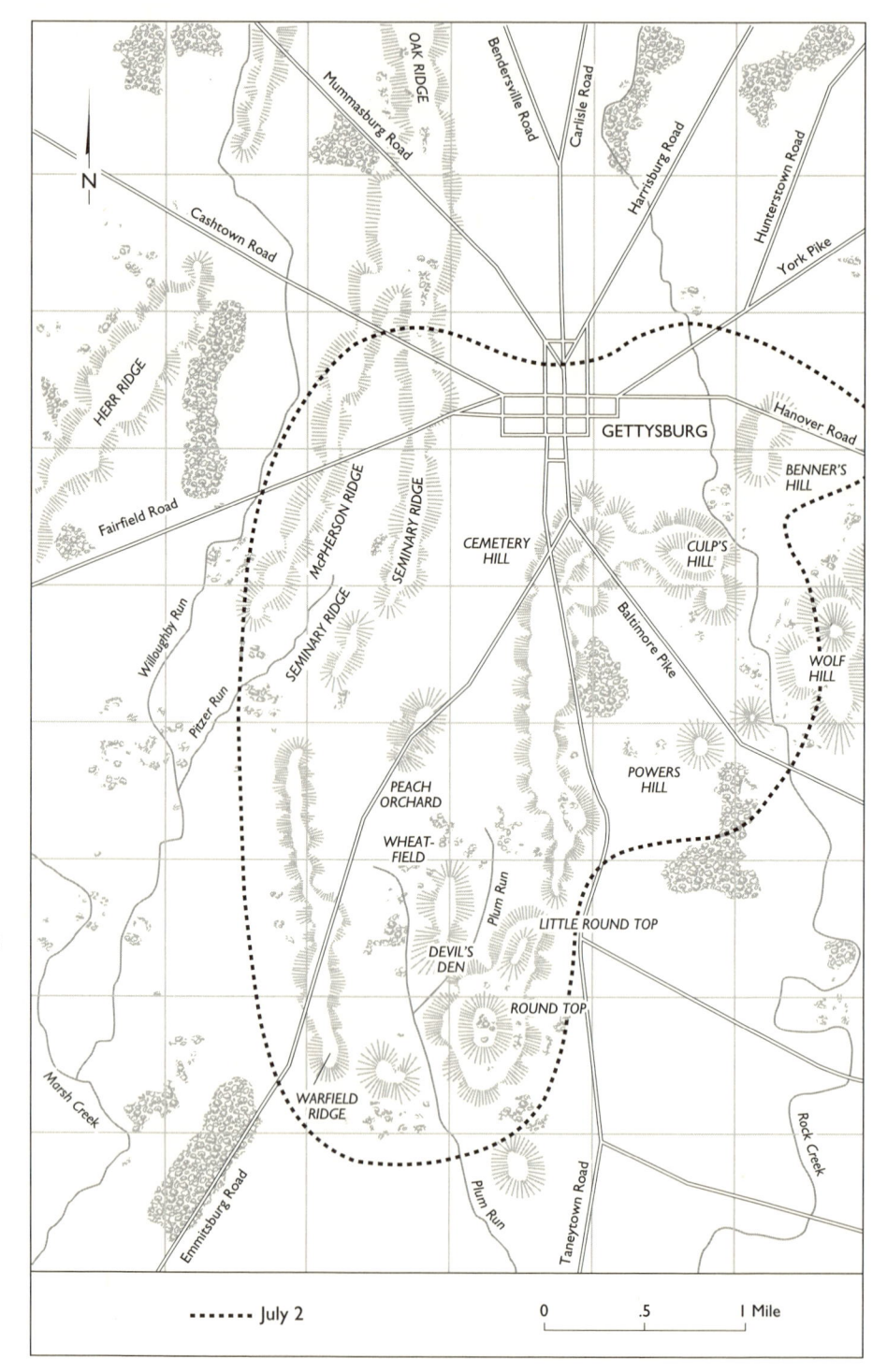

CHAPTER THREE

July 2: The Climax of the Battle

Through these fields of destruction
Baptisms of fire
I've watched all your suffering
As the battles raged higher

—Mark Knopfler

The theater of battle for Thursday, July 2, shifted mostly to the south of Gettysburg as outlined in map 3-1. However, significant fighting occurred on the hills nearer the town—a separate and later conflict not as well known as the battle that raged between the two famous ridges south of Gettysburg. The weather in this part of Pennsylvania was mostly cloudy but with a slightly more seasonable temperature than on the previous day. It was 74° at 7 A.M. on July 2 and rose to 81° by 2 P.M.

When the fighting on this day eventually started, large Confederate units were deployed on and to the east of Seminary Ridge (map 3-1), an unimpressive height that runs from the Lutheran seminary southward, eventually crossing the Emmitsburg Road. The left of the Union line was positioned on Cemetery Ridge, a higher prominence extending south from Cemetery Hill. This hill is high, flat ground in the northern sector of the July 2 theater of battle (map 3-1). However, Cemetery *Ridge* flattens out as it approaches the smaller of two additional hills: Little Round Top and Big Round Top. These anchored the southern end of the battlefield.

A rolling rebel attack commenced in the late afternoon, moving initially toward the Round Tops from Seminary Ridge, and from the projection of it below the Emmitsburg Road, called Warfield Ridge (map 3-1). This attack would achieve a crest of sorts near the center of the shank of the Union's "fishhook" configuration (map 3-4), which curved over Cemetery Hill and Culp's Hill to the north and northeast. The Confederate attack on the northern part of the Union line began as the fighting in the southern and central sectors wound down.

Therefore, the initial series of attacks will be described first, followed by a treatment of the evening assaults on the Union right flank positioned on the northern hills.

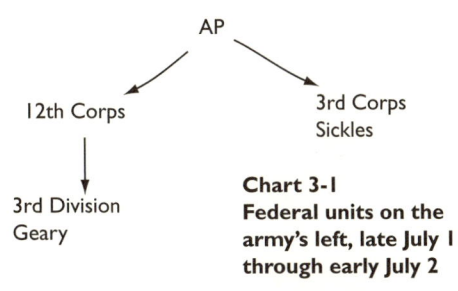

```
            AP
           / \
      12th Corps   3rd Corps
          |        Sickles
          ↓
      3rd Division
         Geary
```

**Chart 3-1
Federal units on the army's left, late July 1 through early July 2**

79

The Armies Move into Position:
The Confederates Deploy Southward with Some Difficulty, and the Federals Solidify Their Fishhook Line with a Reserve Force Placed behind It

On Thursday morning, Gen. Robert E. Lee decided to reinitiate attacks on the Army of the Potomac. However, from the perspective of his right-hand man, Lt. Gen. James Longstreet, Lee had other strategic options. At least that is how Longstreet saw things after the campaign and the war. We will deal with those apparent options in due course, but in the meantime let us try to appreciate why Lee chose to execute a series of frontal assaults. His reasons varied from short-range tactical considerations based on reconnaissance to, from a broader and deeper perspective, aspects of the Army of Northern Virginia's character and recent history.

However, to facilitate planning for the *specifics* of his army's attack on July 2, General Lee sent one of his staff engineers, Capt. Samuel R. Johnston, accompanied by Longstreet's engineer, Maj. John J. Clarke, on a ride to scout the Union left. At about 4 A.M., the officers took off from the position of the Confederate concentration northwest of Gettysburg and rode counterclockwise, down toward the Round Tops (map 3-2). They skirted the face of those two hills and began moving northward, possibly riding up on Little Round Top itself. The small scouting party eventually returned to the commanding general at about 6:30 A.M. Johnston reported that the Union line was arrayed *part way down Cemetery Ridge,* ending not very near to the north face of Little Round Top. This was false, as Maj. Gen. Daniel E. Sickles's 3rd Corps occupied the line in that area. Hours before, Sickles's corps had taken over from Brig. Gen. John W. Geary's 3rd Division, 12th Corps, elements of which were on Little Round Top itself as Wednesday turned into Thursday (chart 3-1). However, the 12th Corps had then been ordered to its final position on Culp's Hill, where it became the principal force in the defenses there. Captain Johnston's reconnaissance was inaccurate, and this led to a flawed Confederate attack plan.[1]

The scouting mistake may have been worse than a case of "I did not see them from up on Little Round Top." Did Johnston and his mates really ride to the vicinity of position occupied by Sickles? It is conceivable that they had ascended the high ground near the southern end of a place called Houck's Ridge (west of Little Round Top) and missed the vicinity of the Round Tops altogether (see the question mark near the bottom left of map 3-2). Captain Johnson's postwar statements about riding onto Little Round Top are not compelling when one projects him back in time to a ride that was both in the dark and in unfamiliar territory.

Possessing this unintelligent intelligence, General Lee formulated the first part of his complicated plan for July 2. General Longstreet was to march his 1st Corps southward from its overnight position on Herr Ridge to the west side of Seminary Ridge (map 3-1). There, two of Longstreet's divisions would form their battle lines in the vicinity of the intersection of Seminary Ridge and the Emmitsburg Road and open the attack.[2] Also, the east-facing Confederate line would by that time have been extended to its left (northward) by brigades from Richard Anderson's and Dorsey Pender's 3rd Corps divisions. These largely fresh troops were to move a relatively short distance into position from north of the Fairfield Road (map 3-3). The 3rd Corps battle lines would then extend southward, with Anderson's right roughly facing the Federal center. Pender's units moved from south of Lee's headquarters (map 3-3) to positions just below the Fairfield Road.

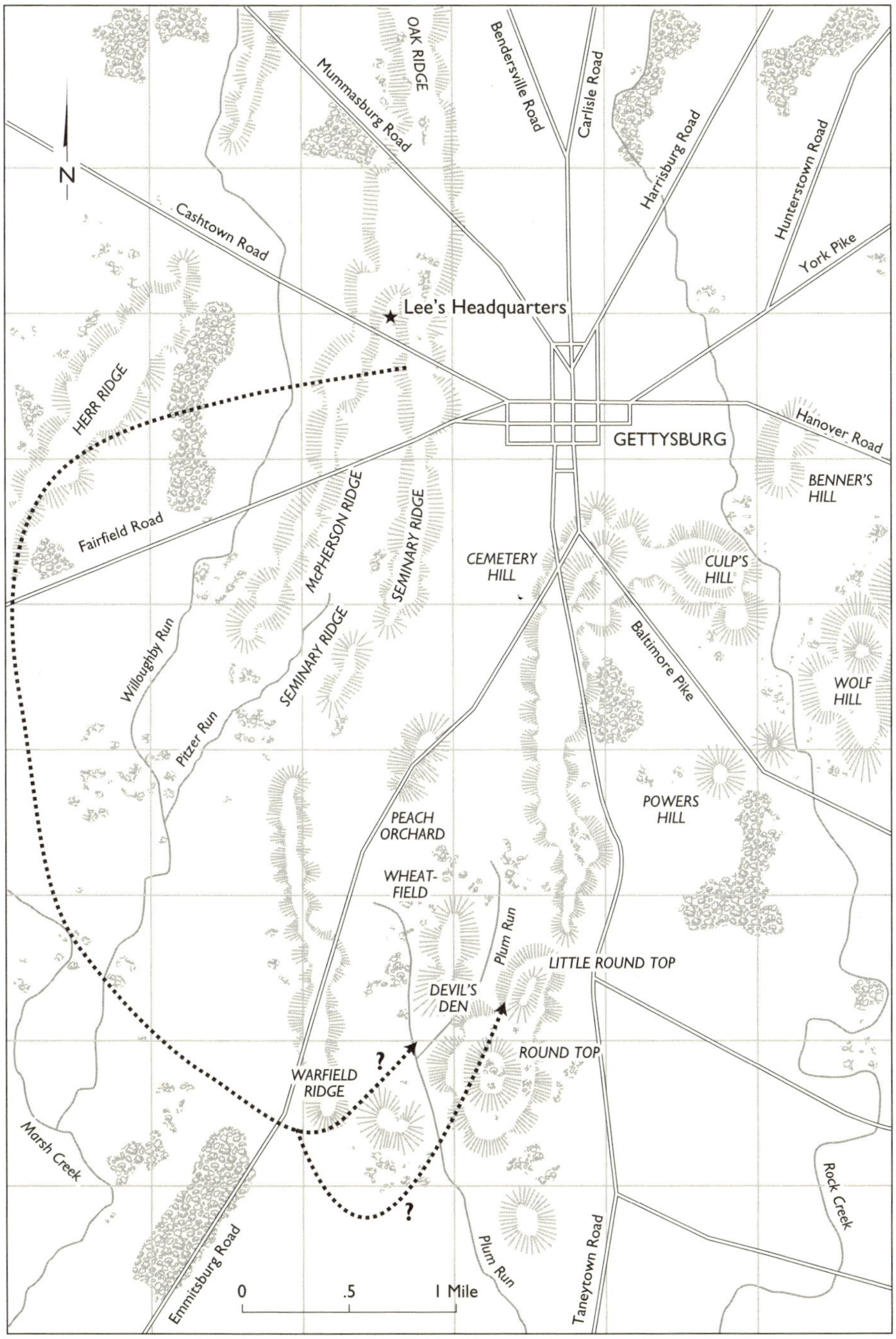

Map 3-2
Johnston's reconnaisance

Anderson's brigades deployed from a starting point farther to the west (up Cashtown Road), marched south (roughly along Willoughby Run), then turned east to form up on Pender's right.

The extreme rebel right would overlap the Union left. Longstreet's attack was therefore to slant in a northeasterly direction, hitting the supposedly short and vulnerable end of the Union line and rolling it up toward Cemetery Hill. By that time, Anderson's units (and almost certainly General Pender's, to his left) would have gone in, adding additional power to the general assault and creating the culmination of an overall *en-echelon* attack (map 3-4). Such a tactical stratagem is designed to accomplish the following: Ideally, from Lee's perspective, the Union response to Longstreet's attack would be to shore up its left by siphoning off

THE CLIMAX OF THE BATTLE   81

**Map 3-3
Confederate 3rd Corps
deployments, early afternoon**

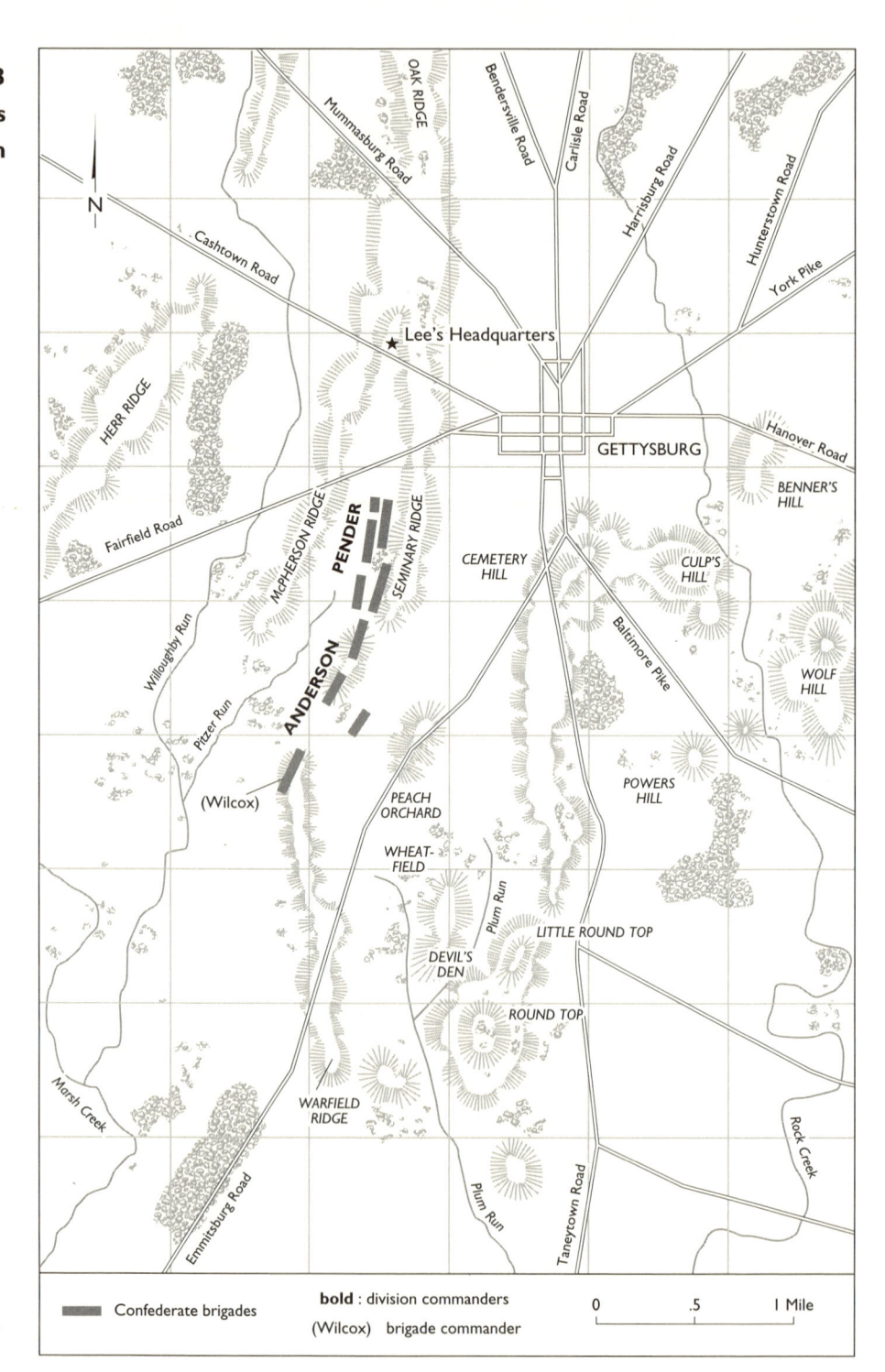

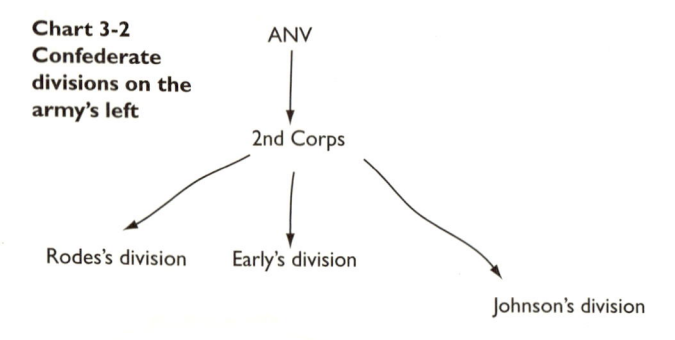

Confederate brigades
bold: division commanders
(Wilcox) brigade commander

**Chart 3-2
Confederate divisions on the army's left**

ANV → 2nd Corps → Rodes's division, Early's division, Johnson's division

82   THE STAND OF THE U.S. ARMY AT GETTYSBURG

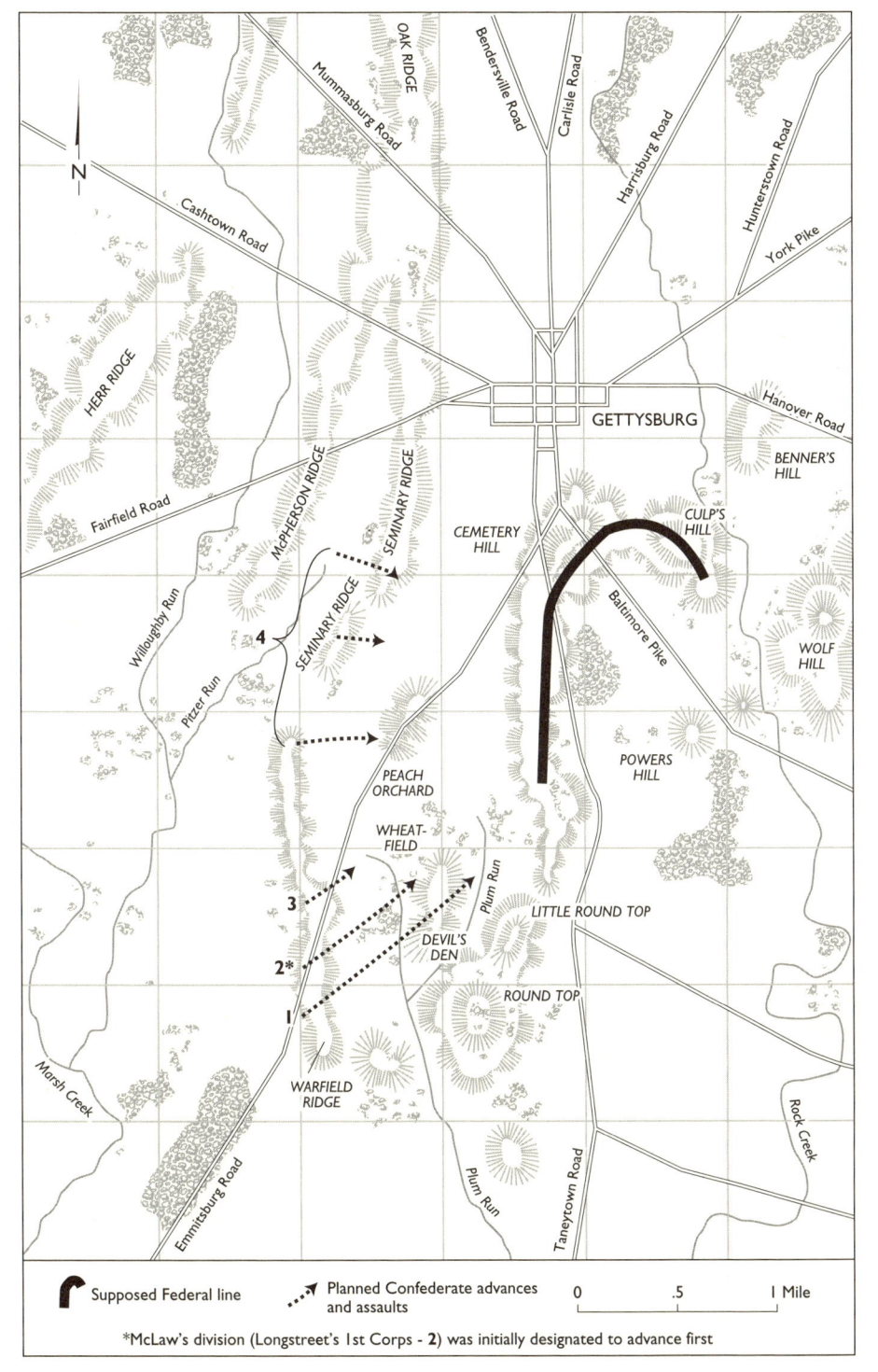

**Map 3-4
How the Confederate *en-echelon* attack was envisioned**

Supposed Federal line

Planned Confederate advances and assaults

*McLaw's division (Longstreet's 1st Corps - 2) was initially designated to advance first

troops from the center, thus leaving it fatally weakened for the subsequent attack by Hill's 3rd Corps divisions.

Moreover, the Federals were soon to be in even worse peril, as they would be caught in a pincer attack. This is because General Ewell's 2nd Corps (map 3-5, chart 3-2) was to "demonstrate" against the Union right in coordination with the opening of Longstreet's assault. Initially, the demonstration would pin down the Federals on the two northern hills so that they could not reinforce the assailed Union units on the left flank. Given the opportunity—that is, if Ewell sensed the

THE CLIMAX OF THE BATTLE   83

**Map 3-5
Confederate 2nd Corps deployments**

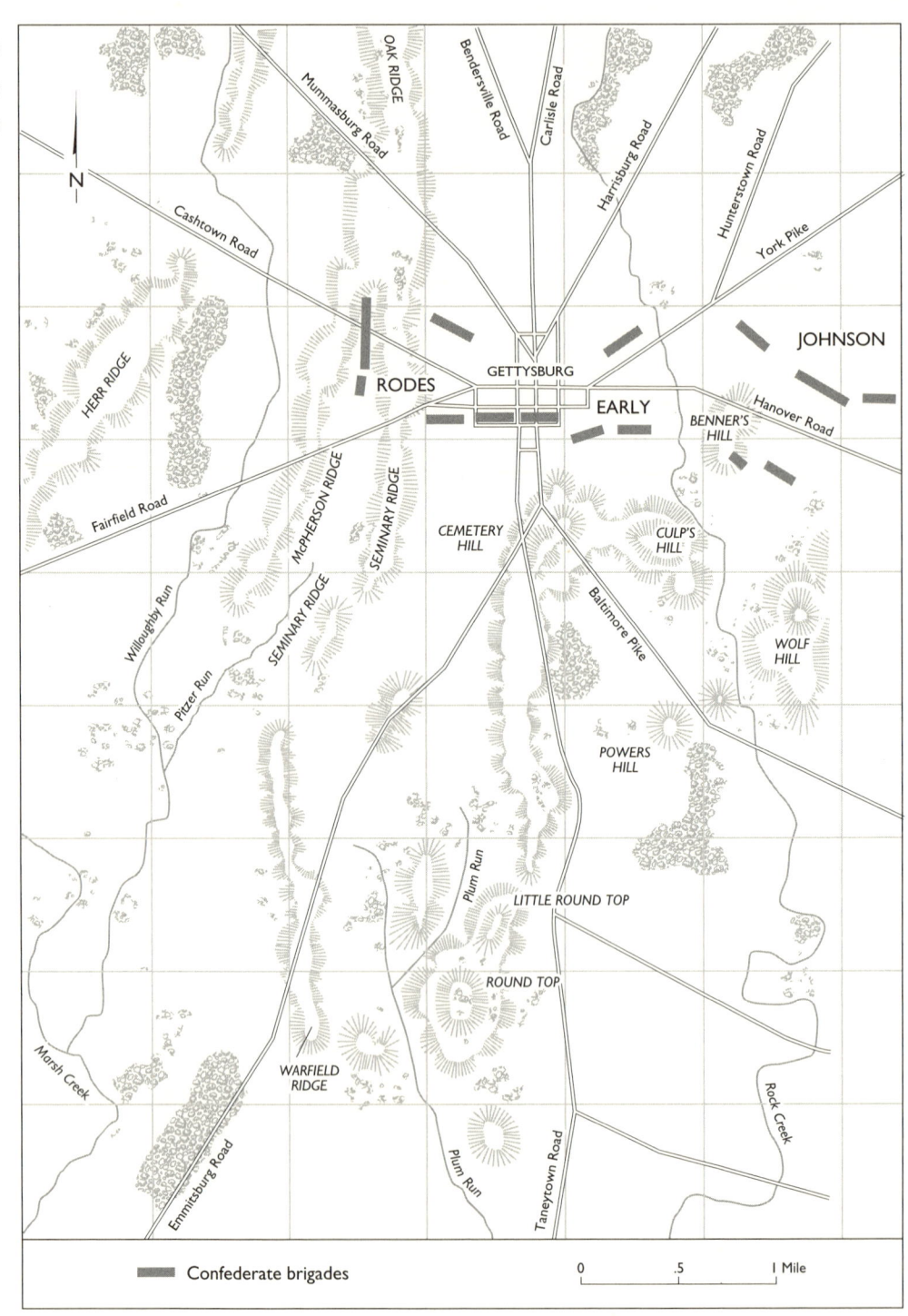

■ Confederate brigades

Union left and center was crumbling—the 2nd Corps would bear down on the Federal right, and the confused, menaced Union position would cave in altogether.[3]

This was a complicated scheme. For instance, it required coordination, especially in terms of Ewell's role, and he was an "untried" corps commander. However, General Ewell had performed well during the long march north from Virginia, although his success at Winchester was against a far inferior Federal force (see Chapter 1). Nevertheless, both of Ewell's divisions engaged by the Federals on July 1 had achieved much—except for the poor performance of Rodes's division

**Map 3-6
Confederate strategic redeployment possibilities**

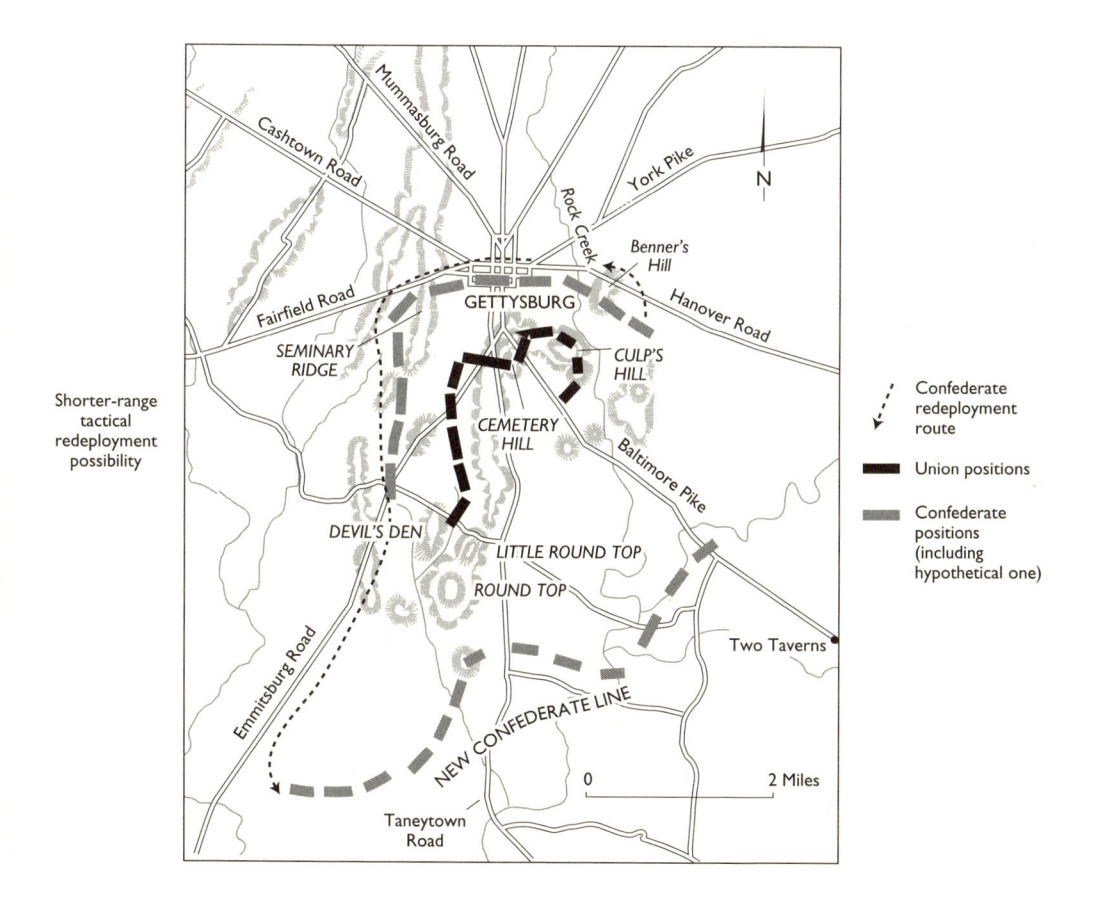

in its early assaults on the Union center north of Gettysburg. To preview the quality of Ewell's actions on July 2, keep in mind that he *seemed* to have demonstrated and attacked too late that Thursday evening. It thus appears that he did fail to coordinate properly. But is this true? We will deal with that issue in detail later, during a treatment of the Culp's Hill controversy (in the section entitled "The Confederate left finally attacks . . ."), one of many that continue to swirl around the second day of the battle.

The principal controversy regarding the events of July 2 involves the attitude and performance of General Longstreet. His strategic plan, which he put to General Lee as early as the evening of the First, was to *redeploy the entire Army of Northern Virginia* (map 3-6). Thus, according to the 1st Corps commander, the army should not have attacked the Federals at Gettysburg. The Confederate success of July 1 had put the Union in a geometrically advantageous position (an irony discussed in the previous chapter): They occupied high ground, with excellent "interior lines." The fishhook configuration, known to the rebel high command by early on the Second, was packed with defenders. The Union defense was replete with artillery as well as infantry. Within the overall confines of the fishhook (as it is roughly diagrammed in map 3-4), two lines of cannon were eventually placed. This was done under General Meade's supervision based upon specific instructions from his artillery chief, Brig. Gen. Henry J. Hunt. One line, running from Cemetery Hill down the ridge to the south, faced west. In mirror image, the second line of artillery batteries was distributed from Cemetery Hill along the Baltimore Pike, facing east. These were "'exceptionally strong lines of artillery and infantry with interlocking fields of fire." The defensive configuration was "rock-solid and as close to impregnable as any line constructed by the Army of the Potomac during the war."[4]

The geometry of the Union positions permitted relatively rapid communication from one end of the Union line to the other, a distance of some three miles from the barb down to the eye of the fishhook. Moreover, Union observers on the *really* high ground—such as Little Round Top, or Power's Hill to the northeast of it (map 3-1)—were provided with fine panoramic views of the armies' positions and movements. If such observers included flag-bearing signalmen, Federal communication possibilities were accentuated—beyond those that would involve couriers moving from one position behind the fishhook to the other, always a manageable distance. General Longstreet and his fellow commanders must have known that Confederate communications would be hampered by the exterior nature of their line, which eventually extended from Warfield Ridge in the south to Maj. Gen. Edward Johnson's positions east of Culp's Hill, a distance of five and one-half miles.

Legend has it that General Longstreet was an emerging "defensive genius" who wished to attack only in specific, tactically advantageous circumstances. In this respect, he supposedly had in mind the Battle of Fredericksburg (December 13, 1862) and his well-timed decisive counterattack at Second Manassas (August 30, 1862). In both of those engagements, the Confederates had been on the tactical defensive. They had not only won those battles, but also had absorbed *relatively* few casualties. Longstreet consistently implied (especially in his writings through the rest of the nineteenth century) that he was a properly conservative tactician who never wanted to risk devastating the army in a given battle or campaign.

What Longstreet wanted General Lee to do was move the Army of Northern Virginia out of the Gettysburg vicinity and establish a defensive position on suitable ground between the Army of the Potomac and Washington, D.C. Longstreet began to urge this strategic deployment in conversations with General Lee on the night of July 1.[5] According to the 1st Corps commander, the move would invite an attack by the Army of the Potomac because General Meade's superiors, believing the nation's capital was in peril, would be screaming at him to evict the invading rebel force.

Longstreet had to be aware of the fact that the Army of the Potomac was, on the morning of July 2, in no position to effect any strategic protection of the Federal capital: Meade's force was arrayed in a *north-south* direction. Why, then, he argued, should the Confederates oblige them by attacking *from the west and north*? Instead: march! Get away from Gettysburg and the formidable Federal position there. Meade would necessarily have to abandon that position and come after Lee's legions.

That the Army of Northern Virginia *might* have moved away in this manner—swinging around the Federal force in a large counterclockwise wheel (map 3-6)—is suggested by events later that day, when thousands of Confederates deployed well south of town, overlapping the Federal force arrayed to the east of them (map 3-4). One result of this was that the rebels gained full control of the Emmitsburg Road near the southern end of the battlefield. However, it is not easy to move an entire army down one road.[6] The Confederates under Longstreet really needed a system of roadways to move a corps or more of men away from Gettysburg to the south. Recall how many different routes the Federal army had followed to get there. Furthermore, the Army of the Potomac controlled the other north-south road, which led to Taneytown, Maryland (maps 3-4 and 3-6, bottom). Also unbeknownst to Longstreet, a Union cavalry force under Brig. Gen. Wesley Merritt (detached from Buford's division) patrolled the region where he wanted to go. These troopers could have harassed the marching rebel columns and provided intelligence about the redeployment to General Meade, who had his 12th and 5th Corps in ready reserve (map 3-7). These units almost certainly could have countered the Confederate move in question and might even have attacked the strung-out columns.

In any case, General Lee would have none of this. Many reasons have been put forward explaining why, including the practical difficulties associated with Longstreet's plan just discussed. Equally important, I feel, were Lee's psychology, his sense of the temper of his army, and his memory of recent events. These factors made it easy for him to decide to remain in place on July 2 and attack from there.[7]

To understand this better, we need to review what happened on the first day of fighting at Chancellorsville two months earlier, when the Army of Northern Virginia pushed back the Army of the Potomac. At the end of that day (May 2), the Federal army was still in a pretty good tactical position (map 3-9). However, the Union high command made further mistakes, which seemed to be its métier. The rebels reinitiated their attacks and General Hooker's units gave up additional large quantities of real estate on May 3. One more push, and perhaps the Army of the Potomac could have been destroyed at Chancellorsville—instead of eventually "escaping across the nearest river" as it eventually did. Thus, General Lee was probably considering that he again had his opponents where he wanted them. This time, however, his army was in an even more favorable situation for resuming the attack because it was not divided as it had been at Chancellorsville (during the early stages of which a considerable force was necessarily left behind at Fredericksburg, Virginia, to guard the main body of the rebel army's rear). Also, the Army of Northern Virginia was bolstered for the Gettysburg campaign in terms of raw numbers, as Longstreet's entire corps was back after having been detached to obtain supplies in the James River region during Chancellorsville. The Confederate army in the East thus was on a roll after its recent success on the battlefields in Virginia.

In this context, one can imagine General Lee saying to Longstreet: "*You* were not present at Chancellorsville. Had you been, you would know that we can accomplish the same and more here. We are in better shape than we were in early

May. And our foe—whose soldiers, certainly their leaders, are inferior to ours—is probably worse off than it was then. Look at how they ran from the battlefield yesterday."

To consider further the reasons why the Confederates attacked on July 2, we now turn to James Longstreet's perspective—how he claimed to argue for an alternative plan and lost. What did Longstreet really say to Lee during the battle, and what was his resulting attitude? We have little to go on in terms of contemporary accounts from the summer of 1863. (This same problem returns with regard to the so-called wrangling over the planning for Pickett's Charge the next day.) Both generals' after-action reports for the Gettysburg campaign are notable for how sketchy and unrevealing they are—not that either man would necessarily have reported on tactical arguments that took place on the field.[8] How about wartime correspondence? There is not much of it from Longstreet or Lee at the time of Gettysburg.

To appreciate what General Longstreet might have argued in terms of a strategic, defensive-minded redeployment of the Confederate army, we must rely almost entirely on retrospective postwar writings. By and about Longstreet, they are legion—including letters, articles, and memoirs written from the 1870s into the first decade of the twentieth century. However, Lee, who died in 1870, contributed little to the debate. Longstreet's paper trail is notoriously polemical and inconsistent about Gettysburg. He wrote three separate versions of the discussions he had with Lee about how to fight the battle after July 1.[9] Was he truly surprised and distressed at Lee's desire simply to attack the Union army where it was by the end of that Thursday afternoon? Or was this largely rationalizing hindsight?—in Longstreet's case, written between the mid-1870s and mid-1890s: I was right at Gettysburg. We should have moved our whole army around Meade's left and taken a defensive position between it and Washington. See what happened as a consequence of not following my plan?[10] Could Longstreet have been covering his tracks by postwar posturing, accentuated by his compulsion to rail against other former Confederates who relentlessly excoriated him for the defeat at Gettysburg?

To be fair, Col. Armistead L. Long, a member of Lee's staff, corroborated elements of Longstreet's plan as he initially proposed them on the afternoon of July 1. However, that man's account of the Wednesday night meeting was written almost a quarter of a century later.[11] More contemporary was General Longstreet's letter to his uncle in late July 1863, in which he said that "the battle was not made as I would have made it. My idea was to throw ourselves between the enemy and Washington, select a strong position, and force the enemy to attack us."[12] Also, Longstreet apparently discussed this defensive strategy with Brig. Gen. William Barksdale of Hood's 1st Corps division, who mentioned their conversation before he died on July 3 after being severely wounded on the Second.[13] The standard account is also supported by Col. E. Porter Alexander, who led an artillery battalion in Longstreet's corps and rose to greater prominence during the third day of the Gettysburg battle. Alexander wrote that his commander had suggested the army execute "a turning movement," but that General Lee rejected this plan.[14] Alexander's memoir, although published early in the twentieth century, is regarded as more reliable than most accounts, probably because this former artillery officer spared none of his fellow officers from criticism in his postwar writings when he believed they deserved it. Soon after the war—possibly before Longstreet's rationalizing mind-set had reached the point that we cannot interpret with any confidence what he wrote later—William Swinton, a Northern

**Chart 3-3
Confederate 1st Division units (vanguard and rear)**

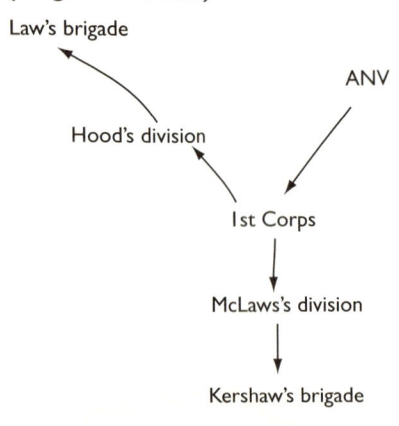

Law's brigade ← Hood's division ← 1st Corps ← ANV
1st Corps → McLaws's division → Kershaw's brigade

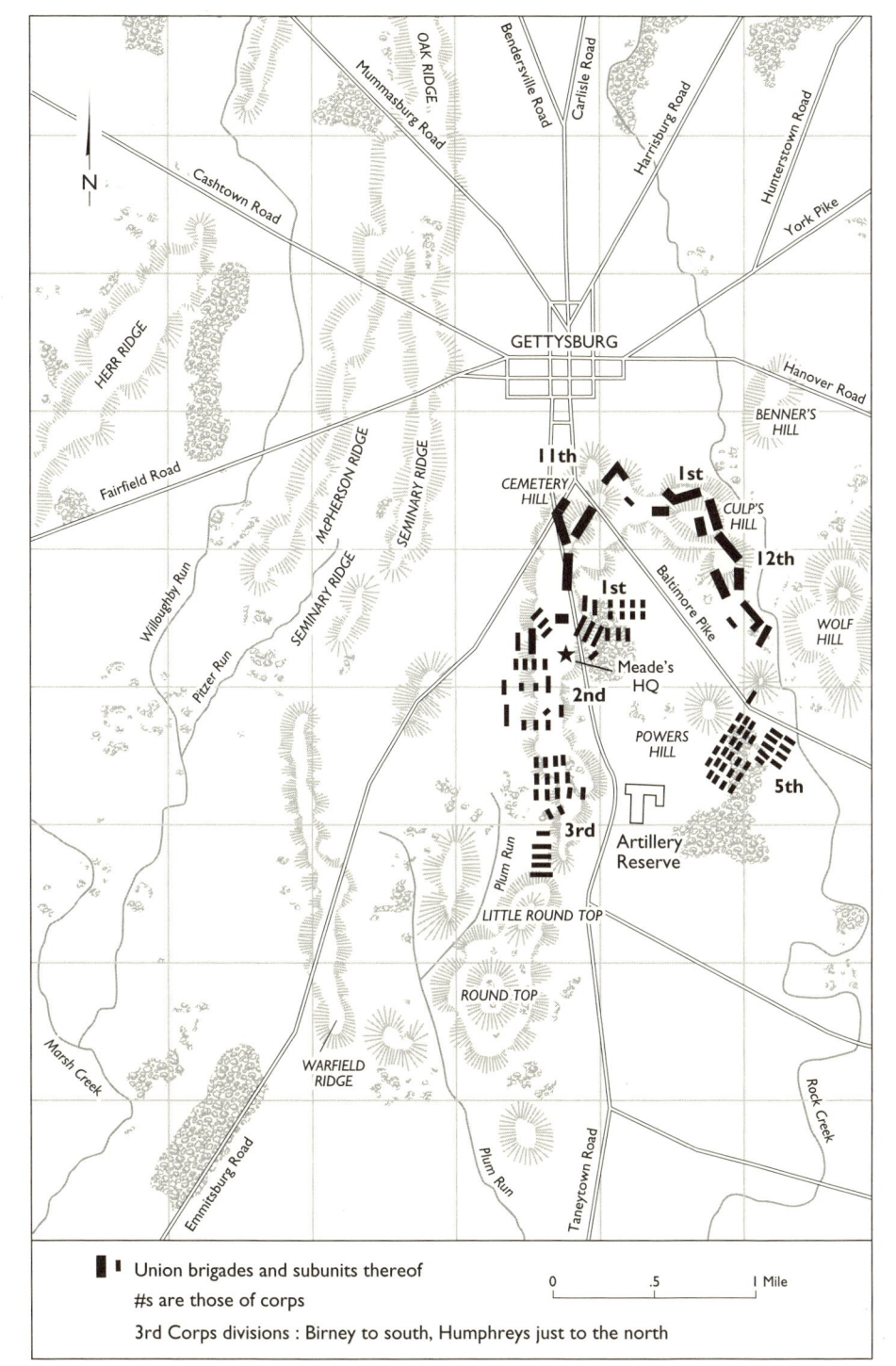

**Map 3-7
The Federal fishhook—and the 5th Corps reserve**

- ▮ Union brigades and subunits thereof
  #s are those of corps
- 3rd Corps divisions : Birney to south, Humphreys just to the north

newspaper reporter, interviewed the former general. The newspaperman paraphrased Longstreet's oral account of how he had "begged in vain to be allowed to execute" the strategic march away from the Gettysburg battlefield on July 2. As for Lee, Swinton says that "contrary to his original intent"—a precampaign "promise to his corps commanders that *he would not assume a tactical offensive,* but force his antagonist to attack him"[15]—the army commander was adamant about offensive tactics.

THE CLIMAX OF THE BATTLE 89

If Longstreet really made this plea and lost the argument with Lee, this would be consistent with the idea that he was in a petulant frame of mind about the specifics of the tactical actions he was "forced" to carry out on July 2—and explains why he dragged his feet. Indeed, Maj. G. Moxley Sorrel, an officer on Longstreet's staff, described the general as failing "to conceal some anger," and said that this displeasure affected his conduct, such that "there was apparent apathy in his movements," which "lacked the fire . . . of his usual bearing on the battlefield."[16] However, Sorrel's remarks were written between 1899 and the time of his death in 1901—exemplifying the hindsight problem mentioned above. To counter the petulance postulate, some modern historians contend that Longstreet performed well on July 2.[17] My main frustration with all of this is that so much of what has been written by both participants *and* those who continue to interpret the campaign today is solely from the viewpoint of what the *Confederates* should have done and could have accomplished. In their view, the Battle of Gettysburg was sitting there for the rebels' taking.

At all events, Lee rejected Longstreet's plan and ordered Longstreet to set in motion the 1st Corps deployment necessary to open an attack on the Federal positions from his lines as they were currently situated. Impersonating a long-gone Union general, George B. McClellan, Longstreet developed on a smaller scale his own case of "the slows" on July 2. The details of this will be developed later, including a further consideration of the possibility that Longstreet had his nose out of joint, which resulted in a desultory performance on his part and helped the Union cause that day.

One thing that is not in dispute is that the commander of the Army of the Potomac did need time—which General Longstreet donated to General Meade, allowing the Union commander to organize and solidify details of the Northern army's position without being rushed. For example, the 5th Corps—the sixth of Meade's corps to arrive at Gettysburg—was able to make its three-mile march to the battlefield that morning without feeling pressured. Meade placed these eleven thousand men on the Baltimore Pike, back behind the fishhook. The 5th Corps thus formed the reserve of the Army of the Potomac (map 3-7), ready to rapidly reinforce any threatened point along the line. Reinforcing movements by the 5th Corps were indeed to occur, some of them with crucial effect. Meanwhile, the 6th Corps—still far away from Gettysburg at this time—was ordered to march from northeastern Maryland (map 2-28) and get to the battlefield before the day was out. Should the 5th Corps be needed, the 6th would become the new reserve if it could get to the battlefield in time. Longstreet gave these marching Federals time enough, and the 6th Corps was to keep its appointment.[18]

Some Southern writers, former military men wielding poisoned pens later in the nineteenth century, reviled Longstreet for not "attacking at dawn" as General Lee supposedly ordered him to do. This is palpably false.[19] Longstreet, however, *was* supposed to begin getting his two divisions into position during the morning. After conferring with Lee about the 1st Corps's impending march, General Longstreet accomplished nothing during the remainder of the morning. Later, when General Lee returned from a conference with General Ewell, he encountered a distressingly *static* situation insofar as his army's right wing was concerned.[20] This was a serious problem—more so than the Confederate high command might have known at the time. After the war, Robert E. Lee wrote, "the battle would have been gained if General Longstreet had obeyed the order given him and attacked early instead of late."[21]

Meanwhile, in the middle of that Thursday in July at Gettysburg, General

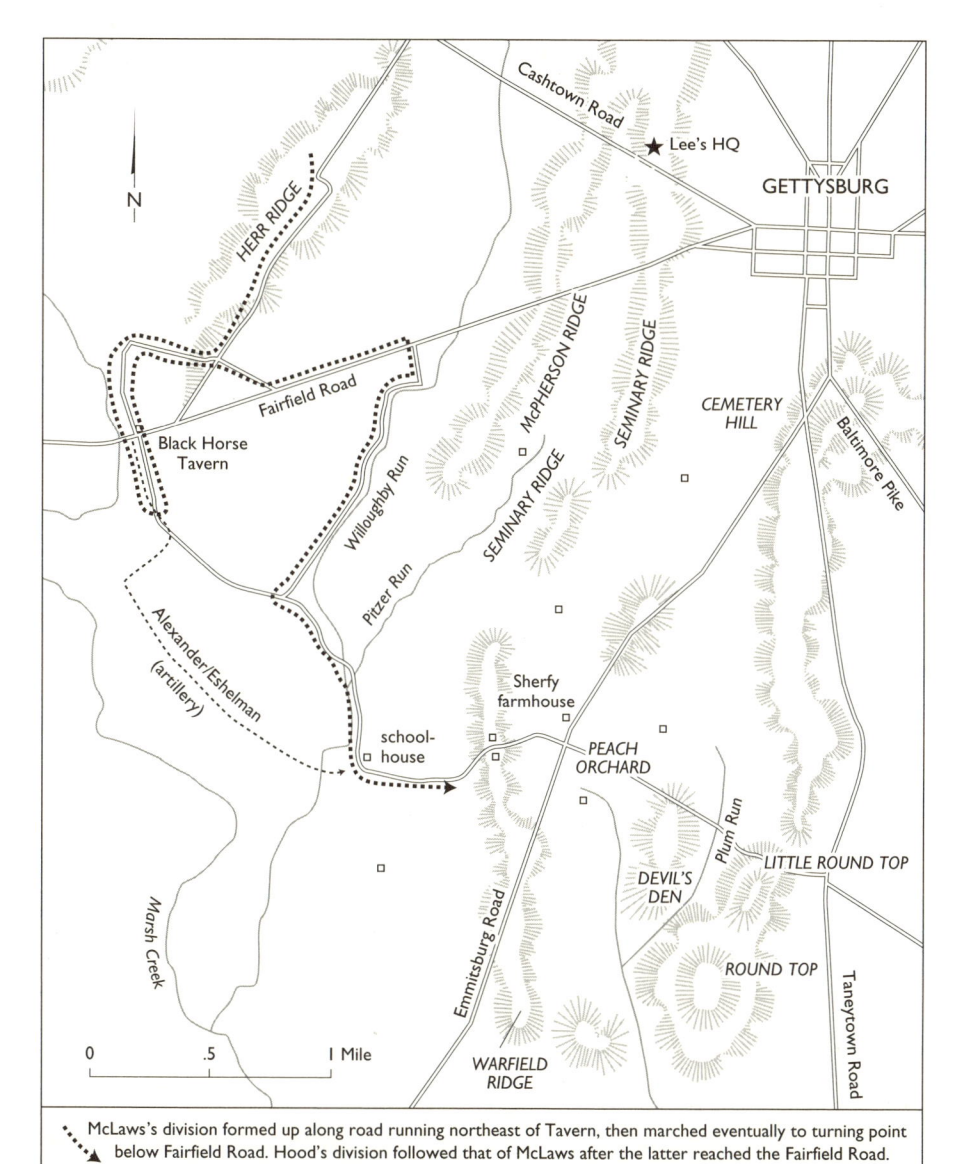

**Map 3-8
Confederate 1st Corps marching and countermarching, early afternoon to 4 P.M.**

• • • McLaws's division formed up along road running northeast of Tavern, then marched eventually to turning point below Fairfield Road. Hood's division followed that of McLaws after the latter reached the Fairfield Road.

Longstreet put forth (poutingly?) the problem of his "last brigade," which still was not on the field. The unit in question was Brig. Gen. Evander M. Law's brigade of Alabamians in Maj. Gen. John Bell Hood's division (chart 3-3). Whereas the tentative plan was for Maj. Gen. Lafayette McLaws's division to open the attack as soon as it was in position on the rebel right (southwest of Gettysburg), Longstreet for some reason wanted to wait until Law's brigade arrived in the vicinity of Herr Ridge (west-northwest of the town) before anyone moved out. This was nonsense, because the deployment from west of Gettysburg down to Warfield Ridge could have been set crisply into motion while Law's brigade was still trudging toward the battlefield from well beyond Cashtown. All Longstreet needed to do to confirm that Law was indeed on his way was dispatch a mounted courier.

Longstreet's two divisions finally began their march soon after Law arrived at about noon—much later than it could have. The van of the column was Brig. Gen. Joseph B. Kershaw's brigade in McLaws's division (chart 3-3). Soon after the

THE CLIMAX OF THE BATTLE   91

marching force snaked its way from Herr Ridge toward the Fairfield Road, crossing it near the Black Horse Tavern (map 3-8), Kershaw's troops came to a piece of high ground. There, the Confederate commanders discerned that their march was almost certainly visible to Federal signalmen on Little Round Top. This led to discord between McLaws and Longstreet and is further evidence that the corps commander was in a sour mood that day.[22]

The outcome of the conversation was that the two divisions abandoned the route they were on and *countermarched* northward to seek a new line of march that would be more protected from Federal eyes (map 3-8). But what if Longstreet or his subordinate commanders had paid closer attention to the route taken by elements of the 1st Corps artillery? Colonel Alexander's and Maj. Benjamin F. Eshelman's batteries found a relatively concealed path that swung *west* of the Black Horse Tavern (south of the Fairfield Road) toward Marsh Creek (left-hand side of map 3-8). They then turned southeast and pulled their cannons to a point near a schoolhouse close to the infantry's eventual objective.[23]

In any case, the long column of Confederate infantry turned around and went back across Fairfield Road, then headed first north and then east, toward the town. It then turned southward again and moved along Willoughby Run (map 3-8). As the Confederates proceeded on low ground near the banks of this stream they came to a point that was less than a thousand yards east of the place where they had turned around. Moreover, they made a roundabout trek that delayed them even longer than would have happened if the column had simply made an about-face (the plan was to maintain McLaws's division and Kershaw's brigade within it at the head of the march). All this reversing and direction changing eventually brought Longstreet's troops tantalizingly near to where they had been a couple of hours earlier. Yet the countermarch seemed to work, as we will learn later when we view it from the Federal perspective.

McLaws's division finally reached the schoolhouse where the artillery batteries were positioned and his brigades marched eastward toward Emmitsburg Road and—between 3:30 and 4 P.M.—deployed to either side of the smaller road that hits it perpendicularly (map 3-8).[24] Union signalmen, who had regained sight of the marching Confederate column, spotted this deployment from Little Round Top. The Federal observers flagged a message up the line, which alerted the 5th Corps (in reserve behind the main line) and set in motion an investigation of the southern sector of the field by a Union general. This was Brig. Gen. Gouverneur K. Warren, who was to become an important player on that day of the battle.

Before these activities of the Northerners came to fruition, the Confederates had to work out the details of their impending assault. This led to another peevish exchange as Generals Longstreet, McLaws, and Hood argued over how the 1st Corps divisions were to be placed and how they would start the attack.[25] This time-wasting, morale-consuming disagreement was intimately associated with a striking change that had come over the entire Federal position at this phase of the battle.

A Union Corps Moves out from Its Line, Breaking the Lower Shank of the Fishhook

Major General Daniel Sickles commanded the Army of the Potomac's 3rd Corps. Only one of his impediments was that he was an inexperienced "political general." He was impetuous and dangerous in a variety of ways, starting well before the war. As a commander, he had exhibited aggressive behavior on occa-

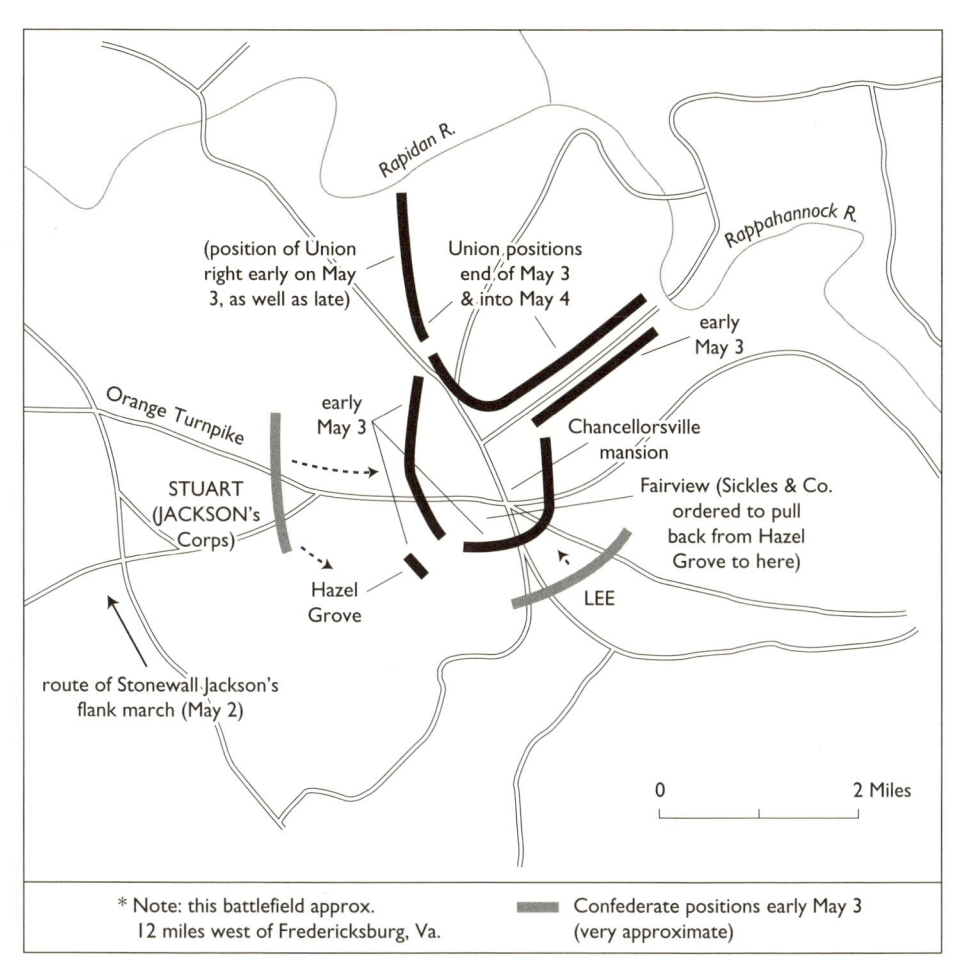

**Map 3-9
Chancellorsville, early May 1863**

sions—such as when he tried to attack the tail of Lt. Gen. Thomas J. Jackson's long flanking march at Chancellorsville on May 2 (map 3-9).

I believe that the memory of that battle is likely to have loomed large in Sickles's mind two months later. His 3rd Corps had been placed at the bottom of the fishhook, as was noted above in conjunction with Captain Johnston's reconnaissance. Sickles's extreme left flank was the fishhook's metaphorical eye (map 3-7). This was low ground, no longer part of Cemetery Ridge. General Sickles fidgeted over this position. The 3rd Corps commander wondered just how vulnerable to a Confederate assault his units might be. Acting upon these worries, he dispatched a scouting party consisting of elements of the 1st U.S. Sharpshooters and some Maine men from the same brigade (chart 3-4).[26] The Sharpshooters and Mainers ranged out across the Emmitsburg Road into Pitzer's Woods (part of which is indicated at the top left of map 3-12). However, before we discuss what they found, note that General Sickles had not sent any of his units to occupy Little Round Top, just to his left. He was supposed to do so, having had

**Chart 3-4
Scouting Federal sharpshooters and the forces they encountered**

ANV → 3rd Corps → R. Anderson's division → Wilcox's brigade

1st U.S. / 3rd Maine ← 2nd Brigade Ward ← 1st Division Birney ← 3rd Corps ← AP

THE CLIMAX OF THE BATTLE 93

that instruction passed along to him by the commander of the previous occupying force—General Geary, whose division, along with the rest of the 12th Corps, had long since been sent northward to Culp's Hill.

In his mind, General Sickles's principal concern was not Little Round Top but the supposed vulnerability of his main line on the low ground. He could discern to his front, in the direction of the Emmitsburg Road, *higher ground* that might be more defensible, or, if occupied by the enemy, the ground near the Peach Orchard along this roadway could become a fine platform for Confederate artillery. To understand how Sickles acted with regard to these considerations, it seems likely that in the early afternoon on July 2 he had a vivid memory of the morning of May 3 at Chancellorsville. At that time, his infantrymen, along with several artillery pieces, held a significant stretch of high ground called Hazel Grove. Their position jutted southward from the main Union line after it had been pushed back into a bowed configuration by Stonewall Jackson's flank attack during the evening of May 2 (map 3-9). Early the next day, Sickles was ordered to withdraw from Hazel Grove. This had several consequences beneficial to the Confederate attacks that soon commenced. One was that the rebels quickly got *their* artillery into Hazel Grove and bombarded the center of the compacted Union line with severe effect in support of Confederate infantry attacks, which met with success on May 3.[27]

Not long afterward on that day of the Chancellorsville battle, the Union center was pushed back even farther, to well north of the Orange Turnpike (map 3-9). If Jackson's surprise attack the previous day had been the beginning of the end, then the Confederate successes and further Federal retreats that day sealed the Army of the Potomac's doom in the Chancellorsville campaign. The Union army's retreat on the Third had pulled it so far northward that General Lee, later that day, was able to ride into the clearing surrounding the Chancellorsville mansion to wild acclaim from his troops—something he may never have forgotten.

General Sickles, for his part, never forgot Hazel Grove. He ached to regain the analog of that ground on the field at Gettysburg. If he did not seize it, he feared the rebels would once again be there with artillery, bombarding his troops.[28]

Meanwhile, some of the Union sharpshooters who had filtered back into the 3rd Corps lines reported that sharp firefights had broken out between their scouting party and Confederate infantry from Brig. Gen. Cadmus M. Wilcox's brigade (map 3-3). Later in life, Sickles claimed that it was he who had revealed the rebel right—Longstreet's force, poised to attack the Union left. However, this was false, and Sickles knew it. Instead, the sharpshooters had run into the right wing of Maj. Gen. Richard Anderson's 3rd Corps line in Pitzer's Woods, which had moved into position before Longstreet's divisions were in place (map 3-3, chart 3-4). The information brought to him by the scouts was enough for Sickles. His corps was about to be attacked and it was geographically vulnerable, so, at about 3 p.m., he ordered the *entire 3rd Corps* to move forward of the Federal line toward the high ground in the vicinity of the Peach Orchard (map 3-10). When one walks eastward from this location and then turns around before disappearing into the trees, the orchard *does* achieve impressive prominence from such a ground-level view.

In Sickles's mind, he was back on the heights of Hazel Grove. To achieve this, he created a salient in his line at the Peach Orchard itself.[30] This was about three-quarters of a mile from the 3rd Corps's initial position, which was a southward extension of the 2nd Corps line.

The new ground at the salient (map 3-10) was occupied by Brig. Gen. Charles K. Graham's 1st Brigade of Maj. Gen. David B. Birney's 1st Division on Sickles's left

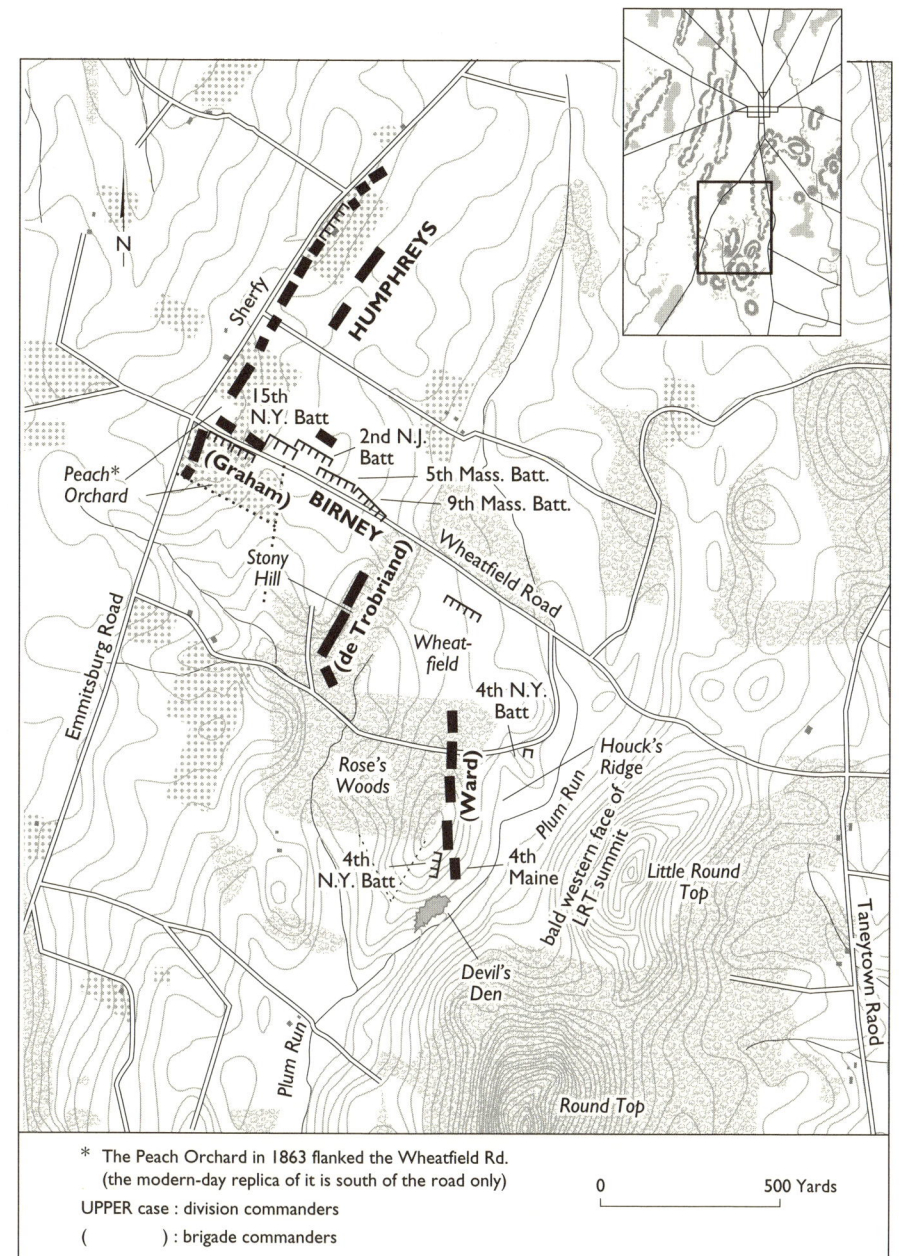

Map 3-10
Sickles's salient at the Peach Orchard plus his left and right wings

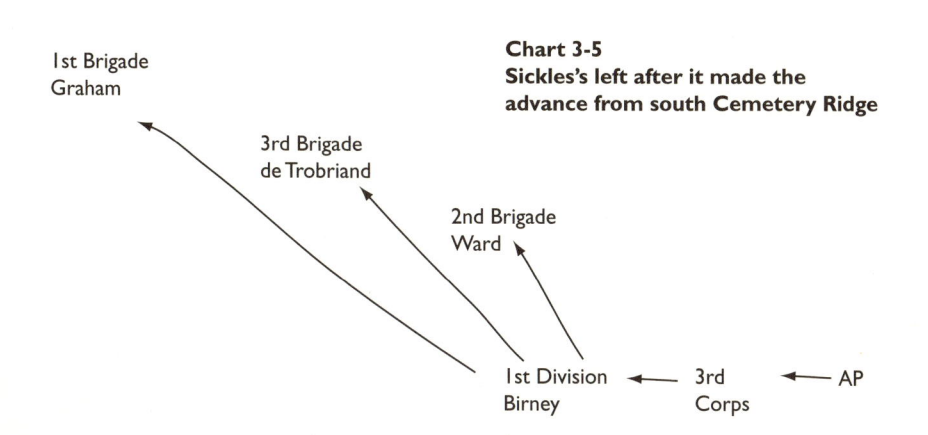

*The Peach Orchard in 1863 flanked the Wheatfield Rd. (the modern-day replica of it is south of the road only)

UPPER case : division commanders

( ) : brigade commanders

Chart 3-5
Sickles's left after it made the advance from south Cemetery Ridge

1st Brigade Graham ←
3rd Brigade de Trobriand ←
2nd Brigade Ward ←
1st Division Birney ← 3rd Corps ← AP

THE CLIMAX OF THE BATTLE   95

**Chart 3-6
Federal artillery batteries in and near the Peach Orchard**

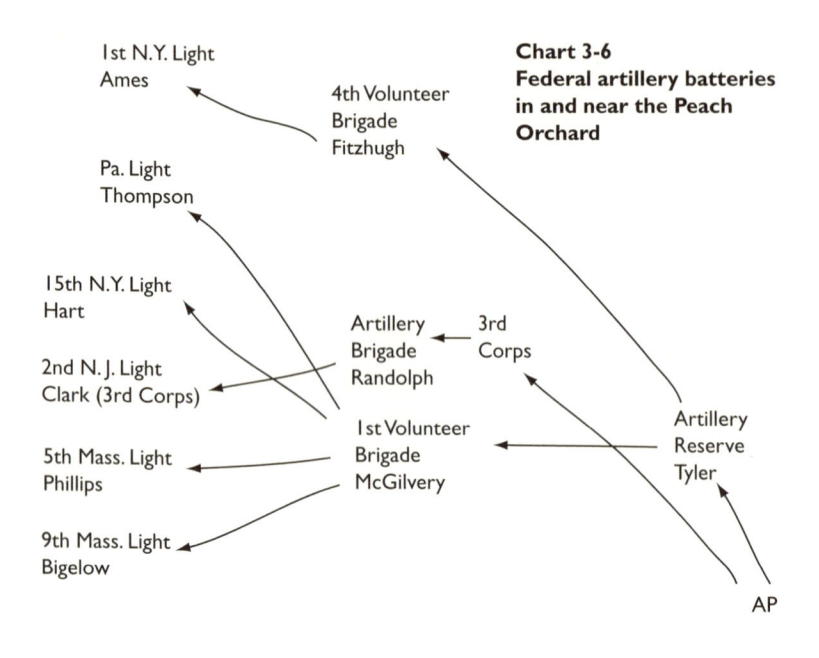

- 1st N.Y. Light — Ames
- 4th Volunteer Brigade Fitzhugh
- Pa. Light — Thompson
- 15th N.Y. Light — Hart
- 2nd N.J. Light — Clark (3rd Corps)
- Artillery Brigade Randolph ← 3rd Corps
- 1st Volunteer Brigade McGilvery
- 5th Mass. Light — Phillips
- 9th Mass. Light — Bigelow
- Artillery Reserve Tyler ← AP

**Chart 3-7
Sickles's right after it made the advance from south Cemetery Ridge**

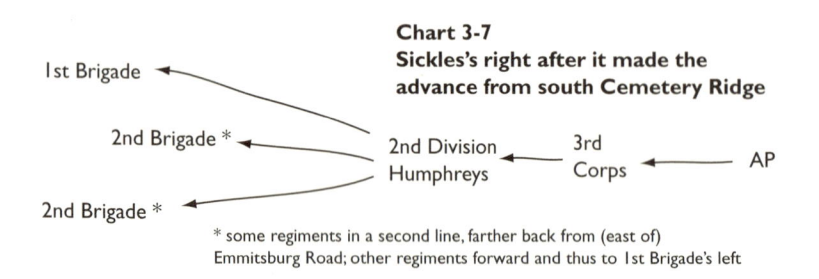

- 1st Brigade ← 2nd Division Humphreys ← 3rd Corps ← AP
- 2nd Brigade *
- 2nd Brigade *

* some regiments in a second line, farther back from (east of) Emmitsburg Road; other regiments forward and thus to 1st Brigade's left

---

wing (chart 3-5). The rest of Birney's division was arrayed in a broken line stretching from the Peach Orchard back toward the famed Devil's Den (map 3-10)—not, mind you, approaching the still woefully unprotected Little Round Top.

That Birney's initial line was a series of fragments is signified by the fact that there was a substantial gap between Graham and the next brigade positioned east of the Emmitsburg Road (map 3-10). This unit—Birney's 3rd Brigade, commanded by Col. P. Regis de Trobriand (chart 3-5)—was placed to the west and a bit to the south of a wheat field that was part of the Rose farm (the buildings of which are indicated on many of the maps in this part of the chapter). Most of de Trobriand's initial position was on a rise that is now called the Stony Hill (map 3-10)—just as the open ground nearby became immortalized as the Wheatfield.

The gap between Graham and de Trobriand was partly filled in by a deployment effected by Lt. Col. Freeman McGilvery of the Federal Artillery Reserve (chart 3-6). He placed a row of guns along the Wheatfield Road where it projects eastward of the Emmitsburg Road (map 3-10).[31] As this was an emergency move, the Federal batteries were unsupported by infantrymen in their immediate vicinity. Nevertheless, these guns would add weight to the imperiled Union defense once Longstreet's right-hooking attacks began.[32]

On the extreme left of Sickles's left wing was Brig. Gen. J. H. Hobart Ward's 2nd Brigade (chart 3-5). It established a defensive line along and to the west of Houck's Ridge, which runs in a northerly direction from the Devil's Den (map 3-10). The ridge is a continuation of the profusion of enormous boulders in the area. No Union units were actually placed among those huge rocks, and few Federal soldiers fought among them. Those who eventually did were from the 4th Maine, one of Ward's five regiments.

Ward's line was anchored at its southern end by Capt. James E. Smith's 4th New York Light Battery. The 4th Maine initially took a reserve position roughly behind Smith's battery (map 3-10). General Ward's westward-facing position was such that a further gap in Sickles's left wing existed between de Trobriand's left, near the Wheatfield, and the right end of Ward's line just west of the northern part of Houck's Ridge (maps 3-10 and 3-14).

The right wing of General Sickles's corps was under the command of Maj. Gen. Andrew A. Humphreys (chart 3-7). His division was positioned in a long line along the Emmitsburg Road northeastward of Graham's position in the Peach Orchard (map 3-10). Humphreys's brigades were not on the road itself, but just east of it.[33]

What had General Sickles accomplished? Eventually—and with extreme, deadly irony—this autonomous, audacious, and arrogant tactical move would devolve to

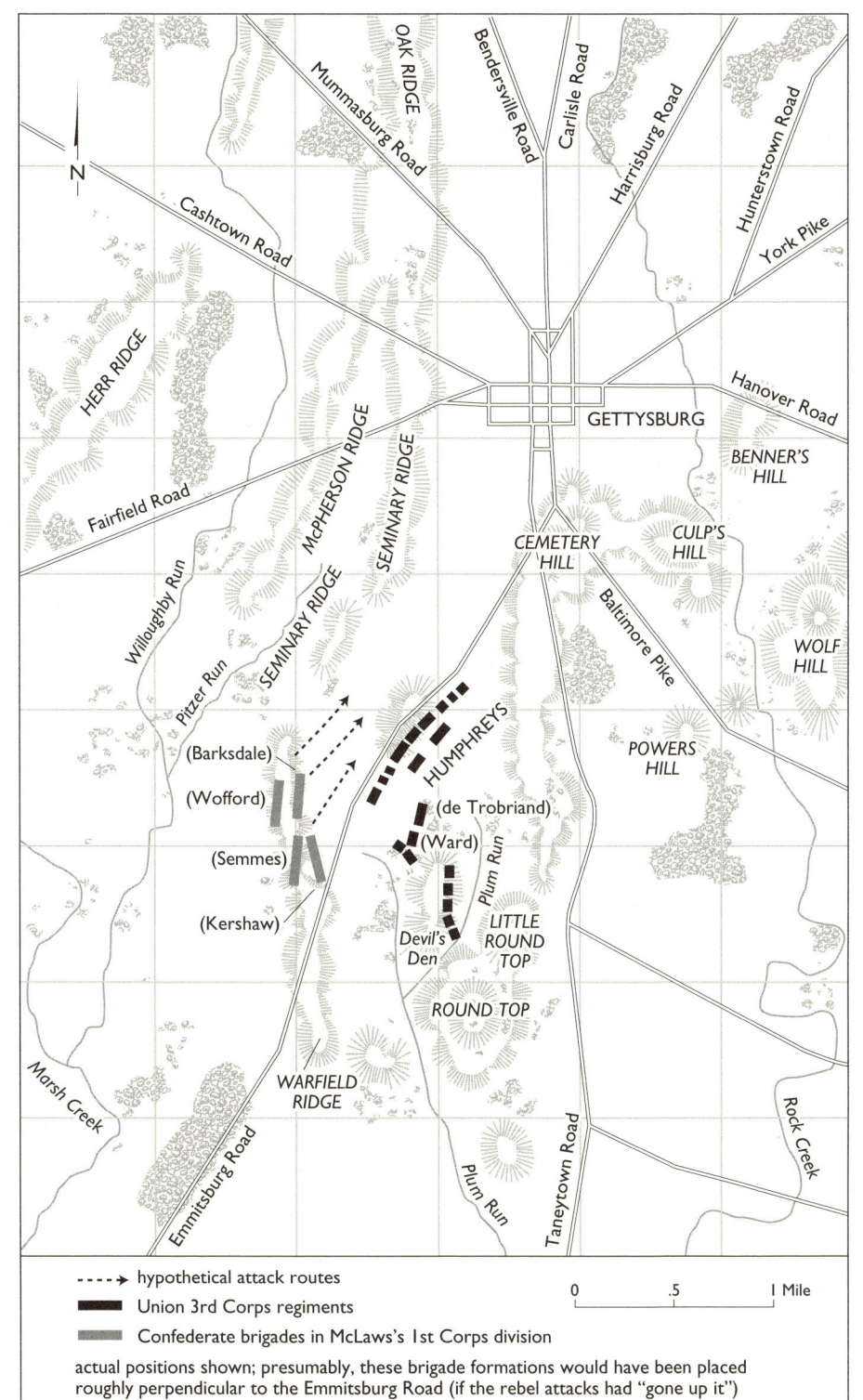

Map 3-11
McLaws's peril (to his right and rear) if he attacked "up the Emmitsburg Road"

- - - -> hypothetical attack routes
▮ Union 3rd Corps regiments
▮ Confederate brigades in McLaws's 1st Corps division

actual positions shown; presumably, these brigade formations would have been placed roughly perpendicular to the Emmitsburg Road (if the rebel attacks had "gone up it")

the Union's *advantage*. That is a tough pill to swallow. For example, in the immediate sense, Sickles had stretched out his already thin line, configuring it to cover one and one-half miles of linear ground, as opposed to about one mile back on southern Cemetery Ridge (compare maps 3-7 and 3-10). It follows that there were gaps in this new series of positions. Just as bad, Little Round Top continued

THE CLIMAX OF THE BATTLE   97

to be bereft of a defensive force. Note that even the base of that hill is a good distance from Ward's line on Houck's Ridge, across a valley that is cut through by Plum Run (map 3-10). Also, Sickles's right wing, in particular the extreme right flank of General Humphreys's division, was "in the air" (a military term meaning unprotected), with no Federal reserve units in sight and thus subject to a flank attack. A corollary to Humphreys's vulnerability was that the left flank of the 2nd Corps line was now exposed on the low ridgeline well north of the Round Tops (map 3-10).

That the advance of Sickles's corps was autonomous speaks to General Meade's preparatory activities during the morning and afternoon. Early that morning, Meade had sent an aide (his son, Capt. George Meade) to find out whether or not Sickles had placed his troops properly in the area previously occupied by the 12th Corps. Captain Meade encountered a grumbling General Sickles, who was already expressing displeasure about the low ground on southern Cemetery Ridge. Later in the morning, Sickles rode north up the Union line to find General Meade. During their brief meeting the army commander authorized Sickles to place the 3rd Corps "within the limits of the general instructions I [Meade] have given you."[34] No doubt that helped Sickles justify (on July 2 and forevermore) moving out to the Emmitsburg Road several hours later—during which time the Confederate foot-dragging had given Sickles more and more opportunity to agonize over the low ground on which he had been initially placed. When the advance occurred, the 2nd Corps soldiers on Sickles's right watched the maneuver dumbfounded. However, General Meade, who was at his headquarters farther north, behind the lines near the Taneytown Road (map 3-7), was unaware of this.

Sometime after 3 P.M., Meade gathered his corps commanders for a "council of war"—not the last of those that would occur that day. In this regard, it is worth noting that Robert E. Lee never met with all three of *his* corps commanders at one place and time during the battle. Meade, on the other hand, wanted all the advice he could get. When Sickles did not respond to the summons to attend the afternoon meeting, General Meade sent another courier flatly demanding the latter's presence at the council. When General Sickles finally rode up, he and his commander could hear artillery fire to the south. This was the prelude to Longstreet's assault, which was finally poised to get under way. There was no time for Meade or Sickles to consider the latter reforming at his original position. General Meade pronounced the council to be over, dispatched Sickles back to his corps, and began at a higher level to deal with what appeared to be an incipient emergency.

How Meade and many of his subordinate commanders responded is the heart of the Gettysburg campaign, because the *climax* of the battle came at the end of this series of attacks, stands, and counterattacks on July 2. For those who infer a Shakespearean meaning to that emphasized word, the turning point occurred in the middle act.

The Confederates Open the Attack with Two Long Right Hooks Moving Eastward against One Federal Corps, Which Is Reinforced by Elements of Another

Before examining the initial phase of Longstreet's assault on the Federal left, we first consider the further wrangling between him and his division commanders.

Thus, we begin with General McLaws, who had moved his division into position west of the Peach Orchard (maps 3-11 and 3-12). Perhaps he was already exasperated by the countermarching, accompanied by much fussing and fuming,

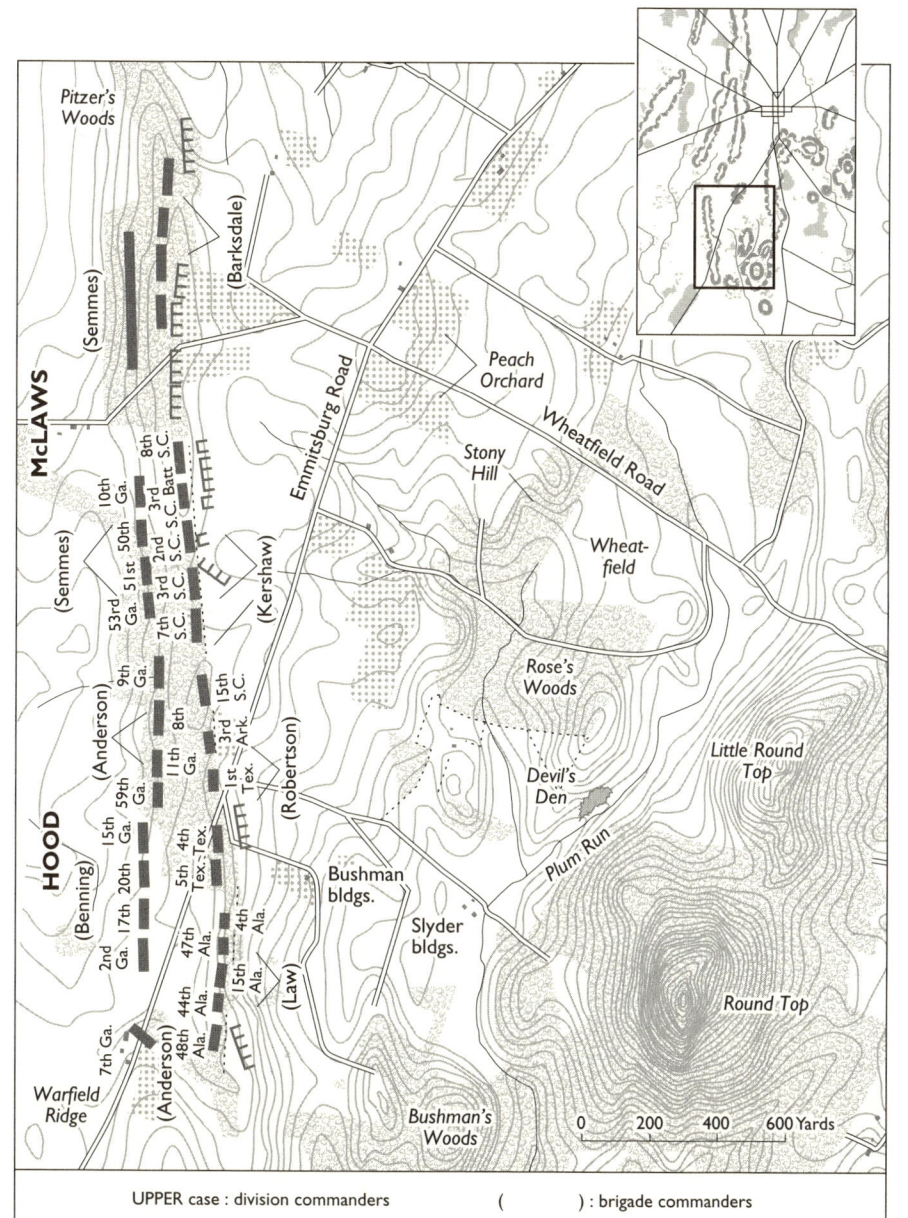

Map 3-12
Attack formations of Hood and McLaws

that preceded his brigades getting into their attack formations. Worse, he could instantly appreciate from the position of the Federal force in front of him—including the nearest portion of it in the Peach Orchard—that the general plan calling for an attack "up the Emmitsburg Road" was no longer sound. To hit the Federal flank well to the north on Cemetery Ridge, he would have to fight his way through the salient or pass along its front, being fired upon all the while. And even if Sickles's corps had not advanced, the Union left extended significantly south of its anticipated location. This would contribute to McLaws's brigades being enfiladed from their right should they begin their advance on a northeasterly course. Moreover, Sickles's left (at least Colonel de Trobriand's brigade) would be in the rebel *rear* as the Confederates' attack angled north and eastward (map 3-11).

THE CLIMAX OF THE BATTLE   99

General McLaws thus got into a verbal row with General Longstreet when his commander sent a courier with a terse message demanding to know why the attack had not started. Longstreet apparently knew that the attacking units would be forced to hit the Peach Orchard, a place crawling with Federal defenders. McLaws responded to Longstreet's question by indicating the distinctly unwise nature of attacking with his flank exposed.[35]

Realize that the Confederates were attempting to update and revise their attack plans *after* moving into battle formation. General Longstreet was probably becoming impatient—or worse, trying to shift the blame to his subordinates. In any case, *he was running out of July 2*. This was so because of the dilatory manner in which he had gotten his two divisions into their attack positions, including the time-consuming countermarch. Thus, Longstreet was *impatiently* late and was probably aware of the fact that his own desultory attitude had contributed to this tardiness. It likely would have been much different if he had provided firm leadership and direction by, for example, prodding his division commanders to get moving sooner and reminding them of the need to find the best march route *before* they moved out. He may have even subconsciously sensed that his corps' dithering had provided the Union defenders valuable time to improve their positions. In this regard, consider that Sickles's decision to move his corps forward was forcing the Confederates to alter their plans at the last minute, and that perhaps it had "foiled Lee's hopes."[36]

Ultimately, after a rapid-fire series of conversations and events, Longstreet changed his mind. He told McLaws to wait for General Hood's division to come into position on the far right (map 3-12, chart 3-8). Thus, Hood would advance first from the southernmost part of the attack formation—roughly facing the extreme left of the Federal position, which now extended southwest of the Peach Orchard (map 3-11).

The Confederate attack plan continued in this state of flux. General Lee himself was aware of the overall nature of this new, unexpected situation involving the Federal left.[37] Given the time of day and the confusion in the Confederate command, one is left to wonder why Lee did not call off the attack altogether. Such an action was not unheard of: The Confederates had first assailed the Union lines at Stones River, near Murfreesboro, Tennessee, on December 31, 1862, yet they did not renew their attack until two days later. Precedent notwithstanding, Lee seemed intent on exploiting the momentum his forces had achieved the previous afternoon. Ewell's and Hill's corps had already made significant deployments in this regard. Now, the majority of Longstreet's corps had at last deployed and was in a position from which it could attack—even if it was late in the day and could no longer employ optimal tactics because of Sickles's move.

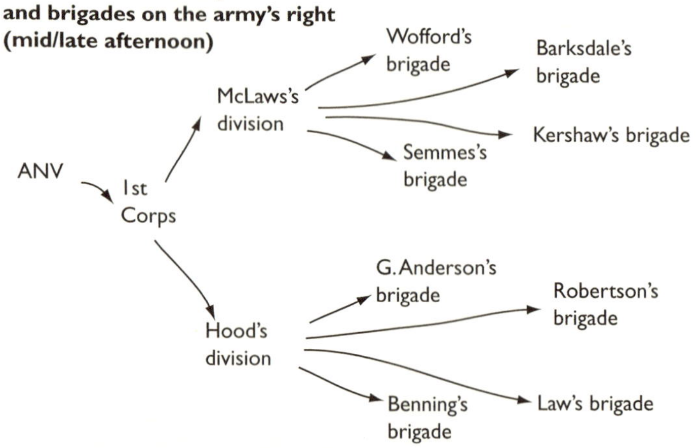

Finally, at about 4 P.M., General Hood was ordered to get ready for the start of the attack. As Hood's units approached their takeoff positions, moving into line to the right of McLaws's division (map 3-12), both General Hood and Brig. Gen. Evander Law, one of his brigade commanders, sent scouts to reconnoiter the Federal left. The scouts scoured the ground well east of the Emmitsburg Road and the Union 3rd Corps positions projecting from there, back toward the rocky regions in the Devil's Den and the Round Tops beyond. The

Chart 3-8
Confederate 1st Corps divisions and brigades on the army's right (mid/late afternoon)

ANV → 1st Corps → McLaws's division → Wofford's brigade → Barksdale's brigade; Semmes's brigade → Kershaw's brigade

1st Corps → Hood's division → G. Anderson's brigade → Robertson's brigade; Benning's brigade → Law's brigade

100   THE STAND OF THE U.S. ARMY AT GETTYSBURG

scouts returned with their intelligence, which soon reached General Longstreet. He thus was aware there was good reason to change the plan. However, he petulantly insisted, at least for the record, that the assault be initiated *en echelon* as earlier directed.

The information from the scouts confirmed to Longstreet and his division commanders the impossibility of attacking in an approximately northeasterly direction as originally planned. Moreover, the three rebel generals knew that the extreme Federal left ended short of the rocky hills. General Hood therefore proposed that his division swing around the Federal left and take one or more of the Round Tops. Longstreet's response, delivered by courier, once again implied impatience and the same rigidity he had previously exhibited with McLaws: "Genl Lee's orders are to attack up the Emmitsburg Road."[38]

It was almost as if Longstreet had noticed that Hood's suggested plan was similar to the one Longstreet had proposed to Lee earlier, and thus his denial of Hood's request was in part due to resentment. Longstreet—or McLaws, Anderson, *someone*—might have done a more careful, thorough job of figuring out the Federals' new position in this southern sector of the field. For example, what if Maj. Gen. Richard Anderson (the division commander nominally in charge of the area in front and to the left of the Peach Orchard) had been more active? He could have gotten word to Longstreet about the *vulnerability of the Union 3rd Corps's right flank,* which was totally exposed. Conceivably, that portion of the Federal line might have been attacked *first,* with Southern soldiers pouring into the large gap between Sickles's right and Brig. Gen. John C. Caldwell's division on the 2nd Corps left back on Cemetery Ridge (chart 3-20). As the day would play out, the gap between the Emmitsburg Road and Ridge behind it was never seriously threatened. Thus, General Sickles got away with the geometrical danger he had created by unhinging the flanks of these two Union corps (maps 3-7 and 3-11).

When Hood finally ordered his infantrymen to attack, the unit that started it all was General Law's brigade of Alabamians (chart 3-8). They were at the extreme right of the Confederate army. Unwisely, it seems to me, General Hood had arranged it so the van of his attack would be the brigade that had made a forced march, starting far away from Gettysburg that morning. Map 3-12 shows the deployment of Hood's troops: a pair of brigades in front, with two more behind them (chart 3-8).

On a larger scale—considering both of the Confederate infantry divisions—the attack involved a series of advances from right to left, south to north. This means that the rebel units did attack in an *en-echelon* manner. This tactical stratagem was discussed above. That Law (and Brig. Gen. Henry L. Benning behind him), then Brig. Gen. Jerome B. Robertson (followed by Brig. Gen. George T. Anderson), and so forth (map 3-12, chart 3-8) would comprise the overall assault as it unfolded is ironic given the initial plan to have McLaws open the attack. However, this was the end result of the wrangling that occurred among the First Corps generals. The saving grace of this lengthy discourse on the details of those exchanges between the corps and division commanders is that it clarifies the manner in which the Confederate attack ultimately unfolded: relentlessly from right to left.

General Hood continued to protest, sending "messengers galloping back and forth . . . while minutes passed and the opportunities slipped by."[39] Despite Longstreet's denials, General Hood ended up having his way: The van of his attack did not move up the road. Instead, as Hood had wanted, it headed south, in a direction that would bring it beyond the southern end of the Federal line. To

Map 3-13

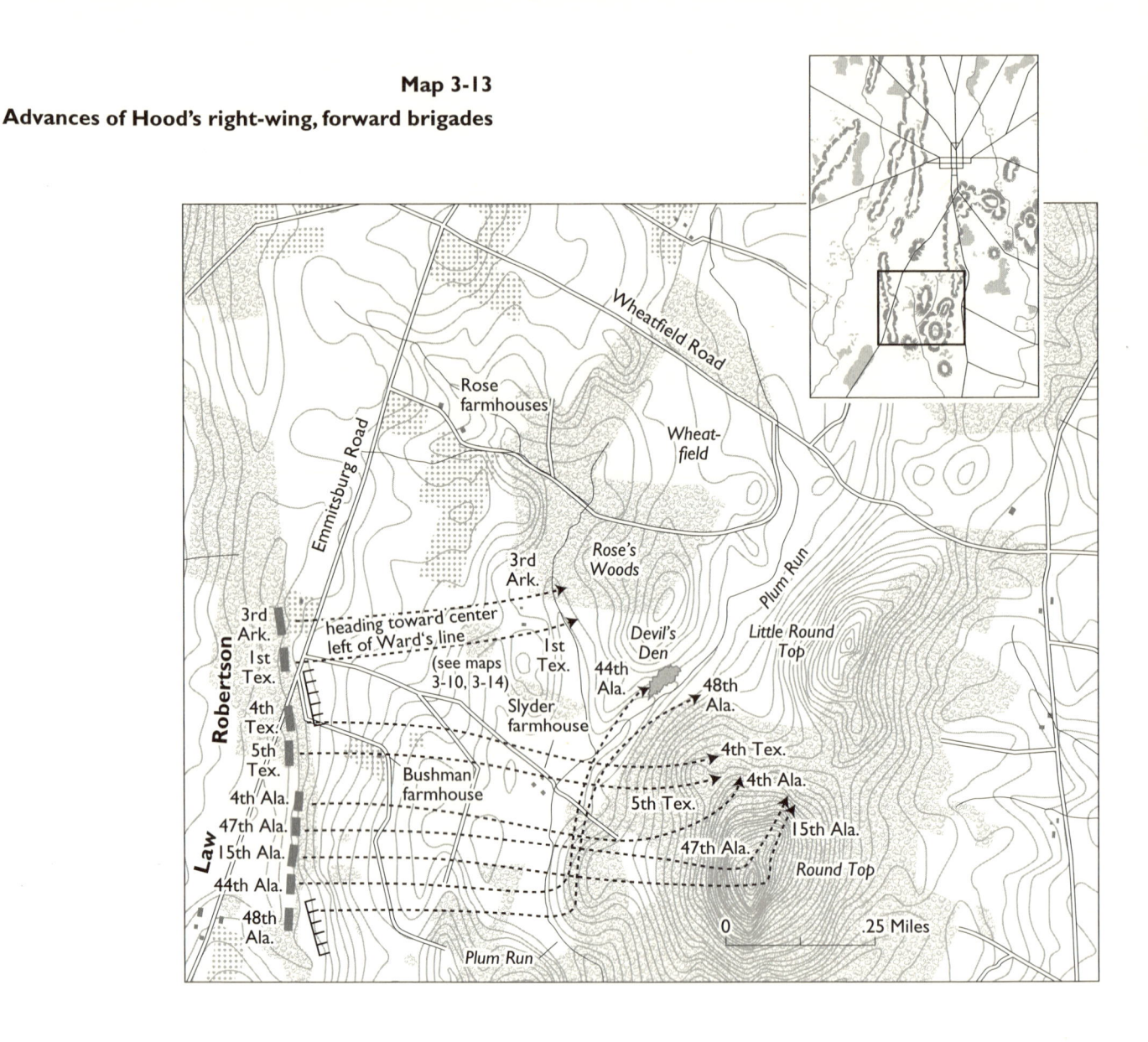

Advances of Hood's right-wing, forward brigades

assault that line would require executing a series of "right hooks" that would swing counterclockwise as the Confederate brigades got about halfway from their jump-off points to the Round Tops.

A problem soon arose: brigade cohesion within Hood's division began physically to come apart. This happened in part because of the Federal shelling raining down on the front and left flanks of the advancing brigades.[40] The fields of fire in this sector were much superior than they are today. When you walk east of Warfield Ridge on the modern-day battlefield, you are in twenty-first-century woods and thus out of sight of where the Union batteries were located. In fact, it is worth pausing to point out that the Gettysburg battlefield is a large one—especially with respect to the fighting that occurred there on July 2. Whether or not a given region of the field was wooded in the 1860s, a large-unit commander who was active there had essentially no view or immediate comprehension of what was happening elsewhere. You can appreciate how isolated such an officer may have felt by walking eastward from Emmitsburg Road toward Big Round Top (maps 3-12 and 3-13). Stop west of Plum Run before you enter the woods that now fill the area between that stream and the big hill and look left (north). From

102   THE STAND OF THE U.S. ARMY AT GETTYSBURG

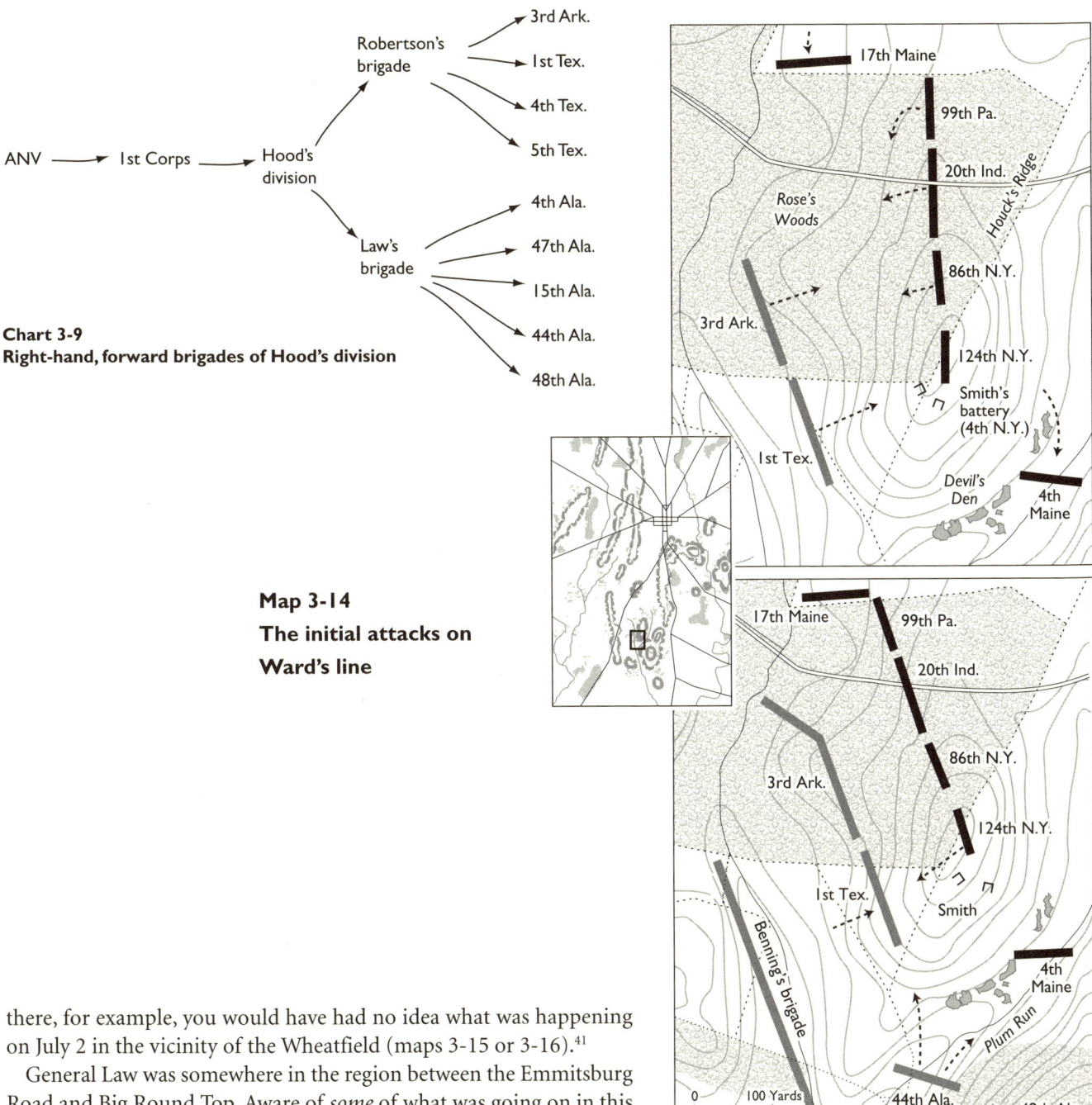

Chart 3-9
Right-hand, forward brigades of Hood's division

Map 3-14
The initial attacks on Ward's line

there, for example, you would have had no idea what was happening on July 2 in the vicinity of the Wheatfield (maps 3-15 or 3-16).[41]

General Law was somewhere in the region between the Emmitsburg Road and Big Round Top. Aware of *some* of what was going on in this sector of the field—such as the Federal fire coming in against Hood's assaulting force—Law had part of his Alabama brigade wheel to the left and head toward the Union artillery blasting away at the first wave of assaulting rebels. Thus, the 44th and 48th Alabama headed toward the Devil's Den and the southern end of Sickles's left wing. As can be seen on map 3-13, this fragmented Law's brigade. The two Alabama regiments that made the abrupt left turn moved northward near Plum Run (map 3-13). An additional rationalization for this move was that the 44th and 48th Alabama would fill up the gap that was opening as the left-hand units drifted to their left during their eastward march, with the right-hand regiments sliding to the right. General Law thus re-routed these two regiments from the brigade's far right, sending them roughly in the direction of Smith's Union battery (map 3-14) at the

THE CLIMAX OF THE BATTLE

southern end of Ward's line on Houck's Ridge. Even though Law was to become the commander of Hood's entire division, this is all that we know of his contribution to the fighting that would soon commence in the vicinity of Houck's Ridge and the Devil's Den.[42]

The 15th Alabama—a regiment previously in the middle of the brigade that initiated the assault (chart 3-9)—now became the extreme right of the rebel force (map 3-13). Just as Law's brigade had split apart, Robertson's regiments did as well. The left wing of his "Texas Brigade" drifted farther north, and its right in effect joined Law's Alabama regiments as they continued advancing due east (map 3-13).

The Confederate attack was losing not only command and control, but also combat power. The advancing lines were thinning out as the brigade components moved apart from each other. The command-and-control problem is illustrated well by General Robertson's actions as he followed his brigade and saw it fan out—two regiments continuing a straight-in advance, the other two angling to the left. General Robertson stayed with his left wing, which was approaching what was then the Union's extreme left flank north of the Devil's Den (map 3-14), while the right drifted off toward Little Round Top—now undefended, but eventually to become the left flank of the overall Federal line.

At the same time General Robertson was losing control of half his brigade, the entire Confederate right wing suffered a severe loss when General Hood was wounded in the left arm by an artillery shell exploding above his head. This occurred not long after the advance commenced, near the Bushman farm (map 3-13). Hood was forced to leave the field, and General Law took over the division in his absence. Perhaps "took over" is too strong a description of his actions, for by the end of the day it became all too clear that Law had exercised little control over the brigades that suddenly came under his command.[43]

The first Confederate regiments to strike the Federal defenders were Robertson's 3rd Arkansas and 1st Texas (chart 3-10). These rebel units had the shortest distance to march toward Ward's line (map 3-13). The Texans approached the left of that line and Smith's 4th New York Battery (chart 3-10) as the Arkansans advanced on Ward's center (map 3-14, top). The rebels' attacking power was less than it might have been because Robertson's other two regiments, the 4th and 5th Texas, were advancing due east with Law's units (map 3-13).

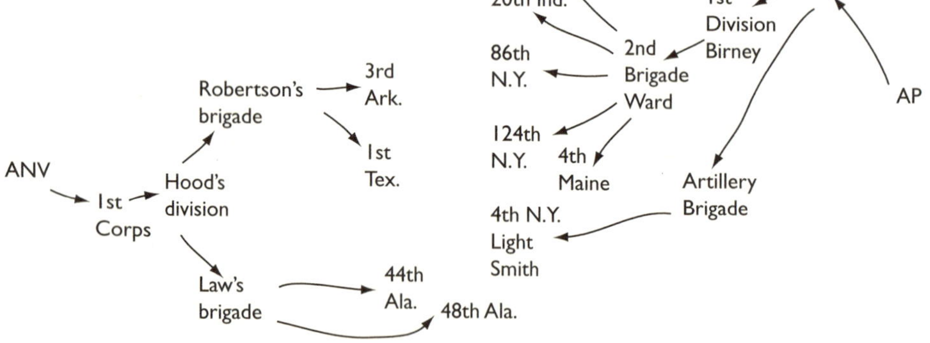

Nevertheless, the fighting became intense on Ward's front. Colonel de Trobriand, whose 3rd Corps brigade was posted to the north (map 3-10), sent one of his regiments in support of Ward (chart 3-10). Thus, the 17th Maine took a position behind a stone fence at the southern boundary of the Wheatfield (map 3-14). The Mainers fired at the exposed left flank of the 3rd Arkansas from a distance of one hundred yards and the Arkan-

Chart 3-10
The initial attacks of Confederate 1st Corps infantry on Ward's Union 3rd Corps defenders (Devil's Den, Houck's Ridge)

sans fell back. This uncovered the 1st Texas's left, leaving it vulnerable to a counter-attack. However, before that occurred, Law's 44th and 48th Alabama (which had made the sharp left turn at Plum Run) began approaching Ward's left flank (map 3-14, bottom; chart 3-10). To counter this threat, Ward ordered the 4th Maine to move from its original position behind and below the left of the brigade line, to a *blocking position in Plum Run Valley* east of Houck's Ridge (map 3-14). To fill the gap created by the 4th Maine's move, General Ward sent the 99th Pennsylvania from the right end of his line (now bolstered by de Trobriand's 17th Maine) toward the left. As the 99th's redeployment was occurring, the 124th New York charged the 1st Texas. The counterattacking New Yorkers swept through the "triangular field" bounded by stone fence lines that gave this open ground its shape (maps 3-12–3-14) and forced the Texans back (map 3-14, bottom). This provided a respite for Ward's defenders. In particular, it allowed Captain Smith to remove one of his guns, which had been disabled by rebel artillery fire. The hiatus was short-lived, however. The 124th New York, which had suffered heavy losses when it charged the 1st Texas, was fired on from the south by the 44th Alabama (map 3-14, bottom). At the same time, that Alabama regiment's right wing tried to advance up the valley. These rebels were met by the 4th Maine, which was by then in position near Plum Run. Some of the Maine men fired down on the Alabamians from atop the rocks in the Devil's Den (map 3-14, bottom).

The fighting near, in, and around Devil's Den was furious. As it escalated, two Union regimental commanders walked to the crest of Little Round Top, some five hundred yards across Plum Run Valley to the east. The officers who looked down upon this frightening melee were Col. James Rice of the 44th New York and Col. Joshua L. Chamberlain of the 20th Maine.[44]

To learn how Chamberlain and Rice came to be on Little Round Top, and about what happened on that hill, we shift our attention back to the right wing of General Longstreet's attack. The story of how the battle for Houck's Ridge and the Devil's Den culminated will be told in the section after the next one.

As Law's Alabamians, joined by the 4th and 5th Texas from Robertson's brigade, continued their eastward advance after the 44th and 48th Alabama regiments made their left turn (map 3-13), an additional right-hooking movement occurred. The subsequent counterclockwise move involved the 47th and 15th Alabama regiments. As previously noted, the 15th was now on the extreme right of the rebel assault, and the 47th Alabama was just to its left (map 3-15). As these units headed toward Big Round Top from Warfield Ridge, the Alabamians took harassing fire from remnants of the 2nd U.S. Sharpshooters (map 3-15, chart 3-15), other elements of which had been deployed to scout the area in front of the south end of Sickles's former line. By late afternoon, a band of these sharpshooters was no longer acting as scouts but as skirmishers, conducting a small-scale fighting withdrawal as they retreated eastward toward Big Round Top (map 3-15).

If the 15th Alabama were to move obliquely to its left toward Little Round Top, the skirmishers' fire would hit the rebels' right flank. That was no good, so Col. William C. Oates, the regimental commander, kept right on going and chased the sharpshooters up Big Round Top. That proved to be tough going, and it carried the Alabamians *away* from the Federal left, which they were supposed to attack.[45] Moreover, the sharpshooters disappeared as they hustled up the big hill—only to reappear in conjunction with the battle for Little Round Top.

One feature of that fight that has been told and retold as one more instance of post-Gettysburg garment-rending anguish involves the extent to which the soldiers in Law's brigade were "dying of thirst." The 15th Alabama was suffering es-

THE CLIMAX OF THE BATTLE

**Chart 3-11
Key elements of the Army of the Potomac's headquarters command and staff**

AP *
↓
Commanding General:
Maj. Gen. G. G. Meade

↙ ↓ ↘

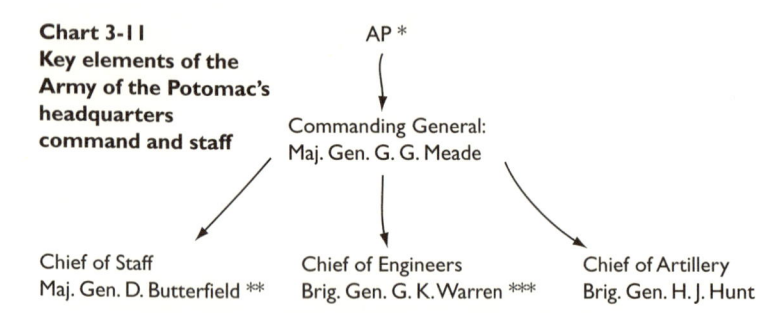

Chief of Staff
Maj. Gen. D. Butterfield **

Chief of Engineers
Brig. Gen. G. K. Warren ***

Chief of Artillery
Brig. Gen. H. J. Hunt

* The generally high-ranking men within Meade's group of staff officers, along with other soldiers under his immediate command, are listed near the beginning of Appendix F.

** Former commander of the 5th Corps brigade led by Col. S. Vincent at Gettysburg (chart 3-12)

*** Former commander of the 5th Corps brigade led by Brig. Gen. S. H. Weed at Gettysburg (chart 3-16)

pecially because a group of infantrymen, detached from the regiment before the assault began to fill the men's canteens, did not return and seemed to have vanished. Ever since, some who marvel at the Confederate struggles on July 2 discuss how awesome it was that this rebel brigade—in particular this regiment within it—made an extended forced march to the field, marched still farther to get into attacking position, went straight into battle, climbed a small mountain, and finally assailed the Federal flank south of Little Round Top. However, there is a problem with this account. Logic dictates that the men in Law's brigade *all* were able to *slake their thirst* as they advanced across Plum Run. It is a significant stream on this part of the field, and the second half of June had been rainy. If any sol-

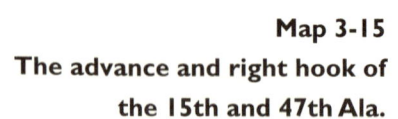

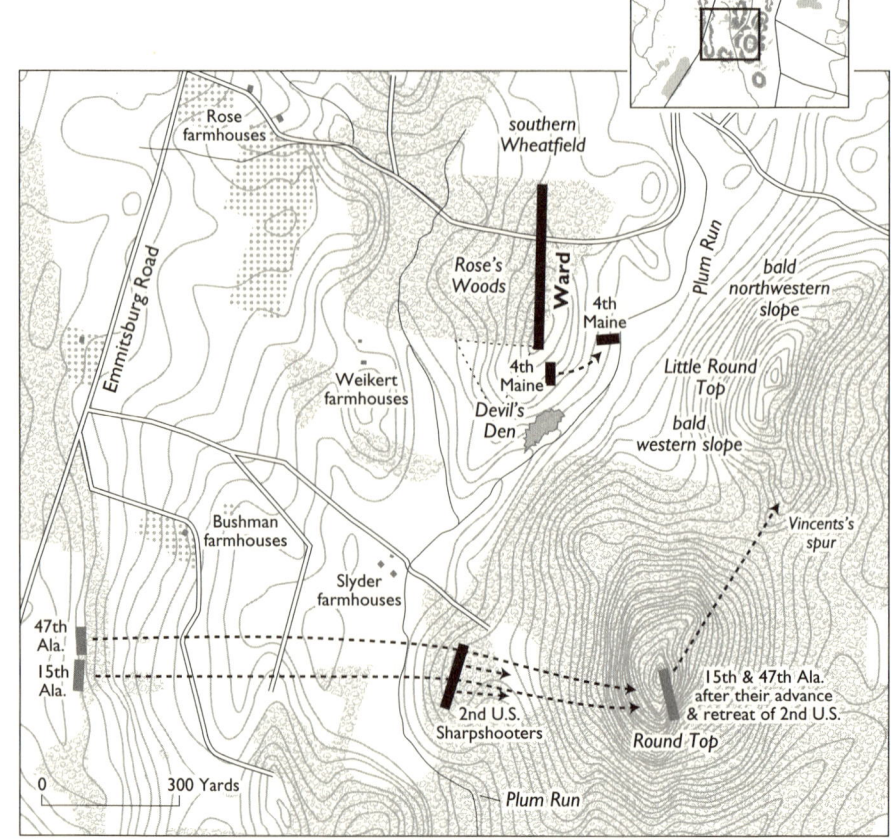

**Map 3-15
The advance and right hook of the 15th and 47th Ala.**

106   THE STAND OF THE U.S. ARMY AT GETTYSBURG

dier was truly "dying of thirst" as he waded through the stream, surely he would have paused to scoop some water into his mouth. He could have done this three or four times in a matter of seconds. One Alabama soldier described how one of his mates accomplished just that as he stood in the middle of the stream.[46] Colonel Oates ultimately passed out on Big Round Top, but that was not until *after* the action on its smaller neighbor to the north. I suspect, however, that Colonel Oates himself drank some water as *he* went through Plum Run. Otherwise, he and many soldiers in his unit might *literally* have died of thirst. Their bodies could not have withstood a waterless day, over the entire course of which they had been subjected to strenuous marching *and* the stress of battle throughout that late July afternoon.

Colonel Oates's troops enjoyed a brief respite near the summit of Big Round Top. Oates later said his 15th Alabama plus the part of the 47th that was now under his command should have maintained their position on the small mountain and converted it "into a Gibraltar."[47] There are problems with this, however. Big Round Top was heavily wooded, and it would have been difficult to get anything but infantry atop it. It would have taken at least a day to drag artillery up the steep slopes and then cut down trees so they would have clear fields of fire. Moreover, there is no large flat area on Big Round Top onto which a significant number of artillery batteries could have been placed.

Meanwhile, Oates being on this hill at the southern tip of the battlefield was doing nothing to the Federals in the short run. Thus, General Law sent a courier to Oates with orders to move to the north and attack any Federal force he might encounter.[48] This meant moving pretty much directly to the north of where Oates and his men now found themselves, such that they ended up at the southward facing slope of the smaller hill. These Alabama regiments will rejoin us in the next section, when the story arrives at Little Round Top, the "smaller hill" in question. (It did not obtain that formal name and the upper-case letters until after the war.)

Note that Oates's force became the *second* in a series of right hooks that describe elements of Hood's and McLaw's assaults on July 2 (map 3-15). The two counterclockwise advances effected by Law's troops (within Hood's division) reveal another way in which the Confederates lost combat power: As units approached the enemy in a right-hooking manner, they separated themselves from the units to their left, some of which moved straight in. It likely would have been very different if Hood's whole division had been able to maneuver in a right hook against the Federal left and possibly gotten into Meade's rear. But there seemed no time to effect such a deployment and advance that late in the day. Thus, the brigades went in piecemeal. Although they did advance in an orderly manner from right to left, they did so in a way that kept spreading the rebel regiments into a south-to-northward line that gradually dissipated the potential force of their attacks.

Sickles could (and did) claim that the advance of his 3rd Corps gave a certain *geometrical advantage* to the defensive deployment along the lower third of the Union line. This retrospectively asserted improvement included the fact that Sickles's portion of the Federal defenses, which mirrored the attacking maneuvers just described, was sticking its westward face into one region of the attack route.[49] The left cheek of that face thus formed the flank that ended up being assailed by the rebel right after it was forced to spread out in a southerly direction. However, the right-center portion of the attacking Confederate line ended up going straight for the nose rather than joining the right-hooking attacks, thus causing the assaults in a given location to fall short of the weight they needed to succeed.

Finally, Sickles could invoke another piece of justification for all of this: He—thus, the Federal left—was *defending out front* in a manner loosely analogous to the way that General Buford had executed his defense the previous day. By defending that way, Sickles would be able to fall back to his initial position—where, if he had simply stayed to absorb the initial blow, a fallback might have resulted in a *breakthrough* of the main Union line, which had nothing behind it, nowhere to fall back and reform. As we shall see, Sickles *did* fall back in time—although not in quite as "good order" as he later claimed was the plan. There is a problem with this explanation, however, and here the Buford analogy is weakened: On the morning of July 1, the Union 1st Cavalry Division commander was only expected to stall the Confederate infantry advance until the van of his army's infantry arrived at Gettysburg. On July 2, Sickles *was* the infantry defense. Who would rescue him if the 3rd Corps's advanced position were imperiled? So far as Sickles knew, no one was available. What if the Union reserve, the 5th Corps, were needed at the north end of the army's line on Culp's Hill (map 3-4)?

As it happened, the outlying Federal left received substantial help from the 5th Corps, as improvised by the Union high command. This saved Sickles to a significant extent. Also, and more interesting, the manner in which high-ranking Federal officers had to *react* to the emergency situation General Sickles had created would end up being an advantage (albeit an arguable one) for that command and for the Union army as a whole. This chapter will close with one side of that argument. For now, consider how much better it might be to react and make decisions without agonizing over them, as opposed to the Federal force being in this kind of situation: "Here we are on this ridge line. Here they come. Where from and how many? When will they get here? Will we crack when they first hit us?"

Earlier in the afternoon than all the activity just described (about three), General Meade sensed that an attack was imminent. Fragments of the relevant information had been reaching his headquarters from the aforementioned signalmen on Little Round Top. This small group of men wigwagged several coded messages to Federal headquarters as the afternoon progressed. One of the signals was sent to Meade's chief of staff, Maj. Gen. Daniel Butterfield (chart 3-11), in the early afternoon. The message from Little Round Top said that a large column of enemy troops was moving west of Gettysburg toward the Union *right*.[50] The signalmen most likely had spotted elements of Longstreet's countermarching corps as they moved east near the Fairfield Road (map 3-8). Not long before the rebel advance began, Meade sent a telegram to Washington saying that the Confederates were moving on *both* of his flanks. That observation was wrong: The initial rebel attacks hit the Union left only. But at least Meade had early warning that Lee was redeploying a significant proportion of his army. Moreover, the commanding general specified in the telegram that he was *anticipating* the possibility that "the enemy is endeavoring to move to my rear and interpose between me and Washington"—and that the Army of the Potomac was ready and in good position to counter such a move.[51]

Finally, between 3:30 and 4 p.m., the nature of the rebel marches became unambiguous: the signalmen on Little Round Top saw many Confederate units moving into the woods in front of them—Longstreet's forces moving into their battle lines. The Federal observers on Little Round Top had not regained visual contact with the Confederates until they were forming up well west of that hill. It follows that the countermarch discussed above was *not* insane. It had *worked* to the extent that the Army of Northern Virginia's 1st Corps's deployment southward went largely unnoticed and created confusion in the Federal ranks.

However fragmented and inaccurate this intelligence was, Meade knew something was up and that Sickles's exposed 3rd Corps was in peril. He responded to the threat by ordering Maj. Gen. George Sykes, commander of the 5th Corps in reserve, to send units to reinforce the 3rd Corps line—if one still existed (map 3-15). Indeed that corps's exposed left was beginning to be assailed near the Devil's Den and along Houck's Ridge, as the rebel artillery fire heard by the Union high command earlier had portended.

Because many additional Confederates were believed to be advancing on the left of the Union army's line, Meade ordered Brig. Gen. Gouverneur K. Warren, his chief engineer, to scout that part of the field. In this respect, it was valuable that the Army of the Potomac possessed several experienced high-ranking staff officers (chart 3-11). These men carried the weight of authority at certain moments—during the battle when they were called upon to make emergency requests of other Union officers.[52]

General Warren first went to Little Round Top accompanied by members of his staff. Although Meade says *he* sent Warren to Little Round Top, Warren later said the idea was his: "Meade sent me to the left to examine the condition of affairs and I continued on till I reached Little Round Top."[53] One reason Warren felt he should go there, or was ordered to do so, involved the very signalmen he soon encountered on the hill. The messages those men had sent up the line, their ambiguities notwithstanding, implied that a Confederate attack was coming. It was much clearer to all in that small cluster of Union soldiers on Little Round Top that it was key terrain. The vulnerability of the position was also self-evident.

Warren supposedly became aware of the impending peril of the Federal position on the hill when he asked that a battery below fire off to the west. This allowed him to spot "the glistening of gun barrels and bayonets of the enemy's line of battle already formed and far outflanking the position of any of our troops" (note 53). Such shoulder arms belonged, of course, to the Confederates who were poised to attack down in the woods. It is just as likely that this part of Warren's account was made up as he wrote this version of the story after the war, to his discredit.[54] Instead, he may simply have been informed of the Confederate units falling into line by the signalmen—who had seen it all by then and relayed the message accordingly.

General Warren did, however, put his life on the line. An artillery shell exploded near the summit of Little Round Top and wounded him, but he retained his senses enough to act as described below. For this he deserves much credit. He was the right officer in the right place at the right time—much as a Confederate major, Henry B. McClellan, had been back on Fleetwood Hill at the Battle of Brandy Station.[55]

Warren sent two messages of alarm. First, he dispatched a mounted courier to General Sickles with orders to send reinforcements (*en*forcements actually) to Little Round Top. Sickles, however, objected, saying that he was already under too heavy an attack. Fair enough. However, another of Warren's messengers found the 5th Corps commander, General Sykes, who had already responded to Meade's orders to send soldiers in support of Sickles. Sykes acquiesced to Warren's emergency request for aid by sending one of his mounted staff officers in search of Brig. Gen. James Barnes, commander of his 1st Division. Elements of Barnes's force were in the van of the reinforcing, westward movement (map 3-16, chart 3-12). It is unclear whether Barnes himself was ever made aware of the threat to Little Round Top. In any case, Sykes's courier found himself in the vicinity of Col. Strong Vincent's 3rd Brigade, which was in the lead of General Barnes's reinforcers (chart 3-12). When

Map 3-16 Federal 5th Corps reinforcing moves

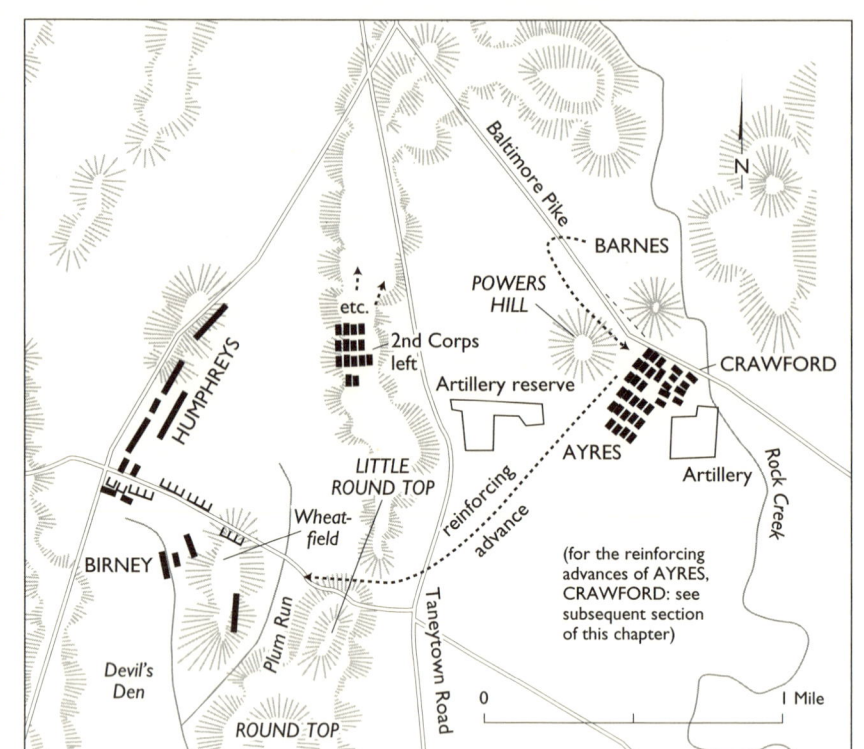

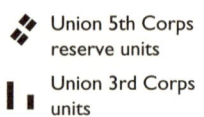

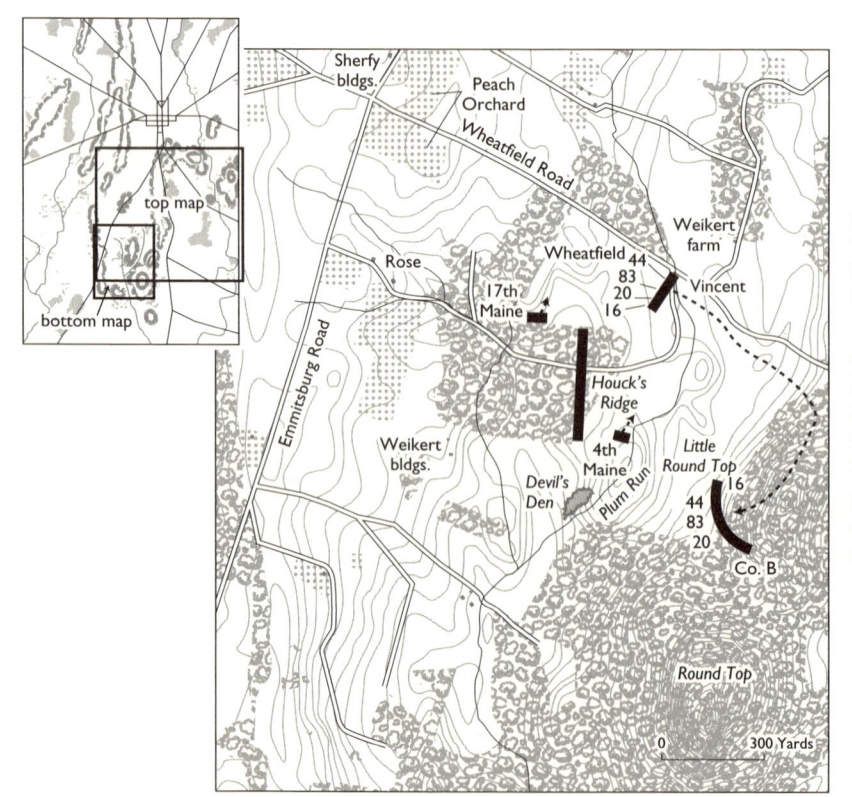

Union 5th Corps reserve units

Union 3rd Corps units

(for the reinforcing advances of AYRES, CRAWFORD: see subsequent section of this chapter)

Regiments within Col. Vincent's 5th Corps brigade: 44th N.Y., 83rd Pa., 20th Maine, 16th Mich.

Co. B = Company B of 20th Maine (which is now left of the brigade line): this Co. detached (see next section of Ch. 3)

line of Gen. Ward's 3rd Corps brigade (vertical) now more in a state of flux

110   THE STAND OF THE U.S. ARMY AT GETTYSBURG

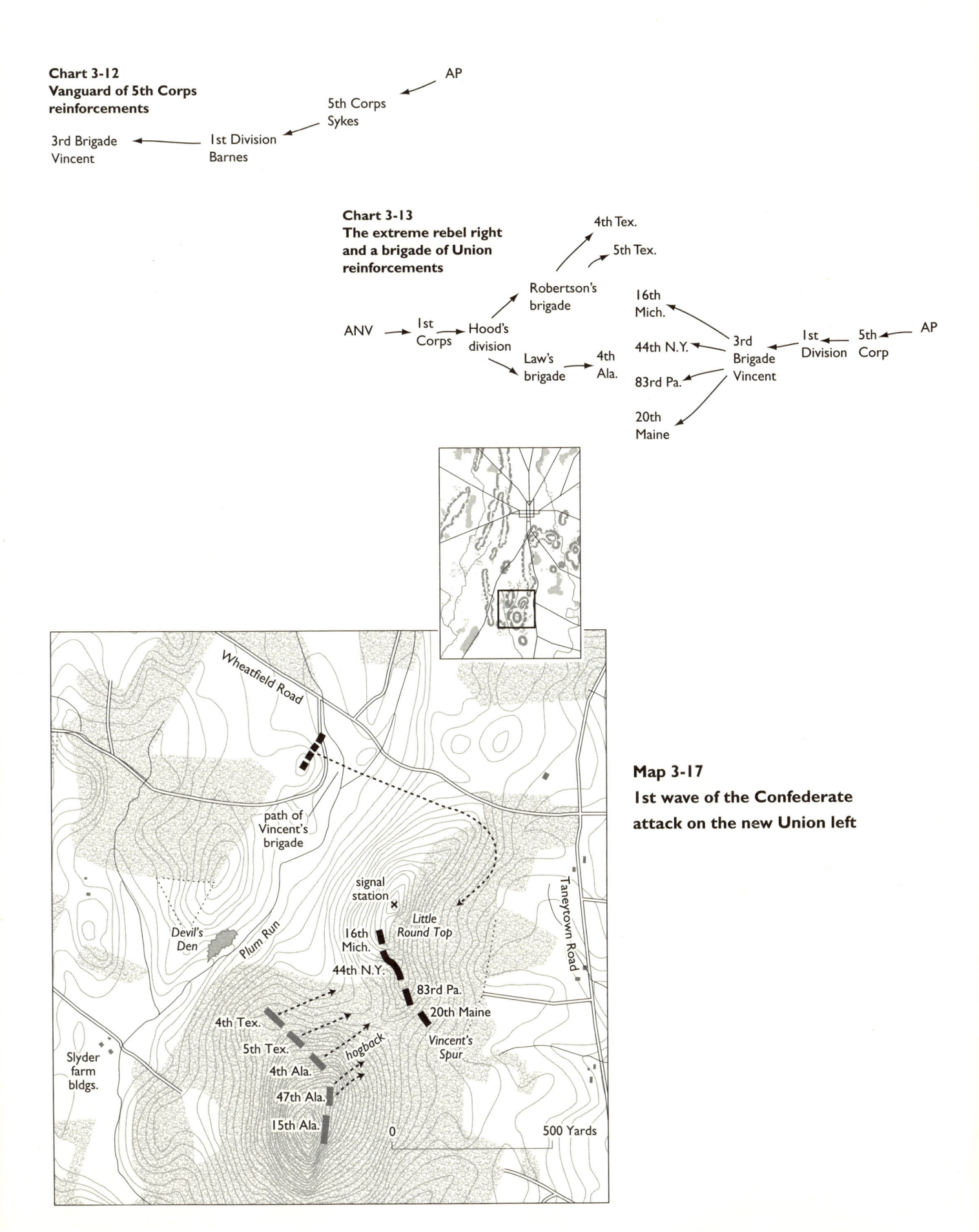

Chart 3-12
Vanguard of 5th Corps reinforcements

3rd Brigade Vincent ← 1st Division Barnes ← 5th Corps Sykes ← AP

Chart 3-13
The extreme rebel right and a brigade of Union reinforcements

ANV → 1st Corps → Hood's division → Robertson's brigade → 4th Tex., 5th Tex.

Hood's division → Law's brigade → 4th Ala.

3rd Brigade Vincent → 16th Mich., 44th N.Y., 83rd Pa., 20th Maine

3rd Brigade Vincent ← 1st Division ← 5th Corp ← AP

Map 3-17
1st wave of the Confederate attack on the new Union left

THE CLIMAX OF THE BATTLE 111

Vincent learned what the staff officer's mission was about, he looked over his left shoulder at Little Round Top. By then, the 3rd Brigade was approaching the vicinity of the Wheatfield, and thus was already west of the rocky hill and to its north (map 3-16).

Seeing that the hill's western face and summit had been cleared of trees and were devoid of troops, Colonel Vincent made a rapid, autonomous, and courageous decision: Contravening his orders and eliminating the middleman (the messenger sent by Sykes to find Barnes), he turned his 1,450-man brigade around and began moving back toward the undefended hill (map 3-16).[56]

This was Strong Vincent's golden moment (it was also one of his last). His decisive action ensured that his brigade got there in the same nick-of-time manner as had happened on the morning of July 1, when elements of the 1st Corps first arrived on McPherson Ridge. The next section describes what happened to Vincent and the troops he commanded on July 2—along with the actions of several lesser-known units of infantrymen who fought furiously for possession of Little Round Top. Later, other Federal 5th Corps will come into play, including those that made the initial reinforcing moves in conjunction with Vincent's brigade.

The Battle for Little Round Top
and the Charge of the 20th Maine

The battle for Little Round Top stirs the soul. The fight that occurred on that hill, and how the opposing forces got there, is believed by many to have been the pivotal moment of the Gettysburg campaign.

What if Gouverneur Warren had not gone to Little Round Top or had not sent for the troops who manned it at the last minute? (We are not done with Warren's actions in this respect.) What if Strong Vincent had not diverted his brigade, which became the first crucial defensive force on the southern half of that hill? And, as we progress into the battle for control of it: What if the 20th Maine, Vincent's extreme left regiment, had not *charged the 15th Alabama,* thus creating the apparent climax within the climax?

Or was it? What if Col. Patrick H. O'Rorke and his 140th New York had not made *their* last-minute rendezvous with the assaulting Texans (described below after the 20th Maine's story), stalling those rebels and saving, it seemed, the central and northern sectors of Little Round Top?

Seen from the other perspective, what if the Confederates *had* seized Little Round Top, fortifying it not only with those victorious infantrymen, but also with artillery? Might they have blasted the entire Union line off of Cemetery Ridge, changing the course of the battle and perhaps altering the history of the American Republic?

The labored questions just posed are not meant to be sarcastic. One can push the arguments about the importance of Little Round Top in either of the directions just implied. Some of the current scholarship about this battle-within-the-battle comes down on the side of its *relative* unimportance.[57] However, the discussion that follows, interspersed with the account of what happened there, will suggest that some of the recent revisionism may have gone too far.

In dealing with the description of what happened, let us bear in mind that the assaults of the Confederate right wing first hit what was *then* the extreme Union left: Ward's brigade near the Devil's Den and along Houck's Ridge (maps 3-10 and 3-14). These impending attacks had triggered the reinforcements from the Federal 5th Corps. The lead unit—Colonel Vincent's 3rd Brigade of the 1st Divi-

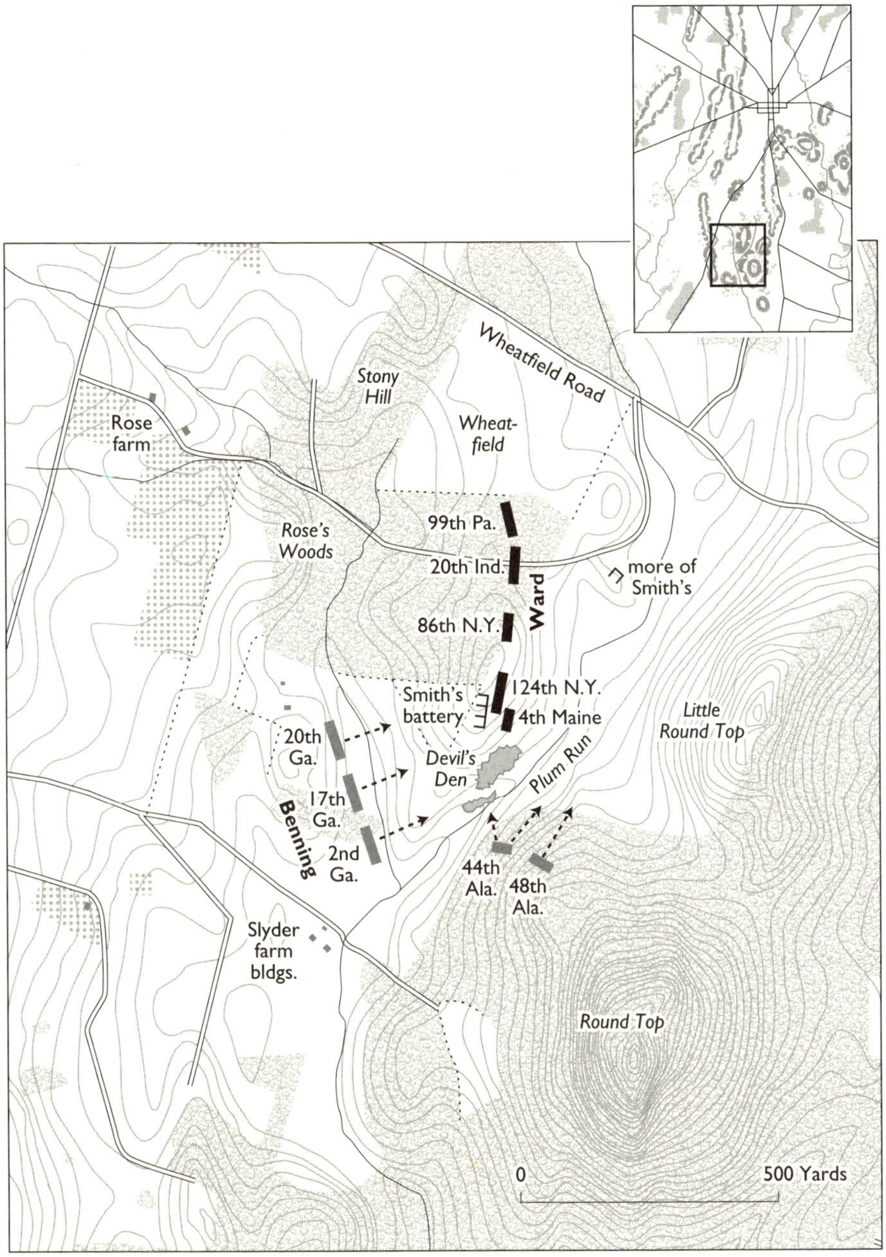

Map 3-18

Elements of the 1st and 2nd waves of rebel attacks threaten the Plum Run Valley

sion—turned 120 degrees to its left (map 3-16, bottom) and rushed up Little Round Top. This helped stall the second wave of rebel attacks as those elements of General Hood's division proceeded farther to the east, passing south of the Devil's Den, in the vicinity of which their comrades were assailing Ward's line (map 3-13).

Thus, the 4th Alabama, along with the 5th and 4th Texas to its left (chart 3-13), headed toward the southwest slope of Little Round Top. This attack group was divided somewhat because there is a hogback feature to Little Round Top's southwestern slope that separated the Alabama troops from the Texans (map 3-17). At any rate, only the southern sector of that slope was defended, such that Vincent's right—the 16th Michigan—manned the rocky ground below the summit, curv-

THE CLIMAX OF THE BATTLE 113

**Map 3-19
Vincent's brigade occupies the lower part of Little Round Top**

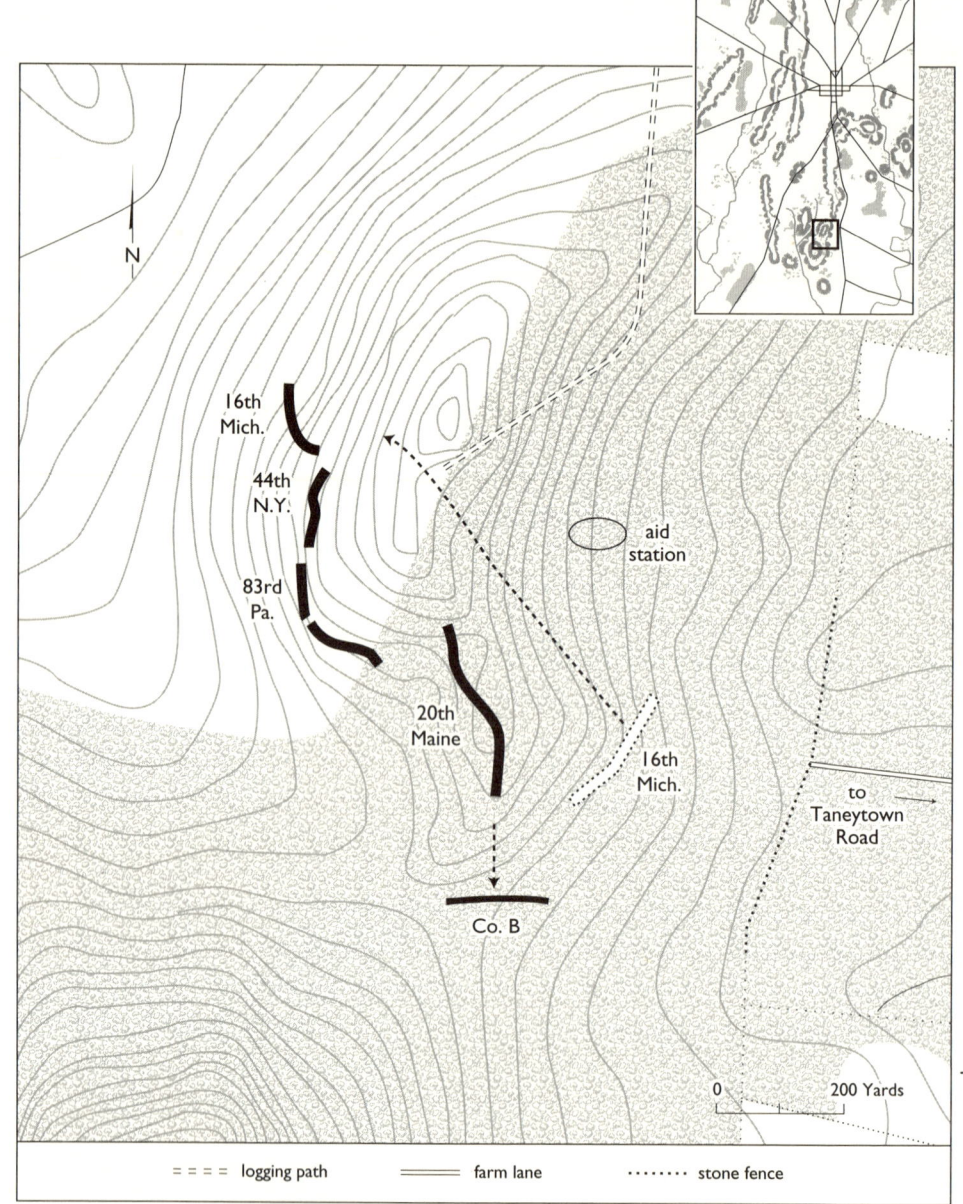

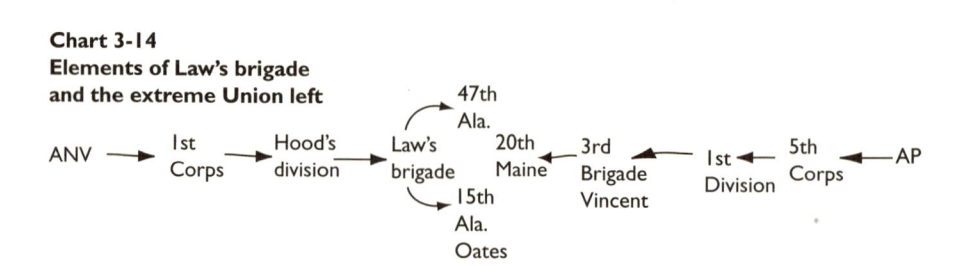

- - - - logging path ═══ farm lane ······ stone fence

**Chart 3-14
Elements of Law's brigade and the extreme Union left**

ANV → 1st Corps → Hood's division → Law's brigade → 47th Ala. / 15th Ala. Oates
20th Maine ← 3rd Brigade Vincent ← 1st Division ← 5th Corps ← AP

114   THE STAND OF THE U.S. ARMY AT GETTYSBURG

ing only partway around the hill in a northerly direction (map 3-17).[58] To the left of the 16th Michigan was the 44th New York. Next, the 83rd Pennsylvania began to curve around the southwestern slope of Little Round Top, connecting with the 20th Maine's right flank. Those Maine men were going into position on a *spur*— a lower part of the hill that projects off its southern edge toward Big Round Top (map 3-17).

As the Confederates engaged Ward's defending force and began to approach the smaller of these two hills, the eastward advancing *and* right-hooking rebels *also* threatened the valley running between Houck's Ridge and Little Round Top (map 3-18). Elements of the incipient Confederate attacks thus menaced Ward's rear and even the left of the Union position on Cemetery Ridge some three-quarters of a mile to the north. A rebel advance up Plum Run Valley (map 3-18) would have dire consequences for the Union positions, especially if Little Round Top were to fall into Confederate hands.

This stage setting is offered to allow an appreciation of the series of attacks, defenses, and counterattacks involving Sickles's left wing and the 5th Corps units that reinforced it (see map 3-10 and the next section of this chapter). For now, we will cope only with the fighting on Little Round Top, as it *became* the extreme left of the Army of the Potomac (map 3-19)—bearing in mind that many components of the action swirling round Sickles's left wing occurred simultaneously.

Thus, the aforementioned 4th Alabama and 4th and 5th Texas approached Vincent's right and center from the southwest (map 3-17) at the same time the 15th and 47th Alabama were advancing toward the southern tip of Little Round Top (map 3-15)—or Vincent's Spur, as it came to be known (map 3-16).[59] The 230-man 47th Alabama was depleted by the disappearance of three advanced companies that had lost contact with the main body. These three units drifted to the right, ending up on the southern end of Big Round Top—yet another instance of the *thinning out and splitting up* of the Confederate lines of advance. In this case, these fifty-five men of the 47th Alabama never got into the fight.

The Texas regiments were able to scale the west face of the hill, threatening Vincent's right (map 3-17) to the extent that several soldiers in the 16th Michigan broke and fell back to the eastern part of Little Round Top. Colonel Vincent was shot in the groin while trying to rally the Michiganders in his vicinity. He died on July 7.

The Confederates made little headway with their frontal assault as the 44th New York and the 83rd Pennsylvania held. Moreover, troops from that Pennsylvania regiment, aided by the right wing of the 20th Maine (map 3-20), blasted the 47th Alabama (chart 3-14), which was approaching the southwestern edge of Vincent's Spur. The Alabamians withdrew from this sector and exited the battle for Little Round Top (map 3-20). Only about 175 of the Alabamians were present on this part of the field to start with (recall that three of the regiment's companies had wandered off to the south earlier). Whatever weight they might have added to the attacks on the Union army's extreme left was gone. Also, the 47th's regimental commander was wounded and fell during the barrage of musketry. But now the 15th Alabama was attacking the 20th Maine (map 3-20, chart 3-14).[60]

It bears repeating that the 20th Maine was on the left flank of the entire Army of the Potomac. The idea is that the 15th Alabama could have pushed the 20th Maine off Vincent's Spur and then rolled up Vincent's entire brigade line from south to north, sending it flying from Little Round Top. This would have given the Army of Northern Virginia's right wing a foothold on this crucial hill.

Most of the 15th Alabama's forces were eventually directed at the 20th Maine's

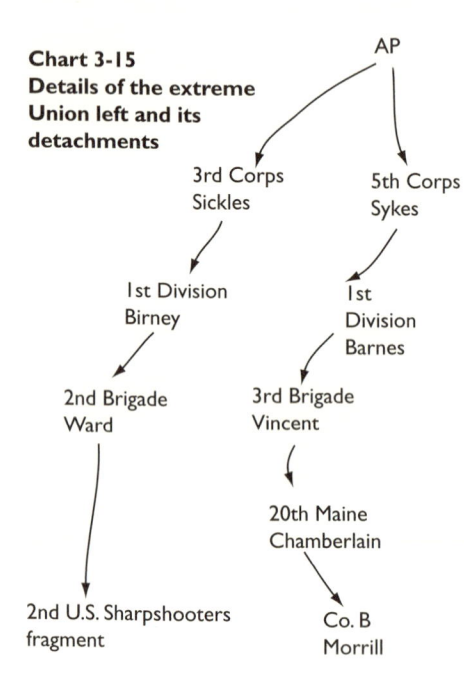

**Chart 3-15
Details of the extreme Union left and its detachments**

```
                    AP
                   ╱  ╲
            3rd Corps   5th Corps
            Sickles      Sykes
               │            │
           1st Division   1st Division
           Birney         Barnes
               │            │
           2nd Brigade   3rd Brigade
           Ward          Vincent
               │            │
           2nd U.S.      20th Maine
           Sharpshooters Chamberlain
           fragment         │
                         Co. B
                         Morrill
```

center and left (map 3-20). Whereas the Maine companies in the center—on either side of the later positions of the regimental colors (map 3-20)—suffered heavy casualties, the part of Vincent's Spur to the left of that point (from the Mainers' perspective) was more vulnerable. Recognizing this, Colonel Oates had the 15th's right (seven companies' worth) shift around farther to their right, aiming to get into the Maine regiment's rear. However, the commander of those Maine men, the legendary Col. Joshua Lawrence Chamberlain, "refused" his line by having his left flank move around counterclockwise (map 3-20). That put the regiment into an L (later a V) configuration. A move of this sort can protect the flank of a defending force—the same kind of protection that might have been afforded the 11th Corps's extreme left the previous day if only its units had achieved a better geometrical configuration.[61]

In contrast, the 20th Maine maneuvered itself into a good defensive position. Although the bent-back left seemed to be the most precarious part of the Mainers' line, there was by then an extra measure of hidden protection. Before the 15th Alabama had struggled down from Big Round Top and along its western face, moving toward but not yet directly threatening Vincent's Spur, Colonel Chamberlain sent a company of skirmishers out to his front (map 3-19). Thus, Company B, commanded by Capt. Walter G. Morrill, moved out toward the saddle between the Round Tops.[62] Soon, the van of the 15th Alabama approached, and the outnumbered skirmishers (a forty-man unit) withdrew eastward out of immediate harm's way. Yet they did not skedaddle. Instead, they took up a position behind a stone fence, hidden down in the trees southeast of the center of the 20th's main line (map 3-20).

Company B was cut off and could not see the rest of the regiment up on the spur. Hearing the heavy fighting that commenced a few minutes later, Captain Morrill might easily have imagined his comrades were being forced from their positions, *completely* isolating his company. Assuming that, he then could have vacated his position behind the fence, moved east to the Taneytown Road (map 3-20), and then set off in search of the army's main body (map 3-7). Morrill instead chose to *hold his ground* behind the stone fence. Whether he knew it or not, he was guarding his regiment's left. He was also reinforced: About a dozen riflemen from the 2nd U.S. Sharpshooters found their way to that stone barrier and put themselves under Morrill's command (chart 3-15). These were the 3rd Corps soldiers who had harassed the Alabamians' advance from Warfield Ridge (map 3-15), and whom Colonel Oates chased up the west face of Big Round Top.

As the fighting on that Thursday afternoon continued to unfold, the 15th Alabama made at least three waves of assaults on the 20th Maine. The brunt of these attacks hit the Mainers' left, although the defenders' center was subjected to pressure as well.

Colonel Oates finally organized a concerted advance by ordering nearly all the men in his seven right-wing companies up the southeastern slope of Vincent's Spur. In this, the most concerted attack on the 20th Maine's center and left, the Alabamians pushed back the already bowed left wing of the defenders, turning their L-shaped position into a hairpin-like V (map 3-20). By then, Oates had given permission to one his officers to take three or four dozen Alabamians beyond the 20th Maine's extreme left (map 3-20). That detached group of rebels got into a position to pour musket fire into the Mainers' left flank. However, as the rest of the rebels pushed toward the 20th's main line, the situation became more dangerous to the defenders in this area. Opposing troops fired away at close quarters and grappled hand-to-hand. One of the rebels hit as he and his comrades got

**Map 3-20
The repulse of the 47th Ala.
and attacks by the 15th**

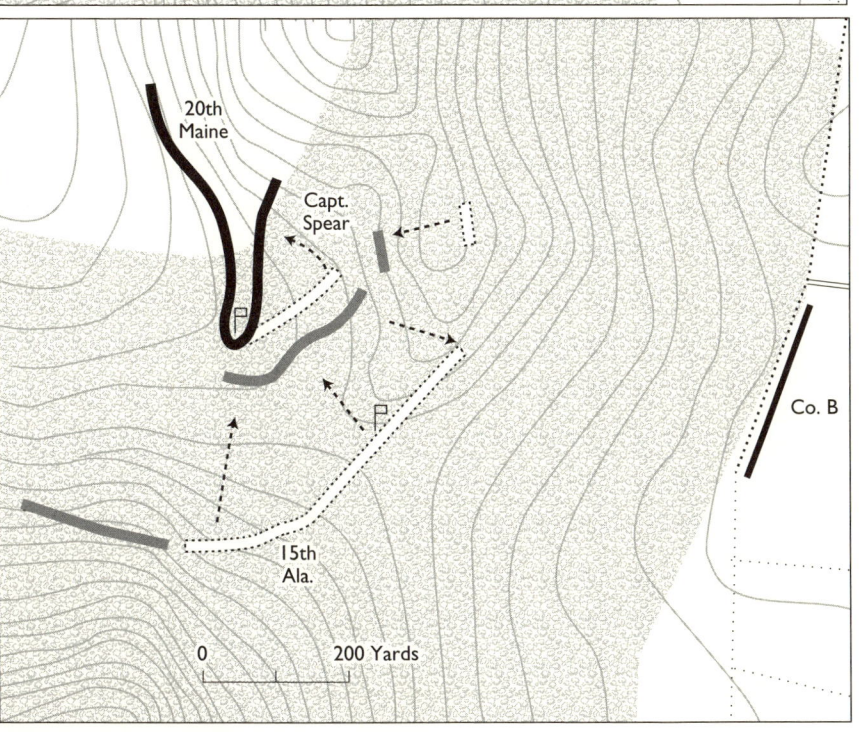

- - - - - - stone fence
▯ regimental colors
⋯⋯ earlier positions of 15th's right and 20th's left

THE CLIMAX OF THE BATTLE 117

into the left half of the hairpin was Colonel Oates's brother, John. He was mortally wounded and died twenty-three days later. A parallel situation existed for Colonel Chamberlain: he had two brothers with him on Vincent's Spur that day (both survived).

Colonel Chamberlain's siblings were but a small part of his concerns out on this hidden corner of the battlefield. His regiment was *isolated*. Much of the 83rd Pennsylvania was out of sight up the slope and off to his right. And this was, in a way, Chamberlain's baptism of fire: Although a participant in previous battles, he was a novice regimental commander who had not yet been engaged in sustained close combat.[63] Moreover, on Little Round Top his regiment was not part of a line of battle, nicely flanked on both sides by other units in his brigade. If that had been the case, he could have conformed to their movements and actions, perhaps under the close control of his brigade commander. Instead, he had to do everything on his own. One of the problems was that he needed to find a way to effect an emergency maneuver involving about half of his regiment, to protect its left flank and rear. Despite all of these pressures, including debilitation and his relative inexperience, Chamberlain remained outwardly calm and in control.[64] This had to have exerted a salutary effect on the soldiers under his command.

Some of the accounts of this action, including Chamberlain's own postwar words, imply that the 20th Maine was severely outnumbered, maybe by as much as ten to one.[65] In reality, the Maine regiment's strength was probably superior to that of the Confederate regiment confronting it.[66] Colonel Oates attacked with about 450 men. For its part, the 20th Maine's line was down (from approximately five hundred) to about the same number when the fighting commenced on the southern spur of Little Round Top, given that Company B had disappeared from there (but not permanently, as we will see). An oft-repeated military truism is that no would-be attacker should undertake an assault unless its forces outnumber those of the defenders by at least three to one.[67] There was no such luck for Oates's Alabamians as they approached Vincent's Spur.

The battle between the roughly matched forces on that low hill raged for at least an hour. By the end of that time, Chamberlain had lost 130 of his men (all but four killed and wounded).[68] Shortly before, he may have heard and at least believed that his troops were "running out of ammunition." This is belied, first of all, by the difficulty of doing that with the rifled muskets of the time (the 20th Maine was armed with muzzle-loading British Enfields). Moreover, consider the account of the officer who commanded the regiment's left wing, Capt. Ellis Spear (map 3-20). He wrote that his companies were *not* out of ammunition, later adding that Colonel Chamberlain could not have known about this anyway as communication between the center and the semi-isolated left was sporadic.[69] However, Spear could not speak for the companies in the center and on the right as those elements of the regiment were out of his sight, given that he was down in the trees in the southeastern sector of Vincent's Spur.

Spear's impromptu command of the left of the 20th Maine speaks to another of Colonel Chamberlain's problems: He had no field officers under him, no experienced lieutenant colonel or major who could have helped him maintain control of the company officers.[70] Whether or not the soldiers of the 20th Maine had enough officers to lead them, they were holding thus far. Yet the rebel attack had begun to make the Mainers' left give way, and the next assault would supposedly have left the defenders unable to fire back. We come, then, to the charge of the 20th Maine. Colonel Chamberlain decided, so the legend goes, to launch a surprise counterattack intended to preempt the next assault upon his lines—which

Map 3-21

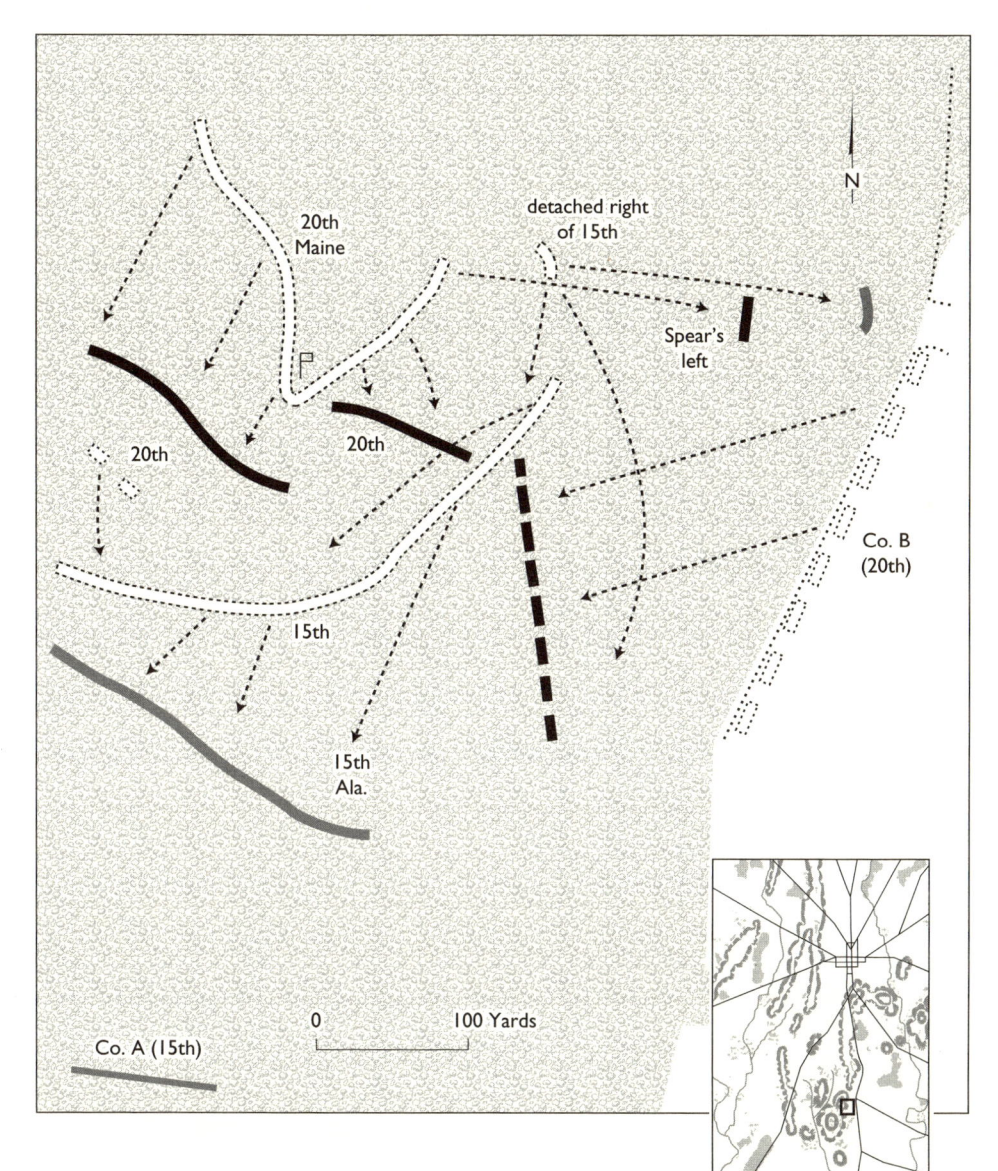

The charge of the 20th Maine

he was convinced would result in the regiment's capture or collapse. After the war, Chamberlain essentially claimed not only to have ordered a charge, but also a "right wheel" forward.[71] This maneuver involved having his left wing swing clockwise as if it were a door on a hinge, catch up with the rest of the charging line, and thus help sweep the rebels down the hill (map 3-20).

The reality is that Colonel Chamberlain—who did have a counterattack in mind—very likely did not order his entire regiment to charge, let alone in the "textbook maneuver" just described.[72] Chamberlain did write that he was about to order the entire regiment forward and that the cry of "'fix bayonets' flew from man to man."[73] However, as the charge unfolded, it was probably more of a spontaneous thing.[74] Some of the Maine men were already filtering down the slope to bring their wounded comrades back into the lines. This seemed to trigger a larger advance and elements of the regiment's center and right began moving toward the Alabamians in front of them (map 3-21). As additional Maine men in this part of the line added their weight to the incipient counterattack, part of the

THE CLIMAX OF THE BATTLE 119

regiment's left saw the move and joined in, aiming to catch up with the advancing center. But the Mainers on the extreme left advanced from their position in the direction they were facing—*not* due south (or wheeling clockwise), but *east.* In fact, the 20th's extreme left went after the detached group of Alabamians (map 3-21) that had earlier moved out beyond the defenders' left flank (map 3-20).

Meanwhile, the 15th Alabama might have been *about to withdraw.* At least that is what William Oates wrote later in life.[75] His regiment had had enough. His men were not about to take the southern spur of the hill, they were exhausted from all their marching that day, and they were "dying of thirst." That Oates was in the process of withdrawing his regiment to a fallback position toward or on Big Round Top to the south does not ring false. For Oates to have written that this was his intention *before* the charge came his way is not a self-aggrandizing claim. Implied in his account is that he had been defeated, whether or not the charge of the 20th Maine is what finally did in his regiment.

As the 20th Maine made its pell-mell charge down the slopes of Vincent's Spur (map 3-21), something else occurred to add the final martial weight to the counterattacking defenders: Company B opened up on the right flank and rear of the 15th Alabama. That isolated company and the sharpshooters who had joined it had been taking potshots at the Alabamians during the time of the rebels' attacks upon the spur. However, Oates and his men did not seem to become aware of them until the time of the charge. This added psychological force to Company B's counterattack.

As the rest of the Mainers advanced on the rebels to their front, Captain Morrill led his approximately fifty soldiers over the stone fence behind which they had stood in a charge of their own. Some members of Company B, moving in a southwesterly direction from the fence, actually passed other members of the Maine regiment—those who had charged down the slope from the extreme left and thus were moving almost in the opposite direction to that of Morrill's men (map 3-21).

At this point, Colonel Oates thought he was surrounded. He believed an entire fresh regiment of Federals had come to this sector of the field. The Alabamians toward the back of the 15th's position here—not immediately threatened by the charging main body of the 20th Maine—might have made a stand with their muskets and perhaps have broken up the charge. But this possibility was ruined by the shock effect of Company B's attack. Oates then gave the order to withdraw, at which time, he later admitted: "we ran like a herd of wild cattle."[76]

Even though the charge of the 20th Maine may have been superfluous—especially if Colonel Oates was about to order the retreat of his regiment anyway—the Mainers caused the precipitous retreat of the 15th Alabama as they scoured the region between Vincent's Spur on Little Round Top and the bigger hill south of it.[77] This might have made it difficult for the rebels to move additional units into this area as a springboard for renewed attacks on the spur. These never happened, so at least the extreme left of the Union line was secure.

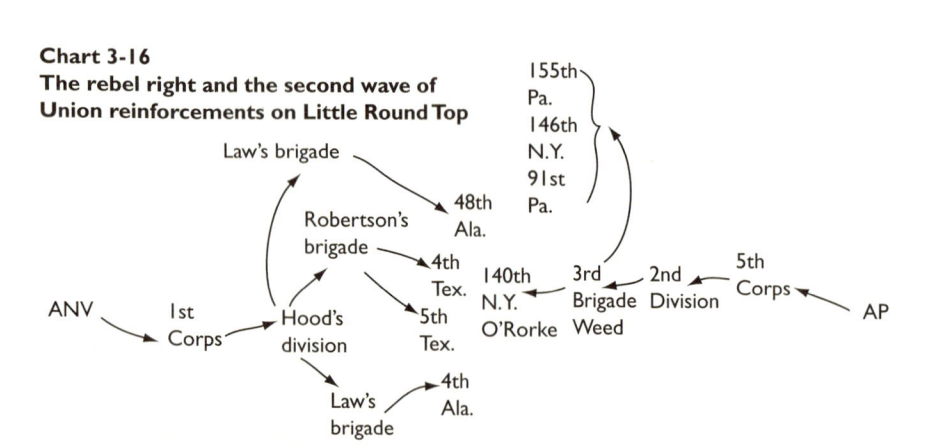

To wind up the Little Round Top story to this point, it is worth asking if

Chart 3-16
The rebel right and the second wave of Union reinforcements on Little Round Top

120   THE STAND OF THE U.S. ARMY AT GETTYSBURG

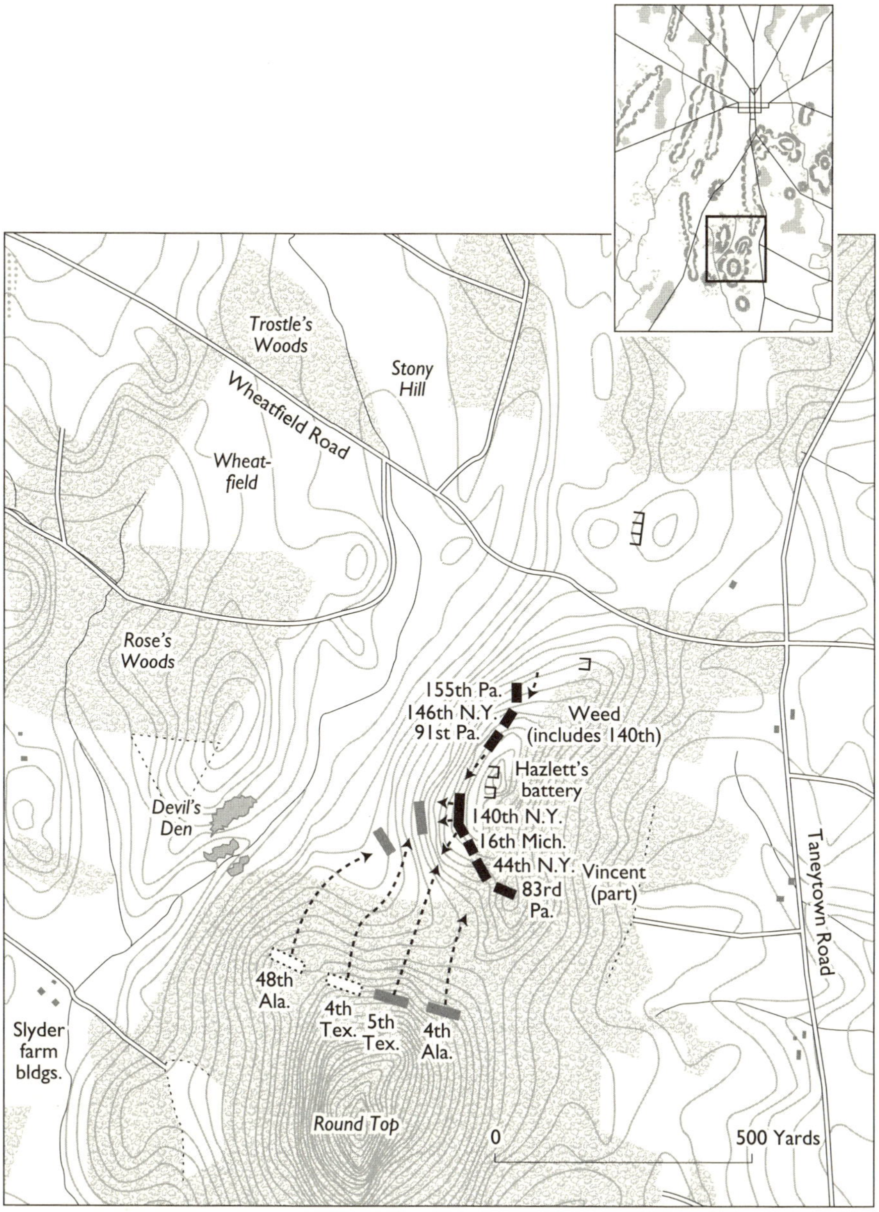

Map 3-22
Texans and Alabamians attack Little Round Top as Weed's brigade arrives

the position at this end of the Federal line was ever in extreme danger. Perhaps not. The 20th Maine was almost certainly not outnumbered, and even before Oates's men went into action against the Mainers, those Southerners would inevitably have a rough go of it. The Alabamians were physically debilitated and they were fighting defenders occupying higher ground that contained appreciable cover in the form of trees and rocks on the spur. Moreover, even if this *one regiment* of rebels *had* pushed the 20th Maine back, it is unlikely that it would have had the strength (numerical or otherwise) to move the rest of the Federal force off of Little Round Top. Unbeknownst to Colonel Oates, at the same time his lone rebel regiment was in the midst of trying to dislodge 20th Maine on the left end of Little Round Top's defenses, the regiments of yet *another* Union brigade were moving in to secure the center and left of the hill (as we will see shortly). Had the Confederates swung the three regiments moving toward the *western* face of Little Round Top (map 3-17) around to the right in a counterclockwise direction to

THE CLIMAX OF THE BATTLE   121

**Map 3-23
The 140th N.Y. ascends and defends Little Round Top**

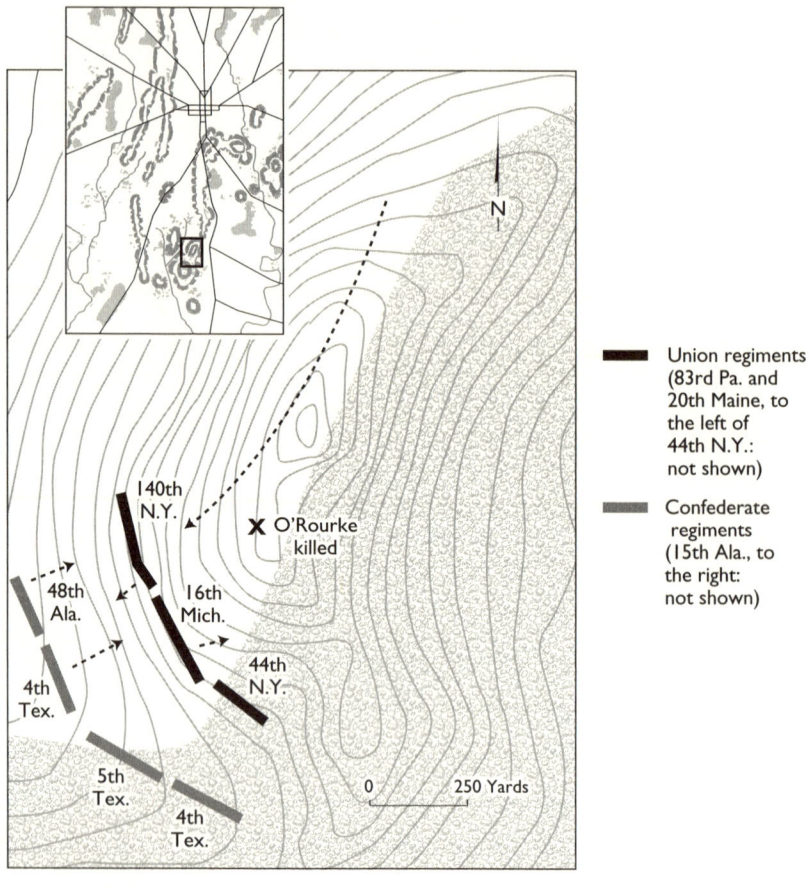

Union regiments (83rd Pa. and 20th Maine, to the left of 44th N.Y.: not shown)

Confederate regiments (15th Ala., to the right: not shown)

140th N.Y.
X O'Rourke killed
48th Ala.
16th Mich.
4th Tex.
44th N.Y.
5th Tex.
4th Tex.

0   250 Yards

**Chart 3-17
Hazlett's battery reinforcing Little Round Top**

5th U.S. Battery D Hazlett ← Artillery Brigade Martin ← 5th Corps ← AP

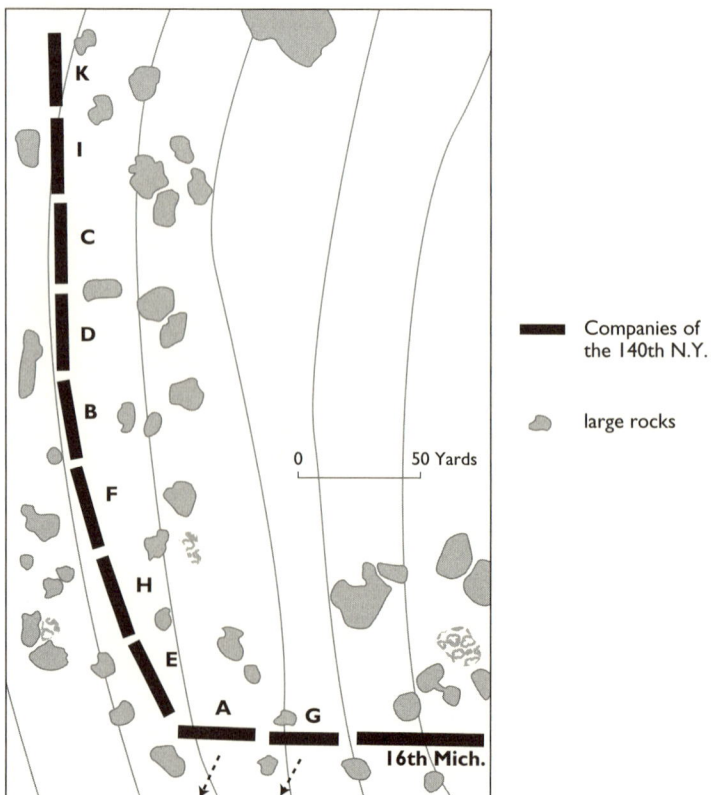

Companies of the 140th N.Y.

large rocks

0   50 Yards

16th Mich.

122   THE STAND OF THE U.S. ARMY AT GETTYSBURG

join or relieve the 15th Alabama in the saddle between the two hills they might have brought enough power to bear on the Union flank at the southern tip of the battlefield. But Colonel Oates was unable even to see any Confederate units to his immediate left during his attacks against the 20th Maine.

Instead, those three rebel regiments—the 4th and 5th Texas and the 4th Alabama—were hitting the Federals on the hill's western slope as Vincent's regiments were being reinforced by the timely arrival of the 140th New York from Brig. Gen. Stephen H. Weed's 3rd Brigade of the 5th Corps's 2nd Division (map 3-22, chart 3-16).

In this regard, Gouverneur Warren's yeoman's work was not done after he got General Sykes to find a force that could occupy Little Round Top. After Warren sent the two messengers in search of such defenders (leading to Vincent's arrival on the hill), the general went looking for more. He found the aforementioned 140th New York regiment north of Little Round Top, moving west to reinforce Sickles. General Warren readily convinced the regimental commander, Col. Patrick O'Rorke, to divert his regiment to the northern slope of Little Round Top.

O'Rorke led the 140th New York onto the rocky hill (map 3-23). His troops had little time to make an organized advance onto these heights, and Lt. Charles E. Hazlett contributed to the confusion by pulling his guns through the strung-out line of New Yorkers as he struggled to get his cannon into position (Hazlett's actions will be described later in conjunction with the events depicted on map 3-22).

As Colonel O'Rorke neared the center of Little Round Top's crest, he could not see Vincent's soldiers fighting on its southern sector. However, he heard firing in that vicinity and went in that direction—where he saw Vincent's right flank regiment, the 16th Michigan, crumbling. The Michiganders were caught in a cross fire coming from the attacking 4th and 5th Texas (map 3-23, chart 3-16). O'Rorke had the two companies nearest him on the regiment's left get ready to advance down the hill in a southwesterly direction (map 3-23), roughly in the direction of Houck's Ridge and the Devil's Den across the valley in front of him.

As Colonel O'Rorke turned to determine how the rest of his regiment (eight companies) was doing, he was shot in the neck and killed (map 3-23, top). His regiment, however, had managed to get itself into line of battle—the right-hand majority of it arrayed in a north-south line near the top of the hill. Companies A and G on the left, hard up against what remained of the 16th Michigan, charged down the slope (map 3-23, bottom), stalling the rebel advance. The rest of the 140th fired at the Texans trying to advance up Little Round Top's western face, driving these Confederates back. Meanwhile, the 48th Alabama from Law's brigade (chart 3-16) had moved in to support General Robertson's two Texas regiments (maps 3-22 and 3-23). However, Warren's and O'Rorke's quick thinking and the counterattack by the two 140th New York companies stabilized the Union position on the central and northern sectors of Little Round Top. At this time the isolated 15th Alabama, on the right wing of the rebel attack against this hill, was still struggling to beat back the 20th Maine, which it never did.

Meanwhile, Lieutenant Hazlett's Battery D, 5th U.S. Artillery, which had been ordered to Little Round Top by his commander (chart 3-17), made its way up the hill at the same time the 140th New York arrived on the scene.[78] Hazlett managed to get four of his six guns up the reverse (eastern) slope of the hill (map 3-22). That he did, and where those pieces were placed, leads to a later discussion of this hill as an artillery position.[79] Lieutenant Hazlett was soon killed by a musket shot—not long before yet *another* Union officer, General Weed, Colonel O'Rorke's brigade commander, met the same fate. General Warren had found

THE CLIMAX OF THE BATTLE 123

Weed and convinced him to send the balance of his unit onto the hill (chart 3-16, map 3-22). Although this cost General Weed his life, the Union army had finally achieved a solid defensive force on the south and west facing portions of Little Round Top. The extreme left of the Federal defense was at last on the verge of security.

Thus, when the Army of the Potomac was agonizingly gaining command of this sector of the battlefield, the Confederate assaults sputtered out as the rebels in this region began to encounter too many defenders. No longer was the Union army's left short of the mark (as it had been when its extremity was merely on Houck's Ridge); nor was there any longer an open route of advance up the Plum Run Valley (map 3-18). The secure occupation of Little Round Top assured that this fine position would be in Union hands for the remainder of the battle—forming an excellent communication point, and anchoring the army's overall position.

How about artillery on Little Round Top? After a struggle, Lieutenant Hazlett did get two-thirds of his battery onto the summit of the hill on July 2. These guns could not help defend against the attacks coming up Little Round Top's western face because it was impossible to sufficiently depress their muzzles, but they could provide longer-range cannon fire against the advancing Confederates farther to the west. That shot and shell was not of great consequence for the overall Union defense during the late stages of that Thursday afternoon. Nevertheless, the case of Hazlett's battery speaks to a more general issue: How many guns could have been placed on Little Round Top? Only two additional pieces of artillery (completing Hazlett's battery) were squeezed onto the hill for the fighting on July 3. Thus, it is unlikely that *enough rebel guns* could ever have been put into position on Little Round Top. The artillery pieces atop the hill would have been insufficient to fire barrages northward that would have been capable of blasting the Federal lines to smithereens. Thus, *if* the rebels *had* taken the hill, it might not have meant as much as we have been led to believe.

All of this is fair enough—and is a more thoughtful, research-based view than "the 20th Maine saved the Republic."[80] But if we are going to play the game of predicting the past, then we might entertain the following scenario: What if the right wing of the overall Confederate assault had achieved better command and control, as those rebels advanced eastward from Warfield Ridge? What if they had circled additional units round to the right, moving in a counterclockwise wheel to join up with Oates's regiment? A rebel force of this kind—in such a right-place, right-time scenario—could have achieved enough attacking power to crumble the Federal flank: the one regiment out there on Vincent's Spur. In turn, this would have presented the Confederate attack in that sector with a relatively vulnerable flank farther up the hill. The Union defense up there might still have been forming, not solidified by the arrival of Weed's brigade, certainly not dug in. Thus, a more massive assault on Vincent's brigade and the van of that commanded by Colonel Weed might have spelled doom for the fortification of this wonderful position. Being in command of it would have allowed the Confederates to advance up Plum Run Valley just as the Union defense to the west of that valley was giving way (as is described in the next section). General Meade might then have seen his army either in immediate peril insofar as the positions along Cemetery Ridge were concerned, or in an untenable position in the long run. "They have got us covered on the entirety of our left flank," he might have concluded. "Will continuous, if not massive, artillery fire from that hill undermine our morale such that I should not continue to try and hold this ridgeline and the

124   THE STAND OF THE U.S. ARMY AT GETTYSBURG

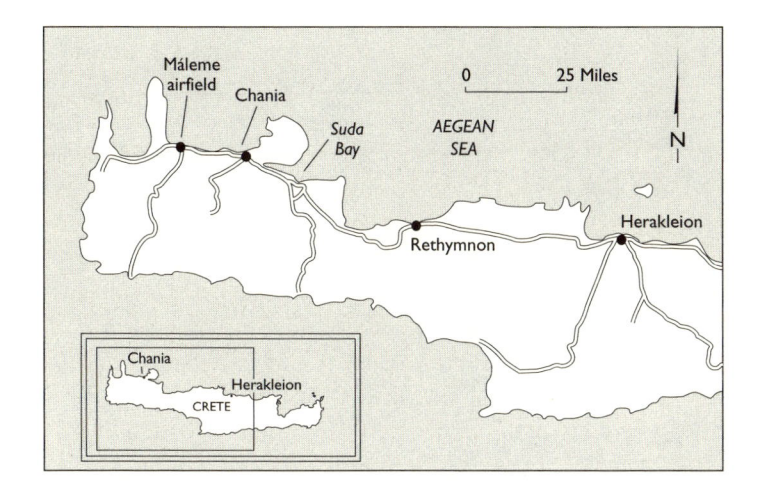

Map 3-24

West end of the island of Crete, May 20, 1941

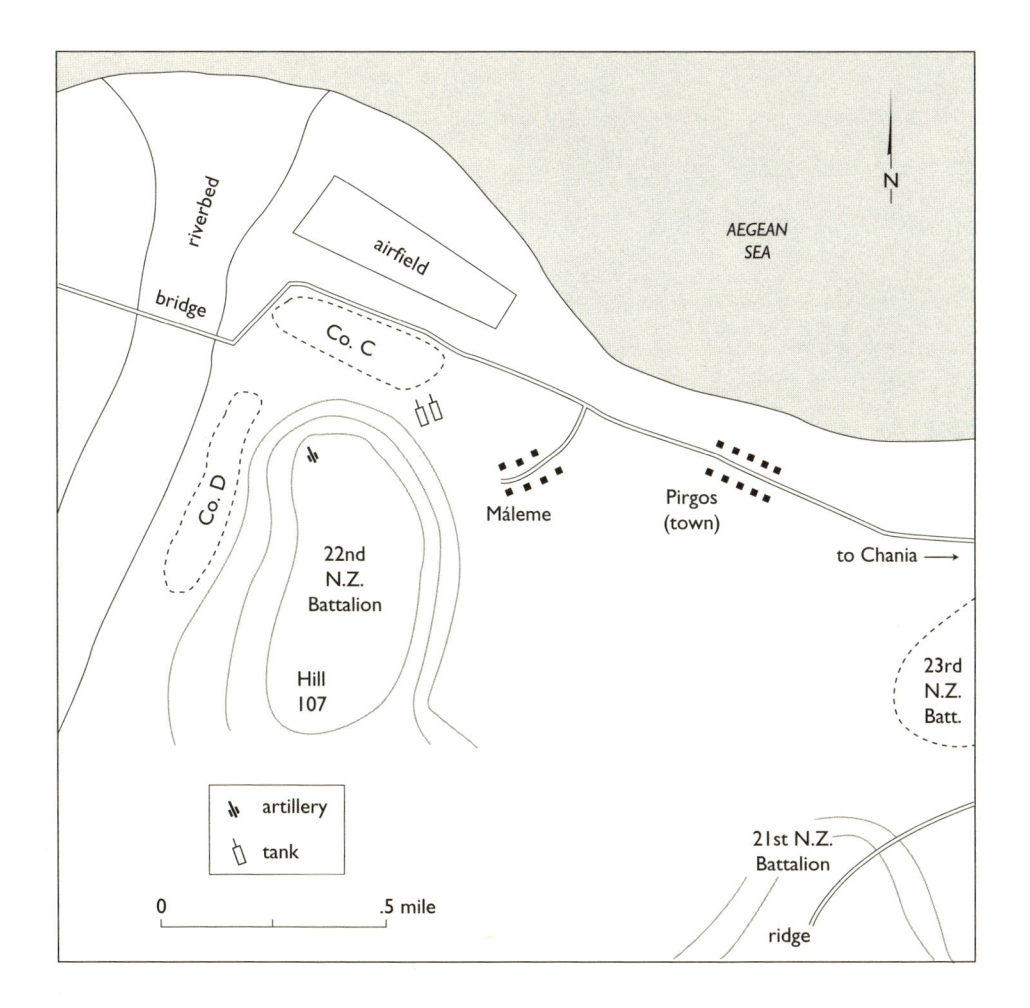

hill [Cemetery] to the north? Will the fine position held by the enemy's right be used as a springboard for an assault on my line tomorrow?" And so forth.

Those who say that Little Round Top could not have been taken, and, if so could not have become the "Hazel Grove of Gettysburg,"[81] might concede that Meade would have given up what remained of his fishhook if the "anchor of the Union left" *had* fallen.[82] Thus, he might have redeployed the Army of the Potomac away from Gettysburg, Pennsylvania—to what potentially dreadful Federal fate, later that month?

THE CLIMAX OF THE BATTLE   125

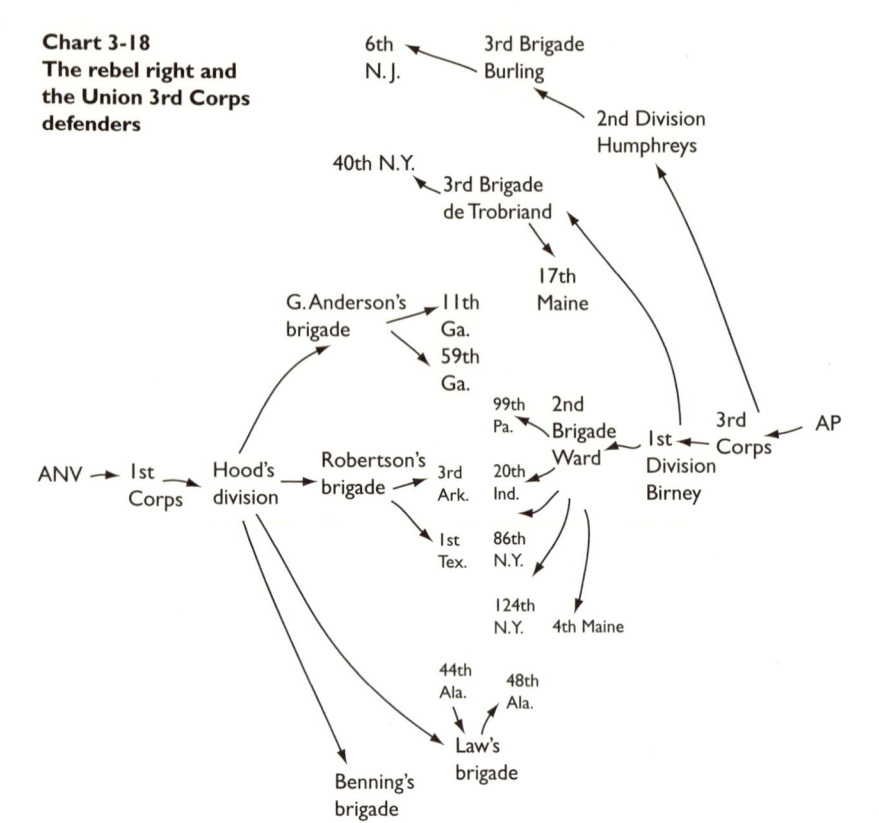

**Chart 3-18
The rebel right and the Union 3rd Corps defenders**

Predicting the past. We're mired in this. How are we going to get out of it? First, let us consider the potential utility of this kind of exercise: Except in the development of computer war games, it might seem useless, because no one can ever know what *would* have happened after a battle event that *didn't* occur. Yet reflecting on such a *what if* sometimes stimulates research. For Gettysburg, wondering about what would have happened if the rebels had captured Little Round Top led historians to scrutinize the *ground* atop the hill.[83] Their survey work led them to conclude that it was a poor place for artillery: only one battery could be placed there, arguably not enough to blast the entire Union army off its fishhook line. (A similar examination of the terrain, in this case south of the Gettysburg battlefield, led to factual knowledge about the aforementioned difficulties facing the Army of Northern Virginia had it tried to redeploy away from the battle lines of July 2.)

Second, we consider an object lesson, which I think speaks to the scenarios at Gettysburg had Little Round Top fallen to the Confederate attacks. For this, we will go forward in time to a more momentous war. What follows is a description of what Stephen E. Ambrose has called the "Little Round Top of World War II."[84] Ambrose was referring to the battle for the Elsenborn Ridge in Belgium during the December 1944 Battle of the Bulge. One of Ambrose's points was that this battle-within-the-battle was a major turning point, in contrast to events like the better known but anticlimactic stand of the 101st Airborne Division at Bastogne to the south.[85] Earlier, near another town in Belgium, one exhausted American division and another that was green accomplished a brilliant fighting withdrawal, ultimately to make a stand on the ridgeline east of Elsenborn. The German 6th Panzer Army was never able to push them off that position despite repeated assaults. This ruined the entire northern sector of the German advance, prevented them from reaching their strategic objective (the port city of Antwerp, Belgium), and doomed the Nazis' last-gasp Ardennes offensive to ultimate failure. We will encounter in subsequent sections certain fighting withdrawals and stands that occurred during the later stages of the afternoon of July 2, 1863.

Meanwhile, a closer World War II analog to Little Round Top comes from the Battle of Crete, which occurred in May 1941, when the Allies in Europe were back on their heels.[86] In particular, they had just yielded the Greek mainland to the invading Nazis. The Allies could have made a last-ditch stand in this part of the Mediterranean theater by destroying the German plan to invade Crete and complete the conquest of Greece. To do that, the Nazis dropped thousands of paratroopers onto the island on May 20. The crucial drop zone, as it turned out, was near its west end. In all three of those zones, arrayed from west to east—near Máleme, Rethymnon, and Hērákleion (map 3-24, top)—the Germans were suffering horrendous casualties at the hands of the Commonwealth and Cretan defenders and making no headway. In the western zone, west of the city of Chania

126 THE STAND OF THE U.S. ARMY AT GETTYSBURG

near the little town of Máleme, the Germans were attempting to seize a crucial piece of real estate: an airstrip near the northern shore of the island (map 3-24, bottom). Once it was in their possession, they planned to land airborne troop-transports to effect a crucial reinforcement of the viciously beleaguered paratroopers. But the airfield was commanded by a *hill* held by Commonwealth infantrymen on the left of the Allied line. This was Hill 107, which was manned by Lt. Col. Leslie W. Andrews's 22nd New Zealand Battalion. Andrews was an experienced soldier who had fought in World War I. His soldiers were holding the hill against German assaults up its northern face, and the New Zealanders' heavy small-arms fire was making it impossible for any airplane to land on the Máleme airstrip. In addition, Colonel Andrews had sent two companies down the hill to his left and front, in part to guard the battalion's left flank (map 3-24). Those soldiers were doing their job. However, the bulk of Andrews's force was under severe duress. They were essentially isolated out there on Hill 107, at the *extreme left of the entire army*. Andrews thought that the 22nd's casualties amounted to half the battalion's strength by the evening of the first day of the battle. Furthermore, he believed that his two left-flank companies had been cut off, possibly annihilated. (Had Col. Joshua L. Chamberlain thought as much about his Company B, seventy-eight years earlier?) Andrews begged for reinforcements. These could have come from eastward of Hill 107, where the main body of the Allied force on this part of the island was arrayed along the northern shore (off to the right of map 3-24), anticipating a German amphibious assault. No such invasion came, and no reinforcements came to the 22nd during the early part of that night.

Not long afterward, Colonel Andrews lost his nerve and *pulled the 22nd New Zealand Battalion off of Hill 107*. He was as psychologically defeated as Maj. Gen. Joseph Hooker had been at Chancellorsville. Even though he encountered a reinforcing Commonwealth company as he withdrew east of the hill, Colonel Andrews kept retreating. When the Germans awakened the next morning and resumed their attacks on Hill 107 they discovered it was empty of defenders. The Nazis seized it, allowing their reinforcing air transports to land at Máleme. This "handed the Germans the key to the battle."[87] With their toehold in this western sector of the battle zone having become a foothold, the Germans were ultimately able to *roll up the Allied line from left to right*, inflicting another horrendous defeat upon the Allies, who were reeling at this stage of the Second World War.

Now comes the lesson: *One small hill fell*. It *did* go over to the control of the attacking force—it was not a question of "What if it had fallen?" The capture of Hill 107 *made all the difference* in the Battle of Crete. "Great events sometimes turn on comparatively small affairs." Those words are especially apt, for they come from William Oates and are about the fighting that occurred on that "hidden corner of the battlefield" at Little Round Top on July 2, 1863.[88]

One final point: When you stand at the summit of Hill 107 and look north, you notice how eerily similar the view is to what you see when looking west from the summit of Little Round Top.

The South-to-North Confederate Attack Continues with a Short Right Hook, and the Federals Counterattack from Cemetery Ridge into the Wheatfield

Now let us return to Gettysburg and turn our attention to what used to be the Army of the Potomac's extreme left, before those two 5th Corps brigades moved onto Little Round Top.

Map 3-25
Summary of Confederate units striking Ward's Union brigade, and Federal countermeasures

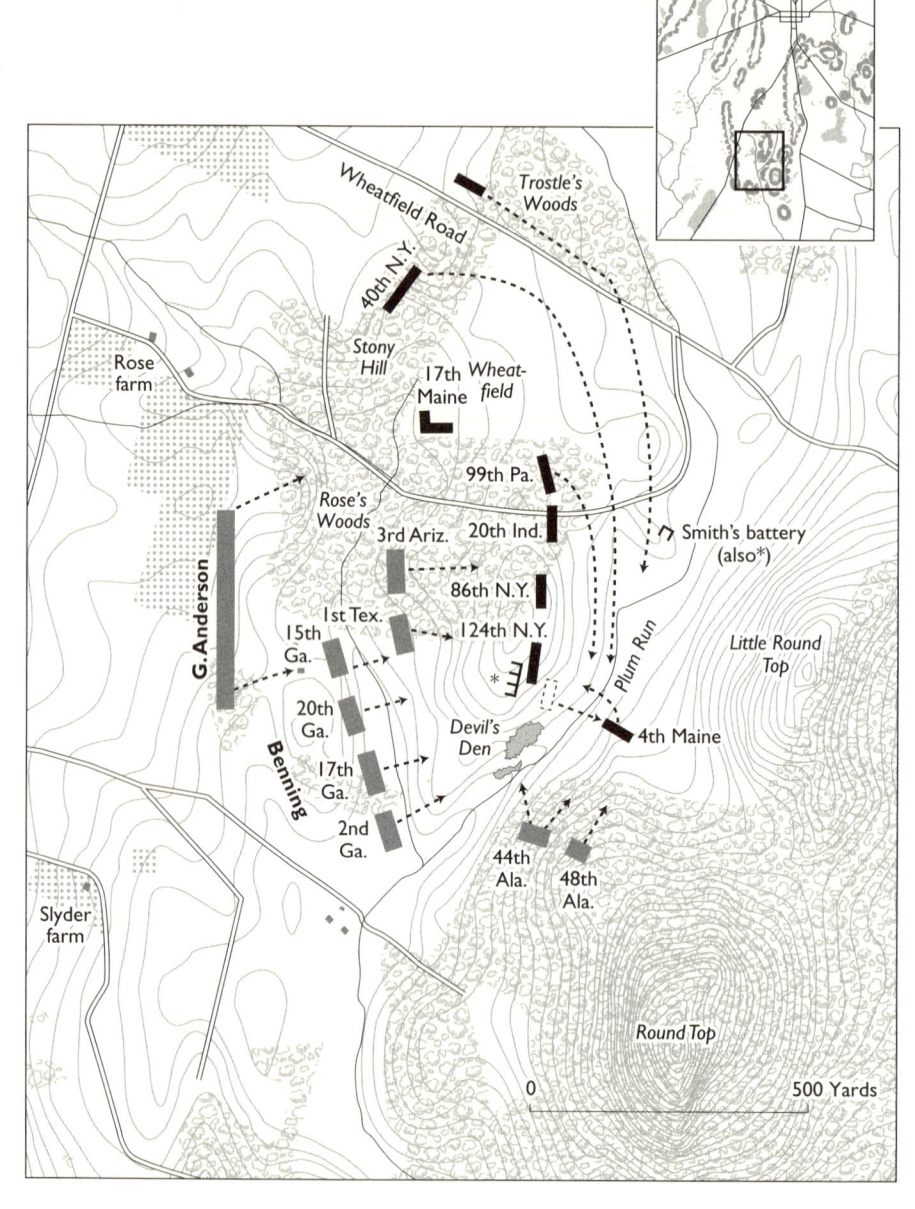

Recall that Ward's brigade (in Birney's 3rd Corps division) was hit before the battle for Little Round Top commenced (map 3-14). Texans and Arkansans from Robertson's brigade (chart 3-18) had attacked Ward's position, moving eastward through the Rose Woods toward the Devil's Den and Houck's Ridge to its north (map 3-25). Alabamians (chart 3-18) had come up underneath Ward's position from the south (maps 3-14 and 3-25). These elements of Law's brigade (another split-up unit) right-hooked counterclockwise toward Ward's left and Smith's New York battery (map 3-14, chart 3-10). They were threatening to get into the rear of Ward's line by advancing up Plum Run Valley between Houck's Ridge and Little Round Top. This would have been an especially dangerous move had Little Round Top not been occupied by the Federal defenders described in the previous section.

128   THE STAND OF THE U.S. ARMY AT GETTYSBURG

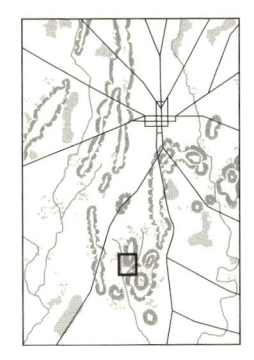

Map 3-26

Continuation of the attacks on Ward's line, and its resurgence

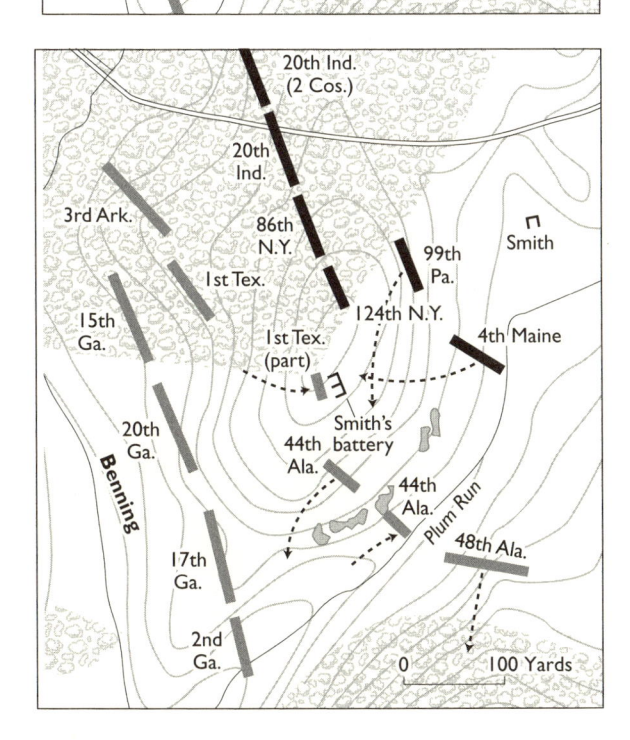

A Unionist among students of the war and of this battle (sparse as their numbers may be) once said to me, "Let's hear it for the Third Corps"—an oddly chosen remark, it would seem, given Sickles's blunder and that his corps was subsequently pushed away from its outlying defensive positions.[89] This is oversimplified, however, because the left wing of the Union 3rd Corps made a stalwart defense for well over an hour of time. Elements of General Birney's division counterattacked while other regiments were redeployed in emergency maneuvers, which was especially important in terms of *blocking Plum Run Valley* (maps 3-26 and 3-27). I say again: If that had not been done, the right wing of the rebel attack would have been in the rear of the Army of the Potomac.

THE CLIMAX OF THE BATTLE   129

Map 3-27
Benning joins the attack against Ward, who is reinforced by other Federal 3rd Corps units

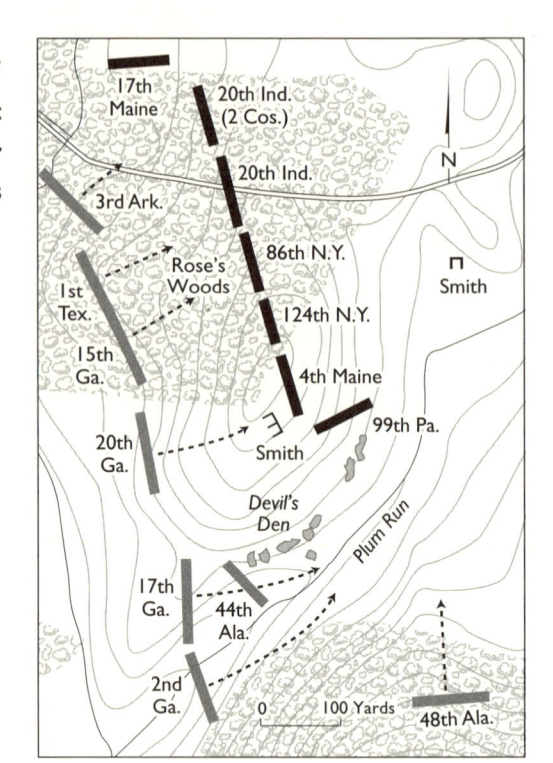

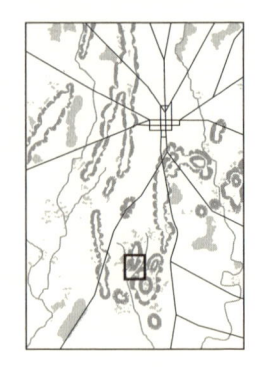

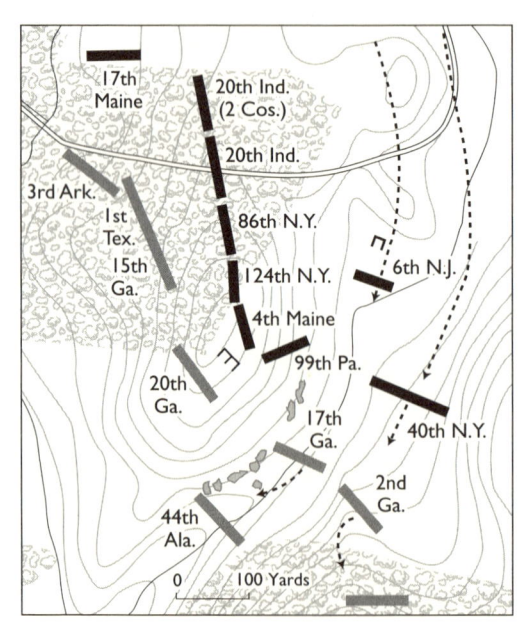

So, we pick up the remainder of the story of Devil's Den and Houck's Ridge. When we left it two sections before, General Ward's positions were being attacked from the west and south (maps 3-14 and 3-25). The Southerners pushed the defenders off the left end of their line where most of Smith's guns stood (map 3-26, top). But Ward's men retook the crest as remnants of the 124th New York, the 99th Pennsylvania, and the 4th Maine counterattacked from the north and east (map 3-26, bottom). Now, the 4th Maine was no longer in a blocking position in the Plum Run Valley, so the 48th Alabama began to advance northward into the gorge (map 3-27, top). Captain Smith had presciently placed two of the cannon from his 4th New York Light Battery in a rearward position. Southward fire from these guns stalled the Alabamians' advance (map 3-27, top).

130 THE STAND OF THE U.S. ARMY AT GETTYSBURG

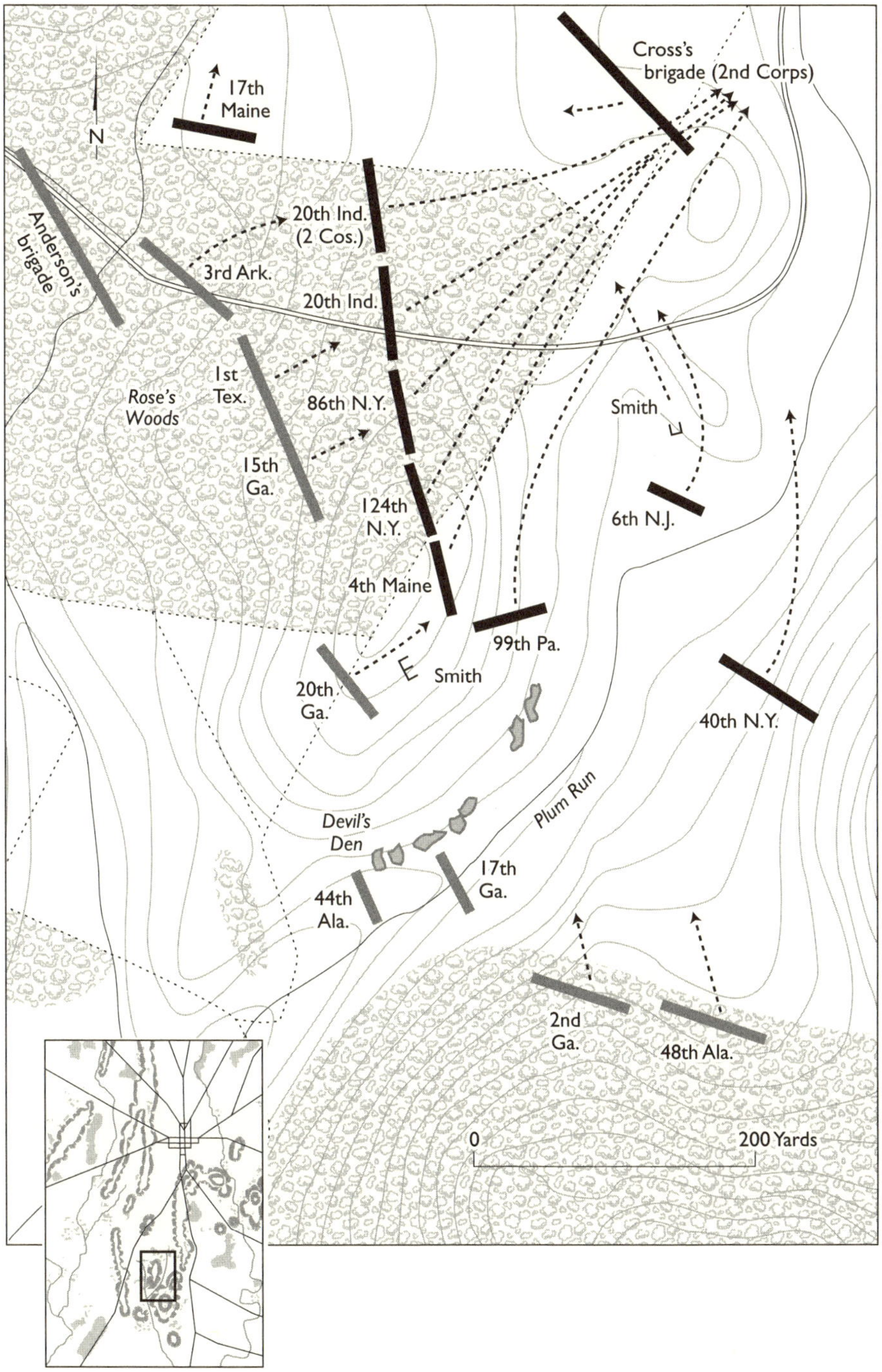

Map 3-28
Ward's retreat

Nevertheless, the beginning of the end was near for Ward's defenders: A brigade of Georgians under Brig. Gen. Henry Benning (chart 3-18) had arrived (map 3-26, bottom) after following the first wave of the assault force (map 3-12). Benning was supposed to follow Law's Alabama brigade but wound up coming in behind Robertson's Texans and Arkansans (that is, Robertson's left wing; recall that his right had veered off toward Little Round Top, as shown in maps 3-13 and 3-17).

Benning joined the rebel attack in this sector, advancing toward Ward's left from the west and south (map 3-27, top). Elements of three Confederate brigades now assailed Ward's positions. As General Benning's right tried to push its way up Plum Run Valley, the 99th Pennsylvania and other of Ward's men on the crest of

THE CLIMAX OF THE BATTLE 131

Map 3-29
The fighting near the Wheatfield, in the Rose Woods, and on the Stony Hill

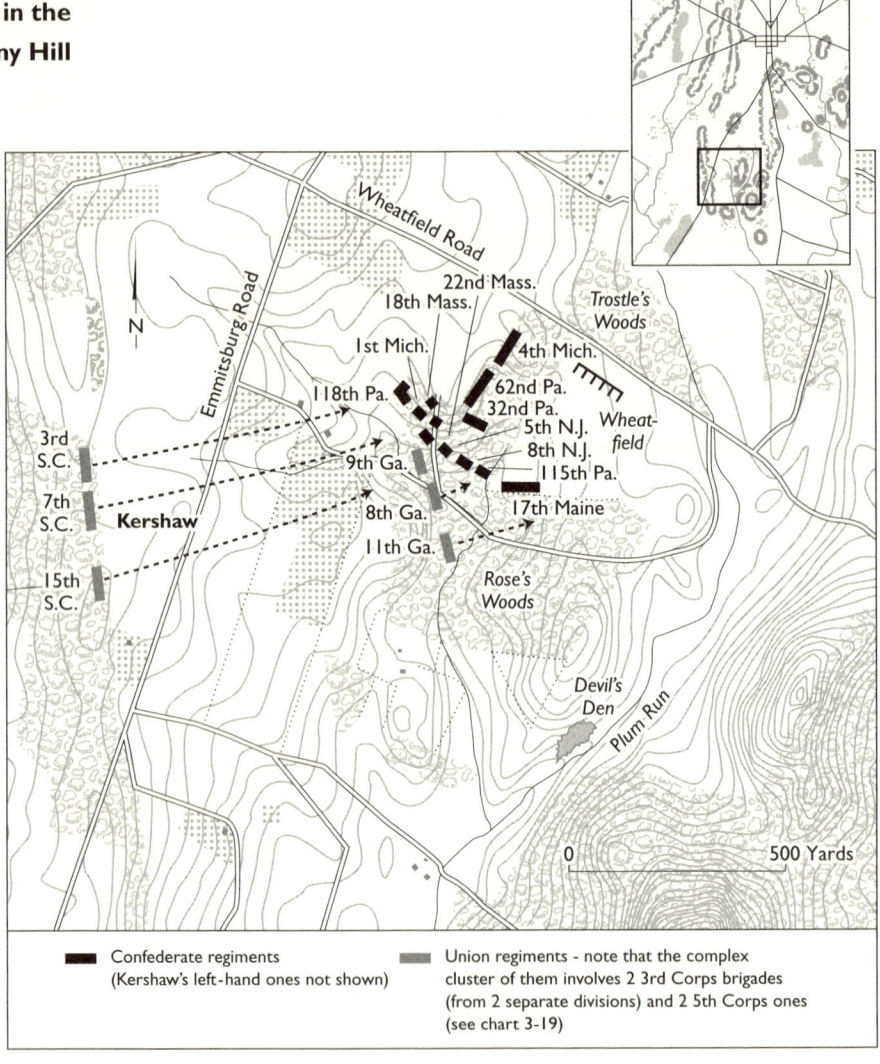

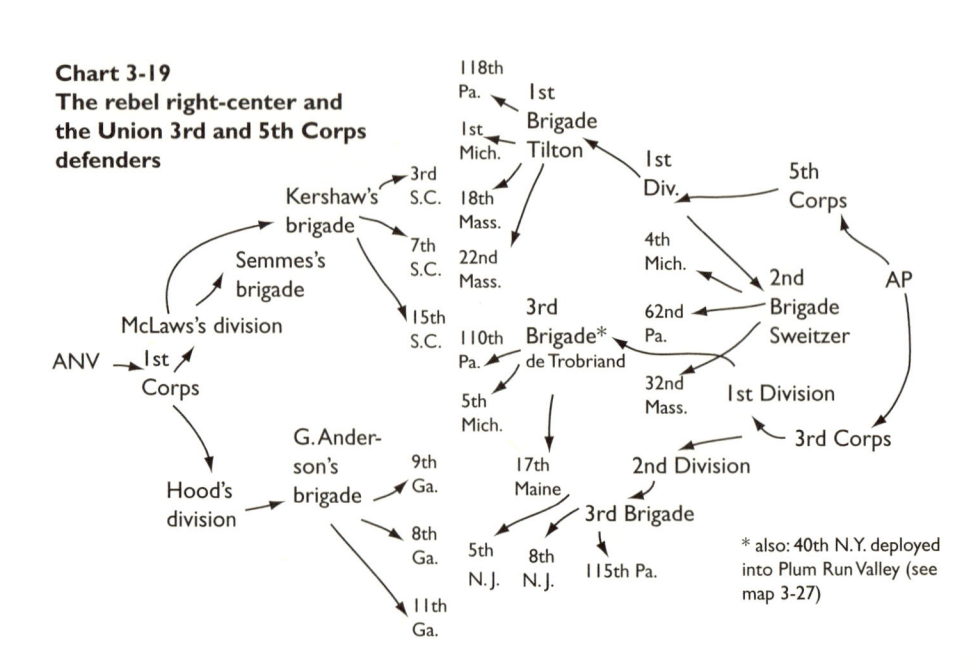

Confederate regiments (Kershaw's left-hand ones not shown)

Union regiments - note that the complex cluster of them involves 2 3rd Corps brigades (from 2 separate divisions) and 2 5th Corps ones (see chart 3-19)

Chart 3-19
The rebel right-center and the Union 3rd and 5th Corps defenders

* also: 40th N.Y. deployed into Plum Run Valley (see map 3-27)

132   THE STAND OF THE U.S. ARMY AT GETTYSBURG

the ridge near the left of the Federal line poured a murderous fire down on the Georgians. But Ward's situation was deteriorating, given that he was outnumbered in this area of the field and being attacked from two directions, so he called for reinforcements. The 6th New Jersey and the 40th New York (chart 3-18) had been posted near the Wheatfield during the fighting to this point.[90] These two regiments circled clockwise (map 3-25) and rapidly marched south, forming yet another blocking force in the Plum Run gorge (map 3-27, bottom).

Brigadier General Hobart Ward now had elements of seven Union regiments defending the area near the Devil's Den and the south end of Houck's Ridge. However, he sensed that the odds were too great against him. In fact, *a further* rebel unit, Brig. Gen. George T. Anderson's Georgia brigade, had arrived on the scene (maps 3-25 and 3-28). Anderson moved in to support Robertson's left. A final Confederate assault advanced toward Houck's Ridge from the west and south (map 3-28)[92] as additional Union reinforcements were beginning to arrive on this part of the battlefield.[93] But these Federal troops were mostly in the Rose Woods to the north and west of Ward's imperiled positions and thus never relieved Ward. As Confederate infantrymen from the 2nd and 17th Georgia (Benning's brigade) and the 44th Alabama (Law's) regiments took the crest, General Ward and his men were being driven from this sector of the field (map 3-28). The Georgians and Alabamians fired on Ward's withdrawing units as they exited the scene to the north and east; the 6th New Jersey and 40th New York held on long enough to help cover Ward's retreat, but they too fell back.

The Confederates were now in control of the Devil's Den area. Three of Smith's artillery pieces had been captured. Ward left eight hundred of his twenty-two hundred men as casualties in the Den, on the ridge, and in Plum Run Valley. The remainder of his retreating 3rd Corps troops ended up on south Cemetery Ridge, north of Little Round Top. They had fought well and in the end were not really routed. The rebel attackers, too, had fought furiously in this sector of the battlefield. However, the attackers were frequently out of control, as the break-up of some of the rebel brigades and fusion of certain regiments suggests. This problem may have prevented the Confederates from more rapidly dislodging General Ward's defenders. And though the rebels now occupied what had been the exposed southern flank of the Army of the Potomac's line, there was a *new* Union left five hundred yards to the east on Little Round Top.

The next Confederate objective was to dislodge de Trobriand's brigade from the areas of the Wheatfield, the Rose Woods, and the Stony Hill (map 3-29). This French-born Union officer waged a hard-fought battle, in contrast to the "many accounts of Gettysburg [which] make the presumption that the men in Sickles' exposed salient fell back without much of a fight."[93] By now, additional 5th Corps units (which had followed Vincent's and Weed's brigades but had not diverted to Little Round Top) manned the Stony Hill (chart 3-18). Colonel de Trobriand needed such reinforcements, because of his regiments that had been redeployed to buttress Ward's position to the southeast (map 3-25). Later, as the 5th Corps troops moved in from the east, many

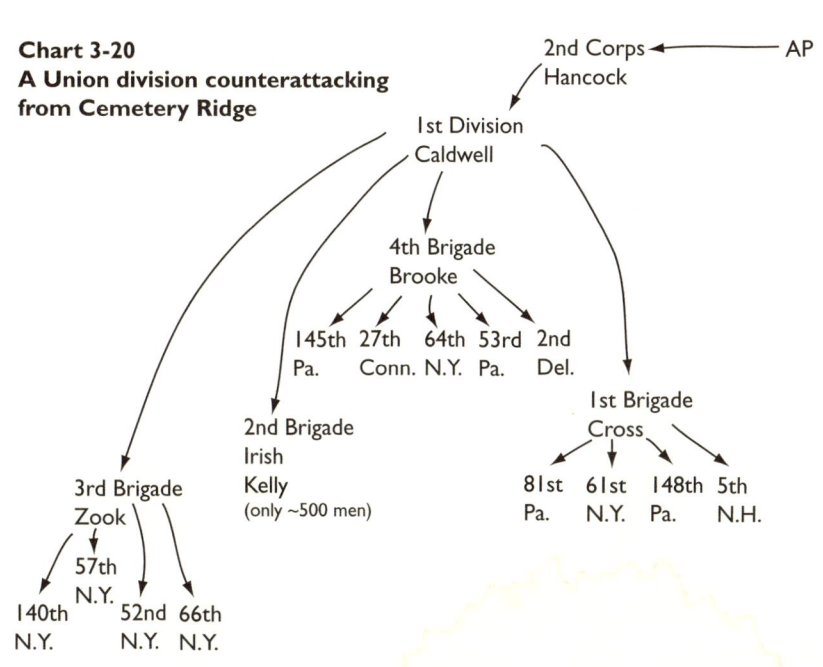

Chart 3-20
A Union division counterattacking from Cemetery Ridge

2nd Corps ← AP
Hancock
↓
1st Division
Caldwell
↓
4th Brigade
Brooke
↓
145th Pa. 27th Conn. 64th N.Y. 53rd Pa. 2nd Del.

2nd Brigade
Irish
Kelly
(only ~500 men)

3rd Brigade
Zook
↓
140th N.Y. 57th N.Y. 52nd N.Y. 66th N.Y.

1st Brigade
Cross
↓
81st Pa. 61st N.Y. 148th Pa. 5th N.H.

THE CLIMAX OF THE BATTLE   133

**Map 3-30
Caldwell's division poised to attack**

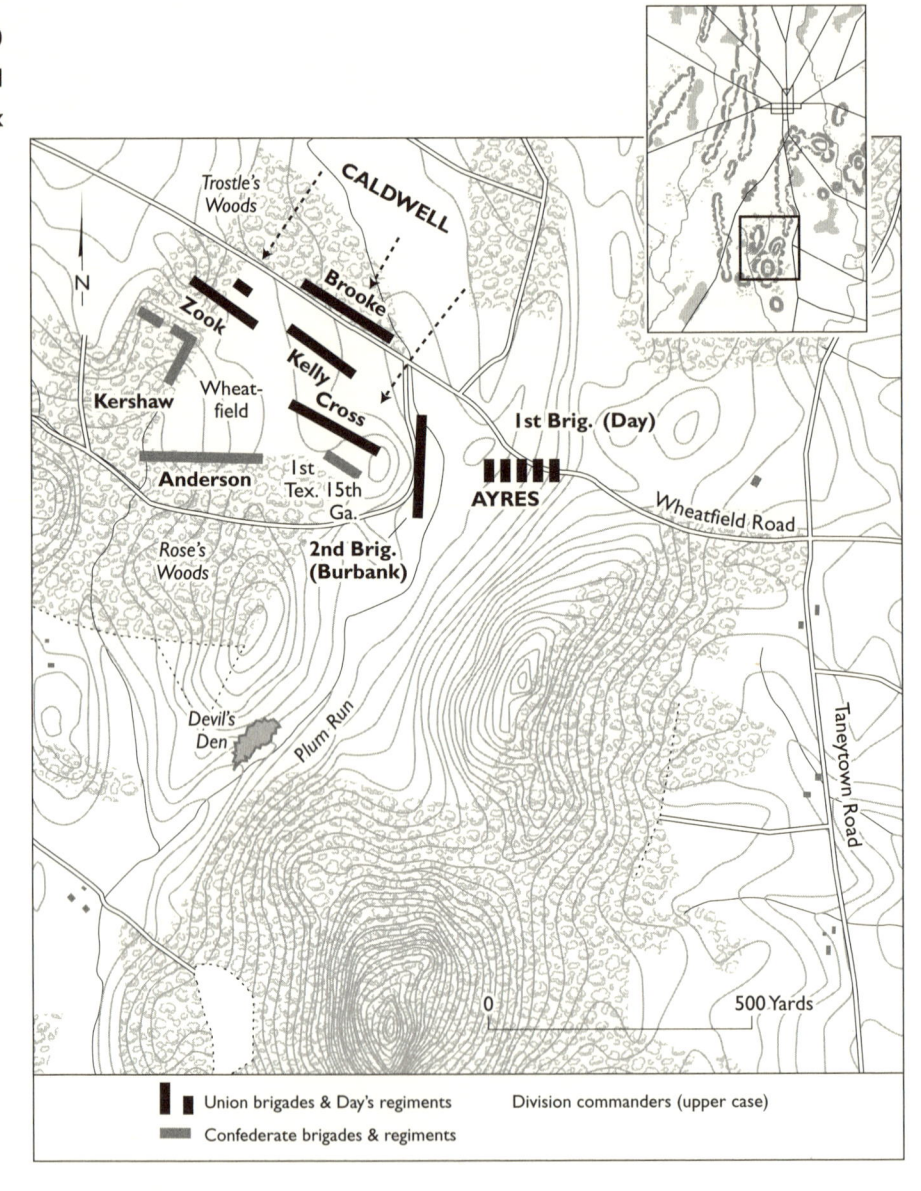

of de Trobriand's infantrymen occupied the stone wall between the Rose Woods and the southern edge of the Wheatfield (map 3-29). General Anderson's brigade (chart 3-19) attacked the Union line behind the wall. George Anderson's Georgians soon were joined on their left by the brigades led by Brig. Gens. Joseph Kershaw and Paul Jones Semmes (chart 3-19). These units were members of Maj. Gen. Lafayette McLaws's division, which had gone in at approximately 5:30 P.M.—more than an hour after Hood's division on the right had initiated the overall rebel attack. As in the case of Hood's assaults, the first phase of McLaws's was in part straight in (west-east in the direction of the Wheatfield) and in part a right hook—albeit a short-punching one owing to the relative proximity of Kershaw's and Semmes's takeoff positions to the central sector of Sickles's left, and to the positions of Federal 5th Corps units that had arrived in this area (map 3-29).

The new Union defenders on the scene feared they would be flanked on their right, as these 5th Corps troops were facing roughly south. Thus they fell back to the north of the Wheatfield Road. This retreat exposed the 3rd Corps line south

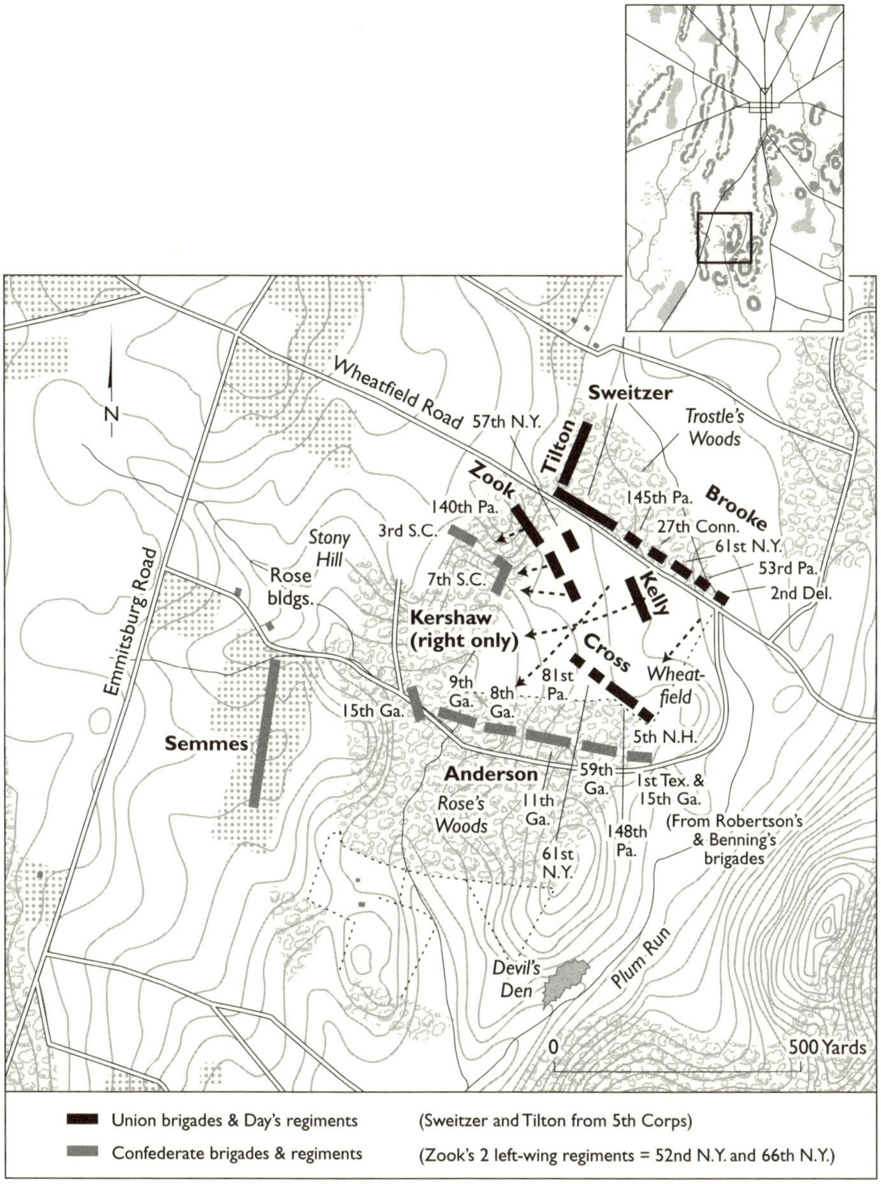

Map 3-31
Caldwell attacks through the Wheatfield

of the Wheatfield to a flank attack, and these Federal units withdrew a short distance as well (map 3-29). The Confederates advanced to the edge of the Wheatfield, which eventually fell entirely under their control—but not without a fight against *additional* components of the active Union defense.

Recall that the left of the 2nd Corps on Cemetery Ridge was exposed thanks to Sickles's advance. Not long after his 3rd Corps was advanced upon, General Meade ordered the commander of the leftmost 2nd Corps division—Brig. Gen. John C. Caldwell (chart 3-20)—to bolster the 5th Corps reinforcing units. Before Caldwell's units advanced, there was a quaint occurrence: The smallest unit in his division—the famed Irish brigade (chart 3-20), whittled down to five hundred men after two years of fighting—knelt on the field at Cemetery Ridge. They did this to receive a blessing from the priest attached to them, Father William Corby.[94]

We now meet Caldwell's division during its advance to the southwest. These 2nd Corps brigades approached the northern edge of the Wheatfield and the area to its east, as the Confederates were driving the aforementioned 5th Corps de-

THE CLIMAX OF THE BATTLE   135

Map 3-32

Kershaw attacks the east of the Peach Orchard

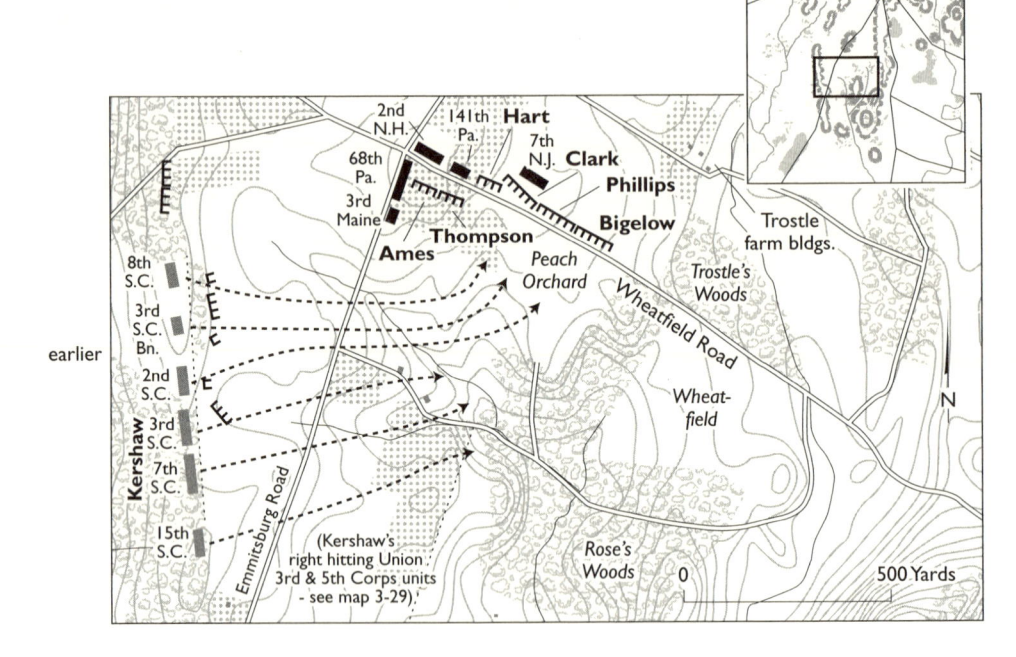

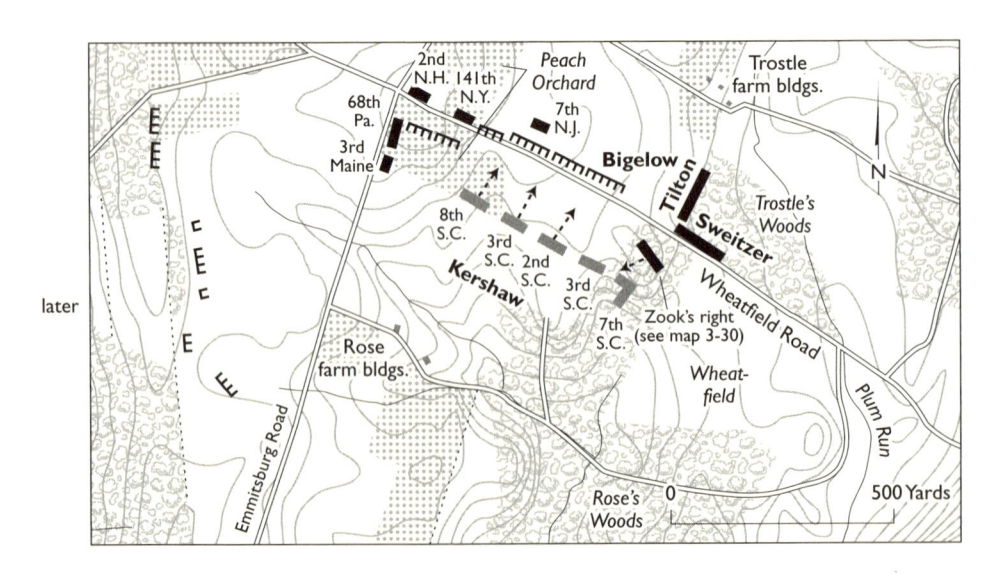

fenders from their positions (map 3-29). Caldwell's brigades formed along the Wheatfield Road (map 3-30). They charged through the Wheatfield (map 3-31), driving the Confederates back. However, Caldwell's brigades counterattacked into this sector with less than full power, the individual units going in piecemeal just as the Confederates had on the day before. Yet General Caldwell did at least get all his brigades into the action.[95] They paid a heavy price including the loss of two of Caldwell's brigade commanders who were killed or mortally wounded.[96]

Recall that the right wing of Kershaw's brigade of McLaws's division was attacking the Stony Hill, west of the Peach Orchard (map 3-29). As this occurred, Kershaw's left wing *wheeled left* and punched—once more as would a boxer's right

136   THE STAND OF THE U.S. ARMY AT GETTYSBURG

Chart 3-21
The rebel right-center and Federal 5th Corps reinforcements

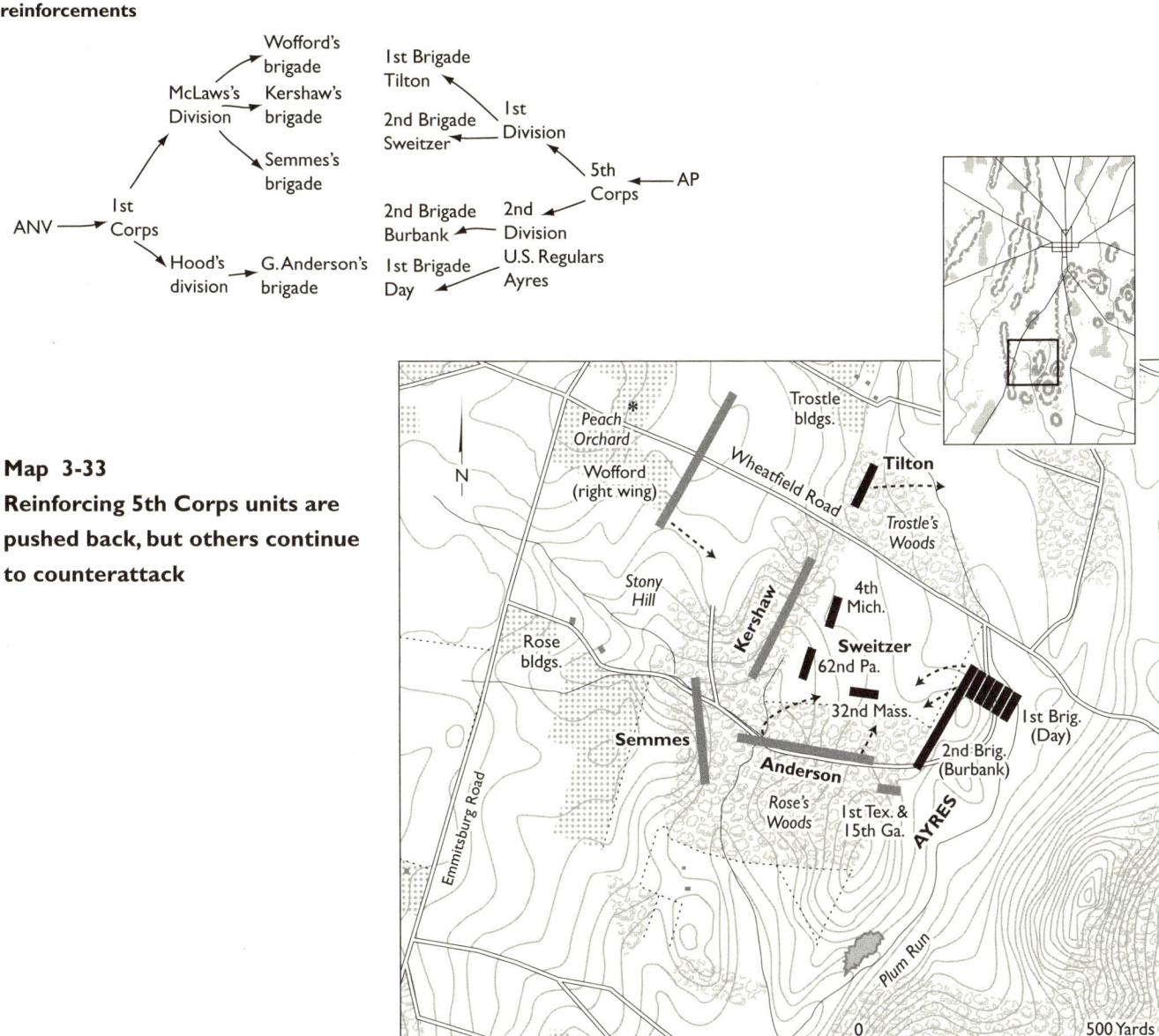

Map 3-33
Reinforcing 5th Corps units are pushed back, but others continue to counterattack

AYRES: division commander   * Federal artillery: gone from the Wheatfield Road

hook—into the infantry gap between the Wheatfield and the Peach Orchard (map 3-32). Thirty cannon from the Federal 3rd Corps and the army's Artillery Reserve were filling this gap as best they could (chart 3-6, map 3-32). These guns blasted away at Kershaw. His men did not get in among the batteries, in part because some of the South Carolinians veered off to the right toward the Wheatfield. This allowed Federal cannon fire to rake Kershaw's left flank. So this sector of the defense along the Wheatfield Road was safe for the moment.

Moreover, the right wing of Kershaw's brigade was soon to be engaged by Caldwell's reinforcing attack. But these four Union brigades achieved only ephemeral success, as the repulsed Confederates (Anderson and Kershaw) re-

THE CLIMAX OF THE BATTLE   137

Chart 3-22
Two of McLaws's brigades against the Union 3rd Corps's right

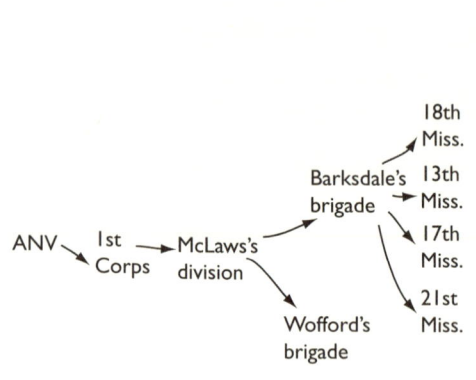

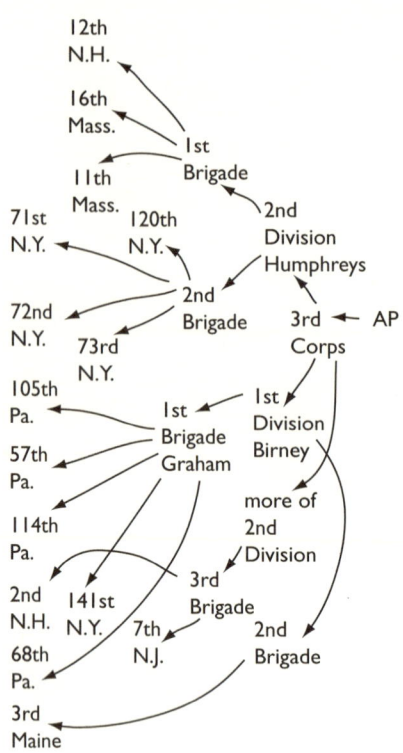

formed and counterattacked after being reinforced by Semmes and by McLaws's brigade of Georgians commanded by Brig. Gen. William T. Wofford (chart 3-21). These rebels helped break the Union salient at the Peach Orchard (as described in the next section) and also swept down the Wheatfield Road on Kershaw's left (map 3-33).[97] Wofford's right-center drove a 5th Corps unit from Trostle's Woods, which abuts the north edge of the Road (map 3-33).

General Caldwell's division fell back in some disorder. The Federal defense gained a bit of time with the move of Col. Jacob B. Sweitzer's 5th Corps brigade from the east into the Wheatfield (chart 3-19). Even though the Union positions in this sector would ultimately crumble, yet another element of the 5th Corps—two Regular Army brigades from Brig. Gen. Romeyn B. Ayres's division (chart 3-21)—added to the defense in this area, approaching the Wheatfield from the east as Caldwell attacked (maps 3-30 and 3-33). Ayres's troops paused at the edge of the Wheatfield when they saw the retreat of Caldwell's division. These Regulars had the task of delaying the Confederate attacks until the retreating 3rd, 5th, and then 2nd Corps troops could fall back to defensive positions on south Cemetery Ridge. General Ayres's soldiers did their job. However, when hit on their left by Kershaw and on their right by Anderson and Wofford's right, Ayres's two brigades were forced to withdraw across Plum Run. They rallied north of Little Round Top, having suffered eight hundred casualties.

Now these attacking Confederates were approaching that stream near the base of the northern half of Little Round Top and on the southern end of Cemetery Ridge. The rebels within the four advancing brigades (including Semmes's) may not have known it, but their attacks were finally running out of steam.

At this point it seems as if the battlefield is in chaos. Therefore, to summarize: (1) The extreme Confederate right and the brigades just to its left attacked the leftmost two-thirds of Sickles's advanced line. (2) Those Federal 3rd Corps units defended, maneuvered, defended again—and were pushed back, notwithstanding (3) the 5th Corps reinforcements arriving on the 3rd Corps's left after advancing from behind the lines on the Baltimore Pike, and (4) the 2nd Corps units coming down from Cemetery Ridge, where they had been near the center of the Union line. (5) This patchwork quilt of counterattacking units was itself counterattacked by the rebels and pushed back to the east.

The South-to-North Attack Continues as a Federal Salient in the Peach Orchard Is Broken, Leading to Fighting Withdrawals Large and Small

The battle on the Confederate right continued to move up the Union line—now proceeding from the Wheatfield and the Stony Hill toward the Peach Orchard. Recall that the right wing of Kershaw's brigade was attacking that hill west

Map 3-34

Barksdale crashes into the Peach Orchard salient

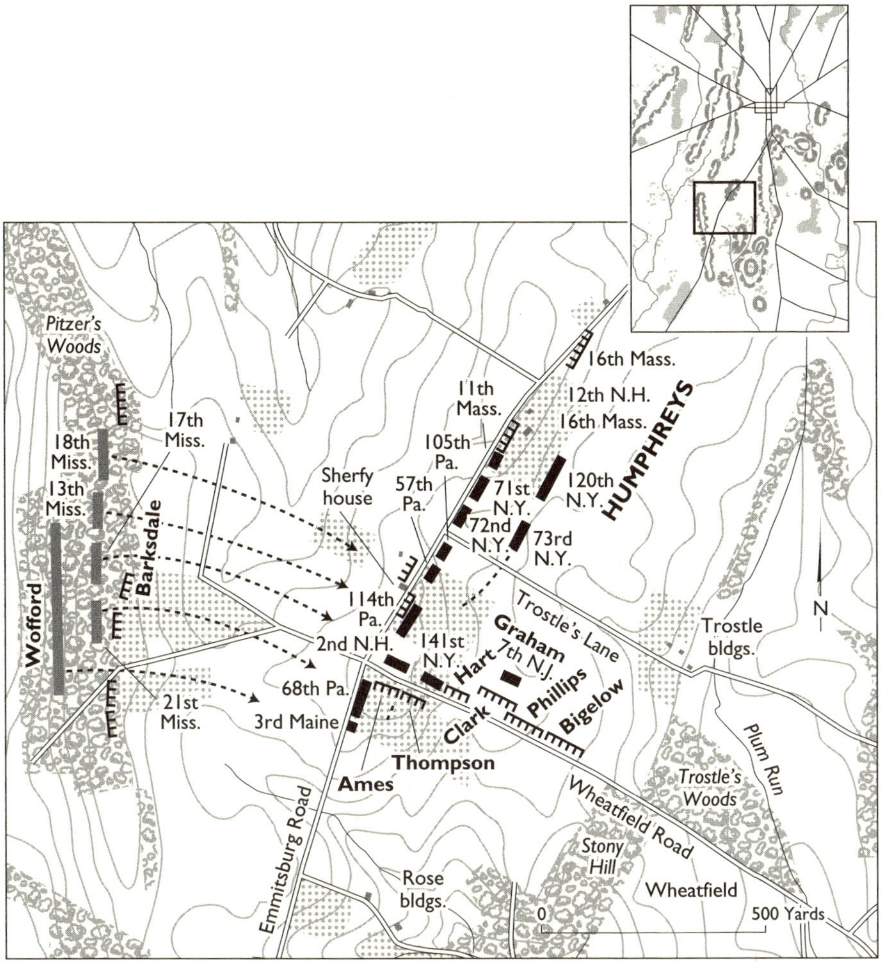

of the Peach Orchard (map 3-29), and his left wing had right-hooked toward the Federal artillery along the Wheatfield Road (map 3-32). But the impending threat to the Union force in this vicinity was just to the west and north, in the Peach Orchard, which was manned in the main by the 1st Brigade, 1st Division, under Brig. Gen. Charles K. Graham, as diagrammed in chart 3-22. Close scrutiny of that chart will reveal the *intermingling* of *other* 3rd Corps units (from more than one division, even). This suggests that the *Federals* in the Peach Orchard had a *similar command-and-control problem* to that faced by the Southerners halfway into their advances toward the Union left.

The regiments of Northerners in the Peach Orchard were not in a very strong position (map 3-34), and no one could have come to their aid during the earlier phases of the battle because the Federal forces were thoroughly preoccupied with the defense of their left on Houck's Ridge, Little Round Top, and the Wheatfield.

Thus, one of the more significant components of the Confederate assault on the Union left occurred when, at about 6 P.M., Brig. Gen. William Barksdale's Confederate brigade charged the Peach Orchard (map 3-34). Barksdale's Mississippians were in turn followed by parts of Wofford's brigade (chart 3-22).[98] The brunt of the attack upon the Federal salient struck Graham's right just north of the Peach Orchard, along the Emmitsburg Road (map 3-34). The defensive line was broken. While Barksdale's right and Wofford's men pushed back Graham's defenders from either side of the Wheatfield Road (where it abuts the northern edge of the Peach Orchard), the left-hand Mississippi regiments turned left and

THE CLIMAX OF THE BATTLE   139

Map 3-35
The fighting withdrawal and stand of the 9th Mass. Light

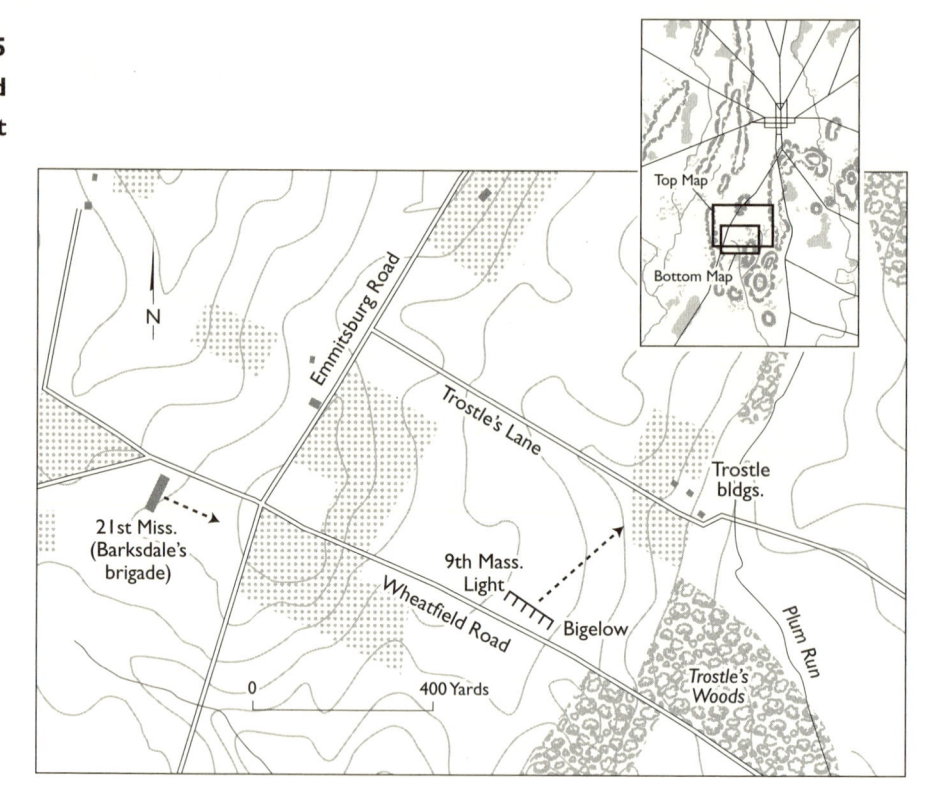

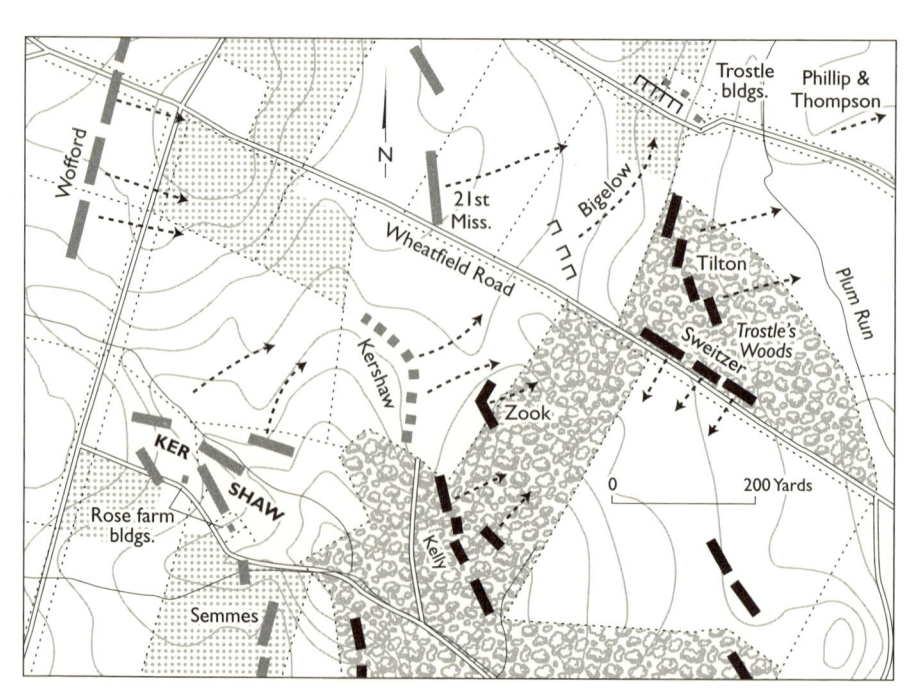

began to assail the Union troops arrayed farther up the Emmitsburg Road (map 3-36). These were the men of Maj. Gen. Andrew Humphreys's 2nd Division, 3rd Corps.

Meanwhile, General Graham's troops were under enormous pressure and did not make a very good fight of it. Some of Graham's men who had turned south to fire into Kershaw's attackers now had to change front to meet the Mississippians. The stand those Federals might have made was ruined by the advance of Wofford's

140 THE STAND OF THE U.S. ARMY AT GETTYSBURG

Georgians (map 3-34), coming toward the Peach Orchard defenders' left and threatening to cut them off. Graham's regiments withdrew in disorder to the east, moving toward the Trostle farm buildings and Cemetery Ridge beyond. General Sickles's headquarters was near the Trostle barn (map 3-35). At the height of this action, a cannonball nearly tore off the bottom part of his right leg. Sickles survived, but he was out of the Battle of Gettysburg and the war.

The shot that struck Sickles was fired from the high ground in the vicinity of the Peach Orchard. After Graham's brigade was pushed back, losing half of its approximately fifteen hundred men, the Confederate gunners turned the Peach Orchard at Gettysburg into another Hazel Grove.[99]

The Union artillery near the Peach Orchard was now retreating as well. Graham's defeat made the positions of the guns along the Wheatfield Road untenable. Some of these batteries had no time to hook up the horses to their pieces (to "limber up"), so the soldiers had to haul the guns away using thick ropes. The withdrawal of Capt. John Bigelow's 9th Massachusetts Light Battery (chart 3-23) is memorable in this regard: As his six Napoleons "retired by prolonge" (pulling the ropes by hand), they stopped and fired at the advancing rebels pressing them from their front and right. Bigelow's men managed to pull their guns some 430 yards northward, reaching the lane near the Trostle house (map 3-35). The battery was preparing to limber up and leave, but the commander of the Union artillery in this sector, Lt. Col. Freeman McGilvery, ordered Bigelow to make a stand amidst the Trostle farm buildings. McGilvery needed to buy time to get the rest of the guns away and set them up along a last-ditch line near Cemetery Ridge. The 9th Massachusetts Light bought them crucial minutes, in particular by stalling Kershaw's brigade (map 3-35, bottom). The artillerymen around the Trostle buildings took horrendous casualties before being overwhelmed by Barksdale's 21st Mississippi (chart 3-23). The Mississippians captured four of Bigelow's Napoleons as they tried to escape through the gate of a fence surrounding the buildings (map 3-35, bottom).

The attack of the right-hand elements of this Mississippi brigade was losing some of its power as it proceeded east toward Cemetery Ridge. The attack, whose real goal was to get into the Federals' main line, had been delayed by the advanced defensive position in the 3rd Corps salient. The attackers also lost their leader when General Barksdale was mortally wounded. His soldiers and the other Southerners all over the place never got to Cemetery Ridge in this relatively southern sector. One move that helped delay the attackers was *the Plum Run line,* consisting of artillery pieces placed along the western slope of the ridge east of the Trostle buildings by Colonel McGilvery.[100] Even so, some of the Union guns on the Plum Run line were overrun, and others suffered heavily from counter-battery fire coming in from the rebel artillery moving into the Peach Orchard (map 3-37).

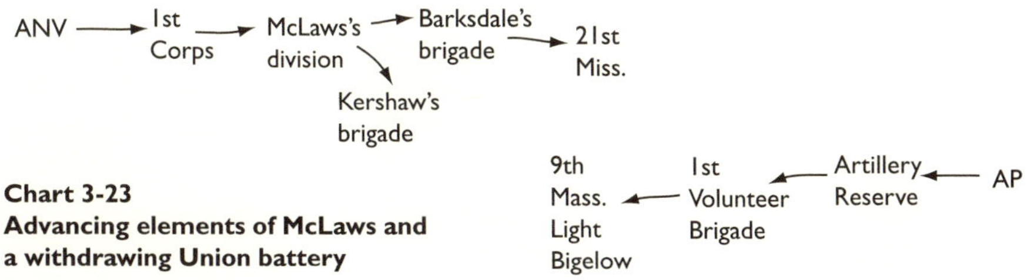

Chart 3-23
Advancing elements of McLaws and a withdrawing Union battery

ANV → 1st Corps → McLaws's division → Barksdale's brigade → 21st Miss.
McLaws's division → Kershaw's brigade

9th Mass. Light Bigelow ← 1st Volunteer Brigade ← Artillery Reserve ← AP

**Map 3-36
Barksdale threatens Humphreys's left, and Wilcox threatens Cemetery Ridge**

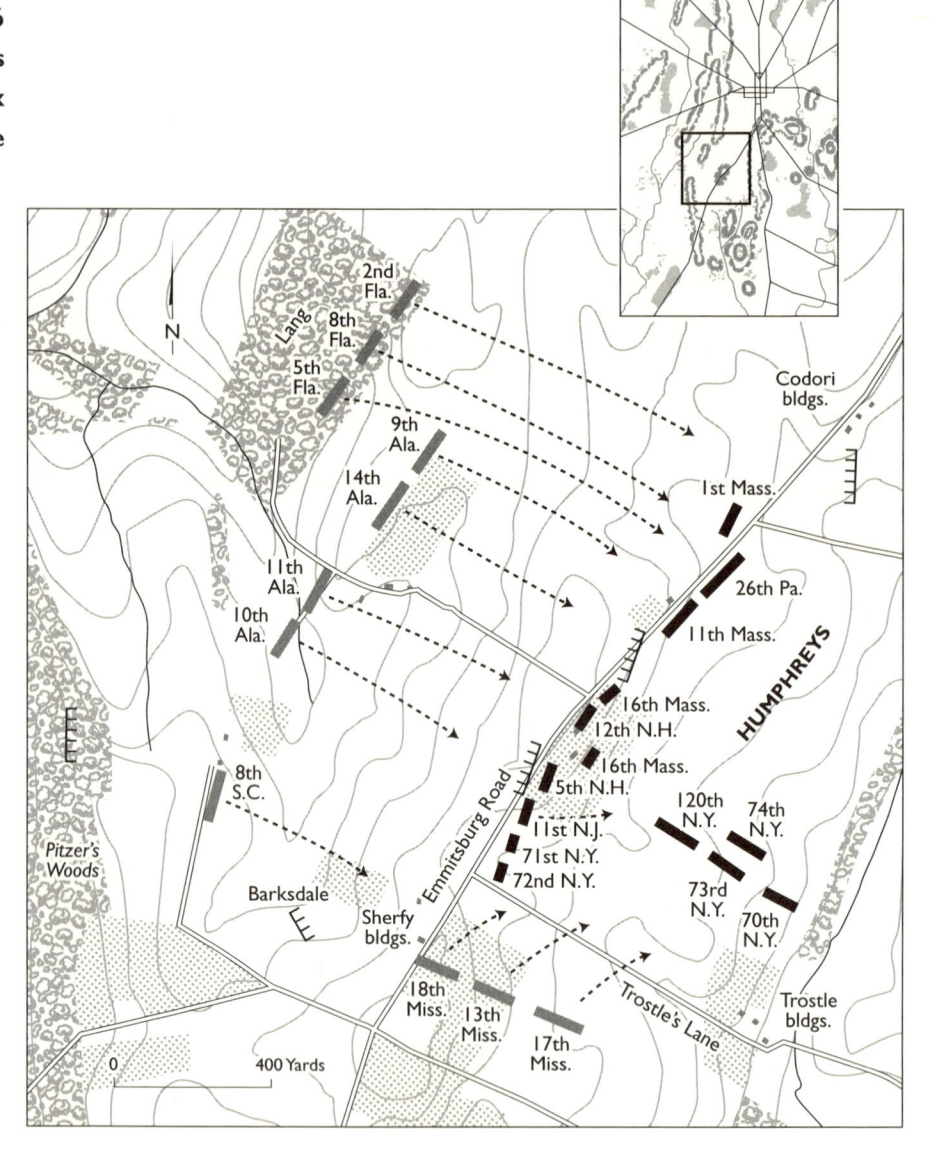

Some of General Barksdale's soldiers were attacking up the Emmitsburg Road at the time in conjunction with the brigade's charge upon the Peach Orchard. Thus, Barksdale's left wing drove into the exposed left flank of General Humphreys's 3rd Corps division (chart 3-24). Although the two regiments on the 2nd Division's left were smashed, Humphreys managed to refuse the remainder of his left wing to stall the attacking Mississippians (map 3-36). However, this now isolated Union infantry unit was soon to be under intolerable pressure. For now, Brig. Gen. Cadmus Wilcox's *rebel 3rd Corps* brigade was going in (chart 3-24). Those scouting Union sharpshooters had found elements of Wilcox's brigade earlier before Sickles's corps advanced to its forward positions. Now, Wilcox was advancing toward the center of Humphreys's line, which ran parallel to the Emmitsburg Road (map 3-36).

Wilcox's Alabamians were supported by Col. David Lang's Florida Brigade, which had formed up just to their left and rear. Humphreys knew that his two exposed and outnumbered brigades could not hold this position, so he ordered his men to retreat—but not without a fight. Commanding his troops on horseback, just behind the battle line, he had them conduct a fighting withdrawal. Several times the 2nd Division's soldiers stopped, turned, and fired at their attackers as this final defending remnant of the Union 3rd Corps retreated to Cemetery Ridge. As Humphreys's withdrawal began, he himself was unhorsed near the Emmitsburg Road. One of his orderlies, Pvt. James Dimond, was nearby and gave the general his horse. Dimond paid for this with his life as General Humphreys rode off to deal with the withdrawal.[101] He kept enough of his men under the iron discipline it takes for a unit to extract itself while fighting, such that the majority of his division rallied back on the ridge.

Meanwhile, infantry units moving in from many directions bolstered the Union defense in this sector (map 3-37). In particular, Col. George L. Willard's 3rd Brigade of Brig. Gen. Alexander Hays's 3rd Division in the 2nd Corps, which had spent the day on Cemetery Ridge, was ordered to reinforce by moving southward (chart 3-25). That division was on the 2nd Corps's right flank, not far below Cemetery Hill. The 2nd Corps commander, Maj. Gen. Winfield Scott Hancock, personally led Willard's brigade down the ridge and into the fight. From *farther* to the north near the right end of the entire Union line, Brig. Gen. Alpheus S. Williams's 12th Corps division was also ordered into the southern sector of the battlefield. Williams, following orders from General Meade himself, marched off Culp's Hill and moved to strengthen the defense of the Union left (chart 3-25).[102]

Note how the Army of the Potomac was continuing to exploit its interior lines. This situation was helped by the fact that the area between Culp's Hill and Cemetery Hill and the northern part of Cemetery Ridge was open and easily traversed. Later, additional Union units were shuttled back and forth across this open ground within the curve of the fishhook-shaped line.[103]

Colonel Willard, however, moved straight down the ridge and counterattacked Barksdale's still-advancing Mississippians.[104] The attack cost Willard his life, but the rebels began to fall back as elements of Williams's division completed the repulse. A regiment from Brig. Gen. Henry H. Lockwood's 2nd Brigade accomplished this (map 3-37, bottom; chart 3-25). The reinforcing units from the north met little resistance (even managing to recapture Captain Bigelow's lost guns), for Barksdale's brigade was on its last legs.

The South-to-North Attack Reaches the Union Center, Is Stalled by a Desperate Counterattack, but Achieves a Mini-High-Water Mark Just to the North

The Barksdale's, Wilcox's, and Lang's brigades had crushed the Union 3rd Corps's center and pushed back its right. Whereas Barksdale's attack had been stopped, the advance of the aforementioned rebel 3rd Corps brigades threatened Cemetery Ridge. Thus Wilcox, trailed by Lang, had gone in shortly after 6 P.M., after Barksdale charged to the Mississippians' left. These brigades, from Maj. Gen. Richard Anderson's division (chart 3-24), were headed toward the left-center of the Union line—or what was left of it, owing to the fact that Caldwell's 2nd Corps division had vacated the region.

Wilcox's brigade neared a swale at the base of Cemetery Ridge. General Hancock himself was up on the ridge in this vicinity, and just about the only troops nearby were from the 1st Minnesota (chart 3-26). They had been detached from Brig. Gen. John Gibbon's 2nd Corps division, which held the center of the Union line. Hancock, seeing one of Wilcox's men carrying the rebel flag as he came out of the swale, ordered Col. William Colvill, commander of the 1st Minnesota, to

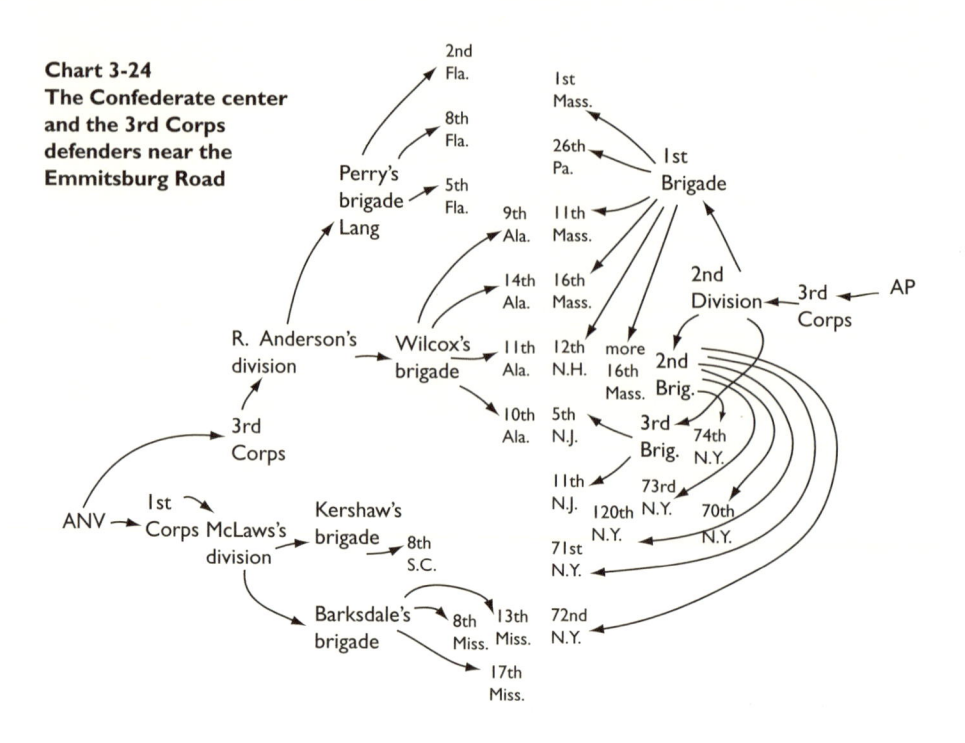

**Chart 3-24
The Confederate center and the 3rd Corps defenders near the Emmitsburg Road**

"take those colors."¹⁰⁵ Voting with their feet in devotion to the Union cause, Colonel Colvill and his small band plunged down the ridge, stalling the rebel brigade (map 3-38).¹⁰⁶ The price for buying these precious minutes was horrendous: more than two-thirds of the Minnesotans were killed or wounded. Legend has it that the regiment lost 215 out of 262 men on July 2, but that is an exaggeration.¹⁰⁷ Yet the time that was bought by the charge of the 1st Minnesota allowed Colonel Willard's right wing, joined by elements of Humphreys's rallied 3rd Corps soldiers, to repel the Alabamians. Those rebels never got onto Cemetery Ridge.

However, the *next* phase of the Confederate's advance would achieve that geographical goal. Brigadier General Ambrose R. Wright's brigade of Georgians from Anderson's 3rd Corps division made this attack (chart 3-27). Wright's brigade started its advance at about 6:30 p.m. and moved toward the Codori buildings on the Emmitsburg Road (map 3-39). The Georgians swept outlying skirmishers from two Union regiments from around the Codori house and barn and captured two batteries in front of a small ridge near those buildings. The shifting to their left of Union units from the center-right opened another gap east of those buildings and south of a copse of trees, which figures prominently in the events of July 3. This hole in the Union line had opened for a reason similar to the one that led to the thin defense in General Caldwell's former position farther down the ridge. This is what an attack *en echelon* is supposed to accomplish.

Wright's Georgians headed for the gap with Colonel Lang's Florida Brigade well to their right (map 3-39, bottom left). Lang's attempt to get onto Cemetery Ridge was pushed back, but Wright penetrated the gap and reached at least to the crest of the ridge (some of his men said they advanced all the way down its reverse slope). The problem with this rebel breakthrough was that it ended up being "unsupported."¹⁰⁸ In particular, Brig. Gen. Carnot Posey's brigade to Wright's left had failed to move with any celerity. For one thing, he got tangled up at the Bliss farm—located in a no-man's-land in the midst of the northern sector of the fields between Cemetery and Seminary Ridges. The Bliss farm was a haven for outposted

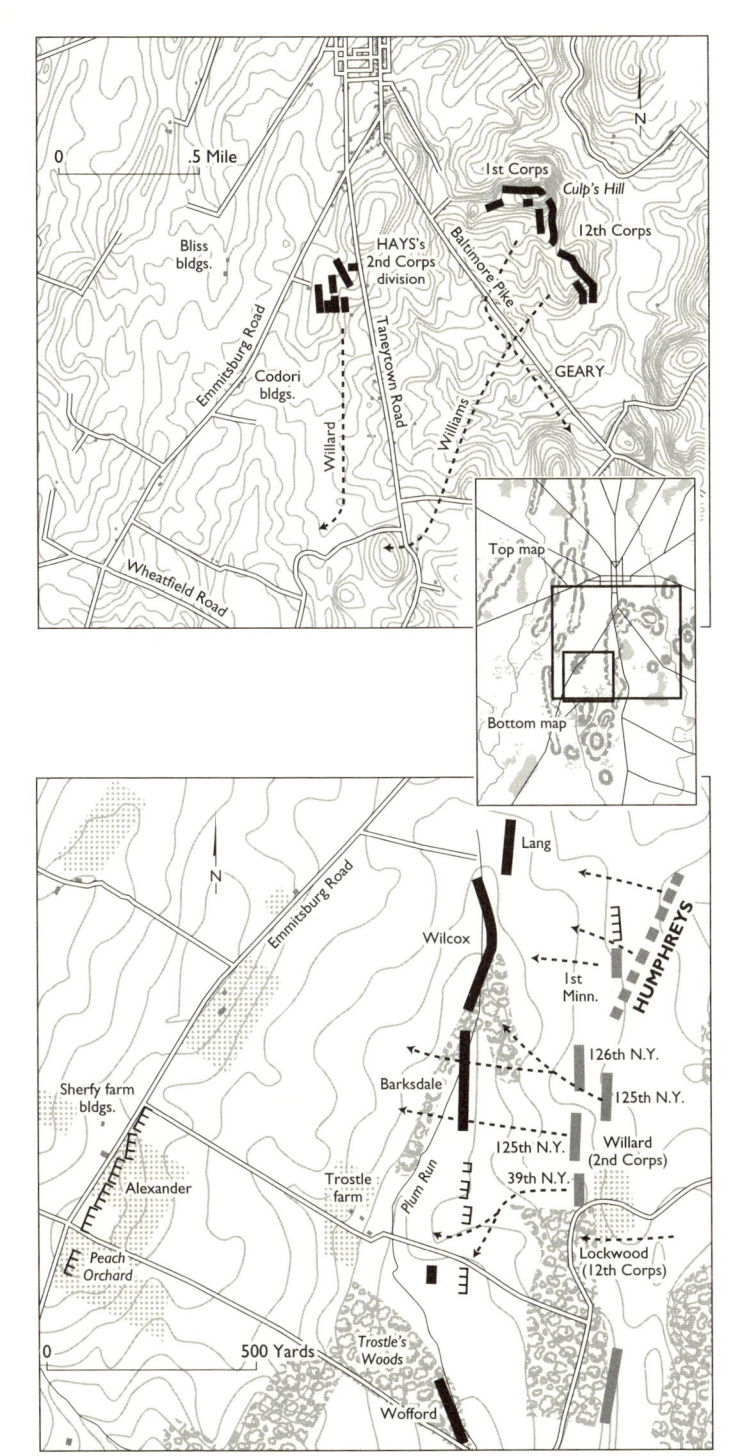

**Map 3-37
2nd and 12th Corps reinforcements and the repulse of Barksdale**

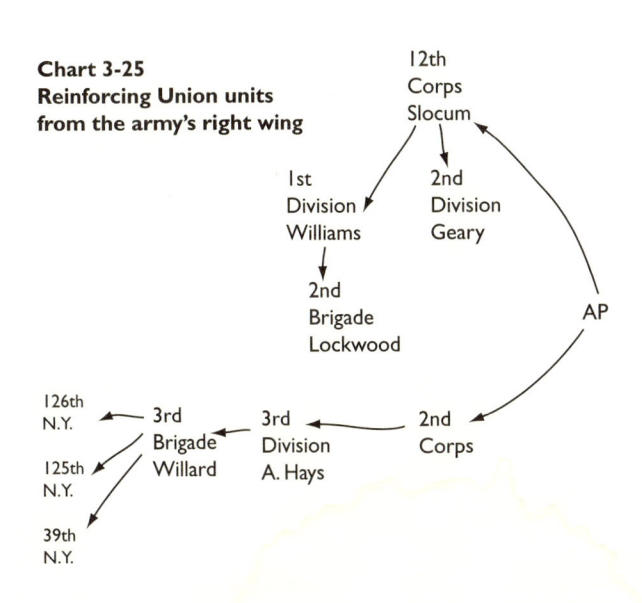

**Chart 3-25
Reinforcing Union units from the army's right wing**

THE CLIMAX OF THE BATTLE

**Map 3-38
The charge of the
1st Minnesota**

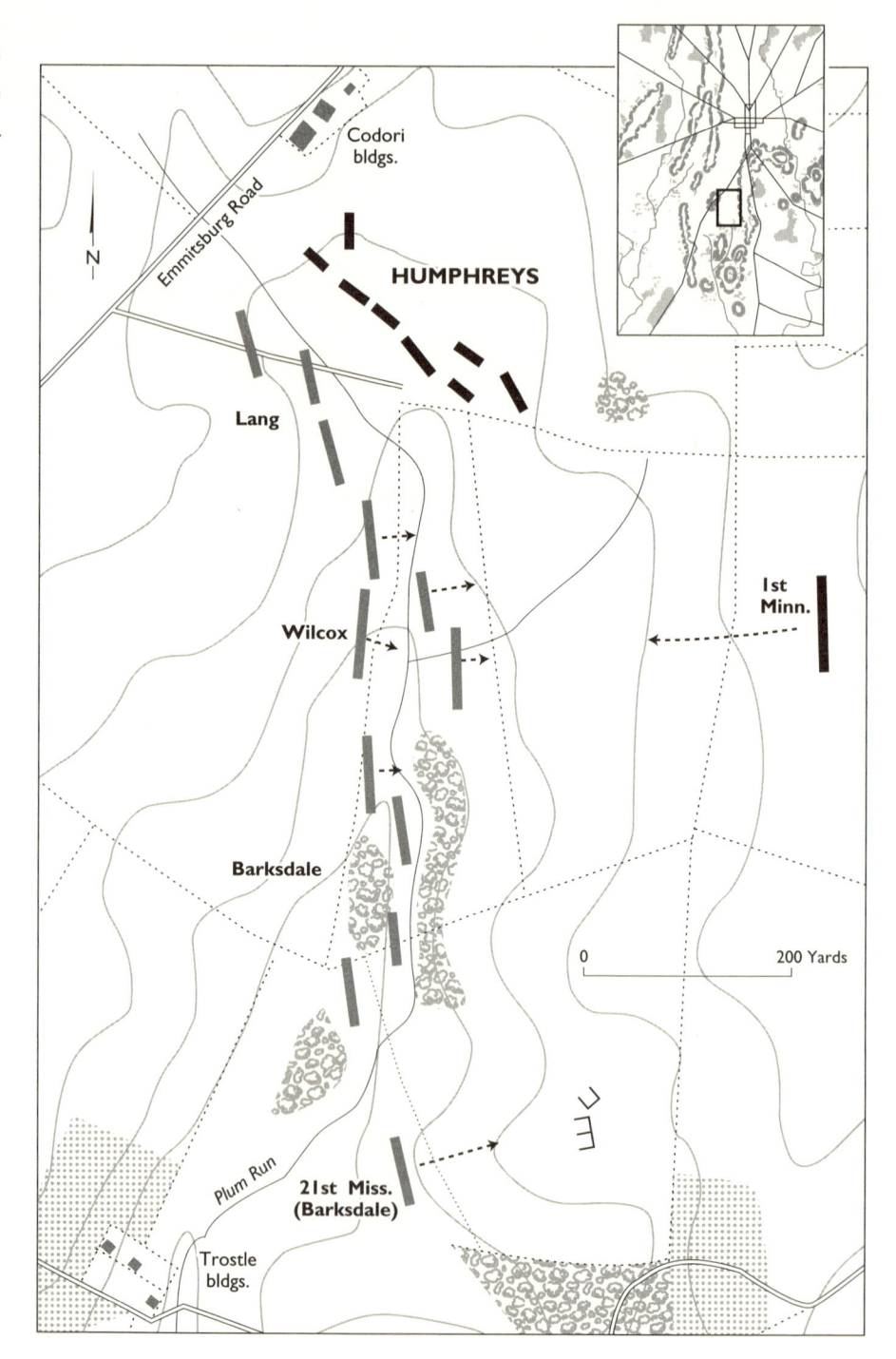

units from both sides, and possession of it kept changing hands (until the Federals had had enough and burned the buildings down late in the morning on July 3). Although Posey's Mississippians captured the Bliss farm (to little purpose), only part of one of his regiments advanced with Wright beyond the Emmitsburg Road (map 3-39).

At this point, the relentless right-to-left advances of the rebel force finally began to peter out. Brigadier General William Mahone's brigade, which had formed to Posey's left, simply did not advance (chart 3-27; map 3-39). Mahone refused to attack without orders from his division commander, Maj. Gen. Richard Anderson. None were forthcoming. The remaining rebel division commander along the

146   THE STAND OF THE U.S. ARMY AT GETTYSBURG

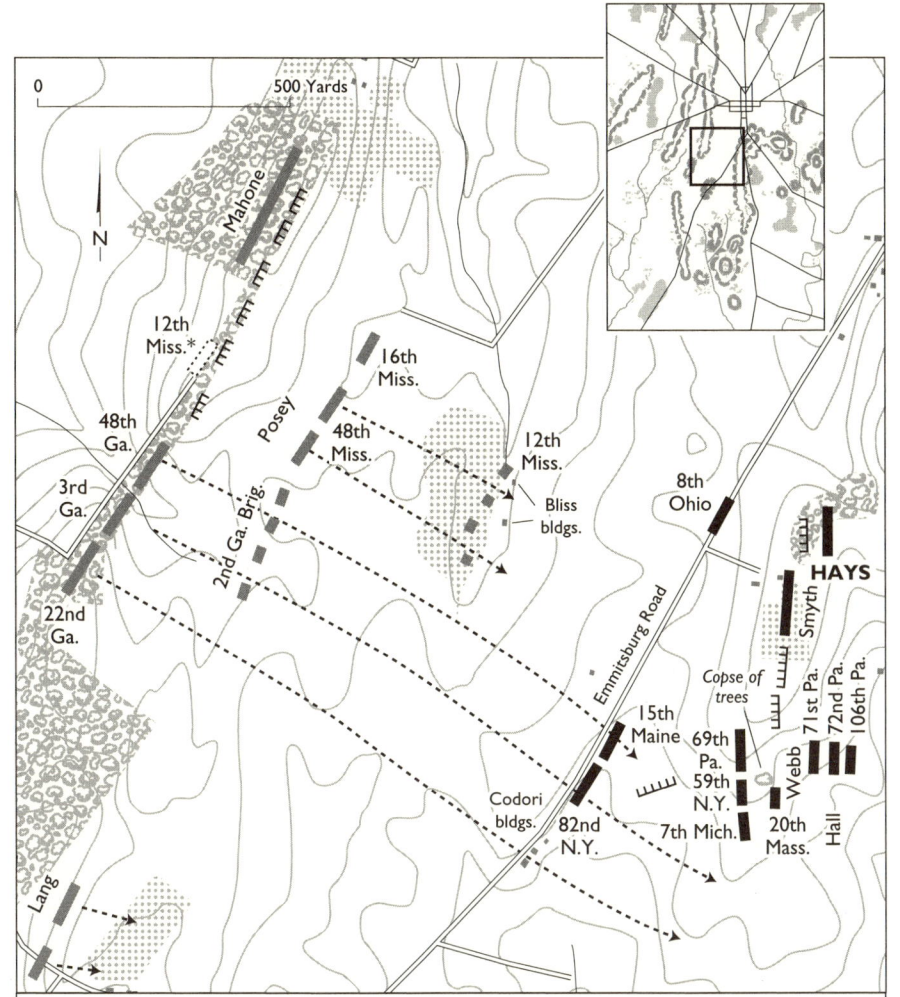

**Map 3-39
Wright's mini-High-Water Mark on July 2**

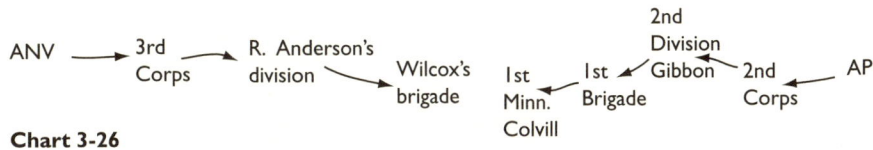

**Chart 3-26
Wilcox's brigade facing the regiment of Minnesotans**

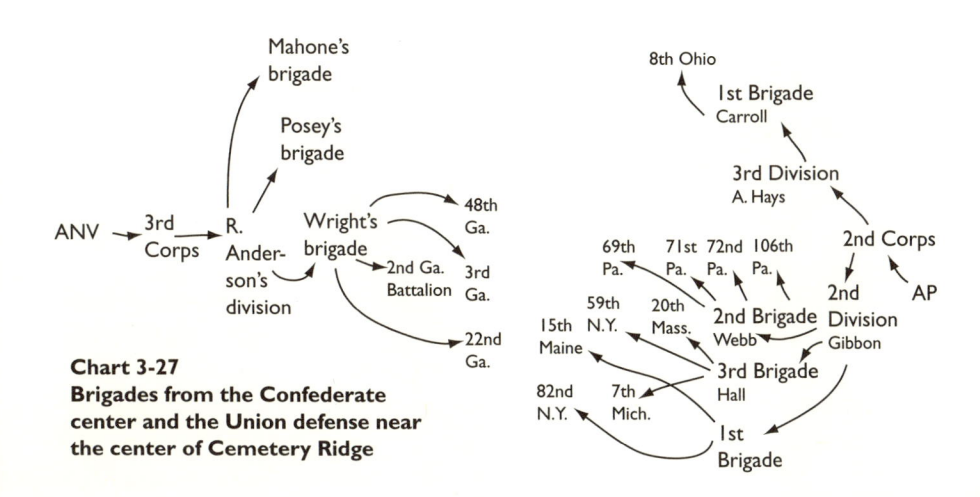

**Chart 3-27
Brigades from the Confederate center and the Union defense near the center of Cemetery Ridge**

THE CLIMAX OF THE BATTLE 147

**Map 3-40
Confederate artillery threatening the Union right**

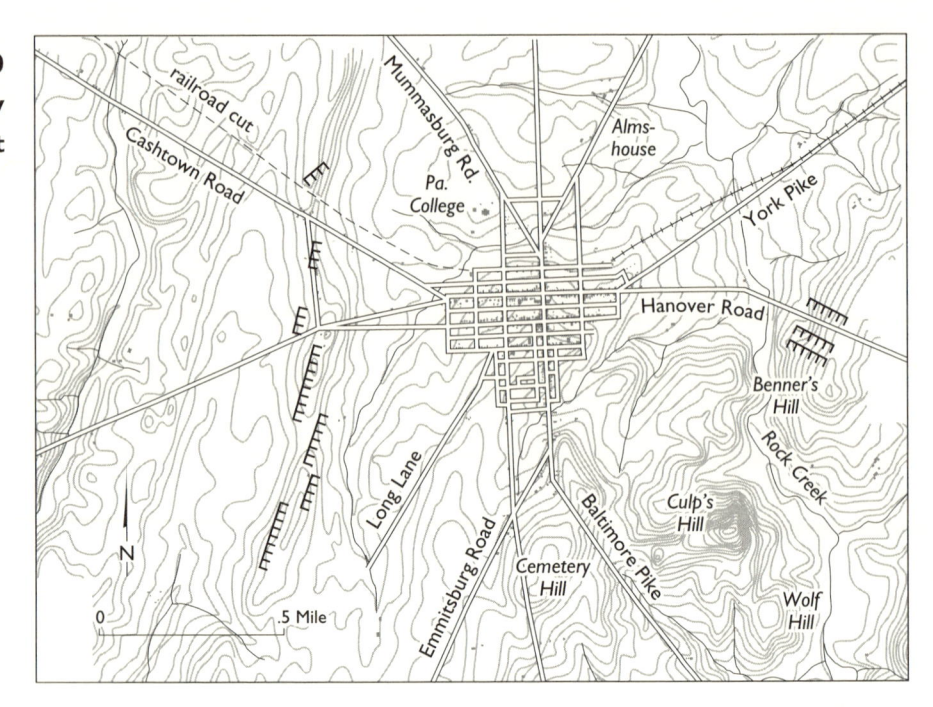

Confederate line, Maj. Gen. Dorsey Pender, tried to shake things loose. Recall that Pender's culminating attack on the previous day had pushed the Federal 1st Corps off the battlefield west of Gettysburg. Now, Pender rode down to General Mahone's takeoff position hoping to get him moving. Pender recognized that *someone* had to act.

Where was Mahone's division commander? Where was A. P. Hill? As General Pender went to find out the reason for Mahone's unconscionable delay, he was hit in the leg by a shell fragment. This took Pender out of the action. Moreover, the wound proved to be mortal; he died back in Virginia on July 18. Late on July 2, the removal of this high-quality general officer from the Confederate cause helped to doom one of the farthest advances achieved by the attacks.

The Confederate Left Finally Attacks Culp's and Cemetery Hills

The entire left wing of the Army of Northern Virginia had been quiet all day. In the morning, General Meade had asked the commander of the army's right wing, Maj. Gen. Henry W. Slocum, to organize an attack against the Confederates along his front.[109] Slocum said that the nature of the ground—hills, rocks, woods—made an attack impossible. When General Warren looked at the topography of Culp's Hills and vicinity and concurred with General Slocum, plans for Union offensive actions in this area were abandoned. That such plans had been set in motion indicates that General Meade was not completely committed to hunkering down on the defense. Eventually, on the morning of July 3, elements of his right wing would initiate an attack in this northern region of the battlefield (see Chapter 4). However, as midday approached on the Second, General Meade may have stored information about the rough high ground on Culp's Hill in the back of his mind. Such terrain can be nicely defensible, allowing Meade to leave it manned by a depleted force should he need to send reinforcements from the Army of the Potomac's right to a more threatened sector.

Map 3-41

Union positions on Culp's Hill

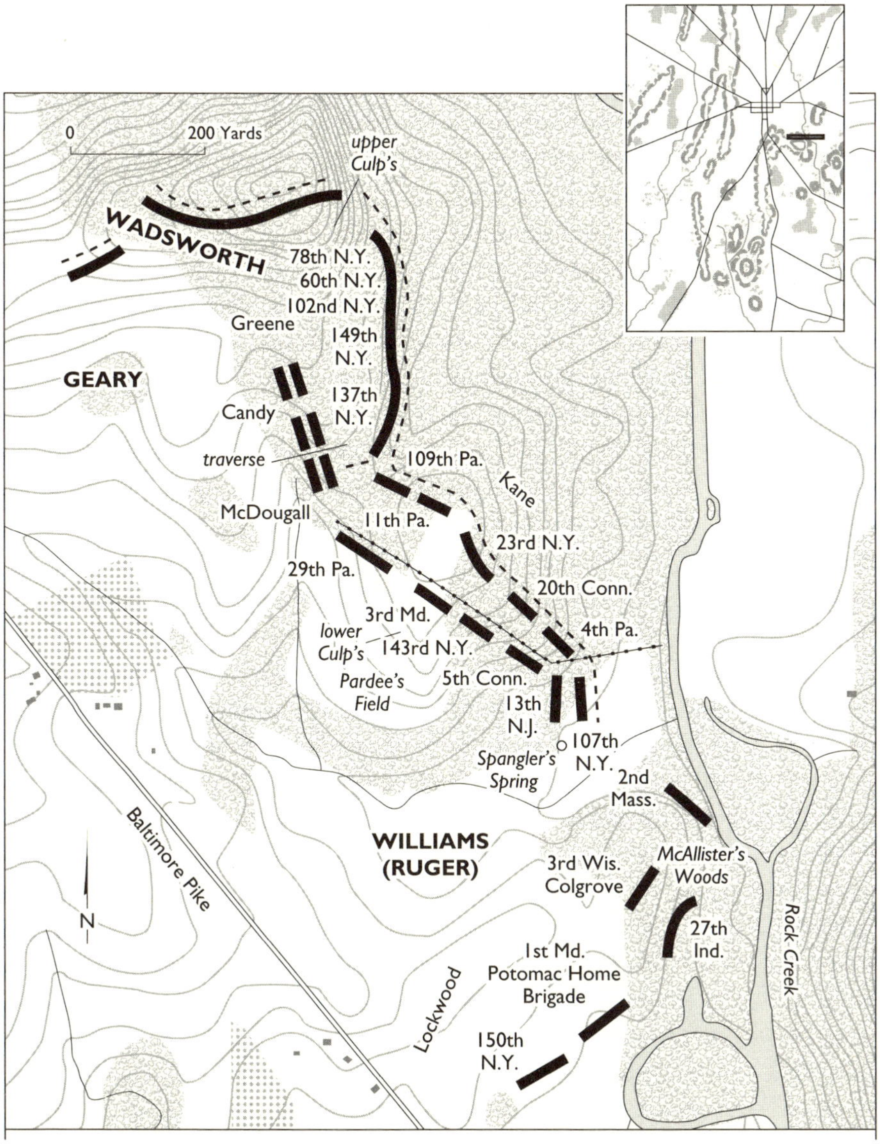

Meanwhile, the Union troops on Culp's Hill were turning their positions into even more defensible ones. They hacked at trees, gathered pieces of cordwood, rolled rocks around, and shoveled dirt, constructing the most formidable breastworks on the field at Gettysburg (map 3-41). This was the only place on the battlefield where defensive fortifications were vigorously constructed.[110] The Confederates gave the Union men essentially all day to build their fortifications along the Culp's Hill line. The defenders would need them.

During the morning and afternoon, the three rebel divisions under Lt. Gen. Richard Ewell formed a static ring around the Federals on Culp's Hill and Cemetery Hill (map 3-5). Ewell's force was supposed to wait until the army's right wing attacked the Federal left before launching a probe at the Union right. Ewell's moves—which he could escalate from a demonstration to a full-scale attack if warranted—were supposed to pin those bluecoats down and not permit them to reinforce their embattled left wing. In the strictest sense, this part of the Confed-

THE CLIMAX OF THE BATTLE 149

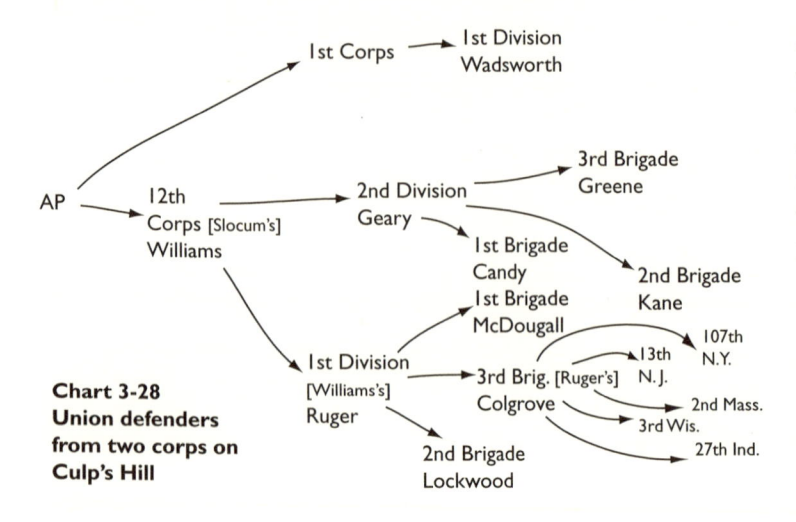

Chart 3-28 Union defenders from two corps on Culp's Hill

```
AP → 1st Corps → 1st Division Wadsworth
AP → 12th Corps [Slocum's] Williams
    → 2nd Division Geary
        → 3rd Brigade Greene
        → 1st Brigade Candy
        → 2nd Brigade Kane
    → 1st Division [Williams's] Ruger
        → 1st Brigade McDougall
        → 3rd Brig. [Ruger's] Colgrove
            → 107th N.Y.
            → 13th N.J.
            → 2nd Mass.
            → 3rd Wis.
            → 27th Ind.
        → 2nd Brigade Lockwood
```

erate plan failed—although the large number of 12th Corps troops from Culp's Hill who departed from there did not contribute significantly to the counterattacks that occurred in the southern sectors of the field. In fact, Brig. Gen. John W. Geary's division took a wrong turn, angling left down the Baltimore Pike and marching entirely out of the fight (map 3-37, top).

Whether any of the 12th Corps should have been ordered off Culp's Hill at all, and whether General Ewell should have (finally) attacked that hill *when* he did is grist for the mill of yet another Gettysburg controversy. Did Ewell receive specific orders about *when* to begin his demonstration against the Union right? This refers to the fact that the plan to attack the Union left did not specifically include a 4 P.M. start, so it might have been necessary to inform the Confederate 2nd Corps commander by mounted courier about when the action commenced on the southern end of the battlefield. Not so: Ewell was only three miles from Longstreet's right wing as the crow flies, so he would have had no problem hearing the 1st Corps's artillery fire as it began in the late afternoon. Thus, General Ewell must have deliberately decided to initiate his demonstration then and *not* to coordinate his own *infantry* attacks with Longstreet's. Ewell would *wait* to send in his 2nd Corps troops, and he may have made the right decision.

Here is what happened along the opposing lines in the northern sector of the battlefield on July 2. Ewell began demonstrating at about 4 P.M., but only with artillery barrages—cannon fire from batteries placed near the Lutheran Seminary and on Benner's Hill, respectively (map 3-40). The bombardment lasted for two hours, but had little effect on the defenders. In fact, the Confederate batteries were outgunned by their Union counterparts on Cemetery Hill, Culp's Hill, the outcropping on Stevens's Knoll, and on Power's Hill to the south (just off the bottom of map 3-40). The Federal counter-battery fire inflicted heavy casualties (fifty-one men and twenty-eight horses killed) and silenced the four rebel batteries on Benner's Hill. This caused all but four of the sixteen rebel guns to withdraw at about 6:30 P.M.

At last, Ewell's infantry attacked from the east. The assault was initiated at approximately 7 P.M. by his extreme left unit, Maj. Gen. Edward Johnson's division, which had not been engaged on July 1. On the evening of the second, Johnson's brigades faced the eastern slope of Culp's Hill, which is less steep than the northern one (map 3-41).

When Johnson began his advance on Culp's Hill he was minus the famed Stonewall Brigade, which had been placed along the Hanover Road guarding the Southerners' extreme left. The Virginia regiments in that brigade fought rearguard actions against detached infantry regiments as well as Union *cavalry* units led by Brig. Gen. David McM. Gregg. Recall that Gregg's division had been riding north toward Hanover Junction, Pennsylvania, and did not turn west toward Gettysburg until July 2. These actions, along Brinkerhoff's Ridge, took place from late afternoon into the evening.[111] The clashes there were significant because they were directly connected with a depletion of General Johnson's infantry force that attacked Culp's Hill. The actions at Brinkerhoff's Ridge on July 2 are described in Appendix C.

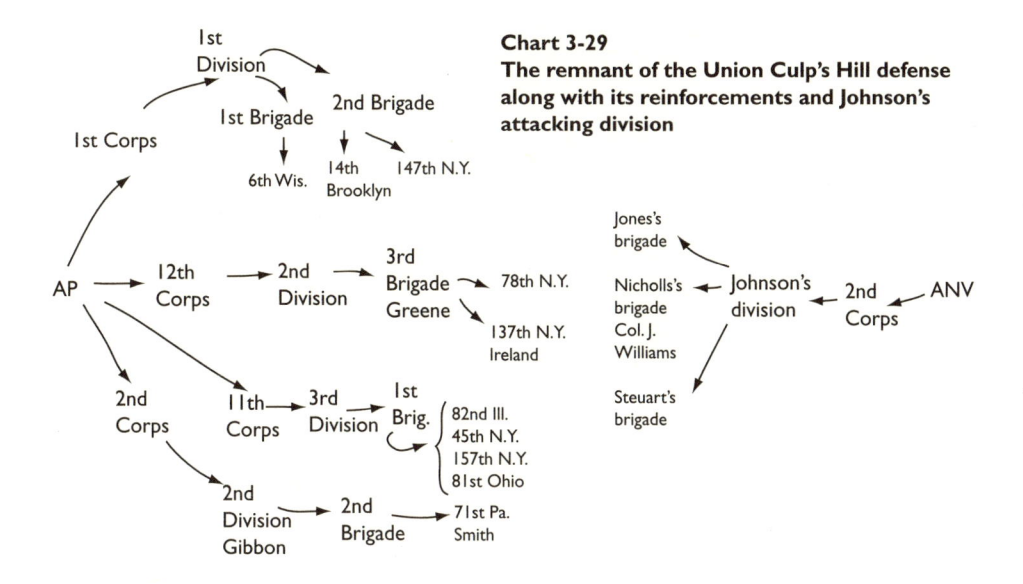

**Chart 3-29
The remnant of the Union Culp's Hill defense along with its reinforcements and Johnson's attacking division**

Ewell's decision to open his infantry attack using his fresh westward-facing division was sound. More important, he had *waited until the defenders to Johnson's front were badly depleted.* The conventional wisdom, which may be wrong, is that Ewell "failed" on July 2 by sending in his foot soldiers too late.

When he did, the only 12th Corps unit left on Culp's Hill was Brig. Gen. George S. Greene's brigade (map 3-41, chart 3-28). Greene was a tough old fighter—and a military engineer. In the Battle of Antietam, his troops had made one of the most impressive advances against the rebel left as they attacked during the morning of September 17, 1862. Nine and one-half months later, Greene again performed well as an engineer during the morning and early afternoon of July 2 by directing his men to build breastworks all along their eastward facing line. The 12th Corps soldiers on Culp's Hill may have remembered their inadequate defensive protection at the Battle of Chancellorsville and hoped to take advantage of their construction this time.[112] Some Civil War officers were opposed to breastworks, however.[113] They believed their men would merely cower there and not go over to the attack with any rapidity. But at sixty-two, General Greene was older and wiser. He insisted that his fourteen hundred men fortify their front. He also ordered the construction of a shorter line of breastworks that ran perpendicular to the main one. This east-west "traverse" would become important (map 3-41).

The Union fortifications were constructed along the *two* hills that comprise the one called Culp's. The more northerly prominence is higher, separated by a saddle from the one below. Both are bounded by the Baltimore Pike to the east and Rock Creek to the west (map 3-40). The smaller hill to the south was flanked by a five-acre field on its northwest slope, and by a meadow and stream just to its south—Pardee's Field and Spangler's Spring, respectively (map 3-41). Below the spring was McAllister's Woods, abutting Rock Creek (map 3-41).[114]

Shifting our attention back to the hill, Federal 1st Corps units to General Greene's left (chart 3-28) had also erected breastworks along their part of the line (map 3-41). The works on Culp's Hill thus extended almost from Spangler's Spring, below the smaller hill, to an east-west line on the upper. Little fighting was to occur on that northward-facing defensive front, manned by troops from Brig. Gen. James S. Wadsworth's 1st Division, 1st Corps (map 3-41, chart 3-28).

However, it was fortunate for the Federals that they fortified their eastward-

THE CLIMAX OF THE BATTLE   151

Map 3-42
Johnson's division attacks Greene's brigade, which is reinforced

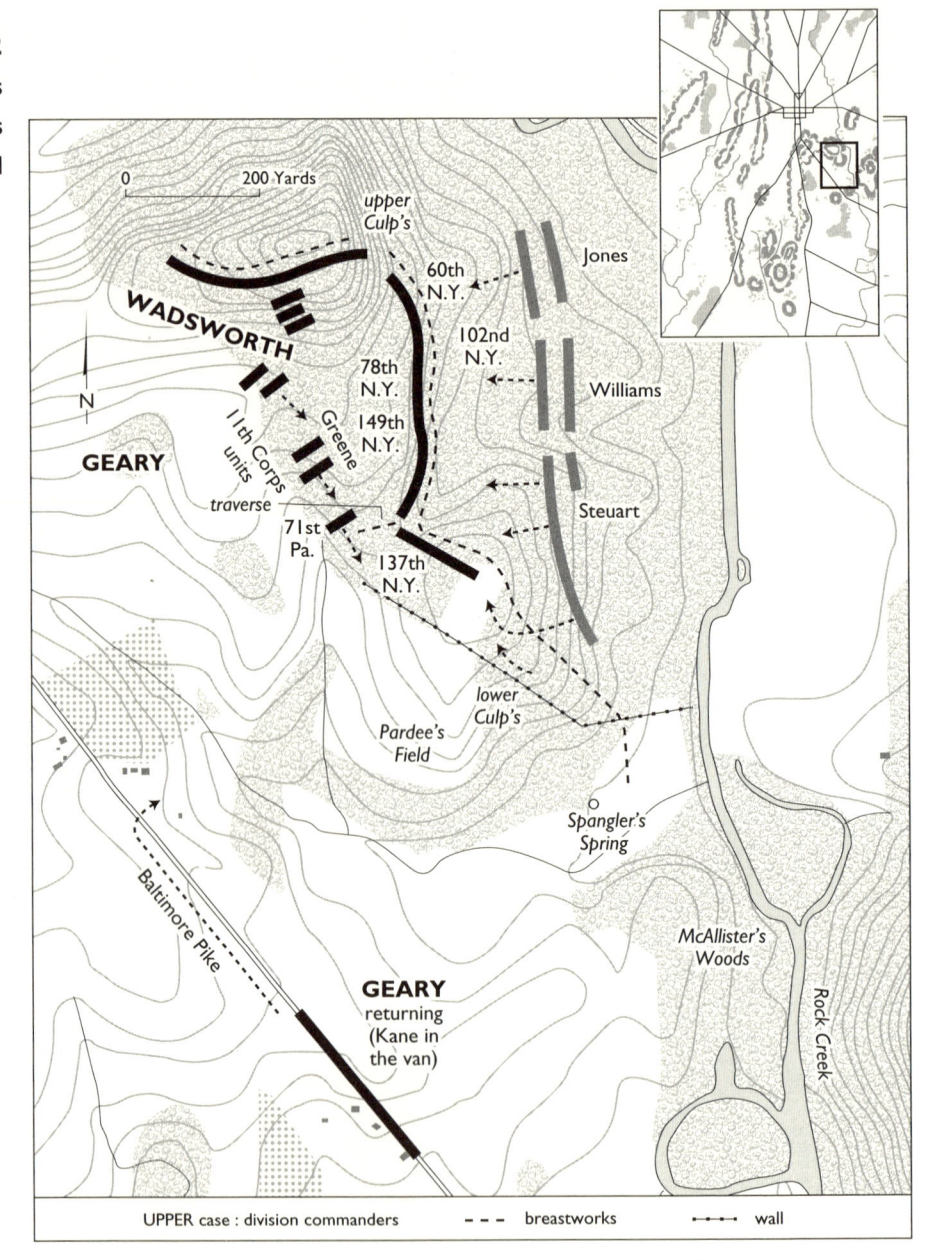

facing line, because so much of the 12th Corps had been redeployed to Cemetery Ridge before Johnson launched his attack. The most salient mistake made by a high-ranking officer in the Army of the Potomac was General Sickles's aggressive westward redeployment of the 3rd Corps in the midafternoon. Yet the removal of most of the 12th Corps from Culp's Hill during the early evening has been called a more serious error.[115] Still, neither move proved fatal. General Ewell's mistake was not so much that he delayed his infantry attacks until 7 P.M., but that he *could* have coordinated his assault so that it would have included all three of his divisions (map 3-5). Then, this Confederate corps might not have run out of daylight. That they did may have been mainly the fault of General Longstreet.

Too late or perfectly timed, General Johnson's division approached the eastern slopes of Culp's Hill.[116] The Confederates could not simply saunter in toward the north-south line of Federal defenders. The rebel infantrymen had to slog through

152 THE STAND OF THE U.S. ARMY AT GETTYSBURG

Rock Creek before approaching the Union line (map 3-41). Moreover, advanced Union skirmishers from the 78th New York, augmented by a company from the 137th New York (chart 3-29), were holding rough ground downslope on Culp's Hill and put up a good fight. General Greene had concentrated the men in his skirmish line where the creek was most fordable (map 3-43). These outlying Union troops were inevitably pushed back. However, by the time the rebels fought their way through the skirmishers, darkness loomed. Perhaps this militated against Johnson being aware of just how few Federals defended in his vicinity. Indeed, General Greene had stretched his main line almost to the breaking point. He thinned and extended it, occupying all the breastworks on upper Culp's Hill and those on the northern part of the lower one (map 3-42).

Just as Greene's right-hand regiment, the 137th New York, reached the trenches that had been abandoned by the left of Kane's 12th Corps brigade, Johnson hit the Federals with three of his brigades (chart 3-29). Two of them struck Greene's line in the works on the main hill. Johnson's left wing, commanded by Brig. Gen. George H. "Maryland" Steuart, advanced against the lower hill and found the breastworks there empty (map 3-42). Thus, Steuart's left-hand regiments occupied the Union works. These Southerners then wheeled clockwise and tried to make their way toward Greene's right flank. Greene's thinned-out brigade was in peril—outnumbered and in danger of being crushed from two directions.

But General Greene was about to be reinforced by troops from Wadsworth's division coming down from their northward-facing line (map 3-41).[117] Elements of the 11th Corps also moved eastward to Culp's Hill from Cemetery Hill (map 3-42, chart 3-29). In all, these reinforcing troops numbered about 750 men. In addition, a regiment from the 2nd Division of the 2nd Corps (map 3-42, chart 3-29) was sent up from Cemetery Ridge to reinforce the depleted force from Geary's division—although the 2nd Corps unit in question would bail out on its 12th Corps mates.

In fact, it was mainly Greene's troops who held their position on Culp's Hill in one of the most dramatic encounters of the Civil War. Some of what happened in the fighting on the attacking rebels' left wing was dreadful: One of General Steuart's regiments, the 1st North Carolina, fired its muskets into another of his units, the 1st Maryland Battalion (chart 3-30).[118] In the warfare of that century, fighting in the twilight or afterward was *not* good.

The imperiled part of General Greene's line turned out to be its right wing when Steuart's Maryland brigade launched its attack in that sector (maps 3-42 and 3-43). There, the 137th New York regiment stood tall. These New Yorkers (chart 3-29) put up a firm defense against Steuart's Marylanders, North Carolinians, and Virginians. The 137th New York's stand was just as impressive and important as the defensive accomplishments of the 20th Maine a short time before at the other end of the Army of the Potomac's line. These Maine and New York regiments had been mustered in during a call for troops in the summer of 1862 (the Mainers entered service in August, the New Yorkers in September). At Gettysburg less than a year later, the commander of the 137th New York was Col. David Ireland, a thirty-one-year-old man of Scottish birth. However, he did not live to tell the tale over and over again, as did Chamberlain of the 20th Maine (Ireland died of disease in September 1864). That may be why the story of this New York regiment has remained as hidden as was its isolated position on the extremity of Greene's line.

This is what happened there: As two of General Steuart's regiments approached the Union breastworks, the 3rd North Carolina was fired on by the muskets of the

Map 3-43
Johnson's left attacks Greene's right: Steuart's brigade against the 137th N.Y.

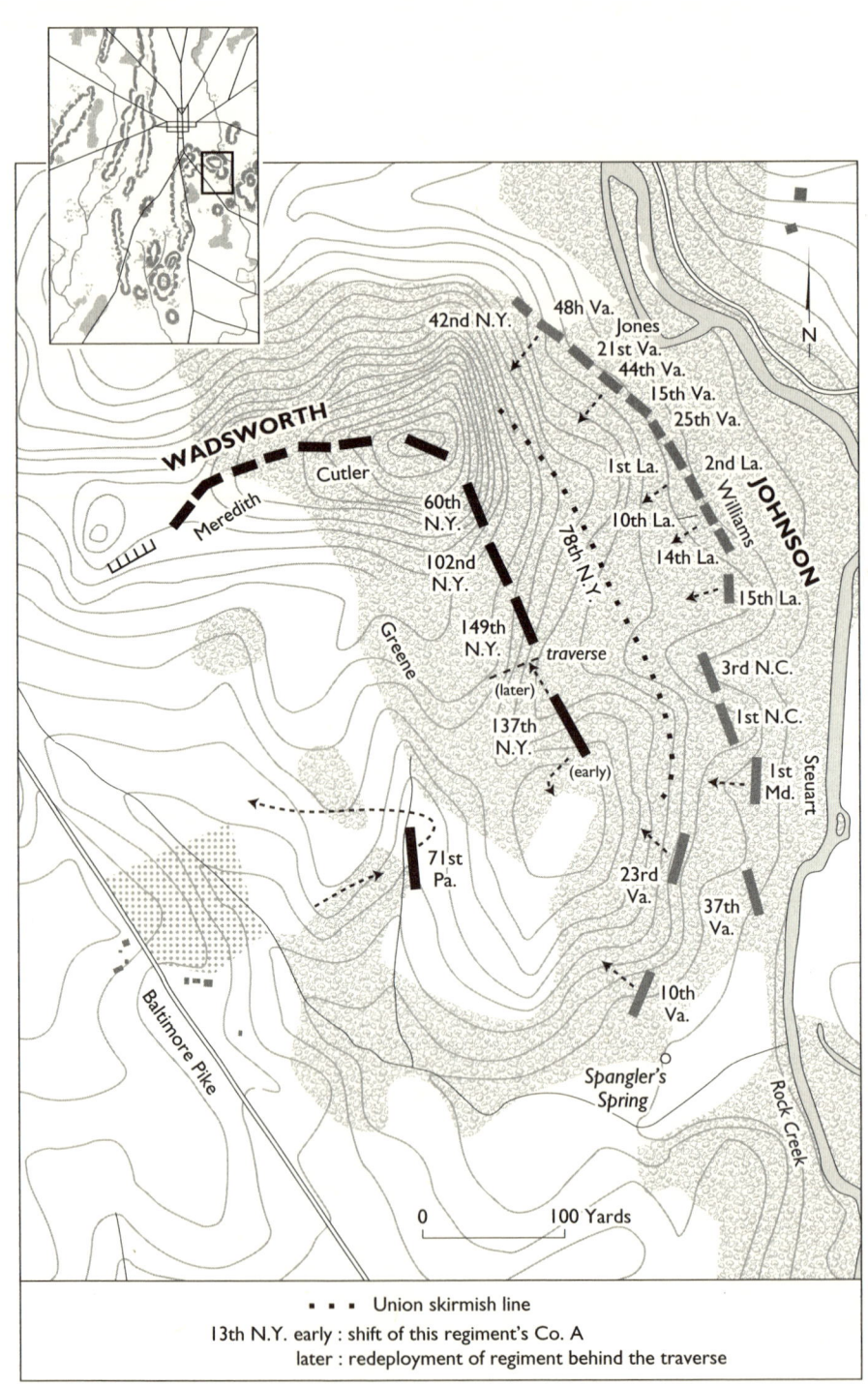

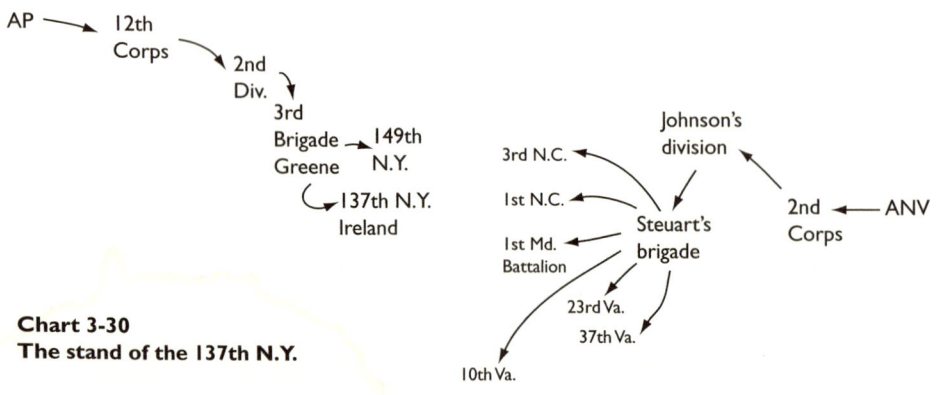

• • • Union skirmish line
13th N.Y. early : shift of this regiment's Co. A
later : redeployment of regiment behind the traverse

Chart 3-30
The stand of the 137th N.Y.

AP → 12th Corps → 2nd Div. → 3rd Brigade Greene → 149th N.Y.
↳ 137th N.Y. Ireland

3rd N.C. ←
1st N.C. ←
1st Md. Battalion ← Steuart's brigade ← Johnson's division ← 2nd Corps ← ANV
23rd Va. ←
37th Va. ←
10th Va. ←

154 THE STAND OF THE U.S. ARMY AT GETTYSBURG

149th New York on Ireland's left (map 3-43, chart 3-30). The men of the 137th New York sent oblique fire into the 3rd North Carolina's right, but at that moment the 3rd North Carolina and 1st Maryland Battalion advanced upon Colonel Ireland's front. This set up an opportunity for the rest of Steuart's brigade to assail the flank of the 137th New York from the south (map 3-43, chart 3-30)—the second of four assaults that would be made on the outnumbered New Yorkers. Unlike the case with the 20th Maine, however, Steuart's approximately two thousand Southerners far outgunned the four-hundred-man 137th. Nevertheless, this second attack receded.

It was now about 8 P.M., time for the antics of one of the reinforcing Federal regiments, the 71st Pennsylvania from the 2nd Corps. General Hancock had ordered Brig. Gen. John Gibbon, his 2nd Division commander, to send reinforcements over to Culp's Hill. Gibbon chose Col. Richard P. Smith's 71st Pennsylvania for the mission (chart 3-29), and General Greene's adjutant met it as it marched in that direction. He directed the Pennsylvanians to the right of Greene's line, and the Pennsylvanians went into position along a stone wall behind the right flank of Colonel Ireland's line (map 3-43). Colonel Smith sent a skirmish party forward, and this score or so of bluecoats ran into the advancing 10th Virginia. That seemed to be enough for the 71st Pennsylvania: Smith ordered his entire regiment to withdraw and it simply went back to the Baltimore Pike (map 3-43). This disturbing performance was a harbinger of things to come for this unit on July 3.[119]

Colonel Ireland and the 137th New York could have used the Pennsylvanians' help on the night of July 2. When the third attack came upon the right end of General Greene's line, Ireland's regiment became almost surrounded, even though by now he had bent back the extremity of his flank into roughly a V configuration (map 3-43). General Steuart's 10th Virginia was at this time circling clockwise and firing into Ireland's right rear, the 23rd Virginia assailed the New Yorker's from the south, and the rest of Steuart's brigade kept up a steady fire from the east (map 3-43).

The position of the 137th New York was untenable, so Colonel Ireland ordered his men to fall back. Withdrawing to the north, they took up a position along the *traversing* breastwork that General Greene had ordered erected at a right angle to the main line of fortifications (maps 3-41, 3-42, and 3-43). The Southern troops were now mainly in the saddle between the upper and lower parts of Culp's Hill. The New Yorkers initially held them off with steady fire from their position along the traverse. Then Steuart's troops made one last advance toward Ireland's line. The attack was repulsed, partly because a group of men from the 137th New York *charged* the advancing rebels to their front. The New Yorkers continued to hold this south-facing position until 10 P.M., when they at last were relieved by reinforcing units.[120] During their stand and active defense, in which the 137th New York withdrew to a protected position and counterattacked from there, the regiment suffered 137 casualties among the approximately 420 men in the regiment. This happened to be almost the same number that was inflicted upon the five-hundred-man 20th Maine at the other end of the Army of the Potomac's line.

The action along the northern (left) sector of the Union's east-facing Culp's Hill line did not involve as serious a crisis as on Greene's right. For example, Jones's Confederate brigade, attacking from the right wing of Johnson's division (map 3-42), suffered the loss of its commander, Brig. Gen. John M. Jones, who was wounded at the onset of the assault. His replacement, Lt. Col. Robert H. Dungan, ordered the brigade to withdraw some two hundred yards a half-hour into the fight, citing heavy losses. The brigade commander to Dungan's left, Col. Jesse M. Williams (map 3-42), fumed that the withdrawal left him unsupported.[121] Jones's (then Dungan's) brigade had been attacking the front manned by the 60th New York near upper Culp's Hill (map 3-42). After the New Yorkers repelled the first wave of the attack, the rebels advanced again on this front and were thrown back in confusion. Precipitating the withdrawal of Jones's Virginians, several of the New Yorkers advanced over their breastworks (countering the anti-fortification theory discussed above) and captured about five dozen of the attacking Southerners.

General Johnson's division—which had been assaulting the Union right wing from two directions, moving in from the east and south—seemed preoccupied with breaking the Federal line on Culp's Hill itself (map 3-42). Because of those concerted attacks and the darkness, the Confederates did not appear to realize that Steuart's brigade on their left could have occupied a crucial sector of the overall Union line on the Baltimore Pike had he wheeled southward during his advance instead of trying to encircle the 137th New York.[122] Confederate possession of the Baltimore Pike might have severed this Union supply route and put the Federal right in danger of being cut off.

That did not happen, however, and Culp's Hill held. As the next section of this chapter will describe, that hill would be reinforced further, and most of Johnson's rebel force would be sent reeling back. Meanwhile, not long after the fighting erupted on the two parts of Culp's Hill, the Confederate *center* in this sector attacked. The assaulting rebel force consisted of Brig. Gens. Harry T. Hays's and Isaac E. Avery's brigades from Maj. Gen. Jubal Early's division (map 3-44, chart 3-31). Early's brigades advanced toward east Cemetery Hill from a ravine south and southeast of Gettysburg with almost no daylight left. As they advanced, they were hit by cannon fire from Stevens's Knoll, an outcropping to the west of upper Culp's Hill.[123]

Struggling through the enfilading artillery barrages, Hays and Avery struck the Union lines at about 8 P.M.[124] The advancing Confederate brigades were moving toward two Federal counterparts, commanded by Cols. Andrew L. Harris and Leopold von Gilsa (chart 3-31). These Union brigades were in the 11th Corps, which had fought (barely, some would say) on July 1 on the Union right. Their division commander, Brig. Gen. Francis Barlow, had been severely wounded then, so Brig. Gen. Adelbert Ames (chart 3-31) now commanded these Federal brigades. His main defenders were at the base of Cemetery Hill. Shortly before the rebels attacked, Ames sent the 17th Connecticut from its position in Harris's line to von Gilsa's left. This shift left a gap in the Union defense. Harry Hays's "Louisiana Tigers" in turn exploited that gap, wheeling in from the right of Early's advancing line of attackers (map 3-44). Elements of Avery's brigade exploited additional weak spots in the Union defense, and some of these attackers were able to get into the defenders' lines.

The opposing forces were by then fighting in the dark. Some of Early's men advanced up Cemetery Hill, threatening the batteries at the top of the slope, but most of this rebel force fought it out at the base of the hill, where four Union regiments were arrayed (map 3-44). Aided perhaps by the uncertainty and confusion created by the darkness, these defenders more or less held their ground. However, some of these Union infantrymen were driven back, and they and their comrades in two artillery batteries fought the Southerners amidst the guns within the main Union line on the Hill. This rebel force would soon be repulsed (as described in the next section).

**Map 3-44
Two of Early's brigades attack east Cemetery Hill**

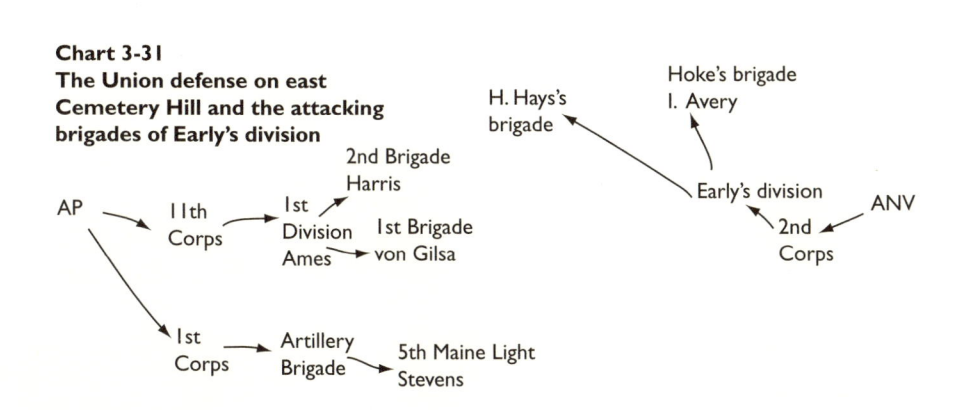

**Chart 3-31
The Union defense on east Cemetery Hill and the attacking brigades of Early's division**

THE CLIMAX OF THE BATTLE

**Map 3-45
Rodes's division advances
toward west Cemetery Hill
then withdraws**

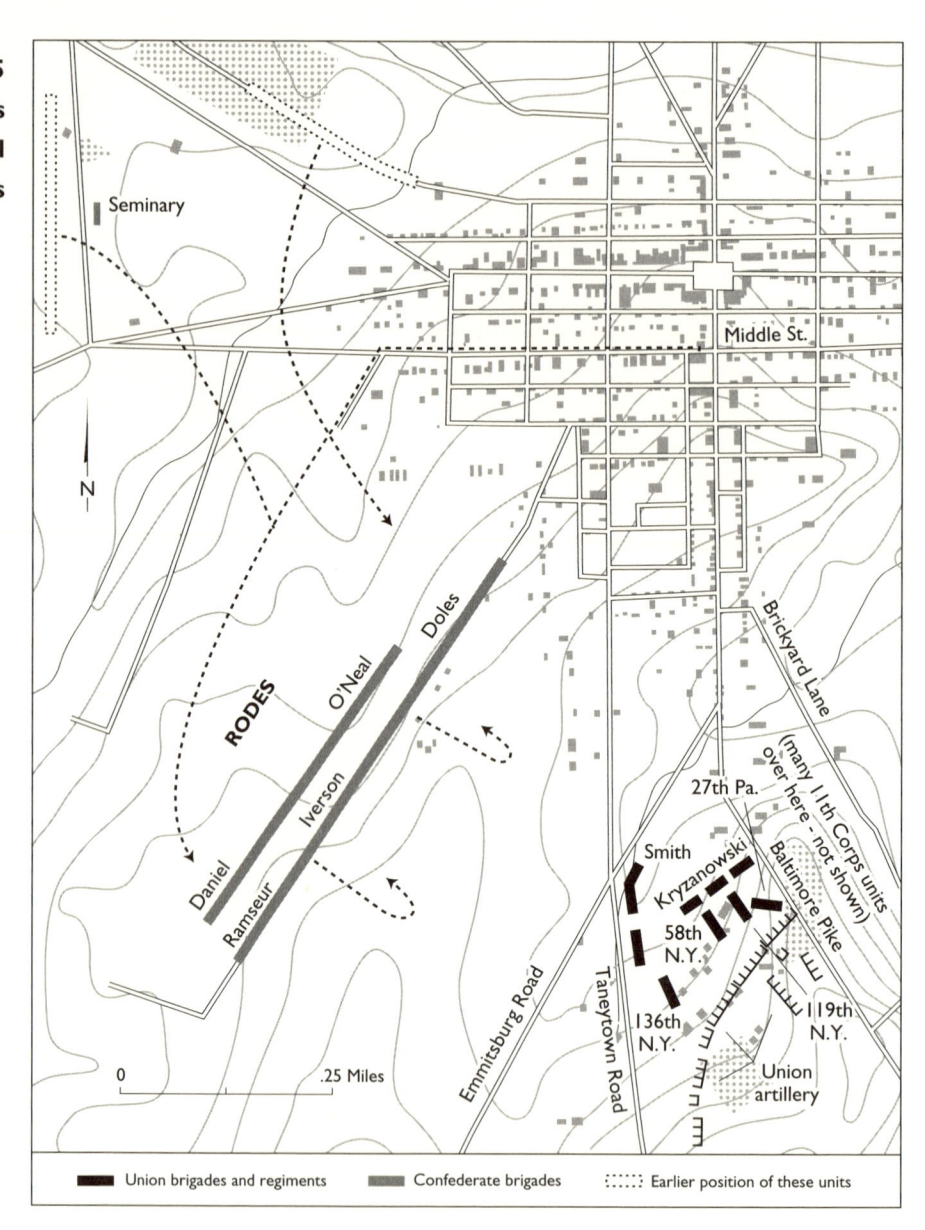

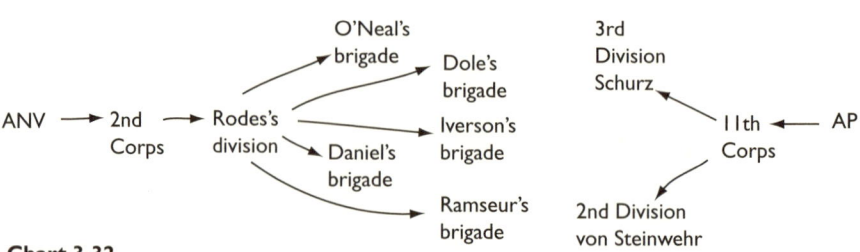

Union brigades and regiments ▮▮▮ Confederate brigades ▮▮▮ Earlier position of these units ⋮⋮⋮

**Chart 3-32
Ewell's right-hand division and the Union defense on west Cemetery Hill**

158   THE STAND OF THE U.S. ARMY AT GETTYSBURG

Meanwhile, although perhaps too many minutes later, Maj. Gen. Robert Rodes's division prepared to continue the rebels' left-to-right assaults. Rodes's division was on the right wing of General Ewell's 2nd Corps (chart 3-32). Although he or Ewell may have considered coordinating this attack with General Early, Rodes was not ready to move until Early's fight on east Cemetery Hill was ending. Furthermore, one might ask why General Rodes left a goodly portion of his division stuck in the streets of Gettysburg during so much of that day (map 3-45). Finally, however, Rodes's infantrymen moved west from their positions in town into the fields northwest of Cemetery Hill.

This rebel division advanced a short distance but then hesitated in the darkness and stopped (map 3-45). It was now after 9 P.M. Sensing the extreme difficulty of an attack under such circumstances, the commander of Rodes's lead brigade, Brig. Gen. Dodson Ramseur (chart 3-32), called a temporary halt to his unit's advance. Ramseur was a tough fighter, as evidenced by his actions on July 1.[125] Wondering if he could nonetheless achieve some sort of an attack, Ramseur went ahead of his brigade, which was formed up on the right end of Rodes's line, to reconnoiter the western slope of Cemetery Hill (map 3-45). Aided by moonlight, he was able to discern a solid line of Federal artillery in his front, heavily supported by infantry of Schurz's and von Steinwehr's 11th Corps divisions (map 3-45). General von Steinwehr's men had occupied this position ever since Maj. Gen. Oliver Howard's golden moment of the previous day.

Ramseur returned to the rebel lines and consulted with Brig. Gen. George Doles (chart 3-32, map 3-45). The two of them then went to General Rodes and explained that a further attack on the hook of the Union right was hopeless. Might these three officers also have been aware of how some of their units, now supposedly ready for battle in front of the northwestern slope of Cemetery Hill, had been so badly brutalized on July 1?[126] In any event, General Rodes accepted the wisdom expressed by these solid officers and gave the order to withdraw back to Gettysburg.

Stands and Repulses All along the Lines

After the close-run fighting began to wane on the eastern and southern slopes of Culp's Hill, Brig. Gen. Thomas Ruger's and Brig. Gen. John W. Geary's 12th Corps divisions returned to this sector of the field.[127] Ruger's troops sealed off the possibility of a further Confederate penetration into the defenses on the lower hill by forming up in the areas of McAllister's Woods and the Baltimore Pike, menacing the left wing of Johnson's Confederate division (map 3-46). General Geary reinforced General Greene's line on the bigger hill with part of his division and dispatched other elements to the southeast to confront the Confederates on the lower hill (map 3-46). The reinforced Federal line in the northern half of this area then pushed back the remnants of General Johnson's attack. Yet the Confederates *had* gained some ground in the southern half of this sector of the battlefield (map 3-46), and heavy fighting would occur there the next morning.

Meanwhile, the Federal defenders on *Cemetery* Hill were in a crisis of sorts as elements of General Early's assaulting force had made it into their lines. As we saw earlier, however, the Confederate attack in this sector had not been all that coordinated and was hampered by the darkness. Reinforcements from Maj. Gen. Carl Schurz's and Brig. Gen. Adolph von Steinwehr's 11th Corps divisions (chart 3-34) moved to the eastern part of Cemetery Hill from their positions across the Baltimore Pike (map 3-47). Moreover, General Hancock sent Col. Samuel S. Carroll's

**Map 3-46
Union 12th Corps units return to Culp's Hill**

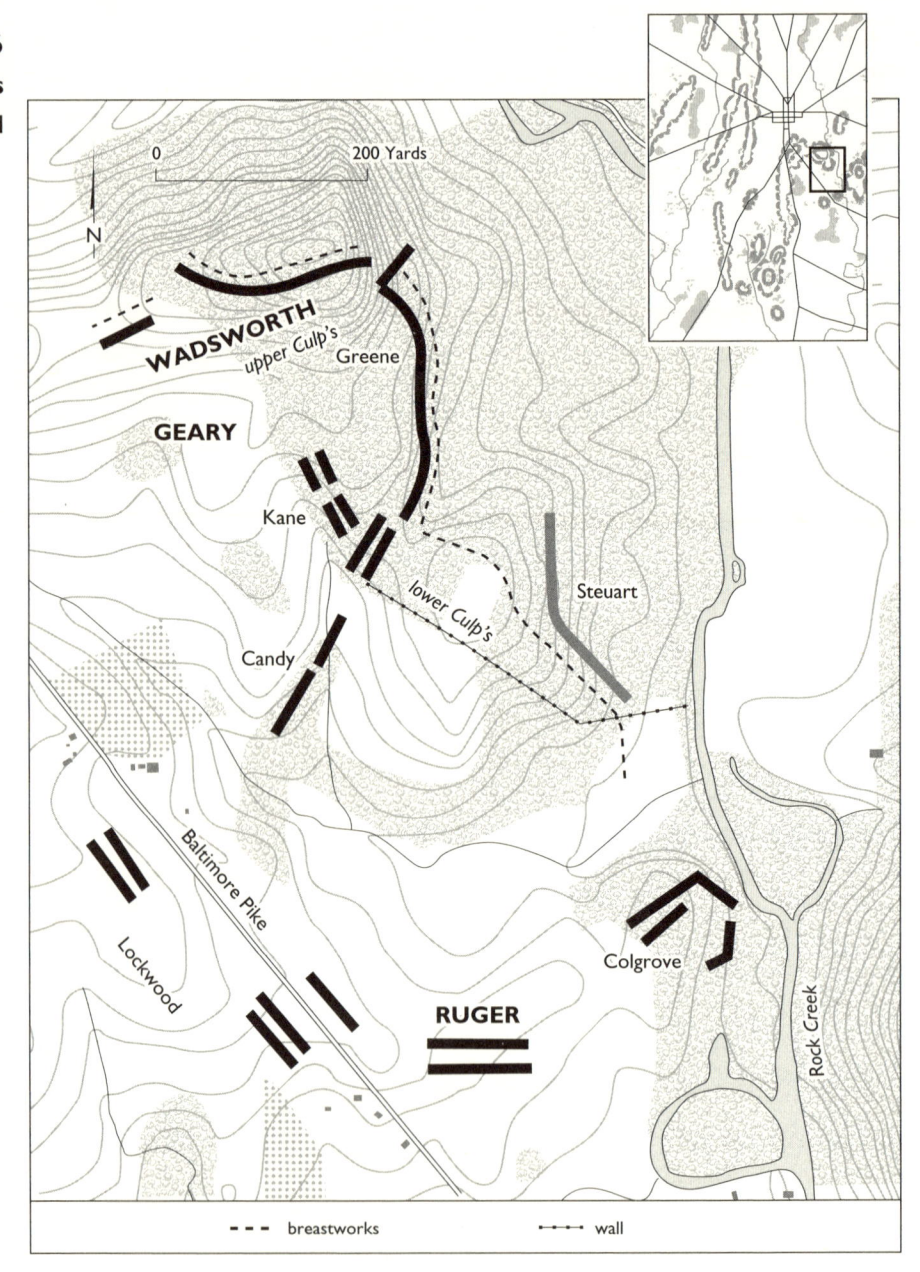

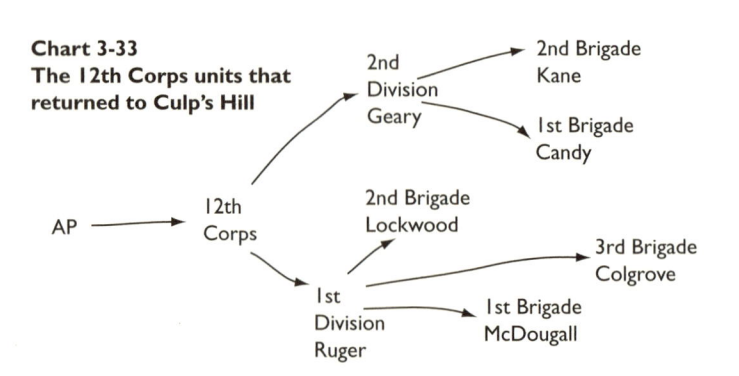

- - - breastworks ——— wall

**Chart 3-33
The 12th Corps units that returned to Culp's Hill**

AP → 12th Corps → 2nd Division Geary → 2nd Brigade Kane
                                      → 1st Brigade Candy
               → 1st Division Ruger → 2nd Brigade Lockwood
                                    → 3rd Brigade Colgrove
                                    → 1st Brigade McDougall

160   THE STAND OF THE U.S. ARMY AT GETTYSBURG

2nd Corps brigade from north Cemetery Ridge (chart 3-33). Carroll was *minus* one of his regiments, the 8th Ohio, which was in a position along the Emmitsburg Road (map 3-39). That this unit was not with him on Cemetery Ridge and then Cemetery Hill late on July 2 will become most significant during the events of the next afternoon. Meanwhile, Carroll marched northeastward in the evening darkness with the rest of his regiments, found the fight on Cemetery Hill, and helped the troops of the 11th Corps repel the left wing of Early's assault (map 3-47).

Below the town and to the south of Cemetery Hill, recall that Brig. Gen. Ambrose Wright's Confederate brigade was isolated in its advance into the Union lines on Cemetery *Ridge*. Even though Wright had initially pushed back a Union brigade on this ridge below the copse of trees—Col. Norman J. Hall's 2nd Corps brigade (chart 3-27)—Wright's position soon became untenable. Hall counterattacked as Brig. Gen. Alexander Webb's brigade of Pennsylvanians circled around counterclockwise, almost getting into Wright's rear. Just to the south, the 13th Vermont, detached into this vicinity from the 1st Corps, advanced upon Wright's right wing (chart 3-35). The rebel brigade was forced back, and many of Wright's Georgians were captured near the Codori buildings (map 3-48).

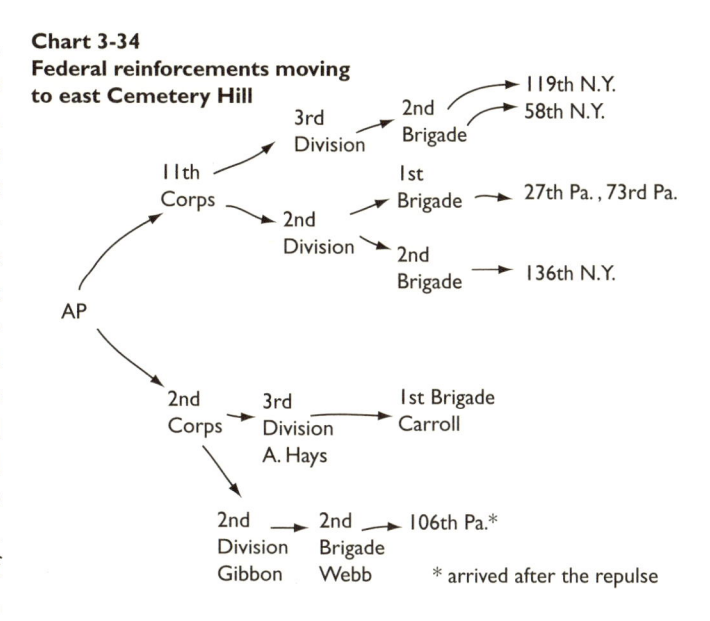

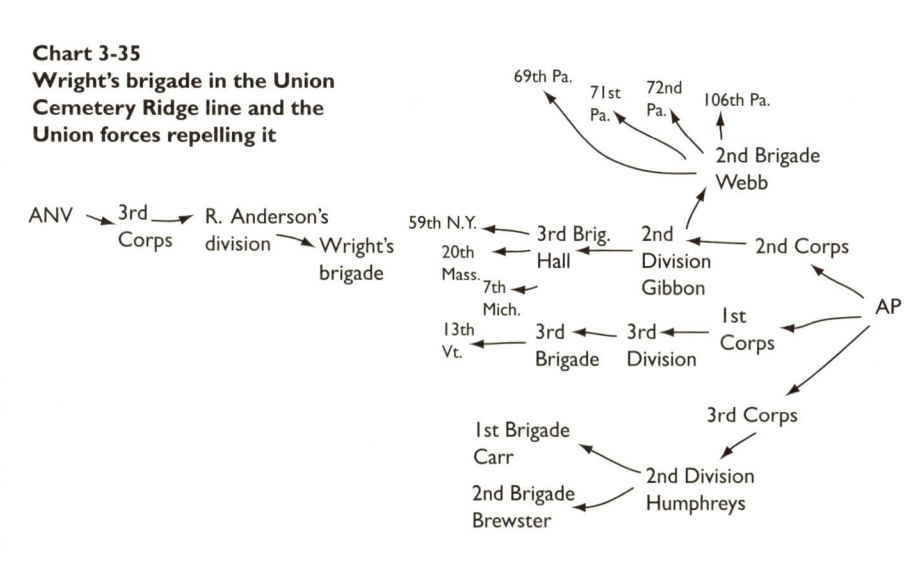

Completing Wright's repulse, additional units from Brig. Gen. John Gibbon's 2nd Corps division moved into this sector (chart 3-35). They were bolstered by rallied elements of General Humphreys's division just to the south. These 3rd Corps bluecoats blocked Lang's tentative advance (map 3-48; the Floridians' initial movements eastward are shown on maps 3-37 and 3-39). Most of the Union units in this area then advanced to the Emmitsburg Road in pursuit of Wright's brigade. Three of the Union guns that had been captured there were recovered. The Southerners were finished in the north-central sector of the field.

Next, recall that other Confederate units were also approaching *Cemetery Ridge well to the south* before the time of Ewell's attacks to the north. On the heels of all those retreating Union units (the entire 3rd Corps, along with elements of the 5th and 2nd Corps), the attacking brigades continued their eastward advance, moving toward the northern section of Little Round Top and to the low ridgeline just above that hill. These Confederates were the remnants of four brigades from Hood's and McLaws's divisions that had assailed the Federal left (chart 3-36).

Chart 3-34
Federal reinforcements moving to east Cemetery Hill

AP → 11th Corps → 3rd Division → 2nd Brigade → 119th N.Y., 58th N.Y.
11th Corps → 2nd Division → 1st Brigade → 27th Pa., 73rd Pa.
11th Corps → 2nd Division → 2nd Brigade → 136th N.Y.

AP → 2nd Corps → 3rd Division A. Hays → 1st Brigade Carroll
2nd Corps → 2nd Division Gibbon → 2nd Brigade Webb → 106th Pa.*

* arrived after the repulse

Chart 3-35
Wright's brigade in the Union Cemetery Ridge line and the Union forces repelling it

ANV → 3rd Corps → R. Anderson's division → Wright's brigade

69th Pa., 71st Pa., 72nd Pa., 106th Pa. → 2nd Brigade Webb
59th N.Y., 20th Mass., 7th Mich. → 3rd Brig. Hall → 2nd Division Gibbon → 2nd Corps → AP
13th Vt. → 3rd Brigade → 3rd Division → 1st Corps → AP
1st Brigade Carr, 2nd Brigade Brewster → 2nd Division Humphreys → 3rd Corps → AP

THE CLIMAX OF THE BATTLE   161

Map 3-47
The Union 11th Corps on east Cemetery Hill is reinforced by 2nd and 11th Corps units

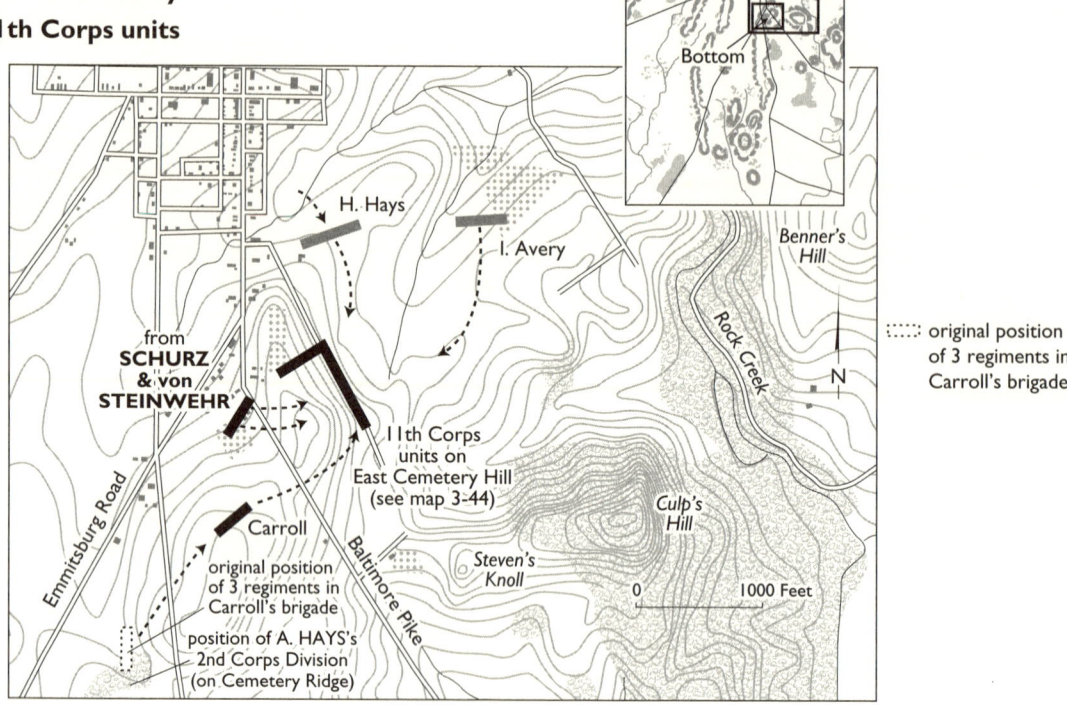

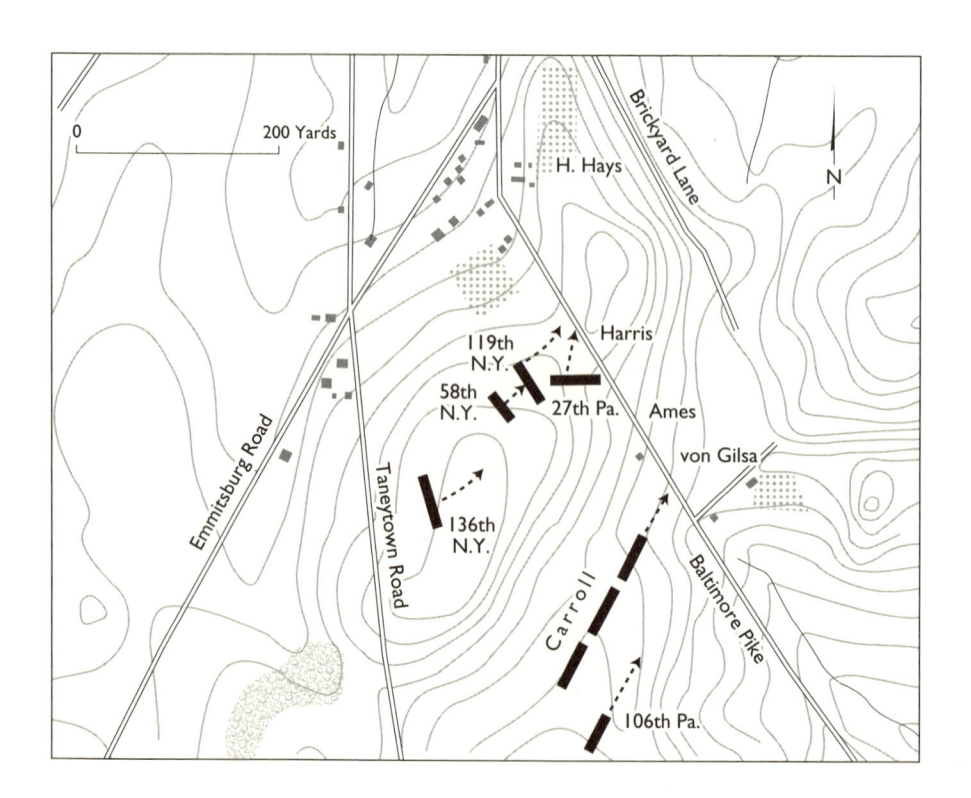

162 THE STAND OF THE U.S. ARMY AT GETTYSBURG

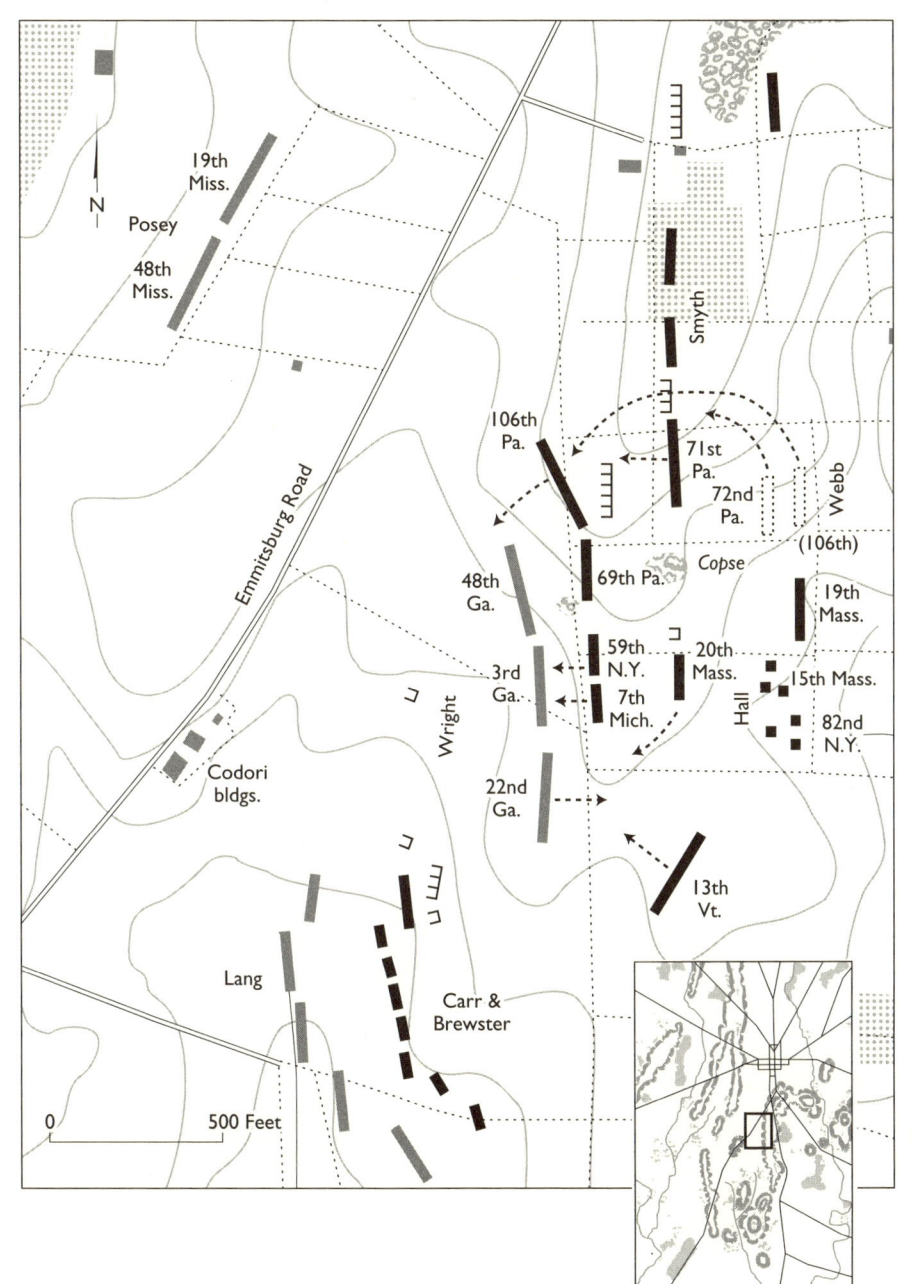

**Map 3-48
The repulse of Wright near the copse of trees**

That they had had to fight their way to this area meant that these Southerners now advanced toward the Federal fallback lines in some disorder.

The Confederates in the brigades led by Brig. Gens. George Anderson, Paul Semmes, Joseph Kershaw, and William Wofford were ripe for a counterattack, and the Pennsylvania Reserves from Brig. Gen. Samuel W. Crawford's 3rd Division, 5th Corps, soon launched one (chart 3-36).[128] One of his brigades, led by Col. William McCandless, formed on the northern slope of Little Round Top (map 3-49). These 5th Corps troops were bolstered by two additional regiments: the 11th Pennsylvania, from the second of Crawford's two brigades, and the 98th Pennsylvania, detached from a brigade of the *6th* Corps (chart 3-36). That large unit arrived at Gettysburg in the late afternoon and replaced the 5th Corps as the Army of the Potomac's overall reserve behind the lines on the Baltimore Pike.

THE CLIMAX OF THE BATTLE

Map 3-49
The repulse of the rebel right near Little Round Top and Plum Run

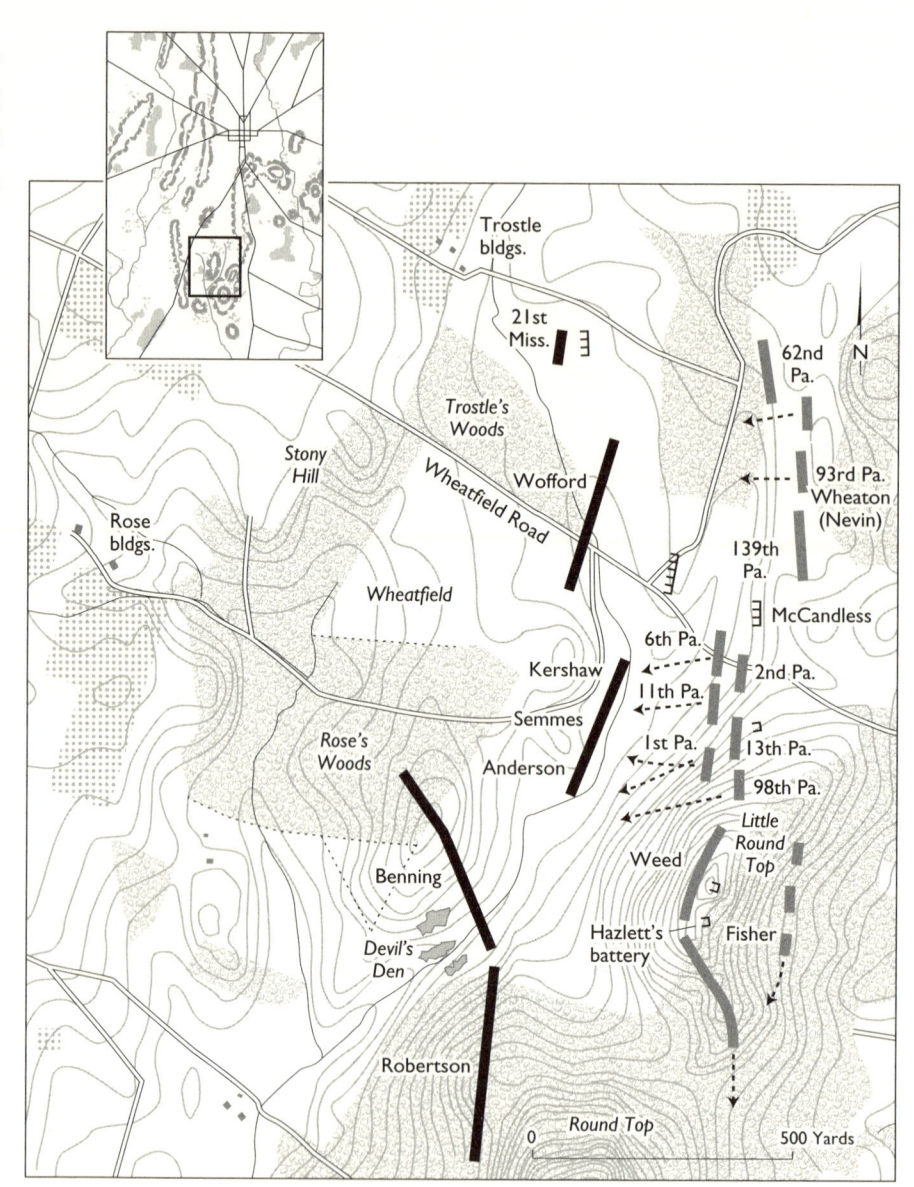

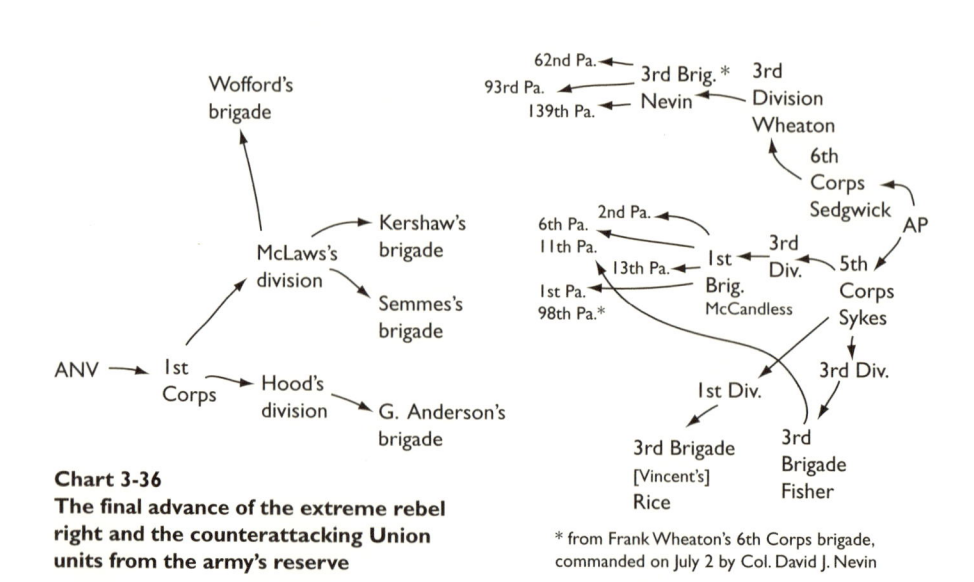

Chart 3-36
The final advance of the extreme rebel right and the counterattacking Union units from the army's reserve

* from Frank Wheaton's 6th Corps brigade, commanded on July 2 by Col. David J. Nevin

164　THE STAND OF THE U.S. ARMY AT GETTYSBURG

With regard to the participation of 6th Corps units in the fighting late on July 2, General Meade first ordered its commander, Maj. Gen. John Sedgwick, to place his men near the army's left wing, in the vicinity of the 3rd and 5th Corps positions. Sedgwick acted quickly, and soon one of his staff officers directed elements of the 6th Corps to advance "toward the heavy firing."[129] General Sedgwick himself came upon one of his brigades and yelled out, "Fall in boys, move quickly!"[130] The result of this flurry of activity was that several 6th Corps troops bolstered the counterattacking force being formed by the Pennsylvania Reserves (chart 3-36, map 3-49).

The Pennsylvanians then charged down the northern slope of Little Round Top, driving the rebel brigades led by Anderson, Semmes, and Kershaw back beyond the Wheatfield. Just to the north of this repulse, most of Col. David J. Nevin's 6th Corps brigade (chart 3-36) advanced against Wofford's brigade, the last of the Confederate units in this area. When Nevin's three regiments moved out from their position on south Cemetery Ridge, Wofford was ordered back. The fourth of Nevin's units, the 98th Pennsylvania, was intermingled with the Pennsylvania Reserves (chart 3-36, map 3-49).

The overall left of the Union line—well beyond Little Round Top—was at last secure. To consolidate that flank, Strong Vincent's 5th Corps brigade—now led by Col. James Rice of the 44th New York—and most of Col. Joseph W. Fisher's 3rd Brigade, 3rd Division, were dispatched to Big Round Top (chart 3-36, map 3-49).

The Climax

The battles south and east of Gettysburg had involved some of the most ferocious fighting of the Civil War (chart 3-37 lists the large numbers of casualties that were suffered on July 2). On a regiment-by-regiment basis, the assaulting Confederates had performed magnificently. Whether the rebel generals had done as well is another matter. Many of the individual Southern units had gained ground—especially in the areas of the *advanced* positions occupied by Sickles's 3rd Corps, and at the southern end of Culp's Hill. Yet the Confederates had failed to dislodge the Union line as a whole. Not only had the Federal defenders been tenacious in *their* overall performance, but they had also yielded almost *no ground* with respect to the *original* fishhook line. The lone exception was the southern sector of the Union breastworks below Culp's Hill. Thus the net gains of the rebel attacks were nearly zero.

This describes the outcome of the battles on July 2 merely in terms of ground and positions. Something else transpired that day: The Union defenders were forced to *respond* to the attacks upon their lines. Sickles's move made them defend in a relentlessly *active* manner. The corps commanders, and General Meade himself, had met most of the Confederate challenges by moving Union units to the right place at the right time—often *just* in time.

The stands and the counterattacks made by the Federal defense worked in the narrow meaning of the term: the rebels were ultimately stalled, frustrated, and forced back. In a larger and subtler sense, the Army of the Potomac seemed to have gained a large measure of *confidence*. By being forced into a frenetic series of positive actions, its overall stand may have resulted in the realization that "We can *do* this. We were made to *act*. We did, and we held."

What if the Union lines had stayed in the fishhook, absorbing the attacks? Even had those all been resisted—the Federals merely holding their positions, as the Army of Northern Virginia had done at Fredericksburg—that kind of result

Chart 3-37
Vanderslice's estimates of casualties for July 2*
(DOES NOT INCLUDE FIGURES FOR CULP'S HILL)

	killed and wounded	missing / captured	total
Confederate	5,660	1,470	7,130
Union	7,890	1,180	9,070

* see chart 2-13

might not have given them the psychological confidence of a significant achievement. The Army of the Potomac thus could thank Sickles for jump-starting a series of defensive *actions* that had a significant salutary effect. Although what General Sickles set in motion stemmed from wrongheaded haughtiness, he deserves ironic credit for *creating a crisis*—albeit a *manageable* one, as the events of that day were to prove.

From the limited perspective of military tactics, it also must be pointed out that a defensive position out in front of the main lines can cause the attackers to expend much of their assaulting power before they approach those lines.[131] That is what happened on July 2 at Gettysburg in several sectors of the battlefield. Sickles may have had this in mind, in spite of his impetuousness and whether or not he was haunted by the memory of Hazel Grove at Chancellorsville. Thus the Army of the Potomac had to give grudging thanks to its strangest corps commander.

But Sickles and his fellow corps commanders also had to thank their commanding general, for General Meade had again *unleashed* them—just as he had begun to do on July 1. During the afternoon of July 2 he had not only helped supervise the active defense, but he also allowed his chief subordinates to respond—often in a manner that forced them to choose a *risky* defensive tactic. They took those risks but won the gambles. Would an earlier commander of the Army of the Potomac (McClellan? Burnside?[132] Hooker?) have given them all this leeway, or even made a decision to do *anything*?

In any case, the rapid series of redeployments of Federal units from many places along the center and right-hand sections of the defensive line were allowed and accomplished. They had been executed in a perilous manner. This opened up the defense to maneuvers that might have broken the Union lines on the left of the Federal 2nd Corps, toward the center of that unit's position, and near the extreme Union right on Culp's Hill. But the Union army had gotten away with it—often by achieving *further* reinforcing moves. These plugged the gaps and bolstered the weakened positions created by the initial shifts.

One of those locations deserves special comment: the place where the depleted defense fought on Culp's Hill. This situation was created when units were pulled from their positions there to support the beleaguered defenders on the Union right. The attack on General Greene's line on Culp's Hill had been a close-run thing. Some believe that the Army of Northern Virginia came as close to winning the Battle of Gettysburg on that hill as it had in any other sector of the battlefield.[133] One of the Southerners' problems in that sector was that General Ewell simply *ran out of July 2.* That darkness fell, thus ending Ewell's attacks late on the Second, speaks to the overall performance of the Confederate high command. Ewell *may,* on one hand, have attacked too late. On the other, he may have waited until almost the right moment—when Culp's Hill had become so poorly defended in terms of troop numbers. If that situation had occurred with enough hours of daylight left, Ewell's force might have had time to overrun the right wing of the Union defense and gain control of the Baltimore Pike. But General Longstreet, given the usual leeway allowed by Lee, had seen to it that the *rebel right* attacked when there was not much of that Thursday afternoon left. General Ewell had been forced to wait until the Union responses to Longstreet's attacks opened up the Federal line to his front. By then, as it turned out, it *was* too late.

Perhaps General Lee should have placed a heavier hand on his "right-hand man," Longstreet, to get that corps commander into his attacking positions earlier. But this was not Lee's style, as has been said many times about the way he commanded in earlier battles.[134] He continued to employ hands-off leadership at Gettysburg. For example, "during the whole time the firing continued [on July 2, Lee] sent one message, and only received one report."[135] Given the complex fighting that day, it was not enough. General Lee might have kept more firmly in mind that two of his corps commanders had just been appointed to those positions. Pertinent to this point is the poor performance of Maj. Gen. Richard Anderson, who failed to manage his 3rd Corps division properly as evening approached. Anderson's obviously desultory activities—at least they seemed so to Dorsey Pender—should have been dealt with by firm orders from General Hill (whose own actions on July 2 were hard to find) or, failing that, from General Lee himself.

For his part, General Meade had much *less* time to work his way into the position of army commander than was afforded Generals Hill and Ewell with their corps. Meade proved, however, that it was sufficient—or perhaps not too much. The time he had, starting on June 28, was not enough for him to brood about or agonize over the question of "Can I *do* this?" Moreover, General Sickles presented him with the sudden crisis of command that took away the last bit of time during which Meade might have thought himself out of a willingness to act and to fight.

Meade called his famous "council of war" on the night of July 2, after it was clear that Culp's and Cemetery Hills were safe. The meeting began about 11 P.M., in Meade's small headquarters building near the Taneytown Road (map 3-7). As a result of this gathering of his large-unit commanders, Meade exhibited a willingness to *keep fighting* the battle.[136] Rather than recount the whole story of that meeting, suffice it to say that General Meade loosely supervised the discussion, which resulted in the assembled officers' unanimous decision that they *remain in a defensive posture in their positions* at Gettysburg.

I believe, however, that they had more than confidence in their *position*—they had gained confidence in their *performance* as well. Juxtaposing remarks made by two of the opposing generals helps reveal this state of mind. James Longstreet wrote after the war that the men in his corps had performed "the best three hours' fighting ever done by any troops on any battle-field."[137] Whether or not this is more self-congratulatory than analytical, a lesser known statement made by Maj. Gen. John Newton, who succeeded General Reynolds as 1st Corps commander, is even more revealing: "General Meade, I think you ought to feel much gratified with today's results." Meade, vividly aware of that day's crises and all the carnage that ensued, replied: "In the name of common sense, Newton, why?" To which Newton responded, "Why, they have *hammered us into a position they cannot whip us out of.*"[138]

That was exactly the case. It also is why the moments when the Union army repelled the final assaults near Little Round Top, below the copse of trees, and from their positions on the two northern hills defined the *climax of the Battle of Gettysburg*. Although they did not know it at the time, in retrospect it seems that the soldiers in the Army of the Potomac had just gained an inner belief that *they* were ones who were invincible. The tables had been turned in the eastern theater of the Civil War. The momentous events of July 3 would prove that this was so.[139]

Map 4-1
Theater of battle, July 3

Phases of Battle:

a. A long unknown battle on the Union right and the Confederate left

b. Lee changes his plan of attack

c. The great artillery bombardment of the Civil War

d. The nine brigades advance

e. The Confederate left wing is counterattacked—and an advancing brigade breaks: envelopment of one rebel flank

f. The Confederate center pierces the Union line: high-water mark

g. Pickett's right is counterattacked: double envelopment

h. The stand of the twenty-six regiments—rejoined by the one that ran

i. Destruction of Pickett's Charge and Union victory at the Battle of Gettysburg

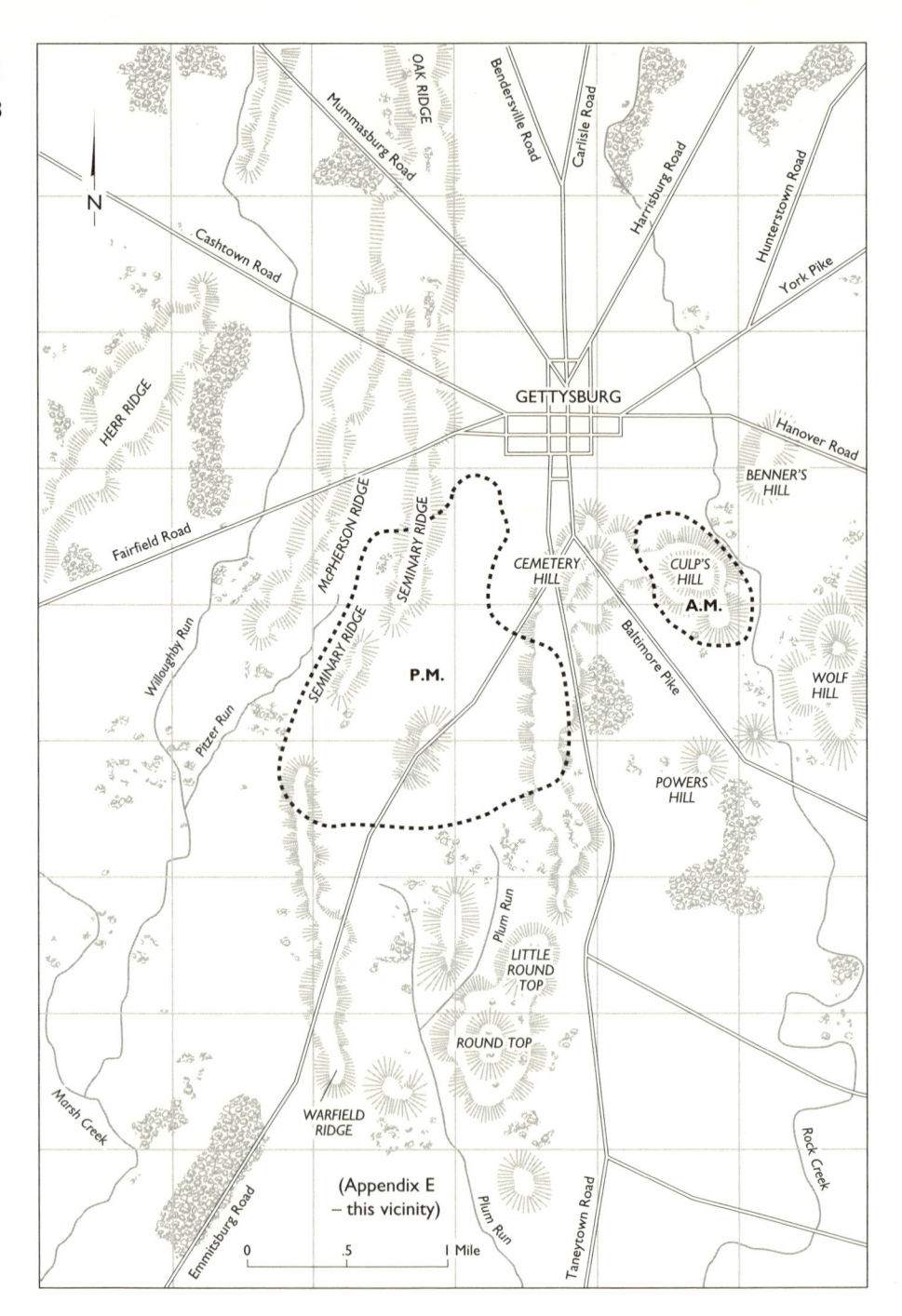

CHAPTER FOUR

July 3: The Great Gamble Lee Could Have Won and the Federals' Finest Hour

> The dead lie in their awkward slumber
> Having answered glory's call
> Lying scattered beyond number
> Piled like cordwood by the wall
>
> —Garnet Rogers

This is July 3 at the Battle of Gettysburg: The story of the nine Confederate brigades that advanced and the one that broke; of the one Union regiment that ran and the twenty-six that stood their ground. Here I paraphrase a passage from a book written by George R. Stewart. The passage rings—although the story from the Federal perspective will involve more than a simple stand by those twenty-six regiments.

For four decades, Stewart's work was the only full account of the third day at Gettysburg.[1] This book is entitled *Pickett's Charge,* although it is about the entirety of this third day of the battle, insofar as actions south of the town are concerned.[2] Another misnomer is that Pickett's Charge was perhaps *neither,* as we shall see when the story unfolds.

The theater of battle for July 3 (map 4-1) is similar to that of the Second (map 3-1). In fact, some of the ground south of Gettysburg involves the same route taken by Brig. Gen. Ambrose R. Wright's Confederate brigade. His attacking troops on July 2 moved to a point along Cemetery Ridge near the most famous location where the fighting occurred on the Third. Note that the area circumscribed in map 4-1 is smaller than the theater of battle for July 2. It does not include Cemetery Hill in the north, and it does not extend as far southward, falling short of Warfield Ridge and its vicinity.[3]

The weather at Gettysburg ranged from cloudy to clear on July 3, 1863. The temperature was seventy-three degrees at seven in the morning and rose to eighty-seven by 2 P.M. After a calm morning and afternoon, heavy clouds appeared and a severe thunderstorm started at six in the evening. A *lot* had happened by that time, both east of the town and to the south of it.

This breakdown of the fighting on July 3 is cutting things pretty fine, for some of these "phases" (d. through i.) proceed rapidly from one to the next within only one hour of time. Thus, Gettysburg's third day might seem relatively simple. Yet there are some intriguing complexities amidst the ostensibly straightforward series of events. The usual maps accompany this account, including some in which the internal geometry suggests simplicity. Once again, this is misleading, and cer-

**Map 4-2
Union guns aimed at the rebel left, early morning, July 3**

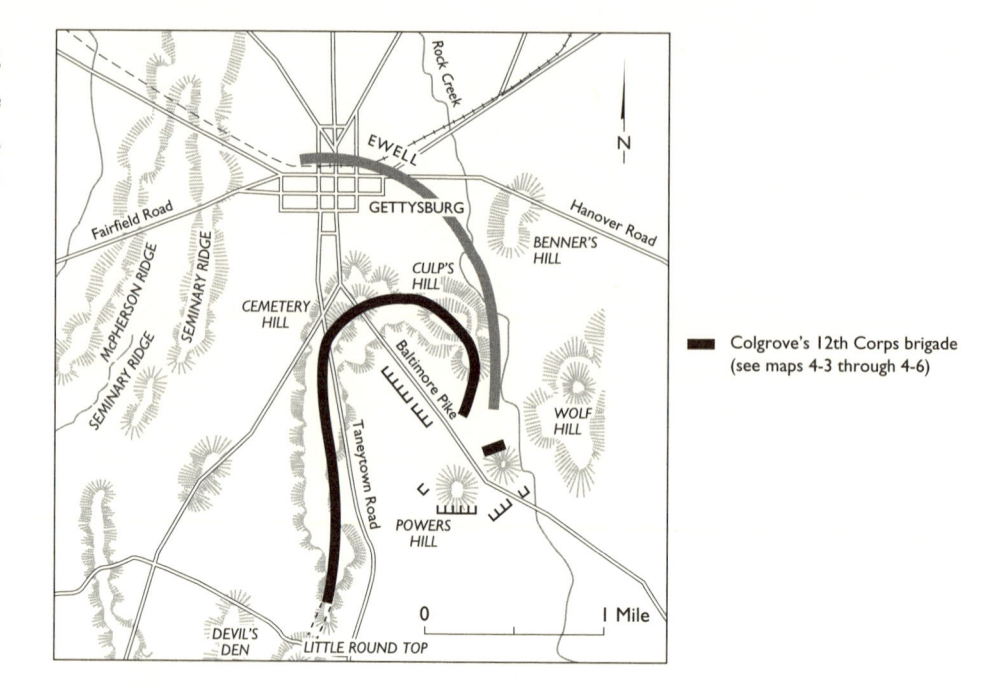

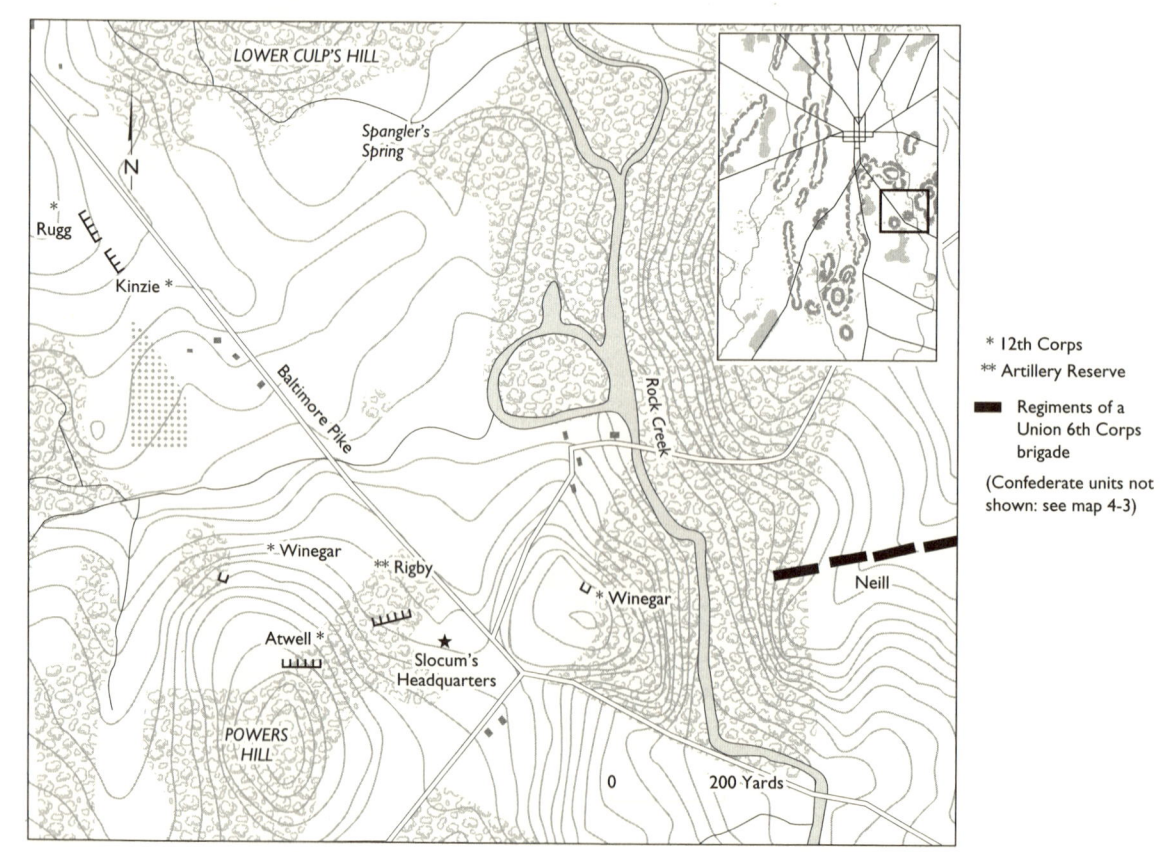

■ Colgrove's 12th Corps brigade (see maps 4-3 through 4-6)

* 12th Corps
** Artillery Reserve

■ Regiments of a Union 6th Corps brigade

(Confederate units not shown: see map 4-3)

170   THE STAND OF THE U.S. ARMY AT GETTYSBURG

tain of the phrases in the listing of phases imply why that is so. Thus, the Union defense against "the Charge" was a very *active* one, as the Federal force continued to perform in this manner. That there *was* a rebel "high-water mark" at Gettysburg on this day might imply that a Confederate tide rolled toward the Union line, crested, and inevitably receded. This further implies that the rebel assault was doomed from the start. That is the conventional wisdom, but it might be wrong. If the Army of the Potomac had not *acted* upon the *confidence* it had gained on the previous day, Pickett's Charge could have succeeded.[4]

A Long Unknown Battle on the Union Right and the Confederate Left

The battle on July 3 started on Culp's Hill. This fight is as unappreciated by the casual battlefield visitor as is the fighting that occurred there the previous evening. Yet the battle for Culp's Hill raged for several hours on the Third. Moreover, *when* the fighting started there significantly impacted on Confederate plans for the day.

Remember that Brig. Gen. George H. Steuart's rebel brigade had occupied a section of the Union fortifications on the extreme right of the defensive line on lower Culp's Hill. Steuart's Virginians, Marylanders, and North Carolinians held those breastworks from the evening of July 2 through the night. Before daylight, the rebel force near both lower Culp's Hill (including the works now possessed by Steuart) and the upper hill was reinforced and significantly stronger than on the previous evening. Nevertheless, the Federals on the army's right wing intended to attack the Confederates in this region of the field, aiming to recapture the works on the lower hill. The Union 12th Corps did not end up attacking, however, because in the meantime, the commander of the Confederate left wing had been ordered to "renew [his] attack at daylight."[5] This led to a long series of assaults on the Northerners' Culp's Hill positions.

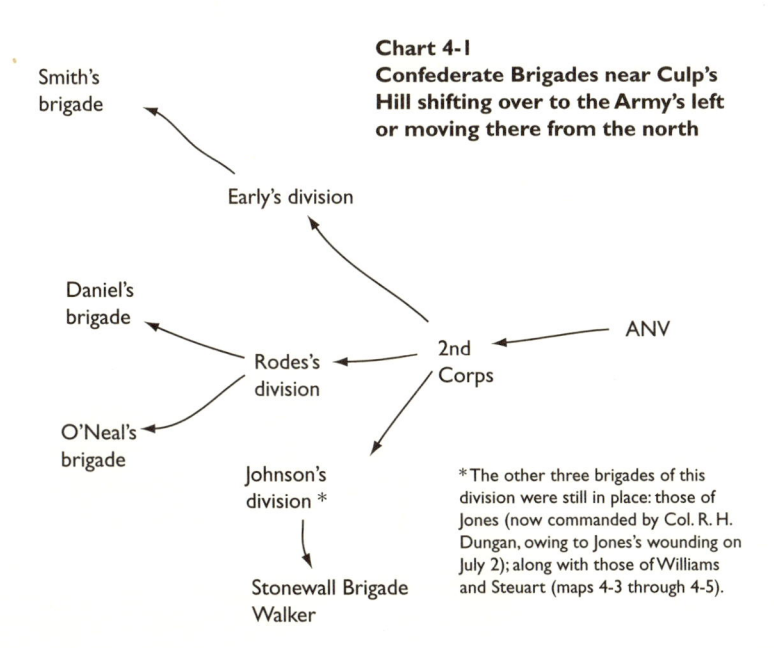

**Chart 4-1
Confederate Brigades near Culp's Hill shifting over to the Army's left or moving there from the north**

- Smith's brigade ← Early's division
- Daniel's brigade ← Rodes's division
- O'Neal's brigade ← Rodes's division
- Rodes's division ← 2nd Corps ← ANV
- Johnson's division * ← 2nd Corps
  - Stonewall Brigade Walker

*The other three brigades of this division were still in place: those of Jones (now commanded by Col. R. H. Dungan, owing to Jones's wounding on July 2); along with those of Williams and Steuart (maps 4-3 through 4-5).

THE GREAT GAMBLE LEE COULD HAVE WON 171

Map 4-3

Johnson's first morning attack on the Union right

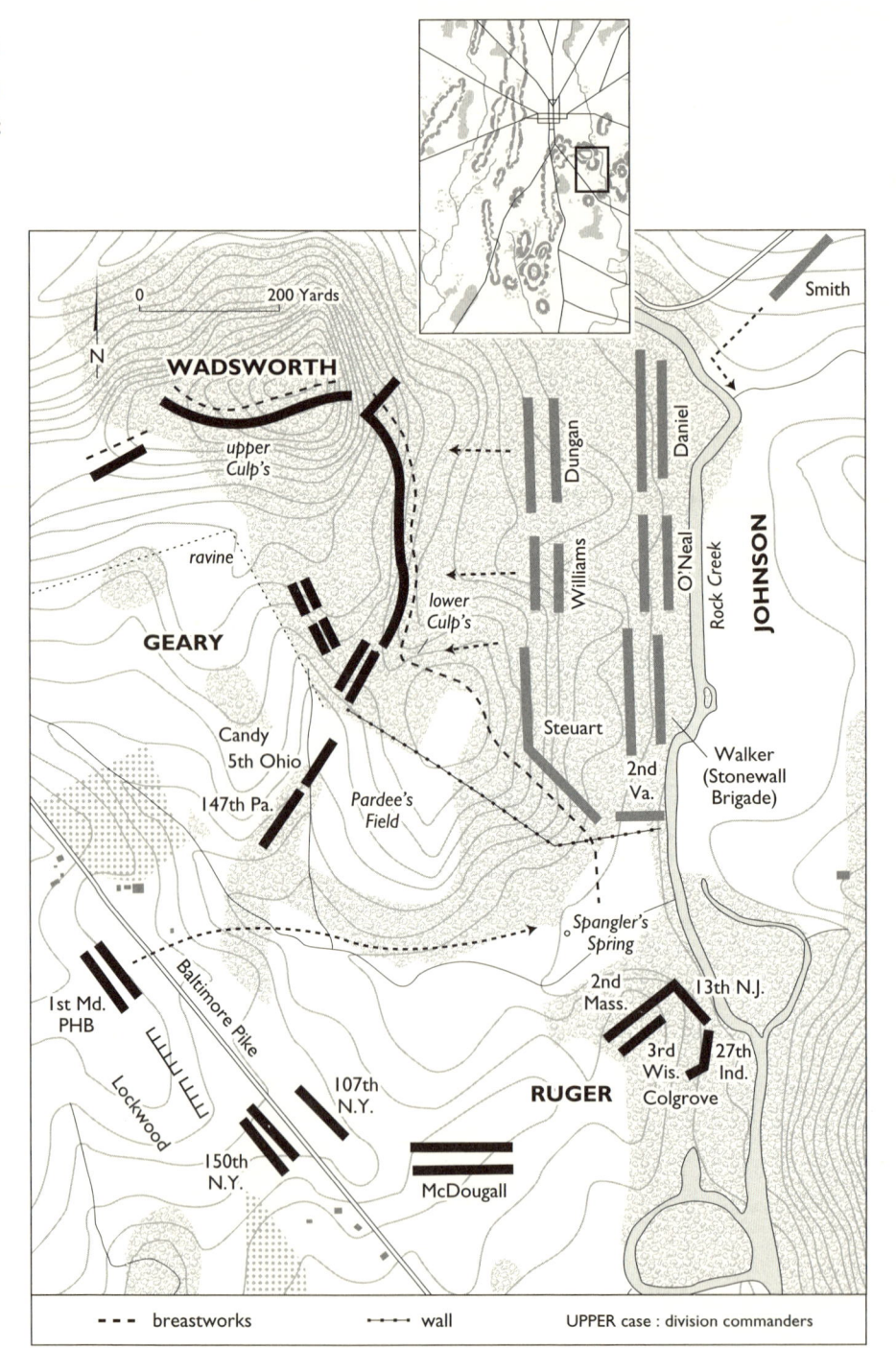

In a way, the Federals in this sector goaded the rebel 2nd Corps units into initiating their assaults.[6] Thus, the action commenced in the early morning hours of July 3 when Federal batteries firing from high ground west and south of the Baltimore Pike (map 4-2) hit the Confederate penetration on lower Culp's Hill (map 4-3). The Federal fire was severe but lasted less than half an hour, until about 5 A.M. This caused the Confederates in this sector to renew their assaults of the previous evening much earlier than Robert E. Lee wanted.

This second battle for Culp's Hill lasted until late morning. The troops of Maj. Gen. Edward Johnson's division and others (charts 4-1 and 4-3) on the extreme left of the Southern army made their first attack westward as they had done on July 2 (map 4-3). However, this assault and the two that followed failed to break the Union line of breastworks (maps 4-3, 4-4, and 4-5). The rebel left wing had been bolstered by the return of the Stonewall Brigade (Johnson's division), elements of which had been tied up in the distracting fight for Brinkerhoff's Ridge during the previous evening (Appendix C). Smith's brigade from Early's division and O'Neal's brigade from Rodes's also joined General Johnson's force (chart 4-1). The assaulting power of the Confederate left wing, amounting to nine thousand men, had roughly doubled compared with the infantry force that had attacked during the evening of July 2. Yet, Johnson had essentially no artillery to support his attacks on the morning of the Third. The Union force in this vicinity, whose infantry component was equal in number to that of the rebels, also included many batteries (map 4-2).[7]

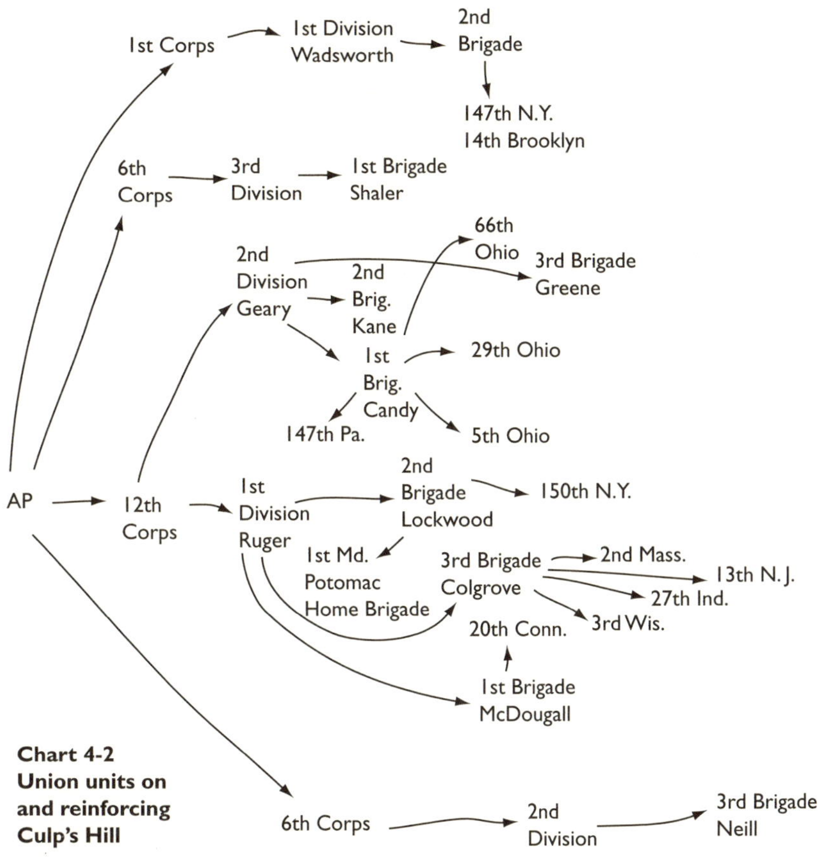

**Chart 4-2
Union units on and reinforcing Culp's Hill**

After they initiated the fighting at dawn, Federal artillery fire continued off and on for five further hours. This provided some extra weight to the defense of Culp's Hill, but the actions of the Union infantry told most of this tale. These Federal units were much more numerous than had been the case the previous evening. The entire 12th Corps was back on Culp's Hill or nearby (map 4-3, chart 4-2), and 1st and 6th Corps units reinforced the Union right before the end of the morning (chart 4-2).[8] The Northerners made use of most of the breastworks they had built on July 2. They also arranged their infantry positions to seal off the Confederate penetration into the lower works (map 4-3). The position on the right of the Federal army's line and the actions of the defending forces there proved too strong for the rebels.

Not long after the action started in the early morning hours of the Third, the Southerners' 2nd Corps commander, Lt. Gen. Richard S. Ewell, learned that the main attack slated to take place in the southern sector of the field would not be launched until 9 A.M. at the earliest. This meant that General Johnson on the rebel left would be fighting alone.

The principal struggle during the fighting at the top of the battlefield on July 3 occurred on upper Culp's Hill, although elements of Brig. Gen. Thomas H. Ruger's Federal division made some probes up the southwestern slope of lower Culp's Hill (map 4-3, chart 4-2). The rebels' first and second attacks occurred along most of this west-facing line, principally against Brig. Gen. George S. Greene's brigade. It was Greene's badly outnumbered soldiers who had borne the brunt of the Southerners' assault on July 2. The stalwart 137th New York Regi-

THE GREAT GAMBLE LEE COULD HAVE WON   173

Map 4-4

Johnson's second attack

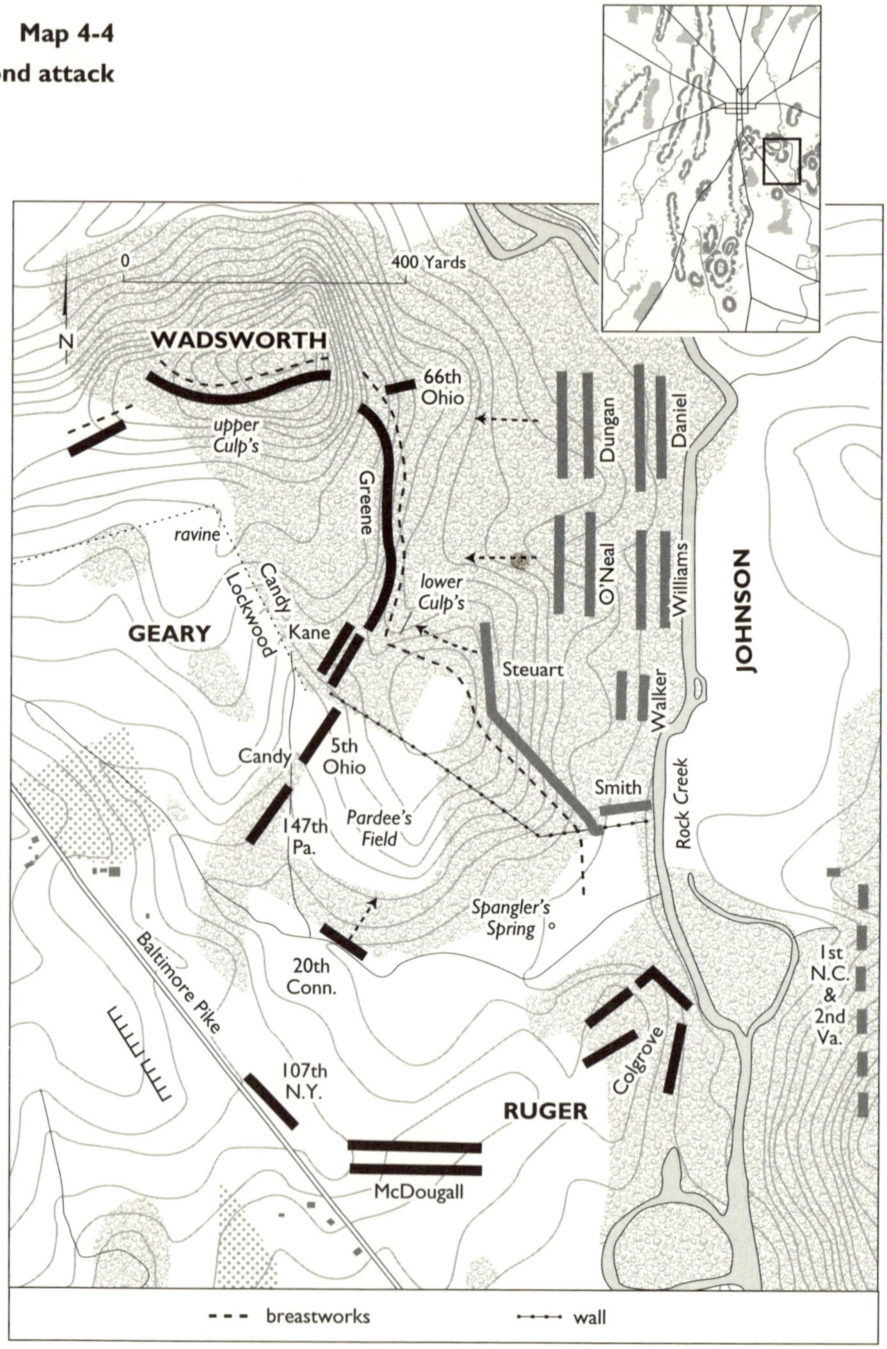

ment, which held the extreme Union right during the twilight hours and nighttime of the previous day, fought hard again on July 3. These New Yorkers, and other Federal regiments in the east-facing line, were relieved at times (exemplified by the 137th New York's position being taken over by the 29th Ohio [chart 4-2] after the former fought along the breastworks for two hours on that Friday morning). In fact, the defenders shuttled back and forth between the front line and a ravine, part of which coursed behind the breastworks (maps 4-3 and 4-4). These bluecoats thus gained respites during the six-hour fight and used these opportunities to clean their rifles.[9]

174   THE STAND OF THE U.S. ARMY AT GETTYSBURG

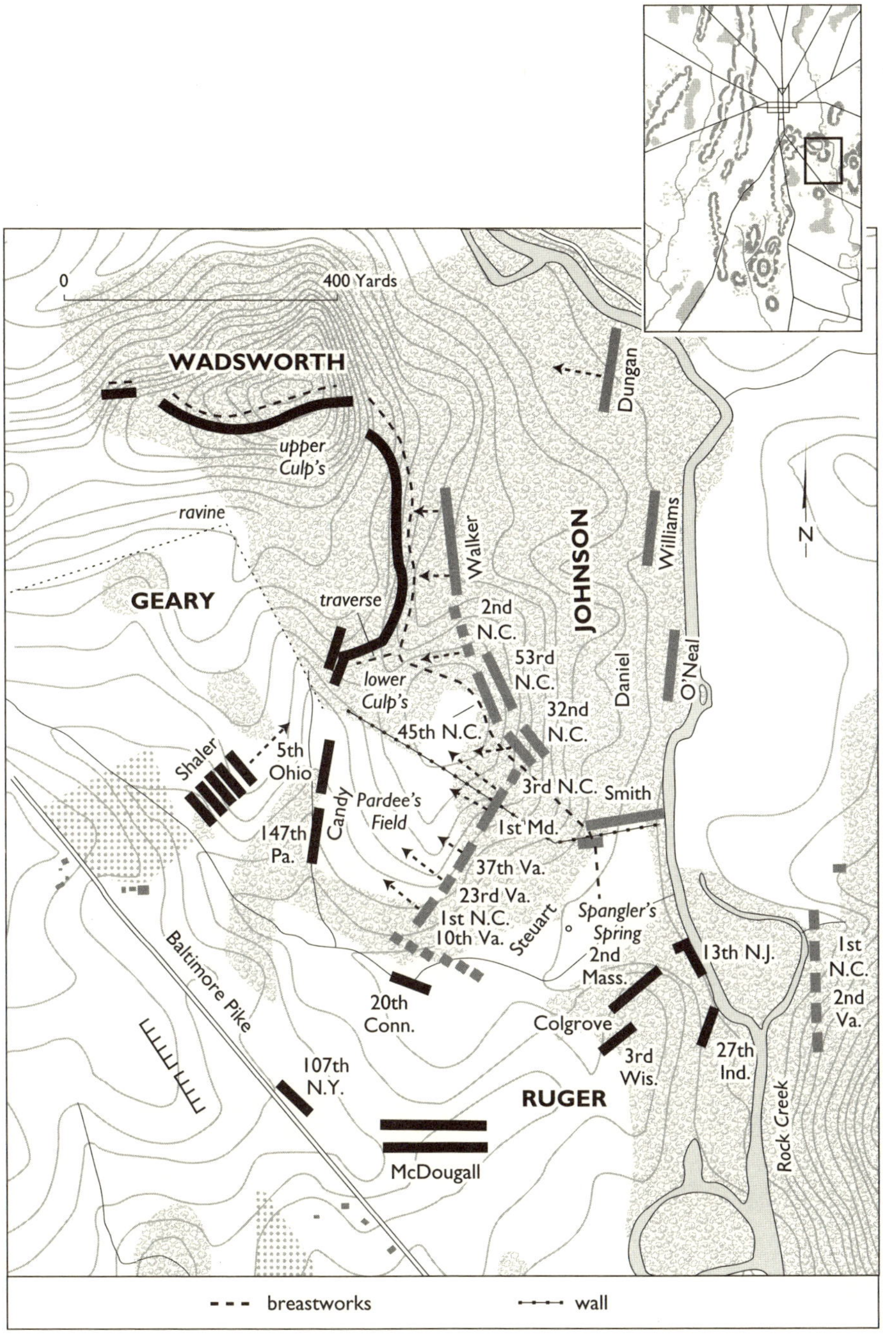

Map 4-5
Johnson's last attack

Some of the shuttling regiments were from Union units other than Greene's. These included the 1st Corps's 147th New York and 14th Brooklyn (the latter was one of the few regiments in either army to see significant action on all three days of the battle). Moreover, Greene's left was bolstered by another of Candy's regiments, the 66th Ohio, which wheeled to face south and enfiladed Johnson's right for much of the morning (map 4-4). The Confederate right wing consisted of Jones's brigade (maps 4-3 and 4-4), now commanded by Lt. Col. Robert H. Dungan, because Brig. Gen. John Jones had been wounded as his soldiers attacked Greene's line on July 2.

Map 4-6

A Union counterattack on Johnson's left fails

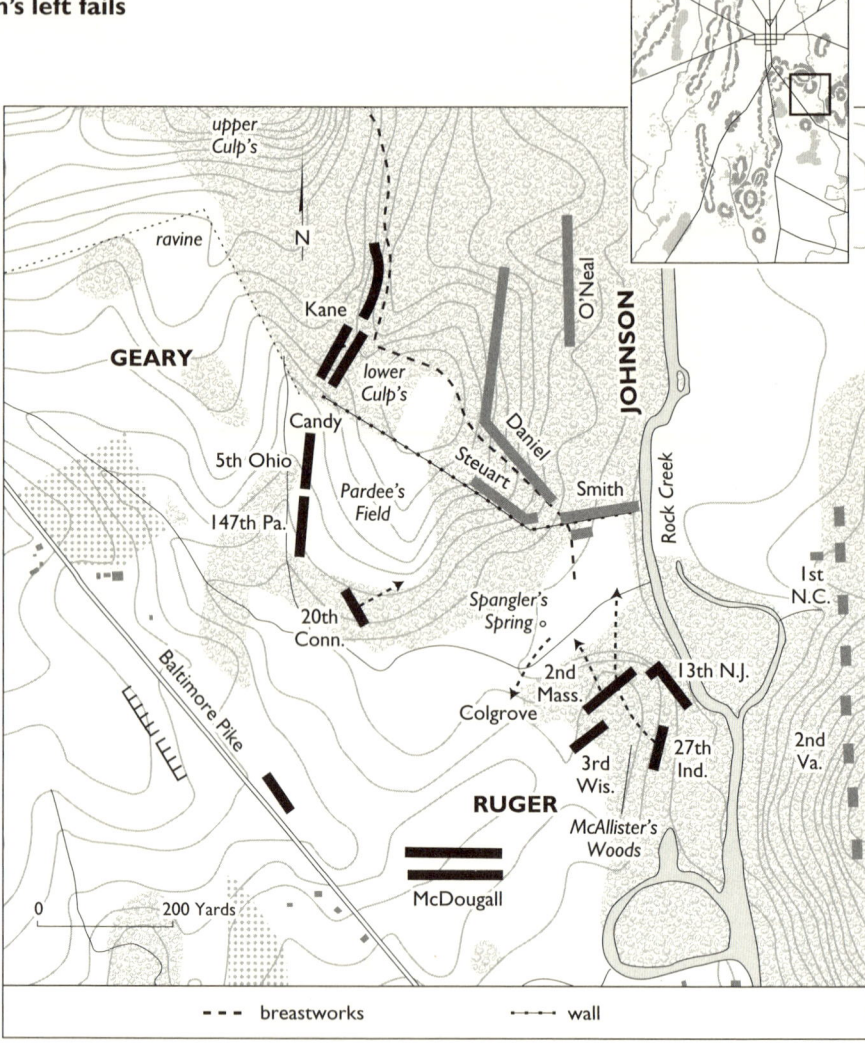

The last of Johnson's attacks came at about 10 A.M. The right and center fronts of the rebel assault force were now composed of Brig. Gen. James A. Walker's Stonewall Brigade and a brigade commanded by Brig. Gen. Junius Daniel (map 4-5). They assaulted Greene's position from the east, while General Steuart's brigade (chart 4-3) advanced over Pardee's Field (map 4-5) in a northerly direction toward the main hill. This two-pronged attack failed. Both attackers and defenders may have been exhausted by this late morning hour. Recall, however, that the Federal commanders kept relieving and augmenting the frontline defenders. Moreover, during the final stages of the action, Union reinforcements from the 6th Corps (the 122nd New York from Alexander Shaler's brigade [chart 4-2]) came to the aid of the 149th New York near the right-center of General Greene's line (map 4-5). The third Confederate attack upon this and the other parts of the Union position lasted until about 11 A.M. As before, the rebels were repulsed. They then withdrew eastward toward Rock Creek (map 4-6).

There was one more small action in this sector. The 2nd Massachusetts and 27th Indiana regiments made a futile attack against Johnson's left across the Spangler Spring meadow (map 4-6, chart 4-4).[10] Although the two regiments were beaten back by Brig. Gen. William Smith's rebel brigade (map 4-6), Ewell's

176   THE STAND OF THE U.S. ARMY AT GETTYSBURG

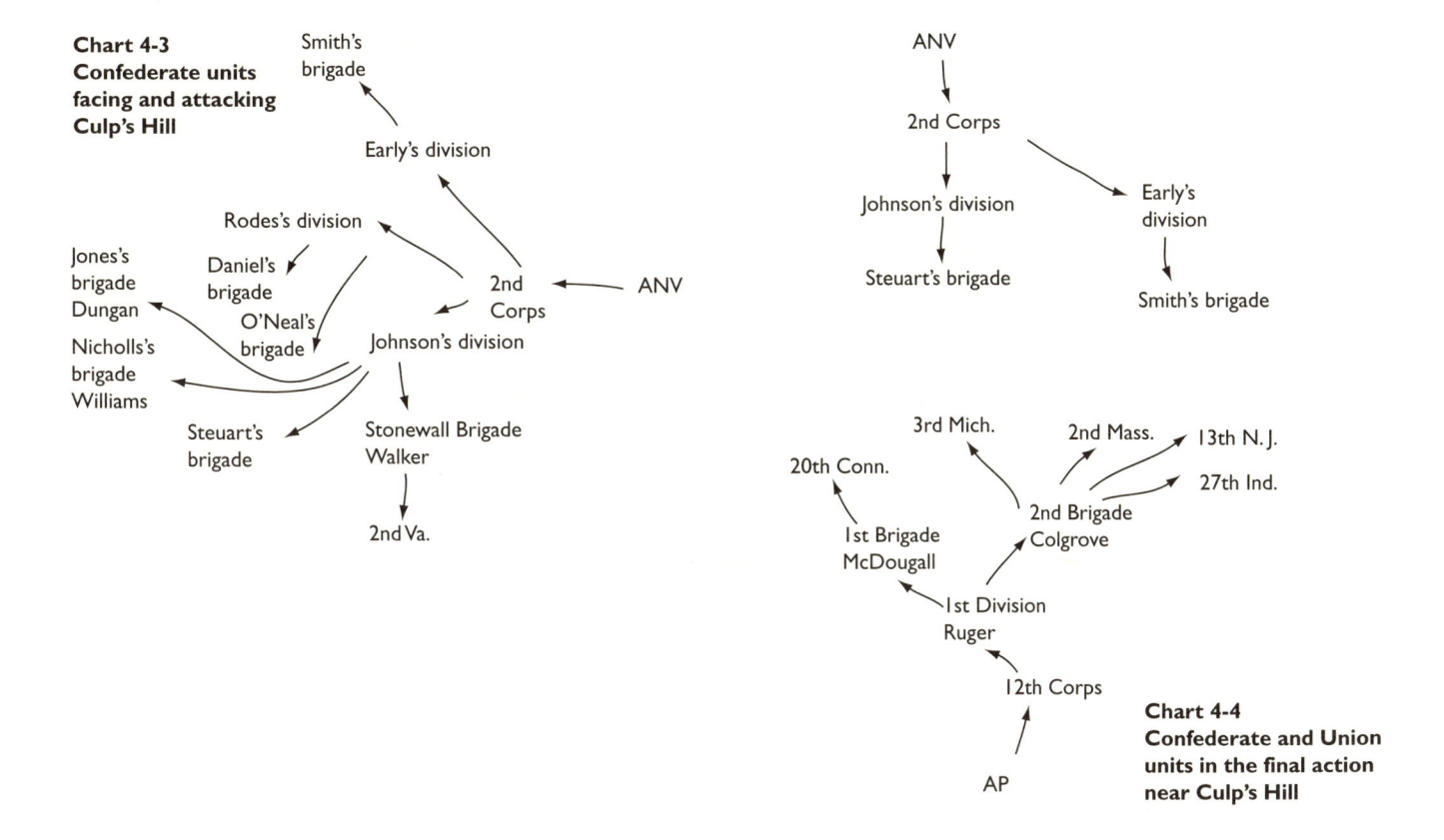

Chart 4-3 Confederate units facing and attacking Culp's Hill

(diagram: ANV → 2nd Corps; 2nd Corps → Rodes's division, Early's division, Johnson's division; Rodes's division → Daniel's brigade, O'Neal's brigade; Early's division → Smith's brigade; Johnson's division → Steuart's brigade, Stonewall Brigade Walker, and Jones's brigade Dungan, Nicholls's brigade Williams; Stonewall Brigade Walker → 2nd Va.)

Chart 4-4 Confederate and Union units in the final action near Culp's Hill

(diagram: ANV → 2nd Corps → Johnson's division, Early's division; Johnson's division → Steuart's brigade; Early's division → Smith's brigade. AP → 12th Corps → 1st Division Ruger → 1st Brigade McDougall, 2nd Brigade Colgrove; 1st Brigade McDougall → 20th Conn., 3rd Mich.; 2nd Brigade Colgrove → 2nd Mass., 13th N.J., 27th Ind.)

failure to dislodge the Federals on the morning of July 3 restored possession of the works on Culp's Hill to Federal hands.

The defenders' casualties numbered about one thousand; those of the attacking Southerners were more than twice as many.[11] The commander of the principal defending unit, Brig. Gen. John W. Geary, said that his 2nd Division soldiers "expended in the fight on July 3, and in subsequent skirmishing, 277,000 rounds of ammunition."[12] This once more speaks to the inadequacy of the would-be wonder weapons of the mid-nineteenth century and the problems that the men faced in using them. These rifled muskets, as intrinsically accurate as they might be, not only fouled readily but also rarely found a target in the hands of inexperienced soldiers who had received little marksmanship training.[13] In the fighting throughout that Friday morning at Gettysburg, Union defenders fired more than a hundred shots for every Confederate killed or wounded.

As the dead and wounded littered the field, the curtain was brought down on this sector of the battlefield—and ended the actions of the Confederate 2nd Corps in the Gettysburg campaign. Recall that the infantry fighting that culminated in this remarkable series of events in American history had been initiated by Ewell's corps when he attacked the Union garrison at Winchester, Virginia, back in the middle of June.

Lee Changes His Plan of Attack

The fact that the Federals took the tactical initiative to reopen the battle on the army's right so early on the morning of July 3 forced General Lee to change his plans for the remainder of that day. The initial planning involved attacks, like those of the previous afternoon and evening, by the Army of Northern Virginia

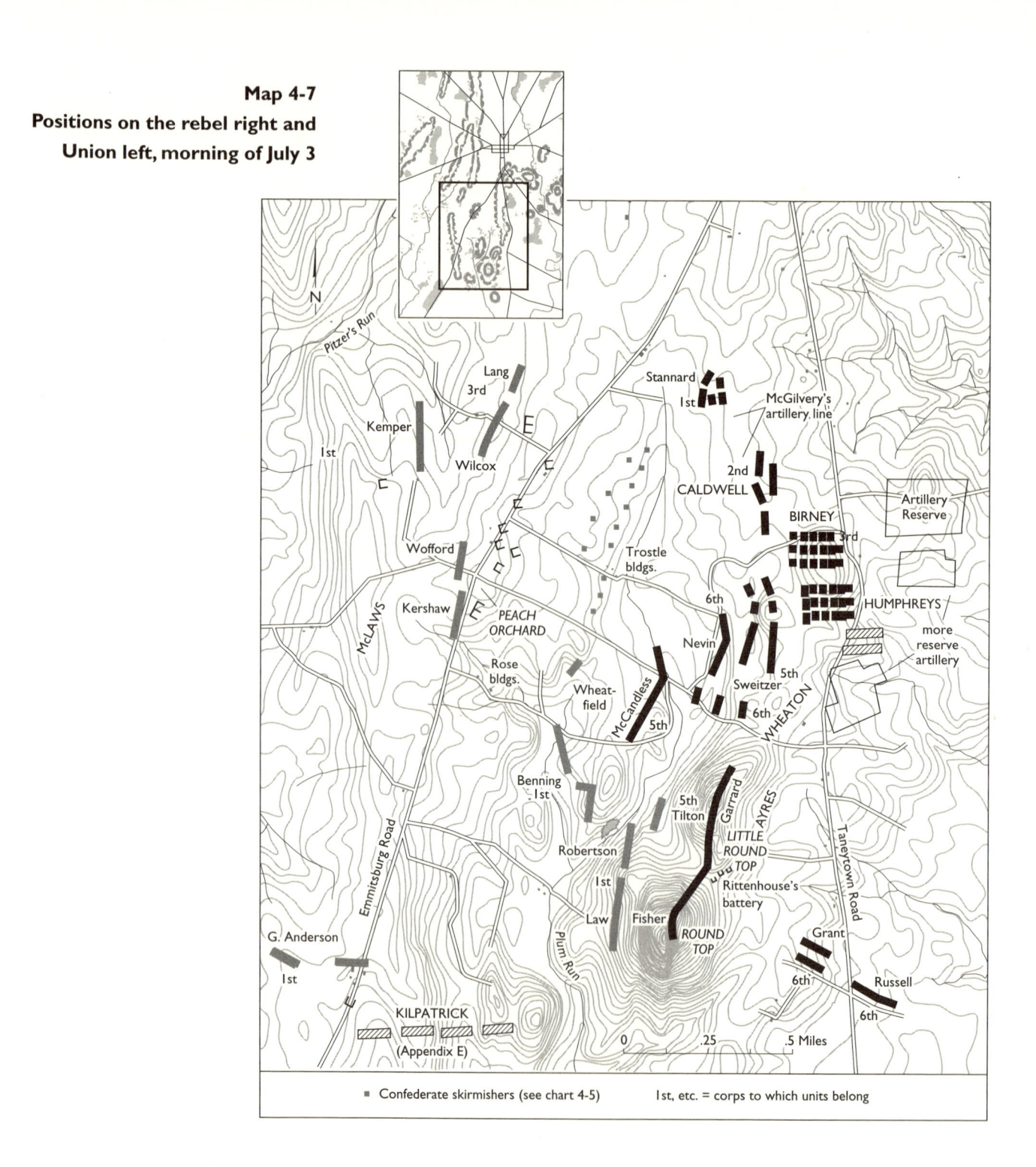

Map 4-7
Positions on the rebel right and Union left, morning of July 3

on the Federal flanks. The assault was envisioned to start much earlier than it had on the Second and, as it took off from the rebel right at the southern end of the battlefield, would include all three of Lt. Gen. James Longstreet's 1st Corps divisions. The one fresh unit of that size in Lee's army—under Maj. Gen. George E. Pickett[14]—was finally to come to Gettysburg to join with the divisions of Hood (now commanded by Brig. Gen. Evander Law) and McLaws, south of the town (chart 4-5). Those 1st Corps troops held several advance positions east of the Emmitsburg Road (map 4-7), which they had gained during the fighting on July 2. Coordinating with the advance of the rebel right on Cemetery Ridge, elements of

General Ewell's 2nd Corps were to hit the Union right on Culp's Hill. Thus the left wing of Ewell's corps, using the positions Johnson's division had gained in the Union works as a springboard, would renew their attacks that had started near nightfall on July 2.

The overall plan for July 3 therefore was much the same as the one the Army of Northern Virginia had tried to carry out the day before. Now, however, the Confederate high command knew where the Union defenders were. There was no problem of stale intelligence and the ensuing foolishness about attacking "up the Emmitsburg Road." Also Lee's army had gained ground on both of the enemy flanks. An analogy to the manner by which the Army of Northern Virginia was poised to renew its offensive at Gettysburg is provided by the positions of the Army of the Potomac at the Battle of Antietam. There, Maj. Gen. George B. McClellan had made gains against Lee's army by the end of the fighting on September 17, 1862. However, he failed to follow up on the eighteenth and thus let Lee off the hook.

A short time after daybreak on July 3, 1863, Lee, Longstreet, and other officers met to discuss the army's plans. Not long before this time, Longstreet "had . . . scouts out all night, and [found] . . . an excellent opportunity to move around to the right of Meade's army" (meaning the Army of the Potomac's left flank, from the Confederates' east-facing perspective).[15] Longstreet made these claims some fifteen years after the battle. General Lee, however, had firmly in mind more local maneuvers at Gettysburg. Lee first issued an order canceling any movement around the Union left, which may have contributed to the delay in the execution of the original flank-attack plan. More serious was the fact that "Pickett's Division was nowhere to be seen."[16]

Longstreet's opposition to the dual flank-attack plan—whether or not Pickett's absence made it moot—seemed to approach insubordination (his own tacit admission in postwar writings). The alternative move he wanted was in line with his constant refrain during this battle. Insubordination is probably too strong a word, however, given the respect Lee had for Longstreet. In fact, Longstreet pointed out to Lee that, were the entirety of his corps to angle toward the Federal left, Law and McLaws would be vulnerable on their right flanks (map 4-8).[17] If Pickett's division formed to the left of the other two 1st Corps divisions, the latter would be attacking in a northeasterly direction (from the army's extreme right) and exposed to dangerous flanking fire from the Federal forces on the Round Tops and in the Plum Run Valley (maps 4-7 and 4-8). Union units near the left of their line might even counterattack. General Lee agreed: The entire 1st Corps would not go in; only General Pickett's division would attack from this sector of the field.

Did this further wrangling within the rebel's high command contribute seriously to stalling the start of a Confederate attack on July 3? More important was "the failure to order up Pickett's Division by daylight," which "wrecked Lee's plan for simultaneous attacks on both flanks of the Union line" (as introduced above). In this context, "no one . . . sent orders for Pickett to have his division on the battlefield by daylight."[18] Pickett's division had halted four miles west of Gettysburg at 6 P.M. on July 2 after marching from Chambersburg. The division encamped near the Cashtown Road's intersection with Marsh Creek—where the Battle of Gettysburg began on July 1 (map 2-4 in Chapter 2; map 4-9).[19]

Instead of this state of affairs being an "oversight or failure of duty," another point of view is that the Confederate high command had Pickett approach Gettysburg in a tentative manner because it was not clear on July 2 where they

**Map 4-8
Hopes and initial attack plans of the rebel high command**

Longstreet's hope for an attack around the flank

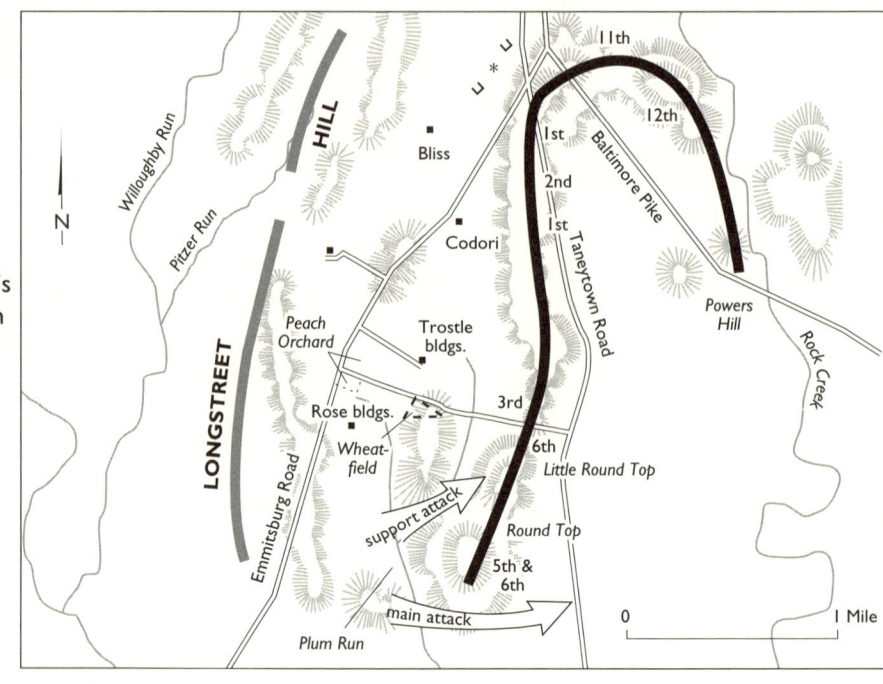

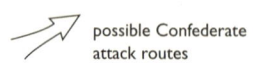

Lee's initial plan for the attack of his right wing

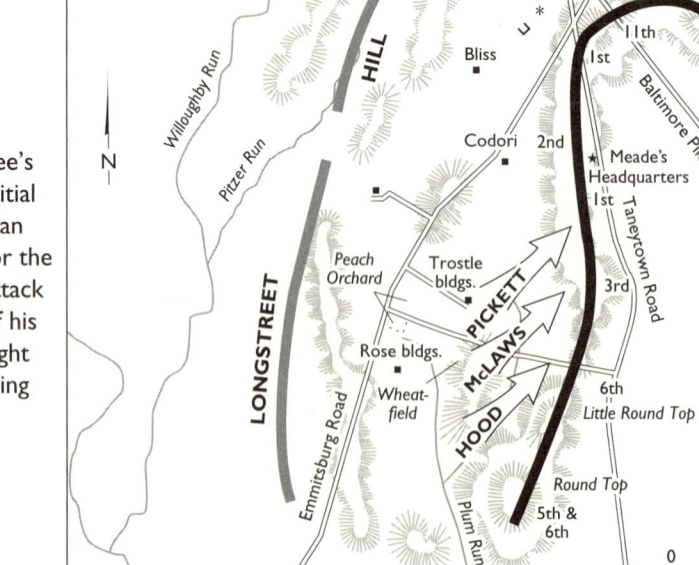

↗ possible Confederate attack routes

▮▮ approximate Confederate and Union main lines

1st, etc. = approximate positions of Union corps

180 THE STAND OF THE U.S. ARMY AT GETTYSBURG

```
                        ANV
                         │
                         ▼
                      1st Corps
                    ╱     │     ╲
                   ╱      │      ╲
          Pickett's       │       McLaws's division
          division        │         ╲
         ╱    │   ╲       │          ╲ Wofford's brigade
        ╱     │    ╲      │           ╲
Armistead's   │     ╲     │            Kershaw's brigade
brigade       │      Garnett's brigade
              │                         Barksdale's brigade
         Kemper's brigade                SKIRMISHERS
                                         Col. B. Humphreys *
                         │
                         ▼
                   Hood's division
                   Brig. Gen. E. Law **
                  ╱      │      ╲
                 ╱       │       ╲
          G. Anderson's  Benning's   Robertson's brigade
          brigade        brigade
                         │
                         ▼
                   Laws's brigade
```

**Chart 4-5
Confederate units:
right wing of the army,
south of Gettysburg**

* Barksdale mortally wounded July 2

** Hood wounded July 2

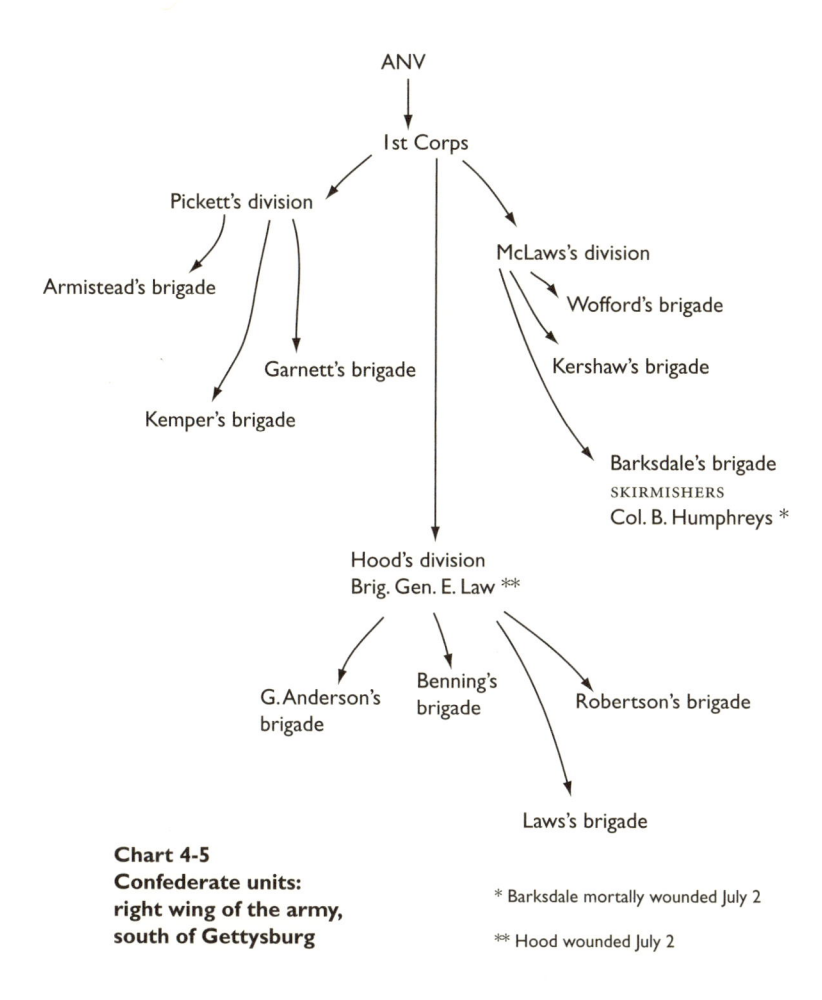

would be needed on the Third. Possibly this 1st Corps unit would be ordered to cooperate with Ewell's 2nd Corps on the rebel left.[20] According to this thesis, Longstreet did not instruct Pickett's division immediately to get closer to the battlefield south of town, where it was to end up. Had Pickett marched there overnight or earlier, this would have increased the chances for a morning attack upon the Union positions. That became moot when Federal forces on the right wing reinitiated the battle during the predawn hours of the Third.

In any event, General Lee was not about to give up and withdraw from Gettysburg after what was an Antietam-like drawn battle to this point.[21] Even though his original plan for assailing the Union army on July 3 was foiled, Lee still seemed to feel that he could achieve a "war-winning Cannae" at Gettysburg.[22] Lee's enemy was *still there*. His own army had one more chance to defeat and possibly rout the Federal force. Withdrawing his army away from the battlefield was out of the question. Longstreet's hoped-for strategic move away from Gettysburg was too risky. This is not meant to infer that Lee thought his army was in peril, but rather that he did not want to risk a scenario in which the Union force could escape. This is an ironic twist on the mind-set of some of the Northern leaders in these circumstances, who thought of turning back the invaders from "our soil."[23]

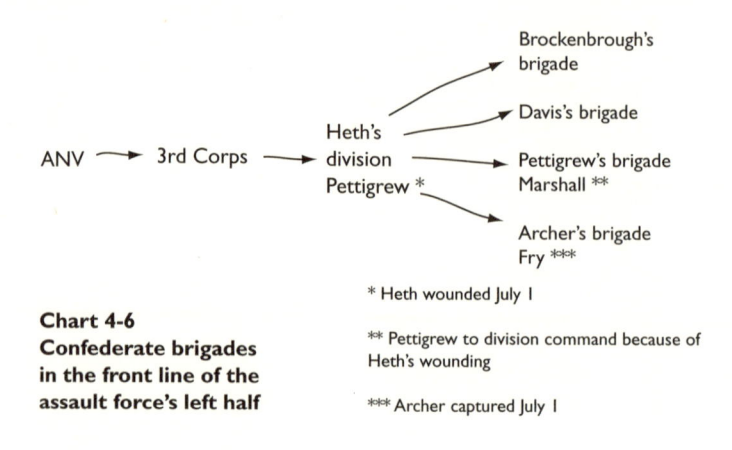

```
ANV → 3rd Corps → Heth's      → Brockenbrough's
                  division       brigade
                  Pettigrew *  → Davis's brigade
                               → Pettigrew's brigade
                                  Marshall **
                               → Archer's brigade
                                  Fry ***
```

* Heth wounded July 1

**Chart 4-6
Confederate brigades
in the front line of the
assault force's left half**

** Pettigrew to division command because of Heth's wounding

*** Archer captured July 1

From Lee's perspective, doing something like "get between the Federal army and Washington" risked failure. Even a more local redeployment could unravel the opportunity that had presented itself to him. After all, who could tell where such maneuvering might lead? A semi-strategic move of this sort had the danger of leading to a disengagement of the two armies, or a situation in which Lee's foe might once again end up in a good defensive position (perhaps at the "Pipe's Creek line" in northern Maryland, as discussed in Chapter 2, note 61). Perhaps General Lee was even secretly pleased that the plans for another complex pair of flank attacks had to be scrubbed. If his "blood was up," something more direct was the best way finally to crush the Northern army in the East.

So General Lee began to formulate a plan to *attack the Union center.* This then was a contingency plan, developed by the Confederates as events played out on the morning of July 3. A rash charge upon the enemy's center was not devised out of impatience, which might have clouded Confederate thinking on the night before, when Lee and some of his commanders might have felt that "We *almost* had them today."[24]

In planning for the frontal assault, General Longstreet performed well during the morning and early afternoon of July 3. He did not exhibit sullen recalcitrance, and the specifics of his tactical design for the attack were of high quality.[25] However, the consequences of his arguably poor performance on July 2 continued to plague the Confederates as the afternoon unfolded on the following day. The Union army was still in strong positions. These included those of the 12th Corps on Culp's Hill, which in the main had not been dislodged. One reason for this outcome was that the delays on Thursday afternoon and evening—with regard to the start of the fighting on the Federal left—had helped the Army of the Potomac hold its ground in the nighttime fighting on the right wing.

As the plan for the frontal assault on July 3 crystallized, Pickett's division was assigned a prominent role. His men were roused from their sleep west of Gettysburg (map 3-9) at about 3 A.M., which would have allowed them to join an early flank attack on the Union left (as discussed above). It would, however, take a unit of that size—about six thousand troops[26]—a few hours to bestir itself, march east down the Cashtown Road, and then deflect southward toward the area of the Confederate army's right. This gave Lee and Longstreet time to choose the other Confederate units that would join Pickett's division in the assault on the

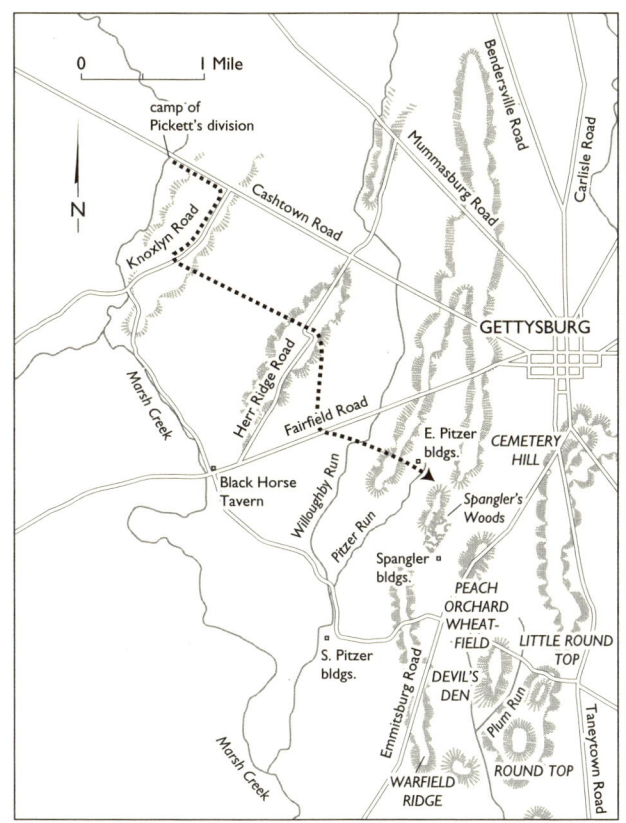

**Map 4-9
Pickett's division marches to the battlefield then deploys near Seminary Ridge**

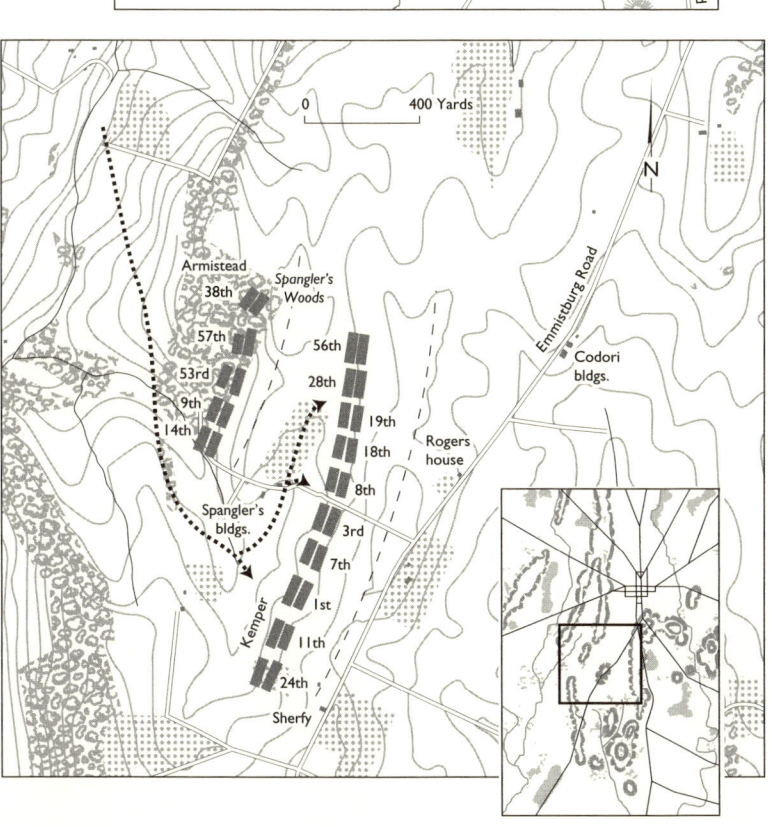

⋯⋯▶ march routes of Pickett's division

▮ Confederate regiments (all #s are for Va. units, each in two lines facing roughly eastward)

┆ intermediate ridgelines (between Seminary Ridge and the Emmitsburg Road)

THE GREAT GAMBLE LEE COULD HAVE WON

Union center. Having agreed with Longstreet that the majority of the 1st Corps would be withheld from the action,[27] it was thus decided that several *3rd* Corps units would form the balance of the attack force. Those units would form up to the *north* of Pickett on his division's left.

The Confederate 3rd Corps troops nominally under Lt. Gen. A. P. Hill had already fought in this battle—but for many of them that meant only on July 1. Also, the left half of Maj. Gen. Richard H. Anderson's 3rd Corps division—which had advanced upon the Union right-center on July 2—had not made all-out assaults. This included the sputtering out of his division's advances —prematurely, some would say.[28] The cessation of the fighting on the previous day contributed to the Confederate 3rd Corps being a relatively fresh unit, even though some of those soldiers were sent back into action less than twenty-four hours after they had fought on July 2.

As Lee and his senior commanders cobbled together a force to form the left wing of the assault, those 3rd Corps troops (chart 4-6) would slightly outnumber the approximately 6,000 men in Pickett's three brigades (chart 4-5). In *Pickett's Charge,* author Stewart underestimated the total number of attackers as about 10,500 infantrymen. Estimates from late-twentieth-century scholarship conclude that at most 12,500 men made the Charge.[29] During the back-and-forth between him and Lee this day, Longstreet apparently guessed that the potential assault force was significantly larger: In his recounting of the high-command conversations that occurred on July 3, the former general claimed in 1877 that he said, "It is my opinion that no fifteen thousand men ever arrayed for battle can take that position."[30] However, considering that he wrote that long afterward, after having been embroiled for years in one verbal wrangle after another about the loss of the Lost Cause at Gettysburg, one might suspect Longstreet of engaging in some breast-beating about how he knew that the attack would fail. It is possible that he did not say this on July 3, 1863, because he seemed to be going about his business in a proper frame of mind, and because the manner in which Longstreet quoted himself is self-serving. *Before* the attack commenced, perhaps he did have faith in it, but then he retrospectively withdrew his support because of the outcome. Yet even if James Longstreet did "see the desperate and hopeless nature of the charge" in 1863,[31] there is reason to believe that *those 12,500 men could have taken the position:* "Every major attack [Lee's] army had mounted against the Army of the Potomac had succeeded, except at Malvern Hill."[32]

At Gettysburg on July 3, when previous Confederate successes could have come to a climactic culmination, it was largely up to General Longstreet to carry out Lee's long-held hopes. The right wing of the impending attack was formally under Longstreet's supervision. With A. P. Hill out of the picture for all intents and purposes, command of the left wing fell to Brig. Gen. J. Johnston Pettigrew and Maj. Gen. Isaac R. Trimble. Recall that Pettigrew had been a brigade commander on June 30, when he marched his men toward Gettysburg but discretely withdrew. He then took over for his division commander, Maj. Gen. Henry Heth, after the latter was wounded on July 1. Two days later, Heth's division was arrayed on Pickett's left, although there was a gap between the two wings of the assault force. General Pettigrew would be in the front of the left wing's assaulting force with four brigades (chart 4-6). All of them had seen action on July 1. Now we come to the smallest of the three components of "Longstreet's assault." It was led by General Trimble, who on July 1 and 2 had been attached to Ewell's corps as acting chief engineer.[33] Trimble was elevated to a field command on the Third and given two brigades from Maj. Gen. Dorsey Pender's 3rd Corps division (chart

4-7). Only Brig. Gen. James H. Lane's brigade was essentially fresh. It had been lightly engaged in the final attacks on the Union positions on Seminary Ridge on July 1 (as discussed in Chapter 2, note 55). On average, however, the units in the left half of the assault force were about 30 percent understrength.

Let us look further at the large-unit commanders within the attack force for the "Pickett-Pettigrew-Trimble assault" (see why it is called Pickett's Charge?). Many observers poke fun at George Pickett because of his flamboyance, his occasionally childlike behavior, and the fact that he graduated dead last in the famed West Point Class of 1846. (Longstreet, by the way, ranked fifty-fourth out of sixty-two in the Class of 1842.) The other two generals were new to the command of large units—Pettigrew in general, and Trimble in terms of Gettysburg. Did they possess the necessary expertise, and did the soldiers in the brigades placed under them (except Pettigrew's from July 1) have sufficient confidence in these unfamiliar leaders? Maybe not. As for the commander of the right wing of the attack—although Pickett may well have been an oddball and a substandard general officer, his performance on July 3 was, at a minimum, a solid one.[34] For their part, the six left-wing brigades led by Pettigrew and Trimble did almost as well. However, we will see that the *extreme left* of Pettigrew's line turned in a flawed performance—the consequences of which might have proved fatal. Perhaps this was not the fault of General Pettigrew or the brigade commander, Col. John M. Brockenbrough (chart 4-6), but rather the somewhat makeshift nature of the Confederate force that was about to be formed in front of the Union lines. This problem was coupled with the fact that many of the assault regiments almost certainly had not recovered sufficiently from the first day's fighting. Additional 3rd Corps units from Maj. Gen. Richard Anderson's division, such as Wright's brigade, had fought more recently and were placed in reserve positions behind the main assault force (map 4-13). As it turned out, none of Anderson's brigades were involved in the fighting, or they barely scraped up against its edges.

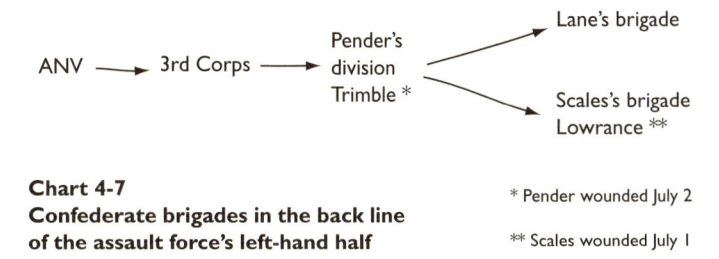

Pickett's division was fresh in terms of fighting if not footsoreness. His three brigades (chart 4-5) approached Gettysburg well before midmorning (again, however, not as early as could have occurred). Then they turned right off the Cashtown Road (map 4-9, top) in order to reach the position from which they would go into action. Much as McLaws and Hood had done on July 2, Pickett moved southeast from a spot west of Gettysburg with General Kemper's brigade in the van.[35] There was no time-wasting countermarch on the morning of July 3 (map 4-9)—even though Pickett's two-mile-long column of marching Virginians endeavored to traverse relatively low ground and stay out of sight of Federal observers on Little Round Top (compare this with map 3-8, which accompanies a discussion of the enervating march made on July 2 by the other two divisions in Longstreet's corps). Indeed, the Confederate high command intended to keep its intentions for the third day of battle as hidden as possible from Federal scrutiny. As we will see, the nature of the ground between the rebel lines and the Union ones south of Gettysburg permitted the Southerners to mask the tactical specifics of their impending assault.

After Pickett's brigades reached their destination southwest of Gettysburg and behind Seminary Ridge (map 4-9, top) at about six in the morning, they remained in columns there for about two hours.[36] During this time—and even before sunrise, but after the battle had resumed on Culp's Hill—General Lee and

Chart 4-7
Confederate brigades in the back line of the assault force's left-hand half

ANV → 3rd Corps → Pender's division Trimble * → Lane's brigade / Scales's brigade Lowrance **

* Pender wounded July 2
** Scales wounded July 1

**Map 4-10
Confederate brigades forming
for the assault**

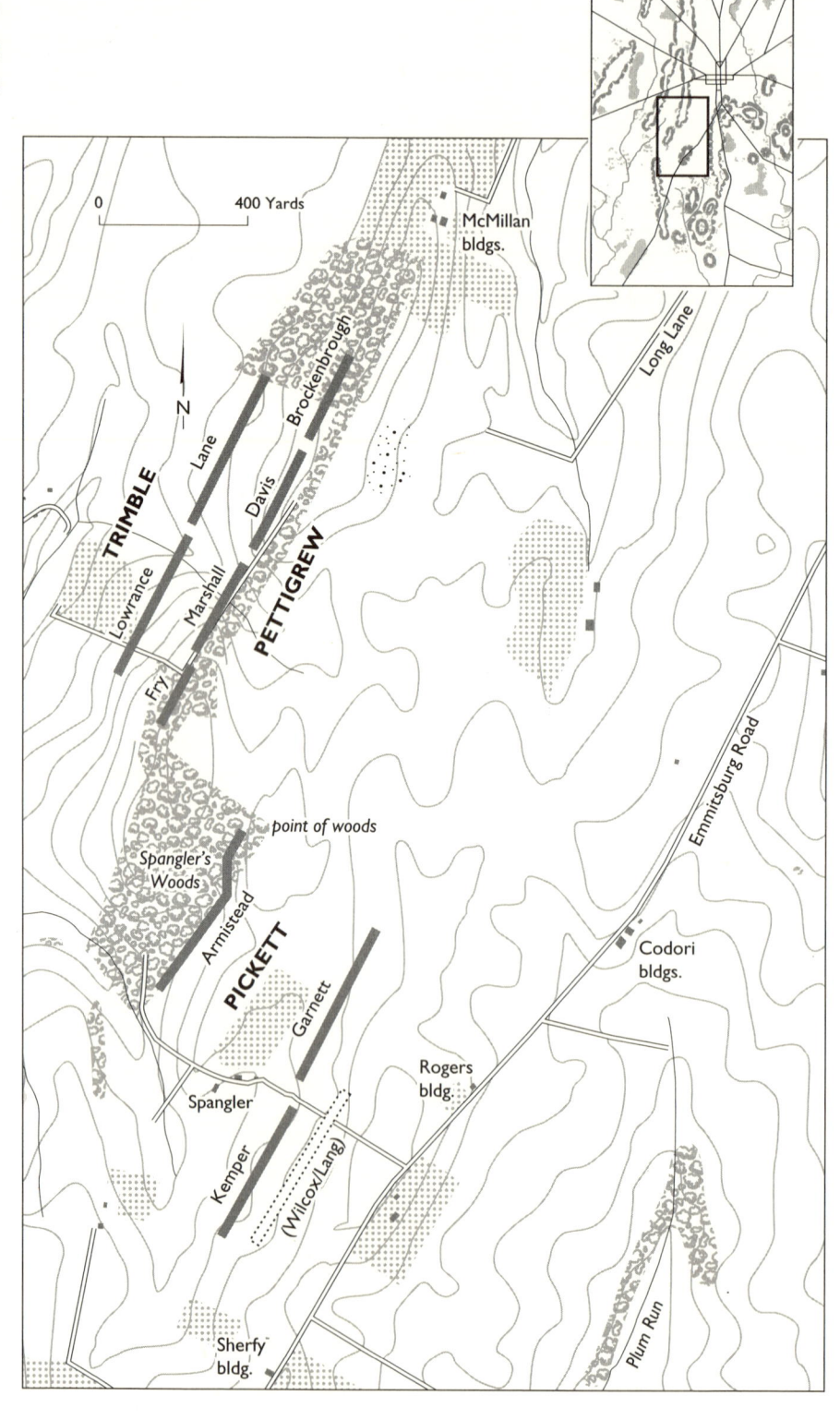

his high-ranking officers were surveying the field in this area and eastward to the Peach Orchard, formulating their plan of attack.[37] Then, at about 8 A.M., the commanders began to deploy the rebel units into a long line of battle. Pickett's brigades were sent to the right from where they were waiting in column just west of Seminary Ridge. The Virginia division marched on a dirt path that coursed through Spangler's Woods so its deployment would *not be visible* to the Union men on Cemetery Ridge or Little Round Top.[38] The brigades commanded by Brig. Gens. James L. Kemper and Richard B. Garnett continued to deploy out of the enemy's sight by going from column into lines in an area *between two elongated rises of ground* west of the Emmitsburg Road (map 4-9, bottom).[39] These elements of Pickett's line did not extend as far to the south as the overall rebel right had stretched the day before. Instead, the right flank of his division was north of the Peach Orchard (map 4-10). Pickett's third brigade, led by Brig. Gen. Lewis A. Armistead, took a hard left as it exited the trees and formed up on the eastern edge of the woods (but not among the trees). Armistead's troops, behind Garnett's line, were protected by the westernmost intermediate ridge (maps 4-9 and 4-10).[40] A total of three ridges run roughly in a north-south direction between Seminary and Cemetery Ridges in this sector of the battlefield, making this ground "a series of rolling undulating swells" that "gave the Southern soldiers (advancing from Seminary Ridge on the south side of the line of battle) protection until reaching the Emmitsburg Road."[41]

To appreciate the deployment of the left wing of the assault formation, consider the ground to the left of General Armistead's line. Here there was a "point of woods" at the eastern extent of the group of trees near Seminary Ridge (map 4-10). The open ground just east of that point is relatively high. Several fence lines divided up the battlefield between that rise and the Emmitsburg Road in July 1863. It has been suggested that Pickett's left could not be juxtaposed with the right wing of the 3rd Corps brigades because of the point of woods or perhaps because of impeding fence lines in this vicinity.[42] However, the problem did not involve the portion of Spangler's Woods that jutted eastward (map 4-10), and many of the fences had already been knocked down during the fighting on July 2. The gap between the two wings of the assault was left open in order that *no part of the overall rebel line would be on high ground in the vicinity of Seminary Ridge, where it would be visible from across the field*.[43] Thus, Pettigrew's right-wing brigade—commanded by Col. Birkett D. Fry, whose importance during the planning of the Charge will be revealed later—was placed north of the high ground.[44] This meant that Fry's right flank was seated in a northern sector of Spangler's Woods, three hundred to four hundred yards above and behind Armistead's left (map 4-10). Colonel Fry's brigade and the rest of Pettigrew's line were therefore hidden from enemy view, with the front of the assault formation's left wing being deployed in a line of woods on the reverse (western) slope of Seminary Ridge (map 4-10).

The Confederate brigades assembled for Pickett's Charge were arrayed over a distance of about one and one-half miles. It was a somewhat ragged line, broken roughly in its center by the aforementioned gap (map 4-10). The southern and northern extremities of the deployment were the right flank of Pickett's division, commanded by Kemper, and the fateful Brockenbrough on Pettigrew's extreme left (map 4-10).

To close up the center gap during the advance, Pickett's division planned to make a series of "left obliques" (diagrammed in map 4-19), so that the Charge that bore his name would have maximal, concentrated attacking power. General Pickett was to achieve these difficult maneuvers superbly, especially when one

**Map 4-11
Confederate artillery positioned for the cannonade**

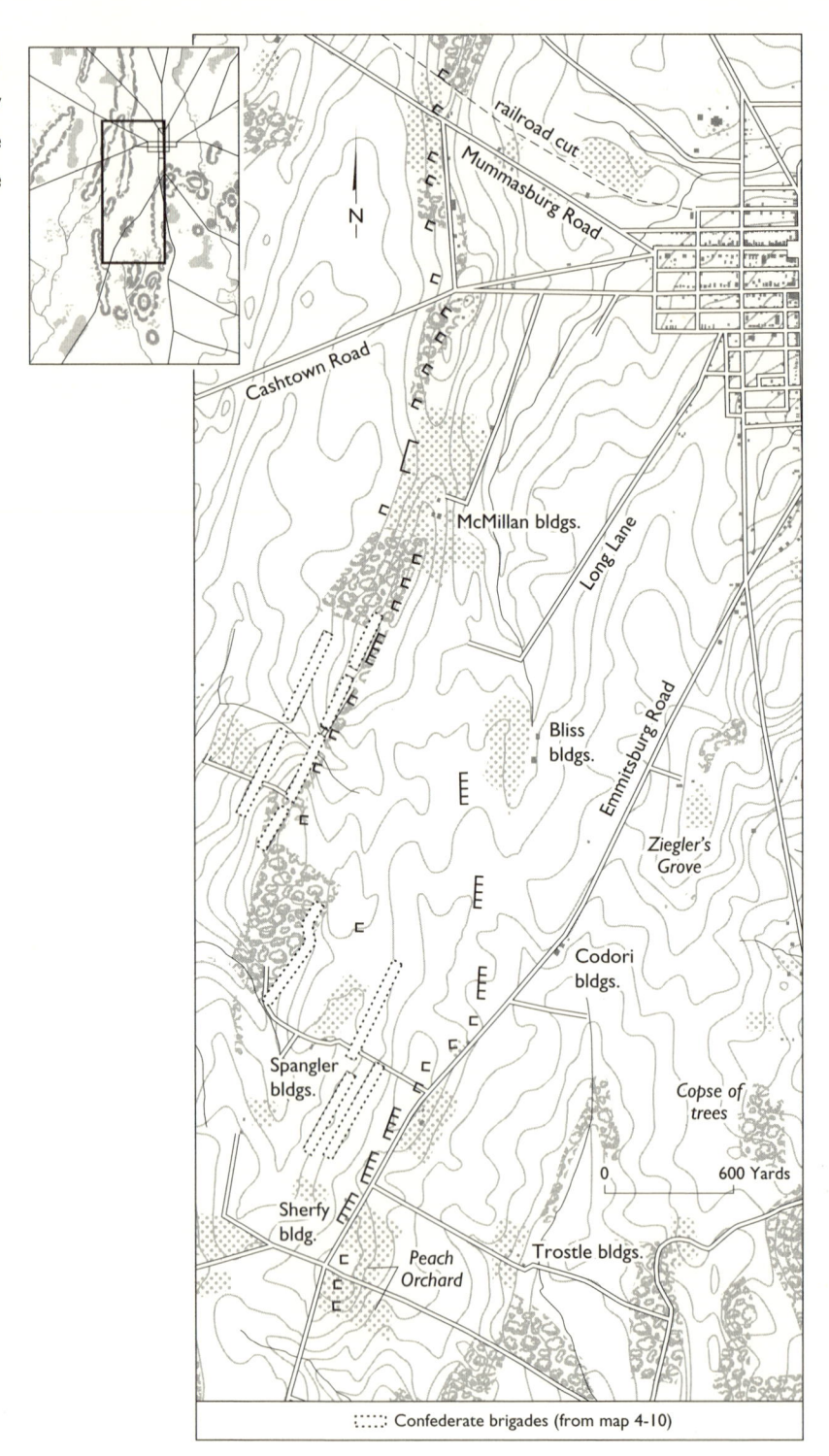

considers that the Confederate line was to come under fire as it advanced. However, the southern half of that line eventually seemed to get carried away in its leftward maneuvers, as we will see.

Indeed, it was not part of the Confederate attack plan to *severely* narrow their attacking front, such that it would *all* converge on the famous copse of trees situated near the center of the Union's positions along Cemetery Ridge (depicted in

188 THE STAND OF THE U.S. ARMY AT GETTYSBURG

map 4-11 and many subsequent diagrams). The so-called copse had many more trees in it than the small number of protected ones on the present-day battlefield. Several years after the battle a farmer leasing that plot of land cut down more than two hundred trees in the copse.[45] This large clump of trees thus served as a readily viewed terrain feature on which the advancing rebel force could guide its movements.

Historian D. Scott Hartwig argues that the attack was supposed to strike Cemetery Ridge over at least a half-mile front—not to converge narrowly in the vicinity of the copse of trees.[46] Countering this view, Wayne E. Motts submits that the left-oblique maneuvers by the rebel right wing were designed to effect a distinct convergence on a *relative* "point" of attack (note 46), and thus accomplish more than just close the gap in the center (map 4-14). Consistent with this analysis is that the Confederate high command designated a unit near the center of the assault force—Colonel Fry's brigade in General Pettigrew's division—to be the "brigade of direction."[47] Fry's brigade was placed almost directly opposite the copse, on the right flank of Pettigrew's front line (maps 4-10 and 4-14). Thus, as Fry's troops advanced straight toward that clump of trees, the other assaulting units were to guide their movements on those Alabama and Tennessee soldiers; most conspicuously, Pickett's brigades would shift to their left accordingly in stages.

Thus, Pickett's left obliques were designed to close up the gap *and* to facilitate the possibility that the Charge would "get mass at a point of attack." However, such an objective did not mean that the whole line was supposed to become a piercing column. It can be argued in this regard that the Confederates' line of battle got squeezed in more than was intended. This was in part because of a *Federal* move opposite Colonel Brockenbrough's brigade on the rebel left. The action near the north end of the lines would have deadly significance for the change in geometry that was to occur within the configuration of the rebel attack.

One further feature of the assault plan: As the attacking line was pushing back the Federal center on Cemetery Ridge, General Stuart and the *Confederate cavalry* would finally enter the fray. Stuart's division had fully arrived by the afternoon and evening of July 2 (as recounted in Chapter 1). Supposedly, his orders for the following day were to swing round Ewell's positions at the northern end of the battlefield, then drop down behind the Union lines—a clockwise maneuver that would bring Stuart's troopers about one and one-half miles east of Cemetery Ridge. Once the infantry breakthrough occurred there, Stuart would complete the incipient rout by assailing the retreating, disordered Federals. This scenario, which did not come close to being played out, is also subject to debate in the cavalry context. The issue is whether Generals Lee and Stuart formulated this specific element of the Confederate offensive on July 3—as cavalierly outlined here. This matter is discussed in some detail within Appendix D.

ANV
↓   ↘
1st Corps   Lee's staff
Longstreet   ↓
↓   Chief of Artillery
Reserve   Pendleton
Artillery
↓
Alexander's   **Chart 4-8**
Battalion   **Confederate artillery**
Alexander   **commanders**

The Great Artillery Bombardment of the Civil War

The Confederate offensive began with a huge artillery cannonade that was designed to soften up the Union line on Cemetery Ridge. This bombardment was aimed at destroying the Federal batteries there so they could not be used against the assault that would come close on the heels of the shelling. If Union infantrymen suffered significant losses from all this artillery fire, so much the better.

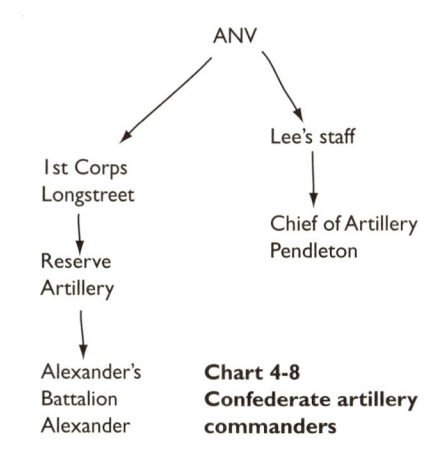

Artillery Brigades
Artillery Reserve
Maj. T. Osborn (11th)

1st Corps
11th Corps

1st U.S., Battery I
Lt. G. Woodruff *
Lt. T. McCrea

Artillery Brigade

1st R. I. Light Battery A
Capt. A. Arnold

4th U.S. Battery A
Lt. A. Cushing *
Sgt. F. Fuger

2nd Corps

1st R. I. Light, Battery B
Lt. T. F. Brown **
Lt. W. Perrin

1st N.Y. Light, Battery B
Capt. J. Rorty *
Lt. R. Rogers

AP

9th Mich. Light, Battery I
Capt. J. Daniels

1st Brigade

Horse Artillery

Cavalry Corps

4th U.S., Battery C
Lt. E. Thomas

1st Regular Brigade

Artillery Reserve

1st, 2nd, and 4th Volunteer Brigades, and others
Lt. Col. F. McGilvery

* killed July 3
** wounded July 2

5th Corps

Artillery Brigade

1st Ohio, Battery L
Capt. F. Gibbs

Chart 4-9
Union artillery, from Cemetery Hill south to Little Round Top

5th U.S., Battery D
Lt. B. Rittenhouse

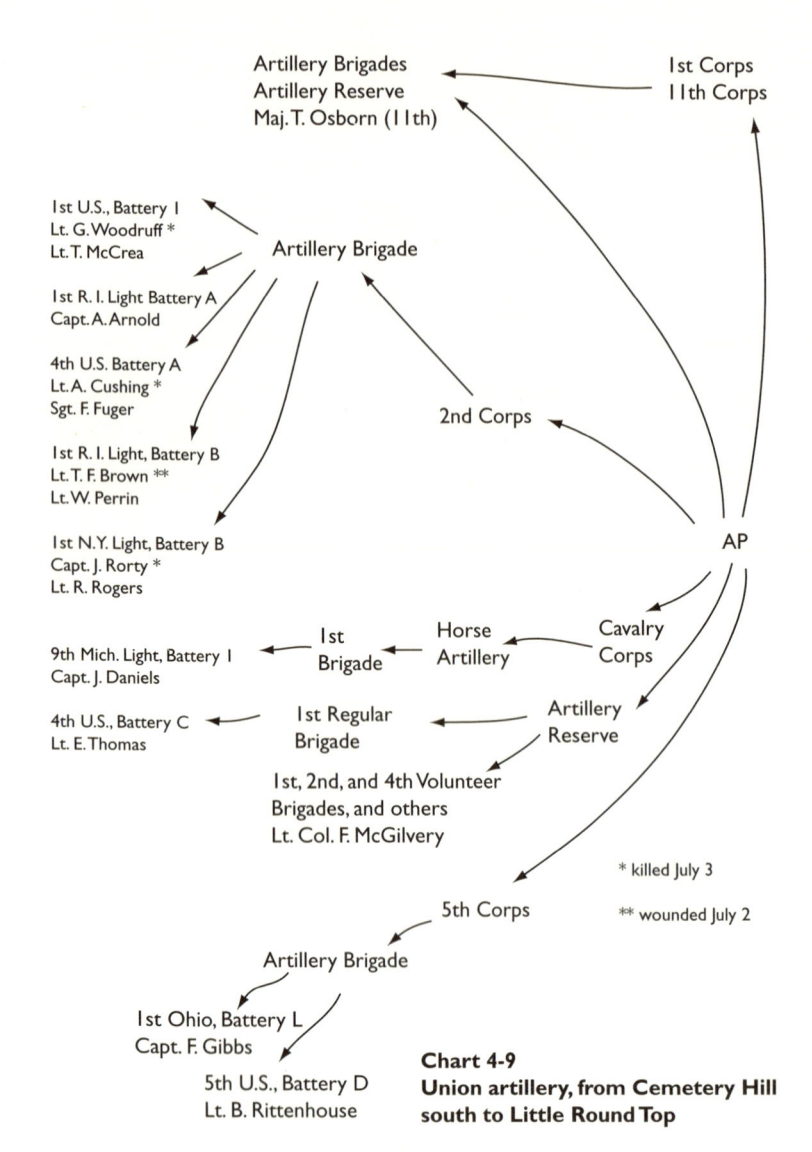

Colonel E. Porter Alexander, commander of the guns in Longstreet's corps, supervised much of the planning for the bombardment. He was a highly competent junior officer, as mentioned before. The officer formally in command of the Confederate artillery, Brig. Gen. William N. "Parson" Pendleton, seemed to be in a stupor of negligence on July 3 (chart 4-8). He is now regarded as a "well meaning but essentially incompetent officer."[48]

The rebels arranged up to 170 guns in a roughly south-to-north line. George R. Stewart gave the lowest estimate, saying there were only 142 artillery pieces, but we will never know the exact number.[49] Alexander's own guns (approximately 75 of them) were arrayed over a distance of more than two thousand yards extending north from the vicinity of the Peach Orchard (map 4-11). Continuing northward, 60 pieces from Lt. Gen. A. P. Hill's 3rd Corps were placed to the left and rear of Alexander's line. This line of guns continued to the north with about 25 guns from General Ewell's 2nd Corps. The broken line of cannon stretched for about two miles from Warfield Ridge in the south to a point west of town in the north. A small number of additional guns were placed separately from the main line, northwest of Gettysburg. These cannon were about a mile and one-half from Cemetery Hill. Other rebel batteries near the center of the long line of guns were within a thousand yards of their targets near the copse of trees (map 4-11).

The alignment of the rebel artillery was suspect, as events would later prove. There is an old military maxim that says that when a line fires at another one parallel to it, a miss is as good as a mile. Perhaps too much of the rough line of Confederate cannon on July 3 was indeed set up to fire perpendicularly to the Federal positions on Cemetery Ridge and the hills that flanked it. Porter Alexander realized as much in retrospect.[50] Following up his insight about the "one single advantage conferred by exterior lines" (discussed in conjunction with the rebel attack plans diagrammed in map 4-8), Alexander bemoaned the fact "that of the 84 guns of the 2nd and 3rd corps to be engaged, 80 were in the same line *parallel to the position of the enemy*" [emphasis Alexander's]. He went on to say that "56 guns [of these two corps] stood idle," and that "it was a phenomenal oversight not to place these guns, and many beside, in and near the town to enfilade the 'shank of the fish-hook' and cross fire with guns from the west."

In addition to acknowledging his point that the cannonade could have been stronger in terms of numbers of batteries, we also revisit the artillery issue introduced in the discussion of Little Round Top on July 2. Enfilading fire *up* the Union line could have been devastating if it had been physically possible to place enough pieces on that southern hill, because a shot that might have been aimed at the middle of the line would still do much damage if it fell short or flew long. Porter Alexander's postwar arguments about July 3 make the same point, al-

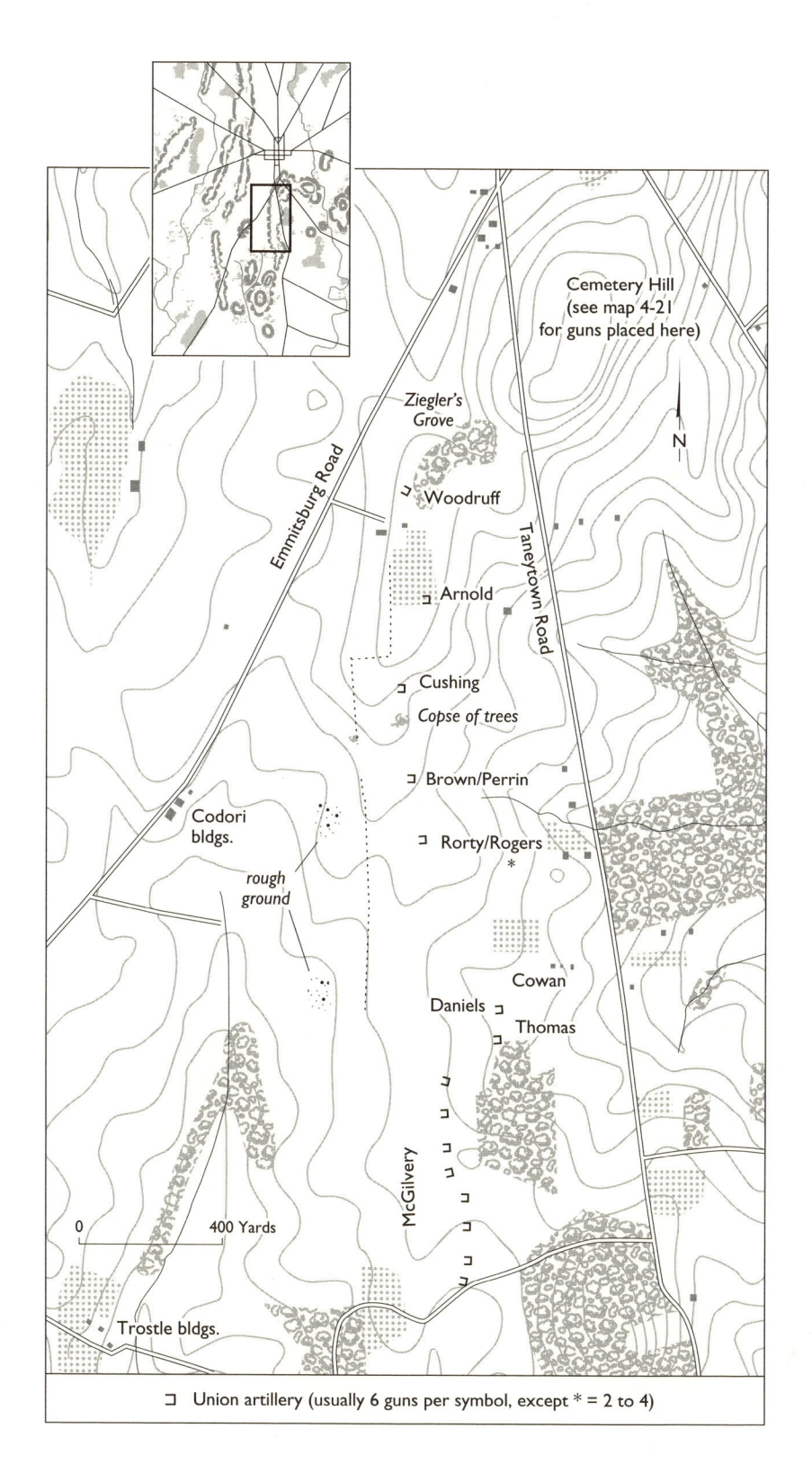

Map 4-12
Union artillery on Cemetery Ridge, late morning

Cemetery Hill (see map 4-21 for guns placed here)

Ziegler's Grove
Woodruff
Emmitsburg Road
Taneytown Road
Arnold
Cushing
Copse of trees
Brown/Perrin
Codori bldgs.
Rorty/Rogers *
rough ground
Cowan
Daniels Thomas
McGilvery
Trostle bldgs.

0   400 Yards

⌐ Union artillery (usually 6 guns per symbol, except * = 2 to 4)

THE GREAT GAMBLE LEE COULD HAVE WON   191

though now we consider artillery fire that would have come from northerly sectors of the field, *down* the Union line on the ridge. Moreover, Alexander specified that it would have been eminently possible to muster and deploy dozens of rebel cannon (not merely six, as in the case of Little Round Top) in the appropriate manner. This would have subjected the northern part of the Federal defense to a *type* of shelling (forget the amount of it for the moment) "so effective that no troops can submit to it long." Or so Alexander wrote after the war. The Confederate fire that was actually aimed to angle in on the Union flanks came from a relatively small handful of batteries placed northwest of the town and in the vicinity of the Peach Orchard (map 4-11). Thus, most of the Confederate bombardment was directed west to east (including some of the guns placed to the south, which fired that way toward Little Round Top).[51]

The cannonade began sometime between 1 and 1:30 P.M.[52] The rebel guns opened fire toward approximately 120 Union ones along the Union line (chart 4-9).[53] The plurality of the Federal artillery (about 40 pieces) was compacted along a six-hundred-yard line on a relatively southern part of the ridge (map 4-12). The commander of this line of cannon was Lt. Col. Freeman McGilvery (he of the Plum Run line from July 2). Only about 35 2nd Corps guns were placed in the Union center. The Northern army could have used more there, as time would tell. Thirty-five to 40 additional pieces faced the Confederate lines from Cemetery Hill. Finally, there were batteries on and near Little Round Top (maps 4-7 and 4-18). One of them was Battery D of 5th U.S. Artillery under Lt. Benjamin F. Rittenhouse (chart 4-9), who had taken over for the slain Lt. Charles E. Hazlett (see Chapter 3). The muzzles of some of Rittenhouse's cannon faced to the northwest, so his battery threatened the right flank of any Confederate infantry that might venture into the open area between Seminary Ridge and Cemetery Ridge. Rittenhouse's guns were bolstered by part of another 5th Corps battery placed near the base of the hill to the north (chart 4-9, map 4-18). But this unimpressive number of Union guns near the southern end of the defensive line gives credence to the notion that that position was not one from which awesome damage could be inflicted upon infantry located to the north—whether it was the main Federal line or a Confederate force moving eastward from Seminary Ridge.

The rebel cannonade was a thunderous affair that lasted between one and two hours.[54] However, one Union soldier called it a "humbug" because in the end it failed to do sufficient damage to the Federal force.[55] Some of the rebel cannon fire was unwittingly aimed too high, and many of the projectiles landed harmlessly on the reverse (eastern) slope of Cemetery Ridge.[56] As for the Union positions on Cemetery Hill, Maj. Gen. Oliver Howard, the 11th Corps commander from whom we have heard nothing since his golden moment on July 1, said that much of the rebels' long-range cannon fire sailed over his positions on the hill.[57] But the potentially most important component of the Confederate fire was that of a hundred rebel guns aimed so that their blasts converged upon the thirty pieces placed near the Union center on Cemetery Ridge. Insofar as a fair fraction of the shot and shell mistakenly landed in regions *behind* the ridgeline, the Federal artillery batteries and infantry units farther to the front (several yards westward) did not have devastating damage inflicted upon them. The infantrymen may have suffered psychologically, but they—along with the Union soldiers in and near the center of the line—were at least encouraged to *hold their forward positions*. With the Confederate shells falling mostly *behind* them, their safest position was to *stay* in their defensive line, poised to meet what might come marching their way.[58]

The general problem was that long-range artillery fire in the Civil War tended not to be as effective as the gunners may have thought it was: Confederate artillerymen especially were woefully short of practice and skill. Also, the shellfire would often explode at the wrong time.[59] Moreover, the staggering amount of smoke created by the black powder as it was ignited into gas obscured the artillerymen's visibility, further limiting accuracy.

Yet the effectiveness of the rebel bombardment on the third day at Gettysburg has been underestimated. Significant damage to Union guns along Cemetery Ridge *was* inflicted.[60] The overshooting also forced Maj. Gen. George Meade from his headquarters behind the right-center of the Union line, near the Taneytown Road (map 4-8).[61] In fact, Meade and his staff officers had to scurry to yet a third location during the cannonade. An additional outcome of all this softening-up fire was not damage as such: the shells landing behind the eastern slope of Cemetery Ridge forced much of the Federal Artillery Reserve to pull back. This would make it more difficult for the gunners in those batteries to rush reinforcing pieces up to the main line.

Meanwhile, the Union 2nd Corps commander, Maj. Gen. Winfield Scott Hancock, demanded that the Federal guns return fire. He wanted the batteries in his corps, which occupied the center of the Union line, not to just take their medicine but to respond—if only to bolster the morale of the men in that sector. Moreover, Hancock rode along Cemetery Ridge during the cannonade hoping to steady the troops by that conspicuously courageous act. Hancock's bravery in the early afternoon of July 3 is a well-known story.[62] Less appreciated is General Longstreet's performance, which mirrored that of his counterpart across the field as Union cannon fire rained down on the Confederate lines waiting in the vicinity of Seminary Ridge. Thus, James Longstreet rode in front of Pickett's soldiers "through the storm of Union fire." General Kemper (who led one of Pickett's brigades) and others said that their corps commander "was unmoved as a statue" and that they would never forget Longstreet's display "of the truest heroism."[63]

During this time, Hancock also verbally sparred with Brig. Gen. Henry J. Hunt, who was in overall charge of the Federal artillery. Hunt wanted to conserve fire for the infantry assault they all knew was coming, and General Hunt did have some say as to how the artillery would perform. But Hancock got his way to a significant degree—even riding down the line to McGilvery's positions and getting that colonel to begin counter-battery fire. McGilvery acquiesced, although he ordered his guns to cease firing once General Hancock departed. Later, however, McGilvery ordered his pieces to resume their counter-battery fire, but at a slower rate this time so as to conserve ammunition to be used against the Confederate infantry, which he knew was coming.

The counter-bombardment from all these Federal guns (ranging from the center down to McGilvery's position) did little damage to the Confederate cannon. The Union fire overshot the mark as well. However, by doing so it did inflict significant casualties on the rebel infantry just farther to the west. In particular, the right wing of the assault force lost three hundred to five hundred men, with Garnett's and Kemper's brigades absorbing most of these casualties. These two of Pickett's brigades were vulnerable because they were behind a large number of rebel batteries on the south end of the long line of guns (map 4-11). Those cannon were relatively near a compact line of Union batteries across the field and were a salient target for return fire from the Federal guns in McGilvery's line (map 4-12).

The cannonade wound down as the Confederates began running short of ammunition.[64] They had fired almost twenty-five thousand projectiles. Colonel

Alexander saw a Union battery being pulled back. This may have been part of Lt. T. Fred Brown's battery from the 1st Rhode Island Light Artillery, commanded on July 3 by Lt. Walter S. Perrin (Brown had been wounded the previous day; see chart 4-9).[65] At the time of this mini-withdrawal, General Hunt ordered a general cease-fire by the guns on Cemetery Ridge. He later said that this was a calculated act, aimed at fooling the Confederate commanders into thinking that their cannonade had done the trick.[66] That Hunt engineered this ploy (at least in retrospect) speaks to the confidence he and his fellow commanders may have been operating under: "We *invited* the attack of the enemy's infantry" (Hunt's postwar words to this effect). The petering out of fire from the Union guns may also have caused Colonel Alexander to overreact, coupling what he ceased to hear with what he thought he saw: the withdrawal of several Federal cannon. It was at about this time that Alexander became embroiled in a flurry of messages exchanged by him and two key infantry commanders.

In the midst of these exchanges, Alexander was under considerable pressure. He not only was involved in combat while supervising the cannonade, but he was also forced to provide crucial pieces of advice to Generals Longstreet and Pickett. Longstreet's messages to Colonel Alexander implied that Alexander was to determine whether the artillery fire would "have the effect to drive off the enemy or greatly demoralize him," and thus decide when and even *if* the infantry assault could commence.[67] The implication is that Longstreet was looking for evidence that could allow him not to attack or to shirk his responsibility for giving the final order for the assault to take off toward the Union line. For his part, Pickett's communications with Alexander implied that he was eager to get going.

Colonel Alexander was understandably unwilling to make such a decision on his own. The pressure he was under may have pushed him into some wishful thinking about the extent to which his fire had potentially ruined the Union's artillery defense. Seeing a Federal battery—or was it two or more?—withdraw, Colonel Alexander sent one more message to General Pickett: "The 18 guns have been driven off For God's sake come quick or we cannot support you ammunition nearly out" (see note 67). Pickett went to Longstreet to extract the order allowing his division, along with the six brigades to his left, to be unleashed. Longstreet nodded his assent. One of the most fateful military actions in American history was about to get under way.

First a pause for some remarks. We are indeed in a slight lull between the end of the cannonade and the beginning of the Confederate advance. General Pickett continued to be active during this time. In fact, there is evidence that he had been sending messages up the line throughout the morning and early afternoon.[68] General Pickett thus was involved in supervising the overall assault force. Perhaps we *should* call the attack that ensued "Pickett's Charge."

Its success or failure might be viewed as hinging on the effectiveness of the bombardment. Yet such preparations are rarely effective. If we shoot forward in time about fifty years, we contemplate one of the most prodigious frontal assaults in all of military history: the beginning of the Battle of the Somme in World War I. In the early summer of 1916, a huge British force in northern France prepared to assault the German line in that sector. As at Gettysburg on July 3, 1863, the Allied offensive force used its artillery to soften up the enemy defense. A colossal cannonade commenced on June 24, and more than 1.7 million shells were fired eastward toward the German defensive positions during the subsequent week. After the bombardment ended, the British soldiers were sent from their trenches into no-man's-land in the early morning of July 1, 1916. This soon became one of the monumental fiascoes in the history of warfare. The British made almost no ground gains and suffered 57,470 casualties on that July day, including 19,240 killed and 35,493 wounded. This exemplifies why, if the American Civil War was the "noblest and least avoidable of all the great mass-conflicts of which till then there was record", World War I came nowhere near displacing it.[69] In particular, the Somme was not only disgusting, but also disastrous in terms of the thinking (if any) and performance of the Allied high command. Frontal assaults against machine guns were preposterous. Moreover, dug-in, hunkered-down defenders were never blown away by the kind of long-range bombardment that we are considering.

In a later world war something analogous would be revealed (in retrospect), when the effectiveness of high-altitude bombing of the enemy army's positions would be called into question—in terms of whether all those tons of bombs would sweep the field and facilitate a strategic move on the offense. The answer was, in the main, "no." This means that it is always the ordinary, beleaguered infantryman who must make an attack succeed by physically taking the ground *on the ground*. The 1991 Persian Gulf War supposedly provides an exception. There, the softening up of a defensive ground force seemed devastating, in part because it went on for a staggering thirty-eight days. Yet the Iraqis still had to be attacked on the ground, and were ultimately defeated in that manner (as is discussed below in another context).

Returning to the nineteenth century, we'll soon learn whether Lee's Confederates at Gettysburg were able to drive the Union army off of Cemetery Ridge after the rebels' artillery bombardment. Its relative ineffectiveness is but one of the issues as to whether or not Pickett's Charge was wrongheaded or insane—such that the Confederate commanders who ordered it and organized it should be subjected to the same kind of denunciation that can be leveled at the British command on the River Somme. As the subsequent sections will argue, the inevitability of the failure of that Charge has been overstated many times. Before the last Confederate assault at Gettysburg commenced, the Union force about to be attacked did not have anything like "machines" that would make their defense impregnable. Moreover, the rebel force was to perform magnificently—not only as it approached its objective but even as some of the attackers came upon the Federal defenders. As this story proceeds, we may infer that the Southerners came within an ace of success. That they did not is related less to the failure of their artillery cannonade, or to the extent that they were sent on a suicide mission, than to the *performance of the men waiting for them on Cemetery Ridge*.

The Nine Brigades Advance

Confederate thinking as the time for the July 3 assault approached was at several levels. At the highest one, Robert E. Lee perhaps may have thought of achieving a Cannae at Gettysburg. By destroying a major Union army in the field he might possibly bring an end to the war as well.[70] Would the North sustain its exceedingly difficult struggle if yet *another* big battle was lost in the East, especially if this devastating defeat occurred on its own soil? Could the South sustain *its* attempt to break free of the United States if the war were to continue to grind it down? In this respect, the Confederate cause was about to absorb an apparently crushing, contemporary blow at Vicksburg.[71] Although the Confederate leaders at Gettysburg on July 3 could not have known about the specifics of this impending defeat in the West, they nevertheless may have sensed that the overall strategic situation required a bold stroke in the eastern theater: "Could [it] all be done by one wild desperate dash?"[72]

But would that stroke be a reckless thrust at the enemy, doomed to fail? First, consider that the Battle of Cannae itself failed to win the war in question. The mighty Romans just kept going against the Carthaginians—as perhaps Lincoln and the United States would have done against the South, a crushing defeat at Gettysburg notwithstanding. Second, the hours of intricate Confederate planning for Pickett's Charge suggest nothing like desperation. Whether or not the final assault at Gettysburg was to be a "dash" (no)—the third point is that a frontal attack supposedly could not win battles in the American Civil War because defensive weaponry was too strong by the middle of that century.

This last consideration is spurious. General Lee was likely to have been cognizant of what frontal assaults had achieved in nineteenth-century wars. Whereas Napoleon's massed frontal attacks at Waterloo had almost entirely failed in 1815, he had previously defeated another enemy using that tactic in the 1809 Battle of Wagram. Near that village northeast of Vienna, an eight-thousand-man French column smashed through the Austrian center. So, it was at worst touch-and-go for the offense in the early 1800s. However, some contend that the rifled musket and supposed advances in artillery made offensive tactics obsolete a half-century later. But this is not universally true: Just four years before Gettysburg, the great Battle of Solferino occurred in northern Italy, seventy-five miles east of Milan. An allied force of French and Piedmontese, attacking up a steep slope, *broke the Austrian center with an assault on its front* and won the battle.[73]

Although General Lee may not have been thinking about what was achieved by European soldiers attacking in 1859 (he never articulated anything of the kind), he conceivably did have these historical perspectives in the back of his mind.[74] Moreover, he may have gauged the Union army to his front to be something of a motley crew. Most soldiers in the Army of the Potomac were Americans as such, but many had been born elsewhere. This was rather unlike the national cohesion that better characterized his own army. Lee had fresh memories of how elements of the Army of the Potomac had broken so badly on May 2 at Chancellorsville, and even on July 1 north of Gettysburg. Did he know that the collapsing flanks in both cases had many German-born soldiers in their units? Perhaps he believed the Federals had been lucky on July 2 and that this polyglot enemy would finally break apart entirely under the pressure of a continuing offensive thrust.[75] In World War II, Adolf Hitler and the German high command were thinking as much while planning the 1944 Ardennes counteroffensive (elements of which were mentioned in Chapter 3). The "mongrelized" Americans would break then collapse if subjected to a severe assault on their front (mainly in Belgium as the winter of 1944 approached). While Robert E. Lee was infinitely superior in his military acumen to Adolf Hitler, both of these leaders seemed similarly to have underestimated the quality of their foes. The ethnically diverse Americans made their great fighting withdrawal to and stand at the aforementioned Elsenborn Ridge in the Battle of the Bulge in December 1944, ruining the Germans' plans. Now we will see how the supposedly too-disparate collection of soldiers in Army of the Potomac would stand on its own ridge south of a town in Pennsylvania.

Still, if the Confederates planned their frontal assault well, who knew what they might achieve on the field and in the eastern theater of the Civil War? The rebel tactical plan was good. The Southerners were also fortunate that the Union center at Gettysburg on July 3 was *not the numerically strongest* Federal position on the field. Only about *six thousand men* held a half-mile-long sector in the Union cen-

**Map 4-13
Confederate reserve units, mainly on the flanks of the Pickett-Pettigrew-Trimble line**

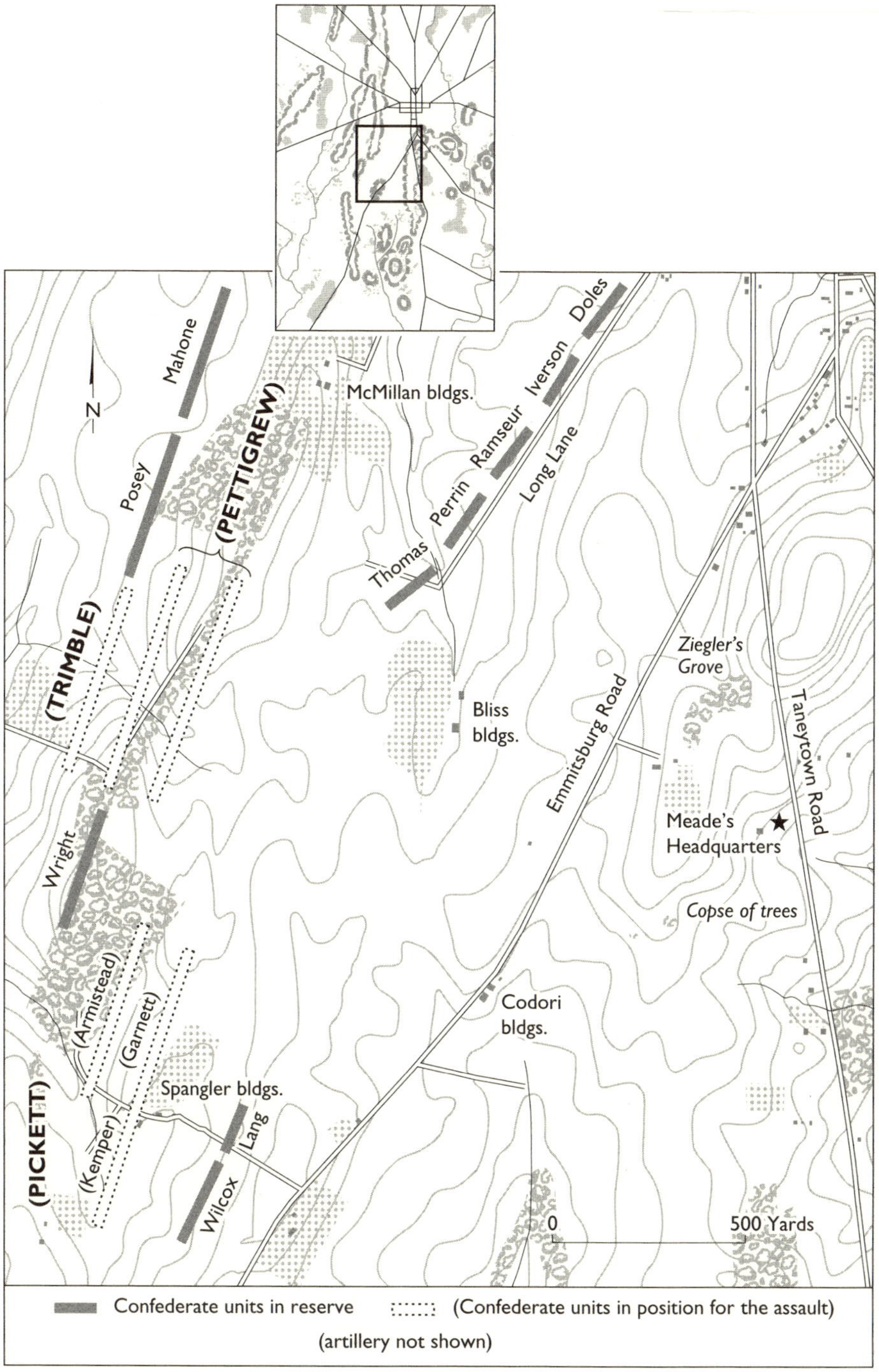

ter,[76] and the artillery defense there was not massive, whether or not the cannonade blew away those guns.

Colonel Alexander and his mates had indeed failed to blow them away, but this did not mean his work was through for the day. The rebels intended to bring elements of his artillery forward as the infantry assault force passed the guns.[77] Thus, the cannon fire support that Alexander spoke of in his frenzied message to General Pickett would be added to the attack. Other components of the support

THE GREAT GAMBLE LEE COULD HAVE WON 197

**Map 4-14
The 9 Confederate brigades poised to attack, and the opening stages of their advance**

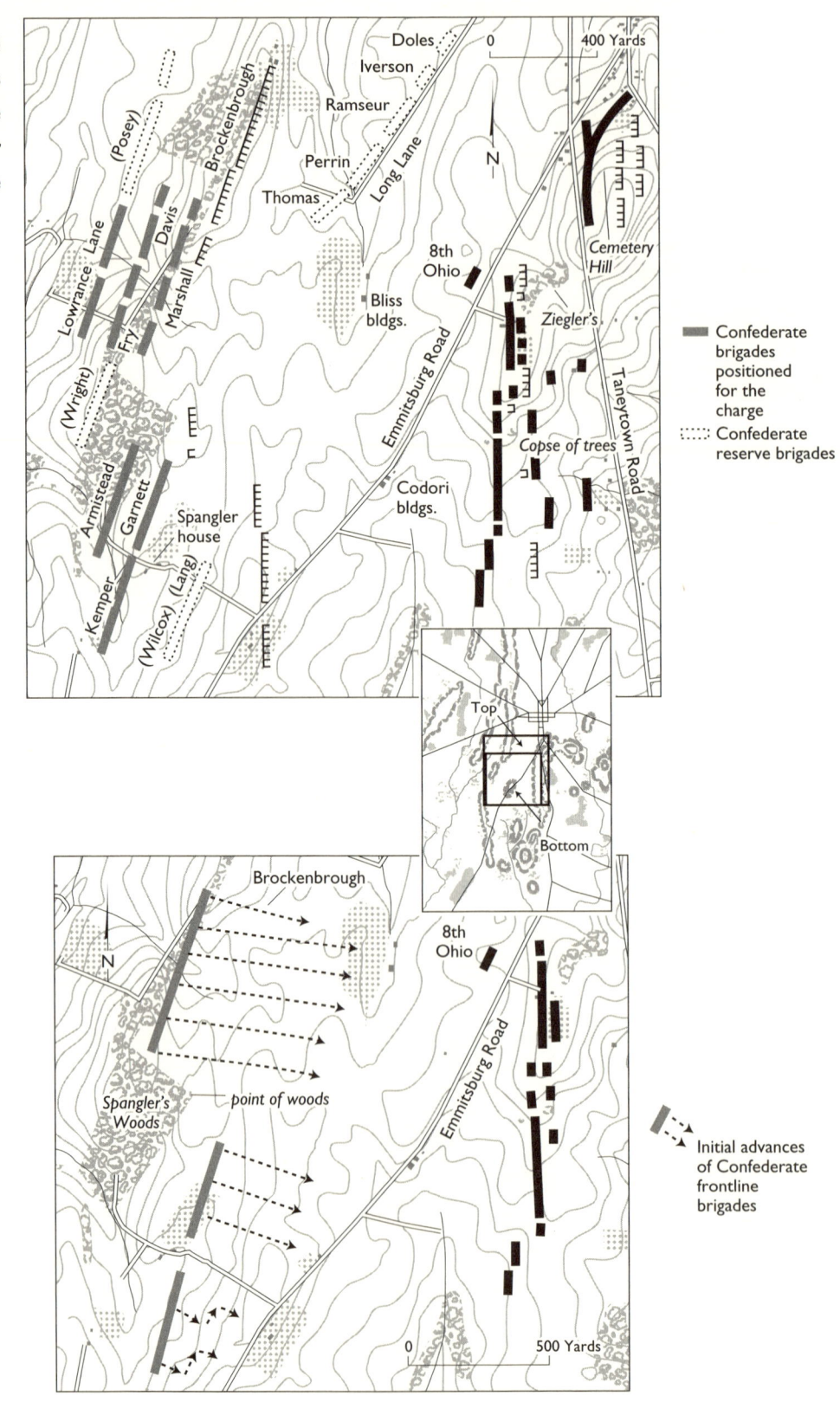

Confederate brigades positioned for the charge

Confederate reserve brigades

Initial advances of Confederate frontline brigades

198   THE STAND OF THE U.S. ARMY AT GETTYSBURG

for Pickett's Charge speak to its high-quality planning. Brigadier General Cadmus Wilcox's brigade was poised in an outward position east of Seminary Ridge. His soldiers (chart 4-10) were to advance if necessary—following Pickett's brigades (map 4-13) if the latter were to get in trouble as they approached the Union line. This right wing of the assault would need all the follow-up infantry support it could get. Near the center of the Confederate line were additional reserve units. A line of infantry made up of men from Maj. Gens. Robert E. Rodes's and Dorsey Pender's divisions (chart 4-10) formed on the rebel left in Long Lane, a sunken road that projects in a southwesterly direction from the town of Gettysburg (map 4-13). Rodes's and Pender's men (the latter led by Brig. Gen. James Lane owing to Pender's wounding on July 2[78]) could provide some long-range musket fire and perhaps move out if the advancing line's left flank became imperiled.

Thus, the Confederate command had established a potential assaulting force of infantry that significantly outnumbered the defenders in terms of the attack force's objective. As the brigades in Pickett's line advanced, they were to effect planned maneuvers that *would* compact the overall line by eliminating the gap between the right and left wings. Artillery and infantry support had been arranged. Thus, Pickett's Charge was to be much more than a mindless mass of men moving eastward. General Longstreet, the soldier formally in command of the attack itself, deserves credit for how he had organized this supposedly impossible attack. And yes, Pickett, too: The prior orders he issued to his three brigade commanders suggest that he had well planned his component of the attack. A short passage of time was to prove that the maneuvers of his men were impressively achieved.

At last Lee's troops moved out from their lines near Seminary Ridge (map 4-14)—focusing on that half-mile of ground centered roughly at the aforementioned copse of trees. The rebels marched steadily forward at about 110 paces per minute, skirmishers to their front. They proceeded through fields of crops, some of them waist-high in the early summer. It thus was difficult actually to "charge" as the Southern soldiers began the advance. More important was that their officers wanted the men to march in a deliberate manner, maintaining the integrity of the lines and unit cohesion therein. Brigadier General Lewis Armistead's brigade was an exception, however. His Virginia regiments had gone into position some two hundred yards behind the front ranks of Pickett's division (map 4-10). The plan was for them to catch up once the advance started, so Armistead's men moved out initially at quick-time.[79] At any rate, the bulk of the Confederate infantrymen would require fifteen to twenty minutes to cross the approximately three-quarters of a mile of open field between the two opposing ridges. Moving deliberately during the early stages of the advance also allowed for the possibility of a final rush at the Union lines: It was well nigh impossible for nine brigades of men to run the entire distance across such a field.[80]

As the rebel force advanced, Pickett's three brigades (chart 4-11) on the right wing (map 4-14) took off from a swale just east of Seminary Ridge, where the

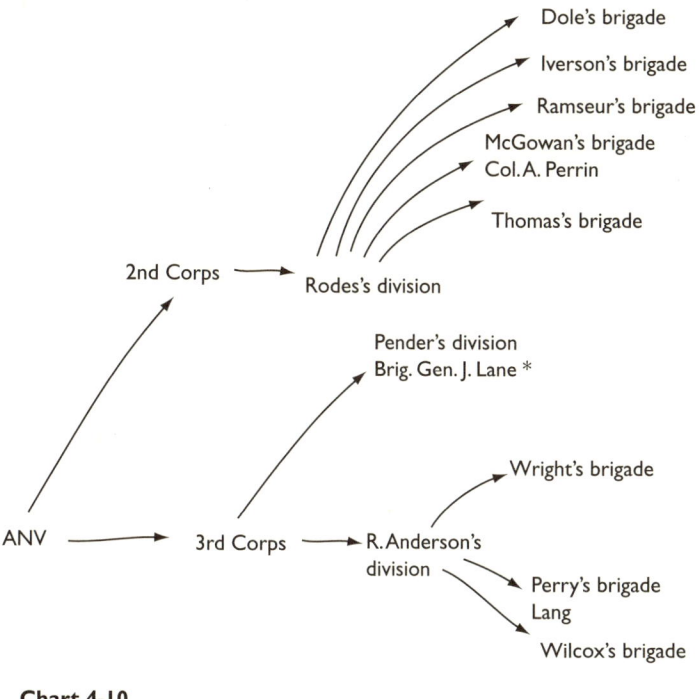

**Chart 4-10
Confederate supporting and reserve Brigades**

* Pender wounded July 2

Map 4-15
Union positions in the center and on the center-left as the assault comes their way

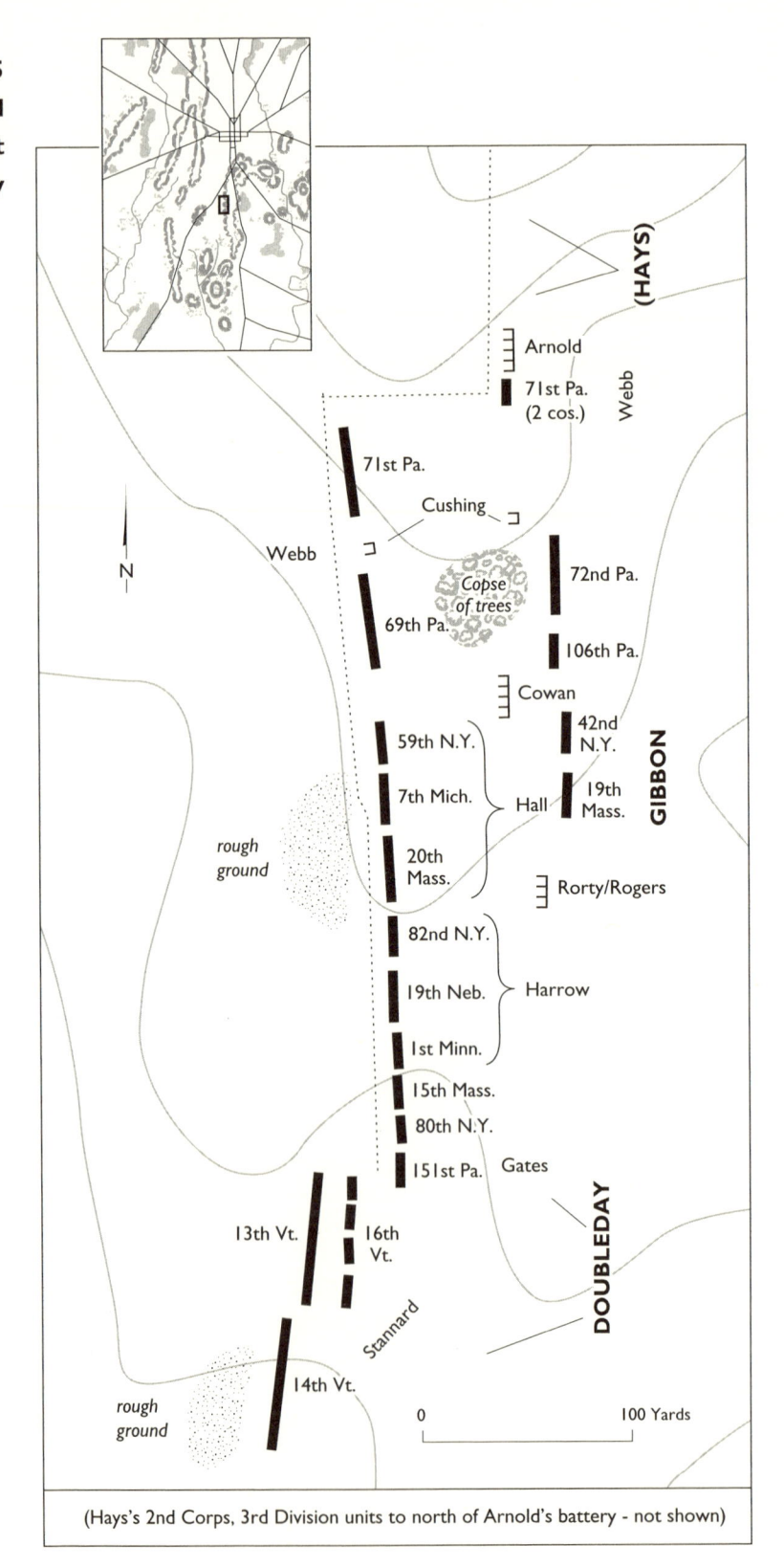

(Hays's 2nd Corps, 3rd Division units to north of Arnold's battery - not shown)

Chart 4-11
Pickett's division and its brigades

ANV → 1st Corps → Pickett's division → Garnett's brigade
→ Armistead's brigade
→ Kemper's brigade

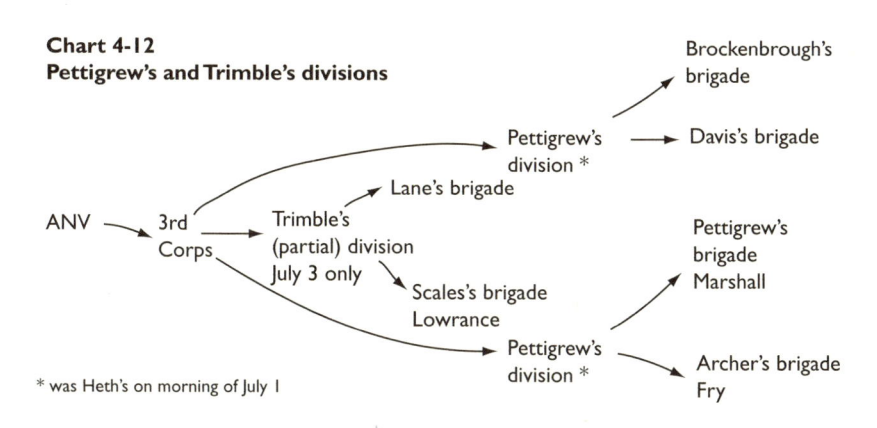

Chart 4-12
Pettigrew's and Trimble's divisions

ANV → 3rd Corps → Trimble's (partial) division July 3 only → Lane's brigade
→ Scales's brigade Lowrance
→ Pettigrew's division * → Brockenbrough's brigade
→ Davis's brigade
Pettigrew's division * → Pettigrew's brigade Marshall
→ Archer's brigade Fry

* was Heth's on morning of July 1

men in the Federal line could not see them. However, the signalmen on Little Round Top spotted Pickett's advancing troops and sent a message up the line. Thus, at least the left-hand portion of the Union's half-mile line in their center was informed of what was coming. The Northerners left in this sector were from a brigade of Vermonters under Brig. Gen. George J. Stannard (map 4-15). The information they received perhaps allowed them some mental preparation and could have provided the impetus for them to make a pivotal maneuver, figuratively and literally, a short time later.

On the Confederate left, the six brigades under Generals Pettigrew and Trimble (chart 4-12) were back in the woods covering Seminary Ridge in this area (maps 4-14 and 4-16). Pettigrew's men came out of those trees after advancing only fifty yards and thus were in plain view of the Union artillery batteries on Cemetery Hill and of the right-hand portion of the central defense near Ziegler's Grove on Cemetery Ridge and just below it (map 4-16). But when he cleared the woods, General Pettigrew could see that his entire line was *not* moving forward in a coordinated manner. Brigadier General Joseph Davis's brigade was still in the woods when Pettigrew's two right-hand brigades came into the open. However, Davis's men soon appeared and rushed to catch up with the rest of the line.

**Map 4-16
Problems with the initial stages of Pettigrew's advancing left wing**

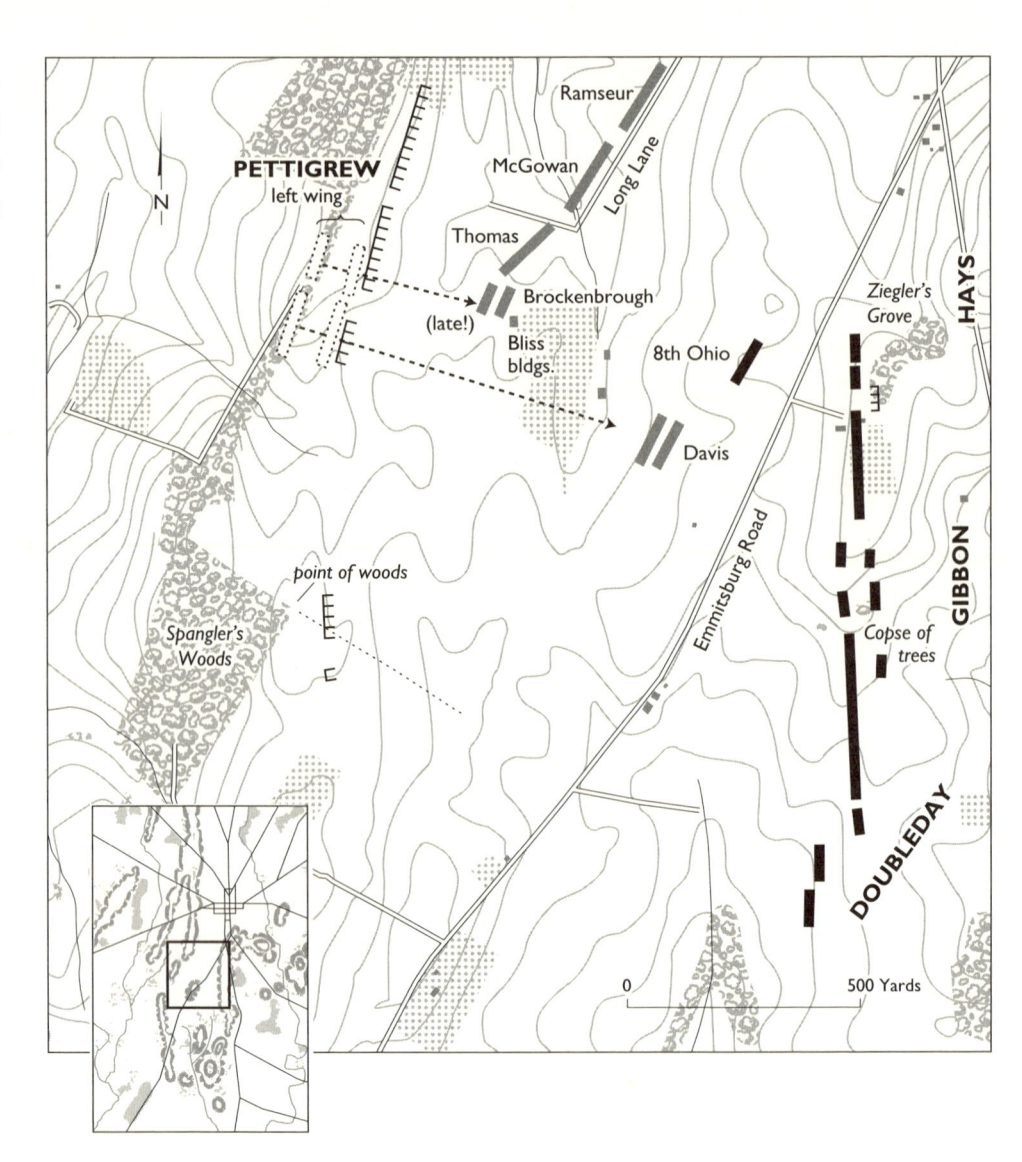

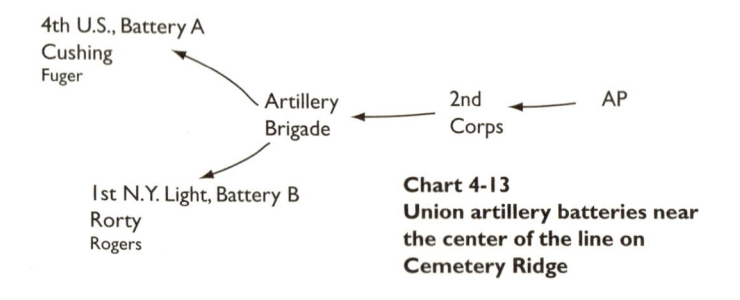

**Chart 4-13
Union artillery batteries near the center of the line on Cemetery Ridge**

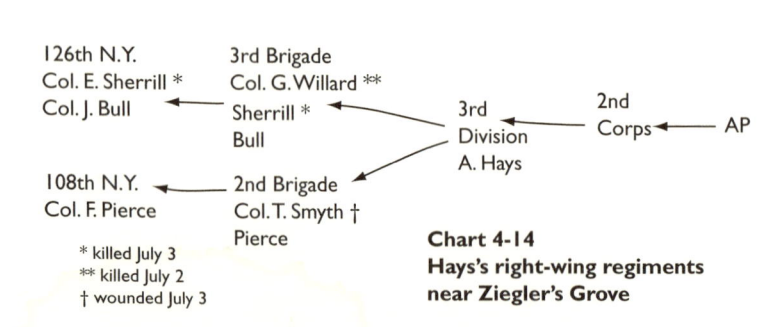

4th U.S., Battery A
Cushing
Fuger
→ Artillery Brigade ← 2nd Corps ← AP

1st N.Y. Light, Battery B
Rorty
Rogers

**Chart 4-14
Hays's right-wing regiments near Ziegler's Grove**

126th N.Y.
Col. E. Sherrill *
Col. J. Bull
← 3rd Brigade
Col. G. Willard **
Sherrill *
Bull
← 3rd Division
A. Hays
← 2nd Corps ← AP

108th N.Y.
Col. F. Pierce
← 2nd Brigade
Col. T. Smyth †
Pierce

* killed July 3
** killed July 2
† wounded July 3

But where was Brockenbrough? His brigade of Virginians formed the left of the entire assault (map 4-14), yet it was not doing its job. This was not necessarily surprising, for John Brockenbrough was a poorly regarded commander, and his men may still have been fought out from their July 1 attacks west of town (his brigade was one of the five participating in Pickett's Charge that had been previously engaged at Gettysburg). Brockenbrough's lateness would have dire consequences.

Meanwhile, the Federal defense was not passively steeling itself against an impending infantry blow. Soon after the Confederate cannonade ceased, the Union officers shifted the positions of some of their batteries. The guns were cleaned and reloaded. The Federals should also have immediately called up reinforcing batteries from the Artillery Reserve (maps 4-7 and 4-18), if only because the defensive cannon

202 THE STAND OF THE U.S. ARMY AT GETTYSBURG

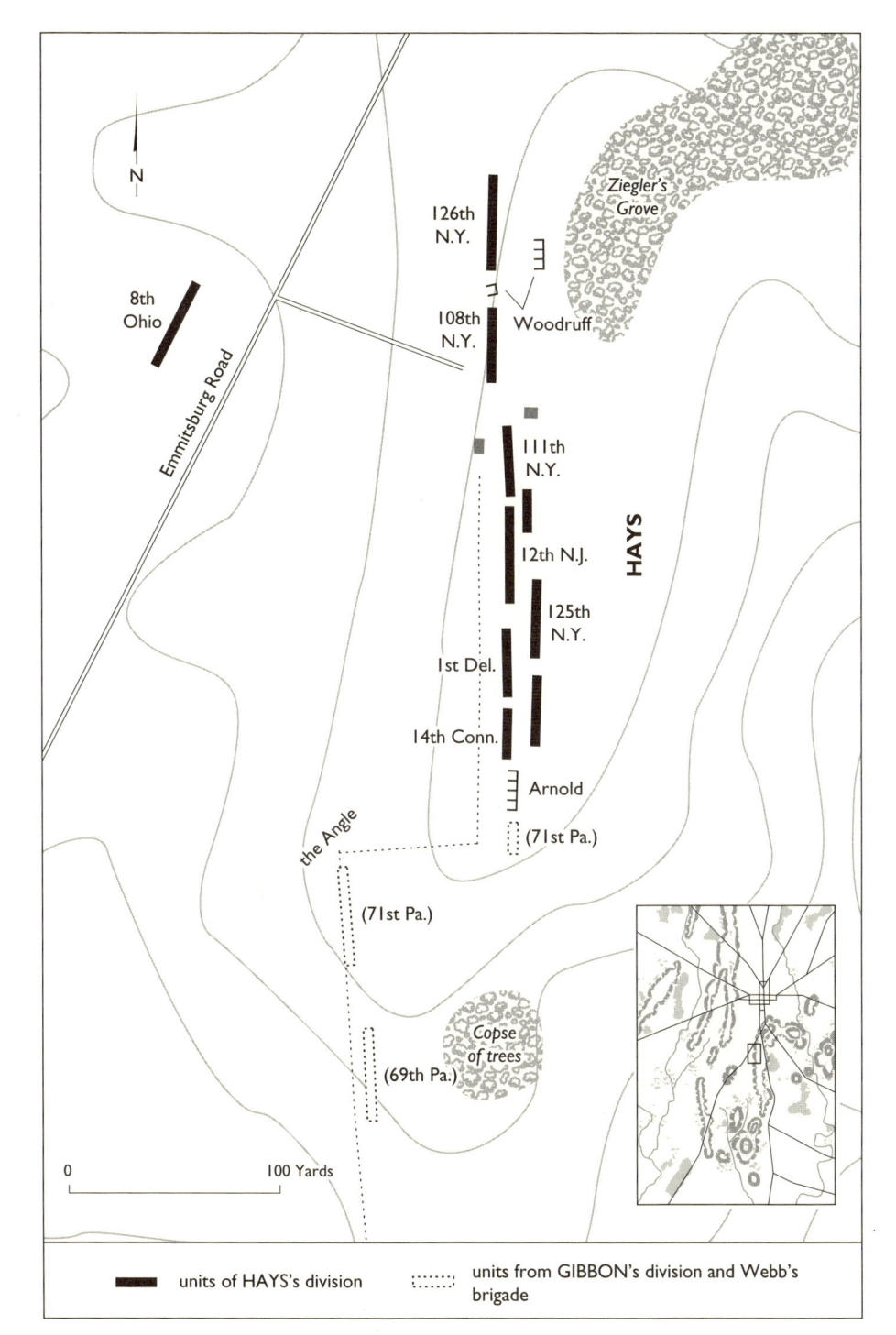

**Map 4-17
Union positions on the center-right as the assault comes their way**

in their center had been depleted. Brown's battery (now Perrin's) was largely gone and Capt. James M. Rorty's (later Lt. Robert Rogers) and Lt. Alonzo H. Cushing's batteries (chart 4-13) were down to a total of 5 guns.[81] Overall, only 23 or 24 pieces remained in this sector, a scant 6 of them still supplied with long-range ammunition. Those guns would not be augmented until after the rebel assault had crested—one of the few instances of sub-optimal Union leadership on July 3. Therefore, the Federal infantry and certain of its commanders would have to outdo themselves.

THE GREAT GAMBLE LEE COULD HAVE WON

Map 4-18
Union artillery positions on the flanks and along south Cemetery Ridge

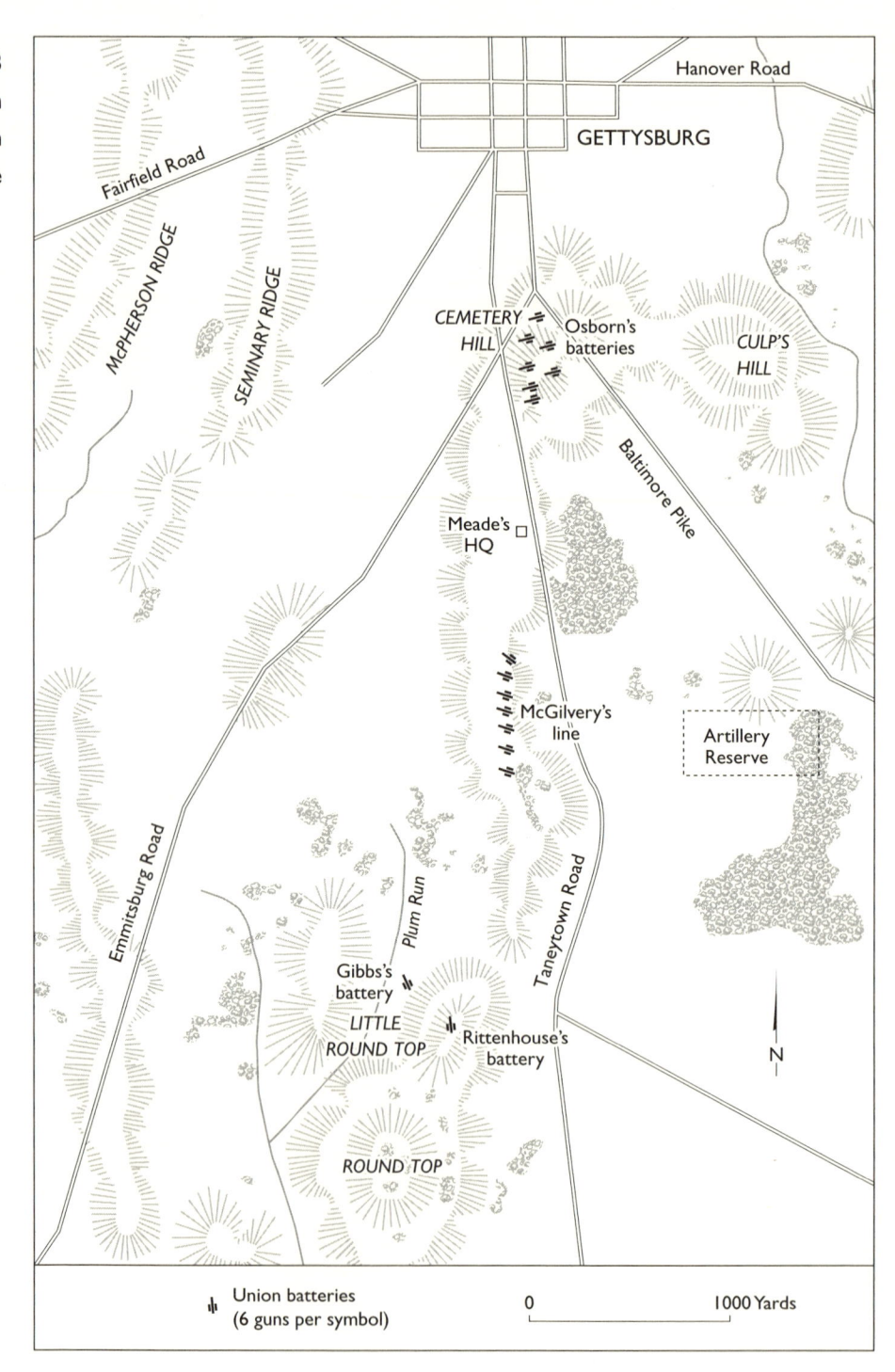

In this respect, and a harbinger of things to come, Brig. Gen. Alexander Hays was active during the post-bombardment lull. Remember that Hays was a division commander whose 2nd Corps unit held the right-hand end of the Union center (chart 4-14). He had been worried to this point about a gap between the end of his infantry line and a battery situated in Ziegler's Grove to the left (northward, but still below Cemetery Hill in map 4-17). General Hays now ordered a regiment of New Yorkers, the 126th, to move to the left and come a bit forward. The 126th New York was thus poised to participate in a key maneuver against the impending attack.

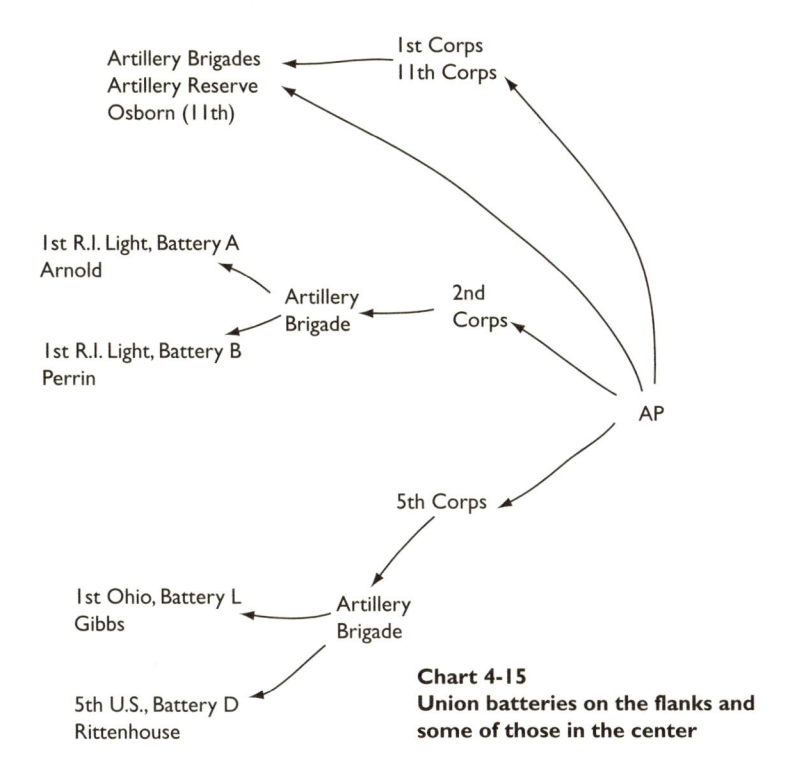

Chart 4-15
Union batteries on the flanks and some of those in the center

THE CONFEDERATE LEFT WING IS COUNTERATTACKED—AND AN ADVANCING BRIGADE BREAKS: ENVELOPMENT OF ONE REBEL FLANK

As the thousands of rebel troops approached the Emmitsburg Road, which slants across the field, they were fired upon by Union guns on Cemetery Hill, by the batteries in the center that still possessed enough ammunition, by McGilvery's larger mass of cannon to the south, and from Little Round Top (map 4-18, chart 4-15). Kemper's men in particular came under fire just as they reached the crest of the easternmost of the intermediate ridges (map 4-9) located between the Emmitsburg Road and Seminary Ridge.[82]

In spite of all the shot and shell that went from east to west, it is not clear that massive damage was done to the attackers. Once again, long-range fire tended to miss the mark. Consider the guns firing from the left end of the Union artillery defense: Lieutenant Rittenhouse's battery on Little Round Top (chart 4-15). His guns had the advantage of enfilading fire against the right and possibly into the center of the advancing rebel line. However, these pieces had to fire more than a mile to land their projectiles amongst the central sector of the assault force (map 4-18).[83] Compounding the problem, the rebels were indeed beginning to compress their line into this region. Rittenhouse had additional problems caused by the rather small area of ground on Little Round Top where his six ten-pound Parrott guns (examples of the rifled cannon described above) could be placed. This meant that "when the enemy got a little more than halfway to our lines, I could only use . . . two pieces, as the others could not be run out far enough to point them to the right" (in a northwesterly direction [map 4-18]).[84] Rittenhouse

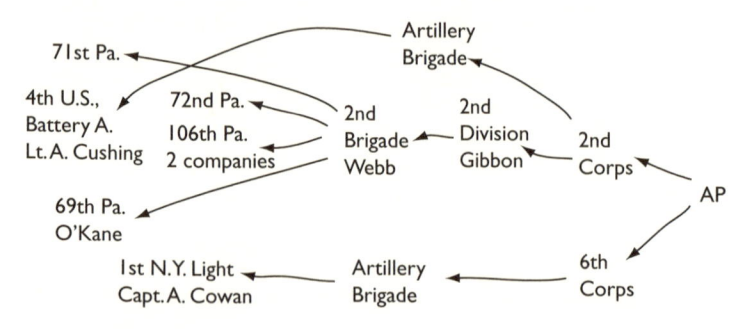

Chart 4-16
Federal forces in the center of the Cemetery Ridge line

thus had only a narrow window of opportunity to do any damage with the bulk of his guns.

The rebel lines moved across the field in fine fashion, regardless of the effect of Union fire upon them. General Pickett's men executed the planned left obliques (map 4-19), as several of the rebel units on the right angled roughly forty-five degrees to the north. Others, in particular General Kemper's regiments on the right wing of Pickett's division, conducted their leftward shifts by making a series of ninety-degree turns northward (maps 4-14 and 4-19) interspersed with straight-eastward advances.[85] Kemper's lines would continue to move in this manner even as they approached the Union positions. Kemper had been the last of Pickett's three brigade commanders to receive the order to move out. Therefore, his first move was a flank march to the left as he endeavored to catch up with Garnett (map 4-19). Kemper's distinctly northward shift was such that his right flank passed near the Rogers houses (map 4-10) as his brigade approached the Emmitsburg Road.

At any rate, the right half of the assault force was beginning to close the gap between it and the advancing elements of General Pettigrew's command. All of this was achieved under fire and under the mental pressure of advancing toward infantry defenders. Several of those Yankees were to remark later how deeply impressed they were by the "splendid sight" of the "long sweeping lines of Confederate infantry advancing" and "parade-ground precision" by which the maneuvers of their enemy were carried out under fire.[86] Many of the Union soldiers gazing at this Confederate display were "Hancock's boys." Although few of the rebels could know this, the Confederate troops probably were not anticipating a cakewalk. They had to have borne in mind how the Federal force had finally stood, all along the line, on the previous day of the battle. Conversely, how much of a psychological jolt had the Union men received as the assault force, more than a mile wide, first came into view? The Confederates had nicely concealed their nine brigades before that moment. Yet the Federals had to know an infantry attack was imminent during the several minutes that passed between the end of the cannonade and the start of the advance.

The leading elements of those rebel brigades covered more than half the distance to Cemetery Ridge in ten minutes or less. Pickett's front line then came to a point of shelter—a swale that straddles the Emmitsburg Road (map 4-19). The Confederate right wing stopped there and many of the units within it dressed their lines by a prearranged maneuver. However, this area of low ground did not extend to where Kemper's men approached the road as they moved east of the second intermediate ridge. The extreme right of Pickett's division thus was unprotected. Nevertheless, they, along with Garnett's regiments, closed gaps created by the Union shelling and got themselves in parallel with the Federal defensive line as Pickett's men further narrowed the distance between them and Pettigrew's troops (map 4-19). The latter's brigades and those of Trimble behind Pettigrew lagged behind Pickett's eastward advance. But the Confederate left wing was catching up, given the redressing actions just described and the fact that Pickett's left obliques required his men to cover a relatively longer distance. So the front of the advancing lines strove to form itself into a powerfully contiguous force. We saw, however, that a portion of the Confederate left had been *really* lagging behind the rest of the line.

206 THE STAND OF THE U.S. ARMY AT GETTYSBURG

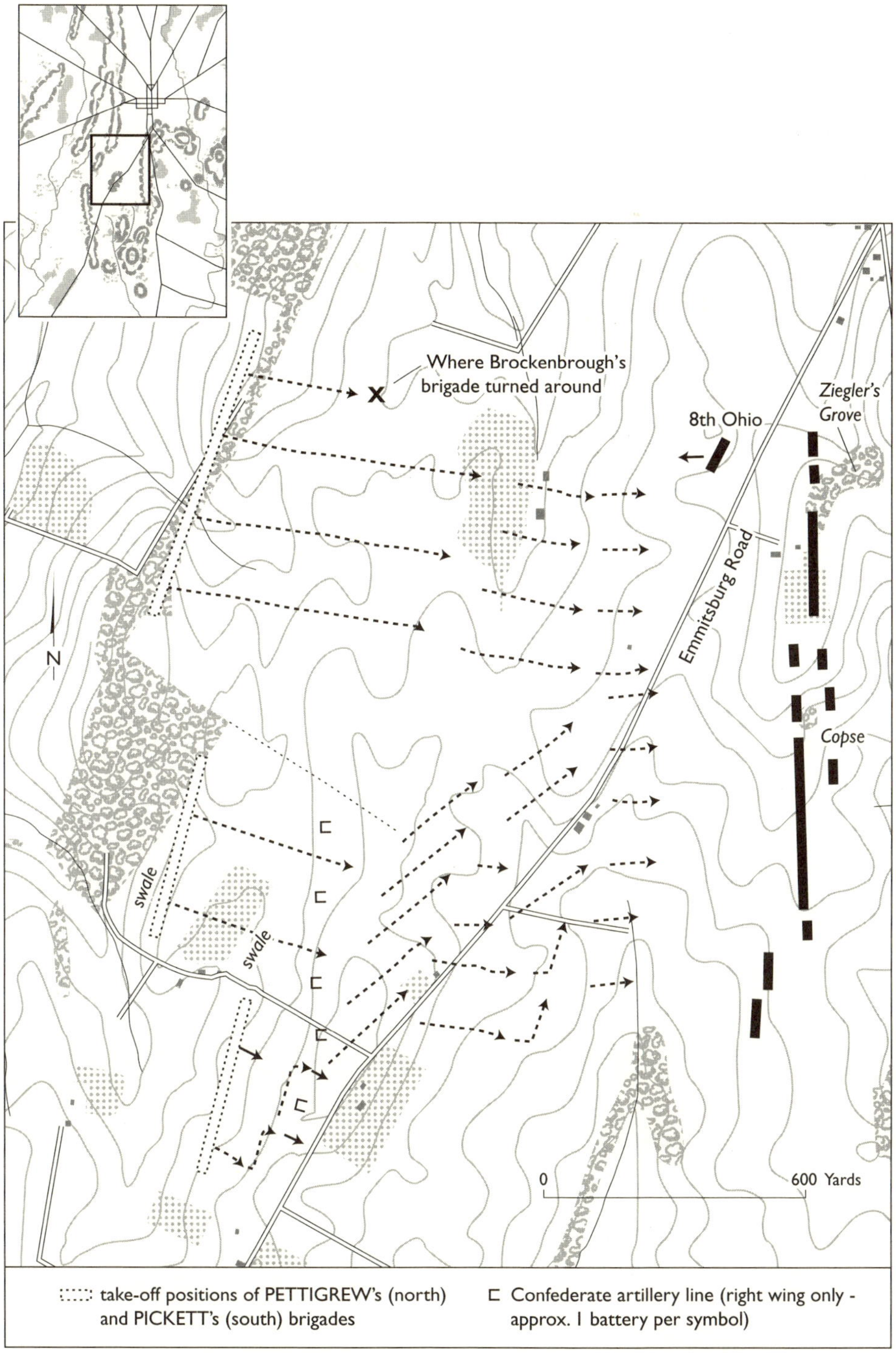

**Map 4-19
Pickett's brigades execute their left-obliques as Pettigrew's front line approaches the Emmitsburg Road**

Meanwhile, we rejoin the further preparations of the defenders, in particular those in the heart of the Union center (map 4-20)—to which an increasing proportion of the Confederate attack was headed. Recall that this was where Brig. Gen. Ambrose Wright's Georgians had broken through briefly on the previous evening. They had been repulsed—in part by virtue of the actions of Brig. Gen. Alexander Webb's "Philadelphia Brigade" (chart 4-16). Webb had taken over that unit just three days before the battle in an effort to try to whip it into shape.[87]

Map 4-20
Webb's 2nd Corps brigade in the Union center during the rebel advance

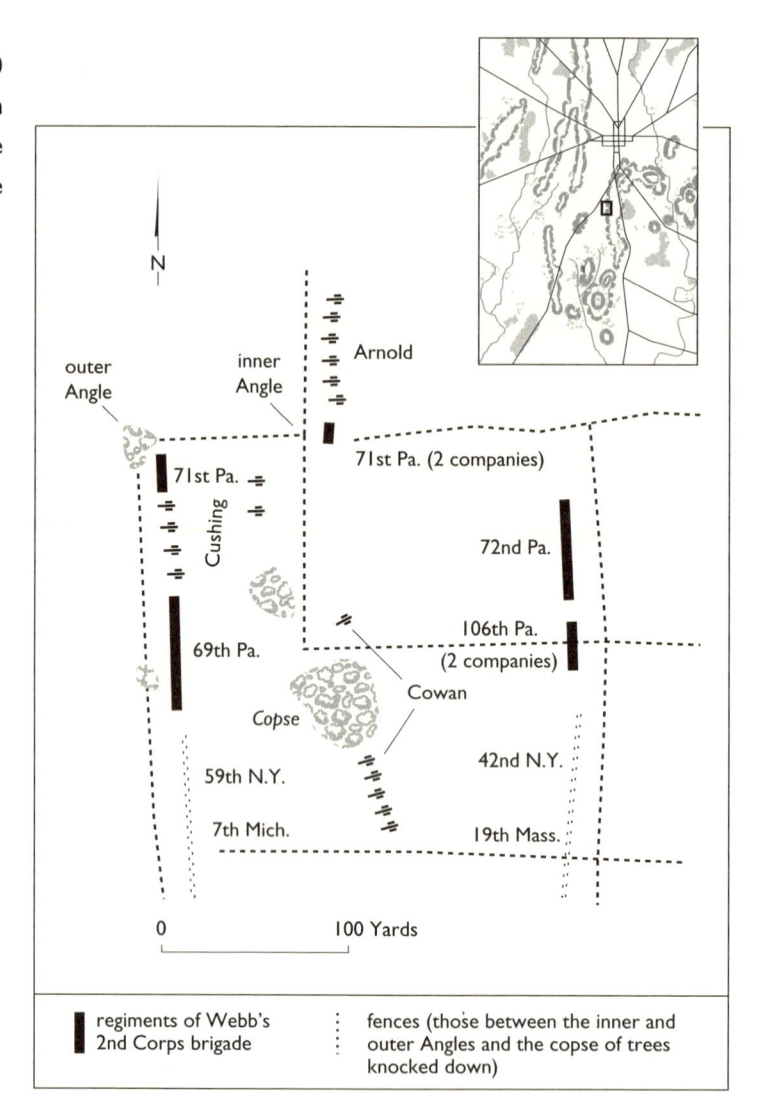

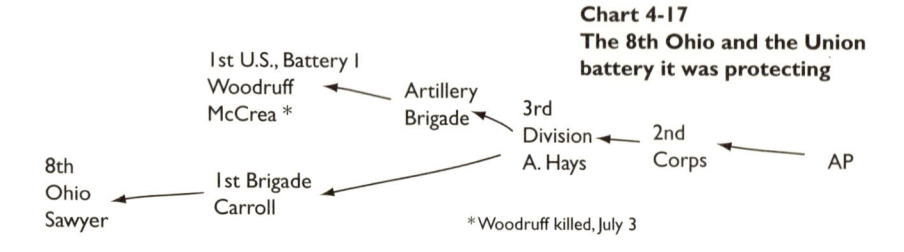

N

outer Angle   inner Angle   Arnold

71st Pa.   71st Pa. (2 companies)

Cushing   72nd Pa.

69th Pa.   106th Pa. (2 companies)

Copse   Cowan

59th N.Y.   42nd N.Y.

7th Mich.   19th Mass.

0   100 Yards

■ regiments of Webb's 2nd Corps brigade

⋮ fences (those between the inner and outer Angles and the copse of trees knocked down)

Chart 4-17
The 8th Ohio and the Union battery it was protecting

1st U.S., Battery I
Woodruff
McCrea * ← Artillery Brigade ← 3rd Division A. Hays ← 2nd Corps ← AP

8th Ohio Sawyer ← 1st Brigade Carroll

*Woodruff killed, July 3

Some regarded the brigade as the caboose of the 2nd Corps's train (as the sorry performance of one of Webb's regiments near Culp's Hill on July 2 seemed to exemplify; see map 3-43 in the previous chapter).[88] That problem was to influence events later on this Friday afternoon. In the meantime, General Webb saw that many of the Confederates seemed headed right at him. He sent a request for the artillery unit on his left (three hundred yards to the south) to come up and bolster the weakened Union center. The battery commander, Capt. Andrew Cowan (chart 4-16), complied and brought his guns to the central sector of the line, unlimbering five pieces roughly behind the positions manned by the 59th New York

208   THE STAND OF THE U.S. ARMY AT GETTYSBURG

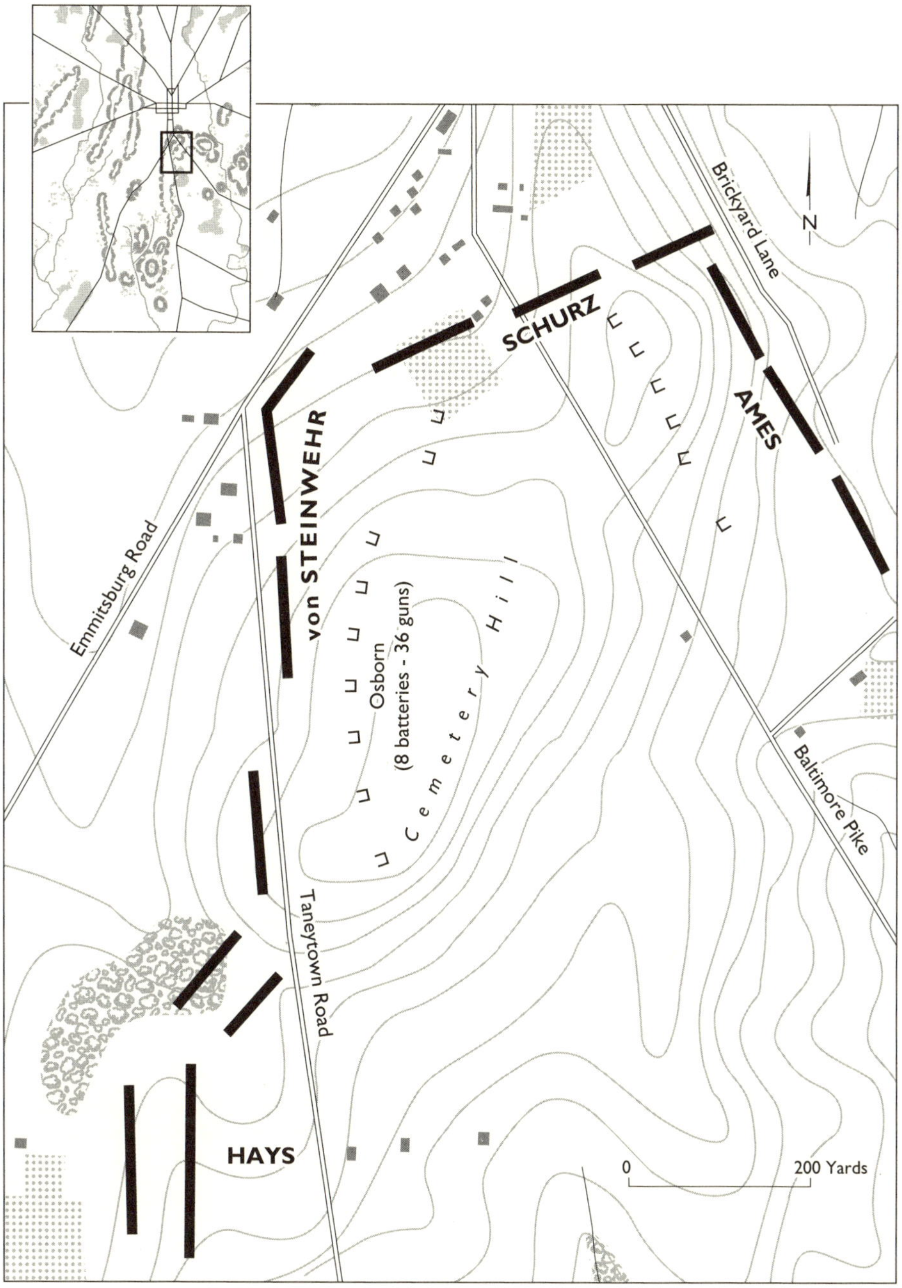

**Map 4-21
The Union right on Cemetery Ridge and Cemetery Hill**

and 7th Michigan (map 4-20). Cowan placed the remaining cannon in his battery just north of the copse of trees near the 69th Pennsylvania (map 4-20). At about this time Lieutenant Cushing (charts 4-9 and 4-16) moved two of his guns forward to the wall (map 4-20). Cushing's battery was posted in a pocket between a region in the center of the Union line called the Angle and the copse of trees (the Angle was introduced in map 4-17, where one sees the north-south fence line extending abruptly westward then angling sharply again to the south).

All the while, the Union artillery on the ridge was lobbing projectiles from a distance, although not *necessarily* with much effect on Pickett's lines.[89] It did, however, influence significant activities occurring on the Confederates' left. Recall in this regard the belated advance of Colonel Brockenbrough's brigade.[90] At

Map 4-22 Pettigrew's left is attacked by the 8th Ohio, which sends it back then wheels to flank the left wing of the assault

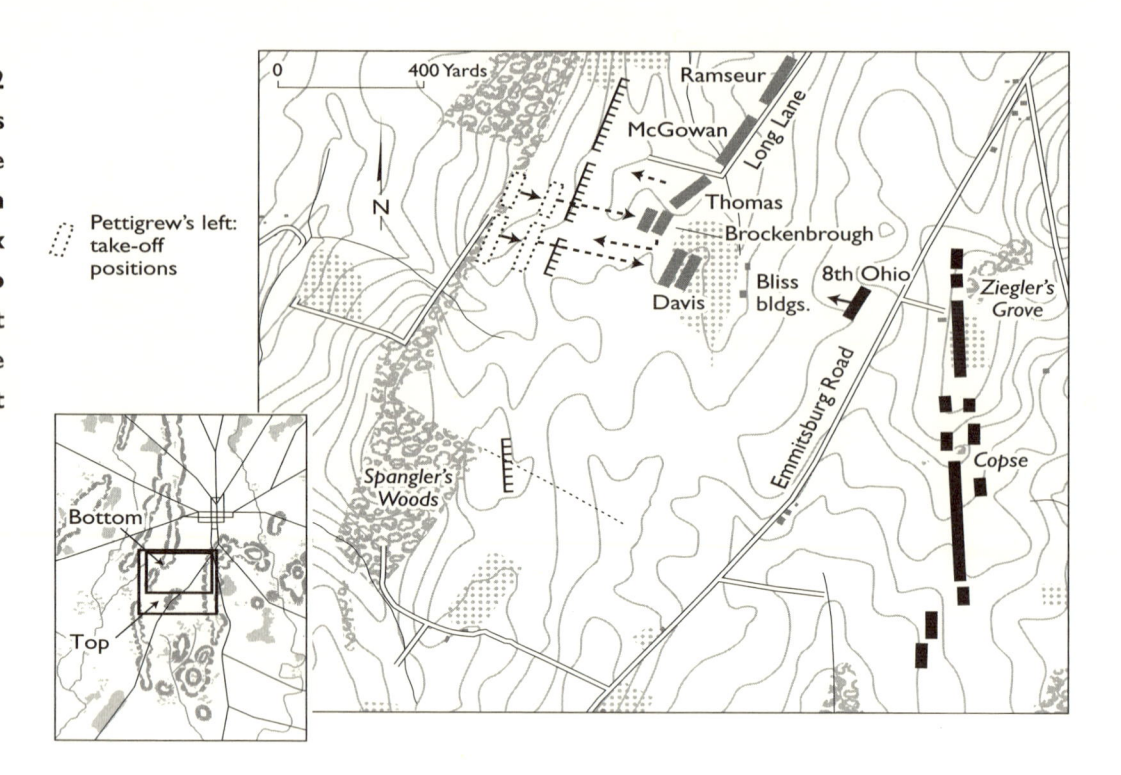

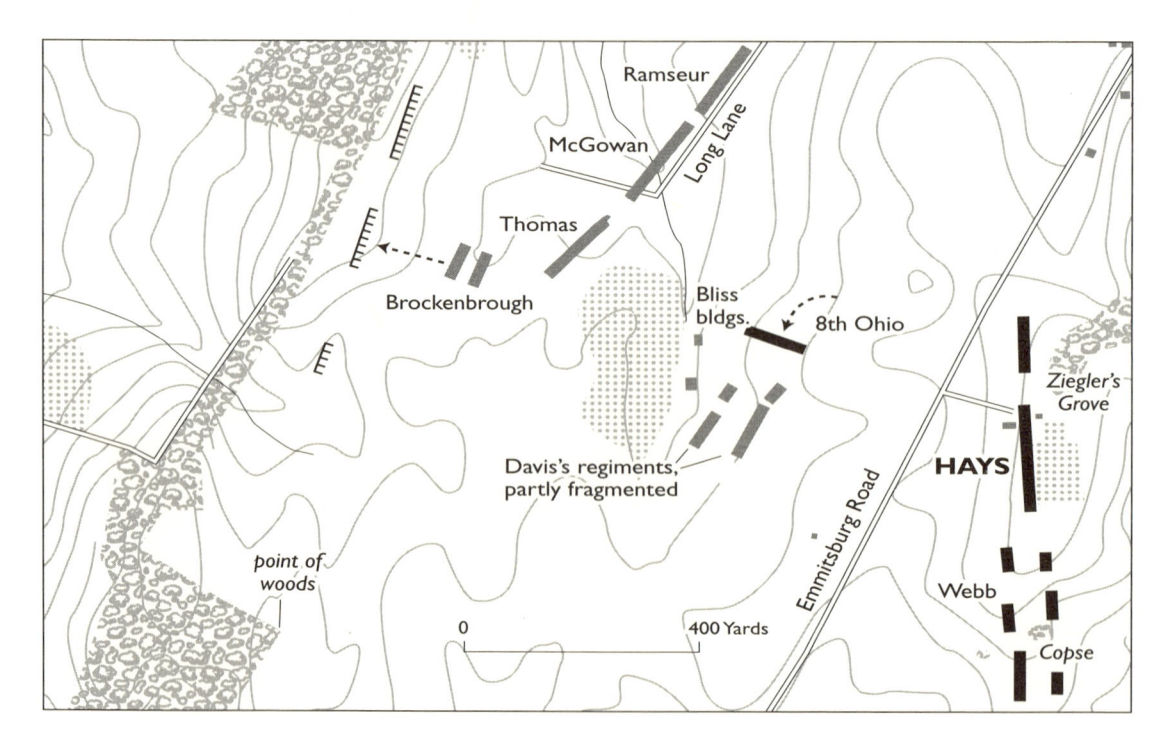

last, these Virginia regiments appeared from amongst the trees and began their eastward advance. They skirted the burned-out Bliss farm buildings and went past the men from Rodes's and Pender's divisions posted in the Long Lane (map 4-16). Brockenbrough's Virginians seemed in no hurry and did not catch up with Davis's brigade at the left end of Pettigrew's line. Thus, Brockenbrough's tentative troops were isolated slightly to the rear. This seemed to cause particularly heavy cannon fire to rain down on them from the Union batteries on Cemetery Hill

210   THE STAND OF THE U.S. ARMY AT GETTYSBURG

commanded by Maj. Thomas W. Osborn from the 11th Corps Artillery Brigade (maps 4-18 and 4-21). The guns assembled on the hill were from this corps and other Federal units (chart 4-15).

Just then, something happened on that part of the field that unlocked the door to Union success. The events involved Lt. Col. Franklin Sawyer's 8th Ohio Regiment (chart 4-17), which had ended up in a forward position the previous day. The Ohioans had initially been sent down the ridge on July 2 to support Lt. George A. Woodruff's battery in front of Ziegler's Grove (chart 4-17). Rebel skirmishers were shooting at the artillerymen from the west side of the Emmitsburg Road. The men of the 8th Ohio drove them off and kept advancing as the Confederates fell back to the Bliss barn (its location, but not any of the actions that occurred there, is depicted on map 4-22). The rebels finally halted Sawyer's attack, but his men *stayed in their advanced position* and set up a skirmish line of their own just west of the road. The line was fired on repeatedly, but the Ohioans continued to hold their ground.

Later that afternoon, most of the 8th Ohio's brigade was sent to reinforce the severely threatened 11th Corps on Cemetery Hill (map 3-44 in the previous chapter). Sawyer's commander, Col. Samuel S. Carroll, had led his 2nd Corps units (a part of Hays's division) from Cemetery Ridge on a short northeasterly march (map 3-47, Chapter 3). Colonel Carroll, it seems, forgot that he had left the 8th Ohio in its by then unnecessarily exposed position.[91] In any case, Colonel Sawyer held firm to his orders and stayed in his advanced location into the night. Sawyer sent a request for reinforcements to join him west of the Emmitsburg Road, but General Hays told him to maintain the position on his own. Hays needed to keep the rest of his men in line (map 4-17, chart 4-14) and had no troops to spare given the departure of Carroll.

On the morning of July 3, small bands of outwardly deployed Confederates hoping to dislodge the Ohioans from their advanced position attacked that small regiment of Union men. Colonel Sawyer did not yield and in fact counterattacked, driving off the mild rebel threat. But his regiment was gradually being whittled down. It had suffered several men killed or wounded on the Second, and two more Ohioans were killed during the Confederate cannonade on the Third. The regiment had gone out to its advanced position with just under two hundred men, but by midafternoon on July 3, the 8th Ohio had only 160 men fit for duty.

Yet they did their duty in spades: As the grand assault approached them, the Ohioans were more or less in the middle of nowhere and obviously imperiled. But they continued holding their ground against the left wing of the rebel advance and then went into action (map 4-22). According to Sawyer, "I advanced my reserve to the picket front, and as the rebel line came within about 100 yards, we poured in a well directed fire, which broke the rebel line, and it soon fled in the wildest confusion."[92]

The rebel unit on the extreme left at the beginning of Pettigrew's advance—Brockenbrough's eight hundred Virginians—had been shaky from the outset and under severe pressure from Osborn's aforementioned artillery fire, which continued to blast due westward from Cemetery Hill. Brockenbrough's brigade probably broke because of this shelling and turned 180 degrees in the vicinity of the Long Lane and went back toward the trees (map 4-22).[93] Sawyer's Ohioans therefore were likely to have fired on what was *then* the Confederate left: Davis's brigade (map 4-22). The combined effect of the artillery fire from Cemetery Hill and the 8th Ohio's counterattack, both directed at the rebels' left wing, was that *the entire Confederate line was in danger.*

Map 4-23
Union moves to envelop the rebel left flank

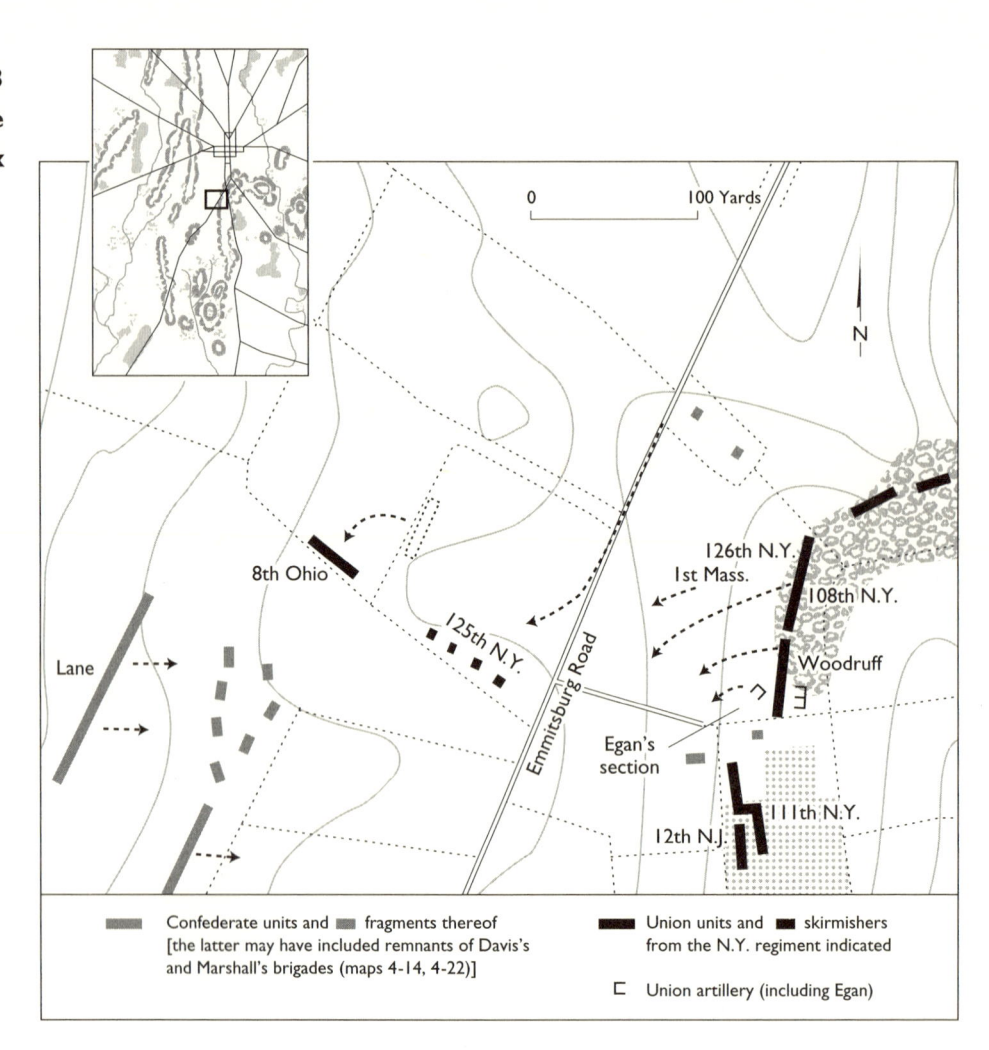

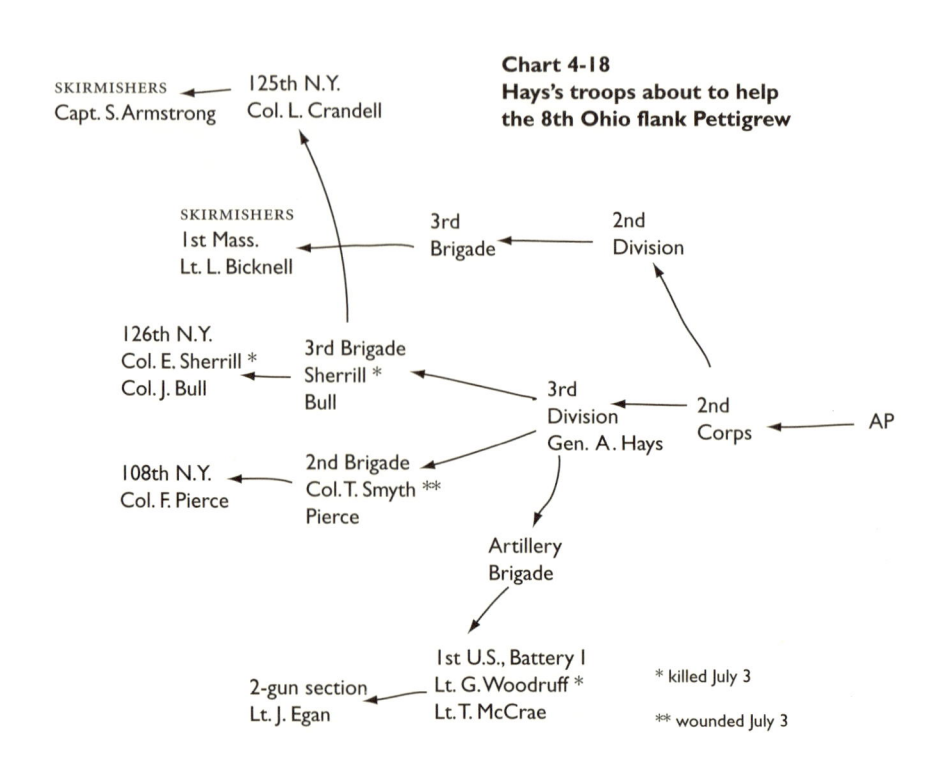

0 — 100 Yards

8th Ohio

125th N.Y.

126th N.Y.
1st Mass.

108th N.Y.

Woodruff

Lane

Emmitsburg Road

Egan's section

12th N.J.

111th N.Y.

▬ Confederate units and ▪ fragments thereof
[the latter may have included remnants of Davis's and Marshall's brigades (maps 4-14, 4-22)]

▬ Union units and ▪ skirmishers from the N.Y. regiment indicated

⊏ Union artillery (including Egan)

Chart 4-18
Hays's troops about to help the 8th Ohio flank Pettigrew

SKIRMISHERS ← 125th N.Y.
Capt. S. Armstrong — Col. L. Crandell

SKIRMISHERS ← 1st Mass.
Lt. L. Bicknell ← 3rd Brigade ← 2nd Division

126th N.Y.
Col. E. Sherrill *
Col. J. Bull ← 3rd Brigade
Sherrill *
Bull ← 3rd Division
Gen. A. Hays ← 2nd Corps ← AP

108th N.Y. ← 2nd Brigade
Col. F. Pierce ← Col. T. Smyth **
Pierce

Artillery Brigade

2-gun section ← 1st U.S., Battery I
Lt. J. Egan ← Lt. G. Woodruff *
Lt. T. McCrae

* killed July 3
** wounded July 3

212 THE STAND OF THE U.S. ARMY AT GETTYSBURG

Here is why. The crumbling of Pettigrew's left flank caused the overall line to compress even further. As Brockenbrough's brigade was faltering, the remaining left-wing units were approaching "the smouldering ruins of the [Bliss] farm buildings" (maps 4-13 and 4-14), and "these obstructions would . . . 'derange' Davis's advancing troops."[94] Thus, "the left flanks of Pettigrew's and Trimble's commands, shifted to the right, or south, thereby producing a gap between Pettigrew's left flank unit . . . and the right flank of Thomas's command at the southern end of the sunken road" (map 4-16). These unfortunate moves on the left wing of the assault therefore *added* to the compression that had occurred as a result of Pickett's left obliques. Whereas those maneuvers had been impressively achieved,[95] Brockenbrough's late start at the other end of the assault, the intense shelling of his brigade that resulted, and the 8th Ohio's attack upon the rebel left combined to set in motion a series of events that foiled the rebels' hopes.

The attacking line was becoming more of a *column,* and while a column can pierce a line, it is vulnerable to being *enveloped*.[96] Colonel Sawyer saw to it that this would occur on July 3. No longer threatened on his front (Brockenbrough was gone, and at least part of Davis's brigade had "fled"), Sawyer wheeled his band of men counterclockwise so that they faced south (map 4-22). Taking a position behind a fence line (map 4-23), the Ohioans raked the squeezed-in left of the advancing line. Their fire caused the men on what was left of this wing of the attack (maps 4-22 and 4-23) to break apart in confusion and terror owing to the deadly effect of enfilading fire on the flank of an infantry line: "Every shot is accurate," in that one which fails to hit someone near the end of that line can do damage farther along.[97]

In this moment, a group of seventy-five skirmishing New Yorkers located to the north ran down the Emmitsburg Road to support the 8th Ohio on its left (map 4-23).[98] This was fortunate for these defenders, because even though the Ohioans "pressed forward" from their position along the fence and captured "a large number of prisoners," they needed help: Sawyer's men "were under a terrific fire from the rebel batteries and infantry," and they absorbed heavy casualties.[99] Colonel Sawyer himself was wounded. Seeing this action against the enemy's flank and that men from his Ohio regiment were continuing to fall, General Hays completed the *envelopment of the Confederate left* by sending the 126th New York along with parts of the 108th New York and the 1st Massachusetts Sharpshooters down Cemetery Ridge (map 4-23). The 126th had been moved to the right a few minutes earlier. It did not have to confront the rebel left, which was no longer in front of it thanks to Sawyer's quixotic attack. The New Yorkers were also perfectly poised to take advantage of this contracting end of the rebel assault. Thus, elements of these two New York regiments, along with about twenty Massachusetts men, filled in most of the remaining area between the ridge and the road (map 4-23). These troops were buttressed by two Napoleons from Woodruff's battery (charts 4-17 and 4-18), most of which had been firing from Ziegler's Grove. However, two of these guns had redeployed earlier to an advanced and slightly more southerly position. These pieces were rolled down the ridge and dropped trail to the left of the 126th New York (map 4-23), pointing their muzzles southward. In this manner, a force of up to four hundred men supported by artillery *covered the north end of Pickett's Charge*.[100]

The Confederate Center Pierces the Union Line:
High-Water Mark

The Confederate attack had nevertheless made impressive progress during the first third of this crucial hour. Elements of the assault force would continue to do so—unaware of the breakdown of their leftmost unit and what flowed from the collapse of that brigade.[101]

While these problems were starting to unfold, the central portion of the Confederate attack was to get *very near its objective.* As a military man might say (and as was previewed above), the technical phrase for the Confederate achievement was that they were able to *achieve mass at the point of attack* (map 4-24). Pickett's Charge was not one of those many events in military history where the men were merely mowed down before they reached the enemy lines—as occurred in the frontal assaults at Fredericksburg in December 1862 and on the Somme in July 1916.

But how many of the rebels reached the enemy defenses on July 3, 1863? This is as good a place as any to discuss the hypothesis of John M. Priest, which is an important theme within his recent book on Pickett's Charge. This author's analysis led him to the conclusion that *only about half* of the Confederate assault force made it even halfway to Cemetery Ridge.[102] Whether or not huge numbers of attacking rebels were mowed down before they reached the Emmitsburg Road, thousands of them did not get that far according to Priest's analysis, mostly because so many of the Southern soldiers *turned back* before they got to the midpoint of the fields between Seminary and Cemetery Ridge. Could this iconoclasm be true? Wayne E. Motts vigorously contends that Priest miscalculated the Confederate strengths and losses for July 3, is wrongheaded about the Southerners' overall attack plan and the manner in which the rebel force approached the Union position, used inadequate or dubious sources, and demonstrably underestimated the morale of the Confederate soldiers.[103]

At all events, an appreciable fraction of the right wing of the rebel assault force came right up to the Union line. These were Pickett's men, who had gone across the Emmitsburg Road with little impediment.[104] The fences in this area were knocked down, whereas those to the north were still standing along the road (map 4-23), forcing Pettigrew's men to climb over them.

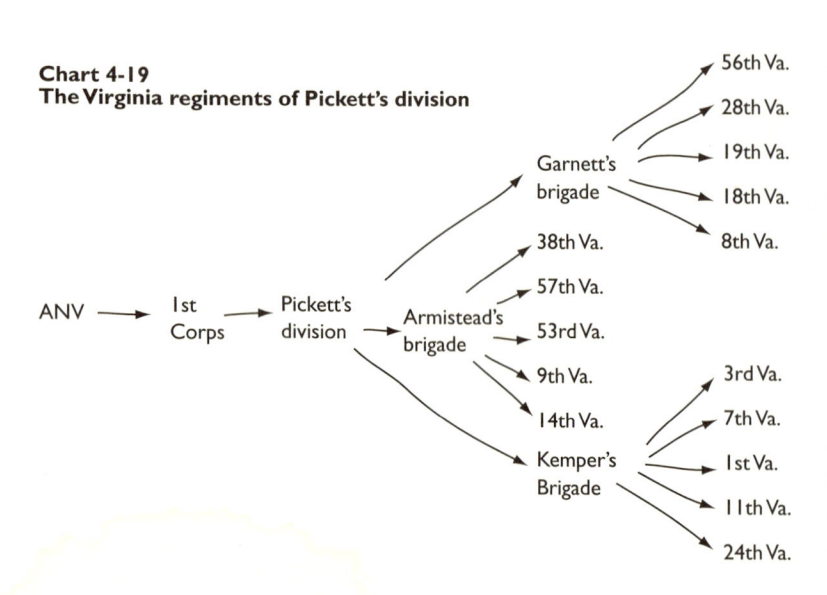

The lead units in Pickett's division advanced up the slope to Cemetery Ridge. The time was about 3:20 P.M. Pickett's troops were, of course, under fire, but parts of the defensive line in front of them were by then thin at best. Also, bear in mind that the slope itself is a rather gentle one. Some of the later Southern accounts of this attack imply that the rebel soldiers strove, in effect, to scale the face of Hoover Dam.[105]

The first small-arms fire to hit Pickett's men was from General Stannard's Vermonters. Some of his men had been uncomfortable about the rather flat nature of Cemetery Ridge in their area, so they occupied some better ground about a hundred yards in front of them (a rough, built-up area that provided some meager protection, as diagrammed in maps 4-15 and 4-25). This is

Chart 4-19
The Virginia regiments of Pickett's division

ANV → 1st Corps → Pickett's division → Garnett's brigade → 56th Va., 28th Va., 19th Va., 18th Va., 8th Va.

Armistead's brigade → 38th Va., 57th Va., 53rd Va., 9th Va., 14th Va.

Kemper's Brigade → 3rd Va., 7th Va., 1st Va., 11th Va., 24th Va.

Map 4-24
Pickett's division masses at the Union center

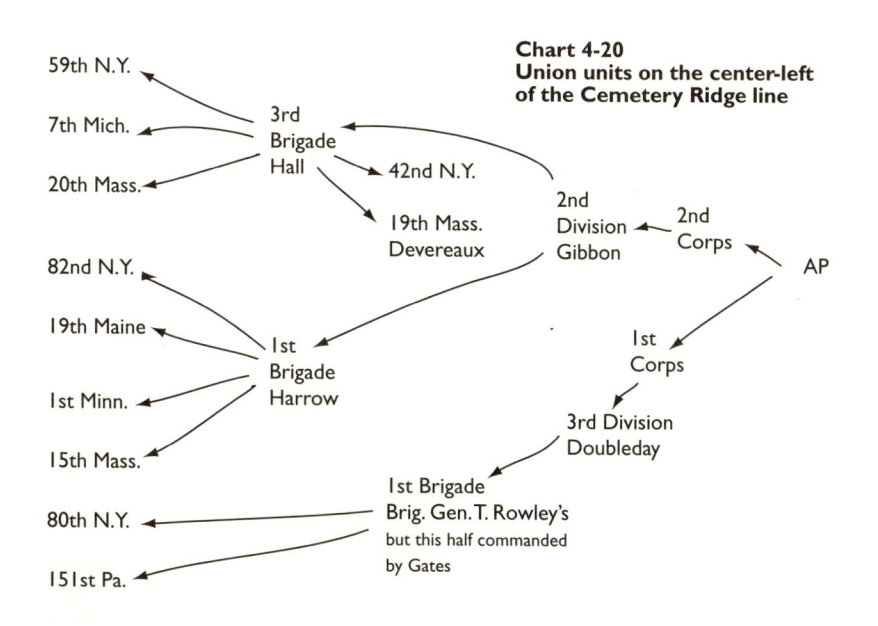

Confederate regiments: northern sector, east of road; not as organized as diagram implies

Chart 4-20
Union units on the center-left of the Cemetery Ridge line

- 59th N.Y. ← 3rd Brigade Hall
- 7th Mich. ← 3rd Brigade Hall
- 20th Mass. ← 3rd Brigade Hall
- 42nd N.Y. ← 3rd Brigade Hall
- 19th Mass. Devereaux ← 3rd Brigade Hall
- 3rd Brigade Hall ← 2nd Division Gibbon
- 82nd N.Y. ← 1st Brigade Harrow
- 19th Maine ← 1st Brigade Harrow
- 1st Minn. ← 1st Brigade Harrow
- 15th Mass. ← 1st Brigade Harrow
- 1st Brigade Harrow ← 2nd Division Gibbon
- 2nd Division Gibbon ← 2nd Corps
- 2nd Corps ← AP
- AP → 1st Corps
- 1st Corps → 3rd Division Doubleday
- 3rd Division Doubleday → 1st Brigade Brig. Gen. T. Rowley's but this half commanded by Gates
- 80th N.Y. ← 1st Brigade Brig. Gen. T. Rowley's
- 151st Pa. ← 1st Brigade Brig. Gen. T. Rowley's

THE GREAT GAMBLE LEE COULD HAVE WON

Map 4-25
Pickett's right-wing units move toward the center, as Stannard's Vermonters are poised to flank them

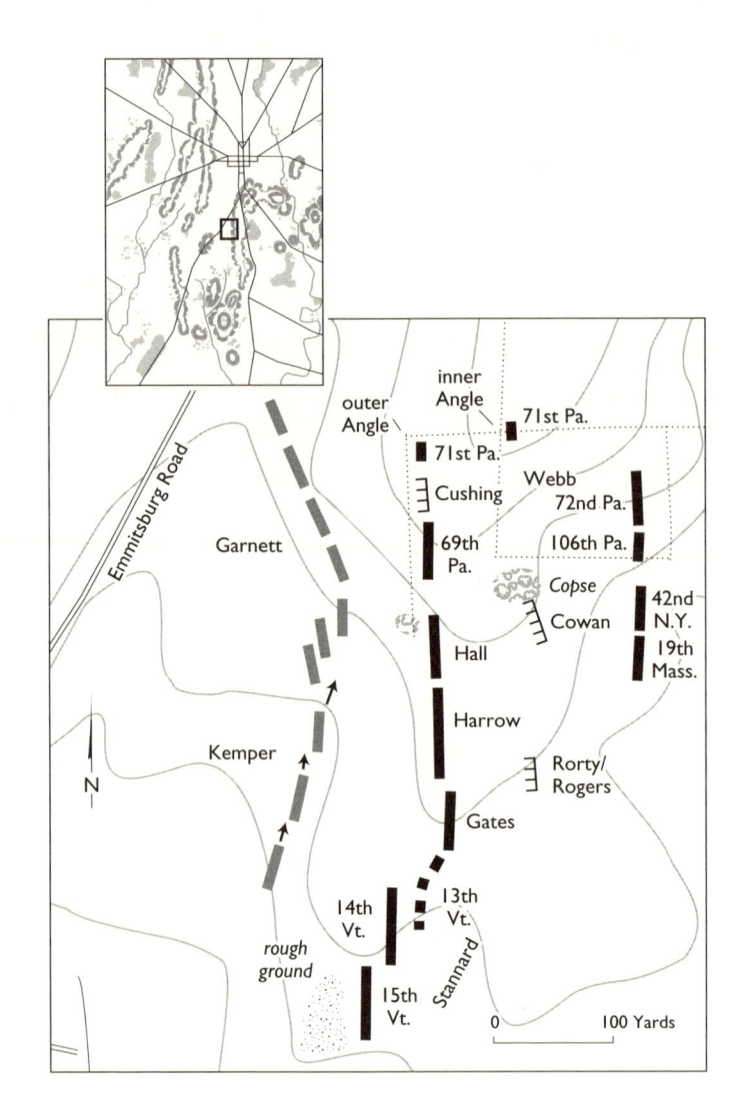

diagram by Col. Norman J. Hall (Army of the Potomac)

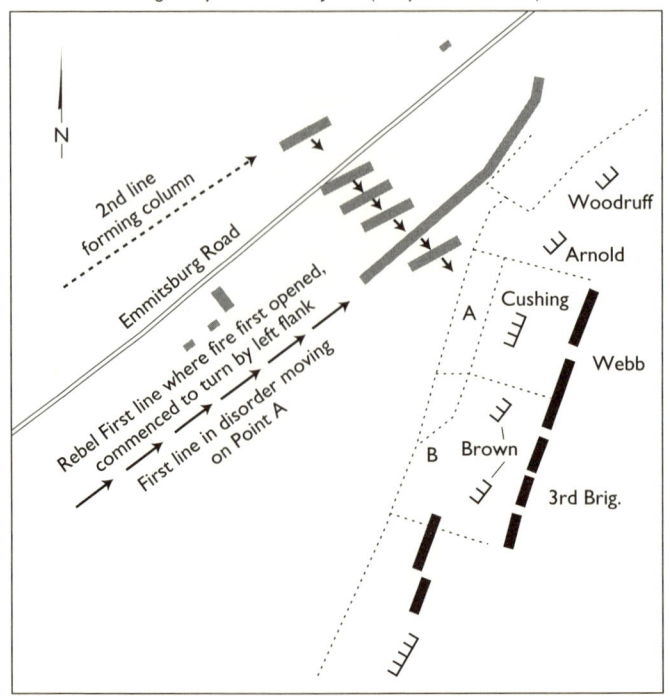

216   THE STAND OF THE U.S. ARMY AT GETTYSBURG

reminiscent of General Sickles falling prey to the instinctive occupation of the higher ground in his front on July 2. In any case, Pickett's right wing absorbed musket fire from the Vermonters. They were lucky that the right wing of the rebel assault did not come right at them. If it had, the Vermonters might have broken, for they were green troops.[106]

Although General Kemper's men (chart 4-19) initially marched directly toward the position of the 14th Vermont (map 4-25, top), these Southerners on the right wing of the assault began slanting across the front of the Vermont brigades (maps 4-24 and 4-25, bottom). That Kemper's Virginians were still shifting to the north as they moved in meant that the musketry to which they were subjected was in part flanking fire. Kemper's men accentuated this danger further when a significant fraction of them fairly rushed farther northward—perhaps having been inadvertently waved in that direction by their commander's exhortations just before he was shot off his horse and severely wounded.[107]

Another interpretation of this event is that the Virginians on the extreme right had *planned* to approach the Union lines after making one more sharp shift to the left. The reading of the Confederate's objectives is consistent with the notion that they intended to compact the assault force, aiming it toward the aforementioned point of attack. A diagram depicting the "unusual nature of the advance of Pickett's men" shows the rebel right well east of the Emmitsburg Road in a line heading toward the Union center.[108] This representation implies that Kemper's men were pointing in that direction of march at this time, not facing forward and making an oblique turn to their left. Colonel Norman J. Hall, whose brigade was in the Union left-center, made the drawing on July 17, 1863 (chart 4-20, map 4-25). Intriguingly, Hall's diagram shows elements of the attacking Confederates "forming column" (map 4-25, bottom). This again suggests a premeditated design on the part of the Confederates to contract toward a relative point of attack.

At any rate, the overall line of attackers was not moving *at* the defense in this sector, but compressing itself ever more into a dense mass, many men deep. It was distributed from the slope below the ridge back toward the road. *Not* a part of the Confederate planning was that elements of the massed formation that was taking shape were getting themselves in trouble—as is implied by an annotation in the map drawn by Colonel Hall: "first line in disorder" (see note 108).

Indeed, as a significant portion of Kemper's brigade angled to the north, these men became intermingled with troops from General Armistead's and Colonel Fry's brigades. Armistead's Virginians had gone to the double-quick once they got within two hundred yards of the Emmitsburg Road (map 4-24; see also note 79). This caused them also to move among Fry's troops. General Armistead's brigade was at the left rear of Pickett's division (chart 4-19) and Colonel Fry's on the right flank of Pettigrew's (map 4-24). These elements of the attacking line were now closing up on each other, which was their short-term goal for the early stages of the advance—although they could not have intended to mix with each other in the confusion that was escalating as Kemper's men arrived in their midst.

Kemper's troops had left the vicinity of Stannard's Vermont regiments and were passing along the front of Brig. Gen. William Harrow's and Colonel Hall's brigades along Cemetery Ridge, south of the copse of trees (map 4-24). Those 2nd Corps soldiers (chart 4-20) added enfilading fire to Kemper's woes, but this soon ceased as the right-wing elements of Pickett's division kept shifting farther to their left toward the center of the Union line (map 4-25).

Considering how those Federal defenders were situated, it is easy to appreciate *their* problems. These difficulties could have proceeded to peril had the rebels

Map 4-26
A portion of the rebel mass in the center enters the Union line, whose center-left moves north to reinforce

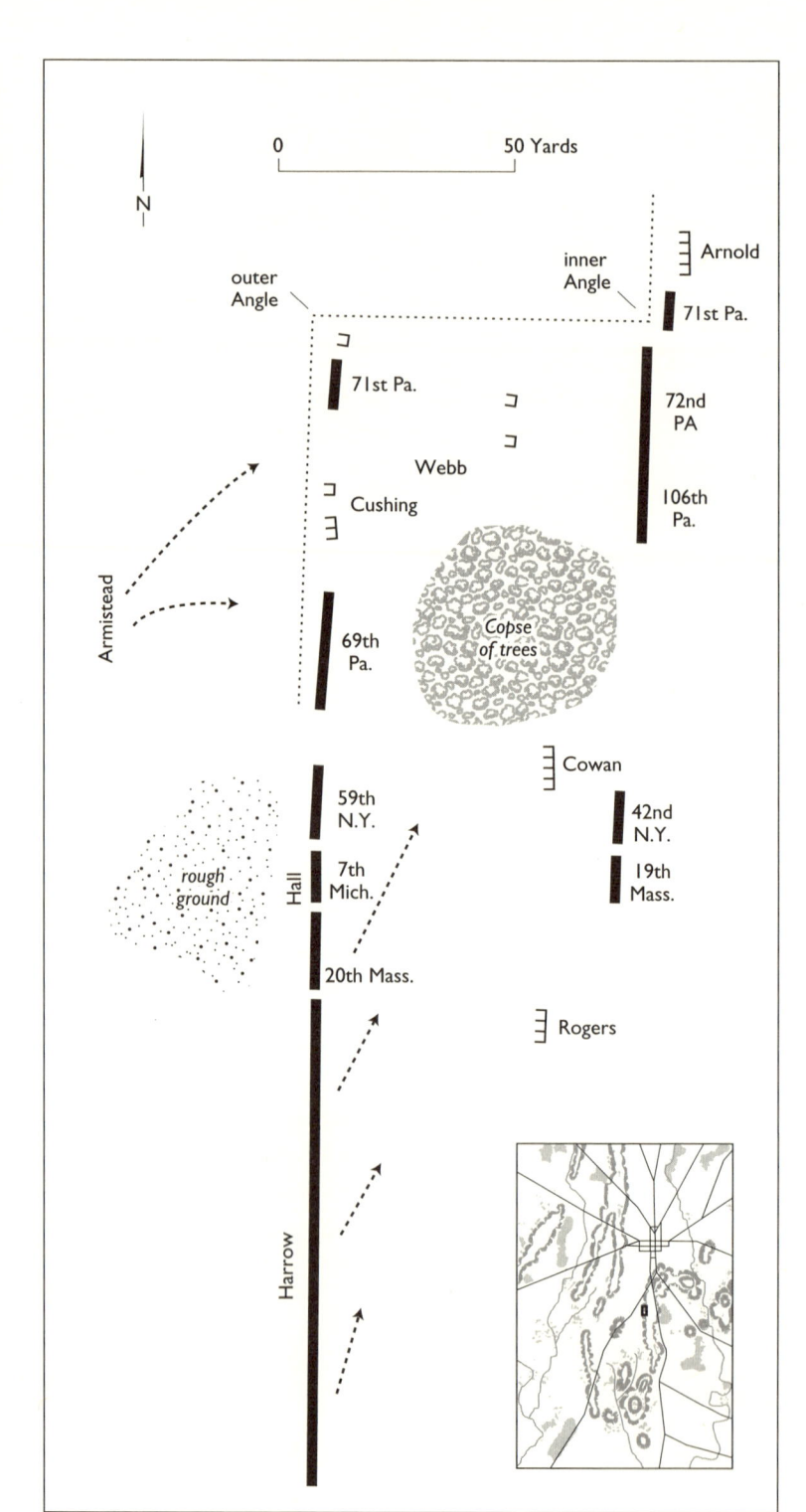

0 — 50 Yards

N

outer Angle
inner Angle
Arnold
71st Pa.
71st Pa.
72nd PA
Webb
Cushing
106th Pa.
Armistead
69th Pa.
Copse of trees

Cowan
59th N.Y.
42nd N.Y.
rough ground
7th Mich.
Hall
19th Mass.
20th Mass.
Rogers

Harrow

Chart 4-21
Webb's Union brigade between the Angle and the copse of trees

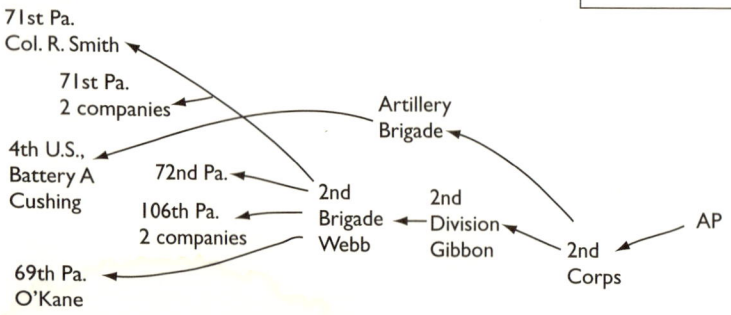

71st Pa. Col. R. Smith
71st Pa. 2 companies
4th U.S., Battery A Cushing
72nd Pa.
106th Pa. 2 companies
69th Pa. O'Kane
2nd Brigade Webb
Artillery Brigade
2nd Division Gibbon
2nd Corps
AP

218   THE STAND OF THE U.S. ARMY AT GETTYSBURG

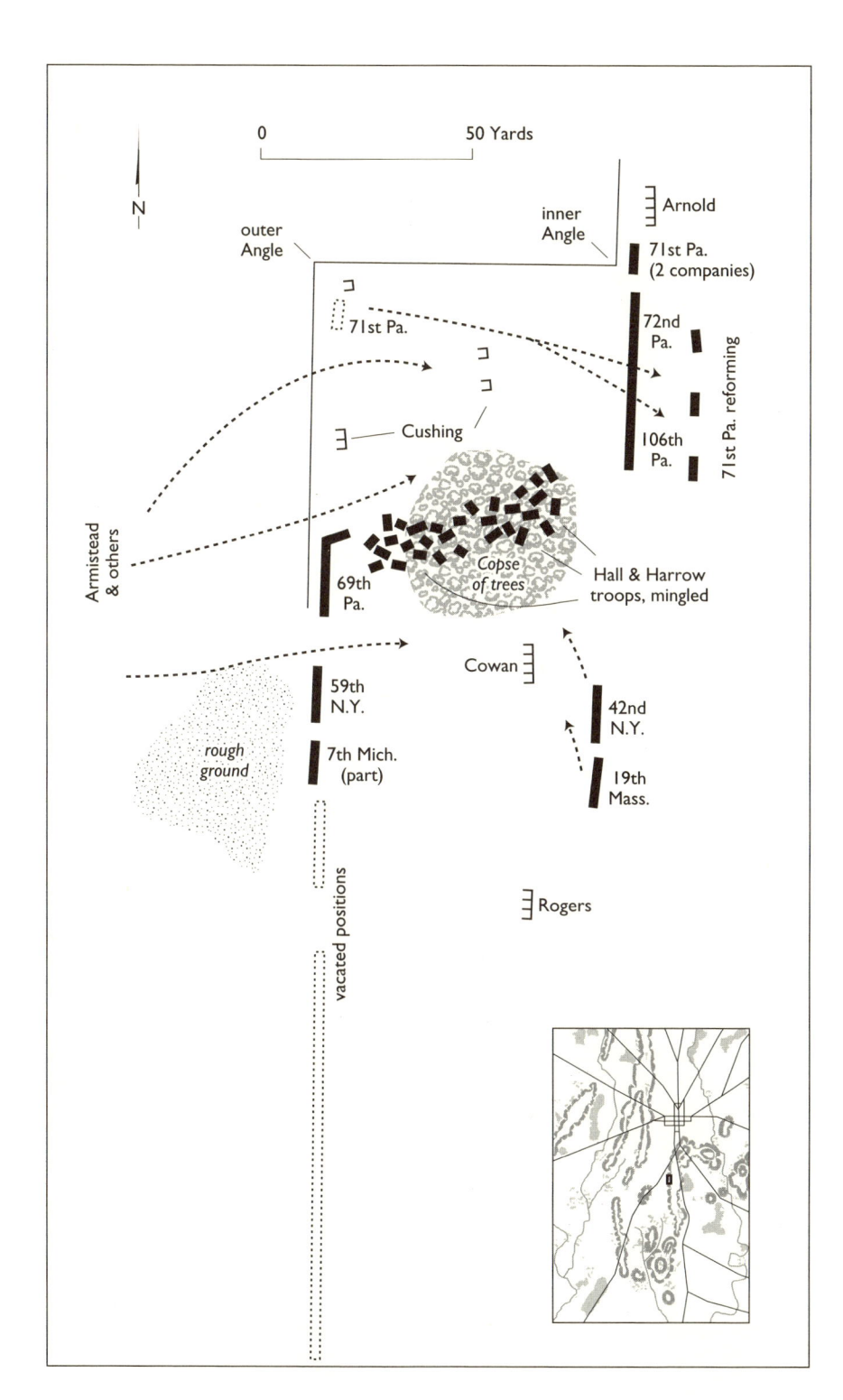

**Map 4-27
The Confederates' mini-breakthrough continues, as the 71st Pa. breaks and other units are poised to reinforce**

THE GREAT GAMBLE LEE COULD HAVE WON

been more organized—that is, had they not found the original geometric features of their attack slipping away. In any case, we have Harrow then Hall to his right along the Federal front (chart 4-20).[109] Then there was a gap between Hall's and Webb's brigades (map 4-25, top). This was filled in part by Cowan's battery, which had dropped trail near the copse of trees once the advance got under way (map 4-26).

The area directly in front of the copse was manned by Webb's 69th Pennsylvania (map 4-26). To the right of the 69th was another gap out at the front of the line, because the 106th Pennsylvania was in a reserve position back toward the east edge of the ridge. To the right of that unit was the 72nd Pennsylvania, also a part of the Philadelphia Brigade. The remaining regiment in that brigade was the 71st Pennsylvania. It had advanced up to the front, behind the low stone wall just south of the "outer Angle" (map 4-26, chart 4-21). Hence, the right of the 71st Pennsylvania hugged a part of this stone fence that ran in an east-west direction for a couple of hundred feet before moving off to the north again.[110]

The 69th and most of the 71st Pennsylvania were lined up behind a north-south line of stone fence that is farther out front than the line manned by Brig. Gen. Alexander Hays's regiments on the far right of the Union center. The two Pennsylvania regiments, smack in the center and in fairly exposed positions, were also vulnerable because of the gap to the right of the 69th Pennsylvania. Similarly, the 69th was not covered on its left by any nearby infantry. The precarious area between the 71st Pennsylvania's left and the 69th's right was bolstered somewhat by Lieutenant Cushing (chart 4-21), who had moved two guns of his battery to the stone fence in front (maps 4-26 and 4-28). Still, only about 375 troops manned the approximately five hundred yards of defensive front in the Union center. The endangered position there may have been the reason that the 71st Pennsylvania was soon to become "the one regiment that ran."

The Pennsylvanians south of the Angle and near the copse of trees faced about three thousand of Pickett's men, a much superior force on paper. But the attackers in the vicinity had become a mingled mass: As they tried to advance toward the crest of the ridge, Pickett's Virginians "merged into one crowding, rushing line, many ranks deep."[111] Several Confederates were to continue the few extra yards necessary, although in the end *not enough of them went forward*. Yet this was not because of mere disorganization or pure loss of will, as I argue in the next section.

Meanwhile, as some of Pickett's Virginians rushed the low stone wall, *most of the 71st Pennsylvania broke*. Although a couple of companies stayed in their forward positions (at the inner Angle, map 4-27), many of these Pennsylvanians ran toward the rear and reformed at the back edge of the ridge behind the position held by the 72nd Pennsylvania.

To take advantage of the fact that the Union front was really thin at this moment, *Brig. Gen. Lewis Armistead led a few score of Confederate troops over the short barrier* (map 4-27). These attackers were from his own brigade, and probably from those of Garnett and Kemper as well (all within Pickett's division). It is likely that some of Fry's 3rd Corps troops (as implied in map 4-24) joined the band that went with General Armistead over the little stone wall.

The attacking rebels pushed back the 69th Pennsylvania's right flank (maps 4-27 and 4-28), capturing several of those soldiers in the process. As they were hit, Col. Dennis O'Kane, the 69th's commander, ordered his right wing to bend back (map 4-28), better to meet the brunt of the attack. These men fell back firing— "not in good order, but in some order," as one of them later recalled.[112] In fact, one of the 69th's companies (the third from the regiment's right, Company F in map 4-28) failed to redeploy because an advancing Southerner killed its captain. Every one of these Pennsylvanians was killed, wounded, or captured. Still, the seven companies on the 69th's left held their ground along the north-south fence line, grappling with their attackers and continuing to fire down into the mass of Confederates on the slope in front of them (map 4-28).

Armistead led his men farther into the Union lines. The rebels overran the guns out near the wall. Lieutenant Cushing, the commander of what was left of this Union battery, had stood by his pieces after being severely wounded earlier. Now he was shot dead by the Confederates storming his position. As General Armistead approached one of Cushing's artillery pieces he, too, was gunned down, mortally wounded. Still, this was the *high-water mark*. The soldiers who had followed their general to the top of the slope and beyond swept past the copse of trees where part of the 69th Pennsylvania had been pushed aside. This opened the gap to the 69th's right even more, and there was still an appreciable one to their left (map 4-27).

According to George Stewart, this moment in the Battle of Gettysburg was a crucial two sweeps of the second hand for the Confederacy.[113] The Southerners in and near the Union center *might have achieved a massive breakthrough.* The small band of rebels that followed General Armistead over the wall were joined by additional Confederate soldiers who broke away from the mass on the slope.[114] Many more could, in principle, have followed. They had the opportunity to pour through the two gaps on the left and right of 69th Pennsylvania (map 4-27). From the Confederates' perspective, the right-hand gap was manned mostly by Cowan's battery, so the first rush there might have been suicidal. However, a second wave of attackers in that sector could have overwhelmed these Union guns. That would have exposed the Federal flanks to being rolled up. Some of the attackers could have wheeled south and hit Hall's flank while others turned to the left and imperiled the 69th Pennsylvania. At this time, an escalating breakthrough at the gap to the north (but still south of the Angle) would have surrounded the 69th Pennsylvania. Moreover, the left flank of Hays's division north of the Angle would have been exposed, so that the Confederates pouring into the gap could have wheeled to the north and tried to roll up Union 2nd Corps units on that flank. That, by the way, is pretty much what happened when Union soldiers attacked the face of Missionary Ridge near Chattanooga in November 1863 (as introduced in Chapter 1, note 46). Elements of the assault force that broke into the defensive line atop the ridge turned left (northward, coincidentally) and then achieved further success by crumpling the rebel flank that had been exposed by piercing the north-south line.

Returning to Pennsylvania: What if a significant Confederate breakthrough near the Angle, which subsequently could have menaced the flank just created, had been *coordinated with a frontal assault by Pettigrew's troops* against Hays? That rebel division was now approaching the right end of the Federal defense, which *could* have been in the process of being cut off. Yet there was better defensive power there than in the Union center: 1,700 of Hays's men supported by eleven cannon. They faced an advancing rebel front of at most 2,500 men (recall that Trimble's two brigades were to the rear of Pettigrew's four [map 4-14]). But the front line of those attackers could have pushed back the 1,700 defenders if the latter's left was caving in.

All of these breakthroughs, subsequent attacking maneuvers, and hypothetical Confederate achievements would have been quite complicated. One can get carried

**Map 4-28
Confederate attacks in the pocket between the Angle and the copse of trees: the 69th Pa.'s right is pushed back**

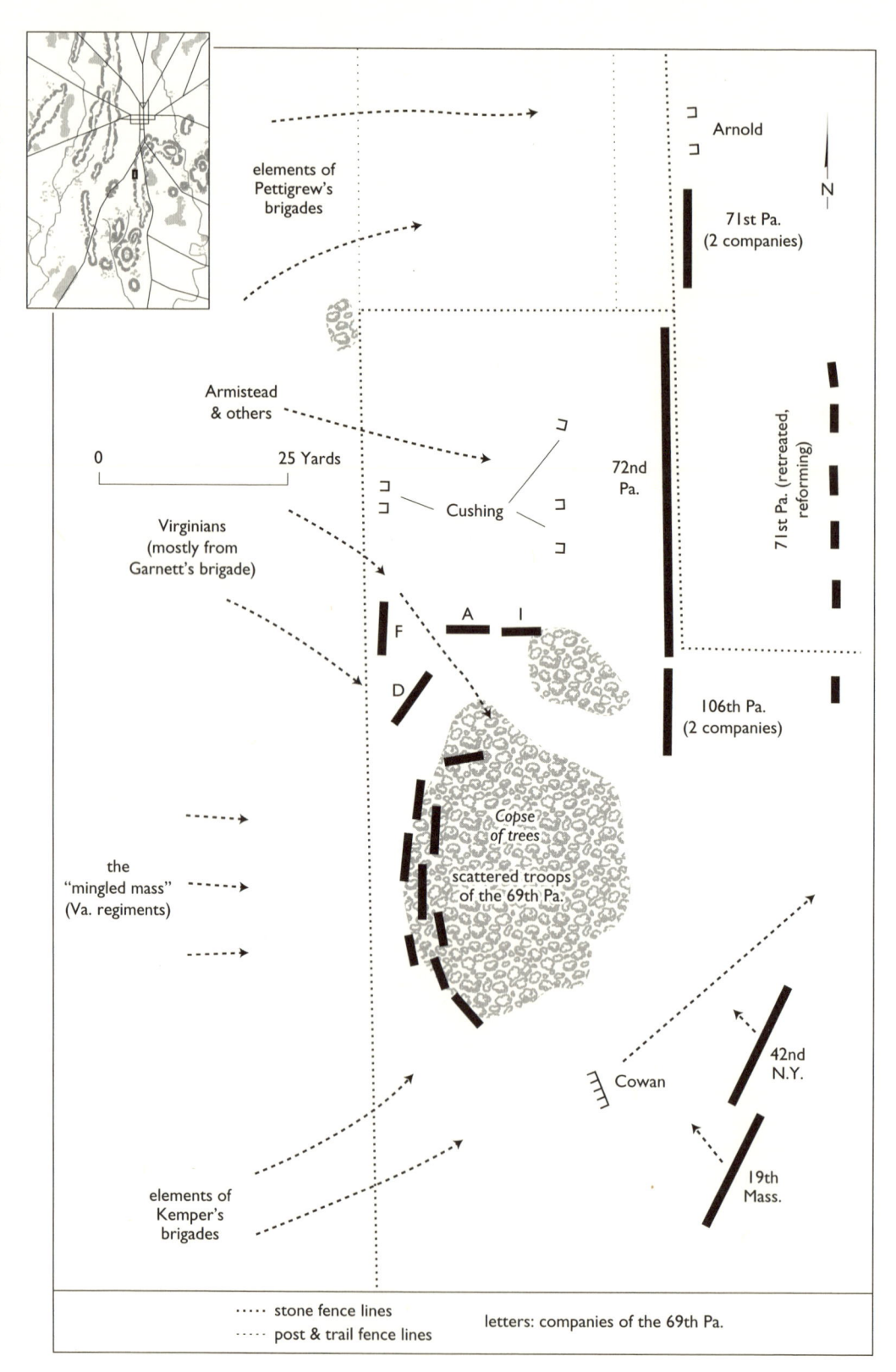

elements of Pettigrew's brigades

Arnold

71st Pa. (2 companies)

N

Armistead & others

0   25 Yards

72nd Pa.

Cushing

71st Pa. (retreated, reforming)

Virginians (mostly from Garnett's brigade)

F   A   I

D

106th Pa. (2 companies)

Copse of trees

scattered troops of the 69th Pa.

the "mingled mass" (Va. regiments)

Cowan

42nd N.Y.

19th Mass.

elements of Kemper's brigades

······ stone fence lines
- - - - post & trail fence lines

letters: companies of the 69th Pa.

222   THE STAND OF THE U.S. ARMY AT GETTYSBURG

Chart 4-22
Examples of losses in the Confederate officer corps:
Pickett's regimental commanders before and during the charge

Armistead's brigade	Garnett's brigade	Kemper's brigade
38th Va. Col. E. Edmonds **k**	56th Va. Col. W. Stuart **mw**	3rd Va. Col. J. Mayo **w** one of if not the mildest wound (hand)
57th Va. Col. J. Magruder **mw, c**	28th Va. Col. R. Allen **k**	7th Va. Col. W. Patton **mw, c**
53rd Va. Col. W. Aylett **w** during the cannonade	19th Va. Col. H. Gantt **w**	1st Va. Col. L. Williams **k**
9th Va. Maj. J. Owens **mw**	18th Va. Col. H. Carrington **w, c**	11th Va. Maj. K. Otey **w**
14th Va. Col. J. Hodges **k**	8th Va. Col. E. Hunton **w**	24th Va. Col. W. Terry **w**

k killed
mw mortally wounded
w wounded
c captured

Two of the cases above involved superficial wounds: Harrison and Busey (1987), in *Nothing but Glory: Pickett's Division at Gettysburg*, indicate that Mayo and Terry survived the Charge unscathed; but Sibley (1996) in *The Confederate Order of Battle* (Vol. I), specifies that they were wounded. The latter is correct according to Wayne E. Motts.

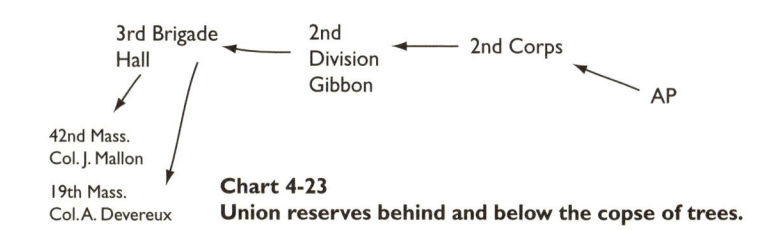

```
                    3rd Brigade    2nd
                    Hall     ←    Division    ←   2nd Corps
                      ↖           Gibbon                    ←   AP
                       ↑
                    42nd Mass.
                    Col. J. Mallon
                    19th Mass.
                    Col. A. Devereux
```

Chart 4-23
Union reserves behind and below the copse of trees.

away with a facile description of this "could-have-should-have" scenario. First of all, the *defensive pressure* to which the assault had been subjected contributed to the disorganization in the attacking center, as the Union men inflicted many casualties. Could the eleven thousand rebels—minus their losses and not including Wilcox's troops—have held the ridge?[115] The number of men organized for Pickett's Charge does not seem to have been enough to attack the six thousand Federals occupying the center of the Cemetery Ridge line. Artillery and musket fire from the Federals during the first twenty or thirty minutes of the rebel advance allowed most of those defenders to hold *their* positions as unit cohesion within the center-right of the attacking force was breaking down. A second point is that the Confederate casualties included many senior officers (chart 4-22). Armistead himself was mortally wounded and Kemper severely so. General Pickett's third brigade commander, Brig. Gen. Richard Garnett, was killed about this time or perhaps slightly later (his body was never identified).[116] Finally, a potentially more severe break in the Federal center—referring to the frontline defenders—might have been mauled by reinforcements: "Union reserves from almost the entire length of the army's line [that] had rushed to the support of the troops on Cemetery Ridge."[117]

Whether or not the defensive line was becoming too strong, and thus whether "we might write of these Hundred Seconds of the Confederacy" (see note 113)—who was going to rally the three thousand troops piled up on the slope below the ridge? Not the regimental commanders, or at least hardly any of them. By the end of the day, all fifteen of these officers within Pickett's division had been killed or wounded (chart 4-22). In fact, of the thirty-two field-grade officers in that division, all but one became a casualty. Perhaps some leadership was left on the slope at the time approximately two hundred to three hundred rebels went over the wall. However, by then that mass of men was most likely too intermixed for an organized attack to be resumed.

For its part, elements of the Union leadership were trying to make it so the mass would not outnumber their defenders to such a dangerous degree. The majority of the men in Hall's and Harrow's brigades were redeploying to their right (map 4-26), aiming to reinforce the center.[118]

Moreover, shortly after the 71st Pennsylvania broke, General Webb tried to get another of his regiments to go forward to fill the gap created by the 71st's abrupt departure and to reinforce the dangerously exposed 69th Pennsylvania (of which 70 percent or so was still in line). However, Webb, who was newly in command of the Philadelphia Brigade, was unable to get the 72nd Pennsylvania to budge from its reserve position near the back (eastern) edge of Cemetery Ridge. The brigade commander and the 72nd's color bearer fairly wrestled each other to the ground in their argument over whether one of them would take the flag forward or the other would hold it in that reserve position. Webb finally gave up and went forward by himself to where the stalwart 69th still stood.

This embarrassing episode proved to be much less important than the manner by which other reserve units of the Federal force joined the fray. Here is what was happening: As the Confederate's mini-breakthrough got under way, Maj. Gen. Winfield Scott Hancock *rode south* along the east side of the ridge. Why will become clear in the next section. Meanwhile, Hancock passed the positions of the 19th Massachusetts and 42nd New York (chart 4-23). They were posted in reserve to the south of the copse of trees and the Angle. Colonel Arthur F. Devereux, commander of the 19th Massachusetts, yelled to Hancock that the rebels were breaking through and asked for permission to attack. With an oath, General Hancock ordered Devereux to counterattack immediately. The colonel led his regiment and the 42nd New York (located on his left) toward the area of the breakthrough as these two reinforcing units turned obliquely to their right (map 4-28). They would contribute important weight to what would ultimately become a repelling force in the Union center. That final repulse will be described after we first consider *why the defenders had to cope with such a small proportion of the potential breakthrough*—and why the Federal actions made this breach of the center so small, dooming Pickett's Charge.

The Stand of the Twenty-Six Regiments—Rejoined by the One That Ran

Winfield Scott Hancock continued his ride southward.[119] He plunged down the ridge behind the lines, because he had *seen Hays's flanking move to the north*. Hancock therefore thought that the *Confederate right wing might also be enveloped*. As he arrived at the relevant spot, the geometry of the situation made it clear that all of this was possible. The assault force was veering off to its left (maps 4-24 and 4-25), leaving open ground in front of the Union men who had been facing Pickett's right. These Federal troops were General Stannard's Vermont regiments,

**Map 4-29
Stannard's regiments move off the ridge to envelop the rebel right**

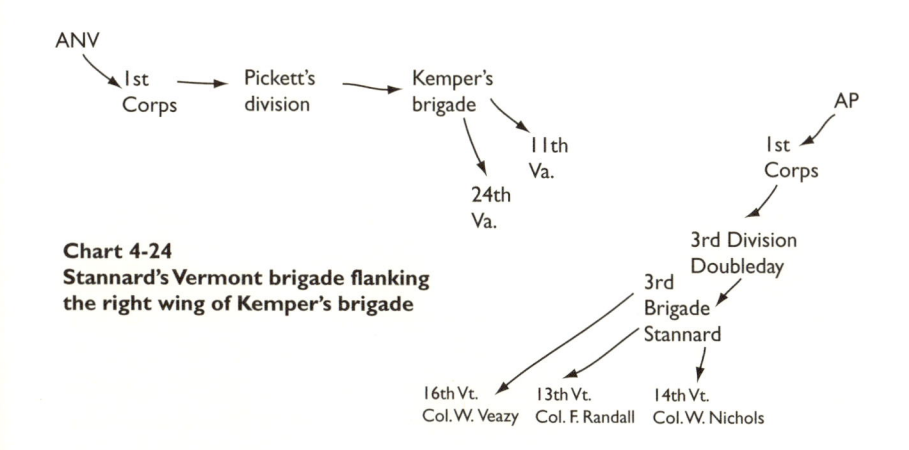

Confederate units (Armistead, Garnett, Kemper's left not as organized as shown)

vacated union positions

**Chart 4-24
Stannard's Vermont brigade flanking the right wing of Kemper's brigade**

ANV → 1st Corps → Pickett's division → Kemper's brigade → 11th Va.
                                                         → 24th Va.

AP → 1st Corps → 3rd Division Doubleday → 3rd Brigade Stannard → 16th Vt. Col. W. Veazy
                                                               → 13th Vt. Col. F. Randall
                                                               → 14th Vt. Col. W. Nichols

THE GREAT GAMBLE LEE COULD HAVE WON

whose earlier actions on July 3 have already been described. By this time, Stannard had his units on the move, and he and Hancock later claimed credit for what was soon accomplished. As the 19th Massachusetts and the 42nd New York were going in (map 4-28), Col. William Harrow's and most of Col. Norman Hall's brigades were also sidling to their right (map 4-27), reinforcing the threatened center. Stannard moved his men in that direction along the front line to occupy the position just vacated by Harrow. This put the Vermonters near Kemper's brigade *on Pickett's wide-open right flank.* The 16th Vermont had been in an advanced skirmishing position to the left of the 14th Vermont (map 4-25, top). Both regiments were pushed back so that the 13th Vermont was farthest forward. Now the 13th, with its right anchored near the ridge, *pivoted clockwise,* swinging out in an east-west line facing to the north (map 4-29). The 16th Vermont swung out behind the 13th, extending the line farther to the west (map 4-29).[120] The Vermonters' deployment placed up to twelve hundred shoulder arms (mostly Springfield rifled muskets) in a position to fire on Kemper's right. The attention of those Virginians, with the 24th Virginia on the flank itself, was focused roughly to their left, as they had been squeezing in toward the center. *Pickett's Charge was double enveloped.*

According to George Stewart, the completion of the twin counterattacks on the wings of the assault occurred just after a band of rebels pierced the front of the Union line (map 4-30).[121] However, it is impossible to know this for certain. The mini-breakthrough described below in conjunction with maps 4-26 and 4-27 may have occurred shortly before Stannard's Vermonters swung out on Kemper's flank. As those Union men did so, the 24th and 11th Virginia tried to turn around and face the counterattack (map 4-29). But this did not stop the two large Vermont regiments from pouring a deadly enfilading fire into the right wing of Kemper's brigade.[122]

This may have been the ultimate pulverizing blow against Pickett's Charge. If the counterattack by the 16th and 13th Vermont Regiments was initiated about the time Armistead and the others went across the low stone wall in the center, the deadliness of the enveloping counterattack on Pickett's right led not only to severe Confederate casualties in that specific sector, but also may have *precipitated panic among the rebel troops massed below the center of Cemetery Ridge.* This militated against those Southerners organizing a significant further push into the Federal lines—a potentially big breech in the center of the Army of the Potomac's west-facing defense, which the Confederates had planned for and were hoping to achieve at this moment.

Just then, a Confederate musket shot crashed into General Hancock's saddle where he sat watching the action a few yards down the ridge, due east of the Codori buildings (map 4-38). Hancock's saddle fairly exploded, and the bullet and saddle fragments ripped into his upper thigh and groin. The wound removed Hancock from the field and limited his action during the remainder of the war. His performance at Gettysburg had been remarkable, starting the moment he arrived on Cemetery Hill during the late afternoon of July 1.

Meanwhile, Colonel Alexander, Longstreet's artillery chief, managed to get a few of his guns forward and fired over the heads of the infantry into the Union lines (map 4-31).[123] These rebel cannon absorbed severe counter-battery blasts from the large number of guns in Colonel McGilvery's command south of the Union center.

Whatever damage McGilvery and the rest of the Federal artillery may have inflicted, it was the *double envelopment that ruined the Confederate attack.* The de-

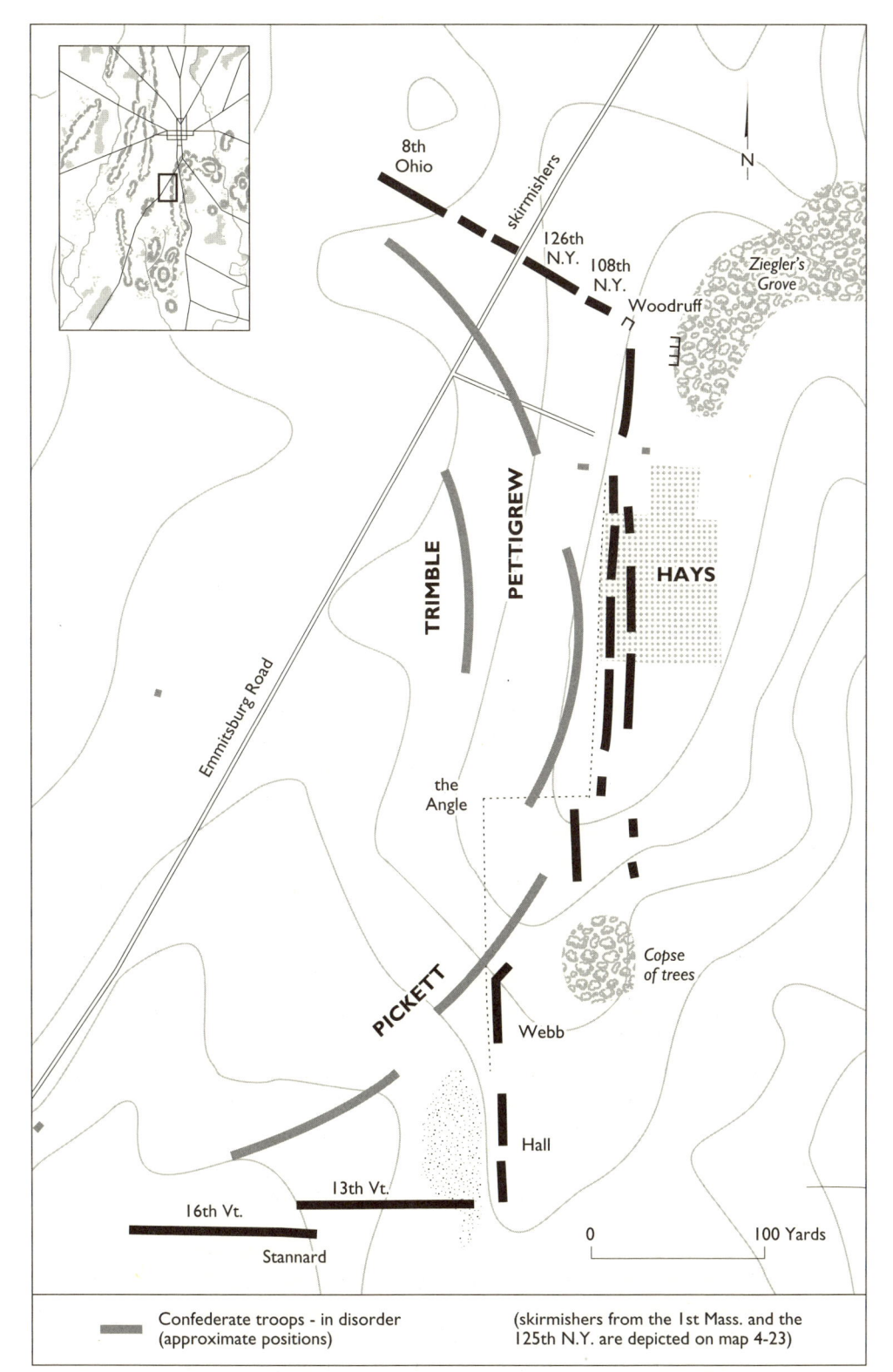

Map 4-30
Double envelopment

8th Ohio
skirmishers
126th N.Y.
108th N.Y.
Woodruff
Ziegler's Grove

TRIMBLE
PETTIGREW
HAYS

the Angle

Copse of trees

PICKETT
Webb

Hall

13th Vt.
16th Vt.
Stannard

Emmitsburg Road

0   100 Yards

― Confederate troops - in disorder (approximate positions)

(skirmishers from the 1st Mass. and the 125th N.Y. are depicted on map 4-23)

THE GREAT GAMBLE LEE COULD HAVE WON   227

**Map 4-31
Elements of the
Confederate artillery
advance in support of
the assault**

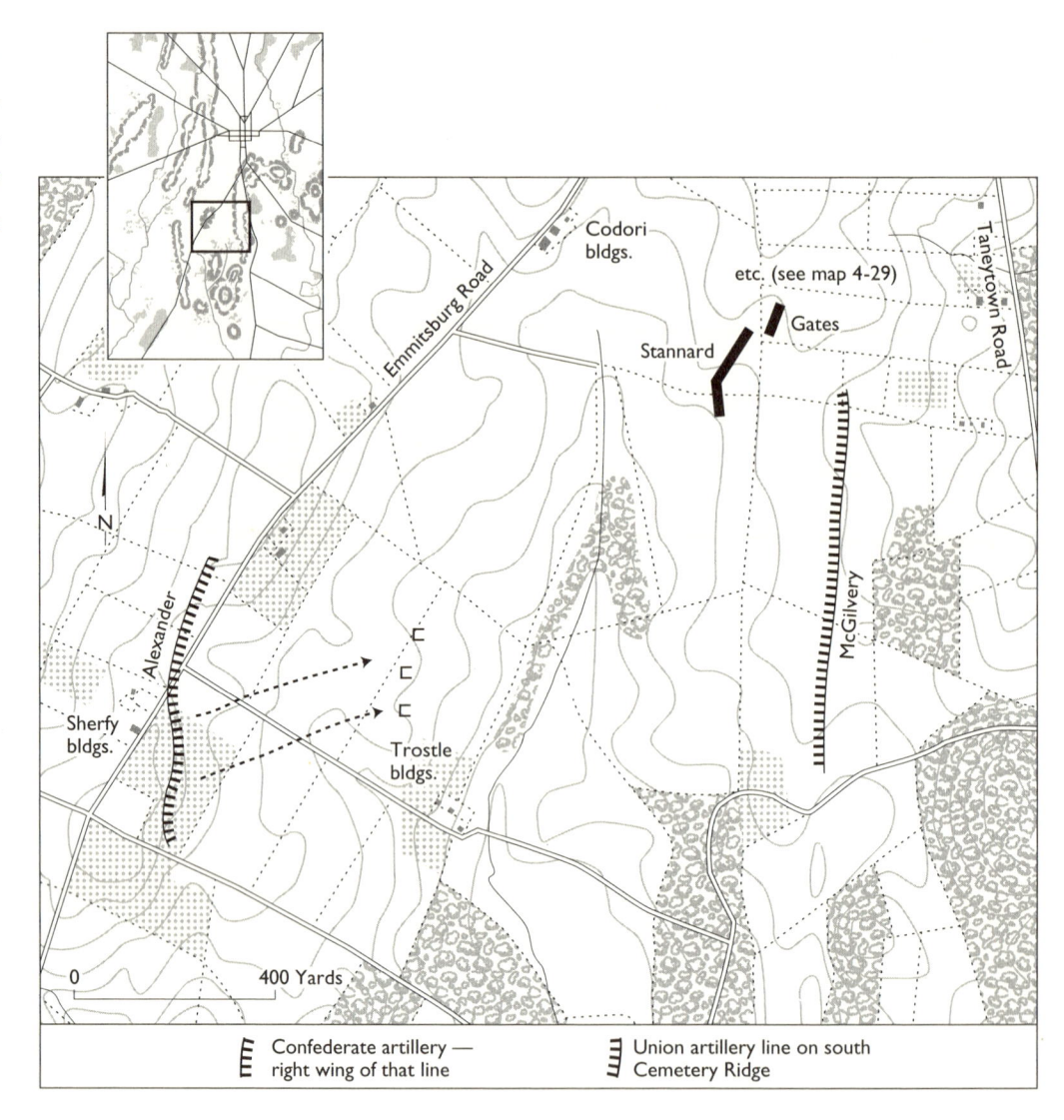

fenders arrayed in the center of the Union defenses had not planned these flanking counterattacks before the assault on their front got under way, but they soon applied a tactical principle that has particularly devastating effects on the attacker. In the center, you present a front that becomes the focus of your adversary's attention. This front is not all that heavy a force. It may not, for example, be composed of a significant defense in depth. Yet you make the enemy believe that your front should be the focus of his attention—either because you may be *threatening him,* or because he is *funneling his force* toward your center. Meanwhile, you retain the tactical ability to maneuver elsewhere on the field—having retained this capability by not massing anywhere near all your troops directly in front of the enemy line. That is what Hannibal did at Cannae, in 216 B.C., sucking the center of the Roman attack toward the front of his defenses. Hannibal's line was relatively weak there, but the thousands of other soldiers thus freed to maneuver worked their way around both of the Roman flanks, precipitating the annihilation of their foe in that ancient battle.

At Chancellorsville, some twenty-one centuries later, Robert E. Lee similarly pinned down the Federal center by presenting a front of defenders—or might

228   THE STAND OF THE U.S. ARMY AT GETTYSBURG

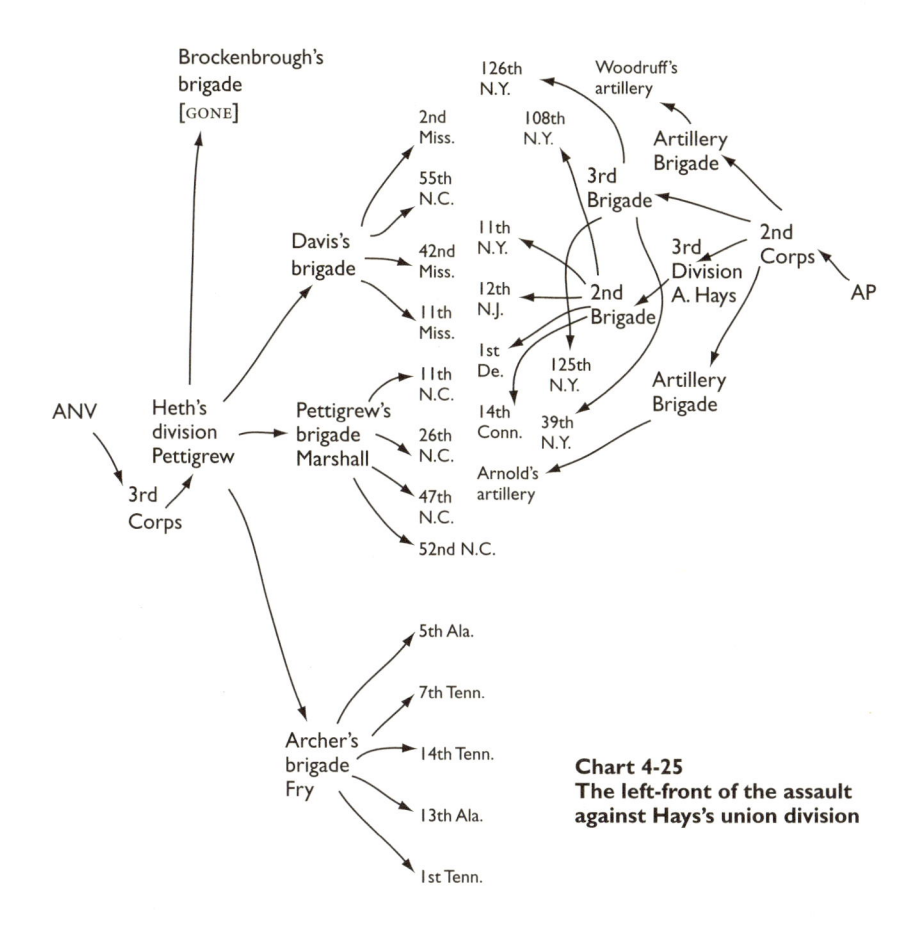

Chart 4-25
The left-front of the assault against Hays's union division

those Confederate units attack? Probably not, because the rebel center was very thin in that sector of the Virginia field (map 3-9, Chapter 3). The Union command at Chancellorsville was unaware of this or unwilling to believe how weak the Confederate force facing them directly was. Yet Lee was still taking an enormous risk by fixing the foe on his weakened center in order to free up Lt. Gen. Thomas J. Jackson's corps, which maneuvered around the Federal flank (also indicated on map 3-9) and crushed it on the evening of May 2. Now, we race forward in time almost 130 years. In the 1991 Persian Gulf War, Gen. H. Norman Schwarzkopf's command was actually outnumbered by the Iraqi forces arrayed along its front. However, Schwarzkopf brought Allied troops and armor forward, facing the Iraqi lines and fixing their attention on that sector. The Allied front was deliberately not of great depth, but it was enough to make the Iraqis believe that an attack upon their center was imminent. Meanwhile, the coalition army, retaining mobility, launched a massive mechanized attack around the Iraqi right flank. This resulted in a complete rout of Saddam Hussein's army from those desert fields.

The Union army at Gettysburg achieved something similar on July 3 in terms of ground tactics. Employing the principle of *economy of force* in the Union center,[124] however unwittingly this may have been done, allowed the Federals mobility elsewhere—such that almost sixteen hundred bluecoats were able to improvise *encircling maneuvers* onto the flanks of the advancing enemy.

This analogy to past and future wars may be overstated. The Federals at Gettysburg were actually rather strong over a *part* of their central defense on Cemetery

THE GREAT GAMBLE LEE COULD HAVE WON 229

**Map 4-32
The Union center-right deploys on north Cemetery Ridge to meet Pettigrew's attack**

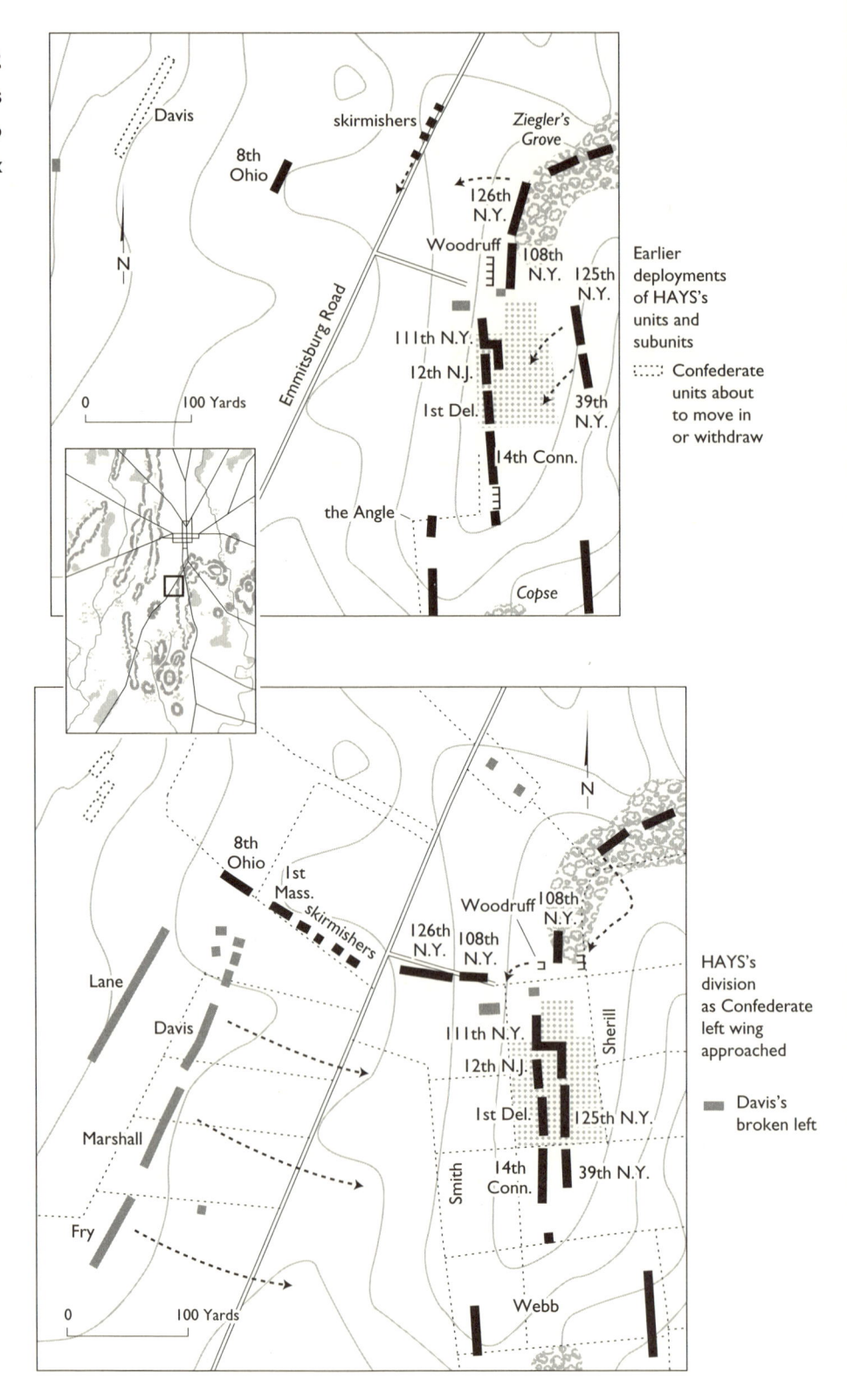

230   THE STAND OF THE U.S. ARMY AT GETTYSBURG

Chart 4-26
Trimble's two brigades crossing the Emmitsburg Road

ANV → 3rd Corps → Trimble's Division July 3

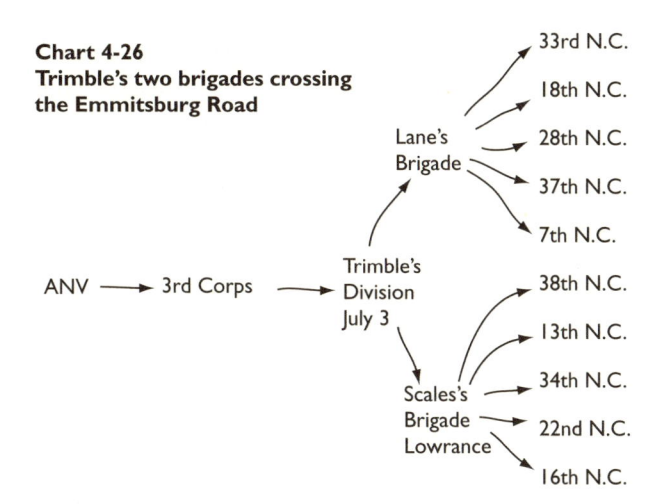

Lane's Brigade → 33rd N.C., 18th N.C., 28th N.C., 37th N.C., 7th N.C.

Scales's Brigade Lowrance → 38th N.C., 13th N.C., 34th N.C., 22nd N.C., 16th N.C.

Ridge. In the region of the center-left, short-range artillery fire from the two batteries there (maps 4-24 to 4-29) inflicted sufficient damage on the Virginians down the slope on Pickett's right wing.[125]

To appreciate further the relative power of the Union defense, we also must focus attention on the *left* half of the assault force. Attacking rebel troops in this subsector were approaching the Union line with less than a 50 percent numerical advantage. In fact, the *right wing of the Union defense* center was relatively strong in the region of Hays's division.

As Pettigrew's shrunken line approached Hays's positions (chart 4-25) and Union musket fire began hitting the rebels' left wing from the front, men of the 126th and 108th New York Regiments, along with the skirmishers to their right (map 4-23), helped Sawyer's 8th Ohio rake the left flank of the assault.[126] Davis's brigade continued to be hit, and several of his Mississippians and North Carolinians fell back. But Union musketry from this north end of the envelopment crashed into Lane's brigade as well. General Lane had hurried his unit (the leftmost of Trimble's two brigades) forward to try to replace the vanished Brockenbrough.

Robert E. Lee acknowledged that the Union's achievement of a double envelopment ruined his assault on July 3. The Gettysburg report he submitted in January 1864 stated that "the enemy was enabled to throw a strong force of infantry against our left, already wavering under concentrated fire from the ridge in front, and from Cemetery Hill, on the left. It finally gave way . . . and was attacked simultaneously in front and on both flanks, and driven back with heavy loss."[127]

General Lee was admitting that *Federal actions* had much to do with the destruction of his army's attack. It is likely that Lee never learned which Union men were responsible for these active defensive moves. Within the left wing of the defensive force, General Hays was one such person. Hays had enough men in his westward-facing line that he could risk deploying part of it down the ridge, achieving the deadly effect just described and acknowledged. The musketry from Hays's main line firing into the attackers' faces was horrendous as well. Union batteries were also in this vicinity (map 4-32). Captain William A. Arnold's battery (chart 4-25), located on Hays's left, fired off its last canister charges at the 26th North Carolina as it advanced up the slope (map 4-33, chart 4-25), then he pulled his battery out of the front line before the North Carolinians approached the stone fence.[128] Indeed, some of Pettigrew's rebels in the van of this advance were able to get within ten paces of the wall where Hays's men stood. But the line

**Map 4-33
The High-Water Mark is passing its crest as the Union center and center-left counterattack**

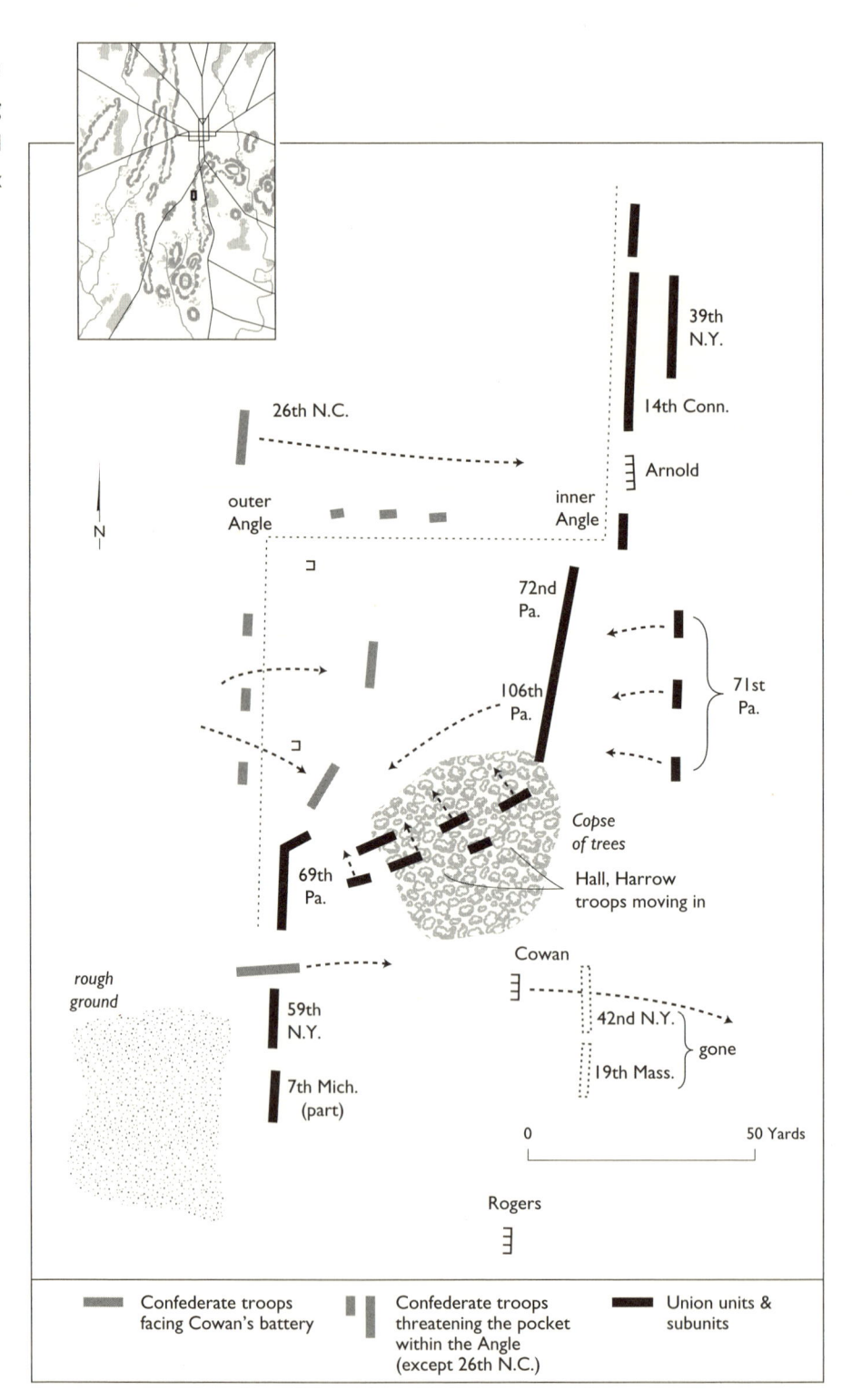

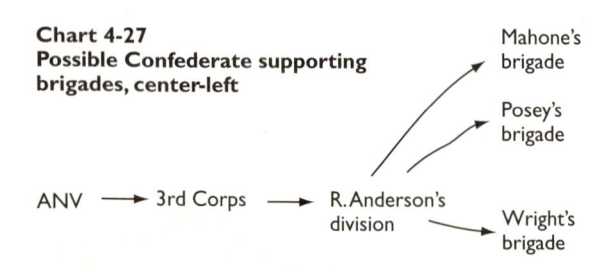

39th N.Y.
14th Conn.
26th N.C.
Arnold
outer Angle
inner Angle
72nd Pa.
71st Pa.
106th Pa.
69th Pa.
Copse of trees
Hall, Harrow troops moving in
Cowan
42nd N.Y.
19th Mass.
gone
rough ground
59th N.Y.
7th Mich. (part)
0   50 Yards
Rogers

Confederate troops facing Cowan's battery | Confederate troops threatening the pocket within the Angle (except 26th N.C.) | Union units & subunits

**Chart 4-27
Possible Confederate supporting brigades, center-left**

ANV → 3rd Corps → R. Anderson's division → Mahone's brigade
→ Posey's brigade
→ Wright's brigade

232 THE STAND OF THE U.S. ARMY AT GETTYSBURG

**Chart 4-28
Federal reinforcements advancing to Cemetery Ridge—late ***

```
                                    A P
         ┌──────┬──────┬──────┬──────┼──────┬──────┬──────┐
         │      │      │      │      │      │      │      │
         ▼      ▼      ▼      ▼      ▼      ▼      ▼      ▼
                            Artillery      Meade's Staff
                            Reserve            │
                                               ▼
                                          Provost
                                           Guard
                                             │
                                             ▼
                                          2nd Pa.
                                          Cavalry
```

11th Corps → 2nd Division → 2nd Brigade → 73rd Ohio
11th Corps → Artillery Brigade → 13th N.Y. Light Lt. W. Wheeler

1st Corps → 2nd Division Robinson → 2nd Brigade Baxter → 88th Pa., 90th Pa., 12th Mass.

2nd Corps → 3rd Division → Provost Guard 10th N.Y. Battalion

Artillery Reserve → 4th Vol. Brigade → 1st N.J. Light Lt. A. Parsons
Artillery Reserve → 1st Regular Brigade → 3rd U.S. Lt. J. Turnbull, 5th U.S. Lt. G. Weir
Artillery Reserve → 1st N.Y. Light Capt. R. Fitzhugh

12th Corps → 1st Division → 1st Brigade McDougall → 123rd N.Y.

3rd Corps → 1st Division → 1st Brigade Tippin * → 114th Pa., 99th Pa.
3rd Corps → 1st Division → 2nd Brigade Berdan ** → 3rd Maine, 4th Maine

1st Corps → 3rd Division → 1st Brigade Rowley † → 121st Pa., 142nd Pa., 149th Pa.
1st Corps → 3rd Division → 2nd Brigade Dana ‡ → 143rd Pa., 150th Pa.

* Graham wounded July 2

** Ward to division command July 2

† Biddle wounded July 1

‡ Stone wounded July 1

*The jumbled nature of this chart connects with the likelihood that its contents are not comprehensive—instead, to give an appreciation of the potpourri of Union units sent in at the last minute.

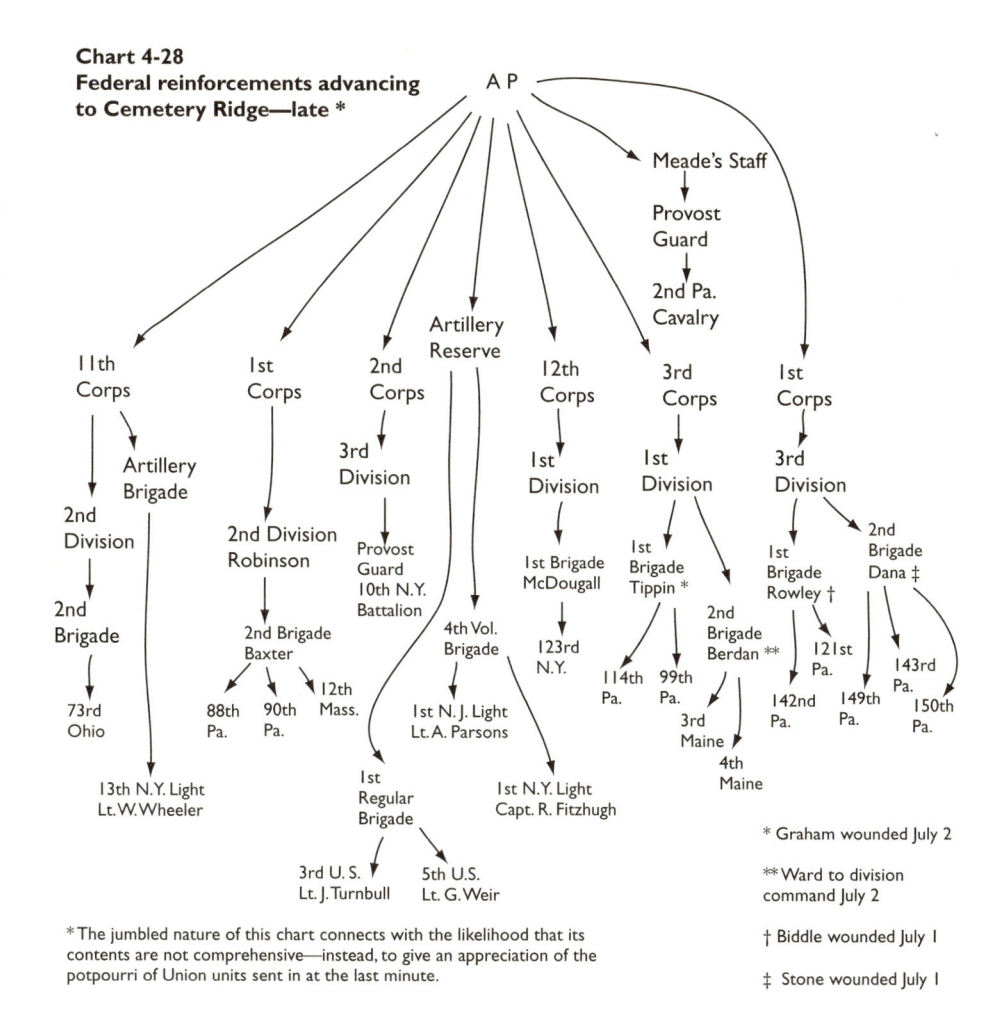

at this stone fence, projecting north from the Angle and farther up the slope because of it, was never breached. Certain Confederate soldiers reached the wall itself and were pulled over it to safety and captivity. As some of the attackers almost got into their lines, Hays's infantrymen were adding sheets of frontal fire to the enfilading musketry, augmented by two guns' worth of cannon fire—all of this being poured into Pettigrew's left. Just before his troops went into action, Hays had been drilling them as Pettigrew's men crossed the field. This was a flamboyant antic on Hays's part, but one that steadied his troops and speaks once more to the confidence with which the Union commanders were operating.

Meanwhile, the Federal defenses to the left of Hays's line were also hotly engaged. The time was shortly after the Confederates in the center swarmed into the Union lines with Brig. Gen. Armistead. Even though their commander, Col. Dennis O'Kane, was mortally wounded, the left two-thirds of the 69th Pennsylvania stood its ground.[129] The regiment's fire may have been furious, because several of these Pennsylvanians had preloaded three or more shoulder arms per man. Just to their left, as the gap manned only by Cowan's battery was threatened by some of Pickett's men advancing up the slope, Captain Cowan let loose his last charges of canister, and those blasts of giant shotgun fire swept most of the ground in his front. Out of ammunition and "with his immediate infantry supports gone, Cowan . . . ordered his guns pulled back by hand."[130]

Over at the part of the Angle where the wall projects westward, two companies of the 71st Pennsylvania were still defending in their forward position. The op-

THE GREAT GAMBLE LEE COULD HAVE WON

posing forces in the area south of the Angle, between it and the copse of trees, engaged in hand-to-hand fighting. This included soldiers from the 19th Massachusetts and 42nd New York coming in from the east edge of the ridge.

At last, the 72nd Pennsylvania and elements of the not-quite-defeated 71st surged forward (map 4-33), moving into the pocket below the Angle to the left of the reinforcing Massachusetts men and New Yorkers (chart 4-20, maps 4-27 and 4-28). Union troops from Hall's and Harrow's brigades near the copse of trees advanced as well. At that moment, elements of Hays's *left wing*—relatively near the center and no longer contending with Pettigrew's retreating units—wheeled south and fired on the flanks of the Confederates holding tenuous positions near the Angle. The Federal soldiers in and near this pocket now outnumbered the attackers amongst them. The remnants of those Confederate troops were cut down, gobbled up, and swept away. Forty-two rebel infantrymen lay dead in the pocket, suggesting that two hundred to three hundred of their mates had broken through.[131] This Union countercharge from the center occurred at 4 P.M., some ten minutes after the double envelopment had been completed.

The Federal position was by then largely safe. General Trimble's 3rd Corps force (chart 4-26) was still advancing in the vicinity of the Emmitsburg Road (map 4-34). But these two Confederate brigades, led by General Lane and Col. William Lee J. Lowrance, went only partway up the slope below Cemetery Ridge, gave up, and streamed to the rear.[132] By then General Trimble was badly wounded, having been shot in the leg near the road. General Pettigrew suffered a severe wound in his hand.

Recall the rebel units posted *behind* Trimble and Pettigrew (maps 4-13 and 4-35). As the left end of Pettigrew's line began to crumble (maps 4-16 and 4-19), General Longstreet sent a staff officer with instructions for Trimble to cover that flank. Potentially as important, he ordered the 3rd Corps division commander, Richard Anderson (chart 4-27), to direct William Mahone, Carnot Posey, and Ambrose R. Wright to advance their brigades in support of the assault's left wing. However, by the time those three units began to move off Seminary Ridge toward the Confederate artillery line east of it (map 4-14), Pickett's and Pettigrew's attackers were being crushed as they approached Cemetery Ridge. At this time, a courier arrived in the vicinity of the guns with an order from Longstreet directing that Anderson's brigades cease their advance (map 4-35).[133]

One cannot help wondering what would have happened to the left wing of the assault, as it approached the halfway point of the advance, had Posey's or Mahone's essentially unbloodied brigades been placed on that flank instead of Brockenbrough's.[134] Neither of those 3rd Corps units had acted in a timely or aggressive manner on July 2, but perhaps they were itching on Friday to atone for having slacked off the day before. At least their brigades were not half-wrecked by having been heavily engaged earlier in the battle. Yet Longstreet did not deploy these units in the first wave of the assault, and his half-hearted order to send them in (along with Wright) in support of Pettigrew and Trimble came too late. A more charitable view is that General Longstreet was following the military maxim that counsels against reinforcing failure. What might the outcome have been if he *had* formulated a plan calling for Wilcox, Lang, Wright, Posey, and Mahone (map 4-13) to advance in a *close-supporting second wave*?[135] That second wave could have received further support from the right wing of the line in the Long Lane (to the north on map 4-13), which was largely quiescent on July 3, and perhaps even from the rebel regiments posted on the left wing of the line of *1st Corps* troops (to the south—at least Wofford's brigade of McLaws's division—on maps 4-7 and 4-36).[136]

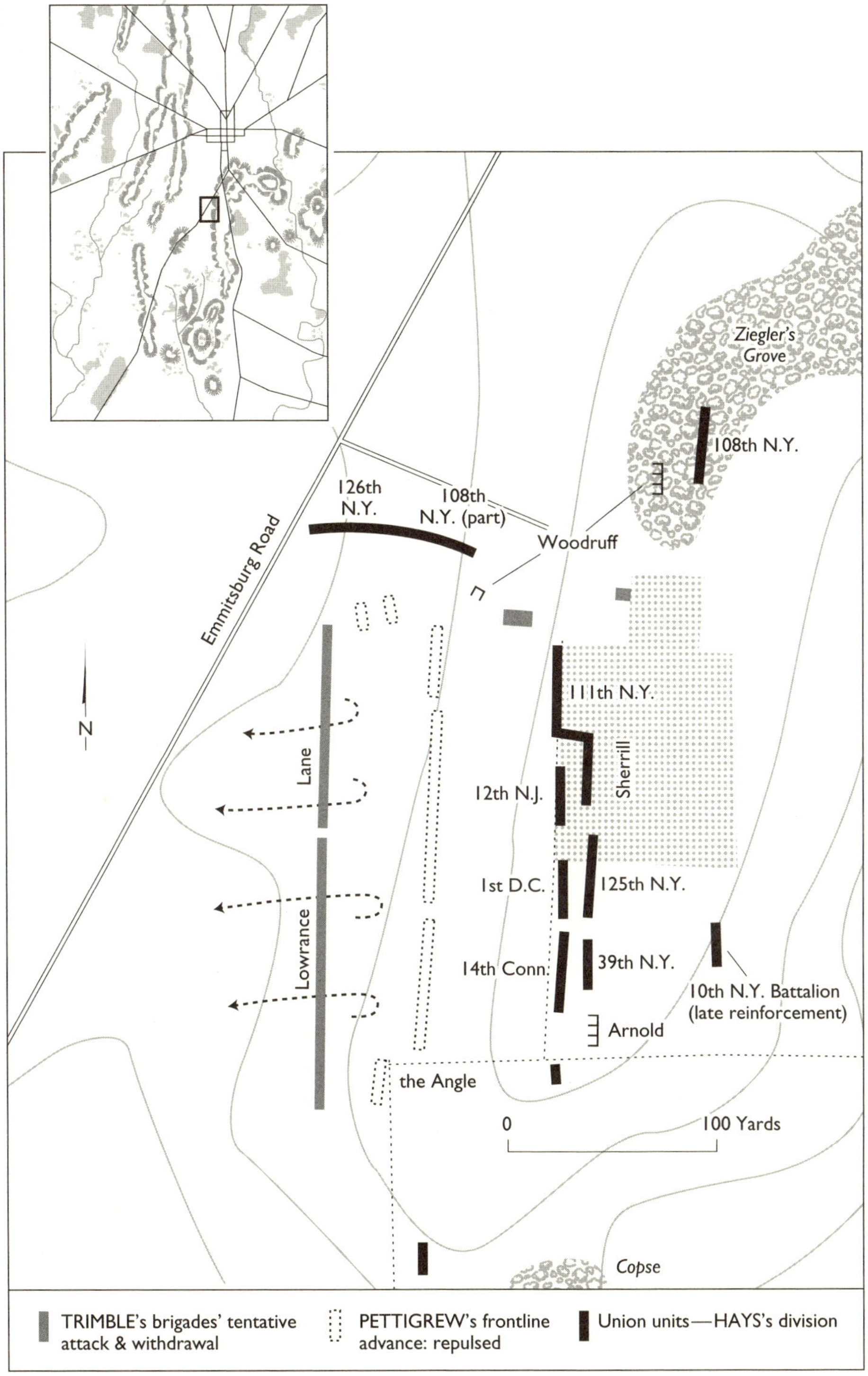

Map 4-34
Trimble's division advances in support of Pettigrew, but gives up the ghost

| TRIMBLE's brigades' tentative attack & withdrawal | PETTIGREW's frontline advance: repulsed | Union units—HAYS's division |

Perhaps the "powerful force" arrayed for Pickett's Charge was *too small*. Even a Confederate cavalryman took it upon himself to say so long after the war: "The divisions of Hood and McLaws, one half of Hill's and the whole of Ewell's stood like fixed stars in the heavens as their comrades marched into 'the jaws of death.'"[137] Yet, by holding all these units back, Lee and Longstreet maintained a significant reserve against the possibility of a Federal counterattack. They also

THE GREAT GAMBLE LEE COULD HAVE WON 235

**Map 4-35
Confederate support units make belated or tentative advances toward the High-Water Mark**

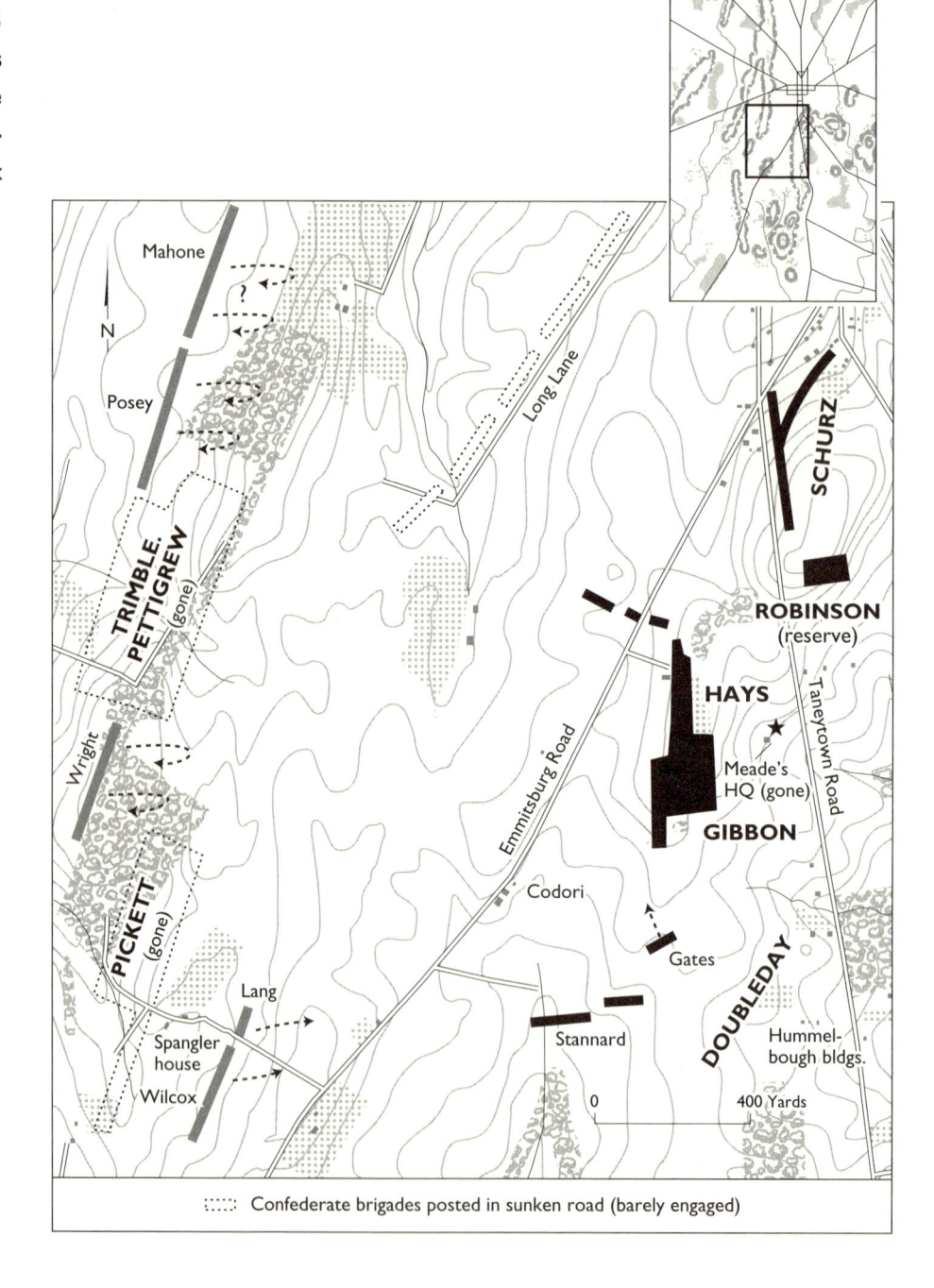

Confederate brigades posted in sunken road (barely engaged)

made their "great gamble" at Gettysburg a conservative one by sending forth only nine brigades of attacking infantry. Incidentally, the 12,500 men in the assault force as originally configured *included* Wilcox's and Lang's brigades (map 4-10), which ended up adding minimal weight to the assault (as we will see). Perhaps as many as ten additional brigades of Southerners posted near Seminary Ridge, or even east of it in the vicinity of the Peach Orchard and along the Long Lane (maps 4-7 and 4-13), could have been rolled into the attack plan.[138] Recall Porter Alexander's postwar argument that the cannonade was *also* understrength. With respect to planning the infantry component of the assault, James Longstreet performed well in terms of how he devised the rebel soldiers' attack geometrically—

236   THE STAND OF THE U.S. ARMY AT GETTYSBURG

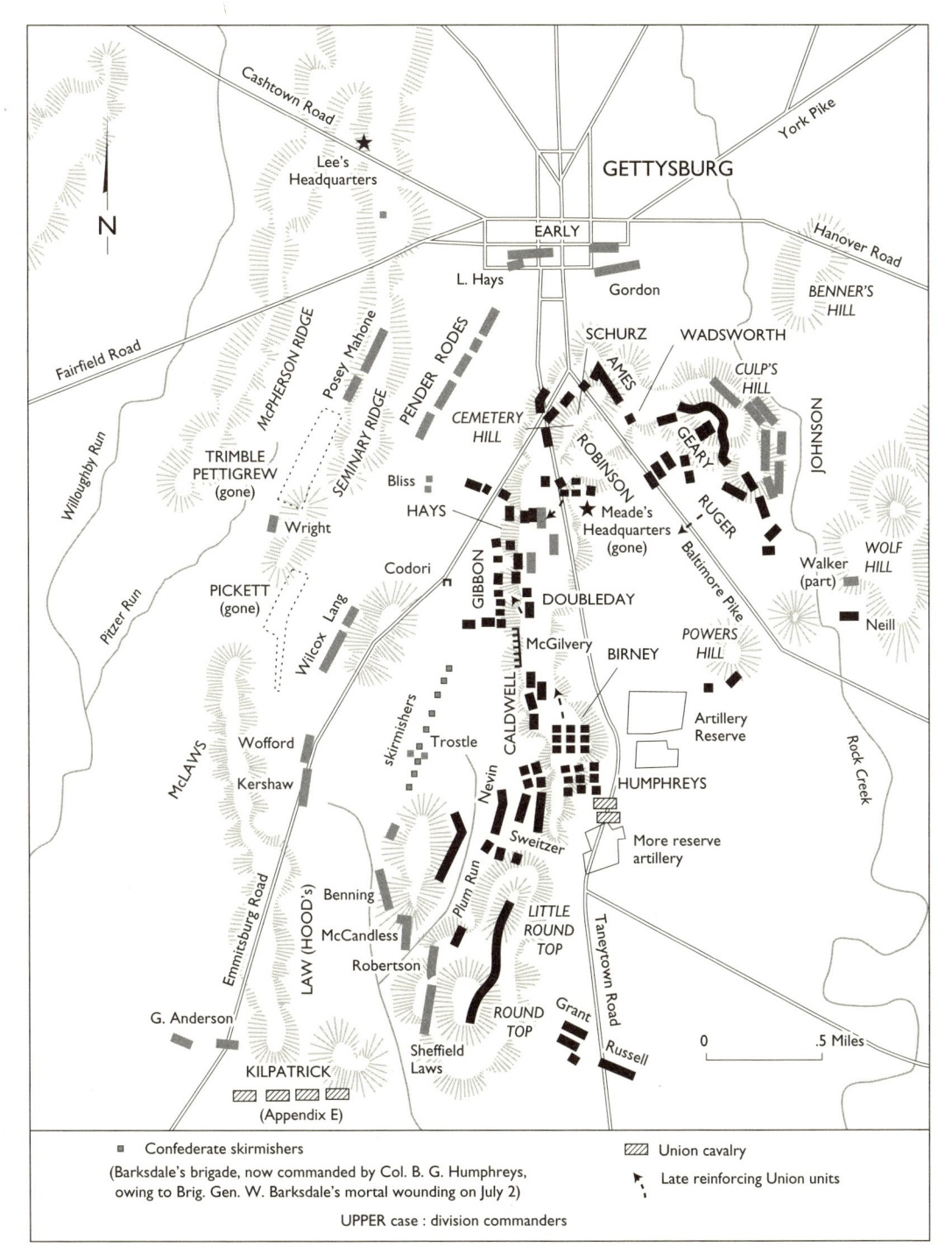

**Map 4-36
Overall position of the opposing forces, late afternoon, including Union reinforcing moves from various corps**

that is, the manner by which these troops were pre-positioned along Seminary Ridge and how the units were to advance across the field, in a manner more interestingly complicated than the aforementioned mindless mass moving across the field. But perhaps he and General Lee did not marshal a large enough infantry force to begin with ("no 15 thousand men..."). Nor was any appreciable second wave thrown in closely to support the two and one-half divisions deployed for the assault.

At all events, the first wave was crushed, and the crisis had passed. Moreover, Federal reinforcements were arriving (map 4-36, chart 4-28), and batteries from

THE GREAT GAMBLE LEE COULD HAVE WON 237

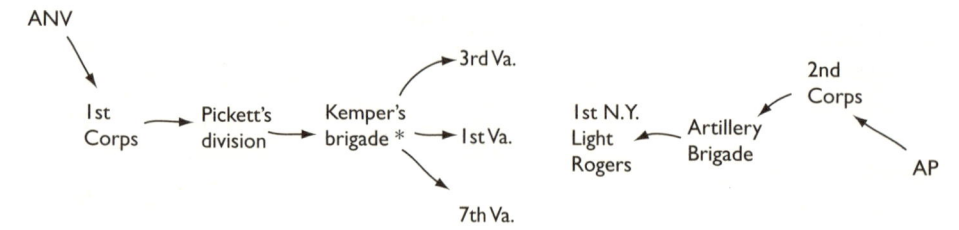

Chart 4-29
A group of Kemper's men rushes Rogers's (formerly Rorty's) Battery

ANV → 1st Corps → Pickett's division → Kemper's brigade * → 3rd Va.
Kemper's brigade * → 1st Va.
Kemper's brigade * → 7th Va.
1st N.Y. Light Rogers ← Artillery Brigade ← 2nd Corps
Artillery Brigade ← AP

* Only small fractions of these Va. Regiments (from Kemper's left) attacked Rogers's battery, and it is not known for certain if the specified units (above) were the ones involved (or at least, were all three of them?). [It is unlikely that any troops from the 24th or 11th Va. advanced against Rogers, because those elements of Kemper's brigade had been tied up trying to cope with Stannard's flank attack (map 4-29).] The Virginians that attacked this Union battery had previously been under a degree of cover in the "rough ground" just west of the ridge (see text). It is also possible that men from the 8th Va. (from Garnett's right) were among the troops who took advantage of that cover.

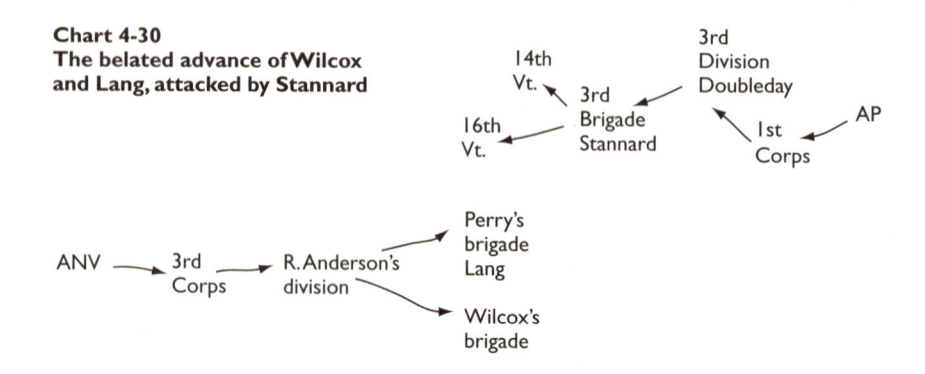

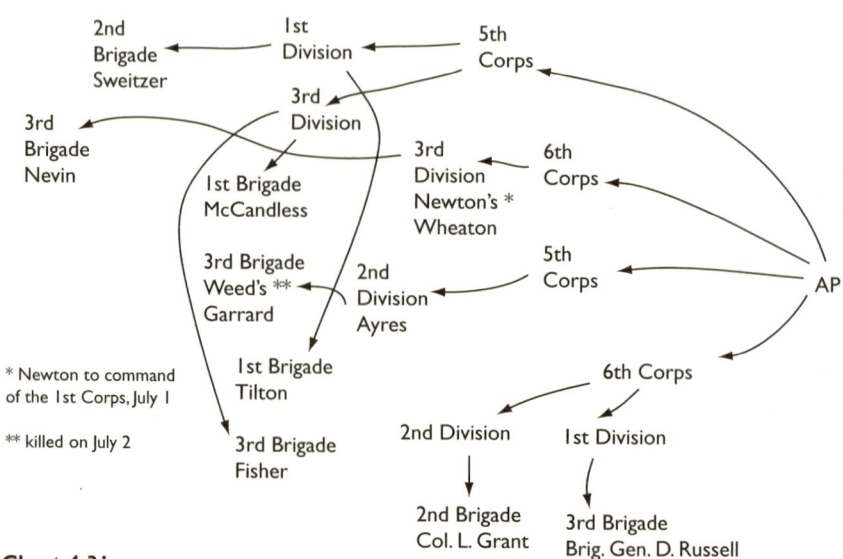

Chart 4-30
The belated advance of Wilcox and Lang, attacked by Stannard

14th Vt., 16th Vt. → 3rd Brigade Stannard → 3rd Division Doubleday ← 1st Corps ← AP

ANV → 3rd Corps → R. Anderson's division → Perry's brigade Lang
R. Anderson's division → Wilcox's brigade

Chart 4-31
Union units in reserve on the Army's left—a possible attack force to follow up the repulse

2nd Brigade Sweitzer ← 1st Division ← 5th Corps
3rd Brigade Nevin
3rd Division
1st Brigade McCandless
3rd Division Newton's * Wheaton ← 6th Corps
3rd Brigade Weed's ** Garrard
2nd Division Ayres ← 5th Corps
1st Brigade Tilton
3rd Brigade Fisher
2nd Division → 2nd Brigade Col. L. Grant
6th Corps → 2nd Division
6th Corps → 1st Division → 3rd Brigade Brig. Gen. D. Russell
AP

* Newton to command of the 1st Corps, July 1

** killed on July 2

238   THE STAND OF THE U.S. ARMY AT GETTYSBURG

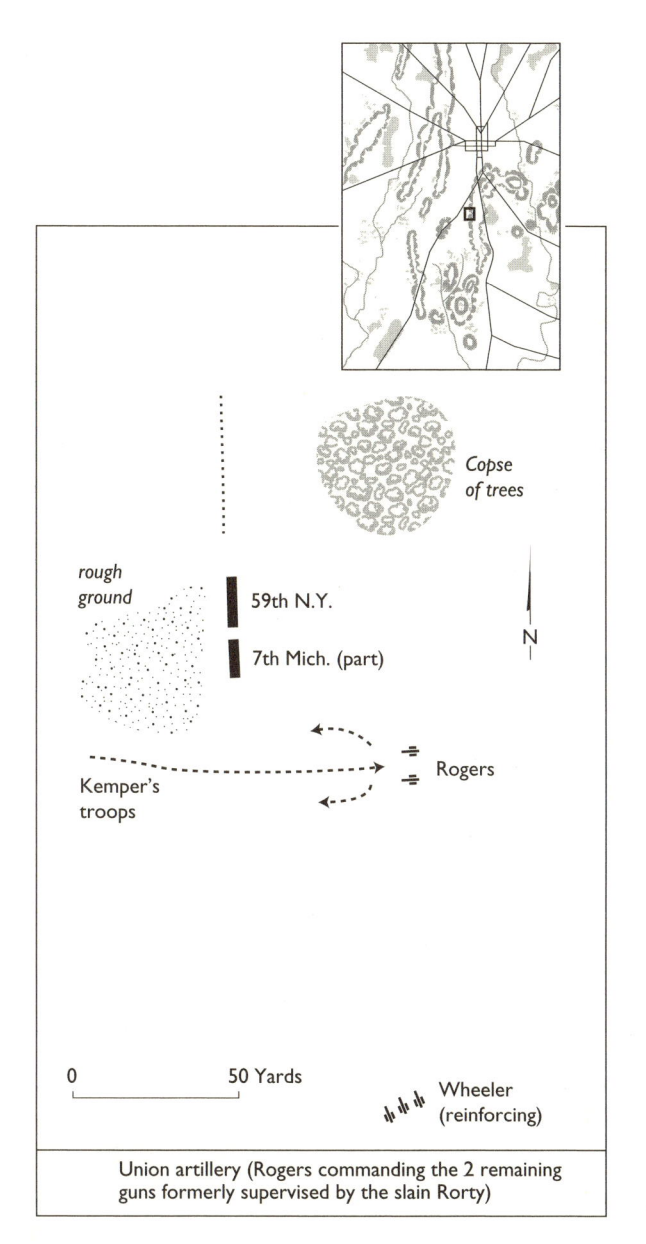

Map 4-37

A group of troops from Kemper's brigade rushes Rogers's guns positioned within the Union center-left

Copse of trees

rough ground

59th N.Y.

7th Mich. (part)

Kemper's troops

Rogers

0 50 Yards

Wheeler (reinforcing)

Union artillery (Rogers commanding the 2 remaining guns formerly supervised by the slain Rorty)

the Artillery Reserve at last came forward (exemplified in map 4-37).[139] Infantrymen from the 1st Corps came in from the north toward Hays's right. Others from that unit, along with 3rd Corps troops, reoccupied the sector of Cemetery Ridge where Harrow's brigade had been. Brigades from the 2nd and 12th Corps (chart 4-28) arrived from the east to bolster the positions along the ridgeline.[140]

As this massed Union defense was about to take command of the field east of the Emmitsburg Road, a band of Confederates made one last futile charge. Some of Kemper's men on the rebel right, who had gotten behind a "brushy knoll about 100 yards in front of the Union works" and had not angled to the north with the bulk of their brigade, rushed the guns of Rorty's battery, which by then was commanded by Lieutenant Rogers (map 4-37).[141] Rogers's front had been uncovered when Harrow's and part of Hall's brigades shifted to their right to reinforce the center (maps 4-26 and 4-28). Now, Lieutenant Rogers's two functioning rifled

THE GREAT GAMBLE LEE COULD HAVE WON   239

**Map 4-38
Wilcox's and Lang's belated supporting advance, repelled by the redoubtable Vermonters**

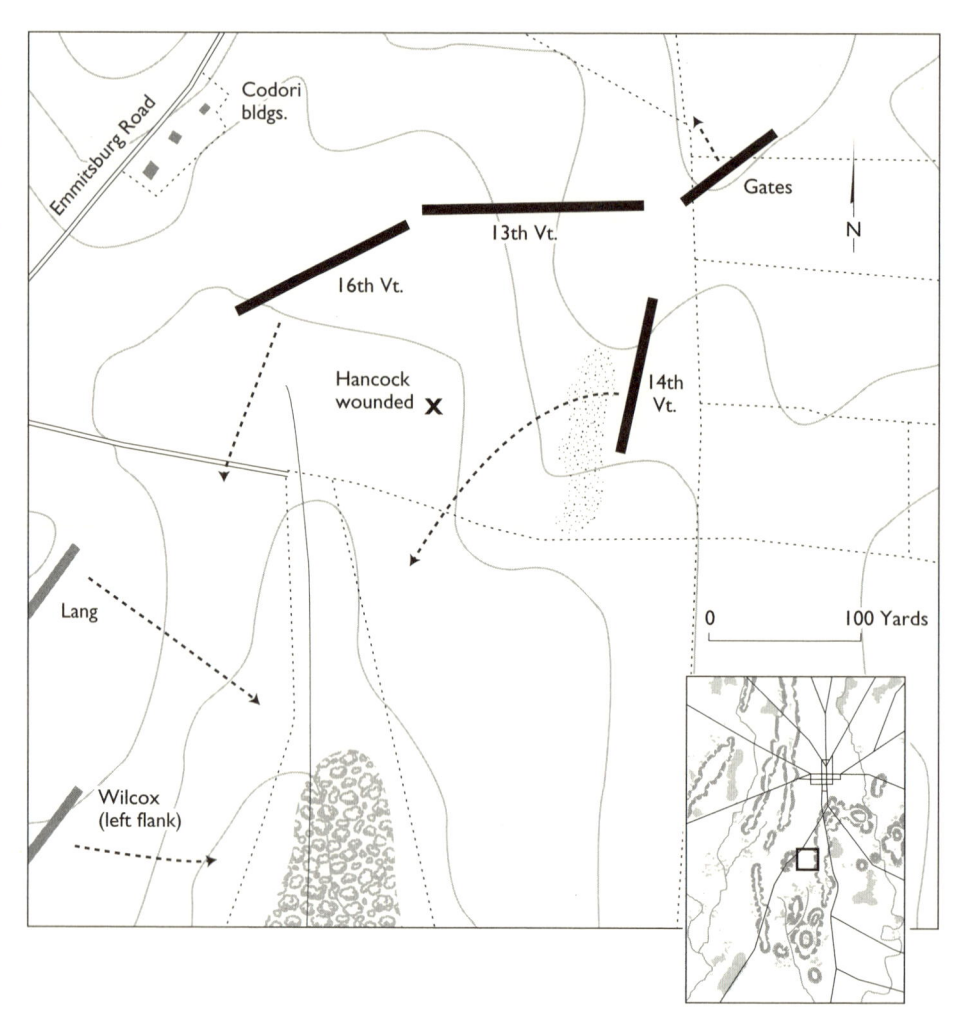

cannon (called Parrotts) and a newly arrived artillery unit (map 4-37, chart 4-28) blasted at the attackers. Some of these Southern troops—probably only ten to twenty men—fought their way into the vicinity of the Federal guns and engaged in hand-to-hand fighting. But the small rebel force that got into the Union lines south of the larger breakthroughs was quickly defeated.

DESTRUCTION OF PICKETT'S CHARGE AND UNION VICTORY AT THE BATTLE OF GETTYSBURG

When Pickett's men were halfway across the field or perhaps a little farther, General Pickett sent one of his staff officers to General Longstreet to urge the release of additional units to support the right wing of the assault.[142] The available rebel units were Wilcox's and Lang's brigades, which had for some time occupied ground near the places where Kemper and Garnett originally formed their battle lines (maps 4-10 and 4-13). But General Wilcox and Colonel Lang held their positions west of the Emmitsburg Road for *too long*, and this was a significant Confederate mistake on July 3. Apparently Longstreet wanted Wilcox (who was in overall command of both brigades) to advance in immediate support of Pickett. These one and one-half brigades (Lang's was very small) were supposed to march right behind Kemper (map 4-13)—*in case the right wing of the main line was flanked*. Did the corps commander fail to get such orders to Wilcox, or had that been Pickett's job? Couriers were sent to General Wilcox *during* the Charge

240   THE STAND OF THE U.S. ARMY AT GETTYSBURG

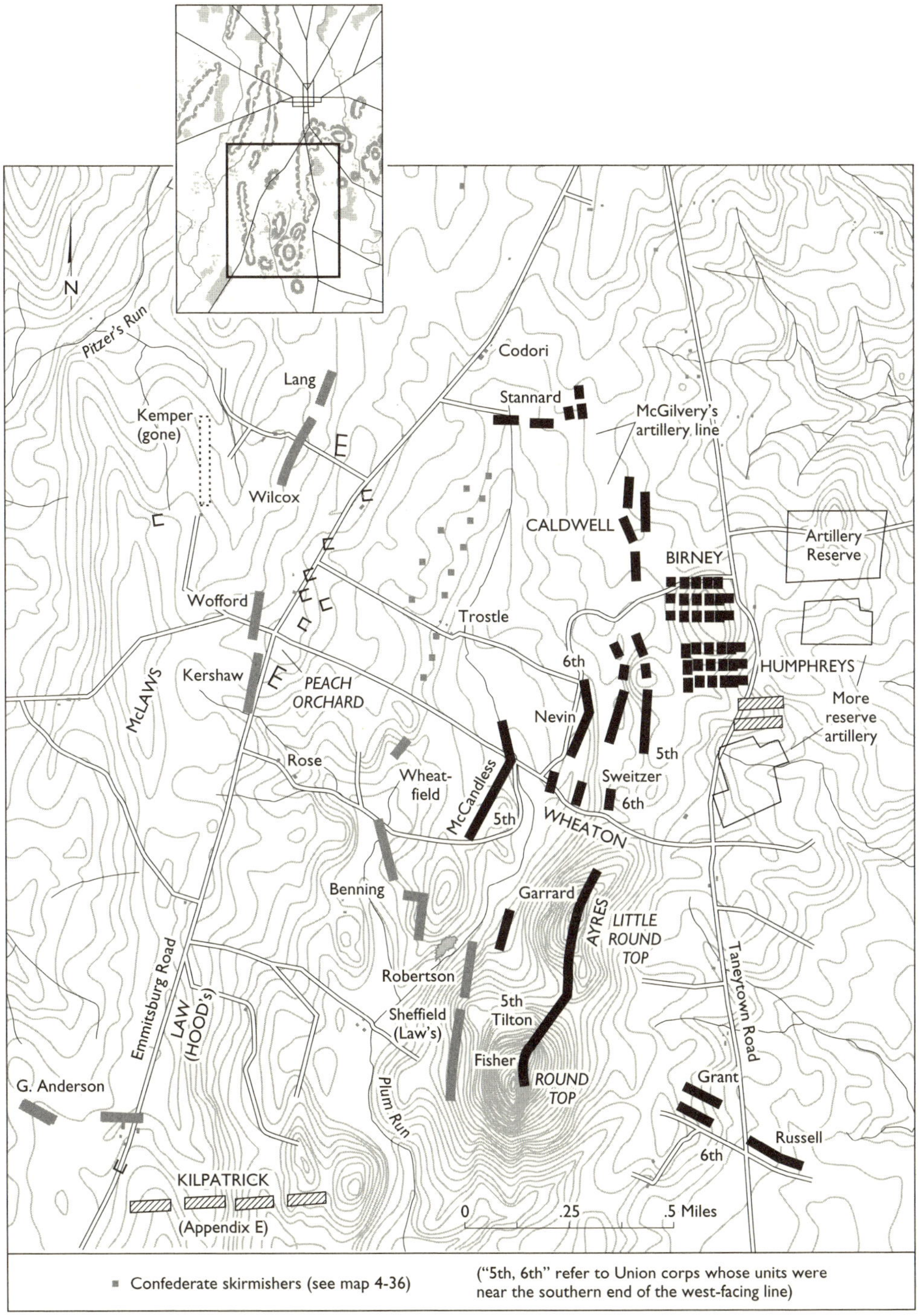

**Map 4-39
The rebel right and the Union left, largely unengaged through the afternoon**

with instructions that he "advance to support Pickett's division," but "it is not known who was responsible for [the] miscommunication" that failed to shake him loose.[143] Or perhaps Wilcox himself had been lethargic. In any case, when he finally began to move westward, it was at least twenty minutes too late. Pickett's Charge was already close to destruction when this belated support approached the fighting, for by then the small bands of rebels in the Federal lines were on the verge of defeat.

Moreover, several men from Stannard's 16th Vermont Regiment changed front, turned 180 degrees, moved slightly southward, and fired into Wilcox's and Lang's

THE GREAT GAMBLE LEE COULD HAVE WON

flank (map 4-38). The 16th was joined by four companies of the 14th Vermont, which until then had remained in the line on Cemetery Ridge (map 4-30). Some of Colonel McGilvery's batteries to the south of this sector fired canister into the tentatively advancing Georgians and Floridians. That was enough for Wilcox's force, which turned and went back toward Seminary Ridge. However, this "ridiculous demonstration" in the waning phases of the Confederate attack, as it was characterized by a Union officer, may have given pause to Federal plans for a counterstroke—an issue that will be taken up more generally in Chapter 5.[144] Meanwhile, the Union officers must have noticed the belated advance of a Confederate brigade, and this could have made them think that their defeated foe was not a routed rabble.

Indeed it was not. The Confederates had considerable reserve forces near the middle of Seminary Ridge. Some of these units, which had barely advanced at all or stood still, were discussed earlier in conjunction with the rebel units that could have been included in the assault but were not. General Lee and his subordinate commanders put three brigades in a defensive position and bolstered it with artillery. However, for this stage of the action on July 3, what we read about the most is Lee moving amongst his men, telling them that the assault's failure "was all my fault,"[145] even though the main feature of Confederate activity at this time was to prepare for a large offensive move on their lines. Gettysburg might have been another Waterloo. There, in 1815, the Allied troops, bolstered by a large Prussian force coming in on the French right flank from the east, rolled down the ridge near the Belgian town of Mont-Saint-Jean, south of Waterloo, and routed the previously attacking Frenchmen.

It was not to be at Gettysburg. A possible contingency plan for a massed counterattack by Union troops primarily from the 5th and 6th Corps never came to pass. We will examine larger issues regarding the fact that the Federals "did not pursue" in the next chapter.[146] For now, consider that Hancock, the overall commander of the Cemetery Ridge line, was down. General Hancock was aggressive and supremely confident. It has been said that he wanted a counterattack to burst forth even as he lay wounded. But the rebel force now converting to a defensive posture was still formidable. Moreover, they were the "indomitable soldiers of the Army of Northern Virginia."[147] Specifically, remember that many units of Hood's and McLaws's 1st Corps troops had been holding good defensive positions on the overall Confederate right, all day (map 4-39). These bloodied units might not have been up to joining the attack, but they retained defensive power.[148] The Union 5th and 6th Corps were positioned in front of these various Confederate 1st Corps units (maps 4-36 and 4-39). Perhaps they could have redeployed north toward the open center, from where they could have followed Wellington's example at Waterloo. But that would have taken time, and there still had to be much confusion and exhaustion along the entire central portion of the Union line.

So the Army of the Potomac demurred. Instead of going over to the attack, the Union men occupied themselves with mopping-up actions: tending to their own wounded and perhaps to some of the Confederates suffering similarly, moving prisoners to the rear, and counting captured battle flags. At least twenty-eight of the thirty-eight attacking regiments (not counting Brockenbrough's) lost their colors.[149] All those captured flags may reflect the glory of it all.

More meaningful than fallen flags were the casualties. The number of Union men who went down may have been more than twenty-three hundred. A contemporary student of Pickett's Charge figures that the number of Union casualties in the center of the line was closer to fifteen hundred.[150] Even the lower estimate implies that the Confederates below Cemetery Ridge, as they approached it after crossing the Emmitsburg Road, were not merely cringing on the slope. They poured significant offensive fire into the Union lines. Later, after some of the rebels got into those lines, some of them had taken positions at the fences within the pocket south of the Angle (maps 4-26 and 4-27) and inflicted further casualties before the final repulse.

On the Confederate side, Pickett's division lost approximately twenty-nine hundred men, and Pettigrew and Trimble suffered up to twenty-five hundred casualties. Overall, Pickett's Charge resulted in a casualty rate of somewhere in the wide range of 45 to 65 percent.[151] Considering the many thousands of men involved in the attack, the Charge was one of the most catastrophic actions in American military history.

Yet the number of Confederates *killed* in the Charge was perhaps between eight hundred and eleven hundred.[152] As horrifying as this may seem, that number does not represent a huge percentage of the assault force. If such a coldly analytical statement is to have any merit, consider the following anecdotal statistic. After the battle, a fence rail along the Emmitsburg Road was supposedly examined for damage. It was near the point where a rebel unit close to the center of the assault force had reached that roadway, and "one board, fourteen inches wide and sixteen feet long, showed 836 bullet holes." George Stewart invoked that image "as evidence of the intensity of the fire." However, that many missed shots implies that the Southern casualty toll could have been far worse.[153]

Nevertheless, the overall Confederate losses in the Charge were staggering. What if an army commander in a circumstance such as this *knew* in advance that such casualties were in danger of befalling an attack he was about to order? Does that make Robert E. Lee a general who was treating his men like cannon fodder? Absolutely not. Even if the 45–65 percent casualties estimated above had been preordained, the commander still could calculate that his force would be able to gain sufficient mass at the objective. That such a body of men got near their objective on the very slopes of Cemetery Ridge means that Pickett's Charge was not annihilated—certainly not before a large fraction of the assault force nearly achieved its geographic goal.[154] At that place and time, the Confederate troops still outnumbered the Union force directly to their front on Cemetery Ridge. A commander *willing to sacrifice half or more of his attack force* might, after a calculated risk-benefit assessment, devise a plan he thought might bring an end to a war. But the grand assault of July 3 only achieved its objective geographically. That it "failed" was "not because of any inherent weakness" or "because the Federals' advantage of position was too great, or Southern leadership faltered." Pickett's Charge "was not a desperate attack as some historians claim." "It failed because the defenders of Cemetery Ridge refused to be defeated and fought with a tenacity they had not exhibited on previous battlefields."[155]

We are not quite done with the Confederate officer after whom the Charge was named. As Robert E. Lee rode amongst his men to rally the defense, he encountered Maj. Gen. George E. Pickett. The commanding general said to his subordinate: "General Pickett, place your division in rear of this hill, and be ready to repel the advance of the enemy should they follow up their advantage." Pickett responded, in tears some reported, "General Lee, I have no division now."[156] His inescapable sadness turned to bitterness after the war. Following a tense visit to Lee in Richmond in March 1870, Pickett turned to his companion and said, "That old man . . . had my division massacred at Gettysburg."[157] This could be invoked as one of the endless number of spoken and written words that Southerners said and put on paper, all of them pointing to the monumental Confederate failure at the climax of their northern invasion in 1863. However, wiser words were uttered at another time and place by the soldier in question. After the war, a newspaper reporter asked the former general why the Confederates lost at Gettysburg. George Pickett looked at the man and replied: "Well, I think the Yankees had a little something to do with it."[158]

Chart 4-32
Vanderslice's estimates of casualties for July 3*
(INCLUDES CULP'S HILL AND THE EAST PLUS SOUTH CAVALRY FIELDS)

	killed and wounded	missing / captured	total
Confederate	4,790	2,710	7,500
Union	3,580	490	4,070

* see chart 2-13

CHAPTER FIVE

Aftermath: The Pursuit and Escape of the Army of Northern Virginia

> Some day you'll return to
> Your valleys and your farms
> and you'll no longer burn
> To be brothers in arms
>
> —Mark Knopfler

The Battle of Gettysburg was over. It had already been subtly won in the waning hours of July 2. The coup de grâce came on the following afternoon. Two cavalry engagements also occurred that Friday (map 5-1). The absence of accounts of them in the previous chapter suggests that those extra actions of July 3 are treated as sideshows in this work (Appendixes D and E), which perhaps is proper.

In the immediate aftermath of the battle as a whole—before we come to the end of the long denouement—let us consider the casualties (chart 5-1). An estimated 24,000 to 28,000 Confederates were killed, wounded, or captured over the course of Gettysburg's three days. However, the Confederates reported "only" 20,451 (chart 5-1), at least in part because of their practice of not counting walking wounded among their casualties.[1] Another factor that runs counter to this deliberate underestimation on the rebels' part is that the approximately 5,000–6,000 of their casualties in the category of "missing/captured" (chart 5-1) was worse than that: "When Lee's army retreated, it left at least five thousand of its wounded, bringing the total number of Southerners who were taken prisoner by the Federals to more than ten thousand."[2] Injured men *not* captured can of course recover to fight again, but the 5,000 "wounded-then-captured" at Gettysburg were lost for the duration of the war.

These losses for the Army of Northern Virginia in the summer of 1863 were horrendous: up to 40 percent, and it would get even worse during the retreat (see below). The Army of the Potomac fared better: 28 percent casualties, a number that nevertheless seems abhorrent. This is the case at least from the perspective of the twentieth century, when the U.S. Army came to regard casualty percentages only a third as high as those suffered at Gettysburg as bloodbaths.[3]

Was the Army of Northern Virginia wrecked by the loss of 40 percent of its men at Gettysburg? The quick answer is "no," for the rebel forces in the East demonstrated resilience and power in the battles beginning ten months later. However, they never again exhibited the attacking élan they had displayed at Chancellorsville and Gettysburg.[4] Perhaps too high a proportion of the Southern soldiers in the East no longer burned to be brothers in arms to quite the extent that their morale over the previous six months had attested. The words of one Georgia soldier who fought at Gettysburg and managed to survive succinctly sum up the state of affairs after and because of that battle: "I am willing to fight them as long

Phases of Battle and Campaign:

a. Late cavalry actions

b. The pursuit

c. The escape

Chart 5-1
Casualties in the Battle of Gettysburg

	killed	wounded	missing / captured	total
CLOSEST TO REALITY *				
Confederate	3,500	14,000–18,000	6,500	24,000–28,000
Union	3,155	14,529	5,365	23,049
**OFFICIAL ** **				
Confederate	2,592	12,709	5,150	20,451
Union	3,155	14,529	5,365	23,049
OTHER ESTIMATES				
Confederate †	4,637	12,391	5,846	22,874
Union †	3,155	14,529	5,365	23,049
Confederate ‡	3,903	18,735	5,424	28,062
Union ‡	3,149	14,507	5,161	22,817
Confederate §	4,485	11,946	5,176	21,607
Union §	3,125	14,412	5,119	22,656

* See T. L. Livermore, *Numbers and Losses in the Civil War in America* (Boston: Houghton Mifflin, 1901), pp 80–81. For an example of the conventional contemporary wisdom about (especially) the Confederate casualties at Gettysburg, see J. MacDonald, *Great Battles of the Civil War* (New York: Macmillan, 1988), p. 111 (here, numbers close to those in the first two rows are given). Also, see note 1 in this chapter.

** These figures are reflected in the casualty estimates for the separate days of the battle (see the final chart in each of Chapters 2 through 4).

† J. W. Busey and D. G. Martin, *Regimental Strengths and Losses at Gettysburg*, 2nd ed. (Hightstown, N.J.: Longstreet House, 1994), pp. 239, 280.

‡ B. Perrett, *The Battle Book: Crucial Conflicts in History from 1469 to the Present* (London: Arms and Armour Press, 1992), p. 194.

§ Figures posted in the Visitors' Center, Gettysburg National Military Park. These estimates were provided by James Roach, a Park Service employee. A historian who works there, D. Scott Hartwig, the results of whose research are mentioned in Chapter 4, disagrees with these posted numbers. He believes that Lee's losses were considerably higher than those indicated in the penultimate row of this chart, and thus more in line with the top row (Hartwig e-mail to author, Aug. 25, 1998).

as General Lee says fight. But I think we are ruined now without going any further with it."[5]

Nevertheless, Gettysburg, according to Southern perspectives in the summer of 1863, may have been a mere setback at a certain moment in the war. Contemporary writings of rebel soldiers and articles in Southern newspapers bear this out.[6] Meanwhile, in the North, the press proclaimed "The Great Victory" and "Waterloo eclipsed!!"[7]

Whether one takes to heart or ignores the public pronouncements from more than 130 years ago, I believe that neither of the armies that faced each other over those three bloody days in July 1863 were ever really the same. Yet there are modern writers who dispute this and argue more generally that the outcome of Gettysburg was not very significant. At the risk of failing to give these military analysts their proper due, let me mention elements of the theses provided by two of them. Chris Perello views Gettysburg as having led to little change in the fortunes of war in America in the 1860s. He claims, for example, that Gettysburg did not "do much to instill any offensive spirit in the Army of the Potomac or its leaders," nor did it "lead to major changes in [Northern] morale."[8] I am not sure that what happened subsequently in the war in the East supports this negativity. At least that is the case if "the morale of the Army of the Potomac sunk to a point perilously close to collapse"[9] during the time of Second Manassas, Fredericksburg, and Chancellorsville (August 1862 to May 1863); and that Northern confidence and resolve surely improved after Gettysburg. A modern articulation of that argument was made by Joseph Glatthaar, who quotes Northern soldiers writing about how "for the first time, they had bested Lee's army in a campaign. The triumph provided proof positive that they were 'good stuff' from which to build an army. With proper . . . leadership, they could defeat the Army of Northern Virginia. This newfound confidence, born of experience, helped to sustain them through [the] last, decisive year of the war."[10] Long before that was to play out, and to signify what Gettysburg in its immediate aftermath meant to the Northern populace, "crowds gathered on the south lawn of the White House" to celebrate Independence Day and "The Great Victory" in Pennsylvania, "where local political figures and dignitaries hurried to join them. . . . People went wild. The city had not seen a celebration of this magnitude in many years. . . . Congratulatory speeches were forthcoming, . . . and church bells peeled throughout the day."[11] Obviously the outbreak of this rejoicing required no knowledge of the fall of Vicksburg, which was coming down on this very day; news about the surrender of the Confederate bastion on the Mississippi River did not reach the East Coast until three days later.

Thus, the citizens of Washington were energized about the dramatic outcome of *Gettysburg*—even though these Americans had no historical perspective about the battle. In this respect, another anti-Gettysburg screed was presented in the 1990s by Richard M. McMurray, who wrote, "no one has made any serious effort to explain how the course of the war after Gettysburg was any different."[12] I suspect that Glatthaar (whose essay appears in the same volume as McMurray's) would disagree in terms of both the explanatory "effort" and the war's "course." Nevertheless, McMurray argues forcefully that the fall of Vicksburg was far more significant than the outcome of Gettysburg. This is a prominent feature of McMurray's thesis and is encompassed within an oft-stated view that "the South lost the Civil War in the West." Some who utter this phrase go on to say: "but they could have won it in the East." McMurry would not so utter; and if it is not the case that "it was all lost at Gettysburg," it is fair to propose that a great opportunity was swept away by the Union army in southern Pennsylvania.[13] As the Southern invasion of that Northern state was being planned in the spring of 1863, Vicksburg was besieged, its fall just a matter of time. Bevin Alexander makes an intriguing point about that Confederate Gibraltar on the Mississippi River: "The threat to Vicksburg aroused fright among Southern civilians but *practically none among Confederate generals*. Lee saw the city only as a means to interdict Federal traffic on the river. Longstreet felt the South would be little worse off if Vicksburg were lost."[14] Alexander is putting some meat on the bones of an interesting question asked by an earlier writer about the relevant importance of the two major theaters of the war: "What benefit could the North gain from Grant's siege of Vicksburg or Rosecrans' capture of Chattanooga if Lee could deliver a crushing defeat to the Army of the Potomac in Pennsylvania?"[15]

Even McMurray believes that, when the Confederate president "sent Lee and the Army of Northern Virginia across the Potomac in June 1863, Davis played his and the Confederacy's strongest hand" (compared, for example, to reinforcing Vicksburg with part of the eastern rebel army).[16] Surprisingly perhaps—at least to the Confederate leadership—the Union held the better cards at Gettysburg with Meade and a resilient army of soldiers. However, Herman Hattaway and Archer Jones contend that not only was the Northern victory in Pennsylvania overblown, the significance of the fall of Vicksburg has also been overstated: "The principal effect was psychological" and, "like the Battle of Gettysburg," involved "the heavy casualties sustained by the Confederates" when Vicksburg capitulated.[17] Indeed, as Alexander wrote, "Lee . . . lost well over a third of his army and had destroyed the last offensive power of the Confederacy. From this point on, the Army of Northern Virginia was a wounded lion. It could only hold on grimly . . . but was unable to effect a decision on its own. . . . The days of the great offensive, of brilliant strikes into the rear of the Union army, of campaigns that could defeat the enemy in battle, were past."[18]

As the Confederates changed their military activities during the final year of the war in the East—shifting to strategic withdrawals and defensive tactics—they were forced to do so because the Yankees had a certain tiger by the tail. The way the Federal forces acted between the spring of 1864 and the spring of 1865 as they advanced into northern Virginia and never let go had as much influence on changing Southern plans as any other factor. Perhaps the relentless determination exhibited by the Army of the Potomac during that period was a reflection of Lt. Gen. Ulysses S. Grant, who, as commanding general of all the Union armies, closely supervised General Meade. But maybe it was the men as well, many having fought at Gettysburg and exhibited during the following year a certain determination of their own. Consider what happened at the end of the Battle of the Wilderness in early May 1864. Soldiers in the Army of the Potomac

> found themselves . . . filing south . . . , and as they marched the men realized they were not headed toward the river crossings but were going . . . toward the lower edge of the Wilderness. . . . As the men trudged along it suddenly came to them that this march was different. . . . A little cavalcade came riding by . . . and there . . . was Grant, riding in the lead . . . heading south. . . . All of a moment the tired column came alive, and a wild cheer broke the night and men tossed their caps in the darkness. They had had their fill of desperate fighting, and [General Grant] was leading them into nothing except more fighting . . . and somewhere, many miles ahead, there would be victory for those who lived to see it. . . . It was the same on other roads. [Another unit of Union troops] backtracked toward Chancellorsville, and as the men reached that fatal crossroads the veterans knew how the land lay and knew that if they took the left-hand fork they would be retreating and if they turned to the right they would be going on for another fight. The column turned right, and men who made the march wrote that with that turn there was a quiet relaxing of the tension and a lifting of gloom.[19]

Was the attitude exhibited by these Union soldiers in the spring of 1864 a reflection of that moment alone, or did this determination and confidence stem in part from memory of their achievements in Pennsylvania ten months earlier?

During the final year of the war, the victor at Gettysburg, Maj. Gen. George Gordon Meade, retained nominal command of the Army of the Potomac. Meade richly deserved this and gained Grant's trust in 1864.[20] In the middle of 1863, General Meade had positioned himself to earn such respect. Recall, for example, how he deployed his units on the Gettysburg field as if they were chess pieces, often anticipating enemy moves. He did not "throw them into battle piecemeal," but eventually got almost all his troops into action and "let the army fight as an army."[21] Yet Meade did not get carried away at Gettysburg; he kept the 6th Corps largely in reserve. Nor was it languishing somewhere on the wings, as so many of Hooker's units at Chancellorsville had done. The 6th Corps at Gettysburg was poised to enter the fray, which some of Maj. Gen. John Sedgwick's units did during the last two days of the battle. In its aftermath, General Meade continued to demonstrate that he was eminently suited for high command. But I am probably getting carried away with admiration for the general's performances from late 1863 to 1865—given the conclusion, by someone who would know, that "George G. Meade was a competent army commander, and Gettysburg was his finest battle."[22]

During the final months of the war, as Grant and Meade operated against Lee in Virginia, many of the Union soldiers who fought at Gettysburg *remained* part of the Union army in the East.[23] Most of the important officers stayed in place within the Army of the Potomac's hierarchy. These men now knew that they could beat the vaunted rebels. Chris Perello—the aforementioned analyst who believes that "Lee's loss at Gettysburg was not the final or even the biggest nail in the Confederate coffin"—said that, after the battle, "the two armies were back in about the same place, and with the same relative strength, as they had been at the outset of the campaign." Moreover, "in the Army of Northern Virginia, the casualties were replaced fairly quickly, with no loss in quality. The Army of the Potomac actually had a much harder time recovering from the losses in the Gettysburg campaign."[24] Really? At the outset of the Battle of the Wilderness on May 4, 1864, the Union force numbered about 120,000, whereas the Confederates could muster only 66,000 (a disparity more than twice as great compared with Gettysburg).[25]

So if the Northern soldiers would continue to perform well in 1864—and would be *allowed* to act as Meade had let them do at Gettysburg—then perhaps these men knew they could not only measure up against Lee's legions, but also defeat them. And even though the Northerners in the army of the East would no longer be fighting "on their own home ground" as the war moved into its penultimate year, if an opportunity presented itself for more active tactical moves, they were willing and able to do that. With many of those counterattacks at Gettysburg working as well as they did, why not go for flat-out offensive tactics?

Let us delve into the eastern campaigning of 1864–65 and reflect further on how things changed after Gettysburg in the context of further analogies to other wars. Such parallels hark back to the labored "last battle" thesis for Gettysburg and the Civil War in the East explained at the beginning of Chapter 1. If we stand back to obtain an overview of the war in that theater, we see its first two years as a series of distinctly separate large engagements. After Gettysburg, however, we see nonstop campaigning, with engagements proceeding almost immediately from one to the next, with the Army of the Potomac driving the Army of Northern Virginia ever southward from a point west of Fredericksburg to one south of Richmond.

This brings to mind an apprehension—based on the same kind of superficial but useful overview—of World War II in the European theater during the last year of that conflict, as the Allies drove the Germans relentlessly eastward. Now, scholars and astute students of either war or both will grumble about these facile overviews: What about the *battles* at Spotsylvania Courthouse (May 1864) and

Cold Harbor (June 1864) on the one hand, and the Falaise Pocket (August 1944) or Arnhem (September 1944) on the other? My point is that the casual observer has no memory of and perhaps never heard of the named engagements that occurred during the second half of 1864 and in 1944. Instead, a person possessing this basic knowledge describes Lee's army in eastern North America and the German forces in western Europe as being pushed ever backward, driven in that direction again and again by the foes that faced them. Such persons, recalling what they learned in classrooms, probably do not know that the Confederates and the Germans resisted furiously in 1864 and 1944, as opposed to the defending forces simply giving up and giving way after Gettysburg and D day, respectively. Nevertheless, the two wars (in these limited but major theaters of them) took on different characters *after* July 1863 and June 1944. To what extent were these significant turns *because* of what happened on the fields of Gettysburg and the beaches of Normandy—not just considering the events as such, but also the nature of the achievements in southern Pennsylvania and northern France?

Such broad analogies between the mid-nineteenth- and mid-twentieth-century conflicts break down in two particular respects. The Confederates, driven from northern Virginia to Petersburg roughly a year after Gettysburg, became bottled up and besieged near that city in eastern Virginia, leading to months of stalemated trench warfare. This was more like the *First* than the Second World War in Europe. Toward the end of the latter one, in late 1944, the Germans launched a huge counteroffensive from the Ardennes Forest near the German-Belgian border (as was mentioned in the Chapter 3 discussion of the Americans' fighting withdrawal to Elsenborn Ridge on the northern shoulder of the Bulge). It put the Allies on the strategic defensive for a month's time, breaking the momentum of their drive across northern Europe toward Germany. Refocusing our attention on the 1860s: The Army of Northern Virginia, in contrast, launched *no appreciable counteroffensive* during the final twenty-one months of the Civil War. The momentum of the war shifted after Gettysburg, and not because Lee's army was fought out or about to give up: "The Yankees had a little something to do with it."

Just as we should view Gettysburg as much from a Northern perspective as a Southern one, what happened after that campaign occurred in large part because of what the Army of the Potomac began to accomplish the moment the war resumed in earnest, in early May 1864. This led not to pell-mell Southern retreats, but to a series of pitched battles in Virginia throughout that spring. Unspeakable horrors accompanied those battles; but just *maybe* the end was in sight, even if it was not yet imminent, subsequent to and because of the campaigns of the previous year. No Northerner would have made a "light-at-the-end-of-the-tunnel" remark after Fredericksburg and Chancellorsville. One could have made a diametrically opposite prediction had the stand of the U.S. Army at Gettysburg failed in the summer of 1863.

For all of this to be played out in 1864 and into the spring 1865, the Army of Northern Virginia first had to *survive* Gettysburg by escaping back into Virginia. Some historians contend that Meade let it do that—tragically prolonging the war. That their interpretation may be incorrect, and that General Meade kept his massive psychological victory intact during the first half of July 1863, is fodder for the final section of this chapter. Before we come to it, however, we will return to the events of July 3 and then examine the two armies' marches and rides away from Gettysburg.

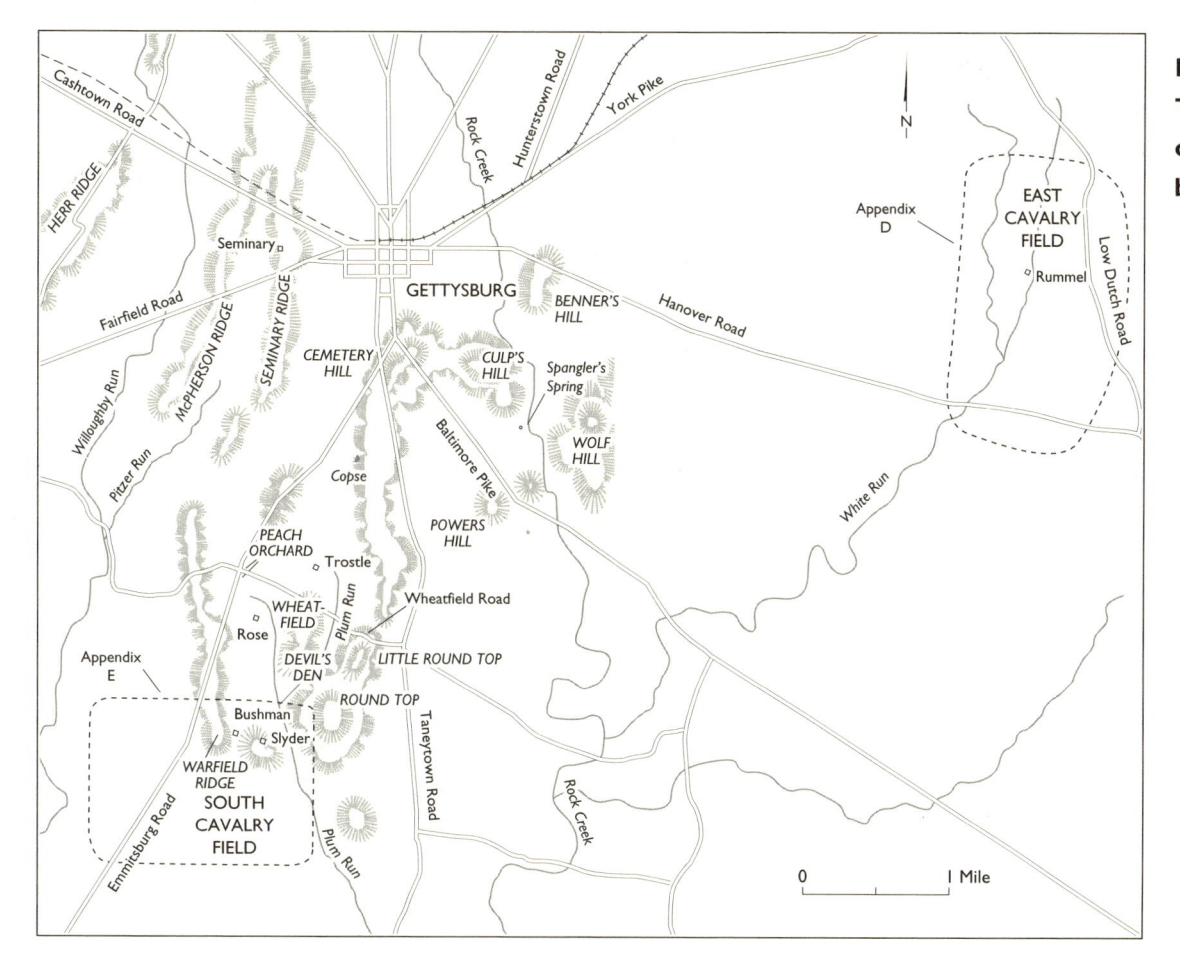

Map 5-1 Theater of cavalry battles, July 3

Late Cavalry Actions

Two cavalry battles within the battle occurred on July 3. Both began before Pickett's Charge and initially involved dismounted troopers. The first action was a clash of cavalry forces east of town to the north of the main infantry action on what is now known as the East Cavalry Field (map 5-1). The second engagement occurred on a southern sector of the main battlefield (map 5-1). That the cavalry battle on the East Field may be *less significant* than some say is suggested by the ambiguous nature of that action—both in terms of how it came to pass and the outcome. For instance, the extent to which the Union cavalrymen "stopped Stuart" (the meaning of which is elaborated on in Appendix D) is difficult to state with conviction and is grist for the Gettysburg controversy mills that keep grinding on.

In contrast, the fighting of mounted Union troopers against Confederate infantry units on the South Field seemed foolhardy and was an unambiguous, albeit small-scale, Union disaster for the Federal horsemen who charged into the rebel right flank. This final sideshow is described in Appendix E.

Chart 5-2
The van of the retreat of Lee's army, and Union cavalry moving westward (early)

ANV → Cavalry Division
- wagon train / Imboden's brigade
- F. Lee's brigade PART
- Hampton's brigade PART / Col. L. Baker *

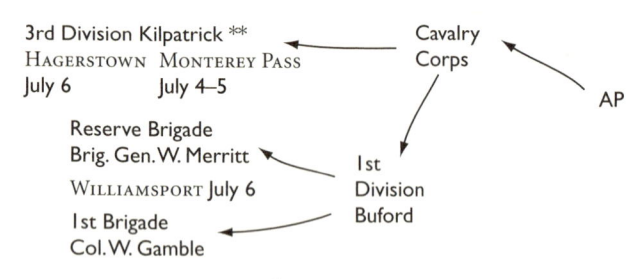

AP → Cavalry Corps
- 3rd Division Kilpatrick ** / Hagerstown July 6 / Monterey Pass July 4–5
- 1st Division Buford
  - Reserve Brigade Brig. Gen. W. Merritt / Williamsport July 6
  - 1st Brigade Col. W. Gamble

* Brig. Gen. W. Hampton was wounded on July 3

** Brig. Gen. J. Kilpatrick's division was bolstered by a brigade under Col. P. Huey detached from Brig. Gen. D. Gregg's 2nd Cavalry Division

The Pursuit

General Lee knew by late on July 3 that he had to get out of Gettysburg. He began preparing to do this by meeting with Brig. Gen. John Imboden that night. This cavalryman and his troopers (chart 5-2), who had been shadowing the Army of Northern Virginia to the west during the campaign, were posted in the rear during the later stages of the battle. Now Lee ordered Imboden to lead the thousands of wagons that would transport the Confederate wounded back to Virginia. Cavalry brigades from Stuart's division led by Brig. Gen. Fitzhugh Lee and Col. Lawrence S. Baker (chart 5-2) accompanied Imboden to guard the flanks and rear of the long train of retreating wagons.

The Confederate cavalry's involvement in the first phase of the rebel retreat signifies that the activities of mounted men were most significant during this stage of the campaign. In fact, almost all the combat actions involved cavalrymen on both sides. General Stuart was as active as could be during the retreat. His troopers did a fine job of screening the infantry's retreat and protecting the Potomac river crossing points from thrusts by Federal forces. As it happened, elements of the Union Cavalry Corps made all of those attacking moves. For Stuart's part, his high-quality performance during the final ten days of the campaign mirrored how well he had done during its first phase, which involved the Battle of Brandy Station and the fights to control the Loudoun Valley (June 9-21).

That seemed like ages ago to the weary survivors of the monumental struggle at Gettysburg as they arose on July 4, 1863. Union skirmishers near the right wing of the Northern army still at Gettysburg reported that the rebel left had pulled back, swinging around from Culp's Hill to Oak Hill—as if the Army of Northern Virginia were preparing to withdraw. Indeed, the retreat began that Saturday when General Imboden's troopers left Gettysburg at 4 P.M. in advance of the seventeen-mile-long column of wagons carrying their human cargo of wounded men headed toward Cashtown and Chambersburg (map 5-2). The Confederates' destination was Williamsport, Maryland (maps 5-2–5-8), one of the places where they intended to cross the Potomac River on their way back to Virginia.

General Meade raised rebel hopes for reaching Southern soil by waiting some forty-eight hours after the Confederates began to leave Gettysburg before the main body of his army began its pursuit.[26] Meade was psychologically exhausted (as some of his post-battle letters to his wife implied), and the Army of the Potomac was physically so. It did not *have* to pursue or otherwise act vigorously, whereas the equally exhausted Confederates were forced to steel themselves for a long and potentially perilous march. Survival of the Army of Northern Virginia was paramount for Southern war aims. Meade may have appreciated this fact, but perhaps from too narrow a perspective.[27] In command for only a week, at the front of his mind was a narrower accomplishment: he had stopped the invasion. "We have done well enough," the general told one cavalry officer.[28] Meade was not the only general officer to express this sentiment. Even before the pursuit began,

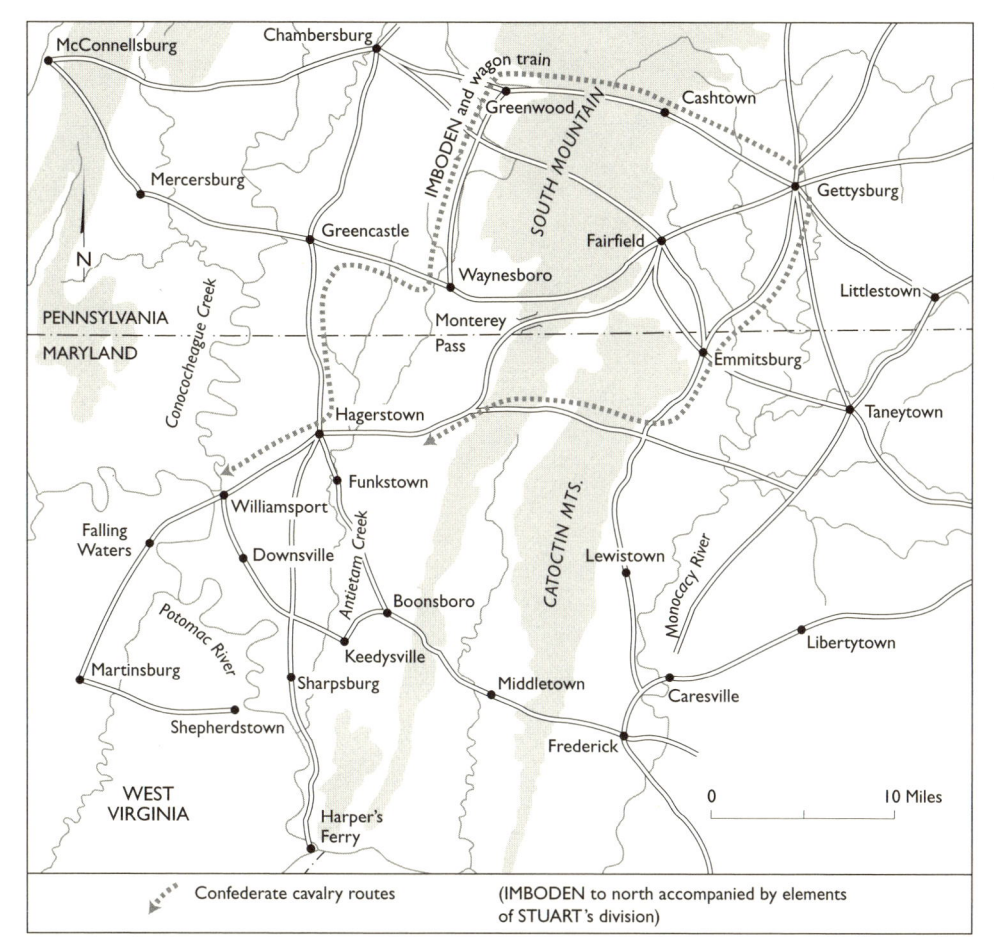

**Map 5-2
The retreats from
Gettysburg of cavalry units
and the wagon train**

Brig. Gen. Gouverneur Warren noted that "the tone among most of the prominent officers was that we had quite saved the country for the time ... that we might jeopardize all that we had done by trying too much."[29] Later, General Meade—still relying on the views of his corps commanders (chart 5-6 and note 32)—would defer to this sentiment.

The Union high command planned the pursuit prudently from another perspective: not to race directly after Lee's army, but in the main to move *south* (map 5-4). A march in that direction would cover Washington (always a concern), shorten the Federals' supply line, and perhaps keep the Northern force within striking distance of the Confederate withdrawal. The problem of Union supply was not a trivial one. Many of the soldiers were without shoes at this time (they were not to be resupplied with them until July 8). Another supply concern was that to follow Lee's army directly would leave the Federals with precious little forage in the rebels' wake.

The cavalry and wagon train led by Imboden approached Williamsport on the afternoon of July 5 (map 5-2). However, some of the wagons did not leave Gettysburg until that day and would not reach the river until the Sixth. It had rained hard on the Fourth, and Federal cavalry twice attacked the retreating column the next day. As the van of this part of the rebel retreat struggled toward the river crossing points, the Southern troopers found the pontoon bridge at Falling Waters (southwest of Williamsport on the West Virginia side) destroyed. This had been done on July 4 by elements of Maj. Gen. William French's garrison force previously stationed at Harper's Ferry, West Virginia, then at Frederick, Maryland

Map 5-3
Union cavalry leaves Gettysburg for the river crossing points

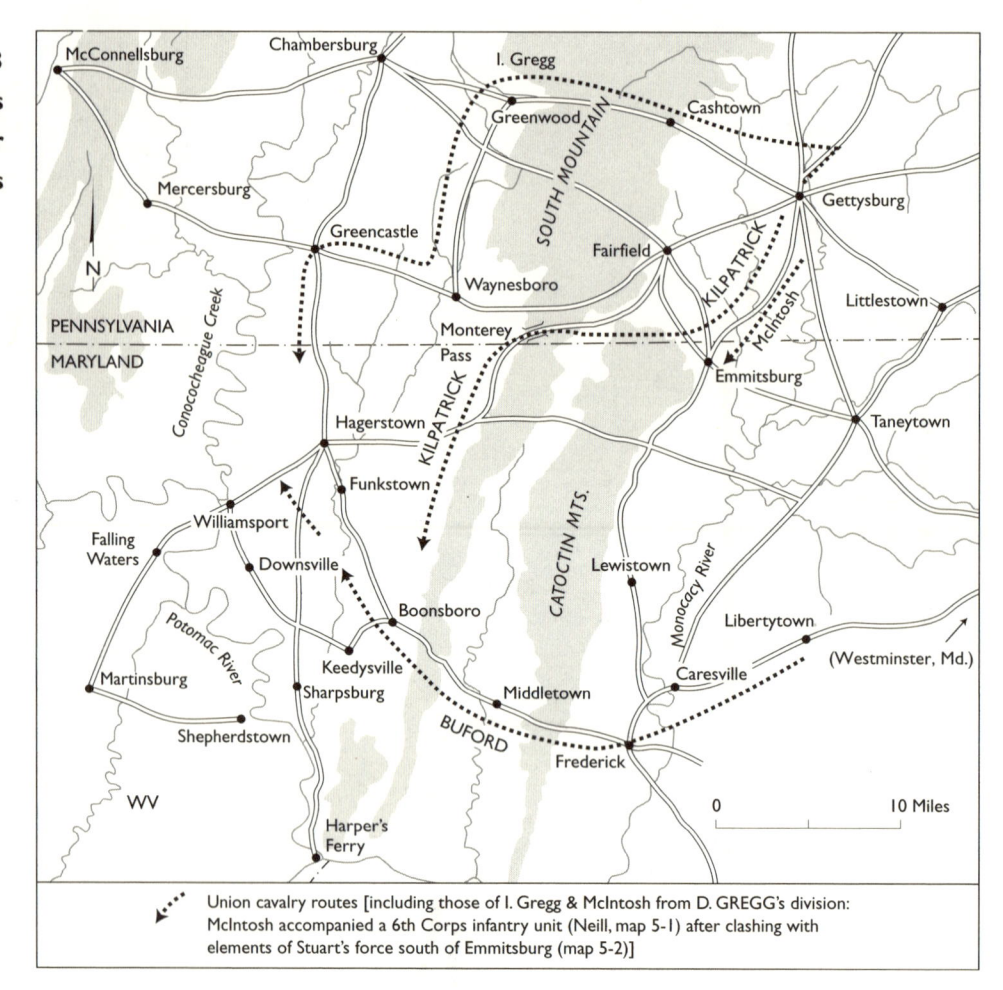

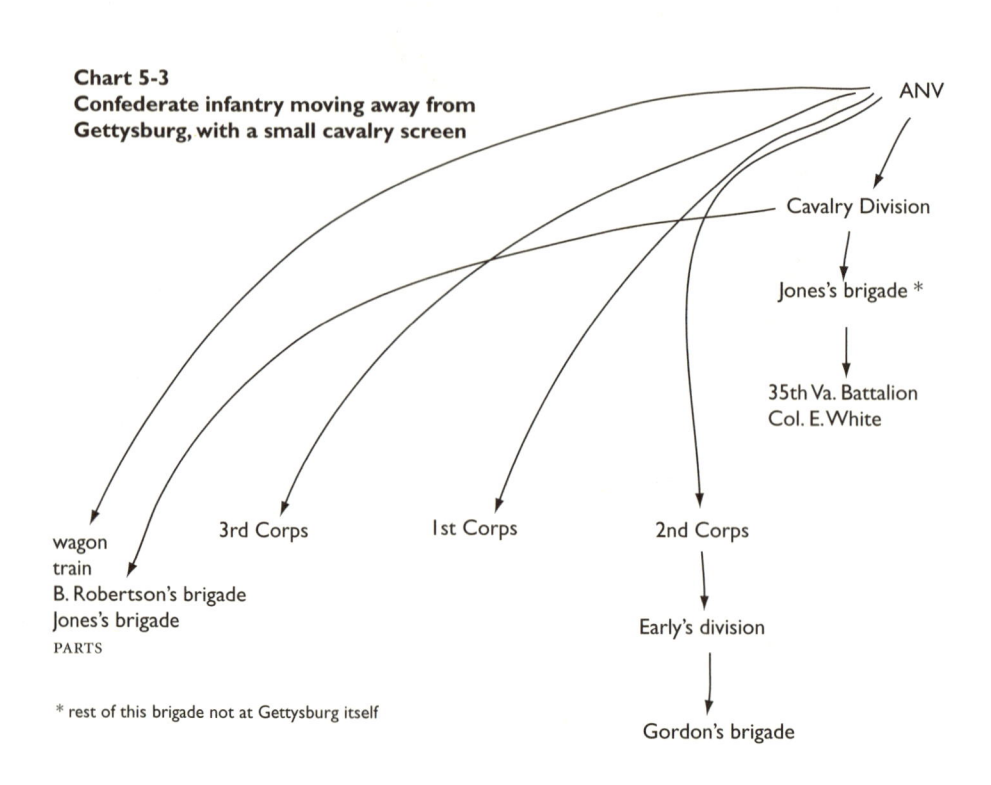

Union cavalry routes [including those of I. Gregg & McIntosh from D. GREGG's division: McIntosh accompanied a 6th Corps infantry unit (Neill, map 5-1) after clashing with elements of Stuart's force south of Emmitsburg (map 5-2)]

Chart 5-3
Confederate infantry moving away from Gettysburg, with a small cavalry screen

ANV
→ Cavalry Division
→ Jones's brigade *
→ 35th Va. Battalion Col. E. White

→ wagon train
B. Robertson's brigade
Jones's brigade
PARTS

→ 3rd Corps
→ 1st Corps
→ 2nd Corps
→ Early's division
→ Gordon's brigade

* rest of this brigade not at Gettysburg itself

254   THE STAND OF THE U.S. ARMY AT GETTYSBURG

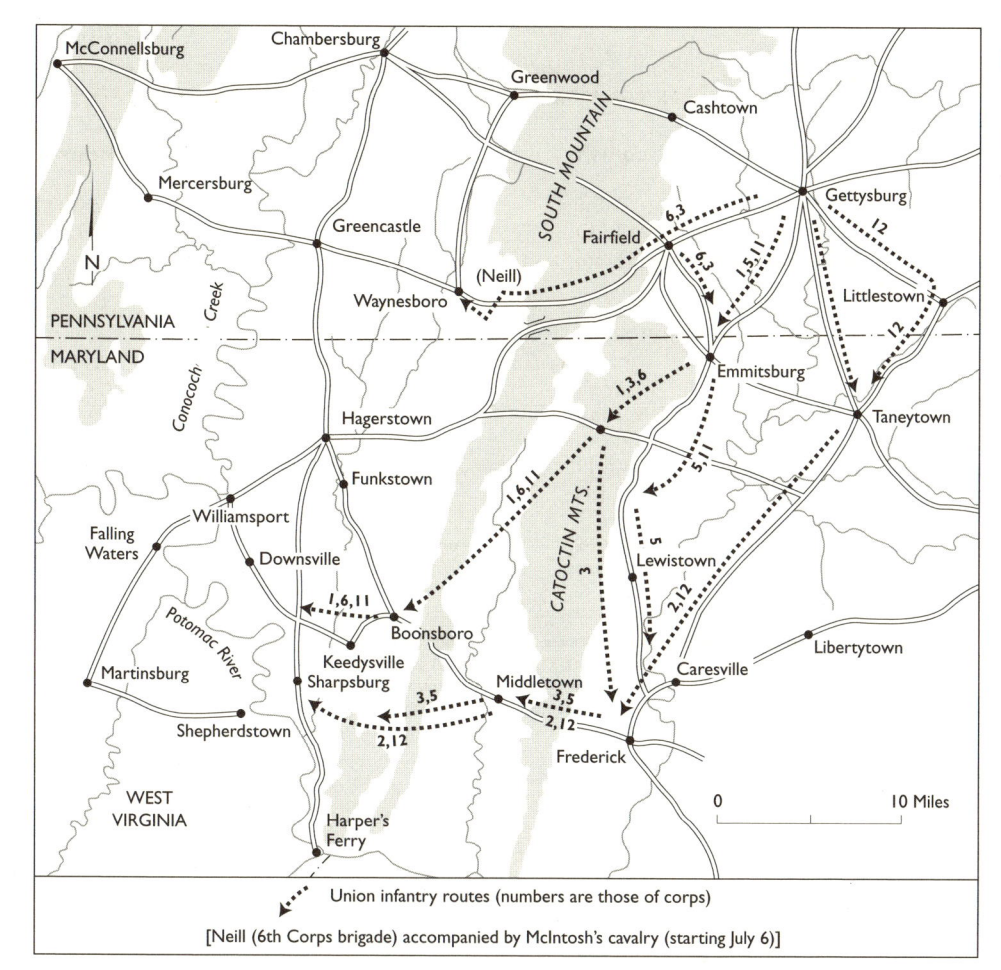

**Map 5-4
The Union infantry pursues Lee, taking the inside track to the south**

(chart 5-6). So the crossing into West Virginia was not going to be quick and easy.

The main body of the rebel army was far from the crossing points on the Fifth. On the Sixth, Imboden was attacked by elements of Brig. Gen. John Buford's cavalry division (chart 5-2), which was heading toward the Potomac River (map 5-3).[30] Supported by additional elements of Stuart's cavalry division (arriving at Williamsport via Emmitsburg and Hagerstown) and by Confederate infantry from Winchester, Virginia, who had just been ferried across the Potomac, the Confederate cavalrymen drove off Brig. Gen. Wesley Merritt's and Col. William Gamble's troopers during a half-hour fight in the early evening on July 6.[31] The twenty-seven-hundred-man Confederate force at Williamsport then prepared to wait for the main body of Lee's retreating infantry.

The Confederate foot soldiers were marching away from Gettysburg by a path that was different from the roads on which the Southern infantry had marched northward in June. Using a route south of that taken by Imboden's train (maps 5-2 and 5-5) and west of the incipient moves by the Union infantry (map 5-4), Lee's main body departed Gettysburg during the afternoon of Saturday, July 4. The Confederates were led by a second wagon train carrying additional wounded men and many of the supplies captured during the campaign. That large fraction of the Army of Northern Virginia initially went west on the Fairfield Road through Monterey Pass and headed toward Hagerstown (map 5-5). Federal cavalry under Brig. Gen. Judson Kilpatrick (chart 5-2) attacked the second Confederate wagon train at Monterey Pass (map 5-3) on the night of July 4–5. This resulted in the destruction of huge numbers of wagons and the capture of more than a thousand rebels. After this engagement, Kilpatrick took the captured men and material about ten miles away to the southwest, across the Maryland border. These Federal troopers thus may have squandered an opportunity to *block* the mountain pass, which was on the route being followed by Lee's main body.[32]

Meanwhile, the weary Confederate infantrymen were marching a shorter route compared with the one they had used in Pennsylvania in June, which took them through Chambersburg. This time, however, the rebel soldiers had to traverse rugged South Mountain. The Confederate wagons and their mounted escort were followed by the infantry corps under Generals Hill, Longstreet, and Ewell in that order (chart 5-3). General Early's division was the last to leave Gettysburg, departing from Seminary Ridge west of town. Brigadier General John B. Gordon's brigade took up the rear, screened by Lt. Col. Elijah V. White's 35th Virginia Cavalry Battalion (chart 5-3).[33] The Confederate columns moved slowly, not clearing the Gettysburg area until the morning of July 5. On that afternoon and into the following day, outlying Federal skirmishers and cavalrymen harassed elements of the retreating rebel force. In particular, General Kilpatrick's division converged on Hagerstown as the Confederate infantry van approached that Maryland town (maps 5-3 and 5-5). In a significant cavalry battle occurring within Hagerstown and its environs on July 6, General Stuart's troopers moving in from the east (map 5-2) cleared this region and Kilpatrick withdrew toward Williamsport late in the day—about the time when General Buford's mounted force was trying to get at the rebel defense ringing that river crossing point (map 5-3, chart 5-2).[34]

General Longstreet had by then taken the lead of the Confederate infantry withdrawal, and his corps reached Hagerstown on the afternoon of July 6. Hill and Ewell, whose corps closed into that area by noon the following day, followed Longstreet. Later on July 7 the van of the retreating infantry approached Williamsport (map 5-5). To facilitate the construction of a new bridge across the Potomac at Falling Waters, West Virginia, General Lee ordered his infantry to deploy in a defensive arc east of the Potomac, which runs north-south at Williamsport and turns westward toward Falling Waters about eight miles downstream (map 5-6).

While cavalry clashed near Funkstown and Boonsboro, Maryland, July 7–10, the Army of Northern Virginia prepared its defenses near the Potomac River, finalizing its positions on the Twelfth. Ewell's corps was on the left end of the line, anchored on a hill one mile west of Hagerstown. Hill's corps occupied the center on high ground extending south and east, and Longstreet's corps was on the right, anchored on the Potomac at Downsville, nine miles from the northern end of the line (map 5-6, chart 5-5). The defensive position was formidable, consisting of a long, broken line of rifle pits and artillery-protecting dugouts formed on high ground and protected over much of its distance by Marsh Creek and soggy bottomland just to the east (map 5-6). There were two roughly parallel lines of entrenchments, that is, a defense in depth; and the frontline defenders had set up their infantry and artillery positions to inflict a deadly crossfire on any attackers that came their way. Perhaps Lee had in mind to invite an attack (map 5-6), the results of which might mitigate the disaster that had just occurred at Gettysburg.[35] Meanwhile, Lee had his troops start rebuilding the pontoon bridge at Falling Waters and hoped the rain-swollen Potomac would recede at the Williamsport ford, which was over thirteen feet deep on July 6.

For his part, General Meade sent a small portion of his infantry away from

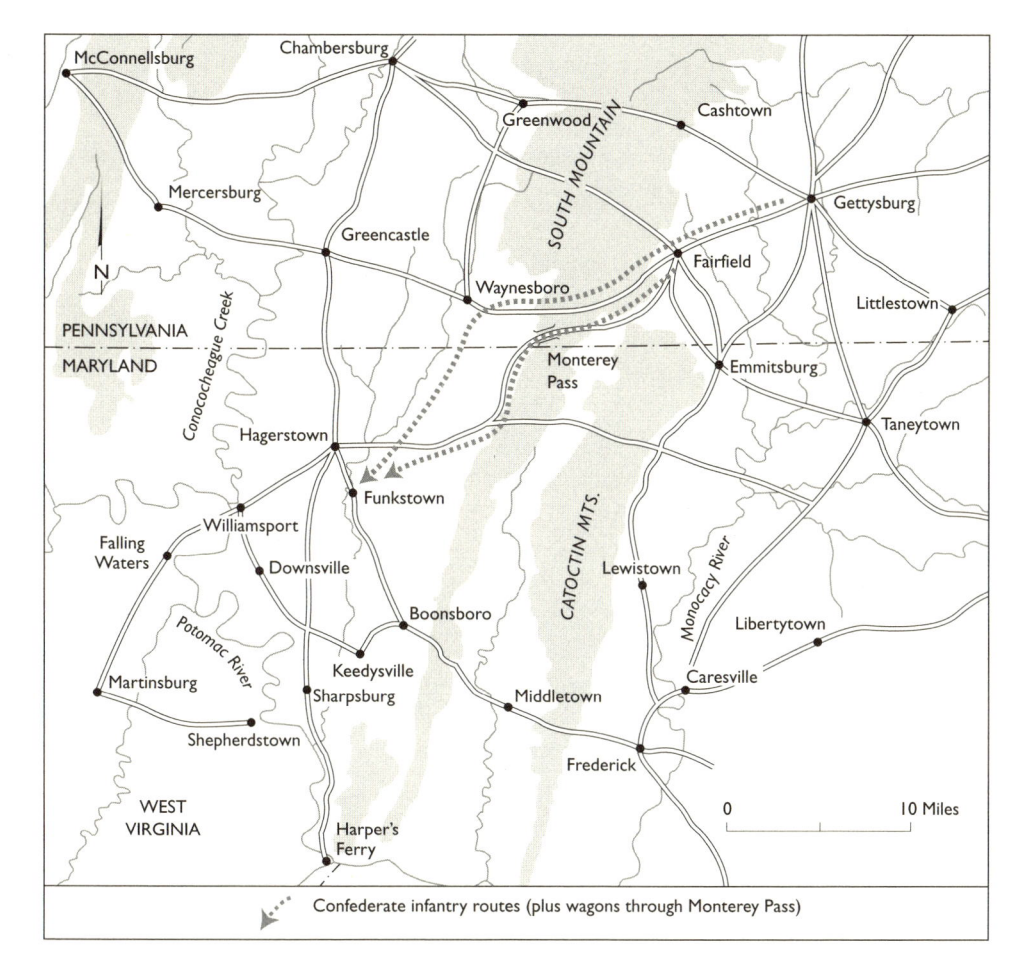

Map 5-5

The Confederate infantry retreats from Gettysburg

Gettysburg in a west-northwesterly direction on July 5 (map 5-3). This may have been a day too late. Meade, however, felt stymied by the heavy rain on the Fourth. Added to this were his exhaustion and a sense that his army was in a similar state.[36] Nevertheless, elements of the 6th and 3rd Corps moved off Cemetery Ridge that Sunday, aiming to follow the line of the Confederates' initial infantry withdrawal (map 5-5).[37] Yet this was only a reconnaissance in force, for it had already been decided that the main body would head south from Gettysburg. The task force that roughly followed Lee's main column of retreating infantry was in part composed of a Union brigade from the 6th Corps. This unit—except for all of its marching, a fresh one that had been lightly engaged at Gettysburg—was commanded by Maj. Gen. John Sedgwick (chart 5-4). On the morning of July 4, Sedgwick sent Brig. Gen. Thomas H. Neill's brigade forward toward a gap in the low mountains west of Fairfield, Pennsylvania (map 5-4), which was held by a group of rebels. A Union cavalry brigade under Col. John B. McIntosh (chart 5-4), which had initially gone south from Gettysburg and tangled briefly with part of Stuart's column of troopers on July 5 (maps 5-2 and 5-3), was ordered to join General Neill's pursuit force the next day.

The remainder of the Union infantry exiting Gettysburg headed in the direction of Fairfield then was rerouted south toward Emmitsburg, where most of the Army of the Potomac was headed (map 5-4). General Meade was planning to

**Map 5-6
Confederate infantry positions near the Potomac River**

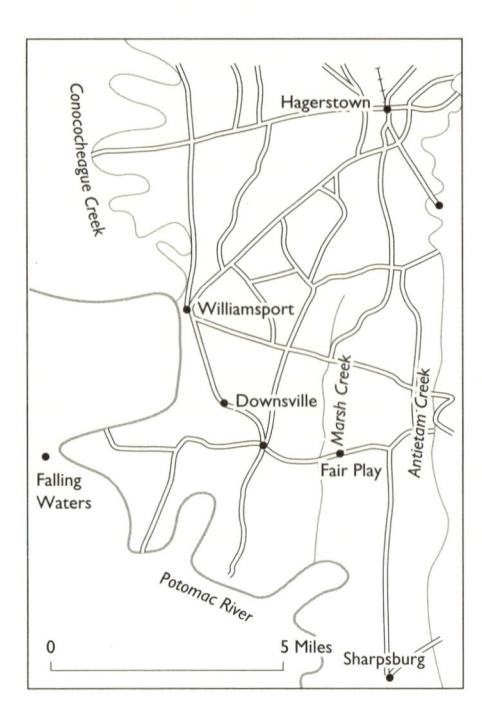

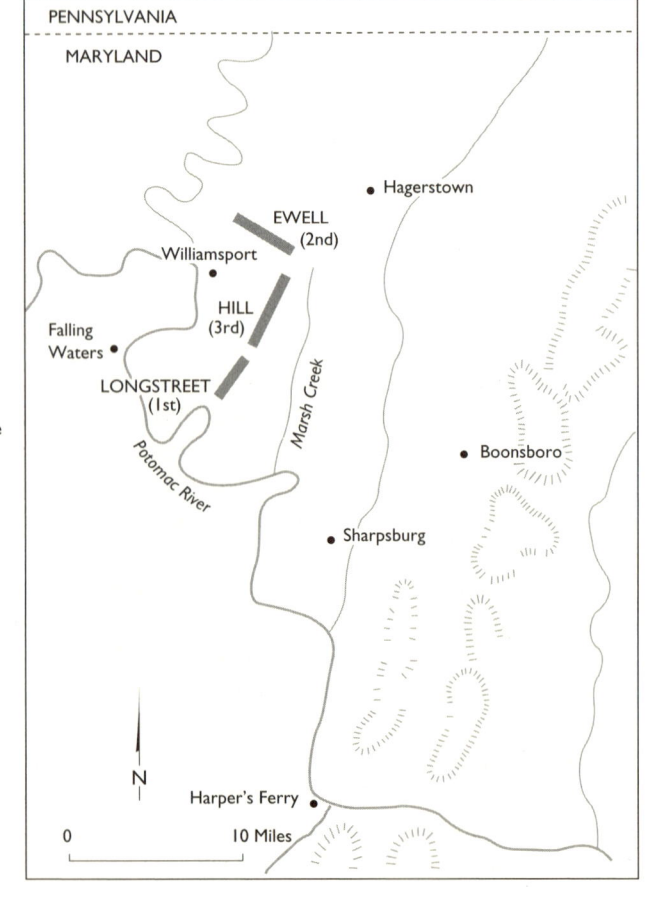

**Chart 5-4
Union units following the Confederate forces westward**

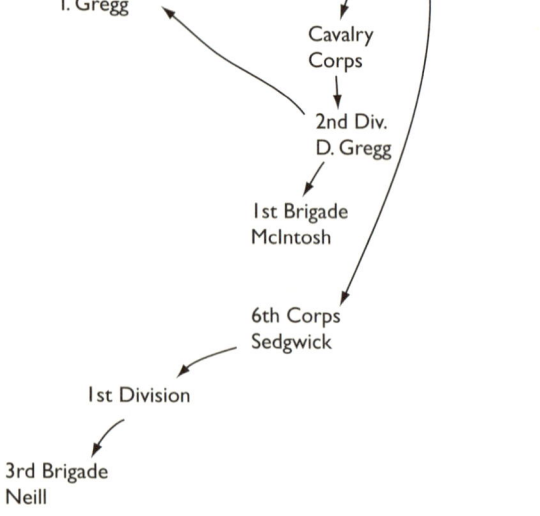

AP → Cavalry Corps → 2nd Div. D. Gregg → 1st Brigade McIntosh
Cavalry Corps → 3rd Brigade I. Gregg
AP → 6th Corps Sedgwick → 1st Division → 3rd Brigade Neill

( ) numbers of Confederate corps

258 THE STAND OF THE U.S. ARMY AT GETTYSBURG

strike west across the Catoctin Mountains, after which his units would rendezvous at Middletown, Maryland (map 5-4). There, the aforementioned shoe problem was alleviated on July 8 by supplies arriving from Westminster and Frederick. From Middletown, the Federals would have to cross South Mountain to get at Lee.

As the Union army marched into Maryland, it proceeded toward the Frederick area over three routes (map 5-4). On July 7, Meade arrived at Frederick, where he had first taken command of the army seemingly a lifetime ago. He expressed that very sentiment and revealed his enervated state in a letter to his wife on July 8.[38]

After moving west toward Middletown as planned, much of the Northern army had crossed South Mountain by July 9 and was headed toward Boonsboro, Maryland, eight miles southeast of Williamsport (maps 5-3 and 5-4). There was an exchange that day between General Meade and Maj. Gen. Henry W. Halleck in Washington in which the latter urged the Army of the Potomac to make "forced marches." Meade replied in an irritated manner that that was exactly what his army was doing.[39] The tone of Meade's message was legitimate, although it is fair to say that his army slowed its pursuit significantly once it reached Frederick and turned west toward where Lee's army was dug in.

The westward route taken by the Army of the Potomac after the Eighth was similar to the one it had followed in the Antietam campaign. Nine months later, the 12th Corps, on the left flank of the pursuing Federal left wing, visited Sharpsburg, Maryland, where the great battle was fought on September 17, 1862 (map 5-4).

As Meade's army marched away from Frederick toward South Mountain, it crept toward Williamsport (maps 5-4 and 5-7). Finally, on July 11 and 12, Meade deployed his forces roughly parallel to the Confederate lines (maps 5-6 and 5-8). The Union 6th and 1st Corps were on the right, the 5th Corps occupied the center, and the 2nd and 12th Corps held the left end of the line to the south. The 11th Corps was placed in reserve (chart 5-4). Two cavalry divisions covered the extremities of the line (chart 5-5)—Buford on the left flank and Kilpatrick on the right, west of Hagerstown (map 5-8).

On July 12, Meade sent a message to General in Chief Halleck in Washington, saying that he intended to attack the Confederate positions. A probing move involving elements of three Federal corps was conducted, but the putative attack was called off when another summer storm erupted. This reconnaissance in force was ordered because Meade and his corps commanders were largely unaware of the enemy's positions. Where exactly were the rebel corps? How good might their defensive positions be? To discuss this situation and come to a decision about a possible action on July 13, Meade held another of his councils of war on the night of July 12. Ten Union generals were present in addition to Meade. The army commander evinced a desire to "do something," despite the fact that he and the rest were still ignorant of the Confederate positions. But General Meade as usual seemed unwilling to act without the approval of his subordinate commanders, who voted seven–three *against* attacking (chart 5-6). Those in the majority believed that the rebel positions were probably too strong, and that if the Army of the Potomac were defeated, the door to Washington and Baltimore would be open.[40] One cannot stress enough that General Meade's frequent consultations with his subordinate commanders during the campaign suggest that he regarded himself as a peer of the men with whom he had so recently been on an equal footing.

Based on the outcome of this most recent conference and to avoid "blindly attacking the enemy," Meade gave conservative orders for reconnoitering the Con-

**Map 5-7
The armies approach the river crossing points**

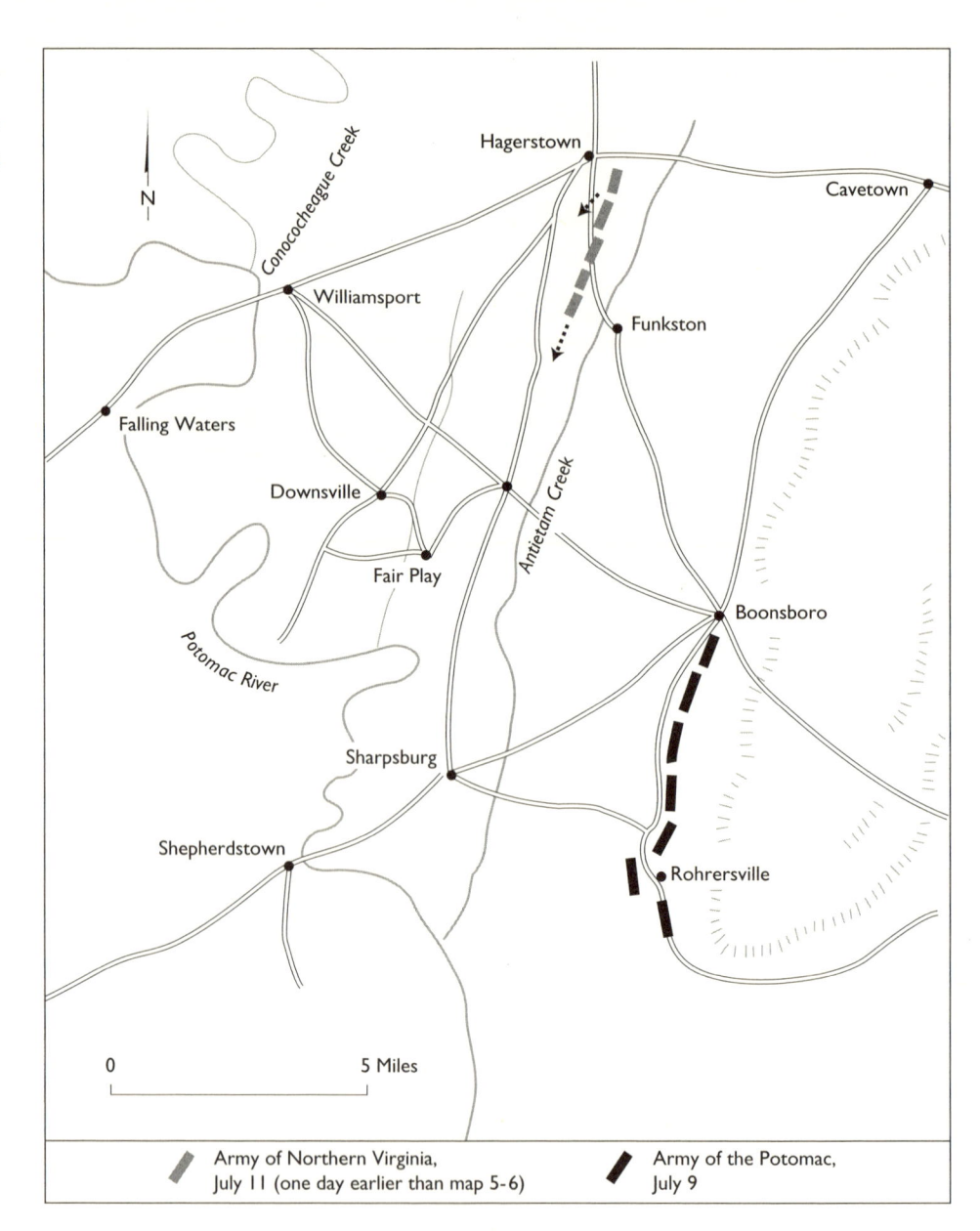

Army of Northern Virginia, July 11 (one day earlier than map 5-6)

Army of the Potomac, July 9

federate lines on July 13.[41] Union men did make reconnaissances that day, with Meade himself participating on horseback. In the evening, Halleck sent Meade a telegram urging an aggressive move against the rebel army: "You are strong enough to attack and defeat the enemy. . . . Do not call a Council of War . . . [which] never fight. Do not let the enemy escape."[42] Halleck's call to battle from afar was, for once, insightful, given what had happened the previous evening. The general in chief may have mainly wanted to go on record as having urged the destruction of the Army of Northern Virginia in Maryland (given that this had not happened in Pennsylvania). However, to cover all his bases, other of Halleck's remarks transmitted to Meade after the battle suggested that the Army of the Potomac act with caution.[43]

Immediately after Gettysburg, when Meade had decided *not* to plunge down Cemetery Ridge after the enemy, President Lincoln was particularly distressed by

Chart 5-5
The two armies facing each other near the Potomac River

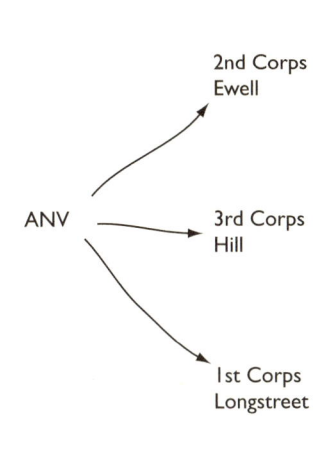

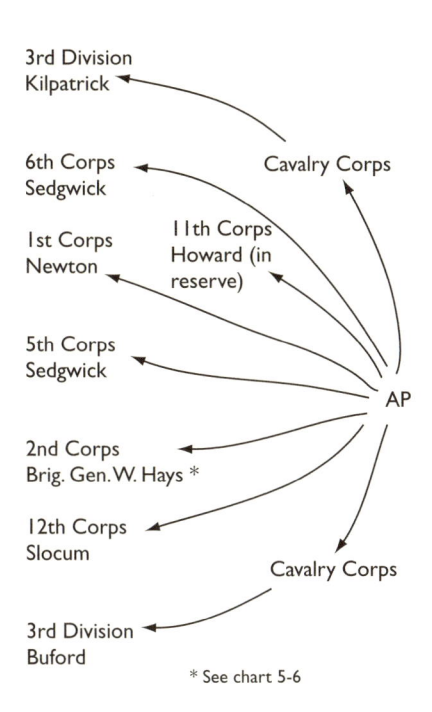

```
                            3rd Division
                            Kilpatrick
        2nd Corps           6th Corps        Cavalry Corps
        Ewell               Sedgwick
                            1st Corps        11th Corps
                            Newton           Howard (in
                                             reserve)
ANV --> 3rd Corps           5th Corps
        Hill                Sedgwick                        AP
                            2nd Corps
                            Brig. Gen. W. Hays *
        1st Corps           12th Corps
        Longstreet          Slocum           Cavalry Corps
                            3rd Division
                            Buford
                                             * See chart 5-6
```

a phrase formulated by the Army of the Potomac's commander. In an order General Meade wrote on July 4, he spoke of how important it seemed to "drive from our soil every vestige of the presence of the invader."[44] Lincoln's fulmination over the worm's-eye-view goal articulated by Meade was perhaps naive. Halleck's cautious words, and Meade's actions that were consistent with them, ran counter to the president's armchair quarterbacking—thankfully so for the Union cause.

The Escape

To appreciate the legitimacy of Meade's prudence, let us look at the situation from the Army of Northern Virginia's perspective on the eve of its departure from the sliver of Maryland it still occupied. Near the Falling Waters crossing point, across the river on the Maryland side (map 5-6), a *third* defensive line of Confederate soldiers had been deployed. This further suggests that even if Robert E. Lee was not necessarily hoping that his foe would attack him, he was really ready for them. However, the Potomac River had subsided enough by July 13 to permit use of the Williamsport ford (maps 5-6 and 5-7). The pontoon bridge also had been rebuilt there and floated downriver to Falling Waters, where it was reassembled. Lee thus exercised some discretion of his own—as opposed to waiting indefinitely at the edge of Maryland for Meade to get his forces together and attack.

The Army of Northern Virginia's commander therefore decided to get out while the getting was good. General Lee ordered Ewell's 2nd Corps to cross over into West Virginia at the ford. The other two corps were to use the bridge, and Longstreet got his troops on the march to cross there at 5 P.M. on the Thirteenth. The bulk of his 1st Corps left its defensive positions at dusk. The rear of Longstreet's corps took until daybreak the next morning to complete its crossing. This component of the escape was unnoticed and unharried by the Union army.

Map 5-8

Two armies facing each other near the Potomac River

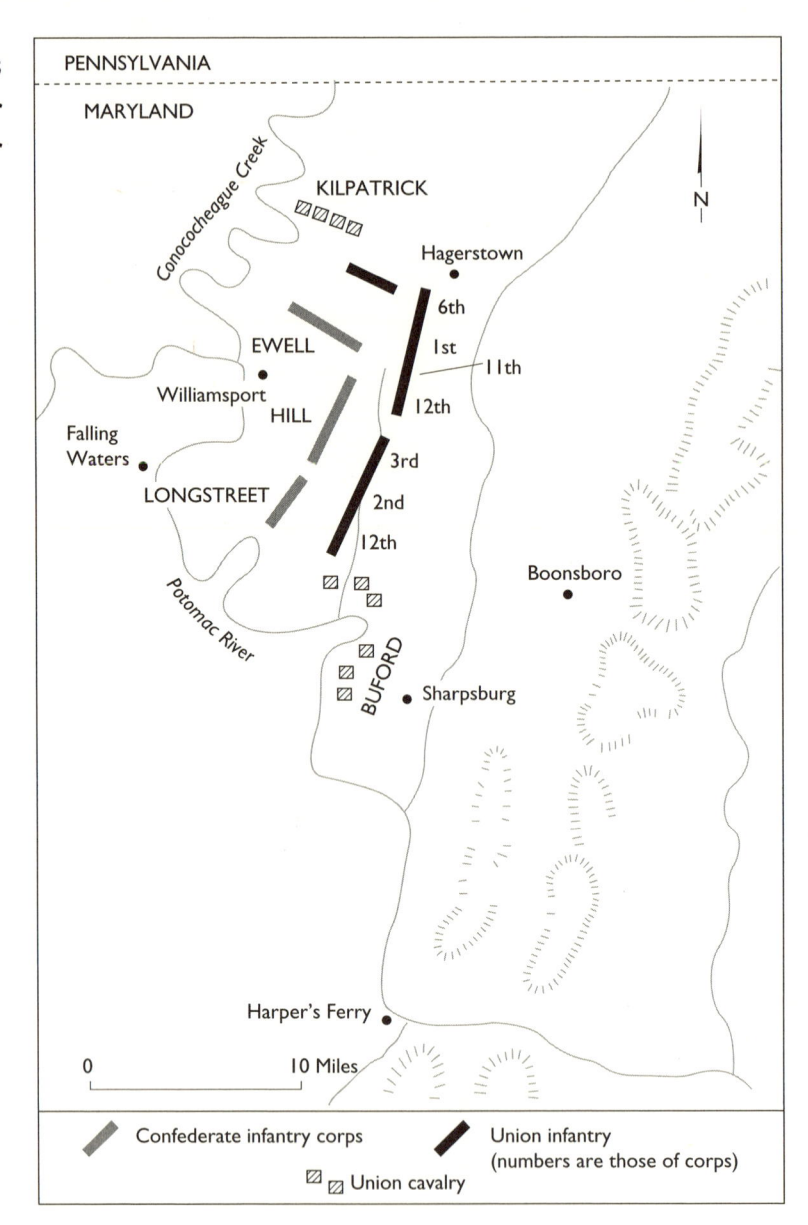

Overnight, the rains came again, making it more difficult for Ewell to ford the river. But cross it he did, with the water often up to the armpits of his 2nd Corps's infantry and artillerymen.[45] Major General Robert E. Rodes's division was the first of Ewell's units to cross, beginning around midnight and finishing at about eight the next morning. A few hours before that time, Hill's corps began to march across the bridge, following Longstreet.

Now, the final scene of this final act of the Gettysburg campaign: Elements of the Army of Northern Virginia seemed ripe for an attack during the early hours of July 14. Ewell could not help defend and Longstreet was barely in a position to carry out such actions; thus, Hill was isolated. This situation was exacerbated by the premature departure of Brig. Gen. Fitzhugh Lee's cavalry brigade (chart 5-7), which crossed the Falling Waters bridge behind Longstreet's corps, thinking that it was the tail end of their army's escaping infantry. It was not, because A. P. Hill's corps was the trailing Confederate unit. The progress of its withdrawal had been slow, as it took twelve hours for that body of men to march seven miles to the bridge (map 5-8).

Union cavalrymen discovered the crossing movements at about 3 A.M. on the Fourteenth, but elements of Generals Buford's and Kilpatrick's cavalry divisions did not begin attacking until about eleven. Those actions were too little, too late—especially in the case of the first of the attacks. The focus of the Union troopers' stabs at the rebels' rear was Maj. Gen. Henry Heth's division (chart 5-7)—which had formed the van of the Confederate advance back on July 1 and now brought up the escaping 3rd Corps's rear. Heth's division, weary from its difficult march to the river, rested in a line it had formed adjacent to the bridgehead behind a screen of Confederate cavalry.

This led to the last-gasp actions within the final act of the campaign. First, a small group of Union cavalry led by Maj. Peter A. Weber of the 6th Michigan advanced toward Heth's line (chart 5-7). The Southerners fired. Bear in mind the deadly effect musketry can have on troopers riding into an attack (as exemplified in Appendix E). Indeed, as Weber and his forty troopers charged into the rebel line, many of the horsemen were shot from their mounts or captured. Only three escaped, and Major Weber was killed. The Confederates suffered only two casualties. One of them was Brig. Gen. Johnston Pettigrew, a prominent figure just before the battle and on July 3, who had succeeded Heth as division commander on July 1. He was mortally wounded during the final action near the river on July 14 and died in Virginia three days later. Lee could ill afford the additional loss of another large-unit commander.

There were to be further losses in Hill's corps. A second, larger wave of Union cavalry began to assail the tail end of the Confederate withdrawal. The latter was now in jeopardy because the supposedly screening cavalry had left prematurely and disappeared across the pontoon bridge. Heth asked for reinforcements.[46] The response was an order for him to fall back toward the river, away from the advancing Union troopers, while a brigade from Lane's 3rd Corps division (chart 5-7) moved a short distance eastward to his aid. The soldiers in Heth's division received this protection from Lane's reinforcing troops and retreated, but the Union cavalry captured several hundred rebel infantrymen in this action.[47] Yet the rebels at the bridgehead were able to conduct a fighting withdrawal to the riverbank, and most of them got away.

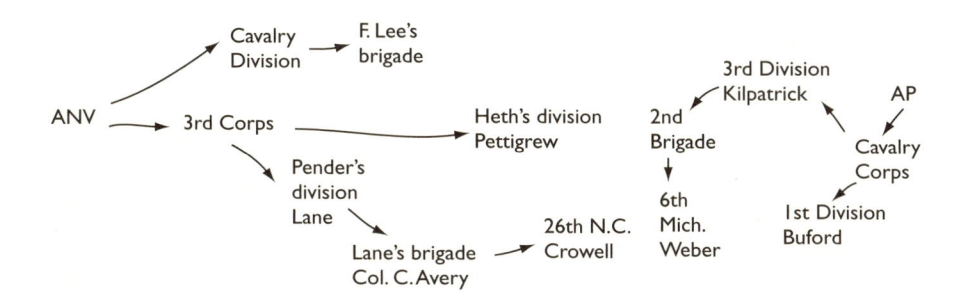

Chart 5-6
Union Council of War, night of July 12

In favor of attacking	Against attacking
Maj. Gen. O. Howard	Maj. Gen. W. French *
Maj. Gen. A. Pleasonton	Brig. Gen. W. Hays **
Brig. Gen. J. Wadsworth	Maj. Gen. A. Humphreys †
	Maj. Gen. J. Sedgwick
	Maj. Gen. H. Slocum
	Maj. Gen. G. Sykes
	Brig. Gen. G. Warren

* Commanding a force garrisoned at Harper's Ferry, W. Va., then Frederick, Md., during the battle. On July 9, two of French's brigades were attached to the Army of the Potomac and he was given command of the 3rd Corps.

** William Hays assumed command of the 2nd Corps July 3, after Gen. Hancock was wounded. William Hays had previously been a brigade commander in the Army of the Potomac's 2nd Corps. He was captured during the Battle of Chancellorsville and when exchanged for a Union-held prisoner on May 15, 1863, he was a general without a job. When Generals Hancock and Gibbon were wounded at Gettysburg, this left Brig. Gen. J. Caldwell as the senior division commander in the 2nd Corps. However, he was a volunteer, and they were frowned upon as corps commanders. Thus, William Hays was summoned to lead the 2nd Corps after the battle. He did not last long in this position, being replaced as 2nd Corps commander by Gen. Warren on August 12, 1863.

† New Chief of Staff. Gen. Butterfield, his predecessor, was wounded July 3.

Chart 5-7
Final actions of the Gettysburg campaign, near the bridge at Falling Waters

ANV → Cavalry Division → F. Lee's brigade
ANV → 3rd Corps → Heth's division Pettigrew
3rd Corps → Pender's division Lane → Lane's brigade Col. C. Avery → 26th N.C. Crowell
2nd Brigade → 6th Mich. Weber
3rd Division Kilpatrick → 2nd Brigade
AP → Cavalry Corps → 3rd Division Kilpatrick
AP → Cavalry Corps → 1st Division Buford

The final body of Southerners to escape across the pontoon bridge was the 28th North Carolina, command of which had devolved to Lt. James M. Crowell (chart 5-7). As the regiment crossed, the ropes attaching the bridge to the Maryland shore were cut, and the pontoons drifted out into the river. The two great armies of the East had finally parted.

Looking back, it might seem as though General Meade let the rebels escape. This began when he failed to go over to the offensive in the late afternoon of July 3. Moreover, he never really menaced his foe during the ensuing eleven days.[48] President Lincoln most prominently led those who verbally assailed Meade for his apparent inaction following the repulse of Pickett's Charge.[49] The various attacks on Meade's performance began in July 1863 and have continued ever since. But some reflection does not leave those criticisms as the *only* voices raised about Meade's actions.[50]

From a tactical perspective, the Army of the Potomac would have had a most difficult go of things if it had assaulted the Confederate positions ringing the crossing points at Williamsport and Falling Waters. Meade must have been vividly aware of the advantages an entrenched force had, and of how well Southern soldiers could perform under any circumstances. Factoring in these concerns, it is likely that he feared his troops would be bloodily repulsed if they launched a counterattack after the destruction of Pickett's Charge on July 3. Whereas these considerations may not excuse Meade's failure to pursue with more celerity in particular, in general he may have decided not to snatch defeat from the jaws of victory. Therefore, Meade's actions (or lack thereof) seem to have been more of a *decision* than a case of timid demurring. He was backed up by the formally voiced opinions of the general officers in his command (chart 5-6). Perhaps Meade was relieved by the caution they too expressed.

Years later, another American military force found itself in a similar situation. The more modern scenario was played out during the Battle of Midway on the morning of June 4, 1942, when dive-bombers from three U.S. aircraft carriers rained bombs on a Japanese carrier task force. In the space of five minutes, three of those ships were burning out of control, and a fourth one was destroyed later that afternoon. The American naval force was a distinct underdog at the outset of the battle, but its stunning victory marked a turning point in that vast theater of World War II. The man in command of the ambushing American aircraft-carrier task force was a junior flag officer, *Rear Adm. Raymond A. Spruance.* He had been thrust into a crucial combat situation with two carriers directly under him just days before the battle. Sound familiar? It was expected that a flag officer senior to Spruance, Rear Adm. Frank Jack Fletcher, would be in charge. Fletcher's carrier did join the two commanded by Spruance before the battle itself came down, but the former's carrier was torpedoed during its later stages (on June 4) and had to be abandoned late on June 4. Therefore, tactical command during the Battle of Midway rested mainly on Admiral Spruance's inexperienced shoulders.

There were many additional Japanese warships steaming eastward during early June 1942—the main body of battleships and their supports. Learning of the catastrophe that had befallen their carriers on June 4, the Japanese commander, Adm. Isoroku Yamamoto, continued his advance, aiming to smash the thin defense of American ships that was now down to Spruance's two aircraft carriers and some smaller support vessels. Admiral Spruance was in fact heading toward the Japanese main body, hoping for a chance to do further damage to the enemy navy. He kept at his foe only long enough to catch the fourth of the Japanese carriers and destroy it. When that had been accomplished, Spruance ordered his outnumbered task force to reverse course, and it steamed eastward away from the enemy. Yamamoto's hope for a deadly nighttime assault against the U.S. ships, when those carriers' planes could not go into action, was foiled. Yamamoto might have sprung such a trap against the American carriers on the night of June 4–5, but this was no longer a serious danger. In fact, Admiral Yamamoto felt that his fleet would be overextended had it continued its eastward advance after its accompanying carrier force had been annihilated. The shock of that total destruction may have made that Japanese naval commander reel psychologically and become overcautious militarily. In any case, Yamamoto turned his fleet around and withdrew to the west, hoping to draw Spruance's smaller force into a trap.

Admiral Spruance did reverse course once more, trying to hunt down the Japanese main body with two further days of westward pursuit. However, after this ineffective action, Spruance broke off the chase, ending the battle. During its fateful opening phase he had made several risky but momentous decisions—especially by committing nearly all his assault planes at the extremity of their range to the possible targets on June 4. It worked, but Spruance's caution in following up the destruction of the Japanese carriers generated much criticism. He was even chided by his superiors during the later stages of the battle. Yet Admiral Spruance had just recently risen to combat command. Perhaps he also acted out of his knowledge that the U.S. Navy was so vulnerable between the time of the disaster at Pearl Harbor and the spring of the following year. Spruance allowed no counterattack from the still-powerful Japanese fleet to reverse the devastating outcome of his surprise attack on that morning in June. Thus, he *sealed the decision* of Midway by ordering the eventual withdrawal of his task force. The great tactical victory on June 4 was secure. In retrospect it was a major strategic victory as well—which would not have been the case had Spruance lost one or both of his remaining aircraft carriers after the Fourth of June.

So, if Spruance of Midway had decided and acted with admirable judiciousness, perhaps something similar can be said about *Meade of Gettysburg*. Yet because of what General Meade did and did not do after that momentous battle in the middle of the Civil War, he has been criticized ever since. He had let Lee go; the war would go on.

That Gettysburg *may* have made the outcome of the Civil War a foregone conclusion is suggested by the manner in which the Union army rose up and stood during those three days in July 1863. The Army of the Potomac showed a truer version of its colors during the Gettysburg campaign than in all its previous battles. After that, Meade's army never let up and finally defeated Lee's battered force in Virginia. Years later, the anguished cries of many former Confederate leaders suggested that the long road to Appomattox had begun at Gettysburg. These erstwhile generals wondered aloud whether the outcome of that battle had started the denouement of the war, although they did not know that in 1863.

Their former commander had little to say publicly after the Civil War, and he certainly did not express a belief that Gettysburg was its climax. However, Robert E. Lee wrote something rather telling in August 1863: a letter of resignation to the Confederate president.[51] Was he grandstanding? Or might he have been acknowledging the magnitude of his defeat at Gettysburg? Many Southern citizens of the time, as well as modern-day essayists, supported the former conclusion by downgrading the significance of Gettysburg amidst the sweep of the Civil War.[52]

Yet it is possible to conclude that the Confederate defeat at Gettysburg dealt a heavy psychological blow to the Confederate cause from which they never really recuperated, a view ratified by so many Southerners throughout the remainder of the nineteenth century. Subsequent attempts to lay the blame for the defeat on *someone* (Lee? Longstreet? Ewell?) confirm the notion that Southern participants in the campaign rhetorically asked over and over again: "My God, was it all lost at Gettysburg?"

What about the other side of the story—told afterward by the words and actions of the Union soldiers who fought there? The extent to which *they* wrote about the campaign and battle with a "Caspian Sea of Ink"[53]—and flocked to Gettysburg in droves, covering the field with monuments like no other ground where men had fought throughout the Civil War—indicates that the Northerners placed the victory in Pennsylvania at the top of their pantheon. And why not? It was the only big battle fought on free soil during the War of the Rebellion. Union soldiers had been defending *their own* home ground for once rather than invading another country and plodding through hostile territory, bearing the burden of a subconscious malaise that troops can carry during such operations. In contrast, at Gettysburg and on the way there, the morale of the Union men was as high as it was among the Southern defenders when the tables had been turned during one southward Federal invasion after another. Confederate combativeness was manifest during those earlier campaigns and would continue to be evident in 1864. But the Northern boys and men in the Army of the Potomac got to grit *their* teeth in July 1863 and achieve a great victory in Pennsylvania.

The stand of the U.S. Army at Gettysburg remains a singular accomplishment in the history of that fighting force. Robert E. Lee may have made a mistake by giving his opponents the opportunity to earn that success. It may have doomed his army and the Confederacy, even though it took twenty-one more months to complete the job.

As we saw at the end of the previous chapter, George E. Pickett knew that the army of which he had been a part did not *lose* at Gettysburg but rather had been on a field where it was *defeated* by its foe. Perhaps the Union army had moved too slowly as it deployed from southern Pennsylvania after making its stand, but in that long-remembered summer of 1863 it was marching on *paths of victory*.

APPENDIX A

The Cavalry Battle at Brandy Station

On June 7, 1863, Brig. Gen. Alfred Pleasonton became the commander of the recently separated Union Cavalry Corps (Appendix F). Under orders from his commander, Maj. Gen. Joseph Hooker, Pleasonton formed his troopers on the northeast bank of the Rappahannock on the night of Monday, June 8—poised to move against whatever Confederates were across that river. Ultimately, two separate Union forces of infantry-supported cavalry planned to move on Culpeper (map A-1), just a few miles away from the river crossings. Why? Intelligence had reached Hooker a couple of days before and indicated that elements of Lee's army, including cavalrymen, had slipped northwest of Fredericksburg into the vicinity of Culpeper. The Federal reconnaissance in force should at least be able to discern the extent of the rebel movements, and possibly harass them as well ("disperse" and "destroy" are words included in Hooker's orders to Pleasonton).[1]

The two groups into which Pleasonton divided his cavalry were the right (more northerly) wing, commanded by Brig. Gen. John Buford; and the left wing commanded by Brig. Gen. David McM. Gregg (chart A-1). Buford's activities, especially, will become important in the Battle of Gettysburg itself. Note that, in addition to his 1st Cavalry Division, Buford led a group of infantrymen under Brig. Gen.

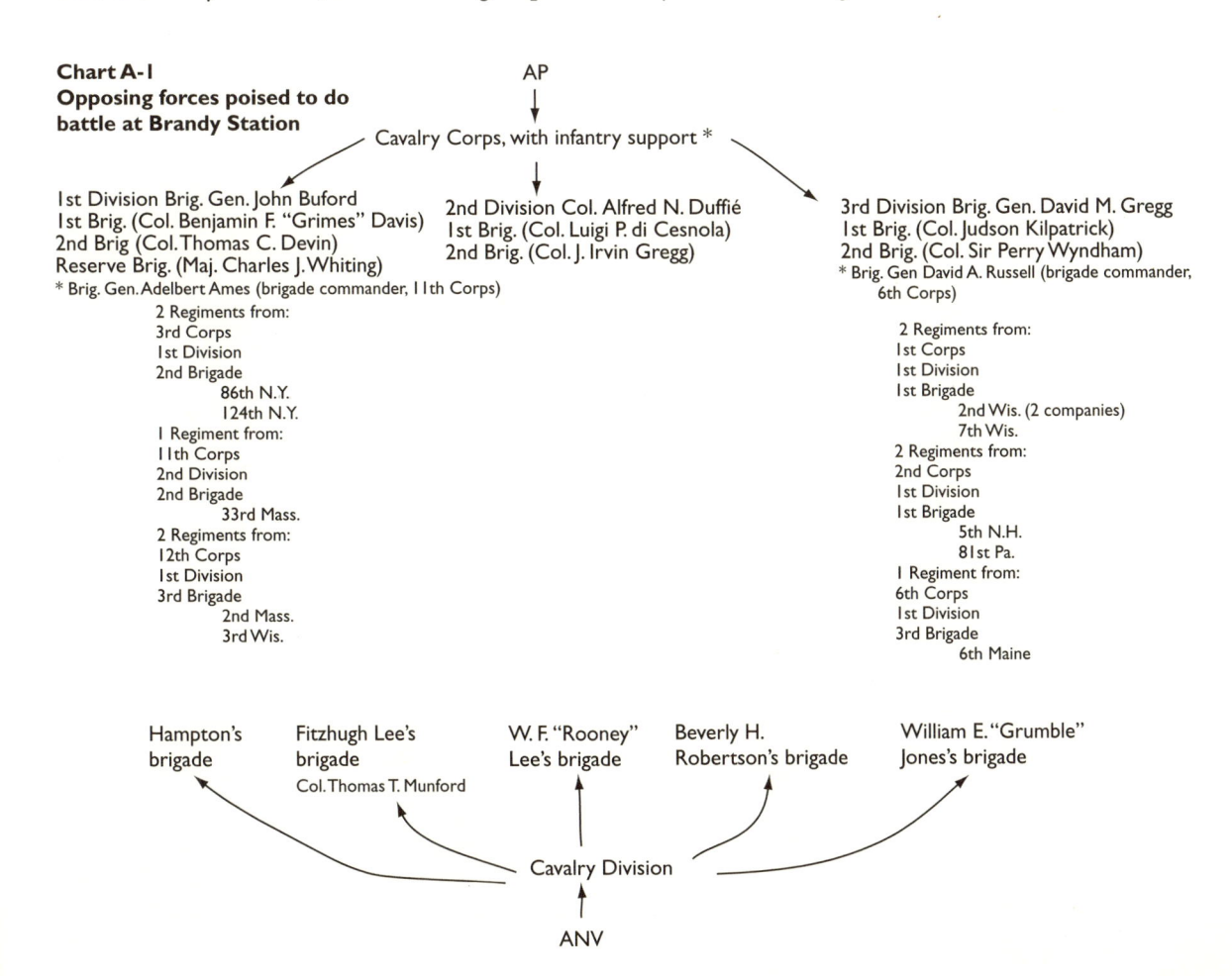

**Chart A-1
Opposing forces poised to do battle at Brandy Station**

AP
↓
Cavalry Corps, with infantry support *

1st Division Brig. Gen. John Buford
1st Brig. (Col. Benjamin F. "Grimes" Davis)
2nd Brig (Col. Thomas C. Devin)
Reserve Brig. (Maj. Charles J. Whiting)
* Brig. Gen. Adelbert Ames (brigade commander, 11th Corps)
   2 Regiments from:
   3rd Corps
   1st Division
   2nd Brigade
      86th N.Y.
      124th N.Y.
   1 Regiment from:
   11th Corps
   2nd Division
   2nd Brigade
      33rd Mass.
   2 Regiments from:
   12th Corps
   1st Division
   3rd Brigade
      2nd Mass.
      3rd Wis.

2nd Division Col. Alfred N. Duffié
1st Brig. (Col. Luigi P. di Cesnola)
2nd Brig. (Col. J. Irvin Gregg)

3rd Division Brig. Gen. David M. Gregg
1st Brig. (Col. Judson Kilpatrick)
2nd Brig. (Col. Sir Perry Wyndham)
* Brig. Gen David A. Russell (brigade commander, 6th Corps)
   2 Regiments from:
   1st Corps
   1st Division
   1st Brigade
      2nd Wis. (2 companies)
      7th Wis.
   2 Regiments from:
   2nd Corps
   1st Division
   1st Brigade
      5th N.H.
      81st Pa.
   1 Regiment from:
   6th Corps
   1st Division
   3rd Brigade
      6th Maine

Hampton's brigade   Fitzhugh Lee's brigade (Col. Thomas T. Munford)   W. F. "Rooney" Lee's brigade   Beverly H. Robertson's brigade   William E. "Grumble" Jones's brigade

Cavalry Division
↑
ANV

Area of detail for map A-1: Fredericksburg and vicinity, early June 1863

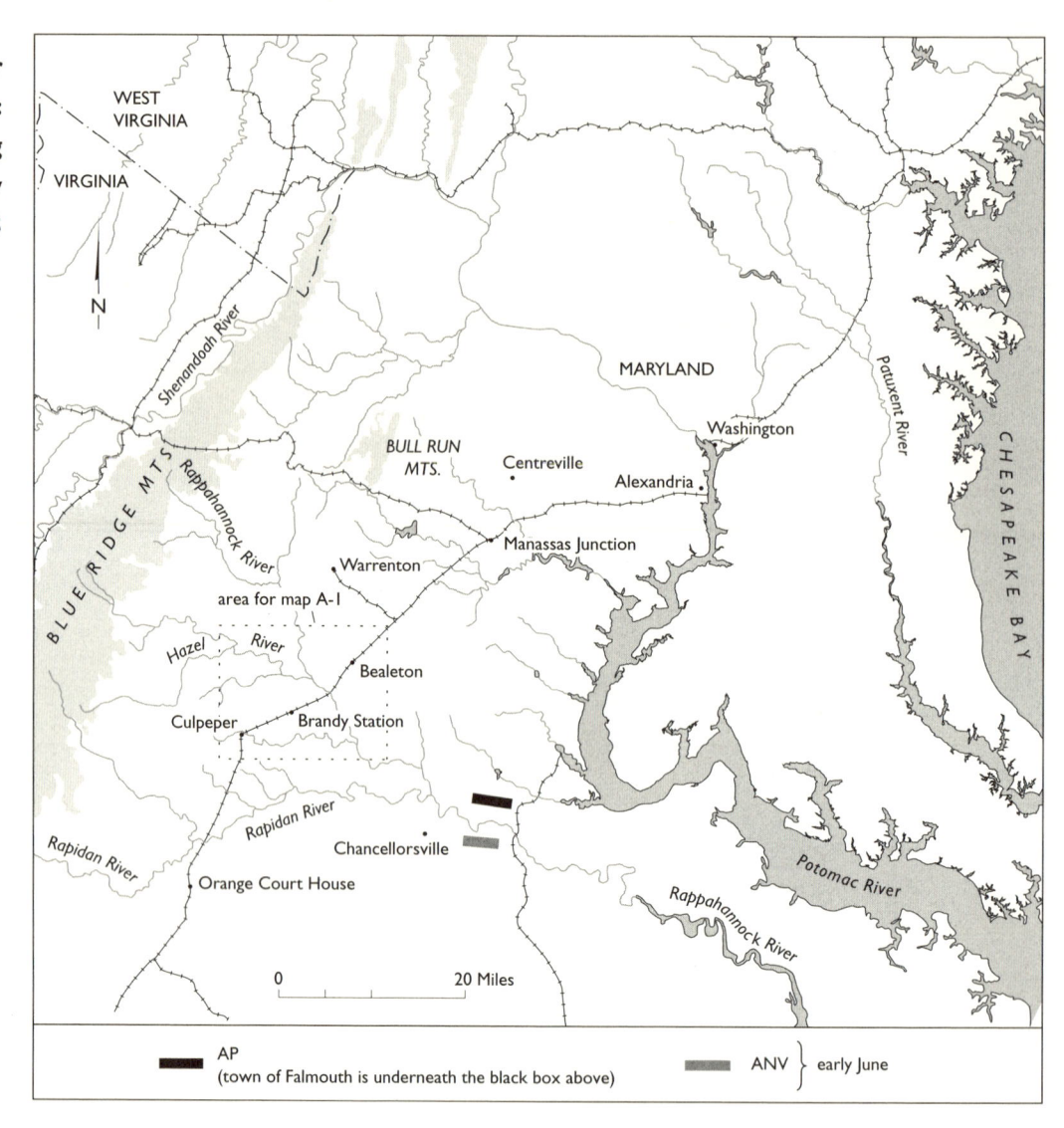

Adelbert Ames, detached from the Army of the Potomac's 11th Corps (chart A-1). Similarly, an infantry unit (chart A-1) under Brig. Gen. David A. Russell (detached from the 6th Corps, the final large unit of Union infantry to arrive at Gettysburg in July) augmented David Gregg's command of troopers from the 2nd and 3rd Cavalry Divisions.[2]

Buford was told to cross the Rappahannock at Beverly's Ford. Gregg was to make the crossing at Kelly's Ford, more than five miles southeast of Buford's intended crossing point (map A-1). The plan was to converge at Brandy Station, a railroad depot situated between the river and Culpeper (map A-1), some four miles southwest of Beverly's Ford and approximately eight miles from Gregg's crossing point. The 2nd Cavalry Division (under Col. Alfred N. Duffié, and in turn under David Gregg) was to head toward Stevensburg, Virginia, located south of Brandy Station (map A-1). Duffié would protect the left flank of the attacking force from any rebel forces that might be on the move, ranging westward from and to the northwest of Fredericksburg.

Meanwhile, the Confederate cavalry under Maj. Gen. J. E. B. Stuart was (indeed) in the vicinity of Culpeper. These troopers were poised to cross the Rappahannock and ride northward to begin their screening duties. Stuart's troop-

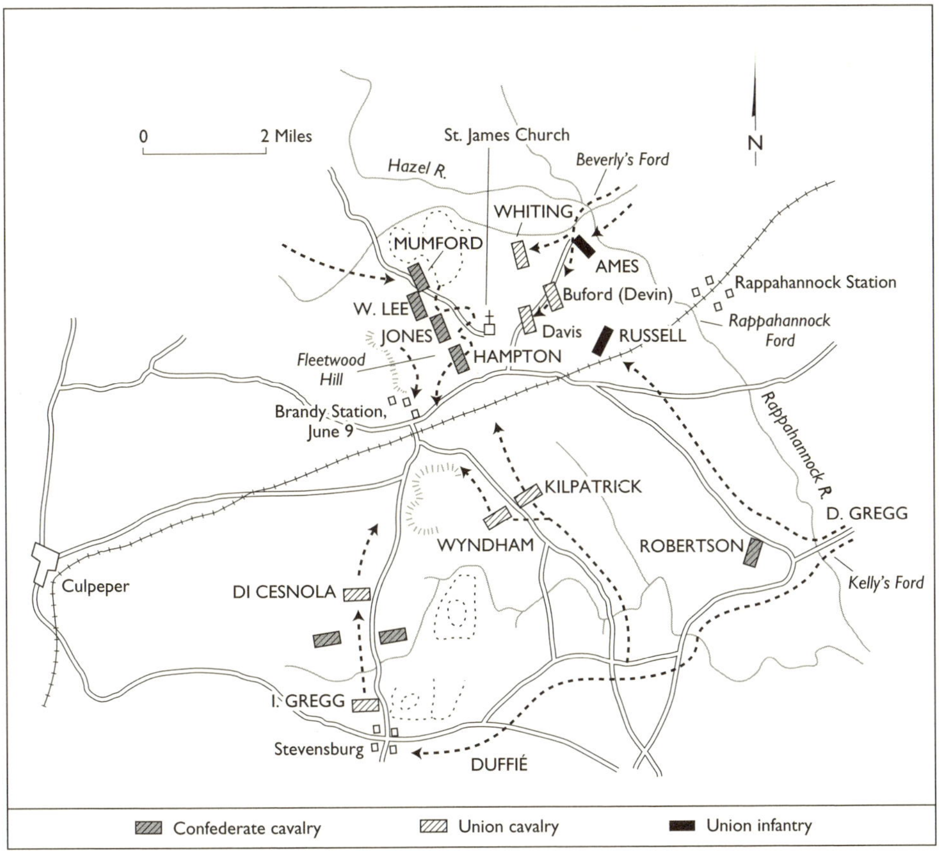

**Map A-1
Brandy Station, June 9**

ers were directed to accompany the Confederate infantry that was about to escape from the confines of Fredericksburg and the Union army facing it across that river by moving upstream along the Rappahannock. This would permit the entire Army of Northern Virginia to slip away into the Shenandoah Valley. The Blue Ridge Mountains guard that valley on its eastern side. The southern entrance to the Shenandoah (map 1-3) is to the west and north of the starting positions of Lee's army (maps 1-1 and 1-2). As the main body, consisting of the bulk of the rebel infantry, entered the valley and marched northward, Stuart would be on its right flank, physically protecting it and keeping it out of sight of whatever Federal forces might be following.

That explains why Stuart's troopers were near Culpeper. At this time, perhaps to preface the impending campaign with some panache, Stuart held reviews of his approximately ninety-five hundred troopers near Culpeper. General Lee inspected the last of these on June 8. The celebratory parades of his cavalry units may have puffed up Stuart into a more strutting posture than usual. Yet he did properly move his horsemen down closer to the Rappahannock River after the review concluded. This put his troopers in a position to initiate the Confederates' second invasion of the North in the eastern theater of the Civil War.

General Stuart himself camped that night on Fleetwood Hill. This prominence was a long, partly wooded ridge running in a roughly north-south direction. The hill itself (on the southern end of the ridge) is on the north side of the tracks about a half-mile east of Brandy Station (maps A-1 and A-4).

Map A-2
Brandy Station, early

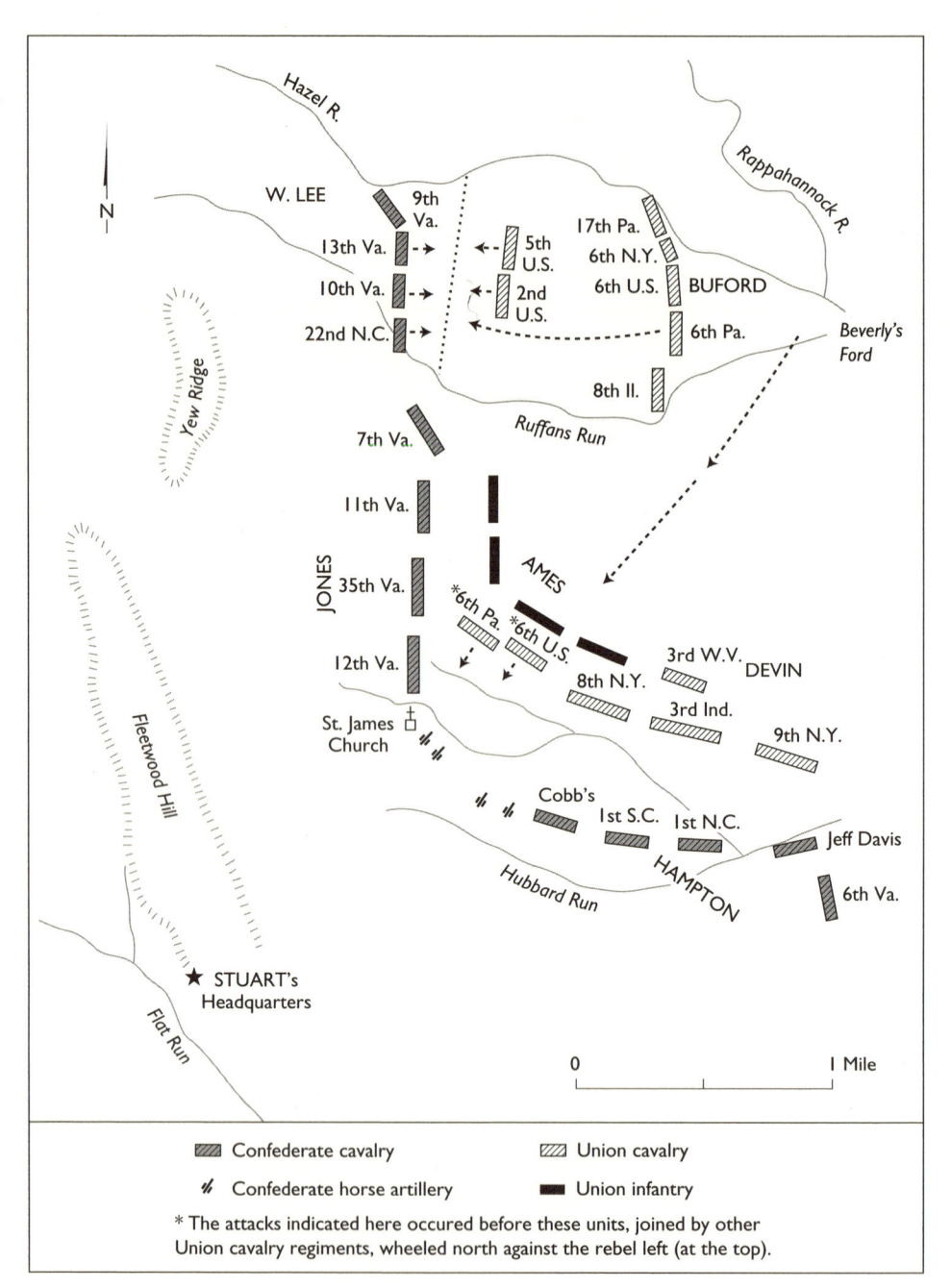

Confederate cavalry — Confederate cavalry
Union cavalry — Union cavalry
Confederate horse artillery
Union infantry

* The attacks indicated here occured before these units, joined by other Union cavalry regiments, wheeled north against the rebel left (at the top).

At 4:30 on the morning of June 9, the van of Buford's force moved across the river at Beverly's Ford. General Buford led forty-five hundred cavalrymen, fifteen hundred infantry troops, and was towing sixteen artillery pieces. The Federals encountered a thin group of Confederate cavalrymen near the river, who were almost certainly startled and got pushed back to an area north of St. James Church (maps A-2 and A-4). Stuart ordered his troopers in the northeast sector to pull back to a low ridge near the church. These rebels, along with the reinforcing 6th and 7th Virginia Cavalry (chart A-2) and a lone cannon, slowed Buford's advance. The ground aided the Confederate defenders by forcing the Federals to go through a swale in order to advance upon this position from the northeast (maps A-2 and A-4).

There was a stalemate and lull in the fighting near the church southwest of

270 THE STAND OF THE U.S. ARMY AT GETTYSBURG

Chart A-2
Brandy Station – early – the field only (not including Stevensburg): thus, vicinity of Beverly's Ford, St. James Church

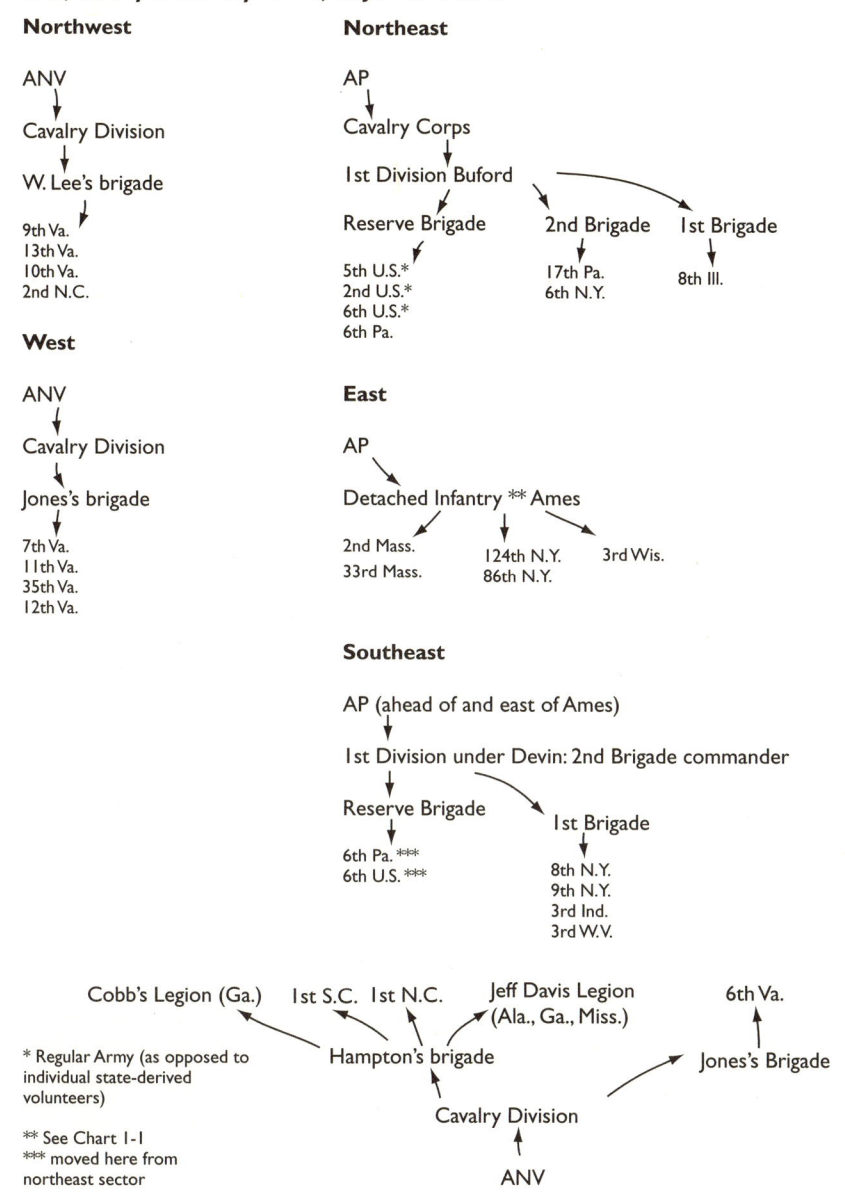

Northwest

ANV
↓
Cavalry Division
↓
W. Lee's brigade
↓
9th Va.
13th Va.
10th Va.
2nd N.C.

Northeast

AP
↓
Cavalry Corps
↓
1st Division Buford ──────────────┐
↓   │
Reserve Brigade   2nd Brigade   1st Brigade
↓   ↓   ↓
5th U.S.*   17th Pa.   8th Ill.
2nd U.S.*   6th N.Y.
6th U.S.*
6th Pa.

West

ANV
↓
Cavalry Division
↓
Jones's brigade
↓
7th Va.
11th Va.
35th Va.
12th Va.

East

AP
↓
Detached Infantry ** Ames
↓   ↓   ↓
2nd Mass. 124th N.Y.   3rd Wis.
33rd Mass. 86th N.Y.

Southeast

AP (ahead of and east of Ames)
↓
1st Division under Devin: 2nd Brigade commander
↓   ↘
Reserve Brigade   1st Brigade
↓   ↓
6th Pa. ***   8th N.Y.
6th U.S. ***   9th N.Y.
                       3rd Ind.
                       3rd W.V.

Cobb's Legion (Ga.)   1st S.C.   1st N.C.   Jeff Davis Legion (Ala., Ga., Miss.)   6th Va.
        ↖   ↖   ↑   ↗   ↑
                        Hampton's brigade   Jones's Brigade
                                ↑   ↗
                        Cavalry Division
                                ↑
                              ANV

* Regular Army (as opposed to individual state-derived volunteers)

** See Chart 1-1

*** moved here from northeast sector

Beverly's Ford (map A-2). Buford was stalled by the confusion of the initial engagement, and his force had to complete its crossing at the ford. Then, at about 8 A.M., Buford's 6th Pennsylvania Cavalry, supported by the 6th U.S. Cavalry (chart A-2), attacked from the right wing of his line. They surged across an open field near St. James Church. The attack was shattered by sixteen Confederate artillery pieces intermingled with five thousand mounted and dismounted rebel cavalrymen. Buford realized the Southerners' defense in this area was too strong (map A-2), although many of the rebel defenders in this sector of the field would be forced to redeploy to meet a Union threat coming in from the south (map A-3).

Leaving four cavalry and two infantry regiments near the church, General Buford took the remainder of his force northward, aiming to work his way round the rebel left flank (near the top of map A-2). But dismounted men from Brig.

Area of detail for maps A-2 and A-3

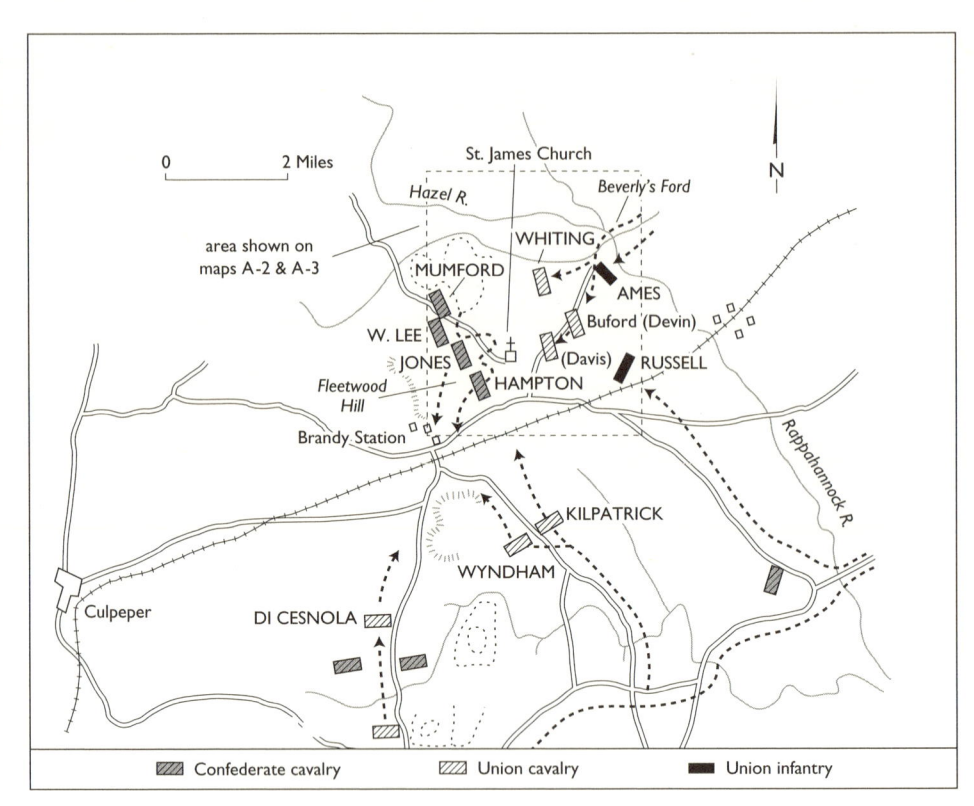

Gen. William H. F. "Rooney" Lee's brigade effectively stopped the Federals there. Rooney Lee (Robert E. Lee's son) had joined the ring of defenders now deployed in a rough arc swinging around (from the east to the north on map 1-4; see also chart A-2.)[3]

Meanwhile, Brig. Gen. David Gregg's attack group, which was about the same size as Buford's command, finally began to press northward. Gregg had crossed the Rappahannock downriver late, not getting all his men across Kelly's Ford (map A-1) until 9 A.M. He had felt compelled to wait for Duffié, whose troopers had gotten lost as they moved westward toward the lower ford (map A-1). Recall that Duffié's job was not to assail the Confederates directly, but to continue in a westerly direction toward Stevensburg (map A-1, chart A-4).

Indeed, Gregg's force soon split off from Duffié. Soon afterward, Gregg crossed the Rappahannock with little opposition. He left several of the infantrymen accompanying him to guard the crossing point. General Gregg then took a right turn with the 3rd Cavalry Division (chart A-1) and headed northwest toward Brandy Station (map A-1). He just missed a Confederate force under Brig. Gen. Beverly H. Robertson, which had moved toward Kelly's Ford to bolster the pickets who had weakly defended that crossing point. Robertson was passive during this stage of the action—reporting the advance of General Gregg's force, but doing nothing to stop its threat to the right flank and rear of the aforementioned ring of Confederate defenders. We will witness Robertson's desultory performance during subsequent stages of the Gettysburg campaign.

Major Henry B. McClellan, Stuart's assistant adjutant general, spotted General Gregg's advance. McClellan had been left alone in charge of Stuart's headquarters (map A-2) while the division commander was at the front near St. James Church. Seeing the impending danger to Stuart's right and rear (map A-3), McClellan sent a courier to his boss. He also had one artillery piece situated on Fleetwood Hill

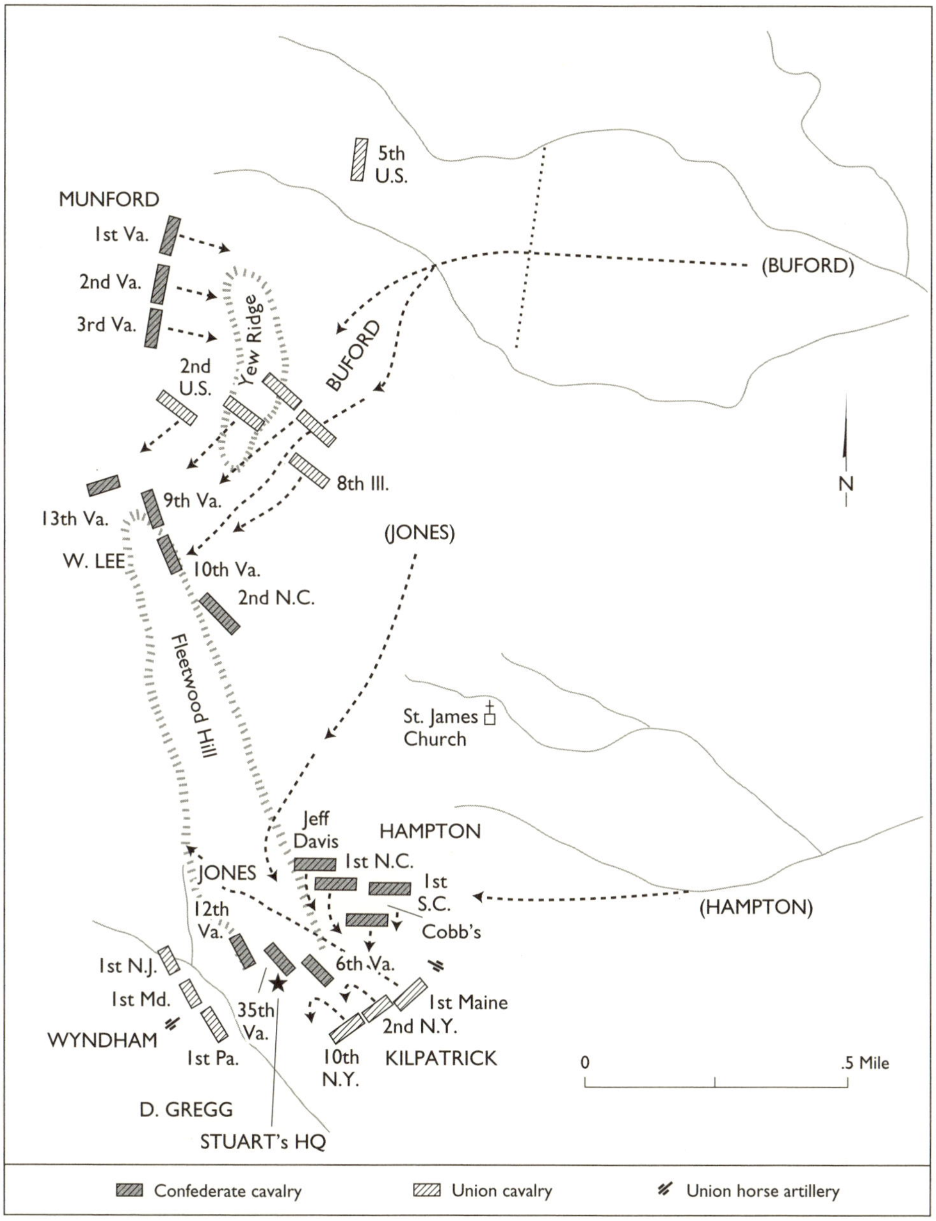

**Map A-3
Brandy Station, late**

fire on General Gregg's horsemen. This caused Gregg to hesitate, and he did not then advance upon this essentially undefended Confederate position. Stuart responded to McClellan's urgent message by pulling most of his regiments from the St. James Church line and sending them galloping to Fleetwood Hill a mile to the south. Thus, when Gregg finally did move toward that position, he found it reinforced by troopers from Brig. Gens. William E. "Grumble" Jones's and Wade Hampton's brigades (maps A-3 and A-4). This Confederate move depleted their defensive positions in the center of the field, where the opposing forces mainly pinned each other down for the remainder of the battle.

As Gregg advanced toward the defenders arriving on Fleetwood Hill (chart A-3), several charges and countercharges occurred in this area (map A-3). During a given part of this battle within the battle, the opposing units often broke down into small subsets of the cavalry regiments. The tide swayed back and forth, with the crest of Fleetwood Hill (at the southern end of the ridge) changing hands

THE CAVALRY BATTLE AT BRANDY STATION 273

Chart A-3
Brandy Station – late: vicinity of Yew Ridge, Fleetwood Hill

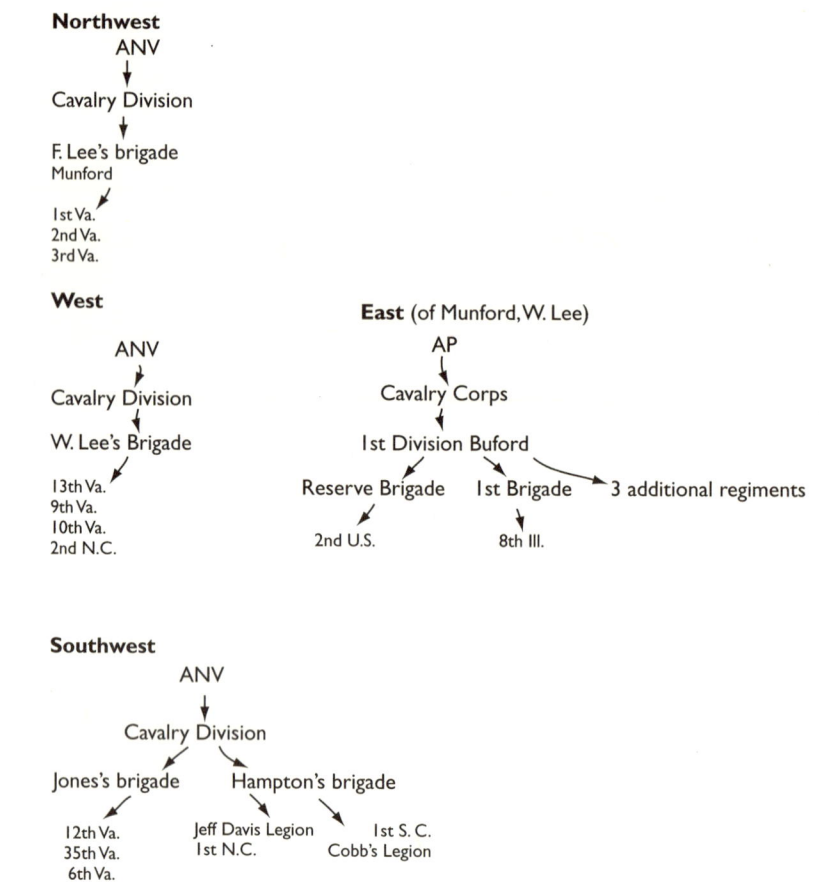

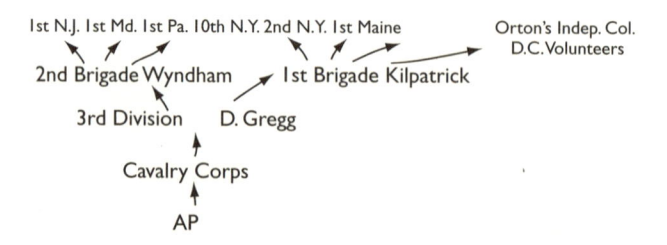

Northwest

ANV → Cavalry Division → F. Lee's brigade
Munford

1st Va.
2nd Va.
3rd Va.

West

ANV → Cavalry Division → W. Lee's Brigade

13th Va.
9th Va.
10th Va.
2nd N.C.

East (of Munford, W. Lee)

AP → Cavalry Corps → 1st Division Buford → Reserve Brigade, 1st Brigade, 3 additional regiments

Reserve Brigade → 2nd U.S.
1st Brigade → 8th Ill.

Southwest

ANV → Cavalry Division → Jones's brigade, Hampton's brigade

Jones's brigade:
12th Va.
35th Va.
6th Va.

Hampton's brigade:
Jeff Davis Legion
1st N.C.
1st S.C.
Cobb's Legion

1st N.J. 1st Md. 1st Pa. 10th N.Y. 2nd N.Y. 1st Maine → 2nd Brigade Wyndham

Orton's Indep. Col. D.C. Volunteers → 1st Brigade Kilpatrick

2nd Brigade Wyndham, 1st Brigade Kilpatrick ← 3rd Division D. Gregg ← Cavalry Corps ← AP

---

several times. This large swirling melee was *the* feature of Brandy Station in which cavalry fighting occurred as one conventionally envisions it (recall that the fight to the north and east often involved dismounted troopers).

General Stuart conducted an *active* defense at Brandy Station. That is the way to do it, as we will see on July 1, 2, and 3 on the field at Gettysburg. The action at Brandy Station provides another preview: During the discussion of the middle of those three days, note that an essentially lone staff officer on a hill south of that Pennsylvania town will summon emergency reinforcing units of soldiers to a certain piece of high rocky ground (Chapter 3). This was analogous to the vigorous performance of Major McClellan on Fleetwood Hill at Brandy Station.

In the meantime, Duffié's two-thousand-man division had encountered two Confederate regiments in the vicinity of Stevensburg (map A-1, chart A-4). Duffié was so delayed by these defenders that, by the time he was able to move north, it

Chart A-4
Brandy Station–late

South – near Stevensburg

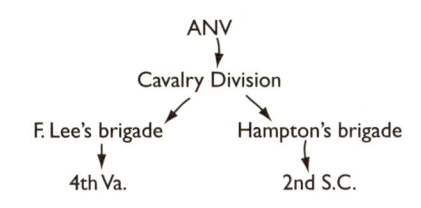

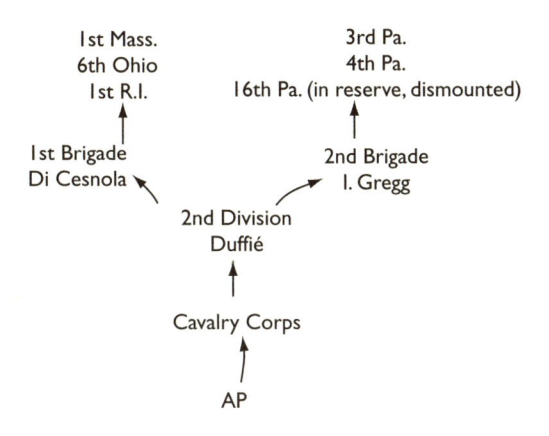

```
            ANV
             ↓
       Cavalry Division
         ↙         ↘
F. Lee's brigade   Hampton's brigade
     ↓                  ↓
   4th Va.            2nd S.C.
```

```
  1st Mass.              3rd Pa.
  6th Ohio               4th Pa.
  1st R.I.      16th Pa. (in reserve, dismounted)
     ↑                      ↑
1st Brigade             2nd Brigade
Di Cesnola  ↖         ↗  J. Gregg
            2nd Division
              Duffié
                ↑
           Cavalry Corps
                ↑
               AP
```

Southwest – near Culpeper

Daniel's brigade (poised to move toward Brandy Station)
↑
Rodes's division
↑
2nd Corps
↑
ANV

was too late to reinforce Gregg in the fight for Fleetwood Hill. Moreover, from the late morning through the midafternoon, Buford was confronted by the Confederates under Brig. Gen. Rooney Lee. These opposing cavalry (and some Northern infantry) units were in the northwest sector (maps A-3 and A-4). Buford gradually forced Lee's brigade back to Yew Ridge and the northern reaches of Fleetwood Hill (map A-4). However, late in the afternoon, a fresh rebel brigade under Col. Thomas T. Munford (chart A-3) arrived in this vicinity to threaten Buford's right flank and rear (maps A-3 and A-4).

At this time in the afternoon (about when Duffié was fitfully coming to the aid of Gregg), the long battle drew to a close. The Federals realized they were not going to take Fleetwood Hill. And before the fighting escalated there, the Confederate units in the center of the field were pressing the line Buford had left near St. James Church (map A-2). The Union command also guessed that Confederate infantry might be at hand. Indeed, Gen. Robert E. Lee accompanied them, arriving near the field that afternoon in time to see his wounded son being carried off by the Federals. The nearest group of Southern infantry was a unit from Maj. Gen. Robert E. Rodes's division of Lt. Gen. Richard S. Ewell's corps (chart A-4), although those soldiers never became engaged at Brandy Station.

THE CAVALRY BATTLE AT BRANDY STATION

**Map A-4
Brandy Station: chronology of Buford's actions**

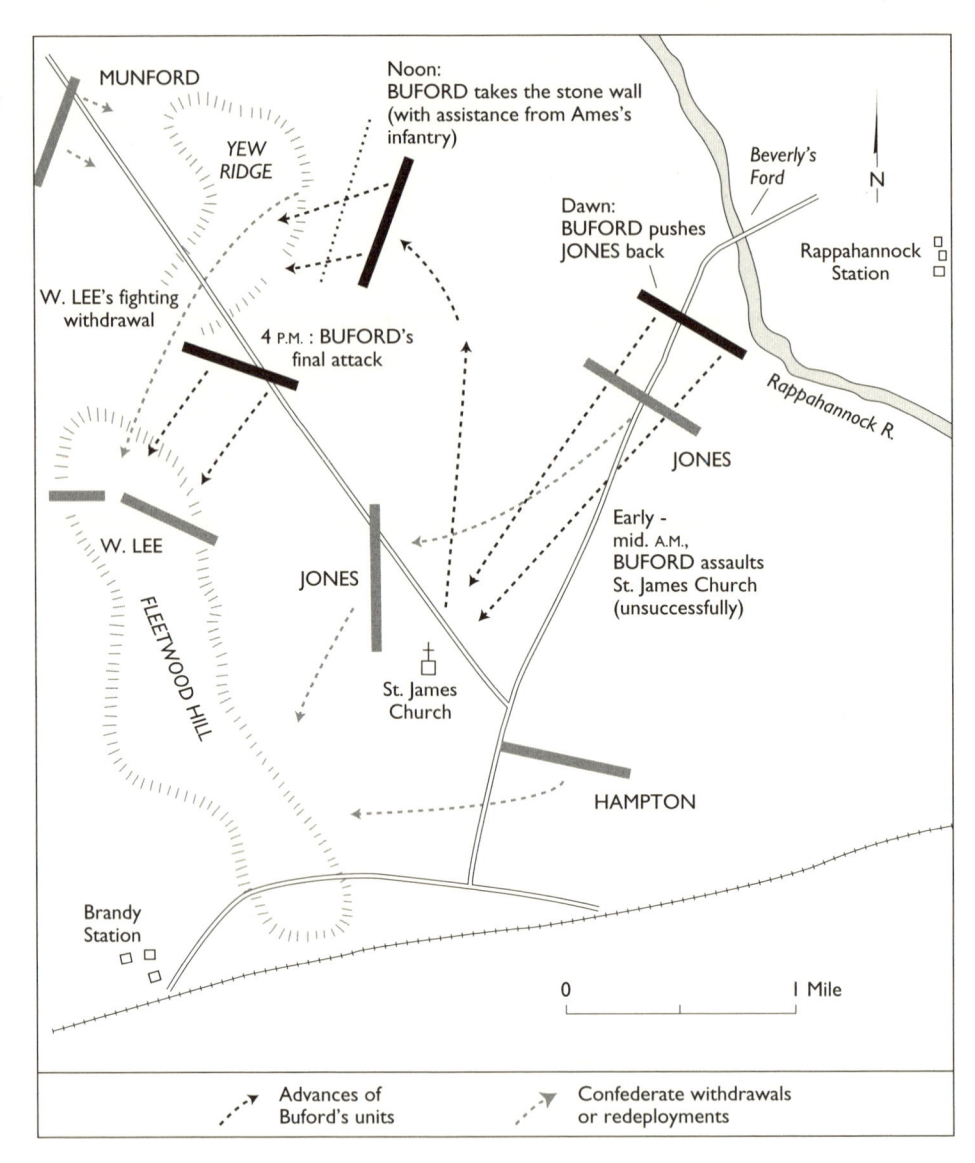

Map labels:
- MUNFORD
- YEW RIDGE
- Noon: BUFORD takes the stone wall (with assistance from Ames's infantry)
- Dawn: BUFORD pushes JONES back
- Beverly's Ford
- Rappahannock Station
- W. LEE's fighting withdrawal
- 4 P.M.: BUFORD's final attack
- Rappahannock R.
- JONES
- W. LEE
- FLEETWOOD HILL
- JONES
- Early–mid. A.M., BUFORD assaults St. James Church (unsuccessfully)
- St. James Church
- HAMPTON
- Brandy Station
- 0 — 1 Mile
- → Advances of Buford's units
- → Confederate withdrawals or redeployments

Noting the proximity of these Southern foot soldiers and the stalemated cavalry fighting, General Pleasonton realized that further efforts would be futile and possibly dangerous. From his vantage point, a hill above the Rappahannock River, he sent word for his two division commanders to withdraw. The Federal forces gradually recrossed the Rappahannock at Beverly's Ford (Buford) and Rappahannock Station (Gregg). The latter crossing point is located between Beverly's and Kelly's Fords (map A-1). General Russell's infantry (chart A-1) came up from Kelly's Ford to help cover the withdrawal. By 9 P.M. the Union cavalry had returned to its bivouac sites near Warrenton and Catlett Station, where it had camped on the eve of the battle at Brandy Station (map 1-4).

APPENDIX B

The Loudoun Valley Cavalry Battles

As the Union cavalry rode northward in mid-June looking for the Confederate army, the troopers never really located its main body—but they did find Stuart's cavalry. This led to the second set of engagements that occurred as the two armies moved from Virginia toward Pennsylvania (the first of these was the Second Battle of Winchester). The Union troopers crossed the Bull Run Mountains into Loudoun Valley (map B-1), moving roughly in a northwesterly direction toward the trio of towns around which the conflicts in that valley would revolve (map B-1).

Those clashes pretty much led to a standoff, as should be evident from the description that follows. Perhaps this increased the Federal cavalry's confidence by another notch. However, those battles did not galvanize the Federal forces as a whole (this would require a new high commander). The fighting in the Loudoun Valley also led to a significant fraction of Stuart's force largely disengaging itself from the Union army between the time of the Loudoun Valley battles (June 17–21) and the end of June (see Chapter 1, section heading "Stuart Leaves Loudoun...").

General Hooker ordered Pleasonton to send elements of his mounted corps in the direction of the marching Confederate infantry. General Pleasonton thus had Brig. Gen. David McM. Gregg order three of his brigades (chart B-1) to ride, on June 17, from the vicinity of Manassas (map B-1) to the town of Aldie (maps B-1 and B-2). They were then to fan out from Aldie and "sweep" the Loudoun Valley, looking for the enemy. Would they find Stuart? If not, could they infiltrate the adjacent valley (the Shenandoah) and gather intelligence about Lee's infantry corps?

As General Gregg proceeded north and west (map B-1), he detached Col. Alfred Duffié and sent him toward Middleburg (map B-1). This was a planned move, part of Gregg's orders from Pleasonton. After Brandy Station, Duffié had been demoted from division command to leader of the 2nd Brigade in David Gregg's division. However, by June 17, the newly promoted Brig. Gen. Judson Kilpatrick had taken over Duffié's brigade, and Duffié was further demoted to command of the 1st Rhode Island Regiment within it (chart B-2).[1] Duffié was directed to swing southward and circle clockwise up toward Middleburg on a route that took him through Thoroughfare Gap, a pass in the Bull Run Mountains (map B-1).

Awaiting Duffié on the Seventeenth were elements of Stuart's cavalry division—who had left the Brandy Station area shortly before this time. Duffié was able to push a small rear-guard force of Confederate cavalry out of Middleburg, but later that day he was counterattacked by two rebel brigades (chart B-2). So, instead of making contact with David Gregg at Aldie, Duffié was mired in a terrible fight near that town. He was not able to escape from the trap at Middleburg until the early morning of June 18. As Duffié's force staggered back toward the Union lines at Centreville on June 19 (map B-1), only about one-third of his three-hundred-man regiment remained.[2]

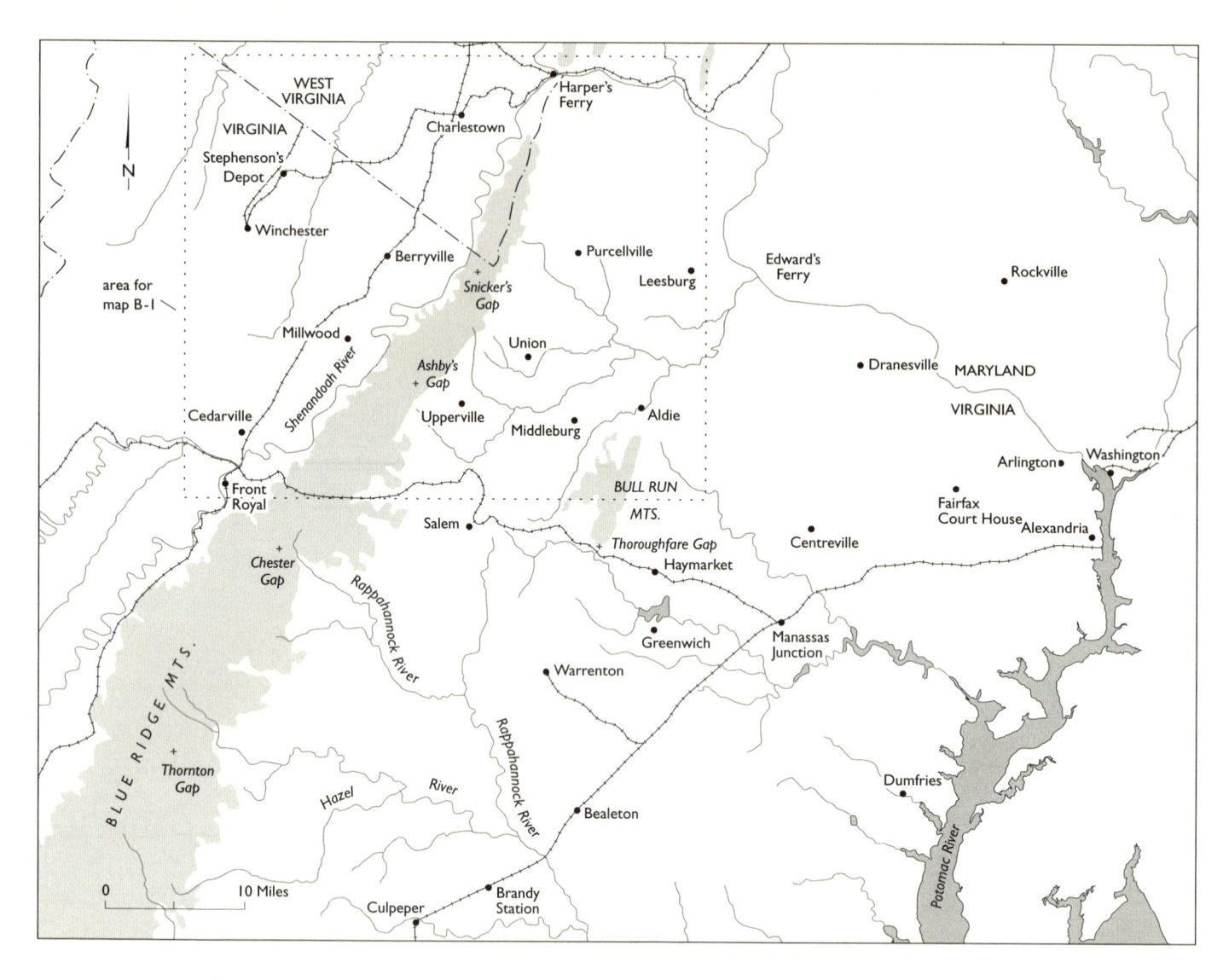

Area of detail for map B-1

Meanwhile, General Gregg's units arrived at Aldie at about 4 P.M. on the Seventeenth. General Kilpatrick's brigade ran into Fitzhugh Lee's brigade—still commanded by Col. Thomas T. Munford, as had been the case at Brandy Station (chart B-1). Kilpatrick attacked piecemeal and was held off by dismounted troopers from the 5th Virginia. This was but one example of the fighting that occurred in a roughly north-south arc just west of Aldie (map B-2).[3] Later that evening, the Confederates withdrew, although they had given at least as good as they got in the fighting near Aldie. Before the outbreak of that battle, Kilpatrick was supposed to have rendezvoused with Colonel Duffié at Middleburg (after Duffié had arrived there and so informed David Gregg by courier). But the engaged Kilpatrick did not come to the aid of the beleaguered 1st Rhode Island, thus helping to seal Duffié's doom.

When General Hooker was informed of the July 17 engagements he ordered General Pleasonton to ratchet up the pressure in the Loudoun Valley. On June 18 the Union Cavalry Corps commander sent additional units past Aldie toward Ashby's and Snicker's Gaps in the Blue Ridge Mountains (map B-1). Meanwhile, Confederate cavalry in the vicinity of Middleburg withdrew from there, but the Union brigade commander, Col. J. Irvin Gregg (David McM.'s older cousin),[4] fell

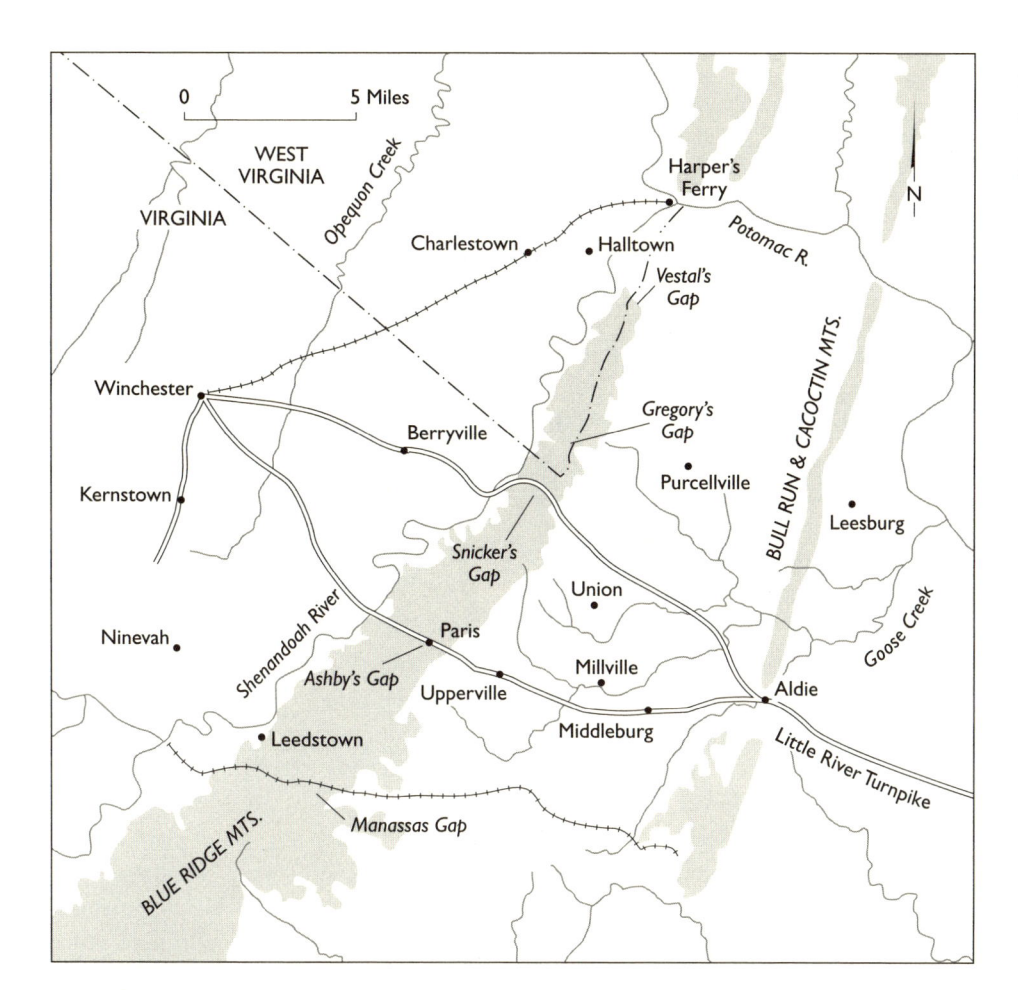

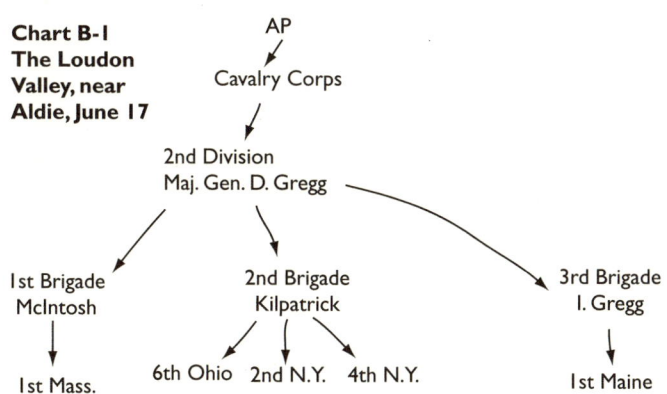

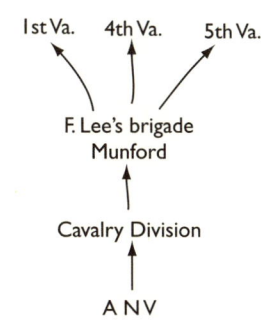

**Map B-1
The Loudon Valley,
June 17–21**

**Chart B-1
The Loudon Valley, near Aldie, June 17**

AP → Cavalry Corps → 2nd Division Maj. Gen. D. Gregg

- 1st Brigade McIntosh → 1st Mass.
- 2nd Brigade Kilpatrick → 6th Ohio, 2nd N.Y., 4th N.Y.
- 3rd Brigade I. Gregg → 1st Maine

ANV → Cavalry Division → F. Lee's brigade Munford → 1st Va., 4th Va., 5th Va.

THE LOUDOUN VALLEY CAVALRY BATTLES

Chart B-2
The Loudon Valley, June 17–18, near Middlesburg

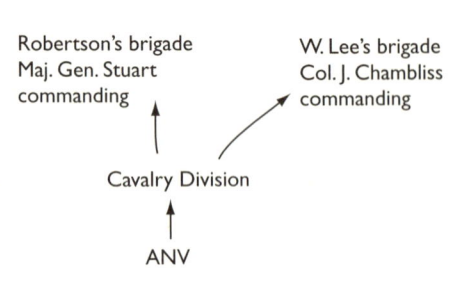

AP
↓
Cavalry Corps
↓
2nd Division
D. Gregg
↓
2nd Brigade
Kilpatrick
↓
1st R.I.
Duffié

Robertson's brigade
Maj. Gen. Stuart
commanding
↑

W. Lee's brigade
Col. J. Chambliss
commanding
↖

Cavalry Division
↑
ANV

back to Aldie, and Stuart reoccupied Middleburg on the night of the Eighteenth. Early the next morning, two of David Gregg's brigades again advanced toward that town in the middle of the valley (map B-1, chart B-3).

Stuart's troopers withdrew to a ridge west of Middleburg (map B-3, chart B-3), where dismounted cavalrymen fought each other into the afternoon of June 19. Rooney Lee's brigade—now commanded by Col. John R. Chambliss Jr. owing to Lee's wounding at Brandy Station—moved southward into this area to bolster the defense. Later that afternoon, Stuart ordered his men back to the next ridge (left side of map B-3), and David Gregg ordered a halt to his attack. Farther to the north, one of Buford's brigades (chart B-3) was trying to move around the left of the main rebel force, aiming to sneak up on Ashby's Gap for the all-important task of learning about Confederate infantry movements. But a unit of Fitzhugh Lee's brigade and elements of the recently arrived force under Brig. Gen. Grumble Jones were sent in that direction to block Federal movement in that area—three miles to the northwest of the main action (map B-3). Heavy rains on June 20 caused a lull in the fighting.

Hoping to increase the westward Union pressure, Pleasonton asked Hooker for permission to send his entire corps toward Stuart's positions. Permission was granted, and General Pleasonton did so on June 21 as the battles in the Loudoun Valley escalated. In that regard, Federal infantry units were detached to advance in support of the Union cavalry. This was the result of orders from Hooker to the commander of the 5th Corps, Maj. Gen. George G. Meade. Thus, three brigades led by one of his division commanders, Brig. Gen. James Barnes, moved into the Loudoun Valley (chart B-4). Two of these infantry units were left in a reserve position at Middleburg; the third, along with five brigades of Union cavalry, assailed Stuart's forces. The advancing infantry was Barnes's 3rd Brigade, commanded by Col. Strong Vincent. We will of course hear more from General Meade later—but also from Colonel Vincent (Chapter 3).

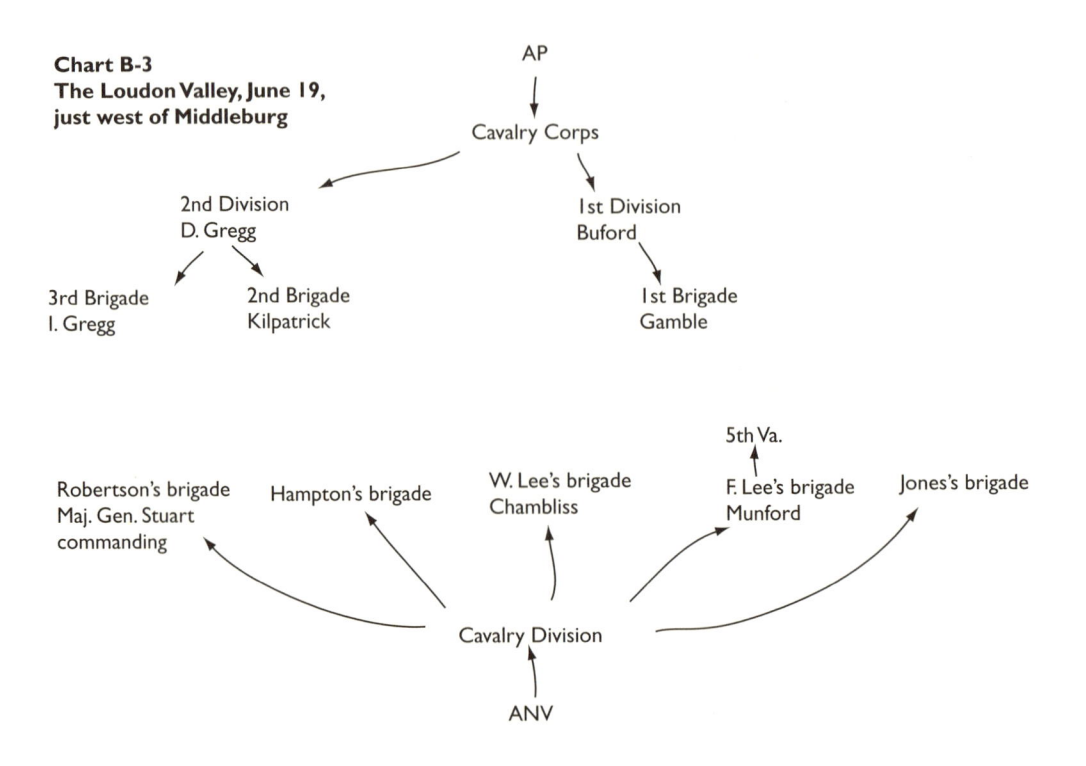

Chart B-3
The Loudon Valley, June 19, just west of Middleburg

AP
↓
Cavalry Corps
↙ ↘
2nd Division   1st Division
D. Gregg   Buford
↙   ↘   ↓
3rd Brigade   2nd Brigade   1st Brigade
I. Gregg   Kilpatrick   Gamble

Robertson's brigade   Hampton's brigade   W. Lee's brigade   5th Va.   Jones's brigade
Maj. Gen. Stuart   Chambliss   F. Lee's brigade
commanding   Munford

Cavalry Division
↑
ANV

280   THE STAND OF THE U.S. ARMY AT GETTYSBURG

Several of the Confederate cavalry units (chart B-5) were driven back from Upperville (map B-4) toward Ashby's Gap (map B-1), where Stuart turned and defended that route of westward retreat. East of Upperville, General Gregg's division (chart B-5) was stalled by the defense and flanking counterattack of General Hampton's Confederate brigade (map B-4). North of that town, General Jones's brigade (map B-4, chart B-6) halted General Buford's advancing division (chart B-5). However, the Union advance resumed, and by 6 P.M. on June 21 Stuart had retreated to Ashby's Gap. This brought elements of the Confederate infantry into the fringes of the engagement. Recall the move of General Longstreet's soldiers back from the Shenandoah Valley toward Ashby's Gap (see Chapter 1, section heading "Ewell Moves North . . . ," and maps 1-4 and 1-5). In particular, Maj. Gen. Lafayette McLaws's division (chart B-6) was directed to hold that position to cover Stuart's retreat. Also, Maj. Gen. Richard H. Anderson's division of Hill's 3rd Corps was ordered to halt on its way to Shepherdstown (chart B-6, map 1-5) and take a defensive position in case of a Federal breakthrough.

Chart B-4
The Loudon Valley, June 21, detached Union infantry

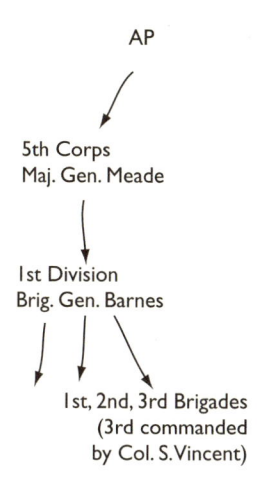

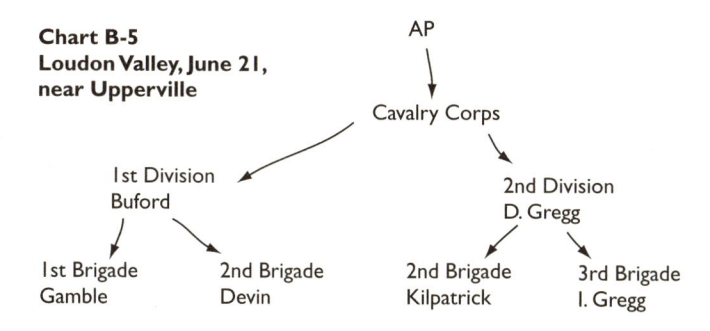

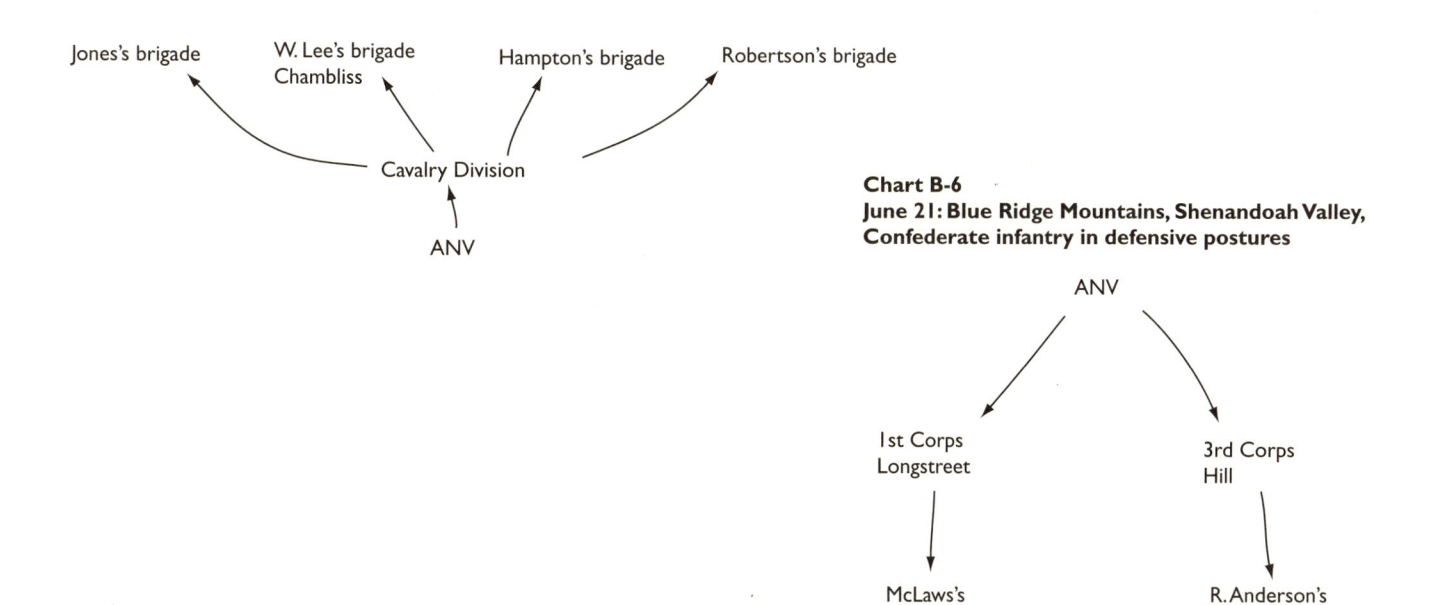

AP
↓
5th Corps
Maj. Gen. Meade
↓
1st Division
Brig. Gen. Barnes
↓
1st, 2nd, 3rd Brigades
(3rd commanded by Col. S. Vincent)

Chart B-5
Loudon Valley, June 21, near Upperville

AP
↓
Cavalry Corps
↙   ↘
1st Division   2nd Division
Buford   D. Gregg
↙   ↘   ↙   ↘
1st Brigade   2nd Brigade   2nd Brigade   3rd Brigade
Gamble   Devin   Kilpatrick   I. Gregg

Jones's brigade   W. Lee's brigade Chambliss   Hampton's brigade   Robertson's brigade
        ↖   ↖   ↑   ↗
                         Cavalry Division
                              ↑
                             ANV

Chart B-6
June 21: Blue Ridge Mountains, Shenandoah Valley, Confederate infantry in defensive postures

ANV
↙   ↘
1st Corps   3rd Corps
Longstreet   Hill
↓   ↓
McLaws's   R. Anderson's
division   division

THE LOUDOUN VALLEY CAVALRY BATTLES

Areas of detail for maps B-2, B-3, and B-4, June 17–21

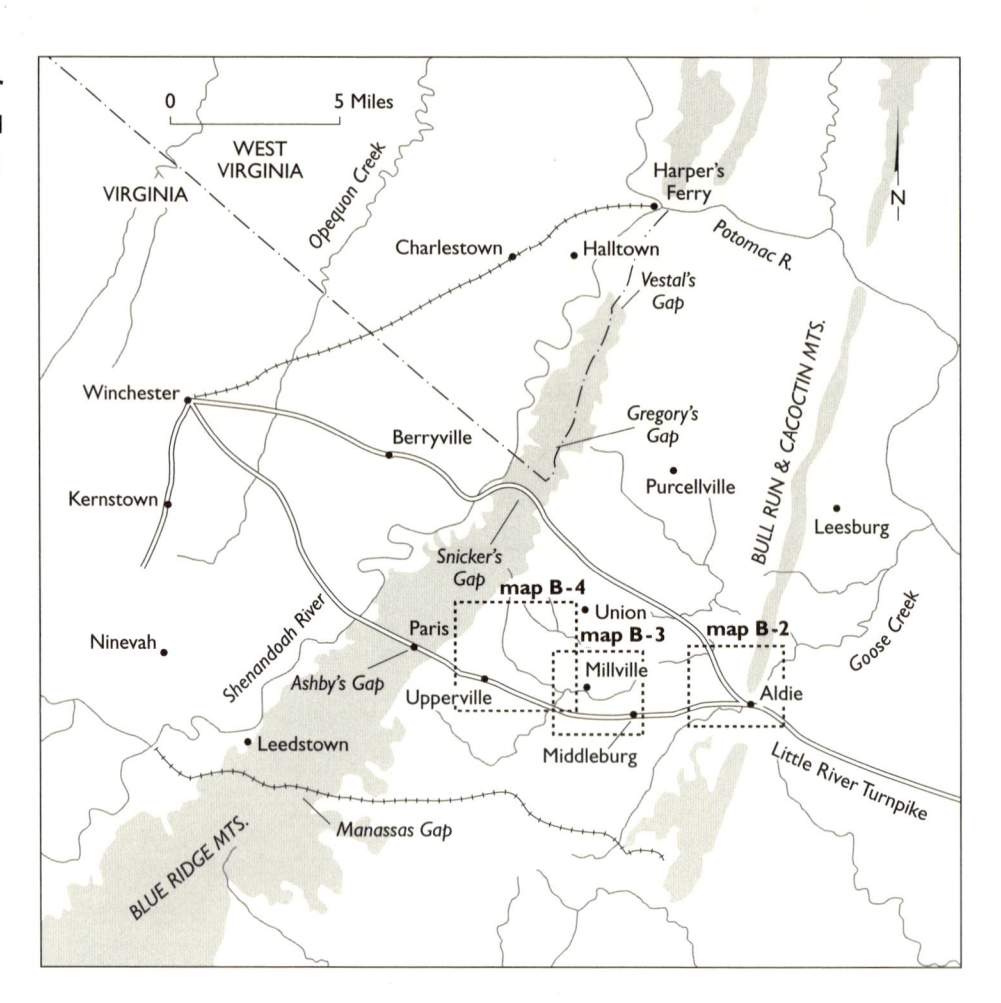

**Map B-2
Action near Aldie, and movements west of there, June 17 (late afternoon)**

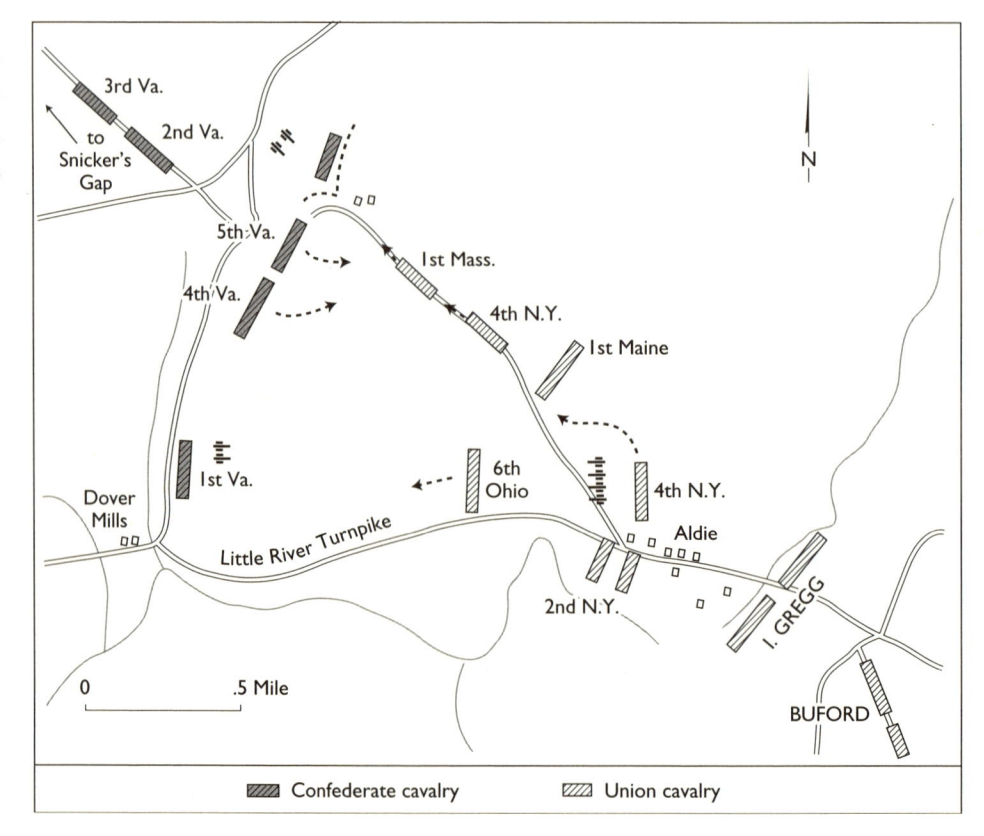

282   THE STAND OF THE U.S. ARMY AT GETTYSBURG

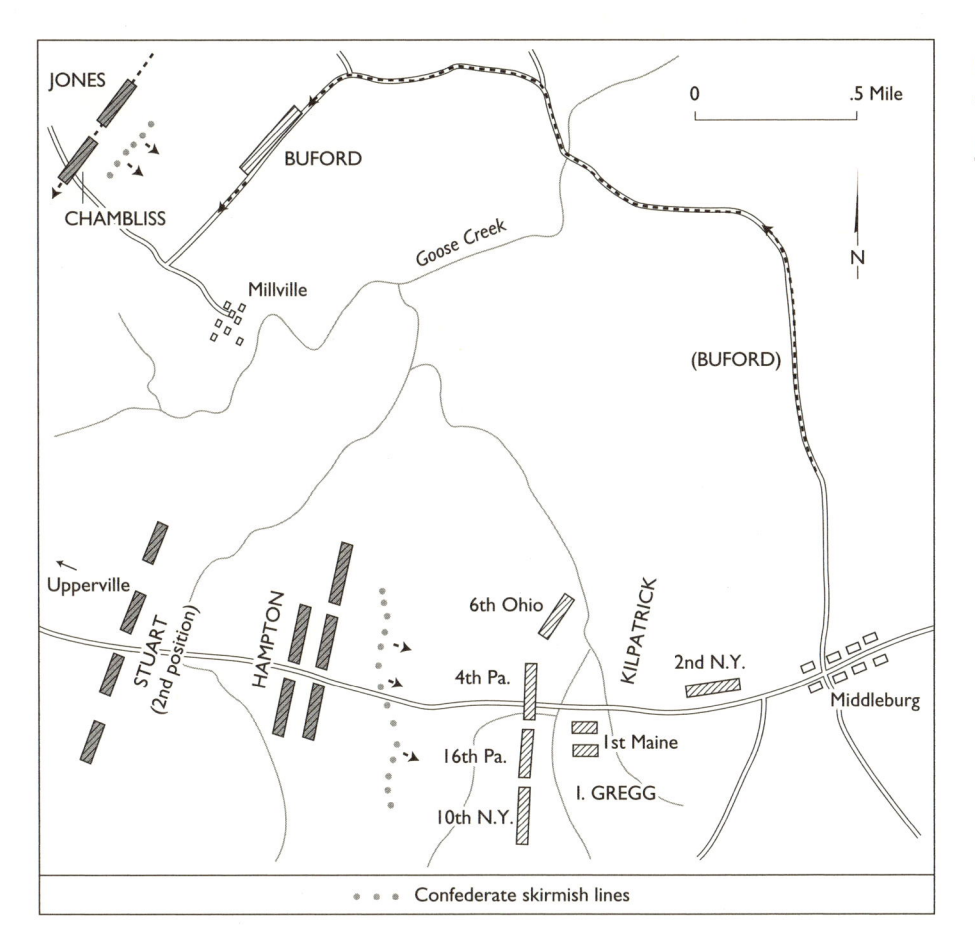

Map B-3
The Battle of Middleburg, June 19 (A.M., P.M.)

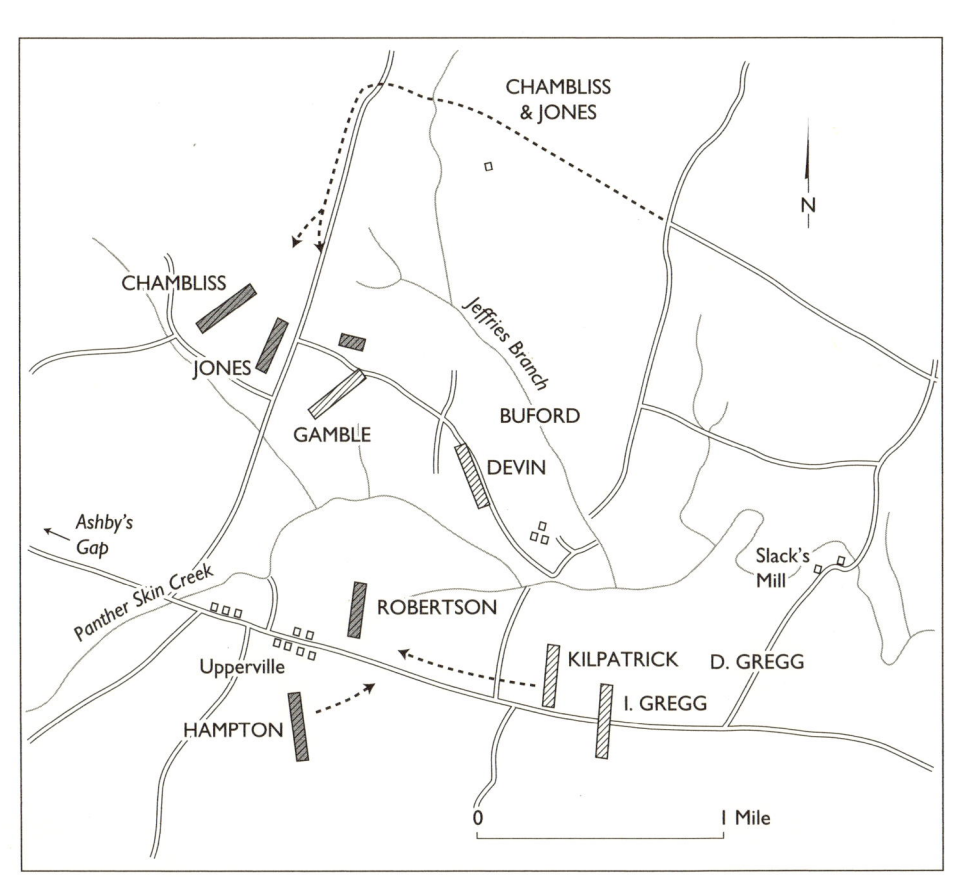

Map B-4
The Battle of Upperville, June 21 (P.M.)

THE LOUDOUN VALLEY CAVALRY BATTLES 283

However, Pleasonton ordered his combined force of Union cavalry and infantry to cease their attempted advance that Sunday evening, ending the Loudoun Valley battles. Over these five days, the Union casualties were 613; those of the Confederates, 510. About half of the latter were captured, and among them was a rebel lieutenant. As Union men were organizing Southern prisoners for their march into captivity, an officer from Colonel Vincent's brigade recognized the Confederate officer. The Union soldier, Capt. Walter G. Morrill from Company B of the 20th Maine, had worked with this Southerner on the Penobscot River in Maine before the war.[5] Morrill will return to the story in Chapter 3 at the battle for Little Round Top.

As a result of the culminating actions in the Loudoun Valley, General Pleasonton was able to report to General Hooker on June 21 and 22 about the large Confederate forces moving northward through the Shenandoah Valley. Pleasonton had to admit that the rebels held all of the mountain passes in the Blue Ridge Mountains, which were therefore serving their purpose of shielding the advancing Confederates from serious scrutiny or impediment. Another Union problem was that Pleasonton's reports were vague and not very accurate. For example, he stated to Hooker that the Confederate 2nd Corps had approached Winchester on June 17, which was off by four days. Pleasonton also indicated that Longstreet's divisions were on their way to join Ewell and that Hill had crossed the Blue Ridge into the Shenandoah. The latter two pieces of intelligence were essentially correct. Yet Hooker remained passive for three more days (see Chapter 1, section heading "Fighting Joe Hooker Fights..."). Meanwhile, the Southern invasion continued.

APPENDIX C

The Fighting Near Brinkerhoff's Ridge

This ridgeline crosses the Hanover Road east of Gettysburg (map C-1). On July 2, Federal infantry units (chart C-1) were situated just east of the ridge and skirmished with Confederate pickets until late afternoon. Meanwhile, Union cavalry was approaching from the east: the 2nd Division under Brig. Gen. David McM. Gregg (minus its fourteen-hundred-man 2nd Brigade, which had been posted to Westminster, Maryland, on July 1).

A Confederate cavalry brigade was supposed to move to this area to guard the overall rebel left. On the way, these horsemen halted as they rode south toward Gettysburg, stopping where Rock Creek intersects the Harrisburg Road (map C-1). The commander of this unit was Brig. Gen. Albert G. Jenkins. He went up nearby Barlow's Knoll (as it is now named) to reconnoiter the situation. There, around midday, he was wounded by an extraordinary long-range cannon shot from a Federal battery on Cemetery Hill.[1] Shoddy staff work caused the orders for Jenkins's mission not to filter down to his subordinate officers. This forced Maj. Gen. Edward Johnson, commander of the Confederate infantry division on the army's left wing (maps 3-5 and 3-42), to deploy the Stonewall Brigade (chart C-1) out the Hanover Road. That deployment depleted Johnson's attack force that assailed the Union right on Culp's Hill in the fighting that started on the evening of July 2 (see Chapter 3, section heading "The Confederate Left Finally Attacks . . .").

On the afternoon of July 2, the van of General Gregg's advance toward Gettysburg tangled with elements of Brig. Gen. James D. Walker's Stonewall Brigade. Colonel J. Irvin Gregg's 10th New York Cavalry (chart C-1) relieved the Union infantry units that had skirmished with the rebels for most of the afternoon.[2] The skirmishing continued, with the Confederate infantrymen now facing a weaker line of dismounted Federal troopers. One of Walker's regiments, the 2nd Virginia, deployed in a line north of the Hanover Road near the base of the ridge. The Virginians advanced and pushed back the 10th New York. At about 7 P.M., the New Yorkers were relieved by two squadrons each (four companies) of the 3rd Penn-

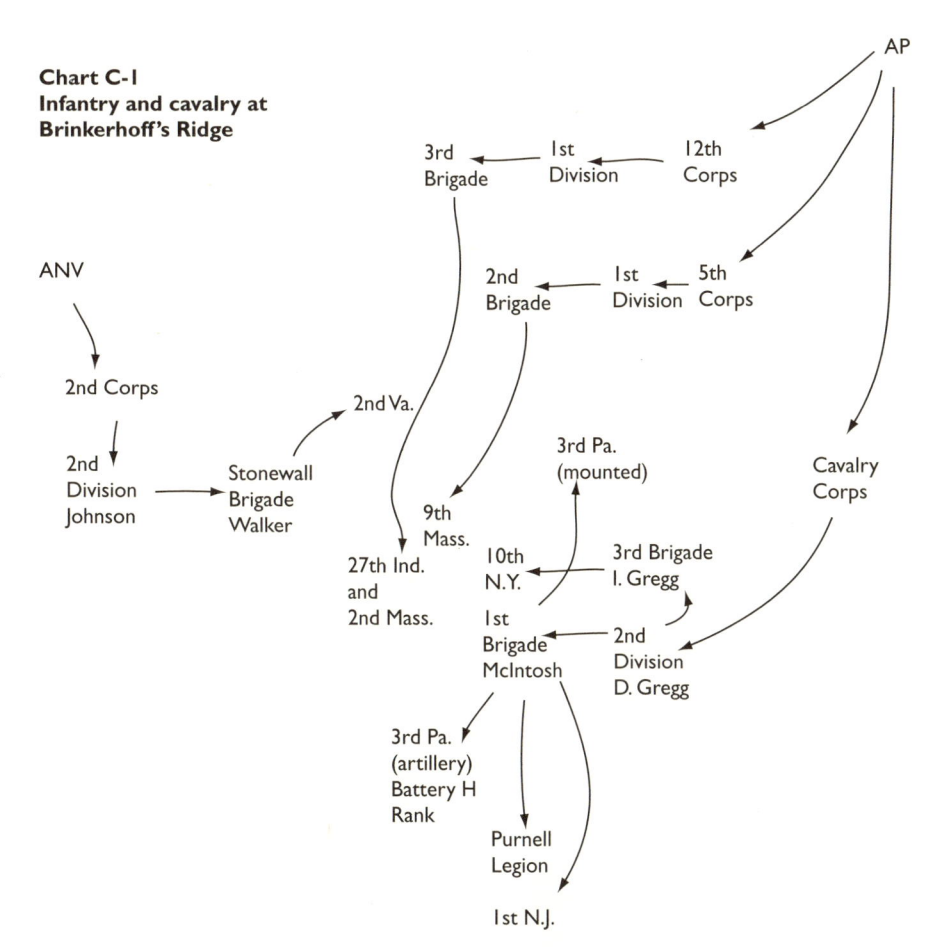

Chart C-1
Infantry and cavalry at Brinkerhoff's Ridge

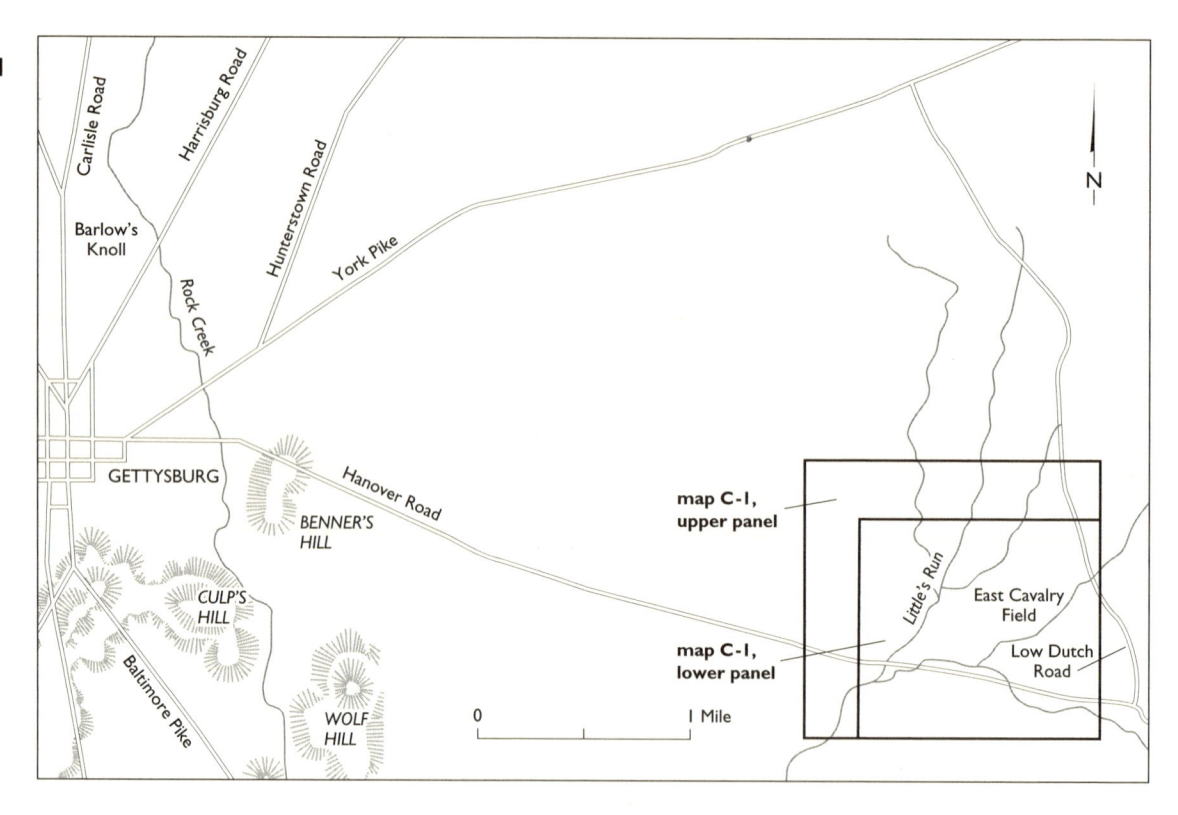

sylvania and 1st New Jersey Cavalry regiments, along with the Purnell Legion of Marylanders (map C-1). North of the road, 2nd Virginia troopers and two squadrons of the 3rd Pennsylvania vied for a stone fence line in the area between Brinkerhoff's Ridge and Cress Run (a stream that forms the approximate west boundary of the East Cavalry Field, where large numbers of troopers fought on July 3 [Appendix D]). Aided by a battery of Federal horse artillery (map C-1),[3] the Pennsylvanians seized the fence line and held it. The right flank of this Union position was dislodged from it but counterattacked and regained the northern part of the stone wall, above the Hanover Road (map C-1, bottom).

The fight near Brinkerhoff's Ridge wound down and ended as darkness approached. The men of the 2nd Virginia withdrew to the west and rejoined the bulk of their 2nd Corps brigade. By the morning of July 3, the Stonewall Brigade had been moved back to rejoin General Johnson's main body and participated in the fighting at Culp's Hill (map 4-3 in Chapter 4). At about 10 P.M. on the Second, Brig. Gen. David Gregg's division was redeployed to the south, toward the Army of the Potomac's left. However, it was to return to the area where it had fought on July 2 and became embroiled in the battle for the East Cavalry Field on July 3 (Chapter 5; Appendix D).

**Map C-1
Fighting near Brinkerhoff's Ridge, east of Gettysburg, July 2, P.M.**

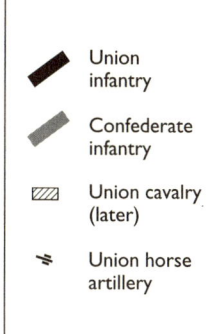

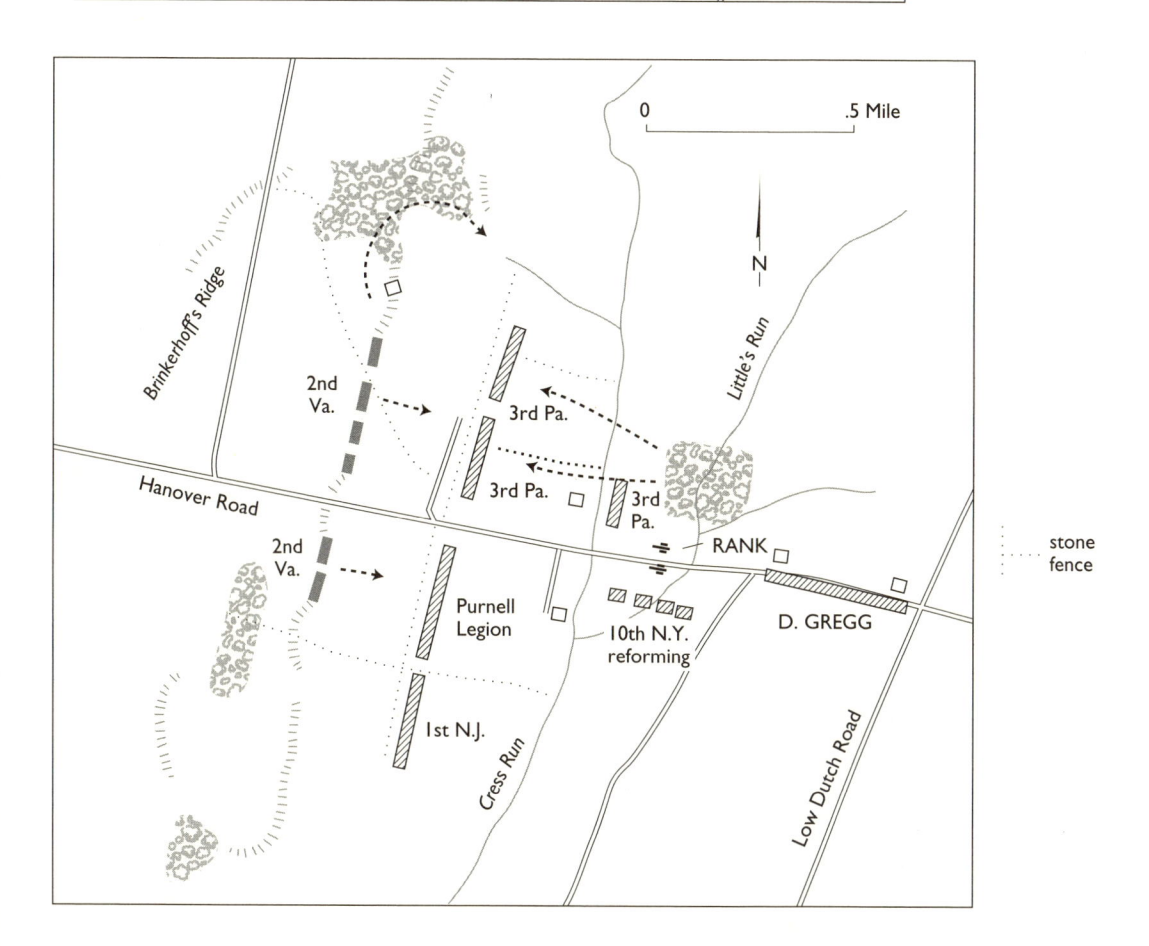

- Union infantry
- Confederate infantry
- Union cavalry (later)
- Union horse artillery
- stone fence

THE FIGHTING NEAR BRINKERHOFF'S RIDGE 287

The timely arrival near Brinkerhoff's Ridge of General Gregg's cavalry force on the afternoon of July 2 tied up the Stonewall Brigade well into the evening hours, forcing it to remain in the area the night of the Second. This drained potential fighters from the attacking force of Southerners that assailed the Union right wing during the evening and nighttime of July 2 (Chapter 3). General Walker, realizing that the "flank and rear [of the Confederate army's left wing] would have been entirely uncovered in the event of my moving with the rest of the division [in the attack on Culp's Hill] . . . deemed it prudent to hold my position until after dark."[4] That position (area-of-detail indicator for map C-1) was well away from the action on the east face of this hill, where Walker's brigade would not join the fighting until the morning of July 4 (Chapter 4).

APPENDIX D

The Cavalry Battle East of Gettysburg

On the morning of July 3, General Lee ordered Maj. Gen. J. E. B. Stuart to protect the rear of the Confederate left flank northeast and east of Culp's Hill (see Chapter 4). No record of these orders exists.[1] Stuart said later that he was instructed only to "move forward to a position to the left of General Ewell's left."[2] It is possible that Stuart's specific job in conjunction with the ordered deployment was to *tie up any Union cavalry force* that he might find.[3] Thus, those Federal troopers would be unable to harass the flank of Pickett's Charge. This presumably meant the right flank of that assault force, for most of the Union cavalry was in the southern sectors of the field. An alternative theory for "what Lee had in mind" is that "the appearance of Confederate cavalry [near the Union rear] . . . would have stirred things up greatly and perhaps distracted Meade from Lee's main plan."[4]

The point is that Stuart's orders *may* not have involved anything about assailing the Army of the Potomac's infantry line by crashing into the Union rear, east of Cemetery Ridge. Also, the hour when Pickett's Charge was to move in and when it might achieve its objective would be difficult for Stuart to know. One is thus left to wonder how he was to coordinate an attack from the rear. Moreover, the ground between the Hanover Road (where Stuart was to be deployed) and the

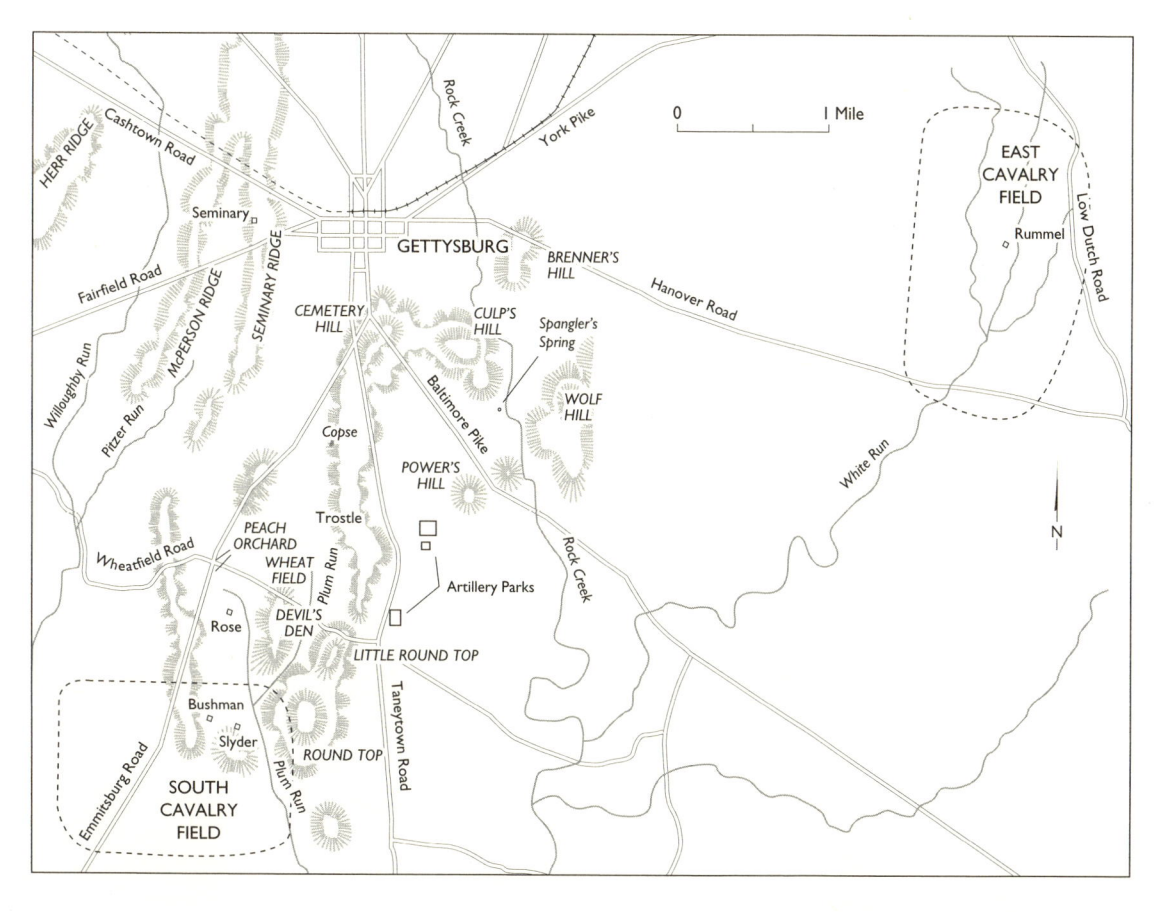

Map D-1 Theater of cavalry battles, July 3

Chart D-1
Confederate cavalry on and approaching the East Field, morning of July 3

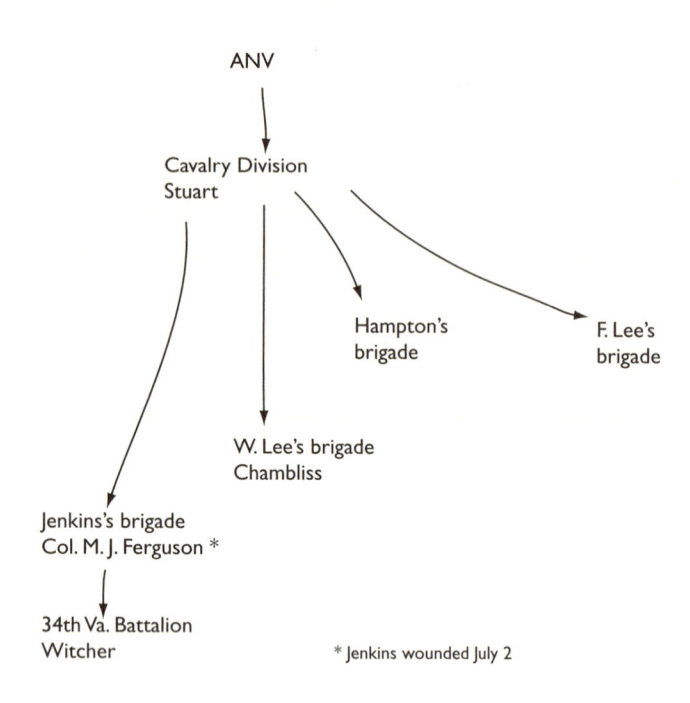

```
                    ANV
                     │
                     ▼
            Cavalry Division
                 Stuart
            ╱       │      ╲
           ╱        │       ╲
          ╱         ▼        ╲
         ╱      Hampton's     ▶ F. Lee's
        │       brigade         brigade
        │           
        │       W. Lee's brigade
        │       Chambliss
        ▼
   Jenkins's brigade
   Col. M. J. Ferguson *
        │                   * Jenkins wounded July 2
        ▼
   34th Va. Battalion
   Witcher
```

Baltimore Pike (in the direction of Cemetery Ridge) seems impassable on maps of that time (cf. map D-1).[5] Even if Stuart had somehow gotten through this area to approach the Union rear, he might then have ridden into the area of the Federal Artillery Reserve (map D-1), where massed fire from the dozens of guns there could have torn the Confederate troopers to pieces.[6] As it happened, Stuart's force got nowhere near Cemetery Ridge. Yet, as his admirers would have it, that was not his mission on July 3. So the best he could have done was "increase the panic of the retreating [Federal] troops, making the victory complete"—if Pickett's Charge had succeeded.[7]

In this regard, General Stuart himself wrote (on August 20, 1863) that "during the day's operations . . . I commanded a view of the routes leading to the enemy's rear"; and that "had the enemy's main body been dislodged . . . I was in precisely the right position to discover it and improve the opportunity."[8] It is not clear what this means. Did he intend to deliver a surprise blow in conjunction with the Pickett-Pettigrew-Trimble assault or perhaps sever a Union line of retreat (see below)? If we take his phrasing at face value, Stuart did not "command" anything except "a view"—given the Federal force nearby (whose presence and actions underlie this appendix). The implication is that *if* the rebel cavalry in this sector "had managed to seize the crossroad [in the upper right corner of map D-1] and march to Two Taverns on Baltimore Pike [see map 2-16 in Chapter 2], they would have been astride the army's main supply line and astride one of its retreat routes"[9]—again, those that the Federals would have scrambled toward if the Army of the Potomac's line had been split in two by the assault on Cemetery Ridge. Stuart's brigades did not manage to secure "the crucial Low Dutch Road–Hanover Road intersection" (map D-1),[10] as we will see when the actions described in this account unfold.

Whatever the mission and goals Stuart had in mind for July 3, he readied his troopers by replenishing their ammunition through part of that morning. Then General Stuart led two of his brigades—under Cols. John R. Chambliss Jr. and Milton J. Ferguson (the latter's unit now attached to Stuart)—out the York Pike (map D-1). They went two and one-half miles east then cut across fields on a lane called the Low Dutch Road, which runs roughly north-south and eventually connects with the Hanover Road (maps D-1 and D-2).

Chambliss and Ferguson were sent to Cress Ridge west of the Low Dutch Road. It overlooks undulating land, including the fields of three farms, between the ridge and the Hanover Road to the south (map D-2). Elements of Jenkins's brigade (now commanded by Colonel Ferguson owing to General Jenkins's wounding on July 2, as described in Appendix C) moved down to positions amongst and near the Rummel farm buildings (map D-2). This was the 34th Virginia Battalion under Lt. Col. Vincent A. Witcher (chart D-1). Stuart was awaiting his trailing units, the brigades of Wade Hampton and Fitzhugh Lee, to come in behind Chambliss and Ferguson on the ridge north of the Rummel farm (map D-2), in the middle of the region that became known as the East Cavalry Field.

Before those units arrived, however, Stuart had an artillery piece fire off four rounds in a variety of directions for a reason that remains unknown—possibly to

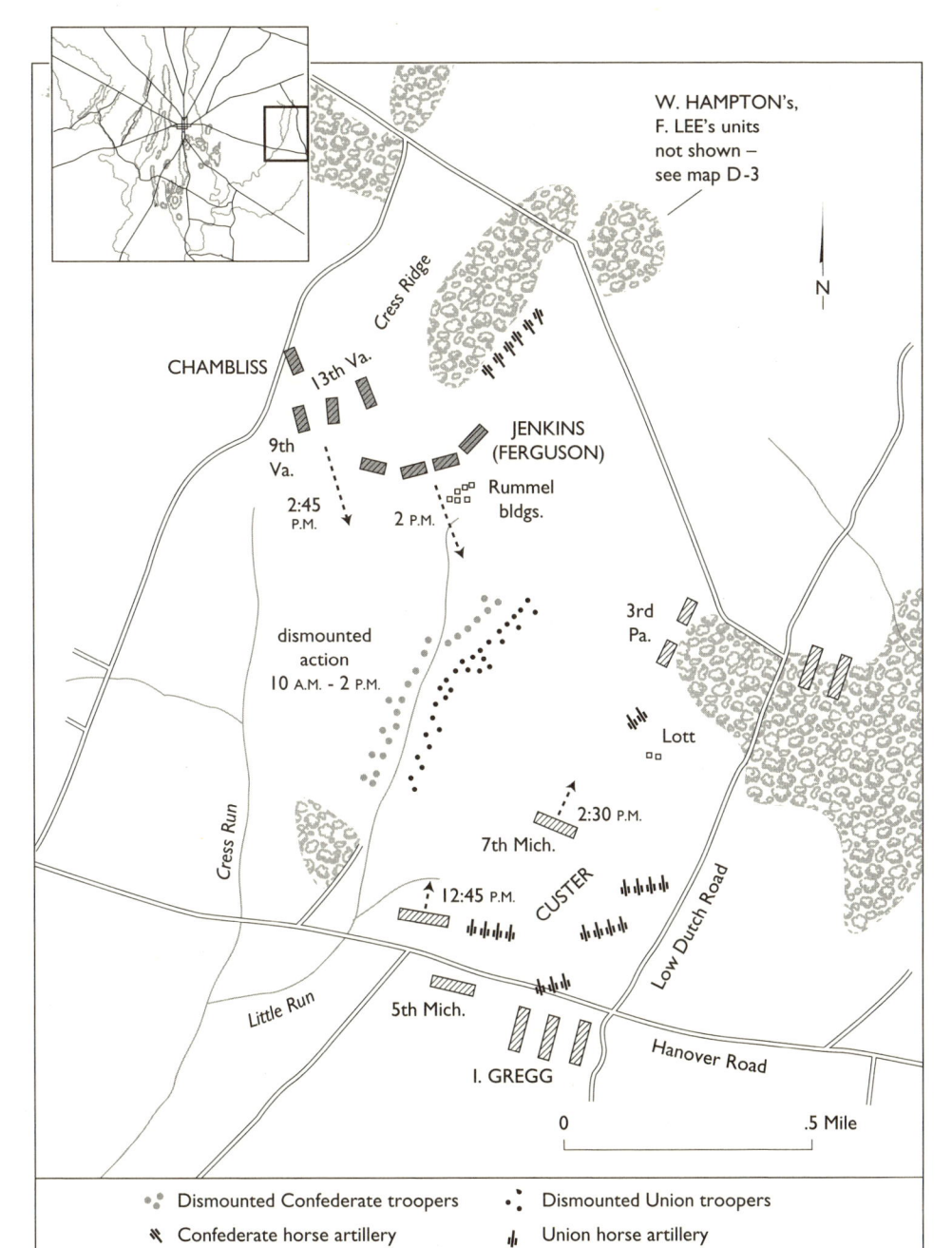

**Map D-2
Early stages of fighting on the East Cavalry Field**

flush out Federal cavalry somewhere in the vicinity (as we continue to bear in mind that the main mission may have been to "tie up" a large number of Union troopers). This noise, and the unconcealed arrival of Hampton and Fitz Lee after noon, brought Union cavalrymen to the area. They approached the intersection of the Low Dutch and Hanover Roads. These Federal troopers were under Brig. Gen. David McM. Gregg, and they had fought in this vicinity on July 2 (Appendix C). To help him guard the Union rear in this northern sector of the field, Gregg had borrowed Brig. Gen. George Armstrong Custer's Michigan brigade from Kilpatrick's division (chart D-1). That brigade and the two formally under Gregg's command had earlier been sent to watch an area near the place where the Low Dutch Road leads to the Baltimore Pike from the Hanover Road (map D-2).

THE CAVALRY BATTLE EAST OF GETTYSBURG

**Chart D-2
Union cavalry on and approaching the East Field from the south, morning of July 3**

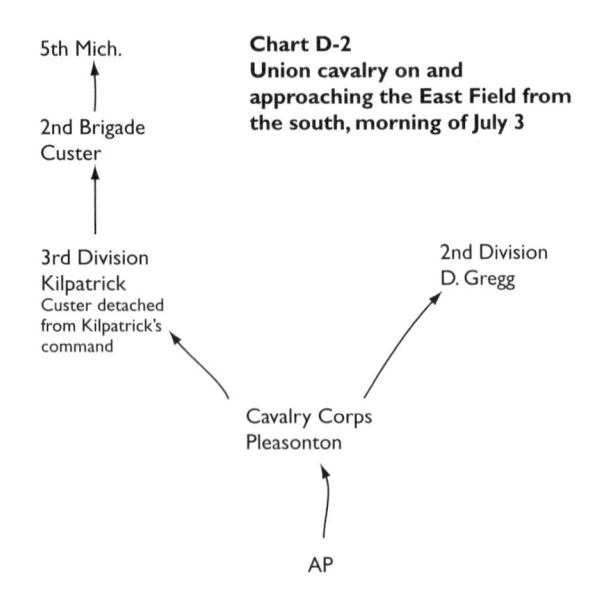

5th Mich.
↑
2nd Brigade
Custer
↑
3rd Division
Kilpatrick
Custer detached from Kilpatrick's command

2nd Division
D. Gregg
↗
Cavalry Corps
Pleasonton
↑
AP

**Chart D-3
Further units of Union cavalry arriving on the East Field**

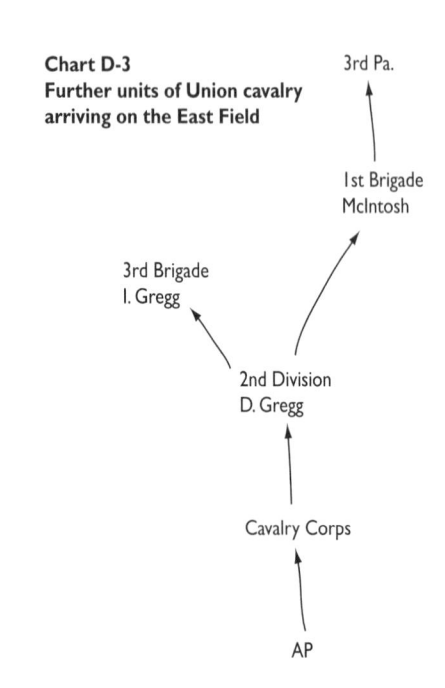

3rd Pa.
↑
1st Brigade
McIntosh
↗
3rd Brigade
I. Gregg
↖
2nd Division
D. Gregg
↑
Cavalry Corps
↑
AP

Custer moved north of there, reaching the Hanover Road at about 9 A.M. His Michigan men were deployed into skirmishing and defensive positions. They had spotted Confederate cavalry to the north, and they might have heard Stuart's signal shots. For its part, Federal horse artillery dropped trail in the area and fired on the Confederate batteries to the north, scoring several hits on the rebel guns along Cress Ridge (map D-2).

However, below the positions of those guns, dismounted Confederate cavalrymen applied pressure to the Federals situated in the south sector of the field. Beginning at about 8 A.M. Witcher's Virginians deployed in the vicinity of the Rummel buildings (map D-2), eventually facing Custer's skirmish line to the south. Before this, Witcher's riflemen had sent long-range fire southward and harassed the Federal troopers manning horse artillery north of the Hanover Road (map D-2).

The fighting between the opposing unhorsed cavalrymen began about 10 A.M. This series of relatively small firefights eventually escalated into large-scale engagements between mounted troopers in the afternoon. Meanwhile, long-range artillery fire crisscrossed the field. The Federals had placed their horse artillery to the south (near the Hanover and Low Dutch Roads). The Confederate guns were lined up along Cress Ridge (map D-2). The ensuing artillery duel involved mostly counter-battery firing. However, the after-action accounts of some Federal officers claimed that the Union guns were also pummeling the Rummel barn. The large building had become a hotbed of Confederate snipers detached from the line of dismounted troopers. The Northerners further claimed that these rebel marksmen were blown out of the barn.[11] This was disputed by some of the Confederates who had been in that vicinity. These Southerners said that Union horse artillery was firing essentially only at Cress Ridge, beyond the area of the Rummel buildings. Some independent accounts from the Union artillerymen largely corroborated these Confederate claims, which are further backed up by modern-day measurements of distances between the relevant locations and considerations of the lines of sight that were likely to have existed in 1863.

This matter is more than a tempest in a teacup, because it relates to *who controlled the center of the cavalry battlefield* in the midst of the fighting and afterward. Part of that issue involves ground troops as well as cannon fire and the extent to which the dismounted troopers held their ground, occupied the protective buildings, and so forth. As the men in this sector exchanged rifle fire during the late morning, Witcher extended his line to the left (east of the Rummel buildings visible in maps D-2–D-4) with troopers from Colonel Chambliss's brigade (chart D-2), who moved in to bolster the dismounted rebel ground force in this area.

Around noontime, Custer's brigade of Federal troopers rejoined its division, nearer to the overall Union left flank. By then, David Gregg's horsemen were also arriving on the field. Earlier, General Gregg, who had heard that more large Confederate cavalry units were coming, stopped Custer as he was moving away to the west, convincing the young general that he (Gregg) might need all the help he could get.

General Gregg kept Col. J. Irvin Gregg's brigade in reserve southwest of the Hanover Road–Low Dutch Road intersection, then moved on past the crossroads with Col. John B. McIntosh's brigade and took up a position south and east of

Custer's units, which were facing roughly northward toward the Confederates deployed in the middle of the field. McIntosh's troopers established a line roughly along the Low Dutch Road (map D-2, chart D-3).

McIntosh's men fired toward the Confederates in the vicinity of the Rummel farm, where Jenkins's dismounted troopers had by then been fighting for more than four hours. Their actions were the yeoman's work of the Confederates on the East Cavalry Field.[12]

As the battle proceeded into the early afternoon, dismounted troopers from Wade Hampton's and Fitz Lee's brigades extended the Confederate line to the east. There were now four rebel brigades in this middle portion of the field, and they had a skirmish line covering the entire front of these south-facing units. Resupplied with ammunition and reinforced, the Southerners in the vicinity of the Rummel farm attacked the line of dismounted Union cavalrymen at Little Run (that stream, most of whose course appears on maps D-2 and D-3, originates at a spring amongst the Rummel buildings).

With the return of Custer's brigade, the Federal troopers on the southern sector of the field had been reinforced by two detached squadrons from the 5th Michigan (map D-2), one unit commanded by Maj. Luther S. Trowbridge and the other by Maj. Noah H. Ferry (chart D-4). As these elements of Custer's force advanced northward toward the 34th Virginia Battalion, Ferry's Michiganders received heavy fire from Witcher's men.[13] Major Ferry's men shot back, and their repeating Spencer rifles did inflict casualties on the soldiers from the 34th. By the end of the day, Witcher's battalion was down to less than a hundred unwounded men. During this particular fight, the Michiganders probably expended their ammunition in an impatient manner and at too long a range (several of Witcher's men suffered wounds to their lower extremities). The advancing line of heavily skirmishing Virginians began to break up the formations of the 5th Michigan squadrons. Major Ferry attempted to rally his men, but he was shot in the head by a rifleman from the 34th Virginia Battalion.

Ferry's Michiganders were driven back at least three hundred yards. But now the southward-advancing rebels absorbed cannon fire from some of Custer's horse artillery. Soon the Virginians were hit by two units of Union cavalry (one of them a regiment from Gregg's division) riding into this part of the field. As the dismounted Michigan men, who by then were out of ammunition, withdrew, Cobb's Georgia Legion (chart D-5) counterattacked the mounted Federal troopers and a saber melee ensued.

This was when Custer's 7th Michigan made its famous but overblown cavalry charge, riding into the fray to stop the Confederate advance. "Come on, you Wolverines!" General Custer was supposed to have shouted.[14] However, as he and his men responded to this battle cry, they did not take account of the many impediments that were on these fields in July 1863. Thus, the charge of the 7th Michigan piled into a rail fence (map D-2).[15] Having completed their repulse of the dismounted troopers from the 5th Michigan, Witcher's 34th Virginia Battalion and other dismounted Virginia troopers enfiladed Custer's charging horsemen. The men of the 7th Michigan dismounted when they were stalled by the

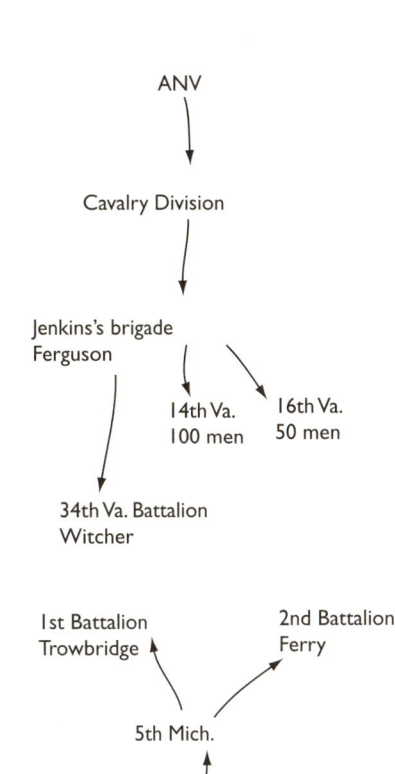

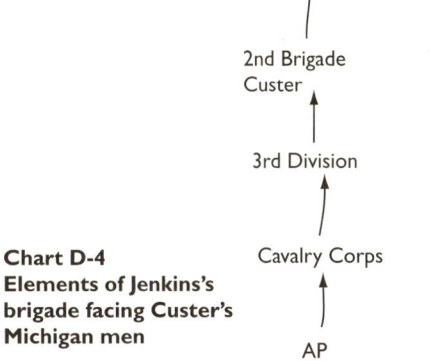

**Chart D-4
Elements of Jenkins's brigade facing Custer's Michigan men**

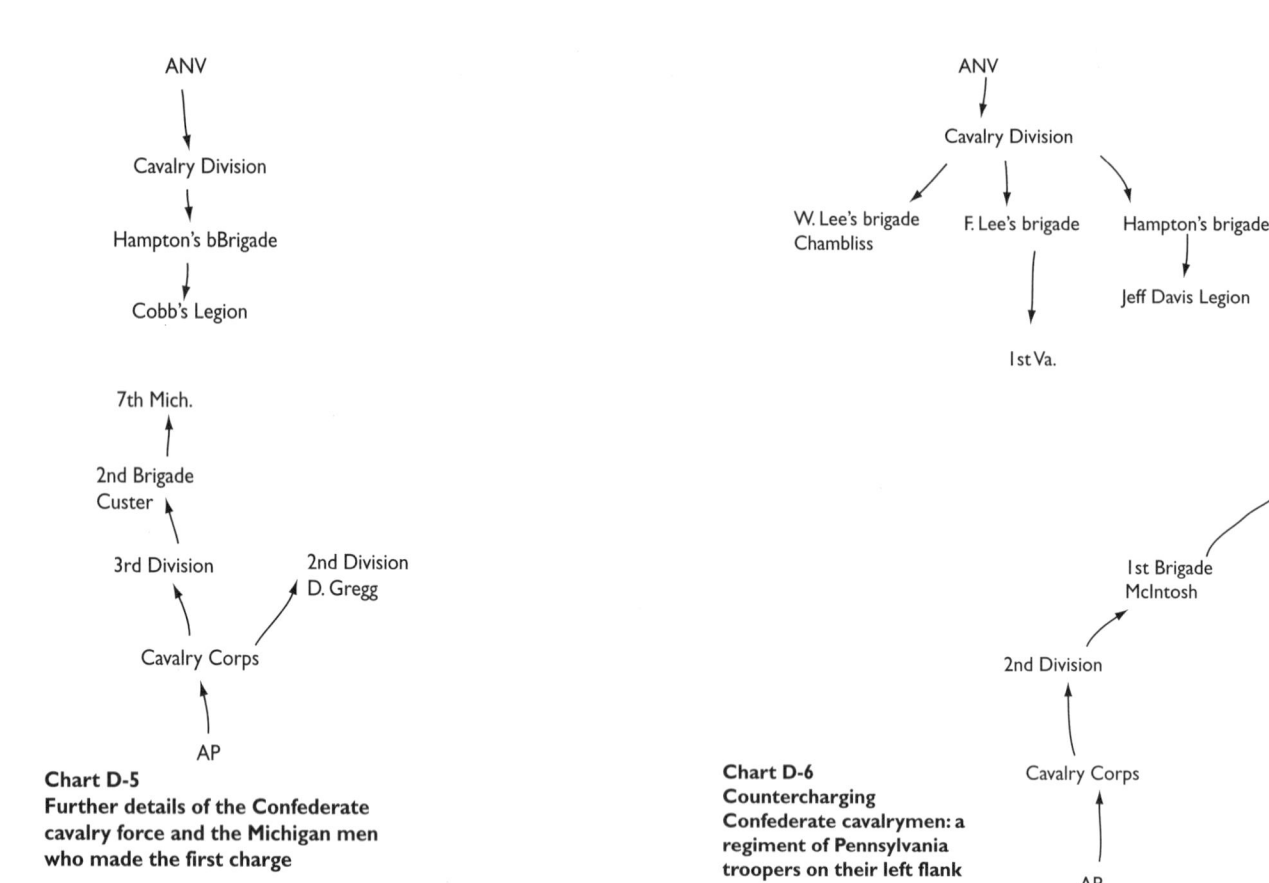

Chart D-5
Further details of the Confederate cavalry force and the Michigan men who made the first charge

Chart D-6
Countercharging Confederate cavalrymen: a regiment of Pennsylvania troopers on their left flank

fence line, but were compelled to fall back under the heavy fire coming on their left and front. The time was between 2:30 and 3 P.M.

Now a series of confused charges and countercharges commenced (exemplified by the dashed arrows pointing south, near the top of map D-2). Some of the Federals managed to remount. They launched two waves of attacks, in part against the still dismounted rebels. The fighting escalated further as regiments from John Chambliss's and Fitzhugh Lee's brigades rode into the fray. Lee's 1st Virginia (chart D-6) made a particularly vigorous charge, supported by advances of the 1st North Carolina Cavalry and the Jefferson Davis Legion. The fighting became hand-to-hand, insofar as this can occur among mounted troopers waving their sabers and wielding their pistols. In any case, the Confederate attacks ran out of steam when the horsemen ran up against one of the other fences in this area (they seemed to be everywhere, although some were deliberately knocked down to clear portions of the field). The rebels were shelled by Union horse artillery; and the 3rd Pennsylvania Cavalry (chart D-6), formed in the aforementioned south-to-north line just west of the Low Dutch Road (map D-2), added flanking fire from its breech-loading carbines. The Confederates were forced back northward past the Rummel buildings.

By then it was after 3 P.M. If Stuart was supposed to ride well west of this field to approach the rear of the Union infantry, he was late. But he did not give up—or at least his brigade commanders did not, because someone in the division ordered one final cavalry charge. There is no record of who gave the instructions for

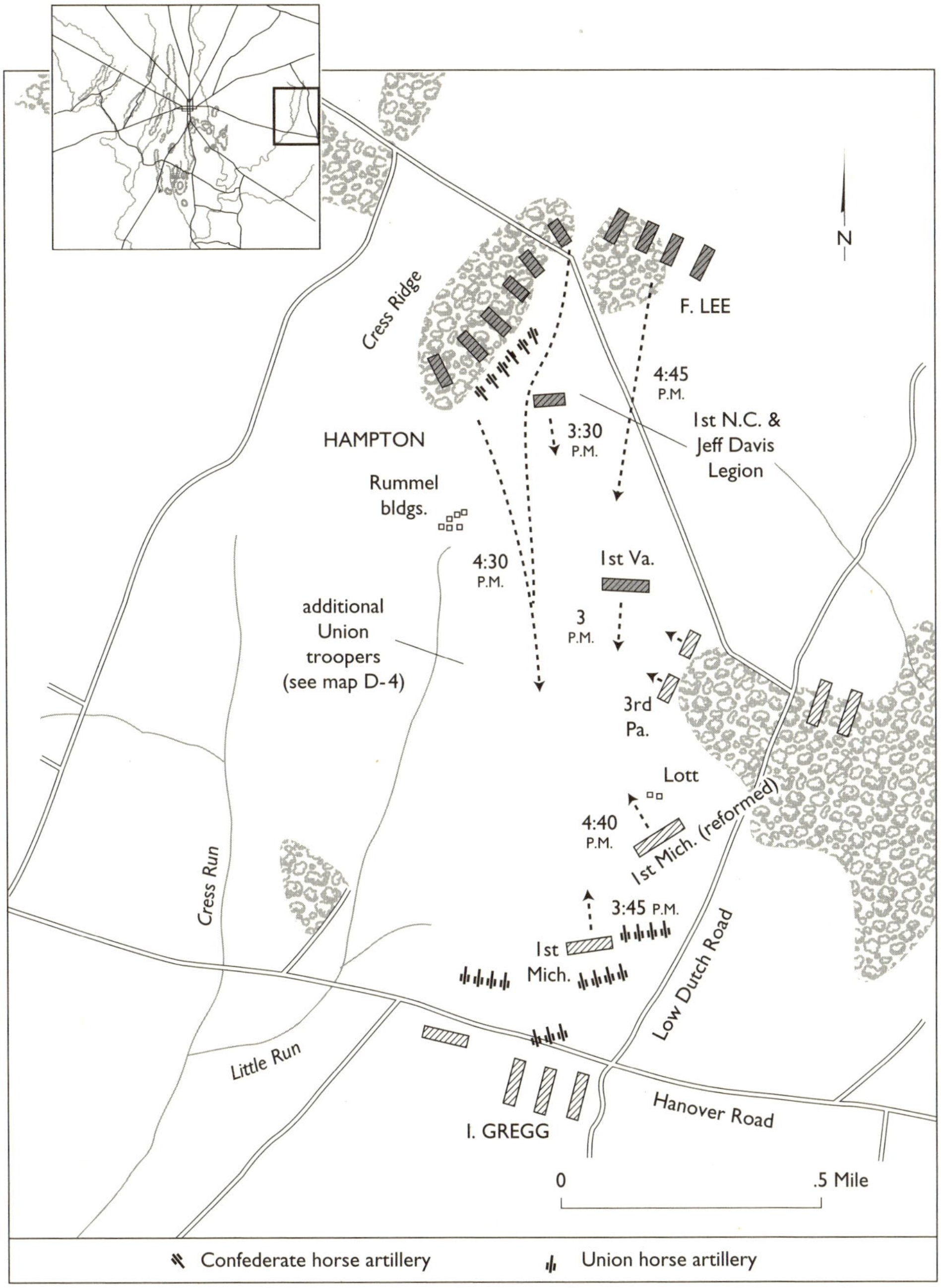

**Map D-3
Late stages of fighting on the East Cavalry Field**

this last mounted attack; Stuart did not mention it in his after-action report.[16] For the final assault, the remaining regiments from Wade Hampton's and Fitzhugh Lee's brigades (map D-3) were gathered (except Cobb's Legion and the 4th Virginia, respectively). These rebel units rode through the woods to advance southward, east of the Rummel buildings. This movement had a grand pageantry to it, as was expressed later by the Federals waiting for them to the south and west (again near the Low Dutch Road).[17]

The mounted rebel force, massed in larger numbers than in the more sporadic and confused fighting earlier, moved south until it was within three-quarters of a mile of the Hanover Road (map D-3). The attackers took heavy fire from Union horse artillery, but the rear ranks closed up and filled the gaps that opened in the

THE CAVALRY BATTLE EAST OF GETTYSBURG

**Chart D-7
The final cavalry charges and countercharges on the East Field**

ANV
↓
Cavalry Division
↙   ↘
Hampton's brigade   F. Lee's brigade

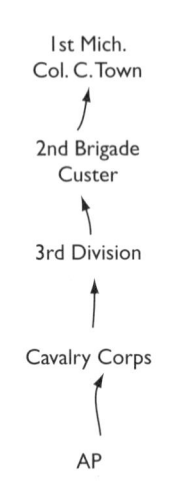

1st Mich.
Col. C. Town
↑
2nd Brigade
Custer
↑
3rd Division
↑
Cavalry Corps
↑
AP

assaulting Confederate force. Behind the Federal batteries was a reserve of troopers in General Gregg's command, the 1st Michigan (chart D-7). Earlier, these mounted men had been drawn up in columns just south of the Hanover Road. Just before 4 P.M., the Michiganders rode forward across the road and past the batteries. They kept advancing and were hit by two regiments from Hampton's brigade (map D-3). Several of the Confederate troopers backed out of this preliminary clash, turning to meet a further Federal advance or to get ready for an attack of their own.

Indeed, the next event was a massed collision of the mounted men in this sector of the field. As in the last stages of the action at Brandy Station (Appendix A), the fight on the East Cavalry Field was a classic cavalry confrontation. Here, the 1st Michigan Regiment was outnumbered by the better parts of two Hampton's and Fitz Lee's brigades. But the Michigan men regrouped and rode northward starting at a walk, then a trot, and finally a gallop. The Confederates in their front did the same. The opposing columns of horsemen crashed into each other (map D-3). Many men and their mounts went down, some tumbling head over heels as riders were crushed beneath the horses. In the resulting melee, the sounds of sabers clashing and pistol shots from the troopers' side arms filled the field east of Gettysburg on that Friday afternoon.

Other Union men in the vicinity came to the aid of the 1st Michigan (chart D-8). Some of these troopers were still in the vicinity of Little Run, threatening the right of the rebel advance (map D-4). While the dismounted Federals fired into that enemy flank, some mounted squadrons of Union men charged sideways into the head of Hampton's attacking column. On the opposite Confederate flank, elements of Colonel McIntosh's command still held the area along the Low Dutch Road, guarding the right flank of the entire Federal position on that field (chart D-8). Two Union officers ordered to hold that position had an opportunity to do something more aggressive. Thus, Capt. William Miller and Lt. William Brooke-Rawle agreed to countermand their standing orders and counterattacked the Confederate left. These men—a portion of the 3rd Pennsylvania Cavalry—fired a volley from their carbines and then rode into the left of Hampton's column. They were joined just afterward by a counterattacking squadron from the 1st New Jersey, which was posted along the Low Dutch Road to Miller's left (map D-4, chart D-8).

The Confederate cavalry's last grand assault lost momentum, attacked as it was on both flanks and in its front. The battle degenerated into small fighting groups as men rode to rescue their imperiled mates in one mini-engagement or another. Finally, the spent Southern horsemen fell back past the Rummel buildings (map D-4). The area south of this farm, down to the Hanover Road where the Union batteries were formed, was in the Federals' possession by late afternoon (Hampton's and Lee's charge having commenced between 4:30 and 5 P.M.).

As evening approached, the Confederates formed a line north of the Rummel farm. Small-arms fire sputtered on, and a half-hearted long-range artillery duel continued into the gathering darkness. However, by then the cavalry battle of Gettysburg was effectively over.

What was the outcome of this battle outside the battle? It can justifiably be summarized as another draw, harking back to similar results in the June cavalry engagements. Moreover, the casualties on the field east of Gettysburg were once

**Map D-4
Final charges on the East Cavalry Field, and Union flank attacks**

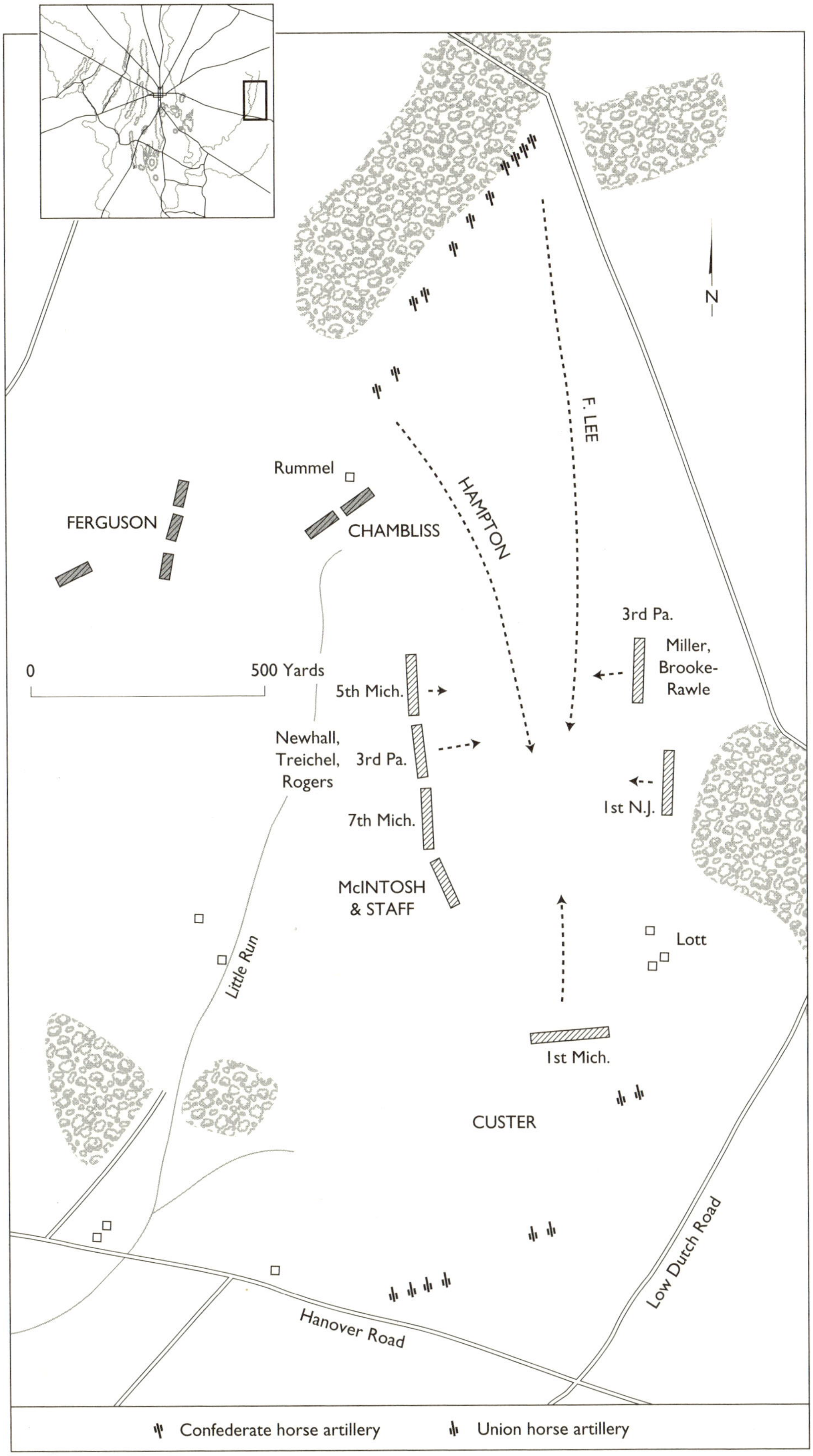

THE CAVALRY BATTLE EAST OF GETTYSBURG

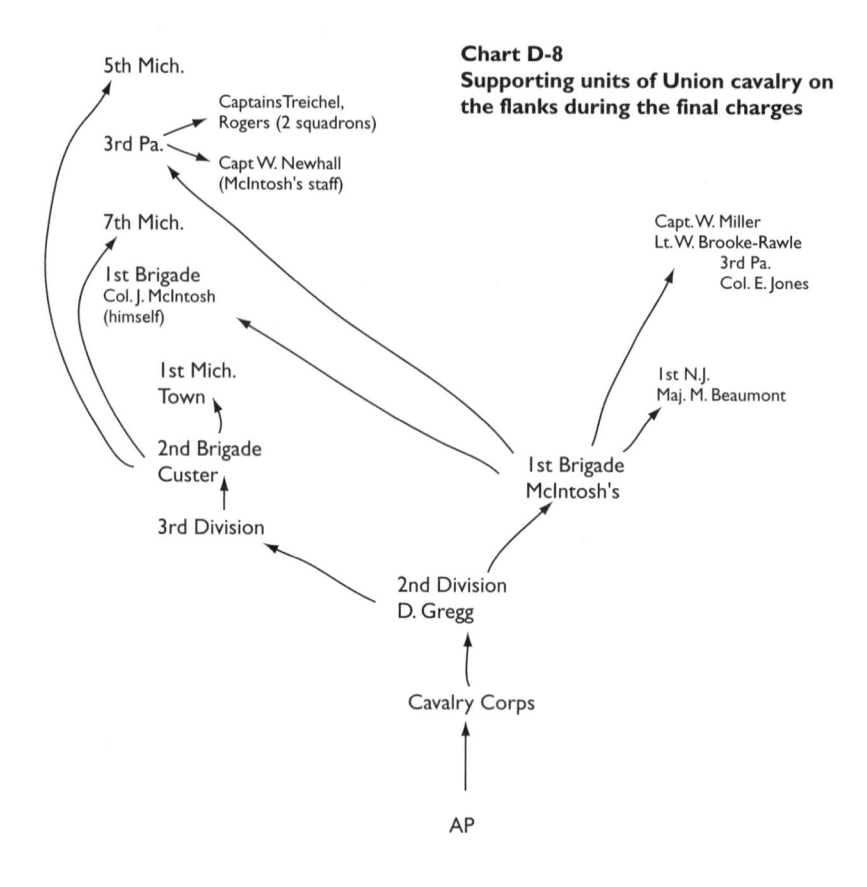

**Chart D-8
Supporting units of Union cavalry on the flanks during the final charges**

again far from brutal: 254 for the Union troopers, 181 for the Confederates,[18] out of approximately nine thousand men present. However, for those who were on the East Field the battle of July 3 was not quite over; for the Southern versus Northern participants continued as verbal adversaries for years: Who commanded the field and who held the Rummel barn after the battle? Both Colonel Witcher of the 34th Virginia Battalion and General Stuart himself recalled walking the field near that barn on the evening of July 3.[19] In their accounts, these two Confederates tacitly argued that the field was theirs. Witcher claimed his men spent the night of July 3 in the Rummel barn,[20] and both officers contended that they had narrowly won the cavalry battle at Gettysburg in the tactical sense.[21]

If the Confederates fighting on the East Cavalry Field had achieved a formal success (accepting the fact that they held significant portions of the field after the fighting), Jeb Stuart had not accomplished very much of large-scale significance. He certainly failed to add a sharp "kidney punch" to his enemy's rear in the area of the main fighting to the west—whether or not that was his objective in the first place. By aggressively continuing an advance clockwise from his starting position west and north of the East Cavalry Field, Stuart did protect the left wing of the rebel army. However, the lengthy series of actions that ensued on that field tied up his force as much as it occupied the Federal cavalry fighting there. And, as the next appendix will reveal, a significant force of Union troopers on July 3 was left to its own devices on and near the South Cavalry Field.

THE STAND OF THE U.S. ARMY AT GETTYSBURG

APPENDIX E

The Fatal Cavalry Charge of Elon Farnsworth

The military action on July 3 that brought the Battle of Gettysburg to its close involved several regiments of Union cavalry.[1] They were guarding the Army of the Potomac's left flank (map E-1). The position of these troopers suggests that they could have attacked Pickett's right flank (map E-4). Where these Federal horsemen were placed and stayed throughout almost all of July 3 reveals that Stuart certainly did not find and engage them to distraction. In this regard, the actions of Brig. Gens. David McM. Gregg, George Armstrong Custer, and the other Union troopers mentioned in Appendix D were successful to the extent that they tied up Stuart — freeing a fellow Union cavalry commander in principle to add counterattacking power against the rebel infantry assault (Chapter 4).

Brigadier General Judson Kilpatrick did nothing of the sort, however. And he was a dubious fellow more generally, as events of that Friday afternoon were to exemplify.[2] Kilpatrick's troopers had fought on the fringes of the Battle of Gettysburg on July 2, clashing with rebel troopers under Brig. Gen. Wade Hampton at Huntersdown, Pennsylvania (five miles northeast of Gettysburg). Late that night, Kilpatrick was ordered to withdraw and ride southward. At dawn on July 3 his division was posted in support of the Union left flank below the Bushman farm southwest of Big Round Top and just east of the Emmitsburg Road (maps E-2, E-3). At 8 A.M., Kilpatrick received an order from Cavalry Corps headquarters to "attack the enemy's right and rear."[3] For this, his depleted division was buttressed by a brigade from Brig. Gen. John Buford's division, the bulk of which was in northern Maryland between the First of July and early on the Third (Chapters 1 and 5).

The cavalry unit ordered to reinforce Kilpatrick was that of Brig. Gen. Wesley Merritt (chart E-1, map E-2). Merritt was instructed in the morning to proceed from Emmitsburg, Maryland, to the battlefield in Pennsylvania.[4] He left northern Maryland (where he was posted about ten miles south of Gettysburg) around noontime and arrived

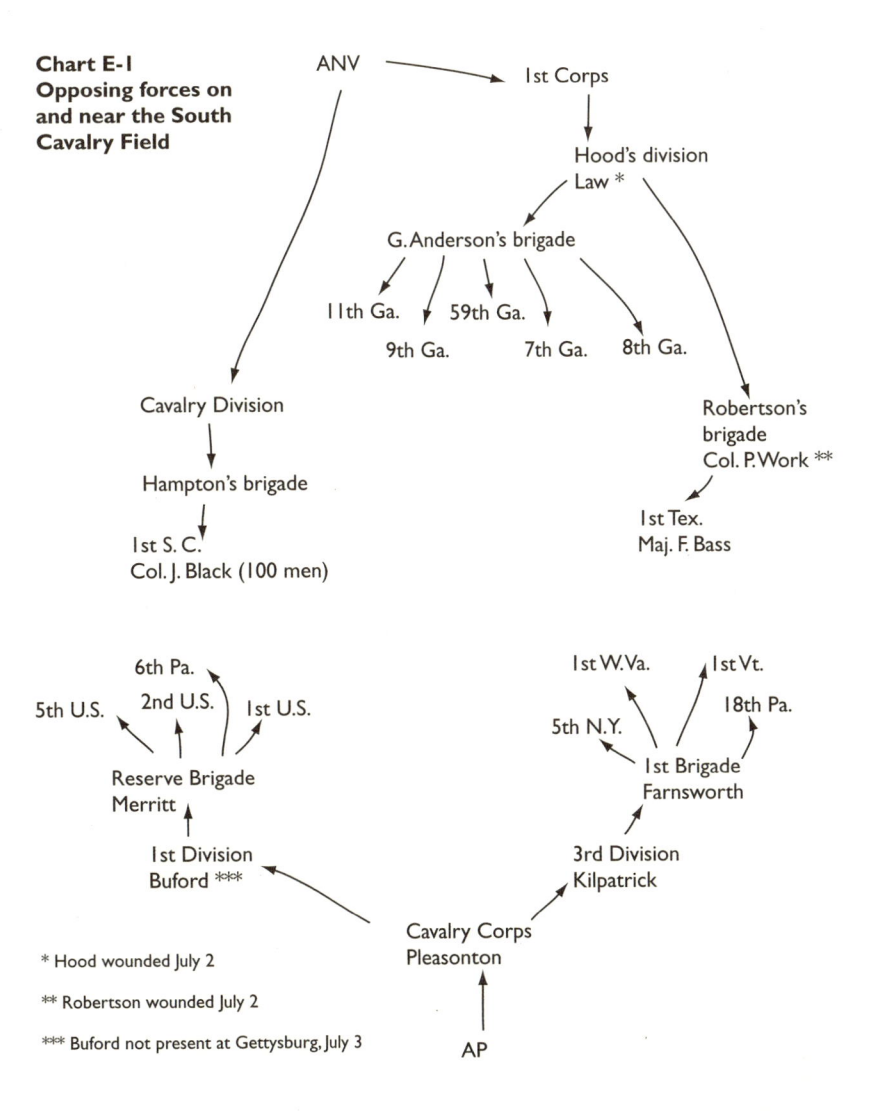

**Chart E-1
Opposing forces on and near the South Cavalry Field**

* Hood wounded July 2

** Robertson wounded July 2

*** Buford not present at Gettysburg, July 3

**Map E-1
Theater of cavalry battles, July 3**

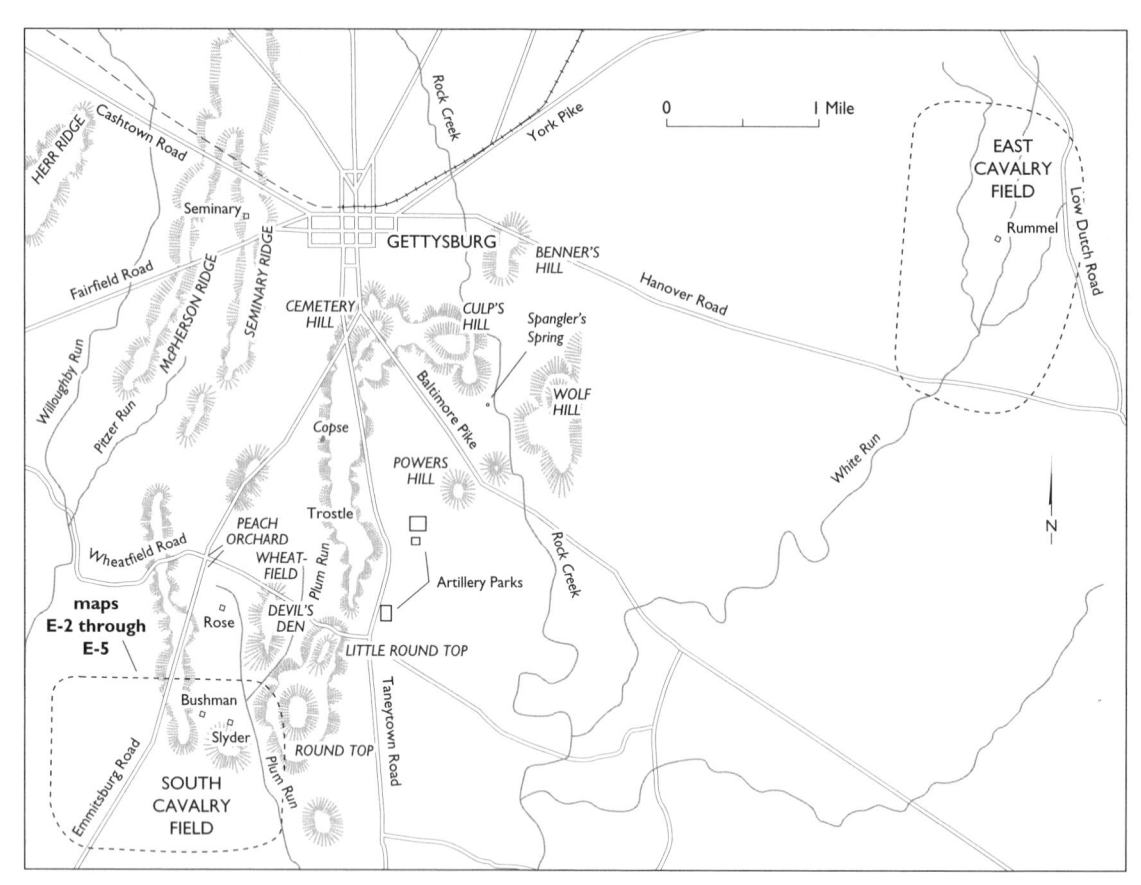

in the vicinity of Kilpatrick's troopers, south of the main battle region (map E-2), in the early-to-mid-afternoon. Remember that Custer's brigade had been detached from Kilpatrick and sent east and north (Appendix D), so Merritt's arrival made up for the part of his force he lost to Brig. Gen. David Gregg.

The troopers under Kilpatrick's command were in a position to support the Union left—but barely, as maps 4-36 and 4-39 reveal: rebel infantry was everywhere in this vicinity. These were mostly the advanced units of Hood's and McLaws's divisions (chart E-1), owing to the ground they had gained near the Emmitsburg Road on July 2. Specifically, Kilpatrick was covered on his left and on his right by brigades from Hood's division. Farther to the north, two of McLaws's brigades occupied the Peach Orchard and vicinity, near the Emmitsburg Road (map E-3, chart E-1).

Kilpatrick's troopers began to demonstrate against the extreme rebel right in the midafternoon on July 3. Merritt's men mainly fought dismounted on the South Cavalry Field (map E-1) as they gingerly advanced up the Emmitsburg Road (map E-2). They were headed toward Confederate troops of Hood's division (chart E-1, maps E-2 and E-3), which by then was led by Brig. Gen. Evander M. Law (recall that the former division commander, Maj. Gen. John Bell Hood, was wounded on July 2). As Merritt approached the Confederate infantry positions, Law moved some artillery batteries to face the dismounted Union cavalrymen and repositioned Brig. Gen. George T. Anderson's brigade (chart E-1) so that most of the ground between the Emmitsburg Road and Big Round Top was covered (map E-2). The advancing Federals increased their pressure. Law, who had received some reinforcements from the 1st South Carolina Cavalry (map E-2,

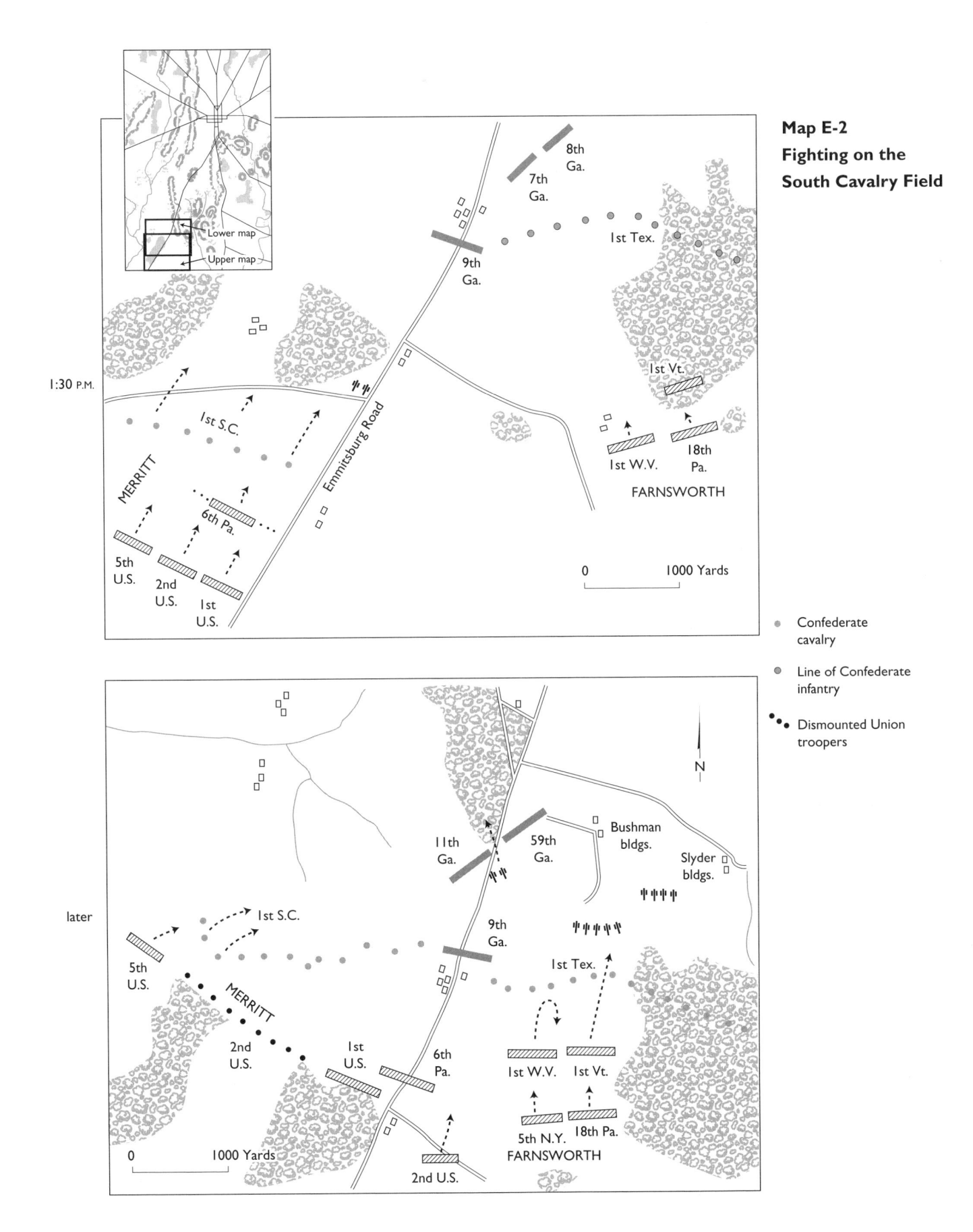

Map E-2
Fighting on the South Cavalry Field

1:30 P.M.

later

- Confederate cavalry
- Line of Confederate infantry
- Dismounted Union troopers

THE FATAL CAVALRY CHARGE OF ELON FARNSWORTH 301

**Map E-3
Farnsworth's charge:
initial stages**

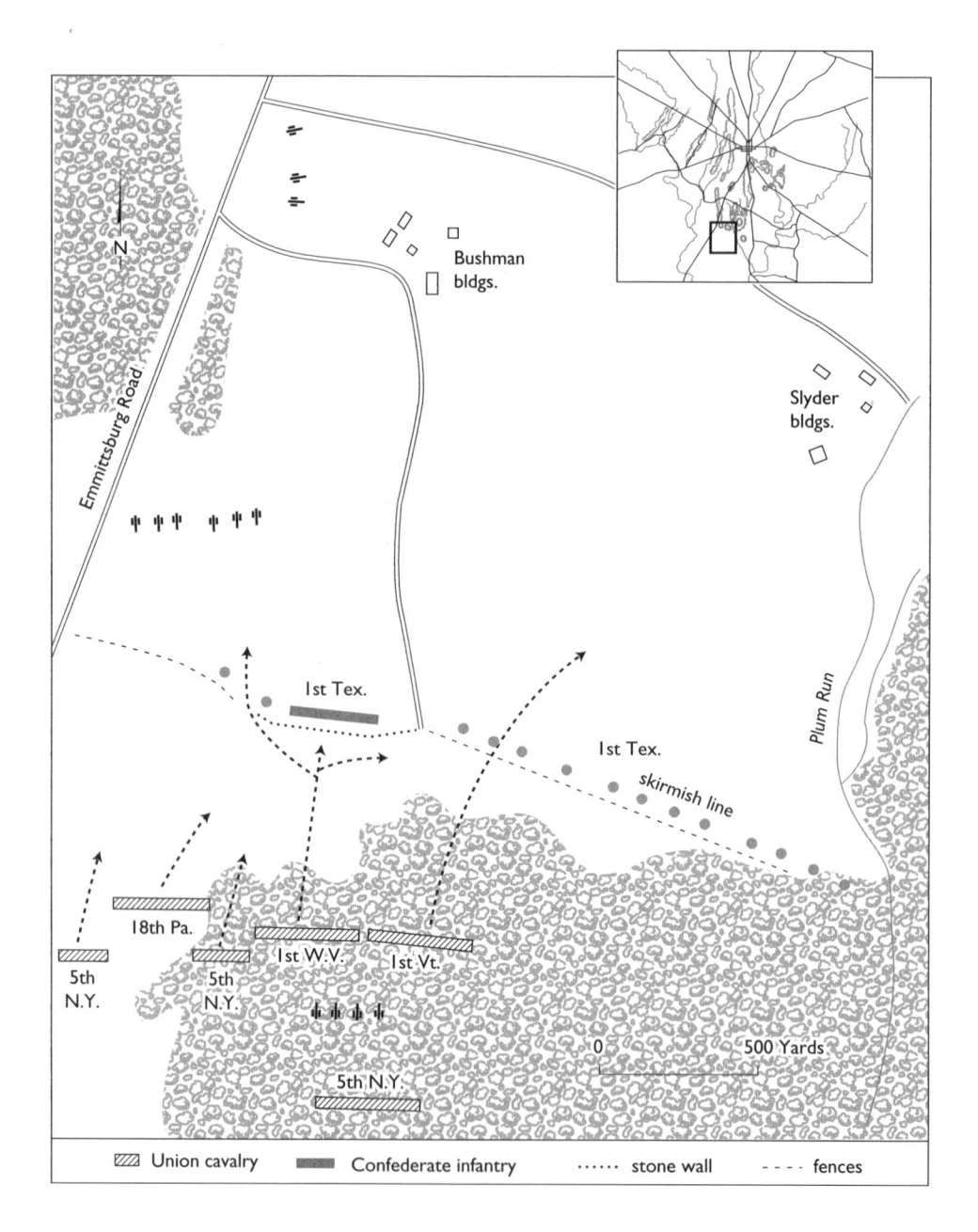

chart E-1), stretched his line farther to his right facing south. Meanwhile, Merritt's men kept progressing toward Law's right (map E-2). This force of dismounted troopers made some headway, but they never pushed the Confederate infantrymen and cavalrymen very far to the north. This was a "feeble effort [that] had ended almost before it began."[5]

This action involving the left-wing regiments of General Kilpatrick's command proceeded for four hours (according to Merritt), out of sight or knowledge of the bulk of the two armies. Finally, at about 5:30 P.M., Kilpatrick received word that the Union center had repulsed a huge rebel infantry assault. This division commander, who came to be known as "Killcavalry," then ordered a more concerted mounted attack, to be executed by the right wing of his force (thus not including Merritt). That the 3rd Division commander ordered this kind of attack seemed to fit with his disparaging nickname, and in this regard he may have been thinking that he could kick the rebels while they were down. However, recall the orders he received that morning.

By the time Kilpatick issued *his* order accordingly, it was too late; Pickett's Charge had ended an hour before. To have threatened the right wing of that rebel assault (Pickett's division itself) meant that Kilpatrick would have had to deploy his troopers much earlier—even in advance of the charge—because these cavalrymen were initially positioned so far to the south, below Big Round Top. *Deploy* meant avoiding the rebel infantry units in this southern sector of the field (maps E-2 and E-4). In this respect, had these Union horsemen launched a late attack due north, it would have meant riding into trouble. General Law by then had neutralized Merritt's threat and shifted Confederate infantry units so that any further attack that came his way would be riding into a trap (maps E-2 and E-3). Playing into this hand, Kilpatrick left Merritt's men dismounted and ordered the remainder of his command to ride directly to the north, into the teeth of the rebel defense at the bottom of the battlefield.

Kilpatrick might have ordered Merritt's men back to their mounts, where—perhaps joined by Farnsworth as well—they could have swung around the rebel infantry's right to get into the defenders' rear. Moreover, Kilpatrick might have tried a move like this *earlier* (as alluded to in the previous paragraph). This could have gotten his troopers around the Confederate 1st Corps defenses, permitting them to assail the southern end of Pickett's advancing infantry division (map E-4).

With Custer gone, Kilpatrick turned to his other brigade commander, the youthful Elon Farnsworth. Legend has it that Farnsworth strenuously objected to the plan for a belated offensive move.[6] In any case, it must have been obvious to him (and General Kilpatrick as well) that this sector of the battlefield was ill suited for mounted operations: The terrain was densely wooded and rolling, dotted with forested knolls, and littered with granite outcroppings. And even the youthful Farnsworth had to know, as did most troopers in the Civil War era, that a cavalry attack on infantry was becoming impossible. Novice and experienced foot soldiers alike were capable of gunning down men on horseback, even from a long distance (if only because of the overall size of the target). Judson Kilpatrick insisted upon the attack anyway, and ordered Farnsworth to take half his brigade and conduct a mounted charge on Law's line.

The rebel defenders to Farnsworth's front were men of the 1st Texas Regiment (chart E-1), which was one of the very first rebel units to engage the enemy on July 2 (near Houck's Ridge in the southern sector of the battlefield). By mid-afternoon of the Third, these Texans had been posted at a stone fence some two hundred yards south of the Bushman farm buildings (map E-2), fronting a large patch of woods. This component of the Confederate defense in this southern sector of the battlefield was established to form a tenuous connection between the Georgia regiments to the west and the Alabamians to the east (maps E-2 and E-5). Indeed, the Texans had to spread themselves thinly to cover this fence line, but in the center of it was a heavier stone wall that provided an excellent ready-made breastwork (map E-3).

The 1st West Virginia Cavalry formed the first wave of Farnsworth's attack. The troopers rode out of the woods across several hundred yards of mostly open ground, heading toward the 1st Texas behind its stone wall. The approximately four hundred West Virginians absorbed volley fire from almost point-blank range. Some of the Union cavalrymen struggled to ride through the line of defenders by jumping the stone fence, but many other of the West Virginia troopers turned to the right and left, trying to outflank the Texan defenders (map E-3).

**Map E-4
Routes that might have been taken by Union cavalry to threaten the right of Pickett's Charge**

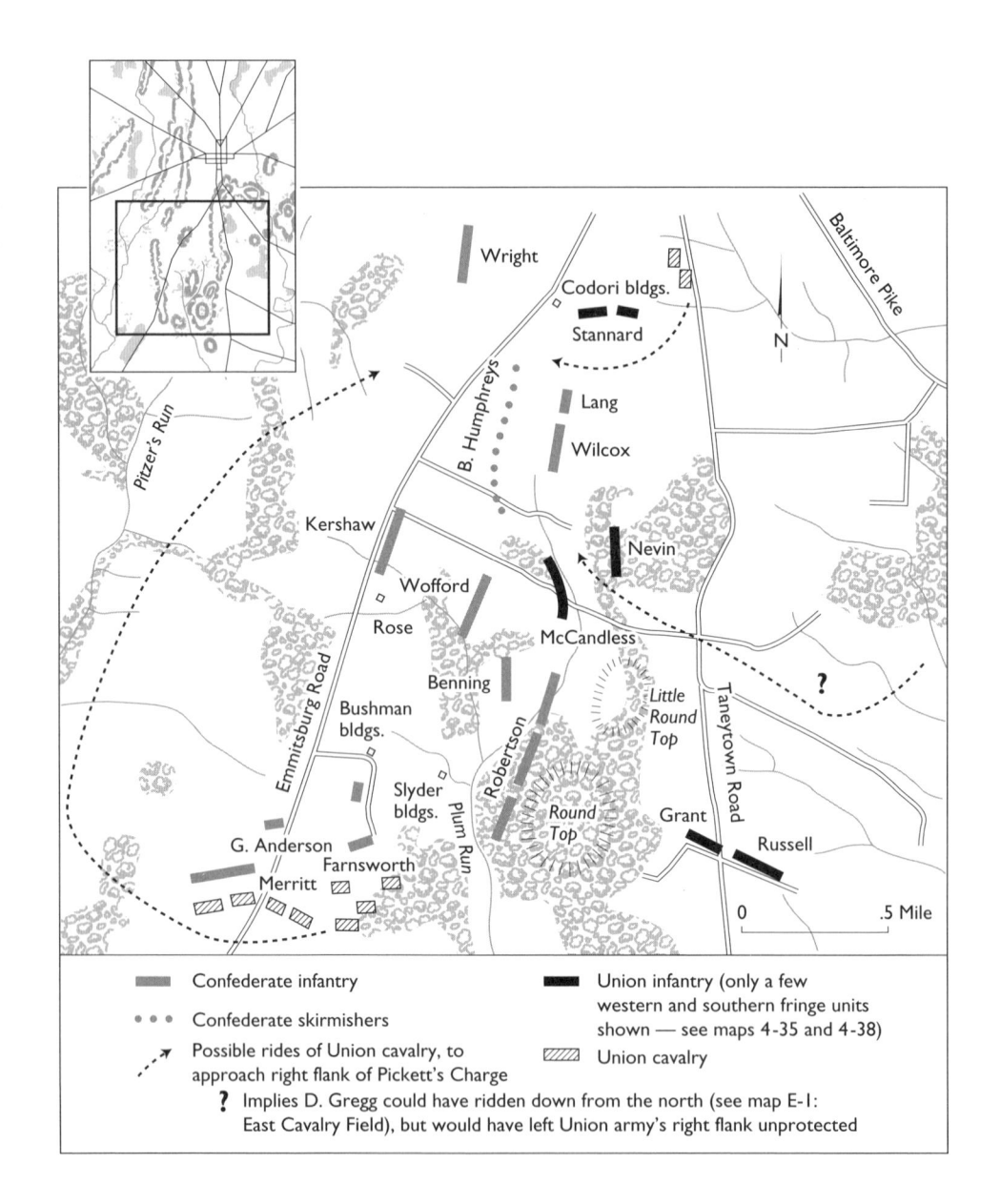

Those Southerners now poured musketry onto the flanks of the riders. Some of the Federal troopers were driven back; but several horsemen, overlapping the most heavily defended position on both sides, gained the area of open fields and woodlots behind the 1st Texas, riding northward from the rear of that rebel unit. Meanwhile, Kilpatrick's 1st Vermont Regiment attacked to the right of the route taken by the 1st West Virginia. Several of the Vermonters were able to crash through the more thinly defended part of the Texans' line, swinging north toward the Slyder farm buildings (map E-3).

Now the second wave of Farnsworth's attack approached—the 18th Pennsylvania supported by part of the 5th New York (map E-3, chart E-1). As the Pennsylvania troopers approached the stone fence, the Texans drove them back with solid volleys of musket fire. The 18th Pennsylvania quickly retreated back into the trees. Half the supporting force of New Yorkers also rode directly toward the fence, while the rest veered left and headed toward Confederate batteries in the sector (map E-3). But these elements of the 5th New York saw that the attack along the front of the wall was collapsing, so the New York troopers hastily withdrew.

Map E-5
Farnsworth's charge and its repulse

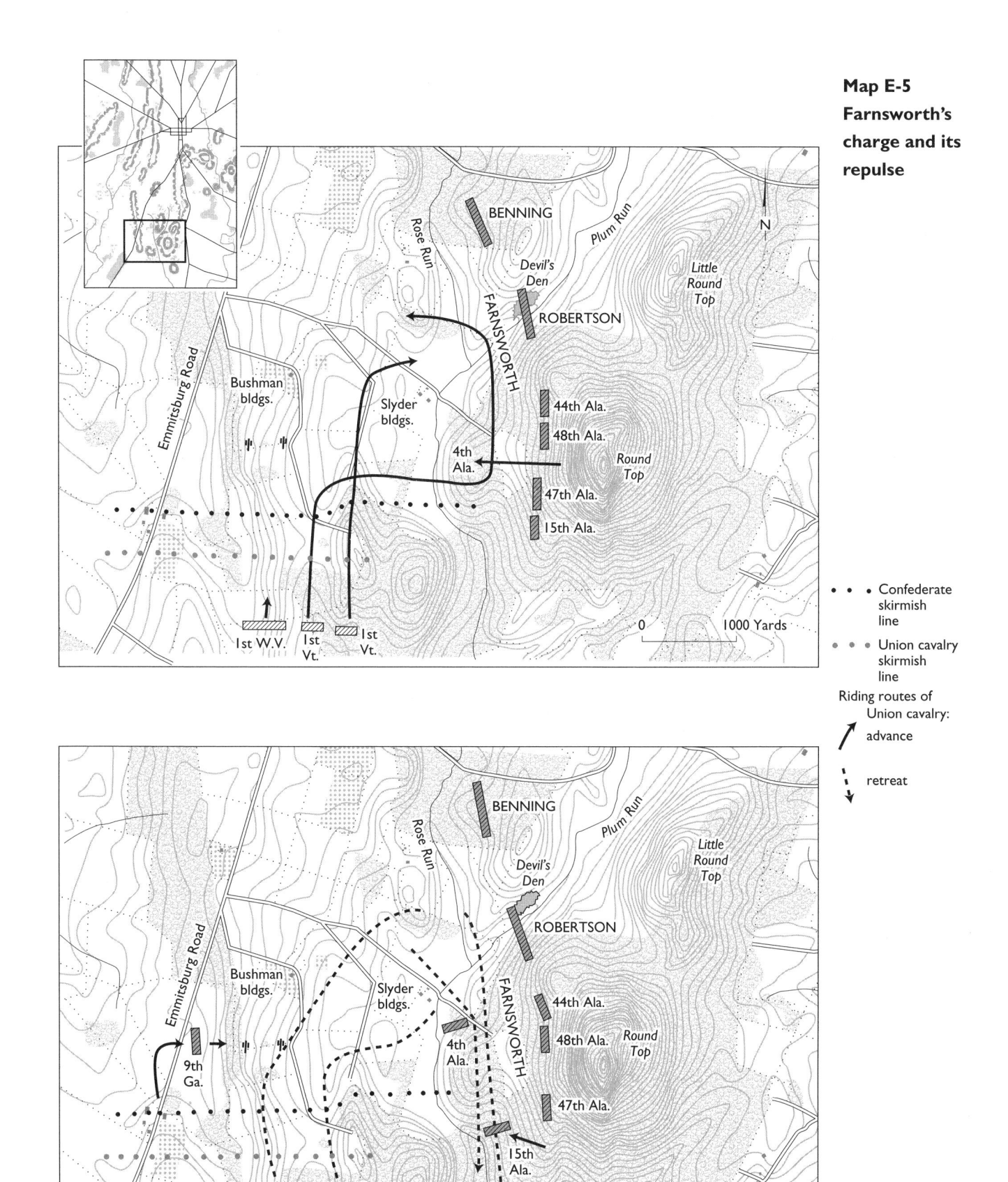

THE FATAL CAVALRY CHARGE OF ELON FARNSWORTH 305

Farnsworth's attack was not over, however. After the repulse of the 18th Pennsylvania and 5th New York, troopers of the 1st Vermont were thundering back toward the backs of the south-facing soldiers in the 1st Texas. Earlier, these Vermonters had ridden northward through the thin skirmish line to the right of the wall and gone past the Slyder farm (maps E-3 and E-5). Some of them rode right past these buildings. Others broke away and wheeled to the east, galloping northward and reaching a place just north of where Plum Run splits off into Rose Run (map E-5). The Vermont troopers were jeopardized by a strong line of defenders arrayed from south to north near the east faces of the Round Tops (map E-5). In addition, a regiment of Alabamians (chart E-1) advanced westward from the main defensive line to confront the Vermonters near the Slyder farm. The rest of the 1st Vermont, led by General Farnsworth himself, swung west (just north of the fork in the aforementioned streams) and came under fire from Brig. Gen. Henry L. Benning's brigade of Georgians (chart E-1; map E-5).

It was now obvious to the Vermont troopers that further offensive action in this area was impossible. The cavalrymen began to turn south, hoping to fight their way back to their takeoff point southwest of Big Round Top. The horsemen split into four groups as they attempted to escape. As they suspected would happen, they were riding into a trap (map E-5, bottom). The main south-to-north line of rebel infantry menaced the troopers' left. The 4th Alabama (facing north, southwest of the Slyder farm on map E-5) fired into one group of retreating cavalrymen. Another Alabama regiment—the 15th, of Little Round Top fame on July 2—swung out from the line to try to block the escape route taken by Farnsworth's own column. A Georgia regiment that had been posted on the Emmitsburg Road (map E-2) moved east to threaten the right-hand column of Vermonters that was retreating from the Plum Run–Rose Run fork (map E-5).

The 1st Vermont was moving southward, essentially through a gauntlet of Confederate infantry units (map E-5). During the Vermonters' frantic attempt to cut their way out of the trap, General Farnsworth was killed as his column of troopers rode into the blocking position held by the 15th Alabama. These desperate Union horsemen were galloping down a farm lane that coursed through the woods southeast of the Slyder farm (map E-5; that dirt path is still present on this hidden part of the modern-day battlefield). As Farnsworth and the horsemen with him approached the 15th Alabama's line, which faced to the south, those rebels turned around and began to fire at the cavalrymen thundering toward them. General Farnsworth turned his mount to the right and headed into the woods in an effort to evade the Alabamians' musketry, but was struck by five bullets and died soon afterward.

Now without their brigade commander, the Vermont men who had managed to retreat farther southward collided with the similarly retreating 1st West Virginia (map E-3). Troopers from these two Union regiments again rode into the line of Texans at the fence. Close fighting ensued, with the cavalrymen and infantrymen bringing sabers, clubbed muskets, and even rocks into play. Ultimately, most of these intermingled Federal horsemen got out, escaping to the south in the same manner that they had broken through.

Farnsworth's quixotic attack was finished. The design and execution of this action was more disgusting than soul stirring—compared, for example, to the suicidal charge of the 1st Minnesota (recall from Chapter 3 why that infantry attack *had* to be made). However, it might be too much to say that General Kilpatrick ordered his 1st Brigade to commit suicide: of the approximately four hundred men who rode north, twenty-one were killed, thirty-four were wounded, and forty-three were captured.[7] In any case, the charge and repulse of Kilpatrick's 1st Brigade ended the third day's fighting at Gettysburg (although probably in sync with the infantry action described in note 1). The Confederates who vigorously repelled this charge were in the main from the 1st Corps (chart E-1)—supposedly fought out from their heavy engagements the day before. Their actions in the late afternoon of July 3 belied this in terms of their willingness to *defend*. Perhaps the performance of these 1st Corps troops on the South Cavalry Field reflected the residual pugnacity of the rebel army as a whole. Perhaps, in turn, the Union high command sensed that that was so, as is discussed in Chapter 5.

Appendix F

Organization of the Union and Confederate Armies at Gettysburg

All the infantry, artillery, and cavalry units that made up the opposing armies in the Gettysburg campaign are listed. A few of the small units that were part of these armies but not present or only partially present at the battle itself are included within various parts of the list. Their status is indicated as follows: (*p*) = only part of unit present; (#) = part of the Army of the Potomac or Army of Northern Virginia, but not present at Gettysburg.

This hierarchical order goes down to regiments as the smallest units listed for the infantry and cavalry, and to batteries for the artillery. An overview of each army's organizational scheme is provided—shortly below for the Union force (chart F-1), and roughly in the middle of this appendix for the Confederates (chart F-2).

Infantry regiments in both armies, and the Confederate cavalry ones, typically were composed of ten companies: A through K, omitting J. Union cavalry regiments normally had twelve companies: A through M, omitting J. Almost all regiments were undermanned in terms of numbers of infantrymen or troopers. Thus, many fewer men were present for duty at Gettysburg than their common mustering-in strength of approximately one thousand. Several regiments were also understrength in terms of numbers of companies present at Gettysburg (thus, fewer than ten or twelve; those companies present in such regiments are indicated by their respective letter designations). This information, as well as most of the numerical data and the artillery battery details, is derived from a book by Alfred A. Nofi.[1]

Commanders and the unit designations of armies, corps, divisions, and brigades appear in standard print, whereas commanders and the designations of regiments, battalions, and separate artillery batteries and companies appear in fine print.

It is frequently the case that two or more commanders are listed for a given unit. This means that the officer noted after the first one assumed command—often because the first was wounded, killed, or captured. These cases are specified within the listings in accordance with the following key:

(*w*) = wounded

(*mw*) = mortally wounded

(*k*) = killed

(*c*) = captured

(?) = unknown as to whether *mw, k, w,* or *c*

The absence of an italicized letter next to a commander's name means he survived the battle, probably unscathed. The source of this information for the Southerners is F. Ray Sibley Jr.'s *The Confederate Order of Battle.*[2] Scrutiny of the listings will reveal that information about casualties during the three days of Gettysburg is more complete for the Army of Northern Virginia, which is why the names of several officers in the Army of the Potomac are followed by a question mark (which in certain instances is annotated by a note revealing that such a soldier was known at least to have lived through the campaign). For Northerners, the information about their fate (*w, mw,* etc.) is contained within the *Official Records* (*OR*) and in some contemporary software files entitled *The American Civil War Resource Data Base.*[3] In the *OR,* the nature of an officer's casualty status can frequently be found within one of the many lists contained in these records, or an after-action account specifies that the officer was killed or wounded (sometimes the relevant account was written by a man who suffered a relatively mild wound). Many other *OR* reports reveal (by their post-battle dates) that the officer in question survived Gettysburg. Reading between the lines suggests that this officer was not wounded during the battle itself, so no italicized symbol follows his name in the listing. For several other Union officers, in some cases neither the fate nor the post-Gettysburg status of men within the Army of the Potomac can be found in the *OR*. The *Resource Data Base* revealed that many of these soldiers were casualties at Gettysburg, or, alternatively, that they at least were not killed during that battle, because they mustered out or otherwise left the army in late 1863 or 1864–1865 (some survived Gettysburg but were killed in later campaigns).

In several instances, more than one officer commanded a given unit. These cases did not necessarily involve battlefield casualties; instead, the original commander (the first one listed) was given a different assignment. For example, a division commander might have temporarily taken over a corps when the commander of *that* unit became a casualty. It was a common occurrence for such an officer to drop back down to his original level of command at a later stage of the battle (as is indicated by the officer's name appearing as the first *and* the third in the string of division commanders, as in this example).

The figures shown are the numbers of men actually engaged during the three days of the Battle of Gettysburg—although several of these figures are doubtful (see, for example, Thomas's brigade in Pender's division of the Army of Northern Virginia's 3rd Corps[4]). Also, no attempt was made to adjust the numerical strength of any unit according to losses that occurred during the battle.

A guide for certain detailed features of this Order of Battle: The staffs of the armies as a whole or those attached to the corps commanders are included in these lists. These staff officers include, among others, chiefs of staff, artillery, engineers, and adjutants. Special groups of men (other than the ordinary fighting units) are designated as an "Escort" or "Provost Guard." These were attached to certain corps commanders' staffs. The types of cannon employed by artillery batteries, mainly "Napoleons" (smoothbores) and two principal types of pieces whose bores were rifled ("rifles," that is, ordnance rifles, or "Parrotts"), are specified. The poundage by which a given piece is often labeled refers to the nominal weight of the projectile it was designed to fire, although many of the pieces could fire a variety of different kinds of shot and shell in general—and did so in this battle.

Chart F-1
General organizational scheme for the Union army in the Gettysburg campaign

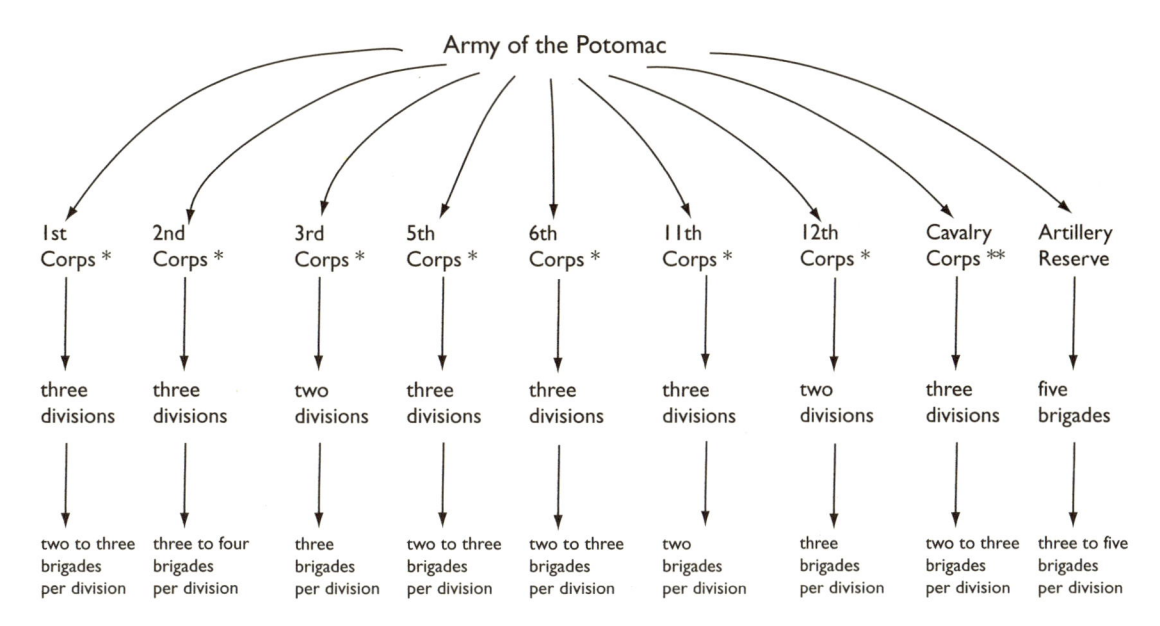

```
                              Army of the Potomac
     ┌────┬──────┬──────┬──────┼──────┬──────┬──────┬──────┐
     ↓    ↓      ↓      ↓      ↓      ↓      ↓      ↓      ↓
    1st  2nd    3rd    5th    6th    11th   12th  Cavalry Artillery
   Corps* Corps* Corps* Corps* Corps* Corps* Corps* Corps** Reserve
     ↓    ↓      ↓      ↓      ↓      ↓      ↓      ↓      ↓
   three three  two   three  three  three   two   three   five
  divisions divisions divisions divisions divisions divisions divisions divisions brigades
     ↓    ↓      ↓      ↓      ↓      ↓      ↓      ↓      ↓
  two to three to three two to two to  two   three  two to three to
   three  four brigades three three brigades brigades three  five
 brigades brigades per div brigades brigades per div per div brigades brigades
 per div per div       per div per div              per div per div
```

* Each infantry corps contained an artillery brigade

** This corps also contained two brigades of horse artillery

Army of the Potomac

approx. 94,000 men[5]

360 artillery pieces

Commanding General: Maj. Gen. George Gordon Meade
Chief of Staff: Maj. Gen. Daniel Butterfield (w)
Chief of Engineers: Brig. Gen. Gouverneur K. Warren (w)
Chief of Artillery: Brig. Gen. Henry J. Hunt (w)
Provost Marshal General: Brig. Gen. Marsena R. Patrick
Assistant Adjutant General: Brig. Gen. Seth Williams
Chief Quartermaster: Brig. Gen. Rufus Ingalls
Medical Director: Dr. Jonathan Letterman
Chief of Ordnance: Lt. John R. Edie (acting)
Provost Guard, 1,365
    93rd N.Y., 371, Col. John S. Crocker
    2nd Pa. Cavalry, 489, Col. R. Butler Price (? unknown if a casualty)
    6th Pa. Cavalry, Companies E, I, 81, Capt. James Starr
    8th U.S. Cavalry, Companies A–G, I, 401, Capt. Edwin W. H. Read (?)
    detachments from 1st, 2nd, 5th, and 6th U.S. Cavalry, 18
    guards and orderlies, Oneida N.Y. Cavalry Company, 42, Capt. Daniel P. Mann (? but survived Gettysburg)
Engineer Brigade (#),[6] Brig. Gen. Henry W. Benham (?)
    15th N.Y. Engineers, Companies A–C, Maj. Walter L. Cassin (? but survived Gettysburg)

    50th N.Y. Engineers, Col. William H. Pettes (? but survived Gettysburg)
    U.S. Engineer Battalion, Capt. George H. Mendell (?)
Signal Corps, 36, Capt. Lemuel P. Norton

1st Corps

12,222
Maj. Gen. John F. Reynolds (k)
Maj. Gen. Abner Doubleday
Maj. Gen. John Newton
    Escort, 1st Maine Cavalry, Company L, 57, Capt. Constantine Taylor

1st Division, 3,857, Brig. Gen. James S. Wadsworth
1st Brigade (The Iron Brigade), 1,829, Brig. Gen. Solomon Meredith, Col. William W. Robertson
    19th Ind., 308, Col. Samuel J. Williams
    24th Mich., 496, Col. Henry A. Morrow (w), Capt. Albert M. Edwards
    2nd Wis., 302, Col. Lucius Fairchild (w), Maj. John Mansfield (w), Capt. George H. Otis (?)
    6th Wis., 344, Lt. Col. Rufus R. Dawes
    7th Wis., 364, Col. William W. Robinson, Maj. Mark Finnicum

ORGANIZATION OF THE UNION AND CONFEDERATE ARMIES AT GETTYSBURG

2nd Brigade, 2,017, Brig. Gen. Lysander Cutler
- 7th Ind., 434, Col. Ira G. Grover
- 76th N.Y., 375, Maj. Andrew J. Grover (k), Capt. John E. Cook
- 84th N.Y. (14th Brooklyn Militia), 318, Col. Edward B. Fowler
- 95th N.Y., 241, Col. George H. Biddle, Maj. Edward Pye
- 147th N.Y., 380, Lt. Col. Francis C. Miller (w), Maj. George Harney
- 56th Pa., Companies A–D, F–K, 252, Col. J. William Hofmann

2nd Division, 2,997, Brig. Gen. John C. Robinson

1st Brigade, 1,537, Brig. Gen. Gabriel R. Paul (w), Col. Samuel H. Leonard (w), Col. Adrian R. Root (w, c), Col. Richard Coulter (w), Col. Peter Lyle, Col. Richard Coulter (w)
- 16th Maine, 298, Col. Charles W. Tilden (c), Maj. Archibald D. Leavitt (? but survived Gettysburg)
- 13th Mass., 284, Col. Samuel H. Leonard (w), Lt. Col. N. Walter Batchelder
- 9th N.Y., 411, Col. Adrian R. Root, Maj. Samuel A. Moffett
- 104th N.Y., 286, Col. Gilbert G. Prey
- 107th Pa., 255, Lt. Col. James MacThompson, Capt. Emanuel D. Roath

2nd Brigade, 1,452, Brig. Gen. Henry Baxter
- 12th Mass., 261, Col. James L. Bates (w), Lt. Col. David Allen Jr.
- 83rd N.Y. (9th Militia), 199, Lt. Col. Joseph A. Moesch
- 97th N.Y., 236, Col. Charles Wheelock, Maj. Charles Northrup
- 11th Pa. (with the 1st Brigade July 1), 270, Col. Richard Coulter (w), Capt. Benjamin F. Haynes (w), Capt. John B. Overmeyer (?)
- 88th Pa., 274, Maj. Benezet F. Foust, Capt. Henry Whiteside
- 90th Pa., 208, Col. Peter Lyle, Maj. Alfred S. Sellers
- Provost Guard, 149th Pa., Company D, 60

3rd Division, 4,701, Maj. Gen. Abner Doubleday, Brig. Gen. Thomas A. Rowley, Maj. Gen. Abner Doubleday

1st Brigade, 1,361, Brig. Gen. Thomas A. Rowley, Col. Chapman Biddle (w), Brig. Gen. Thomas A. Rowley
- 80th N.Y. (20th Militia, Ulster Guard), 287, Col. Theodore B. Gates
- 121st Pa., 363, Maj. Alexander Biddle, Col. Chapman Biddle, Maj. Alexander Biddle
- 142nd Pa., 363, Col. Robert P. Cummins (k), Lt. Col. Alfred B. McCalmont
- 151st Pa. (The Schoolteachers' Regiment), 467, Lt. Col. J. P. McFarland (w), Capt. Walter L. Owens, Col. Harrison Allen

2nd Brigade (Bucktails), 1,317, Col. Roy Stone (w), Col. Langhorne Wister (w), Col. Edmund L. Dana
- 143rd Pa., 465, Col. Edmund L. Dana, Lt. Col. John D. Musser
- 149th Pa., Companies A–C, E–J, 450, Lt. Col. Walton Dwight (w), Capt. James Glenn
- 150th Pa., Companies A–I, 400, Col. Langhorne Wister (w), Lt. Col. Henry S. Huidekoper (w), Capt. Cornelius C. Widdis

3rd Brigade[7] (Paper Collar, arrived July 2), 1,950, Brig. Gen. George J. Stannard (w), Col. Francis V. Randall
- 12th Vt. (#), Col. Asa P. Bluny
- 13th Vt., 636, Col. Francis V. Randall, Maj. Joseph J. Boynton, Lt. Col. William D. Munson (w)
- 14th Vt., 647, Col. William T. Nichols (? but survived Gettysburg)
- 15th Vt. (#), Col. Redfield Proctor
- 16th Vt., 661, Col. Wheelock G. Veazey

Artillery Brigade, 28 guns, 596 men, Col. Charles S. Wainwright
- 2nd Maine Light, Battery B (6 3-inch rifles), 117, Capt. James A. Hall
- 5th Maine Light, Battery E (6 12-pound Napoleons), 119, Capt. Greenleaf T. Stevens (w), Lt. Edward N. Whittier
- 1st N.Y. Light Artillery, Batteries E and L (6 3-inch rifles), 124, Capt. Gilbert H. Reynolds (w), Lt. George Breck
- 1st Pa. Light Artillery, Battery B (4 3-inch rifles), 106, Capt. James H. Cooper
- 4th U.S. Artillery, Battery B (6 12-pound Napoleons), 124, Lt. James Stewart (w)

2nd Corps

11,347

Maj. Gen. Winfield Scott Hancock (w)
Brig. Gen. John Gibbon (w)
Brig. Gen. William Hays

Escorts, 164
- 6th N.Y. Cavalry, Companies D and K, 64, Capt. Riley Johnston (? but survived Gettysburg)
- 17th Pa. Cavalry, Companies E and H, 100 (p)
- Provost Guard, 1st Minn., Company L, 48

1st Division, 3,320, Brig. Gen. John C. Caldwell
Provost Guard, 116th Pa., Company B, 32; 53rd Pa., Companies A, B, and K, 70

1st Brigade, 853, Col. Edward E. Cross (k), Col. H. Boyd McKeen
- 5th N.H., 179, Lt. Col. Charles E. Hapgood
- 61st N.Y., 104, Lt. Col. K. Oscar Broady
- 81st Pa., 175, Col. H. Boyd McKeen, Lt. Col. Amos Stroh
- 148th Pa., 392, Lt. Col. Robert McFarlane

2nd Brigade (The Irish Brigade), 532, Col. Patrick Kelly
- 28th Mass., 224, Col. R. Byrnes
- 63rd N.Y., Companies A and B, 75, Lt. Col. Richard C. Bentley (w), Capt. Thomas Touhy
- 69th N.Y., Companies A and B, 75, Capt. Richard Moroney, Lt. James. J. Smith
- 88th N.Y., Companies A and B, 90, Capt. Denis F. Burke
- 116th Pa., Companies A, C, and D, 98, Maj. St. Clair A. Mulholland

3rd Brigade, 975, Brig. Gen. Samuel K. Zook (k), Lt. Col. John Fraser
- 52nd N.Y. and detachment from 7th N.Y. (15), 134, Lt. Col. C. G. Freudenberg (w), Capt. William M. Scherrer
- 57th N.Y., 175, Lt. Col. Alford B. Chapman
- 66th N.Y., 147, Col. Orlando H. Morris (w), Lt. Col. John S. Hammell (w), Maj. Peter Nelson
- 140th Pa., 514, Col. Richard P. Roberts (k), Lt. Col. John Fraser

4th Brigade, 851, Col. John R. Brooke (w)
- 27th Conn., Companies A and B, 75, Lt. Col. Henry C. Merwin (k), Maj. James H. Coburn
- 2nd Del., 234, Col. William P. Baily, Capt. Charles H. Christman (?)
- 64th N.Y., 204, Col. Daniel G. Bingham (w), Maj. Leman W. Bradley (?)
- 53rd Pa., Companies C–I, 135, Lt. Col. Richards McMichael
- 145th Pa., 202, Col. Hiram L. Brown, Capt. John W. Reynolds (w), Capt. Moses Oliver

2nd Division, 3,608, Brig. Gen. John Gibbon (w), Brig. Gen. William Harrow

1st Brigade, 1,366, Brig. Gen. William Harrow, Col. Francis Heath

19th Maine, 439, Col. Francis E. Heath, Lt. Col. Henry W. Cunningham (*?* but survived Gettysburg)
15th Mass., 239, Col. George H. Ward (*mw*), Lt. Col. George C. Joslin
1st Minn., Companies A–K and 1st Company Minn. Sharpshooters, 330, Col. William Colvill Jr. (*w*), Capt. Nathan S. Messick (*k*), Capt. Henry C. Coates
82nd N.Y. (2nd Militia), 355, Lt. Col. James Huston (*k*), Capt. John Darrow

2nd Brigade (Philadelphia Brigade), 1,224, Brig. Alexander Webb (*w*)
69th Pa., 284, Col. Dennis O'Kane (*k*), Capt. William Davis
71st Pa., 261, Col. Richard Penn Smith
72nd Pa., 380, Col. DeWitt C. Baxter, Lt. Col. Theodor Hesser
106th Pa., 280, Lt. Col. William L. Curry

3rd Brigade, 922, Col. Norman J. Hall
19th Mass., 163, Col. Arthur F. Devereux
20th Mass., 243, Col. Paul J. Revere (*mw*), Lt. Col. George N. Macy (*w*), Capt. Henry L. Abbott
7th Mich., 165, Lt. Col. Amos E. Steele Jr. (*k*), Maj. Sylvanus W. Curtis
42nd N.Y. (Tammany), 197, Col. James J. Mallon
59th N.Y., 152, Lt. Col. Max A. Thoman (*mw*), Capt. William McFadden
Attached: 1st Company Mass. Sharpshooters, 42, Capt. William Plumer (*?*), Lt. Emerson L. Bicknell (some sources say L. E. Bicknall)

3rd Division, 3,644, Brig. Gen. Alexander Hays
Provost Guard: 10th N.Y. Battalion, 82, Maj. George F. Hopper

1st Brigade, 941, Col. Samuel S. Carroll
14th Ind., 191, Col. John Coons
4th Ohio, 299, Lt. Col. Leonard W. Carpenter
8th Ohio, 209, Lt. Col. Franklin Sawyer (*w*)
7th W.V., 235, Lt. Col. Jonathan H. Lockwood

2nd Brigade, 1,103, Col. Thomas A. Smyth (*w*), Lt. Col. Francis C. Pierce
Provost Guard, 36
14th Conn., 172, Maj. Theodore G. Ellis
1st Del., 251, Lt. Col. Edward P. Harris (*arrested by Gen. Hancock and removed from command*), Capt. Thomas B. Hizar (*w*), Lt. William Smith (*k*), Lt. John T. Dent
12th N.J., 444, Maj. John T. Hill
108th N.Y., 200, Lt. Col. Francis E. Pierce (*w*)

3rd Brigade, 1,508, Col. George L. Willard (*k*), Col. Eliakim Sherrill (*k*), Lt. Col. James M. Bull
39th N.Y. (Garibaldi Guard) A–D, 269, Maj. Hugo Hildebrandt (*w*)
111th N.Y., 390, Col. Clinton D. McDougall, Lt. Col. Isaac M. Lusk (*w* [injured]), Capt. Aaron P. Seeley
125th N.Y., 392, Lt. Col. Levin Crandell
126th N.Y., 455, Col. Eliakim Sherrill (*k*), Lt. Col. James M. Bull

Artillery Brigade, 28 guns, 605 men, Capt. John C. Hazard
1st N.Y. Light Artillery, Battery B/14th N.Y. Battery (4 10-pound Parrotts), 117, Lt. Albert S. Sheldon (*w*), Capt. James McKay Rorty (*k*), Lt. Robert E. Rogers
1st R.I. Light Artillery, Battery A (6 3-inch rifles), 117, Capt. William A. Arnold
1st R.I. Light Artillery, Battery B (6 12-pound Napoleons), 129, Lt. T. Fred Brown (*w*), Lt. Walter S. Perrin
1st U.S. Artillery, Battery I (6 12-pound Napoleons), 112, Lt. George A. Woodruff (*k*), Lt. Tully McCrea
4th U.S. Artillery, Battery A (6 3-inch rifles), 126, Lt. Alonzo H. Cushing (*k*), Sgt. Frederick Fuger

3rd Corps
10,675
Maj. Gen. Daniel E. Sickles (*w*)
Maj. Gen. David B. Birney (*w*)
Escort, 6th N.Y. Cavalry, Company A, 51

1st Division, 5,095, Maj. Gen. David B. Birney (*w*), Brig. Gen. J. H. Hobart Ward

1st Brigade, 1,516, Brig. Gen. Charles K. Graham (*w, c*), Col. Andrew Tippin
57th Pa., Companies A–C, E, F, H–K, 207, Col. Peter Sides (*w*), Capt. Alanson H. Nelson
63rd Pa., 246, Maj. John A. Danks
68th Pa., 320, Col. Andrew H. Tippin, Capt. Milton S. Davis
105th Pa., 274, Col. Calvin A. Craig (*w*)
114th Pa., 259, Lt. Col. Frederick F. Cavada, Capt. Edward R. Bowen
141st Pa., 209, Col. Henry J. Madill

2nd Brigade, 2,188, Brig. Gen. J. H. Hobart Ward, Col. Hiram Berdan
20th Ind., 401, Capt. John Wheeler (*k*), Lt. Col. William C. L. Taylor
3rd Maine, 210, Col. Moses B. Lakeman
4th Maine, 287, Col. Elijah Walker (*w*), Capt. Edwin Libby
86th N.Y., 287, Lt. Col. Benjamin L. Higgins (*w*)
124th N.Y., 238, Col. A. Van Horne Ellis (*k*), Lt. Col. Francis M. Cummins (*w*)
99th Pa., 277, Maj. John W. Moore
1st U.S. Sharpshooters, 313, Col. Hiram Berdan, Lt. Col. Casper Trepp (*?* but survived Gettysburg)
2nd U.S. Sharpshooters, Companies A–I, 169, Maj. Homer R. Stoughton

3rd Brigade, 1,387, Col. P. Regis de Trobriand
17th Maine, 350, Lt. Col. Charles B. Merrill
3rd Mich., 237, Col. Bryan R. Pierce (*w*), Lt. Col. Edwin S. Pierce
5th Mich., 216, Lt. Col. John Pulford
40th N.Y., 431, Col. Thomas W. Egan
110th Pa., Companies A–C, E, H, and I, 152, Lt. Col. David M. Jones, Maj. Isaac Rogers

2nd Division, 4,924, Brig. Gen. Andrew A. Humphreys
1st Brigade, 1,718, Brig. Gen. Joseph B. Carr
1st Mass., 321, Lt. Col. Clark B. Baldwin (*w*)
11th Mass., 286, Lt. Col. Porter D. Tripp
16th Mass., 245, Lt. Col. Waldo Merriam (*w*), Capt. Mathew Donovan
12th N.H., 224, Capt. John F. Langley (*w*)
11th N.J., 275, Col. Robert McAllister (*w*), Capt. Luther Martin (*k*), Lt. John Schoonover (*w*), Capt. William H. Lloyd (*w*), Capt. Samuel T. Sleeper
26th Pa., 365, Maj. Robert L. Bodine
84th Pa. (#),[8] Lt. Col. Milton Opp

2nd Brigade, 1,837, Col. William R. Brewster
70th N.Y., 288, Col. J. Egbert Farnum
71st N.Y., 243, Col. Henry L. Potter
72nd N.Y., 305, Col. John S. Austin (*w*), Lt. Col. John Leonard
73rd N.Y., 349, Maj. Michael W. Burns
74th N.Y., 266, Lt. Col. Thomas Holt
120th N.Y., 383, Lt. Col. Cornelius D. Westbrook (*w*), Maj. John R. Tappen

3rd Brigade, 1,365, Col. George C. Burling
2nd N.H., 354, Col. Edward L. Bailey (*w*)
5th N.J., 206, Col. William J. Sewell, Capt. Thomas C. Godfrey, Capt.

Henry H. Woolsey
- 6th N.J., 207, Col. Stephen R. Gilkyson
- 7th N.J., 275, Col. Louis R. Francine, Maj. Frederick Cooper
- 8th N.J., 170, Col. John Ramsey, Capt. John G. Langston
- 115th Pa., Companies A–G, I, and K, 151, Maj. John P. Dunne

Artillery Brigade, 30 guns, 596 men, Capt. George E. Randolph (*w*), Capt. A. Judson Clark
- 2nd N.J. Light Battery (6 10-pound Parrotts), 131, Capt. A. Judson Clark, Lt. Robert Sims
- 1st N.Y. Light Artillery, Battery D (6 12-pound Napoleons), 116, Capt. George B. Winslow
- 4th Battery N.Y. Light Artillery (6 10-pound Parrotts), 126, Capt. James E. Smith
- 1st R.I. Light Artillery, Battery E (6 12-pound Napoleons), 108, Lt. John K. Bucklyn (*w*), Lt. Benjamin Freeborn
- 4th U.S. Artillery, Battery K (6 12-pound Napoleons), 113, Lt. Francis W. Seeley (*w*), Lt. Robert James

5th Corps

11,024

Maj. Gen. George Sykes
- Escort, 7th Pa. Cavalry, Companies D and H, 78 (*p*)
- Provost Guard, 12th N.Y., Companies D and E, 99

1st Division, 3,534, Brig. Gen. James Barnes
1st Brigade, 655, Col. William S. Tilton
- 18th Mass., 139, Col. Joseph Hayes
- 22nd Mass. and 2nd Company Mass. Sharpshooters, 137, Lt. Col. Thomas Sherwin Jr.
- 1st Mich., 145, Col. Ira C. Abbott (*w*), Lt. Col. William A. Throop (*w*)
- 118th Pa. (Corn Exchange Regiment), 233, Lt. Col. James Gwyn

2nd Brigade, 1,422, Col. Jacob B. Sweitzer
- 9th Mass., 411, Col. Patrick R. Guiney
- 32nd Mass., Companies A, B, and D–K, 242, Col. G. L. Prescott (*w*)
- 4th Mich., 342, Col. Harrison H. Jeffords (*mw*), Lt. Col. George W. Lumbard
- 62nd Pa., 426, Lt. Col. James C. Hull

3rd Brigade, 1,453, Col. Stong Vincent (*mw*), Col. James C. Rice
- 20th Maine, 503, Col. Joshua L. Chamberlain (*w* [slightly])
- 16th Mich. and Brady's Company Mich. Sharpshooters, 263, Lt. Col. Norval E. Welch
- 44th N.Y., 391, Col. James C. Rice, Lt. Col. Freeman Conner
- 83rd Pa., 295, Capt. Orpheus S. Woodward

2nd Division, 4,021, Brig. Gen. Romeyn B. Ayres
1st Brigade, 1,574, Col. Hannibal Day
- 3rd U.S., Companies B, C, F, G, I, and K, 300, Capt. Henry W. Freedley (*w*), Capt. Richard G. Lay
- 4th U.S., Companies C, F, H, and K, 173, Capt. Julius W. Adams Jr.
- 6th U.S., Companies D–I, 196, Capt. Levi C. Bootes
- 12th U.S., Companies A–D, and G, 413, Capt. Thomas S. Dunn
- 14th U.S., Companies A–G, 490, Maj. Grotius R. Giddings

2nd Brigade, 958, Col Sydney Burbank
- 2nd U.S., Companies B, C, F, H, and K, 201, Maj. Arthur T. Lee (*w*), Capt. Samuel A. McKee
- 7th U.S., Companies A, B, E, and I, 116, Capt. David P. Hancock
- 10th U.S., Companies D, G, and H, 93, Capt. William Clinton
- 11th U.S., Companies B–G, 286, Maj. De Lancey Floyd-Jones
- 17th U.S., Companies A, C, D, G, and H, 260, Lt. Col. J. Durell Greene

3rd Brigade, Brig. Gen. Stephen H. Weed (*k*), Col. Kenner Garrard
- 140th N.Y., 447, Col. Patrick H. O'Rorke (*k*), Lt. Col. Louis Ernst (? but survived Gettysburg)
- 146th N.Y., 454, Col. Kenner Garrard, Lt. Col. David T. Jenkins
- 91st Pa., 210, Lt. Col. Joseph H. Sinex
- 155th Pa., 424, Lt. Col. John H. Cain

3rd Division, 2,853, Brig. Gen. Samuel W. Crawford
1st Brigade, 1,243, Col. William McCandless
- 1st Pa. Reserves (30th Pa.), 377, Col. William C. Talley (?)
- 2nd Pa. Reserves (31st Pa.), 232, Lt. Col. George A. Woodward
- 6th Pa. Reserves (35th Pa.), 323, Lt. Col. Wellington H. Ent
- 13th Pa. Reserves (42nd Pa. "Bucktails"), 297, Col. Charles F. Taylor (*k*), Maj. William R. Hartshorne

3rd Brigade, 1,605, Col. Joseph W. Fisher
- 5th Pa. Reserves (34th Pa.), 284, Lt. Col. George Dare
- 9th Pa. Reserves (38th Pa.), 320, Lt. Col. James McK. Snodgrass
- 10th Pa. Reserves (39th Pa.), 401, Col. Adoniram J. Warner
- 11th Pa. Reserves (40th Pa.), 327, Col. Samuel M. Jackson
- 12th Pa. Reserves (41st Pa.), Companies A–I, 272, Col. Martin D. Hardin

Artillery Brigade, 26 guns, 432 men, Capt. Augustus P. Martin
- 3rd Mass. Light Artillery, Battery C (6 12-pound Napoleons), 115, Lt. Aaron F. Walcott
- 1st N.Y. Light Artillery, Battery C (4 3-inch rifles), 62, Capt. Almont Barnes
- 1st Ohio Light Artillery, Battery L (6 12-pound Napoleons), 113, Capt. Frank C. Gibbs
- 5th U.S. Artillery, Battery D (6 10-pound Parrotts), 68, Lt. Charles E. Hazlett (*k*), Lt. Benjamin F. Rittenhouse
- 5th U.S. Artillery, Battery I (4 3-inch rifles), 71, Lt. Malbone F. Watson (*w*), Lt. Charles C. MacConnell

6th Corps

13,577

Maj. Gen. John Sedgwick
- Escort, 1st N.J. Cavalry, Company L, 38, Capt. William S. Craft
- Provost Guard, 1st Pa. Cavalry, Company H, 54 (*p*), Capt. William S. Craft

1st Division, 4,207, Brig. Gen. Horatio Wright
- Provost Guard, 4th N.J., Companies A, C, and H, 80, Capt. William R. Maxwell

1st Brigade, 1,319, Brig. Gen. Albert T. A. Torbert
- 1st N.J., 253, Lt. Col. William Henry Jr.
- 2nd N.J., 357, Col. Charles Wiebecke
- 3rd N.J., 281, Lt. Col. Edward L. Campbell
- 15th N.J., 410, Col. William H. Penrose

2nd Brigade, 1,322, Brig. Gen. Joseph L. Bartlett
- 5th Maine, 293, Col. Clark S. Edwards (? but survived Gettysburg)
- 121st N.Y., 409, Col. Emory Upton
- 95th Pa., 308, Lt. Col. Edward Carroll
- 96th Pa., 308, Maj. William H. Lessig

3rd Brigade, 1,480, Brig. Gen. David A. Russell, Brig. Gen. Joseph J. Bartlett (arrived July 3)
- 6th Maine, 377, Col. Hiram Burham (?)
- 49th Pa., 275, Lt. Col. Thomas M. Hulings
- 119th Pa., 403, Col. Peter C. Ellmaker
- 5th Wis., 419, Col. Thomas S. Allen

2nd Division, 3,603, Brig. Gen. Albion P. Howe
2nd Brigade, 1,927, Col. Lewis A. Grant
- 2nd Vt., 443, Col. James H. Walbridge
- 3rd Vt., 364, Col. Thomas O. Seaver
- 4th Vt., 380, Col. Charles B. Stoughton
- 5th Vt., 294, Col. John R. Lewis
- 6th Vt., 330, Col. Elisha L. Barney

3rd Brigade, 1,733, Brig. Gen. Thomas H. Neill
- 7th Maine, Companies B–D, F, I, and K, 216, Lt. Col. Seldon Connor (?)
- 33rd N.Y. (detachment), 60, Capt. Henry J. Gifford
- 43rd N.Y., 370, Lt. Col. John Wilson
- 49th N.Y., 358, Col. Daniel D. Bidwell
- 77th N.Y., 367, Col. Winsor B. French (? but survived Gettysburg)
- 61st Pa., 286, Lt. Col. George F. Smith (?)

3rd Division, 4,731, Maj. Gen. John Newton, Brig. Gen. Frank Wheaton
1st Brigade, 1,766, Brig. Gen. Alexander Shaler
- 65th N.Y., 276, Col. Joseph E. Hamblin
- 67th N.Y., 349, Col. Nelson Cross
- 122nd N.Y., 395, Col. Silas Titus
- 23rd Pa., 466, Lt. Col. John F. Glenn
- 82nd Pa., 277, Col. Isaac C. Bassett

2nd Brigade, 1,591, Col. Henry L. Eustis
- 7th Mass., 319, Lt. Col. Franklin P. Harlow
- 10th Mass., 360, Lt. Col. Joseph B. Parsons
- 37th Mass., 564, Col. Oliver Edwards
- 2nd R.I., 347, Col. Horatio Rogers Jr.

3rd Brigade, 1,368, Brig. Gen. Frank Wheaton, Col. David J. Nevin
- 62nd N.Y., 237, Col. David J. Nevin, Lt. Col. Theodore B. Hamilton
- 93rd Pa., 351, Maj. John I. Nevin
- 98th Pa., 351, Maj. John B. Kohler
- 102nd Pa., 103 (#),[9] Col. John W. Patterson
- 139th Pa., 442, Col. Frederick H. Collier (w), Lt. Col. William H. Moody

Artillery Brigade, 46 guns, 937 men, Col. Charles H. Tompkins
- 1st Battery, Mass. Light Artillery (6 12-pound Napoleons), 135, Capt. William H. McCartney
- 1st Battery, N.Y. Light Artillery (6 3-inch rifles), 103, Capt. Andrew Cowan
- 3rd Battery, N.Y. Light Artillery (6 10-pound Parrotts), 111, Capt. William A. Harn
- 1st R.I. Light Artillery, Battery C (6 3-inch rifles), 116, Capt. Richard Waterman
- 1st R.I. Light Artillery, Battery G (6 10-pound Parrotts), 126, Capt. George W. Adams
- 2nd U.S. Artillery, Battery D (4 12-pound Napoleons), 126, Lt. Edward B. Williston
- 2nd U.S. Artillery, Battery G (6 12-pound Napoleons), 101, Lt. John H. Butler (?)
- 5th U.S. Artillery, Battery F (6 10-pound Parrotts), 116, Lt. Leonard Martin (?)

11th Corps
9,054
Maj. Gen. Oliver O. Howard
Maj. Gen. Carl Schurz

Maj. Gen. Oliver O. Howard
- Escort, 1st Ind. Cavalry, Companies I and K, 50, Capt. Abram Sharra (? but survived Gettysburg)
- Provost Guard, 17th Pa. Cavalry, Company K, 36
- Headquarters Guard, 8th N.Y. Independent Company, 40, Lt. Hermann Foerster (?)

1st Division, 2,459, Brig. Gen. Francis Barlow (w), Brig. Gen. Adelbert Ames
1st Brigade, 1,118, Col. Leopold von Gilsa
- 41st N.Y., Companies A–E, G–K, 218, Lt. Col. Detleo von Einsiedel
- 54th N.Y., 183, Maj. Stephen Kovacs, Lt. Ernst Both (?)
- 68th N.Y., 226, Col. Gotthilf Bourry (?)
- 153rd Pa., 487, Maj. John F. Frueauff

2nd Brigade, 1,337, Brig. Gen. Adelbert Ames, Col. Andrew L. Harris
- 17th Conn., 386, Lt. Col. Douglas Fowler (k), Maj. Allen G. Brady (w)
- 25th Ohio, 220, Lt. Col. Jeremiah Williams (w), Capt. Nathaniel J. Manning, Lt. William Maloney, Lt. Israel White
- 75th Ohio, 269, Col. Andrew L. Harris (w)
- 107th Ohio, 458, Col. Seraphim Meyer, Capt. John M. Lutz

2nd Division, 2,775, Brig. Gen. Adolph von Steinwehr
1st Brigade, 1,156, Col. Charles R. Coster
- 134th N.Y., 400, Lt. Col. Allan H. Jackson (? but survived Gettysburg)
- 154th N.Y., 190, Col. Daniel B. Allen (? but survived Gettysburg)
- 27th Pa., Companies A–E, G–K, 277, Lt. Col. Lorenz Cantador
- 73rd Pa., 284, Capt. D. F. Kelley

2nd Brigade, 1,614, Col. Orland Smith
- 33rd Mass., 481, Col. Aldin B. Underwood
- 136th N.Y., 473, Col. James Wood Jr.
- 55th Ohio, 321, Col. Charles B. Gambee
- 73rd Ohio, 338, Lt. Col. Richard Long

3rd Division, 3,079, Maj. Gen. Carl Shurz, Brig. Gen. Alexander Schimmelfennig
1st Brigade, 1,670, Brig. Gen. Alexander Schimmelfennig, Col. George von Amsberg, Brig. Gen. Alexander Schimmelfennig
- 82nd Ill., 310, Lt. Col. Edward S. Salomon (? but survived Gettysburg)
- 45th N.Y., 375, Col. George von Amsberg, Lt. Col. Adolphus Dobke
- 157 N.Y. 409, Col. Phillip P. Brown Jr. (?)
- 61st Ohio, 247, Col. Stephen J. McGroarty
- 74th Pa., Companies A, B, D–K, 326, Col. Adolph von Hartung (?), Lt. Col. Alexander von Mitzel (c), Capt. Gustav Schleiter (?), Capt. Henry Krauseneck (?)

2nd Brigade, 1,403, Col. Wladimir Kryzanowski
- 58th N.Y., 193, Lt. Col. August Ottom, Capt. Emil Koenig
- 119th N.Y., 257, Col. John T. Lockman (w), Lt. Col. Edward F. Lloyd
- 82nd Ohio, 312, Col. James S. Robinson (w), Lt. Col. David Thomson
- 75th Pa., Companies A–I, 208, Col. Francis Mahler, Maj. August Ledig
- 26th Wis., 435, Lt. Col. Hans Boebel (w), Capt. John W. Fuchs (w)

Artillery Brigade, 26 guns, 604 men, Maj. Thomas W. Osborn
- 1st N.Y. Light Artillery, Battery I (6 3-inch rifles), 141, Capt. Michael Wiedrich
- 13th Battery, N.Y. Light Artillery (4 3-inch rifles), 110, Lt. William Wheeler
- 1st Ohio Light Artillery, Battery I (6 12-pound Napoleons), 127, Capt. Hubert Dilger
- 1st Ohio Light Artillery, Battery K (4 12-pound Napoleons), 110, Capt.

Lewis Heckman

4th U.S. Artillery, Battery G (6 12-pound Napoleons), 115, Lt. Bayard Wilkeson (*mw*), Lt. Eugene A. Bancroft

12th Corps

9,788

Maj. Gen. Henry W. Slocum

Brig. Gen. Alpheus S. Williams

Provost Guard, 10th Maine, Companies A, B, and D, 169, Capt. John D. Beardsley (*?*)

1st Division, 5,256, Brig. Gen. Alpheus S. Williams, Brig. Gen. Thomas H. Ruger

1st Brigade, 1,835, Col. Archibald L. McDougall

5th Conn., 221, Col. W. W. Packer
20th Conn., 321, Lt. Col. William B. Wooster
3rd Md. (arrived July 2), 290, Col. Joseph M. Sudsburg
123rd N.Y., 495, Col. James C. Rogers, Capt. Adolphus H. Tanner
145th N.Y., 245, Col. E. Livingston Price
46th Pa., 262, Capt. James L. Selfridge

2nd Brigade, 1,818, Brig. Gen. Henry H. Lockwood

1st Md. (Eastern Shore), 532, Col. James Wallace
1st Md. (Potomac Home Brigade), 674, Col. William P. Maulsby
150th N.Y., 609, Col. John H. Ketchum

3rd Brigade, 1,598, Brig. Gen. Thomas H. Ruger, Col. Silas Colgrove

27th Ind., 339, Col. Silas Colgrove, Lt. Col. John R. Fesler
2nd Mass., 316, Lt. Col. Charles R. Mudge (*k*), Maj. Charles F. Morse
13th N.J., 347, Col. Ezra A. Carman
107th N.Y., 319, Col. Nirom M. Crane
3rd Wis., 260, Col. William Hawley

2nd Division, 3,964, Brig. Gen. John W. Geary

Provost Guard, 28th Pa., Company B, 37

1st Brigade, 1,798, Col. Charles Candy

5th Ohio, 302, Col. John H. Patrick
7th Ohio, 282, Col. William R. Creighton
29th Ohio, 308, Col. Wilbur F. Stevens (*w* [slightly]), Capt. Edward Hayes
66th Ohio, 303, Col. Eugene Powell
28th Pa., Companies A, C–K, 303, Capt. John Flynn (*w*)
147th Pa., 298, Lt. Col. Ario Pardee Jr.

2nd Brigade, 700, Col. George A. Cobham Jr., Brig. Gen. Thomas L. Kane, Col. George A. Cobham Jr.

29th Pa., 357, Col. William Rickards Jr.
109th Pa., 149, Capt. F. L. Gimber
111th Pa., 191, Lt. Col. Thomas M. Walker, Col. George A. Cobham Jr., Lt. Col. Thomas M. Walker

3rd Brigade, 1,424, Brig. Gen. George S. Greene

60th N.Y., 272, Col. Abel Godard
78th N.Y., 198, Lt. Col. Herbert von Hammerstein
102nd N.Y., 230, Capt. James C. Lane (*w*), Capt. Lewis R. Stegman
137th N.Y., 423, Col. David Ireland
149th N.Y., 297, Col. Henry A. Barnum (became ill July 2), Lt. Col. Charles B. Randall (*w*)

Artillery Brigade, 20 guns, 391 men, Lt. Edward D. Muhlenberg

1st N.Y. Light Artillery, Battery M (4 10-pound Parrotts), 90, Lt. Charles E. Winegar
Pa. Light Artillery, Battery E (6 10-pound Parrotts), 139, Lt. Charles A. Atwell
4th U.S. Artillery, Battery F (6 12-pound Napoleons), 89, Lt. Sylvanus T. Rugg
5th U.S. Artillery, Battery K (4 12-pound Napoleons), 77, Lt. David H. Kinzie

Cavalry Corps

12,101

Maj. Gen. Alfred Pleasonton

1st Division, 4,514, Brig. Gen. John Buford

1st Brigade, 1,600, Col. William Gamble

Headquarters Guard, 6th Vt. Cavalry, Company L, 35
8th Ill. Cavalry, 470, Maj. John L. Beveridge
12th Ill. Cavalry, Companies E, F, H, and I, 470, Col. George H. Chapman
3rd Ind. Cavalry, Companies G–M, 233, Col. George H. Chapman
8th N.Y. Cavalry, 580, Lt. Col. William L. Markell (*?* but survived Gettysburg)

2nd Brigade, 1,148, Col. Thomas C. Devin

6th N.Y. Cavalry, Companies B, C, E–G, I, and M, 215, Maj. William E. Beardsley (*?*)
9th N.Y. Cavalry, 367, Col. William H. Sackett (*?*)
17th Pa. Cavalry, Companies A–C, E–G, I–M, 464, Col. Josiah H. Kellogg
3rd W.V. Cavalry, Companies A and C, 59, Capt. Seymour R. Conger (*?*)

Reserve Brigade (arrived July 3; detached to 3rd Cavalry Division), 1,792, Brig. Gen. Wesley Merritt

6th Pa. Cavalry, Companies A–D, F–H, K–M, 242, Maj. James H. Haseltine (*?*)
1st U.S. Cavalry, Companies A–E, G–M, 362, Capt. Richard S. C. Lord (*?*)
2nd U.S. Cavalry, 407, Capt. T. F. Rodenbough (*?*)
5th U.S. Cavalry, 306, Capt. Julius W. Mason (*?*)
6th U.S. Cavalry, 475, Maj. Samuel H. Starr (*w, c*), Lt. Louis Henry Carpenter, Lt. Nicholas Nolan (*?*), Capt. Ira W. Claflin

2nd Division, 2,664, Brig. Gen. David McM. Gregg

Headquarters Guard, 1st Ohio Cavalry, Company A, 37

1st Brigade, 2 guns, 1,561 men, Col. John B. McIntosh

1st Md. Cavalry, Companies A–L, 285, Lt. Col. James M. Deems
Purnell (Md.) Legion, Company A, 66, Capt. Robert E. Duvall
1st Mass., Companies A–H, 250 (guarding army headquarters), Lt. Col. Greely S. Curtis
1st N.J. Cavalry, 218, Maj. M. H. Beaumont
1st Pa. Cavalry, Companies A–G, I–M, 355, Col. John P. Taylor
3rd Pa. Cavalry, 335, Lt. Col. E. S. Jones
3rd Pa. Heavy Artillery, Battery H (2 3-inch rifles), 52 (*p*), Capt. W. D. Rank

2nd Brigade (#),[10] Col. Pennock Huey

2nd N.Y. Cavalry, Col. Otto Harkhaus
4th N.Y. Cavalry, Lt. Col. Augustus Pruyn
6th Ohio Cavalry, Companies A–E, G–L, Maj. William Stedman
8th Pa. Cavalry, Capt. William A. Corrie

3rd Brigade, 1,263, Col. J. Irvin Gregg

1st Maine Cavalry, Companies A, B, D–K, and M, 315, Lt. Col. Charles H. Smith
10th N.Y. Cavalry, 333, Maj. M. Henry Avery
4th Pa. Cavalry, 258, Lt. Col. William E. Doster

16th Pa. Cavalry, 349, Lt. Col. John K. Robison

3rd Division, 3,902, Brig. Gen. Judson Kilpatrick
    Headquarters Guard, 1st Ohio Cavalry, Company C, 40

1st Brigade, 1,925, Brig. Gen. Elon Farnsworth (k), Col. Nathaniel P. Richmond
    5th N.Y. Cavalry, 420, Maj. John Hammond
    18th Pa. Cavalry, 509, Lt. Col. William P. Brinton (? but survived Gettysburg)
    1st Vt. Cavalry, 600, Col. Addison W. Preston
    1st W.V. Cavalry, Companies B–H, L–N, 395, Col. Nathaniel P. Richmond, Maj. Charles E. Capehart (?)

2nd Brigade (July 3 with 2nd Cavalry Division), 934, Brig. Gen. George A. Custer
    1st Mich. Cavalry, 427, Col. Charles H. Town
    5th Mich. Cavalry, 646, Col. Russell A. Alger
    6th Mich. Cavalry, 477, Col. George Gray
    7th Mich. Cavalry, Companies A–K, 383, Col. William D. Mann

Horse Artillery, 40 guns, 764 men
1st Brigade, 28 guns, 492 men, Capt. James M. Robertson
    9th Mich. Battery (6 3-inch rifles), 111, Capt. Jabez J. Daniels
    6th N.Y. Battery (6 3-inch rifles), 103, Capt. Joseph W. Martin
    2nd U.S. Artillery, Batteries B and L (6 3-inch rifles), 99, Lt. Edward Heaton (? but survived Gettysburg)
    2nd U.S. Artillery, Battery M (6 3-inch rifles), 117, Lt. Alexander C. M. Pennington Jr. (? but survived Gettysburg)
    4th U.S. Artillery, Battery E (4 3-inch rifles), 60, Lt. Samuel S. Elder

2nd Brigade, 12 guns, 272 men, Capt. John C. Tindall
    1st U.S. Artillery, Batteries E and G (4 3-inch rifles), 82, Capt. Alanson M. Randol (? but survived Gettysburg)
    1st U.S. Artillery, Battery K (6 3-inch rifles), 114, Capt. William M. Graham
    2nd U.S. Artillery, Battery A (6 3-inch rifles), 74, Lt. John H. Calef [11]
    3rd U.S. Artillery, Battery C (6 3-inch rifles) (#),[12] Lt. William D. Fuller

Artillery Reserve
110 guns, 2,376 men
Brig. Gen. Robert O. Tyler
    Headquarters Guard, 32nd Mass., Company C, 45, Capt. Josiah C. Fuller
    Train Guard, 4th N.J., Companies B, D–G, I, and K, 272, Maj. Charles Ewing

1st Regular Brigade, 24 guns, 445 men, Capt. Dunbar R. Ransom (w)
    1st U.S. Artillery, Battery H (6 12-pound Napoleons), 129, Lt. Chandler P. Eakin, Lt. Philip D. Mason (?)
    3rd U.S. Artillery, Batteries F and K (6 12-pound Napoleons), 115, Lt. John G. Turnbull
    4th U.S. Artillery, Battery C (6 12-pound Napoleons), 95, Lt. Evan Thomas (?)
    5th U.S. Artillery, Battery C (6 12-pound Napoleons), 104, Lt. Gulian V. Weir

1st Volunteer Brigade, 22 guns, 385 men, Lt. Col. Freeman McGilvery
    5th Battery, Mass. Light Artillery/19th N.Y. Battery (6 3-inch rifles), 104, Capt. Charles A. Phillips
    9th Battery, Mass. Light Artillery (6 12-pound Napoleons), 104, Capt. John Bigelow (w), Lt. Richard S. Milton
    15th Battery, N.Y. Light Artillery (4 12-pound Napoleons), 70, Capt. Patrick Hart
    Pa. Light Artillery, Batteries C and F (6 3-inch rifles), 105, Capt. James Thompson (w)

2nd Volunteer Brigade, 12 guns, 241 men, Capt. Elijah D. Taft
    1st Conn. Heavy Artillery, Battery B (4 4.5-inch rifles) (#), Capt. Albert F. Brooker
    1st Conn. Heavy Artillery, Battery M (4 4.5-inch rifles) (#),[13] Capt. Franklin A. Pratt
    2nd Battery, Conn. Light Artillery (4 12-pound James, 2 12-pound howitzers), 93, Capt. John W. Sterling
    5th Battery, N.Y. Light Artillery (6 20-pound Parrotts), 146, Capt. Elijah D. Taft

3rd Volunteer Brigade, 22 guns, 431 men, Capt. James F. Huntington
    1st Battery, N.H. Light Artillery (6 3-inch rifles), 86, Capt. Frederick M. Edgell
    1st Ohio Light Artillery, Battery H (6 3-inch rifles), 99, Lt. George W. Norton
    1st Pa. Light Artillery, Batteries F and G (6 3-inch rifles), 144, Capt. R. Bruce Ricketts
    W.V. Light Artillery, Battery C (4 10-pound Parrotts), 100, Capt. Wallace Hill

4th Volunteer Brigade, 24 guns, 499 men, Capt. Robert H. Fitzhugh
    6th Battery (F), Maine Light Artillery (6 12-pound Napoleons), 87, Lt. Edwin B. Dow
    Md. Light Artillery, Battery A (6 3-inch rifles), 106, Capt. James H. Rigby
    1st Battery, N.J. Light Artillery (6 10-pound Parrotts), 98, Lt. Augustin N. Parsons
    1st N.Y. Light Artillery, Battery G (6 12-pound Napoleons), 84, Capt. Nelson Ames
    1st N.Y. Light Artillery/11th N.Y. Battery (K) (6 3-inch rifles), 128, Capt. Robert H. Fitzhugh

Chart F-2
General organizational scheme for the confederate army in the Gettysburg campaign

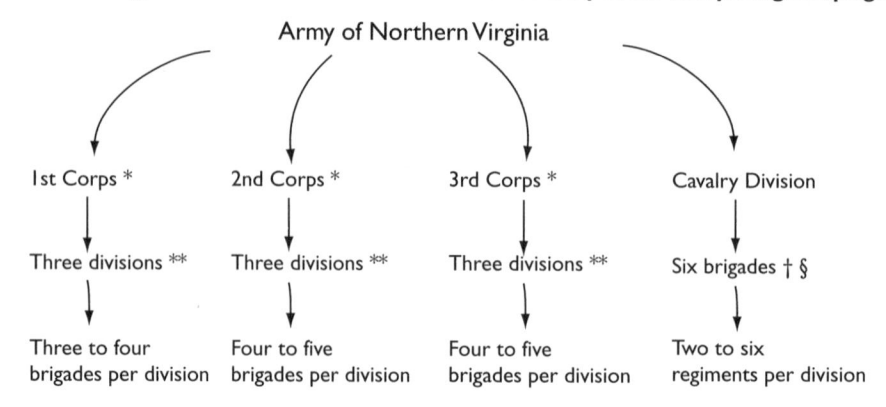

Army of Northern Virginia
→ 1st Corps *, 2nd Corps *, 3rd Corps *, Cavalry Division
→ Three divisions **, Three divisions **, Three divisions **, Six brigades † §
→ Three to four brigades per division, Four to five brigades per division, Four to five brigades per division, Two to six regiments per division

* Each corps had an artillery reserve.

** There was a division artillery within each such unit.

† Only four of these came out of Virginia to Gettysburg itself, although there was one further cavalry brigade (Brig. Gen. J. Imboden's), which was not formally under the division's command, but which accompanied the army into Pennsylvania. One of the four brigades that went into Pennsylvania (under Brig. Gen. A. Jenkins) included a small artillery battery.

§ The further unit within this division was the Horse artillery (six batteries).

Army of Northern Virginia

approx. 72,000 men[14]

280 artillery pieces

Headquarters and Staff, 17
Commanding General: Gen. Robert E. Lee
Chief of Staff and Inspector General: Col. R. H. Chilton
Chief of Artillery: Brig. Gen. William N. Pendleton
Chief of Engineers (acting): Maj. Gen. Isaac R. Trimble (*w*)
Chief of Ordnance: Lt. Col. Briscoe G. Baldwin
Chief of Commissary: Lt. Col. Robert G. Cole
Chief Quartermaster: Lt. Col. James L. Corley
Judge Advocate: Maj. H. E. Young
Military Secretary (acting Assistant Chief of Artillery): Col. Armistead L. Long
Aide-de-camp and Assistant Military Secretary: Maj. Charles Marshall
Aide-de-camp and Assistant Inspector General: Maj. Charles S. Venable
Staff Engineer: Capt. Samuel R. Johnston
Medical Director: Dr. Lafayette Guild
Escort: 39th Va. Cavalry Battalion, Company C, 43, Maj. John H. Richardson

1st Corps

20,811
Lt. Gen. James Longstreet

McLaws's Division, 6,924, Maj. Gen. Lafayette McLaws
Kershaw's Brigade, Brig. Gen. Joseph B. Kershaw, 2,183
   2nd S.C. (Palmetto), 412, Col. John D. Kennedy (*w*), Lt. Col. F. Gaillard
   3rd S.C., 406, Maj. Robert C. Maffett, Col. James D. Nance
   7th S.C., Companies A–M, 408, Lt. Col. Elbert Bland (*w*), Col. D. Wyatt Aiken
   8th S.C., Companies A–M, 300, Col. John W. Henagan, Lt. Col. Axalla John Hoole, Maj. Donald Mc. McLeod (*k*), Col. S. G. Malloy
   15th S.C., 488, Col. William D. De Saussure (*k*), Maj. William M. Gist
   3rd S.C. Battalion (James), Companies A–G, 203, Lt. Col. William G. Rice
Semmes's Brigade, 1,334, Brig. Gen. Paul Jones Semmes (*mw*), Col. Goode Bryan
   10th Ga., 303, Col. John B. Weems (*w*)
   50th Ga., 302, Col. William R. Manning, Lt. Col. Francis Kearse (*k*), Capt. A. S. McGlashan, Maj. William O. Fleming

51st Ga., 303, Col. Edward Ball
53rd Ga., 422, Col. James P. Simms

Barksdale's Brigade, 1,620, Brig. Gen. William Barksdale (*mw*), Col. Benjamin G. Humphreys

13th Miss., 481, Col. James W. Carter (*k*), Lt. Col. Kennon McElroy (*w*)
17th Miss., 469, Col. William D. Holder (*w*), Lt. Col. John C. Fiser (*w*)
18th Miss., 242, Col. Thomas M. Griffin (*w*), Lt. Col. William H. Luse (*c*), Maj. George B. Gerald
21st Miss., Companies A, and C–L, 424, Col. Benjamin G. Humphreys, Maj. Daniel N. Moody

Wofford's Brigade, 1,398, Brig. Gen. William T. Wofford

16th Ga., 393, Col. Goode Bryan
18th Ga., 302, Lt. Col. Solon Z. Ruff
24th Ga., 303, Col. Robert McMillan
Cobb's (Ga.) Legion, Companies A–G, 213, Lt. Col. Luther J. Glenn
Phillips (Ga.) Legion, Companies A–F, L, M, and O, 273, Lt. Col. Elihu S. Barclay

Division Artillery, 16 guns, 378 men, Col. Henry G. Cabell

Pulaski (Ga.) Battery (2 3-inch rifles, 2 10-pound Parrotts), 63, Capt. John C. Fraser (*mw*), Lt. William J. Furlong
Troup County (Ga.) Light Battery (2 12-pound howitzers, 2 10-pound Parrotts), 94, Capt. Henry H. Carlton (*w*), Lt. Columbus W. Motes
1st N.C. Artillery, Ellis Light, Battery A (2 12-pound Napoleons, 2 3-inch rifles), 131, Capt. Basil C. Manly
1st Richmond (Va.) Howitzer Battery (2 12-pound Napoleons, 2 3-inch rifles), 90, Capt. Edward S. McCarthy

Pickett's Division, 5,578
Maj. Gen. George E. Pickett

Garnett's Brigade, 1,459, Brig. Gen. Richard B. Garnett (*k*), Maj. Joseph R. Cabell, Maj. Charles S. Payton

8th Va., 193, Col. Eppa Hunton (*w*), Lt. Col. Norborne Berkeley (*w, c*), Maj. Edmund Berkeley (*w*), Lt. John Gray
18th Va., 312, Lt. Col. Henry A. Carrington (*w, c*), Col. Robert E. Withers
19th Va., 328, Col. Henry Gantt (*w*), Lt. Col. John T. Ellis (*k*), Maj. Charles S. Peyton (*w*)
28th Va., Companies A–G, I–K, 333, Col. Robert C. Allen (*k*), Lt. Col. William Watts
56th Va., 289, Col. William D. Stuart (*mw*), Lt. Col. P. P. Slaughter, Capt. James C. Wyatt (*mw*), Capt. Frank W. Nelson

Kemper's Brigade, 1,634, Brig. Gen. James L. Kemper (*w, c*), Col. Joseph C. Mayo Jr. (*w*), Col. William R. Terry

1st Va. (Williams's Rifles), Companies B–D, G–I, 209, Col. Lewis B. Williams Jr. (*k*), Lt. Col. Francis G. Skinner, Maj. Francis H. Langley (*w*), Capt. George F. Norton (*w*), Capt. Thomas Davis (*w*), Capt. Benjamin F. Howard
3rd Va., 322, Col. Joseph C. Mayo Jr. (*w*), Lt. Col. Alexander D. Callcote (*k*)
7th Va., Companies A–G, I–K, 335, Col. Waller T. Patton (*mw, c*), Lt. Col. C. C. Flowerree, Capt. Alphonso N. Jones
11th Va., 359, Maj. Kirkwood Otey (*w*), Capt. James R. Hutter (*w, c*)
24th Va., 395, Col. William R. Terry (*w*), Capt. William N. Bentley (*w*)

Armistead's Brigade, 2,055, Brig. Gen. Lewis A. Armistead (*k*), Col. William R. Aylett (*w*)

9th Va., Companies A–G, I–K, 318, Maj. John C. Owens (*mw*), Capt. James J. Phillips
14th Va., 422, Col. James G. Hodges (*k*), Col. William White (*w*)
38th Va., 400, Col. Edward C. Edmonds (*k*), Lt. Col. Powhatan B. Whittle (*w, c*)
53rd Va., 435, Col. William R. Aylett (*w*), Lt. Col. Rawley White Martin (*w, c*)
57th Va., 476, Col. John Bowie Magruder (*mw, c*), Maj. Clement R. Fontaine

Division Artillery, 18 guns, 419 men, Maj. James Dearing

Fauquier (Va.) Battery (4 12-pound Napoleons, 2 10-pound Parrotts), 134, Capt. Robert M. Stribling
Lynchburg (Va.) Battery (4 12-pound Napoleons), 96, Capt. Joseph G. Blount
Richmond (Fayette, Va.) Battery (2 12-pound Napoleons, 2 10-pound Parrotts), 90, Capt. Miles C. Macon
Richmond (Hampden, Va.) Battery (2 12-pound Napoleons, 1 3-inch rifle, 1 10-pound Parrott), 90, Capt. William H. Caskie

Hood's Division, 19 guns, 7,375 men, Maj. Gen. John B. Hood (*w*), Brig. Gen. Evander McIver Law

Law's Brigade, 1,933, Brig. Gen. Evander McIver Law, Col. James L. Sheffield

4th Ala., 308, Col. Pinckney D. Bowles, Col. Lawrence H. Scruggs
15th Ala. Companies A–L, 499, Col. William C. Oates, Capt. Blanton A. Hill
44th Ala., 363, Col. William F. Perry, Maj. George W. Cary
47th Ala., 347, Col. James W. Jackson, Lt. Col. Michael J. Bulger (*w, c*), Maj. James M. Campbell
48th Ala., 374, Col. James L. Sheffield, Capt. T. J. Eubanks

Texas Brigade, 1,743, Brig. Gen. Jerome B. Robertson (*w*), Lt. Col. Phillip A. Work

3rd Ark., 479, Col. Vannoy H. Manning (*w*), Lt. Col. Robert S. Taylor
1st Tex., Companies A–M, 426, Col. Phillip A. Work, Maj. Frederick S. Bass
4th Tex., 415, Col. John C. G. Key (*w*), Lt. Col. Benjamin F. Carter (*mw*), Maj. John P. Bane
5th Tex., 409, Col. Robert M. Powell (*w*), Lt. Col. King Bryan (*w*), Maj. Jefferson C. Rogers

Anderson's Brigade, 1,874, Brig. Gen. George T. Anderson (*w*), Lt. Col. William Luffman

7th Ga., 377, Col. William W. White
8th Ga., 312, Col. John R. Towers (*w*), Capt. Dunlap Scott
9th Ga., Companies B–K, 340, Lt. Col. John C. Mounger (*k*), Maj. William M. Jones (*w*), Capt. George Hillyer
11th Ga., 310, Col. Francis H. Little (*w*), Col. William Luffman, Maj. Henry D. McDaniel (*w, c*), Capt. William H. Mitchell
59th Ga., 525, Col. William A. Jackson Brown (*w, c*), Maj. Bolivar H. Gee, Col. Maston G. Bass

Benning's Brigade, 1,420, Brig. Gen. Henry L. Benning

2nd Ga., 348, Lt. Col. William T. Harris (*k*), Maj. William S. Shephard
15th Ga., 368, Col. Dudley Mc. DuBose
17th Ga., 350, Col. Wesley C. Hodges
20th Ga., 350, Col. John A. Jones (*k*), Lt. Col. James D. Waddell

Division Artillery, 19 guns, 403 men, Maj. Mathias W. Henry, Maj. John C. Haskell

1st N.C. Artillery (Rowan), Battery D (2 12-pound Napoleons, 2 10-pound Parrotts, and 2 3-inch rifles), 148, Capt. James Reilly
3rd or 13th (?) N.C. Artillery Battalion (Branch's), Battery F (1 6-pound and 1 12-pound howitzer, and 3 12-pound Napoleons), 112, Capt. Alexander C. Latham
Charleston (S.C.) "German" Light Battery (4 12-pound Napoleons), 71, Capt. William K. Bachman
Palmetto (S.C.) Light Battery (2 12-pound Napoleons and 2 10-pound Parrotts), 63, Capt. Hugh H. Garden

1st Corps Reserve Artillery, 34 guns, 918 men, Col. James B. Walton

Alexander's Artillery Battalion, 24 guns, 576 men, Col. E. Porter Alexander, Maj. Frank Huger
- Madison (La.) Battery (4 24-pound howitzers), 135, Capt. George V. Moody
- Brooks (S.C.) Light Battery (4 12-pound howitzers), 71, Capt. William W. Fickling, Lt. S. Capers Gilbert (w)
- Ashland (Va.) Battery (2 12-pound Napoleons, 2 10-pound Parrotts), 103, Capt. Pichegru Woolfolk Jr. (w), Lt. James Woolfolk
- Bath (Va.) Battery (4 12-pound Napoleons), 90, Capt. Osmond B. Taylor
- Bedford (Va.) Battery (4 3-inch rifles), 78, Capt. Tyler C. Jordan
- Richmond (Va.) Parker Battery (3 3-inch rifles, 1 10-pound Parrott), 90, Capt. William W. Parker, Lt. J. Thompson Brown, Lt. George E. Saville

Washington (La.) Artillery Battalion, 10 guns, 338 men, Maj. Benjamin F. Eshleman
- 1st Company (1 12-pound Napoleon), 77, Capt. Charles W. Squires, Lt. C. H. C. Brown (w, c)
- 2nd Company (2 12-pound Napoleons, 1 12-pound howitzer), 80, Capt. John B. Richardson
- 3rd Company (3 12-pound Napoleons), 92, Capt. Merritt B. Miller, Lt. Andrew Hero Jr.
- 4th Company (2 12-pound Napoleons, 1 12-pound howitzer), 80, Capt. Joseph Norcom, Lt. Henry A. Battles

2nd Corps

20,572

Lt. Gen. Richard S. Ewell
- Escort, 39th Va. Cavalry Battalion, Company C, 31, Capt. William F. Randolph

Early's Division, 16 guns, 5,460 men, Maj. Gen. Jubal A. Early
Hays's Brigade, 1,295, Brig. Gen. Harry T. Hays
- 5th La., 196, Col. Henry Forno, Maj. Alexander Hart (w), Capt. Thomas H. Briscoe
- 6th La., 218, Col. William Monaghan, Lt. Col. Joseph Hanlon
- 7th La., 235, Col. Davidson B. Penn
- 8th La., 296, Col. Travanion D. Lewis (k), Lt. Col. Alcibiades de Blanc (w), Maj. German A. Lester
- 9th La., Companies A–I, 347, Col. Leroy A. Stafford

Smith's Brigade, 806, Brig. Gen. William Smith
- 31st Va., 267, Col. John S. Hoffman
- 49th Va., Companies A–F, H–K, 281, Lt. Col. Jonathan Catlett Gibson
- 52nd Va., 254, Lt. Col. James H. Skinner (w), Lt. Col. John D. Ross

Hoke's Brigade, 1,244, Col. Isaac E. Avery (mw), Col. Archibald C. Godwin
- 6th N.C. State Troops, 509, Lt. Col. Robert F. Webb, Maj. Samuel McD. Tate
- 21st N.C., Companies A, C, D, and F–M, 436, Col. William W. Kirkland
- 57th N.C., 297, Col. Archibald C. Godwin

Gordon's Brigade, 1,813, Brig. Gen. John B. Gordon
- 13th Ga., 312, Col. James M. Smith
- 26th Ga., 315, Col. Edmund D. Atkinson
- 31st Ga., 252, Col. Clement A. Evans (w)
- 38th Ga., 341, Capt. William L. McLeod (k)
- 60th Ga., 299, Capt. Walter B. Jones
- 61st Ga., 288, Col. John H. Lamar

Division Artillery, 16 guns, 290 men, Lt. Col. Hilary P. Jones, Capt. James McD. Carrington, Lt. Col. Hilary P. Jones
- La. Guard Battery (2 3-inch rifles, 2 10-pound Parrotts), 60, Capt. Charles Thompson (k), Capt. Charles A. Green
- Charlottesville (Va.) Battery (4 12-pound Napoleons), 71, Capt. James McD. Carrington
- Richmond (Va.) "Courtney" Battery (4 3-inch rifles), 90, Capt. William A. Tanner
- Staunton (Va.) Battery (4 12-pound Napoleons), 60, Capt. Asher W. Gardner

Johnson's Division, 6,433, Maj. Gen. Edward Johnson
Steuart's Brigade, 2,121, Brig. Gen. George H. Steuart
- 1st Md. Battalion, Companies A–G, 400, Lt. Col. James R. Herbert (w), Maj. William C. Goldsborough (w, c), Capt. John W. Torsch, Capt. James P. Crane
- 1st N.C. State Troops, 377, Lt. Col. Hamilton A. Brown
- 3rd N.C., 548, Maj. William A. Parsley
- 10th Va., Companies A–L, 276, Col. Edward T. H. Warren
- 23rd Va., 251, Lt. Col. Simeon T. Walton
- 37th Va., Companies A–F, G–K, 264, Maj. Henry C. Wood

Nicholls's Brigade (Louisiana Tigers), 1,104, Col. Eugene Waggaman (w), Col. Jesse M. Williams
- 1st La., Companies A–G, I, and K, 172, Lt. Col. Michael Nolan, Capt. Thomas Rice, Capt. Edward D. Willett
- 2nd La., 236, Maj. Ross E. Burke (w, c)
- 10th La., 226, Maj. Thomas N. Powell
- 14th La., 281, Lt. Col. David Zable
- 15th La., 186, Maj. Andrew Brady

Stonewall Brigade, 1,323, Brig. Gen. James A. Walker
- 2nd Va., 333, Col. John Q. A. Nadenbousch
- 4th Va., Companies A–I, and L, 257, Maj. Williams Terry
- 5th Va., Companies A, and C–L, 345, Lt. Col. Hazael J. Williams Jr. (w), Maj. James W. Newton, Col. John H. S. Funk
- 27th Va., Companies B–H, 148, Lt. Col. Daniel M. Shriver
- 33rd Va., 236, Capt. Jacob B. Golladay

Jones's Brigade, 1,520, Brig. Gen. John M. Jones (w), Lt. Col. Robert H. Dungan, Col. Bradley T. Johnson
- 21st Va., Companies A, and C–K, 236, Col. William P. Moseley
- 25th Va., 280, Col. John C. Higginbotham (w), Lt. Col. John A. Robinson
- 42nd Va., 265, Lt. Col. Robert W. Withers (w), Capt. Jesse M. Richardson (w), Capt. Samuel H. Saunders
- 44th Va., Companies B–K, 227, Maj. Norvell Cobb (w), Capt. Thomas R. Buckner
- 48th Va., 265, Lt. Col. Robert H. Dungan, Lt. Col. Oscar White, Lt. Col. Robert H. Dungan
- 50th Va., 240, Lt. Col. Logan H. N. Salyer

Division Artillery, 16 guns, 356 men, Lt. Col. R. Snowden Andrews (w), Maj. J. W. Latimer (mw), Capt. Charles I. Raine
- 1st Md. Battery (4 12-pound Napoleons), 90, Capt. William F. Dement
- 4th Md. (Chesapeake) Battery (4 10-pound Parrotts), 76, Capt. William D. Brown (k), Lt. Charles S. Contee (w)
- Allegheny (Va.) Battery (2 12-pound Napoleons, 2 3-inch rifles), 91, Capt. John C. Carpenter, Lt. William T. Lambie, Capt. John C. Carpenter
- Lynchburg (Va.) "Lee" Battery (1 3-inch rifle, 1 10-pound Parrott, 2 20-pound Parrotts), 90, Capt. Charles I. Raine, Lt. William W. Hardwicke

Rodes's Division, 7,986, Maj. Gen. Robert E. Rodes

Daniel's Brigade, 2,162, Brig. Gen. Junius Daniel
- 32nd N.C., Companies A, B, and D–K, 454, Col. Edmund C. Brable
- 43rd N.C., 572, Lt. Col. Thomas S. Kenan (w, c), Lt. Col. William G. Lewis
- 45th N.C., 570, Lt. Col. Samuel H. Boyd (w, c), Maj. John R. Winston (w, c), Capt. Alexander H. Galloway (w)
- 53rd N.C., Companies A, B, and D–K, 322, Capt. William A. Owens
- 2nd N.C. Battalion, Companies A, B, and D–H, 240, Lt. Col. Hezekiah L. Andrews (k), Maj. John M. Hancock (w, c), Capt. Van Brown

Iverson's Brigade, 1,384, Brig. Gen. Alfred Iverson, Capt. Donal P. Halsey
- 5th N.C. State Troops, 473, Lt. Col. John W. Lea, Capt. Speight B. West (w), Capt. Benjamin Robinson (w)
- 12th N.C., 219, Lt. Col. William S. Davis
- 20th N.C., 372, Lt. Col. Nelson Slough (w), Capt. Louis T. Hicks
- 23rd N.C., 316, Col. Daniel H. Christie (mw), Lt. Col. Charles C. Blacknall (w, c), Capt. William H. Johnston (c)

Doles's Brigade, 1,323, Brig. Gen. George Doles
- 4th Ga., 341, Col. David R. E. Winn (k), Maj. William H. Willis
- 12th Ga., 327, Col. Edward Willis
- 21st Ga., 287, Col. John T. Mercer
- 44th Ga., 364, Col. Samuel P. Lumpkin (mw), Maj. William H. Peebles

Ramseur's Brigade, 1,027, Brig. Gen. Stephen Dodson Ramseur
- 2nd N.C. State Troops, 243, Maj. Daniel W. Hurtt (w), Capt. James T. Scales
- 4th N.C. State Troops, 196, Col. Bryan Grimes
- 14th N.C., 306, Col. R. Tyler Bennett (w), Maj. Joseph H. Lambeth
- 30th N.C., 278, Col. Francis M. Parker (w), Maj. William W. Sillers

O'Neal's Brigade, 1,688, Col. Edward A. O'Neal
- 3rd Ala., Companies A–L, 350, Lt. Col. Charles Forsyth, Col. Cullen A. Battle
- 5th Ala., 317, Col. Josephus M. Hall
- 6th Ala., 382, Col. James N. Lightfoot (w), Capt. Milledge L. Bowie
- 12th Ala., 317, Col. Samuel B. Pickens
- 26th Ala., 319, Lt. Col. John C. Goodgame

Division Artillery, 16 guns, 385 men, Lt. Col. Thomas A. Carter
- Jefferson Davis (Ala.) Battery (4 3-inch rifles), 79, Capt. William J. Reese
- King William (Va.) Battery (2 12-pound Napoleons, 2 10-pound Parrotts), 103, Capt. William P. Carter
- Morris (Va.) Battery (4 12-pound Napoleons), 114, Capt. Richard C. M. Page (w), Lt. Samuel H. Pendleton
- Richmond (Va.) "Orange" Battery (2 3-inch rifles, 2 10-pound Parrotts), 80, Capt. Charles W. Fry

2nd Corps Reserve Artillery, 30 guns, 648 men, Col. J. Thompson Brown

1st Va. Artillery Battalion, 20 guns, 367 men, Capt. Willis J. Dance
- Powhatan (Va.) Battery (4 3-inch rifles), 78, Lt. John M. Cunningham
- 2nd Richmond (Va.) Howitzer Battery (4 3-inch rifles), 64, Capt. David Watson
- 3rd Richmond (Va.) Howitzer Battery (4 3-inch rifles), 62, Capt. Benjamin H. Smith Jr.
- 1st Rockbridge (Va.) Battery (4 20-pound Parrotts), 85, Capt. Archibald Graham
- Salem (Va.) "Flying" Battery (2 12-pound Napoleons, 2 3-inch rifles), 66, Lt. Charles B. Griffin

Nelson's Artillery Battalion, 10 guns, 277 men, Lt. Col. William Nelson
- Ga. Regular Battery (2 3-inch rifles, 1 10-pound Parrott), 73, Capt. John Milledge Jr.
- Amherst (Va.) Battery (3 12-pound Napoleons), 105, Capt. Thomas J. Kirkpatrick
- Fluvanna (Va.) "Consolidated" Battery (3 12-pound Napoleons, 1 3-inch rifle), 90, Capt. John L. Massie

3rd Corps

22,083

Lt. Gen. Ambrose Powell Hill

Heth's Division,[15] 7,461, Maj. Gen. Henry Heth (w), Brig. Gen. James J. Pettigrew (w)

1st (Pettigrew's) Brigade, 2,584, Brig. Gen. James J. Pettigrew (w), Col. James K. Marshall (w, c), Maj. John T. Jones
- 11th N.C., 617, Col. Collett Leventhorpe (w, c)
- 26th N.C., 843, Col. Henry K. Burgwin Jr. (k), Lt. Col. John R. Lane (w), Maj. John T. Jones, Capt. S. W. Brewer (w, c), Capt. H. C. Albright
- 47th N.C., 567, Col. G. H. Faribault (w), Lt. Col. John A. Graves (w, c), Maj. John T. Jones
- 52nd N.C., 553, Col. James K. Marshall (k), Col. Marcus A. Parks (w, c), Maj. John Q. A. Richardson (k), Capt. Nathaniel A. Foster

2nd (Brockenbrough's) Brigade, 971, Col. John M. Brockenbrough, Col. Robert M. Mayo
- 40th Va., 253, Capt. T. Edwin Betts (w, c), Capt. Robert Beale Davis
- 47th Va., Companies A–H, and I, 209, Col. Robert M. Mayo, Lt. Col. John W. Lyell
- 55th Va., Companies A, and C–M, 268, Col. W. S. Christian (c), Capt. Charles N. Lawson
- 22nd Va. Battalion, Companies A, B, D, E, G, and H, 237, Lt. Col. Edwards P. Tayloe, Maj. John S. Bowles

3rd (Archer's) Brigade, 1,197, Brig. Gen. James J. Archer (c), Col. Birkett D. Fry (w, c), Lt. Col. Samuel G. Shepard
- 13th Ala., 308, Col. Birkett D. Fry
- 5th Ala. Battalion, 135, Maj. A. S. Van De Graaff
- 1st Tenn., 281, Lt. Col. Newton L. George (w, c), Maj. Felix G. Buchanan (w)
- 7th Tenn., 249, Col. John A. Fite (c), Lt. Col. Samuel G. Shepard
- 14th Tenn. A–E, G–L, 220, Lt. Col. James Lockert (w, c), Capt. B. L. Phillips

4th (Davis's) Brigade, 2,305, Brig. Gen. Joseph R. Davis
- 2nd Miss., Companies A–L, 492, Col. John M. Stone (w), Maj. John A. Blair (c)
- 11th Miss., 592, Col. Francis M. Green (w), Lt. Stephen Moore
- 42nd Miss., 575, Col. Hugh R. Miller (mw), Capt. Andrew Mc. Nelson
- 55th N.C., 640, Col. John K. Connally (w, c), Lt. Col. Maurice T. Smith (k), Maj. Alfred H. Belo (w), Lt. George A. Gilreath, Lt. M. C. Stevens

Division Artillery, 15 guns, 396 men, Lt. Col. John J. Garnett, Maj. Charles Richardson
- Donaldsville (La.) Battery (2 3-inch rifles, 1 10-pound Parrott), 114, Capt. Victor Maurin
- Norfolk (Va.) "Huger's" Battery (2 12-pound Napoleons, 1 3-inch rifle, 1 10-pound Parrott), 77, Capt. Joseph D. Moore
- Norfolk (Va.) "Light Artillery Blues" Battery (2 3-inch rifles, 2 12-pound howitzers), 106, Capt. Charles R. Grandy
- Pittsylvania (Va.) Battery (2 12-pound Napoleons, 2 3-inch rifles), 90, Capt. John W. Lewis

Pender's Division, 6,735, Maj. Gen. William Dorsey Pender (*mw*), Brig. Gen. James H. Lane, Maj. Gen. Isaac R. Trimble (*w, c*), Brig. Gen. James H. Lane
1st (McGowan's) Brigade, 1,882, Col. Abner M. Perrin
    1st S.C. (Provisional Army), Companies A–C, E–L, 328, Maj. Cornelius W. McCreary
    1st S.C. Rifles, Companies A–H, K, and L, 366, Capt. William M. Hadden
    12th S.C., 366, Col. John L. Miller
    13th S.C., 390, Lt. Col. Benjamin T. Brockman
    14th S.C., 428, Lt. Col. Joseph N. Brown (*w*), Maj. Edward Croft (*w*)
2nd (Lane's) Brigade, 1,734, Brig. Gen. James H. Lane, Col. Clarke M. Avery, Brig. Gen. James H. Lane (*w*), Col. Clarke M. Avery
    7th N.C., 291, Capt. John McLeod Turner (*w, c*), Capt. James G. Harris
    18th N.C., 346, Col. John D. Barry
    28th N.C., 346, Col. Samuel D. Lowe (*w*), Lt. Col. William H. A. Speer (*w*), Maj. Samuel N. Stowe (*w*), Lt. James M. Crowell
    33rd N.C., 368, Col. Clarke M. Avery
    37th N.C., 379, Col. William M. Barbour
3rd (Thomas's) Brigade, 1,326, Brig. Gen. Edward Thomas
    14th Ga., 331, Col. Robert W. Folsom
    35th Ga., 331, Col. Bolling H. Holt, Lt. Col. William H. McCullohs
    45th Ga., 331, Col. Thomas J. Simmons
    49th Ga., 329, Col. S. T. Player, Capt. Charles Mc. Jones (*k*), Capt. Oliver H. Cooke
4th (Scales's) Brigade, 1,405, Brig. Gen. Alfred M. Scales, Col. William J. Hoke, Brig. Gen Alfred M. Scales (*w*), Lt. Col. George T. Gordon, Col. William Lee J. Lowrance (*w*)
    13th N.C., 232, Col. Joseph H. Hyman (*w*), Lt. Col. Henry A. Rogers (*w*), Lt. Robert L. Moir (*w*), Adj. N. S. Smith
    16th N.C., Companies B–K, and M, 321, Capt. Leroy W. Stowe
    22nd N.C., Companies A–M, 321, Col. James Conner
    34th N.C., 311, Col. William Lee J. Lowrance (*w*), Lt. Col. George T. Gordon (*w*)
    38th N.C., 216, Col. William J. Hoke (*w*), Col. John Ashford (*w*), Lt. John M. Robinson, Capt. William L. Thornburg (*w*), Lt. John M. Robinson, Capt. George W. Flowers
Division Artillery, 16 guns, 377 men, Maj. William T. Poague
    1st N.C. Artillery, Battery C (Charlotte Battery) (2 12-pound Napoleons, 2 12-pound howitzers), 125, Capt. Joseph Graham
    Madison (Miss.) Battery (3 12-pound Napoleons, 1 12-pound howitzer), 91, Capt. George Ward
    Albermarle (Va.) "Everett Artillery" (2 3-inch rifles, 1 10-pound Parrott, 1 12-pound howitzer), 94, Capt. James W. Wyatt
    Warrenton (Va.) Battery (2 12-pound Napoleons, 2 12-pound howitzers), 58, Capt. J. V. Brooke, Lt. Addison W. Utterback

Anderson's Division, 7,135, Maj. Gen. Richard H. Anderson
Wilcox's Brigade, 1,726, Brig. Gen. Cadmus M. Wilcox
    8th Ala., 477, Lt. Col. Hilary A. Herbert
    9th Ala., 306, Capt. J. Horace King (*w*)
    10th Ala., 311, Col. William H. Forney (*w, c*), Lt. Col. James E. Shelley
    11th Ala., 311, Lt. Col. John C. C. Sanders (*w*), Lt. Col. George E. Tayloe
    14th Ala., 316, Col. Lucius Pinckard (*w, c*), Lt. Col. James A. Broome

Mahone's Brigade, 1,542, Brig. Gen. William Mahone
    6th Va., 288, Col. George T. Rogers
    12th Va., 348, Col. David A. Weisiger, Lt. Col. Everard M. Feild
    16th Va., Companies A–G, 270, Col. Joseph H. Ham, Lt. Col. Richard O. Whitehead
    41st Va., 276, Col. William A. Parham
    61st Va., 356, Col. Virginius D. Groner
Perry's (Florida) Brigade, 742, Col. David Lang
    2nd Fla., Companies A–M, 242, Col. William D. Ballantine (*w, c*), Maj. Walter R. Moore (*w, c*), Capt. C. Seton Fleming
    5th Fla., 321, Col. Richard N. Gardner (*w*), Capt. Council A. Bryan, Capt. John W. Holleyman
    8th Fla., 176, Lt. Col. William Baya
Wright's Brigade, 1,413, Brig. Gen. Ambrose R. Wright, Col. William Gibson (*w, c*), Brig. Gen. Ambrose R. Wright
    3rd Ga., Companies A–L, 441, Col. Edward J. Walker
    22nd Ga., 400, Col. Joseph Wasden (*k*), Capt. Benjamin C. McMurry
    48th Ga., 395, Col. William Gibson, Capt. Matthew R. Hall, Col. William Gibson (*w, c*)
    2nd Ga. Battalion, 173, Maj. George W. Ross (*mw*), Capt. Charles J. Moffett (*w*)
Posey's Brigade, 1,322, Brig. Gen. Carnot Posey
    12th Miss., 305, Col. William H. Taylor
    16th Miss., 385, Col. Samuel E. Baker
    19th Miss., 372, Col. Nathaniel H. Harris
    48th Miss., 256, Col. Joseph Mc. Jayne (*w*)
Division Artillery (11th Ga. artillery battalion, the Sumpter Artillery), 17 guns, 384 men, Maj. John Lane
    Company A (1 12-pound howitzer, 1 12-pound Napoleon, 1 3-inch rifle, 1 10-pound Parrott), 130, Capt. Hugh M. Ross
    Company B (4 12-pound howitzers, 2 12-pound Napoleons), 124, Capt. George M. Patterson
    Company C (3 3-inch Navy rifles, 2 10-pound Parrotts), 121, Capt. John T. Wingfield (*w*)
3rd Corps Reserve Artillery, 36 guns, 736 men, Col. R. Lindsay Walker, Maj. William T. Poague
McIntosh's artillery battalion, 16 guns, 357, Maj. David G. McIntosh
    Hardaway (Ala.) Battery (2 3-inch rifles, 2 12-pound Whitworths), 71, Capt. William B. Hurt (*w*)
    Danville (Va.) Battery (4 12-pound Napoleons), 114, Capt. R. Stanley Rice
    2nd Rockbridge (Va.) Battery (2 12-pound Napoleons, 2 3-inch rifles), 67, Capt. Samuel Wallace
    Johnson's Richmond (Va.) Battery (4 3-inch rifles), 96, Capt. Marmaduke Johnson
Pegram's artillery battalion, 20 guns, 375 men, Maj. William J. Pegram, Capt. Ervin B. Brunson
    Pee Dee (S.C.) Battery D (1st S.C.) (4 3-inch rifles), 65, Capt. Ervin B. Brunson (*w*), Lt. William E. Zimmerman (*w*)
    Fredericksburg (Va.) Battery (2 12-pound Napoleons, 2 3-inch rifles), 71, Capt. Edward A. Marye
    Richmond (Va.) "Crenshaw" Battery (2 12-pound Napoleons, 2 12-pound howitzers), 76, Capt. J. Hampden Chamberlayne (*c*), Lt. Andrew B. Johnston (*w*)
    Richmond (Va.) "Letcher" Battery (2 12-pound Napoleons, 2 10-pound Parrotts), 76, Capt. Thomas A. Brander
    Richmond (Va.) "Purcell" Battery (4 12-pound Napoleons), 89, Capt. Joseph McGraw

Cavalry Division
8,098
Maj. Gen. James Ewell Brown Stuart

Hampton's Brigade, 1,751, Brig. Gen. Wade Hampton (*w*), Col. Lawrence S. Baker
- Cobb's (Ga.) Cavalry Legion, Companies A–L, 330, Col. Pierce M. B. Young, Lt. Col. William B. Delony (*w*)
- Phillips (Ga.) Cavalry Legion, Companies A–G, 238, Col. William B. Rich
- Jeff Davis's (Miss.) Cavalry Legion, Companies A–F, 246, Lt. Col. J. Frederick Waring, Maj. William G. Conner (*k*)
- 1st N.C. Cavalry, Companies A–K, 407, Col. Laurence S. Baker, Lt. Col. James B. Gordon
- 1st S.C. Cavalry, Companies A–K, 339, Col. John Logan Black (*w*), Lt. Col. John D. Twiggs, Maj. William A. Walker (*w*)
- 2nd S.C. Cavalry, Companies A–K, 186, Col. M. Calbraith Butler, Maj. Thomas J. Lipscomb

Fitzhugh Lee's Brigade, 1,913, Brig. Gen. Fitzhugh Lee, Col. Thomas T. Munford
- 1st Md. Cavalry Battalion, Companies A–E (with 2nd Corps), 310, Maj. Harry W. Gilmour, Maj. Ridgely Brown
- 1st Va. Cavalry, Companies A–K, 310, Col. James H. Drake (*k*)
- 2nd Va. Cavalry, Companies A–K, 385, Col. Thomas T. Munford, Lt. Col. James W. Watts (*w*), Maj. Cary Breckinridge
- 3rd Va. Cavalry, Companies A–K, 210, Col. Thomas H. Owen
- 4th Va. Cavalry, Companies A–H, and K, 544, Col. William C. Wickham
- 5th Va. Cavalry, Companies A–K, 150, Col. Thomas L. Rosser

William H. F. Lee's Brigade, 1,173, Brig. Gen. W. H. F. "Rooney" Lee (*w, c*), Col. John R. Chambliss Jr.
- 2nd N.C. Cavalry, Companies A–K, 145, Col. Solomon Williams (*k*), Lt. Col. William H. F. Payne (*c*), Lt. Col. William G. Robinson, Capt. William A. Graham (*w*), Capt. James W. Strange, Lt. Joseph Baker, Maj. Clinton M. Andrews
- 9th Va. Cavalry, Companies A–K, 490, Col. Richard L. T. Beale (*w*), Lt. Col. Meriwether Lewis (*w*)
- 10th Va., 9 companies, 236, Col. J. Lucius Davis (*w, c*), Maj. Robert A. Caskie
- 13th Va., Companies A–K, 298, Col. John R. Chambliss Jr., Lt. Col. Jefferson C. Phillipps (*w*), Maj. Joseph E. Gillette (*w*), Capt. Benjamin F. Winfield
- 15th Va. (#), Maj. Charles R. Collins

Jenkins's Brigade, 2 guns, 1,126 men, Brig. Gen. Albert G. Jenkins (*w*), Col. James Cochran, Col. Milton J. Ferguson
- 14th Va. Cavalry, Companies A–L, 265, Col. James Cochran, Maj. Benjamin F. Eakle (*w*), Capt. Edwin E. Bouldin
- 16th Va. Cavalry, Companies A–L, 265, Col. Milton J. Ferguson, Maj. James H. Nounnan
- 17th Va. Cavalry, Companies A–K, 241, Col. William H. French
- 34th Va. Cavalry Battalion, Companies A–G, 352, Lt. Col. Vincent A. Witcher
- 36th Va. Cavalry Battalion, Companies A–E, 125, Maj. James W. Sweeney (*w*)

Charlottesville (Va.) Horse Artillery Battalion (2 12-pound howitzers), Capt. Thomas E. Jackson

Robertson's Brigade (#),[16] Brig. Gen. Beverly H. Robertson
- 4th N.C. Cavalry, Companies A–H, Col. Dennis D. Ferebee
- 5th N.C. Cavalry, Companies A–K, Col. Peter G. Evans (*mw*), Lt. Col. Stephen B. Evans, Lt. Col. James B. Gordon

Jones's Brigade,[17] 1,743 men, Brig. Gen. William E. "Grumble" Jones
- 6th Va. Cavalry, Companies A–K, 625, Maj. Cabell E. Flournoy, Lt. Nicholas Nolan
- 7th Va. Cavalry, Companies A–K, 428, Lt. Col. Thomas Marshall
- 11th Va. Cavalry, Companies A–K, 424, Col. Lunsford L. Lomax, Lt. Col. Oliver R. Funston Sr.
- 12th Va. Cavalry (#), Col. Asher W. Harman (*w*), Lt. Col. Thomas B. Massie, Col. Asher W. Harman (*c*)
- 35th Va. Cavalry Battalion, 232, Lt. Col. Elijah V. White

Division Horse Artillery, 15 guns, 406 men, Maj. Robert F. Beckham
- 2nd Baltimore (Md.) Light Artillery Battery (4 10-pound Parrotts), 106, Capt. William H. Griffin
- Ashby's (Va.) Battery (4 guns—type unknown) (#),[18] Capt. Robert Preston Chew
- 1st Stuart (Va.) Horse Artillery Battery (4 3-inch rifles), 106, Capt. James Breathed
- Lynchburg (Va.) Horse Artillery Battery (4 guns—type unknown) (#), Capt. Marcellus N. Moorman
- 2nd Stuart (Va.) Horse Artillery Battery (2 3-inch rifles, 2 12-pound Napoleons), 106, Capt. William M. McGregor
- Washington (S.C.) Battery (2 3-inch rifles, 2 12-pound Napoleons), 79, Capt. James F. Hart

Imboden's command (#),[19] Brig. Gen. John D. Imboden
- 18th Va. Cavalry, Companies A–K, Col. George W. Imboden
- 62nd Va. Mounted Infantry, Companies A–M, Col. George H. Smith
- Va. Partisan Rangers, MacNeil's Company, Capt. John Hance McNeill
- Staunton (Va.) Horse Artillery Battery (6 12-pound Napoleons), Capt. John H. McClanahan

Appendix G

The Potential and Problems of Small-Arms Fire at Gettysburg

A subtext of this work involves my frequent wondering aloud about the difficulties associated with weaponry in the mid-nineteenth century. If the arms carried and operated by Civil War soldiers in general and those who fought at Gettysburg in particular were not all that advanced, then perhaps the men who fought on the defensive did not have all *that* much of a built-in advantage. It would follow that if the defenders succeeded, it was more a matter of their actions and accomplishments than the a priori decisiveness of the arms they carried. At Gettysburg, then, the attacking Confederates could have succeeded. That they in the main did not was the result of a series of Federal successes achieved by the officers and men themselves and not by the mere operation of their advanced weapons.

Irrespective of the quality of those arms in 1863, a defending unit has a certain advantage. Such men are relatively stationary and can operate their weapons at a given moment more readily than can a group of attackers. When you are on the move, firing a shoulder arm accurately is no easy task. Reloading a muzzle-loading long arm in such circumstances (or in other combat situations, as discussed below) is even tougher. A musket, rifle, or carbine in the Civil War was a far cry from the currently reviled "assault rifle" with which a modern-day soldier on the attack can lay down heavy fire by spraying it at the defenders. Moreover, reloading a multi-round magazine on the move causes only a slight hesitation. Firing and reloading a Civil War artillery piece while attempting to advance it in support of attacking infantry is even more problematical, and the addition of such heavy weight to the Confederate assaults at Gettysburg was rare. So, if the Union units being attacked could not only fire their weapons with relative impunity, but also were using vastly improved implements of war, how could a tactical offensive prevail?

Attempts to answer such questions lead us into controversy. The disagreements have been expressed in Civil War literature and by historians who argue these points more informally. It may be useful to discuss the general features of the arguments and then consider how certain events of the Gettysburg battle speak further to these issues.

Was there a "rifle revolution" that had come to the fore by the time of Gettysburg? An affirmative answer is based partly on the fact that rifling the bore of a long arm makes a bullet fired from it more accurate over a longer range, compared with fire from a smoothbore musket. Rifling per se was an invention that predated the Civil War by many decades. However, it was very difficult to load a bullet into a rifled musket because the round was designed to fit snugly in the bore breech so that it would "take" the rifling. This meant that the firer expended a fair amount of time and energy ramming that tightly fitting ball down the barrel until it was firmly settled in the breech. When fired, the bullet would exit the muzzle spinning and be driven through the air, holding its line over a relatively long distance—perhaps several hundred yards. In contrast, a smoothbore bullet is made smaller than the diameter of the muzzle bore so that it is easily seated in the breech. This allows for relatively rapid loading, but the bullet has no particular spin imparted to it when fired, so it behaves somewhat like a knuckleball, resulting in mediocre accuracy and range.[1]

Now comes the revolution. Conical bullets developed in the mid-nineteenth century were smaller than the bore, but their base would expand the instant the powder in the breech was ignited.[2] Thus, the bullet would catch the rifling, exit the weapon spinning, and become an accurate shot that could be effective at distances of well over a hundred yards. A smoothbore shooter, on the other hand, was fortunate to hit a target at that distance or even less.

Specifically, rifled muskets that were mass-produced as the middle of the century approached had grooves cut into the bore of the barrel—one turn per seventy-two inches. That is not very tight rifling, but it was enough to permit a talented, practiced shooter routinely to hit a small target at impressive distances. A modern-day marksman firing a replica of a Civil War rifle, or even an original, can hit a paint can more often than not at 250 yards.[3]

It was not so much the rifling down the bore of these weapons that propelled the revolutionary features of fighting 135 years ago. Instead it was the minié ball—which was neither, actually (see note 2). Thus, as of the mid-nineteenth century, all foot soldiers could in principle be armed with rifled muskets firing easy-loading "minnie balls" (the anglicized form of the term). There was no reason to limit the supply of such shoulder arms to a relative handful of marksmen, whose slowness of loading might be offset by their accurate shooting. Every Civil War infantryman could be equipped with a rifle that had achieved the perfect compromise in terms of reloading rapidity and theoretical shooting effectiveness.

The consequences of these advances in weaponry were that they had the potential to change the nature of warfare in the 1850s and 1860s. Thus, Grady McWhiney and Perry D. Jamieson argue that the long-range accuracy provided by rifling made the tactical offensive dubious.[4] Yet Civil War officers generally failed to appreciate this and kept making attacks—"impossible" ones—because so many defenders were firing rifles.

There are some problems with this thesis, however. In the first place, manufacturing of rifled muskets had not been able to keep pace with the demand, so not all soldiers were equipped with them by the time of Gettysburg. In the Army of the Potomac, for example, approximately 4 percent of the infantry units were armed with smoothbores, and another 7 percent carried a mixture of such weapons along with rifles.[5] Neverthelesss, it is clear from these numbers that the great majority of Union soldiers at Gettysburg carried rifled muskets. But perhaps this did not add massive martial weight to their fighting potential, *if* the effectiveness of all those rifles has been overstated. This and other counterarguments form the thesis of Paddy Griffith, who wonders about the quality of the advanced weapons and how effective the armies were in taking advantage of their long-range capabilities.[6] Summaries of Griffith's position and those of his critics appeared a few years ago in *North & South* magazine.[7] However, these authors mostly recycled their old arguments. I suspect, in any case, that Jamieson and McWhiney have won the debate in the minds of other Civil War historians. Many of them adhere to the perceived wisdom about small-arms improvements impacting on the battles of that war—in which defensive fighting had become dominant in principle, but the generals did not realize this, and so forth. With regard to specific features of the controversy over battle tactics and the rifle revolution, one expert wrote that he does not think Griffith "has made his case that the advent of the rifle had a negligible impact—or *should have had* a negligible impact on tactics. He argues that most infantry firefights in the Civil War, because of the wooded terrain in which most battles occurred, took place at a hundred yards or less—smoothbore musket range—and therefore the greater range of the rifle was unimportant. His evidence for this assertion is extremely thin."[8]

Leaving aside the issue of whether the burden of proof is on those who assert there was a "rifle revolution" or on their embattled critic Griffith, the implications of these components of the dispute are mostly concerned with the manner by which rifled muskets were brought to bear on the tactical situation at hand. This perspective views the events and outcome from somewhat above the battlefield. Just as important in the opinion of other investigators is a consideration of real-world usage of a rifle in the hands of a given Civil War soldier. For this, Joseph G. Bilby provides some valuable information.[9] He is not so much concerned with the effectiveness of a unit of firing men in one tactical circumstance or the other. Instead, he discusses cogently the problems associated with a Civil War shoulder arm as operated by an individual infantryman. Bear in mind that such a man was a "citizen soldier" who, especially in the case of Northerners, had little or no experience with firearms before the war. Bilby describes in rich detail what this inexperience meant: The man who fired was often floundering. The problem was exacerbated by the extent to which Civil War soldiers were trained in the use of small arms and permitted to practice shooting—inadequately and rarely. One problem was that there was not enough small-arms ammunition available to allow an appreciable fraction of it to be spent on target practice.[10] Therefore, if a soldier and his unit stood on the defense, this may have been more a matter of his determination, as opposed to a capacity for mowing down the attackers by skilled usage of modern nineteenth-century weaponry. And such determination was not exhibited by all Civil War soldiers engaged in a given action, an argument that can be made with reference to a twentieth-century conflict: "in the Second World War, as many as 25 percent of American infantry engaged in firefights *did not fire at the enemy!* There is evidence that this was the case in earlier wars, too, including the Civil War; many combatants found ways to avoid firing at the enemy—tending to the wounded, spotting for comrades, running messages, fetching ammunition, or simply firing to miss."[11] Echoing Poulter's remarks, James M. McPherson describes a "consensus [that] existed in many [Civil War] regiments," for which "only half the men did the real fighting.... The rest were known ... as skulkers, sneaks, beats, stragglers, or coffee-coolers.... They seemed to melt away when the lead started flying."[12] It is arguably easier for defenders to shirk their duty rather than stand their ground on the firing line. Men marching forward during an attack, especially over relatively open ground, would be more conspicuous if they gave up. This happens, of course, and may have occurred during Pickett's Charge (recall the Priest versus Motts argument in Chapter 4, referred to in notes 102 and 103 thereof). But what if only half to three-quarters of the outnumbered Union defenders brought their rifles and muskets to bear on that supposedly suicidal assault?

This question brings us to a consideration of additional problems associated with the use of individual shoulder arms in the Civil War. These uncertainties are indeed signified by pulling together some threads from various occurrences during the Battle of Gettysburg. I remind the reader of these events and vignettes, and expand upon their possible significance, in chronological order.

Recall from the account of the fighting on the first day the "lull" that settled over the battlefield after the initial infantry clash in the morning. Not long afterward, the battle resumed in the center of the field, arrayed west and north of the town. However, the rebels' right wing remained quiescent until later in the afternoon. Before these men of the Confederate 3rd Corps were ordered back into action, General Lee arrived on the field, riding down the Cashtown Road. Several colleagues have mentioned their memory of accounts about what Lee saw during his arrival: his 3rd Corps soldiers distributed to either side of the road (maps 2-13, 2-21), many of them tending campfires. None of us can confirm this anecdote. It may not have happened but is worth considering from both sides of a mini-dispute. One such view is that—if the account is true—"the campfires were soldiers boiling water for coffee, which the Confederates were able to obtain in Penna. and greatly relished."[13] Yet I suspect that the water was heated so the soldiers could *clean their weapons.* Why? Even a relatively brief fight—and there had only been one or two morning hours' worth of that in this sector of the battlefield on July 1—leads to enough rounds expended so that the muskets in the hands of a significant fraction of the infantrymen engaged might have *fouled.* Whatever advances had occurred in the design of shoulder arms, those of the mid-nineteenth century still had to be loaded as follows: rip open a paper-covered round that contains black powder and the bullet; dump the powder down the muzzle; drop the bullet in and operate a 3.3-foot-long ramrod to seat the bullet in the breech of the barrel; cock the hammer and place a percussion cap on a nipple, atop the outer end of a short tube that guides the cap's small explosion down into the breech.[14] One implication of these materials and methods is that a filthy mess built up inside the barrel. The unburned carbon *eventually* made it impossible even to ram home a subsequent round. Therefore, Civil War soldiers would take advantage of a lull in the fighting to restore their weapons to optimally serviceable condition.

The extent to which this was a relentless and severe problem in the combat of the time is much disputed. Andrew H. Addoms III, a modern-day Civil War small-arms expert, believes that a rifle or any kind of muzzleloader would become fouled after a dozen or perhaps fifteen shots.[15] He says that restoring the weapon to its pre-battle state of usefulness would have required cleaning it with hot water and not merely dumping the contents of a canteen down the barrel. Countering this view is that of historian D. Scott Hartwig. He believes that "the powder used during the war was generally pretty good and burned well," and even though "after 20–25 rounds a Civil War infantryman was probably not ramming a bullet all the way home with ease . . . a soldier could fire a full ammo load, 40 rounds, without much difficulty." Hartwig went on to say: "if a soldier under normal circumstances could not fire 40 rounds without cleaning his rifle there would be evidence about it in primary documents. I haven't found it. Perhaps it was such a commonplace problem that soldiers didn't bother to even mention it."[16] Occasionally they did, however. Thus, a Massachusetts soldier at Antietam (September 1862) "managed to shoot five Rebels before his rifle fouled . . . [and] he was severely wounded while trying to hammer a ball down the muzzle." In the Battle of Chancellorsville (May 1863), men in a New Jersey regiment "after a few rounds . . . found it difficult to ram minnie balls down the barrels of their weapons." At Chickamauga (September 1863), men in a Confederate brigade trying to load .58-caliber bullets in their Enfield rifles found that, "after the first few rounds," this action was "frequently choking the guns to the extent that they could not be forced down."[17]

Part of the Little Round Top story—involving the 20th Maine regiment and its

Enfields—provides another case in point, as will be discussed shortly. To lead up to it, consider the putative fouling issue that is raised by an event from the afternoon of July 1. Not long after the resumption of hostilities in the center of that day's theater of battle, Brig. Gen. Henry Baxter's Union brigade ambushed the first waves of attackers in Maj. Gen. Robert Rodes's division (maps 2-17, 2-18). Yet the Federal defenders eventually withdrew, and this helped the further waves of Rodes's attacks push back the Union defense in this sector. Why were Baxter's men ordered to pull out? As their commander put it, "we had suffered severely and expended our ammunition."[18] It is possible, however, to take a jaundiced view of such an account. It was *arguably* difficult for a soldier to fire all of his rounds in one action, unless he and his mates were rotated to the rear and allowed to clean their weapons (discussed later in conjunction with the fighting on the morning of July 3). When a commander claims his men were out of ammunition as he describes the withdrawal of his unit, he might instead have meant that his soldiers' weapons were fouled. It also is possible that General Baxter heard *some* of his troops cry out that they had no more bullets, perhaps because they went into action with only a few of them. Other men may have dumped several rounds on the ground, more easily to grab the next one for reloading, and then moved to another spot and lost those rounds. This Federal unit did shift positions in the midst of its aggressive defensive fight on July 1.[19]

It is equally plausible that most of Baxter's men had not fired off all their rounds but felt required to withdraw because of *unusable* shoulder arms.[20] Yet it sounds better for the commander of a Civil War unit to say his soldiers fought so furiously that they discharged all their ammunition. Now, such defenders would have to withdraw for either of the reasons being considered: no more ammunition, or no way to fire their remaining supply. But if the latter occurred frequently, as Addoms would have it, then the defensive capabilities of a Civil War infantry unit such as Baxter's brigade at Gettysburg were less than awesome.

Another group of Northern soldiers more famously ran out of ammunition during the afternoon of the second day at Gettysburg. This was Col. Joshua Chamberlain's 20th Maine Regiment on Little Round Top, which felt compelled to charge the Alabamians attacking it because they could not continue to defend and could not withdraw. The nineteenth-century controversy over this matter was discussed in Chapter 3 (the man in charge of the 20th Maine's left wing said that his soldiers did not expend all their rounds, as cited in note 69 of that chapter). Colonel Chamberlain himself alluded to a rifle-fouling problem that some of his men might have encountered during their July 2 fight: "many of our arms [were] unserviceable" (again, see note 69 in Chapter 3). Had a substantial proportion of the Maine men used up all their ammunition, or did many of them have unserviceable long arms after firing only one or two dozen shots? In either case, they believed themselves unable to continue their purely defensive stand.

Recall that when the 20th Maine charged down the southern slope of Little Round Top (but also eastward of the regiment's position [map 3-21]) at the 15th Alabama, an isolated company of Mainers on the Alabamians' right flank supported the counterattack with a volley of rifle fire (maps 3-20 and 3-21). Extra weight to this flank fire was provided by a group of sharpshooters who had joined Capt. Walter Morrill's Company B. Perhaps their fire into the Alabama men was especially deadly. Other Confederates at Gettysburg may have been subjected to the same kind of accurate rifle fire when a separate subunit of Berdan's Sharpshooters encountered the left wing of the rebel 3rd Corps deployed below the Fairfield Road earlier in the afternoon of July 2 (map 3-3). These men of General

Sickles's Union 3rd Corps had been sent out to learn whether Confederates were deployed in the woods west of the main Union line, waiting to attack it. The sharpshooters did find elements of Brig. Gen. Cadmus Wilcox's brigade (map 3-3) and fired on those Alabamians, possibly with murderous effect.

But how supremely skilled were Colonel Berdan's men, who were formally designated as marksmen? They had been recruited into these elite units of the Union army based on their experience and skill with firearms: "no recruit was to be accepted who at 200 yards was unable to place 10 consecutive shots in a target, the average distance of which was not to exceed 5 inches from the center of the bullseye."[21] This phrase has been repeated many times to describe the sharpshooters' prowess. Here is a reality check, however: Eight of Berdan's companies were practicing on January 13–14, 1863 (an opportunity given to few units of ordinary infantrymen). They fired a total of 531 shots over distances ranging from 180–250 yards, at targets that varied between 2 feet × 2 feet and 5 feet × 5 feet, and *only 57 percent of their shots* hit the targets.[22]

If men like this—who entered the army with a relatively high level of shooting skill and were permitted to practice further—were not devastatingly accurate with their rifles, how about the ordinary infantryman? "Most recruits, especially in Federal ranks, were totally unfamiliar with firearms. . . . Soldiers in action, especially untrained ones, tend to fire high and often wildly."[23] Once a citizen became a soldier, "target practice throughout the Union army was haphazard and lacked preliminary basic marksmanship instruction." Thus, "the inherent accuracy a gun displays under controlled conditions does not predict combat accuracy." Even conditions of the kind enjoyed by Berdan's men when they were practicing early in 1863 did not lead to shooting that was all that "sharp." This was in spite of another factor from which they benefited: the ammunition for the breech-loading Sharps rifles, which were manufactured specially for these sharpshooters,[24] was almost certainly optimal. In contrast, the rounds supplied for a .58-caliber muzzleloader varied in size, just as did the bore size of such a weapon (see note 15). If the minnie ball was slightly too small, the rifle's accuracy and effectiveness at longer ranges was significantly diminished and fouling of the weapon was exacerbated.[25]

The ordinary infantryman's lack of shooting skill and effectiveness in combat showed at other stages of the Gettysburg battle. Remember the aftermath of the fighting at Culp's Hill on July 3. The commander of a principal Union unit there, Brig. Gen. John Geary, claimed that his men expended "277,000" rounds. This implies some seventy shots per defender. That is believable, for the fight at the north end of the field throughout that Friday morning was the most sustained action of the battle. If these 12th Corps men (and the other Union defenders on Culp's Hill indicated in chart 4-2 of Chapter 4) really got off that many shots per man, then they must have replenished their ammunition supply *and* taken time out to clean their rifles.[26] At any rate, the apparent intensity of this sustained Federal fire was wildly out of proportion to Confederate combat casualties near Culp's Hill on July 3 (which Geary overestimated as twelve hundred killed and forty-eight hundred wounded).

The same phenomenon is exemplified by a vignette from Pickett's Charge on the afternoon of the same day: That stretch of fence line at the Emmitsburg Road, some 250 yards west of the Union line's right center, with the "836" bullets embedded in nineteen square feet of wooden fence railing. Once again, this reveals how many times the Union men *missed*. In the hands of Civil War soldiers, the shoulder arms of the time were not weapons of mass destruction.

Yet I claimed in Chapter 4 that Pickett's Charge was "destroyed." For example, the Confederates attacking the Union center and right on Cemetery Ridge absorbed about 23 percent combat casualties. This may not seem a horrendous number, but it is a rather high proportion for an attack in a Civil War battle. Specifically, approximately thirteen hundred men were killed and wounded in Pettigrew's and Trimble's divisions during the charge.[27] However, this is fewer than twice as many as the number of failed rifle shots that crashed into that short stretch of fence line—leaving aside the question of how many men in Pettigrew's and Trimble's commands were hit by artillery fire, which remains unknown. That the percentage of Confederate soldiers in this sector of the charge who were hit can be regarded a *relatively* high one for the times is suggested by one further consideration of the rifle issue in the mid-nineteenth century.

For this, we turn to "another source that supports the position of the limited effect the rifle had in Civil War battles."[28] A component of this analysis contemplates the rifle's effectiveness in other nineteenth-century battles. The source was an officer in the Army of the Potomac, Col. George L. Willard. He commanded a 2nd Corps brigade at Gettysburg, which was deployed from a northern sector of Cemetery Ridge on July 2 to reinforce the army's left wing (map 3-37 in Chapter 3). In February of that same year, Colonel Willard published a document called *Comparative Value of Rifled and Smooth-Bored Arms.* He was a longtime soldier who had served in the Mexican War in the 1840s. That war was fought with smoothbore muskets. Willard's worries about the rise of the rifle may have been motivated by the old maxim "if it ain't broke, don't fix it."[29] Nevertheless, by way of technically insightful detail, he presented arguments that support Joseph Bilby's late-twentieth-century thesis about the real-world problems encountered by rifle-bearing soldiers in the mid-nineteenth century—particularly men who had barely been trained in the use of such weapons. According to Willard, "much has been said during the past few years about the rifled musket and rifled cannon, and the great changes they would effect in the art of war. . . . [But] it is a grave error, to adopt rifled arms, with the elevating sight, to the exclusion of smooth bore." He pointed out that "the particular merits of the new arms lie in their accuracy and in their long range, but these have been purchased at the sacrifice of some important qualities." The student of the Civil War who brought Willard's analysis to light (see note 28) paraphrased that officer by noting that the rifle "comes with an elevating sight that is difficult to manage and easily damaged. Nineteen twentieths of the men who carry the rifle don't know how to use it." The former colonel was then quoted about what can be inferred as the *disadvantage* under which an untrained soldier labored in the mid-nineteenth century:

> In the new arm, the trajectory is very high; at long distances the projectile plunges and the dangerous space (for the enemy) is reduced to a few yards. . . . Thus at 900 yards, an error of 5 yards in the appreciation of the distance, and at 500 yards, an error of 30 yards, would cause to be missed a target 15 feet high, sufficient to entirely over shoot a line of Cavalry. . . . With the rifled musket, the trajectory of the piece sighted for 500 yards gives the following results: at 100 yards the ball passes 7 feet above the line of sight. At 200 and 250 yards, it passes 12 feet above; at 300 yards 12½ feet, to fall suddenly to 0 in the next 200 yards. . . . The sight must be regulated (changed) for every change of 100 paces in the distance. For example, at 400 to 450 paces the aim must be at the waist belt, and from 450 to 500, the aim must be directed to the top of the cap, otherwise the ball will bury itself in the ground at your enemy's feet. The soldier's mind is perpetually occupied in guessing at distances and

in combining them with elevations of the sight, and of the point to be aimed at for each distance.

Colonel Willard may have been cutting things too fine here (and he does not even mention the effect of windage).[30] At least he is losing a modern reader unfamiliar with handling a shoulder arm. But one implication of Willard's points leads to the following question about long-range fire, which suggests itself out of common sense: What if a group of defending Civil War infantry was sending *volley fire* toward an assemblage of *massed attackers,* located two hundred yards or more from them? Even if the defenders could not shoot very accurately in terms of picking out individual enemy soldiers—forming up to assault or already moving toward them from such long distances—the massed fire might still do great damage to the bunched offensive formation. This is because "lateral dispersion" of the defensive fire might not be a serious problem: A two-hundred-yard shot, putatively aimed at one segment of the cohesive attack group, might not hit that particular section but could kill or wound a soldier to the left or right. However, as Willard argues by way of technical language, the ordinary Civil War soldier would often misjudge the *distance* between him and the target—be it an individual infantryman, a packed line of impending attackers, or an artillery battery. Even if lateral dispersion did not create an inaccuracy problem in the case of a large unified target, the defenders' shots would be prone to fall short or fly high. Given the long-distance "effective range" of rifled gunfire, defensive shots falling short may not have been as problematical as those that would zip over the heads of the attackers. This problem was exacerbated by the relatively high degree of finger pressure that was required to discharge a Civil War rifled musket, which was not equipped with a "hair trigger." The effort needed to pull it tended to cause the barrel to be elevated inappropriately, contributing to the likelihood of a misdirected shot that would be fired "wild high."[31] These considerations add further weight to an argument that the principal long arm used in the Civil War did not allow a soldier to be a particularly deadly defensive fighter. In fact, Colonel Willard went on to suggest that an infantryman in that war might have been less effective than if he had been equipped with a more primitive shoulder arm. He "pointed out that in the recent European battles of Magenta and Solferino (1859) the losses were less than during the battles of the Napoleonic era that were fought with smooth bore muskets."[32] This point was echoed many years later by Paddy Griffith: "Was it actually true that casualties were heavier in Civil War battles than they had been in Napoleonic ones? Not really."[33]

You may remember that Col. George Willard was killed at Gettysburg on July 2. This occurred as elements of his brigade withdrew toward Cemetery Ridge, after their reinforcing move had succeeded in repelling the advance of Brig. Gen. William Barksdale's Mississippians in the southern sector of the battlefield (map 3-37). There might have been a deadly irony to Willard's death, had it been a shot from a rifled musket that took him down. That, however, was not the case. He was killed by artillery fire: "just after Willard crossed Plum Run [moving eastward toward the ridge], a shell fragment tore away his face and a portion of his head."[34] Perhaps it was this aspect of a defending army's power that made attacks in the Civil War so problematical. That, at least, is the thesis of those modern historians cited in Chapter 4 who believe that Pickett's Charge was largely destroyed by the Union army's cannons at Gettysburg.[35] Addressing that subject, however, would require another contentious essay.[36]

Notes

Preface

1. Catton was so quoted during an interview he gave about Gettysburg, which appeared in a film written and directed by Kerwin Silfies: *The Last Full Measure* (Santa Monica, Calif.: Ferde Groat Films, 1983). The interview was filmed shortly before Catton died in 1978. Catton's works on the Northern Civil War army in the East are entitled *The Army of the Potomac* and respectively subtitled *Mr. Lincoln's Army* (1951), *Glory Road* (1952), and *A Stillness at Appomattox* (1953), all published by Doubleday of Garden City, N.Y. The title of the last of these books paraphrases words written long after the war by Joshua L. Chamberlain, commander of the 20th Maine at Gettysburg.

2. Prof. James M. McPherson, Princeton University, to author, May 19, 1995. The letter was written in conjunction with the origin of the college course at Brandeis University that gave rise to this book.

3. However, a contemporary historian states that Catton was the writer who "launched the Civil War publishing boom" (Stephen W. Sears, "All the trumpets sounded: Bruce Catton, An appreciation," *North & South* 3, no. 1 [Nov. 1999]: pp. 3, 24–32). One of Catton's works achieved special prominence when *A Stillness at Appomattox* was awarded a Pulitzer Prize. The same honor was later bestowed on McPherson's *Battle Cry of Freedom: The Civil War Era* (New York: Oxford University Press, 1988).

4. Author to McPherson, Dec. 3, 1988.

5. McPherson to author, Dec. 7, 1988.

6. Another recent author avows a somewhat similar purpose, at least in terms of his incorporating many contemporary pieces of scholarship about Gettysburg. That work, Noah A. Trudeau's *Gettysburg: A Testing of Courage* (New York: Harper Collins, 2002), appeared after this one was completed and copyedited—too late to make point-by-point comparisons between the two regarding "what really happened" during the campaign.

7. This dynamic display of what happened on July 1–3, 1863, has been attacked as a sleazy, commercially driven pseudo-summary of the battle. Even though the Electric Map is getting long in the tooth, it still gives visitors a good preliminary feel for the battle. The program consists of a taped narrative describing the movements of the Army of the Potomac and the Army of Northern Virginia, depicted by electric lights on a relief map, as they converged on Gettysburg, and what happened as a result of that "meeting engagement," as it is termed in military jargon.

Acknowledgments

1. This story is recounted in Jonathan Weiner, *Time, Love, Memory* (New York: Alfred A. Knopf, 1999), pp. 240–57.

2. Because of the large numbers of Americans who flock to Gettysburg each year (estimated by the Gettysburg National Military Park as between 1.5 and 2 million per year). Historian Carol Reardon recently pointed out that this designation surfaced long ago, quoting a man who worried about calling "Gettysburg merely a 'Mecca,' a phrase the guide-books and more talkative veterans have got hold of" (*Pickett's Charge in History and Memory* [Chapel Hill: University of North Carolina Press, 1997], p. 129).

3. Adams and Richardson are mentioned in E. J. Coates and D. S. Thomas, *An Introduction to Civil War Small Arms* (Gettysburg: Thomas Publications, 1990), pp. 75–77, 78–81; and in Joseph G. Bilby, *Civil War Firearms: Their Historical Background, Tactical Use and Modern Collecting and Shooting* (Conshohocken, Pa.: Combined Books, 1996), pp. 93–94.

Introduction

1. The first began in early September 1862 and culminated with the Battle of Antietam in western Maryland on September 17. By the time the second ended, the region into which Lee's army withdrew had become West Virginia, President Lincoln having issued a proclamation on June 20, 1863, declaring it the thirty-fifth state.

2. See James M. McPherson, "What's the Matter with History?" in *Drawn with the Sword* (New York: Oxford University Press, 1996), pp. 231–53. McPherson exemplified the problem—as he sees it, that "only the most dedicated buff can wade through all of this prose" about individual battles—by mentioning works devoted to Gettysburg: "We have an 800-page tome on the first day alone plus two volumes by a single author on the second day totaling 725 pages" (p. 244). One feature of that observation is a little off the mark: the second of these works covers elements of the fighting that occurred on all three days of the Gettysburg battle. In any case, one can indeed get into any and all details of the Gettysburg campaign by going to these and a host of other books and to a vast number of shorter articles. Many of these works, with an emphasis on recent ones, are discussed in the Bibliographic Essay.

3. "[U]ntil only about twenty-five years ago the history of slavery, secession, and the Civil War was largely shaped by the losers. Even a cursory perusal of the literature demonstrates that . . . [t]he notion that the winners write the history is largely fabricated by the losers. After all, they have much more interest in explaining why the war turned out as it did than do the victors" (Alfred A. Nofi, "Rewriting History [letter]," *North & South* 2, no. 7 [Sept. 1999]: p. 5).

4. Wilson is quoted on his feelings about the Civil War's outcome in McPherson, *Battle Cry of Freedom*, p. 854.

5. Three of these books (edited by Gary W. Gallagher and published in 1992–1994) cover each day of the battle in turn. The fourth (Gabor S. Borritt, ed., *The Gettysburg Nobody Knows* [New York: Oxford University Press, 1997]) presents essays about several aspects of the Gettysburg campaign. *Gettysburg Magazine*, appearing twice yearly since 1989, is edited by Bob Younger and Dr. Edwin C. Bearss (among others).

6. Champ Clark, *Gettysburg: The Confederate High Tide* (Alexandria, Va.: Time-Life Books, 1985), p. 59.

7. These charts are small subsets of the vast "Order of Battle," military jargon for an organizational listing of all military units that participated in a given battle or campaign. The complete Gettysburg Order of Battle is in Appendix F.

8. California, Kansas, Kentucky, Iowa, Missouri, and Oregon were not formally represented in the Union forces fighting at Gettysburg. Nebraska, which did not become a state until 1867, contributed regiments to the Union armies in the western theater (as did the other states listed above, except Oregon).

9. This unit was also known as the California Brigade. By the time of Gettysburg, its regiments all had Pennsylvania designations, which they assumed after a brief period of sponsorship by the young West Coast state. About five hundred Californians served in the 2nd Massachusetts Cavalry in the Army of the Potomac but did not participate in the Gettysburg campaign.

10. Many of the artillerymen had to be foot soldiers, too. However, some of them got to ride on the ammunition chests. Troopers in the cavalry's "horse artillery" were provided their own mounts.

11. Civil War cavalry regiments were divided into six squadrons, each composed of a pair of hundred-man companies. However, just as with their infantry cousins, the real number was far less than that by the time a given regiment of horsemen went into action in the Gettysburg campaign.

Chapter 1
The Roads to Gettysburg

1. This true story was pieced together from Harry W. Pfanz, *Gettysburg: The Second Day* (Chapel Hill: University of North Carolina Press, 1987), p. 424; Milo M. Quaife, *From the Cannon's Mouth: The Civil War Letters of General Alpheus S. Williams* (Detroit: Wayne State University Press, 1959), pp. 228–29; and "Letter of Brig. Gen. Alpheus Williams . . . Nov. 10th 1865," in David L. Ladd and Audrey J. Ladd, eds., *The Bachelder Papers*, 3 vols. (Dayton, Ohio: Morningside House, 1994), vol. 1, pp. 212–23.

2. Between July 1861 and May 1863 (before Gettysburg), the eastern armies had fought at First Manassas, on the peninsula between the York and James Rivers in the Battles of the Seven Days, then at Second Manassas, Antietam, Fredericksburg, and Chancellorsville. All of these battles except Antietam occurred in northern Virginia. After the Battle of Gettysburg in southern Pennsylvania, the war continued until the spring of 1865. The fighting in the east recommenced in earnest in May 1864.

3. This paraphrases part of a speech delivered by Winston Churchill in 1942. He was in turn paraphrasing an earlier remark by a Greek statesman (J. Bartlett and J. Kaplan, eds., *Bartlett's Familiar Quotations*, 16th ed. [Boston: Little, Brown, 1992], p. 621).

4. Discussed with citations by McPherson in *Battle Cry of Freedom*, pp. 606–607. The Northern armies thus were not quite as much of a "polyglot" as Michael Shaara (see *The Killer Angels* [New York: David McKay, 1974]) and others suggest: 25 percent were immigrants, almost 10 percent less than the foreign-born part of the male populace of military age. Moreover, many of the Northern soldiers who came from abroad spoke English (these men were from Ireland, England, even Canada). Eighty percent of the Army of the Potomac was native born, an appreciably higher percentage than for the Union forces fighting in the West.

5. The York and the James framed the 1862 Peninsula campaign. The Army of the Potomac came to strategic grief there as a result of the Battles of the Seven Days, which led to the emergence of Robert E. Lee, who succeeded Gen. Joseph E. Johnston as commander of the Army of Northern Virginia. On December 13, one of the seven major battles in the East during the first half of the war took place at Fredericksburg, Virginia.

6. Part of it shows that an element of one Federal corps had crossed to the south bank of the Rappahannock. General Hooker's chief of staff, Maj. Gen. Daniel Butterfield, sent an order to the Maj. Gen. John Sedgwick, to "throw your Corps [the 6th] over the river . . . make a reconnaissance . . . and ascertain the position and strength of the enemy. . . . Seize any citizens as prisoners who could give any information." The Union high command had received reports that the Confederates were withdrawing some of their forces from Fredericksburg. In an attempt to keep tabs on these movements, Sedgwick's men manned rifle pits located between the town and the river. These 6th Corps infantrymen exchanged small-arms fire with Confederate pickets and were fired upon by rebel artillery. The order quoted above, written by Butterfield at Hooker's direction, is reprinted in Lt. Col. Robert N. Scott, ed., *The War of the Rebellion: The Official Records of the Union and Confederate Armies*, ser. 1, vol. 27, pt. 3 (Washington, D.C.: Government Printing Office, 1880–1901), p. 12. (Hereafter cited as *OR* followed by the part and page numbers—unless from a source other than ser. 1, vol. 27). The *Official Records* are a treasure trove of primary material about essentially all military activities that occurred during the Civil War: reports by officers, reprints of orders that passed between them, list after list of verbal and numerical data. Records of the Gettysburg campaign are contained in series 1, volume 27, parts 1–3. The majority of parts 1 and 2 consists of reports of Union and Confederate officers, respectively. Part 3, subtitled "Correspondence, etc.," includes orders sent by officers on both sides.

7. The battle of Trevilian Station, June 11–12, 1864, deserves the honor of having been the largest *all-cavalry* engagement of the war. See Eric J. Wittenberg, *Glory Enough for All: Maj. Gen. Philip H. Sheridan's Trevilian Raid and the Battle of Trevilian Station, June 7–25, 1864* (Baton Rouge: Louisiana State University Press, 2001). This significant clash occurred sixty miles northwest of Richmond. It involved an approximately ninety-three-hundred-man Union raiding force commanded by Maj. Gen. Philip H. Sheridan and a blocking force of about sixty-eight hundred Confederate troopers under Maj. Gen. Wade Hampton, who was not quite yet formally in command of all the Army of Northern Virginia's cavalrymen but had effectively taken over after the death of Jeb Stuart on May 12, 1864.

8. The numerical losses at Brandy Station are given in E. G. Longacre, *The Cavalry at Gettysburg* (Lincoln: University of Nebraska Press, 1986), p. 87; and Eric J. Wittenberg, "Brandy Station Seminar" (http://www.gdg.org/brandsem.html), pp. 27, 50. Wittenberg, after scrutinizing *OR* reports, breaks down the Confederate losses at Brandy Station as 51 killed, 250 wounded, and 132 missing, which is in agreement with Longacre's estimate of "fewer than 500 [Confederate] casualties." The overall losses during the two days of Trevilian Station (see preceding note) were between 10 and 20 percent—significantly higher than the approximately 6 percent at the one-day Battle of Brandy Station. The clash of troopers in the 1864 battle resulted in the highest proportion of cavalry casualties during the war.

9. Henry B. McClellan, *I Rode with Jeb Stuart* (Bloomington: Indiana University Press, 1958), p. 294 (emphasis in original). McClellan, a cousin of Union Maj. Gen. George B. McClellan, wrote this memoir between 1880 and 1885.

10. Two final points: The *Second* Battle of Brandy Station occurred on October 10, 1863. *Third* Brandy Station seems to have been won by the American people, who have been purchasing the

battlefield—which came within an ace of being turned into a racetrack in the 1990s.

11. Some regiments were reassigned to different brigades and divisions, vis-à-vis the organization implied in the first four charts in appendix A. Certain Union officers who fought at Brandy Station were sacked (see Appendix A), soon to disappear into the limbo of history before the time of the Gettysburg battle.

12. Mark Nesbitt quotes examples of newspaper attacks about the June 9 surprise, along with Stuart's contemporary denunciation of them (*Saber and Scapegoat: J. E. B. Stuart and the Gettysburg Controversy* [Mechanicsburg, Pa.: Stackpole, 1994], p. 40).

13. The *First* Battle of Winchester—May 25, 1862, part of "Stonewall" Jackson's Shenandoah Valley campaign—had been another Confederate victory. It occurred in conjunction with General McClellan's attempts to get at Richmond by moving up the James peninsula in eastern Virginia. In the Second Battle of Winchester, Ewell may not have performed with as much confidence and competence as his formal success there suggested (that he took the town and all those prisoners). It has been argued that he "faltered" before Winchester (see Michael A. Palmer, *Lee Moves North: Robert E. Lee on the Offensive* [New York: John Wiley and Sons, 1998], pp. 73–76). This sour note is based largely on an 1868 account by General Lee in which he described General Ewell sending him encouraging messages about entrapping Milroy's Federal force. That word was followed by a dispatch in mid-June 1863 stating that "upon closer inspection he [Ewell] found the works [at Winchester] too strong to be attacked" and asked for Lee's instructions. Lee's words were paraphrased by a man with whom he communicated (quoted ibid., p. 76). The conventional wisdom is that Ewell recapitulated this kind of dithering on the evening of July 1 at Gettysburg; it certainly haunted him down the years (as is discussed in the last section of Chapter 2).

14. Three brigades in one of Ewell's divisions—that of Maj. Gen. Robert Rodes—and the cavalry force under Jenkins crossed at Williamsport on the fifteenth. Major General Edward Johnson's division forded the Potomac just downstream of Shepherdstown on June 18, and Maj. Gen. Jubal Early's division crossed there on the Twenty-second.

15. General Stuart ordered Fitzhugh Lee's brigade (with Col. Thomas T. Munford still in command) to "take the advance of Longstreet's column." Beverly Robertson's and W. H. F. Lee's brigades were also sent northward across the Rappahannock, to be followed by that of Jones (the latter was, for all intents and purposes, ordered to lag behind on temporary picket duty). Colonel John R. Chambliss Jr. was in command of Rooney Lee's unit owing to the wounding and capture of the commanding general's son at Brandy Station, and one regiment of it was "left . . . on the lower Rappahannock, co-operating with A. P. Hill" (Stuart's Aug. 20, 1863, report, *OR*, pt. 2, p. 687).

16. Edwin B. Coddington, *The Gettysburg Campaign: A Study in Command* (New York: Charles Scribner's Sons, 1968), pp. 66–67.

17. General Butterfield, Hooker's chief of staff, sent specific marching orders to all Union corps commanders on June 13. Among these instructions were those transmitted to General Sedgwick of the 6th Corps (quoted in note 6 above), whose men were directed to recross the Rappahannock on the bridges they had built for their reconnaissance in force on the south bank (map 1-2).

18. General Hooker took over the Army of the Potomac on January 25, 1863, and whipped it into fine shape during the winter and spring. He then managed—or mismanaged—his army's defeat at the Battle of Chancellorsville (May 2–6), which took place there, about ten miles to the east at Fredericksburg, and between Fredericksburg and Chancellorsville.

19. During June 1863, the various cavalry leaders from both sides were in a state of flux until late June. Promotions and demotions occurred in conjunction with various reorganizations that led to new division, brigade, and regimental commanders—and the correlated disappearance of certain cavalry officers from the campaign. Some were wounded or got captured. Others fell into disfavor and were fired. The cavalry listings in the Order of Battle (see Appendix F) show which regiments and brigades were within which divisions, and who their commanders were, during the Battle of Gettysburg.

20. In contrast to how the opposing cavalry forces met in Loudoun Valley, the trailing Federal infantry would find it difficult to effect an actual collision with their foes or achieve some kind of blocking position—even if General Hooker had been disposed to follow the rebel infantry with dispatch.

21. Coddington, *Gettysburg Campaign*, p. 59.

22. Wilbur S. Nye (*Here Come the Rebels!* [Baton Rouge: Louisiana State University Press, 1965]) and Mark Nesbitt (*Saber and Scapegoat*) will have none of this. In their view, General Stuart was not seeking vindication for Brandy Station by "another ride around the enemy." Nesbitt gives a nod to the standard view that "Stuart, taking a beating from . . . the . . . newspapers, resolved to . . . make the Yankees regret" Brandy Station (p. 181).

23. I was startled to hear this remark in a lecture about the cavalry at Gettysburg, delivered by William O. Adams at a Civil War Roundtable meeting (Worcester, Mass., Oct. 1995). Adams has long researched this component of the campaign in particular (see Bibliographic Essay) and is sympathetic to the Civil War struggles of the Southern forces in general.

24. David Powell, "Stuart's Ride: Lee, Stuart, and the Confederate Cavalry in the Gettysburg Campaign," *Gettysburg Magazine*, no. 21 (July 1999): pp. 27–43.

25. *OR*, pt. 3, p. 923.

26. On the Twenty-seventh, elements of Stuart's Confederate cavalry clashed with Federal troopers near Fairfax Courthouse, Virginia. Stuart enjoyed a short-term tactical success (all but eighteen of the Union cavalrymen were captured), which characterized several of his actions during the campaign. However, the action on this day is also an example of the events that delayed Stuart's northward movement.

27. The most famous of Stuart's circular rides occurred during the Peninsula campaign in June 1862, when Stuart went around McClellan's army. He did so again that October, after the Battle of Antietam, ranging northward to Chambersburg, Pennsylvania.

28. Alan T. Nolan, "R. E. Lee and July 1 at Gettysburg," in *The First Day at Gettysburg: Essays on Confederate and Union Leadership*, ed. Gary W. Gallagher (Kent, Ohio: Kent State University Press, 1992), p. 17; Nesbitt, *Saber and Scapegoat*, pp. 57–73. General Lee's June 23 order to Stuart included some authentic military gibberish: "If General Hooker's army *remains inactive,* you can leave two brigades to watch him, and withdraw with the three others, but should he *not appear to be moving northward,* I think you had better withdraw this side of the mountain to-morrow night" (*OR*, pt. 3, p. 923; emphasis added). It could well be that Lee (more likely one of his staff officers) suffered a slip of the pen when generating this important piece of Gettysburg-campaign correspondence. The first of these related orders from Lee to Stuart, transmitted on June 22, was sent from Berryville, Virginia (maps 1-6 and 1–11), where General Lee himself had arrived on June 20.

29. A preview: The Battle of Hanover on June 30 both stalled and enervated Stuart's brigades to the extent that he drifted farther north in Pennsylvania at a time when Ewell's rebel infantry had already begun moving westward toward Gettysburg.

30. This unit, the 35th Virginia Battalion from Jones's brigade (chart 1-1), first ranged ahead of Ewell after crossing into Maryland and later accompanied Early's division from the 2nd Corps. Imboden and his horsemen were not formally part of the Army of Northern Virginia but under its direction. For example, Imboden was ordered at the outset of the campaign to "cover the movement [of General Ewell] toward Winchester" and "to prevent [Federal] troops guarding the Baltimore and Ohio railroads from those [garrisoned] at Winchester" (*OR*, pt. 3, pp. 305, 313). Moreover, Imboden's men destroyed several bridges along the Baltimore and Ohio's route, northwest of where the rebel main body marched (*OR*, pt. 2, pp. 296–97).

31. Imboden's command did not become closely involved in the Gettysburg campaign until after the battle. Also note that the 35th Virginia Battalion and Jenkins's brigade were out in front, relatively near Ewell's infantry or accompanying it on a given day—hence not in any proximity to General Lee himself. The three brigades Stuart chose to go with him were his main men, in that the commands of Robertson and Jones had recently been ordered to hook up with the bulk of Stuart's division (Robertson coming up from North Carolina and Jones from the Shenandoah Valley).

32. *OR*, pt. 3, pp. 927–28.

33. In David Powell's view, it was *Stuart's job* to be with the main body of the Confederate infantry by riding in a timely manner to where the rebels were marching in Pennsylvania (Powell, "Stuart's Ride," pp. 27–43). Robertson's mission included watching over the supplies captured by the rebels and sent south (p. 41). However, Nesbitt argues that Robertson should have commenced riding northward on June 25, at which time General Stuart assumed those two brigades would follow Lee, move onto the infantry's right flank, and "perform all the tasks Stuart would have if he had been there" (Nesbitt, *Saber and Scapegoat*, pp. 69–70). Thus Robertson would have been "following the Confederate army once the Federals crossed the Potomac, which is what he was ordered to do" by Stuart on June 24 (ibid., p. 152). Powell, however, holds that Lee wanted Robertson in a more southern sector of the theater (to look after the aforementioned supply wagons *and* protect the infantry's rear from a Federal force at Harper's Ferry). Powell goes on to note that it was not until *June 30* that "Lee [sent] orders to Robertson . . . to join the army" ("Stuart's Ride," p. 41). Did the commanding general not summon Robertson as punctually as he might have—once he realized Stuart was not keeping his appointment? By the time three of Jones's regiments (from Robertson's command) managed to trickle into Pennsylvania, June had become July, and the battle was essentially over (see Appendix E).

34. One of Lee's staff officers said after the war that Stuart should have been so charged (Nesbitt, *Saber and Scapegoat*, p. 64).

35. This is fodder for *further* controversy and is discussed in Appendix D.

36. Excusing this sarcasm, check out the first two chapters of Nesbitt's *Saber and Scapegoat*, which describe how Stuart's military training and prewar activities prepared and predisposed him "to use his men like a light saber" (p. xvi).

37. Another argument against the scenario just stated is that if Stuart had tried to stall the Federal infantry marches, he might have been foiled by Federal cavalry, which could have *harassed Stuart* and kept him away from the Union army's northward trek. This counter-scenario is evident from the position of the Federal forces as depicted on map 1-15.

38. Powell, "Stuart's Ride," pp. 34–35.

39. Emory M. Thomas, "Eggs, Aldie, Shepherdstown, and J. E. B. Stuart," in Gabor S. Boritt, ed., *The Gettysburg Nobody Knows* (New York: Oxford University Press, 1997), p. 117. The body of this essay elaborates the stress-fatigue hypothesis.

40. *OR*, pt. 3, p. 914.

41. Baron Antoine-Henri de Jomini was a Swiss citizen who first became a military chronicler then theorist. He served as a staff officer with Napoleon in the late 1700s and early 1800s. Among the many strategic military maxims in his *Précis de l'art de la guerre* (1838) is that "In a war, the capital is ordinarily the objective point" because it is not only "the center of communication, but also the seat of power and government" (Jomini, *The Art of War* [reprint, London: Greenhill, 1992], p. 87). It was not clear that Harrisburg, Pennsylvania, was either in 1863. The extent to which Lee and other Civil War generals were influenced by Jominian principles, as espoused by West Point instructors before the Mexican War (1846–48), is arguable (McPherson, *Battle Cry of Freedom*, pp. 331–32).

42. There was also a bridge at Harrisburg for vehicular and pedestrian traffic. The bridges near the state capital were never threatened. However, a rebel force advancing beyond York toward the Susquehanna River was under orders from General Ewell to demolish a separate bridge that connected Wrightsville to Columbia (map 1-11). Upon their approach to Wrightsville, the rebels (under Maj. Gen. Jubal Early's command) decided not to destroy the span but to use it for crossing the Susquehanna in order to advance farther into Pennsylvania. Ironically, the Pennsylvanians then burned the bridge.

43. Neither Gordon nor Early referred in their after-action reports to having noticed the "great ground" south of Gettysburg in conjunction with passing through that town on June 26. The reports of these generals were submitted on August 10 and 22, 1863, respectively. See *OR*, pt. 2, pp. 491–93 for Gordon's report; and pp. 459–73 for Early's. In his memoirs, Gordon wrote that during the June phase of the campaign he had "expressed . . . the opinion that if the battle should be fought at Gettysburg, the army which held the heights would probably be the victor. The insignificant encounter I had on those hills [on June 26] impressed their commanding importance on me" (*Reminiscences of the Civil War* [1903; reprint, Baton Rouge: Louisiana State University Press, 1993], p. 140).

44. Charles C. Fennel, "The Attack and Defense of Culp's Hill: Greene's Brigade at the Battle of Gettysburg, July 1–3, 1863" (Ph.D. diss., West Virginia University, 1992), pp. 70–71. Fennel deserves this citation for first bringing to my attention this specific feature of General Hooker's activities during June 1863, which imply that his attitude was not one of thoroughgoing passiveness. Additional details about "Hooker's plan for using [the] Harper's Ferry troops and those of his 12th Corps" are in Stephen W. Sears, "Meade Takes Command," *North & South* 5, no. 6 [Sept. 2002]: pp. 12–20 (esp. pp. 18–19).

45. The general was momentarily in shock and consternation during the wee hours of that Sunday. He was not, however, thunderstruck by the promotion. Between the Battle of Chancellorsville and the commencement of the Gettysburg campaign, certain of his peers in the Army of the Potomac had been discussing amongst themselves and with the high command in Washington the possible replacement of Hooker with Meade. The latter was privy to some of these conversations, although he did not actively seek elevation to army command. Sears most recently recounted this story in "Meade Takes Command," pp. 12–16.

46. General Hooker's performance in the battles for Chattanooga in late November 1863 was not unambiguously meritorious. Nonetheless, his troops won the relatively minor Battle of Lookout Mountain (south of that Tennessee city, November 24, 1863) and significantly contributed to the Union victory in the

great Battle of Missionary Ridge (November 25, 1863), when the Federal soldiers under his command attacked the left (south) flank of the rebel line along that ridge east of Chattanooga. These three divisions of Union infantrymen had been sent to the western theater from the Army of the Potomac's 11th Corps (see Chapter 2) and from its 12th Corps (see Chapters 3 and 4). Joseph Hooker's activities, accomplishments, and the lack thereof seem to provide a quintessential example of the "Peter Principle" (Laurence J. Peter and Raymond Hull, *The Peter Principle: Why Things Always Go Wrong* [New York: William Morrow, 1969]). In this instance, Hooker was promoted to the level of his incompetence in early 1863, as was revealed in May of that year. At the end of the next month, when he was booted out, he could have simply vanished into the limbo of history (the Peter Principle operating, as it usually does, in an up then out direction). That is what happened to other Union army commanders who had been fighting in the eastern theater (or trying to anyway). Instead, Hooker reappeared as a corps commander in late 1863 and revealed that he had indeed dropped back to the level of his competence.

47. Quoted in George Meade, *The Life and Letters of George Gordon Meade*, ed. G. G. Meade, 2 vols. (New York: Charles Scribner's Sons, 1913), vol. 1, p. 383 (emphasis added). The editor is the former general's son, George G. Jr., who was at Gettysburg as a captain on the army commander's staff.

48. Mark Nesbitt suggests the Harrison spy story should be relegated to myth (*Saber and Scapegoat*, pp. 79–80). Nevertheless, there are enough explicit mentions of Harrison (no first name given) in the postwar writings of James Longstreet, his staff officer Moxley Sorrell, and Lee's military secretary, Charles Marshall, to allow the conclusion that a scout of this name brought Longstreet information about the Army of the Potomac's movements and positions in late June. However, Harrison never met with Lee himself, as Shelby Foote contends in *The Civil War: A Narrative*, vol. 2, *Fredericksburg to Meridian* (New York: Random House, 1963), pp. 462–63. His report was transmitted orally to the Southern commander.

Who was this Confederate spy? Probably not Mississippi actor James Harrison, as suggested by John Bakeless in *Spies of the Confederacy* (Philadelphia: Lippincott, 1970), and by Nesbitt, who augments his analysis in *Saber and Scapegoat* with a photograph of "James Harrison." Instead, "the fabled agent" was Mississippian Henry Thomas Harrison. See James O. Hall, "The Spy Harrison," *Civil War Times Illustrated* 24, no. 10 (Feb. 1986): 18–25. However, Troy Trimble ("Harrison: Spying for Longstreet at Gettysburg," *Gettysburg Magazine*, no. 17 [July 1997]: pp. 17–20) says that we cannot be sure of the spy's identity, although a man named Harrison assuredly contributed significant scouting results to the Confederate high command.

Nesbitt also believes that there was no surprise (*Saber and Scapegoat*, pp. 79–82), a view that is echoed by Nolan in "R. E. Lee and July 1," pp. 13–14. These authors argue that, irrespective of H. T. Harrison's activities and report, other evidence about General Hooker's intentions and movements was filtering into General Lee's headquarters during the second half of June.

49. Published examples of this back-and-forth about what J. E. B. Stuart did, or should have done, are cited in note 33.

50. This is a rhetorical flourish, because some of the roadways in southern Pennsylvania at the time (such as one that connected York to Shippensburg) bypassed Gettysburg (maps 1-15 and 1-19). Actually, General Lee recommended to his corps commanders that they concentrate at Cashtown, a location closer to the mountains than Gettysburg (map 1-8). Lee had in mind that the Army of Northern Virginia might choose ground there to fight a defensive battle, with good fallback positions in the hills behind them, should it prove necessary to redeploy in that manner. Bevin Alexander recently put forth an intriguing alternative scenario in *Robert E. Lee's Civil War* (Holbrook, Mass.: Adams Media, 1998). Alexander hypothesizes that the Army of Northern Virginia "could have crossed the Susquehanna, seized Harrisburg, broken the bridges . . . and had a long head start down the undefended road to Philadelphia . . . with much industry and [a] location astride the main north-south railroad arteries of the North. The Union army would have been powerless to stop such a movement, but would have been bound to try—compelled to chase after the rebel army in an exhausting, debilitating footrace. Anywhere along the way . . . at any superior position . . . Lee's army could have halted, rested, built formidable entrenchments . . . and waited," as they ultimately did near the end of the campaign, on the banks of the Potomac River (p. 183). See Chapter 5.

51. There are many examples of Northern motivational sentiments that would come under the heading of this phrase, which is not necessarily a direct quote of anybody in the Union army (although novelist Michael Shaara, in the quote from the beginning of this chapter, implies that someone might have said as much). In any case, see the essays by Joseph T. Glatthaar (pp. 13–14, 27, 38) and Carol Reardon (p. 137) in Boritt, ed., *Gettysburg Nobody Knows*. The surging spirits that infected the Union soldiers as they marched north have been mentioned so repeatedly that one wonders if some chroniclers are carried away with the extent to which the phenomenon contributed to the Northerners' determined fight at Gettysburg. Nevertheless, this hypothesis lives on, as exemplified further in D. A. Ward's "Sedgwick's Foot Cavalry: The March of the Sixth Corps to Gettysburg," *Gettysburg Magazine*, no. 22 (Jan. 2000): pp. 43–65. Most of this article consists of quotes from ordinary infantrymen. There was an intriguing twist to the attitude of these Union soldiers, some of whom may have actually welcomed the Confederate invasion: "Many of the men suggested that only a raid by Lee, deep into northern territory, would expose friends and families to the destructive nature of war and thus mobilize all the north's resources" and make "Northern civilians understand the kind of . . . commitment that was needed to crush the rebellion" (pp. 49–50). Ironically, Sixth Corps, the largest corps in the Army of the Potomac (see Appendix F), was not heavily involved in the battle of Gettysburg itself. Its men did, however, make a heroic forced march to the battlefield, the significance of which is discussed in Chapter 3.

52. The Southerners' putative morale problem is a principal theme of Joseph T. Glatthaar's "The Common Soldier's Gettysburg Campaign," in Boritt, ed., *Gettysburg Nobody Knows*, pp. 3–30. The quotes farther down this paragraph of the main text that speak to what certain Confederate soldiers felt about the campaign as of late June are from Brian M. Gottfried, "Mahone's Brigade: Insubordination or Miscommunication?" *Gettysburg Magazine*, no. 18 (Jan. 1998): p. 69. Not everyone buys Glatthaar's thesis. See, for example, Harry W. Pfanz, *Gettysburg: The First Day* (Chapel Hill: University of North Carolina Press), pp. 19, 29. The "you're down here" remark was attributed to a rebel soldier by historian Shelby Foote in Ken Burns, *The Civil War*, episode 2, "A Very Bloody Affair, 1862" (Walpole, N.H., and Washington, D.C.: Florentine Films and WETA-TV, 1990). This declaration seems flippant, but perhaps not: Whether or not an ordinary Southern soldier cared about slavery or "states' rights," he might have been reflexively compelled to fight against invading enemy troops. In contrast, Northerners *did not have to fight at all* (unless they had joined the army and were under orders). In other words, the Union citizenry and government were, in the strictest sense, not *required to do anything* about secession

other than to *let the Southern states go.* This takes us beyond the scope of the book. Bear in mind, however, that the tables were turned during the Gettysburg campaign: a Union soldier might have yelled out in the general direction of the rebel army that "now you're *up here!*"

53. In this campaign, Kilpatrick careened from brigade, to regiment, back up to brigade, and finally to division command. Kilpatrick's 3rd Division was the smallest such unit of Federal cavalry as the Battle of Gettysburg approached and during it (Appendix F). This division, essentially a newly formed one in late June, had a distinctly different composition compared with the "3rd Division" of Union troopers at the time of Brandy Station (see chart 1 in Appendix A). The second incarnation of this division (during June 1863) was a newly created one, as follows: A Union cavalry force had been detached from Washington to screen the Army of the Potomac's left wing as it marched north. General Hooker requested on June 26 that the commander of this mounted force be sent off for another assignment (at Harrisburg, Pennsylvania), which was ordered by the commander in chief (General Halleck) on the Twenty-eighth. On that day, most of the regiments in this screening force of troopers were reassigned to the Army of the Potomac and became Kilpatrick's new 3rd Division (Pfanz, *First Day*, pp. 35–36).

54. On this day, yet another Union cavalry command shift occurred (cf. preceding note) when the recently promoted Brig. Gen. Wesley Merritt took over the Reserve Brigade in Buford's division—replacing a certain ill-starred major (see note 4 in Appendix E). This unit was not to be involved in the fateful action that occurred near Gettysburg on the morning of July 1 (Chapter 2). Merritt's brigade was posted in northern Maryland at that time and did not end up in action at the Battle of Gettysburg until July 3 (Appendix E).

55. Meanwhile, at Westminster and Muddy Branch in northern Maryland, cavalry skirmishes broke out between elements of Stuart's northward-riding brigades and Union forces under Maj. Napoleon B. Knight. The Confederates repelled Knight's attack. Union casualties were nine dead or wounded; the Confederates lost eighteen dead or wounded.

56. Meade had attached Maj. Gen. Alfred Pleasonton, the Cavalry Corps commander, to his staff, so the latter was not autonomously directing the movements of Federal troopers.

57. *OR*, pt. 1, pp. 923–24.

58. Champ Clark, *Gettysburg: The Confederate High Tide* (Alexandria, Va.: Time-Life Books, 1985), p. 44.

Chapter 2
July 1: The Union Suffers a Setback but Gains a Great Position

1. Thomas A. Desjardin, *Legends of Gettysburg: Separating Fact from Fiction* (Gettysburg: Friends of the National Park at Gettysburg, 1997), pp. 2-3. This essay also provides the meteorological information given at the beginnings of Chapters 3 and 4. For further details, see Thomas L. Elmore, "Torrid Heat and Blinding Rain: A Meteorological and Astronomical Chronology of the Gettysburg Campaign," *Gettysburg Magazine*, no. 15 (July 1995): pp. 7–21.

2. This was manifestly the case, as map 1-19 shows. Nevertheless, there is no written evidence that General Lee explicitly ordered his commanders to avoid engaging Union army elements they might encounter (Nolan, "R. E. Lee and July 1," p. 21). However, General Ewell's after-action report states that he "was informed [by General Lee] that, in case we found the enemy's force very large, he did not want a general engagement brought on until the rest of the army came up" (*OR*, pt. 2, p. 444).

3. Desjardin cogently discusses the falsity of this battle having been precipitated because of shoes (*Legends of Gettysburg*, p. 1). However, General Heth made a parenthetical mention of his shoe-gathering mission in the report he submitted on September 13, 1863 (*OR*, pt. 2, p. 637). The importance of the would-be shoes, and that Heth really had to get them because General Pettigrew had failed to do so on the previous day, escalated fifteen years later: "As I opened the battle of Gettysburg—stumbled into it, going to Gettysburg to get shoes, not to fight—I claim I should know as much about the opening operations . . . as any man living" (Henry Heth, "Gen. Lee's Orders to His Cavalry," *Philadelphia Weekly Times*, Mar. 23, 1878). See also J. L. Morrison, ed., "The Memoirs of Henry Heth," *Civil War History* 8 (Sept. 1962): pp. 300–26.

4. Pfanz, *First Day*, p. 26.

5. After the war, Heth remembered A. P. Hill's reply to the question of whether there was "any objection to his taking his [Heth's] division to Gettysburg again to get those shoes . . . 'None in the world'" (Coddington, *Gettysburg Campaign*, p. 264).

6. According to Pfanz, "when the skirmishing began, the [Union] cavalrymen on the forward line [presumably including those ranging out toward Whistler's Ridge (map 2-4)] were mounted. After they fell back on their reserve, horse holders took the horses to the rear and the carabineers fought on foot" (*First Day*, pp. 57–58).

7. Michael Phipps and John S. Peterson, *"The Devil's to Pay": Gen. John Buford, USA* (Gettysburg: Farnsworth Military Impressions, 1995), p. 44. Jones discharged this breech-loading weapon from a point that is 1.8 miles from the back edge of McPherson Ridge (closest to the town—where the modern-day Reynolds Avenue runs from the Fairfield Road and crosses the Cashtown Road on the way to Oak Hill [map 2-5]). The point being reiterated here is that the outer edge of Buford's defensive deployment was a *considerable distance to the west* of where many battlefield visitors sense that that cavalry commander made his "one stand" against the rebels' infantry advance.

8. Well, not really. About an hour and a half previously, pickets from the 17th Pennsylvania Cavalry (Col. Thomas C. Devin's 2nd Brigade; map 2-5, chart 2-1) had encountered advance elements of Ewell's 2nd Corps coming down from the north (Richard S. Shue, *Morning at Willoughby Run: July 1, 1863* [Gettysburg: Thomas Publications, 1995], pp. 54–58). This indicates that Devin's right wing of Buford's defense was well outside of Gettysburg early and on the alert for a Confederate threat from the north, although that was not to be a quite-so-imminent one. As of June 30, the closest known rebel infantry unit was Hill's corps. Yet, firefights between the Union cavalry and rebel 2nd Corps skirmishers began about 6 A.M. on July 1 near the road that runs northward to Carlisle (map 2-5). This roadway is now named Table Rock Road as it draws near Gettysburg. Another modern-day road running parallel to Table Rock is Carlisle Road.

9. Thomas A. Desjardin to author, Nov. 9, 1999. "Shaara's book inflated the story," Desjardin added. The novelist indeed wrote that John Buford "never [received] recognition for his part in choosing the field and holding it, and in so doing saving not only the battle but perhaps the war" (Shaara, *Killer Angels*, p. 373).

10. However, Eric J. Wittenberg, in "John Buford and the Gettysburg Campaign," *Gettysburg Magazine*, no. 11 (July 1994): p. 38, says that General Buford "recognized the significance of the high ground to the south of the town." This is not persuasive, though, because the source cited made such a claim on Buford's

behalf retrospectively. The anonymously authored article in question was written in 1867, probably by one of Buford's former staff officers. See Eric J. Wittenberg, "An Analysis of the Buford Manuscripts," *Gettysburg Magazine,* no. 15 (July 1996): pp. 7–23. This Union officer wrote further about the battle as a whole, with four years of hindsight: "Had it not been for these fortuitous circumstances [the deployments and actions of Buford's troopers on the morning of July 1], the rebels would have occupied the strong positions which they afterward endeavored in vain to make themselves masters of" (p. 18). At least one Union commander on this part of the field during the midmorning hours appeared to have specifically recognized the importance of these "strong positions": General Reynolds sent a courier to Meade's headquarters in northern Maryland. This officer departed at 10 A.M. and reached Taneytown about an hour-and-a-half later—reporting to General Meade that "the enemy was approaching Gettysburg in force and that *Reynolds feared . . . the Confederates would seize the heights on the 'other side' (south or east) of the town*" (Pfanz, *First Day,* p. 74, emphasis added).

11. Gary W. Gallagher, "Confederate Corps Leadership on the First Day at Gettysburg: A. P. Hill and Richard S. Ewell in a Difficult Debut," in Gallagher, ed., *First Day at Gettysburg,* p. 32. However, General Hill's report of his actions at Gettysburg (Nov. 1863, *OR,* pt. 2, pp. 606–609) does not mention orders from Lee proscribing engaging the enemy on July 1, whereas General Ewell's report did (note 2).

12. Phipps and Peterson, *"Devil's to Pay,"* p. 46.

13. Ibid., p. 47.

14. This vaunted unit was not always the 1st of the 1st of the 1st (Appendix F), but was given that numerically exalted position after Chancellorsville (May 1863).

15. Cutler's Brigade was not only the first Union infantry unit to arrive (see the top of map 2-10), it also began to be attacked by Davis's Southerners as the Iron Brigade's column was arriving on McPherson Ridge (bottom of map 2-10). See Pfanz, *First Day,* p. 84.

16. Ibid., p. 96.

17. Flank attacks can be executed with deadly effect on groups of putative defenders or—in the case of a flanking counterattack—to turn the tables on an advancing force. Gettysburg includes other examples of this military geometric phenomenon, including—on July 3—a pair of flank attacks for the ages.

18. Shue, *Morning at Willoughby Run,* p. 242. The numerator and denominator include the men of Lt. John H. Calef's battery (maps 2-7 and 2-10), who were detached from the 2nd Brigade of the Union Cavalry Corps's Horse Artillery (see Appendix F).

19. This has long been regarded as a severe blow to the Union general officers on the field at Gettysburg because of the high regard in which Reynolds was held, including the seeming affection expressed by several soldiers in the context of his untimely death. See Edward J. Nichols, *Toward Gettysburg: A Biography of General John F. Reynolds* (University Park: Pennsylvania State University Press, 1958), pp. 185, 192, 211, 216–17; and Michael A. Riley, *"For God's Sake, Forward!": Gen. John F. Reynolds, USA* (Gettysburg: Farnsworth House Military Impressions, 1995), p. 3. However, I am somewhat at a loss to understand just why he was viewed with such admiration (personally and professionally), because it is not clear how much he accomplished militarily during the first half of the war. Photographs of John Reynolds taken during the early 1860s show a man who *looked* the part of a fine general officer—a consideration that cannot be dismissed out of hand (see note 60).

20. This Wisconsin regiment got well situated in reserve under an order from General Doubleday: As the 6th Wisconsin was advancing to form up on the 24th Michigan's left (map 2-10), an officer from Doubleday's staff arrived with instructions for this regiment of Westerners to halt (Pfanz, *First Day,* p. 102), which they did by occupying the position shown near the bottom left of map 2-10.

21. Archer's advance was unlikely to have occurred without skirmishers "100 yards to the front" (probably from the 5th Alabama battalion noted in chart 2-2)—as Pfanz implies without specifying how cautious or incautious were these rebels' movements into McPherson's Woods (*First Day,* pp. 62–63). For his part, Robert K. Krick opines that Archer's brigade surged forward into an untenable situation without adequate reconnaissance (if any at all) ("Three Confederate Disasters on Oak Ridge: Failures of Brigade Leadership on the First Day at Gettysburg," in Gallagher, ed., *First Day at Gettysburg,* p. 99).

22. This presages the disaster that was about to befall this rebel brigade. The chance that it would happen might have been exacerbated by the less than sterling quality of the unit's commander. In this regard, Joseph R. Davis of Gettysburg was the nephew of Confederate president Jefferson Davis, and the former's generalship was indeed promoted in part by (literal) nepotism.

23. General Doubleday deserves credit for ordering the charge of the 6th Wisconsin, although the Iron Brigade's attack south of the Cashtown Road was not his doing: General Reynolds was exercising the final moments of his command at that time (Pfanz, *First Day,* p. 120).

24. The commander of this regiment, Col. Rufus Dawes, estimated that "160 men of the 6th fell" during their charge (Pfanz, *First Day,* p. 109).

25. In particular, Howard saw Cutler's brigade retreating in disorder toward Seminary Ridge. Howard jumped to a conclusion about this reverse, leading to Doubleday being inappropriately fired from 1st Corps command. Oddly, his replacement was a division commander from the *6th* Corps, Maj. Gen. John Newton, whose units, along with the others from that corps, were nowhere near Gettysburg on July 1 (map 2-28). General Newton's military performance during the remainder of the battle was unremarkable. He will, as it turns out, be best remembered for a fateful phrase he uttered at the end of the fighting on July 2 (see Chapter 3).

26. Making a reconnaissance of the emerging battlefield, General Howard and a staff officer rode to Cemetery Hill to get a good view of the area. Seeing that "the hill commanded the town and the country to the west and north [and] that its gentle slope in those directions made for a good artillery position," Howard said to his staffer: "This seems like a good position, colonel." The man replied, "it is the only position, general." In his 1902 *Autobiography,* "Howard stressed that both [he and his staff officer] had meant *'position for Meade's army' '"* (quoted in Pfanz, *First Day,* p. 136).

27. David L. Shultz and Richard Rollins, "'A Combined and Concentrated Fire': Deployment of the Federal Artillery at Gettysburg, July 3, 1863," *North & South* 2, no. 3 [Mar. 1999]: pp. 39–60.

28. One of these batteries (the one facing northwest in map 2-15) was beaten up during the fighting west of town that morning (map 2-11; *OR,* pt. 1, pp. 349–50). A battery that had gone north of town in the early afternoon was eventually forced back, and a portion of it formed on Cemetery Hill, bolstering the defenses there (*OR,* pt. 1, pp. 754–55). Only about a dozen Federal artillery pieces were available to help withstand an attack on the hill—had the Confederates attempted one on the evening of July 1.

29. The 11th Corps troops moved through the town toward the plain north of it as the lead elements of the Confederate 2nd Corps (Rodes's division) were arriving on the battlefield at Oak Hill (see below and map 2-17). General Schurz, temporarily in control of the

advancing 11th Corps force, wanted his own 3rd Division to form up directly to the right of the Union 1st Corps. Rodes's rebels reached this position first, however, so the bulk of Schurz's division deployed somewhat south of Cutler's 1st Corps brigade—creating a gap on the southern slope of Oak Ridge between that unit and the main body of the 11th Corps's left wing (map 2-21). Schurz nevertheless managed to support the 1st Corps's right flank with a line of skirmishers (men from Brig. Gen. Schimmelfennig's 3rd Division, 11th Corps, as diagrammed in the middle of map 2-21).

30. In this regard, the lull overlapped the resumption of the fighting in the center of the lines insofar as the 11th Corps on the Union right was concerned. Thus, these two of Howard's divisions were not involved in the fighting until well into the afternoon.

31. At sunrise on July 1, Rodes's division began marching toward Gettysburg. General Ewell, Rodes's commander, and Maj. Gen. Isaac R. Trimble, a high-ranking officer attached to the Confederate 2nd Corps who enters the story later on this Wednesday and resurfaces on July 3 as well, accompanied Rodes. The trio of generals accompanied this division of infantrymen as they proceeded toward Cashtown via Middletown, Pennsylvania (a town six miles due north of Gettysburg now called Biglerville). Before the column reached Middletown (map 2-16), Ewell received (at 9 A.M.) a courier from the 3rd Corps commander, A. P. Hill, with an important message that the latter's unit was advancing on Gettysburg. Ewell ordered his divisions to do the same. Rodes turned his division left at Middletown to march down the Carlisle Road toward the now famous town in this region. As Rodes's brigades deployed on and around Oak Hill (maps 2-17 and 2-21), he saw Union troops from the 11th Corps advancing toward him (see note 29), thought he was about to be attacked, and was "determined" to preempt such a possible move with an assault of his own (Pfanz, *First Day*, pp. 161–62). Two further episodes are important to register in this regard: At the time General Ewell redirected the two 2nd Corps divisions in his vicinity toward Gettysburg, he sent a courier to Cashtown to inform the commanding general, Robert E. Lee, that these units were on their way to that Pennsylvania town (ibid., p. 150). When Ewell's staff officer returned to Gettysburg, at about the time Rode's brigades were preparing to attack the Federal center (map 2-17), apparently the gist of Lee's message was that "a general engagement was to be avoided until the arrival of the rest of the army " (quoted without attribution by Pfanz, ibid., p. 161; cf. note 3). But General Ewell was aware of the facts that his 3rd Corps mates had already been engaged earlier on this Wednesday, that a battery in Rodes's division of his own corps was now firing at the Federal lines, and thus "that it was too late to avoid an engagement" (Ewell, as quoted ibid.).

32. Recall that these probing rebels engaged in small firefights early on July 1—encountering only the cavalry pickets in Colonel Devin's command.

33. Rodes in fact felt he should attack because of the putative threat of 11th Corps troops arriving in his vicinity (note 31). The heavy skirmish line just to Baxter's right was composed of men from the 45th New York, a Regiment in Schimmelfennig's brigade within Schurz's 3rd Division of the 11th Corps (see note 29 and map 2-21).

34. Pfanz, however, believes "it may be assumed . . . sharpshooters were posted as skirmishers in . . . front [of O'Neal's Brigade]" as it advanced toward Baxter's position (*First Day*, p. 164). A member of the 88th Pennsylvania (in Baxter's brigade) wrote in 1886 that O'Neal's "line of battle [was] covered by a cloud of busy skirmishers" (quoted by Krick, "Three Confederate Disasters," p. 126).

35. Initially, three of Baxter's regiments—the 12th Massachusetts, 97th New York, and most of the 11th Pennsylvania (cf. map 2-17)—shifted to face west as Iverson advanced. The latter's brigade had begun to move in at the same time as O'Neal, and Baxter's other units were still dealing with the would-be attack of these Alabamians (map 2-17) as O'Neal's North Carolinians approached (Pfanz, *First Day*, p. 170).

36. This brigade of North Carolinians was "marching steadily, without skirmishers and without reconnaissance" (Krick, "Three Confederate Disasters," p. 133).

37. This "out of ammunition" issue, in its Gettysburg context, is discussed at some length in Appendix G.

38. For the sake of continuity, the last phase of the rebel attacks in this area (by General Ramseur) is described here (map 2-19), although this temporarily overlapped with the renewal of hostilities on the Confederate right and Union left (map 2-23, two sections below).

39. The Confederates hitting them from the west were part of the 3rd Corps attack mentioned above and described in detail later.

40. Richard A. Sauers, "The 16th Maine Volunteer Infantry at Gettysburg," *Gettysburg Magazine,* no. 13 (July 1995): pp. 33–42.

41. The fires would have been lit not for a lunch break, but for heating water so these 3rd Corps soldiers could clean their muskets. This points to a problem connected with black-powder-firing muzzle loaders: Did the advances in shoulder arms as of the mid-nineteenth century make offensive warfare so dangerous that it might have been impossible? What happened at Gettysburg on July 2 and 3 might favor this notion, but I do not believe it. On the other hand, the events of July 1 reveal that an attacking Civil War army could succeed, at least in the short run. This issue, a contentious one involving the war in general, is dealt with in Appendix G.

42. While Heth's division was marching toward Gettysburg in the early morning on July 1, "Hill lay at his headquarters contending with an unknown malady" (Gallagher, "Confederate Corps Leadership," pp. 44, 149n22). The standard view of A. P. Hill's generally unwell state during the Civil War is that he suffered chronically from "gonorrhea contracted on furlough" while a cadet at West Point in the mid-1840s—the result of an unfortunate tryst with a prostitute in a New York City brothel (Jack D. Welsh, *Medical Histories of the Confederate Generals* [Kent, Ohio: Kent State University Press, 1996], pp. 78–80). Little could be done during the nineteenth century for victims of this debilitating but not necessarily fatal disease (penicillin was not discovered until 1928).

43. Also see note 31. Two side points are warranted as well: One of Ewell's three divisions was, until late afternoon (map 2-27), actually intermingled with Hill's Corps (maps 2-16 and 2-28); and the concentration point for Ewell's corps, along with the two other ones, was originally planned to be Cashtown (as implied in note 31).

44. Early moved out from his June 30–July 1 bivouac at 8 A.M. on Wednesday morning, intending to march toward Cashtown via Huntertown and Mummasburg, Pennsylvania (which are northeast and northwest of Gettysburg, respectively). Recall from note 31 that it was about 9 A.M. when Ewell turned the two 2nd Corps divisions in his vicinity south toward Gettysburg.

45. A. Wilson Greene, "From Chancellorsville to Cemetery Hill: O. O. Howard and Eleventh Corps Leadership," in Gallagher, ed., *First Day at Gettysburg,* pp. 76–77, 82. According to Pfanz, who reminds us that General Schurz had been put in overall command of the outlying 11th Corps divisions while General Howard was back on Cemetery Hill: "Schurz did not order Barlow to a specific piece of ground, but he did order him to place one brigade on

Krzyanowski's right [map 2-22] and the other . . . behind it." With respect to the rough features of such a potential arrangement, Pfanz also points out the following: Not only might the brick buildings of the almshouse have "provided a strong point along such a line" (whose right flank could have been anchored there), but also that there was a rise of ground just south of this location — "a potential fallback position in case the first line [of the 11th Corps's right wing] did not hold" (*First Day*, p. 230).

46. In contrast, the Army of the Potomac's *left* flank at Chancellorsville was nicely anchored on the banks of the nearest river, providing it with natural protection (see map 3-9 in Chapter 3).

47. To try to keep things straight temporally it is useful to register that, as General Barlow deployed the 11th Corps's right wing onto "his" fateful knoll, the Confederate 3rd Corps was renewing its attacks on the Union left wing (map 2-24).

48. Greene, "From Chancellorsville to Cemetery Hill," p. 79. Moreover, one component of the 11th Corps defense, the 157th New York from Schimmelfennig's brigade, actually counterattacked the rebels advancing in its sector (map 2-22)—a great cost, in that this New York regiment lost three-quarters of its numbers.

49. As Doles's rebel brigade (from Rodes's division) moved to the left and pressed the defenders on the west slope of Barlow's Knoll (map 2-22, top), it is likely that this drew General Barlow's attention away from the threat from Hays's and Avery's brigades along the Harrisburg Road (map 2-22, bottom)—further worsening the chance that Barlow might hold (Pfanz, *First Day*, p. 245). The first Federal force to retreat through the town was Col. Thomas C. Devin's cavalry brigade, whose troopers had been deployed north of Gettysburg back in the early morning (map 2-5). Elements of Devin's unit had been picketing the roads approaching Gettysburg from the north in the midafternoon but had fallen back as Early's division approached (map 2-21). These mounted Union men then took a position just east of town, with Colonel Devin posting vedettes northeastward along the York Pike (map 2-21).

50. The last Union unit to withdraw was the 45th New York—the first 11th Corps troops on the field, who had deployed to a position near the Federal center to support Baxter's brigade near the Mummasburg Road (map 2-18 above). For temporal coordination: as a Union artillery unit that was posted in the vicinity of the 45th New York withdrew southward, the battery commander saw elements of the Union 1st Corps retreating from the vicinity of Seminary Ridge north of the Cashtown Road and the railroad cut (map 2-25).

51. A musket shot hit him in the hat, into which he had stuffed paper to ensure a proper fit. General Heth was wounded—not terribly, but enough so that his division was taken over by Brig. Gen. James Johnston Pettigrew (chart 2-9), who up to this time commanded the center brigade (map 2-13).

52. *OR*, pt. 2, p. 639. Colonel Fry was wounded and captured during Pickett's Charge on July 3 and left no after-action report. Fry's successor, Col. Samuel G. Shepard, provided the official account (*OR*, pt. 2, pp. 646–47) of Archer's brigade's activities on July 1 and does not mention which of these Alabama or Tennessee regiments might have advanced farthest toward the Union cavalry (posted at the bottom of map 2-24).

53. Maj. Gen. Abner Doubleday turned in a reasonably good performance on this day, his later demotion notwithstanding. He had positioned the arriving 1st Corps units well (map 2-13), including those placed in reserve, he committed the reserves to the fighting north of the Cashtown Road in a timely manner (maps 2-16 and 2-18), and arranged for some breastworks to be built at the 1st Corps's final fallback position (on Seminary Ridge, map 2-25).

54. Daniel had made two southward pointing attacks from north of the Cashtown Road (map 2-20). His third one occurred mainly in an eastward direction, coordinated with the attacks of Confederate 3rd Corps units south of this roadway (map 2-25).

55. Union cavalrymen (chart 2-10) guarding the 1st Corps's left flank below the Fairfield Road (map 2-25) stalled the right wing of Perrin's attack. Just as Colonel Fry had done shortly before (map 2-24), Brig. Gen. James H. Lane made a supporting advance in this sector (maps 2-24 and 2-25) and skirmished with troopers from Gamble's 1st Brigade of Buford's 1st Cavalry Division. Gamble's troopers had withdrawn to the south of Gettysburg after their morning fight, but they now returned to this westward sector. Half of these cavalrymen dismounted to form a protective force on the left wing of the army's overall line. This move threatened Lane's flank, making him wary of its security and slowing his advance. By the time Lane's foot soldiers approached Seminary Ridge, Perrin had helped cleared the area of Federal infantry defenders (map 2-26) with his left wing's attack against Federal infantry on Seminary Ridge and his right's advance against Gamble's position. One consequence of these components of the July 1 action (Perrin vs. Biddle and Gamble, as depicted on map 2-25) was that General Lane reported no casualties on this day of the battle. These apparently stray details are significant because Lane's brigade was the *only unbloodied rebel unit,* from the fighting on July 1, on the entire left wing of Pickett's Charge two days later (see Chapter 4).

56. Cutler's Union troops (the first such infantrymen to arrive on the field during the midmorning) were still in this vicinity (map 2-21) and were pushed off the field as well. These 1st Corps soldiers and those in Baxter's and Paul's brigades were unable to resist Daniel's and Ramseur's assaults—which were augmented by reformed elements of O'Neal's and Iverson's shattered brigades—in part because these Federals had no support from their flanks. There was too much pressure on the Union left at this time from 3rd Corps Confederates south of the Cashtown Road and from Early's 2nd Corps rebels attacking the Union right north of Gettysburg.

57. For example, as Barlow was pushed back and to his left, this uncovered Ames's right flank and forced his withdrawal under combined pressure from Gordon, Hays, and Avery (map 2-21). Schimmelfennig's command, which was farther to the left, thus became isolated. However, before the Union retreat became pell-mell, the advances of Avery and Hays were delayed. Von Steinwehr's 1st Brigade, led by Col. Charles R. Coster (charts 2-5 and 2-11) made a counterattack and stand. General Schurz, still the overall commander of the outlying 11th Corps defenders, asked General Howard to send reinforcements when Schurz observed rebels approaching his right along the Harrisburg Road (map 2-22). After two or three such requests, Howard grudgingly detached Coster's brigade from his Cemetery Hill defense (map 2-15) and sent it forward to a point just above Stevens Run near the northern edge of Gettysburg (map 2-23, top) to support Schurz. The reinforcers arrived just as Barlow was being crushed out on the 11th Corps's right flank. Coster, too, soon came under severe pressure from two directions when Avery and Hays attacked (chart 2-11). Coster's command held out long enough for Ames to withdraw in some order (map 2-22) from what had been his forward and threatened position (map 2-21). The reinforcing support and delay achieved (at least modestly) by Coster came at a heavy price in that he lost 550 men from his unit, about the same number of casualties suffered by each of Barlow's brigades.

58. The worst losses for an Iron Brigade regiment at Gettysburg, 363 of 496, were suffered by the 24th Michigan (map 2-10, chart 2-9). Some members of the Iron Brigade remained in the Union army until the war ended, and this unit remained on the rolls until that time. But a succession of replacements (draftees from the East)

resulted in the Iron Brigade's losing its distinctly western identity and praiseworthy qualities.

59. The following example is most instructive in this regard: After the 6th Wisconsin (of railroad cut fame) retreated from Seminary Ridge through the streets of Gettysburg, it "hurried on" south of the town. "Finally its men saw 'the colors of the Union, floating over well ordered lines of men in blue, who were arrayed along the slope of Cemetery Hill.' It was the 73rd Ohio of Col. Orlando Smith's brigade, von Steinwehr's division. The brigade's presence and its flags raised the spirits of the retreating troops" (Pfanz, *First Day*, p. 330).

60. David M. Jordan, *Winfield Scott Hancock: A Soldier's Life* (Bloomington: Indiana University Press, 1988), pp. 2–3, 317. Moreover, like the late General Reynolds, Hancock certainly looked the part: "Conscious of his handsome appearance, he was mindful of his dress and bearing.... Soldiers liked this trait" (Glenn Tucker, *Hancock, The Superb* [Indianapolis: Bobbs-Merrill, 1960], p. 70). Both Jordan and Tucker suggest that Hancock's physically commanding appearance helped steady Union nerves during the late afternoon of July 1 (*Winfield Scott Hancock*, p. 83; *Hancock*, p. 123). By analogy, Robert Krick has said that Maj. Gen. Robert Rodes—who of course figured prominently earlier in the July 1 story—ranks "among the best division commanders in an army full of famous ... men." This historian went on to say that "perhaps his appeal grew in part from a striking martial appearance; a member of Jeb Stuart's staff called Rodes and Pender [more about the latter below] 'the most splendid looking soldiers of the war'" ("Three Confederate Disasters," p. 115).

61. That place (shown on maps 1-13, 1-18, and 1-20) involved a contingency plan of General Meade calling for the establishment of a defensive line along Pipe Creek in the event the concentrating rebels began advancing south before the Army of the Potomac caught up with the Confederates in Pennsylvania. General Meade had sent his artillery chief, Brig. Gen. Henry J. Hunt (see Chapter 3), to reconnoiter northern Maryland on June 30. Hunt found a twenty-mile-long line of high ground behind Pipe Creek that would serve as a superb defensive position, including "a nearly perfect ... artillery platform" (Shultz and Rollins, "'A Combined and Concentrated Fire,'" p. 49).

62. The Hancock-Howard controversy—about who should have commanded the coalescing defense as the evening of July 1 approached—is labored over by Harry Pfanz, who points out that Meade knew Hancock better than Howard, could trust the latter in a crisis, and felt that Hancock could best represent him (Meade) on the field (*First Day*, pp. 337–39).

63. Warren W. Hassler Jr., *Crisis at the Crossroads: The First Day at Gettysburg* (Tuscaloosa: University of Alabama Press, 1970). Given "the petty side of Howard" that manifested itself in this dispute between the two generals, Hassler perhaps goes overboard by writing that "Hancock and Howard worked side by side in a firm spirit of mutual cooperation" (ibid., p. 136).

64. As 1st and 11th Corp troops retreated to this vicinity and joined their mates already in place on the two hills just south of town, approximately seven thousand Federal soldiers occupied Cemetery Hill and the western slope of Culp's Hill (Pfanz, *First Day*, p. 333). That force, even without the reinforcements that soon began to arrive, was potentially formidable enough to repel Ewell's bloodied brigades had they attacked these Union positions. Moreover, "at the retreat's end" there were "twenty-two guns of the two corps [11th and 1st] in the cemetery, and ... twenty-three on East Cemetery Hill and Stevens Knoll [map 2-27 (the latter position rises from the saddle between Cemetery and Culp's Hills)]. All were amply supplied with ammunition from the Eleventh Corps train" (ibid., p. 335). Hancock himself had ordered Capt. Greenleaf T. Stevens's 5th Maine Light Battery (from the 1st Corps's Artillery Brigade) to occupy the knoll that came to bear his name.

65. Ibid., p. 339.

66. Five months after the battle, he reported that "my own two divisions [were] exhausted by six hours' hard fighting, [so] prudence led me to be content with what had been gained, and not push forward troops necessarily disordered, probably to encounter fresh troops of the enemy" (*OR*, pt. 2, p. 607). Timidly "prudent" or spot on?—even though Hill would not have been specifically aware of the "fresh troops" manning Cemetery Hill.

67. General Hill merely ordered a brigade and a battery from Anderson's division to guard the army's right by taking up a position a mile or more to the west of McPherson Ridge. At this time, General Lee ratified Hill's passivity by reporting "that the four divisions present were weakened and exhausted" (Pfanz, *First Day*, p. 320).

68. Anderson's troops were approximately at Belmont Schoolhouse Ridge (map 2-6) by late afternoon, not very far (westward) from the action that led to the Union retreat roughly down the Cashtown Road toward Gettysburg. See Coddington, *Gettysburg Campaign*, p. 316.

69. *OR*, pt. 2, p. 318 (General Lee's report, Jan. 1864). The officer who carried the message from Lee to Ewell was Maj. Walter H. Taylor, who recorded this oral transmission of orders in *General Lee, His Campaigns in Virginia, 1861–1865, With Personal Reminiscences* (Brooklyn: Brounworth, 1906), p. 190.

70. Gallagher, "Confederate Corps Leadership," p. 34. Trimble's claim about how well aware he was of the value and vulnerability of Culp's Hill was written in 1883. Another Confederate general (Harry Hays), who led a brigade in Maj. Gen. Jubal Early's 2nd Corps division, also supposedly urged his commander "to strike Culp's Hill with his entire Division" (ibid., p. 35). Yet, if General *Ewell* were to have ordered an assault on this hill, what he had in mind was to bring up his missing division—that of Maj. Gen. Edward Johnson, who was struggling to reach the battlefield from up the Cashtown Road (map 2-16 above). Johnson had "ridden ahead and met with Ewell and Early" to discuss Ewell's hope that "Johnson should occupy Culp's Hill in order to threaten the Union right and rear on Cemetery Hill." But General Johnson's trailing brigade did not arrive until just before darkness—"two hours or more after" Ewell had been told "that the division was an hour away and would soon be up" (Pfanz, *First Day*, pp. 346–47).

71. Federal guns positioned on Stevens's Knoll, an outcropping of Culp's Hill (map 2-27), came into play on July 2. However, the bulk of the high ground on and around Culp's Hill is not a good artillery platform.

72. For example, "the men of Gordon's brigade [in Early's 2nd Corps division (chart 2-8)] were 'much fatigued' when they reached the field" (Pfanz, *First Day*, p. 239).

73. During the afternoon of July 1, Johnson's division was bottled up on the Chambersburg Pike (map 2-28). Johnson's division and the 2nd Corps's supply wagons were the first 2nd Corps elements to arrive in the Gettysburg vicinity. This occurred in conjunction with the rebel army's efforts to concentrate near Cashtown, where General Lee thought he might engage the Army of the Potomac as it proceeded into southern Pennsylvania. Johnson's division was unable to extricate itself from the traffic jam west of Gettysburg and rendezvous with the rest of the 2nd Corps until dusk. This late arrival of Ewell's third division was another factor influencing his decision not to renew an attack on the Federal force forming south of the town (also see note 70).

74. Some of the Union men approaching Gettysburg at this

time, members of Brig. Gen. Alpheus S. Williams's 12th Corps division, got as far as Benner's Hill near the Hanover Road (map 2-29). They never actually threatened General Ewell's left flank on July 1 because they withdrew from this region (which is due east of the town) toward the Baltimore Pike (map 2-29), where Williams's men spent the night.

75. In fact, a staff officer from Brig. Gen. William Smith's brigade—an element of Early's 2nd Corps division that had not been engaged thus far on July 1—breathlessly reported to General Early, "a large Federal force was approaching over the York Pike against Ewell's left flank." The division commander sent another of his brigades, John B. Gordon's, to support Smith. However, "in doing this he seriously reduced Ewell's ability to capture Cemetery Hill" (Pfanz, *First Day,* pp. 343–44).

76. Lee had by now informed Ewell "he would get no help from Hill and Longstreet" (the latter had specified that his leading 1st Corps division was six miles away), even though "he wished him [Ewell] to take Cemetery Hill if possible" (ibid., p. 345).

77. This recapitulates an e-mail exchange between the author and Michael A. Palmer (June 2–22, 1998) about Ewell's performance during the campaign. Additional aspects of this issue are discussed elsewhere in the main text, based on Alan T. Nolan's analysis in "R. E. Lee and July 1," pp. 25–28. His essay includes details of the Union strengths on Cemetery and Culp's Hills and the difficulties Ewell faced in organizing a force to assault those positions.

78. Stephen W. Sears, *Chancellorsville* (Boston: Houghton Mifflin, 1996), pp. 420–22.

79. Richard A. Sauers, *A Caspian Sea of Ink: The Meade-Sickles Controversy* (Baltimore: Butternut and Blue, 1989). The Pipe Creek element of this controversy is discussed throughout Sauers's book.

80. Words supposedly uttered at Antietam (September 17, 1862) by one of McClellan's corps commanders, Maj. Gen. Fitz John Porter: "Remember, General, I command the last reserve of . . ." (Jacob D. Cox, "The Battle of Antietam," in *Battles and Leaders of the Civil War,* ed. Robert U. Johnson and Clarence C. Buel, vol. 2 [Secaucus, N.J.: Castle, 1888], p. 656). This remark helped McClellan convince himself that he should *not* commit that Army of the Potomac's reserve at one of the moments during the Maryland battle when doing so might have shattered Lee's army.

81. The 12th Corps ended up being to the right and north, forming the principal occupying force on Culp's Hill (see Chapter 3).

82. "When word of the capture of Chancellorsville reached him, General Lee rode toward the day's final battlefield [this was near the middle of the May 3 theater of battle (map 3-9)]. His was a mile-long cavalcade of triumph. . . . Beyond any doubt it was the greatest moment Robert E. Lee had experienced in his military life" (Sears, *Chancellorsville,* p. 365).

Chapter 3
July 2: The Climax of the Battle

1. Harry W. Pfanz analyzes Captain Johnston's scouting mission and whether his "incorrect report to his commanding general . . . was to have serious consequences later in the day" in *Gettysburg: The Second Day,* p. 107. Pfanz is as puzzled as anyone as to "why . . . Johnston and Clarke [saw] no Federal troops in the Little Round Top area" (p. 107). Thomas A. Desjardin, an expert on activities revolving around Little Round Top, put forth the hypothesis that these two Confederate officers might never have reached that hill (map 3-2). In Captain Johnston's words: "When I thought I had gone far enough, I turned back" (Johnston to Lafayette McLaws, June 27, 1892, Container 173, Civil War Sources and Photostats III, Douglas Southall Freeman Papers, Manuscripts Division, Library of Congress, Washington, D.C.).

2. Longstreet's other division, commanded by Maj. Gen. George E. Pickett, was not on the battlefield. Pickett's command was about twenty-five miles away at Chambersburg, destroying railroad tracks. General Pickett was ordered to advance toward Gettysburg on the evening of July 1, and his division began to do so in the wee hours of the Second.

3. Note that Ewell's 2nd Corps was already in position to participate as just described because his troops had ended up in, just below, and to the east of Gettysburg as a result of the first day's fight. Moreover, Ewell's extreme left, commanded by Maj. Gen. Edward Johnson, had swung around clockwise, nearly overlapping the Union right (map 3-5). Recall that Johnson's division was not engaged on July 1 because it had become intermingled with Confederate 3rd Corps units on the Cashtown Road.

4. Shultz and Rollins, "'Combined and Concentrated Fire,'" p. 52.

5. Pfanz, *Second Day,* pp. 25–27.

6. This logistical problem, and several others that would have confronted Lee had he "maneuver[ed] the army to the right beyond the Round Tops around Meade's left flank as . . . Longstreet proposed," are discussed by Scott Bowden and Bill Ward in "Last Chance for Victory," *North & South* 4, no. 3 (Mar. 2001): pp. 78–81. To highlight these problems, the authors point out that "one only need read Major General Lafayette McLaws' narrative [*Southern Historical Society Papers* 7, p. 69] of the difficulties he encountered moving his Southern division from the Hagerstown [Fairfield] Road southward to Pitzer's Schoolhouse (west of lower Seminary Ridge [map 3-8]) to get a rough idea of the difficulty Lee would have faced moving the entire Confederate army across country to get around the right of Meades's forces."

7. Bowden and Ward discuss several "consideration[s] driving Lee's decision to attack on July 2." They include: maintaining the initiative in order to avoid a defensive stalemate (which would not "further his vision for victory or the cause of Southern independence"); that the "relative strengths" of the two armies "might never be closer than on July 1–2" (the rebels had more than decimated two Federal corps on the first of day of the battle, and Meade's army was deemed not yet thoroughly concentrated on the Second); and "the confidence of the Confederate soldier within the Army of Northern Virginia was arguably at its zenith." Thus, in Lee's mind, "there was only one *realistic* course of action possible for July 2, 1863, that was consistent with every principle of war that applied—a resumption of the offensive. That conclusion was consistent with his combative and audacious character" ("Last Chance for Victory," pp. 81–84; emphasis in the original).

8. William G. Piston, "Cross Purposes: Longstreet, Lee, and the Confederate Attack Plans for July 3 at Gettysburg," in *The Third Day at Gettysburg and Beyond,* ed. Gary W. Gallagher (Chapel Hill: University of North Carolina Press, 1994), p. 33.

9. Ibid., p. 39. See also Jeffry D. Wert, 1998. "'No Fifteen Thousand Men Can Take That Position': Longstreet at Gettysburg," in *James Longstreet: The Man, the Soldier, the Controversy,* ed. Richard L. DiNardo and Albert A. Nofi (Conshohocken, Pa.: Combined Books, 1998), p. 96, n12.

10. These pseudo-quotes paraphrase several components of Longstreet's postwar writings, which are actually quoted or referred to by Piston and Wert (see preceding note).

11. Long, Lee's military secretary, was "one of those present [with the commander and Longstreet]. Years later [1886] Long wrote that Longstreet advocated turning the Union left to force the enemy from his position" (Pfanz, *Second Day,* p. 26).

12. Gen. James Longstreet, "Lee in Pennsylvania," in *Annals of*

the War, ed. Arthur K. McClure (1879; reprint, Edison, N.J.: Blue and Grey, 1996), p. 414. Did Longstreet embellish the letter quoted in this article? Robert K. Krick is one contemporary analyst who would probably answer in the affirmative. (See his "'If Longstreet . . . Says So, It Is Most Likely Not True': James Longstreet and the Second Day at Gettysburg," in *The Second Day at Gettysburg: Essays on Confederate and Union Leadership,* ed. Gary W. Gallagher [Kent, Ohio: Kent State University Press, 1993], pp. 57–86.)

13. Piston, "Longstreet, Lee," p. 40.

14. E. Porter Alexander, *Military Memoirs of a Confederate: A Critical Narrative* (New York: Charles Scribner's Sons, 1907), p. 391.

15. William Swinton, *Army of the Potomac* (1866; reprint, New York: Konecky and Konecky, 1995); the quotes are from p. 340 (emphasis in original).

16. Brig. Gen. G. Moxley Sorrel, C.S.A., *Recollections of a Confederate Staff Officer,* ed. Bell I. Wiley (Jackson, Tenn.: McCowat-Mercer Press, 1959), p. 157. An analogous description of General Longstreet's demeanor was made in a description of a dispute he had with General Lee on July 2. It concerned the placement of Maj. Gen. Lafayette McLaws's division for the attack on the Federal left. McLaws was a party to this wrangling and noted that Longstreet was "irritated and annoyed"—or so the former division commander said in an 1879 article (William G. Piston, *Lee's Tarnished Lieutenant: James Longstreet and his Place in Southern History* [Athens: University of Georgia Press, 1987], pp. 54, 231).

17. See, for example, Piston, *Lee's Tarnished Lieutenant,* pp. 53–58.

18. This story is told by Ward in "'Sedgewick's Foot Cavalry,'" pp. 59–65. In the wee hours of July 2, Sedgwick sent a courier to Meade promising that the 6th Corps, then in the vicinity of Westminster, Maryland, would reach Gettysburg by 4 P.M. The 6th Corps troops trudged relentlessly in a northwesterly direction, having to march more than thirty miles because they were rerouted along the way (map 2-28). A number of soldiers straggled or needed medical attention. In the early afternoon, the bulk of the corps reached a location five-six miles from the battlefield after having marched "without meaningful rest for more than fifteen hours" (ibid., p. 63). Sedgwick halted the march briefly, but at "4 o'clock, the vanguard of the long column reached the vicinity of Rock Creek (map 3-7), the march was completed, . . . and the Sixth Corps [was] prompt to the hour" (one of Sedgwick's soldiers, quoted ibid., p. 64).

19. Piston, "Longstreet, Lee," p. 47; Wert, "'No Fifteen Thousand Men,'" p. 92.

20. Time was not so much of the essence for the Confederate 3rd Corps units: Anderson's and Pender's divisions had relatively short distances to march to get into position below Cashtown Road, and they did so early in the afternoon.

21. Lee's remarks were written to the Governor of Maryland, John Lee Carroll, in the late 1860s (quoted in Margaret Sanborn, *Robert E. Lee: The Complete Man (1861–1870),* Philadelphia: J. B. Lippincott, p. 127).

22. Jeffry D. Wert, *General James Longstreet: The Confederacy's Most Controversial Soldier—A Biography* (New York: Simon and Schuster, 1993; rpt. New York: Touchstone, 1994), p. 269.

23. Earlier in the morning on July 2, Colonel Alexander had been "specially cautioned to keep all movements carefully out of view of a signal station whose flags we could see wig-wagging on Little Round Top." He achieved this by turning right (away from the lane that extends south of Fairfield Road [map 3-8]), then "going through fields & hollows" (Gary W. Gallagher, ed., *Fighting for the Confederacy: The Personal Recollections of General Edward Porter Alexander* [Chapel Hill: University of North Carolina Press, 1989], pp. 235–36). These Confederate artillery pieces seem not to have been spotted by Union signalmen as they approached their temporary destination, arriving there much earlier than did Longstreet's divisions, then waiting for the infantry near the schoolhouse. One wonders (as did Jeffry D. Wert in *General James Longstreet,* p. 270) whether the rainy days of late June would not have sufficiently softened the ground to cause the wheels of Alexander's and Eshelman's batteries to make obvious ruts along their route—thus suggesting to the infantry a much better alternative to the long countermarch.

24. The continuation of this avenue is now called Wheatfield Road where it courses eastward of the Emmitsburg Road. At the junction of these two roadways was a peach orchard (map 3-8), part of the Sherfy farm. This grove of trees was three times larger in 1863 than the partial replica that still stands.

25. Pfanz, *Second Day,* pp. 150–54; Wert, *General James Longstreet,* pp. 270–74. The arguments between Longstreet and McLaws were a resumption of the disagreement they had earlier in the afternoon (note 16).

26. These men were members of Brig. Gen. J. H. Hobart Ward's 3rd Corps brigade. However, the sharpshooters, led by the blustery Col. Hiram Berdan, reported directly to Ward's superior, Maj. Gen. David Birney. Ward had asked Birney for permission to reconnoiter his front and detached a hundred riflemen from the 1st U.S. Infantry along with the 3rd Maine. When they eventually fell back (having "discovered" what was then the right flank of the Confederate force deployed below the Fairfield Road [map 3-3, chart 3-4]), they did not join with Ward's brigade in the fight for Houck's Ridge. Later, another group of "Berdan's Sharpshooters" (albeit formally under the regimental commander, Maj. Homer R. Stoughton) would advance as a scouting party on a more southerly sector of the field. These men were from the 2nd U.S. Sharpshooter Regiment and would figure in the rebels' advance toward the Round Tops and the battle that occurred on and near Little Round Top (map 3-15).

27. Led in part by Maj. Gen. J. E. B. Stuart, who had assumed command of the wounded Jackson's corps on May 3 (map 3-9).

28. Several students of the Gettysburg campaign have mused about the Hazel Grove/July 2 connection. The idea struck me during an April 19, 1996, conversation with Prof. Kent Gramm of Wheaton College in Illinois. Later, I discovered that this hypothesis might fall under the heading of conventional wisdom about Gettysburg. Richard Sauers, for example, refers to several previous writers who have espoused it. See Sauers, *A Caspian Sea of Ink,* pp. 147–48, and William Glenn Robertson, "The Peach Orchard Revisited: Daniel E. Sickles and the Third Corps on July 2, 1863," in Gallagher, ed., *Second Day at Gettysburg,* pp. 40, 48. By the way, you can go to Hazel Grove to get an appreciation of what that high ground is like with respect to the pulled-back Union positions to the north on May 3, 1963. However, you should move fast: only shards of the old Chancellorsville battlefield remain because Virginians are developing the site into oblivion.

29. Sauers, *A Caspian Sea of Ink,* pp. 63, 95.

30. This piece of military jargon describes the part of a position that juts out from the overall line of men and artillery. Such a salient might seem to be a pugnacious menace to a line of putative attackers, but it also is vulnerable to assault from two sides. If breakthroughs occur near the base of a salient, on either or both wings, the attackers are in a position to isolate and destroy the outward projecting defenders.

31. As the Union 3rd Corps moved west to its new position, Capt. George E. Randolph, commander of that corps's artillery brigade (chart 3-6), placed one of his batteries a fair distance east of

the Emmitsburg Road. When the Confederate guns opened up on the 3rd Corps between 3:30 and 4 P.M., presaging the rebel infantry attack, Captain Randolph rode to the artillery park (map 3-7) and asked Brig. Gen. Robert O. Tyler, the Artillery Reserve commander, for reinforcements. Tyler ordered Colonel McGilvery, who commanded one of the Reserve's brigades (chart 3-6), to hurry fresh batteries westward. One of them was the 9th Massachusetts Light Artillery (chart 3-6), a memorable unit of volunteer artillerymen (see the section of this chapter ending with the phrase "Fighting Withdrawals Large and Small").

32. Calling these attacks "right hooks" oversimplifies somewhat, but elements of the advancing Confederates circled counterclockwise, as does a pugilist's punch of the same name. Initiating its advance due east from Warfield's Ridge (map 3-12), the rebel right ended up hitting Birney's positions from the south and west (map 3-13).

33. Some of his 2nd Division soldiers were attached to Graham's 1st Brigade over in the Peach Orchard salient (see below, chart 3-22). Additional regiments from Humphreys's division, in particular those from his 3rd Brigade, fought with de Trobriand on the Stony Hill (map 3-25, charts 3-18 and 3-19).

34. U.S. Congress, *Joint Committee on the Conduct of the War: Report of the Second Session, 38th Congress,* vol. 1 (Washington, D.C.: Government Printing Office, 1865), p. 331.

35. Pfanz, *Second Day,* p. 152.

36. This is an enigmatic phrase from McPherson's *Battle Cry of Freedom* (p. 657), in which the author alludes to the possibility that the redeployment of Sickles's corps redounded to the eventual benefit of the Federals. This hypothesis is elaborated later in Chapter 3.

37. On at least two occasions in the late afternoon, Lee rode down from his headquarters northwest of Gettysburg to the middle region of southern Seminary Ridge (Piston, *Lee's Tarnished Lieutenant,* p. 98; Wert, *General James Longstreet,* p. 272; Pfanz, *Second Day,* p. 355). However, he exercised little authority over the details of the rapidly evolving changes in the tactical situation.

38. John B. Hood to James Longstreet, June 28, 1875, *Southern Historical Society Papers* 4 (1877): pp. 149–50. Hood also repeated this quote of Longstreet—which he said had repeatedly been transmitted to him from his commander on July 2—in his memoirs. See John B. Hood, *Advance and Retreat: Personal Experiences in the United States and Confederate States Armies* (Philadelphia: Burke and McFetridge, 1880), p. 58.

39. Pfanz, *Second Day,* p. 165.

40. The Union batteries in question were in the vicinity of the Peach Orchard (map 3-10) and also east of there. They included the guns of Smith and his New Yorkers at the southern end of General Ward's line (map 3-10). Recall that this defined the Army of the Potomac's extreme left at this time.

41. Compare Gettysburg to the battlefield south of Waterloo, Belgium, for example. If you stand in the middle of the ridge up which the French kept attacking from the south, you can take in practically the entire field—where the number of soldiers who fought on that Sunday in 1815 was similar to the forces battling in southern Pennsylvania forty-eight years later.

42. Gary E. Adelman and Timothy H. Smith, *Devil's Den: A History and Guide* (Gettysburg: Thomas Publications, 1997), p. 28. General Law was probably near the right of the assault force during the early stages of its advance, about the time that the commander of his division was wounded and taken from the field (Morris M. Penny and J. Gary Laine, *Struggle for the Round Tops: Law's Alabama Brigade at the Battle of Gettysburg* [Shippensburg, Pa.: Burd Street Press, 1999], p. 42). During the later stages of the action on July 2, Law spent most of his time in the vicinity of the Devil's Den (ibid., p. 61). This is difficult to know, however, because General Law provided no after-action report (at least there is none in the *Official Records*).

43. No one knows for sure when General Law became aware he was responsible for three brigades in addition to his own (Penny and Laine, *Struggle for the Round Tops,* p. 42). Law also delayed telling Col. James L. Sheffield of the 48th Alabama that he was placing Sheffield in charge of the Alabama Brigade. General Robertson, commander of the Texas Brigade, did not learn until late that Law assumed command of the division, forcing Robertson to communicate directly with General Longstreet (ibid., p. 61). In fact, none of the Confederate officers in that sector of the battlefield received orders from General Law until the fighting essentially ended (Adelman and Smith, *Devil's Den,* p. 28).

44. Joshua L. Chamberlain, "Through Blood & Fire at Gettysburg," *Hearst Magazine,* June 1913, pp. 12–13. Although Colonel Chamberlain did not know it, he was staring at some of his former Bowdoin College students serving in the 4th Maine. Colonels Chamberlain and Rice probably walked out of the tree cover where the right of the 83rd Pennsylvania was placed on Little Round Top (map 3-17) by its former commander, Col. Strong Vincent, leader of the brigade that had dashed up the hill (see chart 3-13).

45. How tough was it in terms of casualties inflicted on Oates's men by these Union marksmen? This is not known in the particular, but the question leads to a more general one about the meaning of the word *sharpshooters:* How effective were such men and their weapons? This further feature of the problems with Civil War arms is dealt with in Appendix G.

46. W. C. Ward, "Incidents and Personal Experiences on the Battlefield at Gettysburg," *Confederate Veteran* 8 (1900): p. 347. Ward was a private in one of Brig. Gen. Evander Law's regiments, the 4th Alabama.

47. William C. Oates, *The War Between the Union and the Confederacy and its Lost Opportunities* (New York: Neale, 1905), p. 212.

48. Ibid. That General Law sent this man (his assistant adjutant general, Capt. Leigh R. Terrell) to Colonel Oates indicates that Law *was* exercising a measure of control over the fighting as it unfolded and underwent changes throughout the late afternoon (see notes 42 and 43).

49. Sauers, *A Caspian Sea of Ink,* pp. 62, 64, 131.

50. Capt. James S. Hall of the Signal Corps sent this message at 1:30 P.M. See J. W. Brown, *The Signal Corps, U.S.A., in the War of the Rebellion* (Boston: U.S. Veteran Signal Corps Association, 1896), p. 361. Given the long distance between their vantage point and the area of the countermarch, Hall and his men probably could not discern sufficient details of the Confederates' route and mistakenly concluded that a major enemy force was moving toward Cemetery and Culp's Hills.

51. A. T. Cowell, *Tactics at Gettysburg: As Described by Participants in the Battle* (Gettysburg: Compiler, 1910), p. 48.

52. This contrasts with the manner by which General Lee initially got word to General Ewell about the advisability of the latter assaulting Cemetery Hill on the evening of July 1. It was then that Maj. Walter H. Taylor, a member of Lee's small group of comparatively low-ranking staff officers, delivered the "if practicable" message to Ewell.

53. This quote and the one in the following paragraph are in a letter from Gouverneur K. Warren to a former captain in the 140th New York (which was in the second of the Union brigades that eventually manned Little Round Top), dated July 13, 1872. The

letter has been reprinted several times. See, for example, Oliver W. Norton, *The Attack and Defense of Little Round Top, Gettysburg, July 2, 1863* (New York: Neale, 1913), pp. 308–11. Norton was a private in the 83rd Pennsylvania, part of Col. Strong Vincent's Brigade.

54. For instance, the 1872 yarn about gun barrels "glistening" rings false because the positions of Warren, the Confederate infantrymen, and the sun were wrong in the late afternoon (Desjardin, *Legends of Gettysburg*, p. 7). The U.S. Signal Corps historian said after the war that it was Captain Hall on Little Round Top who, "at 3:30 P.M. on the 2nd, discovered the enemy was massing upon Gen. Sickles's left" (Brown, *Signal Corps*, p. 365). A former Union Signal Corps officer who was not at Gettysburg published this account thirty-three years after the battle. Nevertheless, the author expressed both annoyance and sarcasm about Warren's story: "It was Capt. Hall's announcement that the enemy were moving around Sickles's left that brought Gen. Warren to Little Round Top. . . . Capt. Hall found it very difficult to convince Gen. Warren that the enemy's infantry and artillery were there concealed. While the discussion was in progress the enemy opened on the station. The first shell burst close to the station, and the general, a moment later, was wounded in the neck. Capt. Hall then exclaimed, 'Now do you see them?'" (p. 367).

55. McClellan was the lone staff officer there. It was he who warned General Stuart about the impending advance of Federal cavalry from the south. See Appendix A and map A-3 therein.

56. The standard view regarding Vincent's contribution to Federal fortunes on July 2 was recently ratified by James R. Wright, "'I Will Take the Responsibility': Strong Vincent Moves to Little Round Top: Fact or Fiction?" *Gettysburg* no. 25 (July 2001): pp. 48–60. A key piece of evidence cited by Wright is a letter written in 1888 by Oliver W. Norton (see note 53), long a postwar chronicler of Vincent's actions on July 2. The letter describes how Colonel Vincent indeed took "the responsibility" on his own, absent any communications from General Warren or Brig. Gen. James Barnes (Vincent's division commander). However, Thomas A. Desjardin is not quite so sure about Norton's reliability as a source regarding these events (*From These Honored Dead*, chap. 2: "Infirm Foundations," forthcoming Oct. 2003). As Desjardin would have it, "Norton was inherently and extremely biased toward the story of . . . a man [Vincent] for whom he obviously held great esteem." Moreover, by the time Norton published his book (cited in note 53), in which "he described in heroic detail the actions of Colonel Vincent," he "had been blind for many years" and was very "frail" (Desjardin, *From These Honored Dead*, chap. 2). Wright counters Desjardin by quoting an 1872 letter written by Warren in which Meade's former staff officer corroborates Norton's 1888 account ("'I Will Take the Responsibility,'" p. 57). Unfortunately, no additional material that might have been left by key leaders in the battle for Little Round Top has thus far surfaced. Moreover, there is little likelihood any will: Colonel Vincent was mortally wounded during that fight and his successor—Col. James C. Rice, commander of the 44th New York (note 44) before Vincent was shot—was killed in action in Virginia ten months later. Rice's after-action reports for Gettysburg (July 31 and August 14, 1863, *OR*, part 1, pp. 616–20, 621–22) make no mention of who diverted his brigade from its westward reinforcing move to Little Round Top. Two of the brigade's four regiments were the 44th New York and 20th Maine, alluded to above and indicated on map 3-16 (also see notes 44 and 59).

57. Thomas A. Desjardin forcefully argues this thesis in *Stand Firm Ye Boys from Maine: The 20th Maine and the Gettysburg Campaign* (Gettysburg: Thomas Publications, 1995), which is the source for much of the Little Round Top story as recounted here.

58. The Michiganders had initially been placed on the brigade's left but were soon shifted to the other end of Vincent's line (map 3-19). The 20th Maine made its way toward its position by using a logging trail, part of which is depicted in map 3-19.

59. Just before this fighting started, the aforementioned Colonels Chamberlain and Rice somehow found time to leave their regiments (the 20th Maine and 44th New York, respectively) and join each other at the summit, where they observed the crisis unfolding in Plum Run Valley and on Houck's Ridge above it (Chamberlain, "Through Blood & Fire," pp. 12–13).

60. The 15th Alabama suffered an additional noncombat loss: As Colonel Oates's men moved off Big Round Top toward the smaller hill (map 3-13), he thought he saw Union supply wagons in the vicinity and detached Company A of the 15th to capture them. This did not occur. Instead, this ill-conceived mission cost Oates some three dozen attackers, in addition to the twenty-two men sent off to search for water as the advance began.

61. This is diagrammed in map 2-21. Recall from the previous chapter that, even if Barlow had deployed his men on the Federal right in an intrinsically powerful L or V arrangement near the Harrisburg Road, they were badly outnumbered when the rebel left wing hit them on Wednesday afternoon.

62. As described in Appendix B. Captain Morrill was involved in the Loudoun Valley fighting (chart B-4), supporting the advancing Union cavalry brigades in conjunction with the culmination of the actions that took place in that Virginia valley during June (map B-4).

63. The green 20th Maine was at Antietam but did not go into battle there (September 1862). Subsequently Chamberlain, these Mainers, or both were briefly engaged at Fredericksburg (December 1862) and at Chancellorsville (May 1863); see also note 66. At one point during the latter battle, near the fringes of the main fighting on May 4, Chamberlain had his horse shot out from under him but was unhurt.

64. During the fighting on Little Round Top two months after Chancellorsville, Colonel Chamberlain was battered about and slightly wounded in both legs. Yet, "as the fight continued he stoically demonstrated his own confidence, walking calmly among his men." His demonstration of "personal bravery and coolness in the fight . . . did more for victory on the spur than the legend ever recorded" (Desjardin, *Stand Firm*, p. 155).

65. Rev. Theodore Gerrish, *Army Life: A Private's Reminiscences of the Civil War* (Portland, Maine: Hoyt, Fogg, and Donham, 1882), pp. 107–108. Gerrish was a private in the 20th Maine, and his would-be diary includes a stirring account of the battle for Little Round Top. However, Thomas Desjardin ferreted out regimental and hospital records in the National Archives revealing that Gerrish was in a hospital in Philadelphia at the time of Gettysburg. See John J. Pullen, *Joshua Chamberlain: A Hero's Life and Legacy* (Mechanicsburg, Pa.: Stackpole, 1999), p. 137. Thus, Gerrish's account about "fighting against at least ten times [the 20th Maine's] number" cannot be taken seriously. For his part, Chamberlain claimed in 1913 (see *Through Blood and Fire at Gettysburg*), and perhaps believed until the end of his life in 1914, that the 15th Alabama on Little Round top "buffeted [the 20th Maine] back and forth by superior force" (p. 19); and, even after the initial waves of the Alabamians' attacks, that they "still [had] more than twice our numbers" (p. 21).

66. The 20th Maine had been bolstered back in May by elements of the otherwise disbanded 2nd Maine as a part of a significant reorganization of the Army of the Potomac that occurred after Chancellorsville, in part because many two-year enlistments ran out. It is perhaps worth noting that the approximately one hundred men from the 2nd Maine *did* have significant combat experience

before Gettysburg (see note 63). The regimental strength chiseled into the 20th Maine's monument on Vincent's Spur is an underestimate—possibly a deliberate one (Desjardin, *Stand Firm*, pp. 169–84). This is but the tip of the iceberg of the current controversy and revisionism revolving around this part of the battle. One implied reason for the Little Round Top mythology that has been passed down over the years is this interesting aspect of an important primary source: Joshua L. Chamberlain's after-action report (*OR,* pt. 1, pp. 622–26, with the header "Field near Emmitsburg, July 6, 1863"). In reality, Chamberlain wrote the report in the *1880s,* when the *Official Records* were being compiled. Chamberlain's original report (unearthed from the Maine State Archives in the late 1990s by Thomas A. Desjardin) is a fifteen-hundred-word document whose terseness rings true. What he supplied to the compilers more than twenty years later was a more flowery account—a mini-memoir, really—of twenty-five hundred words. In it, Chamberlain refers repeatedly to "Little Round Top" per se. However, the hill did not take on that name until 1865 (William A. Frassanito, *Early Photography at Gettysburg* [Gettysburg: Thomas Publications, 1995], p. 245). Chamberlain's 1884 pseudo-report goes on to mention that two of his men died as a result of wounds suffered in the fighting on July 2. However, they were *still* alive on July 6 (*OR,* pt. 1, pp. 622–26) and did not succumb until July 15 and July 27, respectively.

67. "It became a rule of thumb that attacking forces must have a numerical superiority of at least three to one to succeed in carrying trenches defended by alert troops" (McPherson, *Battle Cry of Freedom,* p. 476).

68. Desjardin, *Stand Firm,* p. 189. The figures cited specify the 20th Maine's losses for both July 2 and 3, although they almost certainly occurred entirely on the former.

69. Andrea C. Hawkes et al., eds., *The Civil War Recollections of General Ellis Spear,* Orono: University of Maine Press, 1997), pp. 35–36. In contrast, Chamberlain wrote after the war about "our ammunition being totally exhausted and many of our arms unserviceable" (letter to John B. Bachelder, Mar. 10, 1884, New Hampshire Historical Society, Concord, N.H.). The last of Chamberlain's words just quoted suggest to me that these arms were fouled. The question is: Had a substantial proportion of the Maine men expended all their rounds (which was likely to have befouled their rifled muskets), or did many of their weapons become "unserviceable" after firing only one or two dozen shots? See Appendix G for more on this matter.

70. The 20th Maine's field officers were out sick or otherwise indisposed and not present at Gettysburg. Soon after that campaign, Captain Spear was promoted to major. On paper, a regiment was authorized three field-grade officers: the colonel, a lieutenant colonel, and a major. Each company was authorized a captain and a first and second lieutenant. However, the staggering attrition rates in the Civil War—which were principally the result of disease—led to severe depletions in the regimental officer cadres. By 1863, regiments were often led by lieutenant colonels, brigades by colonels, and so forth.

71. Chamberlain's would-be after-action report for Gettysburg: *OR,* pt. 3, p. 624 (see note 66).

72. Burns, *Civil War,* episode 1, "The Cause, 1861." The narrator, historian and biographer David McCullough, went on to say that Chamberlain's impromptu execution of this battlefield tactic "saved the Union army and possibly the Union itself."

73. This quote is from Chamberlain's fifteen-hundred-word account written on July 6, 1863, in which he also states that he "ordered a charge" at the culmination of the fight. However, the accounts of other participants indicate that such an order did not get transmitted to the entire regiment. See Desjardin, *Stand Firm,* pp. 69–70, 156; and Hawkes et al., eds., *Recollections of General Ellis Spear,* pp. 35–36.

74. A key primary source for this reevaluation is a letter written by Ellis Spear to John Bachelder on November 15, 1892 (New Hampshire Historical Society): "These men [to the left of the colors, which were at the apex of the V-shaped line of the Regiment] . . . were only a few feet in advance of the line and one of the men . . . said it is a 'damned shame' to leave those men out there, and proposed to his comrades to advance and cover them. Thereupon they called to their comrades up and down the line and, being pretty good men, they responded to the appeal and started. Stopping such men under the circumstances was quite another affair. I do not vouch for myself, I only say that was the talk among the men. My own recollection is simply this, I heard the shout on the right and I saw the colors move to the front, or start to move, and I joined in the shout, and the left moved at the same time, or immediately followed. This is the story, but I believe it is not wholly in accordance with the fact as related by Gen. Chamberlain, and of course what Chamberlain says must be taken as history. He says I believe that he gave the order himself, I do not know as he was farther to our right and in the uproar a single voice could not be heard. Both might be true—As for myself, I charged with the line and helped gather prisoners. That is all." Was Ellis Spear being a bit too petulant and sarcastic? Perhaps not. Desjardin has marshaled additional evidence that buttresses Spear's account (*Stand Firm,* pp. 69–71 and the map on p. 72, which is the source for map 3-21). More recently, John J. Pullen amplified Desjardin's view, citing sources that include postwar words of Chamberlain himself suggesting that "no order to charge was ever given" (*Joshua Chamberlain,* pp. 139–42). Note 88 reveals the origins of Pullen's interest in this subject.

75. "The historian of . . . [the 20th Maine] regiment claims that its charge drove us from the field. This is not true; *I ordered the retreat*" (Oates, *War Between the Union,* p. 220, emphasis in original).

76. Ibid.

77. The Maine men were not, however, able to swallow up whole the 15th Alabama. As those rebels skedaddled to the south, some were welcomed by a supporting force—the 15th's Company A (map 3-21); it had been sent earlier on the ill-conceived mission to capture Union supply wagons (map 3-20). As the charge of the 20th Maine proceeded, this Confederate company returned toward the central and northern sectors of Big Round Top, providing a buffer that helped the Alabamians' retreat from becoming a thorough-going rout.

78. Capt. Augustus P. Martin, in charge of the 5th Corps's Artillery Brigade, elements of which were moving west to join the infantry's reinforcing advance.

79. For now, register that it was not only difficult for the men to drag these guns up the hill—"it being very steep and too dangerous for horse on top"—but also that "there was only room for four guns, *so we took two of the pieces back again*" (emphasis added). This quotation is from O. W. Damon's penciled "War Diary," an unpublished document that was rewritten in ink (private collection of Thomas E. Singelyn, Grosse Pointe City, Mich.).

80. The arguable thoughtlessness of this phrase is discussed in an essay at the end of Desjardin's *Stand Firm* (see pp. 153–67).

81. The excellent high ground at Hazel Grove in the Battle of Chancellorsville (map 3-9) became a position from which *offensive* artillery fire was used by the Confederates to good effect—a rather rare occurrence in the Civil War, as will be exemplified by the events of July 3 at Gettysburg.

82. Pfanz (*Second Day,* p. 205) characterizes the Little Round Top positions as crucially anchoring the Union left. On March 5, 1864, Meade testified before the Joint Committee on the Conduct of the War: "At the same time that they threw these immense masses against General Sickles a heavy column was thrown upon the Round Top mountain [it was not called Little Round Top yet], which was the key-point of my whole position. If they had succeeded in occupying that, it would have prevented me from holding any of the ground which I subsequently held to the last" (U.S. Congress, *Joint Committee on the Conduct of the War,* p. 332). However, D. Scott Hartwig points out that Meade, "by saying [in his post-battle testimony that Little Round Top] was 'the key' to his entire position . . . strengthened the argument that Sickles had blundered by abandoning it" (Hartwig to author, Nov. 2, 1999).

83. Thomas A. Desjardin and several colleagues investigated the summit, made measurements, and determined potential angles of cannon fire—against a background of what they know about the sizes of Civil War pieces and distances of recoil. Their conclusions about the inadequacy of Little Round Top as an artillery platform are bolstered by the words of a participant in the battle (note 79) and echoed by Pfanz, *Second Day,* pp. 505–506.

84. Stephen E. Ambrose, "The Bulge," *MHQ: The Quarterly Journal of Military History* 1, no. 3 (spring 1989): p. 24.

85. His other point was more specific: Control of Elsenborn Ridge was crucial for whichever side took possession of the ground first. Like Little Round Top, that ridge in Belgium was unmanned as the opposing forces approached it. See Stephen E. Ambrose, *Citizen Soldiers: The U.S. Army from the Normandy Beaches to the Bulge to the Surrender of Germany, June 7, 1944–May 7, 1945* (New York: Simon and Schuster, 1997), p. 211.

86. Antony Beevor, *Crete: The Battle and the Resistance* (London: Penguin Books, 1991), pp. 119–28, 144–55.

87. Williamson Murray, "Crete," *MHQ: The Quarterly Journal of Military History* 3, no. 4 (summer 1991): p. 33.

88. Oates, *War Between the Union,* p. 219. Oates's "great-events/small-affairs" remark follows right on the heels of the former Confederate colonel's evaluation of the regiment he led on Vincent's Spur. Thus, Oates wrote: "There were never harder fighters than the Twentieth Maine men and their gallant Colonel. His skill and persistency and the great bravery of his men saved Little Round Top and the Army of the Potomac from defeat." The "hidden corner" phrase about Vincent's Spur is from John J. Pullen, *The Twentieth Maine: A Volunteer Regiment in the Civil War* (Philadelphia: Lippincott, 1957), p. 113. Pullen's work did more than anything to bring the 20th Maine and Joshua Chamberlain to twentieth-century prominence, with its stirring account of what the author characterized as "one of the world's decisive small-unit military actions" (ibid.).

89. Kent Gramm to author, Dec. 12, 1995. See also Kent Gramm, *Gettysburg: A Meditation on War and Values* (Bloomington: Indiana University Press, 1994), p. 117.

90. Respectively, a regiment detached from Col. George C. Burling's 3rd Brigade in Humphreys's 2nd Division, and a regiment from de Trobriand's 3rd Brigade in Birney's 1st Division, both from the 3rd Corps.

91. Bear in mind how regimental separations and confusion accompanied the overall Confederate attack. Another example of this was when the 1st Texas (in Robertson's brigade) and the 15th Georgia (in Benning's) fused together as they struck Ward's line during the final attack (map 3-28).

92. This is exemplified by the appearance near the top of map 3-28 of Cross's 1st Brigade from Brig. Gen. John Caldwell's 1st Division in the Federal 2nd Corps, which was coming in from the north (map 3-30).

93. Kevin E. O'Brien, "'Hold Them with the Bayonet': de Trobriand's Brigade Defends the Wheatfield," *Gettysburg Magazine,* no. 21 (July 1999): p. 87. O'Brien describes in moment-by-moment detail the actions of the 3rd Brigade (1st Division, 3rd Corps) on July 2, revealing that Colonel de Trobriand 's high-quality performance dovetailed with that of General Ward on Houck's Ridge. The cooperation between these two Union brigades was in part supervised by the 1st Division commander, Maj. Gen. David Birney (chart 3-18), who sequentially ordered de Trobriand to support Ward. Thus, before Colonel de Trobriand came under fire from Anderson's, Kershaw's, and Semmes's brigades, he detached the 17th Maine to connect with Ward's right flank (maps 3-14 and 3-25) and later "rushed his last reserve, the 40th New York, across the Wheatfield into the Plum Run Valley" (ibid, p. 79).

94. A statue of Father Corby stands on south Cemetery Ridge to commemorate that event. There is an identical one on the campus of Notre Dame University, near the administration building. Both statues show this priest raising his right hand heavenward. One does not know how many Notre Dame students are aware of the statue's meaning with respect to the Battle of Gettysburg. Those students are, it seems, more taken by the huge mosaic on the south side of the library, facing the football stadium. This is irreverently called "Touchdown Jesus" because the portrayed figure's arms are raised. Needless to say, the statue of the priest is known on that campus as "Fair-Catch Corby." This digression is not meant to be merely silly, on the one hand, or tension alleviating on the other. In addition, this arcane knowledge about Father Corby may help you avoid befuddlement should you visit Gettysburg and be taken over the field by a pro or semipro. Bear in mind that many who hover around the battlefield (in part for their livelihood) call the Gettysburg version of this statue by the same jocular name used by the college students in Indiana. Thus, your guide might say—in a straight-faced manner—something like, "Caldwell's division formed up to attack over there on the ridge, near Fair-Catch Corby."

95. D. Scott Hartwig argues that Caldwell accomplished at least this much in "No Troops on the Field Had Done Better: John C. Caldwell's Division in the Wheatfield," in Gallagher, ed., *Second Day at Gettysburg,* pp. 169–70.

96. Brig. Gen. Samuel Zook and Col. Edward Cross (chart 3-20, map 3-31). Brig. Gen. Paul Semmes of McLaws's division was also mortally wounded.

97. Recall that Kershaw's right wing had also moved in earlier against de Trobriand and the reinforcements from the Federal 5th Corps (map 3-29).

98. However, Wofford's *right* wing—which overlapped Barksdale's right, hence extending just south of it—had advanced toward the Wheatfield and to Trostle's Woods just north of the Wheatfield Road. Thus, these particular South Carolinians in the main attacked elements of the Federal 5th Corps in those two areas (map 3-33).

99. The placement and actions of these rebel batteries were supervised by the redoubtable Col. E. Porter Alexander (map 3-37), who is best remembered for his activities on July 3 (see Chapter 4). At Gettysburg on July 2, the Peach Orchard batteries amounted to only a mini–Hazel Grove. Colonel Alexander also was in charge of the rebel guns that had replaced those on that abandoned Union position at Chancellorsville, two months before.

100. Part of this line is shown at the bottom of map 3-37. Among the batteries positioned there were those desperately trying

to escape the pocket near the farm buildings (map 3-35, bottom).

101. Desjardin, *Legends of Gettysburg,* pp. 10–11. General Humphreys did not describe giving explicit orders for his withdrawing men to stop, turn, and fire. Rather, "being the only troops on the field, the enemy's whole attention was directed to my division, which was forced back slowly, firing as they receded . . . retiring very slowly, continuing the contest with the enemy, whose fire of artillery and infantry was destructive in the extreme" (*OR,* pt. 1, p. 533). A small but poignant element of this destructiveness involved the fate of Pvt. Dimond. He was already wounded when he graciously and courageously donated his horse to General Humphreys. After the battle, the division commander "inquired as to the fate of the private who had rescued him from the chaos" and perhaps saved "his general's life" (Desjardin, *Legends,* p. 11). But Dimond was nowhere to be found; his body was never located, nor was he ever heard from again.

102. General Williams was introduced in the vignette at the beginning of Chapter 1.

103. On the present-day battlefield, much of this area is cluttered with National Park buildings and parking lots. Plans to move the Visitor's Center and other structures, which would restore much of this part of the field to its original state, are continuing to solidify. However, the wrangling over the economic and political issues associated with this putative battlefield renovation sometimes seemed, at least for a time, to escalate toward the "Second Battle of Gettysburg."

104. Part of the attacking force was the 126th New York (map 3-37), whose actions will loom large on July 3.

105. Robert W. Meinhard, "The First Minnesota at Gettysburg," *Gettysburg Magazine,* no. 5 (July 1991): p. 81. A lieutenant in Company E, 1st Minnesota, remembered General Hancock yelling to Colvill, "Charge those lines!" (quoted in W. Lochren, "Narrative of the First Regiment," in *Minnesota in the Civil and Indian Wars, 1861–1865,* vol. 1 [St. Paul, Minn.: Pioneer Press, 1891], p. 35).

106. Richard Moe, *The Last Full Measure: The Life and Death of the First Minnesota Volunteers* (New York: Henry Holt, 1993). The author quotes Colonel Colvill, who—in response to Hancock's command—"immediately gave the order, 'Forward, double-quick,' and under a galling fire from the enemy [sixteen hundred Alabamians under Wilcox] we advanced" (p. 269).

107. The 1st Minnesota's casualties on July 2 were in the range of 65–70% according to Meinhard, "First Minnesota," p. 83. Robert and William Haiber corroborate this in *The 1st Minnesota Regiment at Gettysburg* (LaGrangeville, N.Y.: Info Devel Press, 1991). The lists of the Minnesotans' losses in Appendix A of that work indicate they were all killed, wounded, or died of wounds after the battle. More than 60 percent of the regiment's small remaining force was killed or wounded on July 3 (ibid., Appendix B).

108. This word, or ones to that effect, appears frequently on metal tablets sprinkled throughout the National Military Park (see George R. Large, *Battle of Gettysburg: The Official History by the National Military Park Commission* [Shippensburg, Pa.: Burd Street Press, 1999]). These are among the monumental number of silent guides on the battlefield, many of them commemorating components of the Confederate attacks that occurred throughout the three days. General Wright's specific complaint about the lack of support he received from Posey's and Lang's brigades is discussed by Brian M. Gottfried in "Piercing the Union Line or Inflated Glory?" *Gettysburg Magazine,* no. 17 (July 1997): pp. 70–82. This article also reviews Wright's claims that his men at least reached the crest of Cemetery Ridge.

109. Slocum was nominally the 12th Corps commander; he also had the 5th Corps reserve under him on July 2, but did not really order it around (that was done by Meade).

110. The others were the relatively modest fortifications erected by Doubleday's men at the last defensive line on Seminary Ridge on July 1, and a few built by von Steinwehr's men on Cemetery Hill that afternoon.

111. That ridgeline is roughly at the west edge of the "East Cavalry Field." See map 3-40, Chapter 5, and Appendix D.

112. A member of Greene's brigade stated, "The boys, remembering Chancellorsville, were determined to have good works this time, and went to work with a will" (quoted in Fennel, "Attack and Defense of Culp's Hill," p. 109). However, events during that battle two months earlier "caused little appreciation of their value. They built impressive entrenchments, only to have the army's flank turned, requiring them to abandon their position and fight in the open" (Richard L. Murray, *A Perfect Storm of Lead: George Sears Greene's New York Brigade in Defense of Culp's Hill* [Wolcott, N.Y.: Benedum Books, 2000], p. 16). During this action, on May 3, 1863, Geary's division was under fire from both flank and front and was shelled from Hazel Grove (map 3-9) by Confederate artillery (Stephen W. Sears, *Chancellorsville* [Boston: Houghton Mifflin, 1996], p. 340). At Gettysburg on July 2, it was most fortunate for Green's brigade and the Army of the Potomac that these new Yorkers did not have to "fight in the open."

113. This included Greene's commander at Gettysburg, General Geary, who "fretted about the loss of morale consequent on fighting behind barricades" (A. Wilson Greene, "'A Step All-Important and Essential to Victory': Henry W. Slocum and the Twelfth Corps on July 1–2, 1863," in Gallagher, ed., *Second Day at Gettysburg,* p. 108).

114. Notice on map 3-41 that the nominal commander of the 12th Corps's right is Brig. Gen. Thomas Ruger (chart 3-28). Ruger took over General Williams's 1st Division when Williams temporarily took charge of 12th Corps because General Meade had placed the corps commander, Maj. Gen. Henry Slocum, in charge of Union troops on the Army of the Potomac's right. As Slocum saw it, he commanded both his corps and the 5th Corps (the latter was at that time back in its reserve position along the Baltimore Pike as shown, for example, in map 3-7).

115. "The removal of the Twelfth Corps represents the single most important mistake committed by the Union high command in the entire Battle of Gettysburg" (Fennel, "Attack and Defense of Culp's Hill," p. 125).

116. To coordinate comprehension of other events occurring at this time: This was about when the Confederate *3rd* Corps units were assaulting Cemetery Ridge from the west.

117. Some of these 1st Corps regiments (chart 3-28) assaulted the railroad cut on the morning of July 1 (map 2-12).

118. However, one of the rebel officers involved in this friendly fire incident "believed that few if any of the men [within his own brigade] were hit," according to Brian M. Gottfried in "'Friendly' fire at Gettysburg," *Gettysburg Magazine,* no 27 (July 2002): pp. 78–84. The unit that at least fired *toward* their brothers in arms was the 1st North Carolina, which was advancing toward the Federal works after the other regiments in Steuart's brigade had moved up the eastern slope of Culp's Hill. From several scattered primary accounts, Gottfried pieced together sixteen instances of friendly fire during the Battle of Gettysburg—a problem that has bedeviled fighting forces down the ages, all the way to the recent conflict in Afghanistan.

119. Brian M. Gottfried, *Stopping Pickett: The History of the Philadelphia Brigade* (Shippensburg, Pa.: White Mane, 1999), pp.

164–66. The 71st's commander, Colonel Smith, admitted in his after-action report that, after "arriving at the front [approaching the position of the 137th New York], I became engaged with the enemy on the front. At the same time he attacked me on my right and rear. I immediately ordered my command to retire to the road in my rear [the Baltimore Pike], when I returned to camp without orders" (*OR*, pt. 1, p. 432).

120. The 14th Brooklyn (chart 3-29) redeployed to this southern sector of Culp's Hill (map 3-42), as did one of Geary's wandering units under Brig. Gen. Thomas L. Kane (chart 3-33). Upon its return to the hill's vicinity, Kane's brigade became the first 12th Corps unit to head back toward its original position (maps 3-42 and 3-46). In fact, "Kane took it on his own authority to return to assist Greene" (Murray, *Perfect Storm of Lead*, p. 38).

121. Dungan, *OR*, pt. 3, p. 533; Williams, *OR*, ser. 1, pt. 2, p. 513.

122. Before the 12th Corps redeployments, a path to the pike had been blocked by Union troops occupying the area just north of Spangler's Spring (on the lower hill), in McAllister's Woods, with the extreme Federal right bending back from there in a southwesterly direction toward that roadway (map 3-41).

123. This knoll was named after Capt. Greenleaf T. Stevens, commander of the 5th Maine Light Artillery (chart 3-31).

124. These officers are not to be confused with a Union division commander (chart 3-25) and a Confederate colonel who came to be in charge of a 3rd Corps brigade in Maj. Gen. Dorsey Pender's division (see Appendix F).

125. The aggressive Ramseur was killed while leading a division at the Battle of Cedar Creek in Virginia's Shenandoah Valley in October 1864.

126. See map 3-45, with reference to maps 2-17 and 2-18 in the previous chapter.

127. Elements of Williams's 1st Division (temporarily under Ruger's command) fought on south Cemetery Ridge while Geary's 2nd Division marched off the battlefield.

128. Wondering whether and where he should advance behind the 5th Corps units that had reinforced Sickles earlier, Crawford was authorized to move westward by General Slocum, who was nominally in command of the army's right wing (note 114). As Crawford led his two brigades toward the faltering 3rd Corps positions, he ran into his own corps commander, Maj. Gen. George Sykes, who told him to place the Pennsylvania Reserves north of Little Round Top. After Sykes went off to supervise the activities of his other divisions, he sent a second message to General Crawford telling him that he was on his own. Thus, Crawford himself arranged his troops for the attack on the four rebel brigades advancing on his front (Pfanz, *Second Day*, p. 393).

129. Ibid., p. 393. General Sedgwick had reached the position of Brig. Gen. Frank Wheaton's 3rd Brigade (map 3-49), now led by Col. David J. Nevin. Wheaton had been elevated to command of the 6th Corps's 3rd Division (chart 3-36) when Maj. Gen. John Newton took over the Army of the Potomac's 1st Corps (see Chapter 2).

130. Ibid.

131. See Gramm (*Gettysburg*, p. 117) for an elaboration of this point, juxtaposed with his mention of the principle that was applied by the Federals northwest of Gettysburg on the morning of July 1.

132. Maj. Gen. Ambrose E. Burnside led the Army of the Potomac from late 1862 until early 1863. He is conventionally viewed as one its most hapless commanders. Certainly he contributed to a severe Union defeat in the Fredericksburg campaign, which culminated in the battle there on December 13, 1862.

133. This is literally the thesis of Charles C. Fennel, who states: "the struggle for Culp's Hill was one of the most significant episodes of the Battle of Gettysburg. If Union forces had lost control of Culp's Hill, it would have seriously compromised the position of the Army of the Potomac and may have resulted in another Union defeat.... [By] defending Culp's Hill against over three times their numbers [on July 2] the men of Greene's brigade saved the Union army and, perhaps, the Union itself" ("Attack and Defense of Culp's Hill," p. 181).

134. This is exemplified by Pfanz's remarks about Robert E. Lee's "concept of command." Thus, on July 2, 1863, "Lee had given his corps commanders their instructions and was not interfering with their conduct of the battle" (Pfanz, *Second Day*, p. 390). Michael A. Palmer presents a broader analysis of Lee's "extremely decentralized system of command and control" (*Lee Moves North*, p. 67; see also pp. 40, 67, 83, 115, and 131).

135. Col. James A. L. Fremantle, *Three Months in the Southern States* (London: William Blackwood and Sons, 1893), p. 262. However, Pfanz points out that this information about Lee's communication activities on July 2 was recounted by Fremantle, a British visitor to the Army of Northern Virginia, who may not have observed additional dispatches that could have been sent by or been delivered to the commanding general (*Second Day*, p. 390).

136. Coddington, *Gettysburg Campaign*, pp. 452–53.

137. Longstreet, "Lee in Pennsylvania," p. 424.

138. Emphasis added. Newton's words, along with what Meade said on the night of July 2, are quoted by Pfanz, *Second Day*, p. 438.

139. Perhaps this goes too far, but others have made similar statements. Bevin Alexander, for example, noted that as "July 2, 1863, ended ... the scales tilted against the South" (*Robert E. Lee's Civil War*, p. 217). The climax hypothesis was also briefly stated by Jeffry Wert: "July 2, not 3, 1863, was the pivotal day of Gettysburg" (*General James Longstreet*, p. 279).

Chapter 4
July 3: The Great Gamble Lee Could Have Won and the Federals' Finest Hour

1. The next book-length treatment of this subject to appear—John Michael Priest's *Into the Fight: Pickett's Charge at Gettysburg* (Shippensburg, Pa.: White Mane, 1998)—includes an iconoclastic thesis about the march of the assault across the field below the town. This will be discussed in the section entitled "The Nine Brigades Advance."

2. Stewart's work—the full title is *Pickett's Charge: A Microhistory of the Final Confederate Attack at Gettysburg, July 3, 1863* (Boston: Houghton Mifflin, 1959)—does not cover the July 3 battle for Culp's Hill (see the first section of this chapter) or the cavalry fighting that occurred on this Friday (see note 3); nor does Priest. The account that focuses most fully on this day of the Gettysburg battle is Jeffry D. Wert's, cited frequently below.

3. A cavalry action that occurred *after* the charge was initiated from south and east of that ridge. The description of this belated cavalry charge is in Appendix E. Appendix D features an account of a larger cavalry battle on the East Cavalry Field, well off the right side of the top of map 4-1. That action involved the supposed plan for General J. E. B. Stuart to get into the rear of the Union lines.

4. One-sided discussions of the doomed nature of Pickett's Charge are too numerous to cite. Among the recent considerations

of "whether the charge could not succeed, but would . . . end in disaster" *or* instead can be judged a "well-conceived effort based on an estimate of the relative strengths and weaknesses of the two armies on the morning of July 3, 1863" can be found in Richard Rollins, "The Second Wave of Pickett's Charge," *Gettysburg Magazine*, no. 18 (Jan. 1998): pp. 101, 112. Later, Rollins paraphrased and quoted various twentieth-century critics of Robert E. Lee, who "all use Pickett's Charge to clinch their case." These "assaults upon Lee" churn the notion—a trite one in my view—that the charge was a "poorly conceived" frontal attack that was doomed to fail (Richard Rollins, "Pickett's Charge and the Principles of War," *North & South* 4, no. 5 [June 2001]: pp. 14–15).

5. Lt. Gen. Richard S. Ewell prefaced this phrase with "I was ordered" (*OR*, pt. 2, p. 447), presumably meaning that he was so directed by General Lee. The other component of Lee's plan failed to be realized (see the second section of this chapter).

6. Brig. Gen. Alpheus S. Williams in effect led the 12th Corps at this time—his superior, Maj. Gen. Henry W. Slocum, being the army's right wing commander. Williams had received an order from Slocum to "drive them out at daylight" (Jeffry D. Wert, *Gettysburg Day Three* [New York: Simon and Schuster, 2001], p. 54), which was ratified by General Meade. Thus, General Williams intended that the Federal batteries in this sector would commence firing about 4:30 A.M., presaging the attacks of his 12th Corps infantrymen.

7. These Union guns comprised "the Baltimore Pike artillery line " and "altogether consisted of 74 guns" (as estimated by David Shultz and Richard Rollins in "'Combined and Concentrated Fire,'" p. 54).

8. One such brigade bolstered the 12th Corps's far right flank (map 4-2) and became involved only in skirmishing. Another 6th Corps unit, Brig. Gen. Alexander Shaler's 1st Brigade of the 3rd Division, came in from the 12th Corps's rear and provided defensive support during Johnson's final attack (map 4-5).

9. The problem implied by this feature of the defenders' activities is detailed in Appendix G.

10. This Union attempt to dislodge the rebels occupying the works on lower Culp's Hill has been variously described as occurring after General Johnson's final attack up the east slope of the hill failed (Harry W. Pfanz, *Gettysburg: Culp's Hill and Cemetery Hill* [Chapel Hill: University of North Carolina Press, 1993], p. 342) and before that action occurred (Wert, *Gettysburg Day Three*, p. 74).

11. According to Pfanz: Union, 1,082; Confederate, 1,823 for Johnson's division, plus casualties suffered by Daniel's, Smith's, and O'Neal's brigades (*Culp's Hill and Cemetery Hill*, p. 352). According to Wert: Union, 950—about 10 percent of the Northern infantry force in this sector; Confederate, 2,400—more than 25 percent (*Gettysburg Day Three*, p. 79).

12. Geary's numbers are from his after-action report (*OR*, pt. 1, p. 833). Given this general's indication of how many infantrymen from his 12th Corps division were in action on Culp's Hill, the average defender (discounting officers) fired seventy-five rounds during the approximately six hours of fighting. General Geary estimated that twelve hundred rebels were killed on the slopes of Culp's Hill on July 3 and four times as many were wounded (p. 831). These are almost certainly overestimates, such that "50 shots per casualty on the ground" is at least a twofold *under*estimate.

13. These features of the "rifle revolution" debate are among the shoulder-arms issues discussed (I say again) in Appendix G.

14. In addition to not having been engaged at Gettysburg thus far, Pickett's division had not fought in the war since the summer of 1862.

15. According to William Garrett Piston (*Lee's Tarnished Lieutenant*, p. 200), Longstreet's memoir is the only source for this morning meeting between him and Lee (*From Manassas to Appomattox* [Philadelphia: Lippincott, 1896], pp. 385–89). However, Longstreet also mentioned the July 3 morning exchange in an 1877 essay (see "Lee in Pennsylvania," in McClure, ed., *Annals of the War*, p. 429)—which is the source of the quote about "moving around to the right." If Longstreet did *not* really urge a redeployment on July 3, which might have been wise, the rebels' failure to make dramatic headway in their attack on the Union left on the Second may have left him somewhat in the dark about the enemy forces in this vicinity. For example, would not his continuing request to be unleashed around the left end of that line have left a long marching column vulnerable to an attack by the 5th and 6th Corps, the large Union units lurking in reserve behind the left center of the Federal line (map 4-7, bottom)? *Lurking* might be a well-chosen word: General Lee and the others may have known little about the Federal defenders in the southern sector of the field (map 4-7). In particular, what Union reserves (including artillery) might be there? In other battles, Lee had shown a distinct willingness to maneuver around an enemy flank. However, at Chancellorsville, when he and Stonewall Jackson devised such a tactic, they knew the ground better and were well aware of the Union positions on it. The two Confederate generals had excellent, locally derived intelligence about a largely hidden march route over which they could redeploy a large force for the famous attack on Hooker's right on May 2, 1863 (as shown in map 3-9 in the previous chapter). Two months later in southern Pennsylvania, the Confederate leaders' knowledge of the local terrain and of the enemy's large-unit deployments was not as good, in spite of the scouting activities claimed by General Longstreet on the morning of July 3.

16. Wert (*Day Three*, p. 98) who notes that when Lee and Longstreet met in the early morning the latter confronted his commander with "news that he had issued orders for a movement around the flank of the Union army." This author adds that Lee "must have been stunned" by the fact that Pickett's troops had not arrived in the vicinity of the other Confederate 1st Corps divisions by the time of this meeting.

17. Longstreet may also have had in mind that Hood's and McLaws's divisions were badly bloodied from all the fighting that had taken place less than twenty-four hours earlier.

18. This factual quote—along with the analytical ones in the previous sentence and at the top of the following paragraph (regarding "the failure" and "oversight")—are from Wert, *Gettysburg Day Three*, pp. 98–99. This author then proceeds to blame General Longstreet for leaving Pickett's men too far from the field when hostilities resumed on July 3.

19. Kathy G. Harrison and John W. Busey, *Nothing But Glory: Pickett's Division at Gettysburg* (Gettysburg: Thomas Publications, 1993), pp. 11, 13.

20. Wayne E. Motts to author, June 1999.

21. On Wednesday the Confederates had carried the field. However, the result was the first phase of—in Maj. Gen. John Newton's words—"hammering" the Army of the Potomac back into its fine positions on Culp's Hill, Cemetery Hill, and Cemetery Ridge. The Army of Northern Virginia then gained ground in two sectors on the Second, but not with respect to the overall integrity of the Federals' fishhook line.

22. As exemplified in McPherson's *Battle Cry of Freedom* (p. 656), "a Cannae" is a proverbial term stemming from a battle between the army of Hannibal and a seventy-thousand-man Roman force in 216 B.C. As a result of a *double envelopment*—a fateful phrase—Hannibal annihilated the Roman legions on a field

near Cannae, southeast of Rome near the Adriatic Sea. At Gettysburg on July 3, Lee wished to "retain the initiative" he had seized on July 1 and strived mightily to exploit on July 2—knowing that "to be successful [to effect a war-winning victory?], a commander must think offensively and utilize offensive maneuvers" (Rollins, "Pickett's Charge," p. 19). Thus, based "on actions flowing from the grand strategic needs of the Confederacy" (ibid., p. 23), and remembering that "he had smashed the Federal lines in previous engagements," Lee seemed to believe on July 3 that he could shatter them utterly in one culminating attack (ibid., p. 22).

23. This paraphrases a regrettable remark made by General Meade, as discussed in Chapter 5 in conjunction with its note 44.

24. Meaning Thursday, July 2. On *that* day or the next, the Confederates might have attacked the Union lines by way of a *fourth* scenario—considering that, on July 3, Plan 1 would involve redeploying around the enemy's left flank; Plan 2, hitting both flanks with the 1st and 2nd Corps; and Plan 3, assaulting the shank of the Union fishhook frontally. The ubiquitous E. Porter Alexander, aided by more than thirty years of hindsight, proposed a fourth option (see Piston, "Longstreet, Lee," pp. 41–42; Alexander, *Robert E. Lee's Civil War*, p. 203). Alexander diagrammed (on p. 250 of *Fighting for the Confederacy*, which he began writing in 1897) a plan for the Confederate infantry to hit the *bend* of the fishhook (map 4-8). The "assaulting line," wrote Alexander, "could not [have been] enfiladed, and . . . the places selected for the assault [could have been] enfiladed, & upon shorter ranges than any other parts of the Federal lines" (*Fighting for the Confederacy*, p. 252). What Alexander had in mind was that Union infantry in the vicinity of the bend could not bring much defensive power to bear on an attack that might have struck them right there because many of the Federal troops nearby were facing north (on Cemetery Hill) or west (the defenders arrayed below the bend). Confederate artillery (see circled cannon symbols on map 4-8) could have raked the Union lines on north Cemetery Hill and north Cemetery Ridge in flank, further "softening up" the defenses prior to such an attack. This hypothetical offensive scheme might have worked even better on July 2, when the Union line was not as strong (at least before the 6th Corps arrived in the afternoon).

25. Colonel Long, Lee's assistant military secretary, said as much many years after the war (Armistead L. Long, *Memoirs of Robert E. Lee* [New York: J. M. Stoddart, 1886], pp. 286–94). That all components of the planning for the Charge—by General Longstreet, carrying out Lee's wishes without any neglect or disobedience—were specific and clear was given its most ringing endorsement by Porter Alexander (*Fighting for the Confederacy*, p. 245). Alexander's account also reveals that the words and activities involved in all this planning were distinctly free of wrangling.

An essay by Wayne E. Motts ("A Brave and Resolute Force," *North & South* 2, no. 5 [June 1999]: pp. 20–35) summarizes further evidence that the Confederate high command in general and James Longstreet in particular made detailed, careful plans for the frontal assault on July 3 (ibid., pp. 31–32).

26. There is some confusion over this number: Appendix F specifies that there were 5,578 troops in Pickett's division, which is an overly precise number. Wayne E. Motts estimates that this Confederate division, including support troops, numbered 6,200. Other calculations: Priest (*Into the Fight*, p. 199) lists 5,820 of Pickett's men "present" for the action on July 3, whereas Harrison and Busey say there were 6,262, based on a nicely researched essay on the strengths of this division (*Nothing But Glory*, pp. 169–73).

27. Should they have been entirely kept out of the fight? As will be discussed later in this chapter, the decision not to mobilize any of Law's and McLaws's brigades may have made for an *insufficient* assault force.

28. In this regard, Brig. Gen. Ambrose Wright might well have chimed in: "I was not supported on either of my flanks and so I could not hold the ground I gained near the copse of trees" (maps 3-39 and 3-48). Wright's brigade *almost* went into the fight one day later, but by then the so-called high-water mark of Pickett's Charge had passed its crest.

29. Carol Reardon refers to recent calculations of "a force numbering between 12,000 and 13,000" ("Pickett's Charge: The Convergence of History and Myth in the Southern Past," in Gallagher, ed., *The Third Day at Gettysburg*, p. 57). Priest comes up with a total of 11,555 men in Pickett's, Pettigrew's, and Trimble's divisions (*Into the Fight*, p. 199). Wayne E. Motts (personal communication, June 1999) estimates 12,500, including the approximately 1,600 men from Wilcox's and Lang's brigades who should have participated (maps 4-10 and 4-13). Stewart's figure (*Pickett's Charge*, p. 173) does not take into account those Alabamians and Floridians (which he says totaled 1,400 troops).

30. Longstreet, "Lee in Pennsylvania," p. 429.

31. Longstreet wrote twenty-five years later that this is what he "saw" at Gettysburg ("Lee's Right Wing at Gettysburg," in *Battles and Leaders of the Civil War*, ed. Robert U. Johnson and Clarence C. Buel, vol. 3 [Secaucus, N.J.: Castle, 1888], p. 343).

32. D. Scott Hartwig, "'The Fate of a Country': The Repulse of Longstreet's Assault by the Army of the Potomac," in *Mr. Lincoln's Army: The Army of the Potomac in the Gettysburg Campaign* (Gettysburg, Pa.: Gettysburg National Military Park, 1997), p. 247. Malvern Hill (July 1, 1862) was the last of the Seven Days battles of the Peninsula campaign. A hundred massed Union cannon blew away the Army of Northern Virginia's frontal attack up this hill southeast of Richmond. Lee's counterpart, General McClellan, retreated anyway (to the James River, well southeast of Richmond) on July 2, one year before Gettysburg.

33. Recall that Trimble had supposedly railed in disgust at General Ewell on the evening of July 1 about the vulnerability of Culp's Hill and the extreme desirability of an attack on the incipient Union position there. Also remember that Pender's ostensibly minor leg wound on July 2 not only took him out of the Gettysburg battle, it also resulted in his death approximately two weeks later.

34. This goes against the grain. General Pickett's activities on July 3 have been characterized in terms of he "himself [playing] no part in choosing the formation or the troops who were to take part in the assault" (Richard F. Selcer, *"Faithfully and Forever Your Soldier": Gen. George E. Pickett, CSA* [Gettysburg: Farnsworth House, 1995], p. 31). Moreover, his "conduct during the charge has ever been a matter of dispute" because of "those who suspected that [he] had not gone in with his troops [and] condemned him" accordingly (E. G. Longacre, *Pickett: Leader of the Charge* [Shippensburg, Pa.: White Mane, 1995], pp. 122–25). Indeed, as we will see later in this chapter, Pickett did not lead from the front as the Charge approached the Union lines. However, the general can be credited for a certain confidence about the prognosis for the assault. In the postwar words of James Longstreet: "When I took Pickett to the crest of Seminary Ridge and explained where his troops should be sheltered, and pointed out the direction General Lee wished him to take and the point of the Federal line where the assault was to be made, he seemed to appreciate the severity of the contest upon which he was about to enter, but was quite hopeful of success" (Longstreet, "Lee's Right Wing," vol. 3, p. 343). This optimism may have flowed down to the men in Pickett's division and contributed to the disciplined manner in which they marched across the field, carrying out coordinated maneuvers in an impressive

fashion as the three brigades came under heavy defensive fire.

35. Harrison and Busey depict the winding route taken by Pickett's division after it turned off the Cashtown Road (*Nothing But Glory*, p. 14). According to this diagram, the Virginians made use of the roadways southwest of the town. A postwar account of the line of march from a former Confederate officer indicated that Pickett's division marched diagonally across open fields, using a more direct route to its destination behind Seminary Ridge (map 4-9). The attackers thus achieved an extra measure of protection from prying Union eyes by eschewing the roads in this vicinity. This information is based on a discussion between the author and Wayne E. Motts (June 1999), who found an article written by former captain William W. Wood, who was in the 14th Virginia at Gettysburg. Wood's piece ("Pickett's Charge at Gettysburg," *Philadelphia Weekly Times*, Aug. 11, 1877) was not included in the aforementioned collection of articles (McClure, ed., *Annals of the War*) from that nineteenth-century periodical.

36. As they waited, the long line of Pickett's men stretched from a location just west of the north end of Spangler's Woods (near the Lee monument on the modern-day battlefield), past the Emmanuel Pitzer farm buildings, all the way to a site south of the Black Horse Tavern (map 4-9); this is where Longstreet's divisions had turned around on July 2 to commence their countermarch (map 3-8).

37. Detailed examples of how thoughtful and intricate was this Confederate planning on July 3 are in Richard Rollins, "Lee's Artillery Prepares for Pickett's Charge," *North & South* 2, no. 7 (Sept. 1999): pp. 41–55. Establishing the layout of the attack force and the design of the assault (including the artillery's salient role) took all morning and into the early afternoon.

38. Wayne E. Motts, personal communication, June 1999.

39. Motts, "A Brave and Resolute Force," pp. 28–34. This feature of Pickett's deployment was specified by General Longstreet (ibid., p. 31). Stewart gives an incomplete version of how Pickett's brigades were arranged in these protected positions (map 4-9, bottom) on p. 47 and pp. 86–87 of *Pickett's Charge*.

40. When you stand in the middle of where Armistead's line was—near Spangler's Woods, facing east—you can see nothing but a steep slope. Wayne Motts made this abundantly clear as we stood together at this place on the field (June 23, 1999). The rest of Pickett's division was completely out of sight, as was the Union defense on Cemetery Ridge. That ridge is nowhere near high enough for the Federals to have observed either of Pickett's two main battle lines. Equally important is the psychological benefit provided to the soldiers in this division of Virginians. What they could *not* see as they waited for hours in their concealed positions was the wide, largely open field between them and the enemy army waiting for them on the next ridgeline.

41. Richard Rollins, "The Failure of Confederate Artillery in Pickett's Charge," *North & South* 3, no. 4 (Apr. 2000): p. 29 (part of a series); Paul Clark Cooksey, "The Plan for Pickett's Charge," *Gettysburg Magazine*, no. 22 (Jan. 2000): p. 70 ("protection").

42. Clark, *Gettysburg*, p. 128; Stewart, *Pickett's Charge*, p. 90.

43. Motts, "A Brave and Resolute Force," p. 31.

44. This rebel brigade was formerly under Brig. Gen. James J. Archer. His men, from Alabama and Tennessee, fought near McPherson Ridge on July 1—during the morning of which Archer was captured.

45. Basil Biggs, who worked a farm that included the copse, performed this tree felling soon after the war. John B. Bachelder "felt a reverence for those trees" and was horrified "while passing them one day . . . to find the owner engaged in cutting them down. Bachelder "expostulated with him" and finally convinced him to stop. In 1887, the Gettysburg historian proposed to the Gettysburg Memorial Association that the trees be enclosed within an iron fence; the motion passed later that year. Bachelder went on to say, "The thought of naming the Copse of Trees the 'High Water Mark of the Rebellion' . . . was mine." See Kathy R. Georg, "'A Common Pride and Fame': The Attack and Repulse of Pickett's Division at Gettysburg, July 3, 1863," 1981, archives, Gettysburg National Military Park, appendix B. Ms. Georg later became Kathy Georg Harrison, coauthor of *Nothing But Glory* (see note 19).

46. D. Scott Hartwig, *A Killer Angels Companion* (Gettysburg: Thomas Publications, 1996), p. 26. However, General Longstreet wrote in his report on the campaign about "the salient of the enemy's position" and how "the center of the assaulting column would arrive [there], General Pickett's line to be the guide, and General Pettigrew . . . moving on the same line . . . to assault the salient at the same moment" (*OR*, pt. 2, p. 359). Motts documents additional pieces of evidence about "the actual target of attack," which may not have been the copse of trees itself, but was arguably a well-defined salient "just north of [there] along Cemetery Ridge" ("A Brave and Resolute Force," pp. 31–32).

47. Fry was wounded and captured on July 3 and thus left no report in the *Official Records*. However, after the war Fry wrote that during the early afternoon conferences with Generals Pettigrew, Pickett, and Garnett, "it was agreed that he [Garnett, on the left front of Pickett's division] would dress upon my command. I immediately informed General Pettigrew of this agreement. It was then understood that my command should be considered the centre, and that in the assault both divisions should align themselves by it" (quoted in Richard Rollins, ed., *Pickett's Charge! Eyewitness Accounts* [Redondo Beach, Calif.: Rank and File, 1994], p. 63). See also Motts, "A Brave and Resolute Force," p. 32. The brigade-of-direction principle is pertinent to the Confederate attack plan on the afternoon of July 2. The unit on the right wing of Maj. Gen. John Bell Hood's division, commanded by Brig. Gen. Evander M. Law (map 3-12), was appointed brigade of direction by Hood (Penny and Laine, *Struggle for the Round Tops*, p. 31). In this case, Law's Alabamians were to lead the attack, and succeeding units would advance in echelon from Law's left.

48. Rollins, "Failure of Confederate Artillery in Pickett's Charge," *North & South* 3, no. 4 (Apr. 2000): p. 37. Rollins adds that Pendleton "did little but serve as a liaison between army headquarters and the corps artillery commanders" (ibid.). Pendleton's offensive activities are remembered mostly for his postwar screeds directed at Longstreet's arguably poor performance at Gettysburg: "Pendleton became increasingly involved in the affairs of Confederate veterans and sought to win in peacetime, as [one of the] defenders of Lee, the reputation that had eluded [him] during the war" (Piston, "Longstreet, Lee," p. 49). "His veneration of Lee and detestation of Longstreet bordered on mental instability" (ibid., p. 47).

49. *Pickett's Charge*, p. 114.

50. Alexander's argument, and the quotes that illuminate it in this paragraph and the next one ("no troops can submit to it"), is in *Military Memoirs of a Confederate*, pp. 417–19. For the "oversight" about the placement of Confederate cannon on July 3, Alexander blamed his superior, General Pendleton (Rollins, "Failure of Confederate Artillery in Pickett's Charge," p. 37). Indeed, "Pendleton . . . simply had not done his job in supervising the placement of *all* the guns. No evidence has been found that he examined the 2nd Corps artillery at any time during the entire battle" (ibid., p. 39).

51. Rollins, "Lee's Artillery," pp. 41–55.

52. It may have begun earlier, in that it ended around 2 P.M. according to Porter Alexander (ibid.). This jibes with the time

estimates of John Michael Priest (*Into the Fight*, pp. 51–85). Those of George Stewart (*Pickett's Charge*, pp. 129, 185) are later: bombardment, approximately 1–2:45 P.M.; commencement of the assault, approximately 3 P.M.

53. Shultz and Rollins, "'Combined and Concentrated Fire,'" p. 54.

54. Colonel Alexander originally intended the bombardment to last 30 minutes or less but indicated that the duration was 45–60 minutes. He may have underestimated by up to an hour (Rollins, "Lee's Artillery," pp. 41–55; and see note 52), but another analyst believes the cannonade did not last much longer than one hour (J. Jorgensen, "Edward Porter Alexander, Confederate Cannoneer at Gettysburg," *Gettysburg Magazine*, no. 17 [July 1997]: pp. 41–53). Priest (*Into the Fight*, pp. 194–98) and Wert (*Day Three*, p. 182) concur with this estimate.

55. From a letter written by Capt. Charles A. Phillips, a cannoneer in the Federal Artillery Reserve, on July 6, 1863, quoted by the anonymous author of *History of the Fifth Massachusetts Battery* (Boston: Luther E. Cowles, 1902), p. 652. Phillips's battery was roughly in the middle of McGilvery's line of guns at the left end of the Federal defense that confronted the Charge (maps 4-12 and 4-18).

56. Richard Rollins asserts that the "Rebel gunners did not simply fire high, as has been so often noted" ("Failure of Confederate Artillery in Pickett's Charge," p. 39), but "high, or low, or otherwise off target on July 3" (p. 30). Why was the aim of so many rebel gunners off? One reason relates to the terrain on this part of the Gettysburg battlefield (introduced in note 40). Rollins points out that "many accounts of Pickett's Charge describe the land traversed by the attackers as a valley, or a long slope." That it was instead "rolling land creates a problem for a gunner firing at long range, amounting to an optical illusion" (ibid., pp. 29–30).

57. Quoted in Stewart's *Pickett's Charge* (pp. 143–44). However, in his after-action report, General Howard described some frightening examples of cannonade damage "hurling into the cemetery grounds" (*OR*, pt. 1, p. 706). Richard Rollins, evaluating the damage more generally, concludes that "the Confederates achieved considerable success," in that "fully one third [of the Federal guns] failed to fire a single shot at the attacking infantry . . . as a result of the cannonade" ("Failure of Confederate Artillery in Pickett's Charge," pp. 39, 40); "but it was not enough to accomplish their goal of stopping federal artillery from decimating the attack" (ibid., p. 26).

58. The Union infantry units along the Cemetery Ridge line were not entirely safe during the bombardment: "A reasonable guess would place their losses at 200 to 300 men, but they may have been higher." This was "equal to a strong regiment on the firing line, at a time when every rifle and musket would be needed" (Hartwig, "'Fate of a Country,'" p. 269).

59. The rebel gunners' lack of "long-range target practice or live firing of any sort outside of combat situations" is analyzed by Richard Rollins ("Failure of Confederate Artillery in Pickett's Charge," pp. 26–29). Rollins also describes problems with "shellfire" as they plagued the Confederate artillery in excruciating detail, at least from a Southerner's perspective ("The Failure of Confederate Artillery at Gettysburg: Ordnance and Logistics," *North & South* 3, no. 2 (Jan. 2000): pp. 44–54. See also Rollins, "Lee's Artillery," p. 47). The ammunition for Civil War cannon—especially those firing at long range—included shells or case shot, which was meant to explode near a given enemy position. Shell casings broke into numerous jagged fragments, whereas case shot blew apart and scattered little metal balls packed inside. Although some rounds in Civil War times exploded on contact, the majority employed a lighted fuse to detonate the powder charge inside. However, even if the gunners chose the correct length of fuse (which was ignited by setting off the initial charge in the breech of the cannon), the powder within the projectile might not go off at all, or it would explode prematurely.

60. Approximately thirty-five Union guns were disabled or withdrawn by the end of the cannonade (Wert, *Gettysburg Day Three*, p. 183), so the majority of the batteries in the west-facing line were those on Cemetery Hill and McGilvery's cannon in the southern sector (map 4-12).

61. With all the shot and shell crashing into this vicinity, Meade's staff officers urged him to evacuate the small house on the east slope of Cemetery Ridge, owned by aged Lydia Leister, whose residence was occupied by the commanding general during the battle. Meade relented when it was agreed that a signalman would be left behind to communicate with the 12th Corps headquarters on Powers Hill (maps 4-1 and 4-2). Members of the headquarters group rode across Taneytown Road and posted themselves in a field. However, when artillery rounds began to rain down on *that* location, Meade rode to Powers Hill. It quickly became evident to him that no signals were being sent from the site of his former headquarters, so the army commander returned to the Leister house. There he discovered that the signalman left behind had decamped. The general then rode "toward Cemetery Hill to get a view of the action, which was now at a crescendo" (Wert, *Gettysburg Day Three*, p. 174).

62. See, for example, Stewart, *Pickett's Charge*, pp. 130–31. As Hancock "rode down the line . . . while the missiles from a hundred pieces of artillery tore up the ground around him" (Abner Doubleday's words from the 1880s), a fellow officer was said to have admonished him: "General, the corps commander ought not to risk his life that way," to which Hancock supposedly answered: "There are times when a corps commander's life does not count" (quoted in Clark, *Gettysburg*, p. 133). No doubt he was thinking that such a "gallant act" was necessary to give "heart to his men, clutching desperately to the ground, . . . to nerve them for the ordeal which still lay before them" (Jordan, *Winfield Scott Hancock*, p. 97).

63. Wert, *General James Longstreet*, p. 290 (also the source of quotes in the subsequent main-text sentence: "unmoved . . . heroism").

64. According to Richard Rollins, this was the result of another of General Pendleton's failings (see note 48). He did not arrange for adequate artillery rounds to be near the frontline guns and, "by the time the cannonade began, . . . compounded the problem by moving the reserve trains to a location that was so far away from the guns that they could not be resupplied with the little ammunition left" (Rollins, "Failure of Confederate Artillery in Pickett's Charge," p. 38). This mismanagement impacted on the rebels' largely failed plan to move their cannon forward in support of the infantry's assault (see note 123).

65. Three of Perrin's six guns were taken to the rear, and one additional Union battery retired at this time.

66. Stewart, *Pickett's Charge*, p. 155. Hunt himself alludes to his ploy in an article he wrote in the 1880s ("The Third Day at Gettysburg," in Johnson and Buel, eds., *Battles and Leaders*, vol. 3, p. 374), although there and in his after-action report Hunt also said that he ordered a cease-fire because "our ammunition was running low" (*OR*, pt. 1, p. 239).

67. This and the other rushed, unpunctuated notes from Alexander to Pickett and Longstreet, along with those sent by Longstreet to Alexander, were paraphrased by Alexander in "The Great Charge and Artillery Fighting at Gettysburg," in Johnson and

Buel, eds., *Battles and Leaders,* vol. 3, pp. 357–68. Exact transcripts of these notes, which survived and are stored in the Manuscript Division of the Library of Congress, were reprinted in *Civil War Times Illustrated* 17, no. 1 (Apr. 1978): pp. 22–25. Alexander also described two messages that were transmitted orally to Pickett at this moment on the afternoon of July 3: "For God's sake hurry up" (letter to John B. Bachelder, May 3, 1876, in Ladd and Ladd, eds., *Bachelder Papers,* vol. 1, p. 489. Wert (*Day Three,* p. 186) estimates that the "moment" in question was 1:40 P.M., which is in line with his view (and others') that the cannonade lasted only about an hour (see note 54).

68. Stewart, *Pickett's Charge,* p. 85. After the war, former Confederate cavalry general Fitzhugh Lee compellingly argued in favor of the Pickett's Charge appellation, because "the operation of a detached force generally takes the name of the commanding officer. Pickett was the senior officer in rank" (quoted in Reardon, *Pickett's Charge,* p. 165). This is certainly true with respect to one other division commander, Brig. Gen. James Pettigrew, who had risen to that level only two days before. As for Maj. Gen. Isaac Trimble, who led a charging "division" consisting of but two brigades, he was given that field command on July 3 itself.

69. Winston S. Churchill, *A History of the English Speaking Peoples,* vol. 4, *The Great Democracies* (New York: Dorset Press, 1958), p. 263.

70. General Lee may have borne such a possibility in mind, starting not long after he took command of the Army of Northern Virginia. In his "Battle Report on the Seven Days" (submitted March 6, 1863), in which he described and evaluated his strategic success during the culmination of the Peninsula campaign in June and early July 1862, Lee expressed regret that "more was not accomplished" and wrote that "under ordinary circumstances the Federal Army should have been destroyed" (Clifford Dowdey and Louis H. Manarin, eds., *The Wartime Papers of R. E. Lee* [Boston: Little, Brown, 1961], p. 221). Lee failed to "destroy" the Army of the Potomac over the course of the ensuing year and may have felt frustrated at the end of each campaign in which he led the Army of Northern Virginia during the first year he commanded it.

71. Vicksburg, Mississippi, was the "Confederate Gibraltar" on the Mississippi River that surrendered to Northern forces the day after the Battle of Gettysburg. However, some have argued intriguingly that the political situation in 1863, and even the geopolitical one, was such that the country, the government, and others abroad just did not care much about the war in the West. Gary Gallagher notes that "evidence of Northern preoccupation with the East abounds" ("Another Look at the Generalship of R. E. Lee," in *Lee the Soldier,* ed. Gary W. Gallagher [Lincoln: University of Nebraska Press, 1996], p. 278), then addresses Lee's fixation on the eastern theater of the war. See Chapter 5 for a more detailed discussion of this issue.

72. C. Vann Woodward, ed., *Mary Chestnut's Civil War* (New Haven, Conn.: Yale University Press, 1983), p. 376. For the sake of full disclosure, these words penned by the Southern diarist are not about Gettysburg because she wrote them in June 1862. She seemed concerned then about whether the Southern soldiers possessed the necessary tenacity and resilience to sustain the vast military enterprise in which they were embroiled—an issue that is taken up in Chapter 5 of the current work. Mrs. Chestnut, by the way, became a much-lionized chronicler of and commentator about the American Civil War, as signified by several twentieth-century analyses of her diary, accompanied by abundant reprinting of it in varying forms (e.g., Ben Ames Williams, ed., *A Diary from Dixie by Mary Boykin Chestnut* [Boston: Houghton Mifflin, 1949]; and http://docsouth.unc.edu/chesnut/maryches.html). Moreover,

certain modern historians have echoed and amplified upon the remark of hers quoted above: "Rebel soldiers became increasingly discouraged when the enemy refused to be beaten" (Grady McWhiney and Perry D. Jamieson, *Attack and Die* [Tuscaloosa: University of Alabama Press, 1982], p. 189), which once again is a harbinger of things to come in Chapter 5.

73. At Solferino, on June 24, 1859, the allies *did,* in effect, win the war. The armies in that battle, including fifty thousand Piedmontese troops fighting for Italian unification, were made up of more soldiers than those facing each other outside Gettysburg. Before the French and Italians attempted to break through, they *bombarded the Austrian center*—located near the town of Solferino itself—with artillery. When the allies subsequently attacked, the rifled muskets in the hands of the defenders were not enough—and conceivably were a hindrance, as is discussed in Appendix G.

74. One analyst of Pickett's Charge suggests that "Lee would have been aware of Napoleon III's victory over the Austrians at Solferino," even though "there are no actual indications that Lee read about Napoleon's attack" against the Austrian center (Cooksey, "Plan for Pickett's Charge," pp. 78–79).

75. There is some evidence that Lee had an attitude of this sort about his Northern foe. Alan T. Nolan observes on page 149 of *Lee Considered* (Chapel Hill: University of North Carolina Press, 1991) that,

> as a Southern aristocrat, he tended toward the belief that the Yankees, at least many of them, were a lesser people. This is reflected in the Reverend John Leyburn's report of his 1869 conversation with Lee. According to Leyburn, Lee then expressed sadness about the "number of noble young men" killed in the war, but he insisted that these losses had been "most unequal" between the sections. The South, he said, had "sacrificed the flower of her land." The North had sent "many of her valuable men to the field; but as in all large cities there is a population *which can well be spared*" [emphasis added]. The North also had recruited "immigrants from abroad." In describing the Leyburn conversation, Freeman [Lee's chief biographer] identifies those who could "well be spared" as coming from "the slums of the city." In Lee's view, the deaths of immigrants and the poor were somehow counted in a different way.

76. Again, an object lesson about the difficulty of making this kind of troop-strength estimate for a Civil War battle: Whereas George Stewart concluded "that the total number of the infantry awaiting the assault on Cemetery Ridge was about 5750" (*Pickett's Charge,* p. 174), Scott Hartwig says that "the strength of [the] infantry line can only be estimated . . . and was probably around 6,500" ("'Fate of a Country,'" p. 4).

77. "The planners envisioned a large number of guns going forward with the infantry: perhaps as many as 100 to 150" [thus from Alexander's line as well as many of the batteries arrayed father to the north] (Rollins, "Failure of Confederate Artillery in Pickett's Charge," p. 39).

78. Note that Col. Abner M. Perrin, who took over after McGowan was wounded at Chancellorsville, commanded McGowan's 3rd Corps brigade in the Long Lane on July 3 (as shown on map 4-13). Most of the Confederate units deployed along this sunken road, including Perrin's, had fought hard on July 1.

79. Harrison and Busey, *Nothing But Glory,* p. 56.

80. However, Armistead not only moved away from Spangler's Woods at an accelerated rate of march (see material cited in note 79), he also ordered his men to the "double-quick" as they approached the fences along the Emmitsburg Road. See Wayne E.

Motts, *"Trust in God and Fear Nothing": Gen. Lewis A. Armistead, CSA* (Gettysburg: Farnsworth Military Impressions, 1994), p. 45; and Harrison and Busey, *Nothing But Glory,* pp. 56–58.

81. As a result of the cannonade, Rorty's battery had one, perhaps two, serviceable pieces; and only 4 of his approximately 65 men were fit for duty. Captain Rorty was killed by a subsequent Confederate cannon shot, and Lt. Robert E. Rogers assumed command of what was left of the battery. Other Union batteries placed north of Rorty's (up to Ziegler's Grove) lost between 25 and 45 men during the bombardment, which severely diminished their effectiveness (Hartwig, "'Fate of a Country,'" p. 267).

82. Harrison and Busey, *Nothing But Glory,* p. 49.

83. Capt. Frank C. Gibbs's battery (chart 4-15) was technically on Little Round Top, but rather low on the northern slope (map 4-18). Gibbs "only occasionally [worked] the battery" on July 3 because it was on too low a piece of ground, and his smoothbore Napoleons had insufficient range to be of much use against Pickett's brigades (*OR,* pt. 1, p. 662). Captain Gibbs's after-action report refers to his guns being placed (in the middle of the afternoon of July 2) "on the right slope of Little Round Top (Weed's Hill)." The report was suspiciously dated July 4, 1863. As in the case of Col. Joshua L. Chamberlain's postwar Gettysburg report (see note 66 in Chapter 3), Gibbs's is also called into question: Little Round Top had no such name in 1863. Moreover, the "Weed's Hill" appellation represents a failed attempt by nineteenth-century Gettysburg historian John B. Bachelder to name the hill after a Federal 5th Corps brigade commander killed there on July 2 (see note 45 above and the essay on sources at the end of the book). Bachelder made his pitch for naming this battlefield landmark in October or November of 1863. The particular problem pointed out here may not affect our comprehension of Captain Gibbs's participation in the battle (although he gave a self-congratulatory description of the damage done by his battery on July 2). Nevertheless, it provides another object lesson about the need to be vigilant about the supposedly rock-solid sources in the *Official Records.* There is another possibility to consider: one of the compilers who edited the report in the 1880s may have changed Gibbs's designation of the hill to the then contemporary name of Little Round Top.

84. Quoted in Gary E. Adelman, "Hazlett's Battery at Gettysburg," *Gettysburg Magazine,* no. 21 (July 1999): pp. 64–73.

85. Harrison and Busey, *Nothing But Glory,* pp. 42–43, 48.

86. Hartwig, "'Fate of a Country,'" p. 271; Stewart, *Pickett's Charge,* pp. 182–83; Reardon, *Pickett's Charge,* pp. 19–20.

87. *OR,* pt. 1, p. 429. Regarding Webb's elevation to command of the brigade, Brian Gottfried notes that "none of the primary sources explain why this change occurred" in conjunction with the former commander, Brig. Gen. Joshua Owen, being arrested on June 28 (*Stopping Pickett,* p. 151).

88. Stewart, *Pickett's Charge,* pp. 57–60. Gottfried agrees that "the history of the brigade is fraught with controversy," although his book provides a more balanced view than does Stewart's of these Pennsylvanians' activities and accomplishments (*Stopping Pickett,* p. 229).

89. That Pickett's Charge was not devastated by Federal fire west of the Emmitsburg Road is argued by Paul Clark Cooksey, who estimates that at least ten thousand rebel troops "would have at least reached the Emmitsburg Road" ("Plan for Pickett's Charge," p. 71). Wayne Motts arrived at the same estimate (personal communication, July 1999). However, other students of the July 3 battle conclude that Union defensive artillery fire had a more significant numerical effect on the attacking force. David Shultz discusses the evidence for this in *"Double Canister at Ten Yards": The Federal Artillery and the Repulse of Pickett's Charge* (Redondo Beach, Calif.: Rank and File, 1995). Shultz's colleague, Richard Rollins, echoed this conclusion: "Perhaps 6000 reached the Emmitsburg Road . . . Henry Jackson Hunt, Robert O. Tyler, Thomas Osborn, Freeman McGilvery, Charles Wainwright [Federal artillerymen all] had done their jobs well" ("Failure of Confederate Artillery in Pickett's Charge," p. 40). The evidence cited by Cooksey and by Shultz and Rollins overlaps, but only in part. The latter authors do not mention Maj. Gen. Winfield Scott Hancock's Gettysburg report. According to Hancock, "No attempt was made to check the advance of the enemy until the first line had arrived within about 700 yards of our position, when a feeble fire of artillery was opened upon it, but no material effect and without delaying for a moment its determined advance" (*OR,* pt. 1, p. 373). Nor do they include E. Porter Alexander's postwar judgment that "the volume of [Federal] artillery fire did not seem great & it failed entirely to check or break up Pickett's advance" (*Fighting for the Confederacy,* p. 262).

90. This officer *did* lead that brigade on July 3, although some charts and maps indicate that a Col. Robert M. Mayo, a regimental commander in Brockenbrough's brigade, was in charge of it. For reasons never explained, Brockenbrough split his brigade so that Mayo commanded two regiments within it (his own 47th Virginia and the 55th Virginia). Colonel Mayo was the senior regimental colonel under Brockenbrough and led his so-called demi-brigade on the left wing of the unit's tentative advance. Brockenbrough himself was in charge of the 22nd and 40th Virginia.

91. Colonel Carroll stayed over on Cemetery Hill after going there on the night of July 2. However, one of Carroll's regiments was to make a belated return to Cemetery Ridge on the afternoon of the Third.

92. *OR,* pt. 1, p. 462. That his outposted regiment counterattacked on Davis's front is the result of Wayne Mott's analysis. If the Ohio men were as near as they thought to the point where Brockenbrough's Virginians putatively came under the Ohioans' rifle fire and turned back toward Seminary Ridge, they would have no doubt been subjected to severe musketry from the 2nd Corps rebels in the sunken road (map 4-22). Michael W. Taylor discusses primary sources that speak to "the real question about how far Brockenbrough's brigade advanced" and tacitly concludes that it probably did not go beyond the Long Lane ("North Carolina in the Pickett-Pettigrew-Trimble Charge at Gettysburg," *Gettysburg Magazine,* no. 8 [Jan. 1993]: p. 68).

93. Wayne E. Motts, personal communication, June 1999.

94. Elwood W. Christ, *The Struggle for the Bliss Farm at Gettysburg, July 2nd and 3rd 1863,* 2nd ed. (Baltimore: Butternut and Blue, 1994), p. 79 (also the source of the "producing a gap" passage in the next sentence).

95. This is mildly disputed by a contemporary expert about the Charge. Thus Carol Reardon is skeptical about whether the "parade-ground" marching—in this case to close up the two wings of the assault—really occurred (*Pickett's Charge,* pp. 6, 8). Her misgivings about this particular detail exemplify her larger thesis: How much of an account by a participant reflects what really happened, and how much mirrors what that person was able to or desired to recall? This history-versus-memory approach to analyzing the American Civil War is a prominent feature of current scholarship (see the essay on sources at the end of the book).

96. This paraphrases a point made by Stewart in *Pickett's Charge,* p. 210.

97. Sawyer gave credit to the additional defensive fire that supported him, including the continuing effect of Federal shelling from the northern sector of the defensive line: After "I changed

front . . . thus presenting our front to the left flank of the advancing rebel column[,] our fire was poured into their flank with a terrible effect before the Second Brigade [behind him on Cemetery Ridge; see maps 4-17 and 4-32, and chart 4-25] . . . opened . . . , [and] almost instantly on the fire from the front, together with the concentrated fire from our batteries, the whole mass gave way, some fleeing to the front, some to the rear, and some through our lines, until the whole plain was covered with unarmed rebels, waving coats, hats, and handkerchiefs in token of a wish to surrender." Colonel Sawyer goes on to report his advance southward into the enemy's actual flank and the "about 200" Confederates his Ohioans captured (*OR*, pt. 1, p. 462).

98. These skirmishers, led by Capt. Samuel C. Armstrong, were from the 125th New York (chart 4-18). They had been posted among the buildings near the top right of map 4-23. The score of men from the 1st Massachusetts who bolstered his reinforcing troops were led by Lt. Emerson L. Bicknell, whose regiment was detached from the 2nd Division, 2nd Corps, and attached to the 3rd Brigade in Brig. Gen. Alexander Hays's 3rd Division, 2nd Corps, on July 3 (chart 4-18). This information is from the Order of Battle for the Army of the Potomac (Appendix F) and *OR*, pt. 1, p. 160.

99. After-action report of Lt. Col. Franklin Sawyer (*OR*, pt. 1, p. 462). The 8th Ohio had moved to its skirmish line on July 2 with approximately two hundred men. Colonel Sawyer wrote on July 5 (ibid., pp. 461–62) that he lost forty-five killed or wounded between the morning of the Second and noon on the Third, then fifty-six additional men (plus one captured) that afternoon. These numbers are close to the casualty figures Sawyer listed in a postwar book in which he added that two of his men were killed during the cannonade (*A Military History of the 8th Regiment Ohio Vol. Inf'y* [Cleveland: Fairbanks, 1881], pp. 130, 132–33). They also jibe with those in a contemporary account by a man who served in Company H of this Ohio regiment (Thaddeus S. Potter, "The Battle of Gettysburg: Valor of the Volunteers—Resisting the Desperate Charge of the Confederates—Terrible Slaughter," *National Tribune*, Aug. 5, 1882).

100. Captain Armstrong of the 125th New York (note 98) estimated after the war that "perhaps two hundred men of various commands closed in upon that ill fated left flank at close range, and helped to cut it to pieces" (Ladd and Ladd, eds., *Bachelder Papers*, vol. 2, pp. 1001–1002). Added to this counterattacking force were Colonel Sawyer's 160 Ohioans.

101. General Longstreet gave commands at the time Brockenbrough's brigade broke, implying he did know about the Federal flank attack from the north. Pickett, too, sent orders over to his left to have the situation rectified at that end of the line (implying once again that this *was* "Pickett's Charge"). At this time, the rebel troops in Long Lane fired their muskets off to the east— and were in turn fired upon by some skirmishers from the 11th Corps (most of whose troops in this general sector of the field were to the north and rear of Hays's division). Whatever adjustments Longstreet and Pickett might have been trying to effect, little support came the way of the imperiled rebel left. This includes the fact that the Confederates in Long Lane did not respond to the 8th Ohio's counterattack (map 4-22). Those units, most of them bloodied from heavy fighting on July 1, stayed down in the depressed roadway on the Third.

102. John Michael Priest, "Lee's Gallant 6000?" *North & South* 1, no. 6 (Aug. 1998): pp. 42–56. Priest tacitly amplifies this thesis in his 1998 book *Into the Fight*.

103. Wayne E. Motts, "A Brave and Resolute Force," *North & South* 2, no. 5 (June 1999) pp. 28–34. Paul Clark Cooksey expressed additional skepticism about Priest's claims in "The Plan for Pickett's Charge," 72–73 (see also notes 41 and 89).

104. This refers to the terrain only; recall that Kemper's brigade on Pickett's right wing was conspicuously unprotected from Federal cannon fire that came its way before it reached the road.

105. The Southerners who made such claims about the supposedly imposing precipice that had been advanced upon by Pickett's Charge included two men who described Cemetery Ridge as "rock walls built on the mountain sides and tops," and the Union position there as "well nigh *impregnable*" (quoted in Gary W. Gallagher, "Lee's Army Has Not Lost Any of Its Prestige: The Impact of Gettysburg on the Army of Northern Virginia and the Confederate Home Front," in Gallagher, ed., *Third Day at Gettysburg*, pp. 10–11, emphasis in original). Another rebel soldier (writing home about a week after the battle) said that the Federals "secured an elevated position and fortified it well which saved them from their usual fate" (quoted in Reardon, *Pickett's Charge*, p. 31). S. Dodson Ramseur echoed these claims by saying, "the Enemy occupied a Gibraltar of a position" (quoted in Gallagher, "Lee's Army Has Not Lost," p. 11). General Ramseur and his 2nd Corps unit were rooted in the Long Lane on July 3 (map 4-13) and not involved in the attack.

106. These Vermont men were among the "nine-month regiments" President Lincoln called up in August 1862 as a "quasi-draft" (Howard Coffin, *Nine Months to Gettysburg: Stannard's Vermonters and the Repulse of Pickett's Charge* [Woodstock, Vt.: Countryman Press, 1997], pp. 7–8, 15–21). Some of Stannard's troops had fought at Gettysburg during the early evening of July 2. Moreover, they were scheduled to be mustered out later that month. Soldiers in this situation call themselves "short" and naturally are extra cautious. It thus is all the more remarkable that these Vermonters put up such a fight at Gettysburg.

107. "It was not a planned move," but "Kemper impetuously . . . rose in his stirrups, pointed to the left with his sword, and shouted, 'There are the guns, boys, go for them!'" (Stewart, *Pickett's Charge*, pp. 204–205). Colonel Joseph C. Mayo, commander of one of Kemper's regiments, wrote after the war that this was an "injudicious" command (Priest, *Into the Fight*, pp. 122–24).

108. Reardon, in *Pickett's Charge*, p. 23, reproduces Colonel Hall's map (which is in *OR*, pt. 1, p. 438). Most of it is duplicated here (although spruced up a bit) in the bottom panel of map 4-25.

109. To Harrow's left was a detached portion of a 1st Corps brigade (maps 4-15 and 4-25), under Col. Theodore B. Gates of the 80th New York (chart 4-20).

110. Two companies from the 71st Pennsylvania were detached to a position from which the fence line ran northward; this point is called the inner Angle. The low stone walls that defined the Angle were backed up by additional fence lines within the pocket fronted by the outer fences. These details are shown in map 4-20, for example, but not in most of the other diagrams. That is unnecessary because the fences east of the stone one in front were almost certainly torn down by the Union defenders in the area. The men used some of this material for firewood. More important, Lt. Alonzo Cushing had to move his guns around within the pocket (maps 4-26 and 4-38).

111. This description of the manner in which "Pickett's separate brigades lost their formation as they swept across the Emmitsburg road" is by a former major from the 19th Massachusetts (Edmund Rice, "Repelling Lee's Last Blow at Gettysburg," in Johnson and Buel, eds., *Battles and Leaders*, vol. 3, p. 387).

112. D. Scott Hartwig, "It Struck Horror to Us All," *Gettysburg Magazine*, no. 4 (Jan. 1991): p. 98.

113. Stewart, *Pickett's Charge*, pp. 211, 220–21.

114. Mott estimates that only about 150 rebels accompanied General Armistead over the low wall in the center (*"Trust in God and Fear Nothing,"* p. 45), the same number guessed by Brig. Gen. Alexander Webb, whose men stood in that sector. Hartwig, who took his title from a letter General Webb wrote to his wife after the battle, cited Webb's estimate ("'Fate of a Country,'" p. 35).

115. Notes 29 and 76 discuss the estimated strengths of the opposing forces. Recall that the current conventional wisdom about the numbers of attackers—12,500—does not include Wilcox's and Lang's 3rd Corps brigades, which were positioned near Pickett's right wing (map 4-10). These two units were either not moving forward or they had barely begun to advance toward the Emmitsburg Road by this time.

116. One other brigade commander in the assault force was killed: Col. James K. Marshall (chart 4-12), who led General Pettigrew's former brigade in the left wing of the attack.

117. Wert, who also says that these reinforcing units (exemplified in chart 4-28) "rushed" to support "*when* the Southern infantry had rolled forward in the charge"; although it was at "the time the attackers *had been beaten back* [when] Meade had eighteen brigades from four corps either close at hand or available" (*Day Three*, p. 253; emphasis added).

118. Note, however, how this widened the gap along the center left of the overall defensive line in this sector (map 4-47). This depletion of the frontline defense in this sector was ameliorated somewhat by Colonel Gates's demi-brigade, which wheeled in a clockwise direction, advanced, and poured musket fire into the rebel right (maps 4-35 and 4-38).

119. This is an important component of the July 3 timeline. Stewart first brought it to light in vivid detail (*Pickett's Charge*, pp. 219–20), and it has recently been ratified by twenty-first-century analysts of action on the third day and of the Gettysburg battle as a whole: General Hancock, shortly before breathlessly pausing where the 19th Massachusetts and 42nd New York were posted, had been checking out "his right flank" (Earl J. Hess, *Pickett's Charge—The Last Attack at Gettysburg* [Chapel Hill: University of North Carolina Press, 2001], p. 275) and "had seen how thoroughly Alexander Hays had disrupted Davis' brigade by flanking it" (Trudeau, *Testing of Courage*, p. 499). Hess adds the detail that Hancock "rode up from the rear . . . just behind Devereaux's command" (the 19th Massachusetts), having just previously "gone to Meade's headquarters to get more help for his right flank"; but, finding "no one at the Leister house [see note 61 for why], . . . he rode directly toward the line of battle" (*Pickett's Charge*, p. 275)—leading immediately to the excited exchange between him and Colonel Devereaux. This preceded Hancock's riding "off to the left" (ibid.), "toward the sector held by the . . . Vermont Brigade" (Trudeau, *Testing of Courage*, p. 499). The sources cited by these authors for these events are, variously, an article written for a magazine by Devereaux in 1887 and a letter from the former colonel to John B. Bachelder in 1889 (reprinted in Ladd and Ladd, eds., *Bachelder Papers*, vol. 3, pp. 1609–10); plus a letter written by Hancock in 1868. Trudeau also cites Jeffry D. Wert (in *Gettysburg Day Three*, p. 229) with regard to the exchange between Devereaux and Hancock at the back of Cemetery Ridge. Accounts in the postwar documents penned by these Union officers are supported by their after-action reports. Colonel Devereaux describes Hancock appearing at his regiment's position as the Union front line just to the north of the 19th Massachusetts "seemed to give way in some confusion" (report dated July 7, 1863, in *OR*, pt. 1, p. 443). General Hancock recounts his corroborating observation of the flank attack against the left wing of Pickett's Charge (report dated 1863, no month given, in ibid., p. 373); and of "the enemy . . . crossing over the breastworks abandoned by the troops [of the 71st Pennsylvania]" plus his "passing at this time, Colonel Devereaux" (ibid., p. 374); then of his subsequent interaction with General Stannard about sending "two regiments of his Vermont Brigade . . . to a point which would strike the enemy on the right flank" (ibid.). As the main text of the current work will be emphasizing, these key features of the timeline can be summarized as: envelopment of the left wing of Pickett's Charge; then Armistead's mini-break into the center (see above); then completion of the double envelopment (see above and soon-to-follow paragraphs in the text).

120. The place where the Vermonters carried out this move is south of where the National Park Service signs say it happened. More correct depictions of the enveloping pivot are given in maps 4-29 and 4-38.

121. *Pickett's Charge*, pp. 214, 228. Evidence in favor of the double envelopment's culmination occurring *after* some Southerners got into the center of the Union lines is provided in note 119. As mentioned in conjunction with the material cited there, Hancock was halted en route by Col. Arthur F. Devereux of the 19th Massachusetts, in a reserve position behind and to the south of the copse of trees, who shouted: "See general . . . They have broken through; the colors are coming over the stone wall; let me go in there!" (ibid., p. 220).

122. Hartwig estimates that the flank regiments in Kemper's brigade absorbed approximately five minutes of fire from the Vermont men, or nearly twelve thousand shots ("'Fate of a Country,'" p. 273). As deadly as enfilading fire can be, the total killed and wounded in this brigade of attackers was about 550 men (Harrison and Busey, *Nothing But Glory*, p. 456). Even though one of the Vermonters wrote that the "withering fire" from his mates "completely destroyed their lines" [Kemper's] and that "great masses of men seemed to disappear in a moment" (quoted in Wert, *Gettysburg Day Three*, p. 227), most of the shots from these inexperienced New England troops had to have missed (see Appendix G)—despite the fact that they were firing from an advantageous position on the rebels' right flank.

123. Stewart (*Pickett's Charge*, p. 230) and Rollins ("Failure of Confederate Artillery in Pickett's Charge," pp. 35, 39) say that Alexander advanced eighteen artillery pieces, but another account specifies that "only five guns were able to move forward at all from the over seventy pieces that Alexander had in his line" (Harrison and Busey, *Nothing but Glory*, p. 61). The Confederates originally intended that many more pieces than that were to have "followed behind Pickett's infantry" (Alexander, *Fighting for the Confederacy*, p. 247). See also Rollins, "Lee's Artillery Prepares for Pickett's Charge," pp. 51–52. That they did not was because "Pendleton [Lee's artillery chief, notes 48, 50] had completely failed to organize this maneuver" (ibid., p. 39).

124. This military principle was elaborated on in a June 24, 1997, letter to the author from Gen. H. Norman Schwarzkopf (USA, Ret.). Richard Rollins discusses the operation of "economy-of-force" principles on July 3 at Gettysburg from a slightly broader perspective. For example, he notes that "Meade's handling of the army" included "contingency plans for anything the enemy might do"; thus, "Meade massed his artillery reserve between the Baltimore Pike and the Taneytown Road [map 4-36], a short ride to any spot in his line [the portion of which near the center of Cemetery Ridge was "economically" thin], and put reserve infantry in the same area" ("Pickett's Charge," pp. 22–23). Whereas Rollins believes that these Federal reserves had a significant impact on the repulse of Pickett's Charge (see below), the economy-of-force principles as they played out on the ridge itself were arguably more consequential: Absent any a priori "contingency plans," the Union

commanders on Cemetery Ridge reacted to the tactical situation, maneuvering their flanks to nearly surround the attacking force and destroy it.

125. The Union batteries on Cemetery Hill at the other end of the line were more limited in their effectiveness. Osborn's batteries (map 4-21) could not "safely fire" on the Confederates advancing beyond the Emmitsburg Road "without endangering Hays's infantry [map 4-14] with short rounds" (Hartwig, "'Fate of a Country,'" p. 5). Nevertheless, David Shultz (the student of Pickett's Charge introduced in note 89) claims that because of the overall destruction done to the attackers by Federal artillery, "*one-third or fewer*" of the advancing infantrymen "made it to the Federal lines" ("*Double Canister at Ten Yards*," p. 67, emphasis added). See also Shultz and Rollins, "'Combined and Concentrated Fire,'" p. 56; and Rollins, "Failure of Confederate Artillery in Pickett's Charge," p. 40. A Union cannoneer, Lt. Tully McCrae (who took over Woodruff's battery, a two-gun section of which helped flank Pettigrew's left [map 4-23]), previewed this analysis when he said that "the artillery has never received the credit which was its due for this battle" (quoted in Reardon, *Pickett's Charge*, p. 237). That the Federal artillery on Cemetery Ridge had to cope with a drastically depleted number of Confederate attackers jibes with the view of John Michael Priest, who also believes that the rebel force actually approaching the Union lines was severely diminished, but for other reasons (see note 102).

126. The 108th New York was in the 2nd Brigade, and the 126th in the 3rd, of the 2nd Corps's 3rd Division. Men from the 3rd Brigade (map 4-23), along with those of the 1st Massachusetts Sharpshooters, later challenged the tacit claims of men from the 8th Ohio that it was they who deserved the credit for wrecking Pettigrew's left (Reardon, *Pickett's Charge*, p. 231). In truth, all the Union men who attacked that flank of the assault are to be commended. However, the initial actions of the 8th Ohio were of paramount importance: by holding their exposed position, then exploiting it, the Ohioans instigated the overall counterattack.

127. *OR*, pt. 2, p. 321. The extent to which these are the general's actual words is questionable because his military secretary customarily wrote his after-action reports, then Lee supposedly "approved and signed" them (Nesbitt, *Saber and Scapegoat*, p. 130).

128. Wayne E. Motts, personal communication, June 1999.

129. On the night of July 2, the men of the 69th and 71st Pennsylvania collected small arms and ammunition from their fallen comrades, enough to equip the men in certain companies with several muskets per man (Hartwig, "'The Fate of a Country,'" pp. 253–54, 271, 275).

130. Ibid., p. 276.

131. Stewart, *Pickett's Charge*, pp. 260–61. However, see note 114.

132. Lowrance took over Brig. Gen. Alfred M. Scales's brigade after Scales was wounded in the attack on Seminary Ridge, July 1.

133. General Anderson wrote in his after-action report (dated August 7, perhaps his only contribution to the campaign and battle) that "I was about to move forward Wright's and Posey's brigades [not Mahone's?], when Lieutenant-General Longstreet directed me to stop the movement, adding that it was useless, and would only involve unnecessary loss, the assault having failed" (*OR*, pt. 2, p. 615).

134. Recall from Chapter 3 that Posey, Mahone, or both could have contributed to Wright's "Mini-High-Water Mark" (map 3-39), during the late stages of Thursday's attacks, but did not. For Wright's part, he and his men may have been none too eager to attack on Friday afternoon, for this brigade had suffered 527 killed and wounded in its advance to Cemetery Ridge on the evening of July 2.

135. This thesis is elaborated by Rollins, "Second Wave," pp. 96–113.

136. The other 1st Corps units deployed on the rebel right would have had to hold that ground in order to keep units in the Federal 5th and 6th Corps (map 4-36) from swinging in a clockwise wheel and crushing Pickett's flank.

137. Fitzhugh Lee, *General Lee* (New York: D. Appleton, 1894), p. 295. Brig. Gen. Fitzhugh Lee was at Gettysburg, but not in the vicinity of Pickett's Charge. He fought on the East Cavalry Field on the afternoon of July 3. See Appendix D.

138. Rollins hypothesizes that "the second wave of troops ready to reinforce a successful charge led by Maj. Gen. George Pickett . . . consisted of at least 11, probably 13 and possibly 14 brigades of infantry" ("Second Wave," p. 113). This scenario speaks not so much to the additional Confederate units that could have been arranged for the Charge per se, but in the main to troops that would have taken off some time after the nine brigades advanced.

139. This is likely to be a pictorial understatement given a recently researched estimate that fifty-nine Union guns were "drawn from the Artillery Reserve and sent to various spots along the Cemetery Ridge line." Some of these batteries (all or parts of eleven of them) were brought forward during the cannonade (Shultz and Rollins, "'Combined and Concentrated Fire,'" p. 56). Certain Federal artillerymen argued that "it was the moral effect" of the *late*-arriving batteries that played a key role in breaking the charge (quoted in Reardon, *Pickett's Charge*, p. 121). Rollins further amplified this view, including ratcheting up the relevant numbers: "The total reinforcements" that "swarmed up Cemetery Ridge" (including sixteen guns "brought from the Baltimore Pike line") amounted to "75 guns . . . equal in size to the entire artillery of Longstreet's Corps. . . . By the time the Confederate infantry reached the wall, 134 guns were firing at them," which "played a vital part in the repulse of Pickett's Charge" ("Failure of Confederate Artillery in Pickett's Charge," p. 40).

140. The 2nd Corps soldiers from Col. Samuel Carroll's 1st Brigade had been on Cemetery Hill the previous night. Also, a 6th Corps unit from Brig. Gen. Alexander Shaler's 1st Brigade, 3rd Division, had been poised near the Hummelbaugh house (near the Taneytown Road, behind Stannard's position [map 4-35]). However, no additional 6th Corps troops arrived as late reinforcements.

141. Hartwig, "'Fate of a Country,'" p. 274. Lieutenant Robert Rogers now commanded the Union cannon east of this rough ground owing to the mortal wounding of Captain Rorty earlier (chart 4-29). The advance of the small groups of Virginians was the *third* and last push into the actual line of Union defenders (maps 4-28 and 4-33 show the first two).

142. Stewart, *Pickett's Charge*, p. 194.

143. General Pickett sent a staff officer to Longstreet, who told him to deliver a message to his superior, allowing Pickett to order up Wilcox's brigade. Upon receipt of the message, Pickett dispatched three couriers to Wilcox with the "get going" directions, hoping that one of them would reach that 3rd Corps brigadier (a further feature of Pickett's supervision of the assault *above* the level of his own 1st Corps division). Wilcox describes these instructions in his after-action report dated July 17: "The advance had not been made more than twenty or thirty minutes, before three staff officers in quick succession (one from the general commanding the division[?]) gave me orders" (*OR*, pt. 2, p. 620). That this was a "miscommunication"—or at least that the trio of identical instructions did not shake Wilcox loose at this moment—is noted by Cooksey (*Gettysburg*, no. 22, p. 78).

144. Stewart, *Pickett's Charge*, p. 252.

145. Ibid., p. 256; Priest, *Into the Fight*, p. 173.

146. *OR,* pt. 2, p. 321.

147. Catton, *Stillness at Appomattox,* p. 6.

148. Sometime earlier, and as if further to demonstrate Union pugnacity on this day, some 5th Corps troops in Col. William McCandless's brigades of the Pennsylvania Reserves (chart 4-31) broke away from their positions toward the south end of the field (map 4-39). The Pennsylvanians came up to threaten Kemper's right, but McCandless's men absorbed fire and suffered losses from rebel skirmishers in Brig. Gen. William Barksdale's brigade. Barksdale had been mortally wounded, and his unit was being led by Col. Benjamin G. Humphreys (map 4-36).

149. Some telling details about certain of the captured flags: Colonel Sawyer of the 8th Ohio said that his men took three "stands of colors" from the attacking rebels (*OR,* pt. 1, p. 462), one "not being remembered" (Sawyer, *A Military History,* p. 132). He did specify in both of the accounts just cited that the other two captured flags were from the 34th North Carolina and the 38th Virginia. However, the North Carolina regiment was in Lowrance's (formerly Scales's) brigade on the right of Trimble's demi-division (map 4-14), far from the 8th Ohio's position (maps 4-22 and 4-23), and the Virginia unit—from Armistead's brigade—was even farther away as it began to advance (map 4-24). Sawyer said that the flags of these rebel regiments were taken at the time Ohioans counterattacked from the south-facing position they assumed after first firing westward toward the left wing of the assault. If the colonel's report was accurate, the implication is that some Confederate regiments got badly intermingled, straying significantly from their initial lines of march.

150. D. Scott Hartwig to author, Aug. 25, 1998: "I lean toward Stewart's figure [1,500, *Pickett's Charge,* pp. 261–262]; Vanderslice [2,300] is much too high." Vanderslice also generated overall casualty estimates for July 3 (chart 4-32). The Union casualties listed are the numbers for Pickett's Charge and the fighting in the morning on Culp's Hill.

151. Wayne E. Motts's research leads him to conclude that Pickett's Charge resulted in up to *eight thousand* Confederate casualties, including the "walking wounded" (an issue taken up near the beginning of Chapter 5). Motts goes on to say that the great majority of the killed, wounded, and captured rebels were lost after they crossed the Emmitsburg Road (personal communication, June 1999). However, in terms of the casualty figures themselves, D. Scott Hartwig has studied this case in depth and arrives at different numbers: Pickett's division—581 killed, 1,207 wounded, 1,078 captured or missing; Pettigrew's division—1,200–1,500 total casualties; and within Trimble's demi-division, Lane's brigade—178 killed, 376 wounded, 238 captured or missing; and Scales's brigade, ca. 200 total casualties. This works out to 5,500–5,800 total Confederate losses in the Charge, approximately 45 percent. Note that 10–15 percent of the Confederate casualties were men captured. The percentage of Union soldiers captured was far lower because of the nature of the engagement (Hartwig, e-mail to author, Aug. 25, 1998).

152. Stewart, *Pickett's Charge,* p. 263: 1,125 killed, 4,550 wounded; Priest, *Into the Fight,* p. 199: 801 killed, 1,237 wounded, 1,234 wounded and captured, plus whatever proportion of the 359 generic casualties listed for Wilcox's and Lang's brigades were wounded, fatally or otherwise.

153. The quotes at the end of this paragraph are from Stewart, *Pickett's Charge,* p. 260. It is not clear from Stewart's notes on p. 341 whether he cited a source for this anecdote, which is recycled in Motts's *"Trust in God and Fear Nothing"* (p. 45). Issues revolving round the intensity and accuracy of fire are addressed in more detail in Apendix G.

154. In the aforementioned Battle of Cannae, more than 70 percent of the Roman army was *killed* on the field.

155. "Failed" is the word invoked by two historians whose intermingled phrases are quoted at the end of this paragraph: Cooksey, "Plan for Pickett's Charge," p. 79 ("inherent weakness," "historians claim"); and Hartwig, "'The Fate of a Country,'" p. 247 ("Federals' advantage," "tenacity"). However, as is previewed in the introduction to this work, "failed" seems to be the wrong verb. In this regard Richard Rollins, echoing Cooksey and Hartwig, states that "Pickett's Charge . . . was a well-developed plan based on sound military principles." However, he goes on to say that "its implementation was flawed" ("Pickett's Charge," p. 23). Yet this perspective seems inappropriately to factor out the other actors in this tragedy—the Federal defenders who did more than benefit from a defective "implementation." Instead, they actively destroyed the assault of July 3.

156. William T. Poague, *Gunner With Stonewall,* ed. Monroe F. Cockrell (Jackson, Tenn.: McCowat-Mercer, 1957), pp. 253–54. This exchange between the commanding general and General Pickett may be one more example of Gettysburg apocrypha: Whereas Longstreet encountered his division commander after the repulse, trying "to console his old friend"—and "although accounts conflict"—"it appears that Lee did not speak personally with Pickett at this time" (Wert, *Gettysburg Day Three,* p. 252).

157. John Singleton Mosby, *The Memoirs of Colonel John S. Mosby,* ed. C. W. Russell (Boston: Little, Brown, 1917), pp. 380–81.

158. *Sunday Magazine,* July 1, 1906. The former Confederate general was so quoted in the early 1870s. See Glenn Tucker, *Lee and Longstreet at Gettysburg* (1968; reprint, Dayton, Ohio: Morningside House, 1982), p. 272; and Richard A. Sauers, "Gettysburg Controversies," *Gettysburg Magazine,* no. 4 (Jan. 1991): p. 120. George Pickett was in Canada at the time. Why? He was in self-imposed exile of a sort, for interesting reasons that are detailed in Gerard A. Patterson, *Justice or Atrocity: General George E. Pickett and the Kinston, N.C. Hangings* (Gettysburg: Thomas Publications, 1998).

Chapter 5
Aftermath: The Pursuit and Escape of the Army of Northern Virginia

1. This meant, for instance, that Maj. Gen. Henry Heth, who suffered a debilitating head wound on July 1, is unlikely to have been listed as a casualty—although he was out of action for the remainder of the battle. (Heth's return to command later in July, as described in note 46 below, may have further encouraged Southern casualty counters not to include him.) Standing back from this example to contemplate the overall Confederate figures for the Gettysburg campaign, the relatively low number of casualties reported by General Lee (top of chart 5-1) stemmed from the general unwillingness of Southerners to count so-called slight injuries: Indeed, well before the (second) invasion of the North commenced, General Lee gave explicit instructions that the number of wounded was to be under-reported, so as not "to mislead our friends and encourage our enemies" (order dated May 14, 1863, *OR,* ser. 1, vol. 25, pt. 3, pp. 798–99). In particular, the Gettysburg casualty reports from some Southern commands were only partial or were missing altogether. The records that eventually landed in the War Department in Washington list 12,227 Confederates captured during the Gettysburg campaign, whereas Lee had earlier admitted to only 5,150 (Fennel, "Attack and Defense of Culp's Hill," p. 21; see also note 2). Moreover, historians have never been able to

gather reliable casualty statistics for many Confederate brigades. All in all, it seems highly improbable that the Army of Northern Virginia sustained fewer casualties at Gettysburg than its counterpart, given that the rebels were on the tactical offensive for almost the entire battle (as argued by Fennel, "Attack and Defense of Culp's Hill," p. 21).

2. Wert (*Gettysburg Day Three,* p. 290). The matter of 5,000–6,000 missing/captured (chart 5-1), plus another 5,000 Confederates wounded/captured during the Battle of Gettysburg speaks to another of the apparent disadvantages of the Southerners fighting in enemy territory: It was especially difficult for the relatively ill-equipped Army of Northern Virginia to care for its wounded in a situation where that also meant getting them back to home ground.

3. Consider, for example, the Battle of Tarawa (November 20–23, 1943) in the Pacific theater of World War II. "American public opinion was seriously shocked by the heavy casualties" suffered by the U.S. infantrymen engaged: 1,885 killed and 2,233 wounded from among the approximately twenty thousand men in a marine division (Bryan Perrett, *The Battle Book* [London: Arms and Armour Press, 1992], pp. 288–89). Historian Ronald H. Spector remarked of the 16–17 percent casualty rate suffered at Tarawa, one of the highest sustained by an American force during that war: "At home in the U.S., they could not believe it" (*Eagle Against the Sun* [New York: Free Press, 1985], p. 266).

During the Civil War the American public may never have truly accepted the battlefield slaughter, but by 1863 people were *used to* a magnitude of casualties far higher than those that would be inflicted on U.S. forces in World War II. Gettysburg presented the country with essentially the highest rate and raw numbers of battlefield losses for the Civil War, due in part to the fact that the fighting lasted for three days, a relatively rare occurrence for the 1861–65 battles.

The poor quality of care casualties received during that conflict is signified by the fate of wounded Civil War soldiers. As an example, consider what happened to the 140 men of the 1st Minnesota who were wounded during the regiment's charge from Cemetery Ridge on July 2. Even though the battlefield hospital situation had improved somewhat by mid-1863, twenty-eight of the wounded Minnesotans died after the battle (see Haiber and Haiber, *1st Minnesota Regiment at Gettysburg,* app. A). This was not atypical; 15 percent of the men wounded in Civil War actions died within a few weeks of the battles in which they fought (McPherson, *Battle Cry of Freedom,* p. 347).

The degree to which such a fate for wounded soldiers became unacceptable in later wars is indicated by the reduction in the died-of-wounds rate for American infantrymen, which dropped to 4 percent in World War II, 2.5 percent in the Korean War, and less than 1 percent in Vietnam (Robert Cowley and Geoffrey Parker, eds., *The Reader's Companion to Military History* [Boston: Houghton Mifflin, 1996], p. 296; Harry G. Summers Jr., *Vietnam War Almanac* [New York: Facts On File, 1985], p. 66). These falling percentages reflect more than improvements in medical practices; the attitudes of military leaders changed, too. They organized increasingly large medical operations and improved evacuation procedures in support of the troops who fought twentieth-century battles. See, for example, Mark Harrison, "Medicine," in *The Oxford Companion to World War II,* ed. I. C. B. Dear (New York: Oxford University Press, 1995), pp. 723–31. Thus, whereas in World War II no aircraft were available to fly wounded Americans from the battlefield, one in seven injured soldiers was evacuated by helicopter to a hospital in Korea, and the majority of wounded men in Vietnam were quickly extracted from the battlefield in medevac helicopters (Summers, *Vietnam War Almanac,* p. 66).

While it may seem ludicrous to compare military medical practices of Civil War times to ones in which mechanization could make such a difference, the army's attitudinal problem in the nineteenth century was perhaps as significant as its lack of medevac capacity and infection-fighting drugs. Civil War armies did not seem to *prearrange* all they could have before a battle in terms of coping with the inevitable casualties.

4. The *beginnings* of certain Confederate offensive thrusts near Bristoe Station and Rappahannock Station in Virginia, in October and November 1863, were vigorously repulsed by elements of Meade's army. They became, in the words of a staff officer in the Army of Northern Virginia, "the saddest chapter in the history of this army" (R. Lockwood Tower and John S. Belmont, eds., *Lee's Adjutant: The Wartime Letters of Colonel Walter Herron Taylor, 1862–1865* [Columbia: University of South Carolina Press, 1995], p. 82). The quote refers to Rappahannock Station in particular and is from a letter written on November 7, 1863, by the man who carried Lee's fateful message about Cemetery Hill to Lt. Gen. Richard Ewell on the evening of July 1.

5. Sydney Richardson to his parents, Aug. 5, 1863, published in Mills Lane, ed., *"Dear Mother: Don't grieve about me. If I get killed, I'll only be dead": Letters from Georgia Soldiers in the Civil War* (Savannah, Ga.: Beehive Press, 1977), p. 259. Richardson was a corporal in the 21st Georgia (Doles's brigade, Rodes's division).

6. Gallagher, "Lee's Army Has Not Lost," pp. 4–6, 8–16.

7. From headlines that appeared on July 6, 1863, in the *New York Tribune* and the *Philadelphia Inquirer,* respectively.

8. Chris Perello, "Gettysburg: Lee's Greatest Gamble," *Command: Military History, Strategy & Analysis,* July-Aug. 1992, p. 32.

9. James M. McPherson, "Failed Southern Strategies," *MHQ: The Quarterly Journal of Military History* 11, no. 4 (summer 1999): p. 61.

10. Glatthaar, "Common Soldier's Gettysburg Campaign," p. 30.

11. Duane Schultz, *The Most Glorious Fourth: Vicksburg and Gettysburg, July 4th, 1863* (New York: W. W. Norton, 2002), pp. 368–69.

12. Richard M. McMurray, "The Pennsylvania Gambit and the Gettysburg Splash," in Borritt, ed., *Gettysburg Nobody Knows,* p. 266.

13. William Oates wrote a reflective letter in 1898 in which he said that Gettysburg was the greatest of the Confederacy's lost opportunities (Glenn W. LaFantasie, ed., "William C. Oates Remembers Little Round Top," *Gettysburg Magazine,* no. 21 [July 1999]: pp. 57–63). The letter previewed Oates's memoirs, which are really more than that, as the book presents an insightful and balanced analysis of the war. Oates encapsulates the significance of the Gettysburg campaign in the context of the simultaneous fall of Vicksburg. The events in July 1863, he observed, tolled "the death-knell of the Confederate cause; but neither its governmental authorities, the soldiers, or citizens would see it or believe it. The Union soldiers were enthused, the Confederates depressed, though still ready to fight and die" (look again at note 5). Indeed, the war was far from over, but the weight of the events of mid-1863 (if not their occurrences as such) "seemed ominous of ultimate success of the Union cause" (Oates, *War Between the Union,* p. 243).

14. Alexander, *Robert E. Lee's Civil War,* p. 169 (emphasis added).

15. Glenn Tucker, *High Tide at Gettysburg* (Indianapolis: Bobbs-Merrill, 1958), p. 19.

16. McMurray, "Pennsylvania Gambit," p. 199. See also p. 185.

17. Herman Hattaway and Archer Jones, *How the North Won: A Military History of the Civil War* (Urbana: University of Illinois Press, 1983), pp. 421–22.

18. Alexander, *Robert E. Lee's Civil War,* p. 235. Alexander pointed out (letter to author, Nov. 12, 1999) that Hattaway and Jones provide an "astute essay that constitutes endnote 91" to chapter 13 of *How the North Won* (pp. 419–23). In seven columns of fine print the authors denigrate the potentially war-ending impact of Gettysburg "following a hypothetical Union disaster" there (p. 420). They similarly downgrade the political and economic significance of the fall of Vicksburg.

19. Catton, *Stillness at Appomattox,* pp. 91–92. The Wilderness battle overlapped the ground of the old Chancellorsville battlefield from a year before.

20. Moreover, Major General Meade (his rank in "the volunteers") was promoted on July 7, 1863, to brigadier general in the Regular Army "for skill, good conduct, and gallantry at the battle of Gettysburg"—words of Abraham Lincoln that are quoted by Jeffry Wert (*Gettysburg Day Three,* p. 299). Wert further notes that Meade received congratulatory letters from General in Chief Henry Halleck (July 28), Maj. Gen. John Pope (July 10), and even from the fallen George McClellan (July 11).

21. Glatthaar, "Common Soldier's Gettysburg Campaign," p. 27. An associated and more specific evaluation of Meade is that he "was the first commander of the Army of the Potomac to understand what the artillery advocates wanted, and to make the artillery a key element of his plans" (Shultz and Rollins, "'Combined and Concentrated Fire,'" p. 40).

22. Pfanz, *Second Day,* p. 426.

23. Reenlistments in the Army of the Potomac in 1864 amounted to a surprisingly high percentage (about 50 percent) of the soldiers who had been fighting since mid-1863.

24. Perello, "Gettysburg," p. 32.

25. A more recent analysis concludes that the Army of Northern Virginia's strength at the beginning of hostilities in May 1864 has been systematically underestimated as approximately sixty thousand, but was in reality closer to the number quoted in this text passage (Alfred C. Young III, "Numbers and Losses in the Army of Northern Virginia," *North & South* 3, no. 3 [Mar. 2000: pp. 14–29]).

26. To be fair, part of the Army of the Potomac took off after Lee's infantry on July 5, following it toward Chambersburg. This is described in more detail below. Part of General Meade's hesitation in moving the majority of his force stemmed from a five-to-three vote of his corps commanders *against* leaving Gettysburg on July 4, absent a clear picture of Lee's intentions (*OR,* pt. 3, p. 517). Colonel Regis de Trobriand, 3rd Corps brigade commander, endorsed the decision of the higher-ranking generals: "General Meade . . . would not take the risk of compromising [the victory] by leaving his position before Lee had abandoned his; . . . he acted wisely, whatever may have been said to the contrary" (quoted in A. W. Greene, "From Gettysburg to Falling Waters," in Gallagher, ed., *Third Day at Gettysburg,* p. 184).

27. General Meade so suggested in a letter to his wife Margaret on July 8: "as I have to follow and fight him [Lee], I would rather do it at once and in Maryland than to follow him into Virginia" (Meade, *Life and Letters,* vol. 2, p. 132).

28. General Meade speaking to a Union cavalry officer, quoted in McPherson, *Battle Cry of Freedom,* p. 663.

29. Quoted in Harry W. Pfanz, "The Gettysburg Campaign after Pickett's Charge," *Gettysburg Magazine,* no. 1 (July 1989): p. 120. The quote is from General Warren's post-campaign testimony before the congressional "Committee on the Conduct of the War" (whose Gettysburg-related activities are nicely analyzed by Bruce Tap, "'Bad Faith Somewhere': George Gordon Meade and the Committee on the Conduct of the War," *North & South* 2, no. 6 [Aug. 1999]: pp. 74–80). Another of Meade's high-ranking staff officers, Brig. Gen. Henry J. Hunt, echoed Warren's view (quoted in Lt. Col. William Terpeluk, "A Lesson in Battle Tempo: The Union Pursuit after Gettysburg," *Parameters: U.S. War College Quarterly* 25, no. 3 [autumn 1995]: p. 79).

30. These Union troopers came toward Williamsport, Maryland, from the west. Recall that two of Buford's brigades had been sent away from the Battle of Gettysburg on the morning of July 2 after their fighting west and north of the town twenty-four hours earlier. Buford had been ordered to Westminster, Maryland, to guard supplies.

31. Imboden's defense was augmented by artillery—six of his own pieces and eighteen additional guns detached from the Army of Northern Virginia proper, which General Imboden hauled from Gettysburg.

32. Troopers from Brig. Gens. Beverly Robertson's and Grumble Jones's cavalry brigades accompanied the wagons (chart 5-3). This and many other details about the Confederates' second wagon train and the fighting at Monterey Pass involving it are given in Eric J. Wittenberg, "'This Was a Night Never to Be Forgotten': The Midnight Fight in the Monterey Pass, July 4–5, 1863," *North & South* 2, no. 6 [Aug. 1999]: pp. 44–54. Wittenberg comes down hard on Kilpatrick, who left Lee's retreat route open. Supposedly, this Union cavalry officer, notwithstanding the rather small force he commanded, could have held the pass long enough for Federal infantry to rush to reinforce him.

33. White's troopers had been in the vanguard of the rebel advance in June.

34. At the end of July 6, both Buford and Kilpatrick withdrew to Boonsboro, Maryland (map 5-3). The actions of the Confederate cavalry that day had secured both Williamsport and Hagerstown—a destination of Lee's main body and a point directly along the line of infantry march toward it. The Union cavalry units in that region then were able only to threaten Lee's flanks.

35. On July 7 and 8 Lee wrote to Jefferson Davis from Hagerstown (the commander was back in touch with the president after a three-day hiatus). On the Eighth, General Lee said that the Army of Northern Virginia was in good condition, "its confidence unimpaired." His delay crossing the Potomac River meant he might have to accept battle from the Army of the Potomac, but he was "not in least discouraged" (Dowdey and Manarin, eds., *Wartime Papers,* pp. 543–44).

36. Greene, "From Gettysburg to Falling Waters," p. 185.

37. Meanwhile, a brigade of Union cavalry (map 5-3) followed the more northerly route taken by General Imboden and the wagon train carrying the Confederate wounded (map 5-2).

38. "George [his son] is very well, though both of us are a good deal fatigued with our recent operations. From the time I took command till to-day, now over ten days, I have not changed my clothes, have not had a regular night's rest, and many nights not a wink of sleep, and for several days did not even wash my face and hands, no regular food, and all the time in a great state of mental anxiety. Indeed, I think I have lived as much in this time as in the last thirty years" (Meade, *Life and Letters,* vol. 2, p. 132).

39. *OR,* pt. 3, pp. 605–606.

40. Pfanz ("Gettysburg Campaign after Pickett's Charge," pp. 122–23) provides details about this council. Greene paraphrases additional features of the Union generals' discussion on the night of the Twelfth—including that a possible probe of the Confederate left flank (which was not all that well anchored [map 5-8]) was rejected: "Rain and fog, together with Confederate mobility and vigilance, would have made that effort problematical" ("From Gettysburg to Falling Waters," p. 189).

41. Meade quoted in Greene, "From Gettysburg to Falling

Waters," p. 188.

42. *OR,* pt. 1, p. 92.

43. Greene, "From Gettysburg to Falling Waters," p. 171; Terpeluk, "Lesson in Battle Tempo," p. 73.

44. Meade, *Life and Letters,* vol. 2, pp. 122–23.

45. With no boats available to carry the artillery caissons, Ewell had to send them down to the pontoon bridge. The guns themselves were dragged across the ford.

46. Recall that General Heth had been slightly wounded during the fighting west of Gettysburg on the morning of July 1 (see note 51 in Chapter 2). Between that time and the end of the battle, Brig. Gen. J. Johnston Pettigrew took over Heth's division. In Heth's *OR* report of his post-battle activities (pt. 2, pp. 639–42) he reveals that he resumed command of his division during the retreat. However, neither he nor his commander (Lt. Gen. A. P. Hill, *OR,* pt. 2, p. 609) says exactly when after the battle General Heth resumed his duties.

47. Estimates range from 750 to 1,500 captured rebels on July 14 (Ted Alexander, "Ten Days in July: The Pursuit to the Potomac," *North & South* 2, no. 6 [Aug. 1999]: pp. 10–34). The total casualty figures for July 4–14 add up to about 1,000 for the Union forces (almost exclusively from cavalry actions) and about 5,000 for the Confederates—mostly *captured* cavalrymen and infantrymen (ibid., pp. 20–21). In any event, they were gone forever from Lee's army, whose total losses for the campaign therefore may have approached an astounding 50 percent of his invading force (chart 5-1).

48. The most recent articulation of this anti-Meade judgment is that of Keith Poulter, "Errors That Doomed a Campaign," *North & South* 2, no. 6 (Aug. 1999): pp. 82–88. Poulter is not even sure that the Confederate defensive positions near the river were all that formidable. However, Ted Alexander argues in "Ten Days in July" that they were—a view echoed and amplified by Kent Masterson Brown, "A Golden Bridge: Lee's Williamsport Defense Lines and His Escape across the Potomac," *North & South* 2, no. 6 (Aug. 1999): pp. 56–65.

49. Several documented examples of the anguished frustration expressed by the president are documented in Frank J. Williams, "'We Had Only to Stretch Forth Our Hands': Abraham Lincoln and George Gordon Meade," *North & South* 2, no. 6 (Aug. 1999): pp. 66–72; and Tap, "'Bad Faith Somewhere,'" ibid., pp. 74–80. Tap's article and an essay by Gabor S. Boritt ("'Unfinished Work': Lincoln, Meade, and Gettysburg," in *Lincoln's Generals,* ed. Gabor S. Boritt [New York: Oxford University Press, 1994], pp. 79–120) review the secondary literature in which various analysts either praise or assail Meade's performance during the period July 4–14.

50. Williams ("'We Had Only to Stretch'") and Tap ("'Bad Faith Somewhere'") are in Meade's camp; A. Wilson Greene's recent analysis revolves entirely around a defense of the general's decisions and actions during the final stages of the Gettysburg campaign (see "From Gettysburg to Falling Waters," pp. 161–201). Terpeluk ("Lesson in Battle Tempo," 69–80) provides a relatively balanced view of General Meade's problems and opportunities during the final ten days of the campaign.

51. Gallagher discusses Lee's resignation gambit in the letter the general wrote on August 8, 1863 ("Lee's Army Has Not Lost," pp. 20–21).

52. Ibid., pp. 1–4, 6–8.

53. The subtitle of this book by Richard Sauers is "The Sickles-Meade Controversy." The title, however, could just as well refer to the vast volumes of postwar ink spilled argumentatively by many Southern and Northern veterans—especially those who fought at Gettysburg.

Appendix A

1. Maj. Gen. Daniel Butterfield, Hooker's chief of staff, wrote this order to General Pleasonton on June 7 (*OR,* pt. 3, pp. 27–28).

2. During the three weeks before the Battle of Gettysburg, several cavalry actions occurred in addition to Brandy Station. As the two armies' main bodies moved northward throughout June and during early July, these engagements took place in all three of the relevant states. In some instances, as at Brandy Station, the force of troopers in question was accompanied by supporting infantry (see, for example, chart B-4).

3. Bear in mind that significant elements of the fighting just described involved *dismounted* cavalrymen on both sides. Moreover, the unhorsed Federal troopers were supported on their flanks by the Union infantrymen indicated in chart A-1.

Appendix B

1. Command changes were extremely fluid. If the overall nature of these reassignments was not confusing enough, note in particular that Kilpatrick, who had himself been reduced from brigade to regimental command after Brandy Station, was elevated to division command just a few days after he was restored to brigade command in late June.

2. General Pleasonton unfairly excoriated Duffié for his actions at Middleburg and asked that he be relieved. General Hooker sent Duffié to Washington and thus out of the Gettysburg campaign.

3. Another detail of this engagement involved an unsuccessful attack by the 4th New York (map B-2), commanded by Col. Luigi P. di Cesnola, who had been demoted from brigade command after Brandy Station. Di Cesnola was captured during the course of the 4th New York's disorganized attack.

4. See chart B-3, which refers to June 19.

5. Desjardin, *Stand Firm,* pp. 11–13.

Appendix C

1. Paul M. Shevchuk, "The Wounding of Albert Jenkins, July 2, 1863," *Gettysburg Magazine,* no. 3 (July 1990): pp. 51–64.

2. Paul M. Shevchuk ("The Fight for Brinkerhoff's Ridge, July 2, 1863," *Gettysburg Magazine,* no. 2 [Jan. 1990]: p. 67) indicates that the skirmishers were from two 12th Corps infantry regiments (chart C-1). Additional details for chart C-1 are from Edmund R. Brown, *The 27th Indiana Volunteer Infantry in the War of the Rebellion* (Baltimore: Butternut and Blue, 1984), p. 368. Harry Pfanz (*Gettysburg: Culp's Hill and Cemetery Hill,* p. 154) says the skirmishers were from the 9th Massachusetts, a 5th Corps regiment, and that they were left alone near the ridge when the 12th Corps departed to rejoin their corps on Culp's Hill.

3. Capt. William D. Rank commanded the small battery of heavy cannon. On July 3, his guns were commandeered by Lt. Col. Freeman McGilvery and formed part of the massed line of Federal artillery on the southern sector of Cemetery Ridge (maps 4-18 and 4-31).

4. *OR,* pt. 2, pp. 518–19.

Appendix D

1. Nesbitt, *Saber and Scapegoat,* p. 95.

2. From J. E. B. Stuart's lengthy after-action report dated August 20, 1863 (*OR,* pt. 2, p. 697).

3. William O. Adams (personal communication, Oct. 1995).

4. Nesbitt, *Saber and Scapegoat,* p. 96.

5. Ibid.

6. The artillery parks (map D-1) were not places merely to collect large groups of massed cannon but consisted of many stand-alone batteries that could be quickly dispatched and employed as needed. The locations of the Union Artillery Reserve could also be a rallying point for retreating infantrymen—if significant numbers had been pushed east of Cemetery Ridge by Pickett. Had Stuart's men managed to reach this area (circling around from the north and eventually moving west), they might not have been able to advance any further against dozens of massed guns at the ready, supported by rallied Union troops.

7. Nesbitt, *Saber and Scapegoat,* p. 96.

8. *OR,* pt. 2, p. 699.

9. Wert, *Gettysburg Day Three,* p. 271.

10. Ibid.

11. For example, the reports of Capt. William Miller (chart D-8) and Lt. James Chester in Ladd and Ladd, eds., *Bachelder Papers,* vol. 2, pp. 1264 and 1079. Chester was in charge of a battery section that fired from its position on the southern part of the battlefield (map D-2). The relevant secondary literature usually says things like "the accurate artillery fire [of Federal batteries firing northward] forced the Confederate troops occupying the Rummel barn to evacuate the building" (Marshall D. Krolick, "Forgotten Field: The Cavalry Battle East of Gettysburg on July 3, 1863," *Gettysburg Magazine,* no. 4 [Jan. 1991]: p. 84). However, a Confederate account seems to call this into question: "The line of fire from the guns which first opened on the Federal side (Pennington's guns, almost certainly) passed to the right of the barn on the plain below, but not very far from the barn" (Maj. Henry B. McClellan, Stuart's assistant adjutant general, in Ladd and Ladd, eds., *Bachelder Papers,* vol. 2, p. 1171). Lt. Alexander C. M. Pennington Jr.'s Battery M, 2nd U.S. Artillery, in the 1st Brigade of the Horse Artillery was among the Union guns on the southern sector of the East Field. Lt. Frank B. Hamilton, who commanded a section of Pennington's battery, seems to concur with McClellan: "We did get a special order to direct our fire on that stone barn [Rummels], which had been taken possession of by rebel dismounted skirmishers and from which they could not be dislodged; and I remember that so far as our shots were concerned we did not appear to make much impression" (letter dated Dec. 12, 1884, ibid., vol. 2, p. 1085). William O. Adams and several colleagues made the field measurements mentioned in the main text (personal communication, Oct. 1995).

12. A fictional part of this story is that the mounted infantrymen under Jenkins had only ten rounds of ammunition per man and hence could not have fought for long (Coddington, *Gettysburg Campaign,* p. 522; Krolick, "Forgotten Field," p. 84). This is false, because these fighters replenished their ammunition during the fighting. Colonel Witcher himself went to the rear on a bullet run (Vincent A. Witcher to Henry B. McClellan, Mar. 16, 1886, in Ladd and Ladd, eds., *Bachelder Papers,* vol. 2, p. 1229). Something else that makes the standard story ring false is the contention that the 34th Virginia Battalion was armed with "Enfields." In reality, its troopers carried the typical potpourri of shoulder arms—being equipped at least with .54-caliber Mississippi rifles (Coates and Thomas, *Introduction to Civil War Small Arms,* p. 92) and other types of muzzle-loading rifles. Witcher's was a large battalion of about 350 men, although only five of his companies fought on the East Cavalry Field. The 34th was eventually reinforced by units from Jenkins's brigade (chart D-4), but one of these was a "skeleton paper regiment" (as Witcher called it) and added only about fifty dismounted infantrymen to his force (two letters by Witcher, both dated Apr. 7, 1886, in Ladd and Ladd, eds., *Bachelder Papers,* vol. 2, pp. 1290 and 1297).

13. This was a relatively rare example of the effectiveness of truly long-range musketry. Witcher's 34th Virginia Battalion had a reputation for accurate shooting with their rifled muskets; and the men of Jenkins's brigade (now under Ferguson) were not only experienced mounted infantrymen, but also the average age of the men in the 34th Virginia Battalion was 27. These were not boys. For their part, the Michiganders with their Spencer rifles were ironically outgunned as this engagement broke out below the Rummel farm. Here are the relevant small-arms facts: The Spencer was rapidly reloaded by shoving a metal tube containing seven "fixed cartridges" (self-contained ones—no percussion cap necessary) up the wooden butt. After that, all you had to do between shots was operate a lever (which also serves as the trigger guard), thus projecting the next round into the weapon's *receiver* (for this advanced weapon, a meaningful small-arms component: the metal unit containing the action, to which the barrel and stock are attached). The Spencer rifle, however, had a shorter effective range than a rifled musket; this was because the former's receiver accommodated a rather small cartridge containing less black powder than got dumped down the barrel of a muzzle loader (see Appendix G).

14. Quoted in Michael Phipps, *"Come On, You Wolverines": Custer at Gettysburg* (Gettysburg: Farnsworth Military Impressions, 1995), pp. 42–43.

15. Col. John B. McIntosh (chart D-8) to John B. Bachelder, Aug. 27, 1885, in Ladd and Ladd, eds., *Bachelder Papers,* vol. 2, p. 1124–25. Vincent Witcher refers to another fence line in this vicinity (Witcher to former Confederate major Henry B. McClellan, Mar. 16, 1886, vol. 2, p. 1229). The former Confederate colonel's account of what happened to Custer's dismounted men is in that letter (vol. 2, p. 1230) and in another one entitled "Gregg's and Stuart's Cavalry Fight" (Witcher to John B. Bachelder, Mar. 19, 1886, in Ladd and Ladd, eds., *Bachelder Papers,* vol. 2, p. 1238).

16. Nesbitt, *Saber and Scapegoat,* p. 105.

17. Krolick, "Forgotten Field," p. 86.

18. Wert, *Gettysburg Day Three,* p. 271.

19. Witcher to McClellan, Mar. 16, 1886, vol. 2, p. 1230; and two letters from Witcher dated July 16, 1886, and Mar. 27, 1887 (possibly 1884), in Ladd and Ladd, eds., *Bachelder Papers,* vol. 3, pp. 1439 and 1482.

20. Witcher to McClellan, Mar. 16 and 19, 1886, vol. 2, pp. 1230–31 and 1238; and a subsequent letter he wrote to Congressman John O. Daniel (Mar. 16, 1906, copy in private collection of William O. Adams, Scotland, Conn.). That these men "held this barn until after night" is confirmed by Capt. Edwin E. Bouldin of the 14th Virginia Cavalry (chart D-4) in a letter to John B. Bachelder dated July 21, 1886 (Ladd and Ladd, eds., *Bachelder Papers,* vol. 3, p. 1447).

21. Witcher to Bachelder, Mar. 19, 1886, vol. 3, pp. 1236–39. Jeb Stuart echoed Witcher's description of a tactical Confederate victory on the East Field (*OR,* pt. 2, pp. 698–99). However, the Confederate cavalry commander could leave no retrospective accounts: he was killed in May 1864. Witcher's postwar accounts, of which there are many, ring true. Although sometimes argumentative, he wrote in a straightforward manner, stuck to his story as originally recounted, and gave more than grudging credit to his foe: "The Federal cavalry on this day behaved splendidly" (ibid., vol. 3, p. 1239). He went out of his way to describe the conspicuous bravery of Maj. Noah H. Ferry and the men of the 5th Michigan Cavalry (Witcher letter dated Apr. 7, 1886, in Ladd and Ladd, eds., *Bachelder Papers,* vol. 2, p. 1293). Ferry died at the hands of Witcher's men on the East Cavalry Field (the main text of this

appendix describes where and when). One of Witcher's Union counterparts, Lt. William Brook-Rawle, made a number of statements that conflict with what Witcher wrote. Brooke-Rawle claimed that the farmer Rummel found several dead horses in his farm lane—all Confederate, thus implying what heavy Federal fire must have come into this area, presumably resulting in many Confederate human casualties as well (Kevin E. O'Brien, "'Glory Enough for All': Lt. William Brook-Rawle and the 3rd Pennsylvania Cavalry at Gettysburg," *Gettysburg Magazine*, no. 13 [July 1995]: pp. 89–107). Yet Witcher recounted that the lane was filled with dead *Federal* horses and their former riders (Witcher to McClellan, Mar. 16, 1886, vol. 2, p. 1230). One's best shot at obtaining Witcher's version of the truth requires going back to the original source. For example, consider the letters solicited and catalogued by John Bachelder. That New Hampshire man chose to edit the letters from the erstwhile Confederate Witcher. William O. Adams (personal communication, Oct. 1995) believes a more complete and probably accurate account of the dismounted fighting in this cavalry battle is in Witcher's hand, but it will take some detective work in the archives of the New Hampshire Historical Society in Concord, where the sources of *The Bachelder Papers* are stored, to ferret out his original letters.

Appendix E

1. Perhaps not quite: Jeffry D. Wert recounts an action in the Rose Woods (see Chapter 3, maps 3-25–3-33) that commenced at about 6 P.M. on July 3: A brigade of Union troops from the 5th Corps was sent to clear this wooded sector and encountered the 15th Georgia Regiment of Benning's brigade in what had become Law's 1st Corps division. The Federals attacked the outnumbered Southerners from two sides, inflicting several casualties and "capturing scores of Georgians" (Wert, *Day Three*, p. 285). He goes on to quote a Union 5th Corps general who "claimed later that his Pennsylvanians had fired the 'last shots at Gettysburg'" (ibid.). This may well have been true, in that the cavalry action described in this appendix probably occurred slightly earlier in the late afternoon of July 3.

2. Moreover, if the officer who gives this appendix its name is indicated pejoratively as one of the "boy generals" of Gettysburg—along with his division-mate Custer—then Kilpatrick can be viewed with the same suspicion. Elon Farnsworth, George Armstrong Custer, and Judson Kilpatrick were born in 1837, 1839, and 1836, respectively.

3. *OR*, pt. 1, p. 992.

4. General Merritt's Reserve Brigade was not at full strength on the South Cavalry Field. His 6th U.S. Cavalry (most of it: approximately 400–475 troopers) was dispatched to Fairfield. This was based on a rumor from a Pennsylvania civilian that a Confederate wagon train was parked near that town ten miles southwest of Gettysburg (maps 5-2–5-5). A potentially more significant opportunity than capturing supply wagons was that the 6th U.S. Cavalry might have held up a retreat by the Army of Northern Virginia were it to leave the Gettysburg area headed in the direction of Hagerstown (which it subsequently did). The result of this Union cavalry mission was the Battle of Fairfield.

The fighting near that Pennsylvania village began auspiciously for the Federals: In a valley north of the town, a Virginia cavalry regiment from Jones's brigade attacked the 6th U.S. and was repulsed. These Virginians were one of three of Jones's regiments that formed part of the rear guard of the Confederate Army (General Imboden's mounted rebels also brought up the rear [see Chapters 1 and 5]). Jones's brigade lagged behind during June (Chapter 1), although it held mountain passes on either side of the Shenandoah as the infantry forged ahead through the Valley on their way into Northern territory.

As the Battle of Gettysburg commenced, Jones finally crossed the Potomac River with about fifteen hundred men in his 6th, 7th, and 11th Virginia Cavalry Regiments. The 12th Virginia was left behind, and the 35th Virginia Battalion had been detached on June 10 to escort Ewell's vanguard as the infantry marched northward (Chapter 1). Jones's three invading regiments reached Cashtown on July 3 and were ordered to Fairfield by General Lee as Pickett's Charge was being planned. The 7th Virginia was in the van of this deployment, which is why that unit (by itself) galloped toward Merritt's 6th U.S. Cavalry. General Jones's 6th Virginia was next to arrive on what was becoming a battlefield north of Fairfield.

The combat that occurred there commenced after Pickett's Charge had been repulsed. At Fairfield, troopers of the 6th Virginia fired on the dismounted Federals with small arms and a battery of Jones's horse artillery. This goaded the 6th U.S.'s commander, Maj. Samuel H. Starr, to order part of his regiment to charge the Virginians. The Union troopers were repulsed. Then Jones ordered a mounted cavalry attack in which the 6th Virginia, along with parts of the 7th and 11th, charged Starr's regiment. The latter's troopers were overwhelmed. Soon, more than half of the 6th U.S. troopers had become casualties—mainly prisoners. The remainder escaped southward toward Fairfield. Jones's Confederate horsemen pursued the fleeing Federals through town but eventually gave up the chase, and what was left of Major Starr's command retreated all the way to Emmitsburg, Maryland. General Jones lost only 4 percent of his force. The forgotten Battle of Fairfield was over.

What could General Merritt have been thinking, deploying but one regiment from his command to block a rebel retreat? As it happened, the bulk of Merritt's Reserve Brigade also met with little success on the South Cavalry Field at Gettysburg (as described in the main text of this appendix).

5. Wert (*Day Three*, p. 275).

6. Andie Custer, an admirer of Judson Kilpatrick, vigorously disputes that there was any contentious disagreement between the two generals at this time ("The Kilpatrick-Farnsworth Argument That Never Happened," *Gettysburg Magazine*, no. 28 [January 2003]: pp. 101–16). A correlative point within this author's polemic is that elements of Kilpatrick's plan for his division's attack against the rebel right were well devised. Thus, he was not trying to "kick them while down" but instead judiciously decided, as the ultimate plan for this ordered attack, to have Farnsworth's mounted force attack Confederate batteries deployed on Warfield Ridge (map E-3, middle left). Merritt's dismounted men were supposedly advancing on the left of Farnsworth's takeoff positions (map E-2) in an effort to tie up the Southern infantrymen in that sector and keep them from moving to support the threatened batteries.

7. John W. Busey and David G. Martin, *Regimental Strengths and Losses at Gettysburg* (Hightstown, N.J.: Longstreet House, 1994), p. 259. This casualty percentage is rather high when compared to the numbers for other cavalry actions in the Gettysburg campaign, which tended to be 10 percent or less (see Appendixes A, B, and section a of Chapter 1 in the current work).

Appendix F

1. *The Gettysburg Campaign: June–July 1863*, rev. ed. (Conshohocken, Pa.: Combined Books, 1993), pp. 235–53.

2. *The Army of Northern Virginia*, vol. 1 (Shippensburg, Pa.: White Mane, 1996), pp. 47–55.

3. www.civilwardata.com. This resource was originated by Dick Dobbins of Duxbury, Mass.

4. The dubious indication of exactly "331" for the strengths of three of these four brigades is included in Nofi's Orders of Battle (note 1, p. 251). Noah A. Trudeau recently reproduced these estimates (*Gettysburg: A Testing of Courage,* New York: Harper-Collins, 2002, p. 592). [Perhaps both of these authors drew on the numbers reported by John W. Busey and David G. Martin, *Regimental Strengths and Losses at Gettysburg,* Hightstown, N.J.: Longstreet House, 1994 (corrected and augmented edition), p. 293 (original edition 1982).] Incidentally, the Orders of Battle for Gettysburg that include regimental commanders typically are blank for the men who led most of the units with this Confederate brigade (Thomas's). Both Trudeau (note 2, p. 592) and Sibley (note 2, p. 53) helped fill out this particular part of the Army of Northern Virginia's listing.

5. If all the individual numbers below are correct, which is impossible to determine, the grand total is 93,667.

6. The Engineer Brigade was at Beaver Dam Creek, Maryland, on July 1 when most of it was ordered to Washington, arriving there on July 3.

7. The 12th and 15th Vermont regiments from this brigade guarded wagon trains during the battle.

8. This Pennsylvania regiment guarded wagon trains at Westminster, Maryland, during the battle.

9. This Pennsylvania regiment also guarded trains at Westminster during the battle. However, a 103-man detachment from this regiment escorting a supply column arrived on the battlefield on July 3.

10. This cavalry brigade guarded trains at Westminster during the battle, but part of it was involved in actions occurring during the post-battle retreat and pursuit of the Army of Northern Virginia.

11. This battery was attached to General Buford's 1st Cavalry Division on July 1. In conjunction with describing Calef's actions on that Wednesday morning, Richard S. Shue indicates that this battery was manned by seventy (not seventy-four) artillerymen (*Morning at Willoughby Run,* p. 242).

12. This battery was attached to infantry and cavalry units guarding wagon trains at Westminster during the battle (see notes 5, 6, and 7).

13. This battery was also attached to infantry and cavalry units guarding wagon trains at Westminster (see notes 8, 9, 10, and 12).

14. If all the individual numbers below are correct, which is impossible to determine, the grand total is 71,624.

15. Unlike other Confederate brigades, the 3rd Corps ones in Heth's and Pender's divisions (see a short distance below for the latter) were numbered.

16. This demi-brigade, which contained approximately 970 troopers, including men from Jones's brigade, spent most of the campaign on security duty along the line of communications with northern Virginia.

17. The first three regiments listed here made it out of Virginia, ranging as far north as Cashtown and Fairfield relatively late in the campaign (see Appendix E). These three Virginia units totaled 1,477 troopers. The 35th Virginia Battalion went north at the *beginning* of the campaign (see Chapter 1). The strength of Colonel White's "Comanches" was slightly higher right before the battle (i.e., 262 on June 30). The total strength of Maj. Gen. Stuart's cavalry division includes that of the first three of Jones's regiments and of White's battalion (as of July).

18. This horse-artillery battery—and the Lynchburg, Virginia, one—were attached to Robertson's and Jones's cavalry brigades.

19. This brigade-sized element, which contained approximately thirteen hundred men, was technically not part of the Army of Northern Virginia. It was ordered to cooperate with it during the Gettysburg campaign. Imboden's units were not engaged at Gettysburg and spent the early weeks of the campaign riding north as they covered the rear of the army against possible threats from West Virginia and western Pennsylvania (Chapter 1). During the latter stages of the campaign, Imboden's cavalry led elements of Lee's army away from Gettysburg toward the river crossing points (Chapter 5).

APPENDIX G

1. In addition to a smoothbore shot's lack of spin there is the problem of windage. This is "not the wind's effect on the projectile in flight, but [in part] the effects of the ricochet of the projectile along the center of the bore and the resistance of the air, [which] produced alteration in the path of flight" (Rollins, "Failure of Confederate Artillery in Pickett's Charge," p. 28). The "alteration" occurred in part because of the ball's bouncing per se off the inside of the barrel. Also, this leads to a slight disfiguring of the round, which was a bit lopsided to begin with because of the way it was manufactured. Thus, when a smoothbore round exited the muzzle, it would tend to bob and weave like a baseball pitcher's knuckleball.

2. A French soldier, Capt. Claude E. Minié, developed a bullet in the late 1840s that was small enough to be easily seated in the breech of a rifle barrel. The key feature of the minié ball—as it came to be known, even though it was conical and not shaped at all like a ball—was that it had a wooden plug inserted in its base. The plug was jammed into the base upon firing, causing it to expand and engage the rifling in the bore, thus imparting spin to the round. Shortly afterward, an American—James H. Burton, acting master armorer at the Harper's Ferry armory, who eventually went over to the Confederacy—improved on Minié's design by hollowing out the base of a rifle round with a cone-shaped indentation. Ignition of the powder below the base of a "Burton ball" had the same expanding effect as did the forward movement of Minié's more cumbersome wooden plug.

3. Personal communication from William O. Adams (Oct. 1995), whose prowess in shooting arms of nineteenth-century design is noted in two works about Civil War arms: Coates and Thomas, *Introduction to Civil War Small Arms,* pp. 78–81; and Bilby, *Civil War Firearms,* pp. 93–94. The kind of accuracy described by Adams may be hard to believe—hitting a small target two and a half football fields away using "open sights" (not a telescopic one, with which almost no Civil War soldiers were equipped). However, I have witnessed such "prowess" on a rifle range. A marksman firing an antique, nineteenth-century muzzle-loading rifle hit a paint-can-sized target two hundred yards away with approximately ten of his thirteen shots (just prior to this feat, he hit the targets all twenty-six times at one hundred and at fifty yards). This fellow is middle-aged and has years of experience shooting black-powder weapons.

4. *Attack and Die: Civil War Military Tactics and the Southern Heritage* (Tuscaloosa: University of Alabama Press, 1982).

5. Dean S. Thomas, *Ready . . . Aim . . . Fire! Small Arms Ammunition in the Battle of Gettysburg* (Gettysburg: Thomas Publications, 1993), pp. 52–58. It is interesting to note that the "aim" component of Thomas's title was not a part of the orders shouted to smoothbore-shooting soldiers in earlier wars, because all one could really do with such weapons was fire—and hope. Information about the shoulder arms with which all Army of

Northern Virginia units at Gettysburg were equipped is not available. However, the Confederate armies tended more than the Union ones to go "into the field armed with every description of guns" (words of an 1860s soldier, quoted in Louis A. Garavaglia and Charles G. Worman, "Arms and the Man," *North & South* 4, no. 6 [Aug. 2001]: p. 51). Additional information on the potpourri of rebel small arms is given by these authors on pages 50–51 and further exemplified by Coates and Thomas, *Civil War Small Arms*, pp. 86–96.

    6. *Battle Tactics of the Civil War* (New Haven, Conn.: Yale University Press, 1989).

    7. Paddy Griffith, "The Myth of the Rifle Revolution in the Civil War," *North & South* 1, no. 5 (June 1998): pp. 16–21; and Grady McWhiney and Perry D. Jamieson, "No Myth! The Rifle Revolution," *North & South* 1, no. 5 (June 1998): pp. 22–30.

    8. James M. McPherson to author, May 19, 1995 (emphasis in original).

    9. Bilby, *Civil War Firearms*, pp. 71–86.

    10. The same problem hampered artillerymen, especially on the Confederate side. Another reason the long-range fire in the July 3 cannonade was not as effective as it might have been was that "The Ordnance department in Richmond could not produce enough ammunition to allow the gunners to practice firing" (Rollins, "Failure of Confederate Artillery in Pickett's Charge," p. 26).

    11. Keith Poulter, "The Civil War and the Evolution of Infantry Tactics," *North & South* 4, no. 6 (Aug. 2001): p. 80 (emphasis in original).

    12. James M. McPherson, *For Cause and Comrades: Why Men Fought in the Civil War* (New York: Oxford University Press, 1997), p. 6.

    13. D. Scott Hartwig to author, Oct. 12, 1999.

    14. Notice how laborious this loading operation is. With practice, one might be able to load and discharge three rounds per minute. Even that does not result in very rapid fire, and such a loading rate could be difficult to achieve in the midst of the movements and stress that accompany combat. A further result of these difficulties is that the soldier might not dump all the powder down the muzzle. This would result in diminished velocity of the shot, thus shortening the range; and the bullet would not expand enough to take the rifling properly, thus decreasing the amount of spin, which lessened accuracy. Garavaglia and Worman describe another related problem: "Haste in reloading[, which] could lead to . . . [failure] to remove the ramrod from the bore before pulling the trigger. A muzzle loader without its ramrod was of little use, and battle accounts of ramrods whirring through the air or thunking into trees are common" ("Arms and the Man," p. 55). In conjunction with this passage, these authors quote a wartime correspondent who asked, "Do our good friends ever reflect that the loss of time in loading is the great cause of haste, and consequent inaccuracy in firing?" (ibid.).

    15. Addom's credentials are described in the Acknowledgments section of this work, which also mentions my attempts to assimilate the results of his research into these matters. Moreover, my limited experiences on (civilian) firing lines have resulted in befouled muzzle loaders well before twenty shots. The matter of "any muzzle loader" encompasses smoothbores, of which there were many at Gettysburg (note 5). In wars fought earlier in the nineteenth century and before, essentially all infantrymen were equipped with such primitive shoulder arms, which were *supposedly* rather ineffective (but see notes 29 and 32). Early-nineteenth-century muskets clearly had problems with sustained fire: "Even in the best of circumstances a piece [meaning a smoothbore muzzle loader as used in the Napoleonic Wars] would begin to foul after ten or a dozen rounds, due partially to the uneven quality of gunpowder and also to the poor fit of ball to barrel" (Albert A. Nofi, *The Waterloo Campaign: June 1815* [Conshohocken, Pa.: Combined Books, 1993], p. 93). One is left to wonder two things. First, how much improvement in black powder occurred over the next fifty years? Second, did the minnie balls of the mid-nineteenth century always "fit" properly in the bore of a rifle? A response to the latter inquiry would be "not always," because of slight but significant variations in muzzle-bore diameters and those of the rifle rounds (Andrew H. Addoms III, personal communication, 2000). These variations were systematic, according to a given manufacturing scheme. At the arsenal in Springfield, Massachusetts, essentially every rifle made during the late 1850s and during the war had a muzzle diameter of .580–.581 inches. But there were twenty-two other "contractors" who produced mimics of the Springfield rifled musket, and the bore sizes of these varied from .582 inches to an extreme of .589 inches. Factor in the hundreds of thousands of imported rifled muskets (e.g., note 25), which widened the range of bore diameters even further. Thus, a unit of Civil War infantrymen could easily be supplied—or resupplied in the midst of a battle—with minnie balls that were of the wrong fit for their rifles. The consequences of this problem are exemplified and discussed in note 24.

    16. E-mail to author, Nov. 11, 1999. Hartwig was able to cite some prewar evidence in favor of firing many rounds from a rifled musket "before the barrel was cleaned" (Officers of the Ordnance Department, U.S. Army, *Reports of Experiments with Small Arms for the Military Service* [Washington, D.C.: A. O. P. Nicholson, 1856], p. 44). Addoms believes this report was deliberately exaggerated in order to expedite governmental authorization of a complete switchover to army usage of rifled long arms.

    17. Bilby, *Civil War Firearms*, pp. 113, 59, and 59.

    18. *OR,* pt. 1, p. 307.

    19. This particular brigade was armed mostly with .577-caliber Enfield rifled muskets, which had been imported from England, along with a few .69-caliber smoothbores. Baxter's regiments (maps 2-17 and 2-18) were first posted behind a stone wall running parallel to a roadway in this sector of the field (the Mummasburg Road). From there these Union men repelled the attack of O'Neal's brigade of Rodes's division. To meet the next wave of the rebel advance (Iverson's brigade) Baxter changed front to his left, deploying his men in a westward-facing line behind another stone fence that intersected the one just south of the Mummasburg Road (Hassler, *Crisis at the Crossroads,* pp. 90–91).

    20. Thomas, *Ready . . . Aim . . . Fire!,* p. 52.

    21. Wiley Sword, *Sharpshooter: Hiram Berdan, His Famous Sharpshooters and Their Sharps Rifles* (Lincoln, R.I.: Andrew Mobray, 1988), p. 11. To obtain enough men who supposedly could shoot this well because of their prewar experience, the Army of the Potomac had to recruit them from all over. Thus, these two regiments at Gettysburg were Regular Army units as opposed to state volunteer regiments. Berdan's Sharpshooters, whose *companies* were uniform in terms of the men's state of origin, were drawn from as far north as Maine, ranging down to Pennsylvania, and from as far west as Minnesota.

    22. Sword, *Sharpshooter,* p. 37.

    23. Bilby, *Civil War Firearms,* p. 72; the subsequent quotes in this paragraph are from pp. 82 and 72.

    24. Sword, *Sharpshooter,* pp. 63–90. The appellation of Berdan's regiments and the name of the rifles are unconnected (an unintended pun). The rounds supplied to these sharpshooters were ".52 caliber linen cartridges," which were loaded at the breech of the Sharps rifles. There was a problem with these rounds in that they

were "nonstandard," such that these skilled shooters "could not be easily resupplied" in the midst of a fight (ibid., p. 82). Here's a resupply vignette from the Battle of Gettysburg itself, although it involves ordinary infantry units equipped with muzzle-loading shoulder arms: As the chaos was escalating among the Federal defenders during the late afternoon on July 1, a group of ammunition-laden wagons was ordered to move through Gettysburg and proceed westward, such that men of the Federal 1st Corps's 1st Division could replenish their rounds: "The ten wagons set off for the division. They rolled fast . . . [as they] passed through the town. When they reached the seminary . . . Confederate cannons opened on the wagons as they crossed the ridge [Seminary Ridge, of course; see, for example, map 2-25 in Chapter 2], but they reached the Iron Brigade line [recall that this unit was the 1st Brigade within the 1st Corps's 1st Division—see, for example, positions of the Wisconsin Regiments at this time and place (map 2-25)]. . . . The men riding in three wagons threw boxes of cartridges from them, and O'Connor [the ordnance sergeant in charge of this resupply mission] chopped them open with an axe" (Pfanz, *First Day*, pp. 287–88). What is the chance—in this *representative intra-battle emergency*—that the rounds so delivered were o*ptimal for the arms carried by the specific soldiers* in this situation and location, given the *variability among muzzle diameters and round dimensions* characteristic of the arms and ammunition manufacturing practices of the time (as discussed in notes 15 and 25, for instance)? Exacerbating the ammunition replenishment problem for this particular Union unit at Gettysburg, three of the Iron Brigade regiments carried .58-caliber Springfields, one was equipped with .58-caliber Lorenz rifled-muskets (note 25), and the fifth had a blend of that Austrian arm plus .54-caliber Lorenz's (Thomas, *Ready . . . Aim . . . Fire!*, p. 52). This kind of mixture was not atypical for Civil War brigades in either the Northern or Southern armies, including the two that fought at Gettysburg.

25. The "standard" rounds for infantrymen equipped with the most commonly used type of muzzle-loading rifle were supposed to be just under .575 caliber (inches in diameter at the base), as recommended by James H. Burton (note 2). This size of a minnie ball was designed to fit easily into a rifle bore that was .580 inches at the muzzle (however, see note 15). But the production of minnie balls by hundreds of separate contractors led to deviations from Burton's norm. Such variations in bullet sizes are repeatedly exemplified in Dean S. Thomas, *Round Ball to Rimfire: A History of Civil War Small Arms Ammunition,* pt. 1 (Gettysburg: Thomas Publications, 1997), pp. 135–52. Additional exemplary information can be found in Garavaglia and Worman's "Arms and the Man." They describe the usage of "Austrian Lorenz" rifles (approximately three hundred thousand of these weapons, which are similar to Springfields and Enfields, were imported during the war): "Any number went into service in their original .54 caliber . . . [but] the calibers of . . . [Lorenz's] sold to the Union [by a certain company in 1862] were recorded as .54, .55, .577, .58, .59, and .60!" ("Arms and the Man," p. 52). The consequences of firing a round that was too small are revealed in a letter written by a Federal ordnance officer in 1863: "At a distance of two hundred yards many of bullets cal. .57 [too small for a rifled musket's bore size (note 15)] fell short several yards. . . . With the cal. .577 at two hundred yards the bullets all reached the target [a four-inch thick pine board] several passing through and the remainder penetrating the plank to a distance of from three to three and a half inches" (quoted in Thomas, *Round Ball to Rimfire*, p. 138). The shots fired with the .57-caliber bullets suffered from the fact that the base might not expand quite enough to take the weapon's rifling optimally. Just as important was the *excess gas* that would escape around an inappropriately small bullet an instant after the powder charge ignited. This "blow-by" robbed the round of its potential effectiveness. Moreover, the excess of exploding powder accentuated the amounts of carbon that got deposited along the length of the bore, which resulted in fouling that was worse than in a case of optimal bullet-to-bore fit. What if a round was bit *larger* than ideal for the particular rifle in the hands of a given soldier? A slightly too-tight fit would not necessarily increase reloading problems caused by fouling: *If* the bullet's *lubrication* were of the highest quality, the shooter would not find himself having to fairly hammer the bullet down into the breech. But the vast majority of bullets manufactured in the North and the South were supplied with mediocre lubrication. Thus, even modest fouling would adversely affect the rifleman's ability to reload rounds that happened to be bit too wide. For example, "during the course of the war, any number of Enfields fired standard minnies instead of Pritchetts [a British-manufactured round]. In itself, this practice did not cause problems; what did cause problems, and in a big way, was the fact that Enfields with .577 bores could fire only a few .58-caliber minnie balls before powder fouling made the bullets too difficult to load. In that case, soldiers had to hold one end of the ramrod against the bullet and hammer the other end against a tree to drive the slug home" (Garavaglia and Worman, "Arms and the Man," p. 53).

26. The principal chronicler of the fight for Culp's Hill—Harry W. Pfanz—makes repeated references to the rifle cleaning that occurred throughout the morning of July 3, as the Union defenders were rotated back behind the firing lines. See his *Culp's Hill and Cemetery Hill,* pp. 294, 297–99, 303, 306, 322. Jeffry D. Wert makes *further* referrals of this sort in his account of that day's events (*Day Three*, pp. 64, 65, 67, 79).

27. The casualty figure for these Confederate units on July 3 was specified as 1,313 by Priest (*Into the Fight,* p. 199).

28. Thomas K. Tate, letter to editor, *North & South* 3, no. 3 (Mar. 2000): pp. 7, 94. Tate quotes extensively from Colonel Willard's piece, which was published in Washington, D.C., February 18, 1863, and reprinted as William C. Goble, ed., *Comparative Value of Rifled and Smoothbore Arms* (Hightstown, N.J.: Longstreet House, 1995).

29. Indeed, "certain authorities both North and South argued that even when rifles were readily available the smoothbore still deserved a place in the ranks. . . . in much of the wooded terrain in the east, shots beyond fifty yards were more the exception than the rule [echoing one of Griffith's arguments], and at that distance the fast-loading [smoothbore] musket, with its buck and ball charge [a brutal round consisting of a .69-caliber conical bullet and 3 buckshot, all wrapped in one paper cartridge], was formidable enough. It could be equally formidable in open terrain once the haze of powder smoke settled over the battlefield, making targets indistinct" (Garavaglia and Worman, "Arms and the Man," p. 47).

30. Another feature of this phenomenon (as introduced in note 2) stems from the spin imparted to a minnie ball by a rifled musket. Most such weapons had a right twist, which imparted a clockwise spin to the projectile. This and other features of the bullet's ballistics resulted in systematic drift of the bullet (also known as windage). Thus, the shooter had to compensate in his aiming, as in the following example: To hit the center of a ten-inch target at a hundred yards, he needed to aim about two inches to the left of the target's center. How many Civil War soldiers do you suppose were trained and practiced accordingly? (See the citation to information provided by Joseph G. Bilby in note 23.) However, problems stemming from "the ricochet of the projectile along the center of the bore" (part of Rollins's definition of windage in note 1) did not occur with rifled muskets and minnie balls (even when the latter were too small). Yet, if the rifle had become appreciably fouled, the

conical bullet would tend to *slide* down the bore—not bouncing off its walls, but also not spinning very well if the grooves were filled with carbon deposits.

31. Bilby, *Civil War Firearms,* pp. 72–73.

32. Quoted in Thomas Tate's letter to the editor cited in note 28 above. The Battle of Solferino (June 24, 1859) was mentioned in Chapter 4 as an engagement in which a frontal assault succeeded—even though "the troops in both armies were armed with rifle-muskets" (Bilby, *Civil War Arms,* p. 75). The casualties there included 11–13 percent killed and wounded among the French and Italian attackers. At the Battle of Magenta (June 4, 1859) in the same war, that allied army had also been on the attack, and the combat casualties (killed and wounded) amounted to 8 percent. In comparison, the ubiquitously mentioned Battle of Waterloo (June 18, 1815), which was fought with smoothbore muskets as noted by Willard, resulted in 35 percent of the attacking French army being killed or wounded. In an attempt to undermine the meaning of the successful tactics at Solferino and Magenta, Keith Poulter points out that the "efficacy of [these] frontal assault[s was] . . . largely attributable to the fact that a large proportion of the French troops were veterans, and that entire rifle-armed battalions were thrown forward as skirmishers" ("Civil War and the Evolution," no. 6, p. 83). Again, the rifles. But how forceful is the first of Poulter's points in relation to Gettysburg—where the majority of the Southern soldiers were manifestly veterans? Moreover, the *circumstances* of this battle, including on July 3, allowed for the possibility that the frontally attacking rebels could have carried the day (an argument that is elaborated in Chapter 4). This speaks to another of Poulter's points, which he bases on Civil War assaults of this sort being "sometimes successful, as at Gaines Mill (June 1862, during McClellan's Peninsula Campaign) or Missionary Ridge (November 1863, during the battles for Chattanooga). These, however, tend to be special cases" (ibid.). Precisely: it depends on the circumstances operating within a given battle.

33. Griffith, "Myth of the Rifle Revolution," p. 17. A longer version of this component of Griffith's arguments appeared in his earlier book on this subject, *Battle Tactics of the Civil War.* Griffith is correct about battles of the American Civil War not being the all-out bloodbaths that some imply—at least when pitted against armed conflicts from earlier times and at many other places. In fact, huge numbers of battles going back to antiquity (well beyond the Napoleonic period) *and* many of those that occurred in the twentieth century involved much higher numbers and proportions of (non-Americans) killed and wounded. This *seems* to contradict what was implied by remarks in Chapter 5 about twentieth- and twenty-first-century Americans finding casualty levels like those that resulted from Civil War battles to be unacceptable. Yet there is no real discrepancy, given the following hierarchy of carnage: Big battles all over the world tended to be bloodier than the ones that erupted between 1861 and 1865 during the War of the Rebellion. Moreover, previous wars involving Americans resulted in relatively small numbers of casualties. This caused those of the Civil War to take on a horrifying character from the perspectives of citizens of that time and of historians who have long chronicled that conflict. Inasmuch as the Civil War was so salient in American history and remains so, we subsequently began to regard casualty figures even approaching the carnage that occurred at Shiloh (Tennessee, April 1862), Antietam, Gettysburg, Chickamauga (northern Georgia, September 1863), and during Grant's Overland Campaign (northern Virginia, spring of 1864) as beyond the pale. In truth, the sufferings of neither those specific Civil War armies, nor of the nineteenth-century American populaces from which they originated, were as grim as the agonies endured by any number of previous or subsequent armed forces (during a given battle or campaign) and by the people that gave rise to them. Consider, for example, the battles of Blenheim (1704), Austerlitz (1805), Waterloo (1814), Balaclava (1854), and Solferino (1859), all *one-day* battles in which casualties ranged from 25 to 240 percent more than were meted out at Antietam on September 17, 1862. Then consider the casualty tolls in World Wars I and II: the number of American battle deaths ranges from roughly one hundred thousand in the former to four hundred thousand in the latter. Compare those figures with the *millions* of fighting men from *each of several other countries* who died in either of those conflicts. This exercise coldly ignores the unbelievable number of deaths inflicted on the European and Asian civilian populations in World War II. Finally, let us remember that "only" 220,000 Americans died on Civil War battlefields or as a direct result of wounds sustained as soldiers in those engagements.

34. Pfanz, *Second Day,* p. 406.

35. One feature of the most recent restatement of this thesis is that the equipment and supplies for Northern artillery *were* quite advanced in their design and manufacture—which contributed to their putatively decisive application at Gettysburg (Rollins, "Failure of Confederate Artillery in Pickett's Charge," pp. 26, 37, 40–41). This essay, however, suggests that such high-quality attributes have been exaggerated insofar as they are applied to the shoulder arms of that era.

36. Paul Clark Cooksey is one who suggests such an essay is warranted by explicitly countering Rollins's and his colleagues' conclusions ("Plan for Pickett's Charge," 72–73).

Bibliographic Essay

There are thousands of books and other works about the Gettysburg campaign. A researcher who contemplates wading into this subject receives an immediate jolt when perusing a book about Gettysburg sources; it is seven-eighths of an inch thick, even though more than twenty years old (Richard A. Sauers, *The Gettysburg Campaign, June 3–August 1, 1863: A Comprehensive, Selectively Annotated Bibliography,* Westport, Conn.: Greenwood Press, 1982).

Much of the source material I used has been published over the course of the previous two decades. In this regard, I say sheepishly—although perhaps defiantly as well—that I have not marinated myself in this literature to the extent that I might have tried to incorporate everything that is knowable ("more and more about less and less"). In this respect further, *The Stand* is not an all-out attempt to mine the complete historical record of Gettysburg, but instead is more of a *synthesis:* two parts history, one part historiography. It is, to a significant extent, about other Gettysburg reference works, weighted somewhat in favor of recent books and articles. What follows is a discussion of the authors upon whom I drew most heavily over the course of this synthetic enterprise.

The Gettysburg Campaign in General

I started in the mid-1980s with Edwin B. Coddington's *The Gettysburg Campaign: A Study in Command* (New York: Charles Scribner's Sons, 1968). This "Gettysburg bible" may never go out of date. It is a massive volume that covers virtually everything. However, many of the events he describes and interprets have been reevaluated during the 1980s and 1990s. Moreover, it seems that Noah A. Trudeau's just-appeared work, *Gettysburg: A Testing of Courage* (New York: HarperCollins, 2002), intends to become the "King James" version, in that this author covers the entire Gettysburg campaign at length.

Nearly all of the recent works I read are referred to in the chapter notes (in conjunction with the information supplied for that part of the chapter). In addition, I might have been able to cite Coddington on nearly every page. A disclaimer about his work, which is mirrored in this book: Coddington evaluates the course of the Gettysburg campaign and its outcome in part from a Union perspective. He suggests that the actions of the Army of the Potomac in general, and its commander in particular, "had a little something to do with" the Union victory. Coddington's study also treats George Gordon Meade favorably, which I think puts him in the minority of Gettysburg evaluators.

General Meade is almost ignored in Michael Shaara's *The Killer Angels* (New York: David McKay, 1974). As a novelist, it was Shaara's prerogative to downplay Meade's role. Instead, he focused on the likes of John Buford and Joshua Chamberlain on the Union side, and Robert E. Lee and James Longstreet among the Confederates. *The Killer Angels* won the Pulitzer Prize in the mid-1970s, but it did not begin to be widely read until later. Its readership continues to grow, and many get hooked on Gettysburg by devouring its pages. Jay Luvaas, a military historian at the Army War College at Carlisle Barracks, Pennsylvania, suggested to me that reading Shaara's novel is a good way to start, adding that he "gave a copy to each of the 15 guys [U.S. Army officers] in my seminar about 8 years ago, and asked them to read the first fifty pages before taking them to Gettysburg."[1] To some extent, I *did* "start" with the Shaara novel, as well as with Coddington, although I devoured the former's work in the late 1980s.

As with any work of fiction, there is a problem with using *The Killer Angels* as an introduction to the story of Gettysburg: Shaara's yarn is both inaccurate and incomplete. The author has taken literary license with events in order to tell his story. An intriguing critique of it is D. Scott Hartwig, *A Killer Angels Companion* (Gettysburg, Thomas Publications, 1996). Hartwig "originally looked down upon Shaara's work" but later "gained a greater respect for this fine piece of literature" (p. v). Thus, this historian's purpose was to "write a primer for people who had read the novel to analyze just how Shaara's version of the Battle of Gettysburg stacked up against a historian's reconstruction of events" (ibid.). In addition to putting *The Killer Angels* in perspective, Hartwig indeed provides a fine introduction to the Gettysburg campaign. For my part, I wonder whether Shaara's story is *no farther from reality than some nonfiction accounts of the campaign.* This is one of the perceptions that prompted the current work. I sensed that the story is worth retelling in its entirety, if for no other reason than to incorporate the results of more recent research that almost certainly brings our appreciation of the events in this military campaign closer to reality than where we were twenty or thirty years ago.

Clifford Dowdey's *Death of a Nation: The Story of Lee and His Men at Gettysburg* (New York: Alfred A. Knopf, 1958) offered an "introduction to Gettysburg with a Southern shading." Here I quote from Kent Gramm's *Gettysburg: A Meditation on War and Values* (Bloomington: Indiana University Press, 1994), p. 261—although this author was referring to an analogous work, Glenn Tucker's *High Tide at Gettysburg* (Indianapolis: Bobbs-Merrill, 1958). As its title implies, Graham's book is more perspective than narrative. I found his work most intriguing, although it is not everyone's cup of tea. Some readers have been turned off by its meditative qualities, whereas others denounce the author as too much of a "liberal."[2] Nevertheless, you can learn the basics of what happened at Gettysburg from Graham's essays if you are also willing to read what he believes it means for twenty-first-century Americans.

Numerous separate articles and essays address other general aspects of the campaign. Many of these are collected in a finite number of source materials. Among these is *Gettysburg Magazine,* published twice yearly by Morningside House of Dayton, Ohio, since 1989. This periodical, edited by Bob Younger and Andrew McMillan, is more a scholarly journal than a magazine. An assistant editor, professional historian Edwin C. Bearss, scrutinizes and writes an Introduction to each issue. Many other professional and amateur historians who have contributed to *Gettysburg* present micro-accounts of specific occurrences in many of the articles and analyses of major events cutting across several days of the campaign in others. All of these articles are replete with citations to primary and secondary sources, and most of them provide beautifully informative maps.

Five essay collections are similarly rich with attributed information, although not quite so well augmented pictorially. These works include articles about each day of the battle in turn, edited by Gary W. Gallagher: *The First Day at Gettysburg* (1992) and *The Second Day at Gettysburg* (1993), both from Kent State University Press, and subtitled *Essays on Confederate and Union Leadership.* The putatively final such volume, *The Third Day at Gettysburg and Beyond,* was published by North Carolina University Press in 1994. However a companion (or competing) collection appeared in 1999: *Three Days at Gettysburg* (again, Gallagher-edited, but this time from Kent State University Press). Here, the essays from 1992 and 1993 are recycled, but those about "the third day" are different from those that appeared in 1994. The fifth essay collection is Gabor S. Boritt, ed., *The Gettysburg Nobody Knows* (New York: Oxford University Press, 1997). It variously treats the June components of the campaign, the days of battle, and its aftermath during the first half of July with mostly evaluative articles as opposed to descriptive ones.

Both kinds of pieces can be found in *North & South: The Magazine of Civil War Conflict* (Tollhouse, Calif.), which first appeared in November 1997. This publication is thoughtfully edited and contributed to by Keith Poulter. Insofar as Gettysburg is concerned, Poulter has solicited many individual articles and also published theme issues containing several related pieces about a major feature of the campaign. Each issue includes formal and informal debates about the Civil War in general and Gettysburg in particular. These appear in titled sections within a given issue and as letters from both readers and authors. Its slick appearance notwithstanding, essentially all the material printed in this periodical is *annotated* with citations. This sets *North & South* apart from almost all other Civil War magazines.

Finally, we come to the *Official Records.* Even I, in assembling a synthesis of sorts, turned to primary accounts in the *OR* again and again. These compilations of documents for the American Civil War were nominally edited by Lt. Col. Robert N. Scott and entitled *The War of the Rebellion: The Official Records of the Union and Confederate Armies.*[3] The three books for the Gettysburg campaign were published in 1989 as volume 1, series 1, parts 1–3. A large proportion of part 1 consists of reports submitted by Union officers who participated in the campaign, the battle, or both. Part 2 includes reports of Southern officers and of certain Union ones who were involved in the fringes of the campaign, but not the Gettysburg battle. Part 3, subtitled *Correspondence, etc.,* includes orders and other correspondence by Gettysburg participants from both sides. One imagines that the reports in parts 1 and 2 are among the best primary accounts (for this or any Civil War subject), because so many of them were written rather soon after the battle or the campaign as "official" documents. Thus, the often dubious value of hindsight did not obtain. And, in principle, a participating officer would not be writing a self-serving—possibly vainglorious—account, but instead a putatively terse description of what really happened. Having said this, I found a large proportion of the after-action reports to be a bit suspicious in their content and tone. This attribute was revealed especially in terms of what seemed to be overreaching praise that a given officer would lavish on the performance and accomplishments of his unit during a particular action within the battle. The writer of such an account (they are legion) would go on to single out for commendation the attainments of several individuals within his unit—often using flowery language. Taken on their face, the ensemble of these accounts could leave one with the impression that "everyone did great" and that no individual components of the action involved the reverse of an attack or the failure to defend a position.

Notes about Maps and Charts

Soon after I first presented a college course on the Gettysburg campaign during the winter and spring of 1996, it occurred to me that students who knew nothing about Gettysburg before the course started would benefit from detailed visual aids. Thus, when I started writing this book in early 1997, I immediately included map after map, along with all the charts that identify the military units and key leaders who participated in a given stage of the campaign or the battle. I also sensed that almost all the maps should contain "area of detail" indicators, because the naive student reader would otherwise be unlikely to pay much attention to a particular high-resolution image. Coincidentally, some of the articles in *North & South* are nicely enhanced by these kinds of map insets and are further supplemented by mini-orders of battle analogous to the charts included here.

Regarding derivations of maps in the current work, I have pictorially paraphrased the images that appear in a large number of Gettysburg books and articles. Attributions to these sources (secondary ones, except for the bottom of map 4-25 and map E-5) are listed at the end of this essay. I should mention an assemblage of Gettysburg maps that's even denser than the corresponding part of the current work: John D. Imhof's *Gettysburg Day Two: A Study in Maps* (Baltimore: Butternut and Blue, 1999), which includes a superb series of maps covering events on July 2. Imhof's maps feature a high degree of spatial and temporal resolution backed up by up-to-date research and much verbal annotation.

A seminal series of Gettysburg maps (less highly resolved than Imhof's, but in the same spirit) was produced by John B. Bachelder and published in 1876. This man was the self-appointed nineteenth-century chronicler of Gettysburg and later became its official historian. How this happened is recounted by Richard A. Sauers in "John B. Bachelder: Government Historian of the Battle of Gettysburg," *Gettysburg Magazine,* no. 3 (July 1990): pp. 115–27; and in David L. Ladd and Audrey J. Ladd, eds., *John Bachelder's History of the Battle of Gettysburg* (1886; reprint, Dayton, Ohio: Morningside House, 1997). This volume—like Ladd and Ladd, eds., *The Bachelder Papers,* 3 vols. (Dayton, Ohio: Morningside House, 1994)—is mostly a compilation of accounts by participants. "The Bachelder Maps" (also available from Morningside House) are twenty-eight in number and depict the position of units on the battlefield as a whole. Bachelder's temporal resolution is good for July 1 (14 maps), but he seemed to run out of steam for the second two days of the battle (5 and 4 maps, respectively). He generated a separate series of 4 maps for the fighting on the East Cavalry Field.

Using Bachelder's images as starting points, Thomas A. Desjardin published 4 large and exquisitely detailed maps covering events at Gettysburg. This project was stimulated and supported by the Friends of the National Park at Gettysburg (FNPG), which is a battlefield preservation organization (and more). Desjardin, who aimed to augment and correct the older maps based on his contemporary research, was assisted in this endeavor by six other Gettysburg historians: Gerald Bennett, Charles C. Fennel, D. Scott Hartwig, Harry W. Pfanz, Timothy H. Smith, and Wayne E. Motts. Desjardin's series begins with a depiction of all the field details as they are currently apprehended (every road, stream, building, and area of ground, whether cultivated or wooded). The starting point for delineating this information was the result of intensive survey work carried out in 1868–69 and 1876 by U.S. military men, including Bvt. Maj. Gen. Andrew A. Humphreys, then a brigadier general and chief of engineers, and Bvt. Maj. Gen. Gouverneur K. Warren, at the time an engineer major. These two officers were both generals at the Battle of Gettysburg and were vigorously involved in it. Lower-ranking officers from the Corps of Engineers conducted the postwar topographical work they directed. The maps they produced are available from the U.S. Department of the Interior's Denver Service Center of the National Park Service. Such surveys were conducted as the surveyors traipsed and rode all over the fields, measuring everything with lengths of chain. Remarkably detailed as the surveyors' maps are, they needed to be enhanced and corrected by Desjardin and his colleagues. These seven researchers went on to amend and rectify Bachelder's troop positions in three further maps, one for each of the three days of the battle. Focusing on Desjardin's fourth map, *The Stand* used (with the FNPG's permission) this exquisitely detailed depiction of terrain features and battlefield landmarks to produce templates for most of the maps in this book.

Chapter 1. The Roads to Gettysburg: Virginia, Maryland, and Pennsylvania in June 1863

The bulk of Chapter 1 is a boiled-down version of Coddington's account of the campaigning during June 1863 found in the first ten chapters of *Gettysburg Campaign*. I also perused Wilbur S. Nye's *Here Come the Rebels!* (Baton Rouge: Louisiana State University Press, 1965) and drew more heavily on Mark Nesbitt's *Saber and Scapegoat: J. E. B. Stuart and the Gettysburg Controversy* (Mechanicsburg, Pa.: Stackpole, 1994), as well as an article by David Powell, "Stuart's Ride: Lee, Stuart, and the Confederate Cavalry in the Gettysburg Campaign," *Gettysburg Magazine*, no. 20 (Jan. 1999): pp. 27–43, for post-Nye and -Coddington analyses of Stuart's ride.

Other recent treatments of what happened in June more generally include Joseph T. Glatthaar, "The Common Soldier's Gettysburg Campaign" and Richard M. McMurray, "The Pennsylvania Gambit and the Gettysburg Splash," both in Borritt, ed., *Gettysburg Nobody Knows,* pp. 3–30, 175–202, respectively; Ronald A. Church's 1997 article, "The Pipe Creek Line: An Overview" (http://civilwarhome.com/pch.htm; accessed Aug. 1999); and Bevin Alexander's *Robert E. Lee's Civil War* (Holbrook, Mass.: Adams Media, 1998). These analyses of events and command decisions underpinned some of my pauses for discursive remarks within this chapter.

Chapter 2. July 1: The Union Suffers a Setback but Gains a Great Position

I began with an account of July 1 that's contemporary with Coddington's: Warren W. Hassler Jr., *Crisis at the Crossroads* (Tuscaloosa, Ala: University of Alabama Press, 1970). Later, and with trepidation, I turned to more extensive works about the first day. The first of these is *Gettysburg July 1* ("Completely Revised Edition") by David G. Martin (Conshohocken, Pa.: Combined Books, 1996). I confess not to have read this 736-page encyclopedia in its entirety, but I mined it many times to dig out details about this day of battle. More recently, Harry W. Pfanz published *Gettysburg: The First Day* (Chapel Hill: University of North Carolina Press, 2001). The author must have intended that his work compete with that of Martin; and his book has been better received. However, most components of Pfanz's *First Day* are exceedingly dense (in the mind of yours truly, who did grapple with all of its pages and used the results of that reading to modify an early-twenty-first-century version of this work's manuscript). For example, the author notes in his preface (p. xiv) that "the battle has spawned a number of suppositions" and that he will "address these and other matters" in *First Day*.[4] However—and this is a crucial feature of many battle books, including those about Gettysburg—Pfanz does not really "address these . . . matters." As one plows through this work, one encounters *descriptions* of the occurrences or non-events in question (those alluded to by the quoted phrases and footnote shortly above); but these are supposed to speak for themselves, somehow. Moreover, *First Day* is too sparse in terms of maps, and regimental designations include numbers only, with no indication of what state raised them. Yet, these maps include excellent captions that give a timeline of the events that are diagrammed (more about this book tactic in the section on July 2).

Even though Pfanz does not mention in his citations Richard S. Shue's *Morning at Willoughby Run: July 1, 1863* (Gettysburg, Pa.: Thomas Publications, 1995), I found it to be a clear and informative rendition of what happened during the early hours that day. Shue, of course, describes in detail what John Buford did during the morning of July 1. Additional information about Buford's activities and accomplishments are provided by Michael Phipps and John S. Peterson, "*The Devil's to Pay*": *Gen. John Buford, USA* (Gettysburg: Farnsworth Military Impressions, 1995), and by Maj. Mark S. Stricker, "Dragoon or Cavalryman? Major General John Buford in the American Civil War" (master's thesis, U.S. Army Command and General Staff College, Fort Leavenworth, Kans., 1994). Opposing infantry units came into play heavily later in the morning on July 1. For descriptions of these actions I delved into Robert K. Krick's "Three Confederate Disasters on Oak Ridge: Failures of Brigade Leadership on the First Day at Gettysburg," in Gallagher, ed., *The First Day at Gettysburg: Essays on Union and Confederate Leadership* (Kent, Ohio: Kent State University Press, 1992), pp. 30–56; and Lance J. Herdegen and William J. K. Beaudot, *In the Bloody Railroad Cut at Gettysburg* (Dayton, Ohio: Morningside House, 1990).

For the fighting that resumed and escalated throughout the afternoon, I benefited from the breakdowns and descriptions supplied by Richard A. Sauers in "The 16th Maine Volunteer Infantry at Gettysburg," *Gettysburg Magazine,* no. 13 (July 1995): pp. 33–42; in Gary W. Gallagher, "Confederate Corps Leadership on the First Day at Gettysburg: A. P. Hill and Richard S. Ewell in a Difficult Debut"; A. Wilson Greene, "From Chancellorsville to Cemetery Hill: O. O. Howard and Eleventh Corps Leadership"; and Robert K. Krick, "Three Confederate Disasters." The latter three essays are in Gallagher, ed., *First Day at Gettysburg,* pp. 30–56, 57–91, and 92–139, respectively. Timothy H. Smith's *The Story of Lee's Headquarters, Gettysburg, Pennsylvania* (Gettysburg: Thomas Publications, 1995) offers a particularly useful description of events that occurred later on July 1. The title of Smith's work may not sound like much, but this author describes a lot more than the Confederate commander's headquarters in the vicinity of the actions on the Federal left and rebel right. Smith also gives fine detail about the Wednesday afternoon actions.

With regard to the "Ewell controversy" that stemmed from events on the evening of the first day, rehashing all the issues as to whether that Confederate corps commander might have taken the hills south of Gettysburg can be a doleful process. I thus trimmed this discussion, relying to a significant extent on Alan T. Nolan's "R. E. Lee and July 1 at Gettysburg," in Gallagher, ed., *First Day at Gettysburg,* pp. 1–29. Part of this author's analysis argues against leaping to the conclusion that Ewell *could* have resumed his corps's offensive in order to capture Cemetery and Culp's Hills—and thus that he *should* have, according to the conventional wisdom. If only to keep the mind alive, I discuss this prominent Gettysburg quarrel in part from Nolan's iconoclastic perspective. This author was also one of the first to write a deeply informative account of a military unit from the Civil War: *The Iron Brigade: A Military History* (1961; reprint, Bloomington: In-

376   THE STAND OF THE U.S. ARMY AT GETTYSBURG

diana University Press, 1994). He thus knows whereof he speaks about several features of the July 1 story (recall that this Union brigade of Westerners fought during both the morning and afternoon clashes). One further component of Ewell's potential attacks upon the hills relates to *prior* fortification of Cemetery Hill by troops from the Union 11th Corps. This element of the Ewell controversy is not factored in by all that many students of Gettysburg. My attention to the Union bulwark on Cemetery Hill (*as of* July 1) was revitalized by a discussion of how General Howard, the 11th Corps commander, augmented his division's worth of infantry defenders by placing artillery among them. This discussion is in Richard Rollins and David Shultz, "'A Combined and Concentrated Fire': The Federal Artillery at Gettysburg, July 3, 1863," *North & South* 2, no. 3 (Mar. 1999): pp. 39–60.

CHAPTER 3. JULY 2: THE CLIMAX OF THE BATTLE

The documented expert for July 2 is Harry W. Pfanz. From reading his book dealing with the attack of the Confederate right wing and the defense by the Federal left, I learned a host of details about the fighting in the *southern and central sectors* of the battlefield. The work in question is Pfanz's tour de force about this component of the battle: *Gettysburg: The Second Day* (Chapel Hill: University of North Carolina Press, 1987). This author's follow-up book tells what happened in the northern sector of the field: *Gettysburg: Culp's Hill and Cemetery Hill* (Chapel Hill: University of North Carolina Press, 1993). Pfanz's maps in these two works—on which many of those in Chapter 3 are based—include his usual and useful captions; he also identified regiments by number and state of origin in the latter book (compared with the more cryptic approach taken in *First Day* and *Second Day*). *Culp's Hill and Cemetery Hill* covers events in the vicinity of those two hills during the late stages of the action on July 1 (thus overlapping his earlier *First Day*), as well as throughout the morning hours of July 3.

A work that focuses on Culp's Hill alone is Charles C. Fennel's "The Attack and Defense of Culp's Hill: Greene's Brigade at the Battle of Gettysburg, July 1–3, 1863" (Ph.D. diss., West Virginia University, 1992). Fennel made me aware of this monograph when he walked me all over the northern reaches of the battlefield. He not only was vividly instructive about what happened on the two hills, he also introduced me to his thesis that General Ewell did not attack "too late" on July 1, in that he waited until only Greene's brigade was defending its eastern slope. Articles that helped me tell Brig. Gen. George Greene's largely unknown story, and that of Col. David Ireland on the right wing of Greene's line, are Wayne E. Motts, "To Gain a Second Star: The Forgotten George S. Greene," *Gettysburg Magazine,* no. 3 (July 1990): pp. 65–75; Thomas L. Elmore, "Courage Against the Trenches: The Attack and Repulse of Steuart's Brigade on Culp's Hill," *Gettysburg Magazine,* no. 7 (July 1992): pp. 83–95; Jay Jorgensen, "Holding the Right: The 137th New York Regiment at Gettysburg," *Gettysburg Magazine,* no. 15 (July 1996): pp. 60–67; and Richard L. Murray, *A Perfect Storm of Lead: George Sears Greene's New York Brigade in Defense of Culp's Hill* (Wolcott, N.Y.: Benedum Books, 2000).

The narrative in Chapter 3 paused to discuss Lt. Gen. James Longstreet's proposals for Confederate strategy on July 2 and how the rejection of his plan may have caused him to perform poorly as the events unfolded (accepting for the sake of argument that he *did* perform in that manner on that day). What Longstreet may have said, what he did, and evaluations of the ensuing controversies are examined by Jeffry D. Wert, "'No 15,000 Men Can Take That Hill': Longstreet at Gettysburg," in Richard L. DiNardo and Albert A. Nofi, eds., *James Longstreet: The Man, the Soldier, the Controversy* (Conshohocken, Pa.: Combined Publishing, 1998). Much the same Longstreet issues spill over into July 3, thus: William G. Piston, "Cross Purposes: Longstreet, Lee, and Confederate Attack Plans for July 3 at Gettysburg," in Gallagher, ed., *The Third Day at Gettysburg and Beyond* (Chapel Hill: University of North Carolina Press, 1994), pp. 31–55. These relatively recent essays refer to previous analyses of Longstreet and Gettysburg that are contained within books by the same authors: Piston, *Lee's Tarnished Lieutenant: James Longstreet and His Place in Southern History* (Athens: University of Georgia Press, 1987); and Wert, *General James Longstreet: The Confederacy's Most Controversial Soldier—A Biography* (New York: Simon and Schuster, 1993). Wert and Piston go back and forth as to whether "Lee's old warhorse" did a good job or not at Gettysburg, depending on the circumstances, and thus achieve some balance. Compare their arguments with Robert K. Krick, "'If Longstreet . . . Says So, It Is Most Likely Not True': James Longstreet and the Second Day at Gettysburg," in Gallagher, ed., *Second Day at Gettysburg,* pp. 57–86. All of these writings go over the familiar primary material, especially that written by Longstreet himself from the 1870s into the 1890s. A source that is not so well known but is nonetheless informative about Longstreet's actions and *attitudes* on July 2 is Brig. Gen. G. Moxley Sorrel, C.S.A., *Recollections of a Confederate Staff Officer,* ed. Bell I. Wiley (Jackson, Tenn.: McCowat-Mercer Press, 1959).

Putting Longstreet's "possible course of action" for the Army of Northern Virginia on July 2 in a larger context, Scott Bowden and Bill Ward published an analysis entitled "Last Chance for Victory" in *North & South* 4, no. 3 (Mar. 2001): 76–85. These authors would count themselves among the quintessential admirers of Robert E. Lee—including how wisely and well he devised his army's offensive tactics during the Battle of Gettysburg as well as how sagely he rejected General Longstreet's proposal to "move to the right" and instead resumed the offensive on July 2. That article previews elements of their book-length thesis about the Gettysburg campaign: "a critical examination of General Lee and *Southern* leadership during it."[5]

I find these revisions of the revisions of Robert E. Lee's performance in the Gettysburg campaign suspiciously intriguing. The first version was that the Army of Northern Virginia *lost* the Battle of Gettysburg principally because Lee's subordinates, most notably Longstreet and Ewell, *failed* him. Revisions of this longstanding view surfaced, or at least picked up overheated steam, during the 1990s. The contentions of these fin-de-siècle authors—some of whom scathingly denounce Lee's determination to invade the North in 1863 and his decisions during the Battle of Gettysburg—are summarized by Richard Rollins in "Pickett's Charge and the Principles of War," *North & South* 4, no. 5 (June 2001): 12–24. Rollins himself counters the anti-Lee theses, submitting an analysis that runs parallel to the more labored one presented by Bowden and Ward. But if Lee's reasons for invading and his tactical executions during the battle were sound (at worst), then the arguments of his counterattacking admirers unwittingly make a point that they might find disorienting, as the final feature of this essay-within-the-essay purports to explain: If we accept the notion that little or no wrongheadedness, inadequacy, or blundering characterized the Gettysburg campaign and battle from the Confederate perspective, then it would seem to follow that George Gordon Meade and the Army of the Potomac *actively and impressively defeated* their foe in Pennsylvania—in a manner that deserves as much admiration as continues to be lavished on the great gray-bearded general of the Civil War.

Much of what happened on July 2 at Gettysburg seems to pivot on the battle for Little Round Top, which many seem to regard as indeed the *point d'appui* of Gettysburg (where, with a push, the whole thing could have tilted one way or the other). The events on that hill, the *what ifs,* and the historiographical issues stemming from the ways that story has been told figure prominently in Chapter 3. One of the best sources of information about events on Little Round Top is Thomas A. Desjardin, *Stand Firm Ye Boys From Maine* (Gettysburg: Thomas Publications, 1995). This book describes and analyzes the activities of the 20th Maine Regiment throughout the Gettysburg campaign. *Stand Firm* dramatically and necessarily retells the Little Round Top story about Colonel Chamberlain and his men, and ends up expressing skepticism about whether Little Round Top was in fact "a *point d'appui* in the battle," even though "Law, Longstreet, Meade, Jeff Davis and others all favored" it as such (*Stand Firm,* p. 157). Desjardin's revisions offer an object lesson: Ongoing research into the Gettysburg campaign *can* uncover previously unappreciated primary material. This surely is no surprise to professional historians, but a student of the battle might imagine that Gettysburg has been researched to death, such that current books on the subject are merely recycling old material.

Desjardin first sensed that something was not right about the standard accounts of Little Round Top when he encountered the writings of Capt. Ellis Spear, who commanded Colonel Chamberlain's left wing on the southern spur of the hill. These documents were buried in a file within the Gettysburg National Military Park's archives. After *Stand Firm* appeared, so did a collection of Spear's writings: Andrea C. Hawkes et al., eds., *The Civil War Recollections of General Ellis Spear* (Orono: University of Maine Press, 1997). Thus, we all can read (pp. 32–41 of *Recollections*) one of the accounts in which Spear disagreed with elements of the long paper trail left by Chamberlain. In such postwar writings, that former colonel (later general) increasingly exaggerated his exploits on July 2. For more on this, see Glenn LaFantasie, "Joshua Chamberlain and the American Dream," in Boritt, ed., *Gettysburg Nobody Knows,* pp. 31–55.

Pitting Spear's side of the story against those of other Mainers besides Chamberlain brings us inevitably to Theodore Gerrish, who was a private in the 20th Maine in 1863. Gerrish's Civil War diary was published as *Army Life: A Private's Reminiscences of the Civil War* (Portland, Maine: Hoyt, Fogg, and Donham, 1882), and its chapter on Gettysburg is an important primary source for Little Round Top. The problem is that Private Gerrish was in a hospital in Philadelphia during the battle, a fact uncovered by Desjardin after *Stand Firm* was published. Desjardin addresses this in *From These Honored Dead: Gettysburg in American Memory,* a forthcoming book that includes a chapter entitled "Constructing the Consummate Gettysburg Hero." Additional research by Desjardin, appearing in *Legends of Gettysburg: Separating Fact from Fiction* (Gettysburg: Friends of the National Park at Gettysburg, 1997), helps debunk other components of the old stories about Little Round Top and other events in the battle.

A broader treatment of Union officers' and their units' accomplishments in saving the hill at the south end of Cemetery Ridge—well beyond the case of the 20th Maine—is given by Alexander W. Cameron in "The Saviors of Little Round Top," *Gettysburg Magazine,* no. 8 (Jan. 1993): 31–42. See also Brian A. Bennett, "The Supreme Event in Its Existence: The 140th New York on Little Round Top," *Gettysburg Magazine,* no. 3 (July 1990): 17–25. A Southern perspective on the fighting in this region, with many details about the actions of the rebel right wing, is provided by Morris M. Penny and J. Gary Laine, *Struggle for the Round Tops: Law's Alabama Brigade at the Battle of Gettysburg* (Shippensburg, Pa.: Burd Street Press, 1999). Another contribution from the Confederate side came from the pertinent sections of Col. William C. Oates's history and memoirs, *The War Between the Union and the Confederacy and Its Lost Opportunities* (New York: Neale, 1905). The former commander of the 15th Alabama offers a reasonably dispassionate rendition of the battle for the southern spur of Little Round Top. Oates's performance and writings are further examined in Glenn LaFantasie, ed., *Gettysburg: Lt. Frank Haskell, U.S.A., and Col. William C. Oates, C.S.A.* (New York: Bantam Books, 1992), pp. 49–140. James R. Wright describes how the initial Union force that reached the hill (and manned its southern sector) got there in "'I Will Take the Responsibility': Strong Vincent Moves to Little Round Top: Fact or Fiction?" *Gettysburg Magazine*, no. 25 (July, 2001): 48–60.

My considerations of Little Round Top in the context of certain battles in the European theater of World War II drew on Stephen E. Ambrose's *Citizen Soldiers: The U.S. Army from the Normandy Beaches to the Bulge to the Surrender of Germany, June 7, 1944–May 7, 1945* (New York: Simon and Schuster, 1997) and Antony Beevor, *Crete: The Battle and the Resistance* (London: Penguin Books, 1991).

With respect to actions of the Federal 3rd Corps on July 2—and sensing that the accomplishments of men in that unit are underappreciated—I drew from the very detailed but lucid accounts of what certain 3rd Corps brigades actually did on that day: Garry E. Adelman and Timothy H. Smith, *Devil's Den: A History and Guide* (Gettysburg: Thomas Publications, 1997); and Kevin E. O'Brien, "'Hold Them with the Bayonet': de Trobriand's Brigade Defends the Wheatfield," *Gettysburg Magazine*, no. 21 (July 1999): 74–87. For analysis of the "Sickles controversy," I turned to Richard A. Sauers's *A Caspian Sea of Ink: The Meade-Sickles Controversy* (Baltimore: Butternut and Blue, 1989); and William Glenn Robertson, "The Peach Orchard Revisited: Daniel E. Sickles and the Third Corps on July 2, 1863," in Gallagher, ed., *Second Day at Gettysburg,* pp. 33–56.

Contributions to the narrative that covers the later stages of the fighting on July 2 came from D. Scott Hartwig, "'No Troops on the Field Had Done Better': John C. Caldwell's Division in the Wheatfield," in Gallagher, ed., *Second Day at Gettysburg,* pp. 136–71; Eric A. Campbell, "Baptism of Fire: The Ninth Massachusetts Battery at Gettysburg, July 2, 1863," *Gettysburg Magazine,* no. 5 (July 1991): 47–77; R. L. Murray, *The Redemption of the "Harper's Ferry Cowards": The Story of the 111th and 126th New York State Regiments at Gettysburg* (New York: R. L. Murray, 1994); Bradley M. Gottfried, "Wright's Charge on July 2, 1863: Piercing the Union Line or Inflated Glory?" *Gettysburg Magazine,* no. 17 (July 1997): 70–82; John M. Archer, *"The Hour Was One of Horror": East Cemetery Hill at Gettysburg* (Gettysburg: Thomas Publications, 1997); and from Gary Lash, *Twenty-Five Minutes of Fighting: The Gibraltar Brigade on East Cemetery Hill* (Baltimore: Butternut and Blue, 1995). One of the regiments at Gettysburg that "achieved lasting fame"[6] was the 1st Minnesota. Information on the sacrifices made by this unit on the evening of July 2 and afternoon of the Third came from Robert and William Haiber, *The First Minnesota Regiment at Gettysburg* (LaGrangeville, N.Y.: Info Devel Press, 1991); Robert W. Meinhard, "The First Minnesota at Gettysburg," *Gettysburg Magazine,* no. 5 (July 1991): 78–88; and Richard Moe, *The Last Full Measure: The Life and Death of the First Minnesota Volunteers* (New York: Henry Holt, 1993).

One further work is worthy of singling out: Elwood Christ's *"Over a Wide, Hot . . . Crimson Plane": The Struggle for the Bliss Farm at Gettysburg* (Baltimore, Butternut and Blue, 1993). This narrative cuts across both the second and third days of the battle. What happened in the vicinity of the Bliss farm buildings, located between Seminary and Cemetery Ridges, is obscure to most, and nothing in the battle turned there. However, Christ's book is a paradigm for a well-researched, vividly written micro-account of a component of the battle.

CHAPTER 4. JULY 3: THE GREAT GAMBLE LEE COULD HAVE WON AND THE FEDERALS' FINEST HOUR

The once and future book about July 3 at Gettysburg is George R. Stewart's *Pickett's Charge: A Microhistory of the Final Confederate Attack at Gettysburg, July 3, 1863* (Boston: Houghton Mifflin, 1959). Stewart's work offers balanced coverage of both North and South and is as readable as can be—too readable, in the mind of one modern analyst of Pickett's Charge. Thus, Carol Reardon, author of *Pickett's Charge in History and Memory* (Chapel Hill: University of North Carolina Press, 1997), says that Stewart should have better informed us about when and why the battle participants told their stories. Reardon's point (on p. 207 of *In History and Memory*) seems a bit much, as is elaborated below. Meanwhile, the reader might ponder how impressive it is that Stewart's work stood for forty years as the major single-volume work on this day of the battle. However, Stewart is in the process of being flanked. Additional book-length treatments of July 3 and the final attack at Gettysburg have at last materialized in the current century or toward the end of the previous one. The most recent works are Jeffry D. Wert's *Gettysburg Day Three* (New York: Simon and Schuster, 2001) and Earl J. Hess's *Pickett's Charge—The Last Attack at Gettysburg* (Chapel Hill: University of North Carolina Press, 2001). The results of these authors' research are intended to replace Stewart's *Microhistory of the Final Attack*—and thus compete with each other to become the standard narrative for this day of the battle (although Wert also covers the Battle for Culp's Hill on July 3 and thus overlaps Pfanz's *Culp's Hill and Cemetery Hill*). A high proportion of Wert's work consists of the words, actions, and fates of huge numbers of individual participants in the fighting on July 3. Perhaps accordingly, *Day Three* lacks discursive passages that might have explained more about what happened and why. Moreover, this battle book is quite thin in terms of diagramming the actions of July 3.[7] Hess's book about the July 3 assault is entitled in an almost appropriate manner, for its four hundred pages cover "the last attack" on that Friday afternoon exclusively and in more detail compared with Stewart's or Wert's three hundred pages each (even though Pickett's Charge itself was not the utterly final attack that day). Hess says at the beginning of his take on Pickett's Charge that he will not only present the results of much primary source research (by mining material that was perforce unavailable to Stewart), but also discuss his analyses of the Charge—its planning, potential, execution, and outcome. Indeed, this battle book contains several such passages and provides an interpretive essay at the end, causing Hess's *Pickett's Charge* frequently to rise above the density that characterizes other works covering a major portion of the three-day battle.

A narrower study of the events on July 3 was performed and documented by Kathy G. Harrison and John W. Busey in *Nothing But Glory: Pickett's Division at Gettysburg* (Gettysburg, Pa.: Thomas, 1993). This book provides details about the right half of the Confederate assault (as the title indicates); 75 percent of *Nothing But Glory* consists of tabulated appendixes that supply gory details concerning the Confederate units and men within Pickett's division.

Then we have John Michael Priest's more idiosyncratic work about events on the third day: *Into the Fight: Pickett's Charge at Gettysburg* (Shippensburg, Pa.: White Mane, 1998). This account is less comprehensive regarding the occurrences throughout July 3 compared with those of Stewart, Wert, or Hess (although Priest provides more battlefield diagrams than do that trio of authors, especially the latter two). One of Priest's intentions was to get quickly to the events of that Friday afternoon without presenting very much background information or discussion of strategy and tactics. Each chapter of *Into the Fight* is written in a deliberately choppy manner, breaking down occurrences of the moment into many small subsections about individual units or subsets of the battlefield. Indeed, none of Priest's treatment is discursive (no such passages front it or appear at the end). However, reading between the approximately 750 lines of *Into the Fight* that cover the first half of the rebel advance, one can extract this author's thesis: As discussed in Chapter 4, Priest's tacit conclusion is that the hearts of many Confederate soldiers assembled for the Charge were not in it. For that reason, along with the effects of supposedly withering defensive fire that swept the field during this stage of the Charge, fewer than half of the rebels ended up threatening the Union position on Cemetery Ridge. Priest presents this argument full-bore in a separate essay: "Lee's Gallant 6000?" *North & South* 1, no. 6 (Aug. 1998): 42–56. Priest's contention about half or more of the assault force streaming to the rear before they approached the Federal lines is vigorously disputed by Wayne E. Motts in "A Brave and Resolute Force," *North & South* 2, no. 5 (June 1999): 29–34. See also Richard Rollins, "Getting Beyond All That: The Past and Future of Pickett's Charge," *North & South* 2, no. 4 (Apr. 1999): 35–39; and Paul Clark Cooksey, "The Plan for Pickett's Charge," *Gettysburg Magazine,* no. 22 (Jan. 2000): 66–79.

Motts began his intensive study of Pickett's Charge in the late 1980s, prompted by his research into the life and Gettysburg activities of Gen. Lewis A. Armistead, the results of which he published in *"Trust in God and Fear Nothing": Gen. Lewis A. Armistead, CSA* (Gettysburg: Farnsworth House Military Impressions, 1994). Much of what I learned about events on July 3 came from personal and e-mail communications with Motts. The former included a high-resolution tour of the field, during which he focused on the ground covered by the Confederate right wing before and during the assault. One hopes that Motts will write his *own* book about July 3 at Gettysburg. Whereas he admires George Stewart's work, Motts has accumulated much updated knowledge. Among his discoveries are Maj. Gen. George E. Pickett's papers at Duke University; a most informative account written by a Confederate officer, Capt. William W. Wood of the 14th Virginia in Pickett's division, for the *Philadelphia Weekly Times* (published August 11, 1877[8]); and notes about correspondence with several such officers written by one Peter F. Rothermel in 1870 that were unearthed recently in the Pennsylvania State Archives. Some of the newly uncovered material about July 3—for example, previously unpublished writings from the men of General Kemper's brigade—has been nicely compiled in Richard Rollins, *Pickett's Charge! Eyewitness Accounts* (Redondo Beach, Calif.: Rank and File, 1994) and accentuated my understanding of the July 3 events.

Carol Reardon's recent book is another treatment of Pickett's Charge that quotes a wealth of primary material—on a broader scale than the documents compiled by Rollins, which are more or less after-action accounts. In the aforementioned *Pickett's Charge in History and Memory,* Reardon offers a wide-ranging critique of what participants wrote about the famous assault. Ultimately, Reardon wonders whether we can know *anything* about Pickett's Charge, and by extension about the battle and war of which it was a part. Reardon worked toward her book-length thesis in two essays: "Pickett's Charge: The Convergence of History and Myth in the Southern Past," in Gallagher, ed., *Third Day at Gettysburg,* pp. 56–92; and "'I Think the Union Army Had Something to Do with It': The Pickett's Charge Nobody Knows," in Boritt, ed., *Gettysburg Nobody Knows,* pp. 122–43.

The history-versus-memory approach is surging in Civil War scholarship (the aforementioned Thomas Desjardin being one of its proponents): How much of what was written by participants is history, how much memory—whether legitimately beclouded by time and distance, or deliberately imbued with selectivity or exaggeration? This did not discourage my work on Chapter 4, and I appreciated being made aware of the sources cited by this skeptical author. Reardon does give a nod to George Stewart's rendition of the July 3 story, but she is not so sanguine about that seminal secondary account: "His work illustrated . . . the ensnaring webs of state pride . . . and dreams of personal glory that dogged objective analysis of the attack since July 1863. [This is part and parcel of the history-versus-memory thesis.] Mostly, Stewart had an eye for catchy vignettes. Unfortunately, it seems he treated all those disconnected threads as equally valid historical sources; readers never learned that it mattered a great deal who told the original story, when he told it, and why."[9] Yet it is worth noting that Stewart—although not a formal scholar like Reardon—not only cited his sources relentlessly; he also provided an extensive annotated bibliography in which he frequently expressed his own skepticism about one primary account or another.

Regarding material that provided details for the July 3 narrative, I found one of the most useful documents to be an essay by D. Scott Hartwig: "'The Fate of a Country': The Repulse of Longstreet's Assault by the Army of the Potomac," in *Mr. Lincoln's Army: The Army of the Potomac in the Gettysburg Campaign, Programs of the Sixth Annual Gettysburg Seminar* (Gettysburg, Pa.: Gettysburg National Military Park, 1997), pp. 247–89. Hartwig has focused much of his research into the events of July 3 on the Northern army at Gettysburg. He gives further details about the Union stand and the fighting near the copse of trees at the apex of the Charge in "It Struck Horror to Us All," *Gettysburg Magazine,* no. 4 (Jan. 1991): 89–100. Additional material about that day's action came from Howard Coffin, *Nine Months to Gettysburg: Stannard's Vermonters and the Repulse of Pickett's Charge* (Woodstock, Vt.: Countryman Press, 1997); and Jay Jorgensen, "Edward Porter Alexander, Confederate Cannoneer at Gettysburg," *Gettysburg Magazine,* no. 17 (July 1997): 41–53.

Alexander generated voluminous material about July 3 in particular and Gettysburg in general that is rich with detail, informed criticism of other officers when warranted, and little self-aggrandizement. This former Confederate artillery officer taught me much about what happened during the fighting on the third day and what the Confederate high command said and did leading up to it. Alexander's writings are found in *Military Memoirs of a Confederate: A Critical Narrative* (New York: Charles Scribner's Sons, 1907), pp. 363–446; and Gary W. Gallagher, ed., *Fighting for the Confederacy: The Personal Recollections of General Edward Porter Alexander* (Chapel Hill: University of North Carolina Press, 1989), pp. 219–283.

Although Porter Alexander dominates discussions of the artillery on July 3, one must also come to grips with the planning and actions of several other men. The best sources for this information are the works of Richard Rollins and David L. Shultz, who have authored or coauthored a running series of articles and a monograph on this subject. Their works include Shultz's *"Double Canister at Ten Yards": The Federal Artillery and the Repulse of Pickett's Charge* (Redondo Beach, Calif.: Rank and File, 1995); Rollins and Shultz, "'A Combined and Concentrated Fire': The Federal Artillery at Gettysburg, July 3, 1863," *North & South* 2, no. 3 (Mar. 1999): 39–60; and three additional articles by Rollins: "Lee's Artillery Prepares for Pickett's Charge," *North & South* 2, no. 7 (Sept. 1999): 41–55; "The Failure of Confederate Artillery at Gettysburg: Ordnance and Logistics," *North & South* 3, no. 2 (Jan. 2000): 44–54; and "The Failure of Confederate Artillery in Pickett's Charge," *North & South* 3, no. 4 (Apr. 2000): 26–42. This trilogy is not solely about the Confederate artillery in the battle, for it in part contrasts the performance of the rebel guns and gunners with those of the Union army at Gettysburg. Rollins and Shultz are leading up to a full-length book about the guns of July 3, which will in effect update Fairfax Downey's *The Guns of Gettysburg* (New York: David McKay, 1958) and say more than did Gregory A. Coco in *A Concise Guide to the Artillery at Gettysburg* (Gettysburg: Thomas Publications, 1998).

It is only natural that several published works about Gettysburg make the artillery their focal point.[10] However, much less of the recent research seems to have been dedicated to an analysis of small arms. Perhaps these weapons are considered too mundane, or the nature of shoulder arms, with their great accuracy and range, is taken as a given. Many accounts suggest that midway through the war almost all infantrymen on both sides were equipped with and skilled in the use of the famed rifled muskets. A subtext of this book, which is brought together in Appendix G, is that this conventional wisdom may be wrongheaded. For example, a surprising proportion of soldiers in the Army of the Potomac were armed with smoothbore weapons, which were as cumbersome as they were inaccurate. Data on this matter were provided by Dean S. Thomas in *Ready . . . Aim . . . Fire! Small Arms Ammunition in the Battle of Gettysburg* (Gettysburg: Thomas Publications, 1993). This monograph is about more than ammunition in that it specifies the various types of small arms carried into battle by every Union unit. Similar but more spotty information on Confederate regiments at Gettysburg was extracted from the tabulated facts in Earl J. Coates and Dean S. Thomas, *An Introduction to Civil War Small Arms* (Gettysburg: Thomas Publications, 1990). These works are among many books and pamphlets that *describe* Civil War small arms. One such book stands above most of the others, however: Joseph G. Bilby's *Civil War Firearms: Their Historical Background, Tactical Use and Modern Collecting and Shooting* (Conshohocken, Pa.: Combined Books, 1996). Bilby offers a critique of the situation revolving around rifled muskets, especially in terms of their actual usage by ordinary soldiers. The results of Bilby's research reveal several of the problems associated with the real-world application of these weapons. Who cares? Consider this: It is possible to extrapolate from a consideration of these mundane issues that the relentlessly repeated notion about the insane impossibility of a frontal assault on July 3 at Gettysburg has gone too far.

With respect to this day of the battle, Richard Rollins and David Shultz supplied information about the events of July 3 beyond the relatively narrow area of their research implied by the referrals above. Thus, I benefited from Rollins's collection of primary sources (cited above); from Schultz and Rollins's "Measuring Pickett's Charge," *Gettysburg Magazine* no. 17 (July 1997): 108–17; as well as from two further articles written by Rollins alone: "The Second Wave of Pickett's Charge," *Gettysburg Magazine* no. 18 (Jan. 1998): 96–113, and the aforementioned "Pickett's Charge and the Principles of War." However, these two researchers seem primarily interested in the use of artillery at Gettysburg. By reading their treatments of this subject I may have been coaxed into overemphasizing the impact of artillery fire, particularly from the Federal perspective, on July 3. In this sense, I gingerly suggest that these experts on this aspect of the Gettysburg battle might have succumbed to a natural tendency to stress the importance of what they know so much about simply because they spent a *lot* of time researching this subject and putting pen to paper. Naturally, therefore, such authors would like the reader to absorb what they learned and concluded about how much the artillery accomplished at Gettysburg (or, in terms of the Confederates, did not). Even if this claim about these authors' motives has little validity, one's enthusiasm for their thesis can be tempered.[11] Counterarguments are presented by Paul Clark Cooksey in "The Plan for Pickett's Charge." His research into the events of July 3 led to skepticism about Shultz's and Rollins's analyses as they "seem to indicate the Union artillery repulsed Pickett's Charge" (p. 72).

For my part, I dwell more on the actions of "ordinary" *infantry* units that fought in the Charge, giving special attention to the 8th Ohio Regiment. Owing to the same kind of preoccupation as discussed in the previous paragraph, I may have exaggerated the meaning of these Ohioans' accomplishments. In any case, sources about this Western regiment include a book by Franklin Sawyer, its former commander: *A Military History of the 8th Ohio Vol. Inf'y: Its Battles, Marches and Army Movements* (Cleveland: Fairbanks, 1882); a paper presented by the son of a former officer in that regiment: "Address by Companion D. H. Daggett," read on May 14, 1901, to the Military Order of the Loyal Legion of the United States (MOLLUS),[12] Minnesota, vol. 5, pp. 349–63; and Eric Campbell's "'Remember Harper's Ferry!': The Degradation, Humiliation, and Redemption of George L. Willard's Brigade," pt. 2, *Gettysburg Magazine*, no. 8 (Jan. 1993): 95–110. Additional information about what happened on the Union right and Confederate left (where the 8th Ohio fought on July 3) came from Rollins's *Pickett's Charge!*

CHAPTER 5. AFTERMATH: THE PURSUIT AND ESCAPE OF THE ARMY OF NORTHERN VIRGINIA

This chapter started with numerical information on the casualties of the Battle of Gettysburg. Thus, chart 5-1 specifies sources for the various estimates of the overall figures. This numerology is especially variable for the Army of Northern Virginia. Additional tabulations of casualties, broken down by units for both sides, are in Gregory A. Coco, *Wasted Valor: The Confederate Dead at Gettysburg* (1990) and *A Strange and Blighted Land—Gettysburg: The Aftermath of a Battle* (1995), both from Thomas Publications of Gettysburg; Robert K. Krick, *The Gettysburg Death Roster: The Confederate Dead at Gettysburg*, 3rd ed. (Dayton, Ohio: Morningside House, 1993); John W. Busey and David G. Martin, *Regimental Strengths and Losses at Gettysburg* (Hightstown, N.J.: Longstreet House, 1994); John W. Busey, *These Honored Dead: The Union Casualties at Gettysburg*, rev. ed. (Hightstown, N.J.: Longstreet House, 1996); and Gerard A. Patterson, *Debris of Battle: The Wounded of Gettysburg* (Mechanicsburg, Pa.: Stackpole, 1997). James S. Montgomery's *The Shaping of a Battle: Gettysburg* (Philadelphia: Chilton, 1959) reprinted attempts made by John M. Vanderslice in *Gettysburg, Then and Now* (New York: G. W. Dillingham, 1899) to list the casualties for each of the three days of the battle in turn. These numbers are charted at the ends of Chapters 2, 3, and 4.

The *Official Records* are replete with quantitative material that contributed to these secondary sources, as is discussed in the section above on Appendix F.

The descriptions and discussions of what happened from July 4 until the end of the Gettysburg campaign ten days later built on an older but recently updated work by John W. Schildt, *Roads from Gettysburg* (1st ed., 1979; rev. ed., 1998), published by Burd Street Press of Shippensburg, Pennsylvania. Results of additional and relatively advanced research about the aftermath were published by Harry W. Pfanz, "The Gettysburg Campaign after Pickett's Charge," *Gettysburg Magazine,* no. 1 (July 1989): 118–24; Lt. Col. William Terpeluk, "A Lesson in Battle Tempo: The Union Pursuit after Gettysburg," *Parameters: U.S. War College Quarterly* 25 (autumn 1995): 69–80; and by A. Wilson Greene, "From Gettysburg to Falling Waters," in Gallagher, ed., *Third Day at Gettysburg,* pp. 161–201. The aforementioned essays by Glatthaar and McMurray in Borritt, ed., *Gettysburg Nobody Knows,* include analyses of the battle's outcome and significance. Glatthaar contends that the battle and campaign meant much, and McMurray chides those who wallow in studies of them.

Fresher perspectives, rich with information and analytical detail, can be found in articles that fill most of *North & South* 2, no. 6 (Aug. 1999). Several of these pieces (all of which are cited in the footnotes to Chapter 5) stress the roles played by Union and Confederate cavalry during the days of the marches and rides away from Gettysburg. The depth of cavalry-related detail presented in this special edition of the magazine is warranted: the many actions of the opposing troopers were tactically, in some ways strategically, more significant than were the activities of the retreating rebel infantrymen and the Federal soldiers marching after them.

Appendix A. The Cavalry Battle at Brandy Station (June 9)

Edward G. Longacre gives an overview of cavalry activities in the Gettysburg campaign in *The Cavalry at Gettysburg: A Tactical Study of Mounted Operations during the Civil War's Pivotal Campaign 9 June–14 July 1863* (Lincoln: University of Nebraska Press, 1986), including a chapter devoted to Brandy Station. Further details about that seminal action in the campaign came from Eric J. Wittenberg's 1996 "Brandy Station Seminar," which was available on the Internet at http://www.gdg.org/brandsem.html. Phipps and Peterson, *"Devil's to Pay,"* focuses on General Buford's activities at the outset of this June 9 battle and toward the end of it. Mark Nesbitt's *Saber and Scapegoat* critically discusses whether Stuart was negatively influenced by "the surprise" at Brandy Station and the reproaches about it that appeared in Southern newspapers.

Appendix B. The Loudoun Valley Cavalry Battles (June 17–21)

As the opposing cavalries moved north, the outcomes of their clashes in the valley between the mountains in northern Virginia were ambiguous tactically, and the Federal horsemen achieved little of strategic value. However, both the Union and rebel troopers fought well, overall, in the three battles of the Loudoun Valley. This was arguably significant from the standpoint of increasing confidence on the part of the Northerners. Both Nye, in *Here Come the Rebels!* (pp. 163–211), and Longacre, in *Cavalry at Gettysburg* (pp. 102–33), say as much. Nesbitt, in *Saber and Scapegoat,* is more favorable to Stuart's activities during the period June 17–21. Nonetheless, he nicely depicts the Loudoun Valley battles in graphical detail (pp. 43–56; see also the section on map sources at the end of this essay).

Appendix C. The Fighting Near Brinkerhoff's Ridge (July 2)

The first significant clashes involving cavalrymen occurring near Gettysburg itself took place near this ridgeline east of town. The description of this action is taken from Pfanz's *Culp's Hill and Cemetery Hill* (pp. 153–67). Paul M. Shevchuk contributed further details that do not always jibe with Pfanz's description in "The Fight for Brinkerhoff's Ridge," *Gettysburg Magazine*, no. 2 (Jan. 1990): 61–73; and "The Wounding of Albert Jenkins, July 2, 1863," *Gettysburg Magazine*, no. 3 (July 1990): 51–64. Both of Shevchuk's articles alert one to the significance of Brinkerhoff's Ridge: how the fighting there drained infantry forces from the left wing of the rebel army before it attacked the Federal right on Culp's Hill.

Appendix D. The Cavalry Battle East of Gettysburg (July 3)

The battle on the East Cavalry Field is recounted somewhat differently from the usual accounts, which are exemplified by Marshall D. Krolick in "Forgotten Field: The Cavalry Battle East of Gettysburg on July 3, 1863," *Gettysburg Magazine*, no. 4 (Jan. 1991): 75–88. Was Maj. Gen. J. E. B. Stuart's plan to swing east of Gettysburg, then south, in order eventually to assail the Union rear on Cemetery Ridge? And did the Federal cavalry that met him on what became the East Field stop Stuart in his tracks? Perhaps not (on both counts), as I learned from conversations with a trio of amateur historians who have been studying this action for several years: William O. Adams, Jack Richardson, and Andrew H. Addoms III. Elements of their descriptions of and views about this portion of the July 3 story can be found in Nesbitt's *Saber and Scapegoat* (pp. 95–106), which they believe helped prompt his revisionist account (owing to communications between said trio and Nesbitt).

This appendix is based in part on the research carried out by these four students of the battle, as written down (so far) by one of them. I felt it would be useful to raise the questions about this cavalry fight, as restated briefly in this section of the essay, instead of merely recycling the more standard accounts. You will notice in the appendix itself that Stuart is viewed favorably in terms of the accomplishments of his troopers on the East Field. Nesbitt is a fan of General Stuart, whereas Adams and his colleagues focus most of their admiration on Lt. Col. Vincent A. Witcher of the 34th Virginia Battalion, whose unit was nominally under Stuart on July 3. I delved into Witcher's postwar writings and those of several others who fought on the East Cavalry Field, by way of *The Bachelder Papers* (principally vols. 2 and 3)—using this collection of letters and reports more than for other sections of the book.

Appendix E. The Fatal Cavalry Charge of Elon Farnsworth (July 3)

The account of the fighting on the South Cavalry Field, which ended the Battle of Gettysburg, was pieced together from several sources. Paul M. Shevchuk, "The 1st Texas Infantry and the Repulse of Farnsworth's Charge," *Gettysburg Magazine*, no. 2 (Jan. 1990): 81–90; and J. Gary Laine and Morris M. Penny, *Law's Alabama Brigade in the War Between the Union and the Confederacy* (Shippensburg, Pa.: White Mane Press, 1996), pp. 112–26, home in on a Confederate infantry unit that defended against the charging Union cavalrymen.

For a focus on certain groups of Union troopers that attacked northward across the South Field, see Eric J. Wittenberg, "Merritt's Regulars on South Cavalry Field:

Oh, What Could Have Been," *Gettysburg Magazine,* no. 16 (Jan. 1997): 111–23; and Harold A. Klingensmith, "A Cavalry Regiment's First Campaign: The 18th Pennsylvania at Gettysburg," *Gettysburg Magazine,* no. 20 (Jan. 1999): 51–74.

Wittenberg has pulled together the results of his research into the cavalry activities on July 3 in *Gettysburg's Forgotten Cavalry Actions* (Gettysburg: Thomas Publications, 1998). Pages 1–67 of this work deal with events on the South Cavalry Field. A further chapter (pp. 68–91) was the main source for a footnote in Appendix E about the cavalry battle at Fairfield, which occurred during the afternoon of July 3 west of Gettysburg. Wittenberg, more than I, discusses the potential significance of this forgotten battle outside the battle. See also Paul M. Shevchuk, "Cut to Pieces: The Cavalry Fight at Fairfield, Pennsylvania, July 3, 1863," *Gettysburg Magazine,* no. 1 (July 1989): 105–17.

Appendix F. Organization of the Union and Confederate Armies at Gettysburg

All battle books include lists of the military units involved. For Civil War engagements such orders of battle are derived, or even lifted, from the *Official Records* (ser. 1, vol. 27). The order for the Army of the Potomac is in part 1, pp. 156–68, and for the Army of Northern Virginia in part 2, pp. 283–91. These lists refer to the compositions of the armies from July 1–3, 1863. There are additional orders among the *Official Records* books devoted to the Gettysburg campaign, which give the organization of the two Eastern armies later in the summer of 1863.

I supplemented the usual type of order-of-battle listing by indicating the numbers of soldiers within each unit—from corps down to regiment, a handful of separate battalions, and artillery batteries. This information was nicely supplied by Albert A. Nofi in *The Gettysburg Campaign: June-July 1863,* revised edition (Conshohocken, Pa.: Combined Books, 1993), pp. 235–53. These strengths for the various military units are salted through the *Official Records* (ser. 1, vol. 27, pts. 1–3). The prime secondary source for such numerology about Gettysburg is Busey and Martin's *Regimental Strengths and Losses.*

Nofi's order of battle—unlike what is found in the *Official Records*—does not name regimental commanders, but he specifies which regimental companies were present at Gettysburg for units that were understrength qualitatively and gives details about the artillery batteries. These data are reproduced in Appendix F of this book.

Whether a given officer was killed, wounded, or captured is also indicated in the order of battle (the prelude to Appendix F describes how the specification of unit commanders includes indicators of who may have taken over a given unit, often because of a casualty). Nofi's book specifies what happened to corps, division, and brigade commanders. F. Ray Sibley Jr. went further by giving similar such indicators for Confederate regimental commanders in *The Confederate Order of Battle,* vol. 1, *The Army of Northern Virginia* (Shippensburg, Pa.: White Mane, 1996), pp. 47–55. Accessory bibliographic information about high-ranking officers and what happened to them after Gettysburg came from two compilations by Ezra J. Warner, *Generals in Gray: Lives of the Confederate Commanders* (1959), and *Generals in Blue: Lives of the Union Commanders* (1964), both published by Louisiana State University Press of Baton Rouge. To supplement further the fine print in Appendix F, I plowed through *Official Records* reports, insofar as they were useful for supplying casualty information about commanders of Union regiments. Dick Dobbins's database ("American Civil War Research and Genealogy," www.civilwardata.com) provided many additional pieces of information about the fates of lower-ranking Union officers who fought at Gettysburg.

Appendix G. The Potential and Problems of Small-Arms Fire at Gettysburg

The several individual sources cited within the essay speak for themselves—or can be found in the main chapter passages that are referred to within this polemically appended article (also, see citations in the previous section about Chapter 4). Two sources for Appendix G are worth stressing. The first, Joseph Bilby's book about Civil War firearms (cited and discussed above), includes elements that should give pause to those who make rote reference to the great defensive power that was supposedly in the hands of Civil War soldiers fighting on the defensive. The other, essentially an entire issue of *North & South* (vol. 4, no. 6), is devoted to "arms and the man" (the title of a valuable article in the August 2001 release of this periodical), as they were actually used and as they really fought in the Civil War.

Map Sources

Most of the maps in this book are based on previously published ones. None was reproduced directly; all were modified with respect to conventions used here to depict military units, march routes, and so forth. Many were modified substantively, based on verbally indicated details in several of the documents I scrutinized. Some diagrams were extracted from a certain part of the published map in question. A few maps are not listed below; these were made essentially from scratch.

Chapter 1

1-2: *The Century,* vol. 11 (New York: Century, Nov. 1886–Apr. 1887), p. 119, on which maps drawn by Jacob Wells are printed within an article bearing the following dual title and authorship: "Maps of the Gettysburg Campaign," by Gen. Abner Doubleday, and "The First Day at Gettysburg," by Gen. Henry J. Hunt. See also Johnson and Buel, eds., *Battles and Leaders,* vol. 3, p. 262.
1-3: Clark, *Gettysburg,* p. 32.
1-4: *Century,* p. 119. See also Johnson and Buel, eds., *Battles and Leaders,* vol. 3, p. 262.
1-5: Clark, *Gettysburg,* p. 32.
1-6: *Century,* p. 122. See also Johnson and Buel, eds., *Battles and Leaders,* vol. 3, p. 264.
1-7: Clark, *Gettysburg,* p. 32.
1-8: *Century,* p. 122. See also Johnson and Buel, eds., *Battles and Leaders,* vol. 3, p. 264.
1-10: Nesbitt, *Saber and Scapegoat,* p. 63.
1-11: Clark, *Gettysburg,* p. 32.
1-12: Ibid.
1-13, top: Nesbitt, *Saber and Scapegoat,* p. 63.
1-13, bottom: Powell, "Stuart's Ride," p. 34.
1-14: Hassler, *Crisis at the Crossroads,* p. 9; Shue, *Morning at Willoughby Run,* p. 20; *Century,* p. 123. See also Johnson and Buel, eds., *Battles and Leaders,* vol. 3, p. 266.
1-15: *Century,* p. 123; Shue, *Morning at Willoughby Run,* p. 34. See also Johnson and Buel, eds., *Battles and Leaders,* vol. 3, p. 266.
1-17: Shue, *Morning at Willoughby Run,* p. 27.
1-18: Ibid., p. 55.
1-19: Ibid., p. 34; *Century,* p. 123. See also Johnson and Buel, eds., *Battles and Leaders,* vol. 3, p. 266.
1-20: Shue, *Morning at Willoughby Run,* p. 55; Phipps and Peterson, *"Devil's to Pay,"* p. 45.

Chapter 2

2-1: Greg Novak and Frank Chadwick, *Battles of the American Civil War: A Sourcebook for Volley and Bayonet* (Bloomington, Ill.: Game Designers' Workshop, 1995), p. 38.
2-3: Shue, *Morning at Willoughby Run,* p. 27.
2-4: Ibid., p. 60.

2-5: Phipps and Peterson, "Devil's to Pay," p. 45.
2-6: Shue, *Morning at Willoughby Run*, p. 60.
2-7: Phipps and Peterson, "Devil's to Pay," p. 45.
2-8: Shue, *Morning at Willoughby Run*, p. 27.
2-9: Martin, *Gettysburg July 1*, p. 103.
2-10: Ibid., p. 150.
2-11: Krick, "Three Confederate Disasters," p. 103.
2-12: Martin, *Gettysburg July 1*, p. 124.
2-13: Ibid., p. 179.
2-14, top: Ibid.
2-14, bottom: Ibid., p. 348.
2-16, top: Coddington, *Gettysburg Campaign*, between pp. 236–37.
2-16, bottom: Shue, *Morning at Willoughby Run*, p. 173.
2-17, top: Ibid., p. 191.
2-17, bottom: Martin, *Gettysburg July 1*, p. 225; and information provided to the author by Thomas A. Desjardin (stemming from his research and consultations with D. Scott Hartwig and Wayne E. Motts).
2-18: Ibid.
2-19: Ibid.
2-20: Ibid., p. 388.
2-21: Clark, *Gettysburg*, p. 63.
2-22, top: Martin, *Gettysburg July 1*, p. 285.
2-22, bottom: Ibid., p. 300.
2-23, top: Ibid., p. 312.
2-23, bottom: Ibid., p. 400.
2-24: Ibid., p. 355; Pfanz, *First Day*, p. 271.
2-25: Martin, *Gettysburg July 1*, p. 421; Pfanz, *First Day*, p. 206.
2-26: Smith, *Story of Lee's Headquarters*, pp. 32–33.
2-27: Ibid., p. 494.
2-28: Coddington, *Gettysburg Campaign*, between pp. 236–37.
2-29: Martin, *Gettysburg July 1*, p. 537.

Chapter 3

3-1: Novak and Chadwick, *Battles*, p. 38. Templates for 3-2–3-5: Ibid.
3-6, bottom: Mark Nesbitt, *If the South Won at Gettysburg* (Gettysburg: Thomas Publications, 1980), p. 54.
3-7: Novak and Chadwick, *Battles*, p. 38.
3-8: Pfanz, *Second Day*, p. 120.
3-9: McPherson, *Battle Cry of Freedom*, p. 643.
3-10: Pfanz, *Second Day*, pp. 170–71, p. 314
3-11: Novak and Chadwick, *Battles*, p. 38.
3-12: Pfanz, *Second Day*, pp. 170–71, p. 314.
3-13: Ibid.
3-14: Adelman and Smith, *Devil's Den*, pp. 30, 34.
3-15: Desjardin, *Stand Firm*, p. 38.
3-16, bottom: Ibid.
3-16, top: Clark, *Gettysburg*, p. 70.
3-17: Pfanz, *Second Day*, p. 216.
3-18: Ibid., p. 180
3-19: Desjardin, *Stand Firm*, p. 43.
3-20, top: Ibid., p. 53.
3-20, bottom: Ibid., p. 66.
3-21: Ibid., p. 72
3-22: Pfanz, *Second Day*, p. 229.
3-23, top: Bennett, "The Supreme Event," p. 16.
3-23, bottom: Ibid., p. 25.
3-24: Beevor, *Crete*, p. 121.
3-25: Pfanz, *Second Day*, p. 180.
3-26, top: Adelman and Smith, *Devil's Den*, p. 36.
3-26, bottom: Ibid., p. 41.
3-27, top: Ibid., p. 47.
3-27, bottom: Ibid., p. 47.
3-28: Ibid., p. 49.
3-29: Pfanz, *Second Day*, p. 246.
3-30: Ibid., p. 229.
3-31: Ibid., p. 272.
3-32, top: Ibid., pp. 246, 314.
3-32, bottom: Ibid., p. 292.
3-33: Ibid.
3-34: Ibid., p. 314.
3-35: Campbell, "Baptism of Fire," pp. 55, 69. Both the top and bottom panels include features presented in the maps on both of the pages cited; the latter is a reprint of a drawing by John Bigelow himself.
3-36: Pfanz, *Second Day*, p. 364.
3-37: Ibid., p. 405.
3-38: Meinhard, "First Minnesota at Gettysburg," p. 78.
3-39: Pfanz, *Second Day*, p. 385.
3-40: Pfanz, *Culp's Hill and Cemetery Hill*, pp. 172–73.
3-41: Ibid., p. 113.
3-42: Ibid., p. 207.
3-43: Jorgensen, "Holding the Right," p. 63.
3-44: Pfanz, *Culp's Hill and Cemetery Hill*, p. 238.
3-45: Ibid., pp. 266–67.
3-46: Ibid., p. 286.
3-47, bottom: Ibid, p. 266.
3-48: Gottfried, "Wright's Charge," p. 78.
3-49: Pfanz, *Culp's Hill and Cemetery Hill*, p. 397.

Chapter 4

4-1: Novak and Chadwick, *Battles*, p. 38.
4-2, top: Piston, "Cross Purposes," p. 36; Pfanz, *Culp's Hill and Cemetery Hill*, pp. 332–33.
4-2, bottom: Pfanz, *Culp's Hill and Cemetery Hill*, pp. 332–33.
4-3: Ibid., p. 286.
4-4: Ibid., p. 301.
4-5: Ibid., p. 311.

4-6: Ibid., pp. 342–43.
4-7: Clark, *Gettysburg*, p. 130.
4-8, top: Piston, "Cross Purposes," p. 36.
4-8, bottom: Ibid., p. 37.
4-9, top: Harrison and Busey, *Nothing But Glory*, p. 14.
4-9, bottom: Based on an unpublished map produced by Wayne E. Motts and the Association of Licensed Battlefield Guides of Gettysburg. See also Motts, "Trust in God," p. 43.
4-10: Thomas A. Desjardin, *The Battlefield at Gettysburg*, map 4, *July 3, 1863—Day Three* (Gettysburg: Friends of the National Park at Gettysburg, 1998).
4-11: Ibid.
4-12: Ibid.
4-13: Stewart, *Pickett's Charge*, p. 163.
4-14, top: Ibid.; Hess, *Pickett's Charge*, p. 49.
4-14, bottom: Stewart, *Pickett's Charge*, p. 185
4-15: Ibid., p. 201.
4-16: Ibid., p. 163.
4-17: Ibid., p. 201.
4-19: Ibid., p. 185.
4-20: Harrison and Busey, *Nothing But Glory*, p. 64.
4-21: Eric A. Campbell, "'A Field Made Glorious': Cemetery Hill: From Battlefield to Sacred Ground," *Gettysburg Magazine*, no. 15 (July 1996): 119.
4-22: Stewart, *Pickett's Charge*, p. 163.
4-23: Campbell, "'Remember Harper's Ferry!'," p. 98; Rollins, *Pickett's Charge!* foldout map at end of book.
4-24: Harrison and Busey, *Nothing But Glory*, p. 64.
4-25, top: Stewart, *Pickett's Charge*, p. 201; Priest, *Into the Fight*, p. 88, bottom.
4-25, bottom: After-action report of Col. Norman J. Hall, July 17, 1863, *OR*, vol. 27, pt. 1, p. 438.
4-26: Stewart, *Pickett's Charge*, p. 201.
4-27: Ibid., p. 215.
4-28: Hartwig, "It Struck Horror to Us All," p. 93.
4-29: Harrison and Busey, *Nothing But Glory*, p. 64.
4-30: Stewart, *Pickett's Charge*, p. 229; Rollins, *Pickett's Charge!* foldout map at end of book.
4-31: Harrison and Busey, *Nothing But Glory*, p. 22.
4-32, top: Campbell, "'Remember Harper's Ferry!'," p. 94; Rollins, *Pickett's Charge!* foldout map at end of book.
4-32, bottom: Campbell, "'Remember Harper's Ferry!'," p. 98; Rollins, *Pickett's Charge!* foldout map at end of book.
4-33: Stewart, *Pickett's Charge*, p. 215.
4-34: Ibid., p. 201; Harrison and Busey, *Nothing But Glory*, p. 96; Campbell, "'Remember Harper's Ferry!'," p. 98.
4-35: Stewart, *Pickett's Charge*, p. 163.
4-36: Clark, *Gettysburg*, p. 130.
4-37: Stewart, *Pickett's Charge*, p. 215.
4-38: Steven J. Wright, "'Don't Let Me Bleed to Death': The Wounding of Maj. Gen. Winfield Scott Hancock," *Gettysburg Magazine*, no. 6 (Jan. 1992): 88.
4-39: Clark, *Gettysburg*, p. 130.

Chapter 5

5-2: Coddington, *Gettysburg Campaign*, between pp. 548–49; Alexander, "Ten Days in July," p. 15.
5-3: Ibid.; Harry W. Pfanz, "The Gettysburg Campaign after Pickett's Charge," *Gettysburg Magazine*, no. 1 (July 1989): 123.
5-4: Pfanz, "Gettysburg Campaign after Pickett's Charge," p. 123.
5-5: Ibid.; Coddington, *Gettysburg Campaign*, between pp. 548–49.
5-6, top:
5-6, bottom: Pfanz, "Gettysburg Campaign after Pickett's Charge," p. 123.
5-7: Coddington, *Gettysburg Campaign*, between pp. 548–49.
5-8: Pfanz, "Gettysburg Campaign after Pickett's Charge," p. 123.

Appendix A

A-1: Longacre, *Cavalry at Gettysburg*, p. 68.
A-2: Association for the Preservation for Civil War Sites, "Brandy Station Contract Signed," *Hallowed Ground*, summer 1996, p. 1.
A-3: Ibid.
A-4: Phipps and Peterson, "*Devil's to Pay*," p. 34.

Appendix B

B-2: Nesbitt, *Saber and Scapegoat*, p. 45.
B-3: Ibid., p. 51.
B-4: Ibid., p. 53.

Appendix C

C-1, top: Pfanz, *Culp's Hill and Cemetery Hill*, p. 155.
C-1, bottom: Shevchuk, "Fight for Brinkerhoff's Ridge," p. 70.

Appendix D

D-2: Nesbitt, *Saber and Scapegoat*, p. 97.
D-3: Ibid.
D-4: Kevin E. O'Brien, "'Glory Enough for All': Lt. William Brooke-Rawle and

the 3rd Pennsylvania Cavalry at Gettysburg," *Gettysburg Magazine,* no. 13 (July 1995): 99; David L. Ladd and Audrey J. Ladd, "Stuart's and Gregg's Cavalry Engagement, July 3, 1863," *Gettysburg Magazine,* no. 16 (Jan. 1997): 101.

Appendix E

E-2, top: Wittenberg, "Merritt's Regulars," p. 113.
E-2, bottom: Ibid., p. 118.
E-3: Klingensmith, "Cavalry Regiment's First Campaign," p. 67.
E-4: Based on conversations between the author and William O. Adams, Oct. 1995, and a diagram supplied by Adams.
E-5, top: Penny and Laine, *Law's Alabama Brigade,* p. 115; H. C. Parsons, "Farnsworth's Charge and Death," in *Battles and Leaders of the Civil War,* vol. 3, ed. Johnson and Buel, p. 394.
E-5, bottom: Penny and Laine, *Law's Alabama Brigade,* p. 117; Parsons, "Farnsworth's Charge and Death," p. 394.

Bibliographic Essay Notes

1. Prof. Jay Luvaas, U.S. Army War College, Carlisle Barracks, Pa., to author, Nov. 15, 1991.

2. Gramm was specifically lambasted in this manner by Mark A. Snell (letter to editor, *Civil War News* 21, no. 5 [June 1995]: 38). Snell went on to say that he has "attended or lectured at dozens of Civil War conferences, seminars, symposia, and Civil War Roundtables over the last two decades [and] during that time . . . come to know many of the people who attend these functions and . . . discovered that many of them tend to be politically conservative" (*Civil War Times* 21, no. 8 [Sept. 1995]: 4). Perhaps this is meant to justify a demonization of Gramm. In any case, the number of current Confederate sympathizers beggars the imagination: "I must agree . . . that a huge proportion of the mail we receive is from the South—the writers still trying to justify the cause. Perhaps they protest too much" (William J. Miller, editor, *Civil War Times,* to author, Oct. 2, 1991).

3. The extent to which Scott "edited" the overall *OR* compilation is overstated. A brief history of the origins of this resource, along with credit given to the several persons who contributed to its production, is in Alan C. Aimone and Barbara A. Aimone, *A User's Guide to the Official Records of the American Civil War Armies* (Shippensburg, Pa.: White Mane, 1993), pp. 1–17.

4. Pfanz, *First Day,* p. xiv. Included are notions that Gettysburg was inevitable because of the concentration of roads there; that Union cavalry delayed the Confederates until the Federal infantry arrived on July 1; that a rebel sharpshooter shot Maj. Gen. John F. Reynolds; that the Union forces were defeated on this day because of the poor performance of the 11th Corps; and that only Lt. Gen. Richard S. Ewell's vacilation about pressing an attack on Cemetery Hill prevented the Army of Northern Virginia from achieving a complete victory.

5. Scott Bowden and Bill Ward, *Last Chance for Victory: Robert E. Lee and the Gettysburg Campaign* (El Dorado Hills, Calif.: Savas, 2001), p. iv, emphasis in original. Although Bowden and Ward deal in part with "the events that spawned the campaign" and the "political and strategic state of the Confederacy" in the spring of 1863 (*Last Chance,* p. iii), they seem most interested in the tactical decisions made by General Lee at Gettysburg and what happened accordingly: for example, how Lee resumed the offensive on July 2 "in accord with every sound military principle of the age"; and how, more specifically, he "carefully modified his original plan of attack that afternoon from a more standard flanking assault into an *en echelon* attack to take advantage of the changed disposition of his enemy" (p. iii). Bowden and Ward regard their "approach and method" to be "radically different from traditional fare" about the Battle of Gettysburg, especially with regard to "the complex series of decisions, movements, and fighting on July 2," which are "*always* [as loudly emphasized by the authors] broken apart and tendered to readers in separate chunks" (p. iii)—inappropriately in the (many further) words of these authors, in conjunction with their elaborately affirmative answer to the question about whether "another book is necessary" to reevaluate Gettysburg (p. i).

6. McPherson, *Battle Cry of Freedom,* p. 659.

7. This visual aid problem is exacerbated by labeling gaffes in which the Battle for the East Cavalry Field (Appendix D) is indicated in a lone map on page 274, which depicts the

cavalry actions that occurred this day in the southern sector of the main battlefield and at Fairfield, Pennsylvania (Appendix E). The map for the latter two fights in Wert's work, which attempts to diagram them both in one image, is entitled "Stuart vs. Gregg, East Cavalry Battlefield" (*Day Three,* p. 259). I have no intention here to smugly poke fun at these howlers; instead, they make me wonder whether the campaign and field maps included within most battle books are inserted not only sporadically but also as an *afterthought.*

    8. This periodical printed a series of articles by participants in the Civil War called *Annals of the War.* The original volume of the same title was published in 1879, when the man who originated the series—Arthur K. McClure, a Philadelphia newspaperman—chose what he judged to be the best fifty-six of them. Unfortunately, *Annals,* reprinted in 1996 by Blue and Grey Press of Edison, New Jersey, did not include Wood's article.

    9. Reardon, *In History & Memory,* p. 207.

    10. Concentrating on the artillery may be particularly engrossing because it "was the most technologically advanced and scientifically demanding aspect of nineteenth-century warfare" (Rollins, "Failure of Confederate Artillery in Pickett's Charge," p. 27).

    11. I got wind of this phenomenon in another Gettysburg context. It involved a book that presaged a distinct upsurge in publications devoted to a particular component of the Gettysburg campaign: The following claim appears on the dust jacket of Lance Herdegen and William Beaudot's *In the Bloody Railroad Cut at Gettysburg:* "In the very opening of the infantry fighting [on the morning of July 1] . . . the successful attack [by the 6th Wisconsin of the Iron Brigade] played a key role in the outcome of the battle." That is too much.

    12. The *MOLLUS,* as these compilations of papers are known, stemmed from an organization of Union veterans founded in 1865. By the end of the century, the organization had eight thousand members, composed of such veterans along with their sons and even grandsons. Several *MOLLUS* accounts about the campaign at hand were compiled and indexed by Ken Brandy, Florence Freeland, and Margie Riddle Bearss in *The Gettysburg Papers,* vols. 1 and 3 (Dayton, Ohio: Press of Morningside Bookshop, 1978).

Index of Military Units

Divisions and brigades are indexed under the respective army corps. Regiments are indexed by state. Military units are indexed from text and charts, but not from maps.

ARMY OF NORTHERN VIRGINIA (ANV) (Lee)
1st Corps (Longstreet), 7–8, 30, 80, 88, 132, 254, 261, 318
    Hood's division, 30, 88, 92, 100, 103, 107, 111, 120, 126, 132, 299, 319
        Benning's brigade, 100, 126, 131–133, 181, 319
        G. T. Anderson's brigade, 100, 126, 132, 133, 134, 137, 164, 181, 299, 319
        Law's brigade, 88, 91, 100, 103, 104, 105, 111, 114, 120, 126, 131, 181, 319
        Texas (Robertson's) brigade, 100, 103, 104, 105, 111, 120, 126, 181, 299, 319
    McLaws's division, 30, 88, 92, 100, 132, 137, 138, 145, 164, 281, 318
        Barksdale's brigade, 100, 138, 139–141, 145, 181, 319
        Kershaw's brigade, 88, 100, 132, 134, 137, 145, 164, 181, 318
        Semme's brigade, 100, 132, 134, 137, 164, 318
        Wofford's brigade, 100, 137, 138, 164, 181, 319
    Pickett's division, 30, 181, 201, 214, 319, 343n2
        Armistead's brigade, 181, 201, 214, 319
        Garnett's brigade, 181, 201, 214, 319
        Kemper's brigade, 181, 201, 214, 225, 238, 319
    Reserve Artillery, 189, 320
2nd Corps (Ewell), 6, 19, 30, 54, 82, 83, 171, 177, 254, 261, 320, 338n8, 340n31
    Early's division, 30, 61, 70, 77, 82, 157, 177, 254, 320
        Gordon's brigade, 61, 254, 320, 342n72
        Hays's brigade, 61, 70, 157, 320
        Hoke's brigade, 70, 157, 320
        Smith's brigade, 171, 173, 177, 320, 343n75
    Johnson's division, 30, 73, 82, 150, 151, 177, 320, 342n73, 343n3
        Jones's brigade, 151, 155–156, 177, 320
        Nicholls's brigade, 151, 177, 320
        Steuart's brigade, 151, 154, 171, 177, 320
        Stonewall Brigade, 150, 171, 173, 176, 177, 285–288, 320
    Rodes's division, 30, 54, 56, 68, 77, 82, 158, 171, 177, 199, 321, 340nn29,30
        Daniel's brigade, 58, 68, 158, 171, 176, 177, 199, 275, 321
        Dole's brigade, 56, 68, 77, 158, 199, 321, 341n49
        Iverson's brigade, 56, 158, 199, 321
        O'Neal's brigade, 56, 77, 158, 171, 173, 177, 199, 321
        Ramseur's brigade, 58, 158, 199, 321
3rd Corps (Hill), 7, 30, 33, 40, 254, 261, 321
    Heth's division, 30, 33, 36–37, 39, 40, 46, 65, 77, 201, 229, 263, 321
        Archer's brigade, 39, 40, 45, 46, 65, 182, 201, 229, 321
        Brockenbrough's brigade, 39, 40, 65, 182, 185, 201, 229, 321
        Davis's brigade, 39, 40, 46, 48, 182, 201, 229, 321
        Pettigrew's brigade, 33, 36–39, 40, 65, 182, 201, 229, 321
    Pender's division, 30, 50, 65, 68, 77, 80, 199, 231, 263, 322
        Lane's brigade, 185, 201, 231, 263, 322, 341n55
        McGowan's brigade, 68, 322
        Scale's brigade, 68, 185, 201, 231, 322
    R. Anderson's division, 30, 80, 93, 145, 147, 185, 199, 232, 281, 322
        Mahone's brigade, 147, 232, 322
        Perry's brigade, 145, 199, 238, 322
        Posey's brigade, 147, 232, 322
        Wilcox's brigade, 93, 145, 199, 238, 322, 352n29
        Wright's brigade, 145, 147, 161, 199, 232, 322

Reserve Division
    Pegram's artillery battalion, 39, 40, 322
Cavalry Division (Stuart), 28, 252, 323
    Division Horse Artillery, 323
    Fitzhugh Lee's brigade, 6, 17, 28, 252, 263, 267, 274, 279, 280, 290, 294, 296, 323, 335n15
    Hampton's brigade, 6, 28, 252, 267, 271, 274, 280, 281, 290, 294, 296, 299, 323
    Imboden's command, 25, 252, 323, 336nn30,31
    Jenkins's brigade, 6, 25, 290, 293, 323, 336n31
    Jones's brigade, 6, 254, 267, 271, 274, 280, 281, 323, 335n15, 365n4
    Robertson's brigade, 6, 254, 267, 280, 281, 323, 335n15, 336n31
    "Rooney" Lee's brigade, 6, 17, 28, 267, 271, 274, 280, 281, 290, 294, 323, 335n15
Alabama
    3rd Ala., 58, 321
    4th Ala., 103, 111, 113, 115, 120, 306, 319
    5th Ala., 56, 229, 321
    5th Ala. Battalion, 46, 321
    6th Ala., 56, 321
    8th Ala., 322
    9th Ala., 145
    10th Ala., 145, 322
    11th Ala., 145, 322
    12th Ala., 56, 321
    13th Ala., 40, 41, 46, 229, 321
    14th Ala., 145, 322
    15th Ala., 103, 104, 105–107, 114, 115–123, 319
        Company A, 347n77
    26th Ala., 56, 321
    44th Ala., 103, 104, 105, 126, 133, 319
    47th Ala., 103, 105, 107, 114, 115, 319
    48th Ala., 103, 104, 105, 120, 126, 130, 319
    Hardaway Battery, 322
    Jefferson Davis Battery, 321
Arkansas
    3rd Ark., 103, 104, 126, 319
Florida
    2nd Fla., 145, 322
    5th Fla., 145, 322
    8th Fla., 70, 145, 322
Georgia
    2nd Ga., 133, 319
    2nd Ga. Battalion, 147, 322
    3rd Ga., 147, 322
    7th Ga., 299, 319
    8th Ga., 132, 299, 319
    9th Ga., 132, 299, 319
    10th Ga., 318
    11th Ga., 126, 132, 299, 319
    11th Ga. Artillery Battalion, 322
    13th Ga., 320
    14th Ga., 322
    15th Ga., 319, 365n1
    16th Ga., 319

17th Ga., 133, 319
18th Ga., 319
20th Ga., 319
22nd Ga., 147, 322
24th Ga., 319
26th Ga., 320
31st Ga., 320
35th Ga., 322
38th Ga., 320
44th Ga., 321
45th Ga., 322
48th Ga., 147, 322
49th Ga., 322
50th Ga., 318
51st Ga., 319
53rd Ga., 319
59th Ga., 126, 299, 319
60th Ga., 320
61st Ga., 320
Cobb's Cavalry Legion, 271, 274, 294, 319, 323
Phillips Legion, 319, 323
Pulaski Battery, 319
Troup County Light Battery, 319
Louisiana
    1st La., 320
    2nd La., 320
    5th La., 70, 320
    6th La., 70, 320
    7th La., 70, 320
    8th La., 70, 320
    9th La., 70, 320
    10th La., 320
    14th La., 320
    15th La., 320
    Donaldsville Battery, 322
    La. Guard Battery, 320
    Madison Battery, 320
    Washington Artillery Battalion, 320
Maryland
    1st Md. Battalion, 153, 154, 155, 320
    1st Md. Battery, 320
    1st Md. Cavalry Battalion, 323
    4th Md. (Chesapeake) Battery, 320
Mississippi
    2nd Miss., 46, 48, 229, 321
    8th Miss., 145
    11th Miss., 229, 321
    12th Miss., 322
    13th Miss., 138, 145, 319
    16th Miss., 322
    17th Miss., 138, 145, 319
    18th Miss., 138, 319
    19th Miss., 322
    21st Miss., 138, 141, 319
    42nd Miss., 46, 48, 229, 321
    48th Miss., 322
    Jeff Davis Cavalry Legion, 271, 274, 294, 323
    Madison Battery, 322
North Carolina

1st N.C., 153, 154, 349n118
1st N.C. Artillery, 319
    Battery C, 322
1st N.C. Cavalry, 271, 274, 323
1st N.C. State Troops, 320
2nd N.C. Battalion, 56, 58, 321
2nd N.C. Cavalry, 271, 274, 323
2nd N.C. State Troops, 321
3rd N.C., 153, 154, 155, 320
3rd or 13th N.C. Artillery Battalion, 319
4th N.C., 58
4th N.C. Cavalry, 323
4th N.C. State Troops, 321
5th N.C. Cavalry, 323
5th N.C. State Troops, 321
6th N.C., 70
6th N.C. State Troops, 320
7th N.C., 231, 322
11th N.C., 229, 321
12th N.C., 321
13th N.C., 231, 322
14th N.C., 58, 321
16th N.C., 231, 322
18th N.C., 231, 322
20th N.C., 321
21st N.C., 70, 320
22nd N.C., 231, 322
26th N.C., 33, 36, 65, 229, 231, 263, 264, 321
28th N.C., 231, 322
30th N.C., 58, 321
32nd N.C., 56, 58, 321
33rd N.C., 231, 322
34th N.C., 231, 322, 360n149
37th N.C., 231, 322
38th N.C., 322
43rd N.C., 56, 58, 321
45th N.C., 56, 58, 321
47th N.C., 229, 321
52nd N.C., 229, 321
53rd N.C., 56, 58, 321
55th N.C., 46, 48, 229, 321
57th N.C., 70, 320
South Carolina
    1st S.C., 68, 322
    1st S.C. Cavalry, 271, 274, 299, 302, 323
    1st S.C. Rifles, 322
    2nd S.C., 318
    2nd S.C. Cavalry, 275, 323
    3rd S.C., 132, 318
    3rd S.C. Battalion, 318
    7th S.C., 132, 318
    8th S.C., 145, 318
    12th S.C., 322
    13th S.C., 322
    14th S.C., 68, 322
    15th S.C., 132, 318
    Brooks Light Battery, 320
    Charleston "German" Light Battery, 319
    Palmetto Light Battery, 320
    Pee Dee Battery D, 322

Washington Battery, 323
Tennessee
    1st Tenn., 46, 229
    7th Tenn., 46, 229, 321
    14th Tenn., 46, 229, 321
Texas
    1st Tex., 103, 104–105, 126, 299, 303–306, 319
    4th Tex., 103, 105, 111, 113, 115, 120, 319
    5th Tex., 103, 105, 111, 113, 115, 120, 319
Virginia
    1st Richmond Howitzer Battery, 319
    1st Rockbridge Battery, 321
    1st Stuart Horse Artillery Battery, 323
    1st Va., 214, 238, 319
    1st Va. Artillery Battalion, 321
    1st Va. Cavalry, 274, 279, 323
    2nd Richmond Howitzer Battery, 321
    2nd Stuart Horse Artillery Battery, 323
    2nd Va., 285, 320
    2nd Va. Cavalry, 274, 323
    3rd Richmond Howitzer Battery, 321
    3rd Va., 214, 238, 319
    3rd Va. Cavalry, 274, 323
    4th Va., 320
    4th Va. Cavalry, 275, 279, 323
    5th Va., 320
    5th Va. Cavalry, 278, 279, 323
    6th Va., 322
    6th Va. Cavalry, 270, 271, 274, 323, 365n4
    7th Va., 214, 238, 319
    7th Va. Cavalry, 270, 271, 323, 365n4
    8th Va., 214, 319
    9th Va., 214, 319
    9th Va. Cavalry, 271, 274, 323
    10th Va., 154, 155, 320
    10th Va. Cavalry, 271, 274, 323
    11th Va., 214, 225, 226, 319
    11th Va. Cavalry, 271, 323, 365n4
    12th Va., 322
    12th Va. Cavalry, 271, 274, 323, 365n4
    13th Va. Cavalry, 274, 323
    14th Va., 214, 319
    14th Va. Cavalry, 293, 323
    15th Va. Cavalry, 6, 323
    16th Va., 322
    16th Va. Cavalry, 293, 323
    17th Va. Cavalry, 323
    18th Va., 214, 319
    18th Va. Cavalry, 323
    19th Va., 214, 319
    21st Va., 320
    22nd Va. Battalion, 321, 356n90
    23rd Va., 154, 155, 320
    24th Va., 214, 225, 226, 319
    25th Va., 320
    27th Va., 320
    28th Va., 214, 319
    31st Va., 320
    33rd Va., 320
    34th Va. Cavalry Battalion, 290, 293, 323, 364nn12,13
    35th Va. Cavalry Battalion, 6, 254, 256, 271, 274, 323, 336nn30,31, 362n33
    36th Va. Cavalry Battalion, 323
    37th Va., 154, 320
    38th Va., 214, 319, 360n149
    39th Va. Cavalry Battalion, 318, 320
    40th Va., 321, 356n90
    41st Va., 322
    42nd Va., 320
    44th Va., 320
    47th Va., 321, 356n90
    48th Va., 320
    49th Va., 320
    50th Va., 320
    52nd Va., 320
    53rd Va., 214, 319
    55th Va., 321, 356n90
    56th Va., 214, 319
    57th Va., 214, 319
    61st Va., 322
    62nd Va. Mounted Infantry, 323
    Albermarle "Everett Artillery," 322
    Allegheny Battery, 320
    Amherst Battery, 321
    Ashby's Battery, 323
    Ashland Battery, 320
    Bath Battery, 320
    Bedford Battery, 320
    Charlottesville Battery, 320
    Danville Battery, 322
    Fauguier Battery, 319
    Fluvanna "Consolidated" Battery, 321
    Fredericksburg Battery, 322
    Johnson's Richmond Battery, 322
    King William Battery, 321
    Lynchburg Battery, 319
    Lynchburg Horse Artillery Battery, 323
    Lynchburg "Lee" Battery, 321
    Morris Battery, 321
    Norfolk "Huger's" Battery, 322
    Pittsylvania Battery, 322
    Powhatan Battery, 321
    Richmond Battery, 319
    Richmond "Courtney" Battery, 320
    Richmond "Crenshaw" Battery, 323
    Richmond "Letcher" Battery, 323
    Richmond "Orange" Battery, 321
    Richmond Parker Battery, 320
    Richmond "Purcell" Battery, 323
    Salem "Flying" Battery, 321
    Staunton Horse Artillery Battery, 320, 323
    Va. Partisan Rangers, 323
    Warrenton Battery, 322

ARMY OF THE POTOMAC (AP) (Meade)

1st Corps (Reynolds), 11, 30, 65–70, 71, 77, 261, 311
    1st Division (Wadsworth), 65, 68, 71, 72, 150, 151, 311
        1st Brigade (Iron Brigade), 43, 46, 50, 65, 68, 71, 72, 151, 311, 339n14, 342n58
        2nd Brigade, 46, 47, 48, 50, 71, 151, 173, 312
    2nd Division (Robinson), 71, 312
        1st Brigade, 50, 58, 69–70, 312
        2nd Brigade, 56, 68, 233, 312, 340n35
        3rd Brigade, 120, 312
    3rd Division (Rowley), 65, 68, 71, 215, 233, 312
        1st Brigade, 50, 65, 68, 215, 233, 312
        2nd Brigade, 50, 58, 65, 68, 233, 312
        3rd Brigade, 161, 238, 312
    Artillery Brigade, 157, 190, 205, 312, 342n64
2nd Corps (Hancock), 11, 72, 98, 206, 261, 312
    1st Division (Caldwell)
        1st Brigade, 133, 312
        2nd Brigade (Irish Brigade), 133, 135, 312
        3rd Brigade, 133, 312
        4th Brigade, 133, 312
    1st Division (Caldwell), 132, 133, 135
    2nd Division (Gibbon), 143, 147, 161, 206, 212, 215, 312
        1st Brigade, 147, 215, 312
        2nd Brigade, 147, 151, 161, 206, 207–208, 218, 313, 356n88
        3rd Brigade, 147, 161, 212, 215, 223, 313
    3rd Division (Hays), 144, 202, 212, 225, 229, 233, 313
        1st Brigade, 147, 161, 208, 313
        2nd Brigade, 202, 212, 229, 233, 313
        3rd Brigade, 144, 202, 212, 225, 229, 313
    Artillery Brigade, 190, 202, 205, 206, 208, 212, 218, 229, 238, 313
3rd Corps (Sickles), 11, 30, 79, 93–98, 129, 138, 261, 313
    1st Division (Birney), 93, 104, 128–129, 138, 233, 313
        1st Brigade, 95, 138, 139, 233, 313
        2nd Brigade, 93, 95, 104, 126, 138, 233, 313
        3rd Brigade, 95, 96, 104, 126, 132, 313, 348n93
    2nd Division (Humphreys), 96, 132, 138, 140–143, 145, 161, 313
        1st Brigade, 96, 138, 145, 161, 313
        2nd Brigade, 96, 138, 145, 161, 313
        3rd Brigade, 126, 132, 138, 145, 313
    Artillery Brigade (Randolph), 96, 104, 314
5th Corps (Sykes), 11, 24, 87, 90, 108–109, 133, 261, 314
    1st Division (Barnes), 109, 111, 132, 137, 281, 314
        1st Brigade, 132, 137, 238, 281, 314
        2nd Brigade, 132, 137, 138, 238, 281, 285, 314
        3rd Brigade, 109–112, 164, 281, 314
    2nd Division (Ayres), 137, 314
        1st Brigade, 137, 314
        2nd Brigade, 137, 314

INDEX OF MILITARY UNITS

3rd Brigade, 238, 314
3rd Division (Crawford), 164, 314
1st Brigade, 164, 238, 314
3rd Brigade, 164, 238, 314
Artillery Brigade (Martin), 122, 190, 205, 314
6th Corps (Sedgwick), 11, 90, 163, 164, 165, 261, 314, 337n51, 344n18
1st Division (Wright)
1st Brigade, 314
2nd Brigade, 314
3rd Brigade, 238, 258, 314
2nd Division (Howe)
2nd Brigade, 238, 315
3rd Brigade, 173, 315
3rd Division (Wheaton), 164, 315
1st Brigade, 173, 176, 315, 351n8, 359n140
2nd Brigade, 315
3rd Brigade, 164, 238, 315
Artillery Brigade, 206, 315
11th Corps (Howard), 11, 30, 50, 52, 53, 62, 70, 71, 77, 153, 261, 315, 340n30
1st Division (Barlow), 30, 52, 53, 61, 70, 71, 315
1st Brigade, 61, 157, 315
2nd Brigade, 61, 157, 315
2nd Division (von Steinwehr), 70, 71, 161, 315
1st Brigade, 52, 70, 161, 315, 341n57
2nd Brigade, 52, 161, 233, 315, 342n59
3rd Division (Schurz), 52, 53, 61, 71, 161, 315
1st Brigade, 61, 151, 315
2nd Brigade, 61, 161, 315
Artillery Brigade, 233, 315
12th Corps (Slocum), 11, 23, 75, 79, 87, 152, 261, 316, 343nn74,81, 349n115, 351n6
1st Division (Williams), 143, 144, 160, 173, 177, 316
1st Brigade, 150, 160, 173, 177, 233, 316
2nd Brigade, 144, 150, 160, 173, 177, 316
3rd Brigade, 150, 160, 173, 285, 316
2nd Division (Geary), 144, 150, 160, 173, 316
1st Brigade, 150, 160, 173, 316
2nd Brigade, 150, 160, 173, 316
3rd Brigade, 150, 151, 154, 173, 316
Artillery Reserve, 96, 190, 205, 316
1st Regular Brigade, 190, 233
1st Volunteer Brigade, 96, 141, 190
2nd Volunteer Brigade, 190
4th Volunteer Brigade, 96, 190
Cavalry Corps (Pleasonton), 40, 252, 261, 263, 299, 316
1st Division (Buford), 27, 28, 33, 40, 252, 263, 267, 271, 274, 299, 316
1st Brigade, 28, 33, 40, 48, 68, 252, 267, 271, 274, 280, 281, 316
2nd Brigade, 28, 33, 40, 48, 267, 271, 281, 316, 338n8
Reserve Brigade, 28, 252, 267, 271, 274, 299, 316

2nd Division (Gregg), 28, 258, 267, 285, 292, 294, 298, 316
1st Brigade, 258, 267, 275, 279, 285, 292, 294, 298, 316
2nd Brigade, 267, 275, 279, 280, 281, 316
3rd Brigade, 258, 279, 280, 281, 285, 292, 316
3rd Division (Kilpatrick), 27, 28, 252, 261, 263, 267, 274, 292, 299, 317, 338n53
1st Brigade, 28, 267, 274, 299, 317
2nd Brigade, 28, 263, 267, 274, 292, 293, 294, 296, 298, 317
Horse Artillery
1st Brigade, 190, 317, 364n11
1st Volunteer Brigade, 317
2nd Volunteer Brigade, 317
3rd Volunteer Brigade, 317
Connecticut
1st Conn. Heavy Artillery, 317
2nd Conn. Light Artillery, 317
5th Conn., 316
14th Conn., 229, 313
17th Conn., 156, 315
20th Conn., 173, 177, 316
27th Conn., 133, 312
Delaware
1st Del., 313
2nd Del., 133, 312
Illinois
8th Ill. Cavalry, 33, 40, 271, 274, 316
12th Ill. Cavalry, 33, 316
82nd Ill., 151, 315
Indiana
1st Ind. Cavalry, 315
3rd Ind. Cavalry, 33, 271
7th Ind., 71, 72, 312
14th Ind., 313
19th Ind., 46, 311
20th Ind., 104, 126, 313
27th Ind., 150, 173, 176, 177, 285, 316
Maine
1st Maine Cavalry, 274, 279, 316
2nd Maine Light
Battery B, 312
3rd Maine, 93, 138, 233, 313
4th Maine, 104, 105, 126, 130, 233, 313
5th Maine, 314
5th Maine Light, 157, 342n64
Battery E, 312
6th Maine, 267, 314
6th Maine Light Artillery, 317
7th Maine, 315
10th Maine, 316
15th Maine, 147
16th Maine, 58–59, 312
17th Maine, 104, 126, 132, 313, 348n93
19th Maine, 215, 313
20th Maine, 105, 111, 114, 115–124, 314, 346n63, 347nn66,68–70
Company B, 116, 120

Maryland
1st Md. Cavalry, 274, 316
1st Md. (Eastern Shore), 316
1st Md. (Potomoc), 173, 316
2nd Baltimore Light Artillery Battery, 323
3rd Md., 316
Md. Light Artillery, 317
Purnell Legion, 285, 316
Massachusetts
1st Mass., 145, 212, 313, 316, 357n98, 359n126
1st Mass. Cavalry, 275, 279
2nd Mass., 150, 173, 176, 177, 267, 271, 285, 316
3rd Mass. Light Artillery
Battery C, 314
5th Mass. Light Artillery, 96, 317
7th Mass., 315
9th Mass., 285, 314, 363n2
9th Mass. Light Artillery, 96, 141, 317, 345n31
10th Mass., 315
11th Mass., 138, 145, 313
12th Mass., 56, 233, 312, 340n35
13th Mass., 58, 312
15th Mass., 215, 313
16th Mass., 138, 145, 313
18th Mass., 132, 314
19th Mass., 223, 224, 226, 234, 313, 358n119
20th Mass., 147, 161, 215, 313
22nd Mass., 132, 314
28th Mass., 312
32nd Mass., 132, 314, 317
33rd Mass., 267, 271, 315
37th Mass., 315
42nd Mass., 223
Mass. Light Artillery, 315
Michigan
1st Mich., 132, 314
1st Mich. Cavalry, 296, 317
3rd Mich., 177, 313
4th Mich., 132, 314
5th Mich., 132, 313
5th Mich. Cavalry, 292, 293, 298, 317
6th Mich. Cavalry, 263, 317
7th Mich., 147, 161, 215, 313
7th Mich. Cavalry, 293–294, 298, 317
9th Mich. Light Artillery
Battery I, 190, 317
16th Mich, 111, 113, 115, 120, 314, 346n58
24th Mich., 45, 46, 65, 311, 339n20, 342n58
Minnesota
1st Minn., 143–145, 215, 312, 313, 349nn105–107, 361n3
New Hampshire
1st N.H. Light Artillery, 317
2nd N.H., 138, 313
5th N.H., 133, 267, 312, 313
12th N.H., 138, 145, 313
New Jersey
1st N.J., 314

398 THE STAND OF THE U.S. ARMY AT GETTYSBURG

1st N.J. Cavalry, 274, 285, 298, 316
1st N.J. Light Artillery, 317
2nd N.J., 314
2nd N.J. Light Battery, 96, 314
3rd N.J., 314
4th N.J., 314, 317
5th N.J., 132, 145
6th N.J., 126, 133, 314
7th N.J., 314
8th N.J., 132, 314
11th N.J., 145, 313
12th N.J., 229, 313
13th N.J., 150, 173, 177, 316
15th N.J., 314
New York
   1st N.Y. Cavalry, 314
   1st N.Y. Light Artillery, 96, 190, 202, 206, 312, 314, 315, 316, 317
   2nd N.Y. Cavalry, 274, 279, 316
   4th N.Y. Cavalry, 279, 316
   4th N.Y. Light Artillery, 96, 104
   4th N.Y. Light Battery, 130, 314
   5th N.Y. Cavalry, 299, 304, 317
   5th N.Y. Light Artillery, 317
   6th N.Y. Battery, 317
   6th N.Y. Cavalry, 271, 312, 316
   8th N.Y. Cavalry, 33, 271, 316
   9th N.Y., 312
   9th N.Y. Cavalry, 33, 271, 316
   10th N.Y. Battalion, 233
   10th N.Y. Cavalry, 274, 285, 316
   11th N.Y., 229
   11th N.Y. Battery, 317
   12th N.Y., 314
   13th N.Y. Light Artillery, 233
   15th N.Y. Engineers, 311
   15th N.Y. Light Artillery, 96, 317
   19th N.Y. Battery, 317
   33rd N.Y., 315
   39th N.Y., 144, 229, 313
   40th N.Y., 126, 132, 133, 313, 348n93
   41st N.Y., 315
   42nd N.Y., 215, 224, 226, 234, 313, 358n119
   43rd N.Y., 315
   44th N.Y., 105, 111, 113, 115, 314
   45th N.Y., 151, 315, 340n33, 341n50
   49th N.Y., 315
   50th N.Y. Engineers, 311
   52nd N.Y., 133, 312
   54th N.Y., 315
   57th N.Y., 133, 312
   58th N.Y., 161, 315
   59th N.Y., 147, 161, 215, 313
   60th N.Y., 156, 316
   61st N.Y., 133, 312
   62nd N.Y., 315
   63rd N.Y., 312
   64th N.Y., 133, 312
   65th N.Y., 315
   66th N.Y., 133, 312
   67th N.Y., 315
   68th N.Y., 315
   69th N.Y., 312
   70th N.Y., 145, 313
   71st N.Y., 138, 145, 313
   72nd N.Y., 138, 145, 313
   73rd N.Y., 138, 145, 313
   74th N.Y., 145, 313
   76th N.Y., 46, 312
   77th N.Y., 315
   78th N.Y., 151, 153, 316
   80th N.Y., 215, 312
   82nd N.Y., 147, 215, 313
   83rd N.Y., 56, 312
   84th N.Y. (14th Brooklyn), 47, 48, 50, 151, 173, 175, 312, 350n120
   86th N.Y., 104, 126, 267, 271, 313
   88th N.Y., 312
   93rd N.Y., 311
   94th N.Y., 58
   95th N.Y., 47, 48, 50, 311
   97th N.Y., 56, 312, 340n35
   102nd N.Y., 316
   104th N.Y., 58, 312
   107th N.Y., 150, 316
   108th N.Y., 202, 212, 213, 229, 313, 359n126
   111th N.Y., 313
   119th N.Y., 161, 315
   120th N.Y., 138, 313
   121st N.Y., 314
   122nd N.Y., 176, 315
   123rd N.Y., 233, 316
   124th N.Y., 104, 105, 126, 130, 267, 271, 313
   125th N.Y., 144, 212, 213, 229, 313, 357n98
   126th N.Y., 144, 202, 204, 212, 213, 229, 313, 349n104, 359n126
   134th N.Y., 70, 315
   136th N.Y., 161, 315
   137th N.Y., 151, 153, 154, 155, 173–174, 316
   140th N.Y., 120, 123, 133, 314
   141st N.Y., 138
   145th N.Y., 316
   146th N.Y., 120, 314
   147th N.Y., 46, 47, 151, 173, 175, 312
   149th N.Y., 154, 155, 176, 316
   150th N.Y., 173, 316
   154th N.Y., 70, 315
   157th N.Y., 151, 315, 341n48
   N.Y. Light Artillery, 315
   Oneida N.Y. Cavalry Company, 311
Ohio
   1st Ohio Cavalry, 316, 317
   1st Ohio Light Artillery
     Battery H, 317
     Battery I, 315
     Battery K, 315
     Battery L, 190, 205
   4th Ohio, 313
   5th Ohio, 173, 316
   6th Ohio Cavalry, 275, 279, 316
   7th Ohio, 316
   8th Ohio, 147, 161, 208, 211–213, 313, 359n126, 360n149
   25th Ohio, 315
   29th Ohio, 173, 174, 316
   55th Ohio, 315
   61st Ohio, 315
   66th Ohio, 173, 175, 316
   73rd Ohio, 233, 315, 342n59
   75th Ohio, 315
   81st Ohio, 151
   82nd Ohio, 315
   107th Ohio, 315
Pennsylvania
   1st Pa. Cavalry, 274, 314, 316
   1st Pa. Light Artillery
     Battery B, 312
     Battery F, 317
     Battery G, 317
   1st Pa. Reserves, 164, 314
   2nd Pa. Cavalry, 233, 311
   2nd Pa. Reserves, 164, 314
   3rd Pa. Cavalry, 275, 292, 294, 296, 298, 316
   3rd Pa. Heavy Artillery
     Battery H, 285, 316
   4th Pa. Cavalry, 275, 317
   5th Pa. Reserves, 314
   6th Pa. Cavalry, 271, 299, 311, 316
   6th Pa. Reserves, 164, 314
   7th Pa. Cavalry, 314
   8th Pa. Cavalry, 316
   9th Pa. Reserves, 314
   10th Pa. Reserves, 314
   11th Pa., 56, 163, 312, 314, 340n35
   11th Pa. Reserves, 164
   12th Pa. Reserves, 314
   13th Pa. Reserves, 164, 314
   16th Pa. Cavalry, 275, 317
   17th Pa. Cavalry, 33, 40, 271, 312, 315, 316, 338n8
   18th Pa. Cavalry, 299, 304, 317
   23rd Pa., 315
   26th Pa., 145, 313
   27th Pa., 161
   28th Pa., 316
   29th Pa., 316
   46th Pa., 316
   49th Pa., 314
   53rd Pa., 133, 312
   56th Pa., 46, 312
   57th Pa., 138, 313
   61st Pa., 315
   62nd Pa., 132, 164, 314
   63rd Pa., 313
   68th Pa., 138, 313
   69th Pa., 147, 161, 206, 218, 220–221, 233, 313, 359n129
   71st Pa., 147, 151, 155, 161, 206, 218, 220–221, 233–234, 313, 349n119, 357n110, 359n129

INDEX OF MILITARY UNITS   399

72nd Pa., 147, 161, 206, 218, 234
73rd Pa., 70, 161, 315
74th Pa., 315
75th Pa., 315
81st Pa., 133, 267, 312
82nd Pa., 315
83rd Pa., 111, 113, 115, 117, 314
84th Pa., 313
88th Pa., 56, 233, 312
90th Pa., 56, 233, 312
91st Pa., 120, 314
93rd Pa., 164, 315
95th Pa., 314
96th Pa., 314
98th Pa., 163, 164, 315, 350n128
99th Pa., 104, 105, 126, 130, 131–133, 233, 313
102nd Pa., 315
105th Pa., 313
106th Pa., 147, 161, 206, 218, 220, 313
107th Pa., 58, 312
109th Pa., 316
110th Pa., 132, 313
111th Pa., 316
114th Pa., 138, 233, 313
115th Pa., 132, 314
116th Pa., 312
118th Pa., 132, 314
119th Pa., 314
121st Pa., 233, 312
127th Pa., 70, 315
139th Pa., 164, 315
140th Pa., 312
141st Pa., 313
142nd Pa., 233, 312
143rd Pa., 58, 233, 312
145th Pa., 133, 312
147th Pa., 173, 316
148th Pa., 133, 312
149th Pa., 58, 233, 312
150th Pa., 65, 233, 312
151st Pa., 65, 215, 312
153rd Pa., 315
155th Pa., 120, 314

Pa. Light Artillery, 96
   Battery C, 317
   Battery E, 316
   Battery F, 317
Rhode Island
   1st R.I. Cavalry, 275, 280
   1st R.I. Light Artillery, 194
      Battery A, 190, 205, 313
      Battery B, 190, 205, 313
      Battery C, 315
      Battery E, 314
      Battery G, 315
   2nd R.I., 315
United States (Regular Army)
   1st U.S. Artillery
      Battery E, 317
      Battery G, 317
      Battery H, 317
      Battery I, 190, 208, 212, 313
      Battery K, 317
   1st U.S. Cavalry, 299, 311, 316
   1st U.S. Sharpshooters, 93, 313
   2nd U.S., 314
   2nd U.S. Artillery, 339n18
      Battery A, 317
      Battery B, 317
      Battery D, 315
      Battery G, 315
      Battery L, 317
      Battery M, 317, 364n11
   2nd U.S. Cavalry, 271, 274, 299, 311, 316
   2nd U.S. Sharpshooters, 105, 116, 313
   3rd U.S., 314
   3rd U.S. Artillery, 233
      Battery C, 317
      Battery F, 317
      Battery K, 317
   4th U.S., 314
   4th U.S. Artillery
      Battery A, 190, 202, 206, 218, 313
      Battery B, 312
      Battery C, 190, 317
      Battery E, 317
      Battery F, 316
      Battery K, 314

   5th U.S. Artillery, 233
      Battery C, 317
      Battery D, 122, 190, 205, 314
      Battery F, 315
      Battery I, 314
      Battery K, 316
   5th U.S. Cavalry, 271, 299, 311, 316
   6th U.S., 314
   6th U.S. Cavalry, 271, 311, 316, 365n4
   7th U.S., 314
   8th U.S. Cavalry, 311
   10th U.S., 314
   11th U.S., 314
   12th U.S., 314
   14th U.S., 314
   17th U.S., 314
   U.S. Engineer Battalion, 311
Vermont
   1st Vt. Cavalry, 299, 304, 306, 317
   2nd Vt., 315
   3rd Vt., 315
   4th Vt., 315
   5th Vt., 315
   6th Vt., 315, 316
   12th Vt., 312
   13th Vt., 161, 214, 217, 225, 226, 312, 357n106, 358nn119–122
   14th Vt., 217, 225, 226, 238, 242, 312, 357n106
   15th Vt., 225, 226, 312
   16th Vt., 226, 238, 241–242, 312, 358nn119–122
West Virginia
   1st W.V. Cavalry, 299, 303–304, 306, 317
   3rd W.V. Cavalry, 271, 316
   7th W.V., 313
   W.V. Light Artillery, 317
Wisconsin
   2nd Wis., 45, 46, 267, 311
   3rd Wis., 150, 173, 271, 316
   5th Wis., 314
   6th Wis., 47–49, 50, 151, 311, 339nn20,23,24, 341n59
   7th Wis., 45, 46, 267, 311
   26th Wis., 315

Subject Index

General subject entries are arranged alphabetically. Subentries under engagements and commanders are arranged in chronological order. ANV and AP, used in subentries, designate the respective armies. There is a separate index for military units.

Abbott, Capt. Henry L., 313
Abbott, Col. Ira C., 314
Adams, Capt. George W., 315
Adams, Capt. Julius W., Jr., 314
Adams, William O., 366n3
Addoms, Andrew H., III, 328, 367n15
"Address by D. H. Daggett" (Daggett), 385
Aiken, Col. D. Wyatt, 318
Aldie, Va., 20
Alexander, Bevin, 247, 361n18
Alexander, Col. E. Porter, 320; and Longstreet's alternative strategy, 88; southward deployment route, 92, 344n23; batteries assault Peach Orchard, 141, 348n99; and artillery placement July 3, 190–92, 353n50; determines Pickett's Charge timing, 194, 354n67; plans for additional guns to join assault, 197, 355n77; limited artillery support for Pickett's Charge, 226, 358n123; proposes July 3 attack plan in memoir, 352n24
Alger, Col. Russell A., 317
Allen, Col. Daniel B., 315
Allen, Lt. Col. David, Jr., 312
Allen, Col. Harrison, 312
Allen, Col. Robert C., 223, 319
Allen, Col. Thomas S., 314
"American Civil War Research and Genealogy" (Dobbins), 310, 388
Ames, Brig. Gen. Adelbert, 156, 267, 315, 341n57
Ames, Capt. Nelson, 317
ammunition issues, 58, 327, 366n10, 367n15
Amsberg, Col. George von, 315
Anderson, Brig. Gen. George T., 319; arrives on field at Devil's Den July 2, 133; Wheatfield attack, 134–38; repulsed, 163, 165; in South Cavalry Field July 3, 300–302
Anderson, Maj. J. Q., 40
Anderson, Maj. Gen. Richard H., 322; not sent onto Cemetery Hill July 1, 72, 342n68; moves into position July 2, 80–81; Union line not carefully scouted, 101; orders not issued to Mahone, 146–48; poor performance analyzed, 167; troops' condition July 3, 184; and Pickett's Charge, 234, 359n133
Andrews, Maj. Clinton M., 322
Andrews, Lt. Col. Hezekiah L., 321
Andrews, Lt. Col. R. Snowden, 320
Antietam, Battle of, 334n2, 343n80
Archer, Brig. Gen. James J., 321; on Cashtown Road, 39, 41, 339n21; captured, 45
Armistead, Brig. Gen. Lewis A., 319; deployment before Pickett's Charge, 187, 353n40; during Pickett's Charge, 199, 217, 355n80; leads attackers over low stone wall, 220–21, 357n114; mortally wounded, 221
Army Life: A Private's Reminiscences of the Civil War (Gerrish), 379
Army of Northern Virginia (ANV): attacking élan compromised by loss, 245, 361n4; casualties/captured in summer 1863, 245–46, 361n2; escapes across Potomac, 261–64; organization of, at Gettysburg, 309–10, 318–23; and outcome's significance to, 247–48, 249, 265–66, 361n18, 362n25; physically exhausted after loss, 252; position in late spring 1863, 3; position morning July 2, 79; retreat of, 255–56, 362n35; small arms distribution in, 366n5
Army of the Potomac (AP): command structure of, 75, 106, 109; confidence gained July 2, 165–66; demographics of, 2, 334n4; Gettysburg outcome's significance to, 247–48, 265, 266, 361n18; June marches, 20; Lee's assessment of quality of, 196, 355n75; Meade retains command of, 248–49, 362nn20–21; morale lift on "home" ground, 25, 337n51; organization of, at Gettysburg, 309–17; physically exhausted, 252; position in late spring 1863, 3; reenlistments, 249, 362n23; small arms distribution in, 326; strong

401

defensive position July 2, 86
Arnold, Capt. William A., 313
artillery batteries, ANV: Alexander's Artillery Battalion, 92, 189, 190–92; deployed to schoolhouse, 92, 343n23; placement and cannonade for Pickett's Charge, 189–94, 226, 353n50, 354nn54–60, 358n123; Washington Artillery Battalion, 92
artillery batteries, AP: Arnold's Battery, 229, 231; artillery parks in rear of line, 290, 363n6; on Cemetery Hill July 1, 339n28, 53, 342n64; on Cemetery Hill July 3, 210–11, 358n125; from Cemetery Hill to Little Round Top, 190, 191, 192; on Cemetery Ridge, 86, 202, 208–209; and Pickett's Charge, 205–206, 208–209, 238–39, 332, 356n89, 359nn125,139, 369n35; Horse Artillery in East Field Battle, 292, 364n11; Plum Run line, 141, 349n100; on Little Round Top, 123–24, 126, 205, 348n83, 356n83; Baltimore Pike artillery line, 172, 173, 351n7; Rogers Battery, 238; on Stevens Knoll July 1, 342n64; near Peach Orchard, 96, 137, 141, 345n40; Woodruff's Battery, 229, 359n125
Ashford, Col. John, 322
Atkinson, Col. Edmund D., 320
"The Attack and Defense of Culp's Hill: Greene's Brigade at the Battle of Gettysburg, July 1–3, 1863" (Fennel), 377
Atwell, Lt. Charles A., 316
Austin, Col. John S., 313
Avery, Col. Clarke M., 322
Avery, Maj. M. Henry, 316
Avery, Col. Isaac E., 320; in first wave of assaults July 1, 65, 341nn49,57; attacks Cemetery Hill July 2, 156–59
Aylett, Col. William R., 223, 319
Ayres, Brig. Gen. Romeyn B., 138, 314

Bachelder, John B., 353n45, 356n83
The Bachelder Papers (Ladd and Ladd, eds.), 374, 387
Bachman, Capt. William K., 319
Bailey, Col. Edward L., 313
Baily, Col. William P., 312
Baker, Lt. Joseph, 322
Baker, Col. Laurence S., 322
Baker, Col. Samuel E., 322
Baldwin, Lt. Col. Briscoe G., 318
Baldwin, Lt. Col. Clark B., 313
Ball, Col. Edward, 319
Ballantine, Col. William D., 322
Baltimore Pike, 90, 151, 159
Bancroft, Lt. Eugene A., 316
Bane, Maj. John P., 319
"Baptism of Fire: The Ninth Massachusetts Battery at Gettysburg, July 2, 1863" (Campbell), 380
Barbour, Col. William M., 322
Barclay, Lt. Col. Elihu S., 319

Barksdale, Brig. Gen. William, 319; and Longstreet's alternative strategy, 88; charges Peach Orchard and Emmitsburg Road, 139–43; mortally wounded, 141
Barlow, Brig. Gen. Francis, 315; decision making of, 53; poor positioning July 1, 62; retreats from Early's attack, 63–65, 341nn48,49
Barlow's Knoll, 63, 341n49
Barnes, Capt. Almont, 314
Barnes, Brig. Gen. James, 314; in Loudoun Valley, 280; reinforces left flank July 2, 109
Barney, Col. Elisha L., 315
Barnum, Col. Henry A., 316
Barry, Col. John D., 322
Bartlett, Brig. Gen. Joseph J., 314
Bass, Maj. Frederick S., 319
Bass, Col. Maston G., 319
Bassett, Col. Isaac C., 315
Batchelder, Lt. Col. N. Walter, 312
Bates, Col. James L., 312
Battle, Col. Cullen A., 321
Battles, Lt. Henry A., 320
Baxter, Col. DeWitt C., 313
Baxter, Brig. Gen. Henry, 312; meets O'Neal's attack from Oak Hill, 56–57, 58, 340nn35,36; ammunition problems, 329, 367n19
Baya, Lt. Col. William, 322
Beale, Col. Richard L. T., 322
Beardsley, Maj. William E., 316
Beaumont, Maj. M. H., 316
Beckham, Maj. Robert F., 322
Belmont Schoolhouse Ridge, 42
Belo, Maj. Alfred H., 321
Bender farm, 47
Benning, Brig. Gen. Henry L., 319; at Devil's Den, 131–33; in South Cavalry Field, 306
Bentley, Lt. Col. Richard C., 312
Bentley, Capt. William N., 319
Berdan, Col. Hiram, 313, 329–30, 344n26
Berdan's Sharpshooters, 330, 367nn21,24
Berkeley, Maj. Edmund, 319
Berkeley, Lt. Col. Norborne, 319
Betts, Capt. T. Edwin, 321
Beveridge, Maj. John L., 40, 316
Beverly's Ford, 268, 270
Bicknell, Lt. Emerson L., 313, 357n98
Biddle, Maj. Alexander, 312
Biddle, Col. Chapman, 312
Biddle, Col. George H., 312
Bidwell, Col. Daniel D., 315
Big Round Top (July 2), 105–107, 165
Bigelow, Capt. John, 141, 317
Bingham, Col. Daniel G., 312
Birney, Maj. Gen. David B., 313; troop deployments, 96, 344n26; counterattack of, 129
Black Horse Tavern, 92
Blacknall, Lt. Col. Charles C., 321
Blair, Maj. John A., 321
Blanc, Lt. Col. Alcibiades de, 320

Bland, Lt. Col. Elbert, 318
Bliss farm, 145–46, 210, 211, 213
Blount, Capt. Joseph G., 319
Bluny, Col. Asa P., 312
Bodine, Maj. Robert L., 313
Boebel, Lt. Col. Hans, 315
Bonaparte, Napoleon, 196
Bootes, Capt. Levi C., 314
Both, Lt. Ernst, 315
Bouldin, Capt. Edwin E., 322
Bourry, Col. Gotthilf, 315
Bowen, Capt. Edward R., 313
Bowie, Capt. Milledge L., 321
Bowles, Maj. John S., 321
Bowles, Col. Pinckney D., 319
Boynton, Maj. Joseph J., 312
Brable, Col. Edmund C., 321
Bradley, Maj. Leman W., 312
Brady, Maj. Allen G., 315
Brady, Maj. Andrew, 320
Brander, Capt. Thomas A., 322
Brandy Station, first Battle of (June 9): Duffié at, 268, 272, 274–75; Gregg at, 267, 268, 272–74; Pleasonton at, 267, 276; Buford at, 4, 267–68, 270–72, 275; casualties, 4, 334n8; description of, 4; McClellan at, 4, 109, 272–73, 334n9, 346n55; Stuart at, 4, 268–69, 270, 273, 335n12; criticism of Stuart at, 13, 335n22
Brandy Station, second Battle of, 334n10
Brandy Station, third Battle of, 334n10
"Brandy Station Seminar" (Wittenberg), 386
"A Brave and Resolute Force" (Motts), 382
breastworks, opposition to, 151, 349n113
Breathed, Capt. James, 322
Breck, Lt. George, 312
Breckinridge, Maj. Cary, 322
Brewster, Col. William R., 313
Briggs, Basil, 353n45
Brinkerhoff's Ridge (July 2), 150, 285–88, 349n111
Brinton, Lt. Col. William P., 317
Briscoe, Capt. Thomas H., 320
Broady, Lt. Col. K. Oscar, 312
Brockenbrough, Col. John M., 321; on Cashtown Road, 39, 41; in Pickett's Charge, 185, 202, 209–13, 356nn90,92; command skills of, 202
Brockman, Lt. Col. Benjamin T., 322
Brooke, Capt. J. V., 322
Brooke, Col. John R., 312
Brooker, Capt. Albert F., 317
Brooke-Rawle, Lt. William, 296
Broome, Lt. Col. James A., 322
Brown, Lt. C. H. C., 320
Brown, Lt. Col. Hamilton A., 320
Brown, Col. Hiram L., 312
Brown, Col. J. Thompson, 321
Brown, Lt. J. Thompson, 320
Brown, Lt. Col. Joseph N., 322
Brown, Col. Phillip P., Jr., 315
Brown, Maj. Ridgely, 322

Brown, Lt. T. Fred, 194, 203, 313
Brown, Capt. Van, 321
Brown, Col. William A. Jackson, 319
Brown, Capt. William D., 320
Brunson, Capt. Ervin B., 322
Bryan, Capt. Council A., 322
Bryan, Col. Goode, 318, 319
Bryan, Lt. Col. King, 319
Buchanan, Maj. Felix G., 321
Bucklyn, Lt. John K., 314
Buckner, Capt. Thomas R., 320
Buford, Brig. Gen. John, 316; at Brandy Station, 4, 267–68, 270–72, 275; in Loudoun Valley, 281; northward advance, 27–28; intelligence of ANV movements near Gettysburg, 32–33; picket vedettes posted, 39–40; and fighting withdrawal, 40–41, 42–43, 338nn9,10; casualties, 45, 339n18; pursues Imboden in retreat, 255, 362nn30,34
Bulger, Lt. Col. Michael J., 319
Bull, Lt. Col. James M., 313
Bull Run, Second Battle of, 334n2
Bull Run Mountains, 277
Burbank, Col. Sydney, 314
Burgwin, Col. Henry K., Jr., 321
Burham, Col. Hiram, 314
Burke, Capt. Denis F., 312
Burke, Maj. Ross E., 320
Burling, Col. George C., 313
Burns, Maj. Michael W., 313
Burnside, Maj. Gen. Ambrose E., 166, 350n132
Burton, James H., 366n2
Bushman farm, 299, 303
Butler, Lt. John H., 315
Butler, Col. M. Calbraith, 322
Butterfield, Maj. Gen. Daniel, 106, 108, 311, 334n6, 335n17
Byrnes, Col. R., 312

Cabell, Col. Henry G., 319
Cabell, Maj. Joseph R., 319
Cain, Lt. Col. John H., 314
Caldwell, Brig. Gen. John C., 312; ordered forward to support 5th Corps defenders, 135–36; falls back in some disorder, 138
Calef, Lt. John H., 317
Callcote, Lt. Col. Alexander D., 319
Campbell, Lt. Col. Edward L., 314
Campbell, Maj. James M., 319
Candy, Col. Charles, 175, 316
Cannae, Battle of: as single decisive stroke, 181, 195–96, 351n22; and double envelopment of attackers, 228; casualties, 360n154
Cantador, Lt. Col. Lorenz, 315
capital cities, capture of, 20, 336n41
Carlton, Capt. Henry H., 319
Carman, Col. Ezra A., 316
Carpenter, Capt. John C., 321
Carpenter, Lt. Col. Leonard W., 313
Carpenter, Lt. Louis Henry, 316

Carr, Brig. Gen. Joseph B., 313
Carrington, Capt. James McD., 223, 320
Carrington, Lt. Col. Henry A., 319
Carroll, Lt. Col. Edward, 314
Carroll, Col. Samuel S., 313; defends Cemetery Hill July 2, 159–61, 356n91, 359n140; and 8th Ohio, 211
Carter, Lt. Col. Benjamin F., 319
Carter, Col. James W., 319
Carter, Lt. Col. Thomas A., 321
Carter, Capt. William P., 321
Cary, Maj. George W., 319
Cashtown Road: Heth advances along, 37–40; engagements south of, 42–45; engagements north of, 47–49, 57–58
Caskie, Maj. Robert A., 322
Caskie, Capt. William H., 319
A Caspian Sea of Ink: The Meade-Sickles Controversy (Sauers), 380
Cassin, Maj. Walter L., 311
casualties, ANV: near Oak Hill (July 1), 56–57; July 1 total estimates, 70, 76; Culp's Hill (July 3), 177, 351n11; in Pickett's Charge, 223–24, 242–43, 244, 331, 360nn150–53, 368n27; in Pickett's Charge (officers), 223–24; in East Field Battle, 298; in Battle of Gettysburg, 245, 246, 360n1, 361nn2–3; in retreat and escape, 263, 363n47. *See also individual commanders in Appendix F*
casualties, AP: Buford (July 1), 45, 339n18; Iron Brigade near Cashtown Rd., 342n58; near railroad cut (July 1), 47, 339n24; north of town (July 1), 58–59, 69–70, 341nn48,57; July 1 estimates, 70, 76, 77; 20th Maine on Little Round Top (July 2), 118, 347n68; on Union right (July 2), 138; 1st Minnesota (July 2), 145, 349n107, 361n3; Culp's Hill (July 3), 177, 351nn11–12; Pickett's Charge, 213, 242–43, 244, 357n99, 360nn150–53; 8th Ohio in Pickett's Charge, 213, 357n99; in Battle of Gettysburg, 245, 246, 360n1, 361nn2–3; in East Field Battle, 298; in Farnsworth's charge, 306–307; in pursuit July 4–14, 263, 363n47. *See also individual commanders in Appendix F*
casualties, Civil War, generally, 332, 361n3, 369n33
Cavada, Lt. Col. Frederick F., 313
cavalry: at Brandy Station, 4, 267–76; and Confederate retreat, 252–53; in disarray before Gettysburg, 335n19; dismounted cavalry, 39–40, 42, 338n6; at Hanover, 15–16, 28–31, 335n29; in Loudoun Valley, 8, 11–13, 277–84; Union, reorganized, 4, 335n11. *See also* Stuart, Maj. Gen. J. E. B.
The Cavalry at Gettysburg: A Tactical Study of Mounted Operations during the Civil War's Pivotal Campaign 9 June–14 July 1863 (Longacre), 386
"A Cavalry Regiment's First Campaign: The 18th Pennsylvania at Gettysburg" (Klingensmith),

388
Cemetery Hill (July 1): artillery batteries on, 339nn28,53, 342n64; Buford's awareness of, 40–41; Howard fortifies, 53, 339n26; Union rallies at, 70, 74, 342n59; defensive positions of Union troops, 71; Confederates' decision not to attack, 72–74, 342nn66–71, 343nn75–76; hypothetical attack of, 74
Cemetery Hill (July 2): Ewell's assault on, 156–59; Union reinforcements, 159–61
Cemetery Hill (July 3): artillery batteries on, 210–11, 358n125
Cemetery Ridge, general: copse of trees described, 189, 353n45; descriptions of, by Confederate soldiers, 214, 357n105. *See also* Cemetery Ridge (July 2); Pickett's Charge (July 3)
Cemetery Ridge (July 2): Sickles occupies, 80, 93; Sickles moves out front of, 93–98; Confederate assault, 143–48; attack repulsed, 161–65
Cemetery Ridge (July 3). *See* Pickett's Charge (July 3)
Chamberlain, Col. Joshua L., 314; experience of, 118, 346n63; scouts atop Little Round Top, 105, 345n44; at battle for Little Round Top, 115–23, 346n65; wounded, 346n64; "right wheel forward" and charge order of, 119–20, 347nn72–74; ammunition problems discussed, 329; revisionism in battle accounts, 347n66; evaluation of, by Oates, 348n88
Chambliss, Col. John R., Jr., 322; in Loudoun Valley, 28, 280, 335n15; in East Field Battle, 290, 292, 294
Chancellorsville, Battle of: ANV's position at Gettysburg compared to, 87; AP's right flank at, 62; AP's left flank at, 341n46; Greene's brigade and fortifications at, 349n112; Lee's assessment of AP at, 61, 77; Lee's weakened center as decoy at, 229; and Lee's triumphant moment, 343n82; Hazel Grove, 93, 94, 141, 344nn27–28, 348nn81,99, 349n112; Hooker's mismanagement at, 335n18, 75; Sickles at Hazel Grove, 93, 94, 344nn27–28
Chapman, Col. George H., 312, 316
Chester, Lt. James, 364n11
Chestnut, Mary, 355n72
Chew, Capt. Robert Preston, 322
Chilton, Col. R. H., 318
Christie, Col. Daniel H., 321
Christman, Capt. Charles H., 312
Citizen Soldiers: The U.S. Army from the Normandy Beaches to the Bulge to the Surrender of Germany, June 7, 1944–May 7, 1945 (Ambrose), 380
Civil War: casualties, 332, 361n3, 369n33; Gettysburg changes character of Eastern theater, 249–50; medical treatment, and wounds, 361n3

SUBJECT INDEX   403

Civil War Firearms: Their Historical Background, Tactical Use and Modern Collecting and Shooting (Bilby), 384, 389
The Civil War Recollections of General Ellis Spear (Spears), 379
Claflin, Capt. Ira W., 316
Clark, Capt. A. Judson, 314
Clarke, Maj. John J., 80
Clinton, Capt. William, 314
Coates, Capt. Henry C., 313
Cobb, Maj. Norvell, 320
Cobham, Col. George A., Jr., 316
Coburn, Maj. James H., 312
Cochran, Col. James, 322
Codori buildings, 145, 161, 226
Cole, Lt. Col. Robert G., 318
Colgrove, Col. Silas, 316
Collier, Col. Frederick H., 315
Collins, Maj. Charles R., 322
Colvill, Col. William, Jr., 143–45, 313, 349nn105–106
"'A Combined and Concentrated Fire': The Federal Artillery at Gettysburg, July 3, 1863" (Rollins and Schultz), 377, 384
"The Common Soldier's Gettysburg Campaign" (Glatthaar), 375
Comparative Value of Rifled and Smooth-Bored Arms (Willard), 331
A Concise Guide to the Artillery at Gettysburg (Coco), 384
"Confederate Corps Leadership on the First Day at Gettysburg: A. P. Hill and Richard S. Ewell in a Difficult Debut" (Gallagher), 376
The Confederate Order of Battle (Sibley), 310, 388
Conger, Capt. Seymour R., 316
Connally, Col. John K., 321
Conner, Lt. Col. Freeman, 314
Conner, Col. James, 322
Conner, Maj. William G., 322
Connor, Lt. Col. Seldon, 315
Contee, Lt. Charles S., 320
Cook, Capt. John E., 312
Cooke, Capt. Oliver H., 322
Coons, Col. John, 313
Cooper, Maj. Frederick, 314
Cooper, Capt. James H., 312
copse of trees, described, 189, 353n45
Corby, Fr. William "Fair-Catch," 135, 438n94
Corley, Lt. Col. James L., 318
Corrie, Capt. William A., 316
Coster, Col. Charles R., 315; positioned on Cemetery Hill, 53; counterattacks Early July 1, 341n57
Coulter, Col. Richard, 312
"Courage Against the Trenches: The Attack and Repulse of Steuart's Brigade on Culp's Hill" (Elmore), 377
Cowan, Capt. Andrew, 208–209, 221, 233, 315
Craft, Capt. William S., 314
Craig, Col. Calvin A., 313

Crandell, Lt. Col. Levin, 313
Crane, Capt. James P., 320
Crane, Col. Nirom M., 316
Crawford, Brig. Gen. Samuel W., 163, 314, 350n128
Creighton, Col. William R., 316
Crete, Battle of (WW II), 126–27
Crete: The Battle and the Resistance (Beevor), 380
Crisis at the Crossroads (Hassler), 375
Crocker, Col. John S., 311
Croft, Maj. Edward, 322
Cross, Col. Edward E., 136, 312, 438n96
Cross, Col. Nelson, 315
"Cross Purposes: Longstreet, Lee, and Confederate Attack Plans for July 3 at Gettysburg" (Piston), 378
Crowell, Lt. James M., 264, 322
Culpeper, Va., 267, 269
Culp's Hill (July 1): troops defending, 72, 342n64; Trimble wants to attack, 72–73, 342n70, 352n33; Confederates fail to attack, 342n70
Culp's Hill (July 2): Union offensive actions deemed impossible near, 148; defensive positions fortified, 149, 151–52; Ewell's attack on, 150–56; Greene's defense of, 151, 153, 350n133; removal of most of 12th Corps from, 152, 166, 349n115; analysis of battle, 166, 350n133
Culp's Hill (July 3): setting in early morning, 171; Union artillery support, 172, 173, 351n7; Johnson's attack, 172–73, 175–77; Union defense of, 174–77; casualties, 177; Confederate casualties, 177, 351n11; Union casualties, 177, 351nn11–12
Cummins, Lt. Col. Francis M., 313
Cummins, Col. Robert P., 312
Cunningham, Lt. Col. Henry W., 313
Cunningham, Lt. John M., 321
Curry, Lt. Col. William L., 313
Curtis, Lt. Col. Greely S., 316
Curtis, Maj. Sylvanus W., 313
Cushing, Lt. Alonzo H., 203, 209, 221, 313
Custer, Brig. Gen. George A., 317; in Battle of Hanover, 28; in East Field Battle, 291–94, 296, 300
"Cut to Pieces: The Cavalry Fight at Fairfield, Pennsylvania, July 3, 1863," 388
Cutler, Brig. Gen. Lysander, 312; first Union infantry unit to arrive, 339n15; defeats Davis north of Cashtown Road, 47–49; pushed back by Early, 341n56

Dana, Col. Edmund L., 312
Dance, Capt. Willis J., 321
Daniel, Brig. Gen. Junius, 321; attack along railroad cut, 57–58; supports attack on Seminary Ridge July 1, 68, 341n54; attacks Culp's Hill July 3, 176
Daniels, Capt. Jabez J., 317

Danks, Maj. John A., 313
Dare, Lt. Col. George, 314
Darrow, Capt. John, 313
Davis, Col. J. Lucius, 322
Davis, Jefferson, 362n35
Davis, Brig. Gen. Joseph R., 321; along Cashtown Road, 39, 41, 47–49; generalship of, 339n22; commences attack July 3, 201–202; flanked by 8th Ohio, 211, 231
Davis, Capt. Milton S., 313
Davis, Capt. Robert Beale, 321
Davis, Capt. Thomas, 319
Davis, Capt. William, 313
Davis, Lt. Col. William S., 321
Dawes, Lt. Col. Rufus R., 311, 339n24
Day, Col. Hannibal, 314
de Trobriand, Col. P. Regis, 313; placement on the Stony Hill, 96; supports Ward, 104, 133, 348n93; attacked near Wheatfield, 133–35; on Meade's hesitation to pursue Lee, 362n26
Dearing, Maj. James, 319
Death of a Nation: The Story of Lee and His Men at Gettysburg (Dowdey), 372
Debris of Battle: The Wounded of Gettysburg (Patterson), 385
Deems, Lt. Col. James M., 316
Delony, Lt. Col. William B., 322
Dement, Capt. William F., 320
Dent, Lt. John T., 313
Devereux, Col. Arthur F., 224, 313, 358nn119,121
Devil's Den, 102–105, 130–33, 345n42
Devil's Den: A History and Guide (Adelman and Smith), 380
"The Devil's to Pay": Gen. John Buford, USA (Phipps and Peterson), 376, 386
Devin, Col. Thomas C., 316; arrives with Buford, 28, 40, 340n32; withdraws July 1, 341n49
died-of-wounds rates, 361n3
Dilger, Capt. Hubert, 315
Dimond, Pvt. James, 143
Dobke, Lt. Col. Adolphus, 315
Doles, Brig. Gen. George, 62, 68, 159, 321, 341n49
Donovan, Capt. Mathew, 313
Doster, Lt. Col. William E., 317
"Double Canister at Ten Yards": The Federal Artillery and the Repulse of Pickett's Charge (Shultz), 384
Doubleday, Maj. Gen. Abner, 311, 312; assumes command of 1st Corps, 45, 50; uses 6th Wisconsin to support north of Cashtown Road, 339nn20,23; falls back to Seminary Ridge, 65–68; withdraws through town, 68–70; performance July 1, 341n53; relieved of command of 1st Corps, 339n25
Dow, Lt. Edwin B., 317
"Dragoon or Cavalryman? Major General John Buford in the American Civil War" (Stricker), 376
Drake, Col. James H., 322

DuBose, Col. Dudley Mc., 319
Duffié, Col. Alfred N.: at Brandy Station, 268, 272, 274–75; at Middleburg, 277, 363n2
Dungan, Lt. Col. Robert H., 155–56, 175, 320
Dunn, Capt. Thomas S., 314
Dunne, Maj. John P., 314
Duvall, Capt. Robert E., 316
Dwight, Lt. Col. Walton, 312

Eakin, Lt. Chandler P., 317
Eakle, Maj. Benjamin F., 322
Early, Maj. Gen. Jubal A., 320; moves north with Ewell, 335n14; passes through Gettysburg in June, 21, 38, 336n43; and Wrightsville bridge, 336n42; arrives, attacks July 1, 62–65; reinforces Smith's brigade, 343n75; attacks Cemetery Hill July 2, 156–59
East Cavalry Field, Battle for (July 3), 251, 289–98
Edgell, Capt. Frederick M., 317
Edie, Lt. John R., 311
Edmonds, Col. Edward C., 223, 319
"Edward Porter Alexander, Confederate Cannoneer at Gettysburg" (Jorgensen), 383
Edwards, Capt. Albert M., 311
Edwards, Col. Clark S., 314
Edwards, Col. Oliver, 315
Egan, Col. Thomas W., 313
Einsiedel, Lt. Col. Detleo von, 315
Elder, Lt. Samuel S., 317
Ellis, Col. A. Van Horne, 313
Ellis, Lt. Col. John T., 319
Ellis, Maj. Theodore G., 313
Ellmaker, Col. Peter C., 314
Elsenborn Ridge, battle for (WW II), 126, 250, 348n85
Emmitsburg Road, 87, 96, 139, 187, 345n31
Enfield rifled muskets, 367n19, 368n25
Ent, Lt. Col. Wellington H., 314
Ernst, Lt. Col. Louis, 314
Eshelman, Maj. Benjamin F., 92, 320
Eubanks, Capt. T. J., 319
Eustis, Col. Henry L., 315
Evans, Col. Clement A., 320
Evans, Col. Peter G., 322
Evans, Lt. Col. Stephen B., 322
Ewell, Lt. Gen. Richard S., 320; at second Battle of Winchester, 335n13; moves north as van of ANV, 6–11, 20–22; engagement orders from Lee, 338n2, 339n11, 340n31; orders divisions to Gettysburg, 61, 340n31; arrives, attacks July 1, 62–65; decision not to attack southern hills July 1, 72–74, 342n70, 343nn75–76; hypothetical attack of Cemetery Hill, 74; Lee's plan for, July 2, 83–84, 150, 343n3; preparations and attack on Culp's Hill, 149–56; attacks Cemetery Hill, 156–59; analysis of attacks on July 2, 166, 350n133; renews attack on Culp's Hill July 3, 171, 351n5; in retreat, 256; crosses Potomac, 262, 363n45

Ewing, Maj. Charles, 317

"The Failure of Confederate Artillery at Gettysburg: Ordnances and Logistics" (Rollins), 384
"The Failure of Confederate Artillery in Pickett's Charge" (Rollins), 384
Fairchild, Col. Lucius, 311
Fairfield, Battle of, 365n4
Falling Waters, W.V., 253
Farnsworth, Brig. Gen. Elon, 28, 303–307, 317, 365nn6–7
Farnum, Col. J. Egbert, 313
"'The Fate of a Country': The Repulse of Longstreet's Assault by the Army of the Potomac" (Hartwig), 383
Feild, Lt. Col. Everard M., 322
Ferebee, Col. Dennis D., 322
Ferguson, Col. Milton J., 290, 292, 293, 322, 364n12
Ferry, Maj. Noah H., 293
Fesler, Lt. Col. John R., 316
Fickling, Capt. William W., 320
field-grade officers, 347n70
"The Fight for Brinkerhoff's Ridge" (Shevchuk), 387
Fighting for the Confederacy: The Personal Recollections of General Edward Porter Alexander (Gallagher, ed.), 383
Finnicum, Maj. Mark, 311
The First Day at Gettysburg (Gallagher, ed.), 372, 376
First Manassas, Battle of, 334n2
"The First Minnesota at Gettysburg" (Meinhard), 380
The First Minnesota Regiment at Gettysburg (Haiber and Haiber), 380
"The 1st Texas Infantry and the Repulse of Farnsworth's Charge" (Shevchuk), 387
Fiser, Lt. Col. John C., 319
Fisher, Col. Joseph W., 314
Fite, Col. John A., 321
Fitzhugh, Capt. Robert H., 317
Fleetwood Hill, 269, 272–74
Fleming, Capt. C. Seton, 322
Fleming, Maj. William O., 318
Flournoy, Maj. Cabell E., 322
Flowerree, Lt. Col. C. C., 319
Flowers, Capt. George W., 322
Floyd-Jones, Maj. De Lancey, 314
Flynn, Capt. John, 316
Foerster, Lt. Hermann, 315
Folsom, Col. Robert W., 322
Fontaine, Maj. Clement R., 319
"Forgotten Field: The Cavalry Battle East of Gettysburg on July 3, 1863" (Krolick), 387
Forney, Col. William H., 322
Forno, Col. Henry, 320
Forsyth, Lt. Col. Charles, 321
Foster, Capt. Nathaniel A., 321

Foust, Maj. Benezet F., 312
Fowler, Lt. Col. Douglas, 315
Fowler, Col. Edward B., 312
Francine, Col. Louis R., 314
Fraser, Capt. John C., 312, 319
Fredericksburg, Battle of, 334n2
Freeborn, Lt. Benjamin, 314
Freedley, Capt. Henry W., 314
French, Col. William H., 322
French, Col. Winsor B., 315
French, Maj. Gen. William H.: Hooker's plans for, 23; destroys pontoon bridge at Falling Waters, 253
"From Chancellorsville to Cemetery Hill: O. O. Howard and Eleventh Corps Leadership" (Greene), 376
"From Gettysburg to Falling Waters" (Greene), 386
From These Honored Dead: Gettysburg in American Memory (Desjardin), 379
Frueauff, Maj. John F., 315
Fry, Col. Birkett D., 321; commands Archer's Brigade, 65; placement before Pickett's Charge, 187; as center of Pickett's Charge, 189, 353n47; troops mingled with Armistead's and Kemper's, 217; wounded, captured in Pickett's Charge, 341n52
Fry, Capt. Charles W., 321
Fuchs, Capt. John W., 315
Fuger, Sgt. Frederick, 313
Fuller, Capt. Josiah C., 317
Fuller, Lt. William D., 317
Funk, Col. John H. S., 320
Funston, Lt. Col. Oliver R., Sr., 322
Furlong, Lt. William J., 319

Gaillard, Lt. Col. F., 318
Galloway, Capt. Alexander H., 321
Gambee, Col. Charles B., 315
Gamble, Col. William, 316; deployed northward, 28; fighting withdrawal along Cashtown Road July 1, 40, 41, 42; skirmish with Lane at Seminary Ridge, 341n55; attacks Imboden in retreat, 255
Gantt, Col. Henry, 223, 319
Garden, Capt. Hugh H., 320
Gardner, Capt. Asher W., 320
Gardner, Col. Richard N., 322
Garnett, Lt. Col. John J., 322
Garnett, Brig. Gen. Richard B., 223, 319
Garrard, Col. Kenner, 314
Gates, Col. Theodore B., 312
Geary, Brig. Gen. John W., 316; wrong turn off field of battle July 2, 150; reinforces Culp's Hill, 159; opposed to breastworks, 349n113; in defense of Culp's Hill July 3, 177, 351n12; ammunition expended, 330
Gee, Maj. Bolivar H., 319
General James Longstreet: The Confederacy's Most Controversial Soldier—A Biography (Wert),

Generals in Blue: Lives of the Union Commanders (Warner), 388
Generals in Gray: Lives of the Confederate Commanders (Warner), 388
George, Lt. Col. Newton L., 321
Gerald, Maj. George B., 319
Gerrish, Pvt. Theodore, 346n65
"Getting Beyond All That: The Past and Future of Pickett's Charge" (Rollins), 382
Gettysburg: A Meditation on War and Values (Gramm), 372
Gettysburg: A Testing of Courage (Trudeau), 371
Gettysburg, Battle of, general: basic nature of battlefield, 35; casualties, 245, 246, 360n1, 361nn2–3; as changing character of Civil War in East, 249–50; defensive fortifications used, 149, 349n110; first shots, 40, 338n8; as "last battle" in East, 2, 249; organization of ANV at, 309–10, 318–23; organization of AP at, 309–17; outcome perceived by Southerners, 246; remoteness of parts of battlefield, 102, 345n41; significance of, 247–50, 265–66, 361nn13,18; small arms problems during, 327–31, 367nn19,21,24, 368n26; terrain knowledge of Early and Gordon, 21, 336n43; tactics (*see* tactics, at Gettysburg)
Gettysburg, Battle of, chronology: **July 1**—early morning, 35–43; infantry clashes mid-morning, 43–49; late morning lull, 49–53; fighting resumes in center, 54–59; infantry action all along lines, 60–62; Union lines pushed back below town, 62–70; Union defense centers on Cemetery Hill, 70–77; **July 2**—armies move into position, 80–92; Union 3rd Corps moves out from line, 92–98; Confederates open attack, 98–112; battle for Little Round Top, 112–27; Confederate attack continues, with Union counter, 127–38; Confederate attack continues, and Peach Orchard salient, 138–43; Confederate attack reaches high-water mark, 143–48; Confederate attacks on Culp's and Cemetery Hills, 148–59; Union stands and repulses all along line, 159–65; climax of day's action and turning point of battle, 165–67; **July 3**—Culp's Hill fighting in early morning, 171–77; Lee changes plan of attack, 177–89; great artillery bombardment of Civil War, 189–95; Pickett's Charge commences, 195–204; Confederate left counterattacked, a brigade breaks, 205–13; Confederate center pierces Union line, 214–24; stand of the twenty-six regiments, 224–40; destruction of Pickett's Charge and Union victory, 240–66; late cavalry actions, 251; **July 4–14**—Union pursuit of retreating Confederates, 252–61; Lee's escape across Potomac, 261–64
Gettysburg: Culp's Hill and Cemetery Hill (Pfanz), 377, 381, 387

Gettysburg Day Three (Wert), 381
Gettysburg: Lt. Frank Haskell, U.S.A., and Col. William C. Oates, C.S.A. (LaFantasie, ed.), 380
Gettysburg: The First Day (Pfanz), 375–76
Gettysburg: The Second Day (Pfanz), 377
Gettysburg, Then and Now (Vanderslice), 385
The Gettysburg Campaign: A Study in Command (Coddington), 371, 375
The Gettysburg Campaign, June 3–August 1, 1863: A Comprehensive, Selectively Annotated Bibliography (Sauers), 371
The Gettysburg Campaign: June–July 1863 (Nofi), 309, 388
"The Gettysburg Campaign after Pickett's Charge" (Pfanz), 386
Gettysburg Day Two: A Study in Maps (Imhof), 374
The Gettysburg Death Roster: The Confederate Dead at Gettysburg (Krick), 385
Gettysburg July 1 (Martin), 375
Gettysburg Magazine, 372
The Gettysburg Nobody Knows (Borritt, ed.), 373, 379, 383, 386
Gettysburg's Forgotten Cavalry Actions (Wittenberg), 388
Gibbon, Brig. Gen. John, 312; reinforces Culp's Hill, 155; reinforces Cemetery Ridge, 191
Gibbs, Capt. Frank C., 314, 356n83
Gibson, Lt. Col. Jonathan Catlett, 320
Gibson, Col. William, 322
Giddings, Maj. Grotius R., 314
Gifford, Capt. Henry J., 315
Gilbert, Lt. S. Capers, 320
Gilkyson, Col. Stephen R., 314
Gillette, Maj. Joseph E., 322
Gilmour, Maj. Harry W., 322
Gilreath, Lt. George A., 321
Gilsa, Col. Leopold von, 156, 315
Gimber, Capt. F. L., 316
Gist, Maj. William M., 318
Glenn, Capt. James, 312
Glenn, Lt. Col. John F., 315
Glenn, Lt. Col. Luther J., 319
Godard, Col. Abel, 316
Godfrey, Capt. Thomas C., 313
Godwin, Col. Archibald C., 320
Goldsborough, Maj. William C., 320
Golladay, Capt. Jacob B., 320
gonorrhea, 340n42
Goodgame, Lt. Col. John C., 321
Gordon, Brig. Gen. John B., 320; aware of Gettysburg terrain features, 21, 336n43; arrives from northeast, attacks, 62–65
Gordon, Lt. Col. George T., 322
Gordon, Lt. Col. James B., 322
Graaff, Maj. A. S. Van De, 321
Graham, Capt. Archibald, 321
Graham, Brig. Gen. Charles K., 94, 96, 139–41, 313

Graham, Capt. Joseph, 322
Graham, Capt. William A., 317, 322
Grandy, Capt. Charles R., 322
Grant, Col. Lewis A., 315
Grant, Lt. Gen. Ulysses S., 248
Gray, Col. George, 317
Gray, Lt. John, 319
Green, Capt. Charles A., 320
Green, Col. Francis M., 321
Greene, Lt. Col. J. Durell, 314
Greene, Brig. Gen. George S., 316; defends Culp's Hill July 2, 151, 153, 350n133; defends Culp's Hill July 3, 173–74, 176
Gregg, Brig. Gen. David McM., 316; at Battle of Brandy Station, 267, 268, 272–74; in Loudoun Valley, 277, 278, 280; northward advance, 27–28; fighting near Brinkerhoff's Ridge, 150, 285–88; in East Field Battle, 291, 292–93, 296
Gregg, Col. J. Irvin, 316; in Loudoun Valley, 278–80, 285; in East Field Battle, 292–93
Griffin, Lt. Charles B., 321
Griffin, Col. Thomas M., 319
Griffin, Capt. William H., 322
Griffith, Paddy, 326
Grimes, Col. Bryan, 321
Groner, Col. Virginius D., 322
Grover, Maj. Andrew J., 312
Grover, Col. Ira G., 312
Guild, Dr. Lafayette, 318
Guiney, Col. Patrick R., 314
The Guns of Gettysburg (Downey), 384
Gwyn, Lt. Col. James, 314

Hadden, Capt. William M., 322
Hall, Capt. James A., 312
Hall, Capt. James S., 345n50, 346n54
Hall, Col. Josephus M., 321
Hall, Capt. Matthew R., 322
Hall, Col. Norman J., 313; defends Cemetery Ridge July 2, 161; in defense of Pickett's Charge, 217–20, 226
Halleck, Henry W., 22, 260
Halsey, Capt. Donal P., 321
Ham, Col. Joseph H., 322
Hamblin, Col. Joseph E., 315
Hamilton, Lt. Frank B., 364n11
Hamilton, Lt. Col. Theodore B., 315
Hammell, Lt. Col. John S., 312
Hammerstein, Lt. Col. Herbert von, 316
Hammond, Maj. John, 317
Hampton, Brig. Gen. Wade, 322; at Battle of Hanover, 28; at Brandy Station, 273; in Loudoun Valley, 280; at East Cavalry Field, 290–91; at South Cavalry Field, 299
Hancock, Capt. David P., 314
Hancock, Maj. John M., 321
Hancock, Maj. Gen. Winfield Scott, 312; military bearing of, 342n60; arrives on field July 1, 72; dispute with Howard, 342nn62,63; urges

Meade to stand at Gettysburg, 74; defends Cemetery Ridge July 2, 143–45; artillery positions prior to Pickett's Charge, 190, 191, 192; line numbers at assault point of Pickett's Charge, 197, 355n76; further defensive preparations as Pickett's Charge commences, 207–11, 356n89; bravery during assault, 193, 353n62; orders Devereaux's counter in center, 224, 358nn119,121; orders Stannard's counter on right flank, 224–26, 358nn119,121; wounded and leaves field, 226; and counterattack, 242
Hanlon, Lt. Col. Joseph, 320
Hanover, Battle of (June 30), 15–16, 28–31, 335n29
Hanover Road, 285–88
Hapgood, Lt. Col. Charles E., 312
Hardin, Col. Martin D., 314
Hardwicke, Lt. William W., 321
Harkhaus, Col. Otto, 316
Harlow, Lt. Col. Franklin P., 315
Harman, Col. Asher W., 322
Harn, Capt. William A., 315
Harney, Maj. George, 312
Harper's Ferry, 22–23, 336n44
Harris, Col. Andrew L., 156, 315
Harris, Lt. Col. Edward P., 313
Harris, Capt. James G., 322
Harris, Col. Nathaniel H., 322
Harris, Lt. Col. William T., 319
Harrisburg, Pa., 20, 336nn41,42
Harrison, James, 337n48
Harrison, Henry Thomas (the spy), 25, 337n48
Harrow, Brig. Gen. William, 217–20, 226, 312
Hart, Maj. Alexander, 320
Hart, Capt. James F., 322
Hart, Capt. Patrick, 317
Hartshorne, Maj. William R., 314
Hartung, Col. Adolph von, 315
Haseltine, Maj. James H., 316
Haskell, Maj. John C., 319
Hattaway, Herman, 248
Hawley, Col. William, 316
Hayes, Capt. Edward, 316
Hayes, Col. Joseph, 314
Haynes, Capt. Benjamin F., 312
Hays, Brig. Gen. Alexander, 313; reinforces Cemetery Ridge July 2, 143; and defense of Pickett's Charge, 204; envelops Confederate left, 211, 213; repulses Pickett's Charge, 231–33
Hays, Brig. Gen. Harry T., 320; joins attack July 1, 65; urges Ewell to strike Culp's Hill, 342n70; attacks Cemetery Hill, 156–59; joins attack July 1, 341nn49,57
Hays, Brig. Gen. William, 263, 312
Hazard, Capt. John C., 313
Hazel Grove (Chancellorsville), 93, 94, 141, 344nn27–28, 348nn81,99, 349n112
Hazlett, Lt. Charles E., 123, 314, 347n79

Heath, Col. Francis, 312, 313
Heaton, Lt. Edward, 317
Heckman, Capt. Lewis, 316
Henry, Maj. Mathias W., 319
Henry, Lt. Col. William, Jr., 314
Herbert, Lt. Col. Hilary A., 322
Herbert, Lt. Col. James R., 320
Here Come the Rebels! (Nye), 375, 386
Hero, Lt. Andrew, Jr., 320
Herr Ridge, 38, 42
Hesser, Lt. Col. Theodor, 313
Heth, Maj. Gen. Henry, 321; shoes needed by, as precipitating event, 38, 338nn3,5; orders brigades into Gettysburg, 39; outnumbers Buford two-to-one, 40; inexperience at division command, 41; engagements south of Cashtown Road, 43–45; engagements north of Cashtown Road, 47; poor performance in morning July 1, 49–50; attacks at McPherson Ridge on afternoon of July 1, wounded, 65, 184, 341n51, 360n1; resumes command of division in retreat, 263, 363n46
Hicks, Capt. Louis T., 321
Higginbotham, Col. John C., 320
Higgins, Lt. Col. Benjamin L., 313
High Tide at Gettysburg (Tucker), 372
Hildebrandt, Maj. Hugo, 313
Hill, Lt. Gen. Ambrose P., 321; moves northward, 7, 9; and Heth's advance into Gettysburg, 38, 50, 338n5; and Lee's orders not to engage enemy, 41, 339n11; informs Ewell of approach to Gettysburg, 340n31; ill state of, 61, 340n42; decision not to attack Cemetery Hill July 1, 72, 342nn66,67; desultory activities July 2, 148, 167; and attack plan July 3, 184; in retreat, 256; crosses Potomac, 262–63
Hill, Capt. Blanton A., 319
Hill, Maj. John T., 313
Hill, Capt. Wallace, 317
Hillyer, Capt. George, 319
Hizar, Capt. Thomas B., 313
Hodges, Col. James G., 223, 319
Hodges, Col. Wesley C., 319
Hoffman, Col. John S., 320
Hofmann, Col. J. William, 312
Hoke, Col. William J., 322
"'Hold Them with the Bayonet': de Trobriand's Brigade Defends the Wheatfield" (O'Brien), 380
Holder, Col. William D., 319
"Holding the Right: The 137th New York Regiment at Gettysburg" (Jorgensen), 377
Holleyman, Capt. John W., 322
Holt, Col. Bolling H., 322
Holt, Lt. Col. Thomas, 313
Hood, Maj. Gen. John B., 319; and Longstreet's attack sequence July 2, 92, 101–102; deployment of troops, 101, 103; wounded and leaves field, 104

Hooker, Maj. Gen. Joseph S.: at Battle of Chancellorsville, 335n18; at first Battle of Brandy Station, 4, 267; and Loudoun Valley campaign, 278; late start northward after ANV, 11; cuts Stuart off from ANV, 14; removal as AP's commander, 22–24, 336n46; in Chattanooga campaign, 336n46
Hoole, Lt. Col. Axalla John, 318
Houck's Ridge, 133, 346n59
"The Hour Was One of Horror": East Cemetery Hill at Gettysburg (Archer), 380
Howard, Capt. Benjamin F., 319
Howard, Maj. Gen. Oliver O., 315; arrives, and deploys, 50–53; chooses Cemetery Hill for position, 53, 339n26; reinforces Schurz, 341n57; dispute with Hancock, 342nn62,63; relieves Doubleday and appoints Newton, 339n25
Howe, Brig. Gen. Albion P., 315
Huey, Col. Pennock, 316
Huger, Maj. Frank, 320
Huidekoper, Lt. Col. Henry S., 312
Hulings, Lt. Col. Thomas M., 314
Hull, Lt. Col. James C., 314
Humphreys, Brig. Gen. Andrew A., 313; commands right wing of 3rd Corps, 96, 345n33; assailed on Emmitsburg Road, 140, 142–43; withdraws in good order, 143, 349n101; rallies and pursues Lang to Emmitsburg Road, 161
Humphreys, Col. Benjamin G., 319, 360n148
Hunt, Brig. Gen. Henry J.: reconnoiters northern Maryland, 342n61; places cannon on Cemetery Hill and Ridge, 86; as Chief of Artillery, 106, 311; and Hancock during Pickett's Charge, 193; cease-fire ruse of, 194, 353n66; approves waiting to pursue Lee, 253, 362n29
Huntington, Capt. James F., 317
Hunton, Col. Eppa, 223, 319
Hurt, Capt. William B., 322
Hurtt, Maj. Daniel W., 321
Huston, Lt. Col. James, 313
Hutter, Capt. James R., 319
Hyman, Col. Joseph H., 322

"'I Think the Union Army Had Something to Do with It': The Pickett's Charge Nobody Knows" (Reardon), 383
"'I Will Take the Responsibility': Strong Vincent Moves to Little Round Top: Fact or Fiction?" (Wright), 380
"'If Longstreet . . . Says So, It Is Most Likely Not True': James Longstreet and the Second Day at Gettysburg" (Krick), 378
Imboden, Brig. Gen. John D., 252, 253–55, 322, 362n31
immigrants, in AP, 334n4
In the Bloody Railroad Cut at Gettysburg (Herdegen and Beaudot), 376

Ingalls, Brig. Gen. Rufus, 311
Into the Fight: Pickett's Charge at Gettysburg (Priest), 214, 350n1, 382
An Introduction to Civil War Small Arms (Coates and Thomas), 384
Ireland, Col. David, 153–55, 316
Iron Brigade: arrives, and attacks, 43–45, 339n23; casualties July 1, 65; ammunition resupply of, 367n24
The Iron Brigade: A Military History (Nolan), 367
"It Struck Horror to Us All" (Hartwig), 383
Iverson, Brig. Gen. Alfred, 56–57, 321

Jackson, Lt. Col. Allan H., 315
Jackson, Col. James W., 319
Jackson, Col. Samuel M., 314
Jackson, Capt. Thomas E., 322
Jackson, Lt. Gen. Thomas J., 93
James, Lt. Robert, 314
James Longstreet: The Man, the Soldier, the Controversy (DiNardo and Nofi, eds.), 378
James River, 334n5
Jamieson, Perry D., 326
Jayne, Col. Joseph Mc., 322
Jeffords, Col. Harrison H., 314
Jenkins, Brig. Gen. Albert G., 322; attached to Ewell's 2nd Corps, 6, 335n14; guards Confederate left, wounded, 285
Jenkins, Lt. Col. David T., 314
"John B. Bachelder: Government Historian of the Battle of Gettysburg" (Sauers), 374
John Bachelder's History of the Battle of Gettysburg (Ladd and Ladd, eds.), 374
Johnson, Col. Bradley T., 320
Johnson, Maj. Gen. Edward, 320; moves north with Ewell, 335n14; not with 2nd Corps July 1, 73, 342n73; and Culp's Hill attack July 1, 342n70; deploys Stonewall Brigade out Hanover Road, 285, 288; attack on Culp's Hill July 2, 150–51, 152–53, 156; attack on Culp's Hill July 3, 172–73, 175–77
Johnson, Capt. Marmaduke, 322
Johnston, Lt. Andrew B., 322
Johnston, Capt. Riley, 312
Johnston, Capt. Samuel R., 80, 318, 343n1
Johnston, Capt. William H., 321
Jomini, Baron Antoine-Henri de, 336n41
Jones, Capt. Alphonso N., 319
Jones, Archer, 248
Jones, Capt. Charles Mc., 322
Jones, Lt. Col. David M., 313
Jones, Lt. Col. E. S., 316
Jones, Lt. Col. Hilary P., 320
Jones, Col. John A., 319
Jones, Brig. Gen. John M., 155, 175, 320
Jones, Maj. John T., 321
Jones, Lt. Marcellus E., 40, 338n7
Jones, Capt. Walter B., 320
Jones, Brig. Gen. William E. "Grumble," 322; at Brandy Station, 273; in Loudoun Valley, 280, 281; in Confederate retreat, 256, 362n32
Jones, Maj. William M., 319
Jordan, Capt. Tyler C., 320
"Joshua Chamberlain and the American Dream" (LaFantasie), 379
Joslin, Lt. Col. George C., 313

Kane, Brig. Gen. Thomas L., 155, 316, 350n120
Kearse, Lt. Col. Francis, 318
Kelley, Capt. D. F., 315
Kellogg, Col. Josiah H., 40, 316
Kelly, Col. Patrick, 312
Kemper, Brig. Gen. James L., 319; maneuvers in good order during Pickett's Charge, 205, 206; approaches Union line, 217, 357n107; enfilading fire on right flank, 226, 358n122; wounded, 217, 223
Kennedy, Col. John D., 318
Kershaw, Brig. Gen. Joseph B., 318; attacks the Stony Hill, 134, 136–37, 438n97; repulsed, 163, 165
Ketchum, Col. John H., 316
Key, Col. John C. G., 319
A Killer Angels Companion (Hartwig), 372
The Killer Angels (Shaara), 1–2, 371–72
Kilpatrick, Brig. Gen. Judson, 317; as "boy general," 365n2; in Loudoun Valley, 278; assumes command of 3rd Division, 27, 338n53, 363n1; in Battle of Hanover and aftermath, 28, 31; on July 2, 299; and clash in South Cavalry Field, 299–307; and Farnsworth, 303, 365n6; attacks Confederate retreat, 255–56, 362nn32,34
King, Capt. J. Horace, 322
Kinzie, Lt. David H., 316
Kirkland, Col. William W., 320
Kirkpatrick, Capt. Thomas J., 321
Knight, Maj. Napoleon B., 338n55
Koenig, Capt. Emil, 315
Kohler, Maj. John B., 315
Kovacs, Maj. Stephen, 315
Krauseneck, Capt. Henry, 315
Kryzanowski, Col. Wladimir, 315

Lakeman, Col. Moses B., 313
Lamar, Col. John H., 320
Lambeth, Maj. Joseph H., 321
Lambie, Lt. William T., 321
Lane, Capt. James C., 316
Lane, Brig. Gen. James H., 322; supports Perrin's Seminary Ridge assault, 341n55; replaces Brockenbrough in Pickett's Charge, 231, 234; unbloodied in Pickett's Charge, 341n55; brigade casualties, 360n151; crosses Potomac, 263
Lane, Maj. John, 322
Lane, Lt. Col. John R., 321
Lang, Col. David, 322; attacks Humphreys along Emmitsburg Road July 2, 142–43; Cemetery Ridge assault repulsed, 145; holds back during Pickett's Charge, 240–41
Langley, Maj. Francis H., 319
Langley, Capt. John F., 313
Langston, Capt. John G., 314
"Last Chance for Victory" (Bowden and Ward), 378
The Last Full Measure: The Life and Death of the First Minnesota Volunteers (Moe), 380
Latham, Capt. Alexander C., 319
Latimer, Maj. J. W., 320
Law, Brig. Gen. Evander M., 319; not on field early July 2, 90–91; and scouting of Union line, 100–101; in van of attack July 2, 101; attacks at Devil's Den, 102–104, 345n42; assumes command of Hood's division, 104, 345n43; orders Oates to Little Round Top, 107, 345n48; attack continues toward Little Round Top, 112–15; and Oates's attack at Little Round Top, 115–23, 346n60; his attack on western face of Little Round Top repulsed, 123–24; excluded from July 3 attack plan, 352n27; in South Cavalry Field July 3, 299–303
Law's Alabama Brigade in the War Between the Union and the Confederacy (Laine and Penny), 387
Lawson, Capt. Charles N., 321
Lay, Capt. Richard G., 314
Lea, Lt. Col. John W., 321
Leavitt, Maj. Archibald D., 312
Ledig, Maj. August, 315
Lee, Maj. Arthur T., 314
Lee, Brig. Gen. Fitzhugh, 322; in Loudoun Valley, 278; Battle of Hanover, 28; on East Cavalry Field, 290–91, 294, 359n137; and Pickett's Charge appellation, 355n68
Lee, Gen. Robert E., 318; and Ewell at second Battle of Winchester, 335n13; his orders to Stuart in June, 14–15, 335n28; summons Robertson June 30, 336n33; intelligence before battle, 25, 337n48; orders convergence at Cashtown, 337n50; engagement orders to Ewell and Hill, 338n2, 339n11; arrives on field and assesses position, 60–62; and failure to attack Cemetery Hill July 1, 72–73, 342nn66,67, 343n76; situational assessment at end of July 1, 75–77; low-ranking staff officers of, 345n52; July 2 strategic plan outlined, 80–85; rejects Longstreet's proposed plan, 87–88, 90, 343n7; on Longstreet's delays and outcome of battle, 90; aware of further delays by Longstreet, 100, 345n37; his concept of command, 166–67, 350nn134–35; July 3 strategic plan outlined, 178–89; morning meeting with Longstreet, 179, 351n15; orders Stuart to protect rear of Confederate left flank, 289; offensive-mindedness of, 181, 352n22; stealthy and intricate preparations for attack, 187, 353n37; thoughts as assault approaches, 195, 355n70;

assessment of AP troop quality, 196, 355*n*75; on Union's double envelopment of Pickett's Charge, 231, 359*n*127; following repulse of Pickett's Charge, 243, 360*n*156; and reporting of casualties, 360*n*1; retreat of, 255–56, 362*n*35; escapes across Potomac, 261–64; resignation letter, 265–66, 363*n*51

Lee, Brig. Gen. W. H. F. "Rooney," 272, 275, 322

"Lee's Artillery Prepares for Pickett's Charge" (Rollins), 384

"Lee's Gallant 6000?" (Priest), 382

Lee's Tarnished Lieutenant: James Longstreet and His Place in Southern History (Piston), 378

Legends of Gettysburg: Separating Fact from Fiction (Desjardin), 379

Leister, Lydia, 354*n*61

Leonard, Lt. Col. John, 313

Leonard, Col. Samuel H., 312

Lessig, Maj. William H., 314

"A Lesson in Battle Tempo: The Union Pursuit after Gettysburg" (Terpeluk), 386

Lester, Maj. German A., 320

Letterman, Dr. Jonathan, 311

Leventhorpe, Col. Collett, 321

Lewis, Col. John R., 315

Lewis, Capt. John W., 322

Lewis, Lt. Col. Meriwether, 322

Lewis, Col. Travanion D., 320

Lewis, Lt. Col. William G., 321

Libby, Capt. Edwin, 313

Lightfoot, Col. James N., 321

Lincoln, Abraham: and Hooker's removal, 22–24; and Meade's apparent inaction, 260–61, 264

Lipscomb, Maj. Thomas J., 322

Little, Col. Francis H., 319

Little Round Top (July 2): Johnston's report concerning, 80, 343*n*1; Sickles fails to occupy, 93–94; signalmen atop, 108, 345*n*50; Warren assesses vulnerability of, 109; Vincent occupies, 109–12, 346*n*56; importance of, 112; battle for, 112–24; relative strength of forces, 118; artillery batteries on, 123–24, 126, 205, 348*n*83, 356*n*83; hypothetical analysis of, 124–27; revisionism in battle accounts, 347*n*66, 356*n*83; Bachelder attempts to rename Weed's Hill, 356*n*83. *See also* Chamberlain, Col. Joshua L.; Law, Brig. Gen. Evander M.; Oates, Col. William C.

Lloyd, Lt. Col. Edward F., 315

Lloyd, Capt. William H., 313

Lockert, Lt. Col. James, 321

Lockman, Col. John T., 315

Lockwood, Brig. Gen. Henry H., 143, 316

Lockwood, Lt. Col. Jonathan H., 313

Lohr's Hill, 40

Lomax, Col. Lunsford L., 322

Long, Col. Armistead L., 88, 318, 344*n*11

Long, Lt. Col. Richard, 315

Long Lane, 211, 357*n*101

Longstreet, Lt. Gen. James, 318; northward movement in June, 7–9, 14; Lee's plan for July 2, 80, 81–83; alternative strategy proposed by, 86–87, 343*n*6; analysis of strategic differences with Lee, 88–90, 343*n*12; apparant apathy of, 90, 344*n*16; delays in deploying, and countermarch, 90–92, 108, 166–67; delays because of Sickles's salient, 92, 98–102, 343*n*25; in plan of attack July 3, 178–79; and strategic plan discussions, 179, 351*nn*15,17; and Pickett's absence at daylight, 179–81, 351*nn*16,18; and implementation of plan, 182, 352*n*25; instructions to Pickett, 352*n*34; bravery in early afternoon, 193; knowledge of Brockenbrough's collapse, 357*n*101; and support of left flank, 234; holds Wilcox and Lang back during Pickett's Charge, 240–41; performance in planning Pickett's Charge assessed, 236–37; later writings concerning July 3 events, 184, 352*n*31; in retreat, 256; crosses Potomac, 262

Lookout Mountain, Battle of, 336*n*46

Lord, Capt. Richard S. C., 316

Lorenz rifled muskets, 368*nn*24,25

Loudoun Valley, cavalry clashes in, 8, 11–13, 277–84

Lowe, Col. Samuel D., 322

Lowrance, Col. William Lee J., 234, 322, 359*n*132

Luffman, Lt. Col. William, 319

Lumbard, Lt. Col. George W., 314

Lumpkin, Col. Samuel P., 321

Luse, Lt. Col. William H., 319

Lusk, Lt. Col. Isaac M., 313

Lutheran Seminary, 58

Lutz, Capt. John M., 315

Lyell, Lt. Col. John W., 321

Lyle, Col. Peter, 312

MacConnell, Lt. Charles C., 314

MacThompson, Lt. Col. James, 312

McAllister, Col. Robert, 313

McAllister's Woods, 151, 159, 350*n*122

McCalmont, Lt. Col. Alfred B., 312

McCandless, Col. William, 314, 360*n*148

McCarthy, Capt. Edward S., 319

McCartney, Capt. William H., 315

McClanahan, Capt. John H., 322

McClellan, Gen. George M., 22–23

McClellan, Maj. Henry B., and Brandy Station, 4, 109, 272–73, 334*n*9, 346*n*55

McCrea, Lt. Tully, 313, 359*n*125

McCreary, Maj. Cornelius W., 322

McCullohs, Lt. Col. William H., 322

McDaniel, Maj. Henry D., 319

McDougall, Col. Archibald L., 316

McDougall, Col. Clinton D., 313

McElroy, Lt. Col. Kennon, 319

McFadden, Capt. William, 313

McFarland, Lt. Col. J. P., 312

McFarlane, Lt. Col. Robert, 312

McGilvery, Lt. Col. Freeman, 317; Plum Run line, 96, 141; and artillery in southern sector, 192, 226

McGlashan, Capt. A. S., 318

McGraw, Capt. Joseph, 322

McGregor, Capt. William M., 322

McGroarty, Col. Stephen J., 315

McIntosh, Maj. David G., 322

McIntosh, Col. John B., 257, 292–93, 296, 316

McKee, Capt. Samuel A., 314

McKeen, Col. H. Boyd, 312

McLaws, Maj. Gen. Lafayette, 318; on Longstreet's demeanor July 2, 344*n*16; southward deployment route, 92, 343*n*23; and Longstreet's attack plan, 92, 98–100, 343*n*25; brigades join attack July 2, 134; excluded from July 3 attack plan, 352*n*27; in South Cavalry Field July 3, 300

McLeod, Maj. Donald Mc., 318

McLeod, Capt. William L., 320

McMichael, Lt. Col. Richards, 312

McMillan, Col. Robert, 319

McMurray, Richard M., 247–48

McMurry, Capt. Benjamin C., 322

McNeill, Capt. John Hance, 322

McPherson Ridge, 38, 41, 42, 47

McWhiney, Grady, 326

Macon, Capt. Miles C., 319

Macy, Lt. Col. George N., 313

Madill, Col. Henry J., 313

Magenta, Battle of (1859), 368*n*32

Magruder, Col. John, 223, 319

Mahler, Col. Francis, 315

Mahone, Brig. Gen. William, 322; refused to advance without orders, 146–48; and Pickett's Charge, 359*n*134

Mallon, Col. James J., 313

Malloy, Col. S. G., 318

Maloney, Lt. William, 315

Malvern Hill, Battle of, 184, 352*n*32

Manassas, Second Battle of, 334*n*2

Manly, Capt. Basil C., 319

Mann, Capt. Daniel P., 311

Mann, Col. William D., 317

Manning, Capt. Nathaniel J., 315

Manning, Col. Vannoy H., 319

Manning, Col. William R., 318

Mansfield, Maj. John, 311

maps, sources for, 389–92

Markell, Lt. Col. William L., 316

Marsh Creek, 40, 41

Marshall, Maj. Charles, 318

Marshall, Col. James K., 321; assumes command of Pettigrew's brigade, 65; killed, 358*n*116

Marshall, Lt. Col. Thomas, 322

Martin, Capt. Augustus P., 314, 347*n*78

Martin, Capt. Joseph W., 317

Martin, Lt. Leonard, 315

Martin, Capt. Luther, 313

Martin, Lt. Col. Rawley White, 319

Marye, Capt. Edward A., 322

Mason, Capt. Julius W., 316
Mason, Lt. Philip D., 317
Massie, Capt. John L., 321
Massie, Lt. Col. Thomas B., 322
Maulsby, Col. William P., 316
Maurin, Capt. Victor, 322
Maxwell, Capt. William R., 314
Mayo, Col. Joseph C., Jr., 319, 321
Mayo, Col. Robert M., 223, 356n90
Meade, Maj. Gen. George G., 311; assumes command of AP, 24, 336n45; moves army further north, 25; and Pipe Creek plans, 342nn61,75, 343n79; and Hancock-Howard controversy, 342n62; decides to fully engage at Gettysburg, 74; command accomplishments July 1, 74–75; council of wars July 2, 98; staff of, 106; anticipation of Confederate attack July 2, 108–109; exploits interior lines to redeploy, 143; knowledge of Culp's Hill, 148; after repulse of ANV July 2, 2; command accomplishments July 2, 166, 167; forced from HQ July 3, 193, 353n61; retains command of AP and earns Grant's trust, 248–49, 362nn20–21; psychological exhaustion of, 252; pursuit of Lee, 252, 256–57, 257–61, 362n26; and council of war July 12, 259, 263, 362n40; and Lee's escape, 264, 265
"Measuring Pickett's Charge" (Shultz and Rollins), 384
meeting engagements, defined, 49
Mendell, Capt. George H., 311
Mercer, Col. John T., 321
Meredith, Brig. Gen. Solomon, 43–45, 311
Merriam, Lt. Col. Waldo, 313
Merrill, Lt. Col. Charles B., 313
Merritt, Brig. Gen. Wesley, 316; assumes command of Reserve Brigade, 338n54; ordered toward Mechanicsville, Va., 28; patrols south of battle area, 87; and Battle of Fairfield, 365n4; reinforces Kilpatrick at South Cavalry Field, 299–307, 365n4; attacks Imboden in retreat, 255
"Merritt's Regulars on South Cavalry Field: Oh, What Could Have Been" (Wittenberg), 387
Merwin, Lt. Col. Henry C., 312
Messick, Capt. Nathan S., 313
Meyer, Col. Seraphim, 315
Middleburg, Va., 277, 280
Midway, Battle of (WW II), 264–65
A Military History of the 8th Ohio Vol. Inf'y: Its Battles, Marches and Army Movements (Sawyer), 385
Military Memoirs of a Confederate: A Critical Narrative (Alexander), 383
militia, Pettigrew spots, 38–39
Milledge, Capt. John, Jr., 321
Miller, Lt. Col. Francis C., 312
Miller, Col. Hugh R., 321
Miller, Col. John L., 322

Miller, Capt. William, 296, 364n11
Milton, Lt. Richard S., 317
Minié, Capt. Claude E., 366n2
minnie balls, 326, 366n2, 368n25
Missionary Ridge, Battle of, 336n46
Mitchell, Capt. William H., 319
Mitzel, Lt. Col. Alexander von, 315
Moesch, Lt. Col. Joseph A., 312
Moffett, Capt. Charles J., 312, 322
Moir, Lt. Robert L., 322
Monaghan, Col. William, 320
Monterey Pass, 256, 362n32
Moody, Maj. Daniel N., 319
Moody, Capt. George V., 320
Moody, Lt. Col. William H., 315
Moore, Capt. Joseph D., 322
Moore, Maj. John W., 313
Moore, Lt. Stephen, 321
Moore, Maj. Walter R., 322
Moorman, Capt. Marcellus N., 322
Morning at Willoughby Run: July 1, 1863 (Shue), 376
Moroney, Capt. Richard, 312
Morrill, Capt. Walter G., 116, 284, 346n62
Morris, Col. Orlando H., 312
Morrow, Col. Henry A., 311
Morse, Maj. Charles F., 316
Moseley, Col. William P., 320
Motes, Lt. Columbus W., 319
Motts, Wayne E., 214
Mounger, Lt. Col. John C., 319
Mr. Lincoln's Army: The Army of the Potomac in the Gettysburg Campaign, Programs of the Sixth Annual Gettysburg Seminar, 383
Mudge, Lt. Col. Charles R., 316
Muhlenberg, Lt. Edward D., 316
Mulholland, Maj. St. Clair A., 312
Mummasburg Road, 56, 58–59
Munford, Col. Thomas T., 275, 322, 335n15
Munson, Lt. Col. William D., 312
muskets. *See* rifles, advances in technology; small arms
Musser, Lt. Col. John D., 312

Nadenbousch, Col. John Q. A., 320
Nance, Col. James D., 318
Napoleon, frontal assaults of, 196
Neill, Brig. Gen. Thomas H., 257, 315
Nelson, Capt. Alanson H., 313
Nelson, Capt. Andrew Mc., 321
Nelson, Capt. Frank W., 319
Nelson, Maj. Peter, 312
Nelson, Lt. Col. William, 321
Nevin, Col. David J., 165, 315, 350n129
Nevin, Maj. John I., 315
Newton, Maj. James W., 320
Newton, Maj. Gen. John, 311, 315; assumes command of 1st Corps, 339n25; assessment of July 2 results, 167
Nichols, Col. William T., 312

Nine Months to Gettysburg: Stannard's Vermonters and the Repulse of Pickett's Charge (Coffin), 383
"'No 15,000 Men Can Take That Hill': Longstreet at Gettysburg" (Wert), 378
"'No Troops on the Field Had Done Better': John C. Caldwell's Division in the Wheatfield" (Hartwig), 380
Nolan, Alan T., *The Iron Brigade: A Military History*, 367
Nolan, Lt. Col. Michael, 320
Nolan, Lt. Nicholas, 316, 322
Norcom, Capt. Joseph, 320
North & South: The Magazine of Civil War Conflict, 373
Northrup, Maj. Charles, 312
Norton, Capt. George F., 319
Norton, Lt. George W., 317
Norton, Capt. Lemuel P., 311
Norton, Oliver W., 346n56
Nothing But Glory: Pickett's Division at Gettysburg (Harrison and Busey), 381–82
Nounnan, Maj. James H., 322

Oak Hill (July 1): Rodes arrives at, 340n29; Rodes's uncoordinated attack from, 54–56, 340nn31,33; Baxter defends at, 56–57, 58, 340nn35,36; Daniels joins Rodes's attack, 57–58
Oates, Col. William C., 319; takes Big Round Top, 105–107, 345n45; at Little Round Top, 115–23, 346n60; withdrawal ordered, 120, 347n75; evaluation of Chamberlain, 348n88; on significance of Gettysburg, 361n13
Official Records. *See The War of the Rebellion: The Official Records of the Union and Confederate Armies*
O'Kane, Col. Dennis, 220, 233, 313
Oliver, Capt. Moses, 312
O'Neal, Col. Edward A., 56, 321
Opp, Lt. Col. Milton, 313
O'Rorke, Col. Patrick H., 123, 314
Osborn, Maj. Thomas W., 211, 315, 359n125
Otey, Maj. Kirkwood, 223, 319
Otis, Capt. George H., 311
Ottom, Lt. Col. August, 315
"Over a Wide, Hot . . . Crimson Plane": The Struggle for the Bliss Farm at Gettysburg (Christ), 380
Overmeyer, Capt. John B., 312
Owen, Col. Thomas H., 322
Owens, Maj. John C., 223, 319
Owens, Capt. Walter L., 312
Owens, Capt. William A., 321

Packer, Col. W. W., 316
Page, Capt. Richard C. M., 321
Pardee, Lt. Col. Ario, Jr., 316
Pardee's Field, 151, 176
Parham, Col. William A., 322

Parker, Col. Francis M., 321
Parker, Capt. William W., 320
Parks, Col. Marcus A., 321
Parsley, Maj. William A., 320
Parsons, Lt. Augustin N., 317
Parsons, Lt. Col. Joseph B., 315
Patrick, Col. John H., 316
Patrick, Brig. Gen. Marsena R., 311
Patterson, Capt. George M., 322
Patterson, Col. John W., 315
Patton, Col. Waller T., 223, 319
Paul, Brig. Gen. Gabriel R., 312; breastworks built at Seminary Ridge, 66; bolsters Baxter near Mummasburg Road, 58; brigade casualties, 69–70
Payne, Lt. Col. William H. F., 322
Payton, Maj. Charles S., 319
Peach Orchard, 92, 94, 138–43, 343n24, 348n99
"The Peach Orchard Revisited: Daniel E. Sickles and the Third Corps on July 2, 1863" (Robertson), 380
Peebles, Maj. William H., 321
Pegram, Maj. William J., 39, 42, 322
Pender, Maj. Gen. William Dorsey, 322; military bearing of, 342n60; supports Heth July 1, 50; attack on Seminary Ridge, 68; moves into position July 2, 80–81; mortally wounded, 148
Pendleton, Lt. Samuel H., 321
Pendleton, Brig. Gen. William N. "Parson," incompetence of, 190, 318, 353nn48,50, 354n64, 358n123
Penn, Col. Davidson B., 320
Pennington, Lt. Alexander C. M., Jr., 317, 364n11
"The Pennsylvania Gambit and the Gettysburg Splash" (McMurray), 375
Penrose, Col. William H., 314
Perello, Chris, 247, 249
A Perfect Storm of Lead: George Sears Greene's New York Brigade in Defense of Culp's Hill (Murray), 377
Perrin, Col. Abner M., 322; flanks Union at Seminary Ridge, 68, 341n55; in support of Pickett's Charge, 355n78
Perrin, Lt. Walter S., 194, 313, 354n65
Perry, Col. William F., 319
Persian Gulf War, 229
Pettes, Col. William H., 311
Pettigrew, Brig. Gen. James Johnston, 321; advances along Cashtown Road July 1, 37–38, 41; assumes command of Heth's division, 65; commands left wing of Pickett's Charge, 184–85; commences attack, 201; approaches Union lines, 213, 231–33, 359nn126,127; division casualties, 243, 360n151; flawed performance in Pickett's Charge, 185; mortally wounded in retreat, 263
Peyton, Maj. Charles S., 319
Phillipps, Lt. Col. Jefferson C., 322
Phillips, Capt. B. L., 321

Phillips, Capt. Charles A., 317
Phillips, Capt. James J., 319
Pickens, Col. Samuel B., 321
Pickett, Maj. Gen. George E., 319; personal characteristics and leadership of, 185; ordered to Gettysburg, 343n2; unengaged in war since summer 1862, 351n14; "nowhere to be seen" by daylight July 3, 179–81, 351nn16,18; in plans of July 3 attack, 182–84; strength of division, 352n26; positioning and troop placement before assault, 185, 187, 353nn35,36,39,40; commences attack, 201; maneuvers in good order, 206, 356n95; knowledge of Brockenbrough's collapse, 357n101; requests right wing reinforcements, 240–41, 359n143; division casualties, 243, 360n151; performance of July 3, 185, 352n34; attributed remarks of following war, 243–44, 360n156. *See also* Pickett's Charge (July 3)
Pickett's Charge: A Microhistory of the Final Confederate Attack at Gettysburg, July 3, 1863 (Stewart), 184, 350n2, 381
"Pickett's Charge: The Convergence of History and Myth in the Southern Past" (Reardon), 383
Pickett's Charge: The Last Attack at Gettysburg (Hess), 381
"Pickett's Charge and the Principles of War" (Rollins), 378, 384
Pickett's Charge! Eyewitness Accounts (Rollins), 382, 385
Pickett's Charge in History and Memory (Reardon), 381, 382–83
Pickett's Charge (July 3): books treating, 350nn1,2; doomed nature of, 350n4; Confederate troop numbers in, 184, 223, 235–36, 352n29, 358n115; deployment and preparations, 187, 199, 353nn36,37,40; planned movement to narrow attack front, 187–89, 217; artillery placement and cannonade, 189–94, 353n50, 354nn54–60; Union counter-bombardment, 193; Union troop numbers at assault point, 197, 223, 355n76, 358n115; support components of, 197–99, 355n77; attack commences, 201–204; Union artillery bombardment of, 205–206, 208–209, 332, 356n89, 359n125, 369n35; Union preparations as Pickett's Charge commences, 207–11, 356n89; Union envelops Confederate left, 211–13, 356nn92,97, 357nn98–100; Confederate center reaches Union line, 214–21; disorder of Confederate lines, 220; Armistead's high-water mark, 221, 357n114; hypotheses regarding assault breakthrough, 221–24, 357n114; losses in Confederate officer corps, 223; Union reserves support line, 223–24, 233–34; Union counterattack in center and right flank, 224–26, 358nn121,122; hypothesis regarding close-supporting second wave, 234; Union

artillery reinforcements arrive, 238–39, 359n139; Confederate right wing reinforcements held back, 240–41, 359n143; Confederate colors captured, 242, 360n149; Confederate reserves form defensive line, 242; casualties, 223, 242–43, 244, 331, 360nn150–53, 368n27; reasons for repulse of, 243, 360n155; Fitzhugh Lee on appellation, 355n68
Pierce, Col. Bryan R., 313
Pierce, Lt. Col. Edwin S., 313
Pierce, Lt. Col. Francis C., 313
Pierce, Lt. Col. Francis E., 313
Pinckard, Col. Lucius, 322
Pipe Creek, 72, 75, 342n61, 343n79
"The Pipe Creek Line: An Overview" (Church), 375
Pitzer's Woods, 93
"The Plan for Pickett's Charge" (Cooksey), 382, 385
Player, Col. S. T., 322
Pleasonton, Brig. Gen. Alfred, 316; and Brandy Station, 267, 276; in Loudoun Valley, 280, 284; moves north, 11, 20; promoted, and reorganizes cavalry, 27; attached to Meade's staff, 338n56
Plum Run, 98, 102, 103, 105–107, 128–29, 346n59
Plum Run (artillery) line, 141, 349n100
Plumer, Capt. William, 313
Poague, Maj. William T., 322
Porter, Maj. Gen. Fitz John, 343n80
Posey, Brig. Gen. Carnot, 145, 322, 359n134
Potomac River, Lee's crossing of in escape, 261–64
Potter, Col. Henry L., 313
Powell, Col. Eugene, 316
Powell, Col. Robert M., 319
Powell, Maj. Thomas N., 320
Powers Hill, 354n61
Pratt, Capt. Franklin A., 317
Prescott, Col. G. L., 314
Preston, Col. Addison W., 317
Prey, Col. Gilbert G., 312
Price, Col. E. Livingston, 316
Price, Col. R. Butler, 311
Priest, John M., 214
Proctor, Col. Redfield, 312
Pruyn, Lt. Col. Augustius, 316
Pulford, Lt. Col. John, 313
Pye, Maj. Edward, 312

"R. E. Lee and July 1 at Gettysburg" (Nolan), 376
railroad cut (July 1): first battle for, 47; second battle for, 57–58
Raine, Capt. Charles I., 320, 321
Ramseur, Brig. Gen. Stephen Dodson, 321; enters skirmish for railroad cut, 58; pushes Union troops back, 65; movement on July 2, 159
Ramsey, Col. John, 314

SUBJECT INDEX 411

Randall, Lt. Col. Charles B., 316
Randall, Col. Francis V., 312
Randol, Capt. Alanson M., 317
Randolph, Capt. George E., 314, 345n31
Randolph, Capt. William F., 320
Rank, Capt. W. D., 316
Rank, Capt. William D., 363n3
Ransom, Capt. Dunbar R., 317
Rappahannock River, 3, 267
Rappahannock Station, Battle of, 361n4
Read, Capt. Edwin W. H., 311
Ready . . . Aim . . . Fire! Small Arms Ammunition in the Battle of Gettysburg (Thomas), 384
Reardon, Carol, 356n95
Recollections of a Confederate Staff Officer (Sorrel), 378
The Redemption of the "Harper's Ferry Cowards": The Story of the 111th and 126th New York State Regiments at Gettysburg (Murray), 380
Reese, Capt. William J., 321
Regimental Strengths and Losses at Gettysburg (Busey and Martin), 385, 388
Reilly, Capt. James, 319
"'Remember Harper's Ferry!': The Degradation, Humiliation, and Redemption of George L. Willard's Brigade" (Campbell), 385
Revere, Col. Paul J., 313
Reynolds, Capt. Gilbert H., 312
Reynolds, Maj. Gen. John F., 311; as van of AP infantry approaching Gettysburg, 32, 33; fears ANV would take heights south of town, 339n10; confers with Buford and joins battle, 43; fatally shot, 45, 339n19; command accomplishments July 1, 75
Reynolds, Capt. John W., 312
Rice, Col. James C., 314; at Little Round Top, 105, 345n44; dispatched to Big Round Top, 165; after-action reports, 346n56
Rice, Capt. R. Stanley, 322
Rice, Capt. Thomas, 320
Rice, Lt. Col. William G., 318
Rich, Col. William B., 322
Richardson, Maj. Charles, 322
Richardson, Capt. Jesse M., 320
Richardson, Capt. John B., 320
Richardson, Maj. John H., 318
Richardson, Maj. John Q. A., 321
Richmond, Col. Nathaniel P., 317
Rickards, Col. William, Jr., 316
Ricketts, Capt. R. Bruce, 317
rifles, advances in technology, 325–27, 331–32, 368n29
Rigby, Capt. James H., 317
Rittenhouse, Lt. Benjamin F., 192, 205–206, 314
Roads from Gettysburg (Schildt), 386
Roath, Capt. Emanuel D., 312
Robert E. Lee's Civil War (Alexander), 375
Roberts, Col. Richard P., 312
Robertson, Brig. Gen. Beverly H., 322; at Brandy Station, 272; screens tail of ANV in northward march, 16–17; in Confederate retreat, 256, 362n32
Robertson, Capt. James M., 317
Robertson, Brig. Gen. Jerome B., 104–105, 133, 319
Robertson, Col. William W., 311
Robinson, Capt. Benjamin, 321
Robinson, Col. James S., 315
Robinson, Lt. Col. John A., 320
Robinson, Brig. Gen. John C., 58, 312
Robinson, Lt. John M., 322
Robinson, Lt. Col. William G., 322
Robinson, Col. William W., 311
Robison, Lt. Col. John K., 317
Rock Creek, 151, 153, 176
Rodenbough, Capt. T. F., 316
Rodes, Maj. Gen. Robert E., 321; military bearing of, 342n60; near Brandy Station, 275; moving north, 335n14; arrives at Oak Hill July 1, 340n29; initiates uncoordinated attack on Cutler, 54–56, 340nn31,33; Daniels supports, 57–58; initiates attack then withdraws July 2, 159
Rogers, Col. George T., 322
Rogers, Lt. Col. Henry A., 322
Rogers, Col. Horatio, Jr., 315
Rogers, Maj. Isaac, 313
Rogers, Col. James C., 316
Rogers, Maj. Jefferson C., 319
Rogers, Lt. Robert, 239–40, 356n81, 359n141
Rogers, Lt. Robert E., 313
Root, Col. Adrian R., 312
Rorty, Capt. James McKay, 203, 313, 356n81
Rose Woods, 133–35, 365n1
Ross, Maj. George W., 322
Ross, Capt. Hugh M., 322
Ross, Lt. Col. John D., 320
Rosser, Col. Thomas L., 322
Rowley, Brig. Gen. Thomas A., 50, 312
Ruff, Lt. Col. Solon Z., 319
Ruger, Brig. Gen. Thomas H., 316; commands 12th Corps's right on Culp's Hill, 159, 349n114; probes southwestern slope of lower Culp's Hill, 173
Rugg, Lt. Sylvanus T., 316
Rummel barn, 292, 364n11, 365n21
Russell, Brig. Gen. David A., 268, 314

Saber and Scapegoat: J. E. B. Stuart and the Gettysburg Controversy (Nesbitt), 375, 386, 387
Sackett, Col. William H., 316
salient: Longstreet delayed because of Sickles's salient, 92, 98–102, 343n25; Sickles's 3rd Corps advances, and effects, 93–98, 100, 107–108, 165–66, 345n36; defined, 344n30
Salomon, Lt. Col. Edward S., 315
Salyer, Lt. Col. Logan H. N., 320
Sanders, Lt. Col. John C. C., 322
Saunders, Capt. Samuel H., 320
Saussure, Col. William D. De, 318
Saville, Lt. George E., 320
"The Saviors of Little Round Top" (Cameron), 379
Sawyer, Lt. Col. Franklin, 313; envelops Confederate left in Pickett's Charge, 211–13, 356nn92,97, 357n99, 359n126; captures colors, 360n149; casualties, 357n99
Scales, Brig. Gen. Alfred M., Jr., 243, 322, 359n132, 360n151
Scales, Capt. James T., 321
Scherrer, Capt. William M., 312
Schimmelfennig, Brig. Gen. Alexander, 52, 53, 315
Schleiter, Capt. Gustav, 315
schoolhouse, 92, 343n23
Schoonover, Lt. John, 313
Schurz, Maj. Gen. Carl, 315; deploys on arrival, 52, 53, 340n29; Barlow compromises defensive plans of, 62, 340n45; requests reinforcements, 341n57; defends Cemetery Hill, 159
Scott, Capt. Dunlap, 319
scouting, on Union left (July 2): Johnston's report on Little Round Top, 80, 343n1; Warren scouts left of Union line, reinforces, 92, 109–12, 123; Ward scouting party, 344n26; Law scouts Union line, 100–101; Anderson's inadequate scouting, 101; Chamberlain scouts atop Little Round Top, 105, 345n44
Scruggs, Col. Lawrence H., 319
Seaver, Col. Thomas O., 315
The Second Day at Gettysburg (Gallagher, ed.), 373, 378, 380
"The Second Wave of Pickett's Charge" (Rollins), 351n4, 384
Sedgwick, Maj. Gen. John, 314; at Battle of Brandy Station, 334n6; in July 2 fighting, 165, 350n129; pursues Lee in retreat, 257
Seeley, Capt. Aaron P., 313
Selfridge, Capt. James L., 316
Sellers, Maj. Alfred S., 312
Seminary Ridge, 65–68, 187
Semmes, Brig. Gen. Paul Jones, 318; attacks near Wheatfield, 134–38; mortally wounded, 438n96; repulsed, 163, 165
Seven Days, battles of the, 184, 334nn2,5, 352n32
Sewell, Col. William J., 313
Shaara, Michael, 2, 371–72
Shaffer, Sgt. Levi, 40
Shaler, Brig. Gen. Alexander, 315
The Shaping of a Battle: Gettysburg (Montgomery), 385
Sharps rifles, 330, 367n24
Sharra, Capt. Abram, 315
Sheffield, Col. James L., 319, 345n43
Sheldon, Lt. Albert S., 313
Shelley, Lt. Col. James E., 322
Shenandoah Valley, 6, 269
Shepard, Lt. Col. Samuel G., 321, 341n52

Shephard, Maj. William S., 319
Sherrill, Col. Eliakim, 313
Sherwin, Lt. Col. Thomas, Jr., 314
Shriver, Lt. Col. Daniel M., 320
Sickles, Maj. Gen. Daniel E., 313; military experience, 92–93; at Hazel Grove in Chancellorsville, 93, 94, 344*nn*27,28; occupies Cemetery Ridge, 80, 93; fails to occupy Little Round Top, 93–94, 348*n*82; salient of, and effects, 93–98, 100, 107–108, 165–66, 345*n*36; wounded and leaves field, 141
Sides, Col. Peter, 313
Sillers, Maj. William W., 321
Simmons, Col. Thomas J., 322
Simms, Col. James P., 319
Sinex, Lt. Col. Joseph H., 314
"The 16th Maine Volunteer Infantry at Gettysburg" (Sauers), 376
Skinner, Lt. Col. Francis G., 319
Skinner, Lt. Col. James H., 320
Sleeper, Capt. Samuel T., 313
Slocum, Maj. Gen. Henry W., 316; command of, 349*nn*109,114; and offensive actions on Culp's Hill, 148; orders Williams to drive Confederates off Culp's Hill, 351*n*6
Slough, Lt. Col. Nelson, 321
small arms: caliber variations among, 368*n*25; cleaning rifles, 328, 340*n*41; Enfield rifled muskets, 367*n*19, 368*n*25; fouling problems, 328, 347*n*69, 367*n*15, 368*n*25; and Gettysburg tactics and events, 327–31, 367*nn*19,21,24, 368*n*26; loading procedure, 328, 367*n*14; Lorenz rifled muskets, 368*nn*24,25; minnie balls, 326, 366*n*2; rifle revolution, 325–27; Sharps rifle, 330, 367*n*24; Spencer rifle, 364*n*13; Springfield rifle, 367*n*15; uses of smooth-bore muskets, 368*n*29; windage, in rifles and muskets, 366*n*1, 368*n*30
Smith, Capt. Benjamin H., Jr., 321
Smith, Lt. Col. Charles H., 316
Smith, Lt. Col. George F., 315
Smith, Col. George H., 322
Smith, Capt. James E., 96, 130, 133, 314
Smith, Col. James J., 312
Smith, Col. James M., 320
Smith, Lt. Col. Maurice T., 321
Smith, Adj. N. S., 322
Smith, Col. Orland, 53, 315
Smith, Col. Richard Penn, 155, 313, 349*n*119
Smith, Brig. Gen. William, 176, 320
Smith, Lt. William, 313
Smyth, Col. Thomas A., 313
Snodgrass, Lt. Col. James McK., 314
Solferino, Battle of (1859), 196, 355*n*73, 368*n*32
Somme, Battle of the (WW I), 194–95
Sorrel, Maj. G. Moxley, 90
South Cavalry Field (July 3), 251, 299–307, 365*n*4
Spangler's Spring, 151, 176, 350*n*122
Spangler's Woods, 187

Spear, Capt. Ellis, 118, 347*nn*70,74
Speer, Lt. Col. William H. A., 322
Spencer rifles, 364*n*13
Springfield rifles, 367*n*15
Spruance, Rear Adm. Raymond A. (WW II), 264–65
Squires, Capt. Charles W., 320
Stafford, Col. Leroy A., 320
Stand Firm Ye Boys From Maine (Desjardin), 379
Stannard, Brig. Gen. George J., 312; on right flank of Pickett's Charge, 201, 214, 217; attacks flank, 224–26, 358*nn*119–22; fires into Wilcox's and Lang's brigades, 241–42
Starr, Capt. James, 311
Starr, Maj. Samuel H., 316, 365*n*4
Stedman, Maj. William, 316
Steele, Lt. Col. Amos E., Jr., 313
Stegman, Capt. Lewis R., 316
Sterling, Capt. John W., 317
Steuart, Brig. Gen. George H., 320; attacks Culp's Hill July 2, 153–55; holds lower breastworks through night, 171
Stevens, Capt. Greenleaf T., 312, 342*n*64
Stevens, Lt. M. C., 321
Stevens, Col. Wilbur F., 316
Stevens Run, 341*n*57
Stevens's Knoll, 342*nn*64,71, 350*n*123
Stewart, Lt. James, 312
Stone, Col. Roy, 58, 312
Stony Hill, the, 133
The Story of Lee's Headquarters, Gettysburg, Pennsylvania (Smith), 376
Stoughton, Col. Charles B., 315
Stoughton, Maj. Homer R., 313
Stowe, Capt. Leroy W., 322
Stowe, Maj. Samuel N., 322
Strange, Capt. James W., 322
A Strange and Blighted Land—Gettysburg: The Aftermath of a Battle (Coco), 385
Stribling, Capt. Robert M., 319
Stroh, Lt. Col. Amos, 312
Struggle for the Round Tops: Law's Alabama Brigade at the Battle of Gettysburg (Penny and Laine), 380
Stuart, Maj. Gen. J. E. B., 322; famous circular rides of, 335*n*27; at Chancellorsville, 344*n*27; at Battle of Brandy Station, 4, 268–69, 270, 273, 335*n*12; public criticism of Brandy Station performance, 13, 335*n*22; covers ANV northward movement, 8, 12, 335*n*15; in Loudoun Valley, 280, 281; rides away from ANV in June, 13–18; stress fatigue of, 17, 336*n*39; Battle of Hanover and aftermath, 28–31; orders to, regarding East Field position, 289–90, 363*n*6; and attack plan on July 3, 189; in East Field action, 290–98; screens infantry retreat, 252–53
Stuart, Col. William D., 223
"Stuart's Ride: Lee, Stuart, and the Confederate Cavalry in the Gettysburg Campaign"

(Powell), 375
Sudsburg, Col. Joseph M., 316
"The Supreme Event in Its Existence: The 140th New York on Little Round Top" (Bennett), 379
Susquehanna River, 20, 336*n*42
Sweeney, Maj. James W., 322
Sweitzer, Col. Jacob B., 138, 314
Swinton, William, 88–89
Sykes, Maj. Gen. George, 314; as reserve of AP, 90; reinforces Sickles's left flank, 109–12

tactics, at Gettysburg: artillery bombardments, 194–95, 327, 366*n*10; breastworks, 151, 349*n*113; defending out in front, 166; economy of force, 229, 358*n*124; in frontal assaults, 196–97, 228–31; refusing a line, 116, 346*n*61; salient, 92–98, 344*n*30; and shoulder arms technology, 326–27
Taft, Capt. Elijah D., 317
Talley, Col. William C., 314
Taneytown Road, 87
Tanner, Capt. Adolphus H., 316
Tanner, Capt. William A., 320
Tappen, Maj. John R., 313
Tarawa, Battle of (WW II), 361*n*3
Tate, Maj. Samuel McD., 320
Tayloe, Lt. Col. Edwards P., 321
Tayloe, Lt. Col. George E., 322
Taylor, Col. Charles F., 314
Taylor, Capt. Constantine, 311
Taylor, Col. John P., 316
Taylor, Capt. Osmond B., 320
Taylor, Lt. Col. Robert S., 319
Taylor, Maj. Walter H., 342*n*69
Taylor, Lt. Col. William C. L., 313
Taylor, Col. William H., 322
Terry, Col. William R., 223, 319
Terry, Maj. Williams, 320
These Honored Dead: The Union Casualties at Gettysburg (Busey), 385
The Third Day at Gettysburg and Beyond (Gallagher, ed.), 286, 373, 378, 383
Thoman, Lt. Col. Max A., 313
Thomas, Brig. Gen. Edward, 72, 322
Thomas, Lt. Evan, 317
Thompson, Capt. Charles, 320
Thompson, Capt. James, 317
Thomson, Lt. Col. David, 315
Thornburg, Capt. William L., 322
"Three Confederate Disasters on Oak Ridge: Failures of Brigade Leadership on the First Day at Gettysburg" (Krick), 376
Three Days at Gettysburg (Gallagher, ed.), 373
Throop, Lt. Col. William A., 314
Tilton, Col. William S., 314
Tindall, Capt. John C., 317
Tippin, Col. Andrew, 313
Titus, Col. Silas, 315
"To Gain a Second Star: The Forgotten George S.

Greene" (Motts), 377
Tompkins, Col. Charles H., 315
Torbert, Brig. Gen. Albert T. A., 314
Torsch, Capt. John W., 320
Touhy, Capt. Thomas, 312
Towers, Col. John R., 319
Town, Col. Charles H., 296, 317
Trepp, Lt. Col. Casper, 313
Trevilian Station, Battle of, 334nn7,8
Trimble, Maj. Gen. Isaac R., 318, 322; approaches town, 340n31; wants to attack Culp's Hill, 72–73, 342n70, 352n33; and command of left wing of July 3 attack, 184–85; commences attack, 201; advances then retreats, 234; division casualties, 243, 360n151
Tripp, Lt. Col. Porter D., 313
Trostle farm, 141, 349n100
Trowbridge, Maj. Luther S., 293
"Trust in God and Fear Nothing": Gen. Lewis A. Armistead, CSA (Motts), 382
Turnbull, Lt. John G., 317
Turner, Capt. John McLeod, 322
Twenty-Five Minutes of Fighting: The Gibralter Brigade on East Cemetery Hill (Lash), 380
Twiggs, Lt. Col. John D., 322
Tyler, Brig. Gen. Robert O., 317

Underwood, Col. Aldin B., 315
Upperville, Battle of, 13
Upton, Col. Emory, 314
Utterback, Lt. Addison W., 322

Veazey, Col. Wheelock G., 312
Venable, Maj. Charles S., 318
Vicksburg, Battle of, 195, 247, 355n71
Vincent, Col. Strong, 314; in Loudoun Valley, 280; reinforces Little Round Top, 109–12, 346n56; mortally wounded, 115, 346n56
Vincent's Spur, 115–17
von Steinwehr, Brig. Gen. Adolph, 315; positioned on Cemetery Hill, 53, 70; defends Cemetery Hill, 159; counterattacks Early on July 1, 341n57

Waddell, Lt. Col. James D., 319
Wadsworth, Brig. Gen. James S., 311; sent to Culp's Hill, 72; defends Culp's Hill, 151–52
Waggaman, Col. Eugene, 320
Wagram, Battle of, 196
Wainwright, Col. Charles S., 312
Walbridge, Col. James H., 315
Walcott, Lt. Aaron F., 314
Walker, Col. Edward J., 322
Walker, Col. Elijah, 313
Walker, Brig. Gen. James A., 176, 285–88, 320
Walker, Col. R. Lindsay, 322
Walker, Lt. Col. Thomas M., 316
Walker, Maj. William A., 322
Wallace, Col. James, 316
Wallace, Capt. Samuel, 322

Walton, Col. James B., 320
Walton, Lt. Col. Simeon T., 320
The War Between the Union and the Confederacy and Its Lost Opportunities (Oates), 380
The War of the Rebellion: The Official Records of the Union and Confederate Armies, 310, 334n6, 373, 386, 388
Ward, Capt. George, 313, 322
Ward, Brig. Gen. J. H. Hobart, 313; position July 2, 96; scouting party sent out from line, 344n26; attacks at Devil's Den, 104–105, 130–33
Warfield Ridge, 169, 350n3
Waring, Lt. Col. J. Frederick, 322
Warner, Col. Adoniram J., 314
Warren, Col. Edward T. H., 320
Warren, Brig. Gen. Gouverneur K.: as staff officer, 106, 311; scouts left of Union line, reinforces, 92, 109–12, 123; approves waiting to pursue Lee, 253, 362n29
Wasden, Col. Joseph, 322
Washington, D.C., 14, 247
Wasted Valor: The Confederate Dead at Gettysburg (Coco), 385
Waterloo, Battle of, 196, 242, 368n32
Waterman, Capt. Richard, 315
Watson, Capt. David, 321
Watson, Lt. Malbone F., 314
Watts, Lt. Col. James W., 319, 322
weapons. *See* small arms; tactics, at Gettysburg
weather: July 1, 35; July 2, 79; July 3, 169
Webb, Brig. Gen. Alexander, 313; supports Wright July 2, 161; requests artillery support against Pickett's Charge, 207–209; in defense of Pickett's Charge, 220–21; Pennsylvania troops break, 220–21; unable to reinforce line, 224; brigade command of, 356n87
Webb, Lt. Col. Robert F., 320
Weber, Maj. Peter A., 263
Weed, Brig. Gen. Stephen H., 123–24, 314
Weems, Col. John B., 318
Weikert, George, 2
Weir, Lt. Gulian V., 317
Weisiger, Col. David A., 322
Welch, Lt. Col. Norval E., 314
West, Capt. Speight B., 321
Westbrook, Lt. Col. Cornelius D., 313
Wheatfield, 133–38
Wheatfield Road, 139
Wheaton, Brig. Gen. Frank, 315, 350n129
Wheeler, Capt. John, 313, 315
Wheelock, Col. Charles, 312
Whistler's Ridge, 40, 41
White, Lt. Col. Elijah V., 256, 322
White, Lt. Israel, 315
White, Lt. Col. Oscar, 320
White, Col. William, 319
White, Lt. Col. William W., 319
Whitehead, Lt. Col. Richard O., 322
Whiteside, Capt. Henry, 312

Whittier, Lt. Edward N., 312
Whittle, Lt. Col. Powhatan B., 319
Wickham, Col. William C., 322
Widdis, Capt. Cornelius C., 312
Wiebecke, Col. Charles, 314
Wiedrich, Capt. Michael, 315
Wilcox, Brig. Gen. Cadmus M., 322; skirmishes with 3rd Corps, 94; attacks Humphreys along Emmitsburg Road, 142–43; continues attack at Union center, 143–45; holds back during Pickett's Charge, 240–41
Wilderness, Battle of the, 248, 249
Wilkeson, Lt. Bayard, 316
Willard, Col. George L., 143, 313, 331–32
Willett, Capt. Edward D., 320
Williams, Brig. Gen. Alpheus S., 311, 316; approaches Gettysburg, 74, 342n74; reinforces left, repulses Barksdale, 143; defends AP's left at Weikert's farm, 1–2; leads 12th Corps on Culp's Hill, 351n6
Williams, Lt. Col. Hazael J., Jr., 320
Williams, Lt. Col. Jeremiah, 315
Williams, Col. Jesse M., 156, 320
Williams, Col. Lewis B., Jr., 223, 319
Williams, Col. Samuel J., 311
Williams, Col. Solomon, 322
Williamsport, Md., 252, 253
Willis, Col. Edward, 321
Willis, Maj. William H., 321
Williston, Lt. Edward B., 315
Willoughby Run, 38, 45
Wilson, Lt. Col. John, 315
Winchester, first Battle of, 335n13
Winchester, second Battle of, 6, 335n13
Winchester, Va., 6
windage, in rifles and muskets, 366n1, 368n30
Winegar, Lt. Charles E., 316
Winfield, Capt. Benjamin F., 322
Wingfield, Capt. John T., 322
Winn, Col. David R. E., 321
Winslow, Capt. George B., 314
Winston, Maj. John R., 321
Wister, Col. Langhorne, 312
Witcher, Lt. Col. Vincent A., 290, 292–94, 298, 322, 364nn20–21
Withers, Col. Robert E., 319, 320
Wofford, Brig. Gen. William T., 319; reinforces at Wheatfield, 138, 438n98; advances in Peach Orchard, 139, 140–41; repulsed, 163, 165
Wood, Maj. Henry C., 320
Wood, Col. James, Jr., 315
Woodruff, Lt. George A., 211, 313
Woodward, Lt. Col. George A., 314
Woodward, Capt. Orpheus S., 314
Woolfolk, Lt. James, 320
Woolfolk, Capt. Pichegru, Jr., 320
Woolsey, Capt. Henry H., 314
Wooster, Lt. Col. William B., 316
Work, Col. Phillip A., 319
"The Wounding of Albert Jenkins, July 2, 1863"

(Shevchuk), 387
wounds, died-of-, rates, 361*n*3
Wright, Brig. Gen. Ambrose R., 322; advances up Cemetery Ridge July 2, 145–46, 349*n*108; repulsed, 161; and Pickett's Charge, 359*n*134
Wright, Brig. Gen. Horatio, 314
"Wright's Charge on July 2, 1863: Piercing the Union Line or Inflated Glory?" (Gottfried), 380
Wrightsville, Pa., 336*n*42
Wyatt, Capt. James W., 322

Yamamoto, Adm. Isoroku (WW II), 264–65
York River, 334*n*5
Young, Maj. H. E., 318
Young, Col. Pierce M. B., 322

Zable, Lt. Col. David, 320
Ziegler's Grove, 201, 202, 211
Zimmerman, Lt. William E., 322
Zook, Brig. Gen. Samuel K., 136, 312, 438*n*96

Jeffrey C. Hall began to study the
American Civil War as an avocation
in the early 1980s. This led to the origination
of a course at Brandeis University about the
Gettysburg campaign, which he has taught
since the mid-1990s. Hall is a biologist
at Brandeis and has done genetic and
behavioral research, publishing papers about
the molecular neurobiology of courtship
behavior and biological rhythms.